MONROE COLLEGE LIBRARY
3246800010950

For Reference

Not to be taken from this room

D1689370

LIBRARY
MONROE BUSINESS INSTITUTE

Civilization of the Ancient Mediterranean

GREECE AND ROME

Civilization of the Ancient Mediterranean

GREECE AND ROME

EDITED BY

Michael Grant and
Rachel Kitzinger

VOLUME I

CHARLES SCRIBNER'S SONS · NEW YORK

Copyright © 1988 Charles Scribner's Sons

Library of Congress Cataloging-in-Publication Data

Civilization of the ancient Mediterranean.
Includes bibliographies and index.
1. Civilization, Classical.   I. Grant, Michael,
1914–   .   II. Kitzinger, Rachel, 1948–   .
DE59.C55   1987   938   87-23465
ISBN 0-684-17594-0 (set)

ISBN 0-684-18864-3 (vol. 1)
ISBN 0-684-18865-1 (vol. 2)
ISBN 0-684-18866-X (vol. 3)

Published simultaneously in Canada
by Collier Macmillan Canada, Inc.

All rights reserved. No part of this book
may be reproduced in any form without the
permission of Charles Scribner's Sons.

1 3 5 7 9 11 13 15 17 19   Q/C   20 18 16 14 12 10 8 6 4 2

Printed in the United States of America

The paper in this book meets the guidelines for permanence and
durability of the Committee on Production Guidelines for Book
Longevity of the Council on Library Resources.

Editorial Staff

BETH ANN McCABE, *MANAGING EDITOR*
ELIZABETH ELSTON, *Associate Editor*
W. KIRK REYNOLDS, *Associate Editor*
PETER C. BENEDICT, *Editorial Assistant*
DANIEL J. CALTO, *Editorial Assistant*
JOHN F. FITZPATRICK, *Associate Editor*
SANDRA D. KNIGHT, *Administrative Assistant*
ANJU MAKHIJANI, *Production Manager*
WILLIAM L. BROECKER, *Copyeditor*
JERILYN FAMIGHETTI, *Proofreader*
WILLIAM H. HARRIS, *Copyeditor*
CAROL HOLMES, *Proofreader*
ELIZABETH C. HULICK, *Proofreader*
ALISON KILGOUR, *Copyeditor*
SYLVIA LEHRMAN, *Map Designer*
WM. J. RICHARDSON ASSOCIATES, INC., *Indexer*
LUCY RINEHART, *Copyeditor*
PATRICIA A. RODRIGUEZ, *Cartographer*
JOHN SCHULTZ, *Photo Researcher*
DEBBIE TAYLOR, *Photo Editor*
TERENCE WALZ, *Copyeditor*
G. MICHAEL McGINLEY, *DIRECTOR, REFERENCE BOOKS DIVISION*

Contents

VOLUME I

Chronological Table · xvii
Introduction · xxv

HISTORY

Historical Summary of Greece
A. R. Burn · 3

Historical Summary of Rome
Arther Ferrill · 45

LAND AND SEA

Land and Sea
J. Donald Hughes · 89

CONTENTS

POPULATION

Races and Physical Types in the Classical World
Peyton Randolph Helm · 137

Early Greek Migrations
Ronald A. Crossland · 155

Late Roman Migrations
E. A. Thompson · 171

Languages and Dialects
David Langslow · 183

AGRICULTURE AND FOOD

Farming and Animal Husbandry
K. D. White · 211

Foodstuffs, Cooking, and Drugs
Don R. Brothwell · 247

TECHNOLOGY

Theories of Progress and Evolution
G. E. R. Lloyd · 265

Greek Building Techniques
J. J. Coulton · 277

Roman Building Techniques
James E. Packer · 299

Engineering
John G. Landels · 323

Transportation
Lionel Casson · 353

Crafts and Craftsmen
Alison Burford · 367

Calendars and Time-Telling
Alan E. Samuel · 389

Alphabets and Writing
Rachel Kitzinger · 397

Book Production
Susan A. Stephens · 421

GOVERNMENT AND SOCIETY

Greek Forms of Government
Oswyn Murray · 439

Alternative Paths: Greek Monarchy and Federalism
Michael Grant · 487

Roman Forms of Government
E. Stuart Staveley · 495

Greek Class Structures and Relations
Stanley M. Burstein · 529

Roman Class Structures and Relations
Richard P. Saller · 549

Slavery
Thomas E. J. Wiedemann · 575

CONTENTS

Greek Law
Douglas M. MacDowell · 589

Roman Law
Alan Watson · 607

Greek Administration
Chester G. Starr · 631

Roman Administration
John Ferguson · 649

Interstate Relations
Shalom Perlman · 667

Wars and Military Science: Greece
J. K. Anderson · 679

Wars and Military Science: Rome
Graham Webster · 703

VOLUME II

ECONOMICS

Greek Trade, Industry, and Labor
M. M. Austin · 723

Roman Trade, Industry, and Labor
Keith Hopkins · 753

Mines and Quarries
John F. Healy · 779

Greek Taxation
Robert J. Littman · 795

Roman Taxation
Brent D. Shaw · 809

Insurance and Banking
Wesley E. Thompson · 829

Piracy
Lionel Casson · 837

RELIGION

Divinities
John Ferguson · 847

Myths and Cosmologies
Michael Simpson · 861

Magic
John Ferguson · 881

Greek Cults
Susan Guettel Cole · 887

Roman Cults
John Ferguson · 909

Greek Priesthoods
Judy Ann Turner · 925

Roman Priesthoods
Mary Beard · 933

Divination and Oracles: Greece
John Pollard · 941

Divination and Oracles: Rome
John Ferguson · 951

CONTENTS

Sacrifice and Ritual: Greece
Michael H. Jameson · 959

Sacrifice and Ritual: Rome
John A. North · 981

The Afterlife: Greece
Emily Vermeule · 987

The Afterlife: Rome
John A. North · 997

Ruler Worship
J. Rufus Fears · 1009

Judaism
Seth Schwartz · 1027

Christianity
Helmut Koester and Vasiliki Limberis · 1047

PRIVATE AND SOCIAL LIFE

Greek Education and Rhetoric
Carolyn Dewald · 1077

Roman Education and Rhetoric
Cecil W. Wooten · 1109

Folklore
William F. Hansen · 1121

Athletics
David C. Young · 1131

Greek Spectacles and Festivals
Robert Garland · 1143

CONTENTS

Roman Games
John H. Humphrey · 1153

Greek Associations, Symposia, and Clubs
Nicholas R. E. Fisher · 1167

Roman Associations, Dinner Parties, and Clubs
Nicholas R. E. Fisher · 1199

Medicine
John Scarborough · 1227

Greek Attitudes Toward Sex
Jeffrey Henderson · 1249

Roman Attitudes Toward Sex
Judith P. Hallett · 1265

Images of the Individual
Peter Walcot · 1279

Prostitution
Werner A. Krenkel · 1291

VOLUME III

WOMEN AND FAMILY LIFE

Women in Greece
Helene P. Foley · 1301

Women in Rome
Sheila K. Dickison · 1319

Greek Marriage
Sarah B. Pomeroy · 1333

Roman Marriage
Susan Treggiari · 1343

Birth Control, Childbirth, and Early Childhood
Valerie French · 1355

Houses
Alexander Gordon McKay · 1363

Clothing and Ornament
Larissa Bonfante and Eva Jaunzems · 1385

LITERARY AND PERFORMING ARTS

Epic Poetry
Bryan Hainsworth · 1417

Greek Lyric and Elegiac Poetry
Joseph Russo · 1437

Roman Lyric and Elegiac Poetry
Gordon Williams · 1455

Bucolic Poetry
David M. Halperin · 1467

Drama
Peter D. Arnott · 1477

Epigrams and Satire
J. P. Sullivan · 1495

Music and Dance
Edward Kerr Borthwick · 1505

Literary Criticism
Frederick T. Griffiths · 1515

Greek Historiography and Biography
Stephen Usher · 1525

Roman Historiography and Biography
Ronald Mellor · 1541

The Novel
John J. Winkler · 1563

Letter Writing
Robert Glenn Ussher · 1573

PHILOSOPHY

Greek Philosophy
G. E. R. Lloyd · 1585

Roman Philosophical Movements
Elizabeth Asmis · 1637

THE VISUAL ARTS

Greek Architecture
J. J. Coulton · 1653

Roman Architecture
Roger Ling · 1671

Urban Planning
Thomas D. Boyd · 1691

Greek Sculpture and Gems
Jerome J. Pollitt · 1701

Roman Sculpture and Gems
Richard Brilliant · 1727

CONTENTS

Greek Painting and Mosaic
Jerome J. Pollitt · 1749

Roman Painting and Mosaic
Roger Ling · 1771

Coins
R. A. G. Carson · 1795

EPILOGUE

The Progress of Classical Scholarship
R. R. Bolgar · 1819

Maps · 1833

List of Contributors · 1845

Index · 1851

Chronological Table

ca. 2000–ca. 1400 B.C.	Minoan civilization flourishes in Crete	
ca. 1400–ca. 1200	Mycenaean civilization flourishes on the Greek mainland	
1183	Traditional date for the fall of Troy	
ca. 1200–ca. 1100	Migrations of Northern peoples ("Dorians") into southern Greece	
ca. 1200–ca. 750	The Dark Age in Greece	
ca. 800–ca. 700	Rise of aristocracies in Greece	
ca. Eighth–ca. Fifth Century	Western Mediterranean divided into three major geopolitical parts: Carthaginian, Etruscan, and Greek Southern Italy and Sicily	
776	Traditional date for the founding of the Olympic games	
753	Traditional date for the founding of Rome	
753–510	Monarchy in Rome	
ca. 750–ca. 550	The Archaic period in Greece	
ca. 750	Writing down of Homeric epics in Ionia	Homer (Eighth Century?) Hesiod (Eighth Century)
ca. 750–ca. 550	Period of Greek colonization	
736–716	Revolt of Messenia	
ca. 700	Lelantine War (Euboia)	
669	Sparta defeated by Argos	

CHRONOLOGICAL TABLE

664	War of Independence—Kerkyra vs. Corinth	
ca. 657–627	Kypselos, tyrant in Corinth	
ca. 650–ca. 590	Age of lawgivers in Greece: Drakon (fl. 620) and Solon (fl. 594–592) at Athens	
ca. 650–ca. 550	Tyrant dynasty of Orthagoras in Sikyon	
ca. 640	Theagenes, tyrant in Megara	
ca. 632	Kylon attempts tyranny in Athens	
625–585	Periandros, tyrant in Corinth	Sappho; Alkaios (ca. 600) Greek Lyric Poets
560–510	Peisistratos and sons, tyrants in Athens	Aeschylus (525–456) Pindar (ca. 518–ca. 438)
510	Tarquin the Proud, last Etruscan king, expelled from Rome	
510–31	The Roman Republic	
508/507	Reforms of Kleisthenes in Athens	
ca. 500–323	The Classical period in Greece	
499–479	The Persian Wars	
499	Ionian Revolt	Sophocles (497–406)
490	Battle of Marathon	Herodotus (ca. 484–420)
483	Themistokles persuades Athens to build a navy	
480	Battle of Thermopylae (death of Leonidas, king of Sparta) Battle of Salamis (Xerxes, king of Persia, withdraws)	Euripides (ca. 480–406)
479	Battle of Plateia (death of Mardonius, Persian general)	
478	Delian League (confederacy of Greek cities under Athenian leadership)	
462/461	Ephialtes abolishes privileges of the Areopagus in Athens	
460–429	The Age of Pericles at Athens	Thucydides (ca. 459–399)
451	Five-Year Armistice between Athens and Sparta	
ca. 450	The law of the Twelve Tables published in Rome	
449	Peace of Callias (between Greece and Persia)	

CHRONOLOGICAL TABLE

447	Revolt of Boeotia	
445	Thirty-Years Peace; Athens gives up land empire	Aristophanes (*ca.* 445–385)
		Isocrates (*ca.* 435–338)
431–404	The Peloponnesian War	
431–421	Archidamian War	
ca. 430	Roman and Latin victory over Aequi and Volsci	
		Xenophon (*ca.* 428–*ca.* 355)
		Plato (428–348)
421	Peace of Nicias	
416	Destruction of Melos	
415–413	Sicilian Expedition	
413–404	Decelean War	
ca. 407–396	Rome defeats Etruscan city of Veii and annexes its territory	
404	Athenian defeat at Aigospotamoi by Spartan Lysander	
404/403	"The Thirty Tyrants" at Athens	
404–371	Spartan hegemony of Greece	
399	Execution of Socrates	
387	Gauls invade Rome	
387–386	"The King's Peace": Artaxerxes II, king of Persia, sets the terms of a general peace for Greece	Aristotle (384–322)
		Demosthenes (*ca.* 384–322)
		Theocritus (*ca.* 380–250)
377	Foundation of the second Athenian Empire	
371	Battle of Leuctra: Epameinondas (Thebes) defeats Kleombrotos (Sparta)	
371–362	Theban hegemony of Greece	
362	Battle of Mantinea; death of Epameinondas	
359–336	Philip II of Macedon; rise of Macedonia to foremost power in Greece	Menander (*ca.* 342–*ca.* 291)
340	Rome's expansionist policy results in military domination of entire Italian Peninsula	
338	Victory for Philip II at Chaironeia	
336–323	Alexander (the Great) of Macedon; expansion of Macedonian empire to the East	

xix

CHRONOLOGICAL TABLE

331	Foundation of Alexandria in Egypt	
327–290	Roman wars with Samnites	
323	Battles of the Successors of Alexander for supremacy; establishment of kingdoms of the Antigonids (Macedon), Seleukids (Syria), and Ptolemies (Egypt)	
323–146	The Hellenistic period in Greece	Hellenistic Poetry Callimachus (*ca.* 305–*ca.* 240) Apollonius (*b. ca.* 295)
287	Hortensian law in Rome	
280–275	Pyrrhic War (Roman victory over Pyrrhus, king of Epirus)	
276–239	Antigonos Gonatas re-establishes Macedon as a nation	
264–201	Roman wars with Carthage	
264–241	First Carthaginian ("Punic") War	Plautus (254–184)
238	Rome seizes Sardinia and Corsica	
227	Sicily becomes first tribute-paying province	
225–219	Gauls defeated, annexation of Cisalpine Gaul	
218–201	Second Carthaginian ("Hannibalic") War	
215–205	First Macedonian War (Rome and Macedonia)	
200–196	Second Macedonian War	Polybius (205?–125?)
197	Philip V of Macedon defeated at Kynos Kephalai	
192–188	War with Seleukids (Rome and Seleukids)	
189	Antiochus III, Seleukid king, defeated at Magnesia	
171–167	Third Macedonian War	
149–148	Fourth Macedonian War	Terence (*d.* 159)
149–146	Third Carthaginian War	
146	Roman Destruction of Carthage and Corinth	
146–131	The Late Republic in Rome	
133	Attalos III of Pergamum bequeaths his realm to Rome	
133; 123–122	Tribunates of Tiberius and Gaius Gracchus	
112–105	Victory of Marius over Jugurtha, king of Numidia	Cicero (106–43)

CHRONOLOGICAL TABLE

102–101	Marius defeats Teutones and Cimbri	
		Caesar (100–44)
		Lucretius (94?–50?)
91	Tribune Marcus Livius Drusus the Younger murdered	
90–88	Social War—Rome's allies revolt	
88	Sulla marches on Rome	
88–84	First Mithridatic War	
86	Sack of Athens by Sulla	Sallust (86–35)
		Catullus (84–54)
82–79	Dictatorship of Sulla	
81	Second Mithridatic War	
81–72	Revolt of Sertorius in Spain	
74–63	Third Mithridatic War	
73–71	Slave revolt of Spartacus	
70	Consulship of Pompey and Crassus	Vergil (70 B.C.–A.D. 19)
		Horace (65 B.C.–A.D. 8)
63	Conspiracy led by Catiline; consulship of Cicero	Strabo (64/63 B.C.–A.D. 21)
60	"First Triumvirate," of Pompey, Crassus, and Caesar	
59	Consulship of Caesar	Livy (*ca.* 59 B.C.–*ca.* A.D. 17)
58–50	Caesar's conquest of Gaul	
		Tibullus (54? B.C.–A.D. 18)
53	Crassus defeated and killed by Parthians at Carrhae	
		Propertius (50? B.C.–A.D. 15)
49–45	Civil War. Caesar's victories at Pharsalus (followed by death of Pompey), Thapsus, and Munda	
44	Perpetual dictatorship and assassination of Caesar	
43	Second Triumvirate, of Antony, Octavian, and Lepidus	Ovid (43 B.C.–A.D. 18)
42	Brutus and Cassius defeated at Philippi	
36	Octavian defeats Sextus Pompeius and Lepidus	
31	Antony and Cleopatra defeated at Actium	
31 B.C.–A.D. 284	The Roman Empire: The Principate	
31 B.C.–A.D. 68	The Julio–Claudian Dynasty	
27	Octavian receives the title Augustus	

CHRONOLOGICAL TABLE

27 B.C.–A.D. 14	Reign of Augustus	
		Seneca the Younger (4? B.C.–A.D. 65)
A.D. 14–A.D. 37	Tiberius	
		Pliny the Elder (23/24–79)
31	Execution of Sejanus	
		Persius (34–62)
37–41	Gaius (Caligula)	Josephus (ca. 37–ca. 100)
		Martial (ca. 38–ca. 104)
		Lucan (39–65)
		Quintilian (ca. 40–ca. 96)
		Plutarch (ca. 40–ca. 120)
41–54	Claudius	
		Statius (45?–96?)
		Epictetus (ca. 50–ca. 120)
54–68	Nero	
		Tacitus (ca. 55–after 117)
		Juvenal (60?–140?)
		Pliny the Younger (ca. 61–ca. 112)
66	Outbreak of Jewish Revolt	Petronius (d. 66)
69	Civil War: "Year of the Four Emperors"—Galba, Otho, Vitellius, and Vespasian	Suetonius (ca. 69–after 122)
		Longinus (fl. First Century)
69–96	The Flavian Dynasty	
69–79	Vespasian	
79–81	Titus	
79	Eruption of Vesuvius	
81–96	Domitian	
96–180	"The Five Good Emperors"	
96–98	Nerva	
98–117	Trajan	
101–102, 105–106	Dacian Wars, annexation of Dacia	
113–117	Trajan's campaigns in the East	
ca. 117	Jews of the Dispersion in revolt in Egypt and North Africa	
117–138	Hadrian	
		Lucian (ca. 120–after 180)
		Apuleius (b. ca. 120)
		Marcus Aurelius (121–180)
		Galen (129–199)

CHRONOLOGICAL TABLE

132–135	Jewish revolt; Jerusalem becomes a Roman colony	
138–161	Antoninus Pius	
161–180	Marcus Aurelius; Lucius Verus (*d.* 169)	Tertullian (*ca.* 160–*ca.* 240)
162–166	Parthian War (Lucius Verus)	
170–174	War with Marcomanni and Quadi	
175	War with Sarmatians	
180–192	Commodus	Origen (*ca.* 185–*ca.* 255)
193–197	Civil War	
193	Pertinax; Didius Julianus	
193–235	Severan Dynasty	
193–211	Septimius Severus (Julia Domna, wife of Septimius, *d.* 217)	Cyprian (*ca.* 200–258) Plotinus (*ca.* 205–270)
211–217	Caracalla and Geta (*d.* 211 or 212)	
212	Edict of Caracalla, conferring general citizenship	
217–218	Macrinus	
218–222	Elagabulus (Julia Maesa, sister of Julia Domna, *d.* 222)	
222–235	Severus Alexander, Rule of Julia Mamaea (daughter of Julia Maesa)	
ca. 227	Rebirth of Persian Empire under Sasanians; overthrow of Parthians	
235–284	The "Barracks" Emperors	
235–238	Maximius I Thrax	
250–251	Decius	
257–260	Valerian	
267	Herulian sack of Greece	
270	Dacia abandoned	
270–275	Aurelian	
284–	The Roman Empire: The Dominate	
284–305	Diocletian	
286	Maximian appointed coemperor	
293	Constantius I (*d.* 306) and Galerius Maximianus (*d.* 311) appointed Caesars	
301	Edict on Prices	
303–311	Persecution of Christians	
312–337	Constantine the Great and Licinius (*d.* 324)	

CHRONOLOGICAL TABLE

312	Constantine's victory in the battle of the Mulvian Bridge	
313	Edict of Mediolanum, granting tolerance to Christianity	
324–330	Foundation of Constantinople	
325	Council of Nicaea	
		Ammianus Marcellinus (*ca.* 330–*ca.* 395)
337	Accessions of Constantine II (*d.* 340), Constans (*d.* 350), and Constantius II (*d.* 361)	
353–361	Constantius II rules as sole emperor	
361–363	Julian the Apostate	
363–364	Jovian	
364–375	Valentinian I	
364–378	Valens, coemperor in the East	
375–383	Gratian, emperor in the West	
375–392	Valentinian II, emperor in the West	
378	Battle of Hadrianopolis	
379–395	Theodosius I, emperor in the East	
395	Sack of Greece by Alaric, king of the Visigoths	
395–423	Flavius Honorius, emperor in the West	
395–408	Flavius Arcadius, emperor in the East	
395–408	Stilicho, commander in chief in the West	
410	Sack of Rome by Alaric	
425–455	Valentinian III	
428–477	Gaiseric, king of the Vandals	
432–454	Aetius, commander in chief in the West	
439	Capture of Carthage by Gaiseric	
451	Defeat of Attila and the Huns at the Catalaunian Plains	
454–472	Ricimer, commander of rapid succession of emperors	
475–476	Romulus Augustulus, last emperor of Rome	
476–493	Odoacer (Herulian), king of Italy	
493–526	Theodoric establishes independent Ostrogothic kingdom in Italy	
529	Justinian (Byzantine emperor, 527–565) orders closing of the pagan philosophic schools	

Introduction

PEOPLE SOMETIMES TALK of the decline of the Greek and Roman classics in popular esteem, and it is true that some of the more technical aspects of this field of study are nowadays receiving less widespread attention than previously. Yet it is not necessarily the rival claims of altogether different disciplines that have reduced their prevalence but rather a demand—and, in our experience, it is a persistent one—for broader and more comprehensive views of the classical world itself. Certainly admirable general surveys of the ancient Mediterranean peoples exist. But we came to the conclusion that the public and private lives and achievements of these peoples deserved closer examination and a wider-ranging treatment than has, in most other such books, been accorded to them. That is one of the principal reasons for the present project: not excluding, but not limited to, technical aspects of the subject matter, it aims at offering an extensive range of general topics, discussed in some detail.

The eighty-eight contributors have written ninety-seven essays on the geography of the area, the physical appearance of its inhabitants, their politics and religions, their languages, arts, and technologies, their social and economic activities, and their personal lives. At the beginning, historical summaries offer a chronological survey of the period, which extends from the early first millennium B.C. to the late fifth century A.D. Thereafter the essays are organized topically in order to bring together, within each of them, information which would be scattered in various parts of a work written soley along chronological lines. The challenge the contributors have had to meet is twofold. They have had to strike an effective balance between concrete facts and notable ideas; and they have also had to strike a balance between individual phenomena and the more sweeping movements and changes that characterize the successive ancient epochs.

INTRODUCTION

This Mediterranean world is so varied and exciting that it deserves to receive attention in its own right, without any thought for the debts that we ourselves may owe to it. Nevertheless it is difficult for us to keep those debts and legacies out of our minds for very long. In the eighteenth century Samuel Johnson observed that "all our religion, almost all our law, almost all our arts, almost all that sets us above savages, has come to us from the shores of the Mediterranean." True, so forthright a pronouncement may seem to need a measure of qualification today, when we are better informed about other early cultures and more conscientiously ecumenical. Therefore, while focusing on the Greeks (of post–Mycenaean times) and the Romans, these essays also seek to place the two civilizations in the context of others that influenced, and were influenced by, them.

We cannot, nevertheless, resist the conclusion that Dr. Johnson was to some extent right. As we read the essays in these volumes, the many significant continuities, as well as the differences, between the ancient and modern worlds became fully apparent. And we shall ignore Dr. Johnson's assessment only at our own cost, since we would then fail to understand where so much of our background lies and, in consequence, we would be ignorant of what we ourselves are. However, it is not only the achievements of the ancient world that need our attention, but also its flaws: the unevennesses, failures, and intolerances that eventually brought it to an end. While criticisms in hindsight of earlier civilizations can easily show our own insufficient understanding of the circumstances and problems that beset them at the time, the shortcomings of the Greeks and Romans, from whom we have taken so many of our fundamental assumptions, cannot fail to cast light on the threats to our own survival.

We are pleased and grateful to have been able to engage the services of authors of such learning and variety. Their qualities, in themselves, contradict the decline of the classics. For we believe that anyone who reads these three volumes will be struck by the vitality of classical scholarship in the twentieth century and by the skill with which its practitioners handle material that, although tantalizingly uneven, is of ever increasing dimensions. Nonspecialists—and it is for them, as well as for specialists, that this work is intended—often express surprise at the rapidity of this increase, and of the massive researches that accompany it, considering that we are dealing with epochs of the distant past. But the abundance of such modern progress, from year to year, is confirmed by the studies that follow. Inevitably some subjects have received less attention than others, owing to the lack of either information or of available experts. Yet in approximate terms these essays can be said to present, and represent, the state of the classics in the mid 1980s. (Indeed, more facts and theories have continued to come to light since preparation began; that regrettably, yet understandably, could not be incorporated in the present work.)

The evidence in question, despite its limits, is remarkably varied, and so, it will be seen here, are the possible approaches to its interpretation. For this reason some of the essays will seem to overlap and contain

INTRODUCTION

material repeated elsewhere in the work. Such repetitions have been retained, since each piece is designed to stand on its own, as well as to add to the picture created by the whole. By the same token, we have not sought to eliminate contradictions and differences of opinion between authors, since it has seemed desirable to show not only the complex character of the material with which scholars have to deal but also the range of opinion and of methodology they employ to interpret it. To help guide the reader through what may be unfamiliar territory, we have included ancient place names on a series of maps at the end of the third volume. Within the text, ancient names are followed in parentheses by their modern equivalents, if they exist. The volumes also contain over 175 photographs and line drawings to illustrate the essays for which visual materials are particularly helpful. One unavoidable aspect of preparing a work so extensive in scope is the variant spellings of ancient names. The authors have used either Greek, Roman, or anglicized forms depending upon which scholarly convention they follow. While this means that consistency of spelling has not been forced on the essays, the reader will find the variant forms listed and cross-referenced in the index; page references follow the spelling that is most frequently used.

Our gratitude to the contributors for what they have written we have already expressed. But we should also like to note that many of them offered additional guidance and advice. We also want to acknowledge assistance from a number of others: Glen Bowerstock, Averil Cameron, David Cohen, Peter Connolly, J. A. Crook, A. M. Davies, Sir Kenneth Dover, Peter Green, Donald Lateiner, Eleanor Leach, J.H.W.G. Liebesschuetz, J. R. McCredie, Herwig Maehler, W. Meeks, Martin Oswald, J. M. Rist, C. M. Robertson, Judith Swaddling, Oliver Taplin, and D. A. West.

We greatly appreciate the help we have received from Charles Scribner's Sons. This work, like *Ancient Writers: Greece and Rome,* was the invention of Charles Scribner, Jr., and he and Jacques Barzun have contributed much invigorating encouragement. Our best thanks go to Michael McGinley, director of the Reference Books Division, and the managing editor, Beth Ann McCabe, who have patiently and effectively seen the project through the press. We have also welcomed the collaboration of Ana Abraldes, Abigail Bok, Marshall De Bruhl, Elizabeth Elston, Laura Gross, Kirk Reynolds, Debbie Taylor, and David Voorhees.

MICHAEL GRANT
RACHEL KITZINGER

Civilization of the Ancient Mediterranean

GREECE AND ROME

HISTORY

Historical Summary of Greece

A. R. BURN

ORIGINS, DARK AGES, AND MIGRATIONS

Thucydides believed that the Greek world he knew had emerged from an age of migrations, after which peace and economic progress were slow to come. People had accounts, going back to oral tradition before Greece had the alphabet, of where their ancestors had come from, but there was little about the older, palace-centered, Bronze Age civilization, except for epic accounts of the great Trojan and Theban wars. In the *Iliad* (perhaps eighth century B.C.) there is a catalog of ships, a list of contingents and their leaders, which shows a "map" of Greece quite different from that of historic times but closely resembling that of Mycenaean Greece as revealed by archaeology. Mycenae is the seat of the high king; Pylos, the very site of which was unknown to classical Greeks, and an apparently unified Crete are important; Athens, not very. Rhodes, Kos, and other Dodecanesian islands send smaller contingents, as does Euboia (Evvia). The Cyclades are not mentioned; Lesbos is attacked during the war; Cyprus sends Agamemnon a famous breastplate, but no troops. Asia Minor is entirely non-Greek and sends contingents to aid Troy.

Homer's genius and his "background" will be discussed more fully in the essay EPIC POETRY; but some features of his work must be mentioned here, as significant for the whole character of the then-new Hellenic civilization. Not only does Homer write (or sing) of a time when there were no Greeks in Asia, and of kings and palaces that no longer exist; he assumes (they were there, part of the furniture) the existence of gods, whom he then uses for comic relief—they fight or cheat each other, or act malevolently. Men try to end the war by a duel between Helen's husband and her lover; but Hera and Athena upset the plan in order to see Troy destroyed—because, it was said, they had lost a beauty contest. Homer's attitude is as irreverent as that of Elijah when he suggests that if Baal does not answer a call, he may be out hunting or having a siesta. But, partly because of Homer's genius, his was the picture of divinity that survived into classical times, to the distress of serious thinkers, and thus it left a field open for rationalist speculation. The fact is that these are Bronze Age gods, made in the image of chariot-driving kings, and although they had failed their worshipers in need, they survived, through the epic, into an age to which they did not belong.

At the same time, Homer's heroes may strike us, as they struck our recent ancestors, as not being "primitive." Truly, they are not. They are not even tribal. They fight for their own glory and for loot; the only men who fight for hearth and home in the *Iliad* are the doomed Trojans. But Achilles, who trades length of life for a glorious reputation, was admired, and not only by fools. Socrates himself is said to have cited his example in not prolonging life at any cost. Homer was indeed a "Bible of the Greeks," if a strange one to our eyes. The Greeks, as Homer starts them off in the first words that we have from them, are not "primitive" (whatever that means) but displaced, detribalized, individualistic, potentially progressive. A whole civilization had lived and perished to produce Homer.

The transformation of Homer's map into that of early historic Greece, nearly complete by 1000 B.C., is the result of the migrations "after the Trojan War," briefly described by Thucydides. Recent archaeologists have devoted much labor to the study of the Dark Age, that of Thucydides' migrations; and in general the considerable light that has been shed supports him, though his view that "the Dorians with the children of Herakles took the Peloponnese eighty years after the Trojan War" at best telescopes into one episode what was certainly a long series of events. There are signs of movement, burning or desertion of settlements, reoccupation apparently by different people, dating from around 1200—when the Hittite Empire in Asia Minor fell, and a great fleet of "sea peoples" threatened Egypt—till after 1100, the general direction of movement being from northwest to southeast.

Only the famous Dorians, absent from Homer but so important in historic times, leave no archaeological trace until much later, when things have settled down. This has caused some scholars to doubt whether there was any Dorian invasion, as accepted by later Greek writers, at all.

There is no convenient evidence, that is to say, of newcomers using pottery (the archaeologist's standby) with northern antecedents. Was the Doric dialect, it has been asked, simply "lower-class" Mycenaean? Was it the proletariat who burned the palaces?

There seems to be no need for this hypothesis. The Dorian cities that in historic times dominated the Peloponnese, except for its center and northwest quarter, and the south Aegean as far as Rhodes, were distinguished not only by dialect but, wherever there is evidence, by the articulation of the people into the same three *phylai* (internal tribes): Hylleis, Dymanes, and Pamphyloi. Sometimes there are additional tribes (to take in "adopted" natives, perhaps), but these differ from city to city. It seems more likely that such tribes existed within a unified *ethnos* or "nation" before it became geographically divided, than—uniformly in all cities—among a Mycenaean proletariat. As to the absence of proto-Dorian pottery, it is important to consider where these people came from (according to the early Spartans, the Pindos Mountains, where a small Doris survived) and what their way of life would have been, if so.

Undoubtedly, they would have been transhumant pastoralists, as in many mountain regions, driving their sheep and cattle up to high alps for pasture in summer and down to the plains in winter. Thus the shepherd tribes of the Pindos, the Vlachs and Sarakatsanoi, live to the present day, reconditioning their round huts in the familiar places at the end of each half-yearly migration. Such a life does not encourage the accumulation of heavy or bulky chattels, and especially not of pottery, which is also breakable. The dwellers in the mountain forests—and even in 1930 these were more extensive than now—made much use of wood for barrels. Skins can hold water or wine, and wooden cups are still used. Thus, though parts of the southern Peloponnese seem to have been uninhabited in sub-Mycenaean times (the transitional epoch after the end of what is generally known as the Mycenaean period), this conclusion does not necessarily follow from the absence of remains. As to weapons and metal adornments, "northwestern bronzes," with affinities in Epeiros and Albania, do occur already in late-Mycenaean contexts, perhaps brought by mercenary soldiers. They also occur out of context, but then they are undatable. Long dress pins, with slight bulges to prevent slipping through—indicating a new and looser type of dress—are found on the shoulders of Dark Age women in burials and survive to classical times. The negative evidence for depopulation of parts of the Peloponnese is therefore insufficient.

Such a mountain pastoral people is, moreover, not incapable of having a national consciousness. Different groups meet in summer at regular resorts on mountain passes, which may give rise to permanent trading settlements, like modern Vlach Metsovor in the Pindos Mountains. They could, if they wished, raise an army for a major migration, and it is not impossible that exiled Mycenaean princes, the Herakleids (children of Herakles) of legend (in whom Thucydides believed), may have resorted to them for aid. It is not impossible that the "Return of the Herakleids" was an important episode in a long and confused migration period. They are said to have been beaten off in a first attempt to return, during which Hyllos, the son of Herakles, was killed, and then to have stayed in the north for three generations. In the army or invading horde of the Return it is not surprising to find Hylleis, the Herakleids and their retainers; Dymanes, with their northwestern tribal name, perhaps the backbone of the horde; and Pamphyloi, a "mixed multitude" of groups, families, and individuals, accepted as recruits for the expedition and only then acquiring a common name.

They came from the northwest, where north–south movement is easiest. An allied people from Aitolia stayed in the fertile land of Walis (the vale), as they called it; in Athenian classical Greek it becomes Elis. Here, in beautiful foothill country below the Arcadian Mountains, they took over a well-watered sanctuary originally of the mother goddess and named it Olympia, after Olympos, the mountain home of their gods in the north. Legend said that they came with the Herakleids, guided them, and were thus rewarded. Perhaps it is more likely that they came in afterward. Their language was like northwest Greek, though without some features of the dialects of the Dorians, the "men of Doris," who stayed together longer. The "Dorians with the children of Herakles" bypassed Arcadia, where there were only other mountain pastoralists, speaking a more "Mycenaean" type of Greek but offering only hard knocks and little loot. They went for the palaces. Pylos fell first—perhaps earlier than the usual archaeological date of about 1200 B.C., for its Mycenaean written tablets, preserved by hard baking in the fierce fire, resemble very closely those from Knossos in Crete, burned earlier still. Mycenae itself, the last major citadel to fall, may have held out until about 1100.

Meanwhile there are constant signs of population movement—mostly eastward, though also out to the western isles—and even northward: a migration of late Mycenaeans from threatened Argolis to the narrow strip of coast between the Corinthian Gulf and high mountains, which continued to bear the name of Achaia. People went to any place that offered refuge from the main thrust from the northwest, sometimes for a generation, sometimes for less. A story known to an Ionian poet, Mimnermos of Kolophon, before 600 B.C. (and thus respectably early) has it that refugee lords of Pylos fled to Athens, and such was the prestige of the family of Nestor that they were accepted into its aristocracy and even married into its royal family. In Attica, northwestern elements occupied parts of the west and the island of Salamis (Koulouri). Thucydides (2.15.1) believed a story that men of Eleusis fought with Eumolpos (later counted as a sea raider) against the early king Erechtheus of Athens; and archaeology shows a local movement toward the east coast, such as the considerable late-Mycenaean site of Perati in Attica.

In the islands, notably on Naxos and Kos, several Dark Age sites show settlements of people, populations trying to keep up old ways of life but not lasting more than a generation or two, and finally, though archaeology has provided dates at only a few places, Greeks occupy many points on the east coast of the Aegean.

Nowhere on all the Greek mainland, except at Athens, can continuity of occupation be traced. "Only after a long time," says Thucydides (1.12.4), "did Greece settle down firmly and, instead of migrations, send out colonies. The Athenians colonized Ionia and most of the islands, and Peloponnesians did most of the colonizing in Italy and Sicily, along with some other places in Greece."

The difference between a migration and a Greek colony is that in the latter case the mother city continued to be occupied and gained, at least in prestige and economically through a limited amount of trade, though seldom exercising any political overlordship. Very likely many eastward expeditions did set out from Athens. Mimnermos is proud of his Pylian ancestry. But Thucydides here probably exaggerates through patriotic pride. In his time Athens exercised overlordship over nearly all the Aegean coasts and islands, and her imperialism (an offense to Greek ideas of freedom at the city-state level) could be justified if she could claim to be not only mistress of Ionia and the Cyclades, but also their mother city. Herodotus, himself a Greek of Asia Minor, from the Dorian city of Halicarnassus in the south, knew some local traditions that made the Ionian migration much less "tidy." Even Miletos, he said, which claimed in Athens' greatest age to be a real colony, bringing its official sacred hearth fire from Athens' own town hall, was founded by a band of men who took for wives native women whose menfolk they had killed. There were also settlers from many other places in the old country; the important island of Samos, for instance, drew some from Epidaurus in the Argive peninsula who were fleeing the Dorians.

North of Ionia proper, the coast and the island of Lesbos were settled from northern Greece, where Iolkos (Volos), legendary base for the quest of the Golden Fleece, had the northernmost Mycenaean-style palace known to us. It was burned about 1150, perhaps when the Thessalians of historic times came from farther northwest and drove other peoples before them into central Greece. The town of Iolkos suffered too, but much less severely. In Asia the Aiolians, as they were called, occupied Smyrna (İzmir); but at some date before recorded history begins, it was taken from them by Ionians under leaders of Pylian descent (Mimnermos tells us) coming from the large settlement of Kolophon.

In such violent and disorderly ways the new map of Greece, bestriding the Aegean, replaced the Mycenaean. In old Greece the last episode is said to have been an attempt by the Peloponnesian Dorians to take Athens, possibly about 1065. It failed but did succeed in winning the northern, broader part of the isthmus. Here the Dorians founded the "city" of Megara (big houses), one of the few Greek cities to bear a Greek name, which attests its newness.

The eleventh century saw the deepest impoverishment of the Dark Age, but also the first signs of recovery. In Argolis, while Mycenae and Tiryns lay waste, some population remained in Argos. Scattered small cemeteries and house remains suggest hamlets, where agriculture and even some bronze-working or reworking continued, along with some professional potters. Dorian chiefs may have been glad to have native peasants to work for them. When the hamlets later drew together to found a city called Larissa (another pre-Greek name) below the citadel, the state of Argos included a fourth tribe, presumably for the pre-Dorians. Pottery, as at Athens, is sub-Mycenaean, a feeble continuation of old styles; but then, perhaps by 1050, and perhaps first at Athens, there is a cultural revolution.

THE RECOVERY PERIOD

Almost overnight, as it looks to us with only archaeological evidence, a new style of pottery and its decoration appears: the Protogeometric. The shapes, simple and pleasing, the painted decoration, also of the simplest—broad and narrow dark bands, often suspending rows of concentric semicircles—will be discussed in detail in the essay GREEK PAINTING AND MOSAIC; but significant for social history is the new confidence suggested by the break with nostalgia for an irrecoverable past. These people did not paint as if they were aware of decadence and ashamed of it, and perhaps this is also a sign that they were confident that they could hold their walls: they were no longer afraid that tomorrow, or next year, they might have to flee from northern invaders. Surprising, too, and still unexplained, is the speed with which the new style spread. V. R. Desborough, who first studied Protogeometric pottery in depth, was sure that it arose first in Athens; but in the thirty years since he wrote, so much of it has been found elsewhere, from Argos to renascent Iolkos, that while Athens still seems most probable, one cannot be dogmatic. Most remarkably, it appears across the Aegean at Smyrna (İzmir), Miletos, and other places, hardly later than 1000, providing evidence that Thucydides was wrong if he meant to suggest that these "Athenian colonies" were not much older than the true colonies in the west.

In the southern Peloponnese, recovery from the lapse into pastoralism was slow. At Sparta, the British excavations before 1914 could find nothing of note before about 950 B.C.; in Messenia, much more recently, the Minnesota-Messenia expedition, after diligent search for a representative Dark Age site, selected one at Nichoria in the southwest. Of old a prosperous township in the kingdom of Pylos, it may have been abandoned after the sack of the palace; and though Protogeometric pottery is found, along with some quite solid stone-built, apsidal-ended buildings, the general effect is crude. The Aegean area is the scene of the first-dawning "renaissance."

On the island Euboia, the British School conducted a similar search for a good Dark Age site in 1966 and was blessed by better fortune. On the ridge of Xeropolis, facing the mainland, between classical Chalkis and Eretria and near the modern village of Lefkandi, there had been, after long prehistoric occupation, a late Mycenaean settlement, perhaps one of those made when attempts to maintain the old ways were moving east. It, like all the others, was abandoned, probably after 1100, but not for long. Cemeteries of individual cist graves nearby show people living in the neighborhood who used first sub-Mycenaean pottery and then Protogeometric, not of the very earliest type. It is impossible to say whether they came from Attica.

What was, in any case, astonishing about the new settlement of Lefkandi itself was its precocity and opulence, unparalleled in tenth-century Greece except in Cyprus, where the palace culture and a pre-Dorian dialect like that of Arcadia survived amid successive Greek immigrations. (In fact, Lefkandi and, for a short time, Athens seem to have remained in touch or regained touch with Cyprus.) The richest burials at Lefkandi even contain some gold jewelry, and excavators have found the buried walls, standing to some height, of a long, apsidal-ended building that is the finest of its age known in Greece. During a religious holiday, it was removed by a bulldozer hired by the local landowner, to whom archaeology represented a menace to his plans for development. He was punished for destroying part of the national heritage—and proved to have done some of the archaeologists' work for them; for immediately under the structure was found the now-famous burial of a prince, still prehistoric, still nameless to us (for ancient legends of Euboia are not preserved), known as the Hero of Lefkandi. The bones of a warrior, wrapped in cloth, lay in a bronze amphora with a shallow bronze cup for lid; preservation was so good that even the weave of the cloth can be studied. It is a curious, body-length gown with a head opening but no sleeves (possibly meant for a shroud, but not so used). Beside the amphora lay a spear and sword of iron. Ironworking was, about then, appearing also at Athens, probably introduced from Cyprus and Euboia. On the other side of the chamber lay the skeleton of a young woman with large gold discs forming the front of her brassiere, gilt hair coils, and large dress pins, some of them also gilt. In an adjacent pit were the bones of four horses. It is the richest grave known since the fall of the palaces.

For a time Euboian traders were penetrating the Levant, with Cyprus their farthest certain goal. The wide distribution of Euboian pottery in the Aegean shows a certain prestige. The prevailing style, with its concentric, pendent semicircles drawn with a multiple brush and geometrically neat, was adopted in the Cyclades in Andros, Tenos, and Delos as well as in Skyros farther north; the fact that it remains standard in Euboia for 200 years may also suggest a society well satisfied with itself.

As to how the cities (Eretria, perhaps still centered at Lefkandi, and Chalkis, where the remains are buried under the modern town) were governed, we have no datable evidence. For that, we must turn to Athens, where its subsequent eminence led to the preservation of a later, antiquarian account of a process widespread in Greece: the change from "Homeric" monarchy to aristocratic republics. Probably monarchy was doomed by the end of migrations and large-scale raiding, when local kings could no longer afford to keep up the personal war bands of "companions" that gave them dominance over the other chief families. Aristotle's *Constitution of Athens* says that the process began when, under a king who was no great warrior, the nobles appointed Ion, an immigrant hero, to command the army. The story, introduced to account for Athens' later claim to be the mother city of the Ionians, remains suspect since there was no Ion named among the mythical kings. However, later tradition went on to say that next (the king having lost control of the army) the nobles appointed an archon (a participle that might be translated "regent") over the king for civil affairs; and this is certainly historical, for archon was still the title of the chief magistrate under the later democracy, when he held office for a year. The year was named after him, and for convenient dating a list was kept. The title of king was also kept for an annual official who conducted the chief yearly sacrifices on the festival days of various gods, on behalf of the people. The gods, it was felt, were used to worship conducted by a king. This official also presided over trials of those accused of offenses against the gods (so Socrates, for his free-thinking, was to appear before a king); these offenses included murder, for the presence of an unpunished homicide brought pollution upon the people, and in turn, as in the story of Oedipus, pestilence. The war chief ranked third—striking evidence that Athens, even so early, considered the headship of state to be a civil affair.

Athenians were always litigious. After 683 B.C., when the written list of annual archons began, there were also six judges, *thesmothetai* (layers-down of the law), who were needed with the growth of population. All nine magistrates were then known as the Nine Archons.

The archons were the judiciary and the executive. (Even the war chief presided over a court in cases involving a foreigner.) But high policy, later the affair of the whole people *(demos)*, was in early times that of a council of the "best people," which met west of the Acropolis on or perhaps just below (which would be less windy) the rock of the war god—in the more familiar Latin, Areopagus. Its members, as in many early Greek republics, were those of a defined list of families, called at Athens Eupatridai (patricians). Some of these early councils, like a later House of Peers, admitted heads of families only, an arrangement that Plutarch, under the Roman Empire, thought extraordinary.

It was also necessary at times for the "best people" to call a town meeting, if only to tell the commons what the lords had decided. Since they made up the army, the commons could not be totally ignored, though the rich, who had armor and the best weapons, were the most important part of it; and if one may judge from the meeting of the army in Homer's *Iliad,* a commoner who raised objections was knocked down at once. In the *Iliad,* the only serious discussions take place separately among the chiefs. At Athens, the aristocratic council (the exact selection process is not known) appointed as successive archons "the best and richest." Aristocratic oligarchy was for a long time naked, unashamed—and taken for granted.

The basis of wealth was land; wealth in precious metals, weapons, and utensils, as revealed to us in grave goods, first at Lefkandi and later at Athens, was slow to accumulate. As A. M. Snodgrass has put it, the percentage of the gross national product that came from agriculture was and remained, even in classical Athens, overwhelming. Industrial workers were only a few skilled craftsmen, especially smiths; on the farms, most people did most things (shoemaking, for instance, as in the *Odyssey*) for themselves. In the circumstances, foreign trade cannot have occupied a high proportion of the population either, even in cities that, like those of central Euboia, passed for commercial. Writers in modern times, with modern industry and commerce in mind, have sometimes forgotten this and given a picture of classical society and its social classes that is far too "modern." Nevertheless, foreign trade, even on a small scale, was very important for the development of Greece; for, like a small root cracking a rock, it cracked open the conservative, defensive-minded, illiterate societies that had consolidated an order, of a sort, in the early Iron Age.

Oriental art, not least the commercial goods of Phoenicia, formed one influence that awoke people in "geometric" Greece to the fact that there existed a wider world and more opulent cultures, though a century passed between the appearance of the trade goods in graves in Crete or Euboia and the decisive moment—or rather, generation—when the more progressive cities seem almost suddenly to have decided that the art of their grandfathers was dull. But the most far-reaching result of quickened contact with the Levant was the introduction of the alphabet.

The syllabic writing of the Bronze Age palaces had been used for keeping palace accounts, not least for keeping a record of raw materials issued to workers for return as finished products. Linear B had some 200 signs. Written by professional scribes, no doubt despised by the kings and resented by the workers, it was an instrument of bureaucratic exploitation, and there is no reason to think that it was ever used for literature. But in the Levant, when the first great empires had passed their acme and the Phoenicians alone were still providing the east with metals, the advantages of being able to read and write for oneself became more widely felt, and this demand produced a supply of easier scripts. The Phoenicians produced the best, with only 22 letters, though it bore the mark of its descent from syllabic writing in its shortage of pure vowels; it was this script that Greece adopted, with many local variations (see also the essay ALPHABETS AND WRITING). Only the Greeks of Cyprus, local rivals of the Phoenicians, refused to be beholden to them for anything important and went on using a simplified version of Linear B, reducing its 200 signs to about 40.

Israel and Syria had their chronicles and written poetry before Greece had the alphabet. Where and when the great borrowing was first made, we do not know; but it was certainly before 750 B.C. and most probably somewhere in the Levant, though we cannot exclude the possibility that Phoenicians brought the alphabet to Crete along with their decorated metalwork. A likely enough place is Al-Mina (its ancient name unknown) at the mouth of the Orontes River (Nahr al-Asi) where Greeks had traded and built warehouses since the ninth century, presumably under the protection of the local Syrian king. The pottery that they brought (for their own use—the trade was in less durable goods, perhaps metal for textiles and luxury objects) gives the approximate date and also shows that prominent among the first Greeks here were Euboians.

Writing spread fast in Greece and was soon being used for more than commercial purposes. Scratches on pottery include frivolous verses; numerous whole alphabets, or fragments of them, seem to show people in the act of learning; and probably about 750 B.C. comes a major event: the writing down, in Ionia, of the Homeric epics. The refugee migrants had carried with them, we presume, ballads of heroic events in the "good old days" of the Mycenaean world, a part of their heritage that weighed nothing in the baggage; in Asia Minor they continued to sing and develop them, changing some of the customs of daily life, such as burial rites, into those familiar in their own days. But some details were faithfully kept as they had always been: no Greeks in Asia Minor, no Dorians anywhere, except in Crete by a probably late "accident," no iron weapons. This last was facilitated by the fact that the word for iron was longer than that for bronze and would not have fitted in the verse. In addition, the *Iliad*'s list of the contingents at Troy, described above, fits the Mycenaean "map" so well as to suggest that it may actually have come down from Mycenaean times. That the epic material came in the mid eighth century into the hands of a poet of genius (perhaps more than one; but classical Greeks spoke of only one Homer) is an early installment of the "Greek miracle."

By about 700, poets were writing sequels and a chronicle prelude to Homer's epic episode of the great war; and, more significant for the evolution of the Greek world, Hesiod in Boeotia was using the epic dialect and meter for an entirely different purpose in his didactic poems on farming and on the "genesis of the gods." Hesiod too is a phenomenon in social history, the first European who speaks to us about himself in his own written words. He is a middle-class farmer, owning a plow ox and a slave or two, and employing a hired man seasonally; he is not afraid to accuse the local chiefs (called "kings") of taking bribes in a land dispute—and his poem survived! In a remarkable display of economic individualism he speaks of "buying another man's farm, not he buying yours" as a reward for good farming. He is not even of a family that has been "always" in the area; his father was a retromigrant, who had been a sea trader of Kyme in Aiolis, north of Ionia, but had failed in this and returned to farm (perhaps clearing a patch of wasteland) in a valley head under Mount Helikon. His knowledge of the newly explored west, such as his mention of a mythical "King Latinos" of the Tyrrhenians (Etruscans) remains vague, but the connection with Kyme is significant of new developments, which were to transform the Greek world.

THE EXPANSION OF GREECE

Kyme was on the coast of a major native kingdom: Phrygia, whose king, Midas, also crossed swords with Assyrian armies in the Taurus Mountains. A King Agamemnon of Kyme is mentioned, whose daughter married a Midas; also a Greek named Midakritos (Approved of Midas), as "the first to bring back tin from a Tin Island" somewhere in the west. Kyme went into partnership with the merchants of Euboia, now embarking on western voyages; and together, about 750, Chalkis, Eretria, and Kyme carried out an epochmaking enterprise: creating the first Greek colony in the west, founded as an advanced base for the metal trade. It was counted a Euboian colony, but Kyme enjoyed the honor, like important secondary partners in some later colonies, of bestowing its name (later famous in Latin as the "Cumae" of Vergil).

Even Cumae was not quite the first venture. A generation earlier, Euboians had made a small but active settlement on an island nearby (north of the Bay of Naples): Ischia, which they called Pithekousai (either, as it was said, from *pithekos,* "monkey"—though no monkey bones have been found there—or from *pithos,* "jar," owing to its potteries). Here they traded with the Etruscans, not yet hostile, and worked iron, probably from the island of Aithalia (Latin Ilva, modern Elba). A few Phoenicians even lived among them, which would have been impossible later. Writing was common and, most dramatic in this remote outpost, included the oldest extant manuscript of Greek verse: three lines on a cup, inscribed by the owner in a bold, confident hand; an iambic line and two hexameters, cheerfully convivial, but including an allusion to Nestor's cup described in the *Iliad.*

Ischia was, in the end, deserted on account of volcanic phenomena, not uncommon around the bay; the people moved over to Cumae. But before that, much had happened.

With the growth of population in Greece, many farms had been subdivided among sons until they were no longer viable, or barely so, and there were many poor men dependent on paid labor and liable to be laid off, like Hesiod's hired man, when the harvest was in. The situation was made worse by the fact that the best land around the cities was held by aristocrats, who might even have enough to pasture a horse. There was discontent among the poor, and a myth grew up that once the land had been fairly divided and that it was time to do so again.

To avert this, the landowner governments were prepared to take trouble; and reports of the good coastal plains that the western traders had seen, followed by the foundation of Cumae, suggested a way out. Land overseas could be found for all who were prepared to go. This situation must account for the fact that in the next fifty years there was an outpouring of colonies, of a quite different kind, to the west. They did not go as far as Cumae, though in that direction. Land, not trade, was what they sought.

The experience of the Euboians was found useful, and Chalkis became the mother city of more colonies than her population can have needed, or supplied. The name of Naxos, the first Greek colony in Sicily (ca. 735), suggests that the island of Naxos provided a contingent, though no extant source says so. It had a constricted position, below later Taormina; but from this "beachhead," after a few years, the founder Theocles, no doubt heavily reinforced, moved out to take the fertile plain of the Anapos, south of Etna: first Leontinoi, at the inland end of the plain, and only after it the port of Katane (Catania). Rhegion (Reggio di Calabria) on the "toe" of Italy may have been earlier than Naxos. Messana, at first called Zankle (sickle) from the shape of its bay, was irregularly occupied by pirates until Chalkis and Cumae reduced it to order.

The Achaians, cramped in their narrow land on the Corinthian Gulf, colonized most of the south coast of Italy with what became great cities by Greek standards: Sybaris, Kroton, and Metapontion, whose badge later, on her coins, was an ear of wheat. In classical times grain imports from the west were important to the Peloponnese. Sybaris pushed out across the "instep" to found daughter colonies on the west coast and, within two generations, Poseidonia (Latin Paestum, famous for its temples), halfway to Cumae. Taras (Latin Tarentum), the sole colony of Sparta, and Lokroi Epizephyrioi, the neighbor of Rhegion, last of this group (676 B.C. traditionally) from north of the Corinthian Gulf, were both results of political disturbances at home. From all these desirable territories the relatively backward native farmers were pushed aside, not without violence and sometimes treachery; Sybaris ruled and exploited four native tribes.

Meanwhile Eretria had planted settlers on the island of Kerkyra (Corfu), an important halfway house to the west; and the name of a spring near Chalkis appears in the more famous Arethusa on the island of Ortygia at Syracuse, though no Chalkidian colony took root there, for reasons that will appear. Euboia was at the height of its fame; and here we see the point of a remark in the *Odyssey*, where the hospitable (but mythical) Phaeacians of the west, who bring home the shipwrecked Odysseus, assure him that their magic ships can get him home overnight, "even if it is farther than Euboia, which they say is the remotest land." The point is that there were no Greeks yet in Asia in Odysseus' time, so Euboia is the remotest land known to westerners. Homer is having a little joke with us.

But at this point came the first of the repeated tragedies in which Greek states and finally Greek civilization itself ruined their already brilliant achievements by internal war.

Late in the ninth century Eretria, perhaps originally centered at Lefkandi, built a new city on its classical site, a fine rocky citadel a few miles to the southeast. Now Lefkandi lay on the opposite edge from Chalkis of a fertile plain bisected by the Lelantos torrent; the two cities had shared the plain's resources peacefully while also collaborating abroad. But now they quarreled. As people moved, it seems, to the new city, perhaps Chalkidians encroached on the plain. In any case, they fought, while the knightly aristocracies still observed a tournament-like military convention "not to use missile weapons." To bring in archers and slingers would have been encouraging the lower classes to kill their betters, and that would have been really dangerous.

With merchants and colonizers now roaming the seas, there was a tendency to seek allies afar, perhaps first chiefly against acts of piracy; and in the end a number of neighborly enmities became involved in the war in Euboia. Most of the Greek commercial world became divided into two camps (to say "leagues" would imply organization). Recorded wars occurred mostly between neighbors in opposite camps, and cases of cooperation, between members of the same camp. For example Samos, whose people were at least somewhat piratical, was an enemy of Miletos; and they aided Chalkis and Eretria, respectively. Miletos had also aided Chios in another early war against neighboring Erythrai, which brought Chios into the Eretria-Miletos camp. Long after, Chalkis and Andros (possibly liberated from Eretria) colonized together in the Thracian peninsula, which became known as Chalkidike, and having had a dispute, they called in Samos, Erythrai, and Paros to arbitrate. Corinth, rising in importance, allied itself with the Samos-Chalkis camp and pushed the Eretrians from Kerkyra, took over Syracuse, "driving the Sicilians first from the island," and, about 704 according to Thucydides, lent Samos a naval architect. The Chalkidian camp even gained the moral support of the rising Delphic Oracle. The tales of its useful advice to colonial founders (not all historical) nearly always refer to Chalkis and her friends, hardly ever to the other side.

In the Lelantine War proper, Chalkis won in the cavalry fighting with the help of allies from the broad lands of Thessaly; but a King Amphidamas of Chalkis was killed; and if this is the Amphidamas at whose funeral games Hesiod says that he won a prize for poetic recitation, it helps to date both of them approximately, to a little before 700 B.C. Eretria lost the plain; Lefkandi was deserted, and a hero shrine before the west gate of the new city suggests a cult, forgotten later, of a hero who led the defense of this last line.

Euboia lost its lead. In the west, Corinth was the chief gainer. Syracuse spread over southeast Sicily, with daughter colonies, and the Dorian element was strengthened by Cretans and Rhodians who, about 690, founded Lindioi (from Rhodian Lindos) on the south coast, commonly called Gela after its "cold stream." There was also a small western Megara (Megara Hyblaia), colonized by Megara in Greece when the latter was a protectorate of Corinth. After a century, boxed in between Syracuse and the Chalkidian colonies and unable to expand, Megara Hyblaia founded Selinus (Selinunte), far west on the south coast, which later produced noble sculptures. Gela finally, as late as about 580, founded, half way to Selinus, Akragas (Agrigento), which became the second greatest city in Sicily. Its splendid temples still stand, preserved by the anopheles mosquito, which deterred later habitation. On the north coast Himera (maybe about 648) was the only Chalkidian secondary colony, made up in part of Syracusan political exiles. Later it produced the earliest of Sicily's fine silver coins. Meanwhile Ionian Phokaia had founded Massalia (Marseilles, about 600), which founded daughter colonies as far as Spain, until Carthage checked Greek expansion.

Reckoning in thousands instead of millions, the west was like an America to Greece's Europe. Many of the cities grew much larger than their parents, and the west made major contributions to Greek art and literature, philosophy, and technology. No other colonial field produced such results, though they were important economically.

Colonization in the north Aegean and the northeast is generally later than in the west.

The prizes were less spectacular, and north winds and the strong Hellespont (Dardanelles) current were impediments. Still, Chalkidike, which contains good grain-growing country though the map would not suggest it, came to contain thirty cities, some of medium-large size, mostly from Chalkis, a few, early but undated, from Eretria, a few later from Andros. Paros colonized the large island of Thasos, which in turn secured gold and silver mining settlements on the mainland, not without struggles against the warlike Thracians; they also colonized the port of Kavalla (Skabala), officially Neapolis (new town). Farther east, Chios colonized Maroneia and fought against the Thasians (they were in opposite camps); but a settlement of Ionians at Abdera was wiped out by the Thracians. A new city on the same site, later the home of Demokritos and his "atomic" school, was not established until about 540, when most of the people of Teos migrated thither to escape Persian rule.

In the northeast, Mytilene, largest of the five cities of Lesbos Island, had farming settlements on the mainland opposite. Their children went to school at Mytilene and were accepted only if their native villages showed respect to the metropolis. The settlements spread north to take in the land of Troy, and to Sestos, across the Hellespont. Then came colonists from Miletos, cramped at home by the new native kingdom of Lydia. Phrygia had been destroyed by migrants from the north, the Kimmerians, before 700; but the new king, Gyges, at Sardis, while attacking Ionia, was content that Ionians should hold the Hellespont for him (whence Milesian Abydos, opposite Sestos, about 670, and Kyzikos [Balkız], on an all-but-island, farther up, of uncertain date). Megara, having fought a war of independence against Corinth, and so excluded from the west, joined in this movement, not clashing with Miletos (the camps again) but hostile to Samos when it came on the scene later (Perinthos on the Propontis, now the Sea of Marmara, 599). Megarians colonized Kalchadon (Chalcedon of the Christian church councils now Kadıköy) east of the Thracian Bosporus, with good land and not too formidable natives, and only later (629 according to a local historian) saw the potentialities of the Golden Horn at Byzantium. These settlements were not so important as harbors, for the northeast trade was only beginning, but as unrivaled fish traps for the shoals of tunny that spawned in the Black Sea and migrated to the Mediterranean, growing on the way. Dried fish from these waters became, for classical Greece, a major import.

By this time the Milesians had entered the Black Sea. They explored all its coasts, claiming to have founded seventy cities. Among those in Asia Minor were Sinope—which, with the only good harbor for a long way, collected local cargoes for transshipment—and Trapezous (Trebizond, Trabzoun), named from its "table mountain" (*trapeza*). Some of the alleged dates are certainly far too early; but when a potter at Smyrna signed his name "Istrokles" (famed from the Istros, that is, Danube) about 650, one may infer that his father had visited the great river and was proud of it. A city of Istria is dated 640, credibly. North of the Danube, colonization would have been impossible without the goodwill of the nomad Scythians, who had come from the east and dislodged the Kimmerians before 700; but the Milesians produced trade goods, including wine and decorative amphorae, which the Scythians were glad to exchange for slaves or hides. Some agricultural people survived in southwest Scythia, and some neighboring Scythians even took to growing grain as a cash crop on the famous black earth of the Ukraine, though their own diet was of milk and meat. Here, on the great *liman* (estuary) of the Borysthenes (Dnieper), Milesians settled on Berezan (Borysthenes) Island and then on the inner estuary. Here they later proudly named their city Olbia (prosperity), though other Greeks continued to call them Borysthenites. A later major success was Pantikapaion (a native name, the modern Kerch), about 600, on the Kimmerian Bosporus, in classical times the capital of a native kingdom of Tauris (the Crimea). Several kings bore the Thracian name Spartokos; Thracian people and speech survived in the Crimea.

Especially after the growth of the grain trade, the Black Sea, or Euxine (kind to strangers), as the Greeks called it in euphemism, was of enormous economic importance. Classical Athens fought many campaigns to keep open the Hellespont (Dardanelles) passage. But the colder climate did not encourage the outdoor way of life of the Greek cities; and young intellectuals, of whom the Euxine cities produced their quota, went to classical Athens for higher education and tended, if academically successful, to stay there. At the same time, the cities clung to their Hellenic heritage. Sinope and Olbia both long fostered Homeric studies. Achilles, thought of unhistorically as having fallen fighting to open up the northeast, was the object of a special cult, and people were named after him. The earliest extant text of a Greek letter, found in 1970 at Berezan, is written by an Achillodoros. He has been taken hostage and his goods seized, perhaps as a pledge in the course of a commercial dispute, and begs his son to come and make representations to his captor. The letter is written on a small sheet of lead, rolled up and stuck into a crack in a wall, perhaps a private "mailbox."

Trade with the Levant naturally took a different course. Assyria ejected the Greeks (no doubt piratical) from Syria and Cilicia about 696, and city-kings of Cyprus, with Greek names, served with their ships in Esarhaddon's invasion of Egypt in 681. With the weakening of Assyria, Greek raiders reappeared in the Nile Delta, as already described in the *Odyssey,* and Psamatik, one of the local chiefs who were fighting for power there, advised by an oracle, took the "bronze men from the sea" into his service. Posing at first as Assyria's man, he ended as open rebel, with more troops sent by Gyges of Lydia, and first king of the Twenty-sixth Dynasty. So began an age of Greek penetration of Egypt, more as mercenaries than as traders, though trade increased.

The chief importance of this event for Greek history lay in the impression that Egypt made on the Greeks by its antiquity and its huge monuments, though the language in which they spoke of these was irreverent. It has given us the words *pyramid,* meaning a bun, *obelisk* (needle), and *crocodile,* after the lizards on the dry stone walls in Ionia. In 592, under Psamatik II, some soldiers returning from an expedition far up the Nile carved their names on legs of Rameses II's colossi at Abu Simbel, adding words that make their vandalism historic:

> When King Psamatichos came to Elephantine, this they wrote, who sailed with Psammatichos [*sic*], son of Theokles; and they went beyond Kerkis, as far as the river let them; and Potasimto led the foreigners, and Amasis the Egyptians; and Archon, son of Amoibichos, and Axe, son of Nobody, wrote us [*sc.* the letters. The stone "speaks" as in many early inscriptions: Archon did it with his hatchet].

Names follow, Ionian and Rhodian. Psammatichos the son of Theokles must be an Egyptian-born Greek, named after his father's royal patron. The tomb of Potasimto, who commands the "foreigners" (perhaps Karians), has actually been found.

Among others who came was Solon, the wise man of Athens, "both to trade and to see the country"; and it was under profound Egyptian influence that Greeks, about 600, began to produce monumental stone sculpture.

Naturally the brash foreigners were not popular, and about 570 there was a revolution. King Apries (Pharaoh Hophra in the Bible) was dethroned for favoring them; but the victor, another Amasis (as he lived till 526, it cannot be the one from the Abu Simbel inscription), while acting to allay discontent, was not going to lose the Greek connection. He only made it less conspicuous, keeping his soldiers largely in the modern Canal Zone and confining traders to one treaty port, Naukratis, near later Alexandria. In the temples of Naukratis, fourteen cities are recorded as taking part: Mytilene; six of Ionia; six of the Asian Dorians (Rhodes had three); and from west of the Aegean, one only, the Dorian island of Aigina. Westward-trading Corinth is absent, though her now ubiquitous pottery was plentiful.

No normal colonization was possible in Egypt, nor indeed anywhere in the civilized east, beyond Phaselis in Lykia, a colony of Rhodian Lindos, though a few earlier settlements survived farther east, half-barbarized or "gone native." But west of Egypt there was successful colonization in Cyrenaica, about which we are peculiarly well informed, with a regular history of Kyrene (or Cyrene, in its familiar Latin spelling) by Herodotus and a fascinating account in a later and lately found inscription of the primitive ceremonies accompanying the organization of the colony. The founders were from the island of Thera in time of famine, according to Herodotus; and, says the inscription, the people made colossi of wax and burned them, while they invoked a curse on themselves that they might waste as this wax melted if they did not keep faith (for example, by allowing the colonists to return and share their lands if the settlement proved untenable). In fact, it flourished; in the third generation it invited new colonists from many cities, a move that led to trouble with the white Libyan natives and intervention by Apries, which led in turn to his downfall (about 570). The foundation, therefore, can be dated around 630, but later chronological tables, of which we have a fourth-century A.D. scholarly version by Bishop Eusebius, give both this date and 760 or 759 B.C. This discrepancy, together with such dates as 757 for Trebizond, itself a daughter colony of Sinope, must serve as a warning that some at least of the literary dates for colonies are far too early.

Cyrene flourished under a monarchy until its eighth king was deposed about 440. (The inflated foundation date may be based on an estimate of forty years per generation.) The fertile land exported grain, wool, and, uniquely, the wild herb *silphion,* valued as a laxative so highly that it became extinct from overplucking. A famous cup dated about 550 depicts Arkesilas II seated under an awning, supervising the loading of merchandise.

RENAISSANCE AND REVOLUTION

The largest colonies had been established as a remedy for overpopulation in some areas and a precaution against popular demands for land redistribution; but the transformation of the Greek world that resulted, although agriculture no doubt remained the largest industry, was revolutionary at a more fundamental level.

First, there was a widespread feeling (as we infer from Greek art) of well-being. There was land for all, food for all. Colonization slackens after about 550, because such emigration as continued could go to existing cities, and also because importing food could be a substitute for exporting hungry people. But art—as we see especially from pottery, which survives even if broken, while textiles perish and metal is melted down—became exuberant. A generation after the great emigration to the west, the respectable, traditional (though not stagnant) Geometric style is given up. Apparently people found it dull. In its place appears, most successfully at Corinth, an orientalizing style, with friezes of animals and filler ornaments after the oriental: rosettes, palmettes, the "tree of life" adorned with ribbons like a Christmas tree, not taken from oriental pottery, but often resembling the jewelry and embroidery seen in the adornments of kings and queens in Assyrian relief sculpture. "Babylonitish garments" were probably the imported medium. Moldings on Greek temples (always picked out in paint at this time) use the Egyptian series of alternate lotus buds and flowers, later conventionalized into the familiar "egg and dart." It was an age of gaiety, expressed in newly opulent festivals, like that which a poet—Homer himself according to classical Greeks—so vividly describes in the *Hymn to the Delian Apollo*. As a matter of social history, it is noteworthy that the Ionians who gathered in Delos brought their families, in contrast to the rising festival at Olympia, where women were debarred on pain of death from watching the games. Women athletes at Olympia had only a much less splendid festival at another time. The difference may be connected with the fact that Dorians, predominant in the clientele of Olympia, were more inclined than other Greeks to homosexuality. Rising to fame also in the age of colonization, the Delphic sanctuary too had its four-yearly great athletic and musical festival, and victories there ranked second only to those at Olympia.

Poetry developed and diversified in a manner parallel to art. It is not true that no more epics were written: rather, none have survived from before 300 B.C., and what we hear of them sounds as if they were not very good. The genre was getting worked out. Still less can it be true that Greece hitherto had had no lyrics, love songs, hymns, dirges, satires; only that they had not been written down. The poet of that age who broke a barrier, whose personal poetry was written down, preserved, and not treated as ephemeral, was the great Archilochos, a nobleman's bastard with a chip on his shoulder, colonist, mercenary soldier—altogether a figure of the new, mobile age.

The next poets who force their way into a chapter on history come not before 600 B.C. They are the Lesbian singers, Sappho and Alkaios; Alkaios especially, because he speaks out of the middle of the revolutions that broke out, like fires in a hot summer, in all the progressive, maritime parts of the Greek world. Alkaios tells how, when he was a child, his elder brothers killed a revolutionary boss named Melanchros. With them was a prominent citizen named Pittakos, curiously, a Thracian name, indicating intermarriage at a high social level. But social peace was not restored. When Alkaios grew up there was another boss, Myrsilos (perhaps an Asian name); and, to Alkaios' fury, Pittakos was on his side. When Myrsilos too was killed, Alkaios rejoices: "Now let us get drunk, for Myrsilos is dead!" But then Pittakos himself took the lead. A crowd, Alkaios says, acclaimed him "Tyrant over our unfortunate city." Some people used a more polite word, meaning something like "arbitrator." Pittakos defeated Alkaios' party and drove them out of Mytilene, out of all Lesbos. Sappho is said to have gone to Sicily, Alkaios to Egypt, his elder brother Antimenidas to the army of Nebuchadrezzar, who broke through to the sea after the Battle of Carchemish (605 B.C.). Perhaps, in defeat, they quarreled. They might have met on opposite sides in battle but did not. In the end they reassembled to have another crack at Pittakos (Antimenidas flourishing a splendid sword of honor won by killing a giant in some hostile army). Lydia supplied them with money, but Pittakos was still too much for them. He captured the whole émigré gang and, to their great surprise, let them live, saying, "Forgiveness is better than vengeance"—a sentiment unfamiliar in Greece.

Pittakos overhauled the laws of Mytilene, held power for ten years as the city's choice (even Alkaios admits that, though he deplores it), and then is said to have lived for ten more in retirement. He was counted one of the Seven Sages of his time. Few Greek stories end as happily as his; and yet much of it is probably true, since a leading contemporary source for it was his enemy.

The word tyrant (*tyrannos*), which Alkaios uses, was relatively new to the language, known to us first when Archilochos makes one Charon the Carpenter say that he cares not for gold or power. It is of obscure, possibly Asian, origin, and meant a despot, unlike the now limited *basileis* of old Greece. Revolutions against aristocracies became common because of a shift in the relative strength of social classes. One result of increased wealth was that more men, especially well-to-do farmers, could afford the expensive bronze armor of round shield, corselet, helmet, and greaves, and became important in their cities' wars. As horses remained rare south of Thessaly, the armored foot, *hoplites,* became the core of armies; and as their numbers increased, the advantage of fighting shoulder to shoulder in a phalanx revealed itself. United, the aristocrats should have been able to hold their time-honored position; but faction among them, such as family feuds, was fatal. An ambitious nobleman, especially if his equals "ganged up" against him, could now appeal to a considerable class outside.

"Tyrant" thus denoted a revolutionary despot; it did not at first imply oppressive government. In modern times, Napoleon or Cromwell would have qualified for it; Washington could have. The importance of the early tyrannies in Greece was that they broke a "cake of custom." The republics restored after them were not always democratic, but they were free to experiment.

CORINTH AND TYRANNY

The early history of Corinth comes the closest to being typical of the evolution of a city-state, though in details, like all history, it is unique. The tradition is also oral, therefore erratic.

First there were kings, descended from the Dorian conqueror Aletes. Under the sixth king, Bakchis, the ruling family excluded their numerous cousins from rights of succession (and presumably from forming the royal council). After five Bakchiad reigns, the tradition shows signs of succession troubles; but this time the whole Bakchiad clan, now some 200 families, resisted exclusion and instead abolished the monarchy (in 747 traditionally) and formed a closed oligarchy, appointing presidents (*prytaneis*) from among themselves. This oligarchy organized the colonies at Syracuse and Kerkyra (Corfu), sent young nobles who were in trouble and liable to vendetta into exile as leaders, and even tried to keep some control, unlike most mother cities, over some smaller colonies in northwest Greece. But Kerkyra, grown powerful and populous, resisted, fought a war of independence, and remained free after the first naval battle known to Thucydides (664). Seven years after that, if the dates are right, the Bakchiads were overthrown. No doubt there was trouble at home too.

Legend, of which the charming details are worth reading in Herodotus (5.92b), told how a Bakchiad girl, whom none of the clan would marry because she was lame, was married off to a farmer of ancient but non-Dorian pedigree. An oracle told the government that her baby would be their bane, and the council sent men to destroy it. But the baby smiled at them, and no one had the heart to kill it; and before they came back, steeled to do it, the mother, forewarned, hid it in a jar or *kypsele.* The tale is obviously invented to explain the boy's odd name,

Kypselos. A later account says that, though not a Bakchiad, he became a general. With popular support he overthrew and drove out the Bakchiads, gave their lands to his supporters, and ruled for thirty years (approximately 657–627) with enough popular support not to need a bodyguard.

His son Periandros did have a bodyguard and became a legendary monster of cruelty. Tradition said that he asked advice on government from Thrasyboulos, the great tyrant of Miletos, who defended his city against Lydia, and that Thrasyboulos led his messenger round a field of wheat while carefully lopping off all the tallest ears with his stick. The messenger was puzzled, but Periandros understood.

Periandros was a great soldier. He reconquered Kerkyra, founded other colonies on the way to it, as well as Poteidaia in Chalkidike, and had a fleet on both seas. The famous road for dragging ships across the isthmus was his. But his reign ended in gloom, around 585. His sons died before him, one in bitter enmity with his father, whom he suspected of having killed his mother; and Periandros' successor, a nephew named Psammetichos (the Egyptian name is noteworthy), was overthrown within four years, probably in 58 B.C. So there was a republic again, not democratic, but probably what Greeks called a timocracy, with a property qualification for voting and higher ones for holding official positions—a system in which men could rise. It is said that there were eight artificial "tribes," according to a proverb, "eight of everything." The Dorian blood must have been much diluted. Kerkyra, independent again, was often hostile.

Only one tyrant dynasty lasted longer than that of Corinth: that of Sikyon lasted 100 years (*ca.* 650–*ca.* 550), by caution and avoidance of tyranny in the modern sense. It too raised the non-Dorians to equality. More often, a self-made tyrant's throne was lost by his son or by the next generation. At Megara, Theagenes, who "slaughtered the cattle of the rich, turned out to graze by the river" (perhaps a sign of strife between rich cattlemen and poor farmers), himself died in exile. In the west the first tyrant rises later, at Leontinoi, dated 608; then, as in Latin America today, coups were frequent. Tyranny was everywhere transitory; but it was important in breaking the "cake of custom." People could now experiment.

SPARTA AND REACTION

Corinth exhibits the stages of "typical" city-state evolution. But the future lay with two states that were not typical: Sparta and Athens.

Other Greek cities expanded by sea; Sparta, by land. She mastered the rich and beautiful vale of "hollow Lakedaimon." Outlying villages that accepted her overlordship were left to manage their own affairs; called *perioikoi* (neighbors), they supplied troops when required and did not take part in major decision making. Residents of those villages that resisted became serfs (Helots, perhaps from Helos, on the south coast), not liable to be sold, but attached to the land. This was divided into hereditary, nonsalable estates held by Spartiates, men of five villages that had grown together to form the ramshackle town of Sparta (the sown land) at the foot of a pass over the Taygetos range. The pass was under Sparta's control; from it, people could see the fertile plain of Stenyklaros in Messenia, farther away and lower down, at sea level. Still greedy, the Spartan landowners coveted it; and after a quarrel at a frontier sanctuary, which led to bloodshed, they conquered it, though resistance in the hills beyond lasted for twenty years (traditionally 736–716). With still more land and more Helots (though some Messenians fled to the western colonies), the Spartans were now among the richest aristocracies in Greece; they imported ivory, amber, and oriental garments.

But events taught Sparta that to hold her wealth she must above all be strong. After a defeat by Argos, dated 669 B.C., came (possibly around 640) a desperate revolt of Messenia, backed by Arcadia, in which the Spartans felt for a time that they were fighting for their lives. It was crushed; the conquest of the southwest Peloponnese was completed; but the Messenians never forgot that they had been a free people, and the Spartans knew that they had not forgotten. It was as though Ireland had been as close to England as Wales.

The Spartans had long since modernized their constitution (see also GREEK FORMS OF GOVERNMENT). The monarchy (that strange, dual monarchy, in two families, said to be descended from twin brothers) was limited by the annual election of five ephors (overseers), before whom the kings swore to obey the laws; while the ephors, representing the people, swore obedience as long as they kept the laws. The kings also had to consult twenty-eight elders, elected for life by the Assembly of Spartiates over thirty from among men over sixty of certain noble families—a Senate or gerontocracy indeed. The kings' chief remaining importance was as judges in property questions (for example, which kinsman should marry a girl without brothers, in order to keep the land in the family)—and as commanders of the army. This role and what went with it, great influence (not power) in decisions on foreign affairs, worked rather well. The kings, brought up from childhood to survey the Panhellenic scene, usually took broader views than other Spartans, and when the ephors and the assembly chose to overrule them, it was often unwise. The assembly, according to an early written law called the *Rhetra* of Lykourgos, had final sovereignty; but a rider to the Rhetra, attributed to King Theopompos, the conqueror of Messenia, said that if it gave "crooked" answers, the kings and elders might dismiss it. This seems to mean that amendments and debate were not allowed. The assembly could only vote on what was put before it, and the method of taking the vote was (Aristotle says) "childish": tellers, shut up in a hut nearby, decided whether the shout of approval for "aye" or "no" was the louder. So, if public opinion was nearly unanimous, it could have its way; but the kings, elders, and ephors, by framing the motions to go before it, could usually have theirs. Even the ephors were elected by the same primitive method of acclamation judged by hearers "off-stage," which must have been much more complicated than judging "aye" and "no" shouts, and given ample scope for official secret influence.

The Rhetra is paraphrased by Tyrtaios ("straight answers" are emphasized). Probably after the crisis of this time, Sparta overhauled not its political constitution but its social arrangements, "freezing" or tightening up what look like primitive arrangements for human life, just when most Greek states were modernizing. Also the basic constitutional law, the Rhetra, early among Greek written laws, was Sparta's last. Henceforth, Sparta relied on oral tradition.

Men's life was lived chiefly in men's clubs or "messes," as among some modern uncivilized peoples; the famous Spartan training led up to it. Babies who did not look promising were put out to die, and men might lend their wives to another for stud purposes. Boys who were reared left their mothers at seven for a "pack" led by an older youth, for whom they "fagged," all the packs being overseen by a handpicked older citizen as "minister for youth training." They wore one tunic, summer and winter. Their beds were of reeds plucked, without knives, from the Eurotas River; their diet monotonous, chiefly a blackish wheat porridge, a more primitive confection than leavened bread, and barely sufficient. They supplemented it by stealing from the farms and were beaten if caught, for bad scouting rather than for dishonesty. They were taught reading and counting, and traditional songs and dances (ordered movement); packs met in ballgames and in organized, unarmed combat. In their teens, military training was added. The end of it was to gain election, unanimously by secret ballot, to a men's club that would also be, for life, their section in the army, and in whose hut they would eat and sleep, normally even after marrying, which they were expected to do at thirty. Men visited their wives by stealth. There was room for all in the clubs; but the fear of being blackballed, which would have been social death, must have kept every boy desperately anxious not to be seen to flinch from any ordeal. Girls also had some athletic training, running and wrestling "naked"— perhaps really in short tunics, which other Greeks thought immodest.

In all this, classical Spartans claimed to be living under the laws of Lykourgos. But Lykourgos came nowhere in the lists of kings; and when they asked the Delphic Oracle about him, Apollo said he was not sure if he was god or man but "rather thought" a god. Perhaps he was a prehistoric god, who had become identified with an Olympian—perhaps Apollo himself. Plutarch (*ca.* A.D. 100) wrote a *Life* of him but confesses the inadequacy of early sources. Most thought that he must be a member of one of the royal houses, but they differed as to which one. Just so, all the law of the Jews was attributed to Moses, and of the Brahmins to Manu.

A similar militarist society, with men's life in clubs, survived in the serf-owning Dorian cities of Crete; some said Lykourgos had copied it. The object was the same: survival as landowners; and so was the result—petrifaction. Crete was quick to adopt oriental art, but after early Cretan sculptors had influenced the mainland, Crete contributed nothing to classical Greece. The only incidents in her history were neighborly wars; but these were kept within bounds by a sense of solidarity (syncretism) and by a gentlemen's agreement that in no circumstances would one tamper with another's serfs.

Mainland Sparta enjoyed no such isolation. In the sixth century she decisively defeated Argos, once mistress of all the east coast beyond the Parnon Mountains; but she failed to conquer Arcadia, or even its nearest city, Tegea. This failure shaped her future. Still more serfs might have been disastrous. She now admitted Tegea to alliance, along with the other Peloponnesian states, especially those of the northeast, liberated from Argos' overlordship, or the fear of it, or from tyrants. The alliance was a factor for stability in Greece, but not for progress. Democracy was not encouraged, though loyal allies could move in that direction. Sparta's alliance, plus Athens, formed the core of Greek resistance to the great menace of the Persian Empire; but on the other hand, Sparta was strong enough to check the best political solution for Greece (since cities would not federate voluntarily): that of unity led by Athens.

ATHENS AND THE MIDDLE WAY

In the main colonizing movement, Athens took no part. Athenians were still extending their farms over their own relatively wide territory, and Attica was becoming more closely united. Eleusis may have joined the centralized state only after about 675 B.C.; the "Homeric" *Hymn to Demeter,* perhaps about then, tells of the goddess visiting a king of Eleusis (but in mythical times), and Athens is not mentioned. After 600, both Alkaios and Solon speak of "Atticans" where we would expect "Athenians"; but that usage, if usage it was, did not last. Attica was also still exporting grain; Solon forbade it, so it was going on.

Signs of change come only after 640. Probably in 632 Kylon, a young noble and Olympic victor, son-in-law to Theagenes, tyrant of Megara, seized the Acropolis with his personal followers and Megarian soldiers in an attempt to make himself tyrant; but the peasants stood by their traditional Eupatrid leaders. Kylon escaped, but many of his followers were massacred after surrendering and taking sanctuary. This left a heritage of blood feud and a curse on the chief archon, Megakles, and his family (the leading Alkmaionid house), the memory of which lingered even after religious purifications. Then, about 620, the laws were published by one Drakon—a sign of the spread of literacy and also of impatience among the commons (now including hoplites) with a system under which oral law, known only to the noble judges, might vary.

That was something. But by 600, Attica was in an economic crisis. Evidently the country, with growing population, could no longer easily feed itself. The rich still had grain for sale; but the poorest peasants, now on marginal land, went hungry. They might borrow in a bad year; but paying back with interest tended to become impossible. The security for debt was their land (if they were not already tenants) and ultimately their persons and their families. Increasing numbers were actually sold abroad as slaves. Among the rest, fear and anxiety grew.

Many of the rich were ruthless; the law was on their side. With the best weapons, they could crush an uprising; but some became anxious themselves about the state of the community. One Solon, of ancient lineage and moderate wealth, wrote poems attacking upper-class greed; and at last enough of his own class agreed, for fear of worse, that Solon should be elected archon with special powers to overhaul the laws. All men swore to obey his laws for ten years after their publication. In 594 he proclaimed that all outstanding debts were canceled and that state funds, which the rich must have provided, should be used to redeem those sold abroad. Most of them must have been in neighboring states. But he did not proclaim that dream of the poor, a redivision of the land; and the poor peasants, whose hopes his poems had raised, were disappointed.

However, in 592 B.C. (according to Aristotle; so Solon's special appointment may have been for ten years, like that of Pittakos) he announced a new constitution. He confirmed that all free men, even the landless, had the right to vote in the assembly, and he greatly strengthened that body by providing it with its own steering committee. A People's Council of Four Hundred (100 from each of the four Ionic tribes), instead of the conservative Areopagus, was to prepare the business; middling or "200-bushel" farmers, roughly the hoplite class, were eligible. Archons still came from the cavalry class; but they had to be elected by the assembly and, after their year, to give it an account of their actions, at which complaints could be raised. Only if their accounts were passed could they then enter, for life, the prestigious Areopagus. This council kept the formidable power of ruling as a supreme court on whether a proposal was constitutional, according to (traditional, but now Solonian) law. But to enter it, at least, a "knight" had to have administrative or legal experience as an archon, and to have been elected to that office and "passed" after it. It was a conservative constitution, but it did provide some rights for the common man. Classical Athens "canonized" Solon as father of its democracy.

At the time, Solon went abroad, to Egypt and elsewhere, to escape (he says) being badgered to alter this or that detail; he left the people, with the usual magistrates, to live under his laws at least for the remainder of his ten years. He had not brought peace; rather, he had institutionalized electoral conflict (especially about the chief archonship), which was often fierce. Leaders organized local or class power bases, and in the end, some fifty years later, there was a tyranny after all: that of Peisistratos, who as a young general with Solon's backing had taken (the Athenians said retaken) Salamis Island from Megara. Standing as the champion of the poor, twice driven out, he ended by reigning, very informally, from about 546 B.C. to his death in 528—a very benevolent and approachable despot. He made loans to farmers to improve their equipment; production soared and repayment was easy. But his sons naturally did not have his prestige; Hippias, the eldest, after his brother Hipparchos had been murdered in a plot fired by homosexual jealousy (apparently the fault of a third brother), became suspicious and tyrannical indeed. In 510 he was driven out by Sparta, prompted by the Delphic Oracle, which was secretly influenced by Kleisthenes the Alkmaionid, a descendant of the archon Megakles.

Then Athens had its real revolution. Kleisthenes, who was named after his mother's father, the tyrant of Sikyon, outdid a coalition of conservative nobles by "taking the people into his club," in the words of Herodotus (5.69). By an act of the People's Council and Assembly in 508/507 he made citizens all free men of Attica, including many immigrants from Ionia, now under the Persian Empire. Solon had allowed the naturalization of useful craftsmen who came with their families, but the conservatives probably disenfranchised many on technical grounds. These conservatives appealed to Sparta to suppress this revolution; but the Athenians resisted intervention, first by the masterful King Kleomenes (who came with only his bodyguard of 300, trusting in his prestige), and then, in 506 B.C., by a large Peloponnesian army. Seeing the Athenian army in united and orderly array, the Corinthians, old friends of Athens against Aigina and Megara, developed conscientious doubts; then Damaratos, Kleomenes' coruler, also queried the object of the expedition; and without a blow struck, the great army went home. Never again were both Spartan kings sent out to war together.

The Athenians turned against the Boeotians and Chalkidians, who, as Sparta's allies, had invaded northern Attica. Getting between them, they smote first the Boeotians, taking 700 prisoners for ransom, and then, on the same day, the Chalkidians; this was the defeat that broke the Chalkidian oligarchy of "knights." The Athenians annexed their wide lands and settled on them 4,000 poor Athenians as smallholders. Chalkis became an Athenian dependency. The élan of the democratic army made a lasting impression.

Kleisthenes reorganized the enlarged Athenian citizen body. The four Ionic tribes were replaced by ten artificial ones, named after ancient kings and heroes. Each tribe consisted of three groups of villages, townships, or city wards, from different parts of the country; it was thus a cross section of the Athenian state. In any future political controversy, whole tribes would never automatically be on the same side. Each tribe provided a battalion for the army, and they competed in athletic and musical festivals, thus gaining some tribal esprit de corps. The constitution was still Solon's, forming a class state in which able men could rise, but with a much larger and more democratic-minded voting body.

THE PERSIAN WARS

This was the Athens of the great Persian Wars.

In 499 B.C. Ionia rose against Persian rule,

exercised through local tyrants who were generally hated. Sparta refused support; but Athens, though not with a unanimous vote, sent twenty ships, and Eretria five. With the Ionians, they took and burned Sardis; but the local Persian forces, which they may have drawn off from attacking Miletos, caught them withdrawing, and their reembarkation was a disaster. The peace party at Athens gained a majority, and in 496 elected as archon Hipparchos (a kinsman, not the brother, of the exiled Hippias), who, with no criminal charges against him, had stayed in Athens. There were still many who felt kindly toward the house of Peisistratos. The Asian Greeks, strung out from Cyprus to Byzantion (Istanbul), were beaten down in a six-year war; and Athens' single but stinging blow had put her high on the Great King's agenda. In 490 a seaborne Persian expedition took Eretria and deported its people (save some who escaped) to the Persian Gulf; but landing in Attica, it was defeated at Marathon. The victorious war archon (who was killed) owed much to the advice of Miltiades, a formidable nobleman whose family had learned war as rulers of the Thracian Chersonese (Gallipoli Peninsula) since the time of Peisistratos.

The Athenian hoplites, justly proud, thought that Athens was saved. It was, but farsighted men saw that it would have to be saved again. None saw further than Themistocles, a man of the Kleisthenic revolution: for though his father was of an ancient and priestly family, his mother was non-Athenian, and he seems to have been in law a bastard. The conservatives would have disenfranchised him. As it was, he was archon in 493 B.C., when Athens was hearing in shame and anger of the fall of Miletos, her men slaughtered, temples burned, women sent to the harem. The poet Phrynichos put on a tragedy (then a kind of oratorio, with costume) about it, at the feast of Dionysos. It stung the peace party, for an oratorio on events of the day was unheard-of. The poet was fined, the piece banned; but people remembered it.

Through the years after Marathon, Themistocles worried and thought about strategy: "Miltiades' trophy would not let him sleep." It was not for jealousy, because Miltiades had died in disgrace, suspected (by a group led by the Alkmaionids and Xanthippos, a brother-in-law of theirs) of thinking to make himself a military tyrant, but because the Persian Empire would certainly try again, with its cavalry and myriad archers and Phoenician sailors who hated the Greeks as pirates. At the end of a long line of communications, and in the dangerous Greek coastal waters, something might be done at least at sea—if only Greece had enough ships to do it.

Meanwhile there was taken what proved, in the long run, to be a major step toward democracy. In 487 the assembly voted that in future the archons should be chosen not by vote but by lot among all candidates— who had to be knights in good standing, with nothing against them. This meant that the war archon in particular would be merely the chairman of ten experts, the generals of the regiments, who were still elected and could be reelected and gain experience. Otherwise, it did not seem to make much difference; but henceforth the Areopagus would be recruited from among the average rich men on whom the lot fell, not from the most respected. How long would people put up with the ancient council's power of veto, when the leading politicians of the past were gone?

As it was, politics were fierce enough. At the end of the sixth century, Kleisthenes (it is said), concerned that many respectable adherents of the Peisistratids remained in Athens with no criminal charge against them, had carried a law providing that in every year the people, by a majority containing at least 6,000 votes, might exile one citizen for ten years, without loss of status or property, simply on the ground that Athens would be better without him. Then, in the dangerous years, few had wanted to apply it. One such as Hipparchos, archon in 496–495, might be useful in making peace with Persia and Hippias. Now, with Persia beaten off and old Hippias dead, they applied it, and Hipparchos went. Then they turned against Kleisthenes' own faction, said to have colluded with the enemy in 490, exiling Megakles, head of the Alkmaionid family, and then his brother-in-law Xanthippos, who had led the attack on Miltiades.

The votes for exile were written on *ostraka,* broken potsherds, so the process was informally called *ostrakismos.* Thousands of these have been found. All the above names are represented; but the highest "scorer," except for Megakles, is Themistocles, presumably because he was at risk every time: Themistocles, the pestilent democrat who wanted to treble the navy to 200 ships. This would cost money and would also make the propertyless sailors at least as important as the armored infantry. Was it for them that the spearmen had won Marathon? The leader of Themistocles' critics was Aristeides the Just, a former supporter of Kleisthenes, who thought things had now gone far enough. If the votes of Themistocles' supporters had been scattered, against many well-known figures, he would probably have been top scorer sometime; but he had enough "canvassers" to concentrate their fire.

In 483 there came a godsend: the concession holders in the state-owned silver mines at Laurion, near Sounion, ran into a rich vein, and the state's royalties amounted to 100 talents. Athens could pay a dividend, at ten drachmas per voting citizen. (So there must have been some 60,000 citizens, including old men.) A drachma was the top daily wage for heavy or skilled manual work. But Themistocles persuaded them to forgo this handsome bonus and vote the whole sum for adding 100 triremes (the 150-oared, three-banked battleships) to the 70 that Athens had; enough to smash the old enemy Aigina, he said. Still, the poorer voters deserve high praise. There was also another ostracism (it was becoming an annual event), and Aristeides went. By 480, Athens had 200 ships: just in time, for reports showed that the Persian Empire was mobilizing on a massive scale.

When King Xerxes "marched his army over the sea" by pontoon bridges across the Hellespont and "sailed his fleet through the land," cutting off by a canal the peninsula of Mount Athos, where an earlier Persian fleet had been wrecked by a storm, later Greeks called it pride, an offense to heaven. Actually, both operations were, considering the resources, practical. So was the forward placement of food dumps, whence ships could move the food farther.

Athens manned her 200 ships with difficulty, using her colonists at Chalkis and even allies from inland Plataia, who had to be taught how to row. Forty thousand men were needed, including marines and deck crew.

Themistocles, now the chief commander of Athenian forces, "sold" his strategy to the alliance that met in 480 at Corinth under Spartan high command—no mean feat, since Greeks were accustomed to fight only near home. Ten thousand armored men, a considerable army, were sent to hold the passes north of Thessaly. The fleet, initially 100 Athenian and 100 Peloponnesian ships, took post at the north end of Euboia, marked by an Artemision (temple of Artemis). Thus the enemy fleet would have to come down the dangerous coast of Thessaly, where anchorages were few and small, all together, not in detachments, or the Greeks could destroy them in detail.

But the Greek land front immediately collapsed. It was found that the mountains west of Olympos were far from impassable; and the Persians—who had reconnoitered far more about the area than the southern Greeks knew and had already hacked a wide swathe through the forest all the way from the Propontis (Sea of Marmara)—would not obligingly confine themselves to the gorge of Tempe. Northern Greece, politically divided, was left open, and Themistocles' strategy was in ruins. The fleet could not stay at Artemision unless its land flank was covered, and thousands of Greeks were assembling—at Olympia for the games and at Sparta for its own festival, a religious duty that was taken very seriously. The Delphic Oracle itself urged the Athenians (it is unknown exactly when) to flee to the west; and their envoys barely extracted, by a threat to fast to death in the temple, permission to put their prepared question. This was probably "Can we successfully give battle at Salamis?"—the last island fortress of Attica. It produced the answer, at worst ambiguous, that "divine Salamis" should destroy the children of men; and Themistocles convinced the assembly with the argument that "divine" was too favorable an epithet to portend disaster.

Greece was saved then by Leonidas, king of Sparta. He could not move the army, but he could move his personal guard of 300, each accompanied by seven Helots, three of whom were probably armed. Picking up volunteers en route, he arrived with some 6,000 armored men in time to block the coast road below the cliffs at the hot springs, which gave the place its name of Thermopylai (hot gates). Local troops held the mountain west of the cliffs.

It took the Persians three days to force Thermopylai, after costly frontal attacks, through a remarkable night march of their guard division with a local guide up the west end of the mountain and, brushing aside the local Greek troops, along the top, much of which is flat. Outflanked, Leonidas stayed and fought to the death with a rearguard: the 300-plus armed Helots (neglected in many books) and 1,100 Boeotians, whose cities were now doomed anyhow. But those three days were decisive; for the Persian fleet, forced to move in mass, was caught anchored overnight off the Thessalian coast by a typical late-summer storm and suffered grave losses. The Greek fleet inflicted more while it was reorganizing; but that done, there were still enough ships left to fight the Greeks (now 324 ships) to a standstill. Their defensive half-moon formation was unbroken; but even Themistocles, before he knew that Thermopylai had fallen, agreed that they were in no state to fight again next day. Nonetheless, the work of the few at Thermopylai had made possible that of the 65,000 at Artemision; the losses inflicted on the imperial fleet in that operation—in battle and still more by storm damage—probably decided the war.

Themistocles got the allies to put into Salamis Sound, first to help the evacuation of Athens, then to defend Salamis itself, which, with Athens' magistrates and land forces, was now an important objective. He wanted to be attacked there, and in the end he was. Xerxes, with winter approaching, was in a hurry. Themistocles sent him a message describing dissensions among the Greeks (which were real; and the Persians would have known about them through the Greek exiles in their camp) and suggesting that they might "escape"; whereat Xerxes ordered his navy first to prevent the escape and then, with oarsmen already tired, to enter the straits at dawn. Here, when they had passed the narrowest point and were trying to fan out, the Greeks enveloped the Phoenicians at the head of their column and largely destroyed them. It was one of the decisive battles in world history.

Xerxes withdrew to Asia; this was only common sense, to be in touch with his empire. He left a selected army under his brother-in-law, the young marshal Mardonios, to complete the conquest. Mardonios tried to win over Athens, having the city itself as a hostage; but in vain, as the Athenians assured the Spartans in the name of "our common Hellenic blood and language and religion and ways of life"—a classic statement of Panhellenic patriotism, which, unhappily, was never to be embodied in an enduring state or federation. Nor were the Athenians amused when Sparta offered them a new home inside the Peloponnese. That would make them Sparta's vassals. At last, by pointing out that they could not hold out forever, they induced Sparta to risk a major land offensive; and after a difficult campaign against his more mobile forces, Mardonios (also in a hurry, through shortage of supplies) was drawn into an attack, defeated, and killed near Plataia. In the same summer, a Greek fleet under King Leotychides of Sparta and Xanthippos of Athens destroyed the imperial naval remnants on the beach south of Mykale, opposite Samos. Ionia revolted again; and while Sparta thought it could not be protected, Athens was willing to try. Thus an empire was born.

CLASSICAL ATHENS AND SPARTA

The year 478 B.C. marks the high point of Greek history. There was a chance of unity. Sparta admired Athens although they were so unlike, and was content with Athenian protection of the liberated Aegean. Athens and her new allies solemnly sank masses of iron in the sea and swore unity "till the iron swam." They held councils at the holy isle of Delos, and under Kimon they winkled out stubborn Persian garrisons on the north Aegean coast and raided Asia for spoil. This situation left Sparta free to win serious wars against jealous Argos and discontented Arcadia. But while the next 150 years saw the culmination of Greek achievements in art and literature, their political history is a sad tale of lost opportunities and internal war.

About 466 Naxos, largest of the Cyclades, resigned from the Delian League. Athens, appealing to the oath sworn, decided not to permit secession, besieged Naxos, and forced her to rejoin, on terms that deprived her of her ships and replaced her contribution of ships by money. Many of the hundreds of small cities, whose quota was a fraction of a ship, or a ship every few years, did the same voluntarily, while young men who wished could serve in Athenian ships for pay. Many were long content thus to pay Athens to police the seas; some of the revolts that did occur were ended by the refusal of the commons to cooperate. But the allies were by no means free and equal.

Both Athens and Sparta became more like the modern reader's idea of them. At Sparta the strong king Kleomenes had been suspected of aspiring to despotism, with the aid of Arcadians and helots. He was declared insane by his half brothers (Leonidas was one) and came to a grisly end (*ca.* 490). About fifteen years later, the victor of Plataia, Pausanias, incurred similar suspicions and was starved to death in sanctuary. To avoid sacrilege, he was brought out to die. Sparta could still use Helot troops on occasion; but the feelings of a class twice disappointed in their hopes for an improved status were nevertheless embittered.

At Athens, the Areopagite Council (still mostly elected archons, kings, and war chiefs) had been important in 480, when the assembly could not meet. Thereafter the great families drew together against Themistocles, though there were exceptions. For instance young Pericles, son of Xanthippos, now dead, paid (spring 472) for the production of a drama by Aeschylus, a veteran of Marathon and not reckoned a radical, about the battle of Salamis—therefore in implicit praise of Themistocles, whose deceitful message to Xerxes is emphasized. It was too late to save him; he was at last ostracized about 471 and went to Argos, where his advice to that and other cities on modernizing their constitutions caused anxiety in Sparta. At last, evidence arising from the Pausanias case was collected and used to accuse him of treasonable communication with Persia. Rather than stand trial at Athens in its present mood, he fled over the mountains, through the Athenian fleet blockading Naxos (he told his skipper that he would implicate him, if he was found), to end his days as Persia's governor of an inland Ionian city.

But the political tide was turning. A new Athenian democratic leader, Ephialtes, eloquent and incorruptible though not rich, fanned the envy of the poor and claimed that the wide powers exercised by the Areopagus rested only on usage, gradually assumed. He successfully challenged the accounts of several ex-archons and then, about 462, carried through the assembly a bill depriving the Areopagus of all its "assumed powers," including that of ruling on whether a bill was constitutional. The people would now decide that for themselves, in the assembly or, for detailed argument, before a large jury, whose decision was final.

The Areopagites were embittered. In the last political bloodshed in Athens for fifty years Ephialtes was murdered by a foreign knifeman, who escaped, and his mantle fell upon Pericles, now only about thirty-four years old.

Democracy was now complete. The Areopagus was left as a court for homicide trials, as Athena, legend said, had founded it; and before long the archonships, no longer politically important, were opened formally to the hoplite class and in practice to anyone willing to give a year for a modest salary.

At about the same time came the almost inevitable breach with Sparta. A catastrophic earthquake in 464 B.C. sparked off a revolt of the helots, even in Lakonia; Sparta, having suppressed that, was still faced by national resistance in Messenia, entrenched in the mountain fastness of Ithome. In 462 Sparta appealed to the Athenians, who were said to be good at siege operations; Kimon, against opposition, carried a motion to send help and was sent with 4,000 hoplites. But he was disappointed. His men, to whom "slaves" meant overseas barbarians bought for money, found themselves fighting Greeks defending (as no doubt they shouted from the walls) their old free homes. The Athenian attack was so feeble that the Spartans feared they might even change sides; so they told them to go, while keeping other allies. Insulted, Athens formally denounced her alliance and formed one with Argos, and Kimon was ostracized (461 B.C.).

While Sparta was thus occupied, Corinth resumed her long course of territorial aggression against Megara; and Megara, in desperation, appealed to Athens, her old enemy. Athens garrisoned Megara and her western port, Pegai (a window on the Corinthian Gulf), and, though half her fleet was away supporting Egypt in its revolt against Persia, defeated Corinth at sea. Aigina, alarmed at Athens' new power, joined Corinth. By calling in allies from her own league and without withdrawing from Egypt, however, Athens beat them both, landed troops on Aigina, and blockaded the town. The Corinthians marched on Megara; calling up men from eighteen to sixty to reinforce her new ally, Athens manned yet a third front and won there too. Aigina was starved out, disarmed, and made tributary. Corinth's hatred of her old friend became pathological.

Ithome too was starved out. Its defenders left the Peloponnese under an armistice, and Athens planted them at Naupaktos (Lepanto), which she had taken from the piratical Lokrians. Sparta, with her hands free, sent an expedition to liberate the northern Doris from attack by Phokis and "incidentally" restored Thebes to presidency in Boeotia, a position that had been lost for siding with Persia. Some Athenian reactionaries even urged Sparta to march on Athens, still committed abroad, before it was made impregnable by the completion of Long Walls down to the sea. Athens hit back with allies from Argos and Ionia. The Spartans won a severe battle at Tanagra (the first between Athens and Sparta), but they gave up hope of attacking Athens itself and marched home, past Megara. When they had gone (winter 458–457 B.C.) the Athenians invaded Boeotia, won a great victory, and dominated it for ten years in alliance with the lesser Boeotian cities. Phokis became an ally, and Athenian power reached as far as Thermopylai. This was the moment when imperial Athens seemed most likely to become a permanent leader of the Greek world.

All was changed in 454 by disaster in Egypt. Persian reinforcements invaded the country; a Phoenician fleet entered the Nile. The Athenian expedition held out on an island in the delta until the Persians diverted a branch of the Nile and stormed it. Many were taken prisoner; only a remnant escaped to Cyrene; and, communication being slow, a relief squadron of fifty ships sailed unsuspectingly into the delta and was captured as well. The ever-optimistic democracy had reached its limits.

Athens went over to the defensive. Pericles brought home a fleet of 100 ships, recently stationed in the Corinthian Gulf, at Pegai. On land, merely to help beat off a Spartan invasion of Argos was reckoned a major success. In 451 a five-year armistice was concluded with Sparta; but no lasting peace terms were reached. Old Kimon, back from exile, once more led a league fleet into the Levant, thus showing Persia (and Greece) that that war was still a reality; but he died before the walls of Phoenician Kition in Cyprus, and a victory over a relieving army and fleet gained the expedition only a safe return. Then, with each side convinced that the other was still formidable, de facto peace was made, even if the "world" empire did not stoop (as some think) to a formal treaty (449 B.C.).

In Greece, revolt broke out in Boeotia in 447, even while Sparta was bound by the truce. An Athenian punitive force was ambushed, cut up, and forced to surrender; local allies seem not to have appeared, and Athens gave up Boeotia to save the hostages.

In 446, with the truce over, the Peloponnesians marched on Athens; Megara massacred her Athenian garrison and went back to the Dorian side. Dorian racism was becoming, more than before, a political force. Pericles apparently bought off an invasion of Attica with a bribe to the Spartan high command (probably also with a genuine promise of peace with concessions), but before a conference could meet, he suppressed a revolt of Euboia. Resistance can hardly have been desperate. A young Spartan king and his chief of staff both fled into exile and were condemned to death. With the Thirty Years Peace of 445, Athens gave up her land empire. She kept her league, but lost that too in the wars of 431–404, narrated by Thucydides.

This history is far better known than any before; but limited space forbids going into detail. Athens, though weakened by a terrible plague, survived to make a not-too-disadvantageous peace in 421; but Pericles was dead (429 B.C.), and in 415 the still-sanguine democracy, now listening to his young kinsman, the gay Alkibiades, once more embarked on empire building in support of allies who proved ineffective—this time in Sicily. A great expedition bogged down before Syracuse, which was reinforced by Peloponnesian volunteers. The assembly voted for additional forces, rather than withdrawal, and finally the whole armament, 40,000 men and 173 warships, was lost in 413 B.C. Even then, with Ionia in revolt and Persia subsidizing a Peloponnesian fleet in the Aegean, Athens fought on, won victories at sea—and refused offers of peace that left her only the "allies" who had not revolted. (It is noteworthy that not all had.) But in 404, her last fleet having been caught on the beach of Aigospotamoi by the Spartan Lysander, Athens was starved out. Corinth proposed its total destruction; but Sparta saw that this move would aggrandize Thebes. A reactionary provisional government, the "Thirty Tyrants," under the poet and doctrinaire Kritias, once a friend of Socrates, was overthrown after one year; and a chastened Athenian democracy survived—among other exploits, to execute Socrates in 399.

Thus ended the Athenian dream of a Greece united under her supremacy, a dream that surely could never have been realized. The assembly, thinking nothing impossible, was doomed to overreach itself, if not when it did, then another time. This was the historical Athenian tragedy.

THE END OF FREE GREECE

As Pericles had said over young men killed in an earlier war, "the spring of the year is gone." Sparta, supreme, failed—more quickly and disastrously than Athens—to make a lasting peace. Spartans abroad proved both arrogant and, once free from the home discipline, avaricious. Sparta became involved in war with Persia to defend Ionia; but Persian money fanned the fire of discontent in Greece. By 395 Sparta was also at war with a coalition of Argos, Corinth, Thebes, and Athens and withdrew her forces from Asia. In 387 war was ended by the (Persian) King's Peace, in which Ionia was sacrificed. Sparta became the king's policeman to ensure that other Greek cities were "free and independent," thus putting an end to power blocs other than Sparta's alliance (which was all that Sparta wanted).

Thebes never willingly agreed to the dissolution of her own Boeotian League. In 382 Sparta broke up a league in Chalkidike, which had dominated faction-ridden Macedonia, and a general en route to that war, treacherously and in time of peace, accepted the offer of an antidemocratic party in Thebes to put the citadel of Thebes into his hands. The Spartan government chose to approve; but Xenophon, an exile from Athens and admirer of Sparta, but a man of simple piety, noted that the gods did not seem to agree. Thebes liberated herself with cloak and dagger within three years (379 B.C.); and though King Agesilaos of Sparta invaded Boeotia repeatedly, it became clear that he was not at all anxious to incur heavy casualties, such as a pitched battle with the Thebans would certainly bring.

The birthrate of the Spartiate aristocracy had long been failing to keep up its numbers, and elder statesmen were growing anxious. Thebes still stayed out of attempted peace settlements, insisting that Boeotia was one state and what she did to her neighbors was an internal affair. At last in 371 King Kleombrotos (Agesilaos had been ill), operating from the west with Phokian and other allies, got past the Theban general Epameinondas by a surprise march through the glens of Mount Helikon, forcing Epameinondas to hurry back to get between him and Thebes. The Spartans with their allies had superior numbers, and clamored for battle; Kleombrotos gave way. But Epameinondas, a great tactician, put his Thebans on the left, contrary to custom, and with them and superior cavalry fell furiously upon the Spartan right, which was broken after a fierce struggle. The halfhearted allies on both sides were not engaged. Some 400 Spartiates, over half those present and a third of all those living between eighteen and sixty, fell with their king. Epameinondas let the remnants withdraw, and no Spartan army ever again operated north of the Isthmus.

Thebes dominated northern Greece, and even intervened in Macedonia, taking Philip, a young prince, as hostage in 367. Epameinondas four times invaded the Peloponnese, liberating Messenia, where the splendid walls of Messene (Ithome) are still his monument, and organizing an Arcadian federation. But he was beaten off from the barricaded streets of unwalled Sparta. Many of Sparta's smaller allies stood by her; even the Lakonian helots did not rebel; and Athens, now afraid of Thebes, went over to Sparta's side. Thebes gained Persian favor and subsidies and with them built a fleet, but she had not the resources to keep it up. Athens, having reorganized a naval league with the built-in safeguard that her allies had to vote in a separate "chamber" on important matters, remained more important at sea. After Epameinondas had fallen in battle in the Peloponnese (362), Thebes proved unable even to coerce her neighbor Phokis, which hired mercenaries by "borrowing" from the Delphic treasury. Greece, despite repeated and genuine efforts by intelligent men to find a basis for a permanent "common peace," could never overcome the incompatibility of neighbors' short-term claims. It was a many-sided stalemate.

In Macedonia, political unity had been restored; but in 359 King Perdikkas was defeated and killed by the marauding Illyrians of modern Albania. All the open country was overrun; rival claimants to the throne appeared, with foreign support; and the 22-year-old Prince Philip, regent for Perdikkas' infant son, had to buy off enemies until he could deal with them one at a time. Then he did—and he did it thoroughly.

That he had known Thebes and its army in the days of Epameinondas, though not unimportant, was less important than the fact that Philip was a genius. Macedonia had fine resources of manpower, and horses from the plain of the Axios River. Philip organized them. In his second year, he smote the Illyrians a shattering blow, using tactics that owed something to Epameinondas. He also found a great tactician of his own. "Wonderful people, the Athenians," he remarked; "they find ten generals each year. I have only found one in my life, and that is Parmenion."

A proper appreciation of Philip would require a book on his reign. The army, in his second year, acclaimed him king, which was not contrary to custom. The young prince Alexander, Perdikkas' son, grew up at his court but was not given military commands. Great as a soldier, ever in the front line, repeatedly wounded, Philip was even greater in diplomacy. His successes in Greece were not won by deceiving the innocent (the Greeks were no innocents), but by exploiting existing enmities and by lavish use of gold. He early gained access to the gold fields of Mount Pangaion by protecting Amphipolis, an Athenian colony lost in the Peloponnesian War, which Athens hoped to regain. North of it he acquired a Thasian inland settlement, which he enlarged and renamed Philippi. With the gold, he also added Greek military and other experts to his entourage. Greece, in his early years when Philip did not seem very dangerous, was paralyzed: Thebes by her war with Phokis, and Athens by the revolt of the strongest members of her naval league, who were alarmed by signs of reviving Athenian imperialism, contrary to promises. In Thessaly the inland barons chose him as their war leader against the tyrants of more urban Pherai, who controlled Thessaly's only port at Pagasai.

The tyrants called in help from Phokis, whose mercenaries beat Philip twice; but in 352, at the "Crocus Fields" near Pagasai, his

Thessalian and Macedonian cavalry turned a flank and drove them into the sea. An Athenian fleet picked up swimmers. Athens had always been friendly to Phokis against Thebes and now garrisoned Thermopylai, saving Phokis for the time. Philip turned north, founding colonies of Macedonian peasants and Greek mine operators, and bringing some order among the warring tribes of Thrace. In 349–348 B.C. he conquered Chalkidike, which he had thoughtfully kept divided from Athens by giving places, which Athens hoped to regain, to the Chalkidian League, re-formed under the presidency of Olynthos. Upon Olynthos' appeal, Athens sent some troops, chiefly mercenaries; but they were too few and too late. It was wise, despite the furious patriotic oratory of Demosthenes, not to commit her main forces on Philip's "home pitch." Olynthos itself was disunited; and, not without treachery, it fell in 348 B.C. and was razed.

Athens now wanted peace, but Philip refused to make it with impious Phokis. It had naturally not escaped his notice that the liberation of holy Delphi would be good for his public image. Meanwhile he was delighted to discuss details. He knew that Athens would not want war again. So for two years (348–346) he let various Athenian envoys follow him wherever he happened to be. He was conquering the central Balkans. Phokis looked on, helpless; and when peace with Athens was agreed, quarrels broke out between the Phokian government and its mercenary commander. Philip let the mercenaries go abroad. Moralists noted that many of them perished fighting in Cyrenaica, and called it a divine vengeance. Phokis collapsed. Philip let Athenian intercession save its people from the extreme penalty of massacre and sale into slavery; but a conference of the sacred Amphictyony, or League of Neighbors, which met at Delphi, had them disarmed and sentenced to repay all that they had taken from the holy treasury, by installments over 200 years. Philip was awarded Phokis' two votes in the Amphictyonic Council. Already controlling those of Thessaly and its surrounding hill tribes, he had a majority. It was something like controlling the papacy in medieval Europe.

With Thebes as ally, he could now invade Attica at any time; but he never did. He genuinely admired Athenian culture. Aristotle, a Chalkidian-born disciple of Plato, was tutor to his son Alexander. Isocrates of Athens, self-proclaimed professor of an education for statesmen (in rivalry with Plato's "academic" idealism), despairing of a union of Greece led by Athens and Sparta, turned to Philip. Let him unite Greece for an attack on Persia. Philip wanted to do exactly that; and for such a purpose the Athenian navy would have been invaluable. But in the end, the fierce patriotism of Demosthenes prevailed. Athens' devotion to liberty (for herself, which might mean ruthless imperialism toward others) would not let her join in an alliance as junior partner.

The peace lasted five years. Then Philip's eastward progress led to "incidents" with Athenian mercenaries holding the Thracian Chersonese. Their general was bellicose, and Demosthenes supported him. In 340 Athens was on the same side as Persia, saving Greek cities on the narrow seas from Philip's attack. He turned away to defeat a nomad horde that had crossed the Danube; but he was wounded and lost most of his Scythian booty while marching home through the land of the still-defiant Thracian Triballoi.

Philip was reported dead. At the least, he had been beaten. Athenian armies liberated Euboia and Megara from his partisans, and even Thebes, his old ally, took from his troops a fortress guarding Thermopylai. But Philip was very much alive. Perhaps it was no coincidence that at the Amphictyonic Council in 339 Amphissa in Lokris, near Delphi, an ally of Thebes, moved to censure Athens for refurbishing, under the impious Phokians, a dedication of arms "taken from the Persians and Thebans when they fought against the Greeks." Athens' delegate, the orator Aischines, hit back with a worse charge against Amphissa, that of cultivating dedicated ground. A mob of Delphians went down to clear (and loot) the farms. The Lokrians chased them out with bloodshed. A holy war was declared against Lokris, and Philip, the protector, was invited to come and settle it.

Philip came. Thermopylai was blocked, but he got his army over the hills farther west, and fortified a forward base on the road not to Amphissa but to Thebes. Demosthenes urged Athens to forget old griefs and join Thebes against the archenemy; and thus took place the campaign that ended in total victory for Philip at Chaironeia in 338.

This battle has often been seen as a victory of the new, long, Macedonian pike over the six-foot Greek weapon. But an Athenian professional soldier had introduced nine-foot spears nearly sixty years before, for mercenary (well-trained, specialist) medium-light infantry. As to how the citizen-soldiers of 338 were armed, we have actually no evidence; but that Athens and Thebes had made no effort to match a weapon that could hardly be kept secret is most improbable. Philip more probably won by the greater professionalism of his men, by tactics (actually giving ground before the charge of the Athenians, he may have drawn the allied line askew and spoiled its "dressing"), and by superiority in cavalry. These he massed on his left (on his right was a rocky hillside) and committed to his beloved and splendid eighteen-year-old son, Alexander, who that day led his first triumphant cavalry charge. Smashing the allied horse and outflanking their infantry line, this decided the fate of Greece: the hammer to Philip's anvil.

Philip still treated Athens extraordinarily gently. He released Athenian prisoners unransomed. He cremated their dead on the field and sent home the ashes, escorted by Alexander. He took the Chersonese, but even gave Athens frontier rectifications at the expense of Thebes. The disloyal ally Thebes suffered much worse: execution of some leaders, prisoners held for ransom or sold as slaves, and a garrison in the citadel.

Greece was united in defeat. At Corinth, once the center of resistance to Xerxes, Philip inaugurated a new League of the Hellenes with its declared purpose, vengeance on Persia. Sparta alone stood out. Philip deprived her of some borderlands, in favor of Argos and Messenia—and then went no further, cheating her even of a glorious end. In about 337 Parmenion crossed the Hellespont to secure a bridgehead in the Troad.

But Philip was not to follow. In 336 he was murdered at a high festival by a young man with an old grievance that he had refused to set right. He had long been on bad terms with Olympias, Alexander's adored and tempestuous mother; and he had lately married (he was polygamous) a daughter of a nobleman and niece of a general. This worthy, speaking at the wedding banquet, prayed that she might bear a legitimate heir to the throne. Alexander, publicly insulted, threw his winecup in the general's face. Philip drew his sword and tried to attack his son but was so drunk that he fell down. Alexander took his mother and fled into exile. Although this quarrel was remarkably soon patched up—for no baby would be a substitute for Alexander—there was an obvious suspicion that Olympias and even Alexander had planned the murder and (very important) the immediate killing of the assassin. This view has been not unpopular among recent writers. One should therefore notice that Aristotle in his *Politics,* the sole surviving contemporary evidence, names Philip among no fewer than nine public personages murdered in purely private quarrels.

Aristotle, then teaching in Athens, would certainly never have said anything offensive to Alexander, if only from prudence; but if he, surely well informed, thought that there was really more to it than that, then, with eight other examples to cite, why name Philip at all?

ALEXANDER'S EMPIRE

Alexander was acclaimed at once by the army (that was what mattered), and liquidated a number of people deemed dangerous, including his cousin, Amyntas, Perdikkas' son. Thoughts of freedom ran through Philip's empire; but a swift march into Greece, cutting steps up Mount Ossa when the Thessalians demurred at letting him through the pass of Tempe, won him succession to the generalship of the Hellenic League. (Philip's friends were in all key positions.) In 335 he swept through the Balkans, routing Thracians on the Shipka Pass, nomads beyond the Danube, and Illyrians in Albania, after being apparently trapped in their hills. He met migrating Gauls, peacefully, somewhere near Belgrade. They did not come farther while he lived. He was reported killed in Illyria, and Thebes revolted; but he was before its walls in sixteen days and inside them in a few more, his men entering on the heels of a sortie. He razed the city (nominally on the sentence of a jury of the neighbors, whom Thebes had bullied) but piously spared the temples and the house of the poet Pindar. Thirty thousand people were sold into slavery. Greece was shocked—and cowed.

Having done in a year what many a good general might have been happy to do in five, Alexander then invaded Asia in 334 with 40,000 men, destroyed the armies of the nearest satraps in a cavalry melee beside the River Granicus (Çan Çayı), in which he came close to being killed, and liberated the eastern Greeks. In 333, on the plain of Issus on the northern border of Syria, he routed King Darius III (new to the throne, after two palace assassinations), who had thought to cut him off by occupying the narrow coastal plain of Issos behind him. Then Alexander secured Phoenicia. Proud Tyre held out through most of 332, while the Persians tried to take the war back to the Aegean; but the other cities (chief among them Sidon, harshly punished for a recent revolt) and Greek Cyprus brought their ships back from the Aegean to join him, and with their help he stormed Tyre from the sea. It suffered the fate of Thebes.

In Egypt, lately reconquered after sixty years of freedom, he won over the priests by respecting their gods. The Persians, with a higher religion (an ethical dualism) and contempt for animal gods, had been hated. He was crowned pharaoh, and the desert oracle of Amon, long identified with Zeus by Greeks, accordingly hailed him as Amon's son. Alexander took it much to heart. He had a pedigree back to Zeus through Herakles; he was conscious of his genius; and there was talk in Greece, even among intellectuals, of whether great men (such as Empedocles or Lysander) were in some way superhuman. But the Macedonians did not like it. In Egypt too he founded the first and greatest of his many Alexandrias, a window toward Greece.

In 331 B.C., having already refused Darius' offer to cede all territory up to the Euphrates, he crossed both the Euphrates and the Tigris and shattered the empire's full strength and superior cavalry, drawn up in open cavalry country, at Gaugamela. In a brilliant tactical maneuver he stalled off masses of outflanking cavalry with aggressive flank guards until, with his heavy cavalry and phalanx of pikemen still intact, he could deliver and lead one deadly thrust to the heart. Darius fled east into Media—his second flight—and loyalty to him began to crumble. Mazaeus, the satrap of Babylon who had fought bravely at Gaugamela, surrendered the city. Alexander rested there for forty days, leaking the rumor that his men were demoralized by wine and women. Then he marched out to the southeast, storming mountain passes in winter, to take Susa, Persepolis, Pasargadai, the huge imperial gold reserve, the Persian homeland and best recruiting ground. He burned Persepolis and sent the young men afar, to be drilled as soldiers of the new king. In the spring of 330, Darius at Hamadan had only 1,500 faithful Greek mercenaries and the troops of the eastern satraps; in retreat they deposed, arrested, and—when the pursuit grew hot—murdered him.

Even then it took four campaigns to subdue the warlike northeastern provinces, where "impregnable" mountain castles had to be taken and mobile forces rose again in his rear; and during these trying years severe tension developed between Alexander and his officers. There were several tragedies. Already late in 330 Philotas, son of Parmenion and commander of the horse guards, had been executed for failing to report a conspiracy; his old father, left at base in Hamadan (not unreasonably, at age seventy) was then murdered, lest he take up the vendetta. Kleitos, Alexander's foster brother, who had saved his life in the first battle, taunted him at a banquet with taking all the glory for the work of the army; and Alexander, after much provocation, slew him with his own hand. This act cost him agonies of remorse, but it was too late. Kallisthenes, the official historian, Aristotle's nephew, perished after a conspiracy among the royal pages. Schoolmaster to these young gentlemen, he had spoken of tyrants and tyrannicide; and Alexander in his eastern robes seemed to be becoming the authentic thing. The tradition of Alexander the tyrant began at that time.

Yet, lavish with spoil, leader in battle, repeatedly wounded, he kept the loyalty of his men. In 326 he crossed the Indus River, still hot for the world's end, which he believed to be within reach. He beat Porus, the rajah of Paurava, the greatest warrior in the Punjab, with his 200 (or more probably about seventy) elephants; but that was his last great battle. The men, at last, refused to march against the Ganges kingdoms, which were reported to have 5,000 elephants.

So he returned, reaching the Indian Ocean via the Indus, after more bloody campaigns and a nearly mortal wound. He built ships to explore the seaway back to the gulf and himself marched with a column (not the whole army) by the desert coast to dig wells and leave food depots for the fleet. It was a disaster; he lost many men and nearly all their wives and children to thirst, exhaustion, and a flash flood that overwhelmed his camp in a wadi. The fleet got through, with much hardship. He executed several satraps and generals who had misgoverned, not expecting to see him again. He organized a new army, two-thirds Iranian, and was about to sail for southern Arabia when, in the spring of 323, he fell sick of a fever at Babylon (perhaps tertian malaria) and died in ten days.

What Alexander did is well documented. The fierce controversies about him are mostly about what he thought he was doing, meant to do, and thought about himself; these are questions for which all answers are largely guesses. Our ancient sources, all secondhand, give portraits of Alexander the hero, Alexander the tyrant, Alexander the megalomaniac who thought he was God; and writers ancient and modern have tended to emphasize one or the other. But we do have some firm evidence on personal choices that he made.

First, his only child—a son—was posthumous, though he had married Roxane, daughter of a baron of Sogdia (modern Tadjikistan) in 328. There is rumor that an earlier baby had died in India. But Parmenion and others had begged him to marry and leave an heir before invading Asia. He would not; he spoke contemptuously of "dallying among women." He was, indeed, in debt, and only conquests could maintain his army for long; but Parmenion probably appreciated that as well as he did. Even one alleged bastard, Herakles, was first heard of (and soon murdered) after the little Alexander had suffered the same fate in 310, amid the wars of the generals. Parmenion had known well what lack of an heir would mean.

Alexander was thus no womanizer. At the same time, he was noticeably chivalrous to women of his mother's age; and Olympias would not have minced her words in the presence of her young son over what she thought of her husband's affairs with other women. The result looks to this writer like a "mother fixation," plus an abnormal, infantile reaction against normal sex. It is more fashionable nowadays to say that he must have been homosexual; but if so, ancient Greek literature being what it is on the subject, it is rather surprising that we do not hear more about it. The furious energy with which he marched and fought seems more indicative of repression.

A second result of a personal choice by Alexander was the attempted march to the world's end and actual conquest of what are now Afghanistan, Pakistan, and part of Turkistan. In all these areas he left considerable garrisons, largely of veteran Greek mercenaries replaced by new ones who came out for adventure and loot, settled in native towns now given the added name of Alexandria. They represented a formidable drain of Greek manpower, and their permanent constructive achievement was not great. Bactria, which soon broke away under its own soldier kings (about 280–130), produced some splendid coins before the nomads overran it. In the Punjab, Greek art may have influenced the beginning of Buddhist sculpture; and a King Menander (*ca.* 155–*ca.* 130), who marched to the Ganges, figures (as Milinda) in a Buddhist classic in which he is converted to that faith. But that is all; and farther west, where there were fewer Greeks, the Arsacids, chiefs of nomad descent, seized the province of Parthia about 250, presently all Iran, and later Iraq. Several Parthian kings used on their coins the evidently prestigious epithet "Philhellene"; but it was essentially an Iranian state, one that restored unity to Iran for 400 years.

The loss of the east was accelerated by the preoccupation of the warring Successors with the west, and not least with access to Greece as a source of military and other expert manpower. The huge empire of Seleukos, last commander of Alexander's foot guards, crumbled while Seleukids fought the Ptolemies of Egypt for Syria in wars more costly than even that prize was worth. When his hands were free, about 210, Antiochos III could still march to the Oxus River, winning nominal and fleeting homage from Parthians and Bactrian Greeks; but Egypt, carefully detached and appropriated by Ptolemy I, Alexander's best intelligence and security officer, was much more stable. It was a purely Greco-Macedonian monarchy, proud of its Alexandrian culture centered in the great library, and squeezing wealth from the peasants through a Greek-writing bureaucracy with Macedonian troops (as many as could be got) to keep order. The kings, like the pharaohs, married their sisters. There was some decline in vigor in two centuries, probably more from palace life than from genetic causes; but the family ability flared again in the last (the famous) Cleopatra VII, the first of her line ever to learn Egyptian. She was fluent in several other languages too; and she tried to save her ancestral heritage by captivating, with her charm and wit—though without great facial beauty, to judge by her coins—Roman generals.

In Asia Minor, which Alexander had crossed, taking all the Mediterranean ports but barely touching the northeast, disintegration also set in. The Seleukids claimed it all; but the Ptolemies, for the sake of access to Greece and the Aegean and to timber for ships, held points on the coast of Cyprus and "protected" a puppet league of the Greek islands. New independent states arose. Bithynia in the northwest, under kings of mixed blood with Greek names, brought in as allies (278) the Galatians, the Gauls whom Alexander had met near Belgrade. Their war band of perhaps 20,000 terrorized and plundered far and wide; but after being fought and bought off from Ionia by the Greeks under the captains of Pergamum, and beaten in the east by Antiochos, son of Seleukos, with elephants in his army, they settled a new Galatia in the center, with Asian subjects. East of Galatia was Cappadocia, under kings descended from the Persian satraps, and northeast, the land of Pontus ("Ocean," or the Black Sea), whose kings, descended from other satraps, also held lands beyond that sea (notably Tauris) and aspired to dominate it. Armenia fell under the influence of Parthia, while the Seleukid Empire kept open a tenuous road, reaching the Aegean around Miletos.

Such was the patchwork into which the Persian Empire, shattered by Alexander, broke up in the two generations after his death. Greek influence was spread far, but thinly—the chief cities of Syria, for example, were renamed after Seleukid kings or places in Macedonia—but all the older names reappeared at once with the Muslim conquest, and very few Greek ones survived except in books. Alexandria provided salaried posts for scientists and scholars, even a few poets. Greek Gadara had poets as well as swine.

Pergamum's Hellenistic baroque sculpture of its huge altar (the "Satan's Seat" of the Apocalypse), produced when its rulers had declared themselves kings, to the annoyance of the Ptolemies, at least has power. But were these royal splendors worth so much blood? And would the poetry have been worse without them? Would it not have been better if Philip, who would have been only fifty-nine when Alexander died, had lived to be sixty and used his middle age to reconcile Greece (if possible) and Hellenize an empire of less monstrous size—stopping at the Euphrates, as Parmenion advised, or perhaps, after occupying its capitals to teach Persia a lesson, retiring magnanimously to the western mountains of Iran?

To go farther was at best a mistake (genius is near to madness); but Alexander's worst crime was his neglect, while continually risking his life, to leave an heir and, in case of a minority, to give clear directions for a regency. He simply gave no sign of caring what happened even to his own country when he was dead.

Macedonia itself suffered worst of all. It had nine rulers in forty-three years, only the first two being legitimate, the regents for the puppet co-kings, Alexander's posthumous son Alexander and feebleminded half brother Arrhidaios (throne name, Philip III). Then came violence, in which perished Olympias (who had seized power and killed Arrhidaios) and, later, the little Alexander. The royal tombs were dug up and plundered by Gallic mercenaries; two, perhaps those of the last kings, miraculously survived at Aigai, the old capital, now Vergina. In 279 the whole land was ravaged by other, independent Gauls or Galatians, who raided far into Greece. It was rescued in 276 by Antigonos Gonatas, grandson of Antigonos Monophthalmos (One-eye), who had been a great marshal and late contender for the empire. Gonatas, a brave and conscientious man and a Stoic, restored order (the Gauls having mostly been killed in Greece) and founded a dynasty that lasted until the Roman conquest in 168 B.C.

GREECE UNDER THE SUPERPOWERS

Athens, on the news of Alexander's death, made a brave effort to recover her freedom; her chief ally was the mountain confederacy of Aitolia, where the population had been increasing. The Greeks were beaten; tragically, they would have done better to wait a year or two, but they could not foresee that by that time the generals would be locked in conflict. Athens, defeated by land and sea (the latter being the more important), was never again a world power; but as the city of the philosophers, where a man might say what he would, without (as at Alexandria) caring about the king, Athens was only just beginning. Plato's school, the Academy, lasted for 900 years.

When the struggle for the empire petered out in its partition into still-hostile succession states, Greek cities regained a measure of independence, but it was never complete. Antigonos and his line could not hope to garrison the whole country; but they garrisoned Piraeus, Corinth, Chalkis, and Demetrias (near Volos, named for Gonatas' father): nodal points of communications, useful against any general Greek rising. They were called the Fetters of Greece. The Ptolemies, with their interest in the Aegean, were always ready to support anti-Macedonian movements; but their powerful fleet and mercenaries never effected much. Thus when Athens rose under Chremonides, a democratic leader (266), the Egyptian fleet only hovered offshore; a king of Sparta was killed trying to force the Isthmus, and Athens was starved out (262). Antigonos refrained from reprisals; but his garrisons stayed until 229, when Macedonia was hard pressed by northern barbarians. Athens then bought out the mercenary commander with a financial effort that included pawning the official texts of the great tragedians to Ptolemy III and survived thereafter in "Swiss" neutrality.

Only Aitolia remained truly free. She dominated central Greece, with Delphi and, through alliance with Elis, Olympia too. She claimed to represent Greek freedom; but her privateers at sea were not easily distinguishable from pirates. Urban southern Greeks disliked these rude highlanders; and after 251 the League of the Achaian cities on the Corinthian Gulf extended its membership and emerged as a conscious rival. This was chiefly the work of Aratos, of neighboring Sikyon, a strange, neurotic hero, visibly afraid before a battle, yet brave enough to liberate his city by cloak-and-dagger methods and wise enough to lead it into the league. Much of Arcadia followed, and in 243 Aratos carried out his greatest heroic coup, scaling the cliffs of Acrocorinth to liberate it from the Macedonians by a night surprise. He now had half the Peloponnese, and the aged Antigonos let him be.

Both leagues were genuine federal states. The Greeks never achieved representative government, not because they were too stupid but (probably) because they did not trust each other enough. But each league elected annually a general as chief executive, eligible for reelection but not in successive years, and an advisory council, important but not sovereign. Sovereignty rested with a general assembly, meeting twice a year and in emergencies, which all free men might attend (but naturally the poor could not do so regularly). Votes were counted not individually, but by communities, with "weightage" according to estimated population. Still there was no federal Greece, for the two leagues, alas, were never friendly.

Aratos' tragedy, and Achaia's, were connected with tragedy at Sparta, which now had a revolution, centuries too late. The number of Spartan peers had continued to decrease; there were now only 700. Their families were, naturally, very rich. Sparta's later wars were fought by paid men. Two young kings, of opposite royal houses, successively thought to restore an ideal Sparta (as they dreamed of it), with equal and inalienable lots of land and thousands of new citizens. The first, Agis IV, was legally outmaneuvered and, when he refused to make civil war, was tried for revolutionary action and hanged. In 227 Kleomenes III, taught by his example, did use force, killing four ephors and ten of their supporters. He carried the land reform and could raise a Spartan army 20,000 strong. A thrill ran through the Peloponnese, where the gulf between rich and poor had widened. It had widened throughout Greece, indeed, ever since the inflation caused when Alexander dispersed the Persian gold reserve. The Achaian League, at war with Sparta (this had given the young king his "revolutionary situation"), seemed about to crumble. But Kleomenes was not a social revolutionary; he was a Spartan king, and his revolution was not for export. He offered to join the Achaian League—if he were made its permanent general. Aratos in desperation appealed to Antigonos III Doson, regent in Macedonia for young Philip V, whose father had fallen in 229; and as the payment for aid he handed back the key of the Isthmus, his own prize, Corinth. Kleomenes, after a brave fight, was crushed at Sellasia, north of Sparta (223). He fled to Egypt in hope of returning with Egyptian aid. Put off with words, in 219 he tried to raise a revolt in Alexandria, of all places; he failed and committed suicide.

Antigonos formed a new Hellenic League, with the Achaian League as a part of it; but Aitolia still stood out. Her "nationalist" privateers in the Aegean became a plague. Both Macedon and Egypt had economized on their fleets, though some policing was done in the south by that of Rhodes, where a merchant oligarchy satisfied the people with social services. It was, says the geographer Strabo, "a welfare state though not a democracy."

Rhodes in 217 offered to mediate in a general war of the two leagues. Agelaos of Naupaktos, welcoming the delegates to a great conference there, spoke of the need for peace, "for if the cloud rising in the west should reach Greece, we shall be praying heaven to give us back the chance to call our very quarrels our own." Hannibal was in Italy, winning his early triumphs; and before that Rome, mistress of Italy, chasing pirates in the Adriatic, had interfered in Illyria—too close for Macedonia's liking. A peace was made; but local causes of friction remained, and at the height of Hannibal's success young Philip V made an alliance with him. It was a fatal mistake. Rome's formidable seapower chased his fleet off the western sea, and Rome made alliance with Aitolia. With modest Roman support, Aitolia waged a new war, until 205; and by that time, Hannibal was a spent force.

Roman contact with Greece was nothing new. The western Greeks, even before Italy was united, had been hard pressed by Italian peoples, who had access to substantial supplies of metal. Cumae and Poseidonia fell to the Lucanians (of Samnite origin) before 400. They continued to exist, with some coarsening of their culture. Greek traders settled in Rome; Greek books were read, Greek art admired and imitated. The southern cities were weakened by the attacks of Dionysios I, tyrant of Syracuse (405–367), who made alliance with their enemies and employed Gauls as mercenaries. Taras survived, still a city of some power but repeatedly calling for help from her mother city, Sparta, or from the newly powerful kingdom of Epeiros. The last such expedition was that of Pyrrhos, grandson of Alexander's sister, who fought the Romans in campaigns of much tactical interest (280–275); but after he retired, defeated, Taras fell (272).

Rome's first Carthaginian or Punic (that is, Phoenician) War (264–241) brought Sicily into Rome's orbit and many works of art to Rome. Massalia became Rome's ally. Then came the war with Hannibal (218–201), and after it the Senate determined to settle with Philip. In 197 Philip was beaten at Kynos Kephalai ("the dogs' heads," a range of hills in Thessaly), where Aitolian cavalry took his phalanx in flank. He was made to withdraw altogether from Greece; but the young consul Titus Quinctius Flamininus announced the withdrawal of Roman troops too: Greece was to be free.

There was great rejoicing; but the Aitolians, dissatisfied with their share in the peace terms, then invited Antiochos III, the great Seleukid, to settle things better. Rome, after two foreign invasions, was nervous, and reacted. Her legions drove his first small army in rout from Thermopylai (191 B.C.), and in 189, with allies from Greece and Pergamum, shattered his main forces in Asia Minor. He was made to retire beyond the Taurus Mountains, with Pergamum receiving territorial gains; and the Aitolians were hammered in two mountain campaigns.

Rome had still taken no territory in Greece; but a miserable feature of the following years was that Greeks complained of their rivals to the superpower. Complaints from Pergamum about alleged expansionist designs of Macedonia led to the destruction of that kingdom (in the Battle of Pydna, 168) and its division into four republics, with reduced taxation; but the Macedonians themselves were not grateful. A thousand Achaians, suspected of Macedonian sympathies, were taken as hostages to Italy, where most of them died (as did Perseus, last king of Macedonia). One of the fortunate survivors was the historian Polybius. Later Sparta complained, with some reason, of Achaian League interference, and a Roman mission went to investigate. "We want you as friends," said an Achaian, "but not as masters." At last, needled to madness, Achaian democrats, of whom Polybius had a poor opinion, resorted to war. At the same time there was a populist-royalist rising in Macedonia. As a result, the league was abolished; the cities remained as separate allies—all except Corinth. That was razed, as an example; its art treasures were shipped to Rome; and the consul Lucius Mummius is said to have insisted on the usual clause in his contract with the shippers, that if any articles were lost in transit, they must be replaced by others "not less good." The site lay waste for a century, probably under a solemn curse like Carthage, destroyed in the same year (146 B.C.), until the irreligious Julius Caesar repeopled both with colonies of his veterans. Macedonia was placed under direct rule as Rome's first eastern province. That of Achaia was established only much later.

The province of Asia followed in 133, when the last king, Attalos of Pergamum, childless and perhaps hoping to avert worse, left his realm by will to the Roman people. His own people did not approve. They rose under an illegitimate brother of Attalos, who proclaimed a utopian "Sun City." Neighboring kings helped Rome to put it down. The province of "Asia" then became the victim of an atrocious system of taxation. Syndicates of rich publicans at Rome bid for the prize of collecting the tribute, paid the treasury, and set out to make a profit, while Roman troops kept order. Swarms of Italian moneylenders, often secretly representing senators (great landowners, nominally forbidden to engage in trade) moved in to provide the people with the money that they had to have (in effect, their own money back again) at exorbitant rates of interest. After a generation of this, when the non-Romans in Italy had risen in arms to demand citizen rights, Mithridates VI of Pontus invaded the province while Rome's hands were tied. The Greeks of Asia joined him in mass, and in a general pogrom 80,000 Italian men, women, and children are said to have been killed—a figure perhaps exaggerated but eloquent of the people's feelings.

Mithridates' armies crossed to Greece; his fleet sacked Delos, which, made by Rome into a free port, had become a horrible slave market. (The rich Roman houses still partly standing there are those of the dealers.) The free port itself was a measure of economic warfare against free Rhodes, which gave no casus belli. Athens rose under a philosopher named Aristion, whom history paints in the blackest colors; but it was written from the Roman side. In Italy, civil war broke out between generals Gaius Marius and Lucius Cornelius Sulla, both wanting the eastern command; but the temporarily victorious patrician Sulla crossed to Greece and besieged Athens. Attempts at relief failed, and Athens fell to starvation, catapult artillery, and finally assault. Piraeus was totally destroyed. In the city, Sulla contemptuously agreed to "spare the living for the sake of the dead"; but Aristion and other leaders were executed. Crossing to Asia and taking over a rival Roman army (its general slew himself), Sulla drove Mithridates out of the province and then made peace; going back to "restore order" in Italy, he drowned the opposing party in torrents of blood. After 74, when Rome annexed Bithynia (allegedly by the will of its last king) there was a final Mithridatic war, ending with the suicide of the king in the Crimea, his last possession.

Gnaeus Pompeius (Pompey), the general who finished the war, did not cross the Black Sea. He turned to settle the east. The Seleukid Empire, reduced to Syria and rent by faction even there, had been overrun by Mithridates' ally, the king of Armenia. Pompey "liberated" but did not restore it. It became the province of Syria, its urban language Greek, the Greek of the Gospels. Of the Succession states of Alexander's empire only Egypt remained and the last Ptolemies, unimpressive characters, survived by bribing top Roman statesmen and exploiting their rivalries, until the deaths of Cleopatra VII and Marcus Antonius (Mark Antony) in 30 B.C.

For Greece, the last century B.C. was a time of humiliation punctuated by wars. Pirates were suppressed by Pompey; but moneylenders, including Marcus Tullius Cicero's friends Atticus and Brutus, remained. Athens, living on its past, drew to its schools of philosophy and rhetoric young Romans, from the sons of consuls, like the younger Cicero, to Quintus Horatius Flaccus (Horace), son of a freedman. But after 49 the Greek world became the battleground of the final Roman civil wars: Caesar versus Pompey; Antony and Caesar's great-nephew and heir Gaius Julius Caesar Octavianus (later Augustus) versus Brutus and Gaius Cassius; the same young Octavian versus Antony and Cleopatra between 32 and 30.

The Roman Empire adorned Greece, as it did even distant Britain, with some notable buildings. Julius Caesar may (it is a guess) have given Athens the water-clock tower known as the Tower of the Winds, to replace one destroyed in the sack by Sulla. Marcus Vipsanius Agrippa donated a handsome covered theater; but his and Augustus' munificence was not disinterested. Planted firmly in the middle of the demarcated ancient Agora, the theater obliterated that site more firmly than war had done. The empire explicitly disapproved of democracy, even municipal. Roman Athens, though nominally a free ally, was not to need such a place. For shopping, Augustus provided a supposedly nicer and smaller market a short distance to the east. It had walls.

Athens flourished as a university; Massalia and Rhodes came second to it. Caesar's Corinth grew rapidly more Greek: the Corinth of St. Paul. Sparta was preserved as a museum piece with its archaic customs. Visitors were provided with a theater in which to view the celebrated boys' whipping contests. In Macedonia, wider plains supported larger cities, such as Philippi and Thessaloniki (Salonica), on the great highway to the east.

In peninsular Greece Plutarch, deservedly the most read of Greek writers of this age, deplored the decline of population and the running down of natural resources. Is the whole universe running down? he asks in one of the dialogues that he wrote before the famous *Lives*. He doubts whether all Greece could now raise 3,000 armored men. Part of Greece, against Xerxes, had raised 38,000 men. Pausanias, rather younger than Plutarch, notes in his still-useful guidebook to Greece's antiquities that he found at Patrai a population two-thirds female, working mainly in the textile industry, and "if ever women belonged to Aphrodite they do." (Many males had emigrated to Rome or the east.)

But care should be taken in interpreting Plutarch. Later, for the Christian fourth and fifth centuries, archaeology has revealed the foundations of numerous and large basilica churches, their superstructures robbed away after they had been wrecked and plundered by various invaders, including the Slavs. Evidently, for an authority that cared for the common people, people were there. What Plutarch is thinking of is armored men, who were landowners, middling farmers or richer; that all Greece, without Macedonia, was now divided into as few as 3,000 estates is something that can easily be believed. Many of them were vast. Very rich Greeks, even in the peninsula, are a phenomenon mentioned by other authors too.

The fact was simply that Roman society was plutocratic. Rich men were literally considered better than poor, so the natural tendency of the rich to grow richer went unchecked. The rich of the later empire were enormously rich; while their corresponding lack of numbers, and the lack of enthusiasm and sometimes physical unfitness of the poor to defend a society in which they had no stake, go far to account for the fall of the empire. The great estates were by no means run without men; but for Plutarch, a humane man personally, such men, quite literally, did not count.

The Greek millionaire of whom we know most was Vibullus Hipparchus Tiberius Claudius Atticus Herodes (Herodes Atticus), with wide lands at Marathon and elsewhere. He was a popular lecturer on history and ethics at Athens. As he did not need money, he must have been a teacher by choice. The emperor Antoninus Pius (A.D. 138–161) picked him as tutor to his adopted son Marcus Aurelius; and in Greek Marcus (reigned A.D. 161–180) wrote his *Meditations,* some of them in camp on the Danube, where, as in the Socratic phrase, he was "holding the line, in the place where God had put him." Herodes was also a great donor. To Athens he gave a great theater, perhaps the one still in use southwest of the Acropolis; and Olympia, Delphi, and other sacred sites also shared in his benefactions. But as Goldsmith wrote in "The Deserted Village,"

> ill fares the land, to hastening ills a prey
> where wealth accumulates, and men decay.

The collapse of the empire was foreshadowed in the third century, when inflation by debasement of the coinage raised prices thirtyfold in thirty years, and some twenty-five emperors perished, mostly in military coups. A Gothic tribe, the Heruli, in southern Russia, took to the sea and, though some of their boats were sunk by naval patrols, sacked Greek cities from Sinope to Ephesos and, in 267, Athens.

Even then Athens and its "university" made a partial recovery. Its students at this time (355 B.C.) ironically included the later canonized St. Basil, who campaigned to save the pagan classics in Christian education, and the later emperor Flavius Claudius Julianus (Julian the Apostate). He was a nephew of Constantine the Great; his father had been liquidated by his Christian cousins to secure their succession. Being also a lover of the classics, he made as emperor a last and foredoomed attempt to restore the outworn Olympian religion. Athens even survived Alaric and his Goths (395), though not without further damage. The inevitable final date for its ancient history must be put in 529, when Justinian, sponsor of the great Church of the Holy Wisdom (Hagia Sophia) in Constantinople, ordered the closing of the pagan philosophic schools.

BIBLIOGRAPHY

Modern English writing on the history of Greece begins with George Grote's twelve-volume *History of Greece*, first published 1849–1856 and often reprinted thereafter. The early volumes have been rendered totally obsolete by the rise of archaeological work in Greece (beginning in the nineteenth century) but volumes five to twelve, dealing with the period 480–323 B.C., are based on the same literary sources as are available to modern scholars, and remain worth reading, especially for the history of Athens.

The standard English one-volume treatment of Greek history throughout the twentieth century has been J. B. Bury's *A History of Greece* (first published in 1900), now skilfully edited and updated by Russell Meiggs, 4th ed. (1975; repr. 1985). Nicholas G. L. Hammond's *A History of Greece*, 3d ed. (1986) is agreeably written, but his dates are not always infallible. *The Cambridge Ancient History*, first edition published in twelve volumes (1923–1939), is currently being rewritten by a powerful team of scholars. With the publication of vol. 3, pt. 3, they reached sixth-century Greece, and with the appearance (out of order) of vol. 7, pt. 1, the Hellenistic world. *The Pelican History of Greece* by A. R. Burn (16th impr.,

1986) has been repeatedly revised to take account of new discoveries since its first edition in 1965. Several older works combined learning and charm and continue to hold their own: they include Alfred Zimmern's *The Greek Commonwealth* (1911, subsequently revised; appreciated for the author's sympathy and familiarity with the Greek countryside and pre-mechanized ways of life); H. D. F. Kitto's *The Greeks* (1951, reprinted many times; contained an original chapter on uncritically accepted views on the position of Athenian women); and (Cecil) Maurice Bowra's *The Greek Experience* (first published in 1958).

GREEK HISTORIANS IN TRANSLATION

Readers wishing to know what the ancient Greeks themselves said—without the rewarding study of the language itself—may read Homer, Herodotus, Thucydides, and Xenophon in modern translations that have been published by Penguin Books. Reliable translations in an older English idiom were published earlier by Dent (in its Everyman's Library) and in series, among them the Bohn series, that favored literalness.

The best translation of the fragments of early Greek lyric poetry, important as historical sources as well as for their literary merit, is the collection edited and translated by Richmond Lattimore, *Greek Lyrics* (1955, subsequently revised and enlarged). The edition of *Hesiod and Theognis* (translated by Dorothy Wender and published in a single volume by Penguin, 1973) should also be consulted.

Plutarch's Athenian *Lives*, translated by Ian Scott-Kilvert, are assembled in a volume entitled *The Rise and Fall of Athens* (Penguin, 1960), while his lives of Alexander, Demosthenes, and three of his warring successors are found in *The Age of Alexander* (Penguin, 1973). The chief sources for the study of Alexander are found in the histories of Arrian, translated by Aubrey De Selincourt and entitled *The Campaigns of Alexander* (1976), and in Quintus Curtius Rufus, *The History of Alexander*, translated by John Yardley (1984).

PREHISTORY AND THE ARCHAIC AGE

John Boardman, *The Greeks Overseas*, 2d ed. (1980); A. R. Burn, *The Lyric Age of Greece*, rev. ed.

(1967); Oswyn Murray, *Early Greece* (1980); Chester G. Starr, *The Origins of Greek Civilization* (1961). See also the bibliographies to the essays on Art and Poetry (Homeric).

THE CLASSICAL AGE (FIFTH AND FOURTH CENTURIES)

Russell Meiggs, *The Athenian Empire* (1973), a work of massive scholarship, discusses the numerous problems arising from the sources, including the Athenian "tribute lists." A. H. M. Jones, *Athenian Democracy* (1957) and W. G. G. Forrest, *The Emergence of Greek Democracy* (1966) both treat with common sense a subject of controversy. See also John K. Davies, *Democracy and Classical Greece* (1978), and A. R. Burn, *Pericles and Athens* (1948; repr. 1960), a biography of this not very well documented central figure.

GREECE AND PERSIA

A. R. Burn, *Persia and Greece* (1962), ending 449 B.C., has been supplemented by David M. Lewis (1984). See also *The Cambridge History of Iran,* vol. 2, chaps. 6 and 8.

ALEXANDER THE GREAT

Hero, saint, or an ancient-day Stalin, the figure of Alexander continues to inspire scholars and writers. The older view of Alexander as hero and saint has been counterbalanced by Ernst Badian in several articles, by R. D. Milns in *Alexander the Great* (1968), and by Peter Green in *Alexander of Macedon* (1974). More charitable views are found in Robin Lane Fox, *Alexander the Great* (1973), and A. R. Burn, *Alexander the Great and the Hellenistic Empire* (1947), reissued with an additional chapter and new title, *Alexander the Great and the Hellenistic World* (1960). Mary Renault's nonfictional *Nature of Alexander* (1975) and romances are all worth reading.

THE HELLENISTIC AGE

The authoritative work is William W. Tarn and G. T. Griffith's, *Hellenistic Civilisation,* 3d ed. (1952). Max Cary in *A History of the Greek World, 323–146 B.C.* (1932); repr. with new bibliography, 1968), covers the same ground, if perhaps in a more historically conventional way. *The Hellenistic Age* (1923; repr. 1968) by J. B. Bury, E. A. Barber, Edwyn Bevan, and William W. Tarn covers in short, brilliant essays Greece's literature, popular philosophy, and revolutions. For translations of the literature of the period, see Richard W. Livingstone's anthology, *The Mission of Greece* (1928); Pliny the Younger's *Letters* (2 vols., Loeb Classical Library series) and the latter half of *Acts of the Apostles* are both excellent sources for daily life in the Greek-speaking world under the Romans.

Historical Summary of Rome

ARTHER FERRILL

ROME'S PLACE IN HISTORY

The history of Rome reveals a native ability, highly pragmatic and tenacious, for the arts of government, law, and warfare. Other ancient peoples in the Mediterranean were skillful warriors, especially the Greeks, who under Alexander carried military ingenuity to unparalleled heights; but the Romans combined their warlike prowess with an equally remarkable capacity for peace, for effective political organization and the rule of disparate nations with varied ethnic backgrounds—in short, a genius for knowing what to do with victory after achieving it on the field. In that respect they far surpassed their neighbors and left a unified cultural legacy of administration and law that has had a forceful impact even on the modern world.

Fortunately Romans developed the aesthetic and intellectual capacity to admire, imitate, and elaborate upon Greek cultural achievements in art, architecture, literature, and philosophy, and therefore Romans served the world as the preservers and transmitters of Hellenic achievement. How they developed the interrelated arts of war and peace and how they used them to shape world history is a story of "immense majesty," to use an expression from Edward Gibbon, and for the most part, despite obvious flaws in Roman character, a story of promise fulfilled. One cannot ignore the warts on Roman civilization—cruelty, rapaciousness, violence, and stubbornness, to name but a few—but in the long sweep of Western history Rome's influence was positive and fundamental.

EARLY ROME

The beginnings of Roman history do not offer the splendor of Mycenaean gold or the glory of Homeric epics, but they do reveal some of the essential ingredients of Roman character. Early Roman monuments were sewers and roads, and unlike the Greeks, the Romans learned to write long before they had a literary masterpiece to put in writing. Their early literate efforts were devoted to legal documents. According to Roman tradition Romulus founded the city on 21 April in 753 B.C., and as the small group of Latins set about the task of building their new settlement on the Tiber, they could not have known (nor could any of their neighbors or the ruling nations in the Mediterranean) the historical significance of their undertaking.

Although later Romans offered a reasonably clear and consistent version of their beginnings, modern historians have been skeptical of the stories in the works of Titus Livius (Livy) and other authors, since the Romans who wrote about the early kings did so hundreds of years after Rome's place in history had been assured. The inevitable tendency of later Romans to see in their origins the signs of subsequent Roman greatness colored their view and led to the insertion into the record of many fabulous and unhistorical episodes.

Yet much remains clear. Archaeologists generally agree that the evidence substantiates the traditional view that an important settlement on the site of Rome occurred in the eighth century B.C. Nor is there any doubt that Rome was ruled originally by kings.

Romans believed that there had been seven kings (or possibly an eighth in the person of Romulus' obscure Sabine colleague, Titus Tatius): Romulus (753–?), Numa Pompilius (*ca.* 700), Tullus Hostilius (673–642), Ancus Marcius (642–617), Lucius Tarquinius Priscus (616–579), Servius Tullius (578–535), Lucius Tarquinius Superbus, or Tarquin the Proud (534–510; these dates are all approximate, due to the uncertainties of early dating). The traditional dates for the monarchy are thus from 753 to 510 B.C. They may be slightly inaccurate—even the Romans could not agree on the precise chronology—but despite some serious modern challenges they have usually been accepted as roughly accurate.

Modern archaeological evidence has been helpful in tracing the outlines of Roman development during the monarchy in ways that later Roman authors could not have noted, though those authors do unintentionally provide some corroborating detail in literary records. It is now known that in the period from the eighth to the fifth centuries Rome and Latium were in the vortex of a great cultural conflict that divided the western Mediterranean into three major geopolitical parts—Carthaginian, Etruscan, and Greek southern Italy and Sicily. In the eighth century all three civilizations set out strong roots in the western Mediterranean, and by 500 they had divided much of the West among themselves, while their competition with one another had led by that time to a quasi-international stalemate in the region. Significantly this development coincides with the period of the Roman kings and provides the background for modern efforts to make some sense of Roman traditions about the monarchy and to understand how Rome was able ultimately to carve a place for herself in an arena of strong competition.

Etruscans

The key to Rome under the kings may be found in her proximity to the powerful Etruscans, who lived right across the Tiber roughly in the area between modern Florence and Rome. These people may have come from the eastern Mediterranean, perhaps Asia Minor as Herodotus indicates, but the evidence for their origins is debatable, and some scholars believe that the Etruscans were indigenous to Italy and that they developed their culture naturally out of the so-called Villanovan culture of prehistoric Italy. Their language, which survives today in thousands of ancient inscriptions, largely defies translation and remains an enigma.

Despite the unanswered questions about their origins and language, the Etruscans played a decisive role in civilizing central Italy and particularly the Romans. Etruscans introduced the city-state form of political organization first in their own territory of Etruria proper, where such city-states as Tarquinii, Veii, Caere, and Vulci prospered in the days of the Roman monarchy (and for some time thereafter), and later in other areas such as Rome, Campania, and the Po valley. For a while in the seventh and sixth centuries the Etruscans were territorially expansive until they were checked first by the Greeks of Cumae in 524 (and again in 474), then by Rome in 509, by the Samnites of Campania around 440, and finally by an invasion of Gauls into the Po valley at the end of the fifth century.

Because the Etruscans maintained a far-flung commercial network in contact with the Greeks of the Aegean, with Phoenicia, and perhaps even with Egypt, they were able to incorporate many of the civilized skills of the eastern Mediterranean into their own culture and pass them on to Romans and other Italians. Romans adopted their alphabet from the Etruscans, who had borrowed it with modifications from the Greeks. Remnants of Etruscan sculpture, metalwork, architecture, pottery, and painting reveal a flourishing, sophisticated civilization that continues to amaze people even in its ruined state. Their religion, with its emphasis on omens and divination, had a profound influence on the Romans.

Politically the impact of Etruria on Rome changed the course of Roman history under the kings. Before Etruscan influences were felt, Rome was simply a hut village. The transformation from village to city-state came late in the monarchy under the last three kings, who were Etruscans either by birth or at least in culture. It was in this period that sewers were built, that paths and roads became streets, that temples arose, and that Etruscan Rome became the dominant city-state in the plain of Latium. Roman territory extended to the mouth of the Tiber and was defended by an army in a phalanx formation introduced by Rome's Etruscan rulers.

Government and Society Under the Kings

The Roman kings were theoretically elected for life to serve as heads of state, war leaders, and high priests. They took the auspices to determine the will of the gods and at least in the field exercised powers of life and death over fellow Romans. Their imperium (the right to exercise the powers of state) ultimately became quite extensive under the last kings. Apparently from the beginning they were obliged to consult an advisory council, the Roman Senate, the creation of which was ascribed by tradition to Romulus, who is supposed to have appointed one hundred heads of great families to the body. In tradition, at least, these men became the original patricians ("fathers," though modern scholars have offered other explanations of the origins of this social order). Although the king was not necessarily required to accept the senate's advice, he was expected to consult it on matters of state. In addition, the constitutional principle of the ultimate sovereignty of the people was reflected in an assembly of citizens organized into thirty groups called curiae. The assembly, Comitia Curiata, met when summoned by the king and acted on matters submitted by him, such as declarations of war.

The patricians of the senate constituted an essentially hereditary aristocracy separated from the rest of Roman citizens, the plebeians. Many plebeians became clients or dependents of the power patricians and relied on them for protection and economic support in return for various services. There were also slaves and foreigners resident in monarchical Rome, but they did not have a constitutional, political role in civic life. All patricians and most plebeians belonged to well-organized clans or family units called gentes.

Because of Rome's critical geographical position, situated on the main line of communication between southern and northern Italy at an important river crossing, the city grew and prospered under the Etruscan rulers. Latin was the official language even under the Etruscan kings of Rome and had reached a reasonably high level of development as a legal and administrative language by the end of the monarchy, but Etruscan influence colored the early native Latin culture and resulted in the creation of a major Italian city-state at Rome.

THE REPUBLICAN CONSTITUTION

A dramatic change took place in about 510 B.C. when the Roman patricians, angered by the arbitrary and tyrannical rule of the last Etruscan king, Tarquin the Proud, rebelled and drove him from the city. They were so determined to prevent the reemergence of a tyrant in Rome that they abolished the monarchy and established a republic conferring most of the king's executive authority on two annually elected patrician consuls (probably first called praetors), each of whom could veto the actions of the other. Apparently from the very beginning the two main constitutional principles of the new republic were practiced: annuality (tenure of office for only one year) and collegiality (the sharing of a single office by two or more colleagues).

Over the next two and a half centuries the Romans developed a constitutional system that was widely praised in antiquity, notably by the Greek historian Polybius, and inspired even the Founding Fathers of the United States, who deliberately tried to imitate many of its features. One step, which occurred gradually, was to expand the executive branch of government as the Roman state grew. Two consuls proved inadequate to deal with all administrative problems, especially since they spent so much time in the field with Roman armies. Therefore, by the beginning of the third century B.C. Romans had created the praetorship (in 367), with the *imperium,* or the right to command armies, and with special authority over the Roman judicial system; the censorship (443), responsible for the census every five years and for awarding public contracts; the aedileship (by 450), a police magistracy with control over the marketplace and the public games; and the quaestorship (by 450), a body of either treasury officials or assistants to the consuls.

One intriguing feature of the Roman constitution is that it provided for the election, in times of crisis, of a dictator who held all power for a limited period not to exceed six months. Otherwise the executive offices were subject to the principles of collegiality and annuality except for the censorship, in which the two censors served for eighteen months but were elected only every five years (presumably because Rome did not need an annual census).

At the same time, the senate survived from the monarchy into the republic. Consisting by the mid-republic of about 300 members, it advised the consuls and praetors on most domestic governmental policies and actions, allocated financial resources, and shaped foreign policy. Actual law could be passed, however, only in an assembly of Roman citizens. The original assembly, the Comitia Curiata, had become essentially moribund by the end of the monarchy, and a new Centuriate Assembly (Comitia Centuriata), associated by the Romans with King Servius Tullius (though there has been much debate about its origins) had taken its place. In the Centuriate Assembly, Romans were organized into classes (subdivided into centuries, originally a military unit of one hundred men) on the basis of wealth (in which senators came first and knights [*equites*] next); and since the wealthiest classes were given far more centuries than the others, they were able to dominate the assembly, where voting was by century. Originally the system had been created to provide for military conscription, and since the state wanted warriors who could afford to own the full panoply of armor, preference was given to the wealthy. Ultimately centuriate organization lost much of its military significance, but the Centuriate Assembly continued to serve for the election of high executive officers, for declarations of war, and for the enactment of law.

Shortly after the overthrow of the monarchy, Romans took the first step in the creation of a new and more democratic assembly, the so-called Tribal Assembly. Ultimately (by the mid third century) this assembly was based on a division of Roman citizens into thirty-five tribes, or extensive districts depending mainly on geographical residence, and voting was by tribe on the basis of "one man, one vote." The Tribal Assembly elected the ten tribunes of the plebs and after a long struggle gained the right to pass binding law.

The Struggle of the Orders

While the Romans were engaged in the creation of their constitutional system, they were also involved—quite naturally under the circumstances—in a domestic rivalry, which centered on the efforts of the vast majority of citizens, the plebeians, to gain political equality with the tiny aristocracy of patricians. Patricians had toppled the monarchy, and they tried to dominate, even to monopolize, the government of the newly created republic. Virtually from the outset there were clashes between patricians and plebeians. Roman historians later emphasized the constitutional aspects of the Struggle, though it clearly had economic and social implications as well.

After 510 the patricians were firmly in control. They held all government offices, including the priesthoods, and collectively in the senate they claimed the right to exercise prior and subsequent approval of all legislation. Through the system of patronage, which involved a strong mutual social and political dependence between rich patrons and their poorer clients, and because of the harsh laws of debt, plebeians (or at least a politically active minority of that social order) began to feel strongly oppressed by their patrician leaders. Before the first generation of the republic had passed, plebeian leaders had secured patrician acquiescence in the annual election of tribunes of the plebs, who claimed the right to forbid unjust actions on the part of patrician governmental officers. With this came regular meetings of what later became the Tribal Assembly, where voting was democratic (though slaves were excluded) and the patricians, when they were finally permitted to attend, were greatly outnumbered. Plebeians took a solemn oath declaring their tribunes inviolable and threatening to kill anyone who violated or harmed them.

About 450, plebeians forced the patrician rulers to put Roman law in writing in a codified form so that it would be equally available to all and would restrict arbitrary interpretation by patrician magistrates. The result, the law of the Twelve Tables, published under the leadership of Appius Claudius Crassus Inregillensis Sabinus (Appius Claudius), retained much of the harshness and severity of earlier law but gave all Romans certain basic political and economic rights. Although intermarriage between plebeians and patricians was forbidden in the Twelve Tables, a few years later in 445 special legislation permitted it. Finally plebeians gained access to the highest offices, including the consulship in 366 and the other offices before the fourth century was over. At the end of that century, in 300 B.C., the priesthoods were opened to plebeians. Along with officeholding came membership in the senate, and in 287 the Hortensian law made legislation in the Tribal Assembly valid without regard to ratification by the senate.

In the battle for constitutional principle the plebeians had won, and, in this constitutional sense, the "Struggle of the Orders" was over. The result was the creation of a democratic government, at least in constitutional theory, although in fact the Roman state continued in practice to be highly aristocratic. A new senatorial aristocracy including plebeian leaders and patricians melded together to dominate the political life of the Roman people.

THE CONQUEST OF ITALY

While the Romans shaped their constitution during the Struggle of the Orders, they were also engaged in a series of military conquests that left them masters of the Italian peninsula. The immediate aftermath of the expulsion of the last king was almost certainly a weakening of Rome's military position in Latium as other Latin settlements tried to take advantage of unsettled conditions in Rome. In 493 the Romans made an agreement with the Latins, who were organized in a Latin League, by the terms of which treaty (the Foedus Cassianum) Rome recognized the league as an equal. The two parties agreed to an offensive and defensive alliance, which involved a shared commitment of troops and an equal division of the spoils. In this way the Romans and their neighbors provided for the defense of the plain of Latium.

The key to Rome's strategic position in the early fifth century was the incipient decline of the Etruscans. Starting with the overthrow of Tarquin the Proud in about 510 the Etruscan sphere of influence in Italy began to shrink, and by the end of the fifth century it was considerably reduced. There is a tradition that some Etruscans had made an abortive effort to restore Tarquin to the throne, a story involving the colorful tale of Publius Horatius Cocles' defending the wooden Sublician Bridge against the invading Etruscan army, but whether this occurred or not, historically the significant point is that Rome not only maintained her independence from Etruscan neighbors but began to fill the power vacuum created by the gradual reduction of Etruscan influence in the peninsula.

Throughout much of the fifth century Rome's task in alliance with the Latins was to defend Latium against the attacks of neighboring hillsmen, particularly the Aequi and the Volsci. By about 430 Roman and Latin arms were triumphant, and by the end of the fifth century Rome found herself at war with the powerful nearby Etruscan city of Veii (*ca.* 407–396) for control of the Tiber crossing into Etruria. After a siege of eleven years, according to Roman tradition, in which Rome began to pay her soldiers in order to keep them in the field year round, Veii finally fell, and her territory was annexed. Marcus Furius Camillus, the Roman leader, emerged as a national hero, and Rome had become the dominant military power in central Italy.

The moment of glory was brief. Rome's elevation to power in Latium and southern Etruria changed her status in the international Italian community of the era and forced Rome's leaders to take a broader strategic view of their role. Gauls who had recently crossed the Alps and overrun the Po valley, driving the Etruscans from the region and making it their own homeland, taught Romans their first lesson of geopolitical leadership. In 387 they poured into Etruria and inevitably moved against the greatest military power in the area, Rome. The Roman army was defeated at the Allia, a small tributary some eleven miles up the Tiber, and Romans evacuated their city except for the fortified Capitol defended by a small force. The Gauls sacked the city but could not take the citadel, and after seven months agreed to withdraw for a ransom of 1,000 pounds of gold. Camillus, the hero of Veii, was instrumental in creating the conditions under which the Gauls agreed to withdraw. Later Romans believed that he had actually defeated the Gauls as they were leaving and saved the ransom money, but this is improbable. Still, because of his success in recruiting an army during the siege Camillus had become Rome's hero again, and his forceful personality helped Rome recover from the calamity of the Gallic invasion.

The withdrawal of the Gauls left the city in shambles, and the blow to Rome's prestige had been great. For the next forty years Romans tried with only partial success to restore their former influence in central Italy. The defeat may have had domestic political repercussions since in the generation after the sacking of the city the patricians were forced (in 366) to allow plebeians to hold consulships. Full revenge against the Gauls came finally in 349 when another raiding party was driven out by Roman arms, and Rome could claim a new role as the defender of central Italy against the northern tribes.

Afterward in a burst of renewed vigor Rome pursued an expansionist policy that led in a relatively brief time—from 340 to 275—to the military domination of the entire Italian peninsula. Rome defeated and dissolved the Latin League in 338. Then, turning her attention south to Campania, where she had already granted Roman citizenship to Campania and Cumae for their support during the war with the Latins, Rome entered a long war of attrition, lasting intermittently from 327 to 290, with the Samnites, the native hillsmen of the southern Apennines who threatened Rome's position in the Bay of Naples. The war proved to be a difficult one, and a Roman army suffered a humiliating defeat at the Caudine Forks in 321. It was probably during this war that Romans abandoned the old phalanx formation of fighting and adopted the more flexible manipular legion (consisting of thirty maniples), although some historians believe that the change should be attributed to the earlier influence of Camillus. Finally, despite the tenacity of their opponents and occasional rebellions in other areas of Italy against Roman rule, particularly in Etruria, Rome subdued the Samnites and brought them into the Roman confederation in Italy.

Rome's victory over the Samnites left the emerging empire in a new role. Just as earlier, after the conquest of Veii, Romans faced responsibility for a broader strategic view in defense of central Italy, now they were required to maintain the military integrity of almost the entire Italian peninsula. Although they proved militarily and economically strong enough to provide that leadership, they were still culturally far behind the other major centers of civilization in the Mediterranean. But their next war brought them directly into the ambit of the Greeks, and direct contact with Greek civilization proved to be a powerful stimulus to cultural development in Roman society.

The Pyrrhic War (280–275)

In 282 Rome accepted an invitation from Thurii (Greek Thourioi), a Greek city in southern Italy, to send troops against the native Italian Lucanians, hillsmen who threatened Thurii, Locri (Lokroi), and Rhegium (Reggio di Calabria). When Roman forces were successful, Locri and Rhegium also became allies, but Tarentum (Taras), angered by Roman intervention in the affairs of the Greek cities, sank a Roman naval squadron in the Gulf of Tarentum and drove the Roman garrison out of Thurii. Tarentum then secured the support of Pyrrhus, king of Epirus (Epeiros), a talented Hellenistic general, who crossed over the sea to Italy with an army of 25,000, including some twenty Indian war elephants, a superbly disciplined force, highly trained in the tactics of Hellenistic warfare (280).

From the outset the Romans realized that they faced a formidable opponent. Pyrrhus defeated them at Heraclea in Lucania (280) and at Asculum (279), but in victory he lost so many men that he is reported to have said, "Another such victory and I am lost." Rome tenaciously refused to come to terms after some initial wavering, and because central Italy remained loyal to the Roman alliance Pyrrhus could do nothing against the city itself. Discouraged, he moved into Sicily to fight for Greeks against Carthaginians, and when he returned to Italy in 275 the Roman army met him at Beneventum, where he was finally defeated. He was able to return to Epirus with part of his forces and later conquered Macedonia before dying in a street fight in southern Greece (272).

The victory over Pyrrhus changed the course of Roman history. In the next few years Romans were able to gain control of the Greek cities of southern Italy and to draw them into the Italian confederation. As the champion of her new allies and as the ruling power of the peninsula Rome now had to deal directly with the great Hellenistic kingdoms of the east and with Carthage in North Africa. Although the Romans could not have known it in 275, their success in the Pyrrhic War forced them to begin their transformation from a land power in Italy into an international power dominating the Mediterranean on land and sea. Culturally they were transformed as well, since direct communication with Greek civilization in southern Italy served as a catalyst for subsequent development of Roman civilization.

Wars with Carthage (264–201)

The most important immediate effect of Rome's victory was the change it wrought in relations with Carthage. The Carthaginian Empire, based in North Africa, had expanded over the centuries to include strongholds in Sicily, Sardinia, and Spain. Originally a colony of the Phoenician city of Tyre, Carthage had broken connections with the homeland and by 265 was the major military power in the western Mediterranean. Until the end of the Pyrrhic War, Rome's dealings with Carthage had been peaceful and cooperative. From 509 to 275 three treaties had affirmed the interdependence of the two states, and the last treaty, negotiated during the Pyrrhic War, had been a psychological boost to Rome. As long as Rome competed on land with Etruscans and Greeks, Carthage, which challenged them on the sea, saw no conflict of interest in Rome's expansion. The Roman move to the sea in southern Italy after the defeat of Pyrrhus changed the situation, and within about ten years Rome and Carthage went to war.

The First Carthaginian War (264–241), sometimes called "Punic" from the Latin word for Phoenician, arose out of controversy between the two empires over Sicily. Hiero II, the king of Syracuse, attacked Messana (Messina; 265), a town on the narrow straits that divide Sicily from the toe of the boot of Italy. The rulers of Messana, a group of mercenaries called "Mamertines" who had seized the city earlier, looked to Carthage and Rome for help. Carthaginians reacted at once and sent a naval squadron with some land troops, but the Mamertines, fearful that their new Carthaginian allies would dominate them, continued to press for alliance with Rome. Initially the Roman Senate was hesitant to become involved, but the people in assembly, persuaded that it would be a mistake to let Carthage control the passage between Sicily and Italy and lured no doubt by the prospect of rich Sicilian booty, decided to intervene.

In 264 a Roman army crossed into Sicily, and after some complicated military and diplomatic maneuvers Rome found herself at war with Carthage. In 263 Romans forced Hiero of Syracuse out of the war and negotiated an alliance with him. Then in the following year, Rome with Hiero's help stormed the Carthaginian stronghold of Agrigentum (Greek Akragas) on the south coast of Sicily in a siege that lasted for seven months and involved armies of approximately 50,000 men on each side. Despite the loss the Carthaginian government showed no willingness to end hostilities, and the Roman Senate faced the fact that, probably for the first time, Rome had become involved in a major overseas war requiring a total commitment of national resources.

As a naval power Carthage had the initial advantage. Over the years Rome's land forces had proved their mettle, but remarkably the Carthaginian mercenary army staved off defeat throughout the long course of the war and occasionally beat Roman legions in the field. To offset Carthaginian naval superiority, in 261 Roman leaders ordered the construction of a fleet of 120 warships, including about 100 heavy quinqueremes. Attached to a special mast on each of the vessels was a large gangplank with a spike at its end. This raven or crow (*corvus*), as the Romans called it, gave them the advantage of surprise against straightforward Carthaginian ramming tactics since it could be swiveled and dropped on the decks of Carthaginian ships to permit Roman soldiers to board from the side. Romans stunned Carthage at the Battle of Mylae in 260 with their new fleet under the consul Gaius Duilius.

Afterward, unable to press the land war in Sicily to a successful conclusion, Rome sent a fleet (256) against North Africa, defeating the Carthaginian navy again off Cape Ecnomus before landing near Carthage; but the Carthaginians, with the aid of a Spartan mercenary general, Xanthippus, defeated the Roman army and took the consul Marcus Atilius Regulus captive (255). In the next few years Rome lost several fleets and 200,000 men in great storms on the sea, though they pursued the war doggedly in Sicily. Once in 249 at Drepana, Carthage actually defeated a Roman fleet, but the war had become a war of attrition since neither side could gain exclusive control over Sicily. Finally, as both powers approached bankruptcy and exhaustion, Rome built one last great fleet with the revenues of a forced loan on Roman senators and in 241 destroyed Carthaginian naval power. Carthage could not continue the war and agreed to evacuate Sicily and pay an indemnity of 3,200 talents. Rome had become the major power in the western Mediterranean.

In the next generation Rome followed an expansionist policy in several directions. In 238 she seized Sardinia and Corsica from Carthage and by 227 had organized Sicily (except for Hiero's kingdom) as the first tribute-paying province. From 225 to 219 Roman arms defeated the Gauls of the Po valley, and Cisalpine Gaul came under Roman rule. Roman armies swept across the Adriatic from 228 to 219 to suppress piracy that had threatened the commerce of the Greek cities of southern Italy, but they incurred the wrath of the king of Macedonia, who believed that Rome was impinging on his sphere of influence.

In Carthage, after first suppressing a rebellion by unpaid mercenaries, the general Hamilcar with his young son Hannibal concentrated on developing Carthaginian resources in Spain. There Carthaginian success finally led to hostilities with Rome, after Hannibal, who had taken command, besieged the city of Saguntum, a Roman ally, in 219. When the Carthaginian government rejected the ultimatum to surrender Hannibal, Rome declared war on Carthage again (218). Before the Romans realized what was happening, Hannibal had departed from Spain with an army of 40,000 infantry and cavalry plus elephants, crossed the Alps, and invaded Italy.

The Second Carthaginian War strained Roman resources to the limit. In the first three years of the war Hannibal delivered staggering blows to Roman armies in the field. Approximately 70,000 Roman and allied troops fell in the battles of the Trebia (218), Lake Trasimene (217), and Cannae (216). The Roman confederation in Italy began to crack as Campania opened its gates to Hannibal. When Philip V of Macedonia negotiated an alliance with Carthage to begin the First Macedonian War (215–205) and Syracuse rebelled in Sicily, Rome found herself by 212 deploying twenty-five legions in four separate theaters of war, since Roman armies were also engaged against the Carthaginians in Spain. For a few years after Cannae Rome's empire was very nearly lost. But the alliance in Italy generally held firm, and Rome retook Campania (211), under Marcus Claudius Marcellus finally stormed Syracuse (211) despite the ingenious war machines invented by Archimedes, and ultimately defeated the Carthaginian army in Spain (by 205) to bring the First Macedonian War to a successful conclusion.

In Italy, Romans had deployed the famous Fabian tactics of delay, named after the dictator Quintus Fabius Maximus Verrucosus, and in 207 they defeated Hannibal's brother Hasdrubal at the Metaurus as he attempted to join his army from Spain with Hannibal. Publius Cornelius Scipio, later called Scipio Africanus, persuaded the Romans to carry the war against Carthage into North Africa, and from 204 to 202 he conducted a successful campaign culminating in a great victory at Zama against Hannibal, who had been recalled from Italy for the defense of the homeland. When the war came to an end in 201, Rome reduced Carthage to a simple city, stripping her of most of her North African possessions, of Spain (which Rome took as a province), and of her fleet and elephants. An indemnity of 10,000 talents was also imposed. Hannibal's brilliance on the field of battle had not been sufficient to overcome the loyalty of Rome's confederation in Italy or the perseverance in desperate conditions of the Roman people.

Conquest of the East (200–146)

After the epic struggle with Hannibal there is evidence that war-weariness swept over the Roman people, but the Senate insisted on evening the score with Philip V of Macedonia for turning against Rome in the dark days after Cannae. Responding to an invitation for help from Rhodes and Pergamum (Pergamon), senatorial leaders cajoled the people into a declaration of war against Macedonia, and in the Second Macedonian War (200–196) the Roman general Titus Quinctius Flamininus soundly defeated Philip's phalanx at Kynos Kephalai (197). Philip kept his throne but agreed to restrict drastically his ventures in the Aegean.

Flamininus announced the freedom and independence from Macedonian rule of the Greek cities, but they proved as incompetent to rule themselves in the early second century as they had been before. Within a few years Roman armies returned to Greece and became embroiled in a war with the Seleucid king Antiochus III, who had tried to take advantage of Philip's weakness (192–188). A Roman army under the effective command of Scipio Africanus, who was ill on the day of the battle, defeated Antiochus in 189 at Magnesia in Asia Minor.

In the few short years from 204 to 188 Rome had defeated Carthage, Macedonia, and the Seleucid Empire, a feat with few parallels in the history of the world. Only one major kingdom remained in the Mediterranean, Ptolemaic Egypt, and the Ptolemies were careful to maintain cordial relations with Rome. Although Rome did not yet rule all the territory around the Mediterranean, she had become by far the leading power. It is perhaps not surprising, though many have found it lamentable, that in the generation from 188 to 146 Romans flexed their newly acquired muscles in a burst of imperialism that resulted in two wars with Macedonia (the Third and Fourth Macedonian Wars, 171–167 and 149–148) and its incorporation as a province; the total destruction of Carthage in the Third Carthaginian War (149–146); and the destruction of Corinth (146) in Greece. Rome had provinces in Spain (soon two), Africa, Sicily, Sardinia and Corsica, and Macedonia.

Roman Literary and Intellectual Development (264–146)

In the period from the Pyrrhic War to 146 B.C. Romans had also taken great strides in their cultural development. Direct contact with Greek civilization in southern Italy, Sicily, and in Greece itself had led to an admiration for Greek art, which was brought back to Rome in quantities by victorious Roman generals. Greek comedy was imitated by Livius Andronicus, Plautus, and Publius Terentius Afer (Terence). Romans began to produce their own epic poetry in the works of Gnaeus Naevius and Quintus Ennius, and their own histories, by Fabius Pictor (who wrote in Greek) and Marcus Porcius Cato (Cato the Elder). Livius Andronicus made a Latin adaptation of the *Odyssey,* and Greek teachers, some of whom came to Rome as captured slaves, taught rhetoric, grammar, and philosophy.

Although some Romans, the so-called Philhellenes, actively promoted Greek influence in Rome and served as patrons for Greek intellectuals, others, such as Cato, scorned Hellenism as a corrupting influence. The resulting tensions led occasionally to censorship of Greek philosophers and religions. Still, the basis for rapid expansion of Roman cultural horizons had been laid, and it was too late, by 146 B.C., to stem the tide.

THE LATE REPUBLIC (146–27 B.C.)

The empire had been shaped under the strictures of a relatively small citizen body. In the century and a quarter after 146 B.C. Romans in a welter of blood and civil war discovered the political price of their far-flung conquests. The republican constitution, shackled by the principles of annuality and collegiality, crumbled as Romans sought to divide the spoils of their victories and as one military crisis after another catapulted great generals into positions of unprecedented power and rivalry. In the end freedom (*libertas*)—the state of affairs in which members of the governing class could conduct an active political life—was lost while a line of emperors emerged, beginning with Augustus, to establish one of the world's greatest absolute monarchies.

But the failure of the Roman Republic is only one theme in the history of the period. Culturally it was a splendid era producing such giants as Titus Lucretius, Gaius Valerius Catullus, and Marcus Tullius Cicero. Economically and socially it witnessed a great rise in the standard of living for all Romans and in the area of foreign affairs there was continued rapid growth of the empire.

The Gracchi

In the year 133 B.C. a young tribune of the plebs, Tiberius Sempronius Gracchus, sponsored a reform program that fractured the Roman political establishment. Tiberius had become convinced that a partial redistribution of land was necessary to reduce the imbalances in Roman society caused by Rome's rise to world dominion. As wealth from all parts of the Mediterranean flowed into Rome in the second century B.C., aristocrats became vastly richer, and they purchased more and more land in Italy for their own estates. In fact senators had been required since the passage of the Claudian law in 218 to invest in Italian land since they were prohibited from owning ships of seagoing capacity for commercial activity. The aristocrats preferred to use cheap slave labor, in abundant supply from captives in Rome's wars, and small farmers were driven from the land and out of agricultural employment altogether. Tiberius, whose motives are highly controversial, seems at least to have been genuinely concerned with the social and economic implications of this agricultural revolution. He was no doubt also troubled that Rome's military conscription was based on land ownership and that the decline of the small farmers meant a significant reduction in the manpower pool for the Roman army.

Whatever his motives, Tiberius merely proposed that government land be divided among the landless citizens in small allotments. Over the years much of that land had also come under the control of Roman aristocrats, and though Tiberius allowed them to retain substantial holdings (up to a maximum of about 600 acres), they resented the reclamation and redistribution of the remainder.

Despite the controversial nature of the proposal it had some prospect of success. Tiberius was a member of one of the greatest senatorial families of his age, and he had close ties to many other prominent senators. Furthermore, his proposal was popular with the people who would vote on it in Tribal Assembly. But one of the tribunes, Octavius, vetoed it, and Tiberius then had him deposed, probably unconstitutionally. Afterward the bill passed, but Tiberius' high-handed methods rankled his opponents. He had secured the appointment of a three-man commission (consisting of himself, his father-in-law, Appius Claudius Pulcher, and his younger brother, Gaius) to implement the new law, and when it needed funds to do its work, he attempted to divert the revenues of the newly acquired kingdom of Pergamum (Pergamon) willed to Rome by its last king, Attalus III. The senate was furious at this threat to its traditional control of finances and foreign policy, and when Tiberius announced that he would stand for reelection as tribune, a group of conservative senators with their followers clubbed him to death along with 300 of his supporters. Their bodies were thrown into the Tiber.

Thus began the violence that characterized the political turmoil of the late republic. Significantly the agrarian reform was left on the books, and the commission continued to function. Ten years later in 123 Tiberius' brother Gaius Sempronius Gracchus was elected tribune and managed to secure reelection the following year, a step made specifically legal in the interval by vote of the Roman people. Gaius, a superb orator, advocated an even broader program of reform than his brother, strengthening the land law and providing for the state distribution of grain to citizens at a guaranteed, stable price. He also sought the support of the emergent equestrian order, a class of wealthy Romans with agricultural and commercial interests, who, unlike the senators, traditionally did not seek elective office and direct participation in Roman government. Gaius tried to drive a wedge into their normal alliance with the senatorial establishment by securing for equestrian corporations the right to collect the taxes of the province of Asia (the former kingdom of Pergamum) and to sit on the juries that tried Roman governors for extortion. As the author of what became the Roman dole and expander of the corrupt system of tax farming Gaius bequeathed an unfortunate legacy to the Roman people.

He sponsored various public construction projects, especially roads, and the establishment of several settlements (*coloniae*) of Romans, one at the site of Carthage. His main objective, however, was to extend the franchise by giving citizenship to the Latins and Latin status to the Italian allies. The senate strongly opposed this and in 122 set up its own tribune, Marcus Livius Drusus, who won the support of the people by offering them in some respects even more than Gaius had, while at the same time opposing extension of the franchise. In the end this worked, primarily because Romans generally were not yet prepared to share the benefits of citizenship.

Gaius failed in his bid for reelection, and during riots in 121 the senate passed the Last Decree (*senatusconsultum ultimum*), a temporary declaration of martial law. The consul Opimius raised a force and killed 250 Gracchans—Gaius himself may have committed suicide amid the violence—and later condemned 3,000 more. Although the senate's right to pass the Last Decree, permitting execution of Romans without benefit of trial, was challenged and remained controversial, the senate had succeeded, again by bloodshed, in maintaining its supremacy.

Whether the Gracchi should be regarded as well-meaning reformers struggling against a corrupt aristocracy or as power-hungry demagogues is difficult to ascertain. The Romans themselves debated the question as vigorously as do modern scholars. Probably the Gracchi were sincere, but their methods were constitutionally and politically questionable. The historical significance of the period, however, was far-reaching. The Gracchi had shown enough success to demonstrate that the senate could sometimes be thwarted; they had raised issues, such as land reform and the extension of the franchise, that would be critical in the future; and they had laid the basis for subsequent leaders, the Populares, to act on behalf of the people in attacking the representatives of senatorial privilege, the Optimates. They had also stirred up violent emotions that eventually destroyed the stability of republican government.

Marius and Sulla

For a while after the overthrow of the Gracchi the senate controlled affairs in Rome, but within a few years it had so discredited itself in the conduct of a war against Jugurtha, king of Numidia in North Africa, that another popular leader, Gaius Marius, was able to rise to power. Marius became consul in 107 even though he was an equestrian or knight (*eques*) by birth; that is, he was a "new man" (*novus homo*), the first member of his family to hold a consulship. He criticized the inept and corrupt management of the war in Africa, and after his election the people in assembly transferred the command against Jugurtha from a senatorial leader to himself.

Marius brought the war to a quick and decisive end, and on his return to Rome in 105 B.C. he found that he had been reelected consul for 104 even though the Romans had traditionally required leaders to wait ten years before reelection to the highest office. At the time Rome faced another great military threat, from the northern (German) tribes of the Cimbri and Teutones. Italy was in danger of invasion, and the people wanted their champion to defend them. They reelected Marius consul every year from 104 to 100 B.C., and he repaid their confidence by crushing Rome's enemies.

In the course of his career Marius undertook several reforms that altered Roman history. He dropped the property qualification for service in the legions and encouraged landless volunteers to serve for pay and the hope of booty. At the end of a campaign he provided land grants for his veterans. The result was the beginning of a professional army and an army intensely loyal to its commander, who provided the rewards. On the tactical level, Marius reorganized the legions into ten cohorts each, replacing the less mobile maniples, and streamlined their logistical system partly by requiring his troops to carry many of their own supplies (they came to be known as Marius' Mules). The reorganized Roman legions, trained in the methods of the gladiatorial camps and armed with new and better weapons, politicized by their new social composition and by the forcefulness of their commander, soon became active participants in Rome's political debacle.

Marius had returned to Rome for the year 100, and his sixth consulship, in triumphant victory. As the champion of the people and leader of the Populares he represented a formidable threat to the Optimates ("best men," the name awarded to themselves by the senatorial establishment); the Populares' leaders were also senators, but they differed from the Optimates by endorsing the spirit of the Gracchan reforms. Unfortunately for Marius the year 100 proved to be a catastrophe, as riots broke out in the streets during the elections and Marius was forced to arrest many of his own associates, who were subsequently murdered by a mob. Although he was an excellent general, Marius showed little competence for domestic politics, and after this disgrace he suffered an eclipse of influence.

The 90s were relatively calm until the end of the decade when, in 91, a tribune, Marcus Livius Drusus the Younger, made an abortive effort to secure citizenship for Latins and Italians and was mysteriously murdered toward the end of the year. Finally the allies revolted in anger at their treatment by Rome, and at the outset of the so-called Social War (90–88) Rome agreed to make them citizens. Some refused to accept the belated offer, so the war dragged on, particularly in the south where a staunch adherent of the Optimate cause, Lucius Cornelius Sulla, won military glory and election to the consulship of 88. Simultaneously Rome faced a serious problem in the east, where Mithridates VI of Pontus invaded Roman territory, inflamed the Greeks of the Aegean against Rome, and executed on one day 80,000 Italians in Asia Minor.

In the face of this threat the senate secured the command for Sulla, but Marius, who had rendered good service in the Social War, persuaded the people in assembly to transfer the command to him. Sulla had already mobilized an army, and against the wishes of his officers he ordered it to move on Rome, which he seized. This was the first time that an army of Roman citizens in defiance of the law struck at Rome itself on behalf of its general. Marius and others sought refuge in Africa while Sulla set out again for the east. Then Marius returned, and with his ally Lucius Cornelius Cinna used force to take Rome. The aging general allowed his army to butcher his Optimate opponents; but shortly after entering on his seventh consulship in 86, Marius died. While Sulla fought Mithridates, Cinna continued as consul in Rome through 84, but on Sulla's victorious return in 83, the Populares were defeated, and Sulla became dictator (82–79)—not for a limited term, as the constitution required, but for an indefinite one.

The new dictator supervised an extensive reform of the constitution. He eliminated his opposition by offering rewards for their heads in infamous proscription lists and he confiscated their property. Perhaps 4,000 wealthy Romans were killed. Sulla added 300 new members to the senate, destroyed the powers of the tribunes, restored the courts to senatorial control, and gave the senate virtually complete sway over legislation. He was the last person until Caesar, a generation later, to have the power to reform the Roman constitution at will, but his strongly conservative changes lasted no more than ten years. To be sure, some of his purely administrative reforms in criminal jurisdiction and in the executive branch survived, but in striking at the heart of popular sovereignty by elevation of the senate, Sulla lost an opportunity to resolve the conflicts of Roman society. More than fifty years of suffering were required before Augustus finally resolved the tensions.

Pompey and Crassus

Sulla resigned in 79 and died the following year. Two of his partisans, the young Gnaeus Pompeius Magnus (Pompey the Great—a title he assumed for his services to Sulla in Sicily and Africa) and the wealthy Marcus Licinius Crassus, rose through military commands in the 70s to positions of leadership. Both had fought for Sulla, and when the senate needed generals to deal with a Marian rebel in Spain, Quintus Sertorius, and with the slave rebellion of Spartacus in Italy, Pompey and Crassus went into the field again to return victoriously with their armies to Rome in 71. They stood together as candidates for the consulship for 70 and were elected despite opposition from the Optimates, who particularly feared the prospect of Pompey—regarded as an upstart because of his abnormally early rise to prominence—running for his first elective office. Pompey repaid them in full by persuading Crassus to join with him in restoring the tribunes and the assembly to their full former powers, thereby undoing Sulla's major constitutional reform.

In the meantime Mithridates had gone to war again, and the senate had sent a trusted commander, Lucius Licinius Lucullus, to deal with him; but Lucullus was a stern administrator and strict disciplinarian who annoyed equestrian tax collectors in the east and angered his own legions. Finally in 66 Pompey was placed in command of the war, after he had first gained additional popularity by clearing piracy from the Mediterranean (67).

While Pompey waged a splendidly successful campaign that culminated in the defeat and death of Mithridates and the annexation of Syria as a province, Rome at home witnessed the emergence of several colorful and important political leaders. Crassus continued his activities in the senate and offered powerful support to a rising young patrician, Gaius Julius Caesar, the nephew by marriage of Marius. Aided by this connection with one of Rome's greatest figures and by his own genius for oratory and political maneuver, Caesar climbed rapidly in the 60s to be elected chief priest (*pontifex maximus*) in 63 and praetor in 62, and to serve as governor of Spain in 61.

He was in some ways overshadowed at this time by his older contemporary, Marcus Tullius Cicero. Cicero, like Marius, was a "new man" of equestrian birth, and the leading orator of his age—indeed, of all Roman history. He had attracted attention in Rome's courts by serving successfully as an advocate in several famous cases. In politics he preferred the middle road, instinctively respectful of the senate while supporting Pompey and cooperating with Crassus. As consul in 63 he suppressed the conspiracy led by Lucius Sergius Catilina (Catiline), a disgruntled, bankrupt, and degenerate aristocrat whose threat to Roman government was probably not as great as Cicero made it appear.

The First Triumvirate

Pompey returned to Rome late in 62 and disbanded his army, expecting the senate to ratify the arrangements he had made in the East and to provide land grants for his veterans. But conservative (Optimate) leaders, especially Lucullus and Cato the Younger, balked and delayed action throughout 61. In 60 Crassus supported some equestrian tax farmers who wanted to renegotiate an unfavorable contract, but Cato obstructed the plan. When Caesar returned from Spain in the same year hoping to celebrate a triumph (an honor legally incompatible with political candidacy), he asked permission to stand for the consulship for 59 in absentia while he waited outside the city with his army for the day of the parade. Again Cato intervened, so Caesar abandoned the triumph, disbanded his army, and entered the city to declare his candidacy.

Late in 60, after his election to the consulship of 59, Caesar approached Pompey, Crassus, and Cicero and asked them to join forces with him to dominate the government for their mutual advantage. Pompey and Crassus agreed. Cicero was not happy with the Optimates but could not bring himself to join such a potentially dictatorial alliance. (Modern historians have called the compact between Caesar, Pompey, and Crassus the First Triumvirate though it was not so called by the Romans and, unlike the Second Triumvirate, was never recognized by law.) Nevertheless, Caesar had engineered a powerful coalition. By driving these three dominant men together, the senate had lost its last real chance to maintain control of Roman politics.

In 59, despite the efforts of Caesar's colleague, Marcus Calpurnius Bibulus, to prevent it, Caesar drove through ratification of Pompey's arrangements, secured land grants for his veterans, and arranged the renegotiation of the tax contract for Crassus. For himself Caesar wanted a major military command, and he took an extraordinary one including Cisalpine Gaul, Illyricum (Dalmatia), and Narbonese Gaul for a period of five years. He showed his ruthlessness by threatening to use Pompey's veterans against anyone who opposed him.

Although Caesar did not originally intend the conquest of all Gaul, he immediately became involved in that project on entering his provincial commands in 58. From 58 to 50 he subjugated the area and fashioned in the process one of the world's greatest armies, decidedly loyal to its commander. As a general Caesar often did not prepare his campaigns well, but his decisiveness, speed, and personal bravery on the battlefield compensated for weaknesses in strategic conception and logistical organization. During the 50s his successes in the field captivated the imagination of the Roman people and created the same basis for political power that Marius, Sulla, and Pompey had used so effectively.

In Rome, Pompey and Crassus found it difficult to cooperate. They never liked each other, and in 56 Caesar was forced to intervene to bring them back into alliance. Pompey and Crassus then served together again as consuls in 55 to implement the earlier agreements with Caesar. Pompey was given Spain for five years but permitted to govern it in absentia through his personal representatives (*legati*). Crassus took Syria, also for five years, and Caesar received a five-year extension of his provincial commands.

Shortly thereafter the First Triumvirate began a process of disintegration that eventually led to civil war. Caesar's daughter, Julia, whom Pompey had married in 58, died in 54, thus destroying a personal bond between the two dynasts. In 53 Crassus left Syria with eight legions to invade the Parthian Empire—the only major power confronting Rome's frontiers—and was defeated and killed at Carrhae in Mesopotamia, with the humiliating loss of legionary captives and standards. In 52, because of electoral violence, Pompey served as sole consul, and the Optimates with whom he had to work began to persuade him to abandon the alliance with Caesar and join them in saving the state from the latter's ruthless ambitions. In 51 and 50 several attacks were openly made against Caesar, who wanted to step directly from his provincial commands into a second consulship. Finally in early January of 49 the senate passed a Last Decree, and Pompey took responsibility for the defense of Rome.

Civil War and Caesar's Dictatorship

Caesar had tried to compromise, but Cato and others were implacably opposed to him and with Pompey on their side thwarted all conciliatory efforts. On January 11 Caesar traversed the Rubicon River—the border of Italy—and in a lightning campaign seized Italy and Rome, while Pompey withdrew across the Adriatic toward Macedonia. Since Pompey controlled Spain, Caesar decided to go there; he rapidly defeated the Pompeian legions at Ilerda. After returning to Italy in a dangerous winter crossing of the sea, Caesar moved in January 48 against Pompey, whose attempt at naval domination was frustrated by his surprise attack. Pompey proved too strongly entrenched at Dyrrhachium (Durrës), so Caesar withdrew into Thessaly to feed his troops. Pompey then surrounded Caesar in hostile territory and might have destroyed him with Fabian tactics, but the senators in Pompey's retinue urged battle, and at the Battle of Pharsalus in 48 Caesar won. Pompey fled to Egypt, where he was killed.

Upon arrival in Egypt, Caesar became embroiled in a dangerous civil war but finally succeeded in establishing Cleopatra VII as effective ruler. Before he could turn his attention to the defeat of the Pompeian army that had regrouped in Africa after the defeat at Pharsalus, Caesar had to suppress a rebellion in Asia Minor under Pharnaces, son of Mithridates. In a five-day campaign (*"Veni, vidi, vici"*) Caesar restored Roman authority (47). Back in Rome he suppressed a mutiny in his army, which was clamoring for discharge, and moved across to Africa, where he defeated the Pompeians at Thapsus (46).

In the following year he totally destroyed his Pompeian opposition in another great victory at Munda in Spain.

Militarily Caesar had been everywhere successful, and he occupied a position in Roman government of unparalleled power. Because he was assassinated so soon after achieving total mastery of the empire, it is difficult to know what plans he had for the resolution of Rome's problems or even for his own place in a reorganized government. He had served briefly as dictator in 48; in 46 he was elected dictator for ten years; and in 44 he became dictator for life. As *pontifex maximus* and augur he controlled the Roman religious machinery, and in 46 he had assumed the title of prefect of morals, an exalted lifetime censorship. Since Caesar's day controversy has raged about whether he intended to abolish the republic and become king, but his untimely death forestalled any possibility of certain knowledge.

Amazingly, although he was primarily concerned with military matters in the period from 49 to 44, Caesar accomplished a wide range of reforms. He increased membership in the senate to about 900 by adding many new members from the equestrian order (knights). This dilution of senatorial stature deeply offended some of the older members of the aristocracy who resented Caesar's upstarts. He controlled the elections for executive offices, which he also greatly expanded (for example, by doubling the number of quaestors). The old, irregular Roman calendar based on the lunar year was replaced by a new, solar (Julian) calendar borrowed from Alexandria.

Economically the Civil War had caused chaos and suffering, and Caesar addressed some of the problems by planning new colonies, requiring large ranchers to use some freemen as shepherds instead of slaves, and reducing prewar debts. He developed plans, not implemented, for the construction of a harbor at Ostia at the mouth of the Tiber and even turned his attention to such matters of detail as traffic regulation in Rome. For his achievements he received far greater recognition than any Roman up to his time. A month, July, was named after him; he received the title *parens patriae* (father of his country); and in 44 his image appeared on Roman coins, the first time in history that a living Roman was so honored.

Caesar's dictatorship differed dramatically from Sulla's in many respects, perhaps the most obvious being that Caesar pardoned his opponents and even found high governmental positions for many of them. He was respected for this, and the Romans even erected a temple to his clemency, but the policy that had helped him win the war contributed also to his downfall. On 15 March in 44 B.C. a band of senatorial conspirators led by Marcus Junius Brutus and Gaius Cassius Longinus (Cassius) murdered Caesar as he was about to leave Rome on an invasion of the Parthian Empire. Some of the conspirators actually liked Caesar personally and had prospered under his regime, but they believed that he was a tyrant, that he had destroyed the republic and intended to become king.

Thus ended the career of one of Rome's most talented figures, a general, a statesman, an orator, and a man of letters. His role in Roman history has been endlessly debated and his reputation over the centuries has vacillated as historians have emphasized either his reforms or his inclination toward personal domination. A confident and arrogant man, often also charming; his greatest flaws were overconfidence, conceit, and an inability to justify personal aggrandizement on any idealistic grounds.

The Second Triumvirate

Caesar's death threw Rome into consternation. Marcus Antonius (Mark Antony), an associate of Caesar's in power, cleverly manipulated the situation to his own advantage but was surprised to learn on reading Caesar's will that the dictator had named as his heir and adopted son his eighteen-year-old grandnephew, Gaius Octavius. Octavius assumed the name Gaius Julius Caesar Octavianus after the adoption and is usually called Octavian by modern historians, but his contemporaries, significantly, called him Caesar.

Antony foolishly offended Octavian in the aftermath of Caesar's assassination by refusing to turn over the dictator's money. A group of senators, led by the aging Cicero, took advantage of this disagreement to attempt the destruction of Antony and were willing to use Octavian in the process. At a great battle in 43 near Mutina (Modena) in northern Italy, the Ciceronian coalition defeated Antony with Octavian's help, but in the enthusiasm of victory Cicero decided that Octavian was no longer needed and rebuffed him. Octavian then joined forces with Antony—who had managed to withdraw from Mutina with his legions intact— and with Marcus Aemilius Lepidus (Lepidus), another associate of Caesar's who commanded legions in Spain. Toward the end of 43 the three men took control in Rome and secured passage of a law naming them triumvirs with power to reorganize the state.

The triumvirs officially made Caesar a god but abandoned his policy of clemency in favor of Sulla's methods when they imposed a savage proscription with Cicero's name at the top of the list. The head of the eloquent orator was displayed publicly in the forum. Antony and Octavian then marched east to defeat at Philippi (42) a large force mobilized by Brutus and Cassius. The dictator had been avenged, and the triumvirate was firmly in power.

Unfortunately the triumvirs found cooperation difficult. Lepidus was clearly outclassed by Antony and Octavian, and the personal animosity of the latter two had only slightly abated. After Philippi, Antony stayed in the east while Octavian returned to Rome, and in 41–40 he had to suppress a rebellion led by Antony's wife, Fulvia, and his brother, Lucius. Tensions were so great that advisers of the two generals arranged a reconciliation in a meeting at Brundusium (40), where Antony agreed to marry Octavian's sister, Octavia (Fulvia had died), and Rome's empire was divided to give the East to Antony, Gaul, Spain, and Illyricum to Octavian, and Africa to Lepidus.

For a while war had been averted partly because Antony wanted to concentrate on an invasion of Parthia while Octavian had to suppress Sextus Pompeius, a son of Pompey the Great, who put together a navy and seized Sicily. At Tarentum in 37 Antony and Octavian met again and agreed to renew the expired triumvirate for five years. Then in 36 Octavian defeated Sextus Pompeius and captured Lepidus, who had turned against him in the war with Sextus, but Antony failed in his attempt to conquer Parthia and only very narrowly managed to withdraw his army into Rome's empire.

Octavian's victory and Antony's defeat set the stage for a showdown between the two dynasts. While preparing for the Parthian War, Antony had resumed an earlier relationship with Cleopatra VII of Egypt, and after the abortive invasion they grew closer together romantically and politically. Antony ceded vast powers to her, including some Roman territory, and in 33 he became her consort although he did not divorce Octavia until 32. This notorious affair was unpopular in Rome, where Octavian used it for propaganda purposes by claiming that Antony intended to subject Romans to the rule of an oriental queen. Finally in 31 at Actium the two leaders met; in the naval battle Antony and Cleopatra were defeated, and Antony's land forces surrendered to Octavian. The lovers escaped only to commit suicide in Egypt the following year: Octavian had become master of the Roman world and his triumph meant the end of republican government and the emergence of the emperorship.

Romans in the late republic had simply been incapable of resolving the problems created by their rise to world power. The tensions generated by the Gracchi were exacerbated by the struggles of the great generals. The distribution of the vast wealth of an empire combined with the limitations of a city-state constitution proved too great a problem. The rule of a strong man seemed the only solution since the republican political system had failed to produce unity and peace. These were finally achieved at the expense of political freedom.

Roman Civilization in the Late Republic

Politically the late republic was an age of violence, but it witnessed a cultural growth that was momentous in its force. Economically there was a vast expansion of Roman activity in commerce as well as in agriculture. Some private fortunes reached staggering heights. The annual revenues of Rome's empire in 63 B.C., the only year in Roman history for which we have a precise figure, were 200 million sesterces, and Crassus had holdings of the same size. Pompey and Caesar produced from booty incomes even larger than that of Crassus. Alongside men of great wealth were the slaves and the poor; 320,000 Romans were on the dole as Caesar fought Pompey. Still, the living conditions of everyone had improved; after all, there had been no dole in the earlier period. Wealthy Romans had great houses in the city and palatial estates in the countryside, especially around the Bay of Naples. Cicero spent about three million sesterces on his house in Rome, and he had at least eight villas outside the city; yet he was not one of Rome's richest aristocrats.

In other ways the city reflected Rome's

new prosperity. Pompey paid for Rome's first stone theater, and Caesar subsidized the construction of a new forum. Sulla had a senate house built, and the gardens of Sallust, Lucullus, Maecenas, and Caesar decorated the capital. Marble was used for the first time in private homes, and frescoes covered the walls.

In literature and philosophy the Romans of the late republic made some of Rome's greatest contributions to the Western world. Cicero towers above all his contemporaries as a prose stylist and philosopher. Sallust and Caesar also produced prose works of considerable power. Titus Lucretius combined poetry and philosophy to produce the masterpiece of Epicurean philosophy, *On the Nature of Things* (*De Rerum Natura*), in beautiful hexameter verse. Gaius Valerius Catullus adapted Latin to the lyric meters of the Hellenistic East in occasionally anguished yet always spirited poetry about his lover, his friends, his enemies, and some of the ranking political leaders of the day. Greek influences in Roman literary and intellectual life remained strong, but Romans of the late republic elevated Latin to the level of Greek as an instrument for the highest expression of the ideals of ancient culture.

THE EARLY ROMAN EMPIRE

The new age ushered in by the Battle of Actium was clearly a boon for the Roman people and for Rome's subjects, since the Pax Romana of Augustus was an empire-wide peace that brought an end to civil war and healed the wounds of the Roman body politic. Prosperity and peace lasted almost unbroken for 200 years; yet as the poet Marcus Annaeus Lucanus (Lucan) wrote in the age of Nero, "With that peace came a master." The emperors gradually assumed all power for themselves, but on balance in the early empire, regardless of their sometimes tyrannical and occasionally nearly insane personalities, they did provide stable and even wise administration of the empire. The loss of liberty seems not to have been mourned by the majority of Romans, who willingly accepted "bread and circuses"—Juvenal's term for the distractions provided for the people by the emperor—in its place, and those republican aristocrats who did object were destroyed by the middle of the first century A.D. to be replaced by a new, acquiescent aristocracy drawn ultimately from all areas of the empire. Gibbon was correct in suggesting that the cultural unity forged by Roman rule amid educated classes around the Mediterranean became in the early empire one of the greatest achievements in the recorded history of man.

Augustus

The chief architect of the new regime was Octavian. Unfettered after Actium by rivalry with political and military opponents, he showed as the sole master of Rome consummate tact and diplomacy and a keen awareness of the need to offer Romans an ideological basis for acceptance of his authority. Determined to avoid the fate of Caesar, he slowly shaped a position for himself that resulted in what we know as the emperorship. When he defeated Antony and Cleopatra, he was in his early thirties. By the time he died almost a half century later in A.D. 14 as Emperor Augustus, Rome had been transformed.

After taking Egypt in 30 B.C. Octavian devoted some time to administrative reorganization of Rome's eastern provinces, shattered by military demands during the Second Triumvirate. When he returned to Rome for a great triumph in 29 he presided over the discharge of the fifty-odd legions that were under arms, reducing the number to about twenty-eight for the defense of Rome's frontiers. Finally, in January of 27, in a famous speech to the Roman Senate, he announced his plans for the future government.

He had decided, or so he said, to give up his power and to turn the government back to the senate and people. His adherents had been carefully briefed, and they led a chorus of protests that the state could not survive without his services. With a show of reluctance Octavian agreed that he would stay on in a limited capacity to serve as consul and as governor of Spain, Gaul, Syria, and Egypt for a ten-year period. Since these military ("imperial") provinces based most of Rome's legions, Octavian in effect remained commander in chief of the Roman army. For this apparent self-sacrifice and in recognition of his achievements, the senate voted him the name Augustus, a word charged with religious significance, suggesting that the gods held him in special favor.

His legal authority was complex and far-reaching. Since the 30s he had had the sacrosanctity of the tribunes. He was given the right to wage war, to make treaties, and to regulate Rome's relations with the client (dependent) kings of states bordering the frontiers of the empire. He styled himself Emperor Caesar Augustus, Son of a God, that is, of his adoptive father (Julius Caesar, who had been deified by the state), and there was no doubt that his control over the government was absolute; but he claimed that he had restored the republic and that he served it as princeps, first citizen among equals. Romans generally accepted this happy lie, grateful that they had a strong ruler who cloaked his monarchy in republicanism. Throughout his reign he avoided the titles that Caesar had assumed, and on several occasions he refused the dictatorship and the lifetime censorship when they were pressed on him.

Over the years he slightly modified the arrangement made in 27. He gave up the consulship in 23 to permit more senators to hold Rome's highest office and accepted in its place the full powers of a tribune for life. He was later allowed to take his place at meetings of the senate between the two consuls and to speak first on matters of debate. In 12 B.C. he became *pontifex maximus,* and in 2 he was declared *pater patriae* (father of his country). The regime he created was called the principate, or government by the first citizen, implying the rule of law in which citizen rights were still respected under beneficent leadership.

He was careful to project the image of a champion of ancient Roman traditions. Vacancies in the priesthoods were filled, and Augustus and his friends restored old temples and built new ones. He sponsored several laws designed to restore the sanctity of family life and to encourage childbirth, laws that made adultery a state crime and discouraged celibacy. There is no reason to assume that his program was the result of pure Machiavellian calculation, as some historians have done. He was in many ways a simple man who lacked the sophistication and brilliant intellect of his adoptive father. He genuinely preferred a relatively abstemious life and the pleasures of his family. He was a stern father and on the whole reflected the various virtues that he preached. His naturally conservative, traditionally Roman personality added to the respect Romans felt for him and helped tremendously in the war he waged for men's minds.

The Empire Under Augustus

In 23 B.C. Augustus had been given an *imperium maius,* a power to command that was greater than that of the other governors of the so-called senatorial provinces—that is, those governed by proconsuls, as in the republic. Although his own proconsular authority was strictly valid only in his own (the imperial) provinces, by virtue of his *imperium maius* he assumed responsibility for extending the benefits of good government to the entire empire, and he put an end to many of the rapacious policies that had characterized provincial rule in the late republic. The worst abuses of tax farming were curbed as the emperor put tax collections largely in the hands of a governmental bureaucracy created for the purpose.

He brought the army under the control of the state, for the first time since Marius, by completing the process of professionalization, setting fixed terms for service for legionaries and auxiliaries and providing a state treasury to pay their discharge bonuses and pensions.

With the legions he achieved numerous conquests along the frontiers, particularly the Rhine and Danube, and he added more territory to the empire than anyone in Roman history had done before. When three of his legions were destroyed in A.D. 9 at the Teutoburg Forest in Germany, he abandoned plans for further conquest and settled for a frontier generally along the Rhine-Danube line. In the East he realized that Rome's dream of conquering Parthia would be too costly, so he negotiated a settlement in 19 B.C. that secured return of the standards captured at Carrhae in 53 and release of the captives. Although there were problems throughout his reign along the Rhine and the Danube, Roman legions held the line and protected the heart of the empire. Never before and never since the days of the early empire has the Mediterranean received so much protection at so little cost.

Roman Civilization in the Age of Augustus

Many of the inhabitants of the Roman Empire, citizens and provincials alike, responded with remarkable enthusiasm to the widespread improvements of the Augustan regime. In art, architecture, and literature the period was a Golden Age that witnessed a veritable gushing forth of released tensions and anxiety. New buildings and monuments went up all over the empire as cities and provinces were interconnected by well-maintained Roman roads and the sea burgeoned with commercial activity. The poet Publius Vergilius Maro (Vergil) served as spokesman for the age in his *Aeneid* when he said that Rome under Augustus had fulfilled her destiny to rule the world in peace and justice. Quintus Horatius Flaccus (Horace) had fought for Brutus and Cassius at Philippi, but he too was gradually persuaded to produce elegant poetry in praise of the new Rome. Titus Livius (Livy), in stately prose, composed a history of Rome from its foundation, which reveals some reservations that Romans "could not suffer our own vices or face the remedies needed to cure them," but he was genially tolerated by Augustus and flourished partly because he almost certainly endorsed the emperor's moral reforms.

Sextus Propertius (Propertius) and Albius Tibullus (Tibullus) were overshadowed somewhat by the greatness of Vergil and Horace, but their poetry bubbles with the spirit of the new age. In Greek the rhetorician Dionysius of Halicarnassus wrote many books on early Rome, and Strabo described the geography of the Mediterranean. Diodorus Siculus published a hodgepodge of material on the history of the world. Augustan Rome was vibrant and creative, and generally optimistic—with reason—about the future.

The Last Years of Augustus

Naturally the emperor suffered some failures in his long career, and the principate revealed, even under its founder, some of the flaws that marred its generally impressive record. Augustus knew that he had to groom a successor in order to avoid renewed outbreak of civil war at his death. His efforts were often frustrated, first by the fact that he had no son of his own, and then because his initial choices—his nephew Marcellus, his lifelong friend and associate in power Marcus Vipsanius Agrippa, and his grandsons Gaius and Lucius—all died prematurely. Augustus was frail and often sick, making his dynastic policy seem all the more urgent, but he was the one to linger on into cranky old age. Finally and probably in some disappointment he selected his stern stepson, Tiberius Claudius Nero, the son of Augustus' wife Livia by an earlier marriage, and from A.D. 4 to the end of the reign in 14, Tiberius worked diligently to earn his place as Rome's next emperor and to relieve Augustus of the most burdensome features of government.

Other problems disturbed the tranquility of the age. As the sponsor of the law against adultery Augustus was humiliated by the sexual license of his daughter Julia and a granddaughter of the same name, both of whom were banished from Rome. Disappointments in the family and the battle with health and old age led the emperor in his last years to ignore or violate the forms of republican government he had so long openly advocated. Elections for office in A.D. 7 were canceled because of disturbances, and Augustus simply appointed officials. He found it difficult to attend meetings of the senate and occasionally allowed treason charges to be lodged against aristocratic opponents whom he might have treated more leniently in earlier years. In A.D. 8 the poet Publius Ovidius Naso (Ovid) was banished to Tomi on the coast of the Black Sea because his amatory verses violated the spirit of Augustan social policy and for some other reason, or "error," that Ovid never revealed. That it could be dangerous to criticize an emperor or his policies was a sign of absolutism that would later contribute powerfully to the stagnation of Roman literary and intellectual development and that had already begun to appear by the time of Augustus' death. On the whole, however, Romans were keenly sensitive to the debt they owed their emperor, and when he died in A.D. 14, he was deified by a mourning senate and people.

The Julio-Claudians

Tiberius succeeded Augustus without difficulty despite minor mutinies in some of the legions of the Rhine and the Danube. He was already fifty-five years old, yet he ruled Rome for more than twenty years in a reign that was unpopular with the senate and the people. Dynastic problems cast a pall over the period as Germanicus Julius Caesar, the heir designate, a popular young prince who was Tiberius' nephew and adopted son, died mysteriously on assignment in the East in A.D. 19, and Lucius Aelius Sejanus, prefect of the Praetorian Guard, ruthlessly destroyed Drusus Julius Caesar (the son of Tiberius), Agrippina (the widow of Germanicus), and her two eldest sons in his effort to become the guardian of her youngest son, Gaius Julius Caesar Germanicus (Caligula) and so, in effect, to succeed to the power of Tiberius. To escape the animosities of the imperial family and the attendant machinations for power, Tiberius retired to the island of Capreae (Capri) in 26 and never again entered Rome.

Under the absentee emperor, Sejanus acquired greater influence in the city, but when Tiberius finally realized in 31 how devious his agent had been, Sejanus was executed. The emperor then launched a reign of terror from his island retreat, charging with treason many senators who had collaborated with Sejanus. The last years of his reign were dark and ugly, and Romans everywhere rejoiced at the news of his death in 37. Crowds formed in the streets chanting "Tiberius to the Tiber," and he was not deified.

Tiberius' reign illustrates one of the fundamental problems of the principate. He had tried to follow Augustan precedents and had indicated at the outset his reluctance to assume imperial authority, but some of his contemporaries found him hypocritical. The Augustan pretense of disinclination to rule required a consummate actor or a genuine believer, and Tiberius certainly was not the former and probably was not the latter. His ineptness as a diplomat created tensions largely because the role of emperor fashioned by Augustus was exceedingly difficult to play.

Modern historians see Tiberius as a tragic figure, talented and hardworking, a wise if sometimes static administrator of the empire. There is no doubt that the provinces continued in the prosperity begun under Augustus and that Tiberius genuinely attempted and normally provided excellent administrative oversight of the empire. He was careful to the point of frugality with Rome's finances and left a large surplus in the treasury. Yet the weakness in his personality—stubbornness, cruelty, and flagrant disregard of public sentiment—ruined his reputation.

On the death of Tiberius, Gaius (Caligula), his grandnephew and grandson by adoption, assumed power at the age of twenty-five amid popular rejoicing inspired by his youth and the fact that he was the son of Germanicus. Gaius fueled Roman expectations by liberally spending the accumulated surplus in the treasury on great public games. It was not long, however, before he revealed a tortured mind, probably insane, in an orgy of cruelty and megalomania culminating in his insistence on being worshiped as a god in his own lifetime. He almost certainly had an incestuous relationship with his sister Drusilla, whom he deified on her death in 38, and he suppressed with brutality a conspiracy led by his other two sisters and their lovers. Fortunately for the empire he was assassinated early in 41 after a brief reign of less than four years.

In the confusion following the assassination, Caligula's uncle Tiberius Claudius Drusus was proclaimed emperor by the Praetorian Guard after he promised them a large reward. Ancient authors depict Claudius as a fool dominated by his wives and freedmen, but modern historians reject that view and argue that the emperor made notable contributions to the development of the empire, including an expansion of the efficient central bureaucracy, an extension of the rights of citizenship to some provincials, and the construction of the harbor Caesar had planned at Ostia. Claudius conquered the southern and eastern parts of England (creating a province of Britain) and revealed in sometimes idiosyncratic ways his lively intellectual interests in law, language, and history.

Crippled from youth (perhaps by polio), the handicapped Claudius was regarded as a buffoon by many of his contemporaries, and there is no doubt that his wives and freedmen manipulated him to their advantage. Valeria Messalina (Messalina) let her sexual appetite lead her into conspiracy and was executed, but Agrippina (the younger daughter of Agrippina, the wife of Germanicus and the emperor's niece, whom he then married) used her influence to advantage by securing the accession of her son (by an earlier husband) Lucius Domitius Ahenobarbus (Nero) on Claudius' death in 54, a death that she probably arranged through poisoning.

At the age of seventeen Nero was happily too young to govern, and his advisers, Burrus, prefect of the guard, and the Stoic philosopher Lucius Annaeus Seneca, offered capable leadership during the new emperor's formative years. When Burrus died in 62, Nero assumed full control of the empire and forced Seneca into retirement, but the emperor was more interested in public performances of poetry, tragedy, dancing, and chariot racing than in the burdens of rule, and his regime quickly deteriorated. Although he suppressed a conspiracy in 65, three years later the legions revolted against an emperor who preferred playing the lyre to attending them in their camps. Nero could probably have clung to power had he responded vigorously, but he panicked at the outset of rebellion and committed suicide in 68.

With the death of Nero the Julio-Claudian line of Caesar and Augustus came to an end. The period was one of the most colorful in Roman history and was testimony to the genius of Augustus. He had created a government so strong and responsive to the needs of empire that it functioned well even under aberrant rulers. The principate had developed into a powerful monarchy, and around the provinces agents did the emperor's work effectively, directed by a central bureaucracy that was attentive to administrative detail. Interestingly, the Julio-Claudian emperors, possibly even including Caligula, were motivated by a strong sense of responsibility for the government that frequently surfaced even in their peculiar personalities.

The Julio-Claudian period on the frontiers was peaceful, though tensions between Rome and Parthia led to occasional conflicts. Several client kingdoms were annexed as Roman provinces, but the conquest of Britain under Claudius required considerable military effort and continued to be a problem for many years. The outbreak of the Jewish revolt in 66 reflected the difficulties of reconciling the Roman system of emperor worship and the state religion with the strong monotheism of politically active Jews in Palestine. Similar difficulties led to the suppression of the druids among the Celts of Gaul and Britain and to sporadic local persecutions of the new religion, Christianity, the most famous of which came under Pontius Pilate in Judaea during the reign of Tiberius and after the great fire in Rome in 64 under Nero.

Roman Civilization in the Age of Nero

Although the Julio-Claudian period was volatile in literature and the arts, many scholars have noted, particularly in literature, a slight deterioration from the Golden Age of Augustus to the Silver Age of Nero and his successors. The deterioration was not drastic and can easily be exaggerated. There was still opportunity for genuine, impressive innovation, as in the case of Petronius' picaresque novel the *Satyricon,* but political absolutism had limited the range of authors by forcing them, at their peril, to avoid criticism of the emperor and his policies. A crude sycophancy appeared in the literature of the period since authors often felt obliged to offer extravagant praise of the ruler.

Still, Seneca, the major intellectual and literary figure of the age, wrote poetry and tragedy of real force, though they are perhaps too aphoristic for the modern ear. He commanded a rich vocabulary, and his philosophical treatises and moral epistles reflect the loftiest ideals of Stoicism. He was remarkably popular as an author in his own day, so much so that Marcus Fabius Quintilianus (Quintilian) considered his influence on young writers damaging, and Christians of all ages have found much to admire in his works.

His nephew Lucan wrote an epic poem, the *Civil War* (known also as the *Pharsalia* after the Battle of Pharsalus in 48 B.C.), that is second in the Latin language only to Vergil's *Aeneid,* and a close associate of the Senecas, Persius, wrote poetic satires that show a combination of the influence of Horace and Stoic philosophy. Other authors of the Julio-Claudian period include the fabulist Phaedrus; Seneca's father, Seneca the Elder, who wrote works on rhetoric; and two minor historians, Gaius Velleius Paterculus and Quintus Curtius Rufus.

In art and architecture the Neronian age reached the peak of Roman classicism. Nero's coins are considered to be aesthetically the finest ever produced by Romans, and his rebuilding of the city after the great fire was so impressive that the emperor Trajan later spoke of an unrivaled *quinquennium* (five-year span) of Nero, which appears to refer to the architectural achievements of that emperor's last years. The ruins of Nero's own Golden House testify to the plausibility of such a tribute, and the remains of Pompeii, destroyed only about a decade after Nero's reign, reveal the rich mastery of artists in painting and sculpture as well as architecture.

THE FLAVIANS

The revolt of the legions against Nero led to a great civil war as armies of the various frontiers struggled with one another to place their own commanders on the throne. They disrupted momentarily the tranquility of the Pax Romana, and the historian Publius Cornelius Tacitus (Tacitus) saw the event as a revelation of the fateful secret of the empire, that "emperors could be made elsewhere than in Rome." Servius Sulpicius Galba, the elderly governor of Nearer Spain, descendant of a famous aristocratic family, seized power on the fall of Nero in 68 but could not hold it. In 69, the Year of the Four Emperors, Galba was murdered and replaced by the Praetorian prefect, Marcus Salvius Otho, who was shortly toppled by the legions of the Rhine under Aulus Vitellius. Before the year was over, Titus Flavius Vespasianus (Vespasian), commander of the Roman army in Judea, secured the support of legions in Syria, Egypt, and the Danube and with their help smashed Vitellius' forces. The senate officially recognized the new ruler.

Vespasian rapidly showed his abilities as an administrator and became one of Rome's best emperors. He brought an end to civil war and created a new Flavian dynasty while attempting dynastic continuity by taking the name Imperator Caesar Vespasianus Augustus. He angered some senators when he openly avowed that his sons would succeed him, abandoning the Augustan pretense of an elected princeps, but his firm and otherwise unpretentious rule was the medicine Rome needed after the extravagances of the Julio-Claudians.

The new emperor came from an equestrian family, and although he had successfully pursued a senatorial career, his rise to the purple reflected a growing shift in Roman society in which men of merit, regardless of birth, had greater opportunities than before to leave their mark. His rustic background made him appear crude at times despite a good education in both Latin and Greek, but it also undoubtedly contributed to the pervasive common sense that Romans and modern historians have detected in his policies. He set the Roman treasury on a sound financial basis by abandoning the luxurious court life of the Julio-Claudians and carefully supervising the collection of taxes and other revenues. His son Titus brought the war with the Jews to a successful conclusion in A.D. 70, and elsewhere in the empire legions returned to their posts in defense of the frontiers.

In Britain, Roman expansion proceeded apace, and in Rome itself Vespasian restored the Capitol, constructed a forum—as had Caesar and Augustus—and began work on the Colosseum. Many have seen in his ten-year reign the work of a second Augustus. Upon his death in 79 he was deified.

The short reign of Vespasian's son Titus (79–81), a popular emperor ("the delight and darling of mankind" according to Suetonius), was marred by several natural calamities, including the eruption of Vesuvius and a fire in Rome, but the emperor won public acclaim for his energetic attempts to provide relief. When he died mysteriously in 81, his younger brother, Titus Flavius Domitianus (Domitian), became emperor, but unfortunately the last of the Flavians exhibited tyrannical traits that made him one of Rome's most hated emperors (except among the soldiers) and a target of assassination.

The reign of Domitian, similar in many respects to that of Tiberius, has had its modern defenders. Cruel and conceited, the new emperor liked to be styled *dominus et deus,* yet he worked hard at the business of government, and senatorial malcontents were often responsible for provoking his wrath, especially during and after the revolt in 89 of Lucius Antonius Saturninus, a legionary commander along the Rhine. Domitian devoted considerable effort to the consolidation of Rome's frontiers, and barbarian pressure on the Danube as early as 85 required his personal presence on more than one occasion. He normally appointed good governors and was able to raise legionary pay, for the first time since Julius Caesar, from 300 to 400 denarii per year, but he clearly infuriated the senate by assuming the perpetual censorship and by consulting his personal council (the *consilium principis*) instead of the whole body. Twice he banished philosophers from Italy because of their objections to his despotism, and in the last years of his reign, 93–96, he undertook a purge of the senate through treason trials. The accumulated hatred of the aristocracy inevitably culminated in a conspiracy that included the prefects of the Guard and even Domitian's wife. The emperor was murdered in September of 96, and the senate officially damned his memory.

Flavian rule had made the military basis of the emperorship more apparent and the recognition of monarchy more direct and realistic. The Flavians had also used censorship aggressively to reorganize the senate and draw into the body new aristocrats of talent who were more generally representative of the Italian municipalities and the western provinces than their Julio-Claudian predecessors. Equestrians were widely used for administrative posts within the empire, and the imperial freedmen who had been so prominent in the central bureaucracy, particularly under Claudius, receded into the background. Under the reasonably high moral standards set by the Flavian emperors, fashionable social life in the capital lost much of the orgiastic and crudely extravagant flavor of Neronian Rome, but the Flavians were not able to assuage the tensions between emperor and senate that raged with great passion throughout much of the first century A.D.

THE FIVE GOOD EMPERORS

The overthrow of the Flavian dynasty resulted in an unbroken series of excellent emperors who ruled Rome throughout most of the second century, from 96 to 180. Nerva, Trajan, Hadrian, Antoninus Pius, and Marcus Aurelius are often called the Five Good Emperors because they succeeded in doing what their predecessors had failed to do, winning the full support and cooperation of the senatorial order. Only Hadrian suffered from occasional bad relations with the senate. The historian and senator Tacitus, writing in the first part of the age, exulted in the new conditions, "Times when we can think as we please and say what we think." Edward Gibbon believed that in the entire history of the world this was the period "during which the condition of the human race was most happy and prosperous."

The first of the emperors, Marcus Cocceius Nerva (96–98), a respected senator in his sixties, had been selected for the throne by Domitian's assassins, and the senate happily confirmed him as ruler. He was not in fact a strong man, and one sage commented that the difference between Nerva and Domitian was that under Domitian no one could do anything and under Nerva everyone could do everything. Domitian had been popular with the military, and the childless Nerva responded to the unrest of the soldiers by adopting as his son and heir a governor of the Rhine, Marcus Ulpius Trajanus (Trajan), a senator with considerable military experience whose selection was popular with the troops. After a reign of only sixteen months Nerva died, and Trajan (98–117) took his place without controversy.

During his long reign Trajan became the most popular of all emperors, and by 114 he was officially styled *Optimus Maximus* (best and the greatest). Much of his popularity stemmed from the respect he showed to the senate and a series of foreign wars leading to Rome's most impressive victories in the field since the days of Augustus. In two Dacian Wars (101–102 and 105–106) Trajan resolved for some time Rome's problems on the Danube, as he finally moved across the river and conquered Dacia (Rumania), which he converted into a new province and colonized with many thousands of Roman settlers.

In the East he abandoned long-standing imperial policy, annexed Arabia Petraea (106), and led a Roman army into Parthia (113–117) all the way to Babylon and the Persian Gulf. Though generally successful in the field, he almost certainly overextended Rome's resources, and by the time of his death the Jews of the Dispersion were in revolt in Egypt and North Africa, while the Parthians had retaken Lower Mesopotamia. Trajan died of a stroke suffered in Cilicia (117) as he was on his way back to Rome.

Romans liked their conquering emperor. His domestic policies, including a reduction of taxes and a program of public works, financed by the gold of Dacia, contributed to the esteem in which he was held. Notwithstanding a foreign policy that was too aggressive and left numerous problems for his successor, Trajan's victories stirred memories of earlier Roman greatness, and it was fitting that his ashes were laid to rest in the base of the towering column in Rome that glorified his conquest of Dacia.

Trajan had no son, and on his death his second cousin and ward, Publius Aelius Hadrianus (Hadrian; 117–138), who had been clearly groomed by Trajan as heir designate, assumed the throne. Whether Hadrian, who was in Antioch at the time, was actually adopted by Trajan on his deathbed, as Trajan's wife, Pompeia Plotina, claimed, is uncertain, but he was the obvious choice. Unfortunately the new emperor's followers in Rome executed some men suspected of plotting against him, including four former consuls, and although Hadrian claimed that it had been done without his knowledge (which some ancient and modern historians have doubted), the senate recoiled in the face of renewed executions. The episode naturally renewed tensions between emperor and senate, but until the last few years of his reign Hadrian treated the senate with deference and respect.

Convinced that Trajan's frontier policy had overextended the empire, Hadrian pulled back from the conquests in the East and adopted a frontier strategy of preclusive security, dropping in some areas (Hadrian's Wall in England is the most famous example) a "stone curtain" between Rome and her barbarian neighbors. He was one of Rome's hardest-working emperors and spent many years traveling from province to province visiting the legions in their camps and dealing with local problems. Like Nero he was an eager Philhellene, but Hadrian did not let his interests in literature and the arts divert him from the responsibilities of government.

He restored the military integrity of the empire and in 132–135 brutally suppressed a revolt of the Jews in Palestine. Jerusalem became a Roman colony, Aelia Capitolina, and Jews were denied the right to enter the city. Otherwise Rome, Italy, and the provinces prospered under his rule, and he too reduced taxes and encouraged public works, including the Pantheon and his own mausoleum, the present Castel Sant'Angelo, on the banks of the Tiber in Rome. He spent as much time as he could at his huge and elaborate country palace, the Villa Adriana, near Tibur (Tivoli) about twenty miles outside Rome.

Near the end of his life Hadrian suffered miserably from a debilitating illness, perhaps tuberculosis, and possibly because of the pain and discomfort his treatment of the senate soured. Like Augustus he suffered frustration in his dynastic policy when he executed his great-nephew Fuscus for conspiracy and adopted Lucius Ceionius Commodus, under the name of Aelius Verus, in 136. Unfortunately, Aelius died early in 138, and Hadrian in the last few months of his own life turned to a respected senator, Titus Aurelius Fulvus Boionius Antoninus. To provide for the future succession Antoninus obligingly adopted his seventeen-year-old nephew, the future emperor Marcus Aurelius, and Lucius, the seven-year-old son of Aelius Verus.

When Hadrian died, the senate breathed a sigh of relief and looked forward to the reign of one of their own reputable members. Antoninus Pius (138–161) forced senators to deify Hadrian and proceeded to govern Rome for more than twenty years in a reign so peaceful and prosperous that the eminent Greek man of letters, Aelius Aristides, claimed in a public oration at Rome in 154 that "the whole inhabited world was one city-state." In fact under Antoninus there were minor frontier problems in Britain, North Africa, and Dacia, but the encomium of Aristides is generally well taken. Antoninus ruled with uncommon concern for the welfare of his subjects and even refused to travel because he did not want to burden the cities of the empire with his retinue.

In some ways the reign of Antoninus was the Indian summer of the Roman Empire. Ominous clouds swept over the horizon in the reign of his successor, Marcus Aurelius (161–180). Problems in the East and on the Danube rapidly became crises, and Rome's philosopher emperor spent most of his reign with the legions on the frontier. Parthia seized Armenia in about 162 and Marcus sent his younger coemperor, Lucius Verus, to the East with a Roman army. Victorious by 166, Verus' troops brought back the plague, which swept through the empire. At the same time, Germanic tribes poured over the Danube as far as northern Italy. The two emperors moved up to Aquileia in 168 and saved the situation, but Marcus had to turn his attention to the Danube. (Lucius died in 169.) Successful wars against the Marcomanni and Quadi (170–174) and the Sarmatians (175) were interrupted by the revolt in the latter year of the Roman general Avidius Cassius in Syria and Egypt, where Marcus visited in 176 after the murder of Cassius. Danubian problems required the emperor's personal attention again in 178, and he remained on the frontier until his death in 180. The *Meditations* of Marcus Aurelius reveal him as a thoughtful and considerate man, devoted to responsible government, but the difficulties of war, finance, and the plague gave Romans a foretaste of the more troubled times of the late Roman Empire.

*Roman Civilization Under
the Flavians and Antoninus*

Over the period of roughly a century from A.D. 69 to 180 the Roman state became more paternalistic and bureaucratic and at the same time more cosmopolitan and less strictly "Roman." Trajan and Hadrian were born in the provinces, in Spain, and they reflected the widening horizons of the Roman aristocracy. Although the Five Good Emperors maintained better relations with the senate than the Flavians and were not considered tyrants, the emperorship had been transformed into an absolute paternal monarchy in which Roman subjects all over the empire expected the emperor to deal centrally with their local problems. He had become all powerful in a more than purely political way. As the organizer of divine and human resources the emperor became the chief and often the only possible solution to man's difficulties around the Mediterranean.

One notable and laudable reflection of the role of the father-emperor was the so-called alimentary institution created by Nerva and expanded by his successors. It involved a gift of money to the cities, first in Italy and then in the provinces, which was lent to nearby landowners for improvements, and the interest was paid back to the cities to be used for the support of poor children. In this way the government funded agricultural productivity, provided relief for the poor, and encouraged childbirth. The younger Pliny's letters to Trajan from the province of Bithynia and the emperor's replies show Trajan's attention to the welfare of his subjects. Hadrian was responsible for important reforms in jurisprudence that made interpretation of the law less arbitrary. Bureaucracy and paternalism were to become oppressive in the late empire; under the Five Good Emperors they merely reflected the increasing responsibility Roman rulers felt for their subjects.

In literature Romans continued to excel, though literary productivity and freshness taper off toward the end of the period. The major epic poets of Flavian Rome, Gaius Valerius Flaccus Setinus Balbus, Tiberius Catius Asconius Silius Italicus, and Publius Papinius Statius, can be boring and pedantic, but the *Epigrams* of Marcus Valerius Martialis (Martial), sometimes too scatological for modern translators, are lively and fascinating when they are not grotesque. Quintilian in *Education of an Orator* is often too technical for modern readers, but his chapters on literary criticism show a keen appreciation for good writing. The elder Pliny's *Natural History* is one of the pioneer encyclopedic works of antiquity, and Pliny's enthusiasm for everything under the sun is fascinating. By contrast, Sextus Julius Frontinus' treatises on tactics and aqueducts will interest only specialists. Flavius Josephus, a pro-Roman Jewish author, produced works in Aramaic and Greek on Jewish history and antiquity that are a major source for the study of the Jews (the Aramaic original of the *Jewish War* has not survived).

Greater works appear in the age of Trajan and Hadrian. Tacitus is one of Rome's most forceful prose stylists, though as a historian he makes little attempt to control or hide his biases. In biography the period produced two of antiquity's foremost practitioners, Lucius (?) Mestrius Plutarchus (Plutarch), who wrote in Greek, and Gaius Suetonius Tranquillus (Suetonius) in Latin. Plutarch was more philosophical than Suetonius, and his *Parallel Lives* are more romantic and moralistic than Suetonius' racy *Lives of the Twelve Caesars*.

Pliny the Younger composed *Letters* of elegant style illustrating aristocratic life in the early Roman Empire, but his *Panegyric* to Trajan rambles and is important mainly as a source of information for the reign of Nerva and the early years of Trajan. Juvenal the satirist wrote poetry with great passion and wit on the evils of Roman society.

Under Antoninus Pius and Marcus Aurelius there is a significant change in Roman literary development. In the first place Greek to some extent regained its primacy as a literary language. Marcus wrote his *Meditations* in Greek, and Lucian the satirist, Aelius Aristides, Galen the physician,

Claudius Ptolemaeus (Ptolemy) the astronomer, Appian the historian, and Flavius Arrianus (Arrian) the biographer of Alexander also anticipated reading audiences outside the Aegean. To be sure, Greeks had written for Romans since the days of Polybius, but the age of the Antonines saw increased activity.

In Latin there is a noticeable decline. Marcus Cornelius Fronto's letters will not stand comparison with those of Cicero and Pliny the Younger, and the *Attic Nights* of Aulus Gellius is a hodgepodge. *The Golden Ass (Metamorphoses)* of Lucius Apuleius is somewhat more promising, but in content it too reveals the revival of Greek. The Silver Age of Latin literature had ended by the death of Hadrian.

THE DECLINE OF ROME

Roman history in the third century is the story of decline, beginning with the reign of Marcus Aurelius' son and successor Marcus Aurelius Commodus Antoninus (180–192) and intensifying in the mid third century to near collapse under the chaos of the "barracks" emperors (235–284), when finally at the end of the period Rome was rescued by the dramatic reforms of Diocletian (284–305) and Constantine the Great (312–337). The recovery of Rome under those two potentates gave the empire another century of vitality, but in the fifth century the Western Empire passed from history altogether while portions of the Eastern Empire maintained their existence under the Byzantine emperors into the fifteenth century.

Just as Rome's rise to world empire had occurred over centuries, so her decline was a drawn-out, gradual process, quickening in pace at times, with occasional periods of recovery before the final onslaught of the barbarian invasions. Historians of Rome's decline are caught between two competing forces: one, to show the ways in which one of the world's greatest empires fell; the other, to emphasize that even in decline the civilization of the late Roman Empire was a marvelously varied expression of some of mankind's most creative forces. The story of survival is as important as the story of the fall.

The Age of Commodus and the Severans

Some historians have said that Marcus Aurelius reintroduced the dynastic principle when he allowed his son to succeed him, but that principle had never really been abandoned. Nerva, Trajan, Hadrian, and Antoninus simply had no sons of their own, and their dynastic policy closely followed that of the Julio-Claudians. Fate, nevertheless, dealt severely with Rome by providing Marcus with a successor who was one of Rome's worst rulers. Commodus, interested more in gladiatorial games than in government, was a cruel and tyrannical spendthrift who abandoned his father's strong position on the Danube and neglected the frontiers. He was finally strangled to death in a drunken sleep by a wrestling companion on the last day of A.D. 192.

The death of Commodus resulted in civil war (193–197) and a rapid succession of emperors, as in the years 68–69. The distinguished senator Publius Helvius Pertinax (193) did not survive a full three months before he was assassinated, and Marcus Didius Severus Julianus, who purchased the empire at an auction held by the Praetorian Guard, lost everything, including his life, in little more than two months. The provincial armies clashed again under Decimus Clodius Albinus in Britain, Gaius Pescennius Niger Justus in Syria, and Lucius Septimius Severus in Pannonia. Out of the chaos emerged a new Vespasian, Septimius Severus (193–211), founder of the Severan dynasty (193–235). Septimius was a forceful ruler who restored order, twice invaded Parthia, and organized northern Mesopotamia as a province. He was a North African by birth and his wife, Julia Domna, was Syrian, so his reign represented continuing growth in the influence of the provinces. Like Vespasian he was the son of an equestrian, but he went far beyond his Flavian predecessor in the use of equestrians in Roman government and also in emphasizing the military nature of his regime. He increased legionary pay, and when he died at Eburacum (York) supervising military operations in Britain, he enjoined his sons to enrich the soldiers and forget about everyone else. One of them, Marcus Aurelius Septimius Bassianus Antoninus (Caracalla; 211–217), shortly murdered the other, Publius Lucius Septimius Geta, and ruled much more brutally than his father. He once again raised legionary pay by one-half, and fought successfully with the armies on the Rhine and the Danube and in Parthia until he was assassinated in the East by disgruntled officers organized by the Praetorian prefect, Marcus Opellius Macrinus.

Macrinus (217–218) seized the emperorship but was toppled after humiliating losses against Parthia. Adherents of the Severans, mobilized by the Syrian Julia Maesa, sister of Septimius' wife, secured the throne for the fourteen-year-old Varius Avitus Bassianus Marcus Aurelius Antoninus (Elagabalus; 218–222), grandnephew of Septimius. Elagabalus ranks with Caligula and Nero in depravity, and his main interest other than sensual gratification was to introduce the worship of his native sun-god, Elagabal, to Rome. He was murdered by his soldiers, who dragged his body through the streets of Rome and threw it into the Tiber. The last emperor of the line (Marcus Julius Gessius Alexianus Bassianus, later Marcus Aurelius Severus Alexander; 222–235), a cousin of Elagabalus' and also a youth of fourteen, was weak and incompetent, dominated by his mother, Julia Mamaea, who was officially styled "Mother of Augustus, of the Barracks, of the Senate, and Fatherland." Unlike Elagabalus, Alexander was studious and of high moral character, and for a while his reign was peaceful and stable; but he lacked military competence and lost the confidence of his troops during crises on the frontiers in the last years of his reign. He was finally murdered on the Rhine by a Thracian general, Gaius Julius Verus Maximinus, who rose from a common soldier to become Maximinus I Thrax, emperor of Rome (235–238).

Despite the bizarre flavor, at times, of Severan rule the dynasty produced profound changes in the Roman Empire. The triumph of the provinces over Italy can be seen in the provincial origins of the emperors themselves and in the famous edict of Caracalla (212) extending the citizenship to virtually all free men in the empire. Oriental influences in the court of Elagabalus were in some ways precursors of eastern fashions that became so prominent late in the century. The militarization of the emperorship and the concomitant decline in the prestige of the senate went hand in hand with the emergence of equestrian influence. Septimius was born an equestrian but followed a senatorial career; Macrinus had been an equestrian throughout his career; and Maximinus began as a commoner. The Severans continued Hadrian's efforts in regularizing law and jurisprudence, and under their rule the Praetorian prefects became important judicial officers responsible for cases from Italy (outside of Rome) and the provinces. Distinguished jurors such as Aemilius Papinianus (Papinian) and Domitius Ulpianus (Ulpian) were appointed to the post.

The period also saw an accumulation of problems that contributed potently to the distress that followed Severan rule. Although Roman coins had been debased by Nero and Trajan, the damage was slight, but

Severan debasement of the silver coin by about 50 percent from Augustan standards gradually caused a great price inflation and threatened the economy of the empire. In foreign affairs the incompetence of Severus Alexander and the rebirth in the East, under the Sasanian dynasty, of the Persian Empire, which had absorbed Parthia by 227, left Rome weakened militarily and at the same time faced with a new and formidable opponent.

The Barracks Emperors (235–284)

In the aftermath of Severan rule Rome very nearly collapsed during a half century of intrigue and civil war when more than twenty emperors and as many challengers tore at the purple. A reign-by-reign account of the age would be tedious and dreary, and it would place too much emphasis on the role of individuals in a period swamped by the weight of historical trends. Early in the period the senate had tried to wrest power from the generals in a struggle against Maximinus I, but in the end, though Maximinus fell, the senate proved too weak to withstand the Praetorian Guard and the frontier legions. During these fifty years, Publius Licinus Valerianus (Valerian; 253–260) was one of only two emperors who died a natural death. Valerian was captured by the Persians, and by the end of his reign he had lost control of Gaul, Germany, and Britain (to Marcus Cassianus Latinius Postumus). Not long afterward the eastern provinces, too, seceded, led by Zenobia of Palmyra. As emperors desperately sought to retain the favor of their troops, barbarians swept across the frontiers, and Dacia was permanently lost, about 270. Plague, the decline of population, total debasement of the coinage, and rampant inflation affected Romans everywhere, particularly in the cities. The urban upper classes avoided membership in their city councils as the central government made them responsible for deficits in tax revenues.

One need not exaggerate the tribulations of the period, for they were obviously great. Naturally there were pockets of prosperity, first in one region and then in another, and occasional moments of peace. There were, moreover, individual emperors whose reigns, while they lasted, seemed to reverse the apparent trend of decline. Some emperors of Danubian origin—Lucius Domitius Aurelianus (Aurelian; 270–275), for example—who recovered the two secessionist states in West and East, retained power long enough to offer a semblance of stability. Roman schools maintained the study of grammar and rhetoric while new public buildings were still occasionally constructed.

Christians faced the time of troubles in greater jeopardy than the rest of the population because one of the easy solutions to Rome's problems was to rally the empire around a new dedication to ancient virtues. Some emperors could not avoid the temptation to stamp out the growing un-Roman religion, and the first empire-wide efforts to destroy Christianity occurred in this period, notably under Gaius Messius Quintus Decius in 250–251 and Publius Licinius Valerianus (Valerian) in 257–260. But the religion survived the attack and in the third century produced some of its greatest early Church Fathers—Quintus Septimius Florens Tertullianus (Tertullian; *ca.* 160–*ca.* 240), Origen (*ca.* 185–*ca.* 255), and Thascius Caecilius Cyprianus (Cyprian; *ca.* 200–258). In the last forty years of the century Christianity openly flourished.

In the religious arena the third century was a swirl of activity, although some of the traditional state cults, modified to meet new tastes and longings, remained strong. Elagabalus introduced an exotic (Syrian) form of sun worship that did not appeal to Romans, but Aurelian established a state cult for the sun (*Sol invictus*), and the Neoplatonist Plotinus (205–270) led a circle of intellectuals devoted to traditional Greek rationalism reorganized into a kind of religious monotheism. "The One" of Plotinus embraced the "World Mind," the "World Soul," and "Nature." The duality of spirit and matter was recognized in several religious and philosophical creeds as the material world of the Roman Empire crumbled to make way for spirituality.

Diocletian

When the Danubian emperor Gaius Aurelius Valerius Diocletianus (Diocletian; 284–305) seized power, there was no reason to believe that he would differ significantly from other rulers of the Barracks period. He was a military dynast who had risen through the ranks, but he proved to be a reformer of abundant ability and launched a program of renewal that restored Rome to stability and power. The fact that he ruled for twenty-one years is itself significant, considering the brief reigns of his predecessors, but his achievement went far beyond simple longevity. To provide greater military and administrative efficiency he appointed as his colleague the general Maximian, first as Caesar (the term now indicating a secondary emperor) in 285 and in the following year to the rank of Augustus. In 293 two Caesars (Constantius I Chlorus and Galerius Maximianus) were named to serve the Augusti. The government of the period has sometimes been called a tetrarchy (rule by four), but Diocletian was always the dominant force.

Under the tetrarchy it was possible to assign a ruler to each of the great strategic areas of the empire, Gaul and Britain (Constantius), Italy and Africa (Maximian), the Balkans (Galerius), and the eastern provinces (Diocletian). In this way, when there were simultaneous threats on the frontiers, a ranking member of the ruling "family" was always on the scene to direct the legions against Rome's enemies or to suppress rebellion within. By the end of his reign Diocletian had restored Rome to its full former extent (except for Dacia), and he gave the empire a new lease on life.

Although the new empire of Diocletian was almost as strong as the empire had been in the days of Septimus Severus, it was vastly different. To maintain the control Diocletian sought and the times required, it was necessary to impose on the ancient Mediterranean civilization an onerous bureaucracy in which the regulation of earlier days finally approached regimentation. There had been about twenty-five provinces under Augustus, forty under Hadrian, and fifty under Septimius Severus, but Diocletian nearly doubled the number to about ninety-six without any significant addition of territory. Existing provinces were simply subdivided so that governors, administering smaller territories, had more effective control. Italy lost its favored status and was treated like the other provinces, while the senate was nearly shorn of its role in the regime—the emperor controlled all appointments and most governors did not come from the senatorial class. Significantly Diocletian did not bother to visit Rome at all until near the end of his reign. Not long after, in the reign of Constantine (320), distinctions between the two orders, based on property qualifications, were abolished and they were administratively intermixed.

Under Diocletian each Caesar and Augustus had his own Praetorian prefect who now served a more civilian than military role acting as the emperor's chief agent in the administration of the empire. In the four great prefectures the provinces were organized into dioceses ruled by vicars, about twelve of them altogether, and the governors of the provinces reported to the vicars, who in turn reported to the prefects who served the emperors. This massive growth of bureaucratic machinery brought the government into closer contact with Romans and at the same time separated them from the emperors, who now ruled in a kind of oriental splendor, appearing before their subjects only on great ceremonial occasions. The emperor of Rome was no longer princeps, first citizen; he had become dominus, lord and master, and the principate yielded to the dominate. In recognition of the important religious role of the ruler, Diocletian took the title Jovius and conferred that of Herculius on Maximian.

Although Diocletian's contributions to Roman resurgence were substantial, not all of his reforms succeeded. Debasement and devaluation of the coinage had caused prices to skyrocket, and the monetary system collapsed as coins became nearly worthless. Barter in kind worked better than we moderns would expect, but the obvious difficulties led Diocletian to attempt a restoration of coinage in 294. This failed because he did not have enough bullion to meet the demands of the economy. Prices continued to rise, and in 301 the emperor tried price and wage controls in the Edict on Prices, which also failed. Somewhat more successfully, to meet governmental needs and to eliminate the arbitrary confiscations of his predecessors, Diocletian reorganized Rome's system of taxation by establishing a new land and poll tax, which had the advantage of regularity if not of equity. An annual budget was also introduced.

The emperor's effort to stamp out Christianity proved a failure. Late in his reign (303) Diocletian launched Rome's most vicious persecution of the religion, which continued for several years afterward. He ordered churches destroyed and the scriptures burned, and Christians were driven from governmental positions while clergy were imprisoned. Under penalty of death Christians were required to sacrifice to the state gods, yet the courage of the martyrs seems to have strengthened the commitment of true believers even though some Christians yielded to the pressure of the state. Finally in 311 Galerius, the most eager of the persecutors, stopped the persecution.

It has always fascinated students of Rome that Diocletian abdicated in 305 at the peak of his success, the first person in Roman history since Sulla to give up power voluntarily. He forced his reluctant colleague Maximian to do the same, presumably because Diocletian wanted to give his new system of succession based on the tetrarchy a chance. The traditional dynastic policy was ignored as the sons of Maximian and Constantius I Chlorus were overlooked in the appointment of new Caesars. Diocletian hoped that the selection of Caesars based on merit to succeed the Augusti would end Rome's crises of succession. In this he was bitterly disappointed.

Constantine the Great

Within two years after the abdication of Diocletian, Rome plunged into the abyss of civil war again. Ultimately Constantine, son of Constantius I Chlorus, gained control of the West with a victory near Rome at the Battle of the Mulvian (Milvian) Bridge (312), and Valerius Licinianus Licinius in the following year secured the East. At Mediolanum (Milan) in 313 the two rulers issued the edict granting toleration to Christianity and specifically recognizing it as a legal religion in the empire. Much more significant is the fact that Constantine had become a Christian himself as a result of a vision or dream before the battle at the Mulvian Bridge. His conversion and his defeat of Licinius in 324 to become emperor of the united empire combined to make Christianity the most important, and before long the official, religion of the era. The transformation from pagan to Christian Rome had begun.

Although in his early career he had benefited from political unrest, Constantine the Great became an agent of reform and stability. During his reign many trends of the past were brought to a kind of official fulfillment. First among them was his conversion to Christianity, but in addition he recognized the growing priority of the East over the West, a feature of Diocletian's reign, by building a new Christian capital, Constantinople, at the site of ancient Byzantium on the Bosporus. Near there at Nicaea in 325 he assembled the first ecumenical council of the church, which rejected the Arian heresy and adopted the Nicene Creed.

His economic policies were more successful than those of Diocletian. Using bullion of which some may have been seized from pagan temples, Constantine issued a new gold coin, the solidus, that returned to the empire, in part at least, a money economy and survived as a medium of exchange for nearly a thousand years. He reinforced a tendency to tie sons to their fathers' occupations, a policy that made tax collections more regular and avoided manpower shortages in critical industries. Some have seen the origins of serfdom in his reign since tenant farmers were no longer free to abandon their fields. The long history of economic crisis may have required such drastic solutions, but most historians undoubtedly feel a tinge of regret in comparing the economy of the second century A.D. with that of the fourth century.

In some ways, however, there were actually improvements over the earlier period in military organization. The army of Diocletian and Constantine was large, about 500,000 men, and had a far better cavalry arm than the legions of the early Roman Empire. Furthermore it was vastly more mobile, including a field as well as a static frontier force, so that central reserves could be sent to trouble spots on the frontiers. Sons of veterans were required to serve, and the government actively recruited barbarian mercenaries, a policy that would lead to barbarization of the army; but in the days of Diocletian and Constantine the Roman army was an effective force. Discipline in the infantry could no longer be maintained in the rigorous ways of earlier times, because rulers were more sensitive to the need to cater to their troops in order to avoid mutiny and rebellion, and military costs were much greater; but the troops demonstrated their ability to defend the empire. Diocletian and Constantine had left the empire infused with a new spirit, by no means as optimistic as the spirit of Augustus, but ready to face the challenge of survival after near collapse.

*The Fourth Century
After Constantine (337–395)*

In history great men are rare, but even so, the period after Constantine seems remarkably deficient in that respect. Although Theodosius I was called Great, he was not (he gained the title because of his piety), and the ability of fourth-century emperors to maintain the military integrity of the empire despite important losses in the field is more a monument to the work of Diocletian and Constantine than to the skill of their successors. In the last half of the fourth century the Roman Empire survived on borrowed time, though contemporaries of the period, except for a few astute observers such as the historian Ammianus Marcellinus and the military analyst Flavius Vegetius Renatus (Vegetius), continued for the most part to bask in a waning Roman grandeur.

After the death of Constantine the army insisted that his sons become the rulers and murdered all who might rival them. Constans I, Constantine II, and Constantius II divided the empire, and it was not long before Constans defeated and killed Constantine (340), leaving the West under his control and the East under Constantius'.

Though aggressive in defense of his frontiers, Constans appears to have been a drunken reprobate and was murdered by his own officers (350). In the ensuing years Constantius secured control of the entire empire and ruled as sole emperor from A.D. 353 to 361, while he placed his younger cousin Flavius Claudius Julianus (Julian) as caesar (355) in command of the Rhine. When Šapur II of Persia invaded Roman territory, Constantius moved against him in 360, but troops along the Rhine took advantage of the crisis to hail their commander, Julian, as emperor. Constantius died the following year as he returned to face Julian, and the young man, about thirty years old, became Rome's ruler (361–363).

Julian was an apostate. Reared as a Christian but widely educated in the pagan authors, he returned to paganism, proclaimed general toleration for all religions, and actively favored pagan cults while rescinding various privileges previously given to Christians. He was an able administrator who streamlined the government and reduced taxes, but his reign was cut short when he was killed during an invasion of Persia (363), His successor, Flavius Jovianus (Jovian; 363–364), accepted demeaning terms imposed by Šapur II and returned the empire to a pro-Christian policy before he died after a reign of only several months.

In the confusion a general, Flavius Valentinianus (Valentinian I; 364–375), seized the throne and ruled in the West while his younger brother Valens (364–378) served as coemperor in the East. Frontier problems dominated their reigns. Valentinian struggled—generally successfully—along the Rhine and the Danube against the barbarian pressures of the Franks, Saxons, Alemanni, and Quadi, and Valens held the Roman East against Persia. In 373 he permitted the Visigoths, who were under severe pressure from the Ostrogoths and the Huns, to settle in the empire south of the Danube, but the Visigoths, resentful of the way they had been treated by Roman officials, went to war in 377. In 378, at Hadrianopolis (Adrianople; Edirne) in Thrace, Valens was killed and the Roman army suffered one of its greatest defeats. Flavius Gratianus (Gratian; 375–383) and Valentinian II (375–392), sons of Valentinian I, succeeded their father as corulers in the West, and Gratian elevated a general, Theodosius I (379–395), as emperor in the East. Theodosius pacified the Visigoths by recognizing them as a sovereign nation under their own kings within the Roman Empire.

When Gratian was murdered in the West in 383 and Valentinian II in 392, Theodosius I attempted to unite the empire and was finally decisively successful shortly before his death in 395. Under Valentinian I, his sons Gratian and Valentinian II, and Theodosius I, the empire had faced grave problems and was again in the throes of decline. Military difficulties mounted everywhere, and Theodosius was the last emperor to rule effectively over the entire empire. By the end of the period Christianity had become Rome's official religion, and pagans were persecuted. The economic and social fabric of the empire collapsed under the growing pressures as taxes rose to become an almost insufferable burden. It was increasingly difficult to find Romans who could meet the property qualification for service in the urban councils, and because of the government's rigid economic policies Roman society came close to the development of a caste system. Cities shrank in size and walls had to be constructed around them for their protection. In some areas of the empire the ravages of invaders and tax collectors meant that even the countryside was abandoned.

Despite the quickening pace of decline, the empire of the fourth century was not devoid of literary, intellectual, and artistic achievement. Some of it was inspired by

Christianity and is best represented in the careers of Eusebius of Caesarea, Eusebius Hieronymus (Jerome), Ambrose, and Aurelius Augustinus (Augustine). But Quintus Aurelius Symmachus and the historian Ammianus Marcellinus showed that pagans still had much to offer though their day was passing. Christian influence in architecture and in art left its most notable signs in the emergence of great churches and in the mosaics and paintings associated with them, but interest in science and experimentation, so much a feature of ancient civilization in the Hellenistic age and the early Roman Empire, was fading into magic and mysticism in the otherworldly epoch of the late Roman Empire.

THE FALL OF ROME

On his death Theodosius I divided the empire between his sons, Flavius Honorius (395–423) in the West and Flavius Arcadius (395–408) in the East. It would never be reunited again except partially and briefly by Justinian in the sixth century. The East survived throughout the Middle Ages, in fluctuating circumstances, as the Byzantine Empire, but in the West the Roman Empire did not outlast the fifth century. It was battered by barbarian invaders, often with the connivance of the eastern emperors, who were determined to hold their nearly impregnable fortress at Constantinople regardless of the fate of their western counterparts.

Ironically, dynastic instability in the West, which had contributed so much to the weakening of the region earlier, was not at this period a major problem until the last years of the Western Roman Empire. Until then, only two emperors, Honorius (395–423) and Valentinian III (425–455), had ruled for almost sixty years (with a brief chaotic interlude between their reigns); and although they were not strong leaders, and Valentinian III was merely six years old at the time of his accession, they were both served by men of ability—Flavius Stilicho and Constantius III under Honorius, and Flavius Aetius, the "last of the Romans," under Valentinian III.

Barbarian invasions simply came too frequently and with greater force than in earlier periods, and the barbarian kings showed a ruthless ability to take advantage of Rome's weaknesses. Early in the period Stilicho thwarted the designs of Alaric, king of the Visigoths, but after Stilicho was executed in 408, Alaric led his forces into Italy and sacked the city of Rome in 410 for the first time since the Gauls had done it in about 390 B.C. Alaric died shortly thereafter. Under his brother-in-law Ataulf the Visigoths moved into Gaul. Later they were forced by Constantius III into Spain, though they were subsequently allowed to return to Gaul, where under Theodoric I they created a strong kingdom in what is now southern France.

In the meantime, by 409, the Vandals had swept through Gaul into Spain and established a Vandal state there. In 429, under Gaiseric, they attacked Africa. By 439 they had taken Carthage, and on the death of Valentinian III in 455, Gaiseric crossed over to Italy, and Rome again fell into barbarian hands. Although he made no attempt to hold Rome, the Vandal kingdom in the western Mediterranean survived until the age of Justinian. That part of Gaul not controlled by the Visigoths was overrun by Franks, Burgundians, and Alemanni, while Angles, Saxons, and Jutes seized Britain.

Throughout the first half of the fifth century Stilicho, Constantius III, and Aetius performed minor miracles in maintaining a vestige of Roman authority and independence in the West. As late as 451, at the Catalaunian Plains (known as the battle of Chalons), Aetius rallied most of the barbarian kingdoms to Rome's standards to defeat Attila and the Huns, but when Aetius was murdered in 454 and Valentinian the following year, Rome virtually died with them. The next twenty years saw a rapid succession of emperors, puppets of Ricimer, a barbarian general in the service of Rome. After Ricimer's death in 472, Odoacer, another barbarian general, forced the last emperor of Rome, Romulus Augustulus, to abdicate in 476, and the Roman Empire in the West disappeared. Odoacer became king, not emperor, and toward the end of the century Theodoric established an independent Ostrogothic kingdom in Italy.

The Causes of Rome's Fall.

Historians will debate the causes of Rome's fall forever simply because they are so manifold and complex. The decline of Rome lasted many centuries, and can be detected in the political, social, economic, and intellectual life of the empire. As a result historians have emphasized, almost willy-nilly, a wide range of factors placing special emphasis, as they see fit, on some particular aspect of the decline. We have nearly reached the stage Mark Twain foretold by saying "we shall soon know nothing at all," because scholars "have thrown much darkness on the subject."

This brief summary of Roman history is not the place for systematic analysis of all the explanations of Rome's fall offered since Gibbon. Readers who are interested must consult the bibliography for some substantial additional reading, but I have tried to make clear in the narrative above some of the elements of the problem and my own view that the decisive period of the fall of the empire must be sought in the fifth century, not earlier as some have argued—in the third and fourth centuries. One can tell the story of the empire as easily from the point of view of survival as of decline. In 395 the empire was still largely intact under one emperor. Within a century the Western Empire had collapsed, never to be restored. The division of the empire into two halves at the death of Theodosius I meant for all practical purposes that the full impact of the barbarian invasions had to be borne by the weaker and poorer half (which was bedeviled by oppression, public hostility to the army and bureaucracy, and the obliteration of its middle classes by taxation), while the eastern emperors with few exceptions, either out of policy or jealousy, or both, conserved the resources of the East and passively observed the fall of the West. Whether the barbarian invaders could have been repulsed by the combined might of the full empire is a question that can never be answered, but obviously the odds of survival would have been much greater in a unified empire. The concept of coimperial rule, introduced by Diocletian to create unity, rejected by Constantine, but reintroduced at his death to accommodate his sons, led after the death of Theodosius to disunity and final dismemberment.

The Aftermath of Rome's Fall

For many centuries Rome had given the civilization of the ancient Mediterranean the protection and leadership it required to develop its full potential. There is a sense in which that purpose had been served by the second century A.D. since the signs of cultural stagnation, some would even say of deterioration, in literature, art, philosophy, and the general standard of living first appear then and intensify thereafter. Some historians have argued that ancient Mediterranean man needed to cast off the shackles of a backward-looking civilization in order to move forward into a new and more creative society. The barbarian invasions freed Europeans of the West from the stagnation of late antiquity, and they proceeded to develop in the Middle Ages the basis of a new civilization that in modern times has been one of the most potent forces in world history.

Ironically, however, one of the major ingredients of western European civilization has been its link with the ancient Mediterranean. The fall of Rome had a tumultuous impact on the West. In some areas, such as Britain, ancient civilization was virtually destroyed; but in much of western Europe the heritage of Rome remained a strong force, though not so overwhelming that it suffocated new cultural forms.

Christianity's strong ties to antiquity could not be severed, and the papacy emerged in the West as a preserver of important features of ancient life, even pagan Latin literature. Through Christianity ancient influences were reintroduced into Britain and spread with the religion far beyond the confines of the Western Roman Empire. The influences of Roman administration and law were preserved by the Byzantines and their Orthodox church in the East, and in the Renaissance Western man turned back avidly for inspiration from both Greek and Roman antiquity, inspiration that helped to fashion the forceful, humanist, secular age of modern times.

The Roman Empire in the West was obliterated in the fifth century A.D., but its civilization has survived indirectly in the countless forms of its influence on those who came after. In the physical and literary wreckage of the ancient Mediterranean, Western man has scavenged for centuries, filled with wonder and amazement at "the glory that was Greece and the grandeur that was Rome."

BIBLIOGRAPHY

GENERAL

The Cambridge Ancient History, VII–XII (1928–1939, repr. 1964–1965); Max Cary and Howard H. Scullard, *A History of Rome down to the Reign of Constantine,* 3d ed. (1975); Michael Grant, *History of Rome* (1978); Howard H. Scullard, *From the Gracchi to Nero,* 5th ed. (1982); William G. Sinnigen and Arthur E. R. Boak, *A History of Rome to A.D. 565,* 6th ed. (1977); Chester G. Starr, "The Roman Place in History," in *Chester G. Starr Essays on Ancient History,* Arther Ferrill and Thomas Kelly, eds. (1979).

ROME TO 146 B.C.

Raymond Bloch, *Origins of Rome* (1960); Sir Gavin De Beer, *Hannibal* (1969); Thomas A. Dorey and Donald R. Dudley, *Rome Against Carthage* (1972); Thomas J. Dunbabin, *The Western Greeks* (1968); Robert M. Errington, *The Dawn of Empire: Rome's Rise to World Power* (1972); Einar Gjerstad, *Legends and Facts of Early Roman History* (1962); William V. Harris, *Rome in Etruria and Umbria* (1971), and *War and Imperialism in Republican Rome* (1979); Jacques Heurgon, *The Rise of Rome to 264 B.C.,* James Willis, trans. (1973).

John F. Lazenby, *Hannibal's War* (1978); Robert M. Ogilvie, *Early Rome and the Etruscans* (1976); Massimo Pallottino, *The Etruscans,* 2d ed. (1975); Edward Togo Salmon, *Samnium and the Samnites* (1967); Howard H. Scullard, *Roman Politics, 220–150 B.C.* (1951), *Scipio Africanus: Soldier and Politician* (1970), and *A History of the Roman World: 753–146 B.C.,* 4th ed. (1980); Chester G. Starr, *The Beginnings of Imperial Rome* (1980); Brian H. Warmington, *Carthage* (1960).

THE LATE ROMAN REPUBLIC

A. E. Astin, *Scipio Aemilianus* (1967); Ernst Badian, *Foreign Clientelae (264–70 B.C.)* (1958), *Roman Imperialism in the Late Republic* (1968), and *Publicans and Sinners: Private Enterprise in the Service of the Roman Republic* (1972); P. A. Brunt, *Italian Manpower 225 B.C.–A.D. 14* (1971); *Social Conflicts in the Roman Republic* (1971); John M. Carter, *The Battle of Actium* (1970); Michael Crawford, *The Roman Republic* (1982).

Emilio Gabba, *Republican Rome, the Army, and the Allies* (1976); Matthias Gelzer, *Caesar,* Peter Needham, trans. (1968); Michael Grant, *Cleopatra* (1972), and *Caesar* (1974); Erich Gruen, *Roman Politics and the Criminal Courts, 149–78 B.C.* (1968), and *The Last Generation of the Roman Republic* (1974); Herbert Hill, *The Roman Middle Class in the*

Republican Period (1952); Eleanor Goltz Huzar, *Mark Antony* (1978); Walter K. Lacey, *Cicero and the End of the Roman Republic* (1978); Andrew W. Lintott, *Violence in Republican Rome* (1968).

Frank Burr Marsh, *A History of the Roman World from 146 to 30 B.C.*, 3d ed. (1963); Claude Nicolet, *The World of the Citizen in Republican Rome*, P. S. Falla, trans. (1980); Elizabeth Rawson, *Cicero* (1975); Robin Seager, *Pompey: A Political Biography* (1979); Richard E. Smith, *The Failure of the Roman Republic* (1955); David Stockton, *The Gracchi* (1979); Lily Ross Taylor, *Party Politics in the Age of Caesar* (1949).

THE EARLY EMPIRE

Barry Baldwin, *The Roman Emperors* (1980); Anthony R. Birley, *Marcus Aurelius* (1966); John Buchan, *Augustus* (1937); John H. D'Arms, *Commerce and Social Standing in Ancient Rome* (1981); Samuel Dill, *Roman Society from Nero to Marcus Aurelius* (1904, repr. 1956); Peter Garnsey, *Social Status and Legal Privilege in the Roman Empire* (1970); Albino Garzetti, *From Tiberius to the Antonines*, J. R. Foster, trans. (1974); Michael Grant, *Nero* (1970); Mason Hammond, *Antonine Monarchy* (1959); Bernard W. Henderson, *Five Roman Emperors* (1927).

Arnold H. M. Jones, *Augustus* (1970); Edward N. Luttwak, *The Grand Strategy of the Roman Empire* (1976); Fergus Millar, *The Emperor in the Roman World* (1977); Arnaldo Momigliano, *Claudius: The Emperor and His Achievement*, 2d ed. (1961); Stewart Perowne, *Hadrian* (1960); Meyer Reinhold, *Marcus Agrippa* (1965); Edward Togo Salmon, *A History of the Roman World from 30 B.C. to A.D. 138*, 5th ed. (1966); Robin Seager, *Tiberius* (1972); Chester G. Starr, *Civilization and the Caesars* (1954), and *The Roman Empire 27 B.C.–A.D. 476* (1982); Sir Ronald Syme, *The Roman Revolution* (1939, repr. 1960); Brian H. Warmington, *Nero: Reality and Legend* (1969); Graham Webster, *The Roman Imperial Army* (1969); Zvi Yavetz, *Plebs and Princeps* (1969).

THE LATE EMPIRE

Anthony R. Birley, *Septimius Severus* (1971); Peter Brown, *The World of Late Antiquity* (1971); John B. Bury, *History of the Later Roman Empire*, 2 vols. (1923, repr. 1958), and *The Invasion of Europe by the Barbarians* (1928; repr. 1967); Edward Gibbon, *The Decline and Fall of the Roman Empire* (many editions); Michael Grant, *The Climax of Rome*, 3d ed. (1974), and *The Fall of the Roman Empire: A Reappraisal* (1976); Richard Mansfield Haywood, *The Myth of Rome's Fall* (1958); Arnold H. M. Jones, *Constantine and the Conversion of Europe*, 2d ed. (1962), *The Later Roman Empire, 284–602*, 2 vols. (1964).

Solomon Katz, *The Decline of Rome and the Rise of Mediaeval Europe* (1955); Ferdinand Lot, *The End of the Ancient World and the Beginnings of the Middle Ages*, Philip Leon and Mariette Leon, trans. (1931, repr. 1961); Ramsay MacMullen, *Enemies of the Roman Order* (1966), *Constantine* (1970), and *Roman Government's Response to Crisis, A.D. 235–337* (1976); Mikhail I. Rostovtzeff, *Social and Economic History of the Roman Empire*, 2 vols., 2d ed. (1957); Joseph Vogt, *The Decline of Rome*, Janet Sondheimer, trans. (1967).

LAND AND SEA

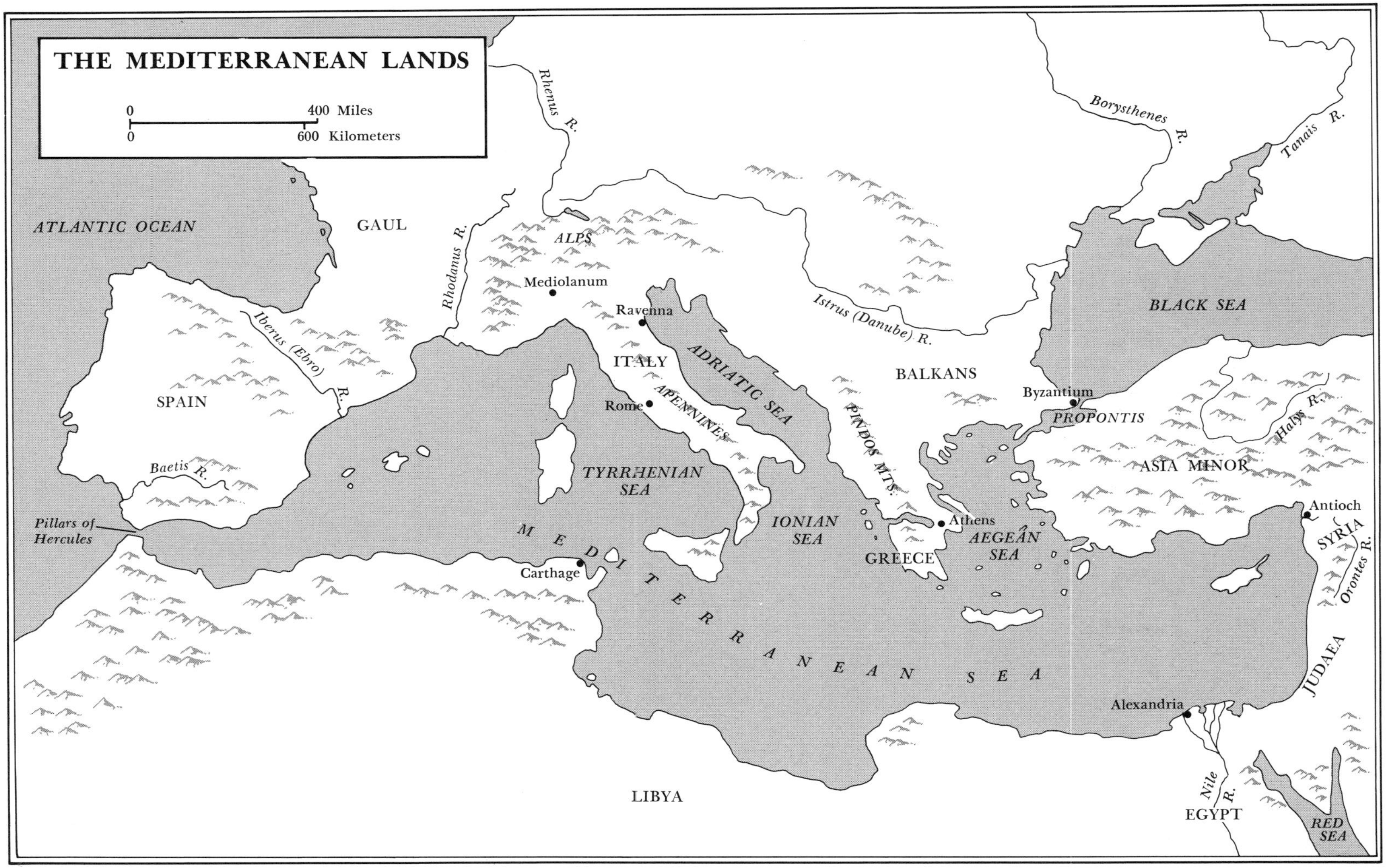
THE MEDITERRANEAN LANDS
0 400 Miles
0 600 Kilometers
ATLANTIC OCEAN
GAUL
Rhenus R.
Rhodanus R.
ALPS
Mediolanum
Ravenna
ITALY
Rome
APENNINES
ADRIATIC SEA
Borysthenes R.
Tanais R.
Istrus (Danube) R.
BLACK SEA
BALKANS
Byzantium
PROPONTIS
Halys R.
ASIA MINOR
PINDOS MTS.
SPAIN
Iberus (Ebro) R.
Baetis R.
Pillars of Hercules
TYRRHENIAN SEA
IONIAN SEA
Athens
AEGEAN SEA
GREECE
Antioch
SYRIA
Orontes R.
Carthage
MEDITERRANEAN SEA
JUDAEA
Alexandria
Nile R.
EGYPT
RED SEA
LIBYA

LAND AND SEA

J. DONALD HUGHES

INTRODUCTION

The Mediterranean region is a cultural, historical, and climatic area that, unlike most others, is defined by the sea that forms its center, rather than by continental or political boundaries. It includes portions of three continents and it stretches from western Europe to the Near East. The Mediterranean climate is what gives the region its special character. Although it can be extremely hot or cold at certain times or places, the overall impression is wonderfully pleasant: sunny, warm, moderated by breezes from the sea. Visitors from northern Europe have often found it seductive. Those who live there have expressed ambivalence about their homelands; Vergil glorified his native earth, Italia, in the *Georgics;* but Hesiod in the *Works and Days* complained about the weather and the soil's infertility in his farm near Askra Pyrgos (Ascra)[1] in Boeotia, mainland Greece.

Another salient feature of the Mediterranean image is the fact that the lands around the central sea have seen the rise, flowering, and fall of great civilizations. Here "grew the arts of war and peace"; here the muses inspired poets, playwrights, historians, astronomers, and dancers. Here laws were promulgated, pharaohs ruled, and both the Athenian democracy and the Roman Empire arose. Here are the regions that are Holy Land for three of the world's great religions. And the monuments of these civilizations still stand, even if often as ruins, around the shores of the sea.

As an environment, the Mediterranean provided unity in the sense of common themes in the lives of those who live around it. The sea itself is perhaps the most important of these themes. As the name indicates, there is the feeling that it is "in the middle," always a presence to be reckoned with. It divides the lands from each other, but it also unites as the highway of trade and travel. Because the Mediterranean lands are mostly mountainous, and those which are not are often rough and forbiddingly dry, it is the sea that in ancient times served as the means of communication as often as, or more often than, the land. But the sea also provides a

[1] For this particular essay, modern place-names appear first followed by their ancient equivalents in parentheses.

seemingly endless diversity. In dividing the land, it has formed it, and itself, into many different shapes. There are huge gulfs, and narrow straits where currents and whirlpools threaten. There are inviting bays and treacherous shallows. None of the larger peninsulas into which the sea cuts the land has an outline similar to any other. The Mediterranean is far from monotonous; there are almost no two places with an exactly similar setting of land and sea, mountain ranges and views.

Another unifying theme is climate; almost everywhere in the region there is a dichotomy between a cool, often rainy winter and a hot, desiccating summer. From one end of the sea to the other, people have found summer the time for travel and war, and winter the season for peace, agriculture, and repair at home. Fernand Braudel said it well in *The Mediterranean and the Mediterranean World in the Age of Philip II* (1972, p. 231).

> That identical or near-identical worlds should be found on the borders of countries as far apart and in general terms as different as Greece, Spain, Italy, North Africa; that these worlds should live at the same rhythm; that men and goods should be able to move from one to another without any need for acclimatization: such living identity implies the living unity of the sea. It is a great deal more than a beautiful setting.

But the climate, too, has diversity. A resident of Gaza, where it virtually never snows, might find the winter unbearably long and cold in Aquila, on the Adriatic shores, where it snows on an average of 17 days between October and April. The island of Cythera (Cerigo) in Greece has perhaps one thunderstorm a year, but Pula (Pola) in Istria (northwestern Yugoslavia) has them on more than 44 days. In Port Said, it rains about 18 days a year; in Algiers, 120 days. These are all Mediterranean places, and the examples could be multiplied ad infinitum. So each town, island, and mountain has its own microclimate, its own pattern of winds, and its own pageant of seasons.

Similarly, the vegetation of the Mediterranean offers a unifying theme. Approaching the shore in locations from one end of the sea to the other, the voyager will see the bluish masses of mountains covered with the brushy growth called maquis, while below in the valleys, blown by breezes, are masses of olive trees like gray but sparkling clouds. But many of the smaller islands are now little more than bare rocks, while the towering cedars, junipers, firs, and pines of fortunately isolated mountains in the Taurus are reminders that the earlier Mediterranean had noble forests.

The earth itself is a document of great importance for the historian, for history takes place within a structured setting. The human actors in the natural scene not only speak and relate to one another; they also react to and impact upon their stage. Therefore to understand the energies and structure of history, it is necessary to begin with the natural environment. With good reason Herodotus inquired about the source and course of the Nile in order to elucidate the life of the Egyptians, and Thucydides described the thin, dry soil of Attica to explain why the Athenians managed to retain their place in their own land while so many others of the old Hellenes had to flee to other shores and islands. The modern historian likewise must consider such questions as the relation of naval affairs to forest resources and the probable extent of deforestation. Thus, the study of the environment can serve as an important key to understanding the human condition.

THE LAND: "THE ELEMENT OF EARTH"

Among the many aspects of the environment that affect human history, the land is of paramount import. It is the place where human beings make their homes, and it provides materials for the architectural expression of their communities. It bears the soil in which crops, grass, and forests grow, supporting people and livestock. Its relief, and its shapes in regard to the sea, determine the kinds of uses to which it can or cannot be put. Colonization, military campaigns, agriculture, communication, and trade all follow patterns shaped by the prior patterns of the land. The Mediterranean basin has some of the most variegated and interesting patterns of land in the world, characterized by high relief, complicated mountain ranges, long peninsulas, deep valleys and embayments, and islands diverse in size and form.

Geographical Survey: Boundaries and Major Provinces

A cultural definition of the region might begin with the areas occupied by the Greeks and Romans. But the Greeks never fully exploited the western Mediterranean, and Alexander's conquests ranged eastward to the Indus Valley, well beyond the Mediterranean world. As for the Romans, they ruled Britain and northern Gaul and for long periods held salients north of the Alps and Danube and east of the Rhine; by no definition can these be called Mediterranean. Contrariwise, a climatic definition seems too narrow, as the true Mediterranean zone is limited to the sea and the lower elevations and leaves in doubt whether areas like western Spain, the Alpine section, Yugoslavia, and the eastern half of the North African coastline belong to it. But the "zone of the olive tree" is certainly the crucial center of the region, and none of it should be arbitrarily excluded.

A more useful definition would be a partly physiographic compromise that takes the cultural and climatic factors into account. For our purposes, then, the Mediterranean region is the Mediterranean Sea with the contiguous lands taken as compact geographical units. The most notable boundaries, therefore, will be the Alps in the north, the Sahara in the south, the Atlantic on the west, and the Arabian and Syrian deserts on the east. This includes parts of three continents and an area stretching 2,800 miles (4,500 km) from west to east and 1,100 miles (1,800 km) from north to south.

The shapes of the Mediterranean lands are complicated and disparate. Their predominant characteristic is an intimate interplay with the sea, a littoral emphasis that is more marine than continental.

Iberia (Spain and Portugal) is the largest of three great peninsulas that extend southward from Europe into Mediterranean climes. Its shape is compact and squarish, with a wedge extending eastward between the sea and the Pyrenees. Offshore are the Balearic Islands, known in antiquity for their cave dwellers and pirates.

Across the Pyrenees is Provence, the Roman Mediterranean province of France (southern Gaul or Gallia Narbonensis), with the rugged Cévennes (Cebenna) Mountains and the Rhône Valley. This has been, historically, an area distinct from the rest of France.

The boot-shaped peninsula of Italy, stretching southeastward for 651 miles (1,050 km), forms the centerpiece of the Mediterranean and, with the triangular island of Sicily, is its major divider. Corsica and Sardinia stand on a north-south line out in the western basin.

The third major peninsula, the Balkan, begins in the north with the ancient lands of Dalmatia and Illyria, extends south through Macedonia and Thrace, and then meets the Aegean Sea in the amazing complex of slender micropeninsulas and hundreds of islands that constitute Greece and the Hellenic Archipelago. This terminates in the line of islands, Crete, Karpathos, and Rhodes, that defines the boundary between the Aegean and the rest of the Mediterranean proper.

Next is the massive, irregular rectangle of the westward-pushing peninsula of Asia Minor or Anatolia (Turkey), with the Black Sea to the north; its surrounding coastlands serve as another adjunct Mediterranean province. At the base of Anatolia, the Mediterranean coastline takes a sharp southward turn, with the important island of Cyprus serving as a turning post. Here is the Levant, a complex province both culturally and physiographically, with a series of ranges and trenches roughly parallel to the coast. There follows the desert triangle of Sinai, its shortest side facing the Mediterranean, which the ancients regarded as the last part of Asia.

Egypt is a province apart, unlike any other. Only Lower Egypt, the delta, is truly Mediterranean, but a historical treatment of the subject can scarcely exclude the narrow valley of Upper Egypt as far as the First Cataract, since Egypt was a single cultural and political unit throughout Greco-Roman times.

West of Egypt, the Libyan Desert stretches 1,200 miles (1,900 km) to the Gulf of Gabès. In this vast province, only the immediate coastal stretch is Mediterranean, with the exception of the fortunate islandlike highland of Cyrenaica and the area around Tripoli, where a range of heights induces a bit more rain.

The western part of North Africa's landmass is a true Mediterranean province. In ancient times, it comprised Africa proper, Numidia, and Mauretania (modern Tunisia, northern Algeria, and Morocco). This rugged landmass, leaving the Atlas Mountains, pushes as far north as Sparta's latitude, and is more or less even with the southern Turkish coast.

These, then, are the major Mediterranean lands. In this study, they shall be the central concern, even if one consideration or another may take us briefly beyond them.

Geology

PLATE TECTONICS. Plate tectonics, as explained below, is the theory that the larger features of the earth's surface, such as continents, mountain ranges, and ocean beds, are the result of interaction between huge, slowly moving segments of the earth's crust. In the late Paleozoic era, perhaps 250 million years ago, all the continents of the earth had their margins joined together. Ancestral Africa was fitted snugly along its northwest continental shelf to the east coast of North America. Europe, from Spain to Norway, also abutted North America from Newfoundland to Greenland. But between Eurasia's southern rim and Africa, of which Arabia was then also a part, yawned the wide gulf of the Tethys Ocean, a tropical sea that has been called the ancestral Mediterranean. Geologists appropriately named this oceanic stretch after a daughter of Ouranos and Gaia (Heaven and Earth) in Greek mythology. She married her brother Okeanos (Ocean), it was said, and had more than 3,000 children, including the Rivers and the Oceanids.

The continental plates were almost never entirely above sea level. Shallow and even relatively deep seas often intruded across the continental surfaces. In these, the sedimentary rocks, particularly the limestone that bulks so large in Mediterranean geology, were deposited, and this deposition continued and accelerated in the next period, the Mesozoic.

The Mesozoic era, often called the Age of Reptiles, began about 230 million years ago and is divided into three periods: the Triassic, Jurassic (beginning about 195 million years ago), and the Cretaceous (from 135 to 65 million years ago). During the early Jurassic, North America began to separate from Africa along a line that has become the Mid-Atlantic Ridge. At first Europe remained attached to North America, but these continents also began separating in the Jurassic. Relative to Eurasia, Africa revolved in a counterclockwise direction, gradually narrowing the Tethys Ocean, and moved to the east. But the eventual collision of Africa with Eurasia was not a simple process. A series of smaller plates split off from northern Africa and southern Eurasia and interacted with the two huge continental masses and with each other. Because of Europe's westward motion relative to Africa, these smaller plates also revolved in a generally counterclockwise direction. The Iberian Peninsula rotated away from western France, opening the Bay of Biscay and eventually pushing up the Pyrenees. Morocco and "Oran" (northern Algeria) may have slid to the east, beginning the process of raising the Atlas Mountains. At the same time, Corsica, Sardinia, and the Balearics nestled against the southern European coast, and "Apulia" (Italy and the Dinaric Alps) stretched near North Africa. Also part of Africa, on the south side of Tethys, were Turkey, part of the Balkans, Iran, and Arabia. By the end of the Mesozoic, the Tethys Ocean had narrowed considerably, and many of the smaller plates had migrated westward.

The Cenozoic era, the Age of Mammals, began about 65 million years ago. It is divided into the Tertiary period and the Quaternary period, the latter including the Pleistocene, or Ice Age, beginning about two million years ago, and Recent, beginning about 11,000 years ago. During the early Tertiary, Apulia revolved about 68 degrees counterclockwise, pushing the Carnics into Europe and beginning the uplift of the Alps. Sardinia and Corsica swung out to near their present positions, performing with the Balearics a graceful counterclockwise dance, following Apulia. Africa began to split from Arabia along the Great Rift, forming the Red Sea and the sunken valley of the Jordan, and Arabia moved northeastward, colliding with Eurasia and closing the Tethys Sea. Three remnants of Tethys survived: the Caspian, the Black Sea, and the Mediterranean. Pushed in front of Arabia, Iran sutured itself to Eurasia, closing off the Caspian basin, and being crushed into the folds of the Zagros Mountains. Turkey moved to the west, isolating the Black Sea basin. Ahead of Turkey, the Rhodope Plate squeezed between Apulia and Moesia, forming the roughly parallel ridges and valleys of the Hellenic peninsula and islands.

At some point in the late Tertiary, these junctures cut off the Mediterranean both in the east and the west. The sea became a lake and began to evaporate. At this time, the level of fresh or brackish water in the Black and Caspian seas was higher, the two were interconnected, and arms of this less saline sea extended into the Aegean and northward across the Balkans. But the inflow from this body of water into the southern and western Mediterranean was not enough to replace the volume lost by evaporation. The Mediterranean gradually disappeared. In its place were thick salt deposits and a few salt lakes. Islands like Cyprus became mountain ranges towering as much as 16,000 feet (5,000 m) above the "dead seas" that remained. Rivers excavated canyons thousands of feet below what is today the surface of the sea. That of the Nile resembled the Grand Canyon in topography, but was even larger.

The salt beds in the Mediterranean depths are too thick to be the result of only one desiccation; water must have entered the basin several times during this period and dried up subsequently. Geologists differ as to whether the source of these incursions was the marine Atlantic or the brackish Black-Caspian Sea.

It is not known how long this condition lasted, but it was certainly longer than a million years, and possibly as much as seven million. Then five or six million years ago, still in the late Tertiary, the Straits of Gibraltar opened, letting in the waters of the Atlantic in a waterfall a thousand times as great as Niagara, but there were as yet no human beings to see it. In a few centuries, the Mediterranean filled, and the world ocean lost enough volume in the process to be lowered 30 feet (10 m). The Nile became an estuary as far upstream as Aswan. The Mediterranean and the outer ocean achieved equilibrium, but not stasis. For a time, the evaporation from the surface of the Mediterranean required a constant inflow from the Atlantic, and the level of the inner sea remained slightly lower than that of the Atlantic. During the ice ages, however, evaporation rates lowered and rainfall and river flow increased. The Mediterranean had a net outflow during the colder times, and as discussed below, its circulation was then quite different from what now exists. A warming trend established something like present conditions around 9000 B.C., and the inexorable pushing of the great continental plates had squeezed the peninsulas and islands into their familiar shapes. These tectonic stresses have not stopped, as the continuing volcanism and earthquakes of the region attest.

A visitor ten million years hence would find the map of the Mediterranean deformed and almost unrecognizable, with the straits perhaps closed again. The patterns of land and sea are like the patterns of clouds, constantly flowing, separating and colliding, over the aeons.

VOLCANOES. Volcanoes, vents where the heated magma of the earth's mantle finds its way to the surface and builds up mountains, are often associated with areas where the continental and oceanic plates separate and collide. This is to be expected, because these are the places where the crust is particularly thin, broken, or under strain. The Mediterranean, which is a complicated region of interacting plates, has many volcanoes, some of which are noted for their frequent activity.

Etna, on Sicily, is the highest volcano in the Mediterranean basin. Its eruptions have been frequent and varied, sending viscous lava flows down its side as far as the sea. There have been explosive events, and cracks and fumaroles have opened in its sides. During intervals between eruptions, gas and dust emerge from its summit, and a pool of lava is often visible. Etna was the goal of many mountain-climbing expeditions in ancient times, including that of the emperor Hadrian, who camped overnight on the summit so that he could view the sunrise from there. Etna has always presented a danger to those who live nearby, although volcanic material may, over a period of time, help to build up fertile soil.

North of Sicily are the Lipari (Aeolian) Islands, a volcanic group. One of them, Vulcano, was named after the Roman fire god Vulcan, and gave its name in turn to this kind of mountain. Vulcano has usually erupted by the violent ejection of solid, very viscous, hot fragments of new lava, rather than continuous lava flows. Farther north in the same group, Stromboli (Strongyle) is the classic example of a volcano in almost constant eruption. Sailors could see afar its glow on the cloud that streamed forth from its crater, where, as Homer said, "thereby not even winged things may pass" (*Odyssey* 12. 62–63).

On the coastal plain of Campania, Italy, rises the most famous volcano of all, Vesuvius. Although it is a fraction of Etna's size, having an elevation of 4,203 feet (1,277 m) as compared with 10,902 feet (3,340 m), it has been even more destructive. In A.D. 79 it exploded in a violent outrush of huge volumes of ash and pieces of stone. Pliny the Younger, who witnessed the event, called the aerial bombs *lapilli,* and this paroxysmal type of eruption has since been named "Plinian" in his honor. Several towns, including Pompeii, were crushed and buried under a thick layer of fallen ash, while nearby Herculaneum was overwhelmed by a pyroclastic (ejected from the volcano) flow of ignimbrite, until recently misinterpreted by archaeologists as a flow of mud. During the explosion, the crater collapsed, leaving a part of the old crater wall that is now called Monte Somma.

There is much evidence of volcanic activity, present and past, all around the Bay of Naples (Gulf of Cumae). The "Phlegraean Fields" behind Pozzuoli (Puteoli), with their volcanic phenomena, provide an example of this, and ancient tradition connects this whole area with the activities of the infernal gods. There are old volcanoes and other plutonic remnants in the rest of Italy, Sicily, Sardinia, and the Balearics, the east coast of Spain, western North Africa, and the Cévennes.

Several of the Aegean islands, such as Melos and Lemnos, are volcanoes or have volcanic components. The most important of these is Thira (Thera), sometimes called Santorini, where the most powerful Plinian explosion known in the history of the Mediterranean occurred during the Minoan Bronze Age. There was a large conical island that completely blew its top, creating a deep crater that was filled by the sea, leaving parts of the crater wall as a circular ring of islands. The explosion, greater than that which destroyed Krakatoa in 1883, must have sent tremendous quantities of tephra into the atmosphere. Marine core samples show that this material settled in the Aegean in an easterly direction from Thira, and archaeological evidence indicates that a relatively light ashfall occurred in eastern Crete. The theory that the eruption of Thira led to the downfall of Minoan civilization has met with popular acceptance, but a tree ring date of 1626 B.C., very likely connected with the Thira event, would present insuperable chronological problems and would indicate that the Minoans recovered from a disaster that struck them at the height of their cultural ascendancy. In addition to the areas already mentioned, there is evidence of volcanic activity in Anatolia, the Caucasus, and the Levant during various periods from the Tertiary to the present.

ROCKS: ORIGINS AND CHARACTERISTICS. The rocks themselves are the tangible record of the process of formation described above. Each of the stages in the movement and interaction of the continental and microcontinental plates can be traced in the very complicated structure of the rocks in the Mediterranean region.

The oldest exposed rocks are segments of the underlying continental blocks that have persisted since the Precambrian era, on the order of a billion years ago or more. These are the crystalline rocks, like granite, formed from molten material intruded at great depths, and they tend to form plateaus where they have not been lifted into more rugged peaks. They can be seen readily in the central and eastern Iberian peninsula, the Massif Central of France, Corsica, Sardinia, Elba (Aethalia or Ilva), Tuscany (Etruria), the Rhodope Mountains, Lydia, and the area around Mount Sinai. Since they have often been subjected to tectonic pressure and to heat, many of these ancient granites have been metamorphosed into gneisses. Much of this stress took place during an earlier period of mountain folding during the Paleozoic era, between 400 and 250 million years ago, when an antecedent of the Alps, called the Hercynian fold belt, was thrust up across the northern and western margins. Signs of the Paleozoic shifts can be seen in sedimentary rocks, volcanic lavas, and beds of coal that derive from buried forests.

Limestone is the most characteristic and widespread rock of the Mediterranean. It is calcium carbonate precipitated from seawater, usually in the form of sea creatures of various sizes, from the microscopic to quite large, and often mixed with varying amounts of sand and mud. In the limestone column drums of the temple of Zeus at Olympia, one can easily see thousands of these shells, concreted together. Much of this limestone was formed during the invasion of the Tethys Ocean during the Mesozoic, and in enormously thick beds. There is a limestone series in the Dinaric Alps in which a total thickness of 23 feet (7 m) can be traced. Associated with the limestones are massive salt deposits from isolated portions of the Tethys that evaporated, as much as 4,900 feet (1,500 m) thick in Greece, for example. Also, red beds formed from sand grains colored by hematite pigment, an iron compound. These represent desert or semiarid conditions when the surface was above sea level. Still more coal seams demonstrate that lush tropical forests flourished in more humid conditions.

Ophiolites, a much-deformed series of rocks, give fascinating evidence of the mechanics of continental drift, and their nature was recognized only recently by geologists. Rich in minerals like serpentinite, spilite, and chert, these are the remnants of the spreading centers, or upwelling cracks and ridges, that appear in the the seafloors when continental plates split apart, and indeed provide the impetus to move the plates. The best known of these today is the Mid-Atlantic Ridge. Since the Mediterranean contains so many small plates, it also exhibits the crushed and inactive evidence of former undersea ridges that have been pushed up by collisions onto continental crust in, for example, the Olympus (Troodos) of Cyprus, Caria in Turkey, Othrys and Vourinos ([Buroinos] southwest of Neapolis) in Greece, and parts of the northern Apennines. These contain the metamorphosed material of sea-bottom sediments, pillow lavas, intrusive dikes, and the mantle of the earth's crust.

Limestone formation continued, and indeed continues, in the Cenozoic era (the latest of the four great eras into which geological time is divided), along with the deposition of such other sediments as shale, sandstone, and conglomerate. Much of this material has been washed down from the land, as in the fan-shaped underwater extension of the Nile Delta (until the construction of the Aswan High Dam). Sedimentary rocks, subjected to pressure and temperature metamorphosis, generally become harder and denser. Shale, for example, becomes slate, and limestone becomes marble. The Mediterranean has many fine marbles of varying colors, patterns, and crystal size. Among the famed ancient quarries were Carrara (Apuania) in Italy, the Aegean island of Paros, and Mount Pentelikon above Athens.

MINERALIZATION. The most valuable metallic ores are associated in the Mediterranean basin with the outcroppings of the older crystalline rocks; generally such materials were brought up from below in the magma. Sometimes they occur in intrusive dikes among the sedimentary layers, or as the result of deposition. The earliest metal to be exploited systematically was gold; it is easily worked and has always been prized for its ornamental beauty. In a few locations it was mined directly from the rock, but most ancient gold mines were placers; that is, gold dust and nuggets were washed from alluvial material, usually in streambeds. The placers did not always last long, and there were "gold rushes" in ancient times. For example, many Roman miners flocked to Ivrea (Eporedia) in the foothills of the Pennine Alps for a few years around 150 B.C. until the gold ran out. There was gold in Spanish Cantabria, in the Pyrenees, the Cévennes, the Styrian Alps, and the Rhodopes. Mount Pangaeus in Thrace was a famous source of placer gold for the Phoenicians, the Greeks, and, from the time of King Philip, the

Macedonians. The Greeks found gold near the Dardanelles (Hellespont) and on the island of Siphnos. The placers of electrum, a gold-silver alloy, in the Pactolus River of Lydia in western Asia Minor encouraged the first coinage in the Mediterranean and enriched King Croesus. In Colchis on the east coast of the Black Sea, it was said, the woolly skins of sheep were used to collect placer gold, giving rise to the myth of the Golden Fleece. There was still gold there in Strabo's time. Egypt had plentiful supplies of gold in the eastern desert, but almost no silver, so that the usual values of the precious metals were reversed there in the days of the pharaohs.

Silver was obtained from the Sierra Morena and the Pyrenees in Spain, the Cévennes, Sardinia, near Sybaris in southern Italy, Illyria, and Cappadocia. The Greeks were the first to coin silver, and the prosperity of Athens, its coins stamped with owls, depended in large measure on the supply of silver from the rich mines at Laurium. The Macedonian foothills were dotted with silver mines.

Lead was widely used in the construction of buildings and aqueducts as a binder, sealer, and waterproofing material, and was also used to make utensils and vessels. It was often found in association with silver; indeed, most silver ores contain more lead than silver. The first metal to be used widely for tools and weapons was copper, and it continued as an essential ingredient in the alloys bronze and brass. It was fairly common in easily worked ores. Among the largest potential sources were southern Spain, the Etruscan area of Italy, Sardinia, Illyria, the Greek island of Euboea, and the copper-rich island of Cyprus, which may have derived its name from the metal. There were spotty deposits in Syria and Lebanon, but very productive mines in the Sinai and elsewhere in the deserts east of the Nile that were worked by the Egyptians. Tin, the other constituent of bronze, was relatively rare in the early centers of metalworking, so a trade developed to bring it from more distant sources. There was a good supply in northwestern Spain and even farther northward, outside the Mediterranean in Brittany and Cornwall. The Etruscans were lucky to find some not too far from the copper ores in their homeland. Zinc, which with copper is used to make brass, was smelted by the Romans from plentiful ores along the Rhine.

The metal that gave the Iron Age its name is fortunately among the most common of the earth's elements, but separating it from its ores was fairly difficult for the ancients, so they sought out the richest and most easily worked examples. The ore called hematite is one of these. Usable iron ore was known in central and northern Spain, the Massif Central and Jura Mountains in France, and the Alps, where it served pre-Roman cultures, Tuscany (Etruria), Elba (Aethalia or Ilva), Sardinia, Dalmatia and the Balkan hinterland, Greece, Pontus, Syria, the mountainous Red Sea coastlands, and parts of the Atlas ranges. Cinnabar, a compound of mercury and sulfur, was valued as a vermilion pigment, and mined in Spain, Tuscany, and Cappadocia. Liquid mercury is easily sweated from this ore and was used in goldsmithing. The fossil fuels were known to the ancients but almost never used. The people of Elis burned lignite coal, which was a remarkable curiosity to others (Theophrastus, *De Lapidibus* 16). The greater deposits of coal in Spain, Asia Minor, and North Africa go almost unmentioned. Asphalt was sometimes used for waterproofing and was known from the Dead Sea; a well of tar on Zante (Zacynthus) is marveled at by Herodotus (4. 195). Seeps of petroleum and natural gas in the Near East burned for years, as the Greeks learned. Alexander the Great watched an experiment with petroleum in which a young man was set on fire with unfortunate results. A good supply of natron was available from the evaporites (sediments deposited when the waters evaporated) in the Egyptian Sahara, and was used to produce dehydration in the process of mummification. Soda, used in the manufacture of glass from silica sand, was also found there.

SOILS. Soil types are the result of several factors: the parent material, that is, the type of weathered rock from which the soil develops; the climate, including temperature and rainfall; the vegetative cover; the topography; and the length of time over which the soil has been developing.

The parent material varies in the Mediterranean basin, following the types of rocks discussed above. Owing to the predominance of limestone, calcareous soils are widespread. The Mediterranean climate is, relatively speaking, a dry one, so the xeromorphic soils (those formed under generally dry conditions) are prevalent. In temperature, the climate is midway between the temperate and tropical zones, so that the soils share some of the characteristics of each. The natural vegetative cover is forest through most of the basin, but deforestation and degraded vegetative cover have been factors since before the rise of Greek civilization, and have critically affected soil formation and erosion. Mediterranean topography is generally mountainous, so that "mountain soils," which tend to be more subject to erosion, thinner, and younger, are important in almost every province. Soil scientists classify the Alps as having "cold mountainous soils," the Pyrenees as possessing "moist mountainous soils," and the other Mediterranean ranges as typically "dry mountainous soils." As a younger region of the earth's topography, the Mediterranean has older soils only in certain relict areas, and even there the impact of human activity has disrupted the soil's structure. In general, Mediterranean soils are rich and well suited to agriculture except in the steeper mountainous zones and in the aridic desert areas.

Two notably typical Mediterranean soils located on limestone rocks are traditionally called *terra fusca* and *terra rossa* (black earth and red earth). *Terra fusca* consists of darker soils, which are usually brown in color. They tend to develop under forest cover on limestone that has a component of siliceous sand. They are not acidic, but vary from neutral to alkaline, since the calcium carbonate that is the major constituent of limestone acts as a buffer against acidity. *Terra rossa* gains its reddish color from iron oxides that are present as impurities in the limestone, and concentrate as the carbonates are leached away during the wet season. During the dry season, the ferric compounds precipitate as minerals like turgite, goethite, and hematite. These soils are heavy with clay, and tend sometimes to be clay-silty, rarely sandy. They are of variable depth and often full of rock debris. The vegetative cover of *terra rossa* is usually garigue or maquis. When *terra fusca* is subjected to deforestation, it tends to leach out to *terra rossa,* but reforestation will often restore it. Another result of deforestation, with evaporation of soil water, is the formation of crusts.

In general, the moister soils of the north are darker in color. In central Yugoslavia and across the northern shores of the Black Sea, there are black soils called chernozems, rich in organic matter, that have developed under the cool grasslands. Southern France has generally well-watered soils of ochroid coloration. In much of Spain, where the rocks are siliceous and crystalline, the soils tend to have a fine sandy consistency. Central Turkey has grassland soil of a dryer type than that of the Ukraine.

Along the desert margins of the south, one finds aridic soils, lighter in color. Here also, due to the prevalent evaporation rates, slaty and crusted soils form. The winds, in the absence of vegetative cover, form dunes. The infrequent rains, with transport of finer material away from some areas by winds, form pavements of pebbles and small rocks over softer materials. The opposite situation, namely saturation with water, occurs mostly in the deltas of the larger river systems, notably the Nile, Po (Eridanus or Padus), Rhône (Rhodanus), and Guadalquivir (Baetis) in southern Spain. Here drainage may be necessary to practice agriculture at all, and a heavily silty soil is discovered.

MOUNTAINS. The voyager around most of its shores will gain the impression of the Mediterranean as a sea backed by mountains. In many places, as at the base of the Maritime Alps, the mountains fall directly into the sea. The barrier character of the land no doubt encouraged some of the Mediterranean peoples, such as the Phoenicians and Greeks, to turn to the sea as an avenue of trade, communication, and colonization.

In the western basin, Spain presents a face of mountainous complexity. The Sierra Nevada rises above the Andalusian coast to an elevation of 11,408 feet (3,478 m), and northward there is a succession of highlands broken only by the valley of the Ebro (Iberus). Next come the Pyrenees, separating Spain and France, whose eastern foothills front the sea. These are more massive than the other Spanish mountains, although the highest point, Pico de Aneto, is slightly lower than that of the Sierra Nevada. Central Provence is a marshy lowland subject to floods, but to the north there are the Cévennes, whose relatively low elevations do not rise above 5,755 feet (1,755 m). But beyond the Rhône are the Maritime and Cottian Alps, rising to 12,602 feet (3,842 m) at Monte Viso. Near Genoa (Genua) the Apennines begin, at first standing with their feet in the gulf but then sweeping across the Italian peninsula to the eastern side, where they present an impressive front to the Adriatic south of the wide Po alluvium, and leave room on the west for the happy hills of Tuscany, Latium, and Campania. "Father Apennine," as Roman poets named this range, reaches his full height in Monte Corno, at 9,558 feet (2,914 m) almost equal to Olympus. Then the mountainous spine of Italy gradually moves back across to the toe of the boot; the heel is relatively flat. The same folded mountains continue in Sicily, overshadowed by the mighty volcanic cone of Etna, rising to 10,902 feet (3,340 m) directly from the sea. The other major western islands are steep, too, Sardinia less so than Corsica. Across North Africa march the roughly parallel ranges of the Atlas Mountains, increasing in height toward the west, where Toubkal (highest peak in the Atlas Mountains) itself rises 13,671 feet (4,168 m) above sea level, but is far inland and cannot be seen from the Mediterranean.

For the eastern basin one can well begin with the Dinarics, which bracket the Adriatic Sea on the east as the Apennines do on the west. They are lower than the Italian range, but more extensive and complicated. Their coastline is a maze of fjords and islands, unlike the relatively smooth coast opposite. The same ranges continue southward to become the Pindus, the backbone of Greece, impressive enough even if its highest peak is only 8,136 feet (2,480 m). Olympus, on a parallel range that almost seals off Thessaly from the sea, rises to 9,568 feet (2,917 m), and its setting above the Gulf of Salonika (Thermaic Gulf) makes it an unforgettable sight. The mountains of Greece finger out into peninsulas and continue as the islands of the Aegean, whose alignment suggests the truth: they are the peaks of drowned mountain ranges. North in Thrace the granitic Rhodope rises to respectable heights to complete the European segment of the tricontinental eastern basin. Turkey has a high central plateau flanked on the south by the

Taurus (Toros) Mountains, a forested range that reaches 12,251 feet (3,735 m) in height above the Cilician coastal plain. Here the coastline turns sharply southward, backed by a series of shorter but important ranges: Nur (Amanus) in Syria, Lebanon of the famous cedars with its summit at 10,129 feet (3,088 m) and Anti-Lebanon as its parallel range inland. The major geological feature south of Lebanon is the rift valley of the Jordan, the Dead Sea, the Wadi el Araba, and the Gulf of ʿAqaba (Elath), which is a northward extension of the Red Sea depression. At 1,292 feet (394 m) below sea level, the Dead Sea is the lowest place on the earth's surface. Mount Sinai, 8,649 feet (2,637 m), rises to the west, and across the Gulf of Suez, there are mountains in Egypt's eastern desert. But the Mediterranean coast from the Sinai westward is devoid of relief all the way to southern Tunisia with two exceptions: the highland of Cyrenaica, 2,880 feet (878 m) above the sea, and another plateau behind Tripoli that rises to 3,175 feet (968 m), but farther inland.

The mountains of the Black Sea area are confined to the south and east coasts. The Pontic ranges stand close above the southern shore and help to enhance the Mediterranean character that the other Black Sea borderlands do not share, with the possible exception of the southeastern Crimea. The eastern end of the Black Sea lies in Georgia, ancient Colchis, which is backed by the great Caucasus Mountains. Here Mount Elburz rises to a spectacular 18,481 feet (5,633 m), higher than any peak in Europe or North Africa, and sets the extreme eastern limit to the Mediterranean world.

Not so much Mediterranean mountains as a physical and climatic barrier that helps to define the Mediterranean world by separating it from northern and central Europe, the Alps deserve discrete description. From their front in the Maritimes, the Alps march northward to their highest point, Mont Blanc between France and Italy, 15,771 feet (4,807 m) above sea level, where the range swings east through Switzerland and Austria, walling Italy from Germany. Some of the High Alps are outcroppings of the old crystalline rocks such as granites, gneisses, and schists (the latter two are much-altered metamorphic rocks); while others are mainly calcareous limestones, dolomites, and marbles. A parallel range to the northwest, the Jura, consists of folded sedimentary rocks prominently including limestone. Toward the east, after sending the lower Dinaric branch southward, the Alps end rather abruptly at the western edge of the Hungarian plain near the Danube. Mountains have marked effects on climate and vegetation, creating distinct regions. This is especially true of the Alps, the largest and highest mountain assemblage in Europe, some 465 miles long and at least 100 miles broad (750 × 160 km). Here is an Alpine world of its own, Mediterranean only in its southern reaches, whose people developed a special character, hardy and defiant, in their isolated valleys.

PLATEAUS, PLAINS, AND LOWLANDS. Scattered among the mountains of the Mediterranean basin are a series of relatively flat areas. These plains and plateaus are not large, but they are quite important as centers of agriculture and cattle breeding. This is the characteristic pattern, at least, in the central Mediterranean, leaving out of consideration for the time being the eastern reaches of the European plain north of the Black Sea, and the stretches of the Sahara Desert, two areas that are atypical of the region as a whole. The Iberian Peninsula has as its central element the Meseta, or Spanish plateau, with an average elevation above 2,500 feet (750 m). This is a dry, rolling plain surrounded and to some extent divided by mountains. The valley of the Ebro to the northeast is a lower plateau screened from the sea by a mountain range. In

France, the valley of the Rhône is open to the south, and served in antiquity as both good farmland and an important avenue of communication. Among Italy's plains, the alluvial Po valley is the largest. This well-watered and even marshy lowland stretches from the terrace of the western Piedmont along the front of the Alps to the head of the Adriatic Sea, where the river continues to extend it by deposition, isolating some of the older ports. Southward, the Arno has a nearly level floodplain in Etruria, and there are important hilly plains on the west side of the Apennines in Latium and Campania. The "heel" of Italy is a rolling lowland, and there are more limited areas of plains in Sicily and Sardinia. The Balkan Peninsula, including Greece, is extremely mountainous, and the "plains" are vest-pocket areas amid the mountains. Macedonia has the largest, but it was restricted in antiquity by an arm of the Thermaic Gulf. Thessaly is an alluvial plain cut off from the Aegean by Olympus, Ossa, and Pelion. Most of the other plains in Greece are limited alluvial valleys like those in Attica, Argos, Laconia, and Elis.

On the other side of the Aegean, Asia Minor has several strips of good alluvial soil extending up the valleys of rivers like the Bakır (Caicus), Gediz (Hermus), Küçükmenderes (Cayster), and Büyükmenderes (Maeander). To detour for a moment into the Black Sea, its northern shore fronts a seemingly endless grassy plain, the ancient land of the Scythians. The other Black Sea coasts are very mountainous, but Colchis has an alluvial plain. On the southern flank of Asia Minor, Cilicia forms a wide coastal plain. The Levant is defined by mountains, but there is a narrower coastal plain in the southern section.

The Nile Delta is a large and important alluvial plain in its own right, the northern extension of the river-valley alluvium that fills the narrow canyon of Upper Egypt. Westward, the first half of the Libyan Desert is low-lying but not without rocky escarpments and other relief. The Qattara Depression and a number of the oases are below sea level. The more easterly parts of the Libyan Desert rise inland into plateaus before there is another gradual sinking below sea level on the central part of the modern border between Tunisia and Algeria. The rest of North Africa, the Maghreb, is predominantly mountainous, but between the ranges it has high plateaus that are long and relatively narrow.

THE SEA: "THE ELEMENT OF WATER"

The sea is the great geographical fact that unites the Mediterranean lands and gives them their common character. From ancient times it has been the highway of trade and warfare. Its presence determines the climate of the region and is the influence that makes the Mediterranean zone extend so far into the three adjoining continents, while everywhere else in the world where that climatic zone occurs it is of quite limited extent. In order to understand the civilization and history of the entire area, it is necessary to understand the sea.

Geographical Survey of the Mediterranean Sea

The Mediterranean has an area of 970,000 square miles (2,500,000 km^2), and the Black Sea an additional 173,000 square miles (448,000 km^2). It stretches 2,232 miles (3,600 km) from the Straits of Gibraltar to the Levantine coast, and 680 miles (1,100 km) from the northern end of the Adriatic to the Gulf of Sidra (Syrtis Major), although its width measured across open water is never more than about 500 miles (800 km). Its mean depth is about 4,920 feet (1,500 m), compared with an average depth of 12,500 feet (3,800 m) for the world ocean, but it cannot be considered a shallow sea, since the areas occupied within it by the continental shelves are relatively small. Its surface hides from view a varied arrangement of trenches, ridges, and deep basins.

SUBDIVISIONS OF THE MEDITERRANEAN. The Mediterranean Sea is divided into two great basins, western and eastern, by the relatively shallow Strait of Sicily, only about 100 miles (160 km) wide, which lies between that island and Tunisia. The western basin comprises three major subdivisions: the Alborán, Balearic, and Tyrrhenian basins, whereas the eastern basin, not so neatly divisible, is dominated by the Mediterranean Ridge, an east-west chain of mountains culminating in the island of Cyprus. A major feature of the southern reaches of this basin is the Nile Fan, a gigantic alluvial deposit extending outward from the delta.

The Adriatic and Aegean seas are also divisions of the eastern basin. The Adriatic is very shallow, much of it less than 328 feet (100 m) deep. The Aegean is relatively shallow but very uneven, filled as it is with islands and underwater ridges and trenches.

The Dardanelles (Hellespont), Sea of Marmara (Propontis), and Bosporus are the relatively shallow access to the Black Sea "annex." The Black Sea has a wide continental shelf in the north and almost none in the south. Its greatest depth, slightly over 7,400 feet (2,200 m), has been found in the approximate center.

The entire Mediterranean is dotted unevenly by hundreds of islands, most mountainous and some volcanic. The largest, Sicily, triangular in shape, is the centerpiece of the Mediterranean. The western basin, generally speaking, has fewer islands, but three are among the largest: Sardinia, Corsica, and Mallorce, or Majorca, of the Balearics. Other important islands of the western basin are Elba, between Corsica and the Italian mainland, Capri, and the volcanic Lipari Islands north of Sicily.

Islands are numerous in the eastern basin. The largest are Cyprus and Crete. To the west, Malta and other islands rise from the shelf east of the Strait of Sicily. But the Aegean Sea is the true home of islands. Scores of them, from wide Lesbos, Rhodes, Chios, and Samos down to mere uninhabited specks, crowd the sea and assure that the sailor is seldom out of sight of land.

Dynamics of the Sea

AN INLAND SEA. The most striking characteristic of the Mediterranean Sea is that, with the single exception of the opening at Gibraltar, it is surrounded by land. But not just surrounded; it invades and interpenetrates the land, separating it into islands and peninsulas. In the Mediterranean, land and sea are in intimate communion. There is no place in Greece more than 68 miles (110 km) from the sea, and Italy has a coastline 21,650 miles (6,660 km) long. Thus, the Mediterranean may truly be called an inland sea. Indeed, it is the largest such sea in the world. For these reasons, it was called by the Greeks *he eso* (or *entos*) *thalatta* (or *thalassa*), and by the Romans *Mare Internum* (or *Intestinum*), all of which mean "the Inner Sea." They also called it "Our Sea" (*he hemetera thalatta* or *Mare Nostrum*). The term *Mare Mediterraneum* was first applied by Gaius Julius Solinus in his *Collectanea Rerum Memorabilium*, as late as the second half of the third century A.D. This now-accepted name literally means "the Mid-Earth Sea." An important result of the landlocked situation of the Mediterranean is the comparative absence of tides, since the gravitational pull of the moon is felt only by the sea itself, without the added pressure of the world ocean. Tides along most Mediterranean shores are less than a meter between high and low. Only in estuaries of special configuration, as in Venice at the head of the Adriatic, are tides occasionally high enough to be troublesome. When the Greeks first passed beyond the Straits of Gibraltar (Pillars of Hercules) to view the outer ocean, they were amazed by the tides, because in their homeland tides were virtually unnoticeable. There is not usually a heavy surf, although storms rapidly build up the waves, especially in winter, and tsunamis, or tidal waves, can be caused by earthquakes and volcanoes.

THE SOURCE OF THE MEDITERRANEAN WATERS. When the Mediterranean basin was opened to the west through the Straits of Gibraltar, water from the Atlantic entered and filled it. Atlantic waters continue to be the major source of the Mediterranean Sea, because there is a constant interchange through The Straits. The Straits of Gibraltar do constrict this interchange, since they are only 9 miles (14.5 km) wide and about 1,200 feet (366 m) deep. But through this aperture flow two currents, one of Atlantic water at the surface moving inward, and the other of Mediterranean water, which is heavier because it is more saline, moving outward in the depths. The exchange is large enough to provide for a complete renewal of the Mediterranean water in seventy-five years. The upper, Atlantic, flow is greater, because the Mediterranean loses a huge amount of water by evaporation, and its average sea level at The Straits is about 4 to 12 inches (10 to 30 cm) lower than that of the Atlantic.

The annual evaporation from the surface of the Mediterranean Sea is approximately 57 inches (145 cm), the equivalent of 150,020 cubic yards (115,400 m³) per second. Only about 27 percent of this is replaced by rainfall, and 6 percent by the inflow of rivers. Another 6 percent comes from the Black Sea through the Bosporus and Dardanelles, leaving the vast majority, 61 percent, of the Mediterranean's water budget to be made up by the Atlantic. Because of the height of the sill at Gibraltar, only the warmer waters near the surface of the Atlantic enter the Mediterranean. In a surface layer, which varies from 260 to 980 feet (80–300 m) thick, these waters are further warmed by the sun, and made more saline as evaporation occurs. Thus, the Mediterranean lacks the temperature gradient typical of other seas, and is the warmest large body of water at its latitude.

SALINITY. The high evaporation rate of the Mediterranean, combined with its enclosed situation, makes it more saline than the outer ocean. As water vapor goes into the atmosphere at the surface, it leaves the salts behind for the most part. However, because thermal currents carry salt out into the ocean, the Mediterranean remains in eustatic balance; that is, the salt being lost is approximately equal to the salt being concentrated in it. The Mediterranean is not becoming saltier. But it is salty enough to make the evaporative manufacture of salt from it easy and economical. The most common salts obtained by evaporation from seawater are chlorides and sulfates of sodium and magnesium. Also present in smaller quantities are bicarbonates, bromides, and salts of calcium, potassium, and strontium. There are also numerous trace elements.

CURRENTS. The only major surface current of the Mediterranean is one that sweeps inward from the Straits of Gibraltar, where it travels at 2 1/2 miles per hour (4 km/h). It slows, but continues along the south side of the western basin, through the Sicilian Strait, and eastward to the Levant. Along this course, increasing salinity causes water from the current to sink, so that it is exhausted in the eastern basin. Each of the smaller basins, the Balearic, Tyrrhenian, Ionian, Adriatic, and the Levantine basin around Cyprus, has a general but somewhat erratic counterclockwise revolution. In general the pattern of currents throughout the Mediterranean is highly localized and regarded by sailors as tricky.

THE BLACK SEA. On the map, the Black Sea looks like a miniature Mediterranean, connected to the larger inland sea by a narrow strait. At its most constricted point, the Bosporus is only 2,100 feet (640 m) wide and 120 to 408 feet (37 to 124 m) deep.

But although evaporation is considerable in the Black Sea, it is not as rapid per unit area as in the Mediterranean because the smaller sea is farther north and therefore receives less solar energy. The total volume of rainfall plus the runoff from the Danube, Dnieper (Borysthenes), Don (Tanaïs), and other rivers is greater than the evaporation, so that the excess surface waters pour outward into the Mediterranean. These waters are brackish rather than salty. In the depths, however, lies a stagnant, salty reservoir where fish life is impossible.

Water on the Land

RIVERS. The Mediterranean proper is not particularly rich in rivers, although from the Nile it receives the waters of earth's longest stream. A more typical Mediterranean river rises in the mountains that rim the basin, is relatively short, carries much less water in summer than in winter, and is navigable only in its lowest stretch near its mouth. In ancient times most rivers were considered to be fresh and potable, although Roman hydraulic engineers recorded variations in temperature, silt load, and taste, qualities that affected their acceptability as sources of drinking water. Rivers carry dissolved material, such as salts, into the sea, and are agents of erosion, transporting rocks, gravel, sand, silt, and organic matter from higher land to lowlands or the sea.

Of the five large rivers of Spain, only the largest, the Ebro (Iberus), flows into the Mediterranean. It drains about 32,800 square miles (85,500 km^2) of largely arid land. Its central basin is relatively level, but above Tortosa it forces its way through a gorge, which bars navigation, and then flows out into its large and fertile delta. South of the Ebro are smaller rivers, the Júcar (Sucro) and Segura (Tader). The Rhône (Rhodanus), which rises in the central Alps, is the only major river originating in non-Mediterranean Europe that flows directly into our sea. It has a large, constant flow, is subject to flood, and in ancient times was too swift for heavy navigation through most of its course. But its valley served as a highway for Greeks and Romans. The huge delta, the Camargue, is noted as one of the wildest areas in Europe, its salt marshes frequented by myriads of flamingos and other water birds, and roamed by herds of wild horses. Another river of Gaul, the Aude (Atax), was used by ancient traffic to reach the Garonne (Garumna) over a portage.

In Italy, there are only short, swift streams along the Tyrrhenian coast until one reaches the Arno, which drains a relatively small basin, is scarcely navigable, and is famous for its destructive floods. Next comes Father Tiber himself, Rome's river, 252 miles (405 km) long and from 6 1/2 to 20 feet (2 to 6 m) deep. It was an important artery for the transportation of grains, timber, and stone below and above Rome, whose port was located near its mouth at Ostia, where siltation was a constantly recurring problem. Draining much of the central Apennines and parts of Etruria and Latium, the Tiber is Italy's second largest river. Smaller streams, the Liri, Volturno, and Sele (Silarus) reach the coast to the south. Several parallel streams enter the Gulf of Taranto; among them the Crati (Crathis) was renowned for its soft water, suitable for washing and dyeing wool. Along the Adriatic coast are many small, short streams, until one reaches the Po (Padus, Eridanus), Italy's mightiest river, 404 miles (652 km) long. Its basin is 27,055 square miles (70,092 sq km), including the widest and most fertile plain in the Mediterranean. Although the Po can be navigated, it is difficult to do so because of the sandbanks. It debouches into the Adriatic through a very large delta with many mouths, which is constantly enlarging due to the heavy silt load of the river. Works to regulate its flow and claim the marshy plain for agriculture began in pre-Roman times and continued throughout antiquity.

The rivers of Greece are storied but not mighty. The landmasses are not large, and the porous limestone allows much of the drainage to seep underground. Worthy of mention, although not major arteries of navigability, are the Achelous in the west, the Alpheus and Eurotas in the Peloponnese, the Peneus, which drains the plain of Thessaly through the pleasant gorge of Tempe, and the Haliacmon (Vistritsa) of the Macedonian mountains. Reaching the northern Aegean from watersheds that lie beyond Greek-speaking lands are the Vardar (Axius), Struma, Nestos, and Évros (Maritsa; Hebrus). The Vardar has been progressively filling the head of the Thermaic Gulf. Pella, Macedonia's ancient capital, was once a port but is now far inland.

On the Asiatic side of the Aegean, valleys of moderate size are drained by the Bakır, Gediz, Küçükmenderes, and Büyükmenderes. The last-named stream has a very winding lower course that gave its name to the noun and verb "meander," and its sediments have isolated Miletus from the sea. On the south coast of Asia Minor, several rivers of no great size flow down the Taurus. Cilicia has at least three of these, including the Cydnus, where Alexander fell ill after bathing in its yellowish waters. The Mediterranean river of Syria is the Orontes, which drains a large part of the northern Levant, including part of the valley between the Lebanon and Anti-Lebanon ranges (Coele-Syria, or Bekaa Valley). Antioch stood on its banks, and Juvenal (3.63) made it a "tributary," cultural if not geographical, of the Tiber. Between the Orontes and Gaza, there are only small streams, many of which flow only in winter. Beyond Gaza, there is nothing until the Nile.

The Nile is in a category by itself. The world's longest river (4,132 mi./6,648 km), it drains an area of about 1.3 million square miles (3,349,000 km²) stretching southward to Kenya, Uganda, Zaire, Tanzania, Rwanda, and Burundi. Its farthest sources lie south of the equator. It has two major branches: the White Nile, the major East African branch; and the Blue Nile, which drains the Ethiopian plateau. There is another Ethiopian affluent, the Atbara, below the junction of the White and Blue Niles. The Nile's annual flood, which moistened Egypt's croplands and renewed its soil, was noted and measured by the ancients. Since the White Nile's flow is regulated by lakes and the great Sudd swamps of the Sudan, it remains relatively constant and free of silt. Thus, the Blue Nile was almost entirely responsible for the flood, whose waters derived from the torrential rains of the western Ethiopian mountains, where average annual precipitation reaches 98 inches (2,500 mm). The start of the flood reached the Sudan in May, Aswan in July, and the head of the delta in August. It took about two months for the flood to reach its maximum, and two more to recede. The black mud that it deposited on the fields was derived almost entirely from erosion in the highlands of Ethiopia. All of the arable soil of Egypt derived from the Nile, which in prehistoric times filled in an estuary of the Mediterranean and then built up the gigantic Nile Delta, after which all the deltas of the world have been called. Named by the Greeks for its triangular shape, like their letter "delta" when viewed, as it was by them, from the north, this vast flat area, twice the size of all the valley land in Upper Egypt, stretches about 100 miles (160 km) from north to south, and about 155 miles (250 km) from east to west. The number of branches and mouths of the Nile in the delta has varied greatly through the centuries. In modern times, the high dam at Aswan has ended both the flood and the deposition of new soil in the delta. The Nile was, and is, navigable to the First Cataract. Once that barrier was passed, in ancient times one could sail on upstream to the Second Cataract at the Sudan border, the Third Cataract in the Nubian Desert, and the Fourth Cataract above Meroë.

From the Nile to Tunis (Carthage), there are no rivers unless a rare and catastrophic rainfall occurs. That it was otherwise in ancient times is shown by the numerous Roman dams and canals whose ruins now mark dry wadis. The Medjerda River (Bagradas) reaches the Mediterranean just north of Tunis, and like many of the rivers of the basin, varies from a respectable flow in winter to a trickle in summer. The other rivers of North Africa west to The Straits behave similarly, or are even less impressive.

The Black Sea, as we have seen, receives more than its share of river water. The Danube, the great river of east central Europe, brings the runoff from 315,000 square miles (817,000 sq km) into the western part of the sea, where it has built a large delta that has many oak forests. The smaller but respectable Dniester and Bug are followed by the Dnieper (Borysthenes), 1,430 miles (2,300 km) long, with a drainage area of 194,208 square miles (503,130 km²). The other great Black Sea river is the Don (Tanaïs), which enters the Sea of Azov (Maeotis) after flowing 1,200 miles (1,930 km), carrying the waters from 194,500 square miles (422,000 km²). Here in the north, the flows are greater in summer because the rivers freeze in the winter. Several smaller rivers drain northward from the Anatolian Plateau into the Black Sea, most notably the Kızıl Irmak (Halys), whose diversion by Thales was reported, but not believed, by Herodotus (1.75).

LAKES. Lakes are features of disparate geological origin, and there are relatively few of any size in the Mediterranean, partly because the limestone strata dissolve easily and form underground drains, called *katabothra* in modern Greek, in many small basins. But the largest and most interesting ones deserve discussion.

The western part of the French Mediterranean coast is lined by a number of large, shallow, brackish lagoons separated from the sea by sand dunes. Some of these intergrade into swamps. Italy has about 1,500 lakes, the majority of them quite small. The largest are those of the Alpine foothills, lying in basins excavated by the glaciers of the ice ages. These are lakes Garda, Maggiore, Como, Iseo, and Lugano. Lago di Garda (Benacus) has an area of 143 square miles (370 km²) and is 33.5 miles (54 km) long. These lakes tend to be narrow, under towering cliffs, especially in their northern reaches, and deep. Como (Larius), the deepest, has a sounding of 1,345 feet (410 m). In ancient times, as in modern, these beautiful blue lakes were resort areas. Como is celebrated in the writings of Vergil, the elder and younger Pliny, and Claudian. Lake Trasimene, in Umbria, is 49 square miles (128 km²) in size, but shallow, with marshy shorelines. Farther south, there are a number of lakes that fill volcanic craters, such as Bolsena, Bracciano (Sabatinus), and Avernus (Lucrinus). The last named has no natural outlet and was regarded by Vergil as the entrance to the underworld. Agrippa made it a harbor by connecting it with the Bay of Naples (Gulf of Cumae). There are also lagoons near the Adriatic Sea in Apulia and the Po Delta.

A number of lakes nestle among the limestone mountains of the Balkans, such as lakes Ohrid (Lychnitis), Prespa, and Castoria (Límni Kastorías). Ioannina, in Epirus, has a lake (Pambotis) with subterranean drainage, and Aetolia has a scattering of them. Greece proper has few lakes. In the Peloponnese, Lake Stymphalus was the site of Hercules' mythical bird hunt, appropriately, but alternate openings and closings of the limestone drain have caused it to fill and almost disappear in different periods. Boeotia's Lake Copais, famous source of eels in ancient Greece, was partly drained by Alexander's engineer, Crates (Strabo, *Geography* 9.2.18), and in the last one hundred years has been converted into farmland.

Asia Minor has a row of lakes south of the Sea of Marmara, but its most extensive ones are found in basins without outlets in the Anatolian heartland. The largest, Tuz Gölü (Palus Tattaeus), is a shallow saline lake about 50 miles (80 km) long and 30 miles (48 km) wide in the winter that recedes each summer, leaving a barren stretch of dried salt, which was collected and served as an item of trade. Israel (Palestine) has two historic lakes, both below sea level: Galilee, or Tiberias, and the Dead Sea. The Jordan River flows from Galilee, which is fresh, to the Dead Sea, which is one of the most saline bodies of water on earth. At about 300 parts per thousand of salts to water, bacteria are the only form of life that survive there. The deep waters have a temperature of about 72° F (22° C). Together the two lakes occupy the Jordan Rift. Galilee has an area of 64 square miles (166 km²) and lies at 686 feet (209 m) below sea level; the Dead Sea has an area of 405 square miles (1,049 km²), is 1,302 feet (395 m) below sea level, and has a depth of about 1,300 feet (400 m).

In Egypt, the Bitter Lakes, with a high concentration of sodium sulfate, filled part of the isthmus between the Gulf of Suez and the Mediterranean. A series of lagoons including lakes Manzala, Burullus, and Maryūt (Mareotis), extend along the outer margin of the delta. In a basin below sea level, Al-Faiyūm (Fayum), seepage from the Nile created a brackish, saline lake, Birket Qārūn (Moeris), about 150 feet (45 m) below sea level and 85 square miles (220 km²) in area. This salt lake has varied in level and area through history. The only lakes of note in the rest of North Africa lie in the system of saline lakes in Tunisia and Algeria, extending 250 miles (400 km) westward from the Gulf of Gabès (Syrtis Minor). In past ages, this may have been a branch of the Mediterranean Sea. In more recent times, it is covered with water only in periods of heavy rains.

MARSHES. Wetlands are not common in the generally dry Mediterranean, and salt tide marshes are absent around the tideless sea. But marshes do develop in river deltas, in lakes that are gradually filled, and along the seacoast where erosional deposition leaves extensive lowlands. The latter persist in the Mediterranean because forces that would wash them away, such as currents and waves, are weak or lacking along with the tides. The most extensive marshes are in river deltas. The Camargue is a marshland in the Rhône Delta, about 300 square miles (780 km²) in area, rich in flamingos, egrets, beavers, and turtles. A famous wetland in Roman history, the Pontine (Pomptine) Marshes in southern Latium extended between the Alban Hills and the Tyrrhenian Sea. Many attempts were made to drain them, both for agriculture and because they were malarial, but these efforts succeeded only in the twentieth century. Today the original aspect of the marshes can be seen only in Monte Circeo National Park. Even small rivers around the Mediterranean had marshy stretches near their mouths, but those most extensive and most often represented in ancient art belong to the Nile. Egyptian reliefs and murals, and Roman mosaics, represent scenes of hunting birds and animals, and fishing in these wild marshes among the papyri and other reeds. But reclamation sharply reduced the area of wetlands, and the papyrus became rare in Egypt. A few of the brackish marshes still exist along the northern margin of the delta. Some may be seen near Alexandria along Lake Maryūt (Mareotis), although in an exceedingly polluted condition.

THE WATERS UNDER THE EARTH. Water flows not only on the surface, but also underground; it saturates certain strata and supplies the wells and springs. Underground rivers are also relatively common in the Mediterranean basin. Limestone, common in the area, dissolves in water containing carbon dioxide and thus allows the formation of solution channels and caves. In a landscape where limestone predominates, much if not all of the drainage will be into underground channels instead of surface streams. Such terrain is called karst, and its type locality is the Karst of the Dinaric Alps, Yugoslavia. There, and in parts of Greece and similar locales, streams and rivers may disappear through open sinks (*katabothra*), only to reappear from springs called karst rises, mostly where a layer of less soluble rock occurs. One river that does this is the Alpheus, the "sacred river" of Olympia, the site of the original Olympic Games, which "ran / Through caverns measureless to man" (Coleridge, *Kubla Khan*).

In many places the solution of limestone by underground water has created caves, some of them of great extent and beauty. These are found in almost all of the lands bordering on the Mediterranean. They have served as dwellings, as folds for sheep and goats, and as religious sanctuaries. Caves on Crete have yielded thousands of votive objects. Some were storied in mythology as places where gods were born or reared, such as Zeus in Crete and Hermes near Pylos. The latter cave has stalactites with a fancied resemblance to the skins of cattle that the infant god stole from Apollo. The Caves of Castellana, in Apulia, Italy, were famous for their beauty. The deepest explored cave system in the Mediterranean drainage is that of Dent de Crolles, Isère, in the French Alps, which is 2,158 feet (658 m) deep. Spluga della Preta, in Venetia, Italy, is almost as deep, 2,089 feet (637 m).

Other types of rock also allow for the passage of water. The oases of the Sahara are fed by waters flowing generally northward through aquifers of permeable sandstone, often for distances of more than 495 miles (800 km). Most of the water that surfaces in Egyptian oases such as Farafra, Baharīya, and Siwa comes through the Nubian sandstone from the northern Sudan and Chad.

CLIMATE: "THE ELEMENTS OF AIR, FIRE, AND AETHER"

Ancient philosophers, geographers, and physicians, such as Plato, Aristotle, Hippocrates, and Eratosthenes, postulated the effects of various climates on the human beings who live under their influence. Although an extreme environmental determinism is not here advocated, few would doubt that climatic effects have been major influences on the development of cultural adaptations.

Mediterranean Climatic Zone

The Mediterranean Sea has given its name to a type of climate that is found in several parts of the world, including California, Chile, western South Africa, and the western and southern parts of Australia. The zone is most extensive in the Mediterranean because the sea extends far inland at just the right latitude, and the mountain ranges to the north offer some shelter from colder air masses.

SEASONAL REGIME. Generally, the Mediterranean climate may be described as a subtropical climate with a cool, moist winter and a hot, dry summer. That is, it has two easily distinguishable seasons rather than four.

The wet season lasts from October to May, longer in the northern and western areas and shorter in the south and east. In most places, the winter months are wettest. But in Spain, southern France, northern Italy, and Macedonia, the autumnal months have the most rain. But the term "wet season" is perhaps misleading. Even during these months, rain is seldom constant and often rare. Nice, France, for example, has 33 inches (838 mm) of rain annually, but only eighty-one rainy days, and it is in the moister half of the basin. The typical Mediterranean rainstorm is intense; on Malta, 11 inches (279 mm) has been recorded in one day. But such storms are brief, leaving most of the winter sunny. The average number of hours of sunshine in Athens is 2,655 per year; Berlin has only 1,614. The amount of Mediterranean rainfall is, however, unpredictable from year to year. One year may provide twice the average; the next only half.

Precipitation is also quite variable from place to place in the Mediterranean; Port Said in the arid east has an average of 2 inches (50 mm) of rainfall, while Crikvenica, a mountainous location near the Yugoslavian coast, receives 181 inches, (4,626 mm), some of it as snow. These are extremes, of course. More typical amounts in the drier eastern basin are Haifa, 27 (679); Athens, 16 (406); Salonika, 21 (545); Alexandria, 8 (217); and Tripoli, 16 (421). In the generally more rainy western basin, some averages are Gibraltar, 36 (909); Valencia, 18 (472); Marseilles, 22 (574); Rome, 36 (923); Palermo, 29 (749); and Algiers, 30 (765). The rainiest area is the eastern coast of the Adriatic. The Black Sea has its heaviest precipitation at the eastern end, where Batum averages 98 inches (2,500 mm); and its lowest in the north, where Kerch has only 13 (330).

Temperatures are regulated by the nearness of the sea, and therefore the winter is not as cold as it is elsewhere at similar latitudes. It seems incredible that Venice is as far north as Ottawa and that Thessalonica is farther north than Denver. Average temperatures in winter are mild. There is no month in Palermo, Sicily, with an average temperature below 50° F (10° C). In many Mediterranean cities, the difference between the warmest and coolest months varies only 25° F (14° C) or so, while day and night differ by something like 14° F (8° C). Near sea level, the temperature only rarely falls below 32° F (0° C). Snow may occur on one or two days in the winter in a locality like Athens, but generally melts in a few hours. One must, however, not overemphasize the pleasantness of the Mediterranean winter. Storms often sweep the sea and raise waves to perilous heights. The ancients avoided sailing at this time.

The dry, hot season lasts from May to October. In Greece, May Day is popularly called the "first day of summer." In most of the Mediterranean basin, the months between June and September are virtually rainless. Thus, this was the season in ancient times not only for voyages but also for military campaigns. The heat becomes unpleasant, and the inhabitants complain that it keeps them awake both during the afternoon siesta and at night. The mean highest temperature in summer in Naples, for example, is 91° F (33° C), and this heat can be oppressive in a maritime situation. On the Libyan coast, temperatures rise above 120° F (49° C), and rain scarcely ever falls. But in more characteristically Mediterranean territory, thundershowers can break the summer drought, especially near the mountains.

WINDS AND WEATHER. On each of the eight sides of the Tower of the Winds in Athens is a relief of a personified wind, portrayed as if flying and bearing some attribute indicating its character. These are: Boreas, North; Kaikias, Northeast; Apeliotes, East; Eurus, Southeast; Notus, South; Lips, Southwest; Zephyrus, West; and Skiron, Northwest. This is a beautiful system, and perhaps fairly accurate for Athens, but unfortunately not even the Athenians agreed on the names and directions of the winds. Aristotle (*Meteorology* [*Meteorologica*] 2.6 363a21) gives a system of twelve winds.

In Italy and elsewhere, other names are given, because the winds themselves differed. One can construct a different "wind rose" (that is, a diagram of the prevailing winds in an average year) for each place in the Mediterranean. But there are some larger wind patterns, and major winds whose names are famous. The Mediterranean is a windy region.

In the winter, the relatively warm Mediterranean causes a series of low-pressure centers to form over it. As part of the world-girdling circulation at these latitudes (30 to 45 degrees north), these lows move eastward. Depressions moving in from the Atlantic are strengthened over the larger sea basins within the Mediterranean, but these basins generate their own lows, particularly in the Gulf of Genoa, the northern Adriatic, and the sea around Cyprus. During this period, moist winds come from the west and southwest bearing rain. Aristotle calls Lips a "wet wind." The jet stream, which guides the depressions, shifts into the Mediterranean in October, bringing the rains. It moves farther south into North Africa in January or February, bringing a decrease of rains in the northern reaches of the western basin. It moves north again between March and May, bringing a second, subdued maximum in the rainfall as it passes, usually exiting from the region in May.

But the Mediterranean lows cause the warmed air within them to rise, drawing in winds from the lands around. When this warmed air comes from the high-pressure dome of air over the European continent, it enters as a series of cold, dry northerlies. Most infamous of these is the mistral, centered in the Rhône Valley, the violent "master wind" (Italian *maestrale*, from Latin *magister*), which sometimes uproots trees and blows vehicles off roads. A cold, descending wind called bora afflicts the Dalmatian coast. Other winds of similar type are the gregale, which sweeps off the Balkan Peninsula across the Ionian Sea, sometimes as far as Tunisia; and the *vardarac*, which comes down into the Aegean along the line of the Vardar River. Cold winds also flow from central Anatolia toward the Aegean, Black Sea, and Mediterranean.

Lows over the Mediterranean also attract winds from the Sahara Desert. These are hot and dry and they bear great quantities of reddish and yellowish dust. Sirocco is the Italian name given this general type of wind, although each of the lands subject to it has given it a name of its own (Spanish *leveche;* Tunisian *chili;* Egyptian *khamsin* from the word for "fifty" because it supposedly blows fifty days in a year). This wind is extremely disagreeable, bringing sandstorms with dust that coats every surface and penetrates every crack and orifice. In the Maghreb it roars down the front of the Atlas Mountains as a foehn (a dry wind that warms as it descends), and gives the effect almost of a blast furnace. As the sirocco crosses the sea, it absorbs moisture and becomes a dusty, muggy wind called the *garbi* in Italy and the Aegean. Clouds generated from this air mass often pour down rain that is red from the dust it contains. Siroccos are particularly common as the seasonal regime changes in the springtime.

In the summer, the North Atlantic mass of high pressure extends over west-central Europe, producing generally northwest winds of continental dry air that move across the Mediterranean toward the African and Asian deserts, where heated air rises. But these winds become northeasterly in some parts of the basin, such as the Maghreb coast and the Aegean. In the Aegean, these relatively steady winds are called etesian (annual, from Greek *etos,* year) or *meltemi* (perhaps from Italian *bel tempo,* good weather). They make sailing easy, at least in a southerly direction, but make it important that harbors be sheltered from the north. From this source, Egypt enjoys almost constant north winds that cool Alexandria and make upstream sailing possible on the Nile all the way to the Sudan. The summer also sees cooler sea air moving in over the larger landmasses, such as Iberia and Asia Minor, to replace the heated air that is rising.

INFLUENCE OF TOPOGRAPHY. Much of what has been said about the Mediterranean climate does not apply to the mountains within the basin. Elevation brings cooler temperatures, a fact appreciated by the ancient epicures who enjoyed summer drinks cooled by snow brought from the peaks. As a rule of thumb, an ascent of 328 feet (100 m) has the same climatic effect as a journey at sea level of 93 miles (150 km) northward. Thus the higher mountains bore forests of cold-loving trees, and winter up there was frigid and snowy. It is with good reason that mountain shepherds in the Mediterranean wrap themselves in goatskin cloaks. But although most of the higher mountains in the region receive coatings of winter snow, very few of them retain it through the summer. Only in the Alps and Pyrenees are there glaciers of any size.

Another function of mountains is to serve as barriers to the movement of air and moisture. The Alps and Pyrenees undoubtedly keep much of the unpleasant weather of maritime Europe from moving south. Also, mountain ranges, by forcing the air flowing over them to rise and cool, cause the moisture in it to fall as precipitation on the windward side. On the lee side of the mountains, the air descends, warms, and dries. Since the flow of moisture-bearing air in the Mediterranean is generally from west to east, the mountain ranges ordinarily have a moister western slope and a drier eastern one. Cities to the west of the mountains, therefore, will have more precipitation, and those to the east, in the "rain shadow," will be shorted of rainfall. This can be illustrated by two places on opposite sides of the Pindus Massif in Greece: Corfu (Corcyra), to the west, receives an average annual precipitation of 52 inches (1,319 mm); Larissa, to the east, gets only 20 inches (522 mm).

CLIMATIC CHANGE. Many ancient writers were aware that the climate does not remain the same. As Plato remarked (*Laws* 6.782, trans. by A. E. Taylor [1961]), "There have ... been, all over the world, ... multifarious climatic revolutions." In recent years, much study has been given to the question of climatic changes in historical periods, so that it is possible to say something about changes before, during, and after the time of ancient Greece and Rome.

The most far-reaching change in the late prehistoric period was the end of the most recent Ice Age, called in Europe the Würm Glaciation. Beginning in about 15,000 B.C., a general warming trend set in, although with many fluctuations. Then the warming became steadier, and the period 6,000 to 3,100 B.C., called the "hypsithermal" or "climatic optimum," had temperatures some 36° F (2° C) higher than now, on the average. Near the end of that period, the Egyptian Sahara had attained its present state of desiccation. The sea rose to a level estimated at 7 to 10 feet (2–3 m) higher than today. There followed a cooling called the "Piora Oscillation," about 3,100 to 2,800 B.C., followed by more variations until a cooling trend brought conditions somewhat colder than in the twentieth century from 1200 to 300 B.C. In Greek Archaic times, 700–500, the average seems to have been 3.6° F (2° C) cooler than now. It must be emphasized that this figure, like all such estimates, is only an average; there were many exceptional years.

After 300 B.C., temperatures warmed and remained relatively similar to those of the present until about A.D. 400. Whether they were in fact not quite as warm as in the twentieth century can be argued, since many parts of the Roman world around the Mediterranean are now under water, indicating a rise of sea level since then. The fact that climatic conditions during the Hellenistic and Roman periods were not all that different from today has led a number of historians of the ancient world to discount climate as a factor in history.

These general, long-term fluctuations of climate were not observed by ancient writers, but they did record local alterations during shorter periods. Theophrastus (*Etiology of Plants* [*De Causis Plantarum*] 5.14.1) observed that when the water was drained from the Thessalian Plain near Larissa, the weather became colder in the winter, and frost more common. Claudius Ptolemy recorded the weather of Alexandria in a journal, noting the frequency of heat, rain, and thunder from year to year.

Open-Air Life in the Mediterranean

The Mediterranean climate encourages outdoor activities in ways that more northerly regimes, with their cold and plentiful precipitation, and more southerly climes, with a blazing sun that must be avoided, do not. Thus, it is understandable that athletes could compete nude in the open, and that various assemblies met under the sky to conduct their business. Open marketplaces, roofless theatres, temples whose altars were outside, and houses centered on courtyards all bear witness to the love of the Greeks and Romans for a life lived out-of-doors.

THE "MEDITERRANEAN LIGHT." One of the climatic elements often noted about the Mediterranean region is the quality of the light. It has a notable clarity, and the shadows a sharp definition, not often seen elsewhere. It was maintained by students of architecture that the Mediterranean light had influenced the development of the Greek orders, with their fluted columns and sculptured reliefs. The radiance can hardly be denied by anyone who has made a comparison with the softer light of places like England.

AIRS, WATERS, PLACES. A work survives from late-fifth- or early-fourth-century Greece bearing the name of Hippocrates, the founder of medical science, and having the title *Airs, Waters, Places*. The author attempts to show that the climate, seasons, and winds of a place, the drinking water found there, and the topography and exposure, affect the physique, temperament, intelligence, and therefore even the culture of the people who live there. As a physician, the author stresses the importance of the effects of a local environment on human health, both physical and mental. By studying the place, he taught, one could learn what diseases to expect among the inhabitants, and what kinds of changes of environment and diet might help patients to find healing. He believed that one must understand nature as a whole in order to understand the human body and soul. He was a pioneer student of the effects of climate and the environment generally upon living organisms.

The Mediterranean seems to have more than its share of pleasant and salubrious "places," to use that word in the sense intended by the ancient book. The Greek word is *topoi* (whence "topography"). It has, after all, the Vale of Tempe and the French Riviera, Majorca and the Isle of Capri, Lake Lugano and the Bay of Pylos, Florence and Rhodes. It also has a few places that have never been attractive, such as the Qattara Depression, or even if attractive, not very safe, such as the volcanic island of Thira (Santorini, or Thera). It should be evident that a general description of the climate can only begin to give an understanding of all these places. Each must be appreciated in its individuality as a single piece of the mosaic that is the Mediterranean.

TREES AND PLANTS

Wild Plant Species

Mediterranean vegetation patterns are varied and complex. The number of species represented greatly exceeds that of the areas immediately to the north and south. Greece, for example, with less than half the area of the British Isles, has three times as many species of wildflowers. Many of these are narrow endemics, plants that grow only in a small area, perhaps only on one mountain or island. Mount Athos, occupying the east end of the Acte peninsula, has sixteen species that grow nowhere else. Of ninety species of centaurea that grow in Spain and Portugal, fifty are limited to the Iberian Peninsula. One reason for the diversity of Mediterranean plant life as compared with more northerly Europe is that the great glacial sheets of the Ice Age, which ended only about 11,000 years ago, scoured the north of much of its vegetation and eliminated many older species, while the south was only cooled. Numerous Mediterranean plants survived in appropriate climatic niches, but the European plain had to be recolonized by species that spread northward as the glaciers melted. Still, many plant species are common both to the Mediterranean and to central Europe. On the southern margin of the region, aridity is the limiting factor. Few plant species can survive the dryness of the Sahara.

The ancients had names for hundreds of plant species, as a scanning of the botanical writings of Theophrastus shows. He mentions more than 600. But there is no point in trying to list the names of the species here. There are at least 1,000 within easy walking distance of Athens, say, or Jerusalem. The best approach, then, is to look at the major kinds of plant associations, or forests, brushlands, grasslands, and deserts, and to mention a few of the most typical species found within each.

Ecosystems and Life Zones

The vegetation covering much of the land surface in the Mediterranean basin is a mosaic of plant communities. Each of these communities is a group of species that are interdependent and interact with each other and the animals, the soil, and the local climate within a large or small area. Such a community can be called an ecosystem, a specific manifestation of the dynamic balance that nature tends to establish and maintain. There is a great number of kinds of plant communities in Mediterranean lands, and to generalize too broadly would be misleading. Theophrastus knew the complexity of Mediterranean plant communities, noting that mountains provide a wide variety of elevations and exposures where many different types of wild trees may find the conditions each prefers.

It is possible, however, to distinguish a number of broadly similar communities whose distribution is determined mainly by elevation, exposure, and rainfall. Biologists in western North America have referred to similar latitudinal and altitudinal belts as "life zones," a concept that may be useful in the Mediterranean area as well.

FORESTS, MAQUIS, AND GRASSLANDS. The vegetation of the Mediterranean basin may be roughly divided into three major altitudinal life zones. The lowest of these contains the typical vegetation of the true Mediterranean climatic zone. This extends from sea level to about 2,130 feet (650 m) elevation in the northern and western mountains, and to above 3,280 feet (1,000 m) in southern and eastern ranges like the Taurus and Atlas. In its natural state this is a land of evergreen forests, dominated by pines and evergreen oaks. The so-called Aleppo pines (*Pinus halepensis* from mainland Greece westward and *Pinus brutia* from the Aegean eastward) form extensive forests at low elevations. Along streams, plane trees and willows flourish. In dryer sections the trees are often widely spaced on account of competition for moisture.

But the most distinctive plant association of the Mediterranean is a hardy brushland of shrubs forming dense and sometimes impenetrable thickets that many observers from other climates would hesitate to call a forest, since it rarely exceeds 23 feet (7 m) in height. It has come to be called maquis, from the French; in Italian it is *macchia;* and in Spanish, *matorral.* Its most important species are broad sclerophylls, that is, evergreen trees with broad leaves that are adapted through thick, hairy, leathery, or waxy coverings to resist drought. Indeed, maquis is not only drought resistant but also adapted to survive fire. After one of the region's common (virtually periodic) fires, the shrubs rapidly reestablish themselves by sprouting from buried root crowns, as the kermes oak and bracken do, or from seeds that germinate in great heat or spread easily or take root in the bare, scorched topsoil. Some, like the cistus, strawberry tree, and thuja, can recuperate after a fire, often accelerating their growth at that time.

Plants of the maquis are adapted to the long, dry Mediterranean summer. They have long root systems and their osmotic pressure (the ability of a root to draw moisture from the soil) is high. As evergreens, they can take advantage of winter moisture and the growth it makes possible. Most of them bloom during the short spring, when the environment is briefly both warm and moist. Forests in this zone, after their removal, may be replaced by maquis, but maquis is a natural climax vegetation in many areas, not just the result of deforestation or misuse. (Climax is the biotic community capable of perpetuation under the prevailing conditions of soil and climate.) Even before human beings began tree clearance in this section, the maquis flourished on lower hillsides all around the Mediterranean. The most conspicuous plants of this community are large shrubs such as holm and kermes oaks, junipers, arbutus, laurel, myrtle, tree heather, rockrose, broom, mastic tree, and rosemary, to name only a few.

After repeated destruction by clearing, browsing, or fire, maquis will be replaced by a low, tough community of often spiny, aromatic shrubs that barely cover the rock, gravel, or sand of the Mediterranean slopes. This association is called *garigue* in French; *tomillares* in Spanish after the thyme that is one of its more notable species; and *phrygana* or "kindling" in Greek because the only wood it supplies is thin, short sticks. No doubt there was some garigue on the rockiest Mediterranean hillsides in prehistoric times, but people and their herds have produced far more of it where there was formerly forest or maquis. Garigue, rarely growing more than 20 inches (0.5 m) high, and often not as tall as the rocks among which it grows, is rich in the plants that are the sources of familiar spices: basil, garlic, hyssop, lavender, oregano, rosemary, rue, sage, and savory. These scents, wafting out to sea, give Mediterranean coasts a pleasant ambience. But they do not exhaust the list of Mediterranean plant species; there are more than 200 common ones, including low junipers, dwarf palms, broom, gorse, gromwell, spurges, heather, rockrose, and daphne. Plants that grow from bulbs and tubers, like asphodel, crocus, hyacinth, iris, tulip, and even some orchid species, also survive in the dry soil among the garigue bushes.

In extremely dry or overexploited areas, not even garigue can survive, and one finds a winter grassland sometimes called "steppe," although the latter term is properly used only for the summer grasslands of continental Europe and Siberia. It contains many annual species that flourish in the moist half of the year (November to May), and also root perennials and tuberous or bulbous plants like asphodel, one of its most characteristic components. In spring, the asphodel steppe produces a colorful but very short display of flowers before the dry winds come: "The grass withers; the flower fades" (Isaiah 40:7–8). The plants that survive best here are those most resistant to grazing, like mullein, sea squill, and thistlelike composites. Members of the rockrose, legume, grass, mint, mustard, pink, buttercup, parsley, and lily families are common.

Above the true Mediterranean zone just described there is, where rainfall permits, a deciduous forest belt extending upward to about 4,430 feet (1,350 m) above sea level, somewhat higher in the south. Commonest in these forests are the deciduous oaks, elm, beech, chestnut, ash, and hornbeams. The deciduous tree communities are most often seen in the northern and western reaches; elsewhere they are limited to moist enclaves or may not appear at all. In earlier times they were much more extensive. This area can be called the upper Mediterranean zone.

Still higher is the Mediterranean mountain zone, which rises to treeline at an elevation of from 7,070 feet (2,150 m) in the Maritime Alps to 7,540 feet (2,300 m) on Mount Olympus and 9,350 feet (2,850 m) in the High Atlas Mountains of North Africa. Its characteristic vegetation is a tall coniferous forest of pines, silver fir, cedars, and junipers, interrupted by open meadows. The cedar forests, most famous in Lebanon, also occurred in the Taurus Mountains, on Cyprus, and along the Atlas ranges. The size of the trees that grow in this higher mountain zone convinced Pliny the Elder that snow is good for trees, unless it comes late in the year. This is a subalpine zone of winter snows and summer thundershowers, where low temperatures limit plant growth to the summer months. That is why Mediterranean shepherds brought their herds to the high mountain pastures then, in the well-known practice of transhumance.

Still higher, where trees cannot grow, is an alpine tundra of dwarfed flowering plants and lichens, and finally the rocky summit peaks where snow lingers for much of the year, but not all through the summer. Neither Olympus nor Etna possesses a glacier. Tiny plants at this elevation are adapted to a short summer growing season; they must flower and set seed within a few short weeks before freezing weather returns.

DESERTS. Life in the deserts on the margins of the Mediterranean basin consists of ecosystems adapted to very severe conditions of dryness. These occur to the south, in the Sahara; to the east, in the interior of Arabia and Syria; and in a more limited area of central Turkey. The rainfall varies from none at all to a maximum of .98 inches (250 mm), and sometimes it is so sparse that no vegetation can be seen. Extensive stretches of bare rock and sand make the Sahara and the Arabian deserts far more desolate than the arid lands of the southwestern United States. In order for higher plants to grow, there must be the equivalent of about 0.2 inches (50 mm) of rainfall in sandy loess, 0.3 inches (75 mm) in sand, and 0.4 inches (100 mm) in rocky terrain; these amounts are often lacking. Fortunately some water is stored in sand from one year to the next, so that the meager winter rains can be used to some extent during the ensuing summer. Surface water flows intermittently in the wadis, streambeds that are dry for most of the year, and more water may flow from underground, where long roots can reach it. Here and there water rises to the surface and provides an oasis; the Nubian sandstone of the eastern Sahara carries water that fell as rain and snow in the highlands of equatorial Africa toward the Mediterranean.

The deserts are therefore not devoid of plants, but those that grow are adapted to aridity. Some are annuals that spend most of their life cycles as seeds, and then when a rain comes, usually in winter, they explode in a brief paroxysm of growth, flowering, and fruiting. Others are low-growing perennials that have various ways of promoting their water intake, reducing water loss, and surviving the long periods of drought. Many have long root systems, especially those that grow in sand; the tamarisk can send its roots 98 feet (30 m) underground, and the retama 66 feet (20 m). During hot and dry periods many plants will reduce their transpiration surface by dropping leaves or failing to grow them. The ephedra has no leaves at all. Studies in the deserts of the Middle East have shown that during the summer scarcity of moisture, desert vegetation will allow only a thirtieth of the evaporation from plant surfaces that occurs in the weeks after a spring rain. The adaptations of these plants are numerous, including thick cuticles and tissue walls, few evaporative stomata, small or inrolled leaves, water-storage cells, and the ability to go into long periods of quasi dormancy. Thorns, strong and unpalatable or even poisonous juices, and other devices that discourage browsing animals also favor survival in the desert ecosystems.

Among the genera of plants seen in relatively favored parts of the deserts that abut the Mediterranean are, in addition to those already mentioned, zygophyllum (caltrop), artemisia (sagebrush), varthemia, centaurea (thistle), origanum (oregano), anabasis, astragalus, convolvulus, atriplex, stachys, and the salt-adapted halogeton and haloxylon. Where the desert receives an average rainfall above that marginal for plant growth, it intergrades into a series of semisteppe associations, where shrubs or grass may cover most of the ground. In the oases and along the better-watered wadis, hydrophytes (plants that thrive in moist conditions) grow and there will even be groves or lines of trees. The palm, so typical of these places today, is a human introduction of historic times.

Plants and Human Use

FORESTRY AND THE TIMBER TRADE. A heavy demand for forest products existed throughout classical times. Since coal, petroleum, and natural gas were almost never used as fuel, wood and its partially oxidized product, charcoal, served to warm buildings; to cook meals; to heat water for the large and popular public baths; to fire the kilns that hardened bricks, tiles, and ceramic vessels; to melt ore in metallurgical processes; and to reduce limestone to fertilizer. More wood was used for fuel than any other purpose, but the demand for building timbers and shipbuilding material, particularly for masts, often required long timbers from large trees. Wood was also used to make carts, chariots, construction and siege machinery, furniture, tools, sculpture, and musical instruments. So many purposes did it serve that in both Greek and Latin the word for "wood" also meant "substance" or "matter" in general: *hyle* or *materia*.

Some forests, including farm woodlots, were privately owned. But the larger forests that clothed the mountain slopes were generally considered to belong to the sovereign power: the city, the king, or in the case of Rome, the "Senate and the Roman people." Important as sources of supply for military purposes, forests often played a role in diplomacy. Treaties exist in which the Macedonian king asserted control over exports from his timber-rich country. The public lands were sometimes leased, granted, or sold to private individuals or consortia who would cut, transport, and sell the forest products.

Ancient loggers were skilled laborers who could take pride in their work; one who worked on Mount Parnes near Athens ordered his tombstone inscribed, "I never saw a better woodcutter than myself" (Zimmern, *The Greek Commonwealth,* p. 278). An experienced forester, says Columella the Roman writer, would take apprentices and teach them "the principle of his art" (*On Country Matters* [*De Re Rustica*] 11.1.12). Such men knew forests well; they knew which species to choose for various uses, and how to judge which trees to cut: location, exposure, age, habit of growth, appearance of the bark, and time of day, month, and year were all considered. Thus selective logging was known, replanting of trees to regenerate the forest was sometimes required, and important tracts of forest could be carefully managed for sustained yield. But as a rule the desire of the contractors was simply to enrich themselves, and if the land was cleared of the forest, it then became available for grazing cattle, sheep, and goats, or less often for farming. As Lucretius said (*On the Nature of Things* [*De Rerum Natura*] 5.1,370–1,371): "They made the woods climb higher up the mountains,/Yielding the lowlands to be tilled and tended." After cutting by the ax and saw, the branches were lopped and the tree trunks pulled out of the forest by teams of oxen or mules. Transport by water was preferred; logs could be floated down a nearby river to a market or shipping post. At some point the logs were sawed into usable sizes. Valuable woods, such as the cedar of Lebanon or the citrus (*thyon*) of North Africa, were often shipped over very long distances.

DEFORESTATION. The cutting of trees just described was one, but not the only, force tending to forest removal. Just as destructive were the wide-ranging herds of goats, sheep, cattle, and swine. While forests and maquis tend to regenerate themselves after fire or other clearing, and are a renewable resource if properly managed, their new growth can be destroyed by overgrazing. Goats, in particular, eat the little trees that would otherwise reestablish a forest, and they enjoy almost every typical woody Mediterranean species. They will even climb trees to browse on the foliage and bark. To the destructive natural fires caused by lightning one must add those set deliberately by shepherds and goatherds to improve the grazing for their animals. Vergil (*Aeneid* 10. 405–408, trans. by Frank O. Copley [1965]) knew this problem: "in the summer, when hoped-for winds arise, / A shepherd fires the woods at scattered points."

Classical writers create the impression, no doubt justified, that deforestation was extensive in their homelands. Although the entire Mediterranean basin was not denuded of its trees, it is possible to identify many sections that were, such as the mountains near Athens mentioned by Plato (*Critias* 111 B–D) and the Ciminian Forest in central Italy recalled by Livy (9.36.1). The desolation of forests began near urban centers and mining districts, and was most serious in areas of low rainfall, generally to the south and east. Lowlands were exploited before mountains, and places near rivers suffered while more inaccessible woodlands survived. The territories most praised as sources of good timber at the height of classical times were usually mountainous regions with heavier than average rainfall, such as Macedonia, the Alps, the Atlas, and the hinterlands of the Black Sea. Lebanon, the source of cedar, was so nearly exhausted by the second century A.D. that the emperor Hadrian had to forbid the felling of the important timber trees there without his express permission, as inscriptions on numerous boundary markers make clear.

The effects of deforestation in the Mediterranean basin were erosion on the hillsides, flooding, disruption of the water supply, and siltation of lowlands and coasts. Farmers in some areas built terraces to retard erosion and conserve soil, and these served well except in time of war, when those who would have maintained such works were conscripted into the military or killed. Erosion seems to have been at its worst during periods of warfare. Dense forests on mountain slopes act as sponges, collecting the rainfall among their roots and the humus they create and allowing it to seep forth in springs lower down. With the removal of trees came the disappearance of springs, a fact noted by Plato in the *Critias* passage cited above. The coastlines of the Mediterranean, where the relative absence of tides permits the accumulation of sediments, show the effects of erosion in wide lowland deposits near the mouths of rivers and intermittent streams. The Sperkhíos River has turned Thermopylae, once a narrow path between the mountains and sea, into a plain five miles wide. Ports like Miletus, at the mouth of the Büyükmenderes, or Ostia, where the Tiber issues into the Mediterranean, had long struggles to keep open in ancient times, and today their port facilities are isolated from the sea by accretions of sand and silt. In the swamps that appeared in such places, malarial mosquitoes multiplied.

Several other effects of deforestation should be noted. In some areas, tree removal changed local climates in the direction of dryness and greater variations of temperature. Agricultural productivity suffered from depleted soils, salinization, and floods. As abundant sources near the centers of consumption disappeared, wood became rarer and increased in price. Diplomacy and military strategy had to be directed toward securing timber supplies and cutting off the enemy's sources. For example, the Spartan general Brasidas captured a port in wooded Thrace during the Peloponnesian War in 424 B.C., and the historian Thucydides (4.108) had no difficulty in determining why. "The Athenians," he reported, "were terribly alarmed by the loss of Amphipolis. The main reason was that the city was essential to them for the supply of timber for shipbuilding."

SACRED GROVES. In discussing forestry and the cutting of trees, it must be noted that trees were regarded as sacred from time immemorial in the ancestral religions of the Mediterranean peoples. Forests were held to be the original temples of the gods, and trees were believed to be inhabited by spirits called dryads by the Greeks. By classical times, such a belief no longer protected trees in general, but certain precincts were set aside to preserve unusually sacred groves. These areas, called *temene* in Greek and *templa* in Latin, were carefully demarcated and protected both by custom and by civil law. Prohibited within the sacred boundaries were unauthorized cutting of trees or branches, removal of dead wood or leaves, pasturing of animals, plowing or planting, hunting or even bringing dogs inside, or fishing. Often the regulations were so strict as to forbid the introduction of weapons or iron tools of any kind. Witnesses were required to report infractions, and local authorities levied severe penalties. Mythology recorded punishments far more terrible than those contained in civil law codes. Erysichthon, who cut down a tree in brazen disregard of the protests of its dryad, was condemned to perpetual, insatiable hunger (Ovid, *Metamorphoses* 8.738–878).

Most sacred groves were small or of moderate size, though some contained gigantic trees. A few groves were of great extent; one at Daphne was ten miles in circumference, and another near Lerna stretched clear down a mountainside to the sea. The original intent seems to have been to keep these precincts in their natural state, but as time went on they gradually assumed the aspect of parks. Tree cutting was permitted, although carefully controlled and only after the prescribed prayers and sacrifices. In one case, the people of Karpathos cut a cypress of remarkable size in their grove of Apollo to send to Athens for the reconstruction of the temple of Athena. First temples, and then public buildings, were erected in groves. Some groves were even leased for private use, and we hear of some that consisted of cultivated fruit trees. After the advent of Christianity, protection was withdrawn from the sacred groves, and many of them were deliberately cut down, while others became enclosed as church cemeteries or monastery gardens.

PLANT INTRODUCTIONS. Many common plant species that today seem typically Mediterranean are actually recent immigrants from distant parts of the earth. The eucalyptus, for example, is an Australian tree; agave, or century plant, originally came from Mexico; the opuntia cactus, the familiar prickly pear, from the West Indies; and the casuarina (beefwood) that today covers the Nile Delta in windbreaks and plantations was brought from the southwest Pacific. The Greeks and Romans themselves introduced many plants into their homelands: the cherry and various kinds of citrus are famous. They spread the olive and vine to their climatic limits. When they established colonies, they tried to take familiar plants with them; they made attempts to grow laurel, Apollo's plant, in the Crimea (Tauric Chersonese) without success. But they did not grow tomatoes, nor have the shade of the eucalyptus to walk in, in spite of its Greek name.

ANIMAL LIFE

Species of Wild Animals

The variety of animals found in the Mediterranean basin is even greater than that of plants. These are components of the ecosystems described in the last section, and in spite of their mobility, tend to be found in one or more of the life zones in broadly defined attitudinal bands. The Mediterranean forests and maquis were a favorable habitat for wild animals. Again, the number of species is so astonishingly large that one cannot even attempt a full list in a work of this kind.

Plants are the food producers of the ecosystems, and all animals, including humans, depend on them. Some animals consume plants directly, while others prey on other animals. All animals and plants, before and after death, may serve as nutriment for the decomposers of the ecosystems, including bacteria, molds, and microscopic animals.

The rich primeval Mediterranean fauna was related to that of the rest of Europe (Palaearctic), with the addition of some animals from the African and Asiatic faunas. There are some endemic species, although a smaller proportion than among the plants.

MAMMALS. Among the wild mammals of the early Mediterranean were such large herbivores as sheep, goats, cattle, boars, horses, and donkeys. Although these were relatives, at least, of domestic animals, the story of domestication belongs with agriculture. The wild, or feral, counterparts of herd animals ranged the less inhabited parts of the Mediterranean then, as they do to the present day. Bison, stags, and red, fallow, and roe deer were common, especially on the European side of the sea. The grassland margins of North Africa possessed a fauna resembling that of East Africa in modern times, with elephants, zebras, and several species of antelopes. The hippopotamus was common in the Nile, and the Arabian desert supported herds of oryx and onagers, or wild asses. Everywhere there were smaller plant eaters like hares, porcupines, squirrels, and mice.

On the next level of the food chain are the carnivores and insectivores. Large predators, such as lions, leopards, lynxes, hyenas, wolves, and the smaller foxes, wildcats, and the weasel tribe, were found in the area. Most, like the jackal, ranged much farther in earlier times than later. The bear's food preferences are so catholic that it must be called an omnivore, along with the Barbary ape. Among the insectivores were the hedgehogs and bats.

REPTILES AND AMPHIBIANS. Snakes play such a prominent role in Mediterranean mythology that it should not be surprising to note that they are found everywhere, that the species are numerous, and that some of them are poisonous. Generally speaking, snakes are carnivores that prey on small animals. The antipathy that snakes aroused, seemingly instinctively, in the ancients, should not blind us to their importance as an integral part of the ecosystem. Several kinds of tortoises, both plant and insect eating, were distinguished by the Greeks and Romans as frequenting the land and freshwater. The carnivorous crocodile was found only near the rivers and lakes of Egypt. Smaller lizards, including the chameleon, the gecko, and a poisonous species (*Tropidosaurus algira*) were abundant.

Among the amphibians, frogs formed choruses in real marshes, not just in plays, like the comedy of Aristophanes named after them. Mistakenly, the ancients considered them to be poisonous, along with toads and salamanders. Most of these water-loving creatures are insectivores.

BIRDS. Birds can be seen everywhere in the Mediterranean, and the ancients knew of scores of species. Most are migratory in varying degrees, and there are species that leave the area entirely for part of the year, so that they are only seasonal parts of the ecosystems in which they live. The nightingale comes to the Mediterranean for the summer half of the year only, as do the swallow, oriole, hoopoe, and several warblers. When they leave, the rook arrives from the north to spend the winter, along with the short-eared owl, brambling, fieldfare, and gulls and many other birds of the sea and the shore. A few, like the avocet, ring ouzel, and wryneck, commute annually between the northern and southern sections of the Mediterranean basin. Thus seasonal transfers of energy are made by the birds into and from local ecosystems. Many are all-year residents; the raven, kingfisher, tawny owl, and great spotted woodpecker, for example. A few, like the cirl and reed buntings, wall creeper, and alpine accentor, have ranges that are predominantly Mediterranean. An offshoot of the rock dove, one of the most Mediterranean of birds, has adapted itself to human structures and spread everywhere as the common pigeon.

Birds were familiar to the ancients, as many of them entered the cities and even nested under the eaves. *Birds,* a play by Aristophanes with an avian chorus, lists many species and shows that knowledge of their appearance and some of their habits was widespread among Greek audiences.

LOWER LAND ANIMALS. The most numerous animals, both in sheer number and in variety of species, are the insects. They are found throughout the ecosystem, at every trophic level. Examples of plant-eating insects are bees, beetles, butterflies, moths, crickets, and the destructive locust. The musical cicada, beloved by poets, spends the early part of its life cycle underground, eating vegetable matter there, and emerges eventually onto the surface; it thus became a symbol of autochthonous birth for the Athenians and others.

Insects that consume animal material include praying mantises, wasps, hornets, and various beetles. Those that like human blood, such as lice, bedbugs, fleas, flies, mosquitoes, and gnats were noted by classical authors with good reason. Ants seem to be omnivorous, although some species specialize in their food sources. Ants from neighboring hills can be observed fighting their miniature wars in the Mediterranean terrain. Many insects aid in the decomposing process; the sacred Egyptian scarab is a dung beetle that lays its egg inside a sphere that it makes of the droppings of some animal, which serves as food for its larvae.

Among other arthropods, the sow bug, or wood louse, is a land crustacean that eats vegetable matter, as does the millipede. The centipedes and the arachnids, that is, the spiders and the scorpions, are mainly insectivorous.

Several species of land mollusks, the snails and slugs, were known to the ancients as destructive of plants. Earthworms were known, but were classed with other worms of unrelated phyla; their useful function in consuming decaying matter, fertilizing, and aerating the soil, is a modern discovery. The freshwater leech was mentioned by the physician Hippocrates, who advised its use for the removal of blood from the back of the head.

Fish and Other Sea Life

The Mediterranean Sea itself is of great importance in the biotic picture of the basin. As seas go, it is not particularly rich in aquatic life, either in number of species represented or in the biomass; that is, the total quantity of living organisms per unit of volume of seawater. This is the result of several factors. Its relative isolation meant that the Mediterranean could be entered only from the Atlantic over the barrier of The Straits. The salinity of the inland sea, increasing to the east, discouraged some less adaptable organisms. The temperature of the Mediterranean varies little with depth, a condition not conducive to the cold vertical currents that favor the growth of plankton, the base of marine food chains. Life in the sea depends upon food producers such as algae and phytoplankton. The cool seasonable north winds common in many parts encourage the mixing of shallow and deep waters, and therefore the growth of plankton, to a limited extent. But in general the Mediterranean is poor in plankton, and therefore its waters are unusually clear and blue, a fact often noted by travelers. The continental shelf, whose shallow waters are the nurseries of fish populations, is very narrow off most of the coasts, with the exceptions of the Adriatic and Black seas, parts of the Aegean, and an area extending eastward from Tunisia. Where the shelf is narrow, currents moving away from the coast can carry millions of tiny fish out into deep water, where they cannot survive. In many parts of the world, organic matter brought into the seas by rivers provides food for marine life. The Nile certainly did this in ancient times; its influence extended as far north as Cyprus. But most of the Mediterranean is poor in rivers.

As we have seen, the underwater ridge between Tunisia and Sicily divides the Mediterranean into two biotic zones, western and eastern. The eastern basin is warmer, more saline, and more isolated than the western. Thus several fish, the sail fluke and Ray's bream, for example, and particularly Atlantic species like the skipjack and pomfret, are limited to the western basin, while others like the rabbitfish and some of the sturgeons are generally found only in the eastern basin. The Black Sea, whose upper cold waters, shallowness, and low salinity combine with great isolation to make it almost a separate ecosystem, contains a number of unique species.

In saying that the Mediterranean is poorer in fish life than other seas, it should not be implied that fishermen of the region found their work unrewarding. On the contrary, fish provided an important part of the diet of ancient Greeks, Romans, and others. The species even of economic importance would make a long list, from the cartilaginous sharks and rays through the small, bony sardines, sprats, and anchovies, and the flying fish, to ample-sized tuna and swordfish. Bream, mackerel, wrasses, mullet, gurnard, and scorpion fish ranged the middle waters, while flounder, sole, and anglerfish lurked on the sea bottom.

The dolphin is a mammal, although ancients and moderns alike often refer to it as a fish. (Unfortunately for nomenclature, there is also a fish [*Coryphaena hippurus*] called, incorrectly, "dolphin"). The true dolphin was regarded as friendly to people and was credited with saving the lives of sailors. Other Mediterranean sea mammals are the monk seal and whales. To complete the vertebrates, there were numerous seabirds such as the cormorants, pelicans, terns, puffins, and grebes. The shearwater was regarded by the Greeks as sacred to Athena. One marine reptile, the sea turtle, was known, and for a time its image appeared on the coins of Aegina.

Among the crustaceans were shrimps, lobsters, and crabs. The numerous mollusks included monovalves like the abalone, limpet, triton, and the murex, or purple shell, the source of the Phoenician dye; also bivalves such as oysters, mussels, and clams. Aristotle noted a bivalve, the pinna, that lived in symbiosis with a small crustacean, the pinna-guardian. The octopus, squids, and nautilus (*Argonauta argo*) are among the cephalopods, as are mollusks.

Still lower in Aristotle's ladderlike arrangements of life forms would have been echinoderms: sea urchins and starfish; and coelenterates: jellyfish, sea anemones, sponges, and coral, some of which were confused with plants.

Among freshwater species the eels of Lake Copais were famous. Fish known in the still and running waters were, along with others, carp, perch, and catfish. The salmon-trout and some sturgeon are anadromous fish that spend most of their life cycles in the sea, but ascend rivers to spawn. The Nile, with its extensive reed and papyrus swamps, was an important freshwater ecosystem that nourished many fish, semiaquatic creatures such as the hippopotamus and crocodile, and the millions of water birds in the celebrated "land of whirring wings" (Isaiah 18:1).

Animals and Human Use

Human beings have found many uses for the animals of the Mediterranean zone. Prominent among these is domestication, but that subject belongs properly with agriculture. This section will be concerned with hunting, the Roman use of animals in the amphitheaters, divination by means of birds, and the inexorable process of extinction during the ancient period.

HUNTING. In the classical world, hunting was engaged in as a sport by the upper classes. Some species, like lions, had traditionally been the game of royalty. The common people hunted where it was allowed, or poached on the great estates and latifundia, to supplement their protein supply or to destroy the predators that raided the herds and the herbivores that plundered the gardens.

But hunting, historically, is not just an activity to be considered alongside other sports and pastimes. It was the aboriginal means of subsistence for all mankind, together with the closely related occupations, fishing and gathering. Hunting was a relic among the Greeks and Romans of the immensely long period during which their ancestors had lived in dependence upon wild animals and plants, before the appearance of domestication and agriculture. The attitudes of the early hunters strongly shaped Mediterranean religion, myth, and ritual.

To these primal hunters, the natural world was alive with spiritual powers. Animals and plants were beings whose cooperation was necessary for human survival. Thus a kind of "reverence for life" was embodied in the hunters' cultural attitudes. In their rituals, they propitiated both the animals themselves and their guardians, deities like Artemis (who was called "mistress of wild animals") and Pan. Long after the old hunting ways had altered, these gods were believed to protect animals in special circumstances. Agamemnon angered Artemis by shooting one of her sacred deer, and the goddess prevented him from sailing on his expedition to Troy until he had sacrificed his own daughter (Sophocles, *Electra* 563–572). Young Athenian maidens honored Artemis by dancing in bearskins. Xenophon advised hunters always to offer some of their prey to the same goddess (*Cynegeticus* 5.14).

Dio Chrysostom, around A.D. 100, described a group of hunters in the wilds of Euboea who still kept the virtues of their ancestors, untainted by the evils of the cities (*Euboean Discourse* 7). Even in Athens the old ways persisted in custom: a law required that anyone who killed a wolf would have to pay for its public burial.

But the surviving writings on hunting form a literary genre that celebrates the manly joys of the chase. These works bear the title *cynegeticus, -a,* because the sport was conducted with packs of dogs ("dog" in Greek is *cyon, cynos*). The species hunted were usually rabbits, deer, and boars, and the hunting was done with nets, snares, spears, and javelins. All this is far from the primal respect for the prey. Still, it is interesting to note that the Pythagoreans, who held that animals have souls like humans, forbade hunting and refused to associate with hunters because they kill creatures who are our relatives.

USE IN ENTERTAINMENT: THE ROMAN ARENA. The Latin word for hunting, *venatio,* referred also to a show held in the amphitheater in which animals were killed by gladiators armed in various ways, or were goaded to fight each other, or were set upon unarmed or lightly armed human beings. Phenomenal numbers of wildlife were killed in this way, often many hundreds in a single day. At the dedication of the Colosseum by Titus, 9,000 animals were destroyed in a hundred days, and Trajan's conquest over Dacia was celebrated by the slaughter of 11,000. Thus the *venationes* represent an important and very destructive use of animals by the Romans.

A vast apparatus existed to collect animals for the many amphitheaters of the Roman Empire. Private consortia made it a business, but were amply assisted by the army. Animals captured for the emperor's own shows were given priority, and the people of the towns through which they passed were required to house and feed them.

If an animal was particularly novel or rare, it might simply be exhibited, but most of the beasts were mutilated and killed. People of every class, from the commoner to the emperor himself, attended the games and indulged their taste for the sight of blood and suffering. Since they had to be visible to thousands of spectators, only the larger animals were displayed, but they were brought from incredible distances. Elephants, first brought to Italy by the invading army of Pyrrhus, were shown in the arena in 275 B.C. During the next century, lions, leopards, and ostriches were seen.

Before the end of the republic, hippopotamuses, rhinoceroses, and crocodiles were brought from Egypt, and Caesar sent a lynx from Gaul. Tigers from Gorgan (Hyrcania), the southern shore of the Caspian Sea, were famous, and Augustus had them brought from as far away as India. Nero flooded an arena so that he could show polar bears catching seals.

DIVINATION BY BIRDS. One of the uses of animals that seemed most important in the context of the traditional ancient religious view of nature—divination—hardly seems a "use" at all to scientifically oriented modern people. Since the ancients perceived the natural world as a scene of the activities of the gods that could be witnessed by human beings, animals and their actions could be studied in order to discern the intent of the divine powers. They regarded the concerns of the gods to be both similar to human concerns and entangled in the affairs of mortals, so the interpretation of signs and omens seemed to be a relevant and prudent pursuit.

Through the medium of natural events, the gods sent warnings to mortals in the form of signs that would prove useful to those who could understand them correctly. A most important way of explaining these was the "science" of augury—the interpretation of the flight and other actions of birds by especially trained seers called augurs. The augur took the auspices (from *avis*, bird, and *specere*, to look) by careful observation of avian behavior.

Eagles, hawks, and herons, singly or in groups, bearing prey or flying free, on the left or on the right, revealed the intentions of the gods through the world of natural phenomena. The augur observed them from a carefully marked spot (*templum, temenos*), facing to the north in Greece, to the south in Rome. Since signs coming from the east were regarded as favorable, the Greeks held the right hand to be the lucky direction, but the Romans preferred the left. Roman augurs divided birds into two types: the *alites*, such as hawks, vultures, and eagles, which gave their meaning by their behavior in flying; and the *oscines*, birds like ravens, crows, and owls, which could also emit meaningful calls.

There were skeptics about augury even in early times, but they were dismissed by most people as improvident fools. Eurymachus, in the *Odyssey*, is made to boast, "Many birds are there that fare to and fro under the rays of the sun, and not all are fateful" (2.181–182), when the learned warrior Halitherses had foretold from a battle between two eagles that Odysseus was on his way home. The outcome of this display of premature rationalism was that Eurymachus failed to heed the proper forewarning and was killed when the vengeful husband returned.

Wild birds presumably did not suffer when used for augury. Chickens and geese, kept in order to observe, for purposes of divination, the way they ate grain, were well fed if captive. But another usual method of observing the gods' will was haruspicy, the inspection of the livers of sacrificed domestic animals. And there were other uses of wild animals that were far more destructive.

THE PROCESS OF EXTINCTION. Readers of ancient literature often find mention of animals in places where they no longer exist. For example, Herodotus (7.126) says that when the Persian army brought camels into Greece in 480 B.C., lions descended from the mountains and attacked them. On the Aegean island of Thira, very early murals have been found of antelopes that today range only in East Africa. While one would not suggest that these animals ever lived on Thira, they must have been found much closer than Ethiopia.

In early times, elephants, antelopes, rhinoceroses, and zebras could be seen in North Africa, while the lion, leopard, and hyena roamed Mediterranean Europe. Ostriches inhabited Syria, and tigers haunted Iran.

Many of these creatures were extirpated in the ancient period, and almost all were seriously reduced in number. Hunters, freed from their primal respect for living things, destroyed the game, especially the large predators, beyond the point where animal populations could renew themselves. The simile of a lion being pursued by shepherds is familiar to readers of the *Iliad*. By the end of the Hellenistic age, there were no lions left in Greece, and wolves and jackals were rarely seen outside the mountains. Hunting reduced wild cattle, sheep, and goats to small relict bands, and eliminated them from some islands. The animal trade for the Roman *venationes* had a disastrous effect on the population of larger mammals, birds, and reptiles. The Hyrcanian tiger was no longer to be found, and hippopotamuses were evicted from the lower reaches of the Nile. The North African herds, once as plentiful as those of present-day Kenya, were devastated.

Professional hunters and trappers also provided wild meat for Mediterranean tables. Songbirds that Americans and English now regard as only ornamental were netted, cooked, and eaten in ancient Italy and Greece. Indeed, that custom has not ceased to the present day. Egyptian art shows marshes thronging with wild bird and animal life, but one searches for it today in vain. The richness of birdlife in more isolated reserves like Las Marismas of Spain and the French Camargue indicates something of what has been lost around the Mediterranean basin. Some species have disappeared entirely, while most others exist with reduced numbers in a portion of their former range. Ancient writers rejoiced at the extirpation of dangerous predatory animals, but could hardly have estimated the extent of other extinctions. Aristophanes did look at the process from an avian viewpoint in his comic play *Birds* and allowed his feathered actors to indict human beings for persecuting them.

HUMAN ECOLOGY AND THE FATE OF CIVILIZATIONS

The history of civilizations in Mediterranean lands can be read as an illustration of the fact that human events do not take place outside the context of the natural environment. Human societies have natural ecosystems as their setting, and cultures are in large measure the adaptations of human groups to the ecosystems within which they live. The health of the first depends on the health of the second. Civilizations flourish only as long as the ecosystems they depend upon. Nowhere is this clearer than in the Mediterranean basin and its environs, where many of the early civilized societies had their origin and ran their course. Many of these societies suffered fates that seem to have visible relationship to environmental factors. Much of the "Fertile Crescent" is desiccated and poor today, North African cities have been buried in the desert sands, and once-thriving ancient ports now lie under strata of erosional sediments. Thus, the question is reasonable: How far was environmental deterioration responsible for the decline of ancient communities, and to what extent were the actions of human beings instrumental in degrading the natural environment and causing the collapse of their own societies?

Human beings have always made changes in the natural environment; it is impossible to live without doing so. But some changes allow a functioning ecosystem to continue in balance with the human societies that depend on it, while changes of a different kind and magnitude hamper and abrade the natural systems that support all living things. Changes of the first kind make human life both possible and pleasant for extended periods of time, while changes of the second kind will eventually render human life unpleasant, difficult, and less sustainable. The history of ancient civilizations provides us with examples of both kinds of interactions.

The ancients often gave voice to an intuitive recognition of the reciprocity in which humankind and the natural world ought properly to support one another. As Xenophon expressed it, "Earth is a goddess and teaches justice to those who can learn, for the better she is served the more good things she gives in return" (*Household Management* 5.12). So a natural law was recognized in which, if human beings treated the world with "justice," they could expect prosperity, but if "unjustly," the environment would respond with disaster—floods and failed harvests being among the most often-mentioned results. The thought occurs in the earliest extant Greek literature (*Iliad* 16.384–392; *Odyssey* 19.109–114) and is repeated by the late Stoics of the Roman Empire. An example follows from the *Epinomis* (979 A–B) of uncertain authorship preserved in the Platonic corpus:

> It is thus that the earth conceives and yields her harvest so that food is provided for all the creatures, if wind and rains are neither unseasonable or excessive; but if anything goes amiss in the matter, it is not deity we should charge with the fault, but humanity, who have not ordered their life aright. (Translated by A. E. Taylor.)

It seemed to many ancient writers that the earth was growing less fertile and less able to sustain human beings. Hesiod recalled a mythical golden age in which crops grew by themselves and humans did not need to labor. There followed ages of silver, bronze, and iron, each less prosperous than the one before. Some, like Lucretius, believed this to be a natural process, in which the earth is growing older. But others, like Columella (*On Country Matters* [*De Re Rustica*], preface 1–3), maintained that environmental deterioration is due to human failures. Earth is not growing old, he said: the blame for her infertility lies in poor husbandry; declining crops are our fault, not hers. Thus earth is seen as responsive to human care or the lack of it, giving rich returns to those who treat her well and punishing those who are lazy or who weary her by trying to wrest from her what she is not ready to give. Environmental problems are, in this view, the passionless revenge of the earth on those who fail, through ignorance or avarice, to practice well the art of the attentive guardian of the land.

This ancient perception appears to be correct. The successive downfalls of former civilizations are associated with environmental collapse. There is a close interconnection between ruined cities and ruined land. Their association with each other is not an accident of history, but a pointed and ironic lesson in ecological imbalance.

The fact of environmental degradation in the Mediterranean basin is quite clear. Olive presses of Roman date have been found in desert areas of Tunisia, where today there are no trees at all, much less olives, in sight. The once-flourishing cedar forests of Lebanon are represented today by a few small groves. And the sediments of rapid erosion still exist and can be studied in the lowlands not far from Rome, and along coastlines all around the inland sea.

Certain prevalent problems of Greek and Roman times must be described in order to appreciate the importance of the environment in the decline and fall of classical civilization. The most noticeable of these is deforestation, with its attendant erosion, which was widespread and damaging in ancient times. Shortages of wood and rising prices were among the debilitating effects, but more important by far was the denudation of steep slopes and their resultant vulnerability to the often torrential rains of the Mediterranean winter. This effect was magnified by the universal grazing of domestic animals wherever there was vegetation, preventing the regrowth of trees and shrubs and periodically destroying the grass where there was overgrazing. Erosion swept away the useful soil, so that trees could not grow again in areas that had been forested before. The soil from the mountain slopes was deposited in low-lying areas, producing poorly drained, silt-choked marshlands. These areas became the haunt of malarial mosquitoes, which forced farm villages to relocate themselves on hills where possible.

A related problem affecting agricultural productivity is salinization. Waters used for irrigation have some salt content, and this is higher when erosion is taking place in the watersheds from which they flow. As evaporation takes place in the fields, the salt is concentrated in the soil, gradually making it more saline. This problem is particularly noticeable in large, flat areas with warm, dry climates where irrigation is practiced, such as the Tigris-Euphrates valley and Al-Faiyūm (Fayum) oasis of Egypt, which is below sea level. In some limited areas it becomes so severe that food crops cannot grow.

Greek and Roman farmers knew agricultural remedies for problems like siltation, salinization, and soil exhaustion through the leaching of essential minerals. But they could not always apply them due to political and military pressures. The tax system bore most heavily on the agricultural sector of the economy, whether the levies were collected in coin or in kind. Farmers were most often pressed into the army, so the manpower available to care for the land declined. Then the theater of war was often the countryside; farm families were killed, their property requisitioned by the troops, their crops, buildings, and terraces destroyed. Deliberate anti-ecological warfare was sometimes practiced in an effort to deny food and other resources to the enemy. Sometimes such damage could be repaired, but often the ecosystems were not given the time to recover. All of these pressures bore more severely on the small farmers, who were ruined and became dependents of great landowners whose large estates, often located in several distant places, survived more successfully.

A typical small Mediterranean farm within the larger landscape, as described by Cato, say, or Pliny, was a relatively complex ecosystem. Many different crops were grown in various parts of the acreage, depending on topography, soil, and exposure. Portions were left in forest as woodlots, and rows of trees were planted for shelter and other purposes. But the tendency in some periods, including later antiquity, was to amass land in larger estates under single ownership. Particularly in Italy and Spain, grazing replaced farming. Where grain was raised, it was planted in vast stretches, a practice called monoculture. All these practices tended to create simplified ecosystems that were vulnerable to factors such as insects and diseases of plants and animals.

The extinction of many species of animals and plants was noted above. This has a negative effect on the total organic system of the environment. Generally speaking, a complex ecosystem is more stable than a simple one. This is because an ecosystem with many species has many more ways of reasserting its balance if it is subjected to stress. As one species after another is removed, the total complex becomes more liable to disaster. Thus by killing off many animals, the Greeks and Romans were unwittingly undermining their economies. This was true even when the species, in a deceptively simple view, seemed harmful. Wolves, foxes, wildcats, and other predators were hunted out because they sometimes raided domestic animals. But Aristotle (*History of Animals* [*Historia Animalium*] 6.36.580) and other ancient writers recorded disastrous plagues of mice that the predators were unable to control, though these writers did not make the connection between the plagues and the reduced number of predators.

Several of the factors noted above affected agricultural productivity in the ancient Mediterranean, where the economy was based on the agrarian sector. The inevitable result of the human failure to support nature was that nature could support fewer human beings. Population decline was a continuing problem in later antiquity. Roman emperors periodically tried to counter it by making marriage and childbearing mandatory. Declining population meant fewer farm workers, so that reductions in population and agricultural production tended to be synergistic. Diocletian's edicts on occupations, requiring men to provide sons to fill their positions, and on prices, setting maximums particularly for food, indicate what was happening at the end of the third century A.D.: food was becoming scarcer, prices were rising, and there was a shortage of labor. Although constant warfare and periodic plagues were also to blame, the chronic agricultural decline was an ineluctable factor deriving from environmental causes.

Industry, although it was not as large a part of the total economy as agriculture, did have important environmental effects in Greek and Roman times. Herodotus (6.46) remarked that a mine operated by the Thasians had thrown a whole mountain upside down, and scars left by ancient mines are still visible today. Mining and smelting operations did more than lay waste to local areas, however. The fuel needs of a large operation like the Athenian silver mine and smelter at Laurium or the Roman iron center at Populonia would consume annually the growth of wood provided by an average forest of a million acres. There were many such centers, and one has to add to their fuel demands the great amounts of wood and charcoal required by the pottery industry.

Pollution was produced by ancient industry. Its extent and importance is a matter of controversy. That dangerous smoke was produced by some operations is a matter of record; Strabo (*Geography* 3.2.8, C147) observed that silver-smelting furnaces in Iberia were built with high chimneys to carry the deadly smoke away from the workers. Lead is the predominant metal in silver ore; it and other poisonous elements like mercury and arsenic were present in industrial processes such as the working of other metallic ores, pottery, leather, and textiles. Workers in these materials were notably subject to poisoning. It is less clear how much the general population was exposed to toxic substances, but it is a public health factor of possibly major proportions. Lead, or silver with high lead content, was used in utensils, dishes, and cooking pots. Sweeteners, jams, and fish sauces contained a high concentration of lead compounds. Water was often conducted through lead pipes or aqueducts sealed with lead, and acidic water can be contaminated by lead. Studies of the ice caps have shown that lead in the atmosphere increased during Roman times. Bones from Roman burials exhibit a variable, but often very high, lead content. The effects of lead poisoning include interference with reproduction, physical weakness, and dulling of the intellectual faculties, and these are cumulative, slow to develop, long lasting, and not easily seen to be connected with the cause. In addition, mercury was commonly used in gold refining, and arsenic appeared in pigments and medicines. It is likely that large numbers of people in the Roman Empire, at least, suffered from varying degrees of environmental poisoning produced by industrial processes.

The poor quality of the urban environment is a subject of frequent comment, particularly by Roman poets of the early empire. Noise pollution and smoke receive the most notice. Air pollution from smoke and dust was undoubtedly bad in the larger cities, judging from the experience of less industrialized cities in the twentieth century as well as contemporary ancient comment. Food was cooked, and rooms were commonly heated, by open wood or charcoal fires. Cities of Roman date had huge public baths whose furnaces and hypocausts were heated with prodigious amounts of fuel. Light was provided by smoky lamps and torches. The air was so polluted in Rome that those who could afford it tried to find relief by frequent trips to the country, in the right direction, and some commented that people coming back from the countryside would lose their tan in smoggy Rome within a few days. Juvenal, in his *Third Satire,* expanded the list of urban ills, complaining of traffic congestion, fires, public works projects that destroyed natural beauty, chamber pots emptied out of upper-story windows, and ever-increasing crime and vandalism.

Garbage and sewage disposal presented a serious health problem in ancient cities. The larger cities had sewers like Rome's *cloaca maxima,* which emptied into the river Tiber, an efficient arrangement except when the not uncommon floods, exacerbated by the deforestation of the Tiber watershed, backed the effluence up into the city. It was said that at these times, the drain in the floor of the Pantheon looked like a fountain. Athens diverted some of her sewage to fertilize the fields in the plain of Attica. The materials collected in latrines were sometimes used in tanneries. Many cities had carts to carry the worst of the garbage outside the walls, but much of it collected in the streets. Pompeii installed "stepping stones" so that pedestrians could cross the muck-filled avenues. The debris of living is, of course, one of the reasons that ancient cities gradually rose above their surroundings on elevations of human origin. The effects on the health of urban populations, with water pollution, vermin, and diseases, are evident. Modern studies show that large cities do not replace their own populations, but to maintain their size are required to draw on in-migration from the surrounding countryside, and this must in all likelihood have been true of ancient cities as well. And the sanitary conditions must have favored the spread of the plagues that swept across the Mediterranean world from time to time.

The conclusion that must be drawn from all the evidence that survives in written records, archaeological sites, and the revealing Mediterranean landscape itself is that environmental factors were of critical importance in the decline of classical civilization. The developments mentioned above weakened the societies, depleting their natural and human resources. Their effects were felt early, but were cumulative, reaching a devastating level by the time of the late Roman Empire.

No people could prosper after their forests had been in large measure cut down, the soil on which they depended for food eroded and salinized, their health undermined by the spreading of malarial marshes, poisonous substances, and the insanitary conditions of urban crowding, their countryside devastated by civil wars and barbarian incursions. It is important to recognize that all these factors were not equally present in all parts of the Mediterranean or in all periods. Industrial pollution, for example, probably reached its height during the second century A.D. in Rome, where at the same time public health measures were as efficient as they ever became in the ancient world. For some locales and in some periods there is enough evidence available to form a confident opinion of what was occurring; for most times and places all too little is known. But further study of this whole question will be rewarding, and it is a question of historical causation that can no longer be ignored.

Since people are not unreasonable enough to want to destroy their own societies and to make life hard for themselves, we can well ask why the ancients acted in ways that produced erosion, exhaustion of resources, debilitating pollution, the spread of disease, food shortages, and ruinous inflation. There is no simple reason, but several parts of a complex answer can be suggested.

The general attitude of the Greeks and Romans toward the natural environment was in earliest times one of worship. Their gods were gods of nature, and were seen as protecting nature from major human injury. But this early worship of nature was subjected to the often skeptical philosophical questioning of the Greeks. Aristotle, most prominently, declared that the highest purpose of everything in the greater order of nature was to serve humankind (*Politics* 1. 3.7). And a certain secular practicality, which did not begin with the Romans but was typical of them, looked at the physical world primarily in terms of its economic value and avoided thinking about the gods at all. Finally, Christianity rose to dominate the last centuries of the ancient world and, while affirming that the natural world is the creation of God, denied it any intrinsic spiritual value. Thus, at few times was there an attitude that would have encouraged a vigorous attempt to guard the integrity of natural ecosystems and to live in balance with them.

The Greeks in particular were interested in learning what makes the world of nature work. Their philosophers and scientists developed many of the ideas that later combined to form the science of ecology. Aristotle himself was important in this way, as was his brilliant student, Theophrastus. But observational and experimental science did not advance far enough in the ancient world to enable a sound theoretical understanding of the web of life. A good practical grasp of what needs to be done existed in agriculture and, perhaps to a lesser extent, in pastoralism and forestry. But economic, political, and military factors intervened to prevent a kind of trial-and-error modus vivendi with the earth. In particular, a balance with nature is a condition of peace and is easily upset by war.

In order to be able to act ecologically, a society must have an appropriate technology. To some extent the ancients did; at least they lacked the more destructive modern inventions. But if their technology was less advanced, it still made major impacts in the long run. The dependence on wood and its derivative, charcoal, as the only major fuel source meant a drain on the forests that alternative technologies might have avoided. Water and wind power were not developed in a major way until the medieval period. Ability to interact positively with the environment also requires a degree of social organization and control. This is true because the community's environmental ends may involve sacrifices on the part of its individual members, sacrifices that they would not make without some degree of social encouragement or coercion. That the ancients had such social control is clear from the works they constructed, including great aqueducts, canals, and roads. These works enabled cities to reach out and draw resources from more distant ecosystems. Technology and social organization can be directed either to conserve or destroy ecosystems. Unfortunately, it seems that their dominant tendency is toward destruction, and only if their use is informed by knowledge and motivated by a positive environmental ethics can this tendency be overcome. Since the peoples of the classical world lacked these for the most part, they set in motion a process best described as the wearing away of the heartlands of Western culture. There was a deterioration at the same time of both environment and people, and it seems clear that it was caused by human beings; that is, to use a term derived from the Greek, it was anthropogenic.

BIBLIOGRAPHY

SOURCES

Herodotus, *The Histories,* A. D. Godley, trans. (1921; repr. 1963); Homer, *Odyssey,* A. T. Murray, trans. (1919); Lucretius, *The Way Things Are: De Rerum Natura,* Rolfe Humphries, trans. (1968); Plato, including *Epinomis,* in *The Collected Dialogues of Plato,* Edith Hamilton and Huntington Cairns, ed., A. E. Taylor, trans. (1961); Gaius

Julius Solinus, *Collectanea Rerum Memorabilium*, Theodor Mommsen, ed. (1587, reproduced in facsimile 1955), A. Golding, trans. (1887; repr. 1955); Thucydides, *History of the Peloponnesian War*, Charles Forster Smith, trans. (1920; repr. 1965); Vergil, *Aeneid*, Frank O. Copley, trans. (1965); Xenophon, *Oeconomicus (Household Management)*, E. C. Marchant, trans. (1923; repr. 1968).

STUDIES

The Mediterranean

Pierre Birot, Pierre Gabert, and Jean Dresch, *La méditerranée et le Moyen-Orient*, 2 vols., rev. ed. (1964); Ernle Bradford, *Mediterranean: Portrait of a Sea* (1971); John Bradford, *Ancient Landscapes in Europe and Asia* (1957); Fernand Braudel, *The Mediterranean and the Mediterranean World in the Age of Philip II*, 2 vols., Siân Reynolds, trans. (1972); Richard Carrington, *The Mediterranean: Cradle of Western Culture* (1971); Max Cary, *The Geographic Background of Greek and Roman History* (1949); Michael Grant, *The Ancient Mediterranean* (1969); Emil Ludwig, *The Mediterranean: Saga of a Sea*, Barrows Mussey, trans. (1942); Jasper More, *The Mediterranean* (1956); John L. Myres, *Mediterranean Culture* (1944); Ehsan Naraghi et al., *Bassin Méditerranéen et Proche-Orient* (1961); Marion I. Newbigin, *The Mediterranean Lands* (1924).

Alfred Philippson, *Das Mittelmeergebiet: Seine geographische und kulturelle Eigenart*, 2d ed. (1907); John H. Rose, *The Mediterranean in the Ancient World* (1933); Ellen Churchill Semple, *The Geography of the Mediterranean Region: Its Relation to Ancient History* (1931); André Siegfried, *The Mediterranean*, Doris Hemming, trans. (1948); Donald S. Walker, *The Mediterranean Lands*, 3d ed. (1965).

Regional Studies. James M. Houston, *The Western Mediterranean World: An Introduction to Its Regional Landscapes* (1964); Marion I. Newbigin, *Southern Europe*, 3d ed. (1949); Catherine D. Smith, *Western Mediterranean Europe* (1979).

Individual Countries or Provinces. Thomas Ashby, *The Roman Campagna in Classical Times*, new ed. (1970); Arnold Toynbee, *Hannibal's Legacy: The Hannibalic War's Effects on Roman Life*, 2 vols. (1965); Henry F. Tozer, *Lectures on the Geography of Greece* (1882; repr. 1974); John B. Ward-Perkins, *Landscape and History in Central Italy* (1964).

History of Geography. Lionel Casson, *Travel in the Ancient World* (1974); F. Lukermann, "The Concept of Location in Classical Geography," in *Annals of the Association of American Geographers*, **51** (1961); James O. Thomson, *History of Ancient Geography* (1948); Henry F. Tozer, *A History of Ancient Geography* (1897; 2d ed. 1964).

The Land

Derek V. Ager and M. Brooks, eds., *Europe from Crust to Core* (1977); Brian T. Bunting, *The Geography of Soil* (1965); John F. Dewey, Walter C. Pitman III, William B. F. Ryan, and Jean Bonnin, "Plate Tectonics and the Evolution of the Alpine System," in *Geological Society of America Bulletin*, **84**, no. 10 (1973); David Neev et al., *The Geology of the Southeastern Mediterranean Sea* (1976); Payson D. Sheets and Donald K. Grayson, eds., *Volcanic Activity and Human Ecology* (1979); Peter Sonnenfeld, ed., *Tethys: The Ancestral Mediterranean* (1981); Brian F. Windley, *The Evolving Continents* (1977).

The Sea

Michelle Bernard, "Recent Advances in Research on the Zooplankton of the Mediterranean Sea," in *Oceanography and Marine Biology*, **5** (1967); Margaret Deacon, *Scientists and the Sea, 1650–1900* (1971), 3–19; Valentin Masachs Alavedra, *Contribution à la connaissance des régimes fluviaux méditerranéens* (1949); Mary Sears and Daniel Merriman, *Oceanography: The Past* (1980), 750–779; Daniel J. Stanley, ed., *The Mediterranean Sea: A Natural Sedimentation Laboratory* (1972); T. Sankey, "The Formation of Deep Water in the Northwestern Mediterranean," in *Progress in Oceanography*, **6** (1973); George Wüst, "On the Vertical Circulation of the Mediterranean Sea," in *Journal of Geophysical Research*, **66**, no. 10 (1961).

Freshwater Hydrography. Cyril E. N. Bromehead, "The Early History of Water Supply," in *Geographical Journal*, **99** (1942); Grahame Clark,

"Water in Antiquity," in *Antiquity*, **18** (1944); Oswald A. W. Dilke and Margaret S. Dilke, "Terracina and the Pomptine Marshes," in *Greece and Rome*, 2d ser., 8 (1961); J. Eubanks, "Navigation on the Tiber," in *Classical Journal*, **25** (1930); Sheldon Judson, "Erosion and Deposition of Italian Stream Valleys During Historic Time," in *Science*, **140** (1963), "Stream Changes During Historic Time in East-Central Sicily," in *American Journal of Archaeology*, **67** (1963), and "Erosion Rates Near Rome, Italy," in *Science*, **160** (1968); Joël C. Le Gall, *Le Tibre dans l'antiquité* (1953); Rushdi Said, *The Geological Evolution of the River Nile* (1981); Leonard J. Snell, "Effects of Sedimentation on Ancient Cities of the Aegean Coast, Turkey," in *Bulletin of the International Association of Scientific Hydrology*, 8, no. 4 (1963); Claudio Vita-Finzi, "Roman Dams in Tripolitania," in *Antiquity*, **35** (1961).

Climate

Edgar Aubert de La Rüe, *Man and the Winds*, Madge E. Thompson, trans. (1955); Erwin R. Biel, *Climatology of the Mediterranean Area* (1944); Keith Boucher, *Global Climate* (1975); Wilfrid G. Kendrew, *The Climates of the Continents*, 5th ed. (1961); Evelyn L. H. Martinengo-Cesaresco, *The Outdoor Life in Greek and Roman Poets* (1911); Masatoshi M. Yoshino, ed., *Local Wind Bora* (1976).
Paleoclimatology. John A. Allan, ed., *The Sahara: Ecological Change and Early Economic History* (1981); Karl W. Butzer, *Environment and Archeology*, 2d ed. (1971), and *Early Hydraulic Civilization in Egypt: A Study in Cultural Ecology* (1976); M. Caputo and L. Pieri, "Eustatic Sea Variation in the Last 2000 Years in the Mediterranean," in *Journal of Geophysical Research*, **81**, no. 33 (1976); Nicholas C. Flemming, "Holocene Earth Movements and Eustatic Sea Level Change in the Peloponnese," in *Nature*, **217** (1968), 1031–1032, and *Archaeological Evidence for Eustatic Change of Sea Level and Earth Movements in the Western Mediterranean During the Last 2000 Years* (1969); H. H. Lamb, *The Changing Climate* (1966), *Climate: Present, Past, and Future*, 2 vols. (1972–1977), and *Climate, History, and the Modern World* (1982); P. A. Pirazzoli, "Sea Level Variation in the Northwest Mediterranean During Roman Times," in *Science*, **194** (1976); T. M. L. Wigley, M. J. Ingram, and G. Farmer, eds., *Climate and History: Studies in Past Climates and Their Impact on Man* (1981).

Trees and Plants

General. Francesco Di Castri and Harold A. Mooney, eds., *Mediterranean Type Ecosystems: Origin and Structure* (1973); L. Emberger, "La végétation de la région méditerranéenne," in *Revue générale botanique*, **32** (1930); G. Kuhnholtz-Lordat, "La *silva*, les *saltus*, et l'*ager* de Garrigue," in *Annales de l'École Nationale d'Agriculture*, **26** (1967); Russell Meiggs, *Trees and Timber in the Ancient Mediterranean World* (1982); Oleg Polunin and Anthony Huxley, *Flowers of the Mediterranean* (1965); Martin Albert Rikli, *Das Pflanzenkleid der Mittelmeerländer*, 3 vols. (1943–1948); UNESCO, *Mediterranean Forests and Maquis: Ecology, Conservation, and Management* (1977).
Floras of Individual Countries. Peter Hadland Davis, ed., *Flora of Turkey and the East Aegean Islands*, 5 vols. (1965–1970); Michael Even-Ari, Leslie Shanan, and Naphtali Tadmor, *The Negev* (1971); Kōnstantinos N. Goulimes and Niki A. Goulandris, *Wild Flowers of Greece*, W. T. Stearn, ed. (1968); Jens Holmboe, *Studies on the Vegetation of Cyprus* (1914); P. Marres, "Les Garrigues languedociennes: Le milieu et l'homme," in *Actes du 86ème Congrès Nationale des Sociétés Savantes* (1961), 201–216; Oleg Polunin and B. E. Smythies, *Flowers of South-West Europe: A Field Guide* (1973); G. Schweinfurth, "The Flora of Ancient Egypt," in *Nature*, **28–29** (1883–1884); Y. Tchou, "Études écologiques et phytosociologiques sur les forêts riveraines du Bas-Languedoc," in *Vegetatio*, **1** (1948); William B. Turrill, *The Plant-Life of the Balkan Peninsula* (1929); Michael Zohary, *Plant Life of Palestine* (1962), and *Geobotanical Foundations of the Middle East*, 2 vols. (1973).
Forest History. H. J. Beug, "On the Forest History of the Dalmation Coast," in *Review of Paleobotany and Palynology*, **2** (1967); W. C. Brice, "The History of Forestry in Turkey," in *Revue de la Faculté des Sciences Forestières de l'Université d'Istanbul*, série A, tome V (1955); J. Donald

Hughes, "How the Ancients Viewed Deforestation," in *Journal of Field Archaeology*, **10** (1983); J. Donald Hughes and J. V. Thirgood, "Deforestation, Erosion, and Forest Management in Ancient Greece and Rome," in *Journal of Forest History*, **26** (1982); Allan Chester Johnson, "Ancient Forests and Navies," in *Transactions and Proceedings of the American Philological Association*, **58** (1927); Marvin W. Mikesell, "Deforestation in Northern Morocco," in *Science*, **132** (1960), and "The Deforestation of Mount Lebanon," in *Geographical Review*, **59** (1969); H. August Seidensticker, *Waldgeschichte des Alterthums*, 2 vols. (1886); James V. Thirgood, *Man and the Mediterranean Forest: A History of Resource Depletion* (1981); H. von Trotha Treyden, "Die Entwaldung der Mittelmeerländer," in *Petermanns Geographische Mitteilungen*, **62** (1916).

Sacred Sites and Enclosures

Carl G. W. Boetticher, *Der Baumkultus der Hellenen nach den gottesdienstlichen Gebräuchen und den überlieferten Bildwerken dargestellt* (1856); Harald Othmar Lenz, *Botanik der alten Griechen und Römer* (1859; repr. 1966); Wilhelm Mannhardt, *Antike Wald- und Feldkulte* (1877); Vincent Scully, *The Earth, the Temple, and the Gods: Greek Sacred Architecture* (1962).

Animal Life

Helena Gamulin-Brida, "The Benthic Fauna of the Adriatic Sea," in *Oceanography and Marine Biology*, **5** (1967); Harry M. Hubbell, "Ptolemy's Zoo," in *Classical Journal*, **31** (1935); Denison B. Hull, *Hounds and Hunting in Ancient Greece* (1964); Otto Keller, *Die Antike Tierwelt*, 2 vols. (1909–1913); Otto Körner, *Die Homerische Thierwelt* (1880); J. M. Pérès, "The Mediterranean Benthos," in *Oceanography and Marine Biology*, **5** (1967); John Pollard, *Birds in Greek Life and Myth* (1977); Thomas Fletcher Royds, *The Beasts, Birds, and Bees of Virgil* (1914); Joceylin M. C. Toynbee, *Animals in Roman Life and Art* (1973); Wilhelm Wegener, *Die Tierwelt bei Homer* (1887).

Human Ecology

Lester J. Bilsky, ed., *Historical Ecology: Essays on Environment and Social Change* (1980); Tom Dale and Vernon Gill Carter, *Topsoil and Civilization* (1955); Bruce Drewitt, "Ecological Factors in the Rise of Civilization," in *Kroeber Anthropological Society Papers*, **27** (1962); Clarence J. Glacken, *Traces on the Rhodian Shore: Nature and Culture in Western Thought from Ancient Times to the End of the Eighteenth Century* (1967); J. Donald Hughes, *Ecology in Ancient Civilizations* (1975), "Ecology in Ancient Greece," in *Inquiry*, **18** (1975), "Early Greek and Roman Environmentalists," in *The Ecologist*, **11** (1981), and "Gaia: Environmental Problems in Chthonic Perspective," in *Environmental Review*, **6** (1982); Edward Hyams, *Soil and Civilization* (1952).

Walter C. Lowdermilk, "Conquest of the Land through 7,000 Years," in *U.S.D.A., Information Bulletin*, **99** (1941), and "Lessons from the Old World to the Americas in Land Use," in *Smithsonian Report for 1943* (1944); Mikhail I. Rostovtzeff, *The Social and Economic History of the Hellenistic World*, 3 vols. (1941), and *The Social and Economic History of the Roman Empire*, 2 vols., 2d ed. (1957); William L. Thomas, Jr., ed., *Man's Role in Changing the Face of the Earth* (1956); Cedric A. Yeo, "The Overgrazing of Ranch-Lands in Ancient Italy," in *Transactions and Proceedings of the American Philological Association*, **79** (1948).

POPULATION

Races and Physical Types in the Classical World

PEYTON RANDOLPH HELM

INTRODUCTION

The Concept of Race and the Evidence for Human Variation in Antiquity

The first, essential task for the student of physical variation among ancient peoples is to appreciate the limitations of the word "race" and to achieve, if possible, a workable definition of this problematic term. If it is used to classify subgroups of the species *Homo sapiens* on the basis of physical appearance, "race" must always be clearly distinguished from other criteria used to classify human beings—criteria such as language, material culture, political allegiance, or other bases for affiliation—since all of these represent independent variables whose geographical boundaries need not be congruent with the territory occupied by a particular "race." This presents special difficulties for ancient historians, since most of the names commonly used to designate ancient peoples are linguistic, political, cultural, or archaeological rather than racial.

Even if this word of caution is rigorously heeded, it is difficult to formulate a workable, useful definition of the concept of "race." Yehudi Cohen (1968) summarized the problem in these terms:

> The concept of race is nothing more than a means for classifying people into different genetic populations. How many genes should be used as a basis for classification? One? If only one, which gene should serve as the criterion for classification? . . . Two or three? Which two or three? And why any particular two or three to the exclusion of others?

Carleton Coon, one of the great defenders of the concept, defined "race" in his *Races of Europe* as "a group of people who possess the majority of their physical characteristics in common." Yet even Coon confessed that there were problems with such a definition, since the different physical traits associated with a particular "race" might have different patterns of distribution. As Bruce G. Trigger observed in 1978:

> While one characteristic may increase in frequency from north to south, another will do so from west to east, or from the center to the periphery of its range. This happens because

natural selection operates upon specific genes, and individual characteristics are selected for or against at different rates and for different reasons in accordance with a wide range of environmental variations.

Defining a specific population as a "race" consequently requires the arbitrary application of two criteria: the selection of genetic traits that will "define" the race, and the imposition of (more or less artificial) geographical boundaries on the distribution of those traits. The dubious validity of such an approach has induced growing numbers of anthropologists to discard "race" as a conceptual tool.

The challenge is even greater for ancient historians because of the scant evidence for ancient human variation. Physical remains are sparse for most times and places and entirely missing for others, depending on such factors as climate, soil conditions, burial customs, and the luck of the spade. When physical remains do survive, they are usually restricted to skeletal material and tell us little about such vital characteristics as pigmentation, eye color, color and texture of hair, and other variables that are obviously necessary for any realistic assessment of racial identity.

Furthermore, ancient historians almost never have the unbroken chronological sequences of skeletal remains from contiguous geographical areas that would be necessary to trace the distribution of particular traits over space and through time. Those conclusions that can be drawn from cranial and skeletal evidence require precise measurements of the remains—measurements that were often not taken or reliably recorded for many early finds. Because of constraints such as these, most anthropologists have abandoned the field of race history.

When the ancient historian turns to literary testimony for evidence of racial classifications, he merely delegates responsibility for selecting "definitive" physical traits to his sources, a risky procedure given the eclectic interests of ancient ethnographers, geographers, and other classical writers who comment on "foreign" (non-Roman or non-Greek) peoples. This is not to say that classical writers were uninterested in foreign peoples. Indeed, even our earliest sources, the poems of Homer and Hesiod, note such far-flung peoples as the Scythians of the south Russian steppe (Hesiod, frag. 150.15–16), the Ethiopians, Pygmies, Libyans, and other peoples of Africa (Homer, *Iliad* 1.423; 3.6; 23.206; *Odyssey* 1.22–23; 4.84–85; 5.282, 287; 14.295; Hesiod, frag. 150.9,15,18), and perhaps even the dark-skinned inhabitants of India (if Homer's eastern Ethiopians are to be equated with Indians). Nonetheless, our earliest sources reveal little about the physical characteristics of these peoples, except what we can glean from the descriptive names the Greeks occasionally attached to them. The name Ethiopian, for instance, means "burnt face"; the ethnic designation Melanes means "blacks." In some cases, however, such made-up names referred not to physical traits of the foreigners, but to other peculiarities of their ways of life, for example the diet of the Thracian Hippomolgoi (drinkers of mare's milk) in *Iliad* 13.5.

We can observe, however, that classical writers never categorized peoples by race. Indeed, language did not support such a system of classification. The available words, Greek *ethnos* and Latin *gens, genus, natio,* implied much more than physical type. The classical ethnographers and geographers display a wide-ranging curiosity about the inhabitants of foreign lands, but physical appearance was not, apparently, of great interest to them unless such peoples were spectacularly different from themselves. The 323 extant fragments of Hekataios' sixth-century B.C. *Journey Round the World (Periegesis)* mention the Celts, Libyans, Ethiopians, Egyptians, Scythians, Syrians, Persians, and Indians, and comment on such diverse topics as dress, diet, flora and fauna, topography, and the etymology of place names. Yet the fragments preserve not a single reference to the physical traits of any of these peoples. The ethnographic digressions in Herodotus' *Histories* (written in the second half of the fifth century B.C.) are among our most valuable sources for the ancient peoples of Europe, Asia, and Africa. Yet Herodotus is clearly much more interested in such topics as climate, religion, burial customs, diet, sexual mores, marriage customs, dress and hairstyle, manner of swearing oaths, and local legends. He comments only occasionally on the genetically determined traits of the peoples he describes. A clue to Herodotus' thinking on the traits that distinguished one people *(ethnos)* from another may be found in the speech he attributes to the Athenians (8.144.2), when they summarize what sets Greeks apart from Persians: "one blood, one language, common shrines and sacrifices to the gods, and a shared way of life." Physical type was only one of several criteria.

The same orientation can be seen in the first-century *Geography* of Strabo, a work based more on library research than on exploration and firsthand observation, which attempted to collate and assess all geographical information about the known world down to that time. Despite his declaration (4.1.1) that "the geographer should relate whatever physical and ethnic distinctions are worthy of note," Strabo does not distinguish peoples on the basis of physical type. Indeed, he rarely records such information and is much more interested in the names of tribes and cities, the location of harbors, relative distances between points, the courses of rivers, natural resources, flora and fauna, social organization and local customs. Perhaps it is fair to conclude that his interests reflect the kinds of information preserved in the earlier works he consulted.

This is not to say that we are completely ignorant of the physical appearance of ancient peoples. In addition to the scraps provided by geographers and ethnographers, there are valuable references to be gleaned from accounts of military campaigns (for instance Arrian's *The March Up Country* [*Anabasis*] or Caesar's *The Gallic War* [*De Bello Gallico*]), from more general histories (such as Diodorus Siculus' *Historical Library* [*Biblioteca Historica*], Livy's *History of Rome* [*Ab Urbe Condita*], Velleius Paterculus' *Roman Histories* [*Historiae Romanae*], Tacitus' *Annals,* and the *History* [*Rerum Gestarum Libri*] of Ammianus Marcellinus), from scientific works (such as Pliny the Elder's voluminous *Natural History* [*Historia Naturalis*], the Hippocratic *Airs, Waters, Places,* and the works of Galen), from poetry (Juvenal, Martial, Lucan, and others), and from other sources. Still, such information is scattered and less complete than we would prefer, and it hardly provides the basis for a comprehensive or scientific analysis of ancient races.

The testimony of ancient sculpture, metalwork, and vase painting sometimes provides a valuable supplement to the literary sources, but ancient art also has its limitations. In many cases, stylistic convention rather than actual fact influenced the depiction of human form and physiognomy. For example, Phoenician and North Syrian artists portrayed the human figure in such different ways that the naive observer might well assume that different races were being depicted. In the case of neo-Assyrian art, where a variety of foreign peoples are depicted within a single stylistic discipline, the sculptors relied on differences in national costume and hairstyle to indicate variety. The same problem is sometimes encountered in Attic black-figured vase paintings depicting Thracians, Scythians, and Persians. Nevertheless, ancient artistic evidence occasionally provides information that we would not otherwise have.

To summarize, it should be clear that the most a modern scholar can hope to provide is an overview of the differences in physical types observed by ancient authors and artists, set against the backdrop of skeletal (usually cranial) variation, which for the most part developed before the beginning of the Iron Age.

THE PHYSICAL REMAINS

If we look for the original ancestors of the Iron Age peoples of North Africa, western Asia and Europe, the search takes us back as far as the Upper Paleolithic period (when the predecessors of modern man replaced the earlier Neanderthal population) and continues through the Mesolithic, Neolithic, Chalcolithic, and early Bronze Ages. From the later Bronze Age down to the beginning of the Iron Age, the popularity of cremation burial makes analysis of physical remains difficult.

The evidence for these periods is purely skeletal, and the racial classifications for such early peoples are based on the relative dimensions of their skulls; in scientific terms this is called "cranial morphology." As remarked earlier, such evidence is of limited value because the osteological evidence, based on the study of bones, is not a reliable guide to other important genetic characteristics.

Physical anthropologists distinguish three major physical types in the prehistory of West Asian, North African, and European peoples: the Mediterranean type, characterized by a long-headed (dolichocephalic) skull, short to moderate stature, and sturdy build; the Nordic type, also dolichocephalic, but of taller stature; and the Alpine type, broad- or round-headed (brachycephalic) with moderate stature and sturdy build. In addition they distinguish various skull types of medium (mesocephalic) proportions, including the Armenoid and Dinaric types.

It should be stressed that these designations do not, so far as we can tell, represent originally distinct races, but are better conceived as categories established by physical anthropologists on the basis of ideal types for the classification of human remains. Furthermore, the distribution of osteological features (and of other genetically determined traits) cannot be assumed to reflect population movements. Mixture, distribution, and change are caused not only by the migration of peoples, but also by local hybridization and mutation and by the dominance of specific genes. The tendency toward increasing brachycephaly and taller stature in the populations of prehistoric and Iron Age Europe seems to have resulted from a combination of such factors.

With these cautionary remarks in mind, we should not be too surprised to discover that even in the Paleolithic to Bronze Age populations of North Africa, western Asia, and Europe heterogeneity of cranial type is the rule rather than the exception, and that it is difficult to draw even the most general conclusions about the "original homes" of different cranial types. Thus, surveys of early physical remains in the ancient Near East indicate the wide distribution of a dolichocephalic "proto-Mediterranean" type, accompanied at many sites by a second long-headed variety that has been variously dubbed "Eurafrican" and "proto-Nordic." Brachycephals characterized by de Vaux as of "the Armenoid or Anatolian race" are attested in the northern Neger, the coastal plain of Palestine, and the Judaean desert caves as early as the mid fourth millennium B.C., and Alpine types begin to appear alongside the more common dolichocephalic skulls in Syria-Palestine, Anatolia, and Iran by the beginning of the Chalcolithic (*ca.* 3600–3300 B.C.).

The population of Europe was, in osteological terms, already physically diverse by the Aurignacian (Upper Paleolithic) period. The earliest population seems to have been dolichocephalic, but by the Neolithic, if not earlier, brachycephalic Alpine types had infiltrated along the central mountain axis, creating what has been referred to as the "Alpine wedge." To the south of this zone, the dolichocephalic Mediterranean type predominates; to the north, the long-headed Nordic type is more frequent. Still, there was so much intermingling of genetic types that by the Iron Age—that is, by about 1200 B.C.—virtually all of the regions known to the Greeks and Romans were inhabited by peoples of mixed dolicho-, meso-, and brachycephalic type. As a survey by Hughes and Brothwell of the physical remains concluded:

> By the time when Neolithic culture was firmly established in Europe, the population responsible for its introduction into the continent was widely distributed but somewhat heterogeneous in so far as this may be gauged from cranial morphology. . . . No doubt there were pigmentary and other genetically determined differences between many of these Neolithic groups, but in osteological terms and with only minor exceptions there is little gross difference demonstrable between the Sumerians of Mesopotamia, the predynastic Egyptians, and the Neolithic inhabitants of Switzerland, except perhaps in stature.

The implications of such results for this study are clear: the physical remains are of little use, by themselves, for reconstructing the different physical types of the peoples of the Greco-Roman world. Such evidence can be useful in supplementing the observations of classical writers about physical types, but even then must be used with caution. Our best testimony for the physical appearance of the different peoples of the ancient world still comes from those who observed them, or who recorded the observations of others: the writers and artists of classical antiquity.

PHYSICAL TYPES IN THE CLASSICAL SOURCES

Greek and Roman interest in foreign peoples dates from the very beginning of the classical literary tradition, as evidenced by Homeric and Hesiodic references to exotic tribes on the fringes of the then-known world. Not surprisingly, Greeks and Romans regarded themselves as the norm, and it is the differences that distinguished distant peoples from themselves that fascinated classical ethnographers and geographers. The foreign peoples whose physical appearance is described most fully in classical literary sources are frequently those most dramatically different in appearance from the Greeks and Romans. Terms such as "short," "tall," "dark," and "fair" are in the classical sources relative to the Greek and Roman physical type, so it is sensible to begin with a description of these peoples. Then, following the sequence usually taken by the ancient geographers, we will survey the peoples known to the classical world beginning with the Iberian peninsula, and proceeding from Europe, to Asia, and back along the coast of North Africa to the Straits of Gibraltar.

Greeks and Romans

Pliny the Elder (*Natural History* 2.80.190) characterizes the inhabitants of the "middle of the earth" (Italy and Greece) as "moderate in the size of their bodies, and of medium complexion" when comparing the various peoples of the earth. Physical anthropologists have characterized the Iron Age inhabitants of these regions as of short to medium stature, of sturdy, though not heavy, build, and with dolichocephalic skulls, becoming more brachycephalic over time. In a "racial analysis" of the ancient Greeks, Angel noted a general increase in height from prehistoric to historic times. Although fair hair and blue or gray eyes were not unknown, dark hair and eyes were more common.

Other peoples of the Balkan peninsula, such as the Macedonians and Illyrians, were not usually considered Hellenes by citizens of the traditional Greek city-states, but the distinction surely reflects cultural rather than physical differences since the Macedonian kings claimed by the fifth century B.C. to be of Argive descent and the Illyrians were regarded as related to the founders of Macedon (Herodotus 5.22). By Strabo's time the Celtic invasions had produced a mingling of physical types that may have distinguished the Illyrians from their Greek neighbors to some degree. Galen's characterization of the Illyrians and Dalmatians as tall, slender, and fair (*On Mixtures* [*Peri Kraseon*] 2.618) presumably reflects Celtic elements.

EUROPE

The Iberian Peninsula

Greek contacts with Iberia date from the late seventh century B.C. when traders from Phocaea (Foça) and Samos in Ionia (western Asia Minor) established contact with Tartessus and several Phocaean colonies were established, including Massilia (Marseilles). Roman interest in Spain assumed an intensive character after Hannibal mobilized the military forces and mineral resources of Iberia for his Italian offensive in the Second Punic War (218–201 B.C.), but the peninsula was not brought fully under Roman control until the early days of the principate.

Strabo devotes the third book of his *Geography* to the Iberian peninsula and its offshore islands, describing its geographical boundaries, coastline, rivers and mountains, major cities, natural resources, economy, mining industry, and the diet, dress, military gear, and personal habits of its population. He neglects to provide a physical description of either the indigenous Iberian tribes or the Celtiberians who occupied areas of central and western Iberia and were the descendants of the Iberians and Late Bronze/Early Iron Age Celtic invaders from the north. Tacitus (*Agricola* 11) fortunately provides a brief characterization of the Iberians as having swarthy skin and curly hair (*colorati, torti crines*), a description that may illuminate Hekataios' reference to a "Libyan *ethnos*" (the Elbestioi) in Iberia (*Journey Round the World* [*Periegesis*] frag. 40), and that is supported by the archaeological and cranial evidence for Neolithic migrations into the Iberian peninsula from North Africa. Martial, of Celtiberian descent, describes himself as hirsute, with unruly (*contumax*) hair, perhaps a result of the Iberian and Celtic mixture (*Epigrams* 10.65). Manilius (*Astronomy* [*Astronomicon*] 4.717) also refers to Iberians' hirsute appearance.

Gaul

The inhabitants of Gaul were variously called Gauls (*Galli*), Galatians (*Galatae*), and Celts (*Celtae/Keltoi*) by classical authors, but all these names were regarded as more or less synonymous, and Caesar remarks that the *Galli* referred to themselves as *Celtae* (*The Gallic War* 1.1). The Greek world knew of the Celts by the late sixth century B.C., when Hekataios (*Journey Round the World* [*Periegesis*] frag. 55–56) placed them in the neighborhood of Massilia and at Nyrax, possibly located in Austria. A century later, Herodotus knew of the Celts as the westernmost people of Europe, except for the Cynetes of southwest Iberia (2.33, 4.49).

They were not restricted to western Europe for long. By about 400 B.C. Celtic invaders entered northern Italy through the Alpine passes, raided south as far as Sicily, and settled in the Po Valley, Lombardy, and Umbria (known thereafter as Cisalpine Gaul). In 387 B.C. a band of these tribesmen sacked Rome itself. Celtic tribes moved eastward as well. In 369–368 B.C. Celtic mercenaries were serving in the Peloponnese. In 335 B.C. envoys from the Celts of the Adriatic Sea paid a call on Alexander the Great during his campaign in Thrace. A band of Celts raided Delphi in 279 B.C. The following year, another group crossed the Hellespont (Dardanelles) to Asia Minor and fought its way inland to northern Phrygia, where it founded its own Celtic state, the later Galatia. By the middle of the third century B.C., then, the Celtic peoples had spread from Spain to Asia Minor. Second and first century B.C. sources reveal that, in northern Europe, the Celts extended at least as far as the Rhine in the northeast and to Britain and Ireland in the northwest.

Although modern scholarship employs the designation "Celtic" as a linguistic term, it is clear that ancient writers considered the Celts—whether they were called *Celtae*, *Galatae*, or *Galli*—a cohesive cultural group united by common customs, beliefs, patterns of social organization, national temperament, and other ethnic characteristics. The ancient sources also agree on the physical appearance of the Celts. Diodorus Siculus (5.28.1) observed: "The Galatae are tall, with pale skin, rippling muscles, and hair which is not only naturally blond, but also bleached artificially to heighten their distinctive appearance." And Ammianus Marcellinus in his *History* (*Rerum Gestarum Libri*) remarked (15.12.1): "Almost all the Gauls are tall, white-skinned, and red-haired, with terrible fierce eyes." Strabo tells us (*Geography* 4.4.6) that the Celts regarded physical fitness as tremendously important, and imposed fines on any of the young men who became fat or potbellied. He also noted that one division of the Gauls—the Aquitani—did not fit this general description but were closer in appearance to the Iberians (4.1.1). Pausanias characterized the Celts as "the tallest of men" (*Description of Greece* 10.20.7), and even Arrian, whose narrative seldom pauses to comment on the appearance of the peoples subjugated by Alexander, commented on the height of the Celtic envoys (*The March Up Country* [*Anabasis*] 1.4.6). Nevertheless, despite their size and generally acknowledged warlike temperament, the Celts were regarded as paper tigers, since their huge physique and love of fighting were not matched by physical stamina or the ability to endure heat and thirst (Livy, *History of Rome* [*Ab Urbe Condita*] 10.-28.3; 27.48.16; 34.47.5; 38.17.3–8; Florus, *Epitome* 20.4).

Depictions of Celts in classical sculpture, most notably the sculptures of Galatians produced by the Pergamene school, support the literary testimony in portraying tall, muscular warriors with round or medium heads and long, flowing hair. A coin portrait of Vercingetorix, king of the Arverni (*ca.* 52 B.C.), depicts the Gallic chieftain with long backswept hair, pronounced cheekbones, and a strong jaw. The physical remains from Hallstatt and La Tène (early and later Iron Age periods, respectively) graves in the areas occupied by the Celts indicate a population consisting predominantly of Nordic dolichocephals mixed with brachycephalic types, prompting Coon to observe that the models for the Pergamene sculptors "may have been drawn from the brachycephalic minority."

Britain

Herodotus, near the end of the fifth century B.C., confessed utter ignorance of the geography and peoples of northern and western Europe (3.115–116). The earliest Greek writer to have left an account of the British isles (*Pretannikai nesoi*) was Pytheas, who visited there around 300 B.C.

That the Iron Age population of Britain was of mixed character seems borne out by the physical remains, which include both dolichocephalic and brachycephalic types, and by Roman and Greek writers from the first century B.C. Caesar (*The Gallic War* 5.12–14) contrasted the indigenous inland dwellers with the coastal inhabitants, who were descendants of Celtic invaders (specifically, the Belgae) and retained many Gallic customs. Strabo (4.5.1) also notes the cultural similarities between Britons and Gauls, but maintains that "the men are taller than the Celts and less blond, and flabbier in the body." A more discriminating account is provided by Tacitus (*Agricola* 11), who distinguishes German traits (red hair and large limbs) among the inhabitants of Calcdonia (the Scottish Highlands), Iberian characteristics (dark pigmentation and curly hair) among the Silures of southeast Wales, and Gallic characteristics among the inhabitants of Kent.

Germany

Traditionally, the Rhine defined the western border of Germany for Roman geographers, although German tribes crossed the river periodically and at least one tribe of Gauls, the Belgae, considered themselves of German racial stock. The origin of the name "Germani" was explained in various ways. Tacitus (*Germania* 2) reports that the Gauls adopted the name of one tribe participating in the third century B.C. incursions along the lower Rhine and applies it to all the tribes across the river. Strabo (7.1.2) suggests that the Romans called them Germani because they regarded these peoples as genuine (*germanus*) Celts.

Strabo's Latin etymology and his remarks on the close kinship of the Germans and Celts (4.4.2) raise the issue of German racial integrity. Tacitus took a firm stand on this question: "I myself agree with the opinion of those who judge the German peoples to be unsullied by interbreeding with any other nation, a pure and unique race" (*Germania* 4.2–3). Nonetheless, Tacitus' own description of the physical appearance of the Germans sounds very much like other classical descriptions of the Celts: "fierce blue eyes, red hair, large stature, . . . although without the stamina for sustained labor and work, and barely able to tolerate heat and thirst." Allusions to Germans by other writers (Juvenal, *Satires* 8.252; 13.164–165 and Seneca, *On Anger* 3.26.3) echo Tacitus' description. Certainly there was considerable mingling of German and Celtic tribes in the areas along the Rhine. Celtic loanwords appear in German, and, although racial conclusions cannot be drawn from linguistic evidence, the combined testimony of archaeology, linguistics, and the ancient descriptions suggest that physically the two peoples may well have had much in common. The most striking physical differences seem to have been that the Germans were taller and had redder hair, as indicated by Tacitus' derivation of the Caledonians from German origins, by Strabo's comment that "the Germans are like the Celts, though larger and fiercer" (4.42), and by a story Suetonius tells about the emperor Gaius, who sought to inflate the number of German prisoners in his triumph by taking the tallest of the Gauls and dyeing their hair red ("Gaius (Caligula)," *Lives of the Twelve Caesars* 47).

The physical remains suggest that dolichocephalic Nordic types perhaps originally from northwest Germany and Scandinavia expanded to the south and west as far as the lower Rhine, mingling with the local populations to produce people typically characterized by dolicho- to mesocephalic skulls.

Thrace

As early as the mid eighth century B.C. the Greeks were aware of nomadic Thracian tribes to their north and west of the Hellespont. Homer apparently regarded them as a far-off people, but he knew them well enough to characterize them as tenders of horses and sheep, who wore their hair in a topknot and fought among the Trojan allies (*Iliad* 2.844; 4.533; 11.222; 13.4–6). In the fifth century B.C. Herodotus placed the Thracians as far west as the Ister (lower Danube), and provided an account of their religious beliefs, sexual mores, and marriage and burial customs (5.3–10). Thucydides' *The Peloponnesian War* (7.29) characterizes the Thracians as "among the most bloodthirsty of barbarians" (meaning non-Greek-speaking peoples).

The physical appearance of the Thracians is rarely mentioned. Around 500 B.C. Xenophanes (frag. 16) characterized them as having blue-gray eyes and red-blond hair (*glaukous kai purrous*); at approximately the same time Hekataios (frag. 180) referred to a Thracian tribe called the Xanthoi (blondes). Nine centuries later, Firmicus Maternus also referred to the Thracians as "red-haired" in the beginning of his astrological treatise *Learning* (*Mathesis*). Whether or not these characteristics were shared by the people of Asia Minor (Anatolia), and, therefore, considered descendants of the Thracians (Strabo, 7.3.2f., mentions the Phrygians, Bithynians, Mariandynians, Mygdonians, and Bebrycians among others) is not clear.

ASIA

Scythia

Although the nomads who roamed the south Russian steppe between the Carpates Mountains (Carpathians) and the Tanaïs (Don) River were known to the Greeks under the single ethnic name "Scythians," they were apparently regarded as a heterogeneous group of tribes. Most scholars agree that they moved into the Pontic region from Siberia early in the first millennium B.C. Hesiod is the earliest classical source to refer to them (frag. 150.15), and they are also mentioned in eighth-century Assyrian inscriptions. Hekataios mentions at least one Scythian tribe whose Greek name was clearly derived from ethnographic observations: the Melangchlainoi, or "black-cloak-wearers." Herodotus (4.20; 100; 107) maintains that the Melangchlainoi kept Scythian customs, but were not of the Scythian race. Herodotus' Scythian ethnography found in the fourth book of *The Histories* remains the most valuable account of Scythian folklore, religious beliefs and rituals, military organization, burial customs, social practices, and attitudes.

Herodotus never describes the physical appearance of the Scythians, although he does describe a neighboring people, the Boudinoi, as having blue-gray eyes and red-blond hair (*glaukos* and *purros*, 4.108), and another neighboring tribe, the Argippaioi, as "bald from birth—both men and women—with snub-noses and large chins" (4.23). The fifth-century Hippocratic treatise *Airs, Waters, Places* characterizes the Scythians as "ruddy" (*purros*) from the cold climate. Galen (*On Mixtures* [*Peri Kraseon*] 2.618) describes them as tall, slender, and "ruddy." Fortunately, we also have depictions of Scythians in sixth- and fifth-century Attic vase paintings and in fourth-century metalwork produced in Greece for the Scythian market. These works depict men, usually bearded, who (when not portrayed in headgear) wear their hair long, flowing, and swept back from the forehead. The faces are characterized by heavy browridges, deep-set eyes, and pronounced noses.

Asia Minor (Anatolia)

The Iron Age population of Asia Minor, excluding the Ionian Greeks, was comprised of diverse *ethnea,* characterized by distinct languages (mostly Indo-European), political systems, and cultures. Some of these, such as the Phrygians, Bithynians, Mariandynians, and others, were considered offshoots of the Thracians. The Galatians who inhabited Cappadocia and Phrygia after the third century B.C. preserved their Celtic appearance. The Carians were considered by Herodotus (1.171) and Thucydides (1.8) to be of Cycladic origin, though they claimed to be indigenous to Asia Minor. Other peoples of Asia Minor were assumed to have had prehistoric Hellenic origins. The original ruling dynasty of Lydia was supposedly descended from Heracles (Herodotus, 1.7). The Lycians were traditionally derived from Crete, an origin also claimed by the Caunians, though Herodotus thought the latter were more probably native to Asia Minor (1.172–173). The Pamphylians and perhaps the Cilicians were also linked to Heroic Age Achaean wanderings (Herodotus, 7.91) after the capture of Troy.

There is no way of knowing with certainty whether these derivations were based on reliable oral tradition, on perceived similarities in language, script, or customs, or on invention. There is certainly no suggestion that such associations were based on perceived physical similarities, because there are hardly any references to the physical appearance of these peoples. Perhaps the most that can be said is that their appearance was sufficiently similar to that of the Greeks themselves that such theories were not considered improbable.

One people who are described in detail were the Colchians, from the region around the mouth of the Phasis (Rioni) at the east end of the Black Sea. Herodotus observed black-skinned and woolly-haired people in this region who practiced circumcision, made linen in the Egyptian fashion, spoke a language similar to Egyptian, and followed Egyptian customs. He concluded that they were descendants of the conquering army of the mythical pharaoh Sesostris (2.104). Although most commentators dismiss this passage, one scholar has tried—not entirely convincingly—to link it to the small community of blacks that still survives in this vicinity today.

Western and Central Asia

For the population of West and Central Asia we are in much the same situation as for Asia Minor. Greek and Roman writers were well acquainted with such diverse peoples as the Phoenicians, Syrians, Jews, Arabs, Armenians, Babylonians, Medes, and Persians, less well acquainted but still knowledgeable about those peoples between Persia and India. China eventually became known, albeit vaguely, to the classical world after the first century B.C. through the silk trade. Ptolemy provides an erroneous description of the Chinese coastline in his second-century A.D. *Geography* (*Geographia* 7.3.1f.; 1.11.7), and Roman missions reached China in A.D. 166 and 284.

Nonetheless, references to physical distinctions among these peoples—with the sole exception of the Indians—are rare and of dubious value. (Herodotus' analysis of the comparative fragility of Persian skulls in the *Histories* [3.12] is an example.) Representations in art rely more on the iconography of clothing, hairstyle, and headdress than physiognomy to convey national differences, and this may reflect the general Roman and Greek perception of Middle Easterners. When Juvenal notes an eastern freedman or a Syrian girl in Rome, it is the pierced ear, heavy perfume, or barbarous turban that draws his fire (*Satires* 1.103–105; 8.160; 3.62f). Third-century A.D. coin portraits of Queen Zenobia and her son Vaballathus Athenodorus of Palmyra show no distinctive Syrian physiognomic traits.

It is probably safe to assume that Chinese conquests in Central Asia during the first century A.D. brought a mingling of the Iranian and oriental physical types in Bactria (northern Afghanistan) and elsewhere, but there is little in the way of explicit description.

India

The Mediterranean world first learned of India through the Persians, who campaigned as far as the Indus under Darius I (521–486 B.C.), unless Homer's mention of eastern "Ethiopians" in the *Odyssey* represents a reference to Indians. Six of the extant fragments (nos. 294–299) of Hekataios' *Journey Round the World* (*Periegesis*) refer to India, and Herodotus added copious ethnographic notes almost a century later (3.94. 98–106). Herodotus was also the first to compare the Indians explicitly with the Ethiopians, maintaining that the semen as well as the skin of both peoples was black. Arrian (*Description of India* [*Indica*] 6.9) elaborated on this comparison, noting that the Indians were neither as snub-nosed nor as curly-haired as the Ethiopians, and that, as in Egypt, the complexion of the inhabitants became darker as one traveled from north to south. In addition, the Indians were tall like the Ethiopians, most of them attaining a height over seven feet (Arrian, *The March Up Country* [*Anabasis*] 5.4). Pliny the Elder (*Natural History* 6.22), Strabo (15.1.13), and others confirm this picture of the ancient Indians, and it seems fair to assume that the contingent of "eastern Ethiopians" that Herodotus musters with the Indian forces in Xerxes' troop roster (7.70) were merely a dark-skinned group of Indian troops.

AFRICA

Egypt

In describing the present-day population of the Nile valley, Trigger in 1978 observed a "gentle gradient" of physical types from the delta to the Upper Nile:

Skin color tends to darken from light brown to what appears to the eye as bluish black, hair changes from wavy-straight to curly or kinky, noses become flatter and broader, lips become thicker and more everted, teeth enlarge in size from small to medium, height and linearity of body build increase . . . and bodies become less hirsute.

A similar continuum of physical variation in antiquity is suggested by ancient Egyptian art and by the observations of classical authors.

The Aegean world had, with few interruptions, maintained commercial and cultural ties with Egypt since the Bronze Age. Depictions of dark-skinned Egyptians or Ethiopians are found in Minoan and Mycenaean palace frescoes at Knossos and Pylos, and Aegean peoples are depicted in Eighteenth Dynasty tomb paintings in Egypt. Homer's references to Egypt preserve both Bronze and Dark Age recollections, and include mentions of Thebes and the "River Aegyptos" (*Iliad* 9.381–382 and *Odyssey* 4.126–127; 14.257–258; 17.427). Hesiod's reference to the "land and city of dark-skinned men" (*Works and Days* [*Opera et Dies*] 527–528) may refer either to Egyptians or Ethiopians. In the former case, this would be the earliest reference in Greek sources to the brown complexion of the Egyptians. Greek familiarity with Egyptians was based on regular direct contact. A Greek trading emporium was established at Naucratis in the late seventh-century B.C.; Greek and Carian mercenaries are known to have served with the Saite pharaohs of this period. Although Herodotus describes the Egyptians as "black-skinned and woolly-haired" (*melangchroes kai oulotriches*), Aeschylus suggests that they were lighter-skinned than their southern neighbors (*The Suppliants* 277–290). Manilius (*Astronomy* [*Astronomicon*] 4.722–730) ranks them as less dark than the Ethiopians, and Arrian also indicates that Egyptians were somewhat lighter-skinned (*Description of India* [*Indica*] 6.9).

Ethiopia and East Africa

South of the first cataract began the land known to the Egyptians as Kush and to the Greeks and Romans as Ethiopia. At least as early as Homer and Hesiod these "burnt-faced" people—and obviously their distinctive dark complexion—were known to the Greeks. Greek and Carian mercenaries in the service of Psammetichus II campaigned against Ethiopians in 593–589 B.C., and the sea captain Skylax of Caryanda, commissioned by Darius I about 510 B.C., sailed from the Indus around the Arabian peninsula and along the African coast of the Red Sea. The *Sea Journey* (*Periplus*) he wrote describing this voyage has not survived, but was apparently available to Hekataios, Aristotle, Strabo, and Avienus. By the end of the sixth century we find, in a fragment (no. 16) of Xenophanes, the first reference to another characteristic of the Ethiopian physical type, the broad, flat nose. Herodotus, whose Egyptian explorations seem not to have reached farther south than Elephantine, near Syene (Aswan), nevertheless gathered much ethnographic information about the Ethiopians and heard reports that they were the tallest and handsomest men in the whole world (3.20.114), an opinion echoed in the fourth-century *Sea Journey* (*Periplus*) of pseudo-Skylax (Müller, *Geographici Graeci Minores*, I no. 112). The presence of Ethiopian troops in Xerxes' invasion force (480 B.C.) gave stay-at-home Greeks an opportunity to see this exotic people at first hand.

Under the Ptolemies, trade routes with the east coast of Africa were reopened as far south as Somaliland. Hellenistic traders could directly observe numerous inland tribes who came to the commercial center at Meroë and hear tales of other tribes that they had not seen, so that various descriptions, some quite fantastic, of East African peoples, all of them lumped together as "Ethiopians," appear in the works of later Greek and Roman geographers. Most of these people, according to the second-century B.C. writer Agatharchides, had black skin, flat noses, and woolly hair (*Geographici Graeci Minores*, I nos. 117–119; 123–156). Strabo mentions the Acridophagoi (Locust-eaters), blacker, shorter, and shorter-lived than other Ethiopians (16.4.12). Pliny the Elder describes the Syrbotae, "who are said to be twelve feet high," as well as tribes without noses, tribes without tongues, and tribes without upper lips—before going on to reject reports of other tribes whose descriptions seemed to him too fantastic to be taken seriously (*Natural History* 6.37.187–195).

Libya and Northwest Africa

The Libyans are mentioned by Homer (*Odyssey* 4.85; 14.295) and Hesiod (frag. 150.15). By the fifth century, Ionian geographers had attached the name Libya to the known part of the African continent west of Egypt, considering it roughly equal in size to Europe. Herodotus (4.42; 4.168–199), though quibbling with his predecessors on the relative size and orientation of Libya, uses the term to describe Africa west of Cyrenaica, including Roman Numidia and Mauretania, and provides a full ethnography of the various tribes of the Libyan seacoast and hinterland. Herodotus characterizes Libyans, along with Egyptians, as black (*melanes*), but Snowden (1983) has collected references that indicate that several northwest African tribes, including the Leukaethiopes of Ptolemy, some of the Gaetuli, and possibly some of the Garamantians, may have been lighter-skinned. The description of the Libyan tribe Gyzantes as *xanthoi* (brown-skinned or, possibly, fair-haired?) by pseudo-Skylax (*Geographici Graeci Minores* I no. 110) may refer to Libyans of a lighter complexion.

Phoenician and Greek exploration of the west coast of Africa began as early as the sixth century, when Phoenician sailors are alleged to have circumnavigated Africa (Herodotus 4.42), and Euthymenes of Massilia sailed as far south, perhaps, as the mouth of the Senegal River. On firmer ground, Herodotus also mentions the Pygmies, whom he characterizes as "black-skinned, and under middle height" (2.32). These diminutive tribesmen had already been mentioned by Homer (*Iliad* 3.6), as well as by Hesiod, who included them in a short list of African tribes (frag. 150.9.18). Yet so fantastic were the descriptions of this people that even Strabo, staunch defender of Homeric geography, questioned their existence (17.2.1). Pliny the Elder, considerably more credulous in this instance, passes along the report of Pygmies in India (*Natural History* 6.22).

FANTASTIC PEOPLES

Perhaps it was the knowledge that unusual tribes like the Pygmies existed that prompted some classical writers to report, however skeptically, other accounts of bizarre peoples from the far corners of the earth. Herodotus (3.116) mentions reports of one-eyed Arimaspians in the extreme north of Europe. Megasthenes, the third-century Seleucid diplomat, claimed to have learned during his trips to India of several wonderful peoples on the borders, including the Enetokoitas, whose ears were so large that they served for sleeping bags; the Okypodes (Swift-feet), who could run faster than horses; the Monommatoi, with dogs' ears and a single eye in the middle of their foreheads; and other wild men whose feet were placed backward on their legs (Strabo 15.1.57). Pliny the Elder reports (*Natural History* 6.35.195) as imaginary (*fabulosa*) several East African tribes, including the Nigroi, whose king was said to have only one eye in his forehead; the Cynamolgi ("Dog-milkers"), with dogs' heads; the Artabatitae, "who have four legs and run around like wild beasts"; and others.

In some instances these tales must surely represent the tall tales of travelers who enjoyed the credulity of their listeners. In other cases they may represent third- or fourth-hand versions of a Greek or Roman etymology for a tribal name or toponym. In some cases they may even derive from reports of encounters with exotic animals.

RACISM AND ETHNIC PREJUDICE

Ethnic prejudice in the Greco-Roman world must be assessed at three levels: the theoretical, the official, and the popular. In addition, we must distinguish ethnic prejudice—the negative treatment of groups or individuals on the basis of cultural or other nonphysical stereotypes—from racial prejudice, which is similar but also directs negative attention to the physical characteristics of the victims. Ethnic chauvinism was the rule rather than the exception in the ancient world. It tended to focus on differences in language, dress, diet, social customs, values, life-style, and, more rarely, religious practices—in short, those very topics that most interested ancient ethnographers. Racial prejudice also existed, but it is more difficult to detect. When it occurs, it usually figures as an element in an existing ethnic bias.

Theories of Racial Differentiation

The most popular explanation of racial differences in classical antiquity attributed physical variations to differences in climate and environment. This belief may be detected in an inchoate form as early as the first occurrences of the name "Ethiopians" (men with burnt faces), but may have been more fully developed by the Ionian thinkers of the sixth and fifth centuries B.C. It is found fully developed in Herodotus, who not only attributes the black complexions of Ethiopians and Libyans to the sun's heat (2.22), but also cites climate as the explanation for the differences between Scythian and Libyan cattle (4.29), and attributes a fanciful difference in the relative thickness and strength of Persian and Egyptian skulls to the effects of the sun (3.12). The theory is articulated in its most extreme form by the fifth- or fourth-century B.C. author of the Hippocratic *Airs, Waters, Places,* who attributed not only physical differences but differences in national character to environmental influences. Onesicritus, Strabo tells us, raised the difficult problem of how unborn infants, presumably unexposed to such influences as the sun's heat, were nonetheless born with the full complement of appropriate racial characteristics (15.1.24). Strabo himself preferred to see these characteristics as inherited.

Such a theory implied, of course, that all races were potentially equal, a position articulated by the fifth-century Sophist Antiphon of Athens. That did not prevent an accommodation with racial chauvinism, however. As the elder Pliny explained (*Natural History* 2.80.189–190), the moderation of the Mediterranean climate not only spared its inhabitants the dark pigmentation of southern peoples and the bleached appearance of northerners, but also provided them with more civilized customs, quicker intellects, and the capacity to rule (*ritus molles, sensus liquidos, ingenia fecunda totiusque naturae capacis, isdem imperia*).

Among Hellenes the environmental theory was less influential than another, more popular way of looking at differences between peoples, the so-called Great Antithesis between Greeks and "barbarians," the development of which was traced by Aubrey Diller. This distinction was essentially ethnic rather than racial, and stands as one of the enduring monuments of cultural chauvinism. Aristotle's belief that "barbarians" were, by nature, slaves (*Politics* 1252b5–9) should consequently be understood as an ethnic, not a racial, judgment. Needless to say, Romans were not pleased to be included within the broad category of "barbarians," and some sympathetic Greek writers tried to remedy the problem by deriving them from Greek, rather than Trojan, origins, or by attempting to restructure the Great Antithesis in such a way that their Italian friends were included on the right side.

It is interesting to note that, despite the fundamental differences Greeks perceived between themselves and "barbarians," one of their earliest mythographic systems for ordering the races of mankind brought the Greeks (specifically the Argives) within a genealogical system that embraced Egyptians, Phoenicians, Cilicians, Libyans, and others who were ethnically distinct from them.

Finally, it is significant that the works of Greek and Roman ethnographers and geographers are not commonly characterized by racial prejudice. Ethnic prejudice is not absent, but when it occurs it is more likely to derive from a country's social customs, political and economic organization, or technology than from the physical appearance of its people. Sherwin-White notes Strabo's approval of those Iberian tribes who had adopted agriculture, settlement in towns, and the rule of law—who had become, as Strabo (3.2.15) describes them, *togatoi,* wearers of the toga, and his "repugnance . . . toward mere differences in way of life such as food, clothing, and domestic manners."

Official Attitudes

In Greece, from the Archaic Age to the middle of the fourth century, citizenship was a jealously guarded privilege restricted to those who could prove citizen descent. In Athens, which provides the most complete evidence for the relative rights and privileges of citizens and foreigners, the Periclean citizenship law of 451–450 B.C. required both parents to be Athenian citizens. Noncitizens might be permitted to live in Athens as "metics" (*metoikoi*, resident aliens), but they were subject to special taxes (in addition to regular taxes), to military conscription, and to other regulations; they could not own real estate, marry Athenian citizens, hold public office, or participate in most public religious observances. Despite these obligations and restrictions, Athens and the Peiraeus bustled with resident foreigners in the fifth and early fourth centuries. Writing in 355 B.C. Xenophon referred to "Lydians, Phrygians, Syrians, and barbarians of all varieties" living as metics in Athens (*Ways and Means* [*De Vectigalibus*] 2.3), and other sources add Thracians, Carians, and Mysians, from northern Greece and Asia Minor, not to mention citizens of other Greek city-states.

Nonetheless, it is clear that the exclusive Hellenic concept of citizenship was not an expression of racial prejudice but a mechanism of political and economic solidarity couched in the outward form of local ethnic chauvinism. When grants of citizenship to foreigners became commonplace (after the fourth century B.C.) it was largely because the autonomous polis was, for most practical purposes, no longer a force to be reckoned with in Hellenistic international relations.

Roman citizenship was gradually extended to all Rome's allies beginning in the fourth century B.C., with the ultimate result that Rome became more nation-state than city-state by the beginning of the principate. Citizenship was extended to the provinces beginning in the late republic and early principate. The *constitutio Antoniniana* bestowed citizen rights on all free inhabitants of the empire in A.D. 212.

Admission to the senatorial class was more jealously guarded. Italians and some provincials were admitted beginning in the late Roman Republic, but they remained a minority until the beginning of the third century A.D. An attempt to introduce new senators from Gaul under Claudius (A.D. 41–54) provoked furious opposition from the existing senatorial class (Tacitus, *Annals* 11.23.3–4). Sherwin-White (1970) observed that the resulting debate, as reported by Tacitus, contained "a remarkable example of the sustained use of racial argument against the equal treatment of foreign peoples" (*alienigenae*). Nevertheless, the imperial civil service offered opportunity and advancement to citizens of virtually all origins and by the end of the century the Iberian-born Trajan had become emperor. Henceforth non-Italian emperors became the rule.

Popular Prejudice

Ethnic chauvinism, dislike, ridicule, and active persecution of other peoples was endemic in the ancient world. Herodotus reports Cyrus the Great's dismissal of the Greeks as a people who "designate a spot in the middle of their cities where they cheat each other and perjure themselves" (1.153). The Romans despised the Greeks of their day, even while revering Hellenic literature, art, and culture. One of the best sources for this antipathy, Juvenal's third *Satire,* makes it clear that the antipathy was based at least partially on competition with clever Greeks for professional advancement in imperial service. Greeks and Jews mutually detested each other in the cities of the eastern provinces, and Josephus reports active Greek persecution of Jewish residents from late republican times through the early principate (*Jewish Antiquities* 16.27–65), but the basis for this hatred was clearly political and religious.

Although ethnic prejudice was, apparently, rife in antiquity, it is difficult to discern how great a role physical differences played in such feelings. Valerius Maximus, who served in Asia during the early first century A.D., compiled a bombastic handbook for rhetoricians contrasting Roman and foreign (*externa*) examples. The simple-minded ethnic stereotypes on which the latter are based focus on differences in national temperament rather than physical appearance. Balsdon (1979) has assembled a collection of Roman ethnic slurs directed at Sardinians, Pannonians, Thracians, Phrygians, Carians, Cappadocians, Paphlagonians, Syrians, Jews, Arabs, and Egyptians; but again the criticisms dwell on such qualities as stupidity, drunkenness, loutishness, illiteracy, cupidity, dishonesty, fickleness, slavishness, and general knavery rather than on their physical characteristics.

Two areas, Europe and Africa, seem to have produced peoples subjected to ethnic prejudice that included an explicit racial element. In Europe, this included the Gauls and the Germans—both physically distinguished by their large stature, fair hair, and pale skin. Sherwin-White notes the absence of citizens from northern Gaul among the upper administrative ranks and in the legions during the early empire and suggests that the Roman prejudice against these northern people was attributable, in significant degree, to their obstinate refusal to assimilate into Roman culture (as the southern Gauls had done), and to the continuing military threat that they posed on the Roman frontier. Velleius Paterculus, who served on the Rhine shortly after the defeat and death of the Roman general Varus in the Teutoburg Forest (Saltus Teutoburgiensis) (A.D. 9) repeatedly alludes to the bestiality (*feritas*) of the Germans (2.106.2; 2.119.5) and suggests that Varus' mistake was in considering the Germans human beings, when in fact they were human only in the sense that they had limbs and voices (2.117.3–4). Ammianus Marcellinus characterizes the Gauls as tall, fair, quarrelsome, and insolent (15.-12.1). The susceptibility of Gauls and Germans to heat, thirst, and drunkenness was proverbial. Martial (*Epigrams* 7.75) pokes fun at a drunken Gaul stretched out full-length in a Roman street, and Florus (*Epitome* 20.4) compares the Insubrian Gauls (in north Italy) to the Alpine snows: massive and white, but quickly dissolved by the heat of the sun.

It should not be surprising to discover that this racial depreciation was mutual. Caesar relates that the German tribe of the Aduatuci, besieged in their strongholds, laughed at the Roman siege preparations, doubting that "men of such puny stature could mount a tower of such weight against their wall" (*The Gallic War* 2.30).

Scholars differ over the existence and degree of color prejudice in the classical world. Snowden has recently argued (1983) that the treatment of Ethiopians in classical literature is "essentially favorable," and that "there was a clear-cut respect among Mediterranean peoples for Aethiopians and their way of life.... Above all, the ancients did not stereotype all blacks as primitives defective in religion and culture."

To the extent that the sources never betray the systematic characterization of blacks as genetically inferior, which is a hallmark of contemporary Western racism, Snowden is correct. Libyans and Ethiopians are attested as freedmen as well as slaves in a wide range of occupations, including professional soldiers, gladiators and charioteers, sailors, actors, dancers, acrobats, caravaneers, boxers, cooks, bath attendants, and other positions.

Nonetheless, most of the occupations attested for Africans in the classical world are of comparatively low social status, and some passages in Juvenal's *Satires* seem to indicate that the physical appearance of blacks was regarded by proper Romans as at best unfortunate, and at worst a perversion of nature. Despite the few exceptional cases of intermarriage cited by Snowden, there is little evidence for participation of blacks in the upper levels of Roman society and government, and it seems not unlikely that an informal color bar existed even if unarticulated in the literary sources.

BIBLIOGRAPHY

SOURCES

Arrian, *Anabasis* (*The March Up Country*) and *Indica* (*Description of India*), T. E. Page *et al.*, eds., E. Iliff Robson, trans., 2 vols. (1929–1933); Julius Caesar, *The Gallic War* (*De Bello Gallico*), René D. Pontet, ed. (1900–1901); Diodorus Siculus, *The Historical Library* (*Biblioteca Historica*) I, T. E. Page *et al.*, eds., C. H. Oldfather, trans. (1933); Galen, *On Mixtures* (*Peri Kraseon*), George Helmrich, ed. (1904); Hanno of Carthage, *Periplus* (*Sea Journey*), in Karl Müller, ed., *Geographi Graeci Minores* I (1855); Hekataios (Hecataeus) of Miletus, *Journey Round the World* (*Periegesis*), in Felix Jacoby, ed., *Die Fragmente der griechischen Historiker* I, pt. 1 (1923); Herodotus, *The Histories* (*Historiae*), Karl Hude, ed., 2 vols. (1908–1911; 3d ed. 1927); Hesiod, *Theogonia* (*Theogony*), *Opera et Dies* (*Works and Days*), and *Scutum* (*The Shield*), R. Merkelbach and M. L. West, eds. (1970); [Hippocrates, attrib.] *Airs, Waters, Places,* in *Hippocrates* I, T. E. Page *et al.*, eds., W. H. S. Jones, trans. (1923; repr. 1939); Homer, *Iliad*, David B. Monro and Thomas W. Allen, eds., 2 vols. (1902; 3d ed. 1920). *Odyssey*, Thomas W. Allen, ed. (1908; 2d ed. 1917).

Josephus Flavius, *Jewish Antiquities* VIII, T. E. Page *et al.*, eds., Ralph Marcus and Allen Wikgren, trans. (1963); Juvenal, *Satires,* in *Juvenal and Persius,* T. E. Page *et al.*, eds., G. G. Ramsey, trans., rev. ed. (1940; repr. 1957); Livy (Titus Livius), *History of Rome* (*Ab Urbe Condita*), Robert Conway and Charles F. Walters, eds., 5 vols. (1914–1965); Manilius, *Astronomy* (*Astronomicon*), Alfred E. Housman, ed. (1903); Ammianus Marcellinus, *Rerum Gestarum Libri qui Supersunt* (*The Surviving Books of the History of Ammianus Marcellinus*), E. H. Warmington, ed., John C. Rolfe, trans. (1935; rev. ed. 1971). Martial, *Epigrams*, E. H. Warmington, ed., Walter C. A. Ker, trans., 2 vols. (1919).

Pliny the Elder, *Natural History* (*Historia Naturalis*), I, II, T. E. Page *et al.*, eds., H. Rackham, trans., rev. ed. (1938–1942); pseudo-Skylax, *Periplus* (*Sea Journey*), in Karl Müller, ed., *Geographici Graeci Minores* I (1855); Ptolemy (Claudius Ptolemaeus), *Geographia* (*Geography*), Karl F. A. Nobbe, ed. (1843–1845; repr. 1966); Strabo, *Geography*, T. E. Page *et al.*, eds., H. L. Jones, trans., 8 vols. (1917–1932; repr. 1960–1967); Tacitus, *The Annals*, E. H. Warmington, ed., John Jackson, trans., 2 vols. (1936–1937), and *Agricola* and *Germania*, E. H. Warmington, ed., M. Hutton, trans., rev. ed. (1970); Xenophanes, *Fragments*, in Hermann Diels, ed., *Die Fragmente der Vorsokratiker* I, pt. 1 (1903; 11th ed. 1964); Xenophon, *Ways and Means* (*De Vectigalibus*), in G. W. Bowerstock, ed., *Scripta Minora* VII (1925; rev. ed. 1968).

STUDIES

John Lawrence Angel, "A Racial Analysis of the Ancient Greeks," in *American Journal of Physical Anthropology*, n. s. **2** (1944); Helen H. Bacon, *Barbarians in Greek Tragedy* (1961); John P. V. D. Balsdon, *Romans and Aliens* (1979); H. I. Bell, "Antisemitism in Alexandria," in *Journal of Roman Studies*, **31** (1941); Stanley Casson, *Macedonia, Thrace and Illyria* (1926); Yehudi A. Cohen, ed., *Man in Adaptation: The Biosocial Background* (1968); Carleton S. Coon, *The Races of Europe* (1939); Simon Davis, *Race-Relations in Ancient Egypt* (1953); Aubrey Diller, "Race Mixture Among the Greeks Before Alexander," in *Illinois Studies in Language and Literature,* **20** (1937).

P. T. English, "Cushites, Colchians, and Khazars," in *Journal of Near Eastern Studies*, **18** (1959); Denise Ferembach, "Le peuplement du proche-orient au chalcolithique et au Bronze ancien," in *Israel Exploration Journal*, **9** (1959); John Ferguson, "Classical Contacts with West Africa," in L. A. Thompson and J. Ferguson, eds., *Africa in Classical Antiquity* (1969); Henry Field, *Ancient and Modern Man in South-Western Asia*, 2d ed. (1961); Herbert J. Fleure, *The Peoples of Europe* (1922); Theodore J. Haarhoff, *The Stranger at the Gate* (1948); Henri Hubert, *The Rise of the Celts*, M. R. Dobie, trans. (1934).

D. R. Hughes and Don R. Brothwell, "The Earliest Populations of Man in Europe, Western Asia and Northern Africa," in *The Cambridge Ancient History* 1, pt. 1, 3d ed. (1970); John P. C. Kent, *Roman Coins* (1978); Alice Littlefield, Leonard Lieberman, and Larry T. Reynolds, "Redefining Race: The Potential Demise of a Concept in Physical Anthropology," in *Current Anthropology*, **23** (1982); James Mellaart, "Anatolia Before 4000 B.C.," in *The Cambridge Ancient History* 1, pt. 1, 3d ed. (1970); Metropolitan Museum of Art [New York] and the Los Angeles County Museum of Art, *From the Lands of the Scythians* (1975); Sabatino Moscati, *The Semites in Ancient History* (1959).

Francis Owen, *The Germanic People* (1960); Thomas G. E. Powell, *The Celts* (1958); Max Radin, *The Jews Among the Greeks and Romans* (1915); Wülf Raeck, *Zum Barbarenbild in der Kunst Athens im 6. and 5. Jahrhundert v. Chr.* (1981); D. B. Saddington, "Roman Attitudes to the 'Externae Gentes' of the North," in *Acta Classica*, **4** (1961), and "Race Relations in the Early Roman Empire," in Hildegard Temporini, ed., *Aufstieg und Niedergang der römischen Welt* II, pt. 3 (1975); A. N. Sherwin-White, *Racial Prejudice in Imperial Rome* (1967); Frank M. Snowden, *Blacks in Antiquity: Ethiopians in the Greco-Roman Experience* (1970), and *Before Color Prejudice: The Ancient View of Blacks* (1983).

L. A. Thompson, "Eastern Africa and the Graeco-Roman World," in L. A. Thompson, ed., *Africa in Classical Antiquity* (1969); Bruce G. Trigger, "Nubian, Negro, Black, Nilotic?" in Sylvia Hochfield and Elizabeth Riefstahl, eds., *Africa in Antiquity: The Arts of Ancient Nubia and the Sudan* 1 (1978); Roland de Vaux, "Palestine During the Neolithic and Chalcolithic Periods," in *The Cambridge Ancient History* 1, pt. 1, 3d ed., (1970); Jean Vercoutter *et al.*, eds., *The Image of the Black in Western Art, I: From the Pharaohs to the Fall of the Roman Empire* (1976); Maria Frederika Vos, *Scythian Archers in Archaic Attic Vase-Painting* (1963).

W. J. Watts, "Race Relations in the Satires of Juvenal," in *Acta Classica,* **19** (1976); Robert E. M. Wheeler, *Rome Beyond the Imperial Frontiers* (1954); David S. Wiesen, "Juvenal and the Blacks," in *Classica et Mediaevalia*, **31** (1970).

Early Greek Migrations

RONALD A. CROSSLAND

THERE ARE TWO GOOD REASONS for considering whether migrations were important in the history of Greece before the ninth century B.C. First, Greek poets and historians of the sixth and fifth centuries B.C. clearly believed traditional stories that such movements had occurred in Greece four or five hundred years before their own times. Second, it is generally agreed that the Greek language was introduced into Greece from some area to the north, or possibly to the east, by the end of the thirteenth century B.C. at the latest. Only the later of these possible migrations, those at the end of the second millennium or later, are directly relevant to Greek history as it is usually defined. But the earlier introduction of Greek into what was later Hellas is also worthy of consideration, because migrations and other events in the early first millennium had their origins in the political and cultural situation of the last centuries of the second. There was no sharp or complete break between the two periods.

THE GREEKS' HISTORICAL TRADITIONS

The Greeks become known to us as a historical people with special characteristics from the seventh century B.C. onward. Their traditions about their own earlier history will not necessarily be reliable, but they should be examined. Historical events might have been remembered in them, even if distorted or fused with myth. The *Iliad* and the *Odyssey*, thought to have been composed about 750 B.C., clearly do not reflect eighth-century Greece as we know it was developing. In particular, the kingdoms of which they tell are not the emerging principal states of that century; the world they depict is either fictitious or largely that of a much earlier period.

A little later Hesiod, or one of his pupils or associates, is familiar with the concept of "Hellenes," that is to say, the whole range of Greek-speaking states or tribes, which he symbolizes by making the main groups within it descendants of a common ancestor,

Hellen (*Eoeae*, "Catalogs of Women," frags. 1, 4). Herodotus, in the fifth century, writes of *tò Hellenikón*, perhaps better translated as "the Greek entity" rather than "Greek community," which connotes some degree of political or social union (8.144). A Greek "ethnic consciousness" had evidently developed in the early to middle centuries of the first millennium, if it did not exist previously, and since all Hellenes spoke dialects of the same language, without significant trace of alien admixture in any of them, on that evidence alone it is likely that they were descended from a linguistically homogeneous population of the late second millennium or the first centuries of the first.

Herodotus believed that the genealogies of some royal families of his time could be traced back more than fifteen generations, that is, to earlier than 1000 B.C. (7.204). Before that, the dominant event in the Greeks' retrospect was the Trojan War, which for the sake of convenience will be referred to as a historical event. Both Herodotus and Thucydides regarded it as historical (Thucydides, 1.8–9), and slightly later Greek historians deduced for it dates corresponding to about 1200 B.C. Tradition set the war at the end of a period in which there had been powerful kingdoms in the Peloponnese, Boeotia, and Crete, mostly not corresponding to the states that were preeminent in the classical period, but the genealogies given for their rulers ran back only for three or four generations before the war.

The Trojan War was thought to have been followed almost immediately by a time of extensive migration and disturbance within Greece, in which many Greek communities, or their aristocracies, moved into their historical territories (Thucydides, 1.12). The movements were believed to have been mainly from northern Greece into the central parts, the Peloponnese, and Crete, with the ancestors of those who regarded themselves as Dorians conquering Greek-speaking predecessors in the first two areas. No Greek author records any tradition that the ancestors of the Hellenes as a whole migrated into Greece from any area outside it, either before the Trojan War or later. At the most, tradition told of the arrival from abroad of the founders of royal or noble families—Pelops, from Lydia or Phrygia, and Kadmos and his followers from Syria. Herodotus and Thucydides apparently believed that the peoples of the pre-Trojan War kingdoms who are mentioned in the Homeric poems, the *Akhaioí* (Achaeans), *Argeioí*, and *Danaoí* (Danaans), spoke Greek, though they do not say so explicitly (Thucydides, 1.3).

By the fifth century B.C. two groups of Greek peoples regarded themselves, and were regarded by others, as closely related among themselves, the Ionians (*Iones*) and the Dorians (*Dorieis*), and the dialects of each group were considered to be similar among themselves. In the third century B.C. Greek philologists recognized three groups of dialects in their language, Ionic, Doric, and Aeolic, the last of which was spoken in Thessaly and the northern Aegean islands. Modern linguists have added a fourth, the classical dialects of Arcadia and Cyprus, and place the Doric dialects, such as Corinthian and Laconian, in a larger "West Greek" group that also includes the dialects of northwest Greece and Elis.

Since Heinrich Schliemann's excavations in the 1870s, modern archaeology has confirmed the tradition that civilized states, mostly larger than those of the fifth century B.C., existed in the Peloponnese eight hundred years previously, but until 1952 there was no direct proof that Greek was spoken in these Mycenaean kingdoms of the Late Bronze Age. It was thought that Greek must have been introduced into Greece at some time during the Bronze Age, probably during the second millennium B.C., but this conclusion was based on its characteristics as a language, which classify it as Indo-European.

At the end of the eighteenth century it was recognized that Greek, Latin, and Sanskrit are so similar in significant respects that they must have developed from dialects of a single prehistoric language, which we refer to as "Indo-European." Since then it has also been shown that almost all the languages of Europe and also Hittite and Luwian, rediscovered in 1906 in the archives of the Bronze Age Hittite capital, Hattusas (at Boğazköy, now Boğazkale, near Ankara), also derive from Indo-European. Dialects of Indo-European were evidently spread by late prehistoric migrations over the lands in which derivative languages were in use early in historical periods, from Ireland in the west to northern India in the east.

The region in which Indo-European developed is thought to have lain to the north of the urbanized regions of the Near East and the eastern Mediterranean of the Bronze Age; opinions differ about its exact location and the date at which the initial "diaspora" took place. The theory of Marija Gimbutas seems the most satisfactory, at least in its earlier and simpler form; this theory concludes that Indo-European evolved among seminomadic peoples of the western steppes of central Asia and was first carried to an area of secondary development in the Pontic region, the lands immediately north of the Black Sea, from which migrants then moved to the areas in which Indo-European languages were in use in early historical times. It is not suggested today that these migrations took place as an "explosion" lasting a few centuries only, or that the migrants were numerous. They appear to have begun about 2500 to 2000 B.C., but no evidence, apart from the archaeological, indicates that Greek was introduced into Greece itself before the second half of the second millennium.

There are strong arguments against the alternative idea that northern Greece, at least, formed part of the region in which Indo-European evolved, so that a dialect ancestral to Greek might have been in use there from as early as the late Neolithic period. Migrations out of the Indo-European homeland well before about 2500 B.C., postulated in Gimbutas' later reconstructions, may be indicated by archaeological evidence, but would not necessarily have been Indo-European in the linguistic sense of the term. That designation should be reserved for deduced prehistoric idioms that are likely to have been dialects of Indo-European as it is reconstructed by comparison of historical Indo-European languages; it is doubtful whether the ancestral language had reached that stage of its development before the first half of the third millennium. Movements out of the steppe region into the Pontic, and beyond it, before about 3000 B.C. are best named after their characteristic cultures, called "Kurgan" from the type of low tumulus that is one of their features.

Proof that Greek was introduced into Greece in the thirteenth century B.C. at the latest, and more probably in the fifteenth or earlier, came with Michael Ventris' decipherment in 1952 of the "Minoan Linear B" clay tablets found in Sir Arthur Evans' excavations at Knossos (1900–1905), in excavations at Ano Englianos in Messenia just before and after World War II, and in small numbers at Mycenae and Thebes. The syllabic script of the tablets had evidently been modeled on the "Linear A" writing also found at Knossos, or on another early Cretan variety. Ventris' conclusion that the Linear B texts were written in a dialect of Greek was surprising at first in the case of those from Knossos, since the Minoan civilization of Bronze Age Crete had apparently developed continuously from a time earlier than any likely date for the arrival of Greek in Greece, and there were good reasons for concluding that the Minoans spoke a non-

Indo-European language. The decipherment has been accepted because it has yielded convincing texts for administrative documents of the Late Bronze Age and a dialect of Greek that was consistent within itself and closely similar to the Arcadian of the classical period.

The use of Greek at Knossos in Late Minoan II (ca. 1450–1380 B.C.) or Late Minoan III has to be explained by conquest or domination by Greek-speaking intruders from the Mycenaean kingdoms of the mainland. (The periods mentioned here are those adopted by Sir Arthur Evans in his reconstruction of the history of Bronze Age Knossos.) Although Mycenaean civilization evolved under strong cultural influence from Crete, it is unlikely that Minoans ever ruled the Peloponnese, and by 1400 B.C. men from the new Mycenaean states were ascendant, trading as far as Syria and settling in Rhodes and at Miletus. About 1400 B.C. may be treated as the definite latest date for the appearance of Greek at Knossos, and so also presumably in mainland Greece, only if Evans' date for the Knossos tablets is accepted. Those from Ano Englianos–Pylos are firmly dated just before 1200 B.C. Leonard R. Palmer found the virtual identity of the script and conventions of the two sets of tablets so remarkable that he doubted Evans' dating of the Knossos group. His arguments that the two sets must be nearly contemporary seemed to have been countered, particularly by John Boardman, but Eric Hallager has revived the question. As a comparison, cuneiform tablets from the Hittite royal archives written at various times between about 1350 and 1200 B.C. show no progressive change in their paleography. However, the dating of the Linear B tablets from Knossos is not vital for the date of the introduction of Greek into the Peloponnese unless one thinks that that might have happened as late as the fourteenth or thirteenth century B.C.

The difficulties of associating archaeological evidence for cultural change with either immigration or change of language are now notorious. It is not possible to deduce accurately how long Greek or pre-Greek was introduced into Greece before the Linear B texts, already in a differentiated dialect of Greek, were written, because no normal speed can be suggested for the development of any language into dialects. However, Mycenaean Greek had already made one phonetic change that sets it apart from the later West Greek dialects and the Aeolic of Thessaly: the change of t to s in most positions. Greek must have evolved into its late prehistoric form (that from which all its known dialects could have developed) early enough for that change to have occurred before the Linear B tablets were written. Nothing indicates that dialects ancestral to, for example, Mycenaean, the Attic-Ionic group, and the West Greek dialects, were brought into Greek by successive waves of immigrants at different times before about 1000 B.C. In most respects the classical dialects and Mycenaean are so similar that we may deduce that they differentiated within Greece, perhaps including Macedonia, after "pre-Greek" had been introduced there. Even if the Linear B tablets of Knossos are dated to the thirteenth century B.C., Greek must have come into use on the Greek mainland at least as early as the fifteenth.

There is no agreement about the date of the first or main immigration of Greek-speaking newcomers into Greece. For some time the appearance of so-called "Minyan" styles of pottery in the Argolid and central Greece about 1900 B.C. was thought to indicate their arrivals. But these new wares have not been shown to have come to Greece from any neighboring region, and they now appear to have been diffused by trade and imitation. A striking cultural change in mainland Greece, accompanied by the destruction of settlements, is now found at the end of the Early Helladic II period, about 2100 B.C., notably at Lerna in the Argolid. A few finds of pottery of "northern" types have also been reported there, supposedly from the central Balkans. A second change in pottery styles has been observed at Lerna between Levels IV and V, apparently early in the second millennium, and Sinclair Hood finds evidence for more substantial intrusions of northerners at the end of the Early Helladic III period, about 2000 B.C. Finally, a temporary fashion of tumulus burial in Attica might show the arrival of invaders about 1700 B.C., though only as a ruling group and in small numbers.

The events at the end of the Early Helladic II period seem the most likely to reflect the arrival of immigrants in numbers large enough to introduce a new language. The strongest argument for deducing that this language was pre-Greek is that Mycenaean and classical Greek appear to have been little influenced by the language or languages they replaced in Greece (apart from the borrowing of place-names and words for local plants and artifacts). If pre-Greek had been brought in by less numerous immigrants between about 2000 and 1700 B.C., the changes would probably have been more fundamental. In any case, it is likely that Greek had been generally adopted in Greece before the sixteenth century B.C. Mycenaean civilization developed directly out of the preceding Middle Helladic culture in that century, stimulated by the higher civilization of Crete. Even if the Linear B texts from Knossos are of the thirteenth century B.C., it is unlikely that Greece changed its language during the early part of the Mycenaean period.

During the thirteenth century the Mycenaean states had a remarkably homogeneous culture, and the use of *Akhaioí* (earlier *Akhaiwoí*) as the most frequent name of all Agamemnon's allies in the *Iliad* suggests that their aristocracies at least regarded themselves as belonging to a single people. The Hittites apparently used the same name, somewhat distorted and written as *Ahhiyawa* or *Ahhiya,* for Mycenaeans with whom they were in contact on their western borders from the early fourteenth to the twelfth centuries. It seems unlikely that the Mycenaean states, even those of the Peloponnese alone, were incorporated into an empire with a central administration. Nothing in the Pylos texts suggests that, and such preclassical roads as have been identified have not been shown to form a planned network. The argument that only an empire could have organized the raids and interventions that the *Ahhiyawa* undertook on the western edge of the Hittite Empire between about 1425 and 1200 B.C., from an area in the Hermos valley to Cyprus in the south, is not decisive. An independent Greek kingdom on Rhodes might well have launched them all, at their widely separated dates, granted an efficient fleet. (The text that records the raids on cities in Cyprus, the so-called Indictment of Mattuwattas, is now dated by Heinrich Otten to about 1425–1400 B.C. instead of to the end of the thirteenth century.) Christian Podzuweit reports that Mycenaean pottery found in Thrace resembles types known from Kos and Rhodes, not those of the Peloponnese or Thessaly, which suggests that it was Greek merchants from the Dodecanese who traded with Thrace, along the coast of Anatolia.

Migrations in Greece at the end of the second millennium must be considered in the context of the collapse or rapid decline of Mycenaean civilization after three centuries of apparent stability. Immigrants might have destroyed it, or simply have profited by the power vacuum it left—if it came to an end for reasons other than attack from outside.

THE LITERARY TRADITION

Herodotus and Thucydides clearly believed the tradition of the Dorian migration.

Their accounts agree in their main lines and some discrepancy is to be expected. Accounts of the migration, if historical, would have been handed down orally during at least two hundred and fifty years. In the seventh century Tyrtaeus knew that the Spartans believed that their ancestors came to Laconia from Doris, in northern Greece (frags. 2, 11). Herodotus refers to the migration only in allusions and in one short discussion (1.56) and Thucydides mentions it in part of his introduction to his history, in which he is primarily concerned to show that the achievements of Greek kings in the legendary past fell short of those of the leading Greek powers of his own century (1.1.12). He seems to assume too close a similarity between conditions in Greece just before the beginnings of history as he knew it and those of his own times. Understandably, he did not realize that the state of affairs out of which the classical city-states evolved represented a regression, or in some places the backwardness of peripheral areas. He describes Hellas as unsettled over the whole of the six hundred years that preceded the rise of the first tyrannies, although this assertion conflicts with what he deduced about the power of Agamemnon. His belief that *stasis*, in the fifth-century sense of civil conflict, was a main factor in the unrest seems anachronistic, though there may have been dynastic struggles within the Mycenaean states (as the story of the Theban War suggests) as well as interstate wars. Fifth-century Greek writers may have been troubled by the discrepancy between the general trend of Greek legends, symbolizing a simple division of the Hellenic race into Dorian, Ionian, and Aeolian branches starting in the reign of Deukalion, and the traditions and genealogies found in the *Iliad*, the *Odyssey*, and lost epics. Hesiod faced the discrepancy when he inserted an "Age of the Heroes" in the otherwise consistent decline of mankind from a Golden Age to the Age of Iron in which he lived (*Works and Days* 156–173).

Classical authors frequently refer to the Dorians' invasion of the Peloponnese as the "return of the *Herakleidai*"—the descendants of Herakles (Hercules). The traditional story was that when Herakles died his sons were exiled from Mycenae by his enemy King Eurystheus and took refuge with the Dorians. One son, Hyllos, became king of one of their tribes (Diodorus of Sicily, 4.37.3; 4.58.6). About a hundred years later his grandsons led the Dorians' invasion jointly with their two other tribal kings to regain their own rights at Mycenae and to win lands for their followers. In recent discussions of these traditions, N. G. L. Hammond argues for their correctness even in detail, Fritz Schachermeyr and Domenico Musti treat them as at least based on historical events, while others explain them as fabrications of the ninth to seventh centuries.

One of Herodotus' longer passages (1.56) tells of the antecedents of the invasion, the movements of the Dorians or their ancestors before their first attempts on the Peloponnese. Thucydides dates two main events in the migrations with reference to the Trojan War (1.12). Details of the final invasion are offered by Pausanias. According to Herodotus, the Dorians were first settled in Phthiotis, in the southern part of Thessaly, "in the reign of Deukalion," the first king to reign after the flood, in Greek mythology, and so, in effect, at the beginning of history. Two generations later they moved to the eastern part of Histiaiotis, in northern Thessaly, near to Mount Olympus. Driven out by the Kadmeians, the followers or descendants of Kadmos (Herodotus, 2.49), which must mean the people of Boeotia before the Trojan War, they then lived "in Pindos," and from there moved to Dryopis, a strip of land between Malis and Phocis, an extension of Doris. Although one of the villages of Doris was named Pindos (Herodotus, 8.43), the area the Dorian people supposedly occupied before moving to Dryopis has usually been identified as the Pindos Mountains, probably because Herodotus adds that while living there they were called *Makednòn* (not the usual word for Macedonian).

This sequence of wanderings may be explained as Herodotus' attempt to reconcile various traditions about the regions of origin of tribes who collaborated in invasions of the Peloponnese at the end of the second millennium B.C. It is unlikely that bodies of migrants numerous enough to undertake such invasions came from Doris and Dryopis alone. Perhaps men from Doris played the leading part, so that their name came to be used for the invaders as a whole, first by the peoples whom they attacked. If so, Herodotus' statement that they came to be called "Doric" only after moving into the Peloponnese will be correct. Hammond considers that Herodotus' account may be correct in detail, recalling the seasonal or occasional migrations of a people who were pastoralists before they moved southward. Perhaps recollections of them influenced Herodotus, even if the itinerary he gave for the Dorians' "long march" is basically symbolic.

The origin of the Dorians in Phthiotis, like the story of the *Herakleidai*, might recall contact with Mycenaean colonists in Thessaly; there was an important Mycenaean settlement at Iolkos, near Pagasai. The Dorians' movement northward is surprising, since archaeological evidence suggests that pressure on them might have come from the north. Their description as *Makednòn*, a name Herodotus also gave to the ancestors of the Sicyonians, Epidaurians, and Troizenians (8.43), need not indicate any kinship with the Macedonians. *Makednoí* may have meant "highlanders" and, if so, might have been used of various tribes. (The little that is known about the language of the Macedonians, the *Makedónes*, suggests that it was not a dialect of Greek.) Schachermeyr thinks that the itinerary represents all the lands that the Dorians occupied before their emigration. Herodotus does not say that they ever lived in Macedonia.

The tradition of the return of the *Herakleidai* may be variously explained. Émigrés from the Mycenaean Peloponnese might have been accepted as rulers among backward tribes of northeastern Greece at the end of the second millennium B.C. Alternatively, the story of the exile of the *Herakleidai* might have been created in the ninth to seventh centuries to express a recollection that Mycenaeans had been present and influential in Thessaly in earlier times. Once it was current the role of the *Herakleidai* would have been magnified by the kings and aristocracies of Sparta and Argos, since it portrayed their ancestors' acquisition of lands in the Peloponnese by conquest as the regaining of just rights. However, one may reasonably conclude that the Dorian migration was historical without accepting that it was led by the *Herakleidai*.

Thucydides treats two movements as main events between the Trojan War and the colonization of Ionia (1.12): the migration of the Boeotians into Boeotia from Thessaly, sixty years after the war, and the conquest of the Peloponnese by the Dorians twenty years later, about 1140 and 1120 B.C. if the war is dated at about 1200 B.C. Herodotus tells of an unsuccessful attempt to invade the Peloponnese by the Heraklid Hyllos a hundred years previously (9.26). Later writers add an expedition under the same leader three years earlier that briefly occupied much of the territory of Mycenae and Tiryns.

Pausanias and Strabo give realistic accounts of the Dorians' final invasion of the Peloponnese. According to these, the Dorians sailed from Naupactus and Molykreion on the south coast of Aetolia to Rhion in Peloponnesian Achaea, the shortest crossing, guided by Oxylos, king of Aetolia. He led them into Arcadia from where they invaded the Argolid (Pausanias, 5.3.6–7), and he subsequently took Elis for himself. This is all plausible. The route through Boeotia would have been barred to the invaders after the Boeotians had migrated there, and the tradition that Hyllos died in battle at the Isthmus of Corinth implies that an earlier attempt to invade through it had failed. Aetolians would have had the seamanship needed to organize the crossing of the Corinthian Gulf, and an initial advance into Arcadia would have left the kings of Mycenae and Sparta uncertain as to which was to be attacked first. In Argos a fortified base was secured near Nauplia, from which the Mycenaean kingdom was presumably reduced. If these are not true details, the author who devised them must have had an excellent capacity for military strategy. The conquest of Laconia was credited to the sons of Aristodemos, one of the Dorian tribal kings who planned the invasion, and so it was presumably thought to have taken place at the same time as the occupation of the Argolid or soon afterward. But there are allusions to prolonged resistance at Amyklai and elsewhere in Laconia.

Recent discussions that treat the whole story of the Dorian migration as fictional emphasize the lack of archaeological evidence that newcomers settled in the Peloponnese either around 1220–1200 B.C. or a century later, and reject the argument that Doric and other West Greek dialects were introduced into the Peloponnese from the north. Nevertheless, archaeology certainly shows that Mycenaean civilization was disrupted by violent events in the last decades of the thirteenth century B.C. and fell into final decline at the end of the twelfth.

Throughout most of the thirteenth century the Mycenaean world was prosperous and apparently secure. Trade between its kingdoms must have been regular and extensive, since the pottery varies little between regions. Destruction at Mycenae followed by strengthening of its fortifications soon after 1250 B.C. is the first sign of war or attack from abroad. About the same time a northward-facing wall was built across the Isthmus of Corinth. Toward the end of the century Mycenae itself, Tiryns, Pylos, and the settlement at Zygouries in Corinthia were destroyed or sacked, and it was perhaps at this time that Gla in Boeotia and Crisa in Phocis were also destroyed. Surveys in Laconia and Messenia have shown widespread abandonment of sites there also at the end of the Late Helladic IIIB period. Drought has been suggested as the cause, but it has not been shown to have been general in countries around the Aegean at that time. Small-scale but continued raiding from the sea might well have caused the depopulation. It is suggested that the palace at Ano Englianos–Pylos was not rebuilt after the sack around 1200 B.C. The northwestern coasts of Greece and those of Illyria have spawned sea raiders at other times in history.

In the twelfth century B.C., during the period of Late Helladic IIIC pottery, the Mycenaean region recovered substantially, though the development of local styles of pottery implies reduction of trade. In the last phase of Late Helladic IIIC, toward the end of the century, Mycenae was finally destroyed as a city and many other settlements were abandoned. In Attica the decline was less severe and a continuous development in pottery styles can be observed, through sub-Mycenaean to Protogeometric and Geometric. The later styles were imitated in the Argolid. This accords well with the idea that Dorians settled in most of the Peloponnese during the eleventh century. But their arrival is not proved by the appearance of new artifacts. Those that are new, like the "Naue II" sword, might have been adopted through trade. Changes in burial customs, with use of cist and pit graves, may show the revival of practices rare but not forgotten during the Mycenaean period.

THE EVIDENCE OF DIALECT

Until recently most modern scholars considered that the hypothesis of a Dorian migration satisfactorily explained the differences between groups of Greek dialects and their distribution in the classical period. Before the decipherment of Linear B it was thought that four dialect groups had begun to differentiate during the Bronze Age, ancestral to the West Greek (Doric and Northwestern), Aeolic, and Ionic groups, and to a dialect group represented by Arcadian and Cypriote. More recently, as an alternative, only two prehistoric groups have been postulated, a northern one ancestral to the West Greek and a southeastern one from which Mycenaean and all classical groups developed. (A third is added if a proto-Aeolic dialect is thought to have become distinct before the first millennium.)

Granted some difference between northern Greek dialects and those of the Peloponnese in the thirteenth century, a Dorian migration would have replaced Mycenaean Greek and perhaps other related dialects with Doric and northwestern Greek dialects throughout the Peloponnese, with the exception of Arcadia, which the immigrants would have left alone as poor, inaccessible, and difficult to conquer. A movement of refugees following earlier colonists would have brought Mycenaean Greek or a similar dialect to Cyprus, where it would have developed directly into the Cypriote of the classical centuries. Attica was bypassed and developed its characteristic dialect, which was taken by colonists to the central Aegean islands and Ionia.

Recently, this reconstruction has been criticized for a number of reasons. First, the division of Greek into four groups of dialects is not clear-cut. Some isoglosses or characteristic features are shared by two or more dialects, which are generally assigned on the basis of other criteria to different groups among the four. This phenomenon, however, is normal in the development of a language into dialects and does not vitiate the accepted general division of Greek into four groups. Second, the ancient Greeks' ability to observe differences between dialects of their own language has been questioned. Their philology was certainly unsystematic by modern standards, but even uneducated, vernacular speakers of a language may have an acute appreciation of similarities and differences between dialects, and we need not reject what ancient Greek authors say about Greek dialects. A general difference between Doric and Ionic Greek seems to have been recognized. In the third century Theocritus presents us with a lady of Alexandria, who was clearly no professional pedant, defending her Syracusan accent as "Doric" (*Idyll* 15.87–93).

Regarding the development of Greek before the first millennium, the present consensus is that pre-Greek was an essentially homogeneous language when it was introduced into Greece, and perhaps remained so as late as the sixteenth century B.C. But two features indicate that Greek had differentiated into northern and southern or southeastern dialect groups by the time the Linear B texts were written. First, Mycenaean, Arcadian, Cypriote, Attic-Ionic, and, in part, Aeolic had all changed original *t* into *s* (as in the change to *didōsi*, "gives," from the earlier *didōti*), while West Greek preserved it. Second, the West Greek dialects developed a characteristic form of the future tense in *-ésō*, changed later to *-éō* or *-â*. Both changes involve innovation in the respective dialects, which shows that the two groups had begun to develop independently.

A radically different explanation of the development of the classical Greek dialects has now been proposed by John Chadwick, in the first place because no convincing archaeological evidence had been found to indicate the arrival of immigrants in the Peloponnese between 1300 and 1000 B.C. It discards the idea that Doric dialects were carried south by migrants and suggests instead that in the fourteenth and thirteenth centuries vernacular Greek was still spoken with little variation throughout Greece, but that a distinct and homogeneous "class" dialect had developed and spread among the rulers of the Mycenaean states, their aristocracies, and their administrators. This is the dialect of the Linear B tablets. The close contacts between the Mycenaean royal houses kept the language of the texts from Knossos and those from Pylos and Mycenae identical. The peasants and artisans of the mainland states, however, continued to speak dialects of "Common Greek" that were little different from those of tribes in the north and northwest who had not adopted Mycenaean civilization.

The disappearance of Mycenaean Greek (which had changed older *t* to *s*) between about 1200 and about 800 B.C. and the appearance of "Doric" dialects (which had not changed *t*) in its place is explained as a consequence of revolts by the lower orders of the Mycenaean kingdoms against their rulers and the resurgence of their vernacular dialects as the sole, and later official, idioms of new states. In Attica, Arcadia, and Cyprus, "standard" Mycenaean survived. The advocates of this explanation claim that the entire classical tradition about a Dorian migration must be regarded as a fabrication designed to associate the new rulers with dynasties of the legendary past, like the *Herakleidai*, and so give them prestige in their own day. Chadwick deduces concurrent use of two dialects of Greek in the Mycenaean palace complexes from "doublets," or variant forms of a small number of words in Linear B texts. In each case the commoner variant supposedly belonged to the standard dialect of Mycenaean while the less common was a corresponding form from the vernacular, which a scribe had introduced into a text by a lapse.

Critics of this theory have pointed out that some migrations in antiquity, which certainly took place, had important effects, and are recorded in literature, left negligible material traces—for example, the movements of the Galatians into central Anatolia and of Slavs into Greece in the sixth century A.D. Moreover, the evidence for use of two dialects at Knossos and Pylos is tenuous. Peter G. van Soesbergen has shown that the doublets, which supposedly indicate such use, could be either archaic and current forms of the same word (for example, the ethnic name *ti-nwa-si-ja* and *ti-nwa-ti-ja-*) or different grammatical formations on the same stem (for example, *pe-ma* and *pe-mo,* representing *sperma* and *spermo,* "seed"). It is hard to assess the new explanation objectively because no communities similar enough to provide analogies survived into modern times, which would permit the development of dialects in their languages to be studied scientifically. But there seems to be no example in the ancient world of the development of a standard or elite dialect across a number of independent communities. Bilingualism seems always to have been a matter of concurrent use of two distinct (if related) languages and to have resulted either from conquest (as in the Roman Empire), infiltration (as of Akkadian into Sumer), or replacement of the language of a small nation by one more important internationally (as of Hebrew by Aramaic). Moreover, it seems unlikely that an aristocracy would develop and preserve a dialect different from that of native subjects in a community as small as a Mycenaean state.

To summarize, attempts to explain the linguistic situation in Greece in the first millennium B.C. and the decline of Mycenaean civilization without assuming immigration from northern Greece are not convincing, and the absence of archaeological evidence for new settlement in the twelfth century B.C. is not decisive. Also there are other arguments for accepting the Greek tradition in its main lines; for instance, many historical communities who regarded themselves as Dorian share a political institution, the division of their citizens into three tribes, Hylleis, Pamphyloi, and Dymanes. Finally, it is difficult to imagine that a narrative as detailed and coherent as the traditional account of the migration was devised for propaganda purposes by a number of city-states that had been established by social revolution. But the story of the return of the *Herakleidai* might have been grafted onto a tradition about a historical migration, and subsequently have been given prominence.

THE "SEA PEOPLES"

Finds of new artifacts made in the past ten years at sites in central Greece and Achaea in the Peloponnese may at last provide convincing evidence for emigration from farther north. But the material must be considered in the wider context of migrations from the Aegean region southward and from the Balkans into Anatolia at the end of the second millennium B.C., particularly those of the so-called Sea Peoples. "Sea Peoples" is the name the Egyptians gave to those who came from lands to the north of Crete and Cyprus. Alliances of Sea Peoples twice attempted without success to invade Egypt: first from the west in conjunction with Libyan peoples in the fifth regnal year of Merneptah (1232 B.C.), then without African allies in Rameses III's fifth year, 1194 B.C. It appears that in the first attempt contingents from Aegean countries sailed directly from them to Libya and joined the Libyans' attack on Egypt with the purpose of winning booty rather than in order to settle in that country. The second attempt at invasion was a migration of whole peoples who emigrated from their homelands under pressure, perhaps of starvation. The Egyptian accounts describe them as overwhelming Hatti, Qode (*Kizzuwatna* in Hittite texts; later Cilicia), Carchemish, Arzawa, and Alasiya (Cyprus, or a kingdom in it). In the first decades of the twelfth century B.C. cities in Cyprus and Syria were destroyed and some, like Ugarit, were never reoccupied. Correspondence between the last known king of Ugarit and the court of Alasiya shows that the two countries had already suffered attacks from the direction of Lycia in southwestern Asia Minor. The course of events from that point is clear. The migrants established a base camp in Amurru (in Lebanon) and from it moved against Egypt, taking their families with them, while their fleet accompanied them along the coast of Palestine. Pottery of Aegean origin appears there in the twelfth century and shows that survivors settled there after their defeat near the Egyptian border.

The unresolved questions about these attempted invasions is whether they were essentially enterprises of peoples of southern and western Anatolia and perhaps the Dodecanese only, or whether they were initiated and perhaps led by northern peoples, or whether there may even have been a concerted plan by tribes of the southern Balkans, with allies on the Aegean coastlands, to attack the heartland of the Hittite Empire, then the cities of Cyprus and Syria, and finally Egypt. If so, attempts by Balkan peoples to invade Greece might be expected at the same time, around 1200 to 1150 B.C.

The names of some of the Sea Peoples may point to their origin, though the Egyptian hieroglyphic script does not indicate vowels and is in other ways not well suited to represent foreign names accurately. It did not distinguish *l* and *r* (since the Egyptian language appears not to have had both sounds) and so does not show whether the names of certain of the Sea Peoples contained an *l* or an *r*. Two of the names may be identified with those of peoples of southern Anatolia known from other sources: *L-k/R-k* should stand for the *Lukka* of the Hittite cuneiform texts, no doubt the ancestors of the Lycians, whose habitat probably extended as far north as

Miletus in the thirteenth century B.C.; *D-n-y-n* (*Denyen*) may be equated with *Dnnym* (*Danunim*), the name of a people of Cilicia in a Phoenician text from Karatepe. The *'I-k-w-š* (*Aka[i]washa* or *Ekwesh*) are thought to be *Akhaiwoí*, Mycenaean Greeks probably from Rhodes. The *T-l-š/T-r-š* (*Teresh* or *Tursha*) may have come from western Anatolia; their name may contain the stem of *Tyrsenoí*, the Greek form of the name of the Etruscans (*Etrusci* in Latin). Herodotus tells that the ancestors of the Etruscans were Lydians who migrated from Anatolia to Umbria, presumably before the Greek colonization of Ionia (1.94). *Š-k-l-š/Š-k-r-š* (*Sheklesh, Shakalsha*) has been compared with *Sikeloí* and *Š-l-d-n/Š-r-d-n* with *Sardoí*, with the suggestion that the two peoples migrated to Sicily and Sardinia after their defeat by Rameses III. One name corresponds neatly with that of a people of northwestern Anatolia: *D-l-d-n-y/D-r-d-n-y* with *Dardanoí*, but *Zeker* or *Tjekker* and *Teukroi* are not so similar. No plausible comparisons have been made for the names of the *W-š-š* (*Weshesh*) or the *P-l-s-t/P-r-s-t* (*Peleset*), who settled in Palestine, their name surviving as "Philistines."

The statement in Rameses' inscriptions that "Hatti" could not stand before the Sea Peoples has commonly been taken to mean that their first success was to sack Hattusas and put an end to Hittite power in Anatolia. Excavations at Hattusas have shown that the city's end was catastrophic. Its archives end abruptly and give no hint about the cause of the disaster, which is dated to about 1200 B.C. or somewhat later, because the last king mentioned, Suppiluliumas II, came to the throne in about 1215 B.C. If the generally held opinion is right, this will imply that the migrations originated in the southern Balkans or northwestern Anatolia. Forces from southwestern Anatolia alone would not have been able to invade the central region successfully through the mountains that faced them, destroy all its main cities, and then march south into Syria. Rameses' statement does not prove that Sea Peoples were directly involved in the sack of Hattusas. "Hatti" was used by the Hittites of all the territory under their sovereignty, not only that of their original kingdom east of the Halys (Kızıl Irmak). Also, the Egyptians might have confused reports of the destruction of Hattusas by invaders from the northwest with what they knew about the actions of the Sea Peoples in southern Anatolia and Syria.

The most probable explanation is that the first attack on a serious scale was an invasion of the Hittites' central territory from the northwest, probably by the ancestors of the Phrygians, though there is also evidence for settlement of Thracian immigrants at Troy in the period of Level VIIB2 (in the appearance of so-called "Buckelkeramik" or "Knobbed Ware"). Herodotus had heard that the Phrygians had migrated to Anatolia from Macedonia (7.73), but no settlement or pottery can be associated with them before the eighth century B.C. Migrations from the southern Balkans probably put pressure on the peoples of western and southern Anatolia, as well as destroying the Hittite state, and caused them to maraud and then to emigrate to the south. The texts from Ugarit before its destruction and Hittite documents of the reign of Suppululiumas II point to sea raids on Cyprus and the Syrian coast. The Sea Peoples whom Merneptah faced must have been experienced seamen to have crossed from the Aegean to Libya (as later Greeks did—for instance, in the voyage of Dorieus; Herodotus, 5.42–43). The Sea Peoples, then, would have come mainly from the southern Aegean and adjacent parts of Anatolia, though they may have accepted some tribes or groups from farther north as allies. The suggestion that the "Sheklesh" came from Italy or the head of the Adriatic rests on a doubtful deduction from their name, though it is interesting that a sword of Italian type with the cartouche of Merneptah has been found at Ugarit.

If there was no large northern element among the Sea Peoples it would be less likely that tribes or large groups from the Balkans entered Greece around 1200 B.C., and much less likely that they conquered Mycenaean states and ruled them during the period of recovery in the Late Helladic IIIC period.

NEW ARCHAEOLOGICAL EVIDENCE

The decline of Mycenaean civilization and the transition to the era of the Hellenic city-states apparently had the following phases: destruction of most main settlements about 1230–1200 B.C., though most were not abandoned; recovery during the Late Helladic IIIC period, though with reduction in interstate trade and contact; then a second phase of destructions followed by a general, more serious lowering of the standard of life, with considerable cultural change; and, finally, the abandonment of Mycenaean sites and the formation of new cities. Pottery had a continuous development from the "granary" style of the Late Helladic IIIC period through the sub-Mycenaean to the Protogeometric and Geometric periods, at least in Attica. Immigration from northern Greece might well have caused the destructions and the changes, but no distinctive new artifacts could be associated with newcomers. Since 1975 archaeologists have made new suggestions about their origin. Part of the evidence lies in sporadic finds of handmade coarse wares at sites where Mycenaean (Late Helladic IIIC) and later sub-Mycenaean or Protogeometric pottery was in use. Jeremy B. Rutter has drawn attention to such "barbarian" pottery among the finds at Korakou near Corinth (excavated in 1921) and considers them most similar to coarse ware found at Troy in Levels VIIB1 (the first after the "Homeric" destruction) and VIIB2, as well as to pottery from south Italy. Sigrid Deger-Jalkotzy reports similar pottery stratified under later Late Helladic IIIC levels at Aigeira (in the Aigion district, in Achaea) and sees the same connections for it; migrants from Illyria would have taken it to Italy.

Coarse ware found at Tiryns, however, is thought to have parallels in northwestern Greece. Gisela Walberg and Nancy Sandars have suggested that some coarse ware for household purposes must always have been made in Mycenaean settlements and that in early Late Helladic IIIC the poorer inhabitants went over for a time to making more for themselves by hand. The excavators claim that the decoration and technique of the wares from Korakou and Aigeira tell against this, and in any case, since pottery was a basic product in Bronze Age communities, it seems unlikely that the art of making it on the wheel would have been lost in villages in the Peloponnese in the twelfth century even if the production of fine wares for the palaces and for export had come to an end. The second recent development is Schachermeyr's conclusion that the spread of two more distinctive wares can be traced from northwestern Greece, mainly Aetolia, to areas in the Peloponnese, those he calls "intermediate ware" (*"Zwischenkeramik"*) and "leather-pouch ware" (*"Lederbeutelkeramik"*). The first he regards as developed from native handmade pottery of Aetolia under the influence of Mycenaean settlers. The second would imitate the kind of vessels used by pastoral nomads. Wares of the two types have been found alongside Late Helladic IIIC and sub-Mycenaean pottery at Corinth, Amyklai, and Sparta.

No one of these newly identified wares can be associated with migrants from Doris and adjacent areas. It appears that the first peoples to profit by the damage done to the Mycenaean cities around 1200 B.C. and the weakening of their rulers' political power were poor tribesmen from the northwest who were now able to settle in their territories. If the coarse pottery of Korakou and Aigeira did come from outside Greece, that would support Schachermeyr's idea that the destructions at the end of the thirteenth century were the work of invaders from the north, if not of Sea Peoples in the strict sense. But the amounts found do not indicate invasion on a large scale, and it is not likely that the intruders became ruling dynasties in Greece in the Late Helladic IIIC period.

The Dorians remain hard to identify in archaeology. Schachermeyr's conclusions about them seem to be the best: that they were a Greek tribe, or group of tribes, who became a militarily efficient people in the Pindus area, Doris, and Dryopis, and finally drove south and conquered the main Peloponnesian states as late as the Protogeometric or the early Geometric period. They assimilated unusually fast and thoroughly in material culture to the other Greeks whom they conquered, and the only material trace of their arrival is in the evident increase in the populations of the Argolid and parts of Crete in the Geometric period. This leaves open the questions whether the tradition of the return of the *Herakleidai* was historical and whether Dorians had made a previous attempt to invade the Peloponnese around 1220 B.C.

MIGRATIONS ACROSS THE AEGEAN AND TO CRETE

Greek tradition held that men of all the three main branches of the Hellenes migrated across the Aegean soon after the Dorians' invasion of the Peloponnese and founded settlements on the islands and the western coasts of Anatolia, most of which became poleis (city-states) from the eighth century B.C. onward. Aeolians from Thessaly and Boeotia supposedly established themselves in the Troad and on the western coast between Kanai and Smyrna. Ionians settled between Smyrna and the Gulf of Iassos. Dorians migrated to Thera, Kos, and Rhodes, and settled also at Halicarnassus and Cnidus on the mainland. The nature of the dialects spoken in the new cities in the fifth century B.C. corresponds to this pattern of migration, except that Smyrna had become Ionian (Herodotus, 1.149–151). Migration to Anatolia from eastern Greece, from Attica northward, was a natural consequence of the pressure put on its peoples by tribes from the north or northwestern Greece. Movements of Dorians to colonize Melos and Thera, and presumably Rhodes and Kos, immediately after their conquest of the Argolid and part of Laconia, are less to be expected. But Herodotus tells that their migration to Thera began in the same generation as their settlement in Laconia (4.147), and the people of Melos believed that their Dorian ancestors had arrived there about 1115 B.C. (Thucydides, 5.112). Archaeology supports these traditions. The early settlements at Smyrna, Klazomenai, and Miletus are dated to about 1000 B.C. by their Geometric pottery, and Dorian Calymna on Rhodes is dated to before 900 B.C.

The Athenian account of the Ionian migration seems to have been that it was organized by Athens, and that the emigrants, including refugees from the pre-Dorian kingdom of Pylos and elsewhere in the Peloponnese, left from Attica (Herodotus 1.145–146; Strabo 14.1.3; Pausanias 7.1.2–4). But the real events in it may have been simplified and Athens' role exaggerated. Herodotus notes that peoples who were never regarded as Ionians took part. But the similarity of Attic Greek to the dialects of Miletus and other cities of Ionia confirms the tradition in its main lines.

Overseas migration would not have been difficult for the Dorians who had conquered the Argolid. The inhabitants of Rhodes were Mycenaean in culture in the fourteenth and thirteenth centuries B.C. and were, in all probability, Greek. The Greeks of the Argolid whom the Dorians dominated would no doubt have been in touch with them and, as seafarers, would have been able to take Dorian colonists to the islands. Homer seems to have known that Dorians lived in Rhodes in his time, but also that it might have been Achaean before the Trojan War. He avoids anachronism by naming Tlepolemus, a son of Herakles, as its ruler and colonizer, and not mentioning Dorians (*Iliad* 2.661–666; Strabo, 14.2.6). Doric Greek was spoken in Crete in the sixth century B.C. but there is no reason to believe that it was introduced there earlier than in Thera and Rhodes. The mention of Dorians in Crete in the *Odyssey* (19.177) is not good evidence that they had arrived there before the eleventh century. Homer, in Ionia, would have known Crete only by hearsay, and so would have been more than usually likely to fall into anachronism and include Dorians among its peoples, as they were in his own day, when making Odysseus describe it. Dorians no doubt settled in Crete in the tenth century, and their coming is shown by an increase in its population.

CONCLUSION

Whatever occurred in Greece during the period of migrations, it created the context in which most of the early city-states began to form. There remains the question of its wider importance in the evolution of Hellenic society and civilization. The disturbances may have had the effect, as a historical accident, of checking the development, which had begun in the Mycenaean period, of larger political units that might have evolved more centrally organized and hierarchical systems of government than those of the poleis, although the economic resources of the Mycenaean states were probably always smaller than those of their contemporaries in central Anatolia and Syria.

Many fifth-century Greeks, including some who did not regard themselves as Dorians, felt that the Dorians were the true Hellenes, while the Ionians, for all their commercial, artistic, and political achievements, and in spite of the Athenians' claim to be autochthonous in Attica, were in some way less pure, both in their origin and in their share of the special Hellenic virtues (Herodotus, 1.56). In Xenophon's case such feelings may reflect nostalgia for a society and an outlook that had changed in Athens by his day, though he thought he still found them in Sparta. But it may be that Greek migrants from the north, especially Dorians, brought with them a well-disciplined and cohesive tribal society, with notable martial abilities that were basic to the strong community spirit that gave the Hellenic city-state its patriotism and sense of identity, along with the feeling that the individual should participate in deciding how its affairs should be run as well as accepting his duty to it.

BIBLIOGRAPHY

SOURCES

The works of Apollodorus, Diodorus of Sicily (Diodorus Siculus), Herodotus, Hesiod, Homer, Pausanias, Pindar, Strabo, Theocritus, Thucydides, Tyrtaeus, and Xenophon are all available in the Loeb Classical Library editions.

STUDIES

Elly Arditis, ed., *The First Arrival of Indo-European Elements in Greece: Acta of the Second International Colloquium on Aegean Prehistory* (1972); Richard D. Barnett, "The Sea Peoples," in *The Cambridge Ancient History,* II, Part 2A, 3d ed. (1975); Oscar Broneer, "The Cyclopean Wall on the Isthmus of Corinth and its Bearing on Late Bronze Age Chronology," in *Hesperia,* **35** (1966); John L. Caskey, "Greece, Crete, and the Aegean Islands in the Early Bronze Age," in *The Cam-*

bridge Ancient History, I, Part 2, 3d ed. (1971); John Chadwick, "The Prehistory of the Greek Language," in *The Cambridge Ancient History,* II, Part 2A, 3d ed. (1975), "Who Were the Dorians?" in *Parola del Passato,* **31** (1976), "The Mycenaean Dorians," in *Bulletin of the Institute of Classical Studies,* **23** (1976), and "I Don' e la creazione dei dialetti Greci," in Domenico Musti, ed., *Le origini dei Greci* (1985); Robert Coleman, "The Dialect Geography of Ancient Greece," in *Transactions of the Philological Society* (1963); John M. Cook, "Greek Settlement in the Eastern Aegean and Asia Minor," in *The Cambridge Ancient History,* II, Part 2A, 3d ed. (1975); Ronald A. Crossland, "Immigrants from the North," in *The Cambridge Ancient History,* I, Part 2, 3d ed. (1971), and "The Mystery of Ahhiyawa," in *Illustrated London News,* **268** (September 1980).

Ronald A. Crossland and Ann Birchall, eds., *Bronze Age Migrations in the Aegean: Archaeological and Linguistic Problems in Greek Prehistory* (1973); Apostolos Basileiou Daskalakēs, *The Hellenism of the Ancient Macedonians* (1965); Ellen N. Davies, ed., *Symposium on the Dark Ages in Greece* (1977); Sigrid Deger-Jalkotzy, *Fremde Zuwanderer im spätmykenischen Griechenland* (1977), and *Griechenland, die Ägäis und die Levante während der "Dark Ages" vom 12. bis zum 9 Jh. v. Chr.: Akten des Symposions von Stift Zwettl 11–14 Oktober 1980* (1983); Vincent R. d'A. Desborough, "The End of Mycenaean Civilization and the Dark Age: The Archaeological Background," in *The Cambridge Ancient History,* II, Part 2, 3d ed. (1975); Edgar J. Forsdyke, *Greece Before Homer: Ancient Chronology and Mythology* (1956); Marija Gimbutas, "Proto-Indo-European Culture," in George Cardona, Henry M. Hoenigswald, Alfred Senn, eds., *Indo-European and Indo-Europeans: Papers Presented at the Third Indo-European Conference at the University of Pennsylvania* (1970); Oliver R. Gurney, *The Hittites* (1975; rev. ed. 1980).

Hans G. Güterbock and Machteld J. Mellink, "The Hittites and the Aegean World," in *American Journal of Archaeology,* **87** (1983); J. B. Haley and Carl W. Blegen, "The Coming of the Greeks," in *American Journal of Archaeology,* **32** (1928); Erik Hallager, *The Mycenaean Palace at Knossos: Evidence for Final Destruction in the IIIB Period* (1977); N. G. L. Hammond, "The End of Mycenaean Civilization and the Dark Age: The Literary Tradition for the Migrations," in *The Cambridge Ancient History,* II, Part 2, 3d ed. (1975); Sinclair Hood, "Northern Penetration of Greece at the End of the Early Helladic Period and Contemporary Balkan Chronology," in *Bronze Age Migrations in the Aegean Region* (1970); William A. McDonald and Richard Hope-Simpson, "Prehistoric Habitation in Southwestern Peloponnese," in *American Journal of Archaeology,* **65** (1961); Karl Otfried Müller, *Die Dorier* (1844); Domenico Musti, *Le origini dei Greci* (1985); Heinrich Otten, *Sprachliche Stellung und Datierung des Madduwatta-Textes* (1969); Leonard R. Palmer and John Boardman, *On the Knossos Tablets* (1963); Christian Podzuweit, "Der spätmykenische Einfluss in Makedonien," in *Proceedings of the Fourth International Congress of Macedonian Studies, Thessaloniki, 1983* (in press); E. Risch, "La posizione del dialetto dorico," in *Le origini dei Greci* (1985).

Zeev Rubinsohn, "The Dorian Invasion Again," in *La Parola del Passato,* **30** (1975); Jeremy B. Rutter, "Ceramic Evidence for Northern Intruders in Southern Greece at the Beginning of the Late Helladic IIIC Period," in *American Journal of Archaeology,* **79** (1975); Michael V. Sakellariou, "Comment on Spyridon Marinatos, 'Mycenaean Culture'" in *Atti e memorie del primo congresso internazionale di Micenologia* in Carlo Gallavotti, ed., *Incunabula Graeca,* **25**, pt. 1 (1968); Nancy K. Sandars, *The Sea Peoples* (1978); Fritz Schachermeyr, *Die griechische Rückerinnerung im Lichte neuer Forschungen* (1983), and *Griechische Frühgeschichte* (1984); Thomas A. Sebeok, *Portraits of Linguists* (1966); Frank H. Stubbings, "The Rise of Mycenaean Civilization," in *The Cambridge Ancient History,* II, Part 1, 3d ed. (1973); Demetrios R. Theochares, "Iolkos, Whence Sailed the Argonauts," in *Archaeology,* **11** (1958); Peter G. van Soesbergen, "The Coming of the Dorians," in *Kadmos,* **20** (1981); Michael Ventris and John Chadwick, *Documents in Mycenaean Greek* (1956); Gisela Walberg, "Northern Intruders in Mycenaean IIIc?" in *American Journal of Archaeology,* **80** (1976); P. A. Wallace, "The Motherland of the Dorians," in *Symposium on the Dark Ages in Greece* (1977); F. A. Winters, "An Historically Derived Model for the Dorian Invasion," in *Symposium on the Dark Ages in Greece* (1977).

Late Roman Migrations

E. A. THOMPSON

MIGRATIONS IN THIS PERIOD resulted in the Germanic peoples founding kingdoms in every part of the Western Roman Empire, and in the year A.D. 476 they caused the deposition of Romulus Augustulus, the last West Roman emperor in Italy.

Before describing the movements of the Germanic peoples, we must note where each of them was living in the middle of the fourth century, on the eve of the migrations. Taking each group from east to west along the northern frontier of the empire: to the north of the Black Sea in what is now the Ukraine were the Ostrogoths; to the southwest in modern Romania lived the Visigoths, the Germanic people about whom we are best informed; and to the west lived the Vandals as far as the northward course of the Danube. On the middle Danube in areas that are hard to define precisely lived the Marcomani, Quadi, and Rugi with the Lombards to the north of them. East of the upper Rhine but south of the Main River were the Alamanni (hence the French "Allemands"). North of the Main dwelled the Franks, and on the upper Main the Burgundians. Finally, on the southern shore of the North Sea were the Frisians, Saxons, and Angles.

THE AGE OF THE MIGRATIONS: BEGINNINGS

Throughout the entire history of the Roman Empire German tribes had been pressing on the northern imperial frontiers, occasionally penetrating them, and even causing their temporary collapse, the aim of the intruders being to collect loot. But the Romans always restored their borders. The external threat to the empire was greatly intensified by the arrival of the Huns in Europe (ca. A.D. 370). No one knew then, and no one is certain now, who the Huns were or whence they came. Excellent, though brief, accounts exist of their pastoral nomadism—they knew nothing of agriculture—and of their rapidly moving horsemen who terrified the settled, agricultural peoples of southeastern Europe. They first appeared east of the Black Sea in the fourth century and drove westward, overthrowing at great speed the kingdom of the

Ostrogoths in the Ukraine and in 376 overrunning the Visigoths. The pursuit of the Visigoths to the north bank of the Danube in the autumn of 376 may be said to have begun the "age of the migrations."

The Roman government admitted panic-stricken Visigoths to the provinces south of the lower Danube, hoping to enlist them into the army. It was estimated at the time that some 200,000 persons crossed the Danube. Owing to gross mistreatment by Roman officers on the spot, these Visigoths revolted, and on 9 August in 378 they won a devastating victory over the army of the Eastern Empire at Hadrianopolis (Edirne, Adrianople) in Thrace, killing the emperor Valens. The view that this was the first victory of cavalry over infantry and that it began the period of the predominance of the horseman in military history is mistaken: the Visigoths were infantrymen like the Romans. The new emperor, Theodosius I, was at first militarily helpless and on 3 October in 382 was obliged to agree to the Visigoths' settling south of the Danube in Roman territory. Theodosius gave them land in Thrace and annual subsidies; in return they were required to keep out the Huns, who now controlled the north bank of the Danube. This was the first occasion in Roman history that a whole barbarian people was permitted to settle inside the empire under the command of its own leaders, not subject to Roman law. This proved to be of great consequence, for the Romans were unable to control them.

The Goths had originated in southern Scandinavia and had crossed to the south bank of the Baltic Sea by the beginning of the Christian Era; Tacitus, a hundred years later, mentions their being in that region. In the mid second century they moved southeastward to the north and northwest shores of the Black Sea, and exerted such pressure on the exposed Roman province of Dacia (approximately Rumania) that in A.D. 270 the Roman government withdrew from the province (perhaps the only case of a voluntary Roman withdrawal in the history of the Western Empire). Those Goths who moved into the abandoned province were the Visigoths (West Goths); those who stayed in the Ukraine were the Ostrogoths (East Goths). Both were overrun or expelled a hundred years later by the Huns.

In the latter part of that century, 275–376, an event of capital importance occurred among the Visigoths. Ulfilas, who became a bishop in 341 and was of a Cappadocian family captured by the Goths, began his great effort to convert the Visigoths to Arian Christianity, and for that purpose carried out his stupendous achievement of translating the Bible into Gothic, a translation of which extensive fragments survive. He began by adapting Greek and Latin letters to invent an alphabet in which to write the work. While the Goths had an alphabet before his time—the early Germanic script known as runes—it was thought to be too closely associated with pagan beliefs to be used for the Bible. The work of conversion was completed after his death in 383 when the Visigoths were living south of the Danube. Visigothic missionaries tried to convert other Germanic peoples, but their successes were slow and far from complete. Even before this there were a number of Catholics living among the Goths, many but not all being Roman prisoners or descendants of prisoners who had been carried off in the third century from Asia Minor. The chieftains of the Visigoths carried out a persecution of the orthodox Christians in 369–372, one of those martyred being Sabas, a Goth and a Catholic. A superb document, the *Passion of St. Sabas,* tells of his death and incidentally gives a vivid description of life in a Visigothic village in peacetime. It records that the villagers, though pagan, did what they could to save Sabas, but were overruled by the central authority (the nature of which is not disclosed). Life in the village itself was regulated by a primitive democracy in which all male villagers had a say.

The arrangement that Theodosius I concluded with the Visigoths in 382 broke up in the year of his death, 395, for the Visigoths claimed that the new Roman government stopped paying their subsidies. Under the leadership of Alaric I they started moving westward. They often acted as a pawn in Roman politics, fighting against one Roman faction in the interests of another, but were not able to obtain further subsidies or land to settle on. In 408 and 409 they invaded Italy, and in 410 they occupied Rome itself, 24–27 August. This event stunned the civilized world: it was the first time Rome had fallen to a foreign enemy in 800 years. (In *ca.* 387 B.C. it had fallen to a force of Gauls led by the perhaps legendary Brennus.) But even this did not bring the Visigoths land and subsidies. They marched to southern Italy hoping to cross to Africa, but failed to do so. Alaric I died in south Italy. His brother-in-law Ataulf led the Goths northward to southern Gaul (France) and northeastern Spain, where he was murdered. At last, in 418 the West Roman government settled them in Aquitania Secunda on the coast between the Gironde and the mouth of the Loire, with Tolosa (Toulouse) as their capital.

The Visigothic kingdom of Tolosa lasted from 418 until 507, when it was overthrown by Clovis, leader of the Franks and founder of the Merovingians, at the battle of Vouillé (outside Limonum [Poitiers]). In this period the nature of Visigothic society was changed radically. A chieftain as late as the time of Alaric I had been able only to advise and hope to persuade his followers: they might or might not follow his lead. But the kings of Tolosa did not try to persuade: they could impose their will on their followers. They used Roman lawyers to draw up a code of laws (written in Latin) for them, and this they imposed on the people at large. They were Arian Christians, but of their church organization little is known. In the main, Arians of this period did not persecute Catholics and pagans, and many Catholic Romans fought with the Visigoths at the battle of Vouillé. One of the most remarkable events of the history of the kingdom of Tolosa occurred in 451, when the aged Visigothic king, Theodoric I, joined forces with the effective ruler of the Western Empire, Aetius, to resist the great invasion of Gaul carried out by their old enemies, the Huns, under the leadership of Attila. In an enormous battle fought on the Catalaunian Plains (the Mauriac plain between Châlons and Troyes in the Champagne region)—often called the battle of Châlons—the allies held Attila, and he retreated into central Europe.

In the kingdom of Tolosa the Visigoths were established as "federates" of the Roman Empire. They lived under their own laws and leaders, using their own law courts and their own (Arian) churches, but had no control over Roman citizens of the region. The Visigoths were established on large Roman estates which the owners divided with them, and had the duty of protecting the estates. The Roman population in the kingdom was still subject to the imperial government in Rome and its appointed officials. Romans, especially Roman lawyers and landed gentry, took an increasing part in the administration of the kingdom, so that when the last Western Roman emperor was deposed in 476 and the Visigothic kingdom became free in name as well as in fact, Romans had a considerable role in administering the kingdom, using their own laws, courts, and churches. Indeed, for the average peasant the transition from Roman to Visigothic rule must have been all but imperceptible. The kingdom expanded in the second half of the fifth century, being bounded by the Loire and the Rhône, and at the end of the century Visigoths began settling in Spain, much of which they then controlled militarily.

After the battle of Vouillé in 507, the Franks won control of the whole of France apart from Narbo (Narbonne) and a narrow strip of territory running along the Mediterranean coast of France to the Pyrenees, which was still controlled by the Visigoths. The first century of Frankish rule is described in the detailed and very lively narrative of the *History of the Franks* by Gregory of Tours (A.D. 538–594).

The Visigoths continued to live in Spain (apart from Gallaecia [Galicia], which was occupied by the Suebi) and maintained a capital at Toletum (Toledo) for several hundred years, until in 711 they were defeated by an army of Moors and Arabs from North Africa.

About the year 550 the Byzantines landed in southern Spain and held a small province around Carthago Nova (Cartagena) and Malaca (Malaga) for three-quarters of a century, when at last the Visigoths expelled them. Visigothic Spain was ruled by Arian Christian kings until in 589 King Reccared announced at the Third Council of Toletum the conversion of himself, his family, and the nobility to Catholicism; Arianism disappeared after only a slight struggle. Although now Catholic, Spanish ecclesiastical contact with the outside world, even with Rome, was exceedingly rare. A series of church councils met throughout the seventh century; their minutes provide much information about conditions in Spain at that time. The law code was often revised and the changes give further information about Spanish life. The seventh century was marked by a sustained attack on the Jews aimed at either converting them forcibly to Catholicism or reducing them to the condition of slaves. None of the kingdoms that developed during the period of migrations shows anything like the ferocity of this persecution. The general impression of Spanish life in the seventh century is one of repression, superstition, gloom, and the gradual breakdown of law and order.

THE SECOND PHASE OF MIGRATIONS

The first great wave of the migrations had begun on the lower Danube and ended in Spain at the other side of Europe. A second wave began on December 31 in 406 when a huge throng of Vandals, Alans, and Suebi broke through the Rhine frontier and entered Gaul. Like the Goths, the Vandals and Suebi were Germanic-speaking peoples who lived by agriculture and fought as infantry; but the non-German Alans were pastoral nomads not unlike the Huns and fought on horseback. When the Huns appeared in Europe about 370 the Alans had been living in the steppe lands east of the Black Sea and north of the Caucasus, where the Huns overran them. How a portion of them managed to appear now on the Rhine is unknown, as indeed are the movements of the Vandals and Suebi from north of the middle Danube. The number of the joint force of men, women, and children that entered Gaul at this time is also unknown but may well have amounted to 100,000 persons. It is sometimes thought that they moved to the Rhine because they were in flight before a major Hun drive to the west from their main territories north of the lower Danube; however, there is no direct evidence for any such movement on the part of the Huns.

About the same time the Burgundians—a German people—moved from the upper Main into the Roman Empire and settled around the city of Augusta Vangionum (Worms). They lived there unobtrusively until in 436 Aetius loosed a force of Huns on them. It is said that no fewer than 20,000 Burgundians were massacred. In 443 Aetius moved the survivors to Sabaudia (Savoy), at that time the name of a strip of land stretching southward from the Lake of Geneva.

There the Burgundians lived as federates of the Romans, sharing the estates with the Roman landowners until the Franks overran them in 534.

In the meantime the Vandals and their allies, having crossed the Rhine, turned northwestward toward the Fretum Gallicum (Straits of Dover), giving rise to a panic in Britain, where it was expected that they would cross the channel. The Britons thereupon elevated a usurping emperor, afterward recognized as Constantine III (407–411). He crossed to Gesoriacum (Bononia, Boulogne) with a sizable force, thus reducing the British garrison and leaving the island almost defenseless. However, the invaders turned away to the southwest, perhaps never having intended to attack Britain. They moved southwest to the western end of the Pyrenees, causing appalling damage as they went. "The whole of Gaul," according to a contemporary, "became one vast funeral pyre." More accurately, they ravaged a huge swath of land across the middle of Gaul from northeast to southwest. They remained in Gaul for three years and then crossed into Spain in the autumn of 409. The Romans were unable to stop them, much less to expel them.

When they entered Spain the Suebi settled in Gallaecia (Galicia) and maintained an independent kingdom there until 585, when the Visigothic king Leovigild (568–586) overran them and incorporated them in the Visigothic kingdom. They had spent the early decades of their independence plundering the western half of Spain, and they appear to have been exceptionally unpleasant and destructive. The Alans invaded Spain in 409 and settled in Lusitania (in the western part of the peninsula). They were all but obliterated by a party of Visigoths acting in the Roman interest in 418.

The Vandals settled in western Spain in 409 and remained there for twenty years. During this period they too seem to have been converted to Arian Christianity, although the names of the missionary or missionaries who accomplished this are unknown. It is likely that they were Visigoths rather than Romans. In 429 the Vandals under King Gaiseric managed to do what Alaric I and his Visigoths had failed to do in 410: they crossed over the Pillars of Hercules (the Strait of Gibraltar) into Africa. The evidence indicates that no fewer than 80,000 persons were ferried across. On arrival in Africa the Vandals marched eastward toward what is now Tunisia, a granary of Rome. The occupation of North Africa by the Vandals caused singular damage to the Romans and constituted a major reason for the empire's fall. It cut off Rome's chief source of supply of grain and oil, and deprived her of control of the central Mediterranean. On 19 October in 439 the Vandals captured Carthage, the second city of the Western Empire. They now began a long series of sea raids on the central Mediterranean coasts and even interfered with the grain route from Egypt to Constantinople. Gaiseric and his men occupied Rome itself for a fortnight in 455, the second time in less than half a century that the great city had fallen to a foreign enemy. The East Romans made several attempts to dislodge the Vandals from Africa but without success. The most calamitous effort was made in 468, when a vast expedition from Constantinople —mounted at a cost in equipment, ships, and supplies that nearly bankrupted the Eastern Empire—ended in total failure. In Africa Gaiseric confiscated the large estates, which were mostly owned by Catholics, and so acquired the deserved name of persecutor. When he died in 477, he was by far the most successful of the barbarian kings of the migration period. His successors showed much less ability and initiative, and indeed many of their followers were enervated by the climate and a slow-paced, highly sensual mode of life in North Africa. The persecution of Catholics continued steadily until 523. The African kingdom of the Vandals collapsed in 534 after a brilliant campaign led by the East Roman general Belisarius, the first step in the grandiose plan of the emperor Justinian I (527–565) to restore the old Roman Empire. The Vandal king Gelimer was taken to Constantinople and was given an estate in Galatia, where he ended his days as a Romanized gentleman and landowner.

THE THIRD PHASE OF MIGRATIONS

In addition to the westward drive by the Visigoths, which began in 376, and that of the Vandals, Alans, and Suebi, which began in 406, there was a third major onslaught of Germanic tribes on the empire beginning in 455, two years after the death of Attila. Under Attila, the Huns had menaced and attacked the East Roman Empire for many years, but following an attack in 447 prolonged peace negotiations took place. One of the East Roman diplomatic missions to the Huns included in 449 the historian Priscus of Panium (in Thrace), who has left a vivid account of what happened. He saw Attila himself several times and observed keenly the life of the Huns at peace. After Attila was defeated by a combined Visigoth and West Roman force in 451, he made an unexpected attack on the north Italian cities the following year, entering Italy from the northeast and plundering cities as far west as Milan. There he was met by a commission of three from the emperor headed by Pope Leo I, who successfully diverted him from Italy. In 453, when planning a further attack on the Eastern Empire, Attila suddenly died in his sleep. His sons divided his great empire between them, but were overthrown by a revolt of their subjects in 455.

It was now that the third great onslaught was launched. A mass of starving peoples were let loose on the middle Danubian frontier, chief among them the Ostrogoths, who since being overrun in the Ukraine ca. 370 had been harshly oppressed by the Huns. They were now settled in Pannonia (roughly Hungary south of the Danube) by the Romans, and it appears to have been now that they were converted to Arianism. But they quickly left Pannonia and for years crossed and recrossed the Balkan provinces trying to wrest land and subsidies from the East Roman government.

In Italy the army, composed almost entirely it seems of a mixed force of barbarians, rebelled and deposed the last of the Western emperors, Romulus Augustulus, replacing him with a barbarian named Odoacer. The issue that had caused the revolt was a familiar one: land for troops and annual subsidies, neither of which Romulus and his advisors was willing to grant. But Odoacer granted them and governed Italy peacefully. He respected the Italian landed gentry and the Catholic church (although he was himself an Arian), and might have ended his days as a respected ruler of Italy had it not been for the turmoil caused by the Ostrogoths in the Balkans.

There the Eastern emperor Zeno (474–491) decided to rid himself of the troublesome Ostrogoths by sending them to Italy to wrest control of the government from Odoacer. The constitutional position of Odoacer had long been a matter of dispute. He was not an independent king like Gaiseric in Africa, and he ruled in name only as an official of the Eastern emperor. In fact, his precise position was never defined, and his rule was none the worse for that. But in 489 Theodoric, the king of the Ostrogoths (afterward "the Great"), invaded northern Italy, and a calamitous war broke out. After fearful loss of life and property Theodoric and Odoacer agreed to rule Italy jointly. However, in 493 Theodoric brutally murdered Odoacer with his own hands in a palace at Ravenna and went on to rule Italy until 526.

Theodoric settled his men on the estates

that had been occupied by Odoacer's troops (who were killed or expelled) and continued the tolerant policies of his predecessor. He exerted himself continuously to prevent outbreaks of anti-Roman feeling among his followers. His constitutional position was undefined, like Odoacer's, but his relations with emperors at Constantinople, whose overlordship he recognized, were uniformly amicable. Unable to pass laws, Theodoric issued "edicts," a collection of which still survives. The edicts maintained the principles of Roman law and were binding on Ostrogoths and Romans alike. No Goth was allowed to sit in the senate or to hold high Roman offices such as the consulship, but Ostrogoths were given important military appointments, and in fact they made up the entire army. Theodoric styled himself "king," but never defined his position further; certainly calling himself "king of Italy" would have been unacceptable in Constantinople. In religious matters he acted on the splendid principle that "no one can be forced to believe against his will."

Under Theodoric's government Italy is said to have enjoyed peace and prosperity such as she had not experienced for many years. The famous church of San Appolinare Nuovo at Ravenna, which still stands, dates from his reign and is remarkable for its mosaics. His tomb in one of the city's most famous buildings also survives, as do a number of manuscripts from this period. They include translations of the New Testament by Ulfilas, and the famous and beautiful *Codex Argenteus*, with a text written in silver ink on purple vellum. (It is preserved in the University Library at Uppsala, in Sweden.) A fragment of a commentary on St. John's Gospel and some lesser writings suggest that Ostrogothic theology was arid and dull, and resembled that elaborated in the Visigothic and Vandal kingdoms.

The end of Theodoric's reign is marked sourly by his execution in 524 of one of his ministers, the Roman statesman and philosopher Boethius, on false charges of treason. As he lay in prison awaiting death Boethius composed *The Consolation of Philosophy,* which became one of the most famous books of the Middle Ages. When Theodoric himself died, in 526, the hostility of the Ostrogoths toward the Romans burst out, and the rank and file objected strongly to the romanized ways of Theodoric's daughter, Amalasuntha, who succeeded him as regent for her son, Athalaric. But Athalaric died in 534, and anti-Roman Ostrogoths murdered Amalasuntha. The great East Roman emperor Justinian I (527–565), his conquest of Africa now apparently complete, took the queen's murder as a pretext for war, and sent Belisarius and his army to Sicily and thence to Italy. The devastating war that ensued (534–553) ended with the virtual annihilation of the Ostrogoths. The destruction of life and property was appalling, and for a period in 536 Rome itself was left almost uninhabited, perhaps for the only time between its foundation, attributed to 753 B.C., and the present.

At the end of the war Justinian, who had now conquered a small part of Spain, set about the reorganization of Italy and its incorporation in the East Roman Empire. Three years after his death in 565, a new enemy entered Italy, the Germanic Lombards (who have left their name in the Plains of Lombardy). They came down from central Europe and entered into an interminable conflict with the Eastern Romans, who proved incapable of preventing them from settling in northern Italy.

EFFECTS OF THE MAJOR WAVES OF MIGRATION

There are additional movements to be considered, but several characteristics of the three phases of migration discussed so far are of major significance, for they produced permanent changes and eventual fusion of the cultures of the migrants and that of the inhabitants of the Roman Empire.

First, there was a strong and lasting tendency, especially among the two branches of the Goths, for leading tribesmen to come to terms with the Roman government whenever they could. On the eve of the battle of Adrianople in 378 the Visigothic leader Fritigern opened secret negotiations with the East Roman emperor Valens, though they came to nothing and so we do not know what he hoped to gain by his treachery. Afterward Theodosius I played on the differences that he detected among the Gothic leaders. This led to a brawl among them, with the result that several went over to the Roman side and received commands in the Roman army. The rank and file of the tribesmen remained hostile to the imperial government. Those who joined the Roman army soon found themselves fighting against their fellow tribesmen, whom they more than once defeated. Alaric's name is associated with one of the great events of history, the fall of Rome to the barbarians in 410; yet he would not be considered among the great men of history. Throughout his career (395–410) he partly supported the West Roman government and partly struggled against it so as to obtain land and subsidies for his people. He was not successful in either policy for long. The reason for this dual policy was stated clearly by his successor, Athaulf, in 413: At first his ambition had been to demolish the Roman Empire but now he wished to preserve it, for if the Visigoths were incorporated in the empire his own position would change. Instead of being a mere tribal leader, able only to persuade and advise his followers, he would be able to impose his will on them, with the machinery of the Roman state to support him. In other words, support for Rome and the strengthening of the Visigothic chieftain's power in his own society were in effect one and the same policy. As long as the Western Empire lasted the Visigoths were divided on this issue.

The Ostrogoths had a similar experience. After Theodoric's death in 526 their leaders successively tried to betray their interests by deserting to the Byzantines. Amalasuntha planned to defect, taking with her the Gothic treasury, amounting to almost three million solidi. Her successor, Theodahad, offered to hand over Tuscany to the Byzantines on condition that he might spend the rest of his life at Constantinople, be made a member of the senate, and be given a substantial income. Later he offered to hand over the entire kingdom in return for an income of about 80,000 solidi (a commoner could live on two solidi or less a year). In fact, in the course of half a dozen years a series of Ostrogothic rulers expressed a willingness to betray the common ranks if the reward were high enough (which usually amounted to a respected position in Roman society and a large income). In settling inside the empire the Ostrogothic nobility thus became markedly romanized.

Since the life of the Roman aristocracy was infinitely richer and more luxurious than anything that could be found outside the northern imperial frontier, it is not surprising that once they had entered the empire the barbarian leaders were tempted to join the nobility, not to destroy it. This tendency can be traced back to the earliest days of the empire.

A second change that occurred in the Mediterranean countries during the migration period concerns warfare and in particular the use of infantry, which had been the dominant military arm throughout the prior course of Roman history. With the arrival of the nomad Huns and their entirely horse-oriented mode of life (it was said that Hun horsemen virtually never dismounted, and even slept on horseback), the Romans might have been expected to review the use of cavalry. The Huns fought exclusively from horseback. How did the Roman infantry engage them? What strategies were adopted at the battle of Châlons in the Catalaunian

Plains in 451 to hold off the Huns? No details have survived for this period, but for the middle of the sixth century, Procopius' *History of the Wars of Justinian* provides vivid descriptions of battle scenes. According to his account, the Ostrogoths' method of fighting differed from that of the Byzantines, a fact noted with satisfaction by the Byzantine general Belisarius when they confronted one another outside Rome in 536. The Ostrogoths had mounted spearmen while the Byzantines —evidently having learned from their experiences against the Huns—had mounted archers. Belisarius' force was able to decimate the Goths without coming within range of their spears. He was also helped by the fact that throughout West Roman history the barbarians never mastered the use of catapults (*ballistae*) to bombard an enemy with rocks, nor did they ever become proficient at siege warfare. The great military innovation of the migration period was the change from infantry to cavalry, and it is unfortunate that we do not know when and by what stages this change came about, or why it led to different results among the Byzantines and the Mediterranean Germans.

A third major change was the eventual conversion of the migrating tribes to some form of Christianity. During the migration period the Catholic church was extraordinarily indifferent to the barbarians, who were viewed as common pagans so long as they remained outside imperial frontiers. A fifth-century West Roman writer relates that Christianity was carried across the frontier in two ways: via barbarian mercenaries in the Roman army who, converted to Christianity, returned home and converted kinsmen and neighbors; and via Christian prisoners, especially clergy, who converted their captors. But neither of these groups, retired veterans or prisoners, can have made a substantial number of converts.

As noted, there were hardly any Catholic missions to the barbarians, St. Patrick's initiative in Ireland in the middle of the fifth century being an obvious exception. The Arians, however, were more active, especially among the Visigoths. The Visigoths themselves, equipped with Ulfilas' Bible, were Christianized to Arianism before the end of the fourth century. In the first quarter of the fifth century the Burgundians and Vandals were also converted, and by the third quarter of the fifth century the Ostrogoths had become Christians. In 465 the Suebi in northwestern Spain were converted to Arianism by Ajax, with the encouragement of the Visigothic government of Tolosa. The contrasting inactivity of the Catholic church among the barbarians remains unexplained.

The migration period, then, transformed the main Germanic peoples from more or less egalitarian tribesmen living east of the Rhine and north of the Danube into a society in which, once they had moved inside the Roman provinces, a landowning, Germanic nobility emerged to govern them. They fought now as horsemen rather than as infantry, and within a generation of their arriving and settling in the provinces they had all become heretical Christians (Arianism was first condemned by the Council of Nicaea in 323). When they became independent of the Western emperors (*ca.* 476), they required many Romans to help them administer their kingdoms, especially in matters of law and tax collection. For this and other reasons many of the great Roman landowners retained possession of some or all of their estates (although not in Africa, where the Vandals expropriated them). The transition from Western Roman Empire to Germanic kingdom was for the most part surprisingly smooth.

BRITAIN AND THE BARBARIAN MIGRATIONS

Britain, which had come under Roman rule in the first century A.D., was left a defenseless imperial province in 407 when the locally proclaimed emperor Constantine III took most of the Roman troops from Britain back into Gaul to forestall a feared move on the part of the migrating Vandals to cross the channel westward. The transition to barbarian occupation of Britain in the next several decades was far from smooth or easy. The invaders, who had been coastal raiders for more than a century, were the Angles from the area of present-day Denmark, and the Saxons from northwest Germany.

The last vestiges of Roman imperial power collapsed in 409 and, according to Procopius, Britain was thereafter ruled by "tyrants," or rulers who usurped the power of the emperors. But Britain had been subject to disasters long before the final collapse. In 368, for example, Theodosius, the father of Theodosius the Great, had been sent to Britain by Valentinian I to expel the Saxons. When he landed in Kent he found that the area was being harried both by Saxons and by Picts from Scotland north of the Firth of Forth.

In the first half of the fifth century, according to Gildas (a preacher who wrote *ca.* 540), Britain was assailed mainly by "Scots" (Irishmen) and Picts. Other sources speak of Saxon raids. Details are lacking, but from incidental remarks it is evident that the country was divided into a number of kingdoms whose kings in Gildas' time were a murderous and tyrannical lot. In 429 Germanus, bishop of Autesiodorum (Auxerre), visited the island, having been sent by the pope to stamp out the heresy of Pelagius (concerned with grace and free will), which had gained a footing. He found that people freely assembled in orderly fashion to listen to a public debate on heresy. But on his journey back to the coast, where he hoped to take ship for France, he witnessed a skirmish between a British force and a mixed army of Saxons and Picts in which the barbarians panicked and fled. Was this clash unusual? It is noteworthy that Germanus and his companions crossed the English Channel four times without ever seeing a Saxon ship and without even considering (so far as we know) that they might see one. There are indications in the sources that the years 446–447 saw a change in the pattern of Saxon behavior from raiding to settlement, and according to Gildas the second half of the century was dominated no longer by raids of Picts and Scots but by Saxons. The tendency in recent British scholarship to argue that the Anglo-Saxon invasions occurred peaceably, before a general coalescence with the native population, and that city life in some places continued unbroken from Roman into Saxon times, can scarcely be reconciled with the facts. What is clear is that in eastern England British place-names virtually disappeared (apart from the names of prominent natural or manmade features—Roman cities, large hills, forests, rivers). The long-established Celtic language itself disappeared in eastern England, and Christianity died out. Only a few words of British Celtic entered the Anglo-Saxon language, none of them derivable from British Latin. The Saxons did not borrow even so simple a device as the potter's wheel from the Britons. Those Britons who survived in the west of Britain conceived a hatred of the Saxons that did not abate for generations, even centuries. They refused to preach the gospel to the Saxons, a fact that shocked the Venerable Bede writing in 731. Contrast this cultural conflict with the course of events in Spanish Gallaecia, where the Suebi settled in 409. There the Latin language, place-names, and Christian religion have survived from that day to this.

As a result of the Saxon invasions of England there was a vast migration of Britons to northwestern Gaul, to what is now called Brittany and had formerly been named Armorica. The influx of Britons reached full flood in the 460s and probably continued into the sixth century. Somewhere in western Britain, in an area the Saxons did not reach before the middle of the sixth century, lived Gildas, whose work of lamentation The Destruction of Britain (*De Excidio et Conquestu Britannia*) is a valuable source for this period of British history.

A final and obscure migration of barbarians involved the movement of the Irish to Scotland in the late Roman period. In the fifth century the Romans called the people in the area of Ireland "Scots" and those in what is now Scotland "Picts" or "Caledonians." But so many "Scots" crossed into the territory of Caledonia that the country came to be called "Scotland." These invasions appear to have begun late in the fifth century, and information about them is based on archaeological and scarce historical evidence that is hard to interpret.

THE FATE OF THE EASTERN EMPIRE

The migrations in the late Roman period left the Eastern Roman Empire, centered on Constantinople, intact. After the death of Muhammad in 632 the astonishing expansion of the Arabs began. In 637 Antioch and Jerusalem fell to them. To the east Ctesiphon surrendered in 641 and Alexandria was handed over in 642. By 650 the great Persian Empire had ceased to exist. The North African coast had been overrun by the end of the century, and in 711 the Arabs subjugated Visigothic Spain. With these conquests the Arabs caused a much greater break with the past than the Germans had. They detached the whole of North Africa and the Near East from Europe, established Arabic instead of Latin or Greek as the dominant Mediterranean language, and reduced Christianity to minority status. Some scholars date the end of the ancient world from the early days of the Arab expansion, not to the invasion of the Germanic tribes from northern Europe.

BIBLIOGRAPHY

John B. Bury, *History of the Later Roman Empire*, 2 vols. (1889); James Campbell *et al.*, *The Anglo-Saxons* (1982); Roger Collins, *Early Medieval Spain: Unity in Diversity, 400–1000* (1983); Christian Courtois, *Les Vandales et l'Afrique* (1955); Jean Hubert *et al.*, *Europe of the Invasions*, Stuart Gilbert and James Emmons, trans. (1969); Arnold H. M. Jones, *The Later Roman Empire, 284–602* (1964), and *The Decline of the Ancient World* (1966); Peter Llewellyn, *Rome in the Dark Ages* (1971); Otto J. Maenchen-Helfen, *The World of the Huns* (1973).

Henry St. L. B. Moss, *The Birth of the Middle Ages* (1935); Ludwig Schmidt, *Geschichte der Wandalen* (1901), and *Geschichte der deutschen Stämme*, 2 vols. (repr. 1970); Ernest Stein, *Histoire du bas-empire*, 2 vols. (1949–1959); E. A. Thompson, *The Visigoths in the Time of Ulfila* (1966); Malcolm Todd, *Everyday Life of the Barbarians: Goths, Franks, and Vandals* (1972), and *The Northern Barbarians, 100 B.C.–A.D. 300* (1975); Erich Zöllner, *Geschichte der Franken bis zur Mitte des sechsten Jahrhunderts* (1970).

Languages and Dialects

DAVID LANGSLOW

INDO-EUROPEAN AND NON-INDO-EUROPEAN

At one time, some 6,000 years ago, a people living in a part of Europe or Asia, perhaps bordering on the Black Sea, spoke a language or a group of closely related dialects now called Indo-European (IE). In the fourth or third millennium B.C. this people migrated in separate groups to all parts of Europe, to Asia Minor, India, even Chinese Turkistan (the Tocharian language from the Tien Shan mountain region). The dialect of each group changed gradually and continually as time passed and as a result of contact with other languages, until any two groups could be found to be speaking mutually unintelligible languages.

The Indo-Europeans were remarkably successful in imposing themselves, their cultures, and their languages in their new territories; the modern-day descendants of IE are spoken in large areas of India, in Iran, and over the whole of Europe (except Finland, Hungary, Turkey, and the Basque lands), from where several have been exported worldwide. Greek and Latin are both IE languages, and many of the lesser-known languages of the ancient Mediterranean, with which the Greeks and Romans had contact, share the same source.

The Indo-Europeans were not the first to bring language to the shores of the Mediterranean, but we know next to nothing of the character and origin of the languages spoken there previously. The occurrence of similar words for wine, for example, in both IE and non-IE languages, in forms that rule out the possibility of borrowing from any known language, and the recurrence of certain names for places, rivers, and peoples throughout the area extending from Spain to the Caucasus have prompted the assumption of variously defined pre-IE substrate languages, termed "Mediterranean," "Ligurian," "Aegean," and so on, according to their supposed area and extent. These have been held to account variously for the non-IE languages of the Etruscans and Anatolians and for the modern Basque, Berber, Georgian, and Dravidian languages. The Cretan pictographic and Linear A scripts may also be written relics of such a pre-IE language; we cannot yet say.

GREEK

Pre-Greek Languages

Greek was not the first language to be spoken in the southern Balkans. Certain features of Greek and Anatolian place-names and Greek nouns, such as the *-nth-* suffix in *Korinthos* or *laburinthos* (labyrinth) and the *-ss-* suffix in *Halikarnassos* or *kuparissos* (cypress tree) have been taken to reflect the earlier existence either of a non-IE substrate language of the "Mediterranean" type or of IE Anatolian settlements in Greece in the Bronze Age.

The Anatolian hypothesis apart, Greek was probably not the first IE language to be spoken in Greece. Some Greek words (such as *purgos,* tower) appear to be IE (compare Sanskrit *bṛhat-,* Avestan *bərəzant-,* Germanic *burg* from IE **bhṛghos*) but may not be explained by Greek sound-changes (IE **bhṛghos* would give Greek **prakhos*. [In linguistic notation, an asterisk precedes a reconstructed form, one that is not actually found in extant sources.]) Such non-Greek IE words, though few in number, have led scholars to envisage one or more of a number of IE languages—"Pelasgian," "Achaean," "psi-Greek," even Luwian (an attested language of the Anatolian group)—as being spoken in Greece before the arrival of the Greeks. "Pelasgian," the most prominent of these hypothetical languages, is named after the *Pelasgoi,* the people who the Greeks themselves believed to have been the autochthonous inhabitants of Greece, to have spoken a barbarian (that is, non-Greek) tongue, and to have survived into classical times in many parts of Greece (Herodotus 1.57; 2.56.1; 6.137–140; 8.44; Thucydides 4.109.4). One should, however, be wary of excessive claims made for these construct languages on very slender evidence. For example, recent studies of the languages of Asia Minor suggest that many Greek words that were previously explained as "Pelasgian" are, in fact, loanwords from Anatolian. We must be no less suspicious of the traditions concerning the ethnography and linguistic geography of Greece before the Greeks that are preserved by ancient historians and geographers, of whom Strabo (64/63 B.C.–A.D. 21) presents perhaps the richest synthesis (*Geography* 7.7.1). Inconsistencies and contradictions in the complex etiological accounts and the impossibility of making any confident connections between the name of a tribe in an ancient source and any linguistic relics render these traditions nearly useless as historical evidence.

The Greek Dialects

It remains difficult to align the linguistic with the archaeological evidence for the arrival of the Greeks in Greece. The bearers of the Early Helladic III and closely related Middle Helladic cultures are often identified as the IE peoples whose language evolved in the Balkans to become Greek, and their arrival is dated accordingly to around the beginning of the second millennium B.C.

Michael Ventris' decipherment of the Linear B script in 1952 proved that Greek was spoken on Crete before the last quarter of the second millennium B.C. and written in a strikingly similar form in Cretan Cnossus and in mainland Pylos, Mycenae, Thebes, and Tiryns. Some 4,800 clay tablets have been recovered, baked and preserved by the very fires that destroyed Mycenaean civilization. The unwieldy syllabic script in which Mycenaean Greek is written tells us much less than we would like to know about the Greek language of that age. For the prehistory of the Greek dialects, and the place of Mycenaean among them, the linguistic evidence underlying ingenious theories and complex debate among scholars is quite inconclusive. The traditional view is that the Mycenaean dialect with the ancestors of Arcado-Cypriot and Attic-Ionic (and perhaps Aeolic) formed in this period, an undifferentiated (south)eastern group (most characteristically developing *-ti to -si) opposed to a (north)western group, the ancestors of Doric and North West Greek, which preserves the sequence -ti. Traditionally, the Dorians (the West Greeks) are held to have appeared in central and southern Greece around the time of the end of Mycenaean civilization (ca. 1200 B.C.), having moved possibly from within northwest Greece itself; their invasion, in this view, is identified with the legendary return of the sons of Heracles to their ancestral homes (Tyrtaeus frag. 1a; Herodotus 1.56.2–3; 8.31; 43; Thucydides 1.107.2). Recently, a quite different view has become prominent. On the assumption that the Linear B tablets show evidence of an upper- and lower-class idiom, it is argued that the Dorians were present all along as serfs in Mycenaean society—there was no Dorian invasion at all—and that the Doric dialects are descended from the lower-class form of Mycenaean.

The Greek dialects of the first millennium, of which Attic alone is well known, present a complicated picture, in which much remains uncertain. A common classification distinguishes East from West Greek. East Greek comprises Arcadian and Cypriot, strikingly similar despite centuries of separation; Aeolic, spoken in Boeotia, Thessaly, and on Lesbos and the neighboring coast of Asia Minor; and Attic-Ionic, Ionic being spoken in the Greek cities on the coast of Asia Minor from Smyrna to Miletus, in the Cyclades, and Euboea, and Attic in Attica. Under West Greek are distinguished Doric, the dialects of much of the Peloponnese, and the dialects of Melos, Crete, Thera, Rhodes, Cyrene in North Africa, and Sicily; and North West Greek, spoken in Elis and Achaea in the Peloponnese, in Aetolia and Epirus, and in the rest of central Greece except for Boeotia and Attica.

The detailed picture, however, is much less tidy. For example, Boeotian and West Thessalian show features of North West Greek and Lesbian shows the influence of Ionic; Pamphylian, a poorly known dialect of southern Asia Minor, shares characteristics with both Arcado-Cypriot and Doric. In short, dialectal fusion, borrowings, and mergers make it impossible to establish rigid classifications of epichoric (locality-restricted) dialects; they demand more particular statements about shared linguistic innovations.

The Literary Dialects

Greek authors, in speaking of "Ionic," "Doric," and "Aeolic" with regard to language, often refer to the literary, not the epichoric, dialects, each being the standard written language of one or more genres of literature. Early Ionic forms the basis of the artificial poetic language of Homer, and hence of elegy and epigram. Ionic is also the language of some personal lyric, of the dialogue of Attic tragedy, and of the prose of Herodotus, Hippocrates, and other medical writers. Doric is the literary dialect of the Pythagoreans and of choral lyric from the time of Alcman (seventh century B.C.). The choruses of Attic tragedy are written in a doricizing Ionic, notably with long *ā* (in, for example, *dustānos*, wretched) for the long *ē* of Ionic Greek (*dustēnos*). Aeolic forms, finally, are scattered throughout Homer, and the dialect of Lesbos forms the basis of the Greek of Sappho and Alcaeus.

The Koine

From about the last quarter of the fifth century B.C., Attic Greek was recognized as the standard dialect for the prose of Sophists, philosophers, and orators. Philip II of Macedon adopted Attic as the official dialect of his court, and Attic came to form the linguistic core of a new *koine glossa* (common tongue) that developed swiftly in the fourth century and was exported and established as far as Egypt, the Pamirs, and the river Jumna by the conquests and foundations of Alexander the Great and his successors.

Between the fourth century B.C. and the sixth century A.D., Greek, once again a single language, was entirely restructured in its phonology, morphology, syntax, and vocabulary, and developed even then many of the characteristics of modern Greek. Among the elements Greek abandoned were diphthongs and distinctions of vowel length; the dual number and the irregular nominal declensions; the *mi*-verbs, the old future and perfect; the dative case; and, in most constructions, the infinitive. Classical words were reused with new meanings (*ariston* came, from meaning specifically breakfast, to denote any meal) and the vocabulary was extended by derivation and borrowing, most loanwords coming from Latin (*patron* from *patronus*, patron; *hospition* from *hospitium*, house).

As the *koine* flourished, so the old dialects died—doubtless more quickly in the towns than in the countryside and sooner in public inscriptions than in family conversation. There are indications that Attic, Laconian, Lesbian, and Rhodian were still used in the second and even the third century A.D. (Philostratus, *Lives of the Sophists* §624, 2.31.1; Strabo 8.1.2; Pausanias 4.27.11; Suetonius, *Tiberius* 56; Dio Chrysostom, *Oration* 1.54), but it seems that to speak in dialect was a sign of a rustic background or lack of education and caused embarrassment even in the home (Aelius Aristides, *Panathenaicus* §326, A.D. 155). These are the last testimonies we have to the classical Greek dialects, save the living Tsakonian dialect of the Peloponnese, which shows links with the ancient Doric dialect, Laconian. (Tsak. *mati*, mother: Doric *mater* vs. *koine meter*.)

The Atticist Movement

Resentment at the domination of Rome; desire to evoke the spirit of the great age of Greece; awareness of the growing discrepancies between the spoken language and that of the texts of education; aesthetic revulsion at the flowery ornate style of the Asianic schools of rhetoric: each of these may have helped to stimulate the Atticist movement of the late Greek world. Influential from the first century B.C. until the third century A.D., Atticists refused to write, some extremists (Athenaeus, *The Learned Banquet* [*Deipnosophistae*] I. 1e) even to utter, a Greek word unless it was attested in the works of a fifth- or fourth-century writer of Attic prose. They used old words in their old senses, resurrected the optative and the Attic dual, and ignored the foundations that had been laid for a standard written *koine* by Polybius (second century B.C.) and Diodorus (first century B.C.). An extensive didactic literature sprang up, the character of which may be indicated in a single sentence from Phrynichus Arabius in the second century A.D.: "Whatever you do, avoid the word *apeleusomai* (I shall go away); neither reputable orators, nor old comedy, nor even Plato uses the word—use *apeimi* instead!" (*Ecloga* 24). While this effortful and often inaccurate prose idiom was well established as the language of belles lettres and oratory before the second century A.D. (Herodes Atticus, Aelian, Aelius Aristides, Lucian, and, in his later works, Plutarch were all careful Atticists), writers of technical literature (the physician Galen, the engineer Hero of Alexandria, the skeptic philosopher Sextus Empiricus) went their own way in the interests of clarity and in order to use new forms of expression for new objects and ideas. Christian writers could have established an alternative written language to the stilted prose of the Atticists; the Septuagint, most of the

New Testament, and the works of the apostolic fathers are written in contemporary colloquial *koine,* in which Atticists like Phrynichus found much to criticize. But as a result of efforts to appeal to educated pagans, by the fourth century A.D. the Attic style became the norm for Christian writers too and, further, "the language of the Fathers of the Church became that of almost all subsequent Greek literature for a thousand years. There was, it is true, an undercurrent of writing in a linguistic form making greater or lesser concessions to spoken Greek, but it remained a humble undercurrent" (Browning, 1983). The distance that lay between the *koine* and the Attic style as early as the fourth century A.D. is well illustrated in the complaint of the woman in the congregation of John Chrysostom that she could not understand the literary language that he was using in his sermon (Cosmas Vestitor, *Life of St. John Chrysostom* 5). In this stark contrast may be seen, already in the first centuries of our era, the diglossy (use of standard languages) that has remained a central feature of Greek down to the present day when the purist *kathareuousa,* though much less common, is no less strongly opposed to the *demotike,* the language of the people.

Greek in Later Antiquity

Greek dominated the eastern Mediterranean world throughout the Roman imperial period, the literary language, at any rate, remaining entirely free of Latinisms: St. Luke, for example, uses, instead of the Latin loanwords *kenturion* (centurion), *kensos* (census), *modios* (bushel), and *titlos* (title), the Greek approximations *hekatontarkhes, phoros, skeuos,* and *epigraphe.* Greek is the language of numerous imperial and magisterial edicts and letters addressed to all parts of the Eastern Empire; Greek is the language, too, of countless private documents written by Egyptians, Jews, Asians, and Iranian Sarmatians and Scythians; Greek is the language of communication between Roman, Jew, and Phoenician and, in the seventh century A.D. in Egypt, between the Arab conquerors and their new subjects.

From the first century B.C. Greek was taught in schools in Rome, in Italy, and in the western provinces. An educated Roman was bilingual in Latin and Greek (Horace's *lingua utraque,* both languages, *Satires* I.10.23). Quintilian, indeed, warned (*Education of an Orator* [*Institutio Oratoria*] 1.1.12–13) against speaking Greek too much lest one's Latin pronunciation and choice of vocabulary become affected.

In the East, Latin prevailed over Greek only as the language of the army (of military commands: Mauricius, *On Strategy* [*Strategikon*] 12 B.14.2–4; of reports of a Greek general, Arrian, *Voyage around the Black Sea* 6.2; 10.1) and of the law (Herennius Modestinus, in Justinian, *Digest* 27.1.1.1.) In all other respects Greek was the lingua franca and the language of administration of the eastern half of the Roman Empire. Until Marcus Aurelius, Greek was the language of culture for the whole of the Roman world—and even beyond its borders, for we hear of Greek tragedies at the Parthian court (Plutarch, *Life of Crassus* 33.2–4) and of Indians who wrote Greek (Strabo 15.1.73), and we may identify Greek loanwords in Georgian and in Ethiopian languages. Then, from the third century A.D. the Greek-speaking area began gradually to diminish; by the fourth century Greek was taught only to the families of the old Roman aristocracy and was almost unknown in the western provinces. In the ecclesiastical sphere, Greek was steadily overtaken by the colloquially based Christian Latin until, under Pope Damasus (A.D. 366–384), even the Roman liturgy was Latinized. Despite a brilliant revival of

Greek in Italy in the works of Symmachus, Boethius, and Cassiodorus, under Theodoric the Great (A.D. 493–526), by the end of antiquity the Greek-speaking area comprised only southern Italy, Greece and the islands, and Pontus and the coast of Asia Minor, with its new political and spiritual center in Byzantium.

LATIN

The Latin language takes its name from Latium and should, strictly speaking, mean the language or dialects of that area. But we have only a few short inscriptions in the dialects of Rome's nearest neighbors—Praeneste (Palestrina), Ardea, Lanuvium (Lanuvio), Norba, and Tibur (Tivoli)—and as Rome came early to dominate the Latian plain, it is to her dialect that "Latin" refers.

Although by early in the second century B.C. Rome had achieved domination over the whole Italian peninsula, along with Sicily, Sardinia, and Corsica, her language remained confined to the city and the colonies until the end of the Social (or Marsian) War (91–87 B.C.). Thereafter, the spread of Latin as the primary spoken language kept pace with Rome's waxing political fortunes and her widening imperial horizons. Especially in the West of the empire, like Greek in the East, Latin became established as the common language of all men.

Latin shows clear evidence of contact with various foreign cultures. While the lexicon is largely inherited from IE (*rex*, king; *agere*, lead, drive) or formed of inherited elements (*regina*, queen; *agitare*, drive, stir), we find many loans: from the "Mediterranean" substrate (*rosa*, rose; *vinum*, wine); from an Italic dialect (*rufus*, red; *popina*, kitchen, beside L. *ruber, coquina*); and from Greek colonies (*talentum*, talent, from Gk. *talanton*). Roman soldiers returning from campaigns brought many foreign words into Latin (Quintilian 1.5.57; Arrian, *Tactics* 33.1): from Gaulish after the invasions of the fourth century B.C. (*essedum*, chariot; *braca*, trousers); from Punic (*avē*, hail!; *mapalia*, huts; *mappa*, napkin); and from Spain (*gurdus*, stupid). From Etruscan, Latin took words both technical (*idus*, Ides) and common (*histrio*, actor) and through Etruscan, Latin borrowed many Greek words (Gk. *prosōpon*, face—Etr. φersu—L. *persona*; Gk. *gnoma*—Etr. **cruma*—L. *groma*, measuring rod).

Archaic Latin

The Latin alphabet was developed from an Etruscan version of the Chalcidic Greek alphabet, although the first writers in Latin appear to have had direct acquaintance with Greek writing habits also.

If, as seems likely, the inscription on the famous Praenestine brooch is a forgery, the earliest evidence of Latin is from Rome itself: the *duenos* inscription and the Forum Inscription, apparently a "sacred law," both of the sixth century B.C. The literary tradition preserves extracts of some very old Latin documents such as the laws of the kings (late sixth century B.C.) and the Twelve Tables (451–450) and, more ancient than either of these, the ritual hymns *carmen Saliare* and *carmen Arvale*, but the original Latin of these has been modernized and/or garbled and Latin inscriptions are by no means common before the second century B.C.

The Latin Literary Language

Over the two centuries from the earliest surviving Latin literature (Livius Andronicus, *ca.* 240 B.C.) to Cicero, we can observe evolution to a highly cultivated written language. At the head of this trend stands Quintus Ennius (239–169 B.C.). Not only did Ennius vastly enrich the resources of Latin in his efforts to adapt the language to Greek literary models, he also encouraged by example the use of regular grammatical forms and normative ideals tending to elegance and economy. The movement was continued by the Scipionic circle, Hortensius, and Caesar, and was perfected by Cicero, notably in his development of the period and of the Latin vocabulary, the latter permitting Latin authors more easily to render Greek works on law and philosophy.

Although Latin knew no such thing as the literary dialects of Greece, a distinction can be made at least between the language of poetry and that of prose, especially in respect of vocabulary: for the word "sword," a poet would use *ensis* or *ferrum* (iron) while a prose writer would say *gladius*. Poetic language was characterized also by archaisms (such as infinitives in *-ier*), Grecisms (for example, *sensit . . . delapsus* for *sensit delapsum* [*esse*], he realized . . . that he had fallen), and neologisms, especially compounds, many modeled on Greek (such as L. *magnanimus*; Gk. *megathumos*, great-hearted).

Spoken Latin and the Romance Languages

Of spoken Latin, often called rather unfortunately Vulgar Latin (*vulgaris*, common, ordinary), our knowledge is very slight. We glimpse the everyday language of the educated Roman in the old Roman comedy (Cicero compares the conversation of the noble lady Laelia with the language of Plautus: *On the Orator* 3.12.45); in Cicero's letters, especially those to Atticus and Paetus (*Letters to His Friends* 9.21.1); in the *Satires* and *Epistles* of Horace; in Vitruvius and the authors of *The African War* and *The Spanish War;* and in the talk of Petronius' Encolpius. Other characters in the *Satyricon*—such as Echion and Habinnas—speak a noticeably more vulgar form of Latin, on a level with, say, that found in Pompeiian wall graffiti. Other, later, sources of this lower *sermo plebeius* (people's talk) are the oldest (from the second century A.D.) translations of the Bible, aimed at the lower orders of society; the *Appendix Probi*, which criticizes the departures of the vulgar tongue from classical norms; and the *Itinerarium Egeriae* (or *Peregrinatio Aetheriae*), an account written by a noble woman of her pilgrimage to the East (*ca.* A.D. 400).

All levels of the colloquial language have in common the use of much freer syntax and of many interjections, Greek words, and expressive forms. Late Vulgar Latin shows an increasing number of features (some of which may be detected as early as Plautus in the early second century B.C.) recognizable as forerunners of the characteristics of the Romance languages. These include the progressive breakdown of the declensional system as a result of sound changes that make originally distinct case forms homophonous: the endings *-us*, *-um* and *-o* all come to be pronounced *o*, for instance; and the consequent use of prepositional phrases: *de* for the genitive, *ad* for the dative. Diminutives are used instead of simple nouns: *oricla* for *auris* (ear). Deponent verbs disappear and intensive and frequentative forms become usual since they are both expressive and regular: *cantare* for *canere* (sing). Homophony, caused again by sound change, leads to the creation of periphrastic perfect and future tenses formed with *habere* (have) and *debere* (must). And old classical words, finally, become obsolete and are replaced by others: *magnus* by *grandis* (big); *ludus* by *iocus* (game); *ferre* by *portare* (carry). It is in this everyday language of merchants, soldiers, and officials all over the empire that the modern Romance languages have their point of departure. The precise nature and manner of their genesis, however, are still far from fully understood.

Even if Latin authors did not make frequent reference to variations in pronunciation, vocabulary, and style of the forms of Latin spoken in different parts of the empire (Cicero, *Brutus* 171–2; Seneca, *On Consola-*

tion, To Helvia 7.9; Quintilian 1.5.8, 56ff.; Pliny the Younger, *Letters* 9.23.2), still common sense would urge belief in many regionally and socially differentiated dialects of Vulgar Latin rather than in a more or less unitary spoken language. But we are still hardly able to pick out from our written sources features by which we may distinguish the common everyday Latin of, say, Spain from that of Africa. In order to explain adequately the great diversity of the modern descendants of Vulgar Latin, we are reduced to dependence upon information about the native language of a given province and, equally important, about the sort of contact it had with Latin.

Clearly, the date of conquest by Rome is significant. Spaniards (from the second century B.C.) will have learned a different Latin from that encountered by the Gauls (from 50 B.C.) or the Dacians (from A.D. 107). Only as a result of early conquest could the dialect of Corduba preserve an archaic lexical feature in the first century B.C. (Varro, *On the Latin Language* 5.162)

Clearly, too, the speed and extent of latinization were critical for the evolution of the colloquial speech of the region. If the process was swift and thorough, as in the case of Baetica in Spain (Strabo 3.2.15), the native language would not influence the Latin of the conquerors; slow or incomplete romanization, seen in northwest Spain, would likely give rise to a highly modified form of Latin.

The rate and degree of latinization would depend in its turn on, among other factors, the type of contact between Latin and the substrate language. Literary Greek, the prestigious language of culture of the whole Roman Empire, resisted latinization completely and, further, colloquial Greek greatly softened the impact of Latin on the languages of Egypt, the Holy Land, and Asia Minor. Punic was for a time the language of trade but was probably always too foreign to allow any Romance language to develop in North Africa. It was Celtic "Old Europe" that had the longest and fullest contact with Latin and where Latin came to replace most successfully its closest relatives among the western IE languages.

Finally, given different degrees of latinization in different regions, historical factors were of primary importance in the development of the Romance languages. By accidental shifts in the centers of political and cultural influence, Italian was born of the Latin not of Rome but of Etruria; French arose not in heavily romanized Narbonensis ("more like Italy than a province," Pliny the Elder, *Natural History* 3.4.31) but in northern France where German influence was strong; Latin was brought back to the south of the Iberian Peninsula after the Arab conquest not by natives of Roman Baetica but by the lately and partially romanized tribes of Gallaecia (Galicia) in the barbarian north.

THE OTHER LANGUAGES OF THE ANCIENT MEDITERRANEAN

The most striking feature of the development of the linguistic map of the Greco-Roman world is the speed and completeness with which, in nearly every corner of the Mediterranean, a host of scrappily attested native languages give place to Greek in the East, Latin in the West, and then disappear from our records. Two written languages—Hebrew and Coptic—have survived as the vehicles of powerful religions. As we shall see in a counterclockwise survey of the Mediterranean, many more survived for a time as spoken languages, especially in more inaccessible, less urbanized regions. Several are attested—in North Africa, Asia Minor, and the Balkans—from late Roman times; Albanian, Basque, and Berber are still spoken today. Neither the successors of Alexander nor the Romans had, as far as we know, any deliberate policy of eliminating native languages or of enforcing the everyday use of Greek and Latin in the worlds they ruled. Nonetheless, Greek and Latin were, for the few, the only languages of education and, for the many, the languages of government and administration, of trade and commerce, and of military service. Accordingly, by the beginning of the Christian Era there can have been very few in the western provinces who did not know at least some Latin, and equally few living in the eastern half of the Mediterranean who did not have some command of Greek.

ITALY

IE Languages of Italy

The linguistic map of ancient Italy before the rise of Rome is complex, an intricate patchwork of diverse languages, some IE, some non-IE, others of unknown affinities. We have good evidence for a number of closely related ancient IE languages: Latin and Faliscan; Oscan, Umbrian, and the Sabellian dialects (the Osco-Umbrian group, to which, confusingly, the term "Italic dialects" is often restricted); and Venetic. Osco-Umbrian clearly stands some way apart from Latin-Faliscan but there remains profound disagreement among scholars as to whether it is the similarities or the differences between the two groups that are more fundamental. That is, did Latin-Faliscan and Osco-Umbrian (and Venetic?) once form a linguistic unity, an Italic group of IE, from which each developed with independent innovations? Or is their period of unity to be ascribed to a much earlier (Italo-Celtic) stage, after which they diverged markedly from each other before becoming more similar again as a result of recent contact within Italy? On present evidence, a choice between the two is a matter of faith.

Of nearly all the other languages of ancient Italy our knowledge is very limited because the inscriptions (apart from glosses, our only evidence), though numerous, are often fragmentary and short, containing only personal names or dealing in a stereotyped manner with dedications or memorials to the dead. The other ancient languages of Italy have in common also the fact that by the first century A.D. they were no longer written, and probably soon after, no longer spoken, having yielded in all their great diversity to the dialect of Rome.

Osco-Umbrian

The best evidence is for Oscan and Umbrian. These two languages and, we suppose on much less evidence, the Sabellian dialects, share so many features that they are generally taken to have formed a linguistic unity in the first part of the first millennium B.C.

In Oscan, we have over 300 inscriptions, from coin legends of 450–350 B.C. to Pompeiian wall graffiti preserved by the eruption of Vesuvius in A.D. 79, written first in the Oscan alphabet of Etruscan type, later in Latin and, especially farther south, in the Greek alphabet. As the chief language (besides Greek, Festus, p. 31 L) of central and southern Italy, Oscan united the lower half of the peninsula while Latin was yet confined to Latium.

To the north lived the Umbrians, who also wrote first in a native alphabet derived from the Etruscan and later in a modified Latin script. Our knowledge of their language derives almost completely from the seven bronze tablets of Iguvium (ca. 200–89 B.C.), which together form an extensive text containing the liturgy and protocol of a brotherhood of priests, the *frater atiieřiur* (in Latin *fratres Atiedii*, Atiedian brothers).

Between Oscan and Umbrian were the so-called Sabellian dialects of central Italy: the languages of the Paeligni, Sabini, Marrucini, Vestini, Hernici, Marsi, and Volsci. We have very little evidence for any of these, and may only tentatively suggest that Marsian and Volscian belong more closely with Umbrian, the rest with Oscan. We can now add to their number the language of the approximately twenty South Picenian inscriptions from south of Ancona (sixth to fifth century B.C.), including the Capestrano inscription (sixth century B.C.).

Most Italians adopted the Latin language along with the Roman franchise at the end of the Social War and all had ceased to write in their native dialects by the first century A.D. The *marones*, Umbrian magistrates, are still heard of in the first century A.D. but their names are Latinized, the Umbrian name *Ner. T. Babr(ie)* (genitive singular [Vetter no. 236]), for instance, appearing in the Latin formula *Ner. Babrius T.f* (Degrassi no. 550). Oscan was spoken until A.D. 79 in Pompeii but we can hardly credit Strabo's claim (5.3.6) that the Oscan farces, the *fabulae Atellanae*, were still performed (first century A.D.) at Rome in Oscan.

Faliscan

Latin's closest relation outside Latium was clearly Faliscan, the dialect of Falerii in south Etruria, of which about 150 inscriptions survive in an archaic alphabet (seventh/sixth to second century B.C.). Important common innovations (such as the **bh*-future: L. *carebo* = Fal. *carefo*, I shall be in need) require the assumption of a stage of unity, although Faliscan developed independently under Etruscan and Sabellian influence.

Venetic

Venetic is the language of nearly 300 inscriptions in a native alphabet of Etruscan type (sixth to first century B.C.) found in an area of northeast Italy around Venice; the evidence of personal names suggests that the language once extended some way south into Yugoslavia (Herodotus 1.196.1; Appian, *Roman History* 12.55,224; Eustathius, *Commentary on Iliad* B 852). Often conservative in its treatment of IE features, Venetic has far more frequent and significant affinities with Oscan, Umbrian, and above all Latin, than with Germanic and Celtic. In common with Latin alone, Venetic develops **bh* and **dh* to *f-* initially but to *-b-* and *-d-* respectively in the middle of a word. Further, Venetic *louderobos* (children: dative plural; Lejeune, no. 26, p. 205) is to be compared with Latin *liberi* (children), both formed on the root **leudh-* meaning "free."

Venetia provides a paradigm case of the process of romanization. In the late second century B.C. Venetic inscriptions came to be written in Latin letters; then for a period (first century B.C. to first century A.D.) Venetic words appeared alongside Latin—or mixed Latin and Venetic—names (Lejeune no. 134, p. 252), and Latin words among Venetic names (Lejeune no. 219, p. 280); and finally Venetic yielded, names and all, to Latin.

Messapian

Some 400 inscriptions (sixth to first century B.C.) in a Tarentine Greek alphabet, the vast majority from the Sallentine Peninsula, attest the IE language of the Messapii, Calabri, Sallentini, Peucetii, and Dauni—the Iapygian peoples of southeast Italy. The language shows IE noun endings (*logetibas*, dative plural) and some IE words (*apa*, from [?], Greek *apo*; *bilia*, daughter, Latin *filia*). Messapian is unlike any other language of Italy in several respects (for example, **o* becomes Messapian *a*), but we are too ignorant to confirm or deny postulated links with Illyrian and perhaps Albanian. Although Messapian names lingered, the language yielded to Latin in the first century A.D., probably latest around modern Lecce, where fourteen late inscriptions are found.

Greek

Greek has been spoken in southern Italy from the second quarter of the eighth century B.C., when the Ionic colony of Pithecousai (Ischia) was founded from Euboea, until the present day. The great Ionic and Doric Greek settlements in Sicily and southern Italy flourished until the fifth century B.C., and even in their subsequent decline, still long resisted romanization. Although Strabo claims (6.1.2) that all of Italy save Taras (Tarentum), Rhegium (Reggio di Calabria), and Neapolis (Naples) is foreign to Greek culture, we find Greek catacomb inscriptions on the east coast of Sicily from A.D. 250–500, and Greek is spoken to this day in parts of the toe and heel of Italy, where the language may reflect a mixture of ancient and later (sixth century A.D.) imported Byzantine Greek.

Minor IE Languages

For the rest of Italy and Sicily we have very slight epigraphic evidence for about a dozen languages. Possibly IE are: the approximately thirty rock inscriptions of Val Camonica, north of Brescia; and, in Sicily, Elymian, represented on a few coins and vase fragments from Segesta in the west, and Siculan, on a few longer but incomprehensible inscriptions from the eastern part of the island.

Non-IE Languages of Italy

Sicily is thought to have been called *Sikanie* before the Sicels (perhaps IE speakers of Siculan) drove out the Sicans. Thucydides, however, states (6.2.2) that the Sicans came from Spain, having been expelled from there by the Ligurians. They inhabit parts of western Sicily to this day. Sicanian, then, or Sican, is the name given to the language (presumed to be non-IE) of a few pieces of graffiti (sixth century B.C.) from Gelo in the southeast.

Also non-IE are the many Phoenician and Punic inscriptions from Sicily and Sardinia, including the famous Pyrgi bilingual in Phoenician and Etruscan, the work of the tyrant of Caere, Thefarie Velianas (fifth century B.C.). The Novilara stele and two or three associated fragments are in an alphabet of Etruscan origin, although, unlike Etruscan, the script contains an *o* sign, besides *u*, and signs for voiced consonants, and the morphology is quite different.

Rhaetic, found in seventy inscriptions in a north Etruscan alphabet from central alpine Italy, may be an Etruscan dialect (Pliny, *Natural History* 3.20.133; Livy 5.33.11). In fact, the link with the Rhaeti implied by the name is quite arbitrary and we know nothing for certain about the language(s) except that it (they) survived at least until Roman domination in the first century A.D.

Etruscan

In Etruscan we have about 13,000 inscriptions (seventh to late first century B.C.) in an alphabet derived from the Chalcidic Greek, most of them from Etruria, but some from Campania, the Po valley, Umbria, and Latium, and one from Carthage. Few are longer than thirty words and 90 percent are for funerary or dedicatory purposes and consist almost entirely of personal names. Our longest document, however, merits mention: it is the inscription of Zagreb, a liturgical text (second/first century B.C.) 1,190 words long, written on a linen book later used in the wrappings of an Egyptian mummy. We know the meaning of some 250 Etruscan words, some explained by Greek and Latin authors: *ais,* plural *aisar* (god; see

Suetonius, *The Deified Augustus* 97.2); some clear from the context: *clan,* plural *clenar* (son). From dice and references to age we can count from one to six: *θu, zal, ci, śa, maX, huθ*. Clearly, Etruscan has borrowed words and names from Greek (Gk. *kothon*, cup; Etr. *qutun*) and other languages of Italy: Umbrian *tota* (people) appears as Etruscan *tuthi;* Latin *magister* (master) as Etruscan *macstre*. We know some Etruscan morphology—such as the genitive in *-al: unial* (of Juno, *Uni*), or in *-us: velus* (of Vel)—but really our understanding of the language remains very poor; even with the aid of the Phoenician parallel text, we cannot read the Pyrgi inscriptions satisfactorily.

The origin of Etruscan was as controversial in antiquity as it is today. Herodotus declared (1.94) that it came from Lydia; Dionysius of Halicarnassus (1.30.1–2) that it was indigenous to Italy, though not like any known language. The modern consensus is that Etruscan is not IE, and that it is related only to the language of the Lemnos stele (sixth/fifth century B.C.; in an archaic alphabet), which bears close comparison with Etruscan morphologically and lexically. This relationship supports Herodotus' view of an eastern origin for part, at least, of the Etruscans of Italy and provides evidence for the traditional identification by Greek authors of the *Tursanoi* or *Tyrrenoi* of Greece and Italy (*Homeric Hymn* 7.6 ff.; Herodotus 1.57; Thucydides 4.109.4).

FRANCE

Greek

Greek was spoken along the coast of southern France and farther up the Rhône Valley from about 600 B.C. when the Phocaeans founded Massilia (Marseilles). It was under this influence that the Gauls of Transalpina, some of whom learned Greek (Lucian, *Herakles* 4), used a variety of the Greek alphabet in inscriptions and commercial documents.

Celtic

Around 500 B.C., while Latin was still a local dialect, Celtic languages were spoken from Britain to Spain and from Spain to the Danube plain. Gaulish (or Gallic), the language of the Celts of France and northern Italy, represents perhaps the most recent Celtic stratum. No literature survives and we depend for our knowledge of Gaulish on personal names, numerous place-names (*Rigomagus*, king's field), loanwords in Latin (*benna, carpentum, carrus, petorritum*, and *raeda*, each a type of carriage, bespeaking an advanced material culture), and fewer than a hundred inscriptions, nearly all of the late republic and early empire. Of these about sixty, in Greek script, are from Gallia Narbonensis, especially around Nîmes and Glanum, and some twenty, in Latin letters, from a little farther north. The others, including the only two (or three) from northern Italy, are in a north Etruscan alphabet.

Additionally, in the same north Etruscan script, from Lugano and the lakes of Lombardy, of the fourth century B.C. and later, come some seventy inscriptions in "Lepontic," a language that may be Celtic or an independent branch of West IE.

Finally, "Ligurian" is used to denote two quite different languages. First, place-name suffixes (*-sco-, -inco-*, and so on) are held to be relics of a pre-IE substrate language of the Pyrenees, southern France, and northern Italy. Second, IE names that are neither Celtic nor Italic, notably in the *sententia Minuciorum* (a Latin inscription from near Genoa, of 117 B.C., Degrassi no. 517) suggest the earlier existence of an independent IE language, perhaps that of the Ligurians, the pre-Celtic people of southern France, east of the Rhone, and of northwest Italy.

Caesar asserts (*The Gallic War* 1.1.2) that each of the three major parts of Gaul had its

NORTH AFRICA

Of the languages brought to North Africa by successive groups of immigrants we are quite well informed. Place-names that appear to be IE are assumed to result from contact with the thirteenth-century B.C. civilizations of Crete and Mycenae. Phoenician activity there, from 1100 B.C., culminated in the foundation of Carthage from Tyre in 814. The Theran colony of Cyrene, founded on the Libyan coast (*ca.* 630 B.C.), remained Greek-speaking until the Arab incursions of A.D. 641. The Carthaginians were keen students of the Greek language and literature: Hannibal knew Greek before he learned Latin (Cicero, *On the Orator* 2.18.75). At the end of the Third Punic War, in 146 B.C., the Roman province was born and romanization begun. Jews of the Diaspora, finally, brought Aramaic to North Africa.

Massylian

Of the native languages of North Africa only Massylian (or Numidian or Old Libyan) is understood at all. Massylian is a Berber language written in a strongly geometrized, (south)west Semitic script and attested almost exclusively in epitaphs but also on the monumental inscriptions of Roman Thugga Terebentina (Tubgag). The Berber languages survived romanization and the Arab conquests, and today preserve many Latin loanwords, some of which do not appear in the Romance languages: Latin *pulcher,* for example, survives to this day in south Morocco as *fulki* (pretty).

Punic

Punic is the name given to the western dialects of Phoenician from the fourth century B.C. until the fifth century A.D. It was the language of the (twelfth to ninth century B.C.) Phoenician colonists of North Africa (especially Utica, Hadrumetum, and Carthage), Malta, Sicily, Corsica, Sardinia, southern France, and Spain. And until the time of Emperor Tiberius (early first century A.D.), Punic—strictly speaking, after 146 B.C., "Late Punic"—was widely recognized, beside Latin, as an official language of North Africa.

African kings minted coins with legends in Punic as well as Massylian; Micipsa of Numidia (148–118 B.C.) wrote his epitaph in Punic; in fact, Punic continued to appear beside Latin on public buildings until the end of the second century A.D. Numerous private inscriptions in Vulgar Punic from Libya (especially Lepcis Magna), Tunisia, Algeria, and Morocco attest the colloquial status of the language in many African towns and reflect the influence of Latin and Massylian on late Punic vocabulary and syntax. In spite of educations in Rome, Juba II of Mauretania (25 B.C.–A.D. 23) used Punic books for his literary compositions in Greek (Ammianus Marcellinus 22.15.8), and the African emperor Septimius Severus (A.D. 211) kept his native Punic and his African accent (Spartian, *Life of Severus* 19.9, in *Scriptores Historiae Augustae*).

Evidence for vowels and pronunciation of Late Punic is offered by the frequent Punic renderings of Latin names, including the proconsul Lucius Aelius Lamia, Horace's friend, and the emperor Macrinus, in the northernmost Punic graffiti, found in the camp of the Twentieth Legion, in Holt, Denbighshire, Wales, from the early third century A.D. More valuable still are the last Punic inscriptions (fourth and fifth century A.D.) in Greek and Latin letters which, incidentally, seem to adhere to the principles of transcription used in one version of the ten lines in Punic of Plautus' *The Little Carthaginian (Poenulus)* (930–939) of 189 B.C. Later indirect evidence for the language is furnished by Augustine, Bishop of Hippo Regius (Bône in Algeria), whose first language was Punic own language, but there is nothing in our linguistic evidence to suggest that the Belgae, to the northeast of the Seine and the Marne, spoke a language different from that of the Celtae of Alsace, Lorraine, and central France to the Atlantic coast (see Strabo 4.1.1). However, the Aquitani in the southwest, between the Garonne and the Pyrenees, may, it is true, have spoken an ancient form of Basque or a related language.

In northern Italy as early as the second century B.C. Polybius notes (2.35.4) only small Celtic settlements on the fringes of the Alps, and these are just a memory by the first century A.D. (Strabo 5.1.6), although the modern place-names *Ponzago* and *Savegnago* may preserve Celtic suffixes, and features of the modern dialects of Liguria and Piedmont may reflect the influence of Celtic phonology. In France, the establishment of Gallia Narbonensis (121 B.C.) and Caesar's conquest of Gaul beyond the Alps (58–51 B.C.) started the steady process of Latinization that by A.D. 400 had banished Celtic from the most thoroughly Celtic country in continental Europe.

SPAIN

There survive around 800 inscriptions in the pre-Roman languages of Spain (fifth–first century B.C.), together with coins from 197 to about 45 B.C. and the names of Spanish people, places, and gods attested in Latin inscriptions and in the writings of Pliny, Strabo, and Ptolemy.

Scholars distinguish three native scripts and two linguistic complexes, the one IE, the other not. A non-IE language, called Iberian and written first in Greek (fifth century B.C.) and later in "Iberian" and Latin scripts, was spoken in the south (east of Obulco), along the east coast, and in the Ebro Valley. The latest mention of the language being in use refers to A.D. 25 (Tacitus, *Annals* 4.45.3); it is presumed to have died soon after and to have left no traces of itself in the modern Romance languages.

Greek and Latin apart (Livy 34.9.1), IE was represented in Spain by Celtiberian and by the language(s) of a "western" linguistic complex. Celtiberian was an independent branch of Celtic and is attested on inscriptions in Latin and Iberian scripts from northern Spain to the west of the Iberian area and in place-names extending farther south.

In northwestern Spain a few documents in Latin letters afford only the haziest picture of one or more IE languages. Archaeology reveals Balkan and Danubian elements beside the Celtic, and evidence of opposing social systems in Galicia and central Portugal may indicate separate IE invasions.

The romanization of parts of Spain was swift and thorough. Even place-names were officially latinized and, after the early principate, personal names are all that survive of the native languages—with the exception of Basque.

Basque

It is unlikely that modern Basque is related to ancient Iberian. The only ancient evidence for the Basques is the name of a people —*Vascones* in Latin authors, *Ba(r̃)scunes* in Iberian—and other names of persons and gods in Latin inscriptions. We may suspect that the Aquitani spoke old Basque or a related language only on such flimsy evidence as the appearance of Basque *aritz* (oak) in the name of a divinity of Aquitaine, *Marti Arixoni* (dative singular). Celtic and Latin names and nouns appear in the Basque area and language but, thanks to late Christianization, successful resistance to the Visigoths, and a language entirely unrelated to Latin, the Basques have retained their ethnic and linguistic identity to the present day and, further, preserve some most striking—presumably pre-IE—lexical correspondences with the Caucasian languages.

(*Confessions* 1.14.23) and in whose diocese Punic was still a popular language (*Epistle 66.2*, Migne, *Bibliotheca Patrum Latina* [hereafter *PL*] vol. 33, col. 236), and, lastly, by Arnobius the Younger, who says (*Commentary on Psalm 104, PL* vol. 53, col. 481B) that Punic was still spoken in the areas toward the Garamantes (*ca.* A.D. 460).

Egyptian

The affinities of Egyptian are not clear. By the two most favored alternatives, it is either a marginal Semitic language or an independent language belonging with Berber, Kushitic, and Semitic to a language family called Hamito-Semitic.

Egyptian was spoken by the native population of Egypt from prehistoric times until the seventh century A.D. One or two foreigners of note learned to speak Egyptian but it was generally not spoken further afield; in connection with exported Egyptian cults, like that of Isis, it is more probable that Greek was spoken in the east and Latin in the west of the Mediterranean world.

Egyptian appeared over the course of history in three native vowel-less scripts. Sacred and otherwise formal documents were carved in the monumental hieroglyphs from the fourth millennium B.C. to our last hieroglyphic text, from Philae of A.D. 394. From hieroglyphic developed (from the Third Dynasty) the cursive writing called hieratic, which was used until the latest period for writing religious texts on papyrus. From hieratic emerged, thirdly (*ca.* 715 B.C.), what Herodotus called (2.36.4) the demotic script. These different writing styles did not replace, but merely restricted, their forerunner(s) and all three were to be found in Greco-Roman times.

In its development from Old Egyptian to Coptic, Egyptian is a single language, although philologists distinguish on linguistic grounds several phases in its history. Old Egyptian (3180–2240 B.C.) differed little from Middle (or "classical") Egyptian, the vernacular (*ca.* 2240–1990 B.C.), which survived as an official and learned language well into the Eighteenth Dynasty (1573–1314 B.C.; "postclassical") and reappeared in archaizing texts as late as the sixth century B.C. Late Egyptian is the vernacular (*ca.* 1573–715 B.C.) and is distinguished from Demotic, the term loosely applied to the language of texts in the demotic script, from about 715 B.C. Although from the second century A.D. the Roman administration no longer recognized the Egyptian language or script on legal documents, we find graffiti in Demotic as late as A.D. 452, on the island of Philae.

Coptic (the name is an Arabic corruption of Greek *Aiguptos*, Egypt) seems to have developed in several dialects from Early Demotic and was the language of Christian Egypt. To some extent, Coptic was a semiartificial literary language elaborated by Egyptian Christian monks and heavily influenced in vocabulary and word order by Greek. From the second or third century A.D. Coptic was written in Greek letters with the aid of seven additional demotic characters; only in Coptic are the vowels of Egyptian written. After the Moslem conquest of A.D. 640 Coptic was gradually replaced by Arabic, but it survived in some parts as a colloquial language until the sixteenth century A.D. and as the liturgical language of the Egyptian church until the present day.

From the time of Alexander, the official language of Egypt was Greek. Its influence upon the native language has not yet been fully studied. Certainly, Demotic borrowed relatively few Greek words, fewer by far than the colloquial language did, as Coptic later showed. Under Diocletian, Latin entered Egyptian documents but was largely restricted to the internal administration of the judicial system.

PALESTINE AND SYRIA

The northwest Semitic languages comprised two main branches: the Canaanite (Amorite, Ugaritic, Old Canaanite, Phoenician, and Hebrew) and the Aramaic (divided into western and eastern groups of dialects).

In Phoenician, we have many thousands of inscriptions dating from the twelfth century B.C. to the fifth century A.D. and covering a vast area, from Ur in Iraq to Mogador in Morocco, and from Aswan on the Nile to Holt in Wales. From 1200 B.C. until Alexander's conquest in 332 B.C., despite successive dominations by the Assyrians, the Babylonians, and the Persians, Phoenician remained an important colloquial and official language of the eastern seaboard of the Mediterranean, from Egypt to Karatepe in Turkey. Between 332 B.C. and Pompey's conquests in 62 B.C., Phoenician gave way to Greek and to an Aramaic *koine,* surviving on only a few inscriptions and coins until A.D. 196 (cf. Lucian, *Alexander the False Magician* 13).

From the end of the Babylonian exile (sixth century B.C.), Hebrew (the Canaanite dialect of the Bible) was ceasing to be the colloquial language of the peoples of Palestine and was becoming first the dialect of Jerusalem and then a sacred language. It yielded, like Phoenician, to an Aramaic *koine* (referred to, rather misleadingly, by Greek authors as "Hebrew") which became, beside Greek, the everyday language of the whole region and remained so from the last centuries B.C. until the end of antiquity.

A western Aramaic dialect was written by the Nabataeans, at least from 312 B.C. (Diodorus 19.96.1) and well into Roman times, their documents occurring all over the Middle East and also in the Aegean and Italy. They may, however, have spoken Arabic rather than the Aramaic that they wrote; at any rate, by the fourth century A.D. the growing number of Arabisms in their documents had practically ousted Aramaic.

Another important (western) Aramaic dialect was that of Palmyra (Tadmor) in northern Syria, which appears in more than 2,000 inscriptions (44 B.C.–A.D. 275) from all over the Roman Empire and, in many bi- and trilinguals, as an official language beside Greek and Latin.

From the eastern Aramaic dialect of Edessa (Urfa) emerged a new Aramaic written language, Syriac, attested from A.D. 6. Under the influence of Christianity, Syriac was the language of a rich literature that enjoyed its first high point in the hymns of the Christian poet-philosopher Bardesanes (second-third century A.D.).

Finally, Greeks and Romans in this corner of the Mediterranean had limited contact with two Arabic languages. Thamudic, a north Arabic language, sparsely attested in Egypt, Sinai, and Palestine, was spoken by nomadic tribes of northern Arabia who drifted across the border of the Roman Empire sporadically and chiefly after the end of Nabataean power in A.D. 106.

Ṣafaitic is the name given (from Mount Ṣafa in Syria) to the Arabic language attested in more than 12,000 inscriptions (first century B.C. to sixth century A.D.) over an area stretching from Palmyra to northern Saudi Arabia.

So thoroughly had Palestine and Syria been hellenized by the Seleucid successors of Alexander that Greek remained the language of education and commerce and a colloquial language beside Aramaic until the end of Roman times. St. Paul spoke both Greek and Aramaic (Acts 21:37–40); the Syrophoenician woman of Canaan in Mark's Gospel (7:26) spoke Greek; the Arab nomads of the Syrian desert scrawled graffiti in bad Greek; Greek was even the language of prayer in some synagogues. It is notable, however, that only Josephus from Palestine and Iamblichus and Lucian from Syria wrote serious works in Greek; as Josephus explains (*Jewish Antiquities* 20.262–5), a Jewish gentleman was more concerned to know the law and the scriptures than to perfect his mastery of a foreign language, a servile accomplishment.

Given the high level of Aramaic-Greek bilingualism in this area in Hellenistic and Roman times, we are surprised not by evidence of mutual linguistic influences but by the fact that these influences are not more extensive and profound. Broadly speaking, we find Aramaisms in the syntax of Greek (for example, *erotan hina* means "to pray that" and *psukhe*, soul, is used for "self," the reflexive pronoun), but no corresponding Grecisms in Aramaic. Conversely, there are countless Greek loanwords in Hebrew and Aramaic, from all walks of life—politics: *bema* (platform) appears as *bymh;* medicine: *splenion* (dressing) as *splnyt;* and clothing: *stole* (garment) as *'s.t.l'*, to give just three examples—but very few Semitic names and words in Greek.

The use of Latin, finally, was restricted, predictably, to the army and the law, the one notable island of Latinity in this ocean of Oriental Hellenism being the famous law school of Berytus (Beirut). From the second century A.D. even Roman milestones and town boundary posts gave distances and administrative details in Greek.

ASIA MINOR

From the cuneiform tablets of the archives of Hattusas (Boğazköy), the Hittite royal capital, we know that both IE and non-IE languages were spoken and written in Anatolia until about 1200 B.C. The IE tongues attested are Hittite, Palaic, Luwian (the Anatolian group), and the language of the kings of Mitanni (an Indo-Iranian language); the surviving non-IE languages are Hattian, Akkadian, and Hurrian.

The Phrygians crossed to Asia Minor from Thrace, perhaps during the chaos of the thirteenth and twelfth centuries B.C., and early in the eighth century founded a wealthy kingdom centered on Gordion (Gordium; Homer, *Iliad* 3.184ff.; Herodotus 7.73; 7.20; 1.6). Old Phrygian (for one Egyptian pharaoh, the oldest human language: Herodotus 2.2), written in an alphabet closely related to the archaic Greek on more than forty inscriptions and some ninety graffiti, and dating from as early as the eighth century B.C., is poorly understood and bears an uncertain relation to Late Phrygian, which is preserved in about 110 inscriptions in the Greek alphabet—mostly curses appended to epitaphs in Greek (which may imply Phrygian-Greek bilingualism)—of the second to fourth century A.D. As with nearly all the ancient languages of Anatolia and the Balkans, we may add testimonies of personal names, place-names, and Greek glosses, but our evidence permits only the most rudimentary sketch of Phrygian phonology and morphology. Herodotus (7.73) links the Phrygians with the Armenians but no innovations common to both languages are known. Phrygian seems to share certain features with Greek, including the temporal augment, the form of the perfect participle passive, and some words, though an apparent *r*-ending of the mediopassive provides an isogloss with Anatolian, Tocharian, Italic, and Celtic. Phrygian has been related also to Thracian and Macedonian, on the one hand, and to Hittite and Luwian on the other; neither thesis can be demonstrated. Phrygian survived the Persian Empire, hellenization, the arrival of the Galatians, and the settlements of the Ostrogoths in the fourth century A.D. (Claudian 20.153–4) into the fifth or sixth century A.D. (Socrates, in Migne, *Bibliotheca Patrum Graeca* [hereafter PG] vol. 67, col. 648A; Sozomenos, *PG* vol. 67, col. 1468A).

Xanthus of Lydia (fifth century B.C.) characterized the Mysian language as half Lydian and half Phrygian (Strabo 12.8.3), and until recently the language of the Üyücek inscription (fourth-third century B.C.) was thought to confirm this and was regarded as Mysian. Now, however, it is thought most likely to be Old Phrygian; for Mysian there remains only the evidence of patristic sources that it was a living language in the sixth century A.D.

From 546 to 336 B.C. all of Asia Minor was part of the Persian Empire and a number of languages were used for different purposes. The language of the law, the army, and the administration was Aramaic, the native Semitic language of the civil servants of the Persian kings. Old Persian was the language of the court and the royal family, and of royal, chiefly monumental, inscriptions most of which, however, also carried versions in Elamite (the language of unknown affinities of the province Susiana) and Akkadian (the East Semitic language of Mesopotamia). All three were written in greatly simplified, quasi-alphabetic cuneiform scripts, and it was Persian trilinguals of this sort that provided Grotefend with the key to the decipherment of this script in 1802.

From the flight of Darius III before Alexander (331 B.C.) until the arrival of the Turks (eleventh century A.D.), Greek was the *synetheia,* the colloquial language, of all Asia Minor. Of course, the languages of Asia Minor exercised an influence, small but noticeable, on Greek: certain phonological peculiarities and many loanwords are plausibly ascribed to Asian influence. This influence was not Iranian—the Persians and their languages were soon forgotten—but came from the descendants of the old Anatolian languages. For, although by the first century A.D. most of the peoples had given up their languages and names in favor of Greek (Strabo 12.4.6), in the south languages survived, some quite late into Roman times, that were related most closely to the Luwian of the monumental "Hieroglyphic" inscriptions erected by boastful kings of the neo-Hittite states of southeastern Asia Minor and northern Syria from the tenth to the seventh century B.C.

Lycian

Two dialects of a Luwian language—Lycian A and Lycian B, or Milyan—are attested in about 180 stone inscriptions and some 150 coin legends found chiefly in the Roman province of Lycia in southwestern Asia Minor. They are written in an alphabet developed from the Greek and date from the seventh to the fourth century B.C. Most of them are grave monuments that are well understood thanks chiefly to a Lycian-Greek-Aramaic trilingual and also to six Lycian-Greek bilinguals. The Xanthus stele, however, is a historical text, and it and a few longer inscriptions are still largely unintelligible. Herodotus records (1.173.3) that when the Lycians came from Crete they were called *Termilai;* strikingly, the Lycians of our inscriptions refer to themselves as *trm̃mili.*

Lydian

Lydian, of which the affinities within Anatolian are highly uncertain, is written in an alphabet of an archaic Greek type on over 100 inscriptions of the sixth to fourth century B.C., mostly grave steles and nearly all from the old Lydian capital, Sardis. Bilinguals, two Lydian-Greek and one Lydian-Aramaic, have helped to a middling understanding of all but three longer sacred prose texts and seven poetic texts that seem to show rhyme at line ends. By Strabo's day there was not a trace of Lydian left in Lydia (13.4.17; see Pausanias 5.27.5–6).

Carian

In Carian we have some glosses and more than 150 inscriptions dating from the seventh to the third century B.C., after which we assume hellenization was complete. These were discovered in Caria itself (fourth-third century B.C.), and in Iasos, Sardis, Athens (a Carian-Greek bilingual, sixth century B.C.), and Egypt (seventh-fifth century B.C., including many graffiti of Carian mercenaries). Of the language and script we know practically nothing for certain, and until something approaching a consensus is reached on how to read the texts, all attempts to place Carian are premature. Of relevance, we may add only that known Carian personal names are devoid of IE characteristics.

Lesser-known Languages

Hard evidence for other languages of ancient Asia Minor is scarce and often ambiguous. Apollonius of Tyana is supposed to have written a book in Cappadocian (Philostratus, *Life of Apollonius* 3.41; 4.19). Patristic sources mention a living language of Cappadocia as late as the fifth century A.D., but we cannot be sure that this does not refer to a local form of Greek, especially as Dioscorides (first century A.D.) mentions as "Cappadocian" a plant name that is clearly Greek.

Again, "Lycaonian," the language in which the crowd at Derbe adored Paul and Barnabus (Acts 14:11), mentioned along with neighboring Isaurian as a living language in the fourth century A.D., may be a Luwian language but could equally well be a local form of Koine Greek.

In Cilicia, Pamphylia, and Pisidia, however, there is better evidence that Anatolian languages related to Luwian survived into Roman times. Cilician personal names from the Greco-Roman period are strikingly similar to old Luwian names: compare *Armasetas* with Luwian *Armaziti*.

Arrian reports (*The March Up Country* [*Anabasis*] 1.26.4, second century A.D.) that some Aeolians who colonized the Pamphylian coastal city of Side promptly forgot their Greek and learned instead an unknown barbarous tongue. This is taken to refer to "Sidetic," the language of five inscriptions (fifth-fourth century B.C.), including two Greek-Sidetic bilinguals, written in a partly unknown alphabet related to the Greek, and presumed on the strength of Anatolian case endings to be a Luwian dialect of Pamphylia.

Strabo mentions (13.4.17) a Pisidian language, which, it is generally believed, appears in sixteen grave inscriptions in Greek letters from Sofular and of which both case endings and personal names appear to be Luwian. Pisidian and the unknown language of the Solymi were spoken, along with Greek and Lydian, at Cibyra in Lycia (Strabo, *ibid.*).

Cataonian, Mariandynian, and Pontic are mentioned by Greek and Latin authors but their origins and affinities are obscure. They might have been aberrant forms of Greek, IE descendants of Palaic, or non-IE descendants of the languages of the Gasga, the wild northern foe of the Hittites.

Galatian

The Galatians, three tribes of Celts settled around Ankara from about 230 B.C., preserved their Celtic language at least until the end of the fourth century A.D. For Jerome, who knew both Ankara and eastern Gaul, said (*PL* vol. 26 §429–430, col. 356–357) that their speech was almost the same as that of the Treveri, a tribe of Celtic Gaul, and his claim is borne out by comparison of Galatian with continental Celtic personal names.

It was from a campaign against the Galatians that Gnaeus Manlius Vulso brought back to Rome in 187 B.C. the very first taste of Oriental luxury and, presumably, the associated words. Later, and uniquely, we can date, to 76 B.C., Lucullus' bringing of the cultivated cherry tree *(cerasus)* from Pontus in Asia Minor to Italy (Pliny the Elder, *Natural History* 15.30.102). But this influence was not mutual; nowhere did Latin become a colloquial language in Asia Minor and it seems from inscriptions that even Roman veterans in their colonies in Pisidia, Asia, Galatia, and Cilicia soon gave up speaking Latin and blended with the local populations.

THE NORTHERN BALKANS

Thracian

The Thracians had certain cultural features in common with those IE invaders identified with the Greeks. At the period of its greatest extent, Thracian was spoken not only as far north as the Danube (Herodotus 5.9) and beyond (Strabo 7.3.10,13), but also perhaps on Samos, Samothrace, and other Aegean islands, and in Bithynia and Mysia, in Asia Minor. Greek authors distinguished many tribes of Thracians (Mysians, Hippemolgians, and Abians, *Iliad* 13.1–7; we read too of Bessians, Bithynians, Dians, Edonians, Getans, Moesians, Odrysians, Trereans, and Triballians) but treated the Thracians as an ethnic and linguistic unity. Of Thracian literature we hear only of the Getan poems of Ovid in exile in Tomi on the Black Sea (*Letters from Pontus* 4.13.19–20; *Tristia* 5.12.58). Our evidence for the language comprises only the Kjölmen tombstone (sixth or fourth century B.C.), the Ezerovo gold ring (fifth century B.C.), personal names and place-names, some sixty glosses and, if they are Thracian, seventy-six inscriptions on pottery fragments and a stone stele from Samothrace (sixth to fourth century B.C.; the ancient native and sacred language of Diodorus 5.47.2–3).

Thracian may well be an IE satem language—(perhaps one in which original palatal stops became fricatives IE *k > Thracian s, for example, in *esbe-?* < IE *$ekwo$-, horse) —although its treatment of IE consonants is uncertain. Indeed, if the etymologies may be trusted, studies of place-names could suggest two IE linguistic strata in the Thracian area, characterized by different suffixes: the one to the north of the Danube, which shows no consonant shift (*Vedea, Salmudessos* from (*wed-/*$udes$-, water), has been called Daco-Mysian; and Thracian proper, to the south of the Danube, which shows a complete consonant shift (*Utus* from *$udes$, water). Place-names apart, the most important source for Daco-Mysian is the list of Dacian plant names in the botanical work of Dioscorides Pedanius of Anazarbus (first century A.D.). For the rest, the Daco-Mysians were so thoroughly romanized that their Vulgar Latin formed, even in the face of strong south Slavic elements, the foundations of modern Rumanian. The Thracians, by contrast, successfully preserved their linguistic identity against the strong influences of Greece and Rome. King Seuthes may have had some Greek in 400 B.C. (Xenophon, *The March Up Country* [*Anabasis*] 7.6.8) but Ovid was not impressed with the standard of Greek spoken in Tomi four centuries later (*Tristia* 5.7.51). Thracian names survive in Latin inscriptions from eastern Dardania well into imperial times and later sources attest Thracian translations of the Gospels (John Chrysostom, *Sermon* 8.1, *PG* vol. 63, col. 501) and the survival of the Bessian dialect of Thracian into the sixth century A.D.

Illyrian

Illyrian, attested only in a handful of glosses and about a thousand personal and geographical names, was spoken over a large area of the northwest Balkans bordering on the Thracian-speaking area to the east, Greek to the south, and Venetic to the northwest. All the glosses and many of the names could be given IE etymologies: with *rhinos*, mist, compare, perhaps, Albanian *re(n)*, cloud; with *Vescleves* perhaps Greek *Euklees* and Sanskrit *Vasuśravas* from IE **wesu-ḱlewes*, "whose fame is good." But none of these equations is at all certain, and without more evidence it is an act of faith to say whether or not Illyrian is IE and, in particular, related to Messapian of southeast Italy. In any case, the real content of the label "Illyrian" has been rendered diverse and imprecise in the extreme by recent studies of Illyrian personal names, which have established not one but four or more name types in this area: Illyrian proper; Pannonian; Dalmatian; and North Adriatic or Venetic-Istrian-Liburnian, the last implying links between Venetic and Liburnian and recalling Herodotus' "Enetoi of the Illyrians" (1.196.1). This obliges us to envisage ethnic and linguistic diversity in the northwest Balkans of pre-Roman times. The emergence of Romance languages in eastern Switzerland, Venetia, the southern Alps, Istria, and Dalmatia implies the complete romanization of the Adriatic coast, while more inaccessible areas harbored safely the ancestor of modern Albanian. It is clear at least that Albanian descends from an ancient language of the Balkans, for it contains loanwords from ancient Greek (for example, *shpellë*, cave, from Greek *spelaion*) but on present evidence it is fruitless to debate the rival claims of Illyrian and Thracian to be that language.

Paeonian

On the evidence of one gloss and of personal names, some Greek *(Ariston)*, some possibly Greek *(Patraos)*, and some non-Greek *(Laggaros)*, the Paeonians (from Paeonia [southern Yugoslavia]), accounted barbarians by the Greeks, cannot be placed linguistically, though scholars have variously held them to be Thracians, Illyrians, Phrygians who did not cross into Asia Minor, or Greeks who did not proceed further into Greece.

Epirote

Although their broad Greek ethnic and linguistic basis is complicated by foreign, especially Illyrian, elements, the Epirotes were probably Greeks who were left behind by the main body of migrants to settle in the inhospitable northwest of Greece. Some place-names of Epirus look thoroughly Greek (for example, *Epeiros*, their homeland, *Thesprotoi*, and *Boion*) and some of the people were recognized as Greeks (Herodotus 7.176; Strabo 9.5.23). On the other hand, Thucydides (1.47.3, 50.3) and Strabo (7.7.1) call the Epirotes *barbaroi*: only two of Thucydides' (2.80) northern chieftains have Greek names and many Epirote tribes did not speak Greek (Strabo 7.7.1) and even enjoyed a tribal form of political life until Roman times (Strabo 7.7.4–5).

Macedonian

The Macedonians, too, may have been Greeks (Herodotus 1.56); again, a Greek basis, seen in Hellenic names of gods and months, is confused by foreign elements, notably Thracian and Illyrian. The ancients themselves were divided on the question of whether the Macedonians were Greek (Isocrates, *Philip* 106–108; *contra* Demosthenes, *Third Olynthiac* 3.16,24); it is likely that Greeks could not readily understand Macedonian (Plutarch, "Alexander" 51.2–4) and a Macedonian claim to be Greek could be seriously challenged in the fifth century B.C. (Herodotus 5.22). Until we discover a text in Macedonian, we can say nothing for certain about the language except that Macedonian names and glosses are either thoroughly Greek (*Alexandros; agema,* a military unit) or clearly cognate with Greek but with systematically different phonological features (*Bilippos* beside Greek *Philippos; kebala* beside Greek *kephale,* head), or they have no known Greek cognates (*abagna,* a type of rose; *aliza,* the white poplar). On present evidence, Macedonian was either a dialect of Greek isolated very early from the rest, or a separate IE language closely related to Greek.

GREEK, LATIN, AND "BARBARIAN"

Even for the languages with which the Greeks had most frequent contact—such as Persian or Phoenician—or which were nearest neighbors and likely closest relatives to Greek—such as Macedonian, Phrygian, or Epirote—information offered by Greek authors is scanty in the extreme. Indeed, throughout antiquity Greek sources display a remarkable lack of curiosity about foreign languages. We hear of not a single grammar of a foreign language written by a Greek, the Alexandrian grammarians contenting themselves with glossing words from Latin, Italic, Celtic, and Iberian. Aristotle, the prolific polymath, says next to nothing about other languages, and even the bilingual Zeno of Citium (335–263 B.C.) wrote a grammar only of Greek and not of his mother tongue, Phoenician. Only exceptionally, and for a particular purpose, did an educated Greek learn another language (Pythagoras learned Egyptian [Diogenes Laertius 8.3] and Themistocles Persian [Thucydides 1.138.1]); otherwise, why should he when it was so evident that Greek was the only language of any worth?

Peoples of non-Greek speech were collectively referred to as *barbaroi*—they seemed to say just "bar bar"—(Cicero, *Republic* 1.37.58), and if at first this term was used quite neutrally to mean simply "non-Greek," it soon came to imply linguistic and cultural inferiority. Foreigners, whether speaking their own language or attempting to speak Greek, and even Greeks who spoke dialects other than Attic, were often the butt of the writers of comedy, and there is no doubt as to the identity of the language that Tereus the hoopoe says he brought to the community of the birds who were previously *barbaroi* (Aristophanes, *Birds* 199–200).

Hand in hand with this lack of regard for other languages went, until Roman times at any rate, the highest possible regard for the Greek language. Epicurus, for example, is said to have placed Greek above all other languages and even to have supposed that the gods spoke Greek (Philodemus frag. 356 Usener).

A few languages, it is true, commanded respect in Greek eyes. Egyptian, for its antiquity (the Egyptians, as Herodotus [2.158.5] informed his Greek audience, also had a word like *barbaroi* for all peoples who did not speak Egyptian); Hebrew and Akkadian, for their associations with the sacred and the magical; and, eventually, Latin.

In 282 B.C., a Roman envoy to Tarentum had been laughed out of court as *barbaros* for his flawed Greek (Dionysius of Halicarnassus 19.5.1). By the Augustan Age, Latin was the language of the rulers of the Mediterranean world and, further, a language with a literature that had won great recognition on its own merits. Plutarch certainly acknowledged this and even felt obliged to excuse himself for not having a greater command of the Latin language (*Life of Demosthenes* 2.2–3). Latin came to hold a special place in

Greek estimation, came even to be regarded as a dialect of Greek (Dionysius of Halicarnassus 1.89f.). Latin could be placed alongside Greek in opposition to all the other, barbarian, languages of the known world (Origen, *Against Celsus* 8.37.3–5, third century A.D.); native speakers of Greek even published history or poetry in Latin (Ammianus Marcellinus and Claudian, fourth century A.D.).

Roman views on the Greek language seem largely to have been complementary to Roman estimation of the worth of Latin. Early on, in the face of the widespread importance and prestige of the Greek language and literature, it was clearly unrealistic for Romans to claim that their language was the only one of any value—though they could insist, until the 80s B.C., that the Senate be addressed only in Latin (Plutarch, *Life of Cato the Elder* 22.4–5). Roman writers were all too conscious of "the poverty of their mother tongue" (*patrii sermonis egestas,* Lucretius, 1.136–9,832; 3.260; see 3.3–7; see also Plautus, *A Comedy of Asses* [*Asinaria*] 11, *Three-Coin Day* [*Trinummus*] 19). An educated Roman spoke Greek before he took formal instruction in Latin, and while Roman officials might refuse from pride to speak Greek in public (Valerius Maximus 2.2.2), and although Cato protested against the corrupting influence of the Greeks, their literature, and their medicine (Pliny, *Natural History* 29.7.14), this inferiority complex was deep-rooted and long lasting. But in the course of the first century B.C., as the Latin literary language neared perfection, Romans' esteem of their native language grew and grew until Cicero could claim that Latin was even richer in linguistic resources than Greek (*On the Chief Good and Evil* [*De Finibus*] 1.3.10; 3.2.5) and Roman orators, following their new demands for the purest *latinitas,* could dub Greek words as barbarisms (Cicero, *On Duty* 1.31.111; Quintilian 11.3.31). The nature of the empire also had a part to play in emboldening speakers of Latin to challenge the supremacy of Greek as *the* language par excellence. The emperor Claudius deprived a Lycian of Roman citizenship on account of the man's ignorance of Latin (Cassius Dio 60.17.4); and the encouragement given by Diocletian and Constantine to the use of Latin in the East is nicely reflected in the Egyptian papyri, which include exercises for Greek-speakers learning Latin and journals of government officials, previously in Greek, written in Latin. A political vision of Rome as ruler of the entire world (Cicero, *Philippic* 6.7.19) led to the view of Latin as the ideal world language extending as far as the frontiers of the empire and uniting all men with a common tongue (Pliny, *Natural History* 3.5.39; Augustine, *City of God* 19.7, with reservations). Finally, at the very end of our period, Jerome, steeped in the works of Cicero, Vergil, and Horace, brought the wheel full circle, in his belief (*Epistle* 50.2) that Latin was the only true language, all the rest, Greek included, being *barbari!*

BIBLIOGRAPHY

SOURCES

Appendix Probi, Sprachlicher Kommentar zur Vulgärlateinischen Appendix Probi, W. A. Bachrens, ed. (1922); Comas Vestitor, *Life of St. John Chrysostom* in Douze récits byzantines sur Saint Jean Chrysostome, F. Halkin, ed. (1977); Dioscorides Pedanius of Anazarbus, *De Materia Medica,* Max Wellmann, ed., 3 vols. (1906–1914); Eustathius, *Commentary on Homer's Iliad,* Marchinus van der Valk, ed., 3 vols. (1971–1979); Sextus Pompeius Festus, *De Verborum Significatu,* Wallace M. Lindsay, ed. (1913); *Itinerarium Egeriae (Égérie, Journal de voyage, Itinéraire).* Introduction, critical text, trans., notes, and maps by Pierre Maraval (1982).

Justinian, *Digest,* in *Corpus Iuris Civilis,* Theodore Mommsen, *et al.,* eds., 3 vols. (1886, repr. 1970–1973); Mauricius, *Strategikon,* George T. Dennis, ed., Ernst Gamillscheg, trans. (1981); J. P. Migne, ed., *Bibliotheca Patrum Graeca [PG],* 163 vols. (1857–1936), and *Bibliotheca Patrum Latina [PL],* 221 vols. (1844–1863); Origen, *Contre Celse,* Marcel Borret, ed. and trans., 5 vols. (1967–1976); Philodemus, fragments in *Epicurea,* Hermann Usener, ed. (1887); Phrynichus Arabius, *Die Ekloge des Phrynichos,* Eitel von Fischer, ed. (1974); Tyrtaeus, *Fragmenta,* Carlo Prato, ed. (1968); Valerius Maximus, *Facta et Dicta Memorabilia,* C. Kempf, ed. (1888).

All other references to Greek and Latin authors are to the editions (with English translations) in the Loeb Classical Library. References to inscriptions are from: Attilio Degrassi, *Inscriptiones Latinae Liberae Rei Publicae,* I (1957; 2d ed. 1965); II (1963); Michael Lejeune, *Manuel de la langue vénète* (1974); Emil Vetter, *Handbuch der italischen Dialekte,* I (1953) [(with P. Poccetti, *Nuovi documenti italici a complemento del Manuale di E. Vetter,* 1979)].

STUDIES

Good starting-points, all with extensive bibliographies, are: J.P.V.D. Balsdon, *Romans and Aliens* (1979), chs. 9, 10; *The Cambridge Ancient History,* II, pt. 1 (3d ed. 1973) chs. 4, 6, 13; pt. 2 (3d ed. 1975) chs. 30, 36, 38, 39; III, pt. 1 (2d ed. 1982) ch. 20c–e; Günter Neumann and Jürgen Untermann, eds., *Die Sprachen im römischen Reich der Kaiserzeit: Kolloquium 8–10 April 1974* (1980).

Indo-European

Henrik Birnbaum and Jaan Puhvel, eds., *Ancient Indo-European Dialects. Proceedings of the Conference on Indo-European Linguistics, April 25–27, 1963* (1966); George Cardona, Henry M. Hoenigswald, Alfred Senn, eds., *Indo-European and Indo-Europeans: Papers Presented at the Third Indo-European Conference at the University of Pennsylvania* (1970); Antoine Meillet, *The Comparative Method in Historical Linguistics,* Gordon B. Ford, Jr., trans. (1967); Oswald Szemerényi, *Einführung in die vergleichende Sprachwissenschaft* (1980).

"Mediterranean" substrate studies. D. A. Hester, "Recent Developments in Mediterranean Substrate Studies," in *Minos,* **9** (1968); Antoine Meillet, "De quelques emprunts probables en grec et latin," in *Mémoire de la Société Linguistique de Paris,* **15** (1908).

GREECE

Pre-Greek

John Chadwick, "Traditional Spelling or Two Dialects?" in A. Heubeck and G. Neumann, eds., *Res Mycenaeae. Akten des VII. Internationalen Mykenologischen Colloquiums in Nürnberg* (1983), a different view of the origin of the Doric dialects; J. B. Hainsworth, "The pre-Greek Place Names," in *Bulletin of the Institute of Classical Studies,* **16** (1969); D. A. Hester, " 'Pelasgian,' A New Indo-European Language?" in *Lingua,* **13** (1965); W. Merlingen, "Fair Play for 'Pelasgian,' " in *Lingua,* **18** (1967); P. G. van Soesbergen, "The Coming of the Dorians," in *Kadmos,* **20** (1981); W.F. Wyatt, "Greek Names in -σσος/-ττος," in *Glotta,* **46** (1968).

Greek

Robert Browning, *Medieval and Modern Greek* (1969, 2d ed. 1983); John Chadwick, *The Decipherment of Linear B* (1958, 2d ed. 1967); Warren Cowgill, "Ancient Greek Dialectology in the Light of Mycenaean," in Henrik Birnbaum and Jaan Puhvel, eds., *op. cit.;* R. A. Crossland and Ann Birchall, eds., *Bronze Age Migrations in the Aegean: Archaeological and Linguistic Problems in Greek Prehistory* (1973); J. B. Hainsworth, "Greek Views of Greek Dialectology," in *Transactions of the Philological Society* (1967); Martin R.P. McGuire, "The Decline of the Knowledge of Greek in the West from *c.* 150 to the Death of Cassiodorus: A Reexamination of the Phenomenon from the Viewpoint of Cultural Assimilation," in *Classical Folia,* **13** (1959); Antoine Meillet, *Aperçu d'une histoire de la langue grecque* (1913; 8th ed. 1975); Leonard R. Palmer, *The Greek Lan-*

guage (1980); J. N. Sevenster, *Do You Know Greek? How Much Greek Could the First Jewish Christians Have Known?* (1968).

ITALY

Latin

Einar Löfstedt, *Late Latin* (1959); Antoine Meillet, *Esquisse d'une histoire de la langue latine* (1928; 5th ed. 1948), with a bibliography by J. Perrot (1966); Leonard R. Palmer, *The Latin Language* (1954); Antonio Tovar, "A Research Report on Vulgar Latin and its Local Variations," in *Kratylos,* **9** (1964).

The other languages of Italy. Giuliano Bonfante and Larissa Bonfante, *The Etruscan Language: An Introduction* (1983); Aldo Luigi Prosdocimi, ed., *Popoli e civiltà dell'Italia antica*, VI, *Lingue e dialetti* (1978).

FRANCE AND SPAIN

Ramsay MacMullen, "The Celtic Renaissance," in *Historia,* **14** (1965); Wolfgang Meid, "Indo-European and Celtic," in *Scottish Studies,* **12** (1968); Antonio Tovar, *The Ancient Languages of Spain and Portugal* (1961), the best general survey.

NORTH AFRICA

Abd el Mohsen Bakir, *An Introduction to the Study of the Egyptian Language* (1978); Sir Alan Gardiner, *Egyptian Grammar* (1927; 3d ed. 1957); Stanislav Segert, *A Grammar of Phoenician and Punic* (1976).

ASIA MINOR

Handbuch der Orientalistik I, Abt. 2, 1 and 2, Lfg. 2: *Altkleinasiatische Sprachen* (1969), with contributions by E. Reiner on Elamite, A. Kammenhuber on Hattian, Hittite, Palaic, Luwian, and Hieroglyphic Luwian, G. Neumann on Lycian, and A. Heubeck on Lydian; Ph. Houwinck ten Cate, *The Luwian Population Groups of Lycia and Cilicia Aspera During the Hellenistic Period* (1961); G. L. Huxley, *Crete and the Luwians* (1961); G. E. Mylonas, "The Luvian Invasions of Greece," in *Hesperia,* **31** (1962); L. R. Palmer, "Linear A and the Anatolian Languages," in *Atti e Memorie del 1° Congresso Internazionale di Micenologia,* I (1968).

THE NORTHERN BALKANS

Giuliano Bonfante, "Note on the Samothracian Language," in *Hesperia,* **24** (1955); Ap. Daskalakis, *The Hellenism of the Ancient Macedonians* (1965); Radoslav Katičić, "Ancient Languages of the Balkans," in *Trends in Linguistics: State-of-the-Art Reports* **4-5** (1976).

AGRICULTURE AND FOOD

Farming and Animal Husbandry

K. D. WHITE

GREEK AGRICULTURE

Town and Country

Aristotle's aphorism "man is a creature of the city" (*politikon zoon*) has often been mistranslated by political scientists as "man is a political animal," and just as often misappropriated by narrowly political historians to justify their concentration on "political" history. However, historians of Greece and Rome have broadened their outlook as the archaeological evidence on settlement patterns has accumulated slowly and has begun to reshape our thinking on Dark Age Hellas and early republican Italy.

The polis and its *chora*, the *urbs* and its *territorium*, are no longer to be conceived as separate entities, the first the province of the political historian, the second the domain of his economic and social colleague. Town and country were not divided politically as they have been in the West since the onset of the Industrial Revolution. The sovereign popular assembly, the ecclesia, at Athens was made up of town and country people, as the official documents testify. An official curse that threatens a bad administrator with a murrain on his cattle and a blight on his crops would be pointless if the majority of those in the ecclesia were townsfolk: they were also peasants. The point emerges clearly from Thucydides' account (2.16–17) of the mass evacuation of the countryside of Attica at the outbreak of war in 431 B.C. and the difficulties encountered by the evacuees in finding lodging in the overcrowded city.

> The Athenians took the advice he [Pericles] had given them, and brought in from the country their wives and children and all their household goods.... Their sheep and cattle they shipped over to Euboea and the islands off the coast. But the move was very difficult for them, since the majority had always been accustomed to living in the country.

For most fifth-century Athenians, their city resembled more what in England would be called a county town than a city; that is, a center to which the inhabitants of neighboring villages, hamlets, or isolated farms came to sell surplus produce, to buy what was needed, and to take part in a variety of community activities, whether political, cultural, or religious. Even after the unification of Attica old habits persisted, as Thucydides (2.17) bears out:

> Most Athenians, both of earlier generations and right down to the present war, were born and bred in the country. . . . It was with a sad reluctance that they now abandoned their houses, . . . leaving behind them what each man regarded as his own city.

Thus we see that even in as sophisticated an urban society as Athens the land and its multifarious activities are of cardinal importance. As M. I. Finley has pointed out (*The Ancient Economy*, p. 23), "The true city of classical antiquity encompassed both the *chora*, the rural hinterland, and an urban center, where the community had its administration and its public cults."

Scope of the Subject

In modern parlance an agriculturist is a cultivator of the soil, one who cultivates field crops to be used either as food for humans and fodder for animals or for industrial or commercial purposes. His occupation is distinct from that of the pastoralist or stockbreeder on the one hand, and that of the horticulturist or silviculturist on the other. In classical antiquity, however, while the above distinction was clearly recognized, the separate activities were nevertheless regarded as parts of a totality of activity on the land; the respective terms *georgia* and *agricultura* were used comprehensively, and the classical usage will be followed here.

Relations between the two major divisions of our subject are, and have been, very close. Most of the surviving writings on agriculture have something to say about human and animal diet, including feeding programs for the latter, and about the methods used in processing foodstuffs, including orchard and kitchen garden products. They also discuss the making of wine and olive oil, which, although not strictly foods, were of vital importance in the economy throughout the period covered by this survey.

Sources of Information

Our knowledge of ancient farming and animal husbandry comes from four sources: literature, archaeological discoveries, surviving implements, and representations in art. Agronomy as a science arrived late on the scene. Its first exponent, according to Columella (*On Country Matters* [*De Re Rustica*]), was the fifth-century philosopher Democritus of Abdera; of the numerous later contributions on the subject scarcely anything has survived. Apart from two works by Theophrastus, there are Hesiod's *Works and Days* (*Opera et Dies*), which although not a farming manual nonetheless provides valuable details on the round of activities that made up the farm year; a few chapters of Xenophon's third-rate work *Household Management* (*Oeconomicus*); and a late and somewhat mediocre compilation, *On Agriculture* (*Geoponica*), that probably dates to the seventh century A.D.

Of outstanding importance are two works by Aristotle's brilliant pupil Theophrastus (ca. 372–ca. 287 B.C.), the *Enquiry into Plants* (*Historia Plantarum*), a classification and description that includes food plants, and the *Etiology of Plants* (*De Causis Plantarum*), on plant physiology, which strongly reflects, for this area of inquiry, the important scientific and technical advances made during the highly innovative Hellenistic period. For the Roman era, by contrast, the literary coverage is extensive and informative, with Cato the Elder and Varro covering the last two centuries of the republic (230–31 B.C.), and Columella and Pliny the Elder the succeeding first century of the empire. A large gap separates these authors from the late-fourth-century writer Palladius, and an even greater interval extends from him to the *On Agriculture* (*Geoponica*). Apart from these technical writings, there are casual but often significant references to agricultural operations and agrarian questions by many other writers, who often supply information on topics not mentioned by the technical writers.

The information provided by archaeological sources has come from the visible remains of agricultural activity on the ground, as revealed by farmsite excavations in Greece (still rare and sporadic, but notably at extensive sites at Metapontum in Sicily and in the Crimean peninsula, with very little on the Greek mainland), and at sites in Italy (specifically at Cosa in Etruria and at several locations in Apulia, Campania, and Basilicata). These investigations are described in various sources listed in the bibliography. Such work has been supplemented and extended by surface surveys based on the identification, by means of aerial photography, of crop marks, vines, trenches, tree holes, and other traces of farming. This method, long established for Roman Italy but comparatively new to Greece, has made it possible to produce detailed sequence maps for single-settlement areas, and shows how patterns of urban and rural settlement can be used to throw fresh light on social and economic changes not clearly revealed in the written records. For example, work in Boeotia has pointed to, among other things, a new site for Ascra, the birthplace of Hesiod.

As for surviving implements, the tally of Greek farm tools is paltry compared to what has been recovered of Roman artifacts. To date, neither mainland nor colonial Greek territories have yielded datable implements comparable to the rich Roman collections in Naples or the superb Gallo-Roman implements at Saint-Germain-en-Laye.

Greek-period vase paintings and terracottas offer representations of a wide variety of agricultural activities. These include plowing, sowing, taking produce to market, picking fruit, kneading dough, and baking. For the Roman period, valuable reliefs depict the earliest known harvesting machines for grain and an array of magnificent floor mosaics from North Africa portraying many aspects of rural life includes a number of pictorial calendars that display seasonal operations. The finest of these, a vast mosaic carpet originally comprising forty panels of which twenty-eight remain, presents in animated style many of the most important activities of a Gallo-Roman estate.

While it is evident from the above survey that the literary and archaeological sources are defective, especially on the Greek side, a great deal of miscellaneous information about farming can be obtained from nontechnical sources, as William E. Heitland demonstrated in his pioneering work *Agricola*.

In evaluating the literary evidence, there is a strong temptation to squeeze a text or an inscription to fit a preconceived conceptual framework designed to bring order out of chaos. It is also tempting to universalize on the basis of a handful of examples. On the archaeological side the possibilities of misinterpretation are of a different order; exclusive reliance on what has been excavated may produce distortion: it is possible to set too high a premium on indestructible material. A good example of this sort of distortion can be seen in the claim made by Mikhail I. Rostovtzeff (*Social and Economic History of the Hellenistic World*) that the impoverishment of Greece in the fourth century B.C. was mainly caused by a decline in industrial activity, and this in turn by a shrinking of the market for industrial products among non-Greek customers. The evidence is almost exclusively archaeological. But pottery, although very important, is not an infallible index of general economic activity.

Rostovtzeff's claim is further undermined by a tendency to which many historians are prone, that of taking evidence confined to Athens and extending it to the whole of Greece. These deficiencies can be lessened by examining the evidence for settlement patterns and agricultural exploitation region by region, and recognizing the sporadic character of the surveys thus far carried out.

CLIMATE, SOILS, AND LAND USE IN GREECE

The basic climatic conditions of the region forming the north shore of the Mediterranean are well known and require only brief mention here. On the Greek mainland, as in peninsular Italy, the chief source of moisture consists of cyclonic storms that originate in the northwest of the region and eastward as centers of low pressure during the colder part of the year. The pattern is reflected in the mythology of Zeus. The "Cloud-compeller" is the god of thunderstorms, and the rain he brings falls much more heavily on the western than on the eastern side of the mainland. (Corfu has more than four times the annual rainfall of Athens.) The distribution of rain, both seasonally and in type of precipitation (heavy downpours as compared to the steady rains of northern lands), makes cereal growing a hazardous undertaking. Since the growing season coincides with the advancing heat of spring and early summer, a delay of the winter rains and the consequent postponement of the growth cycle can expose a maturing crop to excessive heat, resulting in a reduced yield or even total failure. On the Greek mainland, drought and consequent starvation are always in the offing. The low rainfall on the eastern side means that half the arable land must stand idle every year in order to conserve precious moisture. "The fallow," writes Hesiod in *Works and Days* (464), "is the guardian against death and destruction." Some cereals did better than others; in many areas barley flourished where wheat failed to do well. While sown crops (cereals and legumes) were subject to climatic vagaries, some planted crops could survive and even flourish in the long summer drought; these included the grapevine, the fig, and the especially drought-resistant olive. Each of the three played an important role in the diet of all classes. The much wetter western flank provided inland grasslands and coastal meadows that favored the development of animal husbandry; the splendid horses and cattle for which Epirus was famous may be recalled. On the drier flank, sheep raising was possible, and an ancient system of transhumance between lowland and upland pastures evolved.

In tracing the various patterns of land settlement and use from as yet scattered evidence, any notion of geographical determinism must be firmly rejected. While some climatic limitations, such as the northern limit of olive cultivation, are true determinants, there are powerful influences that sometimes reinforce each other, and at other times cancel each other out. As evidence from ground surveys accumulates, preconceptions are refuted by facts, and areas that appear to be ideally suited to one form of exploitation turn out to have been exploited in another. Extending present-day patterns of land use back into antiquity has other pitfalls, most notably that the landscape, and particularly the land profile in the valleys, has undergone considerable change over two millennia and more.

Regional Distribution of Farm Sites

The following account draws on a variety of literary, mythical, and contemporary sources. Here, as in all matters concerning farmers and their ways, it is worth remembering that, land utilization surveys notwithstanding, farmers have often been known to work hard to raise crops unsuited to the soil or climate and to put land under plow that is fit only for pasture.

The northern regions were famous for the raising of horses. The notorious man-eating horses of Greek legend were bred by Diomedes, king of the Thracian Bistones, while the swiftest steeds on the Trojan side were the property of another Thracian, Rhesus. In historic times, the warring states of central and southern Greece—Thebes, Athens, Argos, and Sparta—relied on a heavily armed infantry to win set battles, but to equip their cavalry they imported horses from Macedonia, Thrace, and Thessaly. The best pasture area lay along the southern coastal plain of Thrace, a long stretch of lakes and marshes running between the mouths of the Hebrus (Maritza) and Axius (Vardar) rivers that provided ideal conditions, with summer grazing possible in the mountains of Paeonia, north of Macedonia.

In Greece proper, suitable grazing was scarce, an exception being the almost circular basin of the river Peneus (Pinios, Salambria) in Thessaly, with its high water table and single major outflow. This was the legendary Vale of Tempe lying between Mounts Olympus and Ossa, the site of large estates whose owners had reduced the indigenous population, aptly named "toilers" (*penestai*), to serfdom.

When regarding settlement areas, as far as they can be determined from currently available evidence, it should be emphasized that they did not necessarily conform to present-day preferences (alluvial plains for cereals, hill slopes for sheep, for example), and were presumably established on the basis of quite different criteria. In a recent review of tenth- to eighth-century B.C. Thessaly, Anthony Snodgrass (1982) notes that the clays and marls of the higher ground were preferred to the alluvial soils of the plains, in sharp contrast to southern Greece, where the plains of Argos and Olympia were sown to cereals. Moreover, in many parts of the Mediterranean region effective cultivation is possible only by irrigation, which required techniques that were largely beyond the reach of the ancient inhabitants. The high level of exploitation in Egypt, where the natural inundation of the Nile was harnessed with increasing skill to support a large population, stands in contrast to the underdeveloped conditions of early Attica, where the community lacked the economic strength, as Thucydides recorded (1.2), to put its very light soil to productive use. An additional point, and sometimes overlooked, is that some areas that appear from the map to be part of the Mediterranean region are in fact mid-European in climate. According to *Works and Days* (640), Hesiod's Ascra suffered from extremes of heat and cold, and Vergil's boyhood home in the Po valley was vastly different in climate from the Naples area where his poetic talents developed.

The earliest colonial settlements were made in areas suitable for growing grain: the proverbially "blind" colonists from land-hungry Megara who settled at Chalcedon, on the wrong side of the Bosporus, ignored the rich fishing-grounds of the Golden Horn that lay opposite, so set were they in their agricultural pursuits. The most favored situations were the well-drained lower slopes (the Piedmont, literally meaning mountain foot). In Greece proper, with its narrow valleys and their thin covering of poor soil, such good farmland was rare. Among the handful of fertile valley floors was the plain of Argos, where 30,000 acres (12,141 hectares) seem to have produced only enough wheat to feed the populations of Argos, Mycenae, Tiryns, and Nauplia. The restricted cereal areas were, however, largely given over to the cultivation of barley, which thrives on soils too poor for wheat. Literary sources evidence the preponderance of barley products in the ancient Greek diet, including flat barley cakes (*maza*) and barley porridge (*pollenta*).

Except where irrigation made annual cropping feasible, the land was left fallow in alternate years. Repeated plowing of the fallow, designed to retain the moisture and to reduce the soil to a fine tilth, is reflected in agricultural legend: Triptolemos, "the thrice-plowed" field personified, brings the precious gifts of Demeter (the crops of Ceres, her Roman counterpart) to the world at large. As the fuller Roman record makes clear, the fallow was plowed in early spring, in summer, and again in autumn, at which time it was integrated with the October sowing. According to Hesiod (*Works and Days* 384), this was when the setting of the Pleiades brought on the rainy season. The farmer who delays this final plowing, Hesiod warns (479–482), will "reap sitting down, grasping a thin crop in your hand, you will bring home a complete harvest in a basket, and not many will admire you."

THE GREEK AGRICULTURAL CALENDAR

The start of major farming operations was signaled by the rising or setting of a constellation or an important visible star, or by the behavior of animals or birds; grain, for example, was harvested early in May when the advancing heat of summer caused snails to climb up the stalks (*Works and Days* 571). The rising of Orion in July was the signal for the winnowing and storing of the threshed grain. In Hesiod's calendar the long summer drought is a time for resting until the vintage, when Orion and Sirius, the Dog Star, are at the center of the heavens (in September). As a calendar for the grain farmer, Hesiod's catalog is both rambling and inadequate. Cato's *On Agriculture* (*De Agricultura*), also rambling, is much more informative. In fact, for information on tools and techniques we have to turn to Roman works, which range in scale from the succinct but more than adequate month-by-month calendar of Palladius to the comprehensive treatment by Columella, who follows up his list of the duties of the farm manager with a lengthy catalog of seasonal operations and a timely warning, equally applicable to a Greek farmer, to carry them out "as the weather shall permit." Hesiod reveals nothing about methods of tillage (in contrast to the quite full treatment in Vergil's *Georgics*), but in a delightfully casual way he includes, in a list of farm items that are made of wood, two different types of plow, a "natural" plow consisting of a curved branch of a tree, and a "jointed" plow; the former dragged through the ground like a primitive digging stick, the latter a "three-piece" construction. Hesiod does not describe methods of plowing and sowing or of harvesting cereal crops, but an Attic black-figure cup of the sixth century B.C. portrays the more important stages in a continuous series around the edges.

The degree of effort expended in plowing with a Greek symmetrical ard, a basic soil-breaking plow, would have depended on the condition of the soil and the depth of cut required. Roman agronomists have much to say on soil conditions. Varro, for example, writes (*Country Matters* [*Rerum Rusticarum*]) of heavy soils that break into big clods, so that a broken plow beam abandoned in the furrow was not an uncommon sight. The mainly light soils of mainland Greece would have been easier to work, especially after the first breaking in early spring. Some of the lighter soils could have been worked with a plow light enough to be carried home on the plowman's shoulder, as is still the case in the remoter areas of inland Greece and south Italy.

Sowing was integrated with the final plowing, as shown on the Attic black-figure cup, the sower scattering seed immediately behind the plow as he walks in the footsteps of the plowman. This method of sowing will have required a harrow to cover the seed. A seed drill to keep the seed in the furrow was known to Sumerians by the third millennium B.C., but for some unknown reason the invention failed to reach the Mediterranean. The most efficient method available to the Roman farmer was a final plowing with ears (*aures*) attached to the plow to cover up the seed. This was just one among many repetitive operations that made cereal farming in antiquity so labor-intensive.

Weeding the crop by hand is mentioned by Roman writers and is still practiced in North Africa. Greek sources are silent on the matter, as on hoeing to prevent caking of the surface as well as to promote rapid growth. Greek farmers will no doubt have had difficulty keeping the fields of wheat or barley free of infestation by foreign plants, including the tares of the biblical parable (probably *Lolium temulentum* or darnel). At harvest time there are calls for the whetting of sickles and summoning of reapers: "Rise at daybreak, so that your life will be free from need," says Hesiod (*Works and Days* 573). The harvest is the central episode depicted on the marvelous Shield of Achilles, fashioned by the smith-god Hephaistos. The harvesters are shown at work with sharp sickles in their hands (*Iliad* 18.551–556):

> Armfuls of cut swathes fell to the ground in rows along the furrows, while others were being tied up by the binders with wisps of straw. Three of these stood close up, and the lads who were gleaning at their backs kept up a constant supply, bringing up the bundles in their arms.

Roman peasant farmers had very little leisure; one task followed hard upon another in an endless round of persistent effort (*labor improbus*). In Greece farmers shunned the intolerable heat of midsummer, when the blazing sun scorched the skin and parched head and feet. At this time, Hesiod wrote (*Works and Days* 589 ff.),

> let me have a shady rock, with wine of Biblis, a cake of milk-bread [cheese], and milk from goats just going dry.... So let me sit in the shade, with a bellyful inside me, comfortably sipping the fire-red wine, and turning to face the breeze from the west.

Winters were as harsh as summers were hot. There was no protection from the stormy blasts of Boreas that blew straight down from Thrace. The climate was in fact too harsh to produce quality wines, and this perhaps accounts for Hesiod's almost total silence on the subject of viniculture.

Cultivation of the Grapevine

On this subject, Hesiod mentions only the spring pruning and the vintage; for Greek practice we must turn to other sources, especially Aristophanes, whose play *The Peace* (*Eirene*) has a vinedresser for its hero. And from his *Acharnians* (*Acharneis*) we learn that the three main crop plants—vines, olives, and figs—were grown next to each other. All three were important to the small farmers. The vines were made to climb up the olive or fig trees, to save vital space. The preeminence in Attica of vines over cereal products is well illustrated in a line from Aristophanes' *Women in Parliament* (*Ecclesiazusae*): "I'd sold my grapes, and, my mouth full of coppers, I went off to buy flour in the market." The cultivation of the grapevine and olives is discussed further in the section on Roman agriculture.

Market Gardening

The market gardener who tills his plot intensively is a familiar figure; manuring the soil heavily, he raises successions of vegetables and salad stuffs in season. A well-known bas-relief in Munich shows him on his way to market. A wiry, muscular figure, somewhat bent under the load of produce that hangs from a pole across his left shoulder, he is carrying a basket full of what may well be cheese in his right hand; in front of him walks a cow laden with netted produce carried pannier-wise across her back. This relief seems to be the only archaeological source on Greek market gardening. In literature, the comic poets mention garden produce in great variety, and its importance in the Greek diet is clear. For fuller information on the subject we must turn to the Roman authorities.

Animal Husbandry

The horse played no part in the agricultural economy, being restricted to the battlefield and the arena. Cattle—both cows and castrated bulls—were used only as working animals; milk and its products were obtained from sheep or goats. Pigs and common domestic fowls are normal in subsistence farming everywhere from the tropical belts of Africa and Asia to Europe. Both can survive on scraps, and pigs can be economically integrated with cheese-producing animals, since they thrive on the whey that remains after separation of the curds. References to curd cheese from goats are common from Homer to Theocritus.

When we move from animals that fend for themselves to those that must be closely tended, we immediately come up against the constraints imposed by the fodder supply. Suitable herbage must be looked for. Sheep and goats must be led, not followed; they need to be shepherded to good pasturage and away from the violent heat of midday into cool glades and streams. A good ram was therefore a highly prized possession, as testified in Polyphemus' address to his lagging leader of the flock (*Odyssey* 9.447f.). Sheep and goats were raised over wide areas of Greece. In northern Greece only Thessaly and Boeotia possessed good natural pasture (see Theophrastus, *Inquiry into Plants* 4.10.2). In the south, Elis was more of a pastoral than an agricultural region, while landlocked Arcadia was the legendary abode of shepherds.

ROMAN AGRICULTURE

The prime importance of grain cultivation is reflected in the space devoted to it treated comprehensively by Columella, and at some length by the others; in addition, the elder Pliny devotes his eighteenth book to cereals and legumes, adding some important comments on yeasts and other leavening agents and on the production of meal and flour. Modern historians, in reviewing the agrarian history of Roman Italy, have reached very diverse conclusions about the relationship between practice and theory—in particular about the level of efficiency achieved in cereal cultivation—and have advanced equally diverse explanations for its alleged decline. It was Theodore Mommsen, in his *History of Rome* (*Römische Geschichte*), who first argued that Italian cereal farming was ruined by overseas competition. For Giuseppe Salvioli (*Le capitalisme dans le monde antique*), slave-run plantations were the root of the trouble, a view still widely supported, especially by the Marxist school. Here the traditional position, based on the doctrine that slave-run enterprises are ipso facto inefficient, has been replaced by a more refined analysis, according to which the inherent contradictions of the slave mode of production resulted in the collapse of the intensive plantation, with vines or olives as main crops, and a return to extensive pasturage and cereal cultivation. Earlier, the fashionable view, as advanced by Rostovtzeff (*Social and Economic History of the Roman Empire*), ascribed the decline to competition from provincial grain. Discarded favorite explanations include

Tenney Frank's soil exhaustion theory (*An Economic Survey of Ancient Rome*), and Cedric Yeo's erosion theory ("The Overgrazing of Ranch Lands in Ancient Italy"). The latest exposé by Andrea Carandini and others based on work at Sette Finestre (central Italy, overlooking the Tyrrhenian Sea), seeks to reinforce the orthodox Marxist view with fresh evidence from the spade. With so many wide-ranging interpretations available, it seems that a full investigation of the evidence is overdue; this task has been undertaken by Spurr in *Arable Cultivation in Roman Italy*. He has not only brought both literary and archaeological sources under detailed examination in relation to all the processes involved, but has also brought to bear his own recent experience of farming on Italian soil.

The state of farming in Italy was already the subject of much hackneyed debate when Columella wrote the preface to *On Agriculture;* his list of contemporary explanations for its decline included soil exhaustion. Recently that tedious and nonfactual debate has been renewed with some concentration on selected key periods, such as the Gracchan crisis of 133 B.C. The rival interpreters have fired off quotation and counterquotation from the Roman agronomists rather than carrying out the more sober and possibly more rewarding task of examining the texts, which are plentiful, and the archaeological evidence, which has been scarce but is accumulating rapidly. Molly A. Cotton ("Some Research Work in Roman Villas . . .") provides a useful summary.

The need for this type of inquiry has become more urgent now that the debate has centered on the problem of changes in the pattern of land use and their presumed political effects. To take an extreme example, Toynbee, in a lengthy section of his massive *Hannibal's Legacy*, argued, with copious citations, for a total transformation of the landscape following the Punic Wars, with olive and vine plantations dominating the north and center of the peninsula and a nomadic livestock industry occupying vast tracts of the south. The great diversity of opinion on the question provides a cogent reason for examining what the agronomists have to say and for comparing their statements with other sources of information, dealing with key operations only. By proceeding in this way we may also gain insights into some of the vexing problems of the agrarian history of Roman Italy.

At the outset, the credentials of Roman writers must be examined. Their observations on the general condition of agriculture, if unfavorable to either side of the argument, have been dismissed as optimistic or pessimistic, as trivial commonplaces, worthless rhetoric, or myth. But when a writer reports something he has himself observed, his bona fides must be respected. The relationship between theory and practice must also be clarified. There is always a gap between the two, whatever farming system is under review, whether ancient or modern. Some light has now been thrown on this question by the published results of careful excavations, supplemented by the judicious use of comparisons with current practice in areas not yet affected by major changes in technique. At the same time we must be clear as to what types of agricultural enterprise the various writers are writing about: Do they correspond to any extent with the types of exploitation now being uncovered with the spade?

First, the question of bona fides. The opening paragraph of Cato's *On Agriculture* abounds in commonplaces, and there is so much traditional lore scattered through this remarkable piece of early Latin prose that a casual sampler might assume quite wrongly that the book is little more than an ancient *Old Moore's Almanack*. Yet, in spite of its haphazard form and lack of organic structure, the work is full of shrewd common sense and practical farming knowledge. It also contains valuable chapters on the equipment, organization, and management required to operate estates in which the major products were wine and oil. Especially valuable are the detailed instructions for constructing a press room and olive and wine presses, for assembling a crushing mill, and for estimating the cost of transporting its components from the place of manufacture.

The prefaces to Book Two of Varro and Book One of Columella contain rhetorical exercises on the decline of husbandry. Cato's virtuous yeoman farmer has vanished from the scene, to be replaced by degraded workers hired from town. Farming, which once enjoyed great prestige, is now regarded as a mean occupation:

> Instead of growing our own grain, we import it from our provinces beyond the sea, the while our heads of families have left their sickles and plows, and sneaked within the city walls, preferring to use their hands in the theater and the circus rather than in the cornfields and vineyards. (Varro 2. preface 3; Columella 1. preface 16–18, 20)

These conventional performances are no more to be taken seriously than the introductions provided by Marxist writers; in neither category should they be regarded as an excuse for not giving serious attention to the body of the text.

The problem of gaps between theory and practice will be examined seriatim in the discussion of the various operations. As for the types of enterprise, it is evident from the content of their works that all four writers (the elders Cato and Pliny, Varro, Columella) are concerned with various forms of what may be called investment property, with an absentee landlord, a permanent force of slaves, and hired labor brought in for specific tasks—the main variable being the size of the estate, where this can be established from the information available. By contrast, most of the farms known to us through survey or excavation consist of mixed rather than specialized units, and the majority are modest in size. Two exceptions in the archaeological record are a 200-acre (80-hectare) "plantation" at Gragnano in the Sarno valley, south of Pompeii, and a recently discovered complex at Sette Finestre, near Cosa on the coast of Etruria.

Distribution of Crops and Animals on Farms

The application of more rigorous methods in investigating farm sites in recent years has included the classification and analysis of seeds, bones, and food residues, making it possible to estimate (with some margin of error) what crops were being grown and what animals were kept on a given estate. The recommendations of the agronomists can now be tested and divergences between theory and practice can be noted. We begin with choice of soil and climate. The choice of which kind of crop to plant in which kind of soil depended on the aim of the farmer. This is stated, almost as an afterthought, by Tremellius Scrofa, who was acknowledged by the other speakers in Varro's dialogue (1.3) to be the supreme authority, when he declared that "agriculture is not only an art, but a science as well, which teaches what crops are to be planted in each kind of soil . . . so that the land may regularly produce bumper crops." The importance attached to grain is clear: it is to be grown in soil that is "rich and fat and sweet to the taste" (Columella, 2.2.14). This is only one of many references to the choice of a particular soil variety for a specific crop. All four major writers deal extensively with this topic, and although their treatment is unsystematic, it shows clearly that they were able to distinguish between a wide variety of soil types according to the four recognized categories of structure, texture (degree of sandiness or clay content), moisture, status, and temperature. Varro's discussion of soils is disappointing. The list of soils he classified according to mineral content turns out on investigation to be an ill-assorted jumble of imprecise terms, his grading of soils so rough as to be worthless, his choice of soils for crops amounting to no more than a few random examples. Columella is not much better. Having abandoned a disastrous attempt to adapt Theophrastus' "union of opposites" theory to the classification of soils, he provides a list of combinations of soil qualities that is little better than Varro's; but both he and Pliny are at their best when discussing the regime for particular crops.

Although level plains were regarded as best for cereal cultivation, such land is scarce south of the Po basin; hence the praise heaped on such famous lowlands as the fertile region around Capua or the great tableland, the Tavoliere of Apulia. As in mainland Greece, hill slopes had to be put under cultivation, and here the mattock took the place of the plow, or rather was not displaced by it, as Pliny the Elder explains (18.178). Aspect was also important—a practical point fully understood by farmers, Roman or later, but rarely mentioned in meteorological literature. The process of photosynthesis, of which the ancient farmer was of course ignorant, is essential for growth. Plants, he well knew, could get in each other's shade; where intercultivation of sown with planted crops was practiced, the vines or olives were much more widely spaced than where the trees or vines stood alone.

Terracing, as a means of producing a series of level plots on sloping terrain, has been practiced in the Mediterranean area from prehistoric times; like the lynchets of the Anglo-Saxon farmers of England, terrace remains are easily recognizable. Although obviously outside the agronomist's purview, terracing is likely to have been commonly practiced by subsistence farmers.

Farm Operations: Plowing

With the symmetrical Roman ard plowing was slow and laborious: continuous turning over of the furrow slice requires a turnwrest or moldboard plow; the ard, a simple ground-breaker, had to make a return run, with the plow tilted to undercut and expose the weeds, as Columella is at pains to point out (2.2.25):

> The plowman, moreover, must walk on the broken ground, and in every alternate furrow must hold his plow slantwise, cutting every other furrow with his plow upright and at full depth, but in such a way as not to leave any solid or unbroken ground.

A second plowing at right angles to the first would produce a fine tilth, making an excellent bed for the seeds of wheat or barley. In a well-tilled field it should not be possible for anyone inspecting it to determine which way the plow had gone. Deep plowing with a nine-inch share at full depth is recommended by Columella as part of his standard regime for Italy, where the land, being planted with vine-clad trees (*arbusta*) and olives, needs to be broken and worked rather deep, so that the uppermost roots of vines and olives, which, if left, adversely affect the yield, may be cut off, while the deeper roots get nourishment from the moisture reaching them from deeply worked soil. This operation needs heavy oxen (here Columella disagrees with another authority, Cornelius Celsus), which have to be steered among the trees with meticulous care, and without using the goad, which merely irritates the animal, making him kick.

It would be easy to conclude that in Italy as a whole, cereals were commonly planted in heavy clays. But archaeological evidence from excavated farms in the south does not confirm this. There subsistence farmers were growing several varieties of wheat (husked and naked) on light, sandy soils, as their descendants still do, using small oxen (and even donkeys) and plows that the plowman could easily carry on his shoulder. To illustrate the contrast and emphasize the diversity of practice, even today a heavy white ox drawing a modern all-steel plow could be seen in an intercultivated vineyard in Campania.

The fallowing described previously marks the beginning of a long and fruitful association between crop farming and animal husbandry. The oxen not only draw the plow, but also find grazing in the growth that comes up among the stubble after the harvest and manures the ground for the next crop. The fallow, meanwhile, is not inactive or inert; it is subjected to repeated plowing to remove weeds and prevent evaporation through the surface by capillary action. This is especially important in semiarid areas where moisture needs to be conserved (see White, 1970).

Not all Italian farmers practiced fallowing, as is clear from a casual reference in Pliny the Elder (*Natural History* 18.176): "Spring plowing is equally necessary in the case of fallow land, that is, land sown every other year." A number of spring crops were inserted into the cultivation cycle, and the fact that leguminous fodder plants predominate in the record has led to the assumption that the fallow was being broken by what is now called partial rotation. After mentioning several "succession crops," which may be inserted into a wheat or barley cycle where the soil is rich enough, Pliny refers (18.191) to a shortened fallow of four months after a crop of emmer, followed by spring beans, one of the numerous legumes that were already recognized as soil improvers. Legumes as part of a rotation system appear in a passage in which Columella (2.17) describes the building up of a permanent pasture. The cycle consists of tilled fallow, a root crop, a grain crop, and a final sowing of mixed grass and vetch. An elaborate system such as this (to establish the grass for pasturing cattle would take a further two years) would only be possible for a big landowner; but the assertion of some historians that breaches of the fallow were rare cannot be sustained. If the above recommendations are to be dismissed as counsels of perfection, why does Vergil devote so much space in his *Georgics* to rotation with legumes, concluding with, "rotations lighten the work"? Evidence of attempts to modify the fallow, which halved the annual output of grain, are clear; the motive may have been the increased urban demand for bread. With the decline of Rome, and the reversion from an urban civilization making heavy demands for breadwheat for human consumption, there was a return to the old crop-and-fallow system over most of Europe.

Types of Plow

Variety of soils implies variety in cultivating implements. The best literary evidence on the design of plows comes from Pliny the Elder (*Natural History* 18.171), who lists five types in a developing series, culminating in the "recent invention" of a wheeled plow. This list, which Pliny says refers to types of plowshare, begins with a ground opener, used in advance of the plowing proper, and ends with the wheeled plow to be used on heavy soil.

> There are several kinds of plowshare. The knife [*culter*] is the name given to a curved blade, used for cutting through very dense soil before it is broken, and for marking out the tracks for the subsequent furrows.... A sec-

ond type is the ordinary share, consisting of a bar shaped to a beak-like point. . . . A third type for use in light soils does not extend along the whole length of the sharebeam, but has only a little spike at the end. In the fourth type this spike is broader and sharper, ending in a point, using the same blade to break up the ground and with its sharp sides to cut off the roots of the weeds. Lately a device has been invented in the Raetian area of Gaul, consisting of an attachment of two small wheels to the previous type [of plow]: the local name for this variety is *plaumoratum.*

Pliny's descriptions are valuable on two counts. First, the agronomists ignored the subject, leaving only Vergil's account, which can be variously interpreted. Second, Pliny shows an awareness of technical advance. Note in particular the connection he claims between the double-bladed share and the wheeled forecarriage, a development of profound importance since it made possible the exploitation of very heavy soil without the enormous expense of additional traction animals.

The archaeological evidence on plows is limited but important; surviving iron shares are not plentiful, and Italy has almost none. Plows are not uncommon on the coins of Roman colonies—representing the ceremony of marking out the city boundaries—but the details of design and construction are difficult to make out. Of outstanding importance are the representations of bull-drawn plows on two wall mosaics from Cherchel, Algeria. The plow shown in the upper register is clearly a sole-ard of the type described by Vergil. Next in importance, although not of Mediterranean provenance, are two plow models, one from Roman Germany, the other from Roman Britain. Both have splayed ground wrests for ridging, or for making drainage furrows (Pliny the Elder, 18.179). The second model is fitted with a keel, no doubt to assist the tilting process required to turn over a furrow completely. The range of symmetrical plow types that are still in use is vast (for classification, see Leser, 1931; for distribution, Haudricourt-Delamarre, 1955).

In antiquity and up to the advent of factory production, agricultural implements differed in design not only by region but by individual preference, as did all handmade tools, whether for carpenter or mason: the smith readily makes to order and adapts to individual taste. (For varieties in the design of Roman-period mattocks and hoes, sickles, hooks, and scythes, see White, 1970.) The remarkable variety of type and design is due to the adaptation of a basic design to soil and climatic differences in different parts of Italy, and to the complex regime demanded by such plants as the grapevine and by the different systems of intercultivation of sown with planted crops that prevailed in different areas. Variations in regional technique are frequently mentioned in the texts, while innovations, such as the long-handled Gallic scythe and the improved Italian whetstone, were of special interest to Pliny the Elder.

Extent of Arable Cultivation in Italy

Among the references to the parts of the plow we are told of removable ridging boards, designed to throw up the soil in ridges "between two widely separated furrows, affording a dry bed for the grain" (Columella, 2.4.8). Palladius (1.42) refers to a special type of plow called "eared" from the projections on the share, designed to raise the seed bed and protect it from being rotted by stagnant water in winter. It has been argued that the vernacular word used by Columella for these ridges (*porcae*, sows, as descriptive of the piglike humps) implies the widespread cultivation of land that required being drained. The above procedure would obviously apply to heavy clay soils, which easily waterlog if the ground is level.

Cato's lively description of the effects of heavy storms, "On Ridding the Land of Water in Winter," stresses the importance of drainage ditches. By Columella's time, to judge from the instructions he gives, the science of field drainage had made definite advances. In his usual practical way, he spells out the textbook method for open drains and explains how they must be filled with small stones or gravel; if neither is available, layers of well-trodden brushwood and branches will do just as well.

As archaeological surveys and excavations gradually reveal the pattern of land settlement, it may be argued that wherever traces of Roman settlement are found along alluvial valleys or along the edges of expanses of heavy soils, intensive arable (i.e., plowed or tilled) cultivation occurred. In support of this new argument the rapturous description by the younger Pliny (*Letters* 5.67.7–9) of his Tuscan villa, where the Tiber flowed through meadows and cornfields, may be adduced.

> The countryside round here is really beautiful. Imagine some enormous amphitheater that could only be the work of Nature. The broad, spreading plain is ringed by mountains, their summits topped by ancient woods of tall timber, where there is plenty of mixed hunting. The mountain slopes are covered with plantations of timber, interspersed with large mounds of fertile soil (you would scarcely find any rocky outcrops even if you looked for them), which are just as rich as the most open plains, yielding just as bountiful harvests, but ripening later. Below these the vineyards extend on every side, weaving their uniform pattern far and wide. And where they end, shrubs spring up to form a border at the foot. Then come the meadows and grainfields, which can only be broken by huge oxen and the most powerful plows. The soil is so stiff that at first plowing it rises up in massive clods, needing nine plowings to complete the breaking process.

The allocation of the various crops at different levels is instructive: timber, interspersed with late-ripening crops, is found on the higher slopes; below, the vines (no intercultivation, faster harvesting, and so greater profit) enjoyed first-class drainage.

Hoeing and Weeding

Columella (2.12.8–9) gives the number of days' work needed to produce a crop of grain. If plowing has been done properly (four days per *iugerum*, five-eighths of an acre), no harrowing will be needed. Two days' labor are set down for hoeing, in two phases, one day for weeding, and one and a half for reaping, making a total of nine and a half man-days per *iugerum*, or fifteen days per acre. This compares favorably with current-day manual methods. In Columella's schedule plowing takes up 45 percent of the total work time, and the operations between plowing and reaping require twice as much time as the harvesting itself.

Hoeing and weeding are tedious tasks, but they can easily be done by the subsistence farmer with the aid of his wife and children; indeed, where monoculture of grain is carried on with manual methods, underemployment is still the rule. On the other hand, intercultivation of vines or olives with planted vegetables reduces the need for weeding and makes a profitable pattern of land use, whether for the subsistence farmer or in the slave-run establishment.

Harvesting, Threshing, Winnowing, Storage

The oldest harvesting implement, the sickle or reaphook, appears in its earliest form as a toothed blade with a slight curve, reflecting its development from the animal jawbone used by Neolithic reapers. The strongly curved shape that became dominant enabled the reaper to grasp a handful of stalks with the left hand and remove the heads of grain, with part of the stalk, with a slicing movement that drew the blade toward the worker. The balanced sickle, said to be a Roman invention, was designed to ease the strain on the wrist by setting the haft at an acute angle to the blade.

The long-handled scythe, used in antiquity only for mowing grass at ground level, has an opposite action to that of the sickle: the mower stands up to the work and sweeps the blade into the swathe in a forward arc, the cut grass falling to the left at the end of the stroke. The characteristic curved haft of the English scythe does not appear in the many representations of the classical implement, which invariably display the straight handle still in common use in Eastern Europe.

Variations and improvements in the design of sickles are mentioned by the agronomists and are related either to regional preferences or to the differences in technique reported by Varro (1.50.1):

> There are three ways of harvesting grain. One way, found in Umbria, is to cut the straw down close to the ground, laying each sheaf, as it is cut, on the ground. When a good number of sheaves has been made up, they are gone over again, and the ears are . . . cut off from the straw, sheaf by sheaf. The second method, as used in Picenum, is to use a curved piece of wood with a small iron saw at the end. This grasps a bundle of ears and cuts them off, leaving the straw standing, to be subsequently cut close to the ground. The third method, adopted mainly in the neighborhood of Rome, and at most other places, is to cut the stalk, the top of which is held with the left hand, midway down. . . . That part of the stalk which is below the hand remains fixed on the ground, to be cut later, while the part attached to the ear is carried off to the threshing floor in baskets.

The regional variations in tools and methods are clearly related to the uses to which the straw is to be put, whether for thatching, for litter, or as a fodder supplement for stock. Also, if the ears were reaped separately, threshing time could be saved, and it is not surprising to hear of technical developments and innovations connected with the "heading" process, among them reaping boards and a comb (Columella, 2.20.3), and an animal-powered heading machine described in detail by Palladius (7.1).

The related operations of mowing and reaping have been treated at some length in order to provide an adequate background for two remarkable inventions, or rather an invention and an innovation, that appeared in the Roman period outside Italy, in Britain and in Gaul. The first was a mowing scythe of outstanding design and immense size, while the second was a very interesting attempt at mechanizing the heading process discussed above. Each represents a break in the technical stagnation that is alleged to have pervaded the economy of the Roman Empire. Important too is the fact that they appeared in areas removed from the Mediterranean heartland. As for their distribution, the scythe appeared in several different places within the one province, while the harvesting machine does not appear to have spread beyond a well-defined area.

The so-called Great Chesterford scythe is represented by twelve identical blade specimens discovered more than a century ago in a single group, all bearing signs of considerable wear. Dismissed by some farmers as too heavy to handle and thought by some antiquarians to be blades of scythed chariots, this innovative tool has until recently received no serious attention. Implements of the same type have subsequently been found at other Romano-British sites. Experiments with a replica have shown that with suitable hafting its blade span of about 63 in. (160 cm) could cut a great deal more grass than could a scythe of normal length (about 42 in. [107 cm]). The Great Chesterford estate, in

Cambridgeshire, lies on chalkland very suitable for grass, and an increased demand for fodder may well have arisen from a notable increase in the size of the Roman imperial cavalry at the time these implements were employed in the frontier province of Britain. The use of such implements will have meant a saving in time in a region where haymaking is still affected by summer storms (hence the proverbial English injunction to "make hay while the sun shines").

Once again a passage from Pliny the Elder (18.261) seems to point to an earlier stage in scythe development: "There are two kinds of mowing scythe; the Italian kind is shorter, and handy also for cutting brambles, while the scythe used on the large farms of Gaul is bigger; in fact they economize by cutting through the stalks at middle height, missing the shorter ones." The economizing (Pliny writes *compendium*, saving, shortening) is in time taken at the expense of quantity mowed, which mattered little on a large landed estate, a latifundium. Pliny's implement is not a scythe, but a sort of hybrid of sickle and scythe; it appears in the July panel of a relief of the seasons at Durocortorum (Reims). Pliny's further comment that "Italian mowers use only their right hands to mow" strongly suggests that his Gallic scythe was double-handed, as are the Reims examples.

As for the Gallic grain-heading invention, Pliny concludes his account of different reaping methods (18.296) as follows: "On the large estates [latifundia] of the Gallic provinces very large frames, fitted with teeth at the edge, and carried on two wheels, are driven through the grain crop by a pack animal pushing from behind; the ears are thus torn off and fall into the frame." The writer clearly wishes to point out a very interesting technical development and therefore goes on to explain that "elsewhere the stalks are severed with a sickle, or the ears are stripped off between two boards." More details about this invention are supplied three centuries later by Palladius at the beginning of the August section of his calendar, where a full description makes it clear that there was more than one machine in use, with different types of containers for receiving the ears of grain. The five surviving representations show interesting variations of the lighter of the two machines, including one that may show an intermediate stage of development between the lighter model and the heavy machine Palladius describes (7.2.):

> On the more level plains of the Gallic provinces they employ the following time-saving [*compendium*] method of harvesting. With the aid of a single ox the machine outstrips the efforts of laborers, and cuts down the time of the entire harvesting task. They build a cart mounted on two small wheels. . . .

The body of the text contains details of construction. The models depicted on the monuments are small and pushed by a mule or donkey, but the larger type requires an ox. The actual operation is described in the same passage by Palladius as follows:

> When the driver begins to drive the vehicle through the standing crop, all the ears are seized by the row of teeth, and piled up in the cart, leaving the straw cut off in the field, the height of the cut being controlled from time to time by the cowherd who walks behind. In this way, after a few journeys up and down the field, the entire harvesting operation is completed within a few hours. This machine is useful only on open plains or smooth ground, and where the straw has no economic value.

Unfortunately the writer provides none of the data needed to compare mechanical with manual reaping. Although the directions for building are clear enough, the only attempted reconstruction was a failure. The frame, of the type shown on the monuments, was made of such massive timbers and mounted on such heavy wheels that the donkey was barely able to set it in motion; also, the frame was not splayed at the ends (a very important feature that is clearly visible on the best-preserved relief, from Buzenol). The result was that the stalks wrapped themselves round the advancing axle, bringing the machine to a standstill.

The surviving representations of the harvesting machine come from the same well-defined area, that of the trunk road that linked the Seine at Lutetia Parisiorum (Paris) with the Rhine, passing through Reims and then the southern Ardennes, to Arlon and Augusta Trevirorum (Trier), and down along the Moselle to its junction with the Rhine at Confluentia (Koblenz). This highway traversed a belt of fertile downs south of the Ardennes forest, an area ideal for large estates, such as those of the cloth merchants, the Secundarii, and others who erected lofty funeral towers, like that at Igel, close to Trier.

Why did the harvester fail to spread beyond this region of Gaul? Is this a case of lack of interest in labor-saving devices which, as Heitland and Renard argue, was a "phenomenon accompanying dependence on slave labor"? Or did it not perform significantly better? As we have seen, improvements in the design of manual implements are well attested. The infrequent references in the agronomists to labor shortages are mainly concerned with seasonal operations such as gleaning (Varro, 1.55) and threshing (Pliny the Elder, 18.300). Attention has been drawn to defects in the design, the most obvious of which is the clogging of the comb with chaff. An accurately designed working model might settle the matter.

PLANTED CROPS

The Grapevine

No agricultural regime illustrates more lucidly the meaning of the phrase "careful husbandry" than that of the grapevine, and no combination of technical skill and loving care was more sought after than that to be found in a good vinedresser.

The natural tendency of vines is to sprawl along the ground. The vinedresser's task is to take the vine in hand, taming its wild exuberance, and by pruning and propping to mold and build it into a variety of structures, most of which combine a profitable return with aesthetic satisfaction. Cicero (*On Old Age* [*De Senectute*] 17) has Cato the Elder saying to his young friends Scipio and Laelius, as they walk through his garden,

> The vine, whose nature is to droop, and which falls to the ground unless it is propped, raises itself by means of its fingerlike tendrils, gripping the props . . . and the skilful husbandman checks its growth by pruning with the knife, lest the shoots run to wood, and spread too far. So in early spring, the branches left at every joint produce a bud, from which appears the grape, the scion of this bud, and burgeons with the moisture of the earth and the heat of the sun. . . . Can anything be more delicious to the palate and more beautiful to the eye?

Both moisture and heat are essential for growth, but a promising vintage can be ruined by excessive moisture at the wrong season as well as by the blistering heat of summer winds. Soils are of critical importance. Thus the soils that produce the great wines of France and Germany contain high percentages of stone, gravel, or shale: Château Lafite comes from soil almost three-quarters gravel, and the finest Bernkasteler is from vines planted in shales on clifflike slopes, while the sandy bends opposite produce only ordinary Moselle. The secret is good drainage, and in this regard Vergil advised the wine farmer to "bury in the ground thirsty stones or rough shells; for the water will glide between them and invigorate the plants" (*Georgics* 2.346 ff., based on Theophrastus, *Etiology of Plants* 2.4.3).

Aspect is also of great importance. The simple compass-point rules laid down by earlier writers were rightly rejected by Pliny the Elder, whose treatment of the topic (18.24) gives due weight to a variety of factors, including rainfall, dew formation, and direction and condition of wind. Individual vines have their own preferences, and the grower should rely on experiment.

The various propping systems, which ranged from a simple crossbar to an elaborate structure that resembled the square roof apertures of a Roman house, are discussed in White, *Roman Farming.* In beauty of appearance the palisaded vine on its circular frame and the pergola were outstanding; they may be seen on the upper and lower registers, respectively, of the wall mosaic from Cherchel, Algeria, depicting two of the winter operations.

Vines were planted out from the nursery either in holes or in furrows or trenches. Complete trenching, which ensured both uniform drainage and deep aeration of the whole planting area, was rated the best method. The others were used when labor was scarce or the expected returns could not justify the cost of trenching—no less than 120 man-days per acre. Columella (3.13.6 ff.) gives a complete account of the special trenching called *pastinatio.* Spacing depended on the method of training and the quality of the soil. Ideally, all fruit-bearing trees should have plenty of light, but the heavy initial outlay and high maintenance costs had to be taken into account. Thus the aesthetically pleasing diamond-wise arrangement, still used in olive plantations in parts of Italy, was only recommended for very fertile soils and with vines of very large growth habit (Columella, 3.13.4). The much-favored *arbustum,* where the vines were trained up and "married" to suitable trees (elm or poplar), produced high yields of inferior wine (Columella, 3.3.2). The vinedresser's objective was to control luxuriant growth so that it produced a good number of fruit-bearing shoots at the right time, to remove all dead wood or useless growth, and to train enough bearers to form the shape required by the particular system employed. Attention was thus needed at intervals throughout the year. According to the climate, pruning took place in spring or autumn, and root pruning and cleaning of the vinestock in winter, the vines being staked and tied as they started to develop. With the advance of summer came the trimming of tendrils and leaves, and so on through to the autumn vintage.

Appropriate tools were developed for these varied operations. The two-pronged drag hoe (*bidens*) was for drawing the soil away from the vinestock (a delicate winter task, since neither stock nor root system must be damaged). The multipurpose vinedresser's knife, the culmination of a long process of evolution, was used for a variety of tasks. Columella describes (4.25) the jobs that were done with its various parts:

> Each of these parts performs its own specific task, provided the vinedresser has the skill to use them. When he has to cut something with a thrust of the hand away from him, he uses the *culter* or "knife"; when he is to draw it toward him he uses the *sinus* or "bend"; when he needs to smooth something, the *scalprum* or "paring-edge"; to hollow it out, the *rostrum* or "beak"; when he needs to cut something with a blow, the *securis* or "axe"; when he wants to remove something in a narrow place, he uses the *mucro* or "spike."

Vines were planted, whether in holes or trenches, with ample space for the roots to develop, and at depths varying with the system of training. Trellised vines and vines on trees, both of which were allowed to climb high, needed deep foundations, a minimum of three feet according to Columella, who claimed (3.13.11–12) to have invented an improved device that could spot at once a slovenly trench that tapered to the bottom. (Today, soil that has been disturbed by deep digging, even in ancient times, appears darker in an aerial photograph than the surrounding unbroken or lightly disturbed soil, making it easy to pick out those parts of a farm on which vines or olives were grown.) Columella says that his trench-measuring device was employed "to do away with quarrels and disputes," and the implication is that deep trenching, like the vintage, was put out to contract. Cato's handbook contains specimen contracts for the sale of grapes and for the sale of olives on the tree, but none for trenching. The grape-sale contract called for the provision of forty grape-cutting knives for a vineyard of 100 *iugera* (63 acres or 25 hectares) that had only ten permanent laborers and no specialist vinedresser. Picking grape clusters by hand was not approved, hence the directive that "as many small sickles as possible" should be provided to prevent damage by clumsy hand-picking (Columella, 12.44.4). To ease the pressure on labor, growers were recommended to plant both early and late varieties.

Vintage scenes were popular with fresco painters, but another fine mosaic from Cherchel provides an authentic picture. The center of the floor is taken up with a great trellis from which hang ripe clusters of dessert grapes, while around the sides all the varied activities of the picking season are vividly depicted: the cutting, the placing in baskets, the loaded baskets being carried in a two-wheel farm cart to the press, the pressing, and the pouring.

Wine Production

The series of operations needed to convert wine grapes into wine can be pieced together from a great variety of literary and archaeological sources. The vintager removed ripe clusters from the vine with a small crescent-shaped hook and deposited them in a basket small enough to be carried to the edge of the plantation, where the contents were emptied into larger baskets that in turn were conveyed either by pack donkeys or two-wheel carts to the treading vat for the first stage of the pressing process. Barefoot treading was designed to release some of the juice by means of a gentle squeezing, producing a wet, pulpy mush that was taken on to the next stage, that of pressing by lever or screw press. Some juice from the treading was drunk as new wine; the remainder was boiled down into must (*defrutum*), which was used either as a preservative or to give body to a thin wine (Columella, 12.19). The rectangular treading vats contained outlet pipes leading either into receiving tanks or into pottery containers set beneath the outlets. Treaders worked barefoot, supporting themselves in the slippery conditions by grasping overhead ropes or by using crutched sticks. Both methods are featured on the monuments, the operation being a favorite theme for artists in paint or stone.

On Agriculture ([*Geoponica*] 6.11) contains a lively account of the rules for treading:

> Those who are in charge of the larger baskets called panniers must pick out the leaves and any sour grapes or wizened clusters. Those who tread must pick out anything that has been missed out by those in charge of the baskets, for the leaves, if pressed with the grapes, make the wine rougher and more likely to spoil; great damage is caused by grapes that are dry or sour. Those charged with this task must immediately press with their feet the grapes that are thrown into the vat, and having equally trodden all the grapestones, they must pick up the kernels, that is most of the refuse, so that most of the liquor can run into the channel. . . . The men that tread must get into the press, having scrupulously cleaned their feet, and none of them must eat or drink while in the press, nor must they climb in and out frequently. If they have to leave the press, they must not go with bare feet. The treaders must

also be fully clad and have their girdles on, on account of the violent sweating. It is also proper to have the presses fumigated either with frankincense or some other sweet odor.

The new wine having flowed out of the treading vat, the mush was removed and strained, placed in flexible baskets, and set under the press. The oldest type of lever press was made from the branch of a tree, with one end anchored into the ground, as depicted on a black-figure vase of the sixth century B.C. in which the pull of human muscular energy is helped by the weight of a large stone. A panel from the Vienne mosaic shows a handsome roofed treading vat with dangling ropes; at the press one of the men is forcing the lever down from above while a fellow worker leans outside the vat to obtain a greater purchase on the lever. The constructed (rather than improvised) version is well known from the detailed description given by Cato (18–19), which contains a complete list of the materials needed for building a lever press and the necessary housing to take the counterthrust imposed by the introduction of mechanical traction into the process.

In the squeezing process it is the last few inches that are decisive. Various technical developments aimed at increased efficiency are reported by Pliny the Elder (18.317), who classifies the different types of press and reviews the successive improvements. In Cato's lever press the clumsy stone weights are replaced by a leather rope that draws the pressbeam down by means of a capstan turned by handspikes. As the beam was winched down, the increased counterthrust required the provision of a massive timber frame to secure the fulcrum; in addition, the pressbeam itself took up a great deal of space (a length of 40 feet [12 m] was usual). The first improvement, subsequently refined, was the replacement of the rope and capstan by a wooden spar terminating in a screw fixed into the floor, with a threaded nut above the lever, giving a direct positive thrust. The next improvement, a major change of design, had been introduced, says the elder Pliny, some twenty years before the time of writing (mid first century A.D.); the lever, with its space- and timber-consuming requirements, was now scrapped and replaced by a direct screw press. The earliest form resembled the Victorian letter press, with a single screw bearing down on the mush within a strong frame capable of taking the counterthrust. The subsequent development of a twin-screw model and a more heavily loaded frame follows the pattern of other well-documented inventions. The established lever press will not have been displaced until screw presses of similar capacity had been developed. Large screw presses were in use until very recent times for wine in Sicily, and for oil in North Africa.

To complete the list of presses there is the wedge-and-beam press, not mentioned by any of the authorities but displayed on two well-known wall paintings from Pompeii and Herculaneum. Here a different power source, the wedge, was used. A strong wooden frame like that of the single-screw press is filled with a series of horizontal floors, separated from each other by cone-shaped members, which are driven in by mallets so as to force the floors apart, causing the juice to be expressed into a receiver.

From the pressroom the juice was channeled or piped to the fermentation area for the first stage of vinification; this was usually an open courtyard with a northerly aspect—essential for keeping the temperature from rising too high during the first violent stage of the fermentation process, which lasted nine days (Pliny the Elder, 14.124). Here the must was run off into large earthenware containers (*dolia*), which were pear-shaped, with a deep rebate at the neck to take the lid; in Italy they were sunk up to the shoulder in the ground to obtain another means of temperature control. The ground plan of the farm buildings at a villa at Boscoreale shows the distribution of all the principal activities, which included the pressing of olive oil as well as wine, the wine storage jars being arranged on the north side and the oil containers, which needed warmth, on the south. The jars were buried in four double files, with space left for easy movement around them. As the receivers in the adjoining pressroom filled up, their contents were poured into a large basin with a hole in the bottom, to which was fitted a pipe; this took the liquid across the corridor and, passing through the wall, discharged it into a stone-built vat equipped with holes that corresponded exactly with the rows of jars. At these apertures longer pipes were fitted, which filled up the storage containers in succession. After fermentation ceased, wines were kept thus "in cask" for varying periods. In his inventory for a vineyard Cato calls for enough storage jars to contain the product of five vintages of 800 *cullei* (1 culleus = 168 gal. [636 l]). This, as he has already explained, would give the owner the benefit of higher prices.

Wine held in stock at the vineyard was sold on the spot to the wholesaler, transported in an oxskin to the latter's premises where it was bottled in the familiar amphorae (capacity about 8.2 gal. [31 l]). In the northern provinces of the empire, however, bulk wine was transported, as it has been ever since Roman times, in coopered casks, as the elder Pliny tells us (14.132), adding that in the depth of winter "they even light fires to prevent the wine from freezing."

The next stage, that of delivery to the innkeeper, bar owner, or private consumer, is well displayed on a terra-cotta relief from Pompeii, an inn sign showing two men conveying a full amphora of wine on a pole across their shoulders, the long, pointed jar secured by a rope passing through its handles. Storing containers of fine wines in tiers on specially made racks goes back to Roman times, as we know from the excavated wineshop attached to the House of Neptune and Amphitrite at Herculaneum. Here the amphorae were laid lengthwise on a wooden framework cut to fit their length; they were reached by a wooden ladder.

The Olive

"The cultivation of the vine is more complicated than that of any other tree, and the olive, the queen of trees, requires the least expense of all." So Columella wrote (5.8.1) after completing two books on viticulture, and preparing to dismiss his next subject in a couple of chapters. Vergil believed that olive trees needed no cultivation at all. This is quite incorrect. These slow-growing trees need a good deal of attention in the nursery, where they spend five years before being transplanted. Propagation was normally by slips, which were lightly covered and then identified with a pair of marking pegs "to prevent damage by ignorant diggers" (Columella, 5.9.4). The most important requirement was good drainage; with this provision they will flourish, as Vergil declared, "on the stubborn land and ungracious hills, on the fields of lean marl and pebbly brushwood" (*Georgics* 2.17ff.). Once in their permanent position they still needed at least two plowings a year, the first in high summer to prevent cracking of the surface and exposure of the roots, the second in mid autumn, when they should also be manured and have the moss scraped off their trunks. Pruning was also desirable to build up a good shape and to remove unproductive branches. The proverbially slow growth of the olive, "providing shade for generations yet unborn," meant a long period of no return on a heavy investment. Tax relief for new plantings was given on vines and olives, but the latter qualified for a longer period (seven years compared with three). When Pliny the Elder

(15.2) reported olives that bore fruit while still in the nursery, as compared with the mature tree that took seven years from planting to bear, he did not reveal whether this resulted from improved methods or from the introduction of an early maturing variety (although he does name fifteen varieties compared with Cato's ten).

Large-scale expansion of olive cultivation in areas not hitherto exploited and that today have reverted to desert has been revealed by archaeology in two widely separated areas of the empire. In central and southern Tunisia vast areas have been revealed by aerial photography as parceled out according to the Roman system of rectangular land division known as centuriation, the greater part of which was planted to olives. The other area was in the eastern Mediterranean, east of Antioch. Of the farms once there, Arthur H. M. Jones (*The Later Roman Empire*) writes, "In what is now desert, there are ruins of scores of well-built and evidently once prosperous villages. They were all built in the fifth and sixth centuries A.D." The numerous surviving olive presses indicate that "here at least agriculture advanced, and it may have done so in other areas where the archaeological evidence has been obliterated by later occupation."

The Fig

Figs still rank high in the diet of Mediterranean people, as they did in classical times, for they have a high sugar content as well as important nutritive value. The fig tree thrives on well-drained, sloping ground, with a cover of thin, dry soil such as that of southwestern Anatolia, the home of the Smyrna fig, or of Attica, from which Solon forbade the export of the product. That conditions in many parts of Italy favored the fruit is evident from the number of introduced varieties, which by the elder Pliny's time had reached twenty-nine.

The main obstacle to the successful cultivation of the fig is the habit of premature shedding of the fruit. A remedy, which is correctly explained by Theophrastus (*Inquiry into Plants* 2.8.4), is the process known as caprification: wild figs, which are hosts to gallflies, are attached to the trees to promote cross-fertilization. This procedure is still used today.

ROMAN HORTICULTURE

The Kitchen Garden

By Columella's time the kitchen garden, two of whose main products, vegetables and pulses, had formed the basic diet of early Romans, had fallen into gross neglect. Cato had praised the dietetic and medicinal virtues of the humble cabbage, but Varro, who devotes one-third of his text to the table luxuries of the rich, ignored the subject. Columella filled the gap, and made up for Vergil's neglect of the subject by producing some four hundred uninspired verses that nonetheless represent a well-ordered and comprehensive account. Both he and Pliny the Elder emphasized the need for irrigation. The latter gave first preference to a running stream beside the plots, but cautioned, "if you have only a well, you need a water-lifting device, which may be either a wheel [evidently an improvement on the primitive rope and bucket, consisting of a roller across the wellhead], or a force pump, or by scooping with a swing beam [a shadoof]." Columella called for an enclosure, either a wall or a thickset hedge, to keep out cattle and thieves. One straying donkey could wreak havoc in the kitchen garden. Varro (1.15) recommended planting cypresses on sloping ground and elms to support vines on the level. Supporting both hedge and grapevines, "the elm collects for you many a basket of grapes, supplies sheep and cattle with leaves very much to their liking, and provides boughs for hedges, hearth, and oven." Columella gave excellent advice on digging, manuring, and laying out the beds and access paths (10.77–94). Of the sixty plants named in his poem twenty are herbs; they feature prominently in various seasonal calendars, along with the vegetables and fruit that have always been prominent in the Italian diet. Indeed, the Roman housewife had at her elbow almost all the herbs and spices available to her American counterpart, save only the produce of the New World.

The Orchard

Great importance was attached to the preparation of planting holes for the fruit trees and nut trees with which a Roman orchard was to be stocked. Columella recommended the following (5.10.2 ff.):

> You will dig the plant hole . . . a year beforehand, for then it will be softened by the sun and the rain, and the plant you put in will quickly take root. But if you are in a hurry, dig the plant holes at least two months ahead and warm them by burning straw inside them. The broader and wider you make them, the more luxuriant and prolific will be the fruit you gather. Make your plant hole like an oven, wider at the bottom than the top, to enable the roots to spread more freely, so that the narrow mouth may reduce the penetration of winter cold and summer heat; also, on sloping ground, to prevent the earth heaped up in it from being washed away by rain. . . . In planting cuttings, the shoots should be torn from the stock, not broken off, forming a heel, which will take if thrust immediately into the ground before the sap can dry out.

Under Mediterranean conditions, where propagation is effected by seedlings or cuttings, shallow root systems need frequent watering in the early stages of growth. Too much watering of established trees affects fruit quality. This problem can be solved by grafting on an established stock. Advances in this field had been made by the Greeks, who also made the important discovery that whereas seedlings and cuttings tended to revert to the wild or lose quality, grafted stock produced fruit true to type; it also enabled the enterprising grower to introduce new and improved varieties and to acclimatize them.

The different methods of grafting, which call for a high degree of eye and hand skill, aroused the imagination of two great poets. Lucretius speculated on its origin, while Vergil in a fine passage in his *Georgics* incorporated both natural and artificial methods of propagation into an organic whole. Columella, in his account of grafting, mentions six techniques: crown grafting, side grafting, cleft grafting, patch budding, bore grafting, and a type of approach grafting. In the first method, the scion was grafted not into the hard wood, but between the hard wood and the bark, into the cambium layer, thus making a more effective union. The second method was to make an incision with a saw into the trunk, smooth the cut with a surgical knife, and insert the scion into it. In the third method the stock was cut and cleft, so that it could receive the scion, which had been carefully cut and shaped to match the wedge-shaped cleft. (This simplest of all methods is illustrated on a panel of the Vienne seasons mosaic.) The fourth method involved making identical cuts on stock and scion with a hollow punch. Closely related is shield budding, so called because of the triangular graft inserted into the T-shaped stem incision, but it does not appear in the list. Columella's fifth method, which was suitable only for vines, required a special boring tool, the "Gallic auger" (one of many examples of tools and techniques he describes as being of Celtic origin). The last method, in which branches from adjacent trees were joined, is no longer used and may have been only a limited experiment. However, it enabled Columella to state that any kind of scion could be grafted on to any kind of tree, provided the barks were compatible. On the choice of suitable stock for grafting, there is more information in the later writers. Palladius recommended a stock for every tree he mentions, and *On Agriculture* (*Geoponica*) also indicates an increasing interest in this sophisticated art.

Improved techniques of grafting made it easy to establish new varieties, and Rome's conquest of the eastern Mediterranean brought to the West both new varieties of well-known fruits and several that were previously unknown, including the cherry and the peach. The cherry (*Cerasus*) was brought back from Pontus by Lucullus in 73 B.C. The peach (*Malum persicum*), native to China, was unknown to Cato and Varro and was still rare in Columella's time. Pliny the Elder says the cherry reached Britain soon after the Roman invasion in A.D. 43. This important development reached a peak toward the end of the first century A.D., but interest in new varieties of pears, apples, and figs continued to grow. Macrobius (*fl.* A.D. 400) mentions in his *Saturnalia* more of these fruits than Pliny.

ANIMAL HUSBANDRY

A full treatment of the recommended regimes for the rearing, training, and management of the domestic animals, and of their several roles in different types of enterprise, is beyond the scope of this article. Varro devoted an entire book to the subject, and Columella two. We shall be concerned primarily with those animals regarded as essential to the operation of the farm: the working oxen, mules, and donkeys, whether used for plowing, cartage, or other necessary tasks.

The role of stock raising in an agrarian economy depends on a number of variables, including climate and the size of the farm unit. In Roman times the farm may have been a tiny holding of "four acres and a cow"; it may have included a pair of plow oxen, a cow, a mule or a donkey, a goat, a pig, and farmyard poultry—the latter went with even the humblest subsistence unit. Where sheep were part of an establishment, they may have been kept for their milk, wool, or meat, as well as for manure; this required an enclosure so that sheep could feed and at the same time fertilize the next crop. The cow was primarily a working animal, not a milk producer. When stall-fed, it produced valuable supplies of ready-made manure, its litter providing both dung and urine. A major problem for the ancient Italian farmer was to secure enough fodder to keep his working animals alive through the winter, a problem that persisted into modern times, when the use of root crops for winter feed put an end to the annual slaughter of stock in northern Europe. It was the availability of fodder that determined the choice of animal. As Varro bluntly put it, "For this purpose [plowing] some farmers employ donkeys, others cows or mules, according to the fodder available."

Earlier, Cato had given full lists of the equipment, working animals, and "vocal instruments" (slaves) needed for each of his two standard units. A 100-*iugera* (63 acres [25 hectares]) vineyard needed two oxen and three donkeys, two for transport and one for the grain mill, while his much larger olive plantation of 240 *iugera* (1.51 acres [60 hectares]) needed three pairs of oxen and four donkeys, three for carrying manure and one for the mill. Both units included a swineherd, which meant not just a few pigs living on scraps, but a properly managed herd, such as Varro later described (2.4). Their meat was in great demand; their dung, and especially their urine, was used as a fertilizer for vines. The olive plantation also included a shepherd and a flock of a hundred sheep. Cato's list of contract terms contains one for the lease of winter pasturage; in this case the owner kept no sheep on the place but retained the right to pasture two yoke of oxen and one gelding on the rented pasture. Varro gives a vivid description of the life of the rough type of herdsman who lived and worked in the fields on one of those large-scale ranches that he has already roundly condemned in the preface because "these animals do not produce what grows on the land, but tear it off with their teeth" (2.10). This is quite the opposite of the stall-kept animals, which produce the dung that fertilizes the ground that they prepare by plowing.

Sheep are particularly destructive where pasture is thin; unlike cows, sheep twist and wrench the herbage, and only well-rooted grass can withstand this treatment. Bare patches that emerge are later trampled by their small hooves, and the soil becomes so impacted that it does not reseed itself and erosion develops. Recorded holdings of sheep on large estates in south Italy give some support to the view that they were overgrazed; but it would appear that in many parts of the south ranching was the most efficient way of using the land in an overwhelmingly agricultural economy.

The habitat of goats, those familiar inhabitants of the classical landscape, is the upland maquis: "They prefer thickets to open country," writes Columella (7.6.1), adding that they are particularly fond of such plants as "arbutus, buckthorn, wild trefoil, and young evergreen and deciduous oaks that have not yet attained any great height." Their fondness for succulent shoots makes them the enemy of plantation owners, and they effectively prevent the natural regeneration of forests by eating the growing center of the shoot. A small mosaic panel in Tunis appropriately shows Artemis (Diana) aiming an arrow at a goat stretching up for that very purpose. Nevertheless goats were widely kept, not only for the abundance of their milk yield (more than twice as high in proportion to body weight as from cows), but for a variety of other products. The long-haired Cilician (Angora) goat gave hair for sacking and ropes, especially the twisted skeins used in catapults.

Apart from Cato's gelding (kept for riding), and the stallion or mare kept for breeding hinnies or mules, the horse has no place in the economy of a Roman farm. His place was on the battlefield or in the circus, although he may well have ended his days tramping round the grain mill.

Varro's treatise abounds in money-making (and money-losing) enterprises. Big profits were to be made in stud farming for the production of high-grade mules, which played a leading role in transport. Varro himself ran a stud farm in the Reate district, where meadows were so lush that a stake set in the ground one day could be lost to view next morning.

By far the most striking feature of Varro's work is the attention he gives to the production of table luxuries, from fieldfares and peacocks to fancy ducks and geese. It takes up the whole of his Book Three. The various specialties reserved for the tables of gourmets enjoy an equally exotic environment, being raised in netted enclosures, aviaries, ponds, or warrens, with all the equipment needed to fatten the products for the market.

Varro's preoccupations are a long way from the realities of farming. Columella's account of the difficult but vitally important techniques connected with the breaking and training of the plow oxen is more to the point. The breaking-in regime is based on severe restriction of movement; the steers are tied by the horns to horizontal posts set over a stall in such a way that the ropes give very little play. If they are very wild, they are kept like this for thirty-six hours, until their fury has abated (modern methods are much less brutal). The next stage is to train them to walk at the steady pace essential for pulling plows and heavy wagons. They are tied up tightly in the stalls, so that they can be handled by the oxherd and grow accustomed to the sound of his voice. "After this," writes Columella, "their tongues and mouths should be rubbed with salt, and a pint of wine poured down their gullets, using drinking horns." In training them Columella recommended a system practiced on his own farms, in which an untrained ox is yoked with a fully trained one; a particularly obstinate trainee is attached to the center of a triple yoke and forced along at the correct pace by a pair of veterans.

FOOD

Grains

The predominance of cereals in the diet of ancient Greeks and Romans has been recognized ever since the study of their social and economic history began more than a century ago. The ancient agronomists did not treat the subject systematically, but Pliny the Elder provides (18.94–95) a great deal of information on the methods used in converting harvested grains into meal and flour and in the further processes of kneading, cooking, or baking in order to produce gruel, porridge, bread, or cake. But there are many problems with his account. In place of statistical information, which is wholly lacking, he provides useful information (for example, on extraction rates for wheat) interspersed with tall stories that catered to those readers interested in the unusual and the bizarre, such as accounts of record yields. Many traditional processes were thought to be too familiar to be worth describing. For example, he does not describe breadmaking step by step, but does give a list of fancy breads.

Of the ordinary kitchen equipment used in preparing grains, stones from many different types of handmill have survived in large numbers, but the only account of this very common process of small-scale hand grinding comes from an anonymous poem called *The Country Salad* (*Moretum*). In general, the archaeological evidence falls into three categories: representations of milling and baking, artifacts connected with these operations, and surviving grains and their products. Each category presents its own set of problems. In the first case, the artist, who is not normally interested in technical accuracy, may present a scene in which one object partially obscures another. In the second case, although there is abundant information on hand- and animal-powered mills, there is only one ancient water-driven mill that shows the actual working. In the third case, sizable quantities of preserved food grains have now been recovered, and recent studies have thrown fresh light on the many problems of classification and identification.

A predominantly cereal diet can provide the intake of calories needed to sustain physical strength, but it remains unbalanced unless supported by fruit and vegetables. On current evidence, in antiquity grain products contributed 70 to 75 percent of the calories needed, which corresponds closely with the global maximum for present-day consumption. Certain low-status groups such as chain-gang slaves received a higher percentage of grain products. Populations fed mainly on high-grade cereals (wheat or barley) suffer less from shortages of protein, vitamins, and minerals than those living on polished rice (as in Asia) or on root crops (as in West Africa). Green vegetables featured prominently in the diet of ancient Athenians, and wine and oil probably supplied the rest of the calories required.

The blandness and monotony of such a diet must be modified, and Greek and Roman peasants of the classical period made use of a variety of sharp-flavored condiments, relishes, and sauces, including onions, garlic, pepper, and a very strong sauce made from the fermented entrails of fish (*allec;* the expensive variety was called *garum*). Country folk, as in other ages, used gathered supplements from field and woodland, including wild greens and bulbs.

Barley (*krithe, Hordeum vulgare*) was grown extensively, especially in mainland Greece and the Aegean Islands, where it was eaten in large amounts until quite recently. Widely used as animal feed, it was processed for human consumption in the form of porridge and, more commonly, a flat cake the Greeks called *maza*. Barley was a strong competitor with wheat. It thrives on poor soils, where its yield, which is only 10 percent higher than wheat on rich soils, advances to as high as 50 percent. On the other hand, it is 10 percent less nutritious than wheat by weight and 35 percent by volume. It also takes more time and trouble to convert into meal. Barley groats (*alphita;* particles of the hulled, cracked grain) were sprinkled over meat and issued as rations (Thucydides, 4.16). The corresponding grain used for porridge in Italy was a husked wheat called emmer, which produced highly prized groats called *alica. Alica* was also used as a base for many different dishes and in cakes that, if unattractive to a modern palate, were highly nutritious, as was barley water, produced by boiling and steeping the grain. Both barley and emmer continued in favor long after the introduction of the naked wheats (durum or macaroni wheat) and the softer common bread wheat (*Triticum vulgare*), which proved much more suitable for baking into bread. Common bread wheat, which in early republican Italy had been a spring-sown crop, gradually advanced at the expense of emmer, so that by imperial times it had become the main autumn-sown crop. The bad effects of a mainly wheaten diet have been exaggerated (as by Rickman, *The Corn Supply of Ancient Rome*). The nutritional value of wheat differs according to the different ways the grain is milled and the various grades of bread it is made into.

Whole Meal and Flour Production

The introduction of rotary motion into the milling process was the first of a series of inventions that culminated in the highly efficient water mill. Cato's inventories mention both the ancient up-and-down pounding mill and the rotary grinding handmill, but not the earlier Greek improvement on the older type, the side-to-side rubbing-action hopper.

Milling wheat with any of these devices produces whole meal, retaining the indigestible outer coat of the grain, the bran. In the modern machine process, the grain is split, the bran shaved off, and the remainder sifted to produce flour. On the basis of earlier experiments with a rotary handmill it has been shown that four grades of product could be made that correspond fairly well with the archaeological evidence. To produce the top-grade flour known as *flos* or *pollen* would require two grindings and two siftings, using a coarse and a fine sieve.

In classical times, each of the major species of food grains—barley and the two varieties of wheat, husked and naked—required different treatment and different equipment. Without getting submerged in technicalities, three principal questions must be addressed: What sort of end product was produced by the different milling or pounding devices, and by the processes of roasting, parching, and sifting? What were the nutritional values of these products? And what categories of persons consumed the various products?

The processing of the different food grains, whether to produce porridge, pulse, or bread, involved a number of tedious tasks that varied with the particular cereal. Before the introduction of animal power the operations were all carried out by hand, usually by women. The Greek poet Semonides of Amorgos includes in his list of objectionable females those "who will not handle the mill, nor lift the sieve, nor throw the refuse out of doors, nor sit by the oven, afraid of the soot" (*Greek Anthology,* frag. 7.58–60). His verses identify three basic processes: milling (with a handmill), sieving (probably to remove weed seeds and other impurities), and bread baking. If the grain was husked (barley or emmer) two processes preceded the milling, first, roasting or parching, then hulling with mortar and pestle (in large-scale operation a task usually assigned to chain-gang convicts —see Pliny the Elder, 18.109 f.). If groats were required, the different grades were produced by repeated pounding and sifting of the hulled grain. For bread, the hulled grain was milled to produce whole meal. White bread required a special sifting to remove the bran from the meal. It seems clear from the evidence that in classical Greece sieves were inefficient; according to Moritz (1958), "even purified flour . . . must have been very dark indeed by our standards." The recorded improvements in sieve design indicate that the best Roman flour was lighter.

Although barley does not produce good bread, it was long the dominant cereal in Greece, being dislodged but not ousted, according to literary sources, by wheat by the fourth century B.C. Barley continued to be eaten by the poor and by slaves. In Italy, a different change occurred. There the dominant cereal in early times was not barley (which was grown mainly for fodder) but the husked grain called *far* (emmer), which was normally consumed as porridge (*puls*). Pliny the Elder says (18.83),

> Emmer is the hardiest of all grains, and the one that stands winter conditions best . . . it was the first food of the Latium of olden days [and] it is evident that for a long time the Romans subsisted on porridge [*puls*], not on bread [*panis*], since even today foodstuffs are known as "porridge stuff" [*pulmentaria*].

Barley bread, even in Greek times, may have been despised (an early Greek writer rated it "food fit only for slaves"), but proverbs such as "a barley cake is the next best thing to a loaf," and its use as rations, albeit for Spartans, show how widely it was consumed. The porridge made from barley probably continued to be consumed by country folk and "porridge munching" Romans. Their Italian descendants, however, used polenta made from a New World cereal, maize—Indian corn or milo.

So too with the Roman equivalent of barley porridge. At the end of a lengthy discussion of the varieties and properties of wheat, the elder Pliny offers a few tantalizingly brief observations on breadmaking, and then proceeds to devote a great deal of space to emmer groats (*alica*), which he praises as a first-class food with a high nutritive content. He supplements this recommendation with a recipe (18.109 ff.):

> The grain is pounded in a wooden mortar (a stone mortar would reduce it to powder) . . . [and] after the emmer has been stripped of its coat, the bared kernel is again broken up with the same implements. This produces three grades of *alica:* very small, seconds, and very large (the Greeks call it "select"). The groats have yet to acquire the whiteness that is their outstanding quality, though even at this stage they are preferred to the Alexandrian variety. By a subsequent process chalk is added and incorporated into the grain to give it color and fineness. The chalk is found at a place called White Earth Hill, midway between Pozzuoli and Naples.

Breadmaking and Bread Consumption

In his brief reference to breadmaking, Pliny the Elder declares that quality depends on two factors: quality of grain and fineness of sieve. (He does not include either the quality of the leavening agent or the efficiency of the kneading as having significant effect on quality, although both are mentioned.) From this passage we can see that improvements in bread production have taken place with the use of a fine sieve or bolter for flour (a Gallic invention) and brewer's yeast as a leavening agent. In a recipe for inferior groats Pliny the Elder mentions three different kinds of sieves, the last of which is described as extremely fine, letting only sand through (18.115). A reference to Gallic sieves made of horsehair shows that fine flour could be produced. Unfortunately, although we have accurate information from the numerous surviving millstones at Pompeii to reconstruct a mill for experimental purposes, this has yet to be done, and experimental grinding has been confined to handmills. There is some doubt about the number of grindings needed to produce the grades of flour mentioned by Pliny, but we must assume that two would be needed to produce flour on a Pompeian type of animal-powered mill. The use of the term *secundarius* (seconds) does not prove that such flour was produced by a second grinding, but it would be appropriate if it did.

The only surviving account of handmilling comes from the anonymous poem of the late republican period called *The Country Salad* (*Moretum*). With down-to-earth detail, the poem describes part of a day in the life of a peasant smallholder, from the moment he rises in pitch dark to hitching up the plow team. Once he has managed to resuscitate the fire from its embers, his first job is to take from his scanty store a day's supply of grain.

> From this he helps himself to as much as his measure, which runs up to sixteen pounds weight, can take. And now, moving off, he takes his stand at the mill, and on a tiny shelf, fixed firmly for the purpose to the wall, he sets his trusty light. Then he slips both arms out of his tunic and, dressed in a shaggy goatskin, he carefully sweeps clean the stones and bosom of the mill with a tail. Next he summons his two hands to the work, dividing them between the dual task; the left is bent on feeding in the grain, the right on driving the mill. This, on its endless circuit, turns the mill at speed. The grain, pounded by the stones' swift blows, trickles down; the left hand from time to time supports her wearied sister and takes its turn. At last, when the task of turning has reached its appointed end, he transfers the [pounded?] meal into the sieve, and shakes it, and the refuse remains on the top of the sieve, while the pure flour sinks down and, cleansed of impurities, filters through the holes. (22–29; 38–42)

The poet does not tell how many grindings were made, but the language he uses confirms the method established by experiment with hand querns.

Pliny the Elder lists six kinds of leaven (*fermentum*), ranging from millet dipped in unfermented wine to a piece of leftover dough from yesterday's baking (18.102 ff.). Earlier in the book he casually mentions, in a discussion of imported wheats, that "Gauls and Spaniards, when they soak grain in winter to make beer, use the froth that forms on the surface as leaven; that is why their bread is lighter in weight than anyone else's." This seems to be the first mention of brewer's yeast, which in powdered form has long enjoyed the highest favor. Pliny concludes by saying that people who eat fermented bread have "weaker constitutions. Indeed, in the old days, the heaviest wheats were thought to be the most wholesome." Tastes and constitutions differ; light breads are now popular, but in many parts of southern Europe the less carbonated loaf, which keeps much better, is still preferred. Flour, when worked into a nice glutinous paste with water and the yeast incorporated, becomes dough ready for kneading, which captures the carbon dioxide and enables the dough to rise when set in a warm atmosphere. Crumb-Snatcher, the champion mouse in the Greek mock epic *The Battle of the Frogs and Mice*

(*Batrachomyomachia*), boasts of his high standard of living: "I never want for a thrice-kneaded loaf in its neat round basket." Indeed, three kneadings produce a splendid loaf.

The type of ovens attached to the milling and baking establishments of ancient Pompeii and used for commercial production survives unaltered in the pizza establishments of the back streets of Naples. On a small Roman farm or in a cottage the low hearth will have favored the method of baking on leaves or tiles (see Ovid, *The Roman Calendar* [*Fasti*] 6.315–316). All the agronomists mention baking on leaves in the ashes. An improved method was to place an earthenware crock (*testum*) over the loaf, and this seems to have originated with the use of tiles or potsherds for baking.

The evidence for Greek bread is very sparse. There are far more references to barley cake than to wheaten bread, and there are few indications of variation in the quality of the product. It would, however, be unwise to assume either that more barley was consumed than wheat, or that those who ate wheaten bread ate only the best quality. It is typical of the situation that the greatest source of information on this topic occurs in a list of fancy breads in a vast and erudite compilation entitled *The Learned Banquet* (*Deipnosophistae* 3.113) by the Greek grammarian Athenaeus (*fl.* A.D. 200). After placing wheat well above barley for producing bread that is both more nutritious and more digestible, the author proceeds to list wheaten products in ranked order:

> Loaves made of bread wheat flour are superior to those made of groats; next come those made from sifted meal, and then those made from unsifted meal. But the rolls made from bran give a much less wholesome juice. . . . All bread is more digestible when eaten hot. . . . Nevertheless, hot bread is apt to cause flatulence, though it is none the less digestible for that, while cold bread is filling and indigestible. But bread which is very stale and old is less nutritious and is apt to cause constipation.

From the above we may deduce that the learned professors showing off their learning in banquet conversation had very confused notions about the processes of digestion. Their comments reflect only too well a gross ignorance of biochemistry that hampered ancient medicine, as does a typically inconclusive reference (21.2) to the subject in *Problems,* which is spuriously attributed to Aristotle: "Why is food from wheat better suited to the body and more nutritious than food made from barley? Because it has a moderately glutinous character?"

The technical writers have little to say about the quality of Roman bread, but casual comments are frequent in other writers. Passing references in the comedy writers Plautus and Terence should be treated with reserve; in the case of the satirists, even greater caution should be exercised, for the essence of good satire lies in extravagance and exaggeration. As Moritz (1958) has shown, Roman *farina,* the meal normally used in noncommercial baking, will have been poorer in quality than than that of a similar long-extraction flour of 85 to 90 percent produced by modern milling and sifting methods. Of the various types of flour and meal produced by Roman methods (and there is need of careful experiment here), we can reasonably assume that what was called "secondary" (*secundarius*) bread was eaten by the majority of the population, only a minority enjoying the higher grades. There are no statistics, so we do not know what proportion of the urban or rural populations had to subsist on the lower-grade product, which may well have been healthier than the more refined product. But numerous literary references support the view that the lower classes ate low-grade bread. Dictionaries show that adjectives meaning dark, black, and dirty-looking were applied to "ordinary" bread; an exhaustive study of this kind of evidence would be rewarding. Among casual references may be mentioned an opinion given by the great jurist Ulpian (d. A.D. 228) (Justinian, *Digest* 23.9.3.8) on what items of property should pass to the heir as being essential to the running of the deceased owner's estate: "Item: the barley in store for the household (that is, the slaves)." By contrast, four centuries earlier slaves were fed on rations of wheat or wheaten bread (although the grade or quality is not known). Other casual references reflect on the quality of Roman bread. Writing about sensation, the poet Lucretius (*On the Nature of Things* [*De Rerum Natura*]) supports his argument by referring to what was evidently a common experience, that of the unsuspecting person who encounters a stone in the bread he is eating. Horace, describing a journey from Rome to Brundusium (Brindisi) (*Satires* 1.5), condemns the local bread at Canosa in Apulia as "gritty": the wise traveler stocks up with a double supply of better bread at the previous stop. Alfred Ernout, editor of the Budé edition of Horace, discussing this passage in a note, says that Roman milling techniques did not reduce the grain to flour, but broke it into fragments, which were then passed through sieves to divide it into different qualities of bread. "The loaves found at Pompeii," he adds, "are very dense in texture, and very compact in structure; hence an encounter with a stone against a tooth would have been a common occurrence."

In distinguishing between the diet of different classes, we should notice that in Rome high-quality bread was not exclusive to the upper classes; provision of acceptable bread to the general populace was part of the price the emperors had to pay if they were to sleep soundly in their beds. The three references cited above are a mere handful among a great number; a further example shows the need for systematic examination of the evidence on bread quality. In the Brothwells' *Food in Antiquity* (p. 211) the following passage from Pliny the Elder (18.115) is quoted and described as being a recipe for bread made from husked wheat:

> Pound the wheat-grain with sand to remove the husks, the grain then being one-half of its former measure. Then 25% of gypsum is added to 75% of the meal, and the flour is bolted.

This paraphrase refers, however, not to bread, but to what Pliny the Elder considered a cheap substitute for *alica*, the fine porridge meal, and the authors rightly call attention to the deleterious effects of using sand to remove the husks. The need for research into the whole question of food grains and their use as staple foods in classical antiquity is further emphasized by Foxhall and Forbes (1982).

In the important matter of preferences for one food grain over another we need to look more closely at the references to processing techniques and to consider the evidence now coming forward as a result of experimental growing. Emmer, it is said, was displaced as a bread producer by common breadwheat and was restricted to porridge. Yet its actual advantages, especially for the small farmer, were considerable: first, it thrived on poor soils; second, experimental cropping on a simulated Iron Age farm in England produced high yields; third, if only the ears are reaped during harvest, leaving the straw, it can be taken straight into store without the labor of threshing or winnowing. On this Varro commented (1.63), "Emmer which you have stored in the ear at harvest time and wish to prepare for food, should be brought out in winter to be ground in the mill and roasted." Note also that Pliny (18.298) says that emmer is difficult to thresh. The frequent references to emmer in the agronomists show that it was widely grown.

Other Foods

As for meat, vegetables, fruit, and other items in the Roman diet, the best documented sources relate to the diet of Roman soldiers. The results of work on animal bones from thirty-three sites in the provinces of Britain and Germany do not support the popular view that Roman soldiers, like civilians, ate little meat; rather, they show that, in order of popularity, beef, mutton, pork, and goat's meat were principal items of the soldier's diet. Veal, lamb, and sucking-pig were also eaten. Hunting for the pot was popular, with venison, hare, and wild boar appearing frequently; fish, seafood, and poultry were in evidence on many sites, together with fruit and nuts in considerable variety. That fruit was recognized as important for health is shown in a passage in one of the four *Books of Military Matters* (*Epitoma Rei Militaris* 4.7) by Vegetius, a fourth-century writer, in which the camp commandant is advised to arrange for the collection and storage of large quantities of fruit in the event of there being any prospect of a siege. Food remains found at the fortress of Vindonissa (Windisch) in Switzerland prove that the troops garrisoned there ate apples, plums, cherries, peaches, grapes, and elderberries, as well as sweet chestnuts, hazelnuts, walnuts, and beechnuts. Analysis of vegetable matter from the station of Novaesium (Neuss) on the lower Rhine, mostly dated to the first century A.D., reveals large quantities of wheat, barley, and wild oats (probably used as fodder), as well as broad beans, lentils, garlic, sorrel, nipplewort, grapes, elderberries, and hazelnuts. Particularly prominent were four plants that the Romans had introduced into Germany: rice, chickpeas, olives, and figs.

Food Shortages

Failure of the staple crop was an ever-present threat to the Mediterranean farmer, since delay in the arrival of the autumn rains (the "former rains" of the Bible) meant delayed planting and consequent exposure of the maturing grain to the dreaded mildew or rust (*robigo*). Vergil wrote in *Georgics* (1.150–154):

> Soon, too, on the corn comes dreaded mischief, the blighting rust, feeding on the stems, and the lazy thistle bristling in the fields; the crops die off, and in their place springs up a prickly growth, burrs and calthrops, and amid the burgeoning corn the luckless darnel and barren oats hold sway.

Light spring showers helped to mature the crop, but heavy downpours were not uncommon, causing severe damage to a heavy crop already in the ear. Vergil continued:

> Often, as the farmer was bringing his reapers into the yellow fields, and stripping the yellow-stalked barley, my own eyes have seen all the winds clashing in battle, tearing up the heavy crop far and wide, from its deepest roots, and tossing it on high. Then with its dark whirlwind the storm would sweep off the light stalk and the flying stubble. Often, too, . . . clouds mustering from on high roll up a murky tempest of black showers; down falls the lofty heaven, and with its soaking deluge washes away the smiling crops and the labors of the oxen.

In the light of such weather changes, it is hardly surprising to learn that local famines were frequent.

A full-scale study of famines, long called for and now being undertaken by Peter Garnsey, will underline the difficulties involved in maintaining food supplies to the large urban centers, as well as the effects of famine on Greek and Roman diet. That crop failures leading to food shortages were common is clear from the writings of the agronomists, who often referred to substitute foods. Columella, at the start of a chapter on growing barley, wrote (2.9.14) that "six-rowed barley is a better food than wheat for all farm animals . . . and in times of scarcity there is nothing better as a protection against want." At the beginning of a chapter on legumes he gave first place to the lupine, "as it requires the least labor, costs least, and is of all crops the most beneficial to the land. It makes an excellent fertilizer for worn-out vineyards and arable fields. It flourishes even on exhausted soil, and is long-lasting when stored in the barn. In the case of humans too it serves to ward off famine if successive years of crop failure occur."

Chestnuts, which can be made into bread, were a well-known famine food substitute. Xenophon's troops found a hoard of them in Armenia; "baking them into loaves, they made the bread which they used most" (Xenophon, *The March Up Country* [*Anabasis*] 5.4.27). Chestnut bread has been a staple among poor village communities down to modern times. Wild herbs and weeds were used as food when man was a food-gatherer. We may fittingly conclude with a moving passage from the historian Procopius writing of the agonies suffered by the population of Rome when besieged by the Goths in A.D. 537 (*The Gothic War* [*De Bello Gothico*] 5.19.19 f.):

> As long as there was ripe grain in the fields, the most daring of the soldiers, inspired by greed, used to go to the nearby fields on horseback, and leading other horses. There they cut the heads of grain . . . and sold them at a very high price to wealthy Romans. The rest of the population lived on a variety of herbs which grow in profusion both on the outskirts of the city and inside the fortifications. The territory of the city of Rome is never short of herbs either in winter or at any other season: they flourish abundantly all the year round.

BIBLIOGRAPHY

SOURCES

Greek

Aristophanes, *Acharneis* (*The Acharnians*), B. B. Rogers, trans. (1910), and *Eirene* (*The Peace*), B. B. Rogers, trans. (1930); *Geoponika, sive Cassiani Bassi Scholastici De Re Rustica Ecologae* [*On Agriculture*], H. Beckh, ed. (1895); Athenaeus, *Deipnosophistae* (*The Learned Banquet*), Charles Burton Gulick, trans., 7 vols. (1927–1941); Hesiod, *Opera et Dies* (*Works and Days*), Richmond Lattimore, trans. (1959); Homer, *Iliad*, W. R. Paton, trans., *The Greek Anthology*, 5 vols. (1956–1960); Theophrastus, *Historia Plantarum* (*Enquiry into Plants*), Arthur Hort, trans. (1916), and *De Causis Plantarum* (*Etiology of Plants*), Benedict Einarson and George K. K. Link, trans. (1976); Thucydides, *Thucydides' History of Peloponnesian Wars*, Rex Warner, ed. (1954; repr. 1967); Xenophon, *Oeconomicus* (*Household Management*), J. Thompson and B. J. Hayes, trans. (1925).

Roman

Marcus Porcius Cato (the Elder), *De Agricultura* (*On Agriculture*), Ernest Bréhaut, trans. (1933); Marcus Tullius Cicero, *Cicero's Selected Works*, Michael Grant, ed. and trans. (1960); Lucius Iunius Moderatus Columella, *De Re Rustica* (*On Country Matters*), Harrison B. Ash, Edward S. Forster, Edward H. Heffner, trans., 3 vols. (1945–1948); Rutilius Taurus Aemilianus Palladius, *De Re Rustica*, trans. as *Palladius on Husbondrie* by Barton Lodge, 2 parts (1873–1879); Gaius Plinius Secundus (Pliny the Elder), *Historia Naturalis* (*Natural History*), Hugh Rackham, trans., 10 vols. (1938–1963); Pliny the Younger, *The Letters of the Younger Pliny*, Betty Radice, trans. (1963);

Procopius, *De Bello Gothico* (*The Gothic War*) in his *History of the Wars,* H. B. Dewing, trans., vols. 3–5 (1919–1928); Marcus Terentius Varro, *Rerum Rusticarum Libri Tres* (*Country Matters, in Three Books*), Lloyd Storr-Best (1912), and Bertha Tilly, trans., *Varro the Farmer* (1973); Publius Vergilius Maro (Vergil), *Georgics,* Cecil Day Lewis, trans. (1940, 1947).

For other translations of Cato and Varro: *On Farming,* William D. Hooper, trans., rev. ed. by Harrison B. Ash (1960); Virginia Farmer, *Roman Farm Management* (1913). For another translation and a critical survey of Vergil: Patrick Wilkinson, *The Georgics of Virgil* (1969). For bibliographies of Roman sources: Kenneth D. White, *A Bibliography of Roman Agriculture* (1970); René Martin, *Recherches sur les agronomes latins et leur conceptions économiques et sociales* (1971).

GENERAL

Ester Boserup, *The Conditions of Agricultural Growth* (1965); Geoffrey W. Dimbleby, *Plants and Archaeology* (1967); Stephen L. Dyson, "Archaeological Survey in the Mediterranean Basin, A Review of Recent Research," in *American Antiquity,* **47** (1982); Moses I. Finley, *The Ancient Economy* (1973); William E. Heitland, *Agricola* (1921; repr. 1968); Theodore Mommsen, *Römische Geschichte* (*The History of Rome*), William P. Dickson, trans. (1911–1931); Colin Renfrew and Malcolm Wagstaff, eds., *An Island Polity* (1982); Giuseppe Salvioli, *Le capitalisme dans le monde antique* (1906); John T. Schlebecker, "Farmers and Bureaucrats: Reflections on Technical Innovation in Agriculture," in *Agricultural History,* **51** (1977); Ellen Churchill Semple, *The Geography of the Mediterranean Region: Its Relation to Ancient History* (1932); Claudio Vita-Finzi, *The Mediterranean Valleys* (1969); Kenneth D. White, *Country Life in Classical Times* (1977), and *Greek and Roman Technology,* (1984), with extensive bibliography.

GREEK AGRICULTURE

Michel Austin and Pierre Vidal-Naquet, *Economic and Social History of Ancient Greece* (1977); Hendrik Bolkestein, ed., and E. J. Jonkers, annotat., *Economic Life in Greece's Golden Age* (1958); Joe C. Carter, "Rural Settlement at Metaponto," in Graeme Barker and Richard Hodges, eds., *Archaeology and Italian Society, British Archaeological Reports, Intl. Ser.,* **102** (1981); Victor Ehrenberg, *The People of Aristophanes* (1951; repr. 1974); Sarah C. Humphreys, *Anthropology and the Greeks* (1978); Michael H. Jameson, "Agriculture and Slavery in Classical Athens," in *Classical Journal,* **73** (1977); William A. McDonald and George R. Rapp, Jr., *The Minnesota Messenia Expeditions: Reconstructing a Bronze Age Regional Environment* (1972), with extensive bibliography.

Louis-Henri Parias, ed., *Histoire général du travail,* I (1959); Mikhail I. Rostovtzeff, *The Social and Economic History of the Hellenistic World,* 3 vols. (1941; repr. 1953); Anthony M. Snodgrass, "Archaeological Survey in Greece and the Mediterranean Area," in *Annales (Economies, sociétés, civilisations),* **37** (1982), and "Central Greece and Thessaly," in *Cambridge Ancient History,* 2d ed., III, pt. 1 (1982); E. M. Staerman and M. K. Trofimova, *La Schiavitù nell' Italia Imperiale,* 1–3 sec., Rome (1975).

ROMAN AGRICULTURE

Raymond Billiard, *L'agriculture dans l'antiquité d'après les Géorgiques de Virgile* (1928), and *La vigne dans l'antiquité* (1913); John Bradford, *Ancient Landscapes,* Studies in Field Anthropology (1957); Henriette Camps-Fabrer, *L'olivier et l'huile dans l'Afrique romaine* (1953); Andrea Carandini, "Il vigneto e la villa del fondo di Settefinestre nel Cosano," in *Memoirs of the American Academy in Rome,* **36** (1980); Andrea Carandini and A. Ricci, *Settefinestre: Una villa schiaristica nell-'Etruria romana,* 3 vols. (1985); Molly A. Cotton, "Some Research Work in Roman Villas in Italy, 1960–80," in *Rome and Her Northern Frontiers,* Papers Presented to Sheppard Frere (1983); Joseph J. Deiss, *Herculaneum* (1966).

Aage G. Drachmann, *Ancient Oil Mills and Presses* (1932); Tenney Frank, ed., *An Economic Survey of Ancient Rome,* 5 vols. (1933–1938); Joan M. Frayn, *Subsistence Farming in Roman Italy* (1979); Peter Garnsey, "Peasants in Ancient

Roman Society," in *Journal of Peasant Studies*, **3** (1976); André G. Haudricourt and Mariel J-B. Delamarre, *L'homme et la charrue à travers les âges*, 3d ed. (1955); Arthur H. M. Jones, *The Later Roman Empire, 284–602: A Social, Economic, and Administrative Survey* (1964); Jerzy Kolendo, *L'agricoltura nell' Italia romana* (1980); Paul Leser, *Entstehung und Verbreitung des Pfluges (Origin and Spread of Plows)*, (1931); Ramsay MacMullen, *Roman Social Relations, 50 B.C. to A.D. 284* (1974); Thérèse Précheur-Canonge, *La vie rurale en Afrique romaine d'après les mosaïques* (1962).

Marcel Renard, "Technique et agriculture en pays trevire et remois," in *Latomus*, **18** (1959); Mikhail I. Rostovtzeff, *The Social and Economic History of the Roman Empire*, 2d ed., P. M. Fraser, ed. (1957); Emilio Sereni, *Storia del paesaggio agrario italiano* (1961); Alastar Small, ed., "Monteirsi" in *British Archaeological Reports, Supp. Ser.*, **20** (1977); Stephen Spurr, *Arable Cultivation in Roman Italy*, Roman Society Monographs No. 3 (1986), and "The Cultivation of Millet in Roman Italy," in *Papers of the British School at Rome*, **51** (1983); Kenneth D. White, *Farm Equipment of the Roman World* (1975), *Roman Farming* (1970), *Agricultural Implements of the Roman World* (1967), and "Wheat-Farming in Roman Times," in *Antiquity*, **37** (1963); Cedric A. Yeo, "The Overgrazing of Ranch Lands in Ancient Italy," in *Transactions of the American Philosophical Association*, **79** (1948).

FOOD

Jacques André, *L'alimentation et la cuisine à Rome* (1961); Don R. and Patricia Brothwell, *Food in Antiquity* (1969); Dorothy J. Crawford, "Food: Tradition and Change in Hellenistic Egypt," in *World Archaeology*, **11** (1979); R. W. Davies, "The Roman Military Diet," in *Britannia*, **2** (1971); J. K. Evans, "Wheat Production and Its Social Consequences in the Roman World," in *Classical Quarterly*, **31** (1981); Robert J. Forbes, *Studies in Ancient Technology*, 9 vols. (1955–1964); Lynn Foxhall and H. A. Forbes, "*Sitometreia*: The Role of Grain as a Staple Food in Classical Antiquity," in *Chiron* (Munich), **12** (1982); Peter Garnsey, "Grain for Athens," in *CRUX: Essays Presented to G.E.M. de Ste. Croix*, Paul Cartledge and David Harvey, eds. (1985); Peter Garnsey, Tom Gallant, and Dominic Rathbone, "Thessaly and the Grain Supply of Rome," in *Journal of Roman Studies*, **74** (1984).

Naum Jasny, "Competition Among Grains in Classical Antiquity," in *American Historical Review*, **47**:4 (1941), and "The Daily Bread of the Ancient Greeks and Romans," in *Osiris*, **9** (1950); Edward J. Kenney, ed., *Moretum*, Appendix Vergiliana (1983), and *Moretum = The Ploughman's Lunch: A Poem Ascribed to Virgil* (1984); L. Alfred Moritz, *Grain-Mills and Flour in Classical Antiquity* (1958); Geoffrey E. Rickman, *The Corn Supply of Ancient Rome* (1980); Kenneth D. White, "Food Requirements and Food Supplies in Classical Times in Relation to the Diet of the Various Classes," in *Progress in Food and Nutritional Science*, **2**:4 (1976).

Foodstuffs, Cooking, and Drugs

DON R. BROTHWELL

PACKAGED PRECOOKED FOODS and microwave cooking in modern societies provide great contrasts with the food selecting, cooking, and eating habits of peoples of early Mediterranean societies, yet many traditions of today's kitchen and table stem from the ancient world. The peoples of that time mainly prepared their food in technologically simple ovens, or by boiling and roasting; other items were eaten raw. A variety of caldrons, saucepans, bowls, frying pans, large platters, pestles, and strainers was developed. Knives and spoons were important, although it is likely that a much wider variety of food was eaten with the fingers than is customary in most societies today.

During the period considered here, changes occurred at a dietary level. Some new foods appeared, and by Roman times there was far more use of sauces for meats and vegetables. The eating habits of rich and poor Athenians or Romans could be similar in some basic respects, but probably the major difference was in the amount of animal protein available. Earlier Greek and later Roman society probably contrasted somewhat in attitudes to eating and amounts eaten, the former eating more sparingly. A substantial Roman dinner consisted of three parts, the appetizer (*gustatio*), main course (*mensae primae*), and dessert (*mensae secundae*). In the first were egg dishes, vegetables (including asparagus, pumpkins, and mushrooms), seafood, and snails. The main course concentrated on red meats and poultry, and a dessert of fruit or sweet foods followed. A wine and honey mix (*mulsum*) could be available to begin the meal, but most wine was consumed after the courses were finished. In order to give an idea of the variety of foodstuffs available, and of food changes that took place through time, some of the more important categories of food are considered separately.

Cereal Grains

Without doubt, the major carbohydrate foods of Greece and Rome were derived from cereals, supplying perhaps 70 percent of most individual calorie needs. Various graminivorous species have a long history of domestication in the Mediterranean area back to the Neolithic, although not all were equally adapted to the variable environments or were viewed equally favorably by earlier human communities. Limited evidence suggests that early Greek localities grew predominantly barley and less wheat, while Roman preferences appear to have been the reverse. This difference was dictated by poor crop rotation practices, too little manure, and poor soil. The earlier, less developed spelt, emmer, and einkorn wheats eventually gave way to bread wheat. Pliny the Elder refers to the barley grain pastes made by the Greeks, and by classical times the peasant diet also consisted of bread and barley gruel, to which would probably have been added some dairy products, olives, figs, or to a lesser extent meat and salt fish. By the fifth century B.C., food for rich and poor was becoming more differentiated; with the emergence of Athens' greatness, meals for the rich there became more exotic and the importance of cereals was demoted. Aristotle recorded that to protect the poor and impose some economic control, grain guardians were created to control market prices in relation to meal and bread. Serious and extensive shortages occurred in parts of Greece about 330 B.C. and this resulted in the free distribution of large amounts of grain in various parts of the mainland and on the islands.

In contrast to many localities, Athens by the time of Solon (about 590 B.C.) was probably forced to import foreign grain, and markets for wheat were explored in Sicily, Pontus (northern Asia Minor), Cyprus, Egypt, and Thrace. Other areas of Greece, such as grain-rich Boeotia, did not have this problem. Many varieties of bread evolved, and the bakers of Athens were reputed to make the finest. Forms of biscuit and other foods with flour as a major component were also produced, sometimes with the addition of honey, cheese, milk, wine, and other ingredients.

By Roman times in Italy, wheat was the favored cereal, and except in times of shortage, barley was used more to feed farm livestock. Several varieties of wheat were evolved. In terms of output, the lowlands of the Po valley were an important grain-producing area. Because of the vast quantities produced in some areas and the need to store the surplus for eventual use or trading purposes, grain stores were developed. Rome in particular drew on the grain surplus of various areas, and by the end of the first century B.C., about a third of its supply of grain was being shipped from Egypt and Africa. Estimates of wheat yields are given by early writers, the average probably being between 7 1/2 and 22 1/2 bushels per acre (five and fifteen quintals per hectare)—or around a third of the yields produced in Italy and other parts of Europe today.

If one considers that the population of Rome may well have been 750,000 by the first century B.C. and was to increase considerably over the next few centuries, and that each individual used around 440 pounds (200 kg) of grain a year, then the overall grain needs for Rome probably increased to somewhere between 110,200 and 220,500 tons (100,000–200,000 t) a year. No wonder then that large quantities of surplus grain were transported to Rome from grain-producing areas: Etruria, Umbria, and Campania in the vicinity of Rome, as well as farther afield from Sicily, Sardinia, North Africa, and Egypt. Feeding the large numbers in Rome, especially the poor and the growing numbers of slaves, became an increasing problem. This was resolved by the creation of the grain dole, and it has been estimated that by 46 B.C. over 300,000 people in the city were probably collecting free rations of grain, although numbers may have been limited. This form of public assistance fluctuated in extent over the years. In the third century A.D., oil became part of the dole, and for a time bread replaced grain. Even pork fat and wine were added to the basic cereals for a time, but in the late empire these free food distributions came to an end.

Although milling and baking were originally separate occupations and baking was done commercially by the sixth century B.C., there was an increased merging of these jobs by the second century B.C., and the whole process of bread production from start to finish became a major industry in Rome. Leavened bread replaced unleavened, and the distribution of this and other cereal products demanded some organization. Bread from refined wheat flour was considered superior to unsieved wholemeal bread, and barley bread was considered to be less nourishing or digestible. Pliny the Elder states that Picentine bread (made by the inhabitants of Picenum, eastern Italy) was made from spelt grits that were initially soaked for some days and then mixed with raisin juice to form a dough. This was then oven-baked in earthenware pots that broke during the heating. Galen (d. A.D. 199) especially recommended bread baked in large ovens as being the most digestible and tasty. The richer members of society had a range of breads, some prepared with milk, eggs, suet, honey, or cheese, as well as sweeter cakes and pastries. The poorer members of the community were more likely to have eaten coarse, high fiber bread, as well as grain pastes and possibly millet porridge. Salt was not always used in breadmaking.

Legumes (Pulses)

These high-protein vegetables have a long history of cultivation and use in various parts of the world. About twenty different species have been utilized; however, only a restricted number of leguminous plants were important in the Mediterranean. They were used as food crops for both men and cattle, and by Roman times were being used in crop rotations with cereals. Their edible portion was the seed (bean, pea, lentil, etc.).

The broad bean (*Vicia faba*) probably has a Neolithic center of origin in the Near East, with the expansion of its use down the Nile, toward India, and along the Mediterranean coasts. It had spread into more northern parts of Europe by Iron Age times, and there are numerous references to it in classical Greek and Roman literature. Anecdotes suggest that the Greeks and Romans did not view legumes as very important foods, and it may be that they suspected that legumes could have toxic effects. Favism, which can result in anemia and jaundice, is produced in some people by the consumption of broad beans. Pythagoras probably suffered from a hereditary disposition to favism, and was certainly against the eating of beans. Similarly, the paralytic disease lathyrism, which resulted from the overconsumption of the pea from the small hardy vetch plant *Lathyrus sativus*, was known by the time of Hippocrates (469–399 B.C.).

Greek and Roman writers also mention the pea (*Pisum sativum*), another legume species with a history dating to Neolithic times, but it did not appear to be popular. Peas were cooked from the dried form, usually by boiling and with the addition of other foods such as leeks, coriander, pepper, lovage, oil, eggs, birds, Lucanian sausages, and cuttlefish. Lentils also became a common food and were especially esteemed by the Egyptians, and indeed a reference in Martial (ca. A.D. 40–ca. 104) shows that the Romans regarded it as an Egyptian food plant. It is recorded that in the reign of the emperor Gaius (Caligula), an Egyptian obelisk was transported to Rome, using lentils as a packing. Like the seeds of other varieties of pulse, lentils were boiled and could be used as a principal food with mussels or chestnuts or on their own with flavoring. In general, legumes have been the "poor man's food," but nevertheless a nutritious one.

AGRICULTURE AND FOOD

Garden Vegetables and Salad Plants

Except for pulses, the majority of vegetables eaten by Greeks and Romans provided variety and taste rather than high nutritional value. However, their value in providing vitamins and essential trace elements should not be underestimated when considering the diet of ancient peoples. Certain vegetables were used differently in the past; for instance, the Greeks believed in the medicinal value of asparagus and carrots. Also, in pre-Christian times in southern Europe only the leaves of beet were used as a potherb, and in fact it was not cultivated to any extent until the third century A.D. On the other hand, the Spanish salsify was used as a root crop by the ancient Greeks but is uncommonly cultivated and used now. Moreover, in Greek and Roman times certain vegetation was used as a wild food resource, such as alexanders (a pot herb or vegetable), bryony (root having a purgative quality), and butcher's broom (wild myrtle of Dioscorides), as well as parsnip, which did not become cultivated until later medieval times. In the case of lettuce, its cultivation may extend back nearly 6,000 years, and it was probably a common crop in early Egypt, eventually spreading widely in the Mediterranean and becoming popular with Greeks and Romans, possibly moving north with Roman legions. Nevertheless Pliny the Elder refers to at least five wild varieties of lettuce with tougher, more strong-tasting leaves, which seemed mainly of medicinal value. Of root, stem, and leaf crops used in the classical world, onion and its relatives leek and garlic have been of special value. The antiquity of these food species of *Allium* extends back to the First Dynasty in Egypt. There is a biblical reference to them, and Bronze Age remains have been found in Jericho (Ariba). By the time of Theophrastus (fourth century B.C.) and Pliny the Elder (first century A.D.), several onion varieties had been named. Leeks were also cultivated early in the Near East. Remains of garlic at the Roman legionary fortress of Novaesium (Neuss, in western West Germany) would support the contemporary comments that it was a military food and encouraged warriors to be courageous; in general, the Greeks and Romans did not use it domestically. Radish may have been used as a food in the eastern Mediterranean as early as the third millennium B.C., and both Greek and Roman writers refer to regions that produced particularly good varieties. Marcus Gavius Apicius, the first-century A.D. Roman gourmet, suggested that it be served with sauce made from fermented salt-fish liquid (*liquamen*) and pepper. Living at the time of Tiberius, Apicius was known even in his day as an inventor of tasty culinary items. His book is the only one to survive of this early period, and in fact is represented by ninth-century, not Roman, manuscripts. Oil of radishes is mentioned in Roman supplies; it was used for cooking purposes instead of olive oil. And a letter of a Roman soldier records that one type of radish was used as a purge or emetic.

The turnip and related species may initially have been attractive for their oil-seed potential, and are thought to have been domesticated in more than one center between the Mediterranean and India by about 2000 B.C. However, in at least some parts of Europe the turnip may have been first used for food, being taken north for that purpose by the Romans. It was considered in Athens that the best came from Thebes. The Romans, who also appreciated certain regional varieties, boiled turnips and flavored them with a mixture of cumin, rue, asafetida, honey, vinegar, *liquamen,* boiled-down grape juice (*defrutum*), and a little oil.

Without doubt one of the most important green foods was cabbage (*Brassica oleracea*), and although there is little archaeological evidence of it, it is thought to have been in widespread use in the Middle East by 2000 B.C. Not only was it appreciated as a food, but both Greek and Roman writers attribute medicinal qualities to it in preventing drunkenness, in treating colic and paralysis, and even in preventing plague. A variant of this species is the cauliflower, which may not have been developed into a large-headed variety until the Middle Ages. White mustard, also a *Brassica* species, is used today not only as a condiment but also for salad leaves, and both may have been so used in the past. From the Late Helladic site of Marmariani, Thessaly (northeastern Greece, northeast of Larissa), a bag of these seeds has been found. Letters by Roman troops with references to food make mention of jars of mustard and bundles of cabbages.

Greek words for such plants as cucumber, pumpkin, chicory, celery, and leek suggest a Bronze Age or earlier origin for these plants. Other than the cucumber seeds found at ancient Calah (Nimrud, in Iraq), little is known archaeologically. There is little doubt that the use of cucumber spread widely in Europe and Asia in pre-Christian times, being known to the Israelites. The Greeks record that Antioch cucumbers were especially good. Apicius recommends that peeled cucumber be served with *liquamen;* it was also served in a stew with boiled brains, honey, and other foods.

The artichoke appears to be native to the Mediterranean area and was domesticated and spread in pre-Christian times. Mentioned by Dioscorides Pedanius (*fl.* first century A.D.), its food value was doubted by Galen but recommended by Columella in his *On Agriculture,* and perhaps inevitably included in Apicius with the additions and dressings usual to his descriptions and instructions.

Nuts

The wild harvest of nuts, high in protein and oil, has been used by man since prehistory, and the main changes during classical times were in the distribution of the trees and the way in which they were used. The sweet almond grows in frost-free climates and is a native of parts of the Mediterranean. Well-cultivated and mature trees can produce as much as half a ton of nuts per acre. It is thus no wonder they have a long history of use, and were once called the "Greek nut," their antiquity in this area being established to the Neolithic age. The southern part of Italy was similarly ideal for this tree, and it became important to the Romans, who were probably responsible for its gradual extension into northern Europe.

The walnut, originating probably in the Middle East, became extensively cultivated in southern Europe. The Greeks called it the "royal Persian nut" and other names. From Attica, the trees were eventually established in Italy. Hazelnuts also acquired regional and other names, being referred to by the Greeks as "Pontic nuts." The tree was frequently mentioned in Roman literature, and from careful observations on the growth of the hazel in the spring, predictions were made about the success of the cereal harvest.

The sweet chestnut had a more restricted distribution in the European area prior to the Romans, who were probably responsible for its planting in more northern countries to some extent. It is uncertain whether the generic name for this tree, *Castanea,* comes from the town of that name in Thessaly, since its original homeland was probably Asia Minor. Pliny the Elder was aware of nine varieties and noted that when roasted and ground, the nut provided an alternative form of flour, not a food for the more prosperous members of the community. According to Apicius, various nuts were included in sauces for birds, and for certain other meats. Chestnuts were also cooked with lentils. In one way or another, all parts of Roman society consumed nuts, and it is known that the army made good use of these foods too. Archaeological evidence shows that the legionaries of Vindonissa (Windisch, in Switzerland) ate sweet chestnuts, walnuts, hazelnuts, and beechnuts.

Herbs and Condiments

Although not essential from a nutritional point of view, there is no doubt that natural food additives have a long history and have assisted the tastiness of food. Early Assyrian and Babylonian gardens grew such plants as cumin, sesame, mint, basil, coriander, anise, thyme, bay, fennel, saffron, and sage. Other spices such as sage and rosemary were also used by the early Egyptians, so that early Greek and Roman cooking were influenced by a variety of earlier experiments with such additives. Silphium was one herb that was costly and prized, and it became a scarce item by Pliny the Elder's time (first century A.D.). Juice was extracted from the stem and root, and was only used in very small quantities to flavor food. Greek and Roman spice imports included myrrh, cinnamon, cassia (oil-producing Chinese cinnamon), and cardamon. *Liquamen* (or *garum*) was invented by the Greeks about the fourth century B.C. A clear, golden liquid derived from fish fermented in brine, it was a salty sauce with a fishy-cheesy edge that was used in a variety of ways. A number of towns, including Pompeii, were famous for the *liquamen* produced there. Salt was widely valued from Neolithic times, and vinegar may well have appeared on the scene naturally, as a result of soured wine. Both were seen to be valuable for preserves. Vinegar was also diluted as a refreshing drink and was used by the Roman army.

Medicinals and Drugs

A wide range of organic substances were considered to have prophylactic, curative, or healing value, and some plants have already been mentioned in this respect. Watercress was considered to have medicinal value from the first century A.D. until quite recent times. Initially the Greeks used celery medicinally, but later it was seen to be of value in flavoring. The *Iliad* refers to various substances derived from plants that could remove pain or had other medical qualities. While the Hippocratic writers were interested in such substances, it was Theophrastus who produced a more systematic and critical evaluation of these plants. Thus, he considers the potential value of peony, but rejects some of the stories associated with it; also he makes favorable comment on the use of mandrake to prevent pain and in so doing perpetuated the myth of its drug value. Certain plants were seen to affect the personality; strychnos was believed to induce madness, while the root of oleander in wine made an individual cheerful and relaxed. Bryony root was recommended as a depilatory and to remove freckles, and the root of male fern was used normally as a drug and anthelminthic. Cyclamen root was used for boils, and "wild cucumber" for leprosy and sheep mange.

The use of other plants is uncertain. Herodotus was aware that the Scythians used hemp for narcotic effects, but its use as a narcotic elsewhere in Europe is uncertain, even though prehistoric hemp seeds have been found at various European sites. Similarly, opium poppy occurs at various sites, and from the Late Minoan III site at Gazi (on the northern coast of Crete) a terra-cotta statuette was found of a goddess with opium poppy capsules on a head decoration. By Roman times, opium was used in wine to induce sleep or as dried latex lozenges for swallowing.

The culmination of Greek and Roman inquiries into and experimental use of a wide variety of plants and drugs was the five-volume work of Dioscorides Pedanius. Incorporating Indian and Egyptian pharmacological knowledge, this mid-first-century book became a valued reference work for the next fifteen hundred years.

Fruit

The cultivation of the fleshy fruits developed naturally from their exploitation as an attractive wild food resource. While they vary in calorific value, their generally sweet tastes are universally attractive. Some are important sweetening agents and are used in alcohol production; others are largely of nutritional value for their vitamin content. Early Greek and Roman communities, at all levels of society, used fleshy fruits, either raw, dried, in cooked dishes, or as some form of preserve. Some wild fruits continued to be used long after the domestication of other species. For example, the strawberry tree (*Arbutus unedo*) and its edible fruit is mentioned by Theophrastus, and in Roman Italy strawberries formed part of the wild food resources of the forest.

In contrast to most other fruits, dates are low in water and high in sugar content. They were used in the eastern Mediterranean by about 4500 B.C. (on the evidence of Egyptian date pits), and Pliny the Elder states that they were valued in the classical world, a number of varieties coming from Judea. Dates were used at times in bread and the sweet syrup was mixed into sauces. Species of *Prunus* provide the sweet cherry, plum, peach, and apricot, and probably had their origin in Asia. The cherry was known to Theophrastus, but it is uncertain when it first became domesticated. It was certainly valued and spread during the expansion of the Roman Empire; then it appeared to decline during medieval times. Apricots and plums arrived late in Rome, and do not appear to have become important. Similarly, peaches were not widely used and were extremely expensive.

On the other hand, apples and pears, which are botanically related, appear to have considerable antiquity in Greece and Rome, and were cultivated there since at least early historic times. Archaeological evidence of wild pear extends to the Neolithic in Greece, and Theophrastus was impressed by the amount of fruit even the wild tree produced. Domestic forms of apple became a popular source of food.

Except for those discussed below in more detail, no other fruits seem to have been of major importance to the early Mediterranean societies. Raspberry gets brief mention, and strawberry was probably only cultivated sporadically until the fifteenth century A.D., although wild strawberry was to be found in Roman gardens as far back as 200 B.C. The Roman army seems to have been well supplied with fruit when the seasons permitted, and at Vindonissa apples, pears, plums, cherries, peaches, grapes, and elderberries were all being eaten.

Figs

The fruit of the fig tree has been eaten since ancient times either fresh or dried and as a preserve. The dried fig can have a sugar content of over 50 percent, and was thus an important sweetening agent. Cultivation from seed was early recognized as not ideal, and figs have usually been propagated by grafting or from cuttings. Fig trees, bushes, and vines can grow on stony ground and in thin soil cover, and grow best on well-drained slopes. Early archaeological evidence of the fig has been found at Neolithic Jericho and at several Greek Neolithic sites, although its center of origin was probably more southerly, in the fertile region of southern Arabia through to India.

A variety of references to the fig occur in Greek and Roman literature. Greek mythology records that the goddess Ge transformed her son Sykeus into a fig tree to save him from Zeus. Ficus, the generic name of the tree, comes from the name of a sacred fig tree *Ficus ruminalis*, which Roman legend states was the one that sheltered the infants Romulus and Remus (*ca.* 746 B.C.) while they were protected by a she-wolf and a woodpecker (Pliny the Elder, *Natural History* 15.18).

In the diet of ancient Rome, the three important trees were olive, vine, and fig, and these were symbolically planted in the Forum Romanum. Columella points out that the dried fig was of particular value as a food during the unproductive winter period, and Cato reduced the bread ration to his slaves when the figs were ripe. Pliny the Elder records twenty-nine varieties in Italy, a reflection not only of their popularity, but also the fact that various parts of the country were ideally suited to this plant. Apicius relates that figs were boiled with ham, a delicious combination; also that they could be preserved in honey.

Citrus Fruits

It tends to be forgotten that citrus fruits, widespread, high-vitamin-C foods today, were greatly restricted in distribution in classical times, and were not regarded as important. Indeed, there is clear evidence that orange, lemon, and lime only became common in the Middle Ages as a result of Arabic influence. A late Roman mosaic, possibly removed from Tusculum (near Frascati, southeast of Rome) shows that they were at least known earlier, and they appear in frescoes and mosaics at Pompeii, but probably as imported exotic fruits. Only the citron became important in the early Mediterranean, being probably first cultivated in the Near East and known to the Greeks as the "Persian apple." This small evergreen tree is influenced by frosts or high temperatures and thus tends to be restricted to coastal regions. Most important in the distribution of citron has been its association with the religious practices of the Jews, and although there has been some dispute as to when citron might first have been used in the Sukkoth (Feast of Booths), it is certainly likely by the fifth century B.C. A model of a citron from twelfth-century B.C. Egypt provides archaeological evidence of its earlier move westward into North Africa. By the first century A.D. Jewish communities had established its use along the Mediterranean coast, and these areas are today the ones that tend to be important citrus-growing areas.

Non-Jewish peoples remained for some time unimpressed by citron, and at the time of Theophrastus the Greeks viewed it as inedible. Pliny the Elder had the same opinion, but citron gradually became recognized not only for its possible medicinal but also food value. Jewish communities may well have encouraged the early use of other citrus fruits as well, and indeed the Talmud refers to the "sweet citron" (orange). By early Christian times, oranges and lemons appear in Hellenistic and Roman art and literature, but their cultivation may not have been fully established then. With the decline of the Roman Empire, these fruits may have become rare again, only later to be reintroduced by the Arabs.

Olives

One of the most important crops of the Mediterranean area for some millennia has been the olive, which thrives in relatively dry calcareous soil and matures in such conditions within about eight years. Although now in decline, it has been estimated that there are still over 500 million trees. Since its increasing cultivation by Bronze Age times in Greece, it has in fact changed little as a plant. Two varieties are recognized in this area, a cultivated *sativa* and a "wild" or less developed oleaster form. In fact there are about thirty-five species in the world as a whole, and sometime in the fourth millennium B.C. in the eastern Mediterranean, two of these probably gave rise to the cultivated forms. This supposition is based on the fact that the considerable variation in the olive kernels from the site of Byblos (Jubayl, in Lebanon) suggests that more than one species was involved. From these early beginnings, the value of the olive was increasingly seen by peoples in more and more easterly areas, with further diversification occurring in the Aegean and in southern Italy. Once established, olive groves were usually long-lived, and each tree could be relied on to provide a considerable amount of edible oil; in fact 110 pounds (50 kg) of fruit is produced by the mature plant. Archaeological evidence for the early use of olives comes from various sites. From Bronze Age Crete, olive stones and vats for separating the oil have been found (the process being one of crushing the fruit, immersing it in hot water, and separating off the oil). By the sixth century B.C. it was realized that the olive tree produced a good crop in alternate years, and the early Greek economy had to adapt to this cycle accordingly. The Cretan palaces with their storage areas and large storage jars bear witness to the careful plans to keep olive oil in regular supply. If calculations are correct, the storage capacity of the west magazine of the palace of Knossos could alone have been in the region of 16,000 gallons (60,549 l).

Not only did olive oil become an important food commodity, it was also drawn into religious rituals. Viewed through time, olives probably fluctuated in importance, with a marked decline in the Greek Dark Ages and subsequent improvement by classical times. With an increase in Greek colonial activity, the olive followed the movement of wine westward. Writings confirm that by 600 B.C. the olive was well established in Italy. Not all parts of Greece were equally involved in colonization, and Athens together with Attica specialized in olive and wine production to the extent that these items could be marketed for wheat, without the necessity to colonize.

Eventually, the growing, gathering, and processing of olives became a fine art, as Varro relates. He recommends careful picking for the best oil yields, with the best class of olive for eating and the seconds for oil production. The olives for oil were placed in a single layer on shelves until reasonably soft; they could not be left in heaps to go soft as the oil could then become rancid. Ideally ripe olives were then submitted to the *trapetus,* a milling and crushing device of hard and rough stones. Varro noted that the watery residue left after collecting the oil, called *amurca,* could be used as a low-grade fuel, a manure, and as a form of natural weedkiller. Thus, it was used to keep weeds down around the olive trees. The Romans were well aware of the tolerance of the olive to rock terrain and poor soils, and Cato gave explicit instructions as to the type of olive to plant in the different soil types.

Apicius points out that green olives are ideal for oil production, and that an ideal way of preserving green olives is to immerse them in oil. He mentions salted olives in relation to boiled chicken, and chopped fresh olives as stuffing in birds to be boiled. Olives were also added to vegetables, and could be used as an accompaniment in the preparation of cabbage or leeks. The oil was also of value in the manufacture of perfume, as a body lotion, and even as a lamp fuel.

Grapes and Grape Products

The grapevine has been one of the most important cultivated plants of man for the last three thousand years, and its domestication dates from about 4500 B.C. This perennial woody plant is ideally suited to a Mediterranean climate at lower altitudes, and the first center of domestication was probably in southwest Asia. The juicy nature of the berry fruit is ideal for beverage-making, and natural fermentation is usual as the wine yeast occurs inevitably on the skin of the grape. As the juice contains between 15 and

25 percent sugar (dextrose plus levulose), fermentation results in a moderately alcoholic drink. Raisins are the natural consequence of the fruit being sun dried. Literally thousands of varieties of grapevine have evolved, but initially there was only one wild species, *Vitis vinifera.*

Archaeologists have found grape pips at the eastern Macedonian site of Sitagroi or Photolivos (*ca.* 4500–2000 B.C.), the earlier vines probably being wild and the more recent ones cultivated. Pips from fourth-millennium B.C. grapes have also been found in Egypt and Syria, and may indicate cultivation. Finds of pips, stalks, and dried skins provide clear evidence that viticulture was well established in the Aegean in the Bronze Age. Gradually the domesticated vine extended westward to Phoenician settlements, as well as eastward, and it is thought to have been cultivated in parts of Italy by Etruscan times. Further movement of the vine was influenced by Roman conquests of Italy's main river valleys. The spread of early Christianity also helped to consolidate its importance, as the consecration of the Mass demands an availability of wine.

Theophrastus and other Greek writers were well aware of the water, soil, and climatic needs of the vine, as well as the best way of propagation and the need in some cases for pruning. The religious views of the Greeks demanded the ritual use of wine. Dionysius, the wine god, is a suitable reminder of the important links between wine and religious beliefs. Epic literature also provides considerable evidence of the place of wine in Greek culture, the *Iliad* and *Odyssey* providing plenty of bibulous comment. The great variety of wine jugs (amphorae) bowls (kraters), beakers (kotylai), and shallow drinking cups (kylikes) provide material evidence of social drinking. Water was normally mixed with wine in a krater before being poured into a drinking vessel. Greek amphorae for containing and transporting wine were large, fine-quality vessels. For the wealthy, there were also superior molded wine glasses to be purchased by the fifth century B.C., and by the end of the first century B.C. the invention of glass blowing enabled glassware to become common in the classical world.

With the development of Roman vineyards, domestic wine became a common Roman drink, but Greek wine continued to be highly prized. (It is recorded that Lucullus distributed after a voyage no fewer than 100,000 amphorae of Greek wine to the Romans.) Eventually Roman wines improved. Cato makes the point that wine production was a profitable part of agriculture, and gives good advice to wine growers. To increase the range of tastes, various substances were added to the wine in one way or another. An amphora from Carpow (Caledonia, Scotland) had wine flavored with horehound. The Greeks added small amounts of salt water. *Mulsum* was a honeyed wine, sometimes recommended medicinally. Wine could be infused with aniseed, treated with pomegranates, or have rose leaves steeped in it. At times a little myrrh was added, for it was considered to help to preserve the wine. Boiled-down must (unfermented grape juice) was used by both Greeks and Romans in food preparation, two strengths being usual, *sapa* and *defrutum* (half and one-third the original volume). Both Greeks and Romans looked to the north for potential wine markets. By the sixth century B.C., the Gauls were drinking Greek wine, although barley beer was their indigenous and established drink. Roman wine boats were relatively small and could carry up to 3,000 amphorae. Eventually, wooden casks replaced the ceramic amphorae in the transport of wine; the changeover appears to have happened in Pliny the Elder's time (first century A.D.).

Wine was not only exported for commercial reasons, but it also helped sustain

Roman armies outside Italy, where both officers and men consumed it. From the information on amphorae at the legionary fortress of Vindonissa, it is clear that wine had come from southern Italy, Sicily, southern Gaul (France), and Spain. Possibly as a result of Roman occupation, sheltered vineyards may have been developed even as far north as Britain.

Red Meat Animals

By the dawn of the classical age, in the Mediterranean, most animals valued for food had been undergoing some degree of domestication for 4,000 to 8,000 years. Great changes had occurred in the general body size of livestock and in other morphological respects, and the knowledge of animals and the husbandry of those on the farm had become considerable. This can be judged from the *History of Animals* of Aristotle, who gives a wealth of biological and stock-breeding facts and is in serious error with only a modest number of observations. The four major food-producing animals in the ancient world were cattle, sheep, goats, and pigs.

By post-Mycenaean times, both long- and short-horned forms of cattle were kept in Greece. Homer gives the impression that cattle were numerous at the time, but in some parts of Greece herd densities decreased as human populations increased. Epirus became famous cattle country, and Aristotle was so impressed with the animals there that his account gives somewhat distorted facts about size and milk yield. In contrast, few cattle were raised in Attica. Cattle were important in certain temple rituals, and the best were selected for this sacrificial purpose. Of the dairy products butter appears to have been unimportant, and although some cheese may have been produced, this was mainly prepared from the milk of sheep and goats.

Romans prized cattle more than other large livestock, and they were seen to be more expensive animals to keep than sheep or pigs. Although present archaeological evidence represents all too few sites, there is growing evidence that beef was more important than previously believed and was eaten as often as pork in some areas. Probably most of this meat would have come from older animals, both cows and oxen, that had been used as traction animals. It is interesting to note that Apicius mainly excludes beef from his account, although he mentions a number of fried and boiled veal dishes. Possibly this was because older animals were more commonly killed and were then eaten by the less privileged levels of society.

Pigs, both wild and domestic, were being consumed in the Aegean by Neolithic times. Greater forestation during later phases of prehistory would certainly have encouraged the survival of wild pigs and ensured the availability of forest resources (especially acorns and beechnuts) as food for the domesticated variety. Roasting was probably the commonest way of cooking the meat in early days, but Romans later boiled it in sea water and served it with hot or cold sauces. Roman domestic pigs were smaller than the wild species, although both must have been available at times in much of the empire. As shown by the number of pig bones found at archaeological sites, pigs usually made up between 50 and 75 percent of the sample; large collections from Roman and Pompeiian sites contain just over 50 percent of pig bones. Young pigs were well in evidence, and this clearly relates to the succulent nature of the meat (Apicius gives various recipes for sucking-pig.) As well as keeping them for home consumption, farms would supply pigs to butchers in the local town, to be rendered into pork joints, hams, bacon, and sausages. Like cattle, pigs were used for ritual sacrifices. And for the Roman military diet, Vegetius Renatus recommended that wine, cereals, fruits, and bacon should be stored in forts if there was the possibility of a siege.

Archaeologically, it is far from easy to distinguish between fragmented remains of sheep and goat, so these will be discussed together here. Sheep were very important in early Greece, not only in comparison with goats, but with other domesticated mammals as well. This is not to deny that in the days of Homer, meat from the goat was not a delicacy, and goat's milk was rightly valued for cheesemaking. By classical times, as revealed by art evidence, sheep had noticeable variations. Local stocks may well have been added to by imports on more than one occasion, and Homer refers to good milking sheep that were long-wooled, fat, and long-tailed and that came from Syria or Arabia. Greek farmers clearly undertook some selection of this stock, and Herodotus noted differences between the modified sheep and the original Arabian form. Much of the Greek countryside at this time provided an ideal environment for sheep. Varro and others refer to no fewer than three varieties of Attic sheep, and in other areas local varieties were clearly evolving.

Sheep were generally preferred to goats by Roman farmers. Although goats were used for sacrifice, they were generally less profitable to the farmer and could be more difficult to handle and more destructive of vegetation. One advantage was that goats could survive better on very poor farm land. Roman art commonly depicts goats being milked, and there is no doubt that it was their milk and cheese that made them a worthwhile animal to keep. Columella provides most of the information on Roman sheep husbandry, and it appears that wool was its most important commodity, followed by milk and cheese, with flesh least valuable of all. Nevertheless, archaeologically, Italian samples from both town and country sites suggest that sheep and goats made up a quarter to a third or more of the meat diet.

Few other mammals were regularly as important for food as cattle, pigs, goats, and sheep. As regards wild species, various kinds of deer were hunted widely, and venison was well liked. Deer bones have been found in the food debris at Roman sites at Sette Finestre (in central Italy, overlooking the Tyrrhenian Sea), Ostia, Rome, Pompeii, and Pizzica-Pantanello (southern Italy). A number of these Italian sites also provided evidence of the consumption of hare, and the Romans were responsible for the spread of rabbits in Europe. Apicius provides plenty of ideas for cooking and serving both venison and hare, as well as the most diminutive of all mammal foods, the dormouse. Dormice, he suggests, should be stuffed with minced pork and other minced dormice, pounded with pepper, pine kernels, asafetida, and *liquamen,* and cooked in the oven.

Birds as Food

From the evidence of art, literature, and archaeological food debris, the Greeks and Romans ate numerous species of bird, although there would seem to be some preference for the less strong-tasting land species. There was a variety of devices for catching them, including nets, snares, and cages; and in the case of some species, such as quails, advantage was taken of their migratory behavior. The Greek menu included not only large birds such as swans, ducks, geese, pelicans, cranes, and owls, but also those with smaller body size (pigeons, thrushes, larks, jays, wagtails, and nightingales), of which quite a number might be needed to make a meal.

Romans were similarly inclined, and direct archaeological evidence is provided for example at Sette Finestre where, at the second occupation level, fifteen bird species occur, mainly as food debris. In the case of smaller birds, the Roman meal was "expanded" by the liberal use of condiments, including cheese and silphium. Although nightingales were valued for their singing, Horace and others make it clear that they were also eaten, and in fact a number of kinds of small birds were used both as pets and as food, whereas some of the larger birds were kept specifically to be fattened up for the table. Plutarch mentions cranes and swans in this respect, and geese were similarly fattened. It is debatable whether only the more privileged levels of society ate such a range of birds. Nonetheless, Apicius provides cooking instructions for more than ten different species, and he gives recipes for two sauces for boiled ostrich.

There has been some debate as to how early fowls, ducks, and geese were domesticated in the eastern Mediterranean. Certainly by classical times there were domestic forms, and in the case of the fowl skeletal remains show that there was noticeable variation in body size, suggesting different "breeds." Poultry seem first to be referred to in Greece by Theognis (sixth century B.C.); he and others refer to them as "Persian birds." Some doubts were expressed by Plutarch as to the food value of eggs, but Dioscorides Pedanius thought they had medicinal value. By the second century B.C., cockfighting was established as a sport in Italy, while Varro and Columella show clearly that poultry farming could be very profitable. Cocks in particular were also used as sacrificial animals.

Fish

It would be surprising indeed if the peoples of the classical world had not taken full advantage of the fish resources of the Mediterranean. There are in fact numerous references to fish and fishing in art and literature; archaeology provides additional evidence. The nature of the fish caught and the extent of fishing depended initially on the development of boats to work beyond the coasts, but by classical times this presented no problems. There has been some debate as to whether Homeric literature shows that fish was in preclassical times considered a despised article of food. While the ruling nobles may have viewed it as an inferior food, the Greek populace as a whole is unlikely to have turned away from this important food resource, especially the coastal peoples. Later, there is no doubt that the Greeks had a relish for fish, shellfish, and even marine mammals. The great variety of species eaten, and the ways of cooking them, are detailed in the third book of Athenaeus' *The Learned Banquet*. All kinds of fish, ranging from common to scarce species, were preserved, dried, or pickled. Fish curing became important at centers such as Dioscurias (Sukhumi, on the Black Sea), where there was a good salt supply. Tuna, sprats, mullet, sea bream, mackerel, sturgeon, and other fish were sent back to Greek markets, especially from the Euxine (Black Sea) and Maeotis (Sea of Azov). Strabo gives details of the migrations of the tuna and of its feeding habits, and of the continuation of fishing in winter. He and other writers record that the fishing industry was extended by Greek colonies into parts of the western Mediterranean.

Archaeological evidence of fishing and fish is available from various sites. One of the earliest is Knossos, where fish bones were found in a cooking pot and fish appear on seals, on faience, and on gold models (on which men are depicted holding fish on a line); there are also representations of flying fish. From Thebes, there are not only fish vertebrae but also bronze fishhooks (which have been found at other sites beyond the mainland). By Hellenistic times, fish plates occur of a characteristic type: they contain a central small cup for oil or fish sauce that often shows representations of seafood.

Italy was no less interested in fish as food, and its western coasts were famous for tuna. By Roman times, there is a great variety of art evidence that depicts fish of all kinds, fishing from the shore, and large-scale fishing with nets in the open seas. Later, during the second century B.C., fish were kept in *piscinae* or *vivaria,* artificial ponds, although this was more often for pleasure than to ensure a supply of fresh fish. The fish that were favored for the table or were expensive were not necessarily the fish most commonly valued and eaten today. Sturgeon, Martial tells us, was fit for the emperor's table. Turbot, mackerel, gudgeon, tuna, mullet, bonito, conger eel, moray, sea bream, and the spiny wrasse (or at least its organs) were eaten. Various kinds of fish sauce (*garum* or *liquamen*) were prepared and varied in price. Over a dozen varieties of freshwater fish were also used as food.

Fish were prepared for cooking with or without the vertebrae removed. Some were stuffed with such mixtures as cumin, mint, pennyroyal, peppercorns, nuts, and honey. Various seasoning and dressings could also be added. Fish could be oven-cooked in its own juice, boiled, fried, or grilled.

Other Sea and Shell Foods

Although not as important as other foodstuffs, squid, octopus, and shellfish were eaten to some extent. Mollusks were certainly exploited by Neolithic times, as demonstrated by the discovery of oyster, limpet, and other species at various Greek sites. Squid and octopus also appear in Minoan art. The Romans probably developed a taste for these foods to a greater degree than the Greeks. Oysters were cultivated, and special ponds were constructed called *ostrearia.* Mosaics at Pompeii depict lobster, prawn, and squid. Varieties of land snail were also eaten by all sections of Roman society, and special snail enclosures were created for keeping and "fattening" them.

Apicius provides a range of cookery instructions for such foods. Grilled crayfish, stuffed cuttlefish, boiled sea urchin, squid rissoles, and cooked mussels were a few of the dishes, served with dressings and sauces. A dish called *Embractum Baianum,* after the town of Baiae on the Gulf of Cumae (Bay of Naples), consisted of mussels, minced oysters, jellyfish, toasted pine nuts, Jericho dates, olive oil, *liquamen,* celery, coriander, pepper, and rue. Edible land snails were fried or roasted, used in a vegetable stew, or included in a stuffing for sucking pig. In this, as in various other aspects of cooking, Apicius provides a description of the haute cuisine of the empire, which cannot be considered representative of the food habits and attitudes of all levels of Roman society through time.

Honey

While honey, even of wild bees, would have been appreciated in prehistoric times, domestication of the honey bee probably did not occur in Greece until perhaps the sixth century B.C.; two centuries earlier Homer appears not to know of domestic honey. Yet honey from domestic hives was available in Egypt by the third millennium B.C. and in Mesopotamia by the second millennium. There is clearly much to be established still as regards the spread of domestic hives into Greece and westward. In fact archaeological information of relevance continues to appear, and at a Greek country house near Vari in Attica, late fourth- to early third-century B.C. elongated beehive pots have now been identified. Confirmation of this was obtained by the detailed analysis of pottery residues, which were demonstrated to be beeswax. Attic honey was especially famous, and thyme together with certain other aromatic plants of the Greek uplands resulted in some distinctive flavors.

Various early classical writers make comment on bees, beekeeping, and honey, especially Varro, Columella, and Pliny the Elder. Honey was the most important sweetening commodity available in classical times and was thus economically important, although it is debatable what proportion of these early societies would have had common access to it. At least in some Roman households, honey was sufficiently common to be used in cakes, to be used to cover meat as a short-term preservative, and as a preservative for figs, apples, plums, pears, and cherries.

BIBLIOGRAPHY

Herbert W. Allen, *A History of Wine* (1961); Jacques André, *L'Alimentation et la cuisine à Rome* (1961); Apicius, Barbara Flower and Elizabeth Rosenbaum, *The Roman Cookery Book: A Critical Translation of the The Art of Cooking by Apicius for Use in the Study and the Kitchen* (1958); John Boardman, "The Olive in the Mediterranean," in *Philosophical Transactions of the Royal Society,* Ser. B, **275** (1976); Don Brothwell and Patricia Brothwell, *Food in Antiquity* (1969); R. W. Davies, "The Roman Military Diet," in *Britannia,* **2** (1971); Joan M. Frayn, "Wild and Cultivated Plants," in *Journal of Roman Studies,* **65** (1975), and *Subsistence Farming in Roman Italy* (1979); Peter Garnsey, "Grain for Rome," in Peter Garnsey, Keith Hopkins, and C. R. Whittaker, eds., *Trade in the Ancient Economy* (1983); Erich Isaac, "Influence of Religion on the Spread of Citrus," in *Science,* **129** (1959); John Ellis Jones, "Hives and Honey of Hymettus," in *Archaeology,* **29** (1976); Humfrey Michell, *The Economics of Ancient Greece,* 2d ed. (1957).

Pliny the Elder, *Natural History,* H. Rackham, trans., 10 vols. (1938–1963); John R. T. Pollard, *Birds in Greek Life and Myth* (1977); William Radcliffe, *Fishing From the Earliest Times* (1921); Jane M. Renfrew, *Palaeoethnobotany: The Prehistoric Food Plants of the Near East and Europe* (1973); Charles T. Seltman, *Wine in the Ancient World* (1957); Norman Wilson Simmonds, ed., *Evolution of Crop Plants* (1976); Catherine Delano Smith, *Western Mediterranean Europe: A Historical Geography of Italy, Spain, and Southern France since the Neolithic* (1979); W. B. Storey, "Fig," in Simmonds, ed., *Evolution of Crop Plants* (1976); Reay Tannahill, *Food in History* (1973); Theophrastus, *Enquiry into Plants,* Arthur Hort, trans., 2 vols. (1916); Jocelyn M. C. Toynbee, *Animals in Roman Life and Art* (1973); K. F. Vickery, "Food in Early Greece," in *Illinois Studies in the Social Sciences,* **20** (1936); Giovanna Vitelli, "Grain Storage and Urban Growth in Imperial Ostia," in *World Archaeology,* **12** (1980); Kenneth D. White, "Wheat-Farming in Roman Times," in *Antiquity,* **37** (1963), and *Roman Farming* (1970).

TECHNOLOGY

Theories of Progress and Evolution

G. E. R. LLOYD

It is often assumed that there were two main notions of the past competing in Greco-Roman antiquity: a major, if not a majority, view and a minor one. The overwhelmingly dominant conception, according to this schema, is that the present represents a decline from a Golden Age; the minor view puts the emphasis rather on progress from a primitive stage in the development of human society. Some critical comments concerning this schema will serve to introduce its background.

Myths of the Golden Age are of considerable variety and often great complexity, there being no single, "orthodox" version. Some late literary representations picture the Golden Age, or Age of Cronos, as nothing more than a pastoral idyll. The time before Zeus came to power, and before the world order as we know it now was instituted, was envisioned as one in which there was no need for work, no need in particular to cultivate the land, no marriage, no pain, and no disease. However, two influential Greek accounts—one archaic, the other from the classical period—suggest a degree of ambivalence with regard to the age of Cronos.

Hesiod's (fl. 8th century B.C.) myth of the metals is our earliest extant detailed account. In this, there is a clearly defined sequence of ages, starting with a golden age and proceeding down through silver, bronze, and an age of heroes to the age of iron. Hesiod makes plain his view of the trouble and toil of the world he lived in; it is a world of unremitting labor and pain. Yet the way he expresses his distaste at living in it should be noted (*Works and Days* 174–175): "Would I had died before, or been born later," he writes. The statement holds no tangible hope that better times will come, but merely serves to emphasize the nadir that the present age represents. It may be that the remark reflects the notion that such ages are subject to a cyclical return, but, again, no such idea is elaborated here.

Beyond the question of explicit prophecy, two features of Hesiod's attitudes bear stressing. One is his constant criticisms of the bribe-devouring kings, which would be pointless were he entirely resigned to every aspect of the current miseries and misfortune. Those criticisms presuppose, rather, that the kings have it in their power to pay more, or less, attention to justice, and, up to a point, that presupposition runs counter to Hesiod's statements foretelling doom. Against the pessimism of the myth overall, one should consider Hesiod's express confidence that a just ruler is rewarded by prosperity: his people flourish, mothers bear children who take after their fathers, and the crops are abundant (*Works and Days* 225 ff.).

The second feature germane to the notion of progress is that Hesiod's characterization of earlier ages far from shows a uniform, straightforward decline. Inhabitants of the silver age, for example, remain as children for 100 years and then have only a short maturity. This is hardly a picture of an unequivocally enviable existence, nor one that is intended to seem transparently preferable to the lives of those born into the age of heroes. Although the general superiority of earlier ages to Hesiod's time is clear enough, it is not as if Hesiod could be said to look back at each and every one of them with unqualified nostalgia. Rather, it seems truer to say that one of the morals to be drawn from these contrasts, both among the earlier ages and between them and Hesiod's present, is that we should come to terms with the way we actually are. Human beings were originally made by Zeus; but however much a misfortune womankind might be—and Hesiod is quite uncompromising on the topic—women, like agriculture, are necessary for the race to continue. Similarly, there are disadvantages to marriage, but disadvantages, too, in staying unmarried, mainly the prospect of a lonely old age with no one to care for you.

An appreciably more complex version of the Golden Age motif is found in Plato's *Statesman* (*Politicus*) (269c ff.), offering another example of the ambivalence possible in ancient views about the past. Our age, says Plato, is an age when the cosmos is running in reverse. Originally, the Divine Pilot guided the world by turning it in one direction; when he withdrew, the world, conceived as a living creature, moved in the contrary sense. The picture given of the Age of Cronos presents a world with no sexual reproduction, no agriculture, no political societies, and therefore no wars. Whatever its pacific virtues, the Age of Cronos is an age that again cannot wholly be said to be desirable, at least not one that we as human beings can and should desire. The expressions Plato uses are guarded. If those who lived in those times engaged in philosophy, then indeed they may be deemed to have been most blessed (272bc). But the conditional is to be noted, for the possibility is not asserted as a fact. As in Hesiod, the idea of the Golden Age may be a device used to stress some of the miseries, or at least the shortcomings, of the present age. Yet the kind of life it pictures is not one to which we can aspire and still be the human beings we are.

What was presented as the minority view, in the schema sketched above, turns out, upon analysis, to be anything but a homogeneous position asserting a belief in constant and continuous change for the better. Just as some myths of the Golden Age are vehicles for conveying morals about the present, so stories about the rise of man or of civilization often serve a similar function, and the chronological framework of their expression cannot be held to carry literal historical implications. Descriptions of utopian political arrangements may be presented as the goals we can and should set before ourselves, but more often this blessed state is not an envisageable future; it is placed in a mythical setting lacking concrete connections with, and applications to, the present.

Three further distinctions are necessary. First, when reference is made to past advances, the question arises as to what respect or respects the advances are claimed. We must ask whether we are dealing with progress in, broadly speaking, the technological domain (the invention or discovery of practical techniques and skills), or with refinement of intellectual grasp or understanding, with development in morality, or with some combination of more than one of these. Second, we must distinguish between a general reference to the past rise of civilization and the additional idea of continuing progress; many of those who asserted the former had no conception of the latter. Third, ideas about change for the better may or may not be undercut by beliefs in the cyclical nature of time or by an idea of eternal recurrence (the progress being in those cases just a temporary phase in that cycle). Not that those beliefs are uniform or all-pervasive among the Greeks and Romans: the contrast sometimes drawn between Greco-Roman cyclical ideas of time and Judaic linear ones is generally oversimplified.

Finally, among these preliminaries we should point out that while various ideas of progress can be illustrated from antiquity, the notion of the continuous and ongoing evolution of animal species does not appear as a biological theory. It has, to be sure, been claimed that Anaximander, in the sixth century, and Empedocles, in the fifth, adumbrated some such notion. Thus, Anaximander seems to have seen the lack of self-sufficiency of young humans as posing a problem: How did the first babies survive? The solution he proposed was that the first men were born in some kind of fish. Again, Empedocles wrote of various monstrous creatures—ox-faced men and man-faced oxen—generated at one stage in the cosmic cycle caused by the struggle between the principles he calls Love and Strife, although it should be stressed that this refers to a different stage in that cycle from the one we live in now; how far he would carry a claim that similar processes continue to operate in the world we know is unclear. But while both these philosophers and others, especially the Epicureans, had some idea of the need for animal species, including humans, to be well adapted in order to survive, none saw the whole of the animal kingdom as the product of a single and continuing series of changes controlled by the principle of the survival of the fittest. Meanwhile, the majority view in antiquity was that the animal and plant species we are familiar with are fixed and eternal. Some examples of hybridization and cross-breeding were well known, but their end products were generally deemed to be counternatural.

Hesiod provides one of the strongest statements of the idea of a decline from a past Golden Age; yet he also offers expressions of certain notions of the betterment of the human conditions. The figure of Prometheus in Hesiod is not, to be sure, the culture hero of Aeschylus' *Prometheus Bound.* Yet he did steal fire from heaven and give it to men, and that brought with it certain technological changes. Again, what distinguishes man from an animal is justice, practiced under the auspices of Zeus. It is not that Hesiod places emphasis on a contrast between a pretechnological, presocial state of man and his current position, nor that he approves of much that falls under the head of technological change (he has caustic remarks to make about the follies of seafaring, for example), but, implicitly, the contrast is there.

For statements about the rise of one or another constituent of civilization in the past, and for conjectures about what lies ahead in the future, we have to turn to later authors. In the late sixth century, Xenophanes of Colophon offers a clear, if isolated, statement of the idea that discoveries depend on man's own endeavor. "The gods have not revealed everything to mortals from the beginning: but in time by inquiry men discover what is better" (frag. 18). Still, evidence that would provide the background or frame of this remark is lacking, and we cannot say whether or how far it may have formed part of an explicit and fully elaborated conception of progress.

In the fifth century, much clearer expressions of ideas relevant to one or another notion of progress are to be found in the dramatists, in the evidence for the work of some of the later Presocratic philosophers and early Sophists, and in the historians. The diversity of their views, and the different contexts in which they were developed, should not be underestimated.

Passages in Aeschylus and Sophocles develop the idea that man has emerged from a more primitive past, though in *Prometheus Bound* (442 ff.) this is thanks to the intervention of Prometheus himself, while in Sophocles' *Antigone* (332 ff.) the emphasis is on man's ingenuity. The items chosen to illustrate this emergence should also be noted. Aeschylus mentions man's mastery over the animals, his ability to conquer the sea, his exploitation of metals, and especially his intellectual achievements in mathematics, astronomy, and divination, the interpretation of bird signs, dreams, and so on. In Sophocles, the examples given to illustrate man's cleverness include his conquest over the animal kingdom and the sea, and his development of speech, thought, and the social arts. The effect created by this celebration of the marvelous successes attributable to man's intelligence is then, however, somewhat undercut by the next choral lyric (583 ff.), which develops just as eloquently the themes of human frailty and man's powerlessness in the face of the gods.

These and other passages from Greek tragedy of course present no theories of progress; yet they do indicate a thematic interest in the range of man's capacities and some recognition that the level of achievement deriving from these capacities has not always been constant. For more systematic and coherent accounts of the rise of civilization we may turn to fifth-century prose writers, especially the philosophers and Sophists, though reconstructing their ideas from the scanty and biased sources available to us is in every case problematic. Thus our evidence for Anaxagoras, his pupil Archelaus, and Democritus suggests that all three emphasized that it was man's superior intelligence that set him apart from the other animals. Anaxagoras in particular pointed to the special adaptability of the human hand and argued that because of this man is the most intelligent of creatures.

With the Sophist Protagoras, the problem is not so much one of a lack of evidence, as that of gauging the extent to which what we are told by Plato remains faithful to Protagoras' own ideas. The so-called Great Speech set out in Plato's dialogue the *Protagoras* (320c ff.) gives an elaborate account of man's progress from a primitive state to one of civilization. Some of the ideas it contains are probably original, but there is no doubt that Plato has reworked others. From one point of view, however, that issue is of secondary importance, since the dialogue remains unimpeachable evidence for ideas discussed in the fourth century, whether or not they are the views of the historical Protagoras in the fifth century.

In the Great Speech, Protagoras is made to stress the poverty of man's physical endowments: the other animals are far better equipped by nature to survive, and it was only because of man's capacity to use fire and develop technological skills that the human race has not been eradicated. But the first human gropings, the story continues, led to the brink of disaster, for squabbling and fighting developed, and the survival of the race was once again in jeopardy until shame and justice were sent by Zeus. One of the few things we know with reliability about the historical Protagoras is that he said he knew nothing about the gods; therefore, any reference he might have made to Zeus in such a story would have to be interpreted as part of a mythical framework. Stripped of the reference to divine intervention, the story indicates that the qualities needed to survive within society are to be seen as distinct from, and in addition to, the mere gregariousness that prompts social groupings in the first place. The additional point that is given great stress in the speech is that these necessary political qualities, shame and justice, are distributed to everyone alike, not just to a minority: an idea that shows democratic, or at least antielitist, tendencies, with which Plato himself violently disagreed.

Here, then, is a clear and sustained statement of the rise of man from a primitive existence to civilization. Yet we are still given no suggestion of further advance in the future (the institutions of the city-state are, implicitly, the pinnacle of achievement). Moreover, despite the narrative framework of the story, it is an analytic account rather than a literal and historical one. No doubt Protagoras believed in certain advances that had been made in technology and in the intellectual and sociopolitical domains. But we should interpret his chief concern to be those points he makes about the best regulation of the city-state. He is not offering a serious, detailed reconstruction of man's prehistory.

The fifth-century historians, first Herodotus and then Thucydides, do, of course, attempt realistic and objective accounts of events in living memory, and in both cases they refer more or less directly to the beginnings of Greek and of non-Greek society. The comparison between present-day barbarians and probable past circumstances in Greece itself occurs in writings of both historians. Thucydides (1.6) suggests that in the beginning the Greeks, too, probably carried arms as a matter of course, just as many present-day barbarians do—until the security of the city-state rendered this unnecessary. He also puts into the mouth of a Corinthian addressing a Spartan audience the general dictum that in all the arts, politics included, the latest inventions are an advantage (1.71). Yet neither historian gives a clear sense of the possibility of future progress for Greek culture, let alone for humanity as a whole. Herodotus does celebrate the successes of the Greeks in resisting the threat from Persia. He also expresses his admiration for certain aspects of Near Eastern, especially Egyptian, civilization, from which he believes the Greeks derived many of their ideas and customs. Although this gives concrete expression to certain past advances, neither he nor Thucydides entertains a notion of future progress. Indeed, in Thucydides' discussion of the disasters that had befallen Greece in the war between Athens and Sparta, special emphasis is given to the idea of the moral degeneration that flows from political upheaval, especially from civil war. It is not that Thucydides, in recognizing a certain ebb and flow of cultures, is engaged in a purely mechanical view of the cyclical nature of human history; that would be far too strong an inference to draw, despite his statement that his book should prove useful to subsequent generations, thanks to the way in which history repeats itself. The manner in which that statement is expressed allows, even if it does not presuppose, differences in events between which generic similarities may be recognized. Clearly, the very idea of individuals in the future making use of the lessons Thucydides conveys presupposes the possibility of influencing events, even if he repeatedly stresses both the difficulty of predicting the outcome of events and the general instability of human fortunes.

The contrast with some later historians is marked. Polybius in the second century conveys a definite sense, not just of human technological progress, but also of certain ways in which the Roman republic represents advances on Greek institutions. He is clearly impressed by the Roman rise to power, not just in terms of military and political might, but also in terms of the quality of the ascendant civilization. While some texts revert to the idea of cyclical recurrence in human history, Polybius puts far less emphasis on the inevitability of human decline than many other writers had done. In the next century, Diodorus Siculus prefaces his *Universal History* with a detailed discussion of a quasihistorical kind devoted to the early stages of the development of the world and of human civilization (1.7–9). He tells us that his account draws on earlier writers, and scholarly attempts have often been made to identify likely candidates, Anaxagoras, Archelaus, and Democritus all having been suggested. However, it is probably fairer, certainly safer, to suppose that the account is an amalgam of ideas from different originals, and it may itself go beyond any of them.

So far, our survey of the early Greek sources yields fairly substantial evidence that at least certain aspects of the past progress of human civilization were recognized, but little or none concerning the recognition of future advance as a possibility. The chief context in which the latter idea comes to be developed is in discussions of the growth of the *technai,* which would embrace the arts and the sciences. As we should expect, observations on their past progress are quite a common occurrence, a notable example being the words of the Sophist Hippias of Elis, as represented by Plato in the *Greater Hippias* (281d ff.). There, the claim is made that in every art the best practitioners of the past have been outdone by those at work in contemporary society. But clear expressions of future developments appear as well, especially in the work of the medical writers.

By far the most impressive early statement of this idea comes in the treatise *On Ancient Medicine,* a composition that has been dated variously to the late fifth century or to the early fourth. The writer argues that medicine itself has developed from dietetics, having its origin, indeed, in the need we have to cook our food. He is severely critical of some newfangled speculative theories introduced by doctors who attempt, he says, to found medicine on arbitrary hypotheses or postulates. But the present state of medicine does not represent the highest point it can reach, and will reach, the writer claims, by using the tried and tested methods by which discoveries have been made in the past. Medicine is not, and cannot ever be, an exact science; but it is able to reach a high degree of accuracy, and the expectation is that more discoveries can and will be made.

Many themes in this work can be paralleled in other medical literature. Thus, expressions of the idea that advances are continuing to be made in medicine can be found in Hippocratic works of different types. The writers represented in the surgical and the dietetic treatises, especially, often refer to innovations both in medical theory and in practical modes of therapy. The Sophistic work *On the Art* underlines the general point that intelligence is particularly exhibited in the discovery of what is useful: that application being, for this writer, the mark of true cleverness.

The evidence from the Hippocratic corpus relates in many cases to the fourth century, not to the fifth, and the question of whether, or to what extent, there was a general change of mood or of intellectual climate after the Peloponnesian War has been much debated. It is, however, clear that many of the themes found in fifth-century texts are repeated later. In fact, the idea of the primitive origins from which human civilization sprang becomes commonplace, although it is a theme that is put to different uses and is compatible with very different attitudes toward the possible future course of civilization. Thus, Plato in both the *Republic* (2) and *Laws* (3) develops what are presented as quasihistorical accounts of such a development, notably of the rise of technology and the spread of the arts (accompanied by the spread of luxury). There can, however, be no question of pressing the literal details of these stories. Aristotle, too, picks up the theme that the early stages of human society were largely ignorant and foolish compared with the present day, in a notable text in the *Politics* (1.2, especially 1268b38 ff.). Neither philosopher, however, produces any clear statement of any overall optimism regarding the future moral progress of mankind.

We have already noted a certain ambivalence in Plato's treatment of the theme of the Golden Age in the *Statesman* (*Politicus*). In the *Republic,* his concern throughout is to make recommendations about such matters as the nature of moral and political knowledge, the relationship between knowledge and virtue or excellence, the need for reason to rule both in the state and within the individual, and the importance of training and education. The extended account in books eight and nine of the *Republic* showing the way in which one constitutional type degenerates into the next, each worse than its predecessor, supports these moral and political recommendations, but is in no way intended to incorporate predictions as to what is likely to happen in fact (even though Plato no doubt saw Athenian democracy as increasingly degenerate, and not just because it put Socrates to death).

But here, again, the sequence of events described provides a narrative frame for what is essentially an analytic study; indeed, in this case one designed to be rhetorically persuasive, if not also polemical. In regard to the possibility of implementing Plato's ideal state, the claim is that the *Republic* does not deal in impossibilities. Yet the state it pictures is obviously in many respects impractical. On the other hand, we must remember first that colonies continued to be founded in the fourth century, and constitutions changed, and the opportunities for trying out new measures, or at least new political principles, were therefore far greater then than we are used to or can readily imagine in the modern world. Even without the evidence we have that Plato attempted to win over Dionysius the Elder, tyrant of Syracuse (though these attempts were a series of unmitigated disasters), we may imagine that he might well have entertained some active hopes of the practical application of some of his ideas. The *Laws* contains a set of proposals that could more easily lend themselves to actual implementation. However, he wrote it at the end of his life, and it may be that then he was anything but optimistic about his recommendations being carried out in detail. The important point is that the ideal that Plato described is of a *static* society. If he did not despair of improvements being introduced in the existing order of things, at Athens or elsewhere, it was no part of his thinking that these improvements should be open-ended. The best state, once formed, must be preserved from all future change.

Aristotle firmly rejected the absolutism represented by Plato's theory of forms in the moral and political field, as elsewhere. Yet he shared with Plato a conviction that change, as such, is to be avoided. So far as political-constitutional arrangements go, the city-state represents for Aristotle the culmination of possible progress (he had no inkling of the profound changes introduced in his lifetime by the conquests of Alexander). That does not mean, of course, that he is wanting in suggestions about how actual city-states can be improved. He, too, repeats the theme of past progress that mankind has achieved in the technological and, indeed also, the political spheres. And even though Aristotle, like Plato, makes recommendations whose purpose is to improve education, ensure greater stability in the state, and the like, the city-state is always represented as the best possible type of human community.

Where further advance is possible, and to be expected, is in the realm of theoretical studies, in philosophy and in science. He believes that discoveries have been made many times in the past and then lost. To that extent, the background to his thought is one of a belief in cycles of recurrence in a world itself believed to be eternal (cycles that are mirrored also in the physical domain by the changing relationships between land and sea for instance). He also states (e.g., *Politics* 1264a1 ff.) that nearly all possible discoveries and knowledge have been secured. Yet this naive optimism is rather belied, in practice, by the frequent references in the physical and especially the zoological works to areas where further research needs to be undertaken, either to secure the facts of the case or to resolve continuing theoretical difficulties. He allows, also, that his own results are in many cases provisional and explicitly remarks that they may be modified by work done by his successors.

His immediate successors in the Lyceum, among them Theophrastus and Dicaearchus, were successful in carrying through programs of research that Aristotle had planned and initiated. Theophrastus, especially, often echoes the foward-looking remarks in Aristotle, expressing hopes for further advances, not just in the theoretical domain but also in the practical one. His extant mineralogical treatise, *On Stones*, records various recent discoveries—ways of obtaining pigments or of extracting cinnabar, for example—and he mentions the possibility that other such discoveries may be made (para. 59). Art, he says, both imitates nature and produces its own effects. This view is echoed in the Peripatetic work *On Mechanics* (1), which is generally agreed not to be by Aristotle himself, although it is included among his works, where a dictum of the poet Antiphon is cited that "by art men conquer where by nature they are overcome."

Yet, at least according to reports in Porphyry, both Theophrastus and Dicaearchus took a very different line from Aristotle's on aspects of the early stages of mankind's development. In a work in which he deplored animal sacrifice, Theophrastus saw man as originally living in innocence, only later to be corrupted as famine and wars led to bloodshed. He is, however, quoted by Athenaeus (*The Learned Banquet* [*Deipnosophistae*] 12.511d) as recognizing that life in his own day is much more comfortable materially than it had been in the past, but such a stance is not entirely at odds with a notion of decline. Dicaearchus, too, pictured mankind as declining from an existence where it was better endowed by nature, closer to the gods, and happier than the men of his own day.

The main Hellenistic philosophical schools with dogmatic programs, the Stoics and Epicureans, disagreed on a series of fundamental issues relevant to our subject. The Stoics were determinists (though they did not deny moral responsibility), while the Epicureans were antideterminists. The Stoics believed in Divine Providence, while the Epicureans held that the gods live a blissful life in the space between worlds, entirely indifferent to what happens in any world. The Stoics held that the world is subject to periodic destruction, and, while the Epicureans believed in innumerable worlds, they held no belief in cycles ending in cosmic conflagrations. Yet the Epicurean poet Lucretius and the Stoics Posidonius of Apamea (Syria) and Seneca the Younger produced eloquent and diverse statements of man's technological advance in the past, even if none of these statements holds out any great hopes of general moral progress being in store for man.

Book Five of Lucretius' *On the Nature of Things* (*De Rerum Natura*) pictures the gradual advance of man in some detail. Some of the arts have already reached perfection, but others are still growing: shipbuilding, music, and philosophy are all cited as recently improved. Yet the account of the corruption that material advance has led to is just as vivid, as is the description of aspects of the moral degeneracy of his contemporaries. Men grew tired of acorns and of clothing themselves in the skins of wild animals. With the development of more and more luxurious tastes, envy and greed have spread, and wars are fought to satisfy new demands. For Lucretius, the one ray of hope is represented by the philosophy of Epicurus of Samos, for this can save mankind, if only it listens to his wise teachings. Yet, even here, further advances in understanding are not envisaged. On the contrary, Epicurus has already discovered the truth. While some passages refer to the world as still in its infancy (e.g., 5.330 ff.), the emphasis in other sections is rather on the decline in nature's powers (e.g., 2.1150 ff., 5.826 ff.). Despite the text in which the continuing growth of some arts is referred to, Lucretius can in general hardly be said to present an optimistic view of the future except in the single respect that those who follow Epicurus can expect to find happiness.

In Stoic writers, too, a similar ambivalence may be found. Despite their determinism, many are reported to have laid some stress on the possibilities for moral improvement that are open to us as human beings, even though this is often combined with rather gloomy views of the prospects of the ordinary run of men and is in any case somewhat undercut by the Stoic commitment to the doctrine of cosmic periodicities. One who certainly developed the theme of the technological advance of man with some sophistication is Posidonius, a far from orthodox Stoic of the first century B.C. whose ideas are reported and criticized by Seneca, writing a century later, in the nineteenth letter of his *Letters*. According to Posidonius, man's original state was primitive and nasty, but wise men came on the scene who invented a whole series of useful arts and were benevolent rulers: that, then, was the true Golden Age. Among the useful arts, considerable emphasis is placed on practical skills, on developments in architecture, weaving, milling, and the like, but, as many others did, Posidonius associated technological advance with moral decline. It was with the spread of vice and the perversion of kingship into tyranny that laws became necessary.

Seneca rests his case for the benefits of philosophy on the growth of theoretical knowledge and moral understanding. He contrasts true wisdom with the cleverness seen in the development of practical skills, even while he acknowledges that great changes have occurred in the latter. In the *Natural Questions* (7.25), he speaks of the discoveries that will be made in the future, when the ignorance of his own times will be found amazing. Much remains to be done, and later generations will have opportunities to add to knowledge (*Letters* 64.7). Yet all of this has to be seen against the background of the usual Stoic belief in the periodic, catastrophic destruction of the world as we know it, described in almost lurid detail in the *Natural Questions* (3.27 ff.). In passages in the nineteenth letter of his *Letters* he makes clear his view of the decline of nature as well as of the moral degeneracy of man.

For less qualified expressions of the hope of future advance, we have to turn back to the scientists. It is most prominently in discussions of the development of pure science that the idea of ongoing progress is elaborated. In mathematics, astronomy, medicine, and biology, most of the great names in Hellenistic and later science show clear signs both that they recognized what they owed to their predecessors and that they saw themselves as belonging to a continuing tradition, although, naturally enough, the optimism they show concerning the possibilities of future advance varies. We may end this brief survey with some examples from mathematics and astronomy.

In mathematics, Archimedes, in the third century, is keen to give credit where credit is due to earlier mathematicians, noting, for example, who first discovered particular theorems, and who first produced their proofs. Moreover, in presenting his *Method* to his contemporaries he explicitly underlines his hope that it will prove useful to others, and that by this means additional discoveries will be made in mathematics. Archimedes tells us that he himself discovered the theorem for the area of a parabolic segment by means of this method (which assumes that plane figures, thought of as composed of their line segments, can be balanced against one another and investigated mechanically), even though he insists that theorems brought to light by such a method should thereafter be demonstrated by the orthodox procedures of Greek geometry.

Similarly, the gradual advance of astronomy is a frequent theme in Ptolemy in the second century A.D. He points to the improvements that had taken place in the quality of the observational data collected first by the predecessors of Hipparchus, and then by Hipparchus himself, who is often singled out for special praise as having provided the foundation and basis for Ptolemy's own work. In theoretical understanding, too, where Hipparchus had left many of the problems unresolved, Ptolemy is confident that his own solutions represent an improvement but recognizes explicitly that many difficulties remain. He is certain that later astronomers, working with a greater time span and with better data, have an advantage over their predecessors, and he writes on the assumption that the tradition he belongs to will continue. It is, of course, no reflection on the sincerity of his beliefs that, in practice, there were few astronomers who lived up to these hopes after the second century. Certainly by the sixth century, in this as in other fields, the optimism that had so often been expressed concerning the growth of science had largely given way to a certain resignation, and efforts came to be concentrated, not so much on new advances, as on the attempt to keep alive the knowledge that had been discovered by the great minds of the past.

It is, then, we may conclude, in science especially that a sense of ongoing progress is most fully developed, from the classical period down to the second century A.D. While similar attitudes are sometimes expressed in relation to particular topics in philosophy, philosophers from the Hellenistic period were more prone to emphasize contemporary moral corruption, and the solutions they favored were not deemed likely to leave many opportunities for future moral or political development. As far as technological progress goes, some recognition of the emergence from primitive beginnings is standard in many writers, both in prose and poetry, although, again, there are more frequent and more confident expressions concerning what had happened in the past than statements predicting that such advances would continue in the future. The fact that technological progress leads to improvements in the material conditions of human life was often viewed not so much with satisfaction and hope for the future as with anxiety, the alarming suspicion being that such developments were a prime source of degeneracy and corruption.

BIBLIOGRAPHY

SOURCES

The most important texts will be found in the standard editions of the major Greek and Latin authors as follows: the relevant texts of Anaxagoras and Anaximander in Hermann Diels and Walther Kranz, eds., *Die Fragmente der Vorsokratiker*, 3 vols., 9th ed. (1959–1960); Aristotle,

Politics, William D. Ross, ed. (1957), Ernest Barker, trans. (1946); Empedocles (relevant texts), Diels and Krantz, eds., *Die Fragmente der Vorsokratiker* (1959–1960); Hesiod, *Works and Days,* Friedrich Solmsen, Reinhold Merkelbach, and Martin L. West, eds. (1970), Richmond Lattimore, trans. (1959); "Hippocrates" in André M. J. Festugière, ed., *Hippocrate, L'ancienne médecine* (1948); Lucretius, *On the Nature of Things (De Rerum Natura),* Cyril Bailey, ed., (1947); Plato, *Statesman (Politicus),* John Burnet, ed. (1900 and 1903), Joseph Skemp, trans. (1957), and Alfred E. Taylor, trans. (1961), and *Protagoras,* John Burnet, ed. (1900 and 1903), William K. C. Guthrie, trans. (1956), Gregory Vlastos, trans. (1956), and Christopher C. W. Taylor trans. (1976); Polybius, William R. Paton, ed. and trans., 6 vols. (1922–1927); Seneca, *Epistulae Morales (Letters),* Leighton R. Reynolds, ed., 2 vols. (1965), Richard M. Gummere, trans., 3 vols. (1961–1962), and *Naturales Quaestiones (Natural Questions),* Thomas H. Corcoran, ed. and trans., 2 vols. (1971–1972); Diodorus Siculus, *Universal History,* Immanuel Bekker, Ludwig Dindorf, and Friedrich Vogel, eds., 6 vols. (1888–1906); Xenophanes (relevant works), Diels and Krantz, eds., *Die Fragmente der Vorsokratiker* (1959–1960).

STUDIES

The most important studies of aspects of ancient views on progress are the following: John B. Bury, *The Idea of Progress* (1920); Thomas Cole, *Democritus and the Sources of Greek Anthropology* (1967); Jacqueline de Romilly, "Thucydide et l'idée de progrès," in *Annali della Scuola Normale di Pisa,* **35** (1966); Eric R. Dodds, *The Ancient Concept of Progress* (1973); Ludwig Edelstein, *The Idea of Progress in Classical Antiquity* (1967); William K. C. Guthrie, *In the Beginning* (1957); Bernhard A. van Groningen, *In the Grip of the Past* (1953); Jean P. Vernant, *Myth and Thought among the Greeks* (1983).

Greek Building Techniques

J. J. COULTON

VERNACULAR CONSTRUCTION

The decline of the palace cultures of the Greek Bronze Age (the Minoan and Mycenaean periods) involved the loss of a number of sophisticated techniques, including those of monumental architecture. There is no evidence for their continued use in the tenth, ninth, or eighth centuries B.C., and techniques die if they are not practiced. The survival of some Bronze Age buildings through these centuries may have provided a stimulus to the new monumental building that developed during the seventh century. However, between about 1100 and 700 B.C. the building methods used in Greece were essentially vernacular; that is, they used locally available materials in a skillful and workmanlike manner, but without any special search for a spectacular or everlasting effect. The buildings produced were mainly houses, from which the few temples can barely be distinguished on grounds of form or construction. Toward the end of this period some fortification walls were also built, but apart from the scale of operations involved, they made little impact on building practice.

In many areas mud-brick was the normal material for walls. To make the bricks, clay was mixed with water and a suitable temper, such as straw, and worked to a suitable consistency. It was then pressed into rectangular molds of a convenient size, usually 1 to 1 1/2 feet (0.3 to 0.5 m) to a side and 3 to 4 inches (7 to 10 cm) thick, and left to dry. Mud-brick walls were typically 1 1/2 to 2 feet (0.5 to 0.6 m) thick and were set on a few courses of rubble stonework to raise the brick clear of damp ground. Sometimes timber lacings or reinforcements were used to strengthen the wall or help carry the roof; but more recent traditional building shows that such timber work is not necessary, although it may increase earthquake resistance.

In some areas, such as the Cycladic islands, stone was more readily available than clay for bricks, and rubble stonework was used for the full height of the walls. The rock was quarried to provide pieces of appropriate, but not accurately predetermined, sizes and shapes. The effect of the masonry varied, therefore, with the nature of the local stone—neat and regular where the stone was regularly bedded or easily split, but more rugged where the stone broke irregularly. There was little shaping of the stone after quarrying except for special purposes, such as thresholds or post bases; and almost all this work could be done with wedges and a mason's pick hammer. Each side of a wall was built of pieces of stone set with their best face showing, so that a wall consisted for the most part of two more or less interlocking skins, with few pieces running through from side to side. There was no attempt to make tight joints, except at the faces; and the gaps between the main blocks were filled with small stones and mud. The pieces of stone were normally about 6 to 18 inches (15 to 46 cm) long, so that there was no difficulty in raising them into place. Larger stones might sometimes be used low down, where lifting was not needed.

For roofing there were also two main methods: the steeply pitched thatch roof and the more or less flat clay roof. Ancient models of buildings, such as those from Perachora (near Corinth, fig. 1), Samos, and the temple of Hera at Argos, provide firm evidence for the use of thatch, which is not often identifiable in excavated remains. They also demonstrate the pitch that was used and some of the technical details, such as a twisted rope binding the thatch along the ridge. So where we find a freestanding building with a rather long, narrow plan, a central row of posts, and perhaps an apsidal end—one with a semicircular or curving extension, like the Perachora model—we may conclude that it too had a thatched roof. Apart from the evidence of the models, nothing is known of the details of this thatching technique. But once again, recent traditional methods employed by modern builders provide useful suggestions.

Flat clay roofs are still used in traditional building in some parts of present-day Greece and were certainly used in antiquity. The outer waterproofing layer of clay, about 6 inches (15 cm) thick, was carried on a layer of reeds or, in the example of eighth-century houses at Zagora on Andros, thin stone slabs; these in turn were supported by closely spaced wooden crossbeams. Since flat roofs can be extended as easily in breadth as in length, they tend to be associated with rather squarer plans. Flat-roofed buildings can also be more easily built directly against each other, since there is no problem with valley gutters.

The flat clay roof was substantially heavier than thatch, but both types needed internal support over a room of any size. For this purpose wooden posts were used, either set firmly into the ground—as at Lefkandi, on Euboea, and at Nichoria, in the southwest Peloponnese—or supported on bases of stone—as at Zagora, on Andros, and Emporio, on Chios. Most of these posts were probably just trimmed tree trunks, but some were cut to a rectangular shape (at Lefkandi and Samos). Floors were of stamped earth, and doorways were framed in wood or, where the stone split easily, in stone slabs.

All of these materials and techniques already had a long history in Greece, so there is no need to look for an external source for them; their use continued in buildings of no great pretensions long after 700 B.C. Mud-brick and rubble walls were customary for classical and Hellenistic houses (sometimes built on a footing of finer masonry) and were also used for some public buildings: mud-brick for the mid-fifth-century council chamber and Tholos, or council rotunda, at Athens, rubble for the Hellenistic stoas (porticoes) of Delos. Wooden posts were rarer but did occur, and flat clay roofs also continued where the climate was suitable. Thatch, however, was avoided except for the most ephemeral structures. Where these vernacular materials continued in use the associated techniques were little changed, but there was perhaps more trimming of stones for rubble masonry and more standardization of mud-brick sizes.

GREEK BUILDING TECHNIQUES

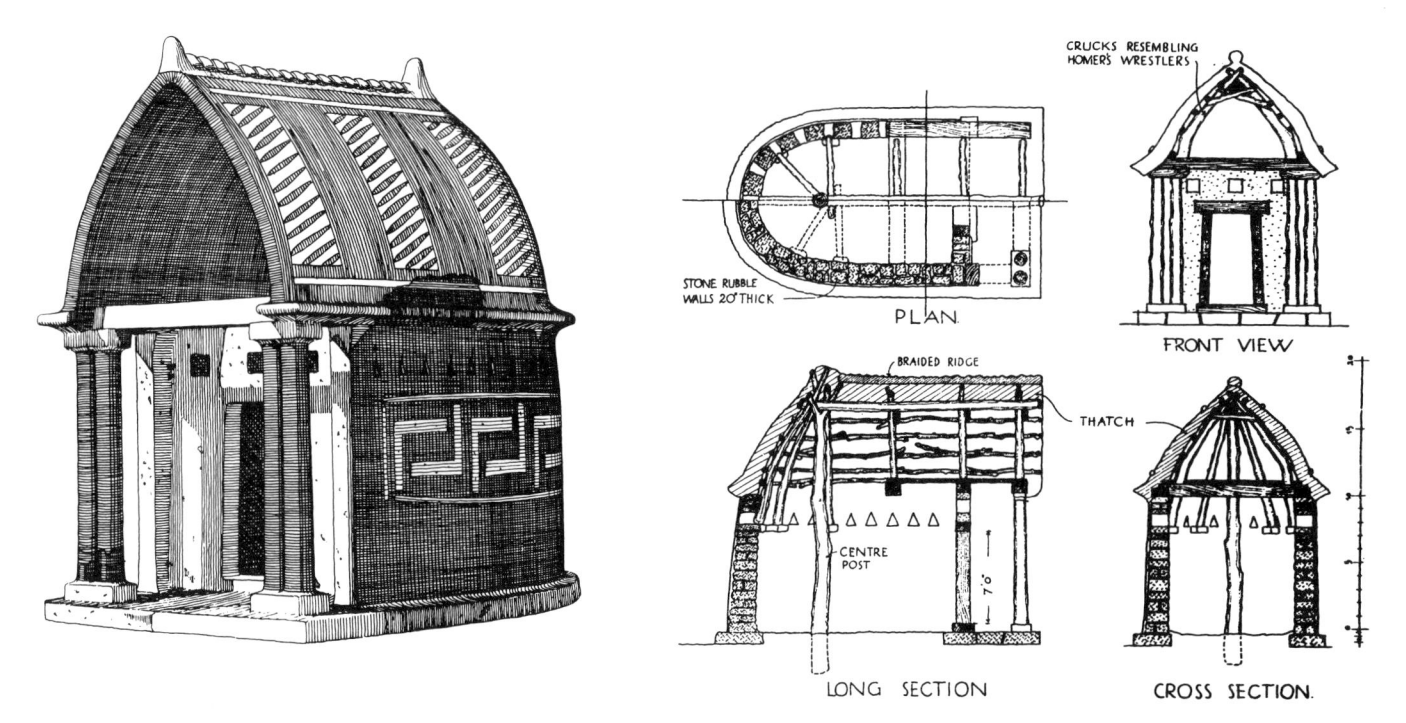

Figure 1. Construction techniques suggested by the restored model of a temple or house from Perachora, *ca.* 750–725 B.C. *Reproduced from Humfry Payne,* PERACHORA I (1940). BY PERMISSION OF OXFORD UNIVERSITY PRESS

MONUMENTAL CONSTRUCTION

During the seventh century a whole new system of building was introduced, initially for temples and then for other important public buildings. In the course of several centuries its use spread to more or less all other classes of building. For walls, carefully dressed stone blocks replaced rubble and mud-brick; and stone replaced wood for columns and the beams they carried. The roof structure normally remained of wood, but instead of thatch or clay, large terra-cotta tiles kept out the rain. It is this monumental building system (rather than the vernacular one) that is associated with the characteristic forms of Greek architecture. Before we look at its origins it is helpful to detail the construction procedures in order to illuminate the technical changes involved. To some extent this approach is anachronistic, since the evidence for the fifth and fourth centuries is often clearer than for the seventh and sixth. But basic construction procedures, once adopted, remained comparatively unchanged.

At the quarry it was no longer sufficient to induce the native rock to break naturally to produce the required quantity of stone in roughly suitable sizes. Large blocks of a defined size and shape were needed for columns and architraves, so that each block needed to be quarried separately. If a block 5 × 3 × 2 feet (1.5 × 0.9 × 0.6 m) was required, for instance, an area of rock larger than 5 × 3 feet would be outlined by a channel; the channel would then be cut down with a pick hammer to a depth of more than two feet; and the block thus defined would be separated from its bed by wedges, either iron wedges driven in by heavy hammers or wooden ones soaked in water so as to swell. Early quarries often exploited isolated outcrops of rock, but later quarries, such as the one at Syracuse, were very deep; and a special marble vein at Paros was exploited by tunneling.

The stone was normally quarried in rectangular blocks and then trimmed roughly to shape at the quarry, although column drums were sometimes cut from the rock as cylinders. However, blocks were always delivered to the builders somewhat larger in all dimensions than the specified size. This additional mantle of stone—the *apergon*—served as protection against accidental damage in transit, but it also helped to avoid the production of blocks slightly but disastrously too small.

Wagons had presumably been used to bring the stone for rubble walls from the quarry, where the terrain was suitable (although pack animals would have been necessary at some sites), and there would have been no difficulty in loading or unloading them. The much larger blocks for the new monumental masonry were much harder to handle. They could be moved for short distances on rollers at either the quarry or the building site. But during the classical period at least, wagons drawn by large teams of oxen were used for overland transport from the quarry to the site. This was adequate for blocks weighing up to ten or twelve tons, the

Figure 2. Cross-section through the temple of Zeus at Olympia, ca. 460 B.C. *Reproduced from Ernst Curtius, Friedrich Adler, et al, OLYMPIA, DIE ERGEBNISSE DER VON DEM DEUTSCHEN REICH VERANSTALTETEN AUSGRABUNG (1890–1897).* THE NEW YORK PUBLIC LIBRARY

largest needed in most classical temples, but may not have been for the twenty- or thirty-ton blocks used in some archaic and Hellenistic temples. The column drums for the temple of Artemis at Ephesus, built in the second half of the sixth century, were pulled to the site like giant rollers; the architrave blocks, which were rectangular in section, had huge wheels built round each end so that they too could be rolled. This method was certainly applied slightly later at Selinus in Sicily, but there is no evidence that it was widespread.

Overland transport of heavy blocks was both difficult and expensive, especially if they had to be brought uphill, so where possible a local stone was used, even if to do so meant opening a new quarry. In some cases the parts of a block that would not be visible were hollowed out to save weight. Apart from the difficulties of loading and unloading, transport by sea was much easier. Limestone from Corinth, for instance, was brought to the sanctuary of Asclepius near Epidaurus largely by sea, reducing arduous overland transport by about two-thirds; and the marbles of Naxos and Paros in the Cyclades could be exported widely in part because the quarries were close to shore.

Monumental masonry also required new skills in constructing foundations. Earlier walls had been built on any existing compacted surface with little or no foundation, for mud-brick and rubble, being slightly yielding, could adapt to minor settlement. The new system of construction was not only heavier but also less tolerant; even a small amount of settling could produce unsightly gaps between blocks and, worse still, could lead to uneven weight distribution on the stone, with attendant risks of fracture. Monumental buildings therefore have substantial foundations (usually one-and-a-half to two times the width of the upstanding parts), which rest either on rock or on undisturbed subsoil. It is rare to find a solid masonry raft beneath a whole building, as at the fourth-century Tholos at Delphi. Usually, each wall or colonnade was given an independent foundation (fig. 2), which was not necessarily laid at the same time. Like a wall, an outer colonnade was usually given a continuous foundation, for it stood on a continuous stepped platform. But more widely spaced inner columns often had individual foundations, and in some large Ionian temples the same was true for the outer columns.

The top of the foundation was marked by a more carefully laid course, the *euthynteria*, whose upper edge was accurately dressed to serve as a guide for setting out the lines of the building proper, whether walls or colonnades. The steps for a colonnade or the lower courses of a wall would then be set back slightly from this edge, leaving it as a visible base line for the building above. The lower part of a wall normally consisted of two rows of blocks set on edge, the *orthostates* (fig. 3d), which were often about three feet

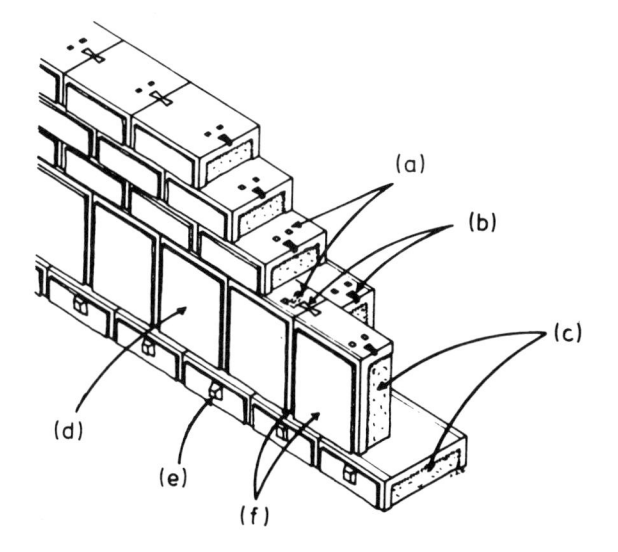

Figure 3. Features of early Greek monumental masonry: (*a*) U-shaped hole used to adjust blocks into place; (*b*) dovetail clamp; (*c*) band *anathyrosis*; (*d*) *orthostate*; (*e*) handling boss; (*f*) preliminary dressing. Reproduced from J. J. Coulton, ANCIENT GREEK ARCHITECTS AT WORK (1977)

(1 m) tall. The normal wall blocks, which were about a third to half as tall and often ran the full thickness of the wall, were then laid above in more or less regular courses, with the vertical joints staggered from course to course.

Whereas the mason's pick hammer was sufficient for the little shaping of stones that was needed in previous vernacular architecture, the more complex and accurate shaping entailed by monumental architecture required a richer tool kit. Squares, rules, and levels were needed for setting out and for testing surfaces; a variety of coarse and fine single-point chisels was needed for the initial shaping; chisels of various widths and straight, curved, or toothed edges were used for the finer and more accurate shaping; and then rasps and abrasives for final surface finishing. Saws were occasionally used, but they were not characteristic tools used in Greek masonry.

Before each wall block was laid in position, the end and bottom faces and the bed on which it would rest were prepared, but the top face was not given its final dressing until the whole course was in place, thereby producing a continuous surface to take the blocks of the next course. These horizontal joint faces, carrying the whole weight of the wall, were normally dressed accurately to a plane to make the top and bottom of each block uniform bearing surfaces. The rising joints, which were structurally less important, were more economically treated. In the foundations, which were invisible, they were often left quite open, but in the visible wall, where the closest possible jointing was wanted, a technique known as *anathyrosis* was employed (figs. 3c, 10, 11). Only a narrow band along the top and sides of the joint face was dressed smooth to make tight contact with a similarly dressed band on its neighbor; the remainder was just cut roughly back out of the way. A similar process was occasionally used in horizontal wall joints, but more widely (although no more appropriately) in the joints between drums that were stacked one on another to form columns (fig. 9).

In rubble walls the mud between the stones served more as a packing than as an adhesive. No packing was needed between the carefully fitted blocks of a monumental wall, and no cement was used to hold them in place. To a large extent their weight and good jointing kept them in place, but these were often reinforced by clamps and dowels, or tenons, which fastened a block to its neighbors in the same course and to those above or below it. Both clamps and dowels varied in shape with time and place, but the earliest clamp type was the dovetail clamp (figs. 3b, 8a). It was normally made of lead or wood shaped like an elongated bow tie, and hammered into corresponding cuttings in the two blocks to be joined.

The drums of a column were much more exposed to sideways movement than the blocks of a coherent wall, and so from the first they were doweled to each other, although not to the stylobate, the stone course on which the column rests. The usual method was by means of a substantial wooden peg, commonly about 2 to 2 3/4 inches (5 to 7 cm) square (less often cylindrical), which fitted into sockets cut in the center of the matching faces of adjacent drums. The natural resilience of the wood allowed the peg to fit tightly in the sockets without preventing a proper contact between the drums, so that there was no need for the lead sealing that an iron or bronze dowel would have required.

The use of very large blocks of stone well above ground level also involved new skills in lifting heavy weights. Inscriptions show that from the late fifth century onward builders lifted large blocks with hoists based on multiple pulley blocks and winches, and their use is attested earlier by numerous cuttings made in the stone to take the various devices for attaching blocks to a hoist (fig. 7). However, evidence for such hoists is generally lacking before the late sixth century, and since earlier builders sometimes used blocks too large to be handled by simple hoists, a different method must have been used by them; there is some evidence that it was based on temporary ramps.

The complex blocks of the upper parts of a building were normally shaped on the ground and set in place in a finished state, except for any carved moldings, stuccoing, and painting. But wall blocks and column drums went into place with a good deal of the *apergon* left on them. Before columns were erected the fluting was cut only for a few inches at the foot of the column and the neck of the capital; the rest of the shaft was left cylindrical. Similarly, wall and step blocks were set with the intended outer faces finished only along narrow vertical and horizontal bands sufficient to define the lines and planes concerned. The *apergon* served as a protection against accidental chipping during the later stages of construction (to which the upper parts were less exposed). It was also easier to achieve smooth, unbroken surfaces in wall, step, or column shaft if the shaping and dressing to final size and contour took place when the building was structurally complete. This procedure was most obviously important in fluted column shafts, where even slight discontinuities in the fluting, which would be inevitable if each drum were fluted separately on the ground, would be visually disastrous. Marble surfaces were given a final smoothing, while other stones were usually coated with a hard white stucco. It was at this stage that any decorative carving was added to moldings, and alternating elements and fine details were picked out in color, applied either directly to the marble or onto the stucco coating.

The general replacement of thatch and flat clay roofs by terra-cotta tiles has already been mentioned. Greek tiling consisted of two main elements: large, fairly flat pantiles, usually about 2 to 3 feet (0.65 to 0.95 m) long and 1 1/2 to 2 feet (0.50 to 0.65 m) wide, which formed the main roof surface; and to cover the joints between the pantiles, narrower cover tiles, matching the pantiles in length but only 8 to 10 inches (20 to 25 cm) wide. These two elements appear in two main forms, known in antiquity as Laconian, as shown in figure 4a (with slightly concave pantiles and strongly convex cover tiles), and Corinthian, as shown in figures 4b and 5 (with flat pantiles and angular cover tiles). The names derive from the areas where the two types seem to have been developed, but the distinction later became rather one of context; Laconian tiles, being simpler to make, were commonly used for houses, while Corinthian tiles were preferred for public buildings.

In addition to the basic tile forms, special forms were made either for special types of roof, such as hipped and conical roofs, or for special parts of a roof, such as the ridge, eaves, and gable ends (fig. 5). Although initially required for making a more weatherproof roof, these last three special tile forms soon developed into more or less elaborate decorative forms. Together the tiles made up an interlocking system, but except at the eaves they were rarely fastened to the building below. Individual tiles were held in place by their weight, assisted sometimes by a bed layer of clay between them and the roof planks. As a result, tiled roofs, which were characteristically ten to fifteen degrees in slope, had to be much less steep than thatched roofs.

The wooden beams that supported the tiling have of course vanished in extant buildings, but the cuttings made for them in the surviving stonework can, with the help of inscriptions and other sources, show the normal procedure. The essential timbers were the ridge beam, which ran the length of

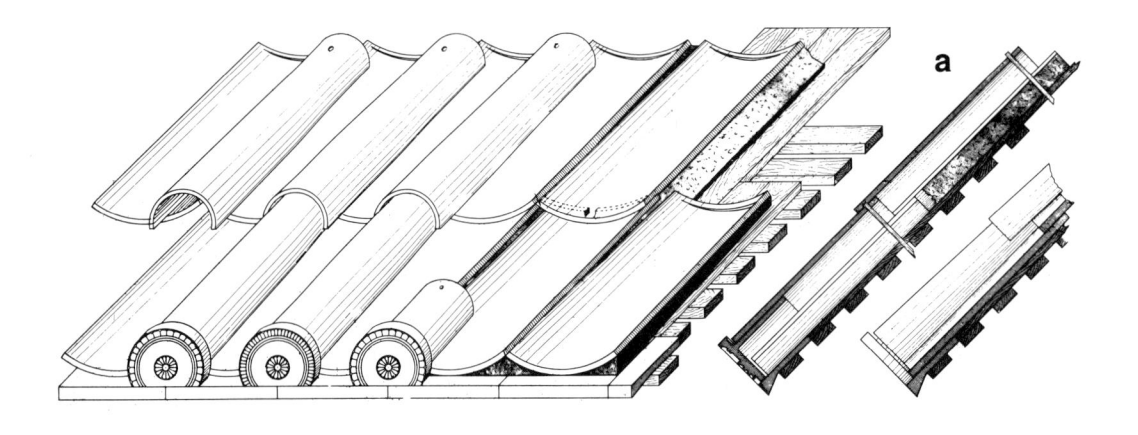

Figure 4. Greek tile roofing systems: (*a*) Laconian type from the temple of Hera at Olympia, *ca.* 600 B.C.; (*b*) Corinthian type from the temple of Zeus at Olympia, *ca.* 460 B.C. *Reproduced from Ernst Curtius, Friedrich Adler, et al.,* OLYMPIA, DIE ERGEBNISSE . . . (1890–1897). THE NEW YORK PUBLIC LIBRARY

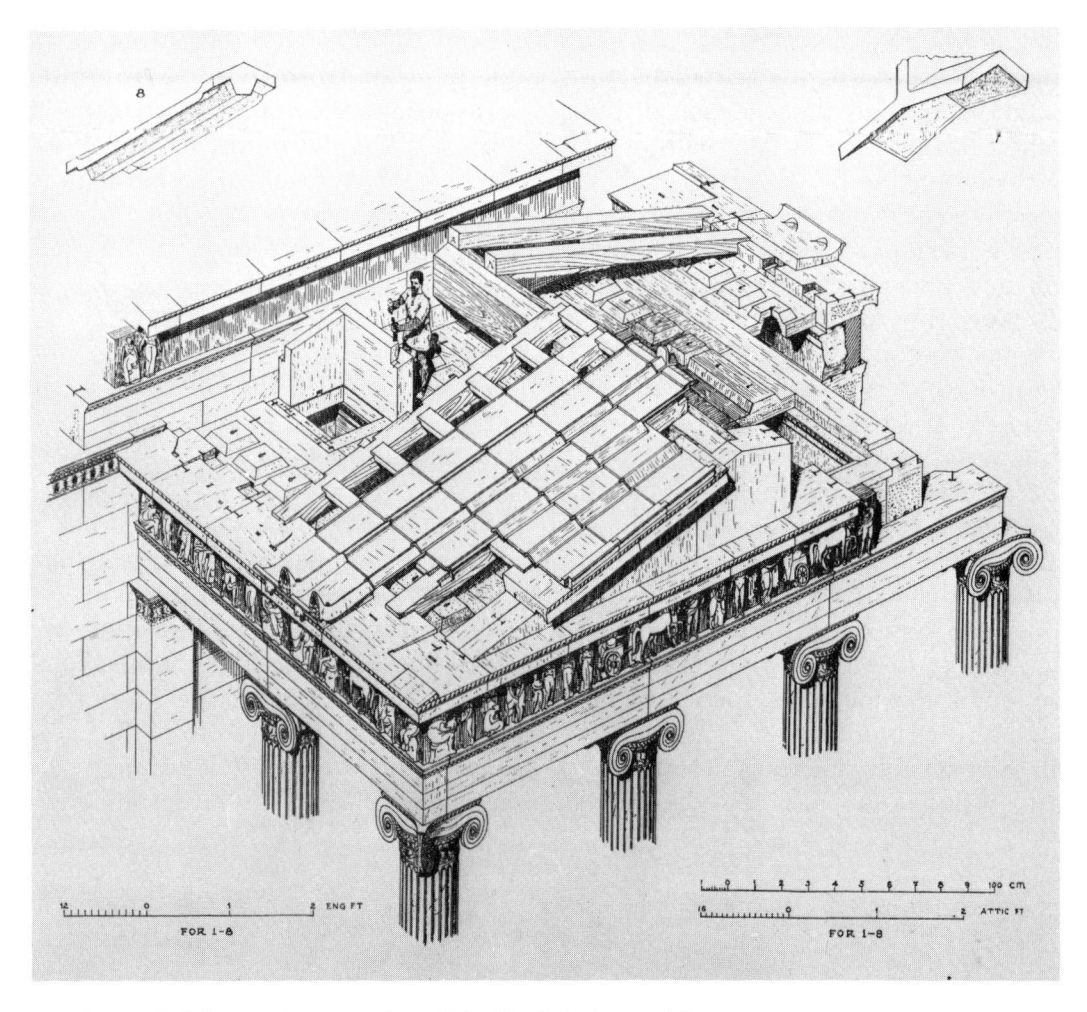

Figure 5. The roof of the northern portico of the Erechtheion at Athens, ca. 421–405 B.C. as reconstructed by Gorham Phillips Stevens: Corinthian tiles are laid directly on battens rabbeted to rafters laid on top of the ridge beam; enlarged details show the undersides of ridge tiles. *Reproduced from James Paton, THE ERECHTHEUM (1927).*
THE NEW YORK PUBLIC LIBRARY

the building at the peak of the gable ends; rafters, which ran at right angles from the ridge beam, sloping down to the eaves at the sides; and purlins, beams running the length of the building parallel to the ridge beam but spaced down the slope of the rafters (fig. 6). Where the span between gables was not great, the roof might be constructed without rafters, using only the ridge beam and purlins between the end walls. Over longer spans direct support for the ridge beam was provided by a central colonnade or wall where that was convenient, as often in stoas. In temples, an uninterrupted center interior space was preferred, and the ridge beam was carried on heavy cross beams supported either by the walls of the cella—the inner structure that housed the image of the deity (fig. 2)—or by internal colonnades along either side of the center space (fig. 6). In some buildings the rafters ran unaided from the ridge to the eaves (fig. 5), but where there were suitably placed walls or inner colonnades, as in temples, those were normally used to support heavy purlins, which could then carry lighter rafters (fig. 6). The rafters were quite closely spaced, but above them there were usually battens or planks to support the tiling (figs. 4, 5, 6).

Although Greek carpenters used a variety of joints in furniture-making and joinery, the principle underlying their roof woodwork is much the same as in stonework: heavy beams were simply laid one above the other, a procedure that was encouraged by the shallow roof pitch. This led to a lavish use of timber, with major beams often 16 to 32 inches (0.40 to 0.80 m) square—squarish sections were normally preferred, perhaps because this entailed the least removal of timber from the natural log. Despite this generous size, spans were normally kept to 16 to 23 feet (5 to 7 m). The larger spans that are found in some areas, such as Sicily, or in some special buildings, such as the Parthenon, are probably due to the availability of unusually large timbers, not to the use of a more sophisticated roof structure, such as the tie-beam truss, in which two rafters and a tie beam are carefully jointed together to form a triangular frame, with the horizontal tie beam in tension. (See fig. 9 in ROMAN BUILDING TECHNIQUES.) But the nature of the evidence makes certainty here impossible.

TECHNICAL DEVELOPMENTS IN
THE ARCHAIC PERIOD
(*ca.* 700–480 B.C.)

This generalized account of Greek monumental techniques should serve to show the changes necessitated by the development from vernacular to monumental architecture. These changes did not all take place at once, but within about a century the development seems to have been effectively complete. The northeast Peloponnese played an important early role, but by the end of the

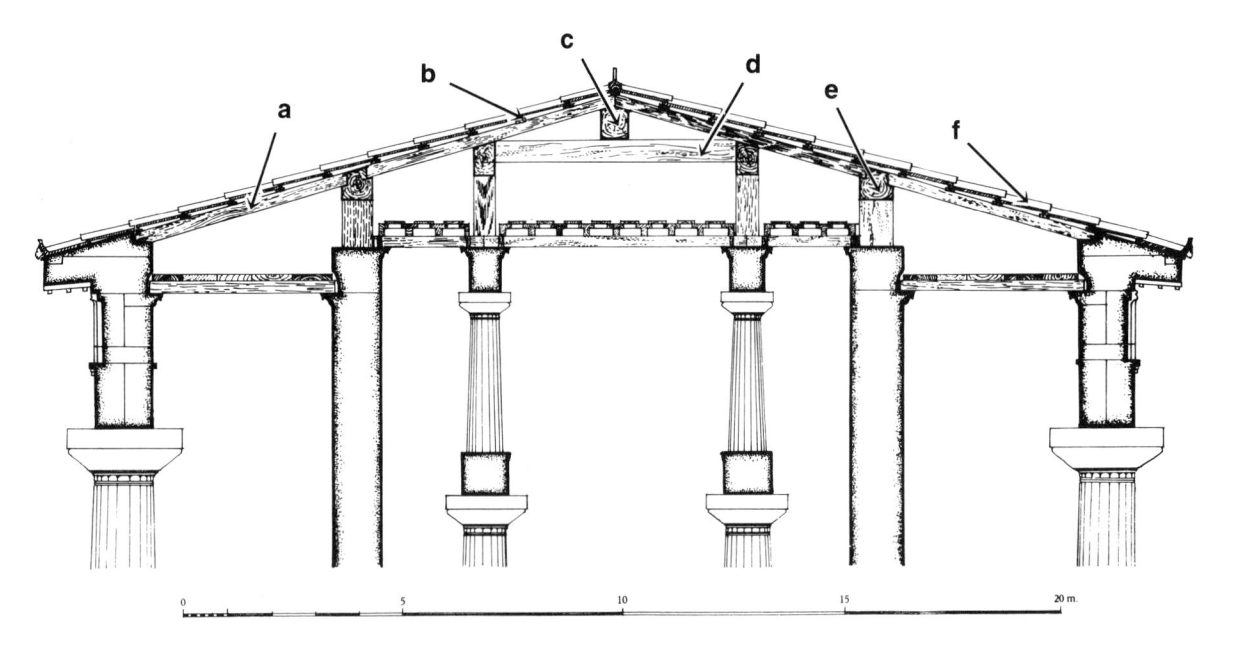

Figure 6. General restoration of the roof of the temple of Poseidon at Paestum, *ca.* 460 B.C.: (*a*) rafters; (*b*) battens; (*c*) ridge beam; (*d*) cross beam; (*e*) purlins; (*f*) terra-cotta tiles. *Reproduced from A. Trevor Hodge,* THE WOODWORK OF GREEK ROOFS (1960). BY PERMISSION OF CAMBRIDGE UNIVERSITY PRESS

seventh century the monumental techniques were being used in other parts of mainland Greece, in the Cyclades, and in Asia Minor. The earliest buildings to display them are the seventh-century temples of Poseidon at Isthmia (near Corinth) and (less well preserved) Apollo at Corinth, both datable to the first half of the century. Their walls were of well-dressed ashlar (square-shaped) blocks, and at Isthmia there are substantial foundation trenches; but the wall blocks are still comparatively small, presenting no major problems of transport or lifting. No clamps or dowels were used to hold the blocks together, but some of the rising joint faces were slightly hollowed in a way approaching *anathyrosis*. Whether the walls were given their final dressing after erection is uncertain, but they were in part stuccoed and painted, and the associated cornice in the structure at Isthmia may have been clad in wood. No remains were found of the outer columns or the beams they carried; it is likely that they were all of wood. Both temples had tiled roofs, the earliest known; yet the sophisticated tile system, with cover tiles joined to pantiles and with special tile forms for eaves, ridge, and hipped ends, suggests that these were not the first such tiles to have been made.

These two temples therefore represent an intermediate stage in the development of monumental techniques, and this continues into the early sixth century, when the temple of Hera at Olympia was built with mud-brick walls on a protruding foot, or socle, of dressed stone, and columns originally of wood, which were progressively replaced by stone. Shortly thereafter, however, temples were being built completely of stone, except for the ceiling and roof, marking the end of this transitional phase.

The sources of this monumental architecture are debated, and one may note a similar argument over the origins of Greek monumental sculpture, which emerged at about the same time and required many of the same techniques. The transitional stage represented by the early temples at Isthmia and Corinth could well have resulted from local development. Stone sarcophagi had been produced in the area from the late eighth century, so the techniques of quarrying and dressing blocks of a desired size and shape in the soft Corinthian stone must have been mastered already. There are no parallels elsewhere for the system of grooves used for lifting or carrying the wall blocks (fig. 7), and tiled roofs seem to have been a Greek invention. So, too, the use of terracotta as an important material in the seventh-century temples at Thermon and Kalydon (in northwest Greece) is largely or wholly a Greek development.

By the end of the transitional period, however, there are a number of additional features that are found also in Egyptian architecture: projecting knobs (fig. 3e) and U-shaped holes (fig. 3a) used in adjusting blocks into place (perhaps occasionally for hoisting them, as has sometimes been suggested), dovetail clamps for holding them together, the process of final dressing after erection, and the same range of tools for working the stone. Harder types of rock, such as marble, were now being worked (although not as hard as many Egyptian building stones), and the transport and handling of very heavy blocks, which the Greeks quickly mastered, probably followed the Egyptian system of sledge, rollers, and temporary ramps. Since we know that from about 660 B.C. the Greeks were in fairly regular contact with Egypt and that the pharaoh of the time, Psamtik I (Psammetichus), was actively engaged in monumental architecture, it seems unreasonable to explain all these similarities as mere coincidence.

The period of closest similarity to Egyptian techniques is the late seventh and early sixth centuries, for although the basic methods of building remained relatively unchanged for the next five hundred years and more, innovations and variations were introduced from time to time, and for most of these no outside influence needs to be sought. At least by about 560 B.C. the Greeks had devised an addition to the mason's tool kit, the toothed chisel, with a serrated cutting edge that combined the advantages of the point and the flat chisel, thus allowing the more rapid production of plane surfaces. At about the same time the initial type of dovetail clamp, normally of wood or lead that could hardly resist the movement of a really heavy block, was reinforced by the addition of a ⊓-shaped piece of iron (fig. 8b), whose crossbar stiffened the dovetail and whose ends hooked into the adjacent blocks of stone; the remainder of the dovetail cutting continued to be filled with lead. This reinforced dovetail was especially favored for marble, which could better stand up to the more concentrated strain, and for situations, such as corners, where stability was particularly crucial.

Builders in mainland Greece and the western colonies worked mainly or entirely in various local limestones during the sixth century, but from the late seventh century builders in the Cyclades were using native marble for monumental buildings, and during the sixth century the Ionians and Samians did so, too. The Naxians in particular seem to have been so proud of their fine marble that they sometimes used it to replace wood not only for the exterior columns and beams, but also for the beams of the ceiling and roof as well; and archaeology supports the comment of Pausanias (5.10.3) that the use of marble tiles, laboriously cut in imitation of the clay prototypes, was also a Naxian invention. The use of marble for roof beams placed too great a restriction on the spaces that could be covered and it was not accepted elsewhere. Marble tiles, however, were sometimes used for important buildings, and from the mid fifth century onward the Athenians adopted marble ceilings for the outer porticoes of their temples, and the fashion was followed somewhat later in the Peloponnese and Ionia.

A similar reveling in megalithic stonework is displayed by the conspicuous use of very large blocks in a number of buildings of the first three-quarters of the sixth century—huge monolithic door jambs at Naxos and Paros and monolithic column shafts in the temples of Apollo and Zeus at Syracuse, standing on stylobate blocks that incorporate the step below in the same block. The use of stones weighing twenty tons or more stops fairly abruptly in the last quarter of the sixth century and is probably to be associated with a general change from the use of ramps and rollers for raising blocks toward the use of a hoist with multiple pulley blocks and a winch. At any rate it is only from this time on that we find in building blocks the cuttings for the various devices that linked the block to a hoist: loops of rope, lifting tongs and hooks (fig. 7), and the lewis iron (an iron plug wider at the bottom than the top, like a half-dovetail, which was placed in a similar-shaped cutting and then wedged or packed so that it could not pull out when the block was lifted by a ring on the plug, as shown in figure 6 in ROMAN BUILDING TECHNIQUES).

The multiple-pulley hoist (see fig. 5 in ENGINEERING), seems to be another Greek invention, and although it restricted the loads that could be raised, it removed the need for a massive short-term labor force, which did not suit the organization of Greek society. These hoists seem to have had a limited ability to move their load horizontally, so they were usually set up at a point midway along the length of a wall. Since the laying of each course was begun at the two ends, this meant that successive blocks could be lifted onto the middle of the course below, then rolled, skidded or levered to their places in either direction, until the last block was lowered into place in the middle.

In the second half of the sixth century

GREEK BUILDING TECHNIQUES

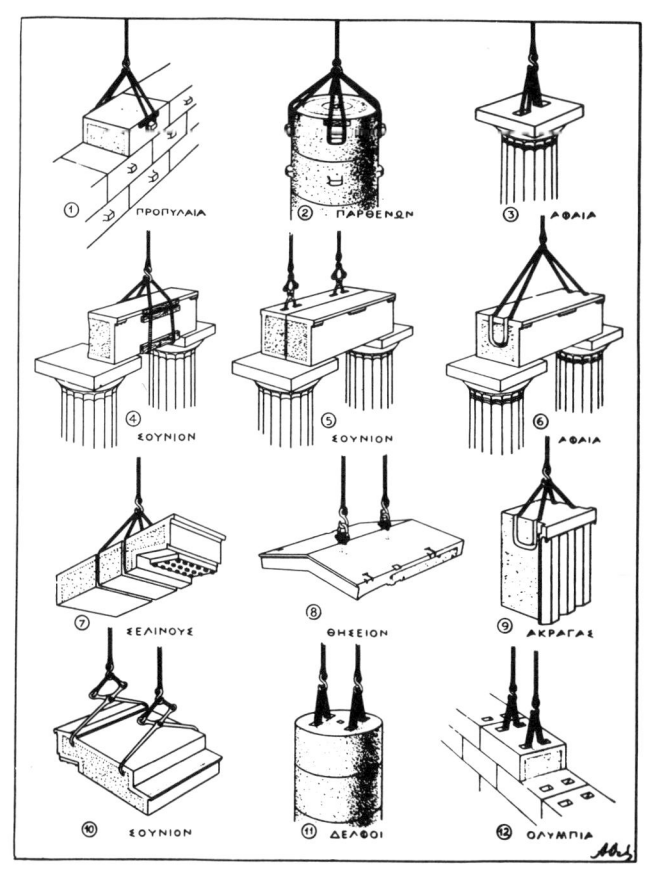

Figure 7. Various devices used by the Greeks for attaching stone blocks to a hoist. *Reproduced from Anastasios Orlandos,* LES MATÉRIAUX DE CONSTRUCTION ET LA TECHNIQUE ARCHITECTURALE DES ANCIENS GRECS (1966–1968). BY PERMISSION OF ÉDITIONS E. DE BOCCARD, PARIS

there were further improvements in the means of holding blocks in place. Soon after 550 B.C. builders in Ionia and the Aegean islands sometimes used square wooden dowels as tenons at wall corners and ends to hold blocks in alignment with those above and below. Similar dowels continue to occur in this area, although more rarely elsewhere, into the Hellenistic period, as for instance in the temple of Apollo at Didyma. Dowels of this type were usually sealed in place with molten lead, but since they were commonly set back from any vertical face of the block, it took much effort to place the molten lead into the dowel cavities. Considerable ingenuity was often required to devise concealed holes or channels for this purpose.

Slightly later, around 525 B.C., a new type of clamp was introduced, apparently from Athens, and although it spread rapidly from there to Delphi and the Peloponnese, it scarcely appears east of the Aegean or west of the Adriatic. It consisted of a piece of iron in the shape of an H with an elongated center bar, like two T's joined base to base (fig. 8f). It was sealed with molten lead into a corresponding cutting in the two blocks to be joined. This lead jacket was important not only in holding the clamp in place, but also as a protection from corrosion and as a cushion to equalize stresses between iron and stone. The H (or double T) shape was perhaps seen as giving more direct anchorage than the simple dovetail clamp (fig. 8a), and at the same time as spreading the strain over a broader surface than the ⊓-shaped reinforcement (fig. 8b), so that it was less likely to fracture the stone. At any rate the H-clamp became a characteristic device in mainland Greek masonry of the fifth century, including the buildings of Periclean Athens (fig. 5).

TECHNICAL DEVELOPMENTS IN THE CLASSICAL PERIOD
(*ca.* 480–323 B.C.)

During the second half of the fifth century Athenian buildings exhibited a number of technical improvements that accompanied the very high standards of masons' work. A more complex system was employed for joining column drums. As shown in figure 9, instead of a simple wooden peg between adjacent drums, a roughly cubical plug (*empolion*) was hammered into the cutting in each of the two drums concerned; in the middle of this plug was a carefully bored circular hole. A cylindrical peg (*polos*) fitted accurately into the two *empolia* to hold the two drums in alignment. At first these

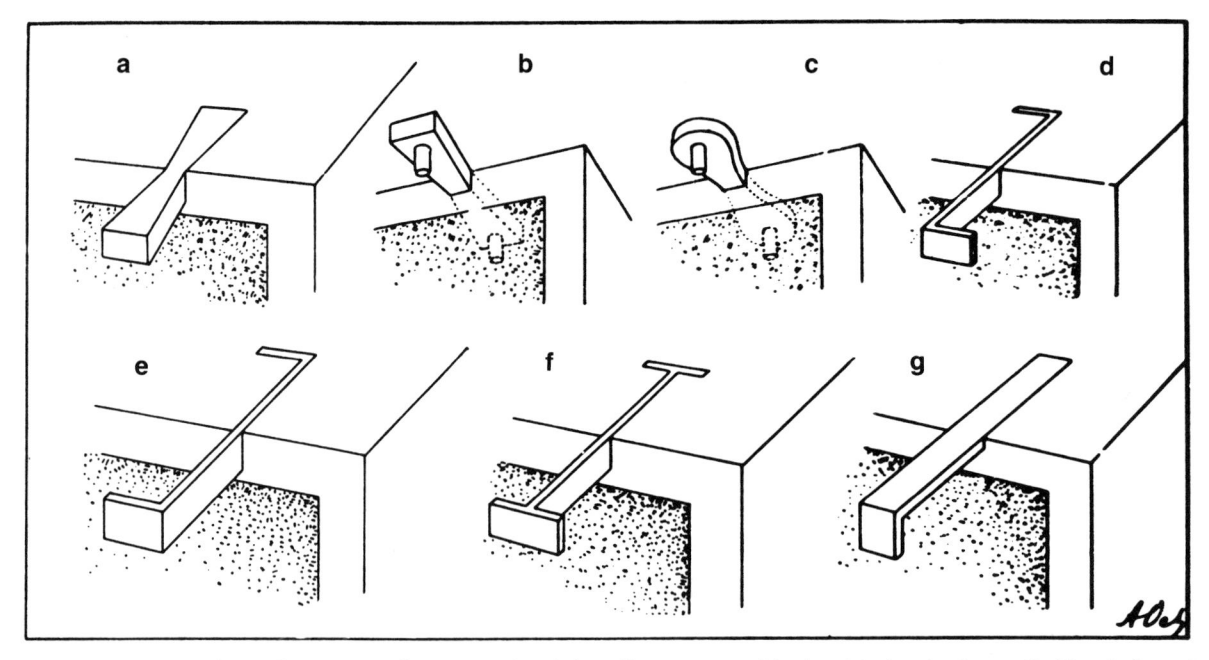

Figure 8. Types of Greek masonry clamps used to join adjacent stone blocks: (*a*) simple dovetail; (*b*) reinforced dovetail; (*c*) reinforced curvilinear dovetail; (*d*) Z-shaped; (*e*) U-shaped; (*f*) H-shaped (or double T); (*g*) flat staple clamp. *Reproduced from Anastasios Orlandos,* LES MATÉRIAUX DE CONSTRUCTION . . . (1966–1968). BY PERMISSION OF ÉDITIONS E. DE BOCCARD, PARIS

fittings were made in wood, the advantage being that since they were made as a set, the two *empolia* could be hammered into place beforehand in the knowledge that when the drums were brought together there would be a perfectly accurate fit between *polos* and *empolia*. However, since the *poloi* and *empolia* could be accurately matched to each other beforehand, they also could be made of bronze, as is specified in a fourth-century inscription from Eleusis. The two bronze *empolia* could be sealed in their cuttings with lead, and the previously tested fit would avoid either sticking or looseness in the dry joint of peg and socket.

The builders of Periclean Athens were also more consistent in their use of dowels in walls than their predecessors. Since quite early in the sixth century flat metal dowels had sometimes been braced diagonally against the free end of a newly laid block, and it was this type of dowel, not the square wooden one, that Periclean builders used. Where possible they placed it at the free end of the block, so that there was no difficulty in pouring the lead sealing and the dowel was now set upright, to give a better purchase in all directions. Dowels of this type were characteristically used for each wall block, but in the last quarter of the fifth century dowels with a T-section, which gave added stiffness in both directions, were used at angles and wall ends.

WALL CONSTRUCTION

The fifth century saw an increase in the construction of public buildings other than temples. Even in the sixth century many secondary buildings in sanctuaries had been constructed making use of the full range of monumental techniques, particularly in the small but elaborate treasuries set up at Delphi and Olympia by individual city-states. Even less important buildings might have

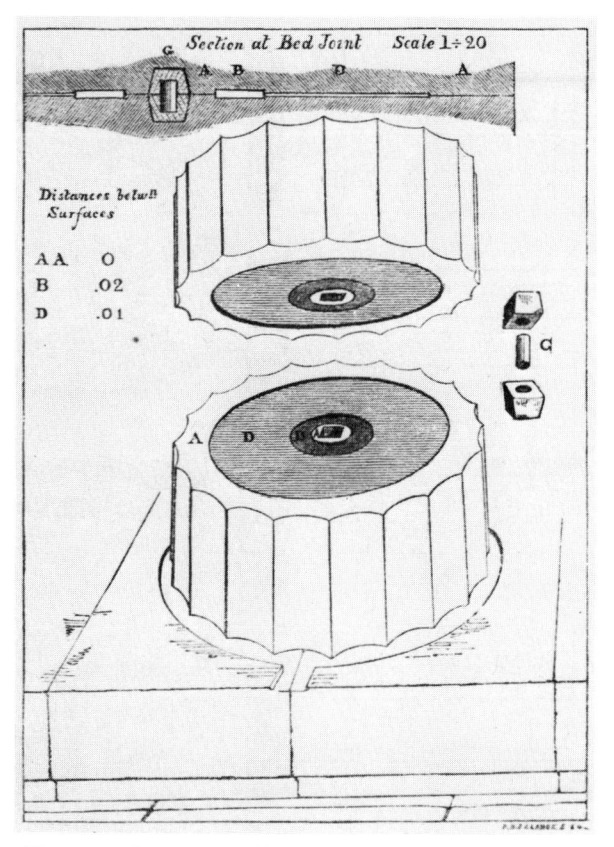

Figure 9. System used by the Greeks for joining stone column drums: cross-section at bed joint shows a *polos* fitted into two *empolia* and the varying degrees of band *anathyrosis* employed between the drums. *Reproduced from Francis Penrose,* AN INVESTIGATION OF THE PRINCIPLES OF ATHENIAN ARCHITECTURE (1851). THE NEW YORK PUBLIC LIBRARY

had mud-brick walls on a dressed stone base or stone columns carrying wooden beams. The same applies to the civic buildings that began to appear in the fifth century, particularly at Athens—stoas, council chambers, a recital hall, and so on. Also becoming increasingly elaborate in the fifth century were the fortification walls built for a city's defense. In the fifth century and earlier many of these walls had been built largely of mud-brick (for instance, the walls built around Athens after the Persian destruction of 480–479 B.C.). However, from the fourth century onward, most fortifications were built entirely of stone, and their masonry employed a variety of joint systems and surface finishes to create a greater range of effects than were normally applied to buildings (fig. 13). For both independent walls and buildings the choice of masonry type might have depended on place, period, building type, and stone type. Only the main variations will be covered here.

In major buildings coursed masonry had been the norm at least from the early sixth century, and usually a more or less regular arrangement of blocks was aimed at. The most regular system, known as "isodomic" (figs. 10, 12a), has all the courses above the orthostates of equal height, and in the best examples all the blocks are of the same length, so that the rising joints in alternate courses come exactly above each other (figs. 10a, b). Isodomic masonry was popular for temples and similar buildings from the early sixth century onward, particularly in mainland Greece and the western colonies. In less regular examples the height of the courses varied slightly, often decreasing toward the top. The blocks of isodomic masonry in a building characteristically ran the full thickness of the wall (fig. 10a), a sort of fossilization of brick construction.

The geographical division is not absolute, but in the Cyclades and east of the Aegean, a more economical system was often used that retained the two-skin construction of vernacular rubble walling. In some cases the inner face consisted of smaller blocks than the visually more important outer face, or it may even have been of a different, less prestigious stone, with only occasional through courses to bind the two faces together (fig. 11d). But a characteristic pattern for important buildings is to have courses consisting of two rows of blocks set on edge so that their broader sides face outward, alternating with courses of a single row of through blocks laid with narrower faces showing (fig. 11a). This usually results in the

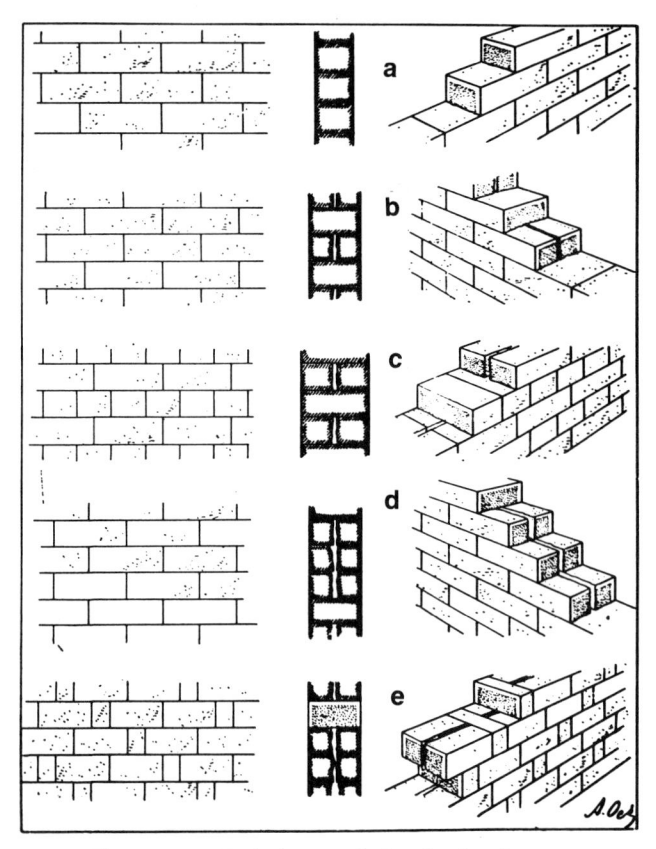

Figure 10. Variations of the isodomic system of coursed masonry. *Reproduced from Anastasios Orlandos, LES MATÉRIAUX DE CONSTRUCTION . . . (1966–1968). BY PERMISSION OF ÉDITIONS E. DE BOCCARD, PARIS*

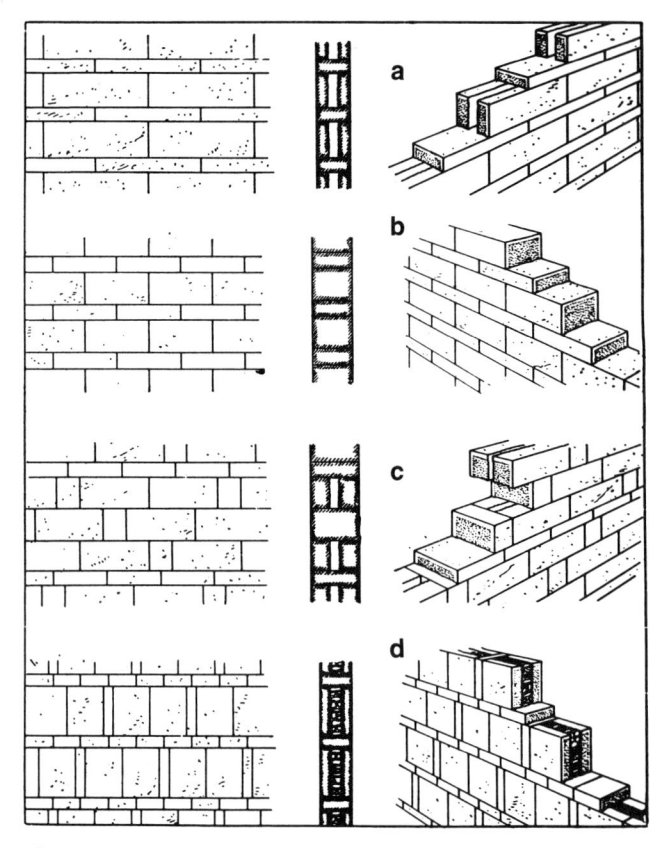

Figure 11. Variations of the pseudoisodomic system of coursed masonry. *Reproduced from Anastasios Orlandos, LES MATÉRIAUX DE CONSTRUCTION . . . (1966–1968). BY PERMISSION OF ÉDITIONS E. DE BOCCARD, PARIS*

alternation of high and low courses, the pseudoisodomic system (figs. 11, 12b), and it was sometimes applied with as much regularity in the jointing as the isodomic system. Appearance and construction were not always so connected, however; walls of uniform course height might consist of alternate two-row courses and through courses (fig. 10b), as in the Parthenon, or walls with alternating course heights might consist entirely of through blocks (fig. 11b). Both variants combine blocks of more than one size, allowing a more economical exploitation of the quarry.

Coursed masonry was also very common for retaining walls and fortification walls. The two faces of a fortification wall are in effect retaining walls holding up a looser filling, for there is rarely jointed masonry through its considerable thickness. In these contexts, particularly in the fourth century, the rising joints may be not vertical but sloping, so that the blocks are trapezoidal (fig. 12c); such blocks may be laid with very little attempt at coursing. Polygonal masonry—in which the visible block faces are polygons (fig. 12d)—was also popular in many areas and periods, although it rarely occurs in buildings. The most striking style of polygonal masonry uses curved joints, known in antiquity as Lesbian (fig. 12e), which necessitated the use of lead strips as flexible tem-

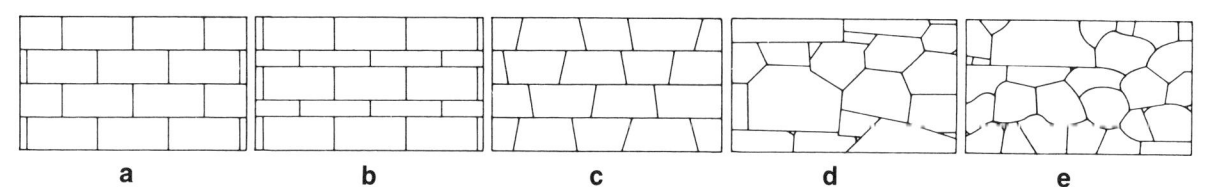

Figure 12. Athenian masonry styles: (*a*) isodomic (ashlar); (*b*) pseudoisodomic; (*c*) trapezoidal; (*d*) polygonal; (*e*) Lesbian polygonal. *Reproduced from John Camp and William B. Dinsmoor, Jr.,* ANCIENT ATHENIAN BUILDING METHODS © 1984 BY THE AMERICAN SCHOOL OF CLASSICAL STUDIES AT ATHENS

plates to transfer the curves required to the block being worked. It was popular mainly in the eastern and northern Aegean areas, although one of the best known examples retains the temple terrace at Delphi, and it is restricted to the archaic period. Much more widespread both in space and time was polygonal masonry with straight joints, which continued in use from the early fifth century though the Hellenistic period, though with an increasing tendency toward rough coursing. This too required each block to be specially shaped for its place, but since the joints are tight only at the wall face, the work involved is not as great as might appear. Polygonal masonry is sometimes combined with coursed masonry in ways that suggest that it was found particularly suitable for certain kinds of stone and was regarded as a more strongly interlocking system of masonry.

Fortifications and retaining walls also showed more variety in surface treatment than buildings did. They might be dressed to a flat face like the walls of most buildings, although not to the same degree of smoothness. But the visible block faces were often left more or less rough, or rusticated. In some cases this effect arose partly from the mason's normal procedures. A smooth band might be dressed around three or more edges of the visible block face, to maintain the vertical and horizontal alignment of the wall, while the rest of the face was never worked smooth, since the context did not require it. But often the roughness was not just an economy of labor; it was intended to enhance the effect of rugged strength appropriate to a fortification wall. A growing range of rusticated effects was evolved (fig. 13). The face might be left roughly projecting from the mason's initial hammer work, for instance, or worked flatter but striated with a heavy punch; it might be given beveled edges or a dressed margin all around, or it might be worked to a careful convex profile, this last being a Hellenistic feature. Particularly from the fourth century onward there were highly sophisticated variations in the surface treatment of different parts of the same wall.

Buildings commonly had smooth wall faces. When smooth margins around raised panels are found (fig. 3f), it is often hard to

Figure 13. Contrasting surface treatment on the rusticated wall of a circular tower at Eleusis, *ca.* 453–310 B.C. *Reproduced from Walther Wrede,* ATTISCHE MAUERN (1933)

293

know whether this is an effect resulting from the mason's work sequence that was simply allowed to remain, or whether it was positively desired. However, even in the sixth century, some surface textures were certainly intentional—for instance, the more or less regular honeycomb pattern on some eastern Greek and Cycladic walls; and in the fifth century we find obviously intended panel effects that emphasize the jointing. Elaborate systems of recessed margins were particularly popular on steps in the fourth-century Peloponnese, and in Asia Minor during the Hellenistic period the marble wall blocks of several temples have smooth margins around equally smooth but slightly raised panels. It is not surprising that in buildings of cheaper materials this last effect was reproduced in stucco.

The H-shaped clamp (fig. 8f) that had been the dominant form of masonry tie in the fifth century continued well into the fourth, but early in the fourth century, Peloponnesian masons began to replace it with the simpler ⌐⌐-shaped clamp (fig. 8g). This clamp was not set in a large dovetail cutting like the reinforced dovetail clamp (fig. 8b), but leaded into a cutting of the same shape as itself. This form, which became almost universal during the Roman Empire, spread to all areas of mainland Greece during the fourth century and also to Asia Minor and the islands. In these last areas, however, the influence of archaic architecture was in many ways strong, and the archaic type of reinforced dovetail clamp remained popular throughout the Hellenistic period, when it was sometimes left intentionally visible. Peloponnesian masons seem also to have been responsible for a change in the system of joining column drums. From the middle of the fourth century the usual square *empolion* cutting was accompanied by additional cuttings, usually for flat or square metal dowels, and it became increasingly common for the bottom drum to be doweled to the stylobate, as it never had been previously.

TECHNICAL DEVELOPMENTS IN THE HELLENISTIC PERIOD
(*ca.* 323–31 B.C.)

The fourth century and Hellenistic period saw the building of a number of colossal temples, several of them succeeding archaic temples of similar size, which they more or less copied. This activity reintroduced the need to lift blocks much heavier than the ten or twelve tons to which classical builders had restricted themselves, but by now that was achieved by multiple-pulley hoists of improved design. The Roman architect Vitruvius describes two devices, the compound winch and the treadwheel, which would allow extra power to be applied (see figs. 3, 4 in ENGINEERING).

Royal patronage of architecture, which was a feature of the Hellenistic period, brought new scope for elaboration in some buildings, including the use of variegated stones and precious metals. However, the aspect of Hellenistic architecture that affected building techniques most widely was the sheer quantity of it. Large numbers of new cities were founded, all requiring defensive walls, agoras, and sanctuaries. Cities both old and new, large and small, expected to have a wide range of civic buildings—stoas, council chambers, theaters, gymnasia, and stadia. Even houses imitated as best they could the columns and masonry of public buildings. It is therefore no surprise to find features that represent economies in labor or materials. In the ubiquitous porticoes of the period a slightly more complex roof structure required fewer large beams for a given span and area, and the very large clear spans in some Hellenistic meeting halls suggest that the advantages of the tie-

Figure 14. Corbeling used to form triangular stepped archways in the dividing walls of a cistern found in the ruins of a Pelasgic city near Mesolongi. *Reproduced from Edward Dodwell, VIEWS AND DESCRIPTIONS OF CYCLOPIAN OR PELASGIC REMAINS IN GREECE AND ITALY (1834).* THE NEW YORK PUBLIC LIBRARY

beam truss may occasionally have been recognized. As for stone work, the continued lightening of the proportions of columns and entablature and the growing preference for textured wall surfaces were probably justified at the time on aesthetic grounds, but would certainly have cut costs as well. More obvious economies are the less careful finishing of individual elements such as column capitals, and the general adoption of the horizontal pour-channel, a shallow groove cut in the top of a block to allow molten lead to be run to a dowel hole. This was a simple method but necessarily left one end of the channel visible.

Throughout centuries of development the structural system of Greek building based on vertical supports carrying horizontal beams remained largely unchanged. There are occasional elaborations such as the hidden fins of stone ribs on the ceiling beams of the Hieron at Samothrace, which increase the effective height of the beams and their strength, or the skillful cantilever balance in the main frieze of the Propylaea at Athens, which reduces the load on the long central architrave, but they make little impact on structural practice in general. Another structural principle well known to the Greeks was that of corbeling where successive horizontal courses overhang one another, projecting farther and farther outward from the two sides of an opening until they meet, forming a stepped arch (fig. 14).

It had been most skillfully used in Bronze Age Greece and was used for tombs in areas near the fringes of the Greek world (Thessaly, Thrace, and Etruria) from the seventh century or earlier. But corbeling required massive supports, and the high curving underface did not fit well with Greek architectural forms. For the Greeks it belonged rather to the realm of civil engineering, to be used in drains, cisterns, underground tombs, fortifications, and such.

More might have been expected from a knowledge of the true arch, constructed with wedge-shaped blocks (voussoirs) and radiating joints between them (fig. 15), and the extension of an arch in the formation of a vault. These had been used in the brick architecture of Egypt and the Near East for centuries, and their widespread appearance in Greek architecture from about 325 B.C. onward may well be due to the experience gained by Greek architects and engineers working in these areas as a result of the eastern campaigns of Alexander the Great. Some evidence suggests, however, that the principle may have been known to the Greeks earlier (presumably from the same source), although scarcely applied. From the late fourth century on the true arch and vault quickly established themselves in much the same contexts as corbeling, and they appear in the substructures of several buildings, particularly those of Pergamene inspiration. But they seldom play an important visible part in buildings (among partial exceptions are the gate to the agora at Priene and the stoa of Attalos at Athens). Nor were the structural advantages of the arch fully exploited. The usual gap spanned was 10 to 16 feet (3 to 5 m) and the largest known clear span was less than 24 1/2 feet (7.5 m). This contrasts strikingly with Roman architecture of a similar period, where substantial vaulted buildings are dated from the early second century onward, and the masonry arches of the Milvian

Figure 15. The true arch as found in the substructure of the east hall of the gymnasium at Pergamum, third century B.C.: (*top*) restored view based upon (*bottom*) existing architectural remains. *Reproduced from Paul Schazmann,* ALTERTÜMER VON PERGAMON VI (1923). THE NEW YORK PUBLIC LIBRARY

(Mulvian) Bridge at Rome (109 B.C.) span about 59 feet (18 m). Vaulting in fact revolutionized the whole nature of Roman architecture.

Two reasons for this difference may be

suggested. First, the elaborate formal patterns of column and entablature, so deeply rooted in Greek architecture, did not mix easily with arches and vaulting; in many contexts, although not for temples, Roman builders were less reluctant to abandon or adapt these patterns if that seemed advantageous. Second, by the early second century B.C. Roman builders had developed a concrete of rubble laid in strong mortar as a major building material. In this medium the curves of arches and vaults were much more easily executed than in the careful mortar-free masonry that Greek builders wished to use. Under the Roman Empire Greek builders also adopted rubble and mortar vaulting for some buildings, notably baths, but their architecture continued to depend heavily on columns and beams, and on dry-laid megalithic masonry. If the Roman architects were masters of vaulting, the Greeks remained masters of construction in finely worked stone.

BIBLIOGRAPHY

Thomas D. Boyd, "The Arch and Vault in Greek Architecture," in *American Journal of Archaeology*, **82** (1978); Alan C. Brooks, "Stoneworking in the Geometric Period in Corinth," in *Hesperia*, **50** (1981); Alison Burford, "Heavy Transport in Classical Transport," in *Economic History Review*, **13** (1960); J. J. Coulton, "Lifting in Early Greek Architecture," in *Journal of Hellenic Studies*, **94** (1974), and *Greek Architects at Work*, 2d. ed. (1982); William B. Dinsmoor, "Structural Iron in Greek Architecture," in *American Journal of Archaeology*, **26** (1922), and *The Architecture of Ancient Greece* (1950); Heinrich Drerup, *Griechische Baukunst in geometrischer Zeit*, Archaeologia Homerica, II (1969).

A. Trevor Hodge, *The Woodwork of Greek Roofs* (1960), and "Bevelled Joints and the Direction of Laying in Greek Architecture," in *American Journal of Archaeology*, **79** (1975); A. Trevor Hodge and Richard A. Tomlinson, "Some Notes on the Temple of Nemesis at Rhamnous," in *American Journal of Archaeology*, **73** (1969); Wolf Koenigs, "Beobachtungen zur Steintechnik am Apollon-Tempel von Naxos," in *Jahrbuch des Deutschen Archäologischen Instituts*, **87** (1972); Robert Koldewey and Otto Puchstein, *Die griechische Tempel in Unteritalien und Sizilien* (1899); Roland Martin, *Manuel d'architecture grecque*, 1: *Matériaux et techniques* (1965).

Anastasios K. Orlandos, "Preliminary Dowels," in *American Journal of Archaeology*, **19** (1915), and *Les matériaux de construction et la technique architecturale des anciens Grecs*, Vanna Hadjimichali and Krista Laumonier, trans., 2 vols. (1966–1968); James M. Paton, ed., *The Erechtheum* (1927); Robert L. Scranton, *Greek Walls* (1941); Richard A. Tomlinson, "*Emplekton* Masonry and 'Greek *Structura*,'" in *Journal of Hellenic Studies*, **81** (1961); Arnold Tschira, "Die unfertigen Säulentrommeln auf der Akropolis von Athen," in *Jahrbuch des Deutschen Archäologischen Instituts*, **55** (1940), and "Keildubel," in *Mitteilungen des Deutschen Archäologischen Instituts, Athenische Abteilung*, **66** (1941).

ROMAN BUILDING TECHNIQUES

JAMES E. PACKER

REPUBLICAN CONSTRUCTION (509–31 B.C.)

From their ancestors of the Iron Age (which began in central Italy around 900 B.C.), republican builders inherited a variety of techniques. Wattle-and-daub still appeared in the rustic huts of shepherds—and sometimes even in more sophisticated urban buildings. In these structures, as in the early Iron Age huts on the Palatine Hill in Rome, floors were often sunken slightly below ground level. At the corners, vertical wooden beams supported both the walls, of interlocking branches (the wattle) protected with mud (the daub), and a sloping thatched roof. Yet, as noted by Vitruvius, the famous Roman architectural theorist of the late first century B.C., while these buildings were easy to construct, their wooden frameworks expanded and contracted with moisture, breaking off the daub; and they were "like torches ready for kindling."

Mud-brick buildings with wooden roofs protected by fired clay tiles were safer and more durable. Dating from the early second century B.C., utilitarian structures of this kind bordered the forum at the Roman colony of Cosa (located about sixty-five miles [105 km] northwest of Rome). Of squared limestone blocks, their stone foundations supported walls of brick dried in the sun. Limestone quoins protected corners and doorways, and coats of external and internal plaster beautified the walls and insulated them from the elements.

The republican temple, which followed Etruscan models, was of similar construction. Its walls (in earlier times of stuccoed mud-brick; later, of regular stone slabs) stood on a stone platform (the podium). At each of the short ends the walls supported a triangular pediment, which, at the front of the building, rose above the stuccoed stone columns of the front porch. The gabled roof consisted of wooden beams, rectangular in section, protected above by terra-cotta tiles and embellished with terra-cottas: brightly colored plaques on the sides and ends of the temple and statuary in the triangular pediments and on pedestals along the ridge of the roof.

THE PRINCIPAL MATERIALS

Tufa and Travertine

Thus, for the builders of the early and middle republic (*ca.* 509–146 B.C.), in utilitarian buildings, in temples, in city walls, the most important long-lasting material was stone. For their early monumental structures, the inhabitants of Rome used the sedimentary tufas found in and around the city.

Later builders obtained their materials from more distant sources, but the techniques of quarrying, which the Romans probably learned from the Etruscans, changed very little over the centuries. Using hammers and picks, laborers partially separated a block from its bed with four vertical cuts. Then, along the zone still attached to the bed, they inserted the horizontal wedges used to free the piece completely. The resulting rectangular block was transported either on a sledge or a two-wheeled cart pulled by a team of oxen. Sometimes the stone was rolled on wooden wheels attached to the short ends.

In the century after 50 B.C., tufa, a stone formed by calcareous and siliceous deposits of springs, lakes, and ground water, was one of the commonest stones used in construction. One variety, salmon-colored with reddish brown and white inclusions, came from the south bank of the Anio (Aniene) River, about three miles (5 km) east of Rome, not far from modern Tor Cervara. Peperino, a light, porous volcanic rock famous for its fire-resistant character, enjoyed even greater popularity with late republican and early imperial builders. Quarried near Lake Albano, this hard, grayish stone with black and white inclusions retained crisp architectural detail. Builders used it in a variety of monuments for columns, entablatures, and walls like the impressive ones that served as firebreaks around the imperial forums of Augustus, Nerva, and Trajan in Rome.

After the beginning of the first century A.D., builders frequently combined peperino with travertine, a limestone formed in the hot springs connected to the prehistoric volcanoes of Latium. Quarried near Tibur (Tivoli), which gave the stone its name, this cream-colored rock occurs in regular horizontal strata broken by hollows left by the disintegration of organic materials. Despite these imperfections, its attractive color and great strength made travertine popular with late republic and early imperial architects. Readily carved, it resisted the vicissitudes of ordinary weathering for long periods, although it chipped and flaked when exposed to fire. Travertine quarries lay twelve miles (20 km) from Rome and transportation costs rendered the stone relatively expensive; masons most frequently employed it in areas subject to weathering or hard usage: corners, podiums, even whole facades of important monuments such as the Theater of Marcellus and the Colosseum.

Unfortunately, granular tufa and porous travertine did not permit precise execution of the smooth architectural profiles the Romans had observed on the Greek buildings of southern Italy and the Hellenistic East. Consequently, builders usually concealed these stones under layers of a fine white stucco composed of plaster and marble dust in which skilled artisans executed the decorative details. Such work initially had the appearance of marble, but it weathered easily, and the resulting breaks, cracks, and chips necessitated frequent restorations. Worse yet, buildings of stuccoed tufa and travertine were deemed not worthy of an imperial capital.

Marble and Granite

For such reasons, the Romans began to import marble on a large scale early in the first century B.C., and by the reign of Augustus (31 B.C.–A.D. 14) many important buildings—like the temple of Mars Ultor in Augustus' new forum or the temple of Apollo Sosianus near the Theater of Marcellus—had marble walls or marble veneers. The colony of Luna (near modern Carrara) on the border between Liguria and Etruria, nearly 200 miles (322 km) northwest of Rome, became the most accessible source of white marble. Laborers transported blocks of this local, fine-grained, pure white or bluish white stone a few miles to the coast where, loaded on ships, the cheapest form of transportation, the stone blocks were carried to Ostia, the port at the mouth of the Tiber River. From there, rafts floated them up the river to Rome's Marmorata, the marble yards lying in the plain along the east bank of the Tiber between the Aventine Hill and Monte Testaccio, that enormous mound of potsherds (the remains of broken *dolia,* or storage jars, and amphorae, or wine jars). Other excellent white marbles originated in Greece on Mounts Hymettus and Pentelicus near Athens and on the island of Paros. Yet, while these stones were prized for color and texture, high cost restricted their large-scale use.

Economic considerations did not, however, limit the importation of colored marbles. By the end of the first century B.C., several types from all parts of the empire were readily available. Giallo antico, purple-veined and golden, came from Chemtou in Numidia (modern Tunisia); cipollino, greenish with black-and-white veins and deposits of mica, from Karystos on the Greek island of Euboea; africano, brightly colored with reds or pinks, whites, and grays on a dark background, from Teos (Kara Göl) on the coast of Asia Minor; pavonazzetto, white with purple veins, from Docimeum (Esçekarahisan) in Phrygia (central western Turkey); calcite and aragonite alabaster, intricately veined in gold, brown, and white, from sites near Tell al-'Amarna in Egypt and Damascus in Syria. To this already varied palette, the emperors of the first century A.D. added several new discoveries. Claudius (41–54) introduced gray granite from Mons Claudianus in Upper Egypt. Nero imported porphyry, an exceptionally hard, white-flecked purple stone from quarries near the Red Sea; and, between A.D. 70 and 75, Vespasian brought red granite from Syene (Aswan) in Upper Egypt to Rome.

These stones were carved into decorative moldings or, sawn into slabs, were used as pavements and veneers. Thin sheets of alabaster were even used to glaze windows that provided the kind of richly subdued golden light still to be seen today in the nineteenth-century Basilica of St. Paul's Outside the Walls. Columns were also of colored marbles. Those of giallo antico, pavonazzetto, and africano were normally fluted; those of alabaster and the harder stones, porphyry and red and gray granite, were plain. Owing to the great compressive strength of granite, columns intended to carry heavy loads were often cut from this stone. Once smoothed and polished, granite retained its finish after centuries of exposure to the weather.

Construction in Stone

The Romans probably learned from the Etruscans to fashion walls from rectangular blocks of stone laid in regular courses; and certainly the fully developed technique, which appeared in Rome in the late sixth century B.C., suggests that, following Greek techniques, Etruscan craftsmen trained local apprentices. Late republican and early imperial walls of squared stone displayed several different bonds. In one type, the joints of one course appear above the centers of that below. In another (fig. 1a), headers, blocks laid with the short ends exposed on the face of the wall, alternated with stretchers, blocks positioned with the long sides visible. In still another (fig. 1b), according to a peculiarly Roman system, courses of headers and stretchers alternated. Doors or windows were generally arches in which wedge-shaped voussoirs rose in a curve from either side to a keystone.

Concrete

Another material widely used in the Rome of the first several centuries of the Christian era was concrete. In his advice to builders of harbors, Vitruvius describes (5.12.5) the composition of this concrete as "stone [rubble, crushed, gravel], lime, and sand"; and, in his view, pozzolana, the volcanic sand that worked best (named for the Pozzuoli region in Campania), came from Baiae (Baia, a luxurious seaside resort just north of the Bay of Naples) and from around Mount Vesuvius. But pozzuolana also occurred in Latium, and by the late first century B.C., foundations, walls faced with squared stone, and even whole buildings were constructed in concrete—a revolutionary change in Roman architectural practice.

Since concrete weathers easily, both sides of exposed walls had outer skins of small stones. Each was rectangular with one end square and the other pointed. The square end showed on the face of the wall; the point bonded the stone to the concrete interior. By the middle of the first century B.C., the facings on these walls had assumed the appearance of the regular netlike pattern today called reticulate (fig. 1c). Until the beginning of Claudius' reign, such overall stone facing remained fashionable. Thereafter, re-

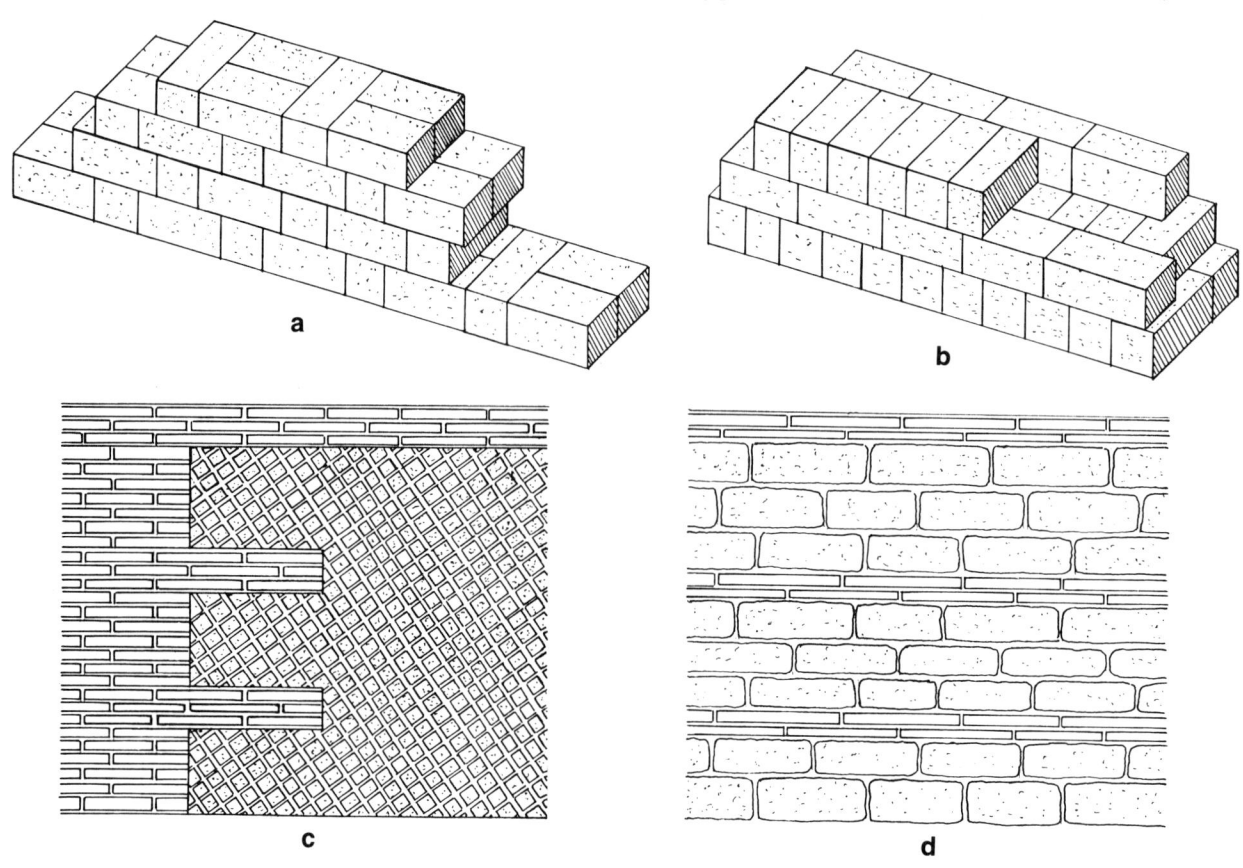

Figure 1. Different bonds of construction in squared stone: (*a*) alternating headers and stretchers in the same course; (*b*) headers and stretchers alternating in different courses; (*c*) concrete wall faced with reticulate divided into sections by brick courses and quoins; (*d*) concrete wall faced with courses of reused brick and tufa blocks.
ALL DRAWINGS BY THE AUTHOR UNLESS CREDITED OTHERWISE

ticulate faced the broad wall surfaces while blocks of tufa or brick were used as quoins at exterior corners. By the latter part of the first century A.D., brick courses also divided the faces of concrete walls, framing sections of reticulate. In all such construction, the bricks were *bipedales,* tiles two Roman feet square halved to form triangles laid with their apexes facing the interior of the wall. (A Roman foot was approximately 11 2/3 in., or 29.6 cm.)

About the beginning of Hadrian's reign (A.D. 117), brick completely supplanted reticulate as a facing, and until the end of the century, concrete walls were sheathed only in brick. Sometimes these walls were stuccoed; often the bricks were clearly visible with designs picked out in yellow, white, or the natural grayish purple of volcanic pumice. After the death of Commodus in A.D. 192, however, the large-scale building projects of the second century had few successors. With a few exceptions, like the new walls built around the city by Aurelian (A.D. 270–275) and the Baths of Diocletian, dedicated by his colleague Maximian in A.D. 305 or 306), the emperors did not undertake major new public works. In consequence, the brick industry declined, and most concrete walls were faced with quoins and courses of tufa blocks with stretches of reused brick (fig. 1d). Dating walls of this period is extremely difficult, but in general the less regularly shaped the tufa blocks and the wider the joints of the mortar that held them, the later the wall. Theodoric I, Ostrogothic king of Italy (A.D. 493–526) after the collapse of the Roman Empire in the West, was the last to construct and repair buildings in Rome with faced concrete.

Architectural Terra-cottas

Although late republican and imperial builders no longer made the large, brightly colored terra-cotta (fired clay) reliefs and full-size statues of Etruscan and early Roman temples, they still manufactured a number of specialized terra-cotta items. Unglazed tiles were the most ubiquitous. The usual covering for roofs, Roman tiles, which copied Greek models, were of two types: pan and cover tiles. Typically rectangular or trapezoidal, the flat pantiles had flanges on the long sides. The cover tiles were semicircular (figs. 2a, 2b) or triangular. Linked by flanges, pantiles lay either on the narrow planks that constituted the uppermost section of the underlying wooden roof (figs. 2b, 2c) or were attached with nails to the battens on which the planks rested. Cover tiles concealed the flanges and, more important, sealed the open joint between them.

Pipes were also frequently made of terracotta. In section, they were either circular or rectangular. The former were drains; the latter, chimneys for ovens, kilns, or hot-air ducts built into the floors and walls of rooms heated by subterranean furnaces (like baths and the more elegantly appointed chambers in palaces). Other specialized tiles, the so-called *tegulae mammatae,* had knobs that kept the tile away from the face of the wall against which it was laid and prevented moisture from reaching the stuccoed surface finish. Some tiles were even cast into the conventional profiles of stone moldings, and in many cases these terra-cotta surfaces displayed the appropriate decoration (for example, an egg-and-dart enrichment on an ovolo, an egg-shaped curve). And finally, masons might carve courses of corbeled brick jutting out from the walls into decorative moldings.

Wood

Little wood survives from imperial Roman times, although it was a common construction material. As late as the first century A.D. many tenement houses were built with wooden frames filled with concrete and rubble. In Herculaneum, destroyed by the eruption of Mount Vesuvius in A.D. 79, the skele-

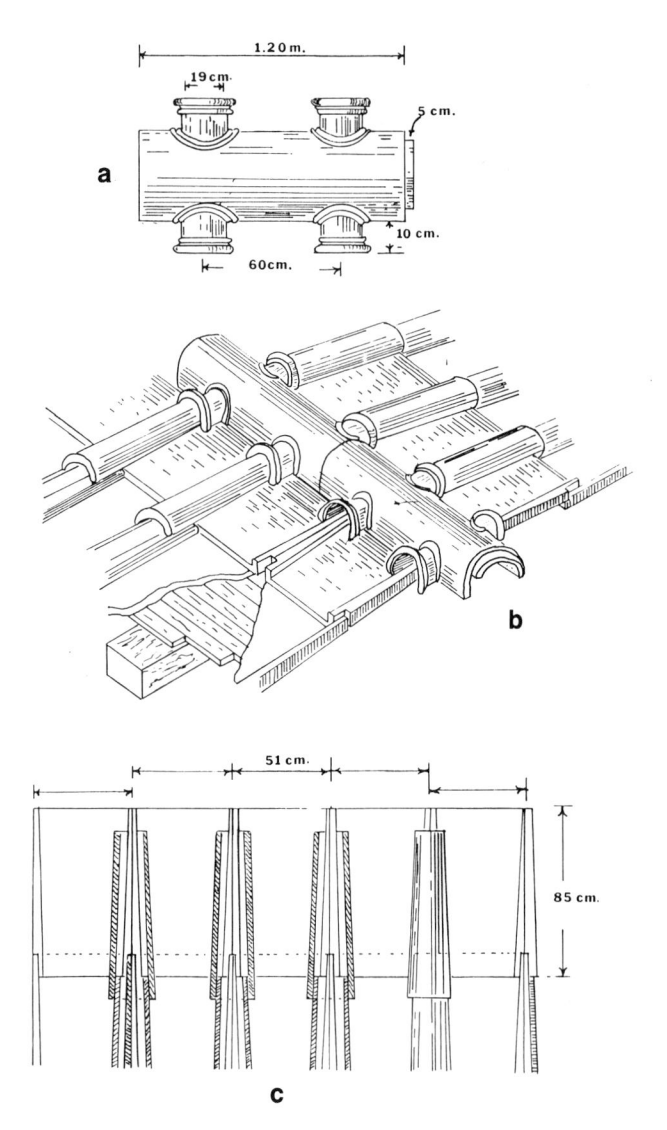

Figure 2. Roof tiles: (*a*) cover tile for ridge pole; (*b*) pantiles and cover tiles in position; (*c*) cover tiles sectioned to show flanges on pantiles underneath (*after Durm, 1905*).

ton of one such tenement, the "House of the Wooden Frame," has been restored by modern excavators; two of the original three or four stories are still standing.

The better-constructed tenements of the second and third centuries A.D. in Ostia and Rome had walls of brick-faced concrete, but many of the floors consisted of wooden joists and planking, while virtually all buildings of every period had wooden door frames and window frames, doors, and shutters. In public buildings wood appeared chiefly in roofs and ceilings, although the latter were stuccoed and/or gilded to conceal the beams. Wood also played an invaluable role in concrete construction. Wooden beams and boards served as forms for walls, simple and coffered vaults, and domes.

The most common varieties of wood were fir and pine, both easily sawn. The lowland fir was in particular demand for its great durability and size—fir achieved lengths of over 100 Roman feet (97 ft./30 m); and even pines were usually at least 60 Roman feet (58 ft./18 m) high. Oak was much prized for its strength, and although no longer than 30 Roman feet (29 ft./9 m), oak boards were of sufficient size for door frames and window frames. Elm served the same purpose and was also sawn into beams. Despite the high cost of transportation to Rome, Alpine larch was sought after for its fire-resisting characteristics; cedar and juniper, for their ability to withstand rot. Indeed, Vitruvius notes (2.9.13) that for this reason the statue of the goddess and the coffered ceiling in the famous temple of Artemis (Diana) at Ephesus were constructed of these woods.

Bronze

The Romans learned from the Greeks and Etruscans to work bronze. Most items were cast in molds. Smaller objects were normally solid; larger pieces were hollow-cast around a sand or clay core that was later partially or completely removed. Bronze was used in construction largely for utilitarian items such as hinges, keys, and handles. On a larger scale, it was used for sheathing, like that of the beams in the porch of Hadrian's Pantheon, and for gilded tiles, like those on the roofs of the temple of Jupiter Optimus Maximus on the Capitoline Hill, on the Basilica Ulpia, and on Hadrian's temple of

Venus and Rome (and also on his Pantheon). Some architectural bronze was purely decorative. Gilded bronze statues and reliefs embellished major public buildings; some luxurious private mansions and public buildings included Corinthian columns with capitals of gilt bronze. Bronze screens, grills, and balustrades were common. Bronze rosettes adorned coffered ceilings, and there were monumental doors fabricated from large sheets of bronze nailed to wooden frames. Some bronze doors, including those of the Pantheon, the curia or senate house (now in the main entrance of St. John Lateran), and the temple of Romulus in the Forum Romanum still survive.

TECHNIQUES OF CONSTRUCTION

The Architectural Programs of the Julio-Claudians and Flavians in Rome (A.D. 14–96)

The materials described above were employed in the large-scale reconstruction of Rome that, beginning in the late first century B.C., continued for nearly three centuries. Ambitious to increase the splendor of the capital, Augustus impressed upon it the stamp of his own personality, building on a grand scale. His famous statement that he found Rome a city of brick and left it one of marble was no idle boast. By 28 B.C., he had reconstructed no fewer than eighty-two temples; before his death in A.D. 14, he had overseen the total renovation of two of the most important shrines in the Forum Romanum: the temples of Castor and Concord. His new forum (figs. 3, 4), which adjoined the Forum Romanum, bore his own name; and under the guise of private munificence, his son-in-law Marcus Agrippa erected an entire new quarter in the Campus Martius, the field that for centuries had been the parade ground of the Roman army.

Lacking Augustus' good sense, his Julio-Claudian descendants disdained his affectedly modest style of living. Yet, their fondness for grandiose new buildings nonetheless proved them his true heirs. Tiberius and Gaius (Caligula) added a new imperial residence on the Palatine Hill. Claudius built several aqueducts and a new harbor at the mouth of the Tiber. After the great fire of A.D. 64, Nero had the opportunity to rebuild the greater part of Rome, and while his housing projects alleviated the suffering caused by the fire and he also sensibly insisted that new tenements be solidly constructed in fireproof, brick-faced concrete, his appropriation of a vast plot in the center of the city between the Palatine, Esquiline (Oppian), and Caelian hills for the site of a luxurious palace generated widespread criticism. The name alone, the "Golden House," commemorates the splendid appointments of this structure, but only a part of the domestic wing survives today, embedded in the substructures of the Baths of Trajan.

Like Nero the Flavians, the dynasty founded by Vespasian in A.D. 69, built much. Vespasian inherited a capital still largely in ruins from the Neronian fire and again partially destroyed in the fighting that had established his regime. The most urgent need was to restore the official state sanctuary, the temple of Jupiter Optimus Maximus, which had burned in the civil war. After rededicating that shrine in A.D. 75, Vespasian turned to other projects: the Temple of Peace, a sanctuary with a large-scale colonnaded precinct, which, despite its name, was an addition to the growing numbers of imperial forums (figs. 3, 4), and a grandiose new amphitheater in concrete and travertine, the Amphitheatrum Flavianum, today better known as the Colosseum.

Titus' short reign allowed him time only

Figure 3. General view of the imperial forums as restored by Italo Gismondi: (1) Forum of Trajan with (2) Temple of Trajan and its precinct, (3) Greek and Latin libraries, (4) Column of Trajan, (5) Basilica Ulpia, (6) east and west colonnades and (7) hemicycles; (8) Forum of Caesar with (9) Temple of Venus Genetrix; (10) Forum of Augustus with (11) Temple of Mars Ultor; (12) Forum-of-Transit (Forum of Nerva); (13) Temple of Peace; (14) Basilica Aemilia facing into (15) Forum Romanum. Reconstruction model by Pierino di Carlo. ROME, MUSEUM OF ROMAN CIVILIZATION

to dedicate the Colosseum and the adjacent public baths, probably also under construction during his father, Vespasian's, last years. Domitian, his younger brother and successor, displayed a mania for building. With his architect Rabirius, he terraced the southwest slope of the Palatine Hill to erect a handsome new imperial residence. He restored the temple of Jupiter Optimus Maximus after it had again burned in A.D. 80; and, in the narrow space between the Temple of Peace and the Forum of Augustus, he installed a new forum, the so-called Forum-of-Transit (Forum Transitorium, later known as the Forum of Nerva) (figs. 3, 4). But, since the space available in that narrow piazza limited the range of architectural possibilities, Domitian began a second large forum for which, just prior to his assassination in A.D. 96, he had purchased and cleared a site just north of the Forum of Augustus.

The Roman Construction Industry

The demands of imperial construction projects, succeeding one another for over a century, created a sophisticated industry that was supervised by an imperial ministry of public works. Made up of numerous and specialized employees and bureaucrats (like those attested in the office of the superintendent of the public water supply), its staff was responsible for overseeing the supply of vital building materials.

The manufacture of brick, that all-important facing for concrete walls, long in hands of several well-to-do families whose names are known for having been stamped on the products of their yards, became an imperial monopoly in the third century A.D. In the imperial brickyards, workers dug and prepared the clay, forced it into molds—adding straw as necessary—then stored and inventoried each day's production. The yards manufactured *bipedales,* somewhat smaller *sesquipedales* (square tiles with sides of 1 1/2 Roman feet [17.5 in./44.4 cm]), different kinds of tile for roofs, drains, and flues, and smaller profiled tiles for decorative moldings. In order to keep track of production, at specified intervals of every so many bricks, workers stamped individual pieces with standardized patterns that included the name of the brickyard and its supervisor. By the early second century, the names of the consuls, the state's ancient republican magistrates, also appeared. From this evidence modern scholars can easily work out the date of a building.

Supplies of marble were no less important, and so Tiberius and his successors expropriated the major quarries for the state. Greeks in the classical period had frequently paid for quarried marble block by block. Under the Romans, quarries that exported popular marbles increased their output, turning out such mass-produced items as monolithic column shafts with standardized heights of 24, 30, 40, even 50 Roman feet (23, 29, 39, 49 ft./7, 9, 12, 15 m). Frequently, artisans skilled in working a local marble accompanied shipments to their final destination, and thus introduced Rome to foreign styles and techniques. This system assured those in charge of the quarries a regular market for their products and provided builders with abundant materials for shafts, veneers, and pavements, a regular inventory that did not require months or years for delivery.

In the late first and second centuries A.D., Rome absorbed most of this marble, although occasionally other cities or private individuals might purchase some either at the quarries or at the ports where the marble was loaded for shipment to Rome. But, by the late second century, the stockpiles of foreign marbles at the Marmorata had increased to the point where some blocks and shafts were not used for years—or even centuries. Indeed, when the Marmorata was excavated in the nineteenth century, a few pieces were retrieved and later sold to J. Paul Getty for his elaborate reconstruction of a Roman villa (the Villa dei Papiri, outside Herculaneum) in Malibu, California. The great abundance lowered the cost of imported marbles, and in the late second and early third centuries, individuals and cities all over the empire could afford them.

Enormous numbers of skilled workers transformed the raw materials into finished buildings. These men belonged to guilds, which were not unions in the modern sense, but associations of specialists in the same trade that offered their members financial benefits such as assistance with funerals and the construction of tombs. The variety of the guilds demonstrates the high degree of specialization that characterized the work force. There were experts in demolition, lime carriers, cutters of stone, marble workers, brickmakers, bronze and iron smiths, layers of pavements (mosaicists and those who installed marble floors), plasterers, painters, pipemakers, and common laborers. Some craftsmen were free, others were slaves; the relative number of each group remains a mystery.

All craftsmen worked under the supervision of an architect, an honored professional whose colleagues came from varied backgrounds. Some were ex-slaves, others were Greeks; some specialized in military engineering, others worked in the imperial service or practiced privately. Whatever his sphere of activity, each architect had served a long and thorough professional apprenticeship that tempered and refined his natural abilities. "For," in the words of Vitruvius (1.1.3) "neither talent without instruction nor instruction without talent can produce the perfect craftsman . . . a man of letters, a skillful draftsman, a mathematician, familiar with historical studies."

Among the famous imperial architects were Severus and Celer, who designed Nero's Golden House and perhaps many of the new brick-faced tenements that replaced the blocks of flats destroyed in the great fire. Rabirius drew up the plans for Domitian's palace on the Palatine Hill and was probably responsible for the spectacular design of the Forum Transitorium and a grandiose suburban villa at Albanum (Albano). Apollodorus of Damascus, Rabirius' successor, achieved an even greater reputation; his works for Trajan included an impressive military bridge across the Danube, a concert hall, a set of baths built over the remains of Nero's Golden House on the Esquiline Hill, and the splendid Forum of Trajan—the completion of Domitian's project north of the Forum of Augustus.

THE FORUM OF TRAJAN

Ancient sources single out the Forum of Trajan (figs. 3, 4, 10) as the most impressive monument in imperial Rome. Summing up the opinion of late antiquity, Ammianus Marcellinus described it in the fourth century as "a construction unique under the heavens, as we believe, and admirable even in the unanimous opinion of the gods . . . a gigantic complex beggaring descriptions and never again to be imitated by mortal men" (10.10.5). With its size and elaborate, unified design, the varied functions it fulfilled, the large number of materials displayed in its buildings, and the multiplicity of crafts involved in its construction, this forum was a characteristic example of an important imperial project, and a closer examination of how it was constructed will illustrate the many different facets of Rome's construction industry in imperial times.

Rabirius had probably completed a set of designs for a new imperial forum before Domitian's death in A.D. 96. Like the grand residences he had built for the emperor on the Palatine Hill, the forum would have stressed Domitian's power and majesty—had it been finished in his lifetime—and would probably have emphasized his military conquests on the northern frontiers. Rabirius may also have considered more mundane matters: it may have been his idea to separate the Market Place on the slopes of the Esquiline Hill from the public buildings in the forum proper, the structures that were to provide dignified settings for the meetings of lawyers, politicians, and common citizens. Certainly, work to clear the site had begun. Demolition workers probably had already torn down most of the buildings whose foundations are today exposed just north of Trajan's Column, and the slopes of the Esquiline must have been cut back into four grandiose terraces. But Domitian's murder delayed further work for ten years, during which the imperial succession passed briefly to Nerva, then to Trajan.

After his conquest of Dacia (Romania, in A.D. 101–102, 105–106), Trajan returned to Rome and commenced his building projects, among them an elegant set of public baths on the Esquiline Hill and a new concert hall. He also decided to complete Domitian's forum, and chose as architect a member of his military staff, Apollodorus of Damascus, the talented designer of the new Roman buildings and an impressive bridge across the Danube, built during the campaigns in Dacia.

Working closely with the emperor, Apollodorus clarified the chief objectives of the design that would first and foremost exalt the emperor by graphically illustrating various aspects of his power. Trajan was to be projected as a benefactor of the needy, a victorious general, a wise lawgiver, and, after his death, a superhuman hero and acknowledged divinity. Each of the forum's sections would illustrate one of these elements.

Apollodorus accepted Rabirius' earlier decision to restrict commercial activities to a completely separate complex of several stories on the terraces of the Quirinal Hill. In this section Trajan was the Great Provider, the source of imperial munificence. In the spacious court in the center of the forum, he was the majestically omnipotent conqueror of Dacia. To the south, the entrances, three grandiose triumphal arches, announced this theme, which continued in the decorations of the flanking colonnades and across the facade of the great basilican law court along the north side of the piazza. Inside the basilica, named Ulpia after Trajan's family, the emperor appeared as a gracious judge; behind it, in a rectangular, colonnaded court, flanked to the east and west by Greek and Latin libraries that symbolized his patronage of learning, he would be entombed after death in the base of a marble column, the shaft of which was over one hundred Roman feet (97 ft./30 m) high, on which a continuous spiral frieze commemorated his martial exploits (the famous Trajan's Column, still standing). The plan also envisaged that, after the requisite vote of the senate, the dead emperor would be worshiped in a grandiose temple atop a high podium just north of the column.

A clear expression of these themes was only one of Apollodorus' problems in working out his design. He had also to relate his creation to the functional layouts of the earlier imperial forums. To achieve this objective, he assumed that, just as the nearby Temple of Peace was the last of those squares to the south, the Forum of Trajan would close the sequence to the north. Extending the axis of the Temple of Peace north to his site, he organized his own complex around it; taking the older forum as his model, he expanded and amplified its scheme. The plan of the bilaterally symmetrical Temple of Peace centered on the sanctuary and adjacent halls that fronted on a broad, rectangular court framed on three sides by colonnades (figs. 3, 4). Similarly, Apollodorus' court was a wide rectangle delimited by porticoes. But, for the colonnade that separated the Temple of Peace from the open enclosure in front of it, Apollodorus substituted the laterally positioned Basilica Ulpia; for the small sanctuary of Peace, the vast temple of Trajan and its surrounding precinct (finally completed by his successor Hadrian).

If this plan thus recalled and enlarged ideas inherent in the Forum of Peace, the individual elements both of the design and of the carved decorations were to constitute recognizable quotations from the other imperial forums. The grand hemicycles behind the east and west colonnades recalled the hemicycles in the Forum Augustum (fig. 4), which also provided the pure profiles and chastely classical architectural details. The statues of Dacian prisoners of the facades of the colonnades (fig. 7) reminded visitors of the caryatids on the attic facade of the Basilica Aemilia in the Forum Romanum and of those on the lateral colonnades in the Forum of Augustus; and the ornamental shields between Trajan's Dacians followed the same sources. Finally the projecting columns on the facades of the triumphal arches

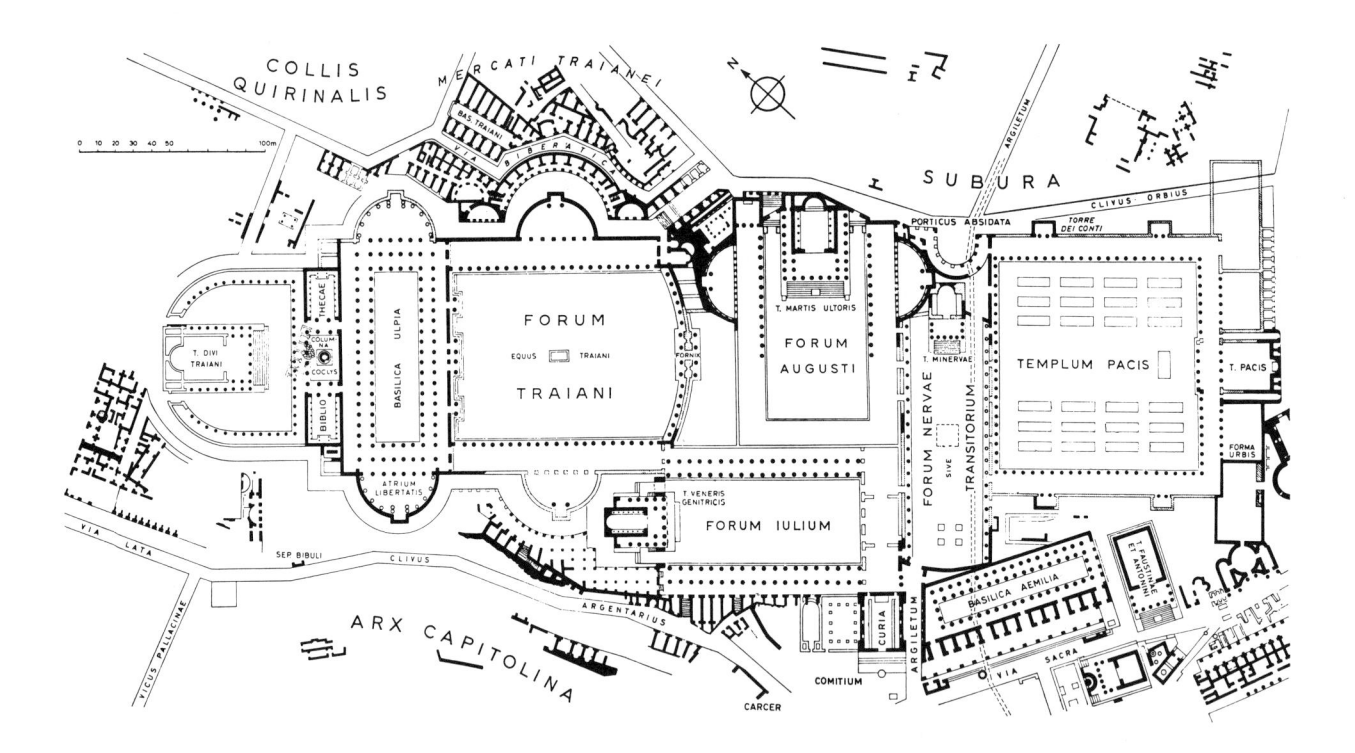

Figure 4. Plan of the imperial forums by Italo Gismondi. *Reproduced from Paul Zanker,* FORUM AUGUSTUM © 1968 ERNST WASMUTH, TÜBINGEN

recalled the nearly identical columns that flanked the entrance to the Forum of Peace (fig. 3).

Apollodorus worked out the general conception and details of this complex and rational plan the same way a modern architect would. Using techniques mentioned by Vitruvius, he drew plans, sections, and colored elevations, and perhaps even constructed wooden models, to establish the general proportions of the forum. Its open court had a length just over 2 3/4 times its width (378 × 136.5 Roman feet, or 367 × 133 ft./112 × 40.4 m). The interior lengths of the flanking colonnades were somewhat under 8 1/2 times their width (388.5 × 46 Roman feet, or 377 × 45 ft./115 × 13.7 m), and the length of the nave in the Basilica Ulpia was about 3 1/2 times its width (299 × 84 Roman feet, or 291 × 82 ft./88.5 × 24.9 m).

The heights of the Corinthian columns and their entablatures (fig. 5a) depended on the standardized lengths of the column shafts: 24 Roman feet (23 ft./7.1 m) in the colonnades, 30 Roman feet (29 ft./8.9 m) in the Basilica Ulpia, and probably 50 Roman feet (49 ft./14.8 m) in the colossal temple of Trajan. Within the orders, the heights of the components (bases, shafts, capitals, architraves, friezes, and cornices) followed a system mentioned by Vitruvius in which the diameter of the lowest shaft section served as a module for determining the dimensions of the other elements. Thus the height of a column base was one-half the lower shaft diameter. The shaft was about eight diameters high; the capital, 1 1/4 diameters; the entablature, between 2 1/4 and 2 1/2 diameters.

Sometimes, Apollodorus used entirely Vi-

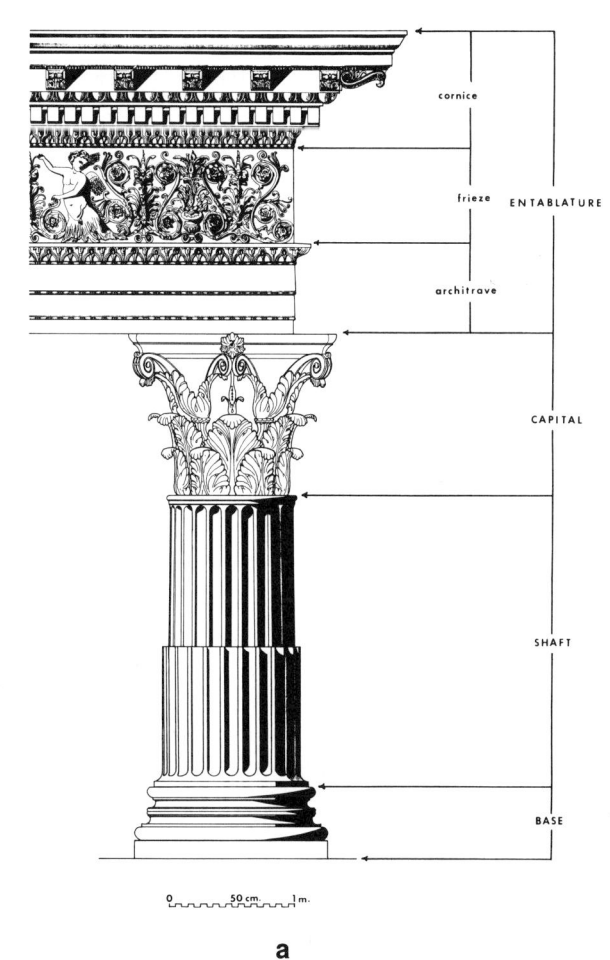

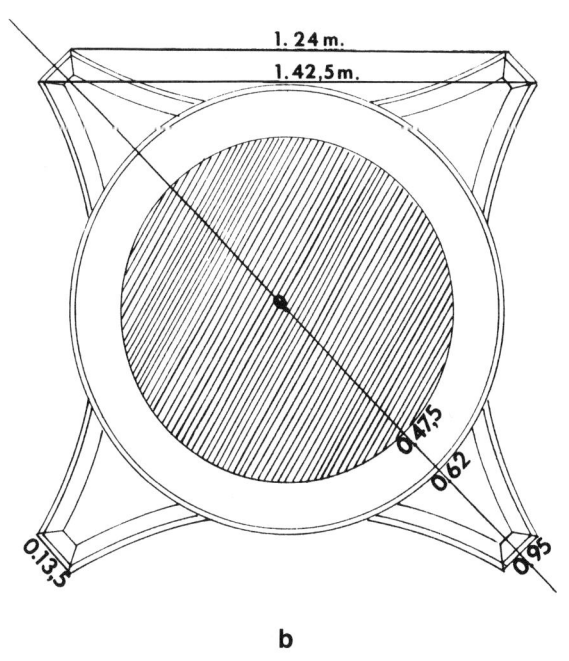

Figure 5. The Corinthian order in the Forum of Trajan (corner from one of the porches of the south facade of the Basilica Ulpia): (a) complete order; (b) capital from east colonnade, looking up: shaft appears in sections; bell without scrolls and acanthus leaves; diagonal across the top of abacus (corner to corner) equals the lower diameter of shaft.

truvian proportions. The diagonals from corner to corner of the tops (abaci) of his Corinthian capitals (fig. 5b) are exactly twice the diameter of the shaft below and the columns of an upper story are three-quarters the height of those of the order below. Yet, many of his proportions vary from the recommendations of Vitruvius, who for basilicas advised (5.1.4–5) "their breadth should be fixed at not less than a third nor more than half their length.... The columns ... are to be of a height equal to the width of the aisle. The aisle is to have a width one-third of the nave."

The measurements of the Ulpia are very different from these proportions. Aisles are 20 Roman feet (19 ft./5.9 m) wide, but columns are 36 1/5 Roman feet (35 ft./10.7 m) high; and with a width of 84 1/2 Roman feet (82 ft./25 m), the nave is 4 1/5, not three times wider than the aisle. However, with the lapse of nearly a century and a half between Vitruvius' time and the building of Trajan's forum, such changes, on a building much larger than any Vitruvius had envisioned, were natural enough. The significant fact is that the same proportions Vitruvius used were still popular in the early second century. His manual thus preserves a generally recognized system of proportions to which later architects referred even while varying them to account for contemporary fashions and their own tastes.

While Apollodorus completed the final

311

drawings, work on the foundations began. He closely supervised the surveyors as they laid out the levels and lines on the four terraces on the Quirinal and in the forum. The latter was excavated to a level several feet below the final elevation. Workmen poured tons of concrete over the rock to form an even stratum to support the pavement of the open court. The foundations of walls, the sides of elevated platforms, were rectangular blocks of travertine held together with ⊓-shaped clamps.

In the section of the forum south of Trajan's Column, the highest podium was that of the Basilica Ulpia, rising 6 3/4 Roman feet (6.6 ft./2 m) above the pavement of the open court. The two platforms for the colonnades were somewhat lower (2 3/4 Roman feet, or 2.7 ft./0.81 m). The structures of all three were identical. In each, the lowest and thickest stratum consisted of mortar uniformly mixed with broken tiles. Above was a layer of mortar mixed with pieces of travertine (or, as in the Ulpia, with fragments of imported colored marbles) on which the bedding mortar for the slabs of the pavement was laid.

With the foundations in place, the masons assembled the walls of the colonnades and the basilica. The walls of the former were made up of rectangular blocks of peperino, externally rusticated so that the stones' projecting centers remained rough while the margins at the joints had a smooth finish. On their inside faces, the blocks were smoothed to receive a marble veneer. Although executed in travertine, the walls of the basilica were identically finished, except that on the side toward the colonnaded court around Trajan's Column, they were smooth-finished rather than rusticated.

Whether of peperino or travertine, these blocks were massive. In the colonnades, a typical stone measured in length, height, and width 2 3/4 × 2 1/2 × 3 4/5 Roman feet (2.7 × 2.4 × 3.7 ft./0.81 × 0.76 × 1.15 m).

With heights of 2 3/4 Roman feet (2.6 ft./0.81 m), the basilica's blocks were slightly larger. Handling these heavy masses of fragile stone demanded great technical skill. The blocks arrived in Rome already roughly shaped. Before positioning, masons smooth-finished the butt ends with mallets, chisels, "claws" (toothed chisels), rasps, and files. Then they painstakingly rubbed powdered emery over the surface to remove the marks of the rasps, and the block was ready to lift into position.

On the top and bottom of each block, masons cut several holes. The lower ones were "set-holes," usually roughly square with sides of 2 to 2 1/3 inches (5 to 6 cm). These sockets were for iron pins. Corresponding sockets in the top of the stone already laid received the pins, which thus served to position each successive block. Once the block was in place, a channel previously cut into the surface of the lower block permitted the masons to pour the molten lead which, when cool, locked in place and protected the lower half of the pin from moisture. Although the archaeological remains of these pourings are often full of air pockets, this problem apparently did not weaken the bond between the pin and the surrounding stone. Since ⊓-shaped iron clamps set in lead also attached the veneer to the walls, workmen installed the veneer as the walls went up. After the outer wall was nearly complete, the monolithic marble pilaster shafts (each positioned by iron pins) were lowered into place.

Cranes hoisted the blocks into position; and the ones employed in the Forum of Trajan were probably much like those described by Vitruvius. The simplest was a jib consisting of two timbers connected at the top (fig. 6). The opposite ends were spread apart, giving the crane the appearance of an inverted V. On all four sides, ropes held the jib at an angle of 45 degrees; and, suspended from the top, another rope (called in Greek

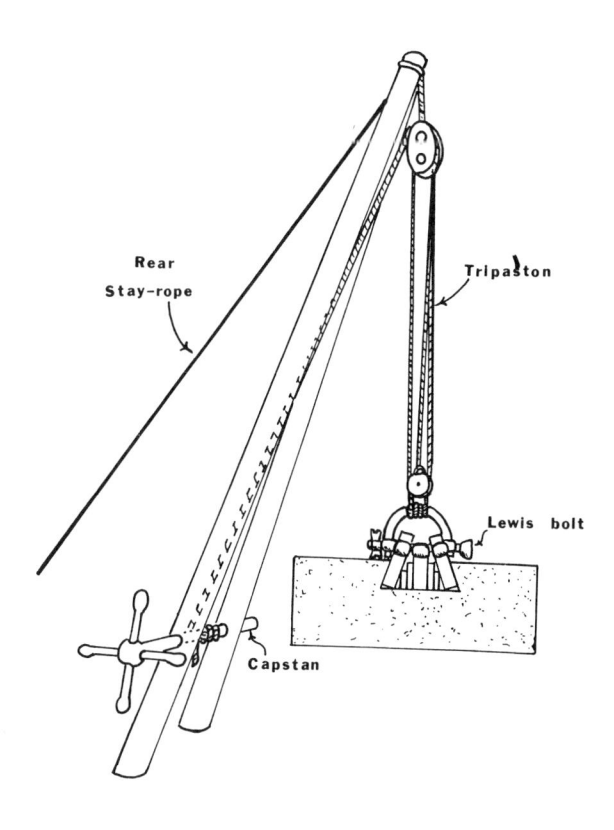

Figure 6. Simple crane showing lewis bolt and sectioned block of stone (*after Landels, 1978 and Crema, 1959*).

tripaston) supported two wheels, one above the other. The lower one was attached to a lewis. That device, which held the block to be lifted, consisted of several iron pins that fit into the set-holes, wedge-shaped in section, cut into the top of the block. (Larger blocks had two such generously proportioned sockets at opposite ends.) After inserting the outer bolts into the socket, the masons wedged them into position with several additional pins. From the lewis, the lifting rope passed around the two wheels above, returning to a capstan that, in rotating, wound up the rope and raised the block. For heavy loads, the beams of the winch were more massive; and the capstan was a large hollow wheel turned inside by as many as three men (see fig. 4 in ENGINEERING).

The walls and facades of the colonnades and the basilica went up simultaneously. Although the basilica was larger than the colonnades (fig. 10), the facades of all three buildings, with adjoining continuous foundations, were constructed as a single unit. First the masons installed the white marble pavement in the open court. Next, they positioned the giallo antico blocks of the stair treads. The two lower treads were bedded in concrete; those above fitted into slots cut in the blocks of the travertine foundations. The top treads were slabs as high as the other treads but 1.2 inches (3 cm) wider than the plinths of the columns that rested on them.

The column plinths and bases were cut from single blocks of white marble turned on lathes. Once the bases were in position, cranes lowered the monolithic pavonazzetto shafts into place by ropes attached to bosses that were later removed. As in the construction of the walls, iron pins at the bottom of each shaft ensured accurate installation. When the shafts had been erected, carpenters put up wooden scaffolding; and, using templates, masons established the correct profile for every shaft (including top and bottom moldings). Then, after preliminary smoothing, they cut twenty-four vertical flutes into the surface of each shaft. When this work was complete, they spent laborious hours finishing the stone, rubbing it first with powdered emery, then with crushed pumice.

In order to avoid damaging the delicate carving on the capitals, journeymen sculptors roughed out the shapes of the leaves and scrolls on the ground and then lifted the pieces into position on the tops of the shafts. Occasionally, however, the tip of an acanthus leaf did break, necessitating repairs. At the top of the broken leaf, the mason cut a rectangular socket. Inserting in it a separate piece of marble, he carved it to its final shape and filled the joint between the old and new marble with stucco.

Even the monolithic shafts of pavonazzetto (in the colonnades) or gray granite (in the Basilica Ulpia and the temple of Trajan) —items too expensive to abandon—were sometimes repaired. In the pavonazzetto shafts, broken fragments were pieced together from two separate drums joined at one-third the height of the shaft at a point where the cabling (partially filled flutes) ended and the complete flutes began. When a gray granite shaft broke or developed a flaw, the ends of the two pieces were shaped into corresponding "keys," undulating projections around the circumferences of the mating surfaces. The two pieces were fitted together, and the joint was filled with stucco colored gray and then polished to the same high gloss as the rest of the shaft.

With the columns in place, assembly of the entablatures began. Their components were in two pieces: architrave/friezes and cornices. Both were as long as the distances between the centers of the columns (18 Roman feet, or 17.5 ft./5.3 m in the basilica; 12 Roman feet, or 11.7 ft./3.6 m in the colonnades).

On the facades fronting the open court, both the colonnades (fig. 10) and the basilica had high attics (the wall above the cornice of the facade). Above each column the masons installed a molded base onto which they hoisted a statue of a Dacian prisoner (fig. 7). With the statue anchored to the base, the workers rested on the figure's head a projecting cantilevered cornice. Iron clamps joined the back, shaped as a tenon, to the flanking stones, and the weight of the masonry above the tenon subsequently stabilized the piece. When all the statues and cornices were complete, the masons set in place the impressively proportioned blocks of the cornice that crowned the attic. To drain water into a semicircular gutter hollowed out just behind the profiled face of this cornice, apprentices cut the fronts of the blocks at a raking angle. Finally, with the

Figure 7. Restored elevation and section of a bay from the facade of the east colonnade in the Forum of Trajan. ITALO GISMONDI

roughed-out elements of the lower orders and the attics in place, master sculptors, specialists in capitals, friezes, and the decorative elements of cornices, gave all the carved surfaces their final profiles and finishes.

In the colonnades, the tie beams of the roof rested in slots cut into the blocks of the cornice (fig. 8). In section these beams were rectangular, 1 × 2 Roman feet (about 1 × 2 ft./30 × 60 cm), and they had a length of 53 Roman feet (51.5 ft./15.7 m). After the beams were in place, the last decorative blocks of the facade were installed: a row of pedestals centered over the Dacian statues. Continuous with each of the pedestals a tenon interlocked with the adjoining blocks to form a continuous parapet at the top of the building.

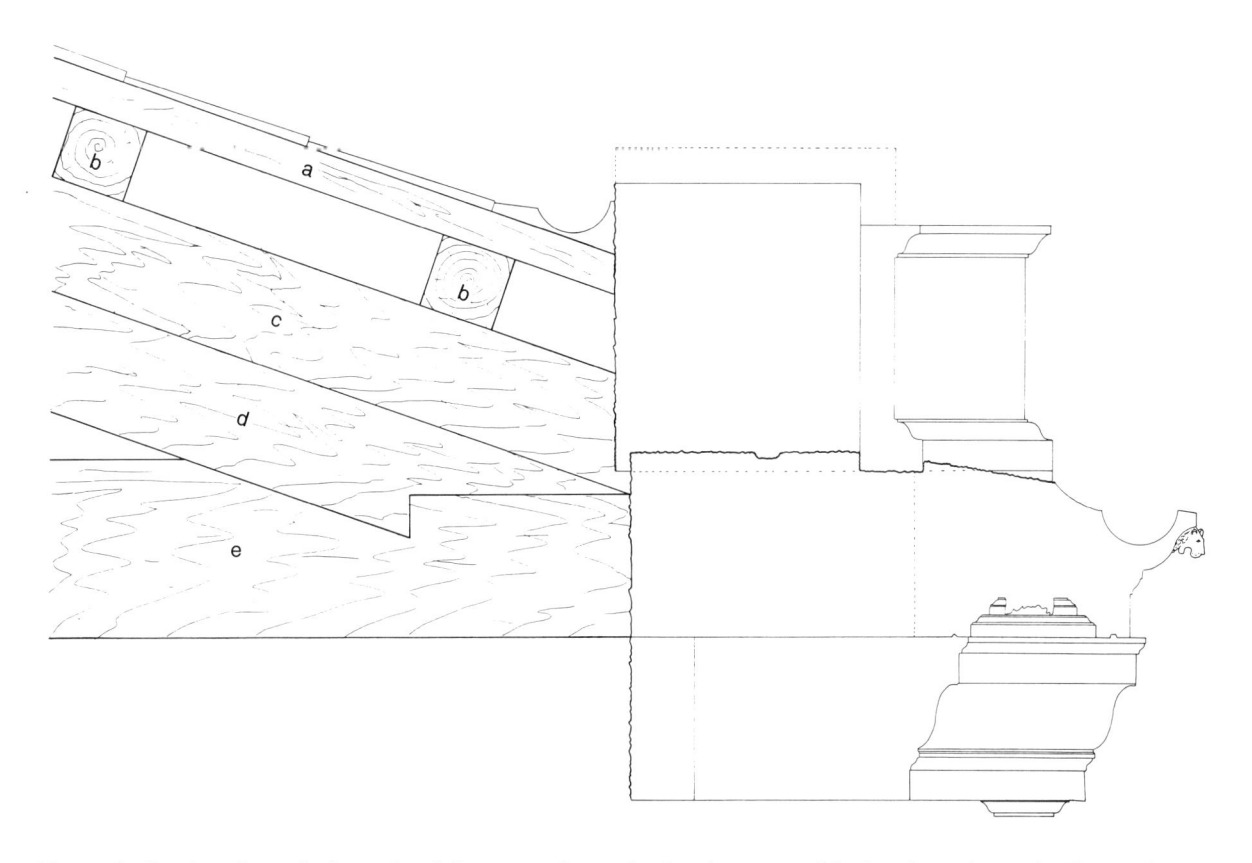

Figure 8. Section through the attic of the east colonnade showing upper blocks of cornice and adjacent beams of timber truss roof: (*a*) batten; (*b*) purlins; (*c*) common rafter; (*d*) principal rafter; (*e*) tie beam.

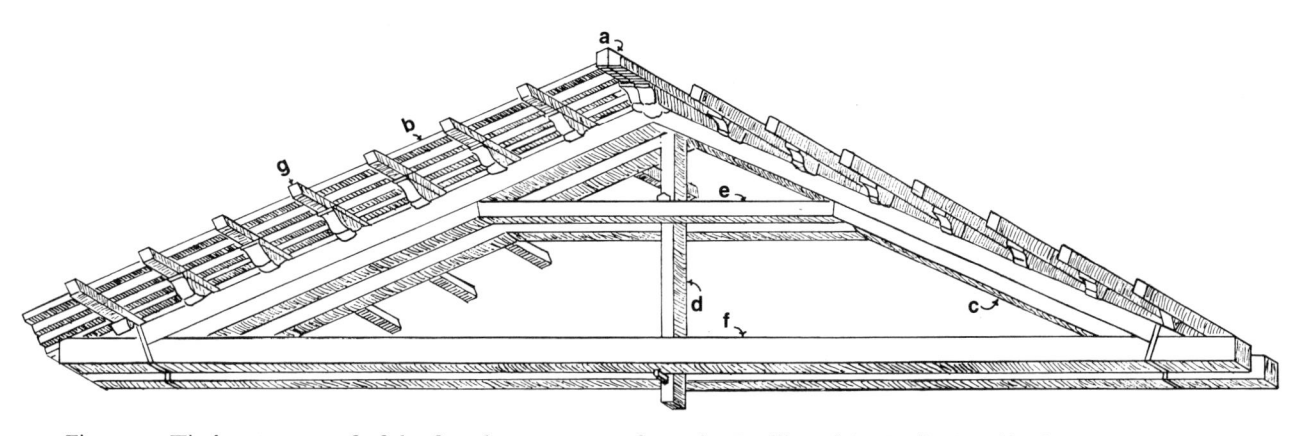

Figure 9. Timber truss roof of the fourth century A.D. from the Basilica of St. Paul's Outside the Walls: (*b*) ridge pole; (*b*) batten; (*c*) principal rafter; (*d*) king post; (*e*) collar beam; (*f*) tie beam; (*g*) purlin (*after Sakur, 1925*).

With the facades of both colonnades finished, carpenters worked on the roofs. Rafters were inserted in slots cut into the tie beams and butted against the backs of the pedestals and the parapet between them (fig. 8). In each truss (fig. 9), two principal rafters, joined by a collar beam, supported the common rafters. Square in section, with sides of three-quarters of a Roman foot (8.7 in./22 cm), purlins were nailed over the rafters, paralleling the facade; at right angles to these, battens supported the plank deck—its boards parallel to the facade below—which in turn carried the tiles.

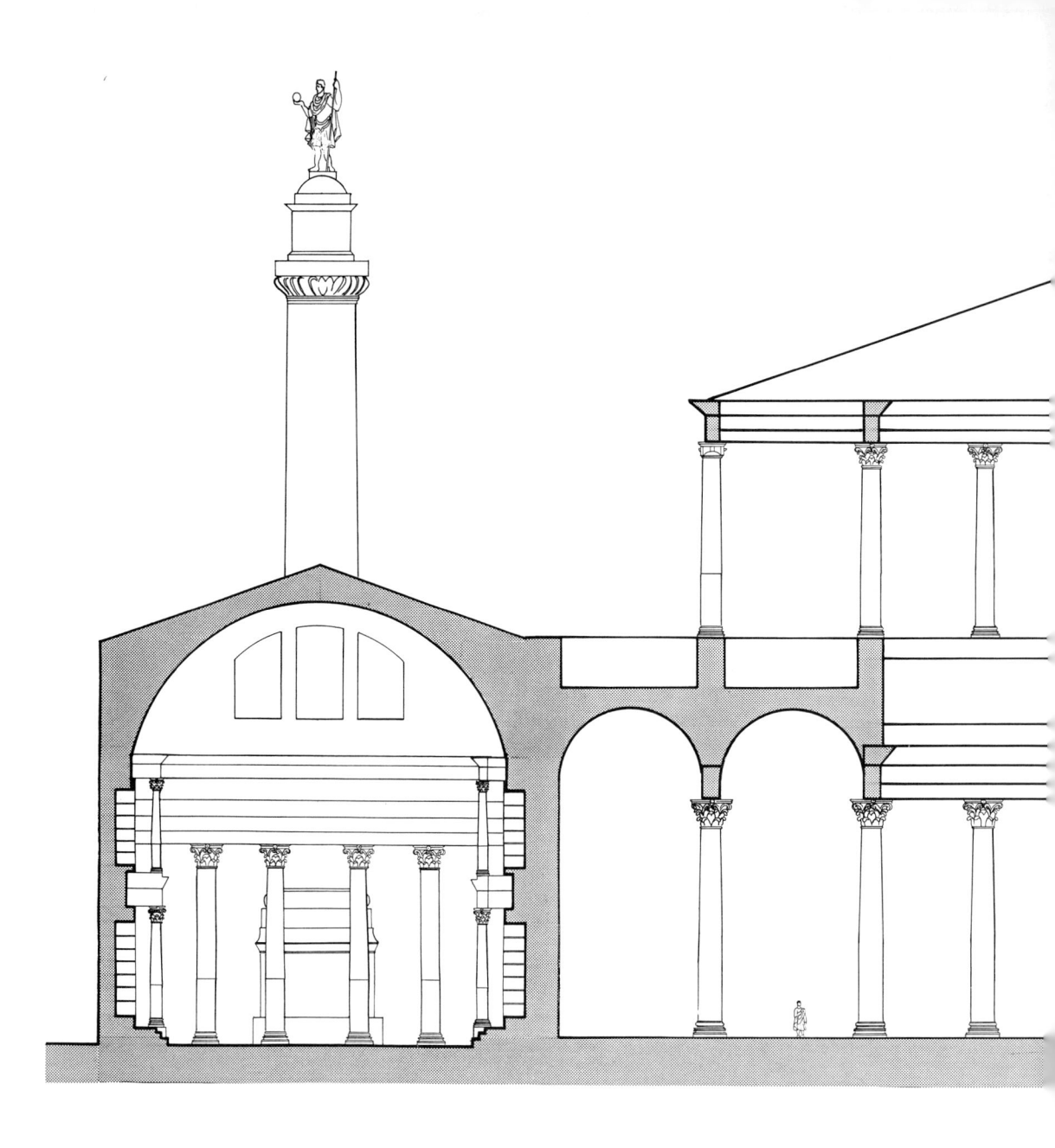

In some respects the methods used in the construction of the Ulpia repeated those in the colonnades. The facade of the basilica was larger (figs. 3, 10) and its individual architectural elements were, consequently, more elaborately decorated, but most of its various features had exact counterparts in the colonnades. As in the latter, the pavonazzetto columns of the facade rested on the heavy travertine blocks of the foundation.

Internally, the basilica's design (fig. 10) was considerably more complex than those of the colonnades; the differences necessitated significant changes in the methods of construction. The gray granite columns of the first order rested on courses of travertine blocks, which enclosed the nave and side aisles in successive frames. Facing the nave, the lower order had a complete entablature. On the aisles, the columns carried only architraves. Left in a rough state, the tops of these blocks served as the footing for

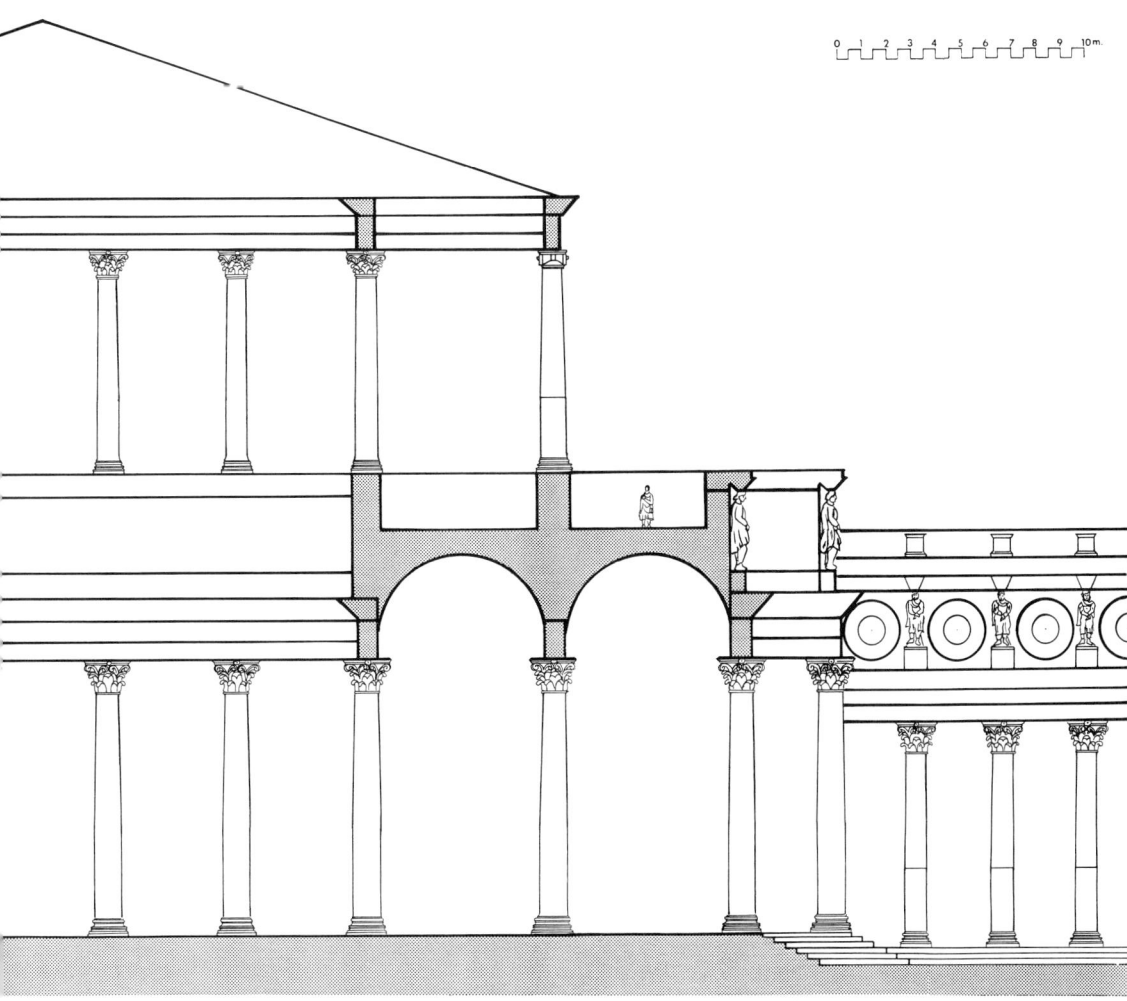

Figure 10. Forum of Trajan. Schematic restored north-south section through the west library and the Basilica Ulpia with part of the facade of the east colonnade.

concrete barrel vaults, supported by temporary wood framing until the concrete cured to full strength. The vaults exerted only vertical thrusts on the columns below; nonetheless, to minimize their weight, when mixing the concrete the builders employed extremely lightweight aggregate consisting of terra-cotta shards and pieces of pumice.

Once the vaults had cured to sufficient strength, the construction crews used winches to lift the components of the second order atop the vaults. As Vitruvius prescribes, the upper Corinthian columns flanking the nave were three-quarters the height of the columns of the lower order. The corresponding columns on the facade were of the same height, but Ionic in style. Together these orders supported a timber truss roof (fig. 9), an enlarged version of the systems in the colonnades, externally covered with thin tiles of gilt bronze.

In structure, the libraries to the north of the basilica (fig. 11) and the multistoried shopping arcade behind the east colonnade (christened by its modern excavator the "Markets of Trajan," fig. 12) differed radically from the colonnades and the basilica. As in those buildings, the foundations were

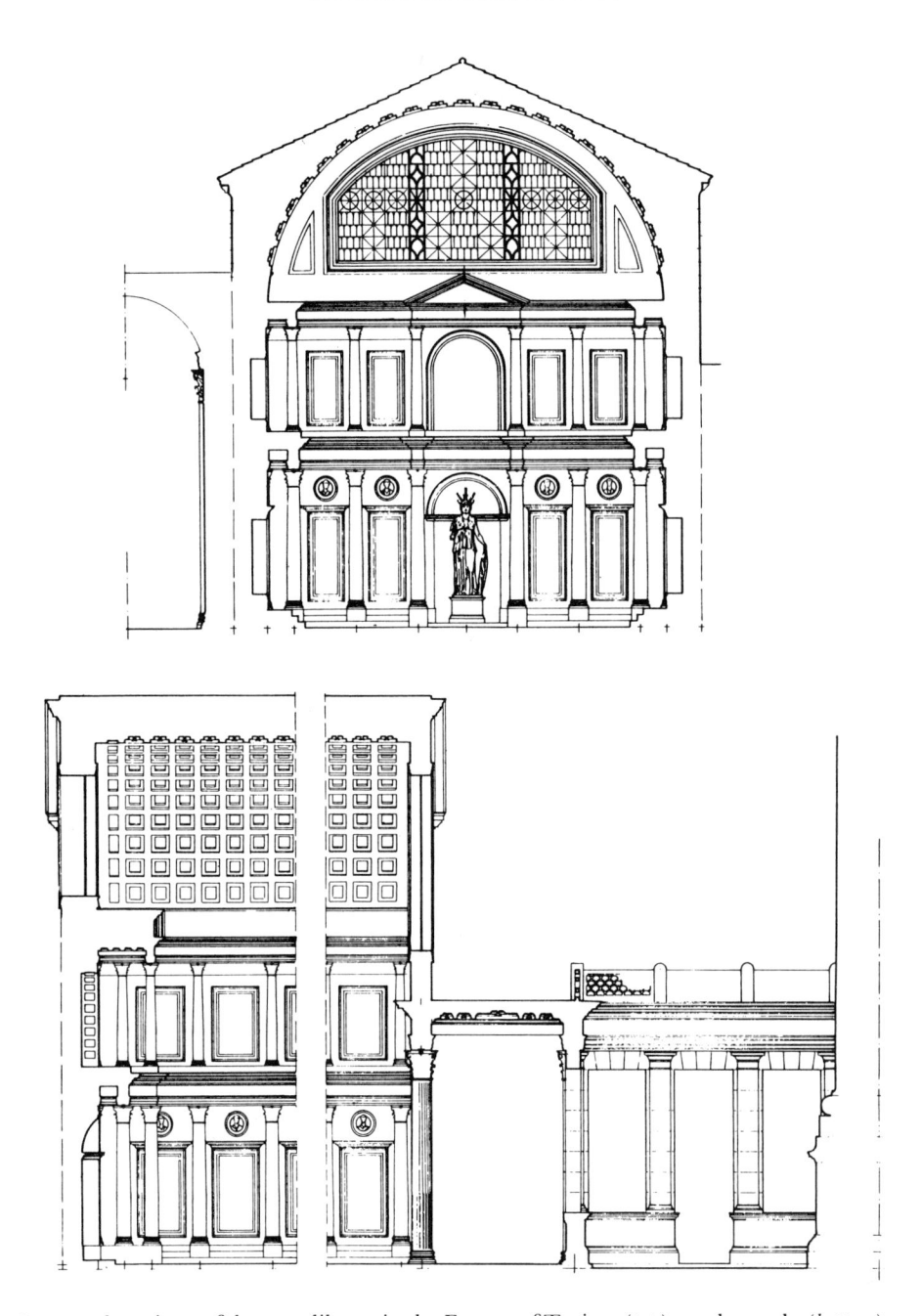

Figure 11. Restored sections of the west library in the Forum of Trajan: (*top*) north-south; (*bottom*) east-west. ITALO GISMONDI

concrete platforms, but the walls and vaults were also of concrete. The walls went up in sections the height of twenty to twenty-five courses of *bipedales*. Between these terracotta frames, the laborers poured concrete; and when it had cured sufficiently to support both its own weight and that of the next section above it, the process was repeated. As the wall rose in height, the workmen rested the planks of the scaffolding on beams set into sockets in the wall. Once a section of the wall had been completed, the

Figure 12. Markets of Trajan during excavation and restoration, ca. 1929. COMUNE DI ROMA, ARCHIVIO FOTOGRAFICO, PALAZZO BRASCHI

workers removed these beams and inserted them in the next section of wall above. On the ground, carpenters nailed together the wooden forms for the barrel vaults and then raised them to the tops of the walls. The concrete for the vault was poured on these forms; when it had cured the framework below was moved to a new position. Domes differed from vaults only in the complexity of the required forms, which were also probably composed of reusable sections.

The construction of the west facade of the markets, the hemicycle in back of the forum's east colonnade, included molded bricks used as decorative moldings and travertine for the jambs and lintels of the entrances to the shops, the bases and Tuscan capitals of the pilasters, and simplified brackets.

Although in the markets painters decorated the stuccoed interiors of the shops only with simple designs, the fine rooms located on the fifth floor received more elegant appointments: veneers of colored marbles in the niches and apses. Similarly, each of the libraries (fig. 11) had pavonazzetto revetments and pavements, the latter laid in designs composed of giallo antico rectangles framed by gray granite borders. The fluted shafts of the columns of the upper and lower orders were also of pavonazzetto, although the bases, capitals, and entablatures were executed in white marble.

The spectacular character of the Forum of Trajan amazed contemporaries, and the monument became one of ancient Rome's chief attractions. Yet, only elegant design and vast scale distinguished this complex from other important monuments. The methods used in its construction were widely employed elsewhere in Rome and central Italy for both public and private buildings: the tenements, mansions, villas, temples, baths, large and small theaters, amphitheaters, circuses, triumphal arches, and tombs were the achievements of vast numbers of highly skilled craftsmen who had been meticulously organized into a disciplined and extremely effective work force. At the command of the emperors, these men transformed Rome, creating the large-scale, richly articulated, elaborately ornamented structures that were three-dimensional expressions of imperial power. These buildings survived for centuries—Hadrian's Pantheon is still intact today—and, even in their final ruin, others remained stimulating, persuasive models for generations of artists, architects, and scholars.

Never has any architectural technology successfully achieved so much for so long for so many.

BIBLIOGRAPHY

SOURCES

Ammianus Marcellinus, *History* (*Rerum gestarum libri qui supersunt*), John C. Rolfe, trans., 3 vols. (1935–1939); Vitruvius Pollio, *On Architecture*, Frank Granger, trans., 2 vols. (1931–1934).

GENERAL

Frank E. Brown, *Roman Architecture* (1961); Filippo Coarelli, *Guida archeologica di Roma antica* (1974), and *Roma* (*Guide archeologiche Laterza*, 6 [1980]); Luigi Crema, *L'architettura romana* (*Enciclopedia classica*, 3, 12,1 [1959]); Giuseppe Lugli, *Roma antica* (1946), and *Itinerario di Roma antica* (1970); William L. MacDonald, *The Architecture of the Roman Empire*, I, 2d ed. (1982); Ernest Nash, *A Pictorial Dictionary of Ancient Rome*, 2 vols., 2d ed. (1968); Samuel B. Platner and Thomas A. Ashby, *A Topographical Dictionary of Ancient Rome* (1929); John Ward-Perkins, *Roman Architecture* (1977), and *Roman Imperial Architecture*, 2d ed. (1981).

STUDIES

Michael H. Ballance, "The Origin of *Africano*," in *Papers of the British School at Rome*, **34** (1966); Marion E. Blake, *Ancient Roman Construction in Italy from the Prehistoric Period to Augustus* (1947), *Roman Construction in Italy from Tiberius through the Flavians* (1959), and *Roman Construction in Italy from Nerva through the Antonines*, Doris T. Bishop, ed. (1973); Auguste Choisy, *L'Art de bâtir chez les Romains* (1873); Giuseppe Cozzo, *Ingegneria romana* (1928); Josef Durm, *Die Baukunst der Etrusker. Die Baukunst der Römer*, 2d ed. (1905); Raniero Gnoli, *Marmora romana* (1971); John G. Landels, *Engineering in the Ancient World* (1978); Giuseppe Lugli, *La tecnica edilizia romana*, 2 vols. (1957); William L. MacDonald, "Roman Architects," in Spiro Kostof, ed., *The Architect: Chapters in the History of the Profession* (1977); Russell Meiggs, *Trees and Timber in the Ancient Mediterranean World* (1982); James Packer, "Roman Imperial Building," in Carl Roebuck, ed., *The Muses at Work* (1969), and "Structure and Design in Ancient Ostia," in *Technology and Culture*, **9** (1968); John Ward-Perkins, "Tripolitania and the Marble Trade," in *Journal of Roman Studies*, **41** (1951), "Quarrying in Antiquity," in *Proceedings of the British Academy*, **57** (1971), and "Nicomedia and the Marble Trade," in *Papers of the British School at Rome*, **48** (1980).

The Forum of Trajan

Carla Maria Amici, *Foro di Traiano: Basilica Ulpia e biblioteche* (1982); Maria Bertoldi, "Ricerche sulla decorazione architettonica del Foro Traiano," in Università di Roma, *Seminario di archeologia e storia dell' arte greca e romana, Studi miscellanei*, **3** (1962); Luigi Canina, *Gli edifizi di Roma antica*, 6 vols. (1848–1856), esp. vols. 1 and 2; Hectoire d'Espouy, ed., *Monuments antiques*, 3 vols. (1910–1912); Attilio La Padula, *Roma 1809–1814* (1958); Christoph Leon, *Die Bauornamentik des Trajansforums* (1971); Jean Baptiste Lesueur, *La Basilique Ulpienne (Rome). Restauration executée en 1823* (1877); James Packer, "Some Numismatic Evidence for the Southeast (Forum) Facade of the Basilica Ulpia," in Lionel Casson and Martin Price, eds., *Coins, Culture, and History in the Ancient World* (1981), and with Kevin Sarring and Rose Mary Sheldon, "A New Excavation in Trajan's Forum," in *American Journal of Archaeology*, **87** (1983); Marina Pensa, "L'architettura traianea," in *Atti del Centro Studi e Documentazione sull' Italia romana*, **2** (1969–1970); Corrado Ricci, *Il Mercato di Traiano* (1929); Paul Zanker, in *Archäologischer Anzeiger, Jahrbuch des deutschen Archäologischen Instituts*, **85** (1970–1971).

ENGINEERING

JOHN G. LANDELS

THIS EXAMINATION of Greek and Roman engineering covers four areas: mechanical, military, hydraulic, and miniature engineering. These areas have been chosen because they illustrate both the versatility and the limitations of Greek and Roman engineering. Among the literary sources two writers are particularly important. Vitruvius Pollio, who lived in the last century B.C. and worked under Augustus, wrote a Latin treatise in ten books, *On Architecture* (*De Architectura*). This title is to be taken in a broader sense than our word "architecture," since it embraces basic science, materials technology, hydraulics, stylistics, public health, and other topics. Hero of Alexandria, who lived a century or so later, was a Greek writer whose works were not particularly outstanding, but who has considerable interest and importance for us because by the accidents of history his treatises—*Pneumatics, Mechanics,* and *Catapult Design*—make up a large proportion of the very small group of works on engineering that have been preserved.

MECHANICAL ENGINEERING

From the late sixth century B.C. onward the Greeks had a working acquaintance with many of the basic principles of mechanics, though it was not until the third century B.C. that they tried to arrive at a full theoretical understanding of them or to construct a technical terminology.

The simplest of these principles was the lever, known from remote antiquity in the form of the crowbar. Archimedes' famous boast, made in his lost work on levers, that if he had somewhere to stand (in the heavens), he could move the whole earth, was the ultimate statement of the theoretical possibilities, given the force that could be applied by one man and the capability of an enormous lever to multiply it.

One particular version of the lever, the winch, consisting of a wooden cylinder of small radius turned by handspikes to reel up a rope or chain, was also known from very early times; this was the device by which

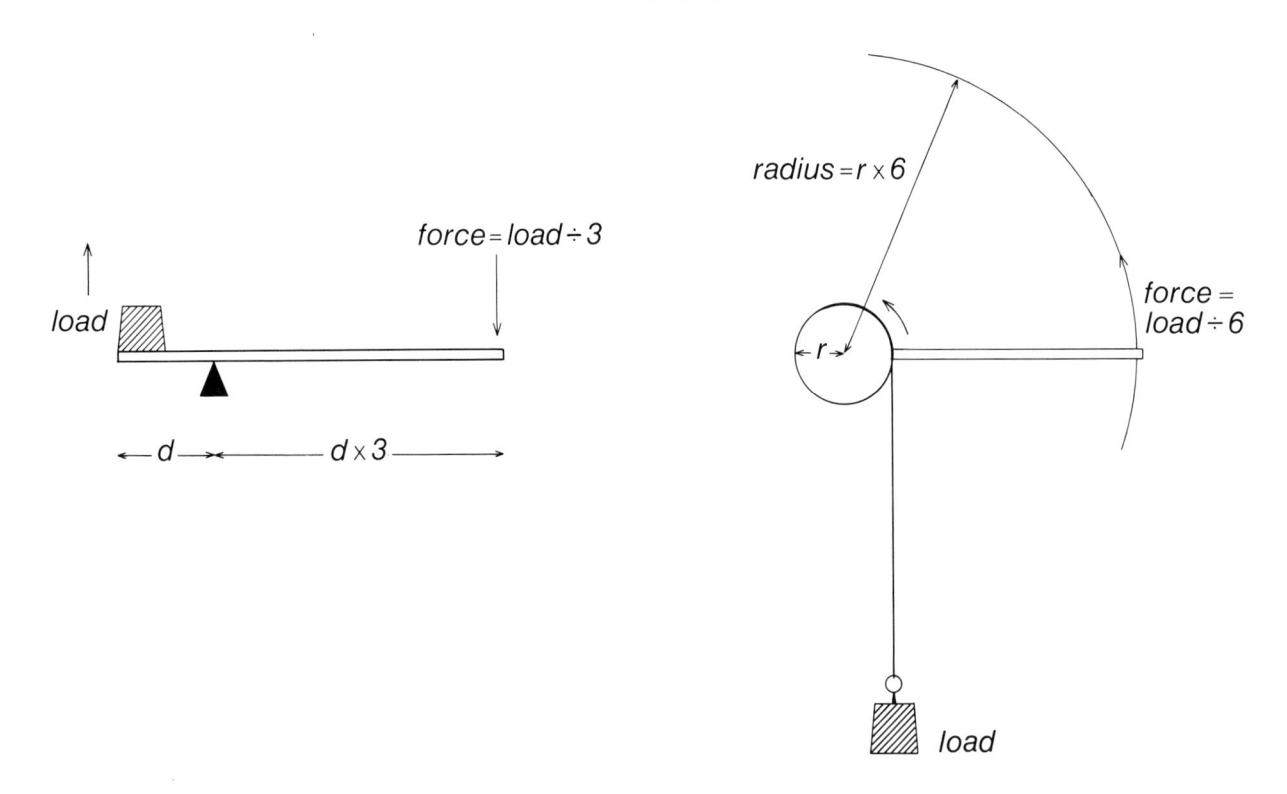

Figure 1. Winch as rotary lever. ALL DRAWINGS BY BRIAN WILLIAMS

manpower was used to operate cranes and hoists and to drag heavy objects over soft ground (for example, a ship over sand). In the theoretical writers this was regarded as a rotary lever (fig. 1), and just as the shorter part of the lever could support a weight greater than the force applied to the longer section, so, as they expressed it, "the smaller circle overpowers the greater," for the weight on the rope from the winch may be many times greater than the force on the handspike needed to raise it.

However, one element of this type of device that is very familiar to us seems to be altogether missing from the ancient picture: the crank handle. Although some passages in Hero have been interpreted as referring to a crank and although some suspect archaeological evidence has been put forward for its use, there is no convincing proof that the ancients knew about it. This failure of invention is very curious, and it has not been satisfactorily explained.

The use in temple construction of columns built up from a number of drums instead of the older monolithic columns is first attested in the late sixth century B.C., and it is probably to be connected with the introduction of effective cranes in the construction process. At first the column drums were quite small, but gradually, as better equipment became available, greater weights could be tackled—three or four tons before the middle of the fifth century and ten to twelve tons in the Hellenistic period. Eventually, in the heyday of Roman engineering in Hadrian's time (early second century A.D.), architects were able to revert to monolithic columns, since their cranes could handle up to thirty-five tons or more.

Our evidence on these improvements in crane design comes mainly from Vitruvius and Hero. Primarily, it was a matter of making the cranes bigger and stronger, using heavier beams for the load-bearing arms and thicker ropes, which were made from hemp or papyrus fiber, with greater safe working loads. But on the mechanical side, several new principles were involved. It is not certain precisely when multiple pulleys were introduced; it is difficult to imagine the column drums and architraves of the Parthenon (mid fifth century B.C.) being hoisted into position without them, and it is clear from Vitruvius that there was an established Greek terminology relating to them, which must date at least to the fourth century. The generic term for a multiple pulley was *polyspaston* (multiple-haul) and the most commonly used forms were the *trispaston* and the *pentaspaston*—the triple- and quintuple-haul (fig. 2).

Another development was a kind of double winch. One winch was used to draw a rope from around the perimeter of a fairly large wooden wheel, which in turn operated the main lifting winch, which had a double set of pulleys and ropes (fig. 3). In combination with the multiple pulleys this device could bring about a reduction ratio of the order of two hundred to one, enabling a small team of three to four men to hoist, albeit rather slowly, a load of several tons.

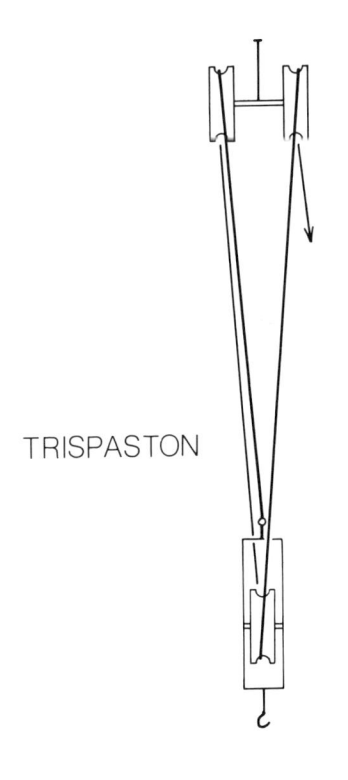

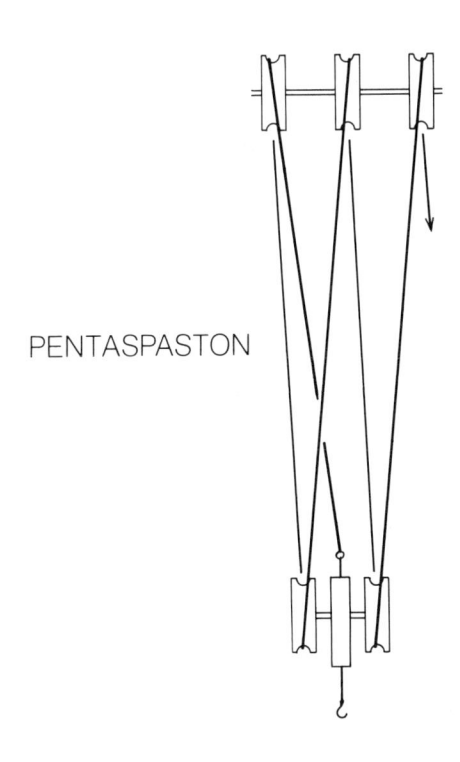

Figure 2. Multiple pulleys.

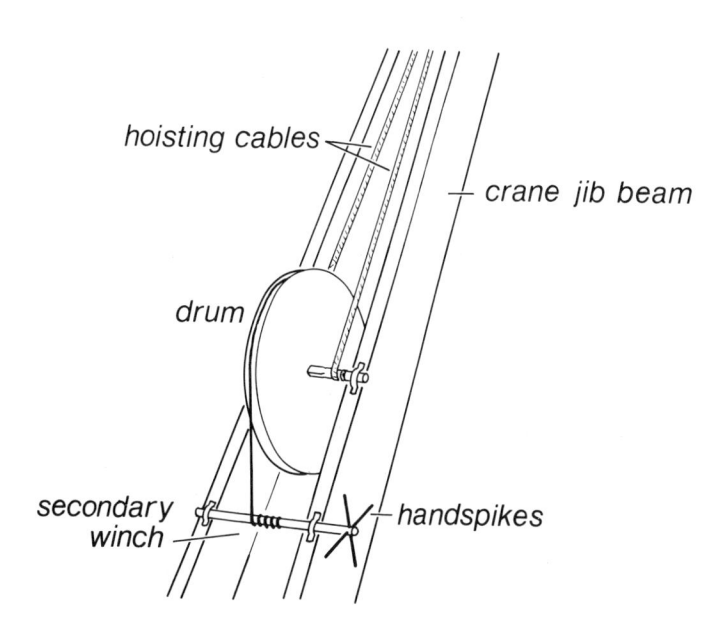

Figure 3. Double winch.

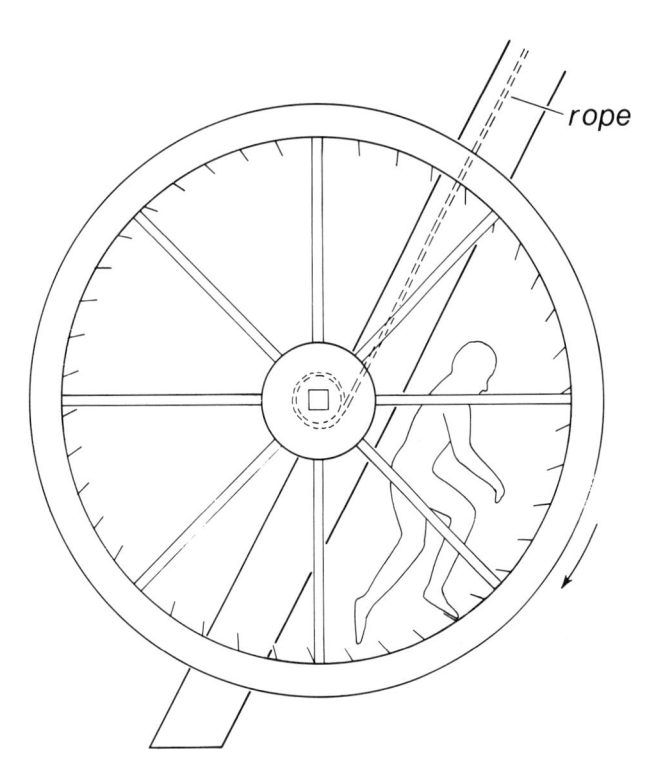

Figure 4. Crane driven by treadmill.

Our evidence on the design of one particular type of crane is exceptionally good. A detailed description in Vitruvius is supplemented by a carved relief on the tomb of the Haterii family (probably early second century A.D.), who were engaged in the construction business. This was the shear legs, a type that could handle very heavy loads but whose jib movements were limited to a small swing forwards and backwards. The illustration agrees with Vitruvius' account (10.2.7) in showing the crane operated by a treadmill instead of a winch; it consists of a large wheel with widely spaced spokes, worked by two or three men walking on slats fixed to the inside of the rim (fig. 4).

Another type mentioned by Vitruvius is "the horizontal, with revolving *carchesion*." This seems to have been the ancient equivalent of the tower crane, with a vertical post or small tower fixed on a firm base and a swivel joint, the *carchesion*, at the top that enabled the jib to be swung around sideways and, possibly, up and down (fig. 5). There is evidence to suggest that the jib was balanced by a counterweight, which may have been adjustable within limits so that variations in the loading could be compensated for.

This type of crane was perhaps the most versatile of all; it was used as a dockside crane for unloading ships and as a war weapon against troop landing craft and against seige engines. It was also probably the one used in the ancient Greek theater for a special effect that was required in a small number of the surviving plays. If a deity or supernatural being had to make a sudden appearance, the actor playing the part was hoisted up from behind the stage set into view of the audience "on the machine" (*mechane*); the Romans called the effect *deus ex machina*. When appropriate, it could be accompanied by a clap of thunder produced by the sound-effects department, using a metal barrel full of stones.

In addition to multiple pulleys and capstans, the Greeks and Romans also made use of gears. They were made of bronze, the ancient technology being inadequate to make them from cast iron or milled steel; this would obviously limit the strength of the teeth on the cogwheels and consequently the loading that a geared winch would be able to bear. A very full understanding of complicated gear ratios, including the use of differentials, is amply proved by the miniature engineering of the Antikythera mechanism described in the section on engineering in miniature.

Hero also discussed screws and various applications of the screw principle, giving detailed advice of a kind that suggests a good deal of practical experience. As part of a press or lifting device, the screw was mounted vertically, and some form of collar, with an internal hole of clearance size, was made to slide along it. Hero probably used the word *knemis* (shin guard) for this part of

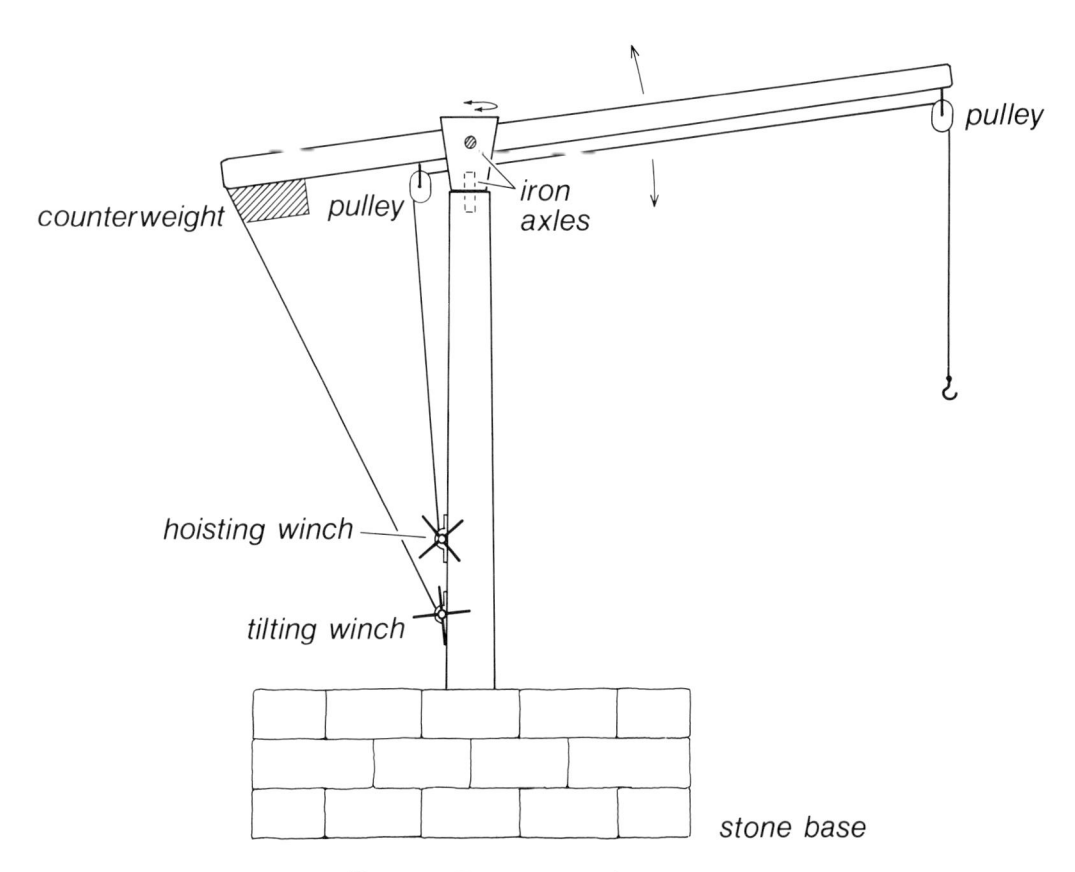

Figure 5. Tower crane with *carchesion*.

the mechanism, which would suggest the shape shown in figure 6. It was attached to one end of a beam, which could operate a press or, if the screw were turned the opposite way, act as a lifting device.

Alternatively, a cogwheel could be used to engage with the screw and form a reduction gear system for a winch. Hero fully understood that each revolution of the screw moved the cogwheel around by one tooth, so that the reduction ratio was equal to the number of teeth, which, given a particular pitch (the space between the threads of the screw), determines the diameter of the cogwheel. He gives instructions on how to mark out a blank wheel for cutting the teeth in it and notes that the profile of the teeth may be rectangular or lentoid (*phakodes*, fig. 7) and that the teeth are not to be cut square across the rim of the cogwheel but diagonally, sloping at the same angle as the gradient (the rake angle) of the screw.

As for the making of the screw itself, Hero actually describes a machine for cutting a female thread in a wooden block that will accurately fit a given male thread. The design is shown in figure 8. The pattern (male) thread passes through a block with a hole of clearance size, with two pegs that engage with the thread, so that as the shaft is turned it advances toward the material to be cut. The remainder of the pattern rod is slightly smaller in diameter than the hole in which the female thread is to be cut. The cutting tool, made of wrought iron, has a cutting edge of the right profile for the thread and projects from a square hole in the side of the rod. As the thread could not possibly be cut

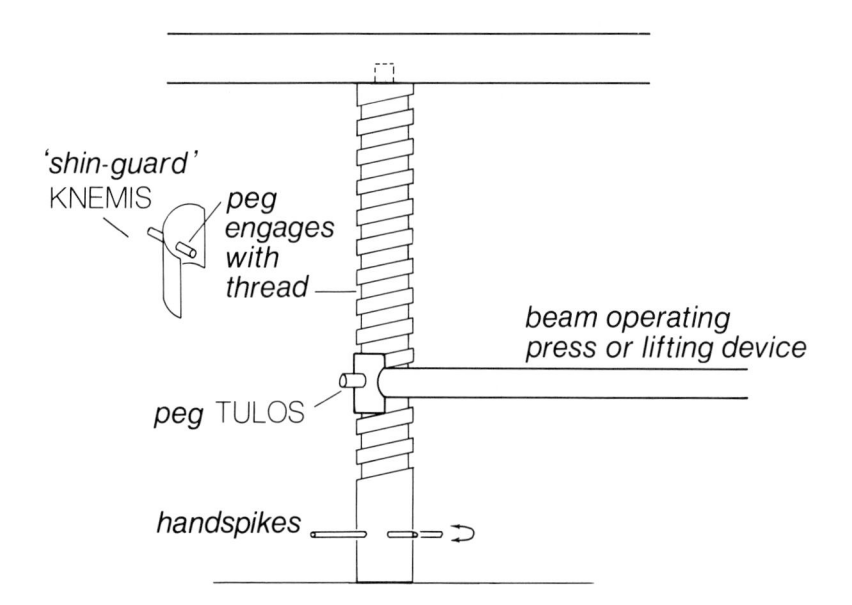

Figure 6. Screw and *knemis*.

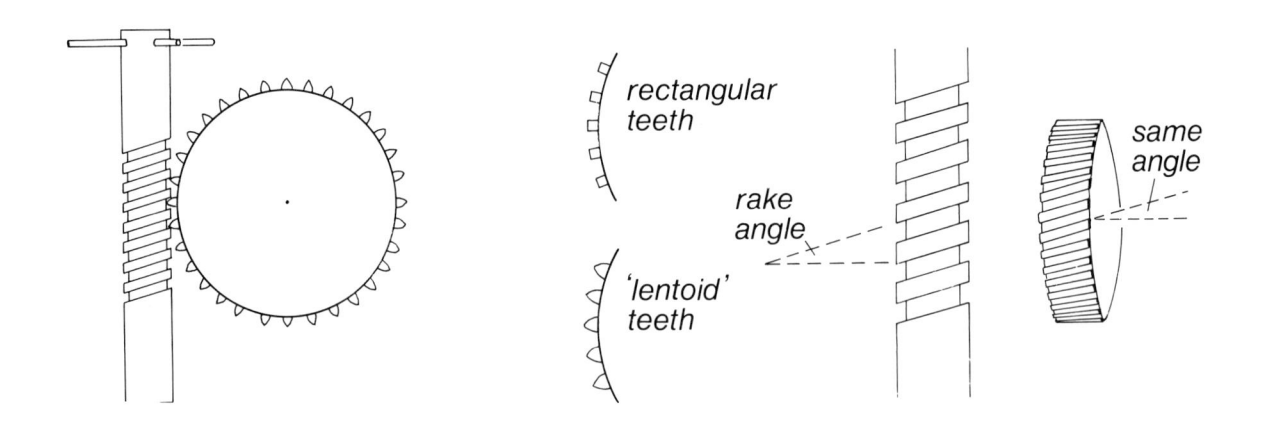

Figure 7. Screw engaging with cogwheel.

in a single operation, a wedge is used to extrude the cutting tool a little farther each time it is driven through the block, until eventually the depth of the thread it has cut matches that of the male thread, and the two will engage very firmly. This would be a great improvement on the "shin guard."

Hero also notes a very useful feature of the screw (*Mechanics* 2.19), namely, that it does not require a locking device to prevent it from being driven backwards.

It must be noted that all the mechanical devices so far described were operated by manpower, either directly or by the use of the windlass or the treadmill. Animal power was used in agriculture and heavy transport, the animals being mainly oxen, and occasionally for milling and water pumping; but manpower was clearly the mainstay of most machinery. It has been argued that the availability of slave labor throughout antiquity relieved engineers from the need to seek or

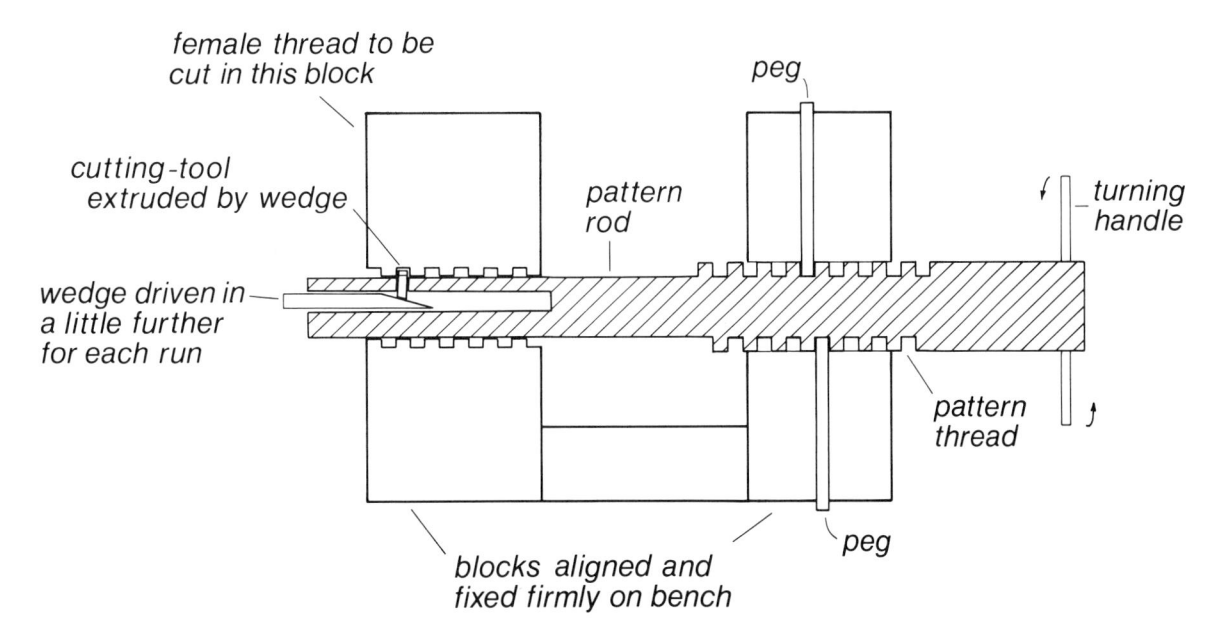

Figure 8. Hero's screw cutting device (cross section).

exploit any other power source. But it is very difficult to sustain this argument from the evidence that is available to us; there were certainly shortages of manpower at various times, but these do not coincide with technological developments and, conversely, slave labor was fairly plentiful at the time when the only other important power source began to be exploited.

This was the waterwheel, and it affords a striking example of the slow spread of technological innovation in the ancient world. It was first used in northern Asia Minor and was known to Roman theoretical writers such as Vitruvius by the mid first century B.C. But, despite what we would regard as its great usefulness, it was not generally exploited until about one hundred years later. Various reasons for this time lag have been offered, but none of them is wholly satisfactory.

Vitruvius describes only one type of waterwheel: the undershot (fig. 9a). The paddles, which he calls "wings" or "feathers" (*pinnae*), project into the water, and the power generated by this type of wheel depends on three factors: the number of paddles, the area of each paddle on which the water impinges (which varies with the depth of the water), and, most important, the speed of flow of the water. As a result, it tends to be rather inflexible, only operating when the water supply is exactly right and becoming virtually unusable if the water level falls even by a small amount. Vitruvius does not mention any need to manage the water supply by making a reservoir higher up the stream or by funneling it into a narrow channel so that its velocity could be increased and a greater proportion of its energy transferred to the wheel. He may not have known about such methods, or he may have regarded them as not being strictly a part of the machinery he was describing.

A more efficient type of waterwheel, the overshot (fig. 9b), can be identified from a small number of archaeological sites, notably Barbegal near Arelate (Arles) in southern France, and in a corner of the Athenian agora near the now reconstructed Stoa of

(a) undershot *(b) overshot*

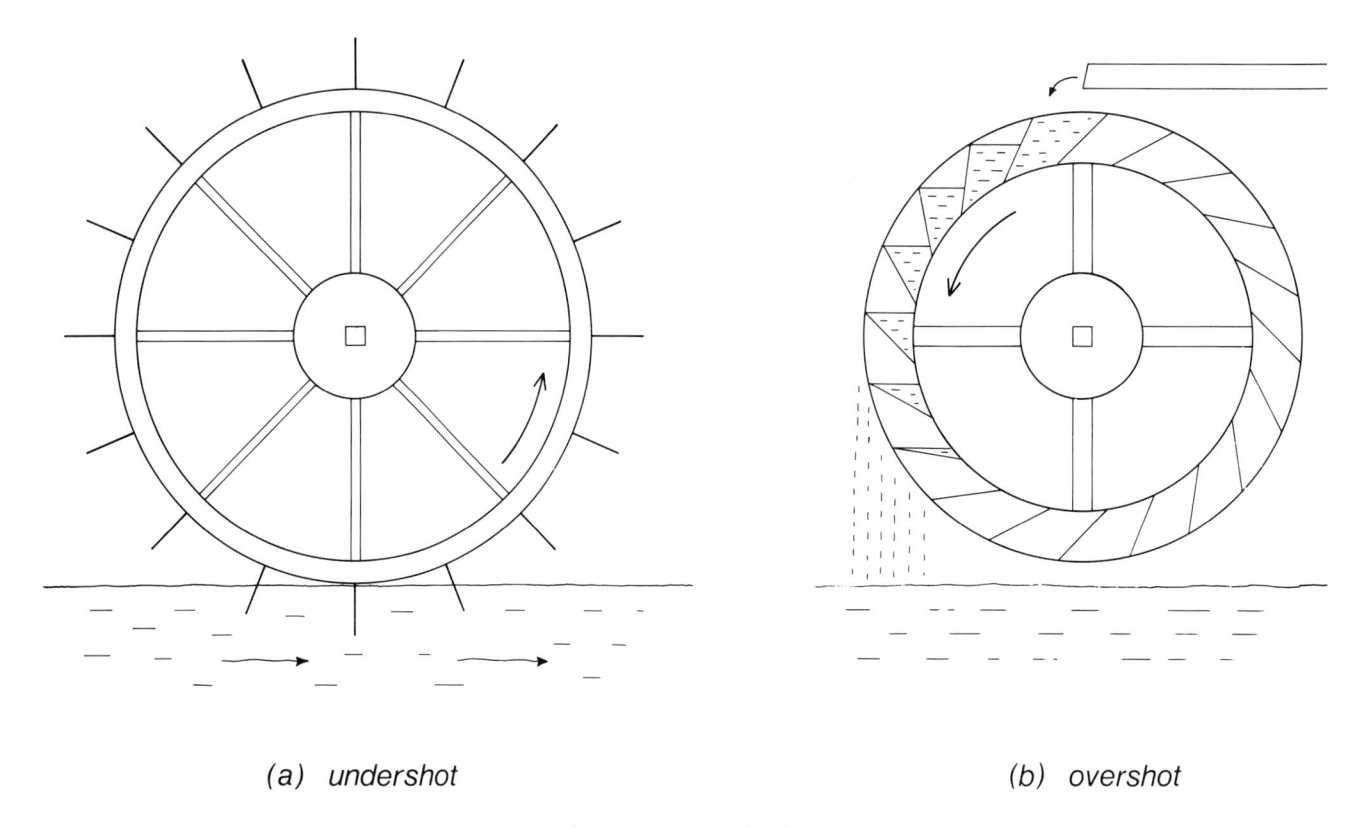

Figure 9. Waterwheels.

Attalus II. This evidence dates mainly to the fourth and fifth centuries A.D.; it lies mainly in the construction of the wheel pit, which has a characteristic form of its own and in some cases bears marks where the pit wheel has rubbed against it.

The overshot wheel generates its power from the falling weight of the water delivered to it, and the output can be estimated very roughly from the quantity of water delivered in a given space of time and the length of the fall, which may be taken as roughly equal to the diameter of the wheel. Thus a wheel of 8 feet (2.44 m) diameter, supplied with water at 5 cubic feet (142 l) per second, is theoretically capable of producing about 4.5 horsepower. In practice, as an overshot wheel is on average about 60 to 70 percent efficient (as compared with about 20 to 25 percent efficiency for the undershot), its actual output might be about 2.7 horsepower. This means that it would do the work of about twenty-five men, without any shift reliefs.

Waterwheels were used for two purposes: for lifting water by means of a bucket wheel or bucket chain and for milling grain. In order to drive horizontal revolving millstones, gears were used, apparently of the "crown wheel" type (fig. 10). In addition to changing the direction of drive, these could also serve to speed up or slow down the rate of drive so as to match the power available from the wheel to the size of the millstones.

MILITARY ENGINEERING

It is a sad reflection on human nature that throughout the whole of recorded history inventors have been required to devote much of their ingenuity and artisans much of

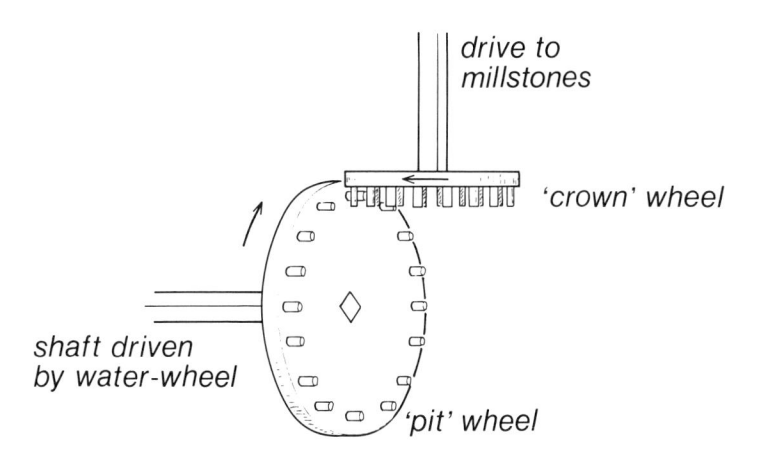

Figure 10. Gearing for water mill.

their skill to the development of weapons of war. The civilizations of the ancient Mediterranean, being no exception, offer many examples of military and naval technology, much of it the result of inspired improvisation but some of it planned and financed by rulers who fully appreciated its value. The most striking instances of this are to be found among the successors of Alexander the Great, kings of small independent states who vied with one another and joined in an arms race that encompassed warship design, the development of siege engines, missile projectors, and various other military machinery.

The attitude of the ancient historians to these developments varies between aristocratic indifference and the almost schoolboyish interest in gadgets and machines that Thucydides displayed in a number of contexts, notably when describing (4.100) the siege of Delium by the Boeotians and their allies in 424 B.C. The defenders had used wood (including, it was alleged, some sacred olive trees) to fortify part of the wall, and the device used by the Boeotians in their attack was perhaps the earliest recorded example of a flamethrower. To make it, they sawed a ship's yardarm in half lengthwise, gouged out a groove along each half, and then put them back together to form a round pipe. From the far end they hung a caldron with an iron pipe curving down into it, and covered part of the wooden pipe there with iron cladding (fig. 11). The other end was mounted on wagons, with a pair of blacksmith's bellows connected to it. The caldron was filled with "burning charcoal, sulphur, and pitch," and when it was brought close to the wooden fortifications, a blast of air from the bellows produced a great sheet of flame, which drove the defenders back and destroyed part of the fortifications. Thucydides' account has an interesting implication. The choice of wood for the air pipe suggests that there was no other material available from which a pipe could be made in a single section, rigid enough to support on its end a caldron weighing perhaps 50 to 60 pounds (23–27 kg). The ship's yardarm would be the most quickly available piece of that material, and protecting it from the heat of the flame was clearly a problem. It might perhaps appear that the Greeks at this point had come close to the invention of gunpowder; the charcoal and sulphur mixture needed only the addition of saltpeter (potassium nitrate, KNO_3) to make it explode. But though they knew and used a substance that they called *nitron*, this was in fact a harmless form of soda, which they used as a detergent. The name "niter" was transferred to saltpeter in the sixteenth century.

There are many other descriptions of

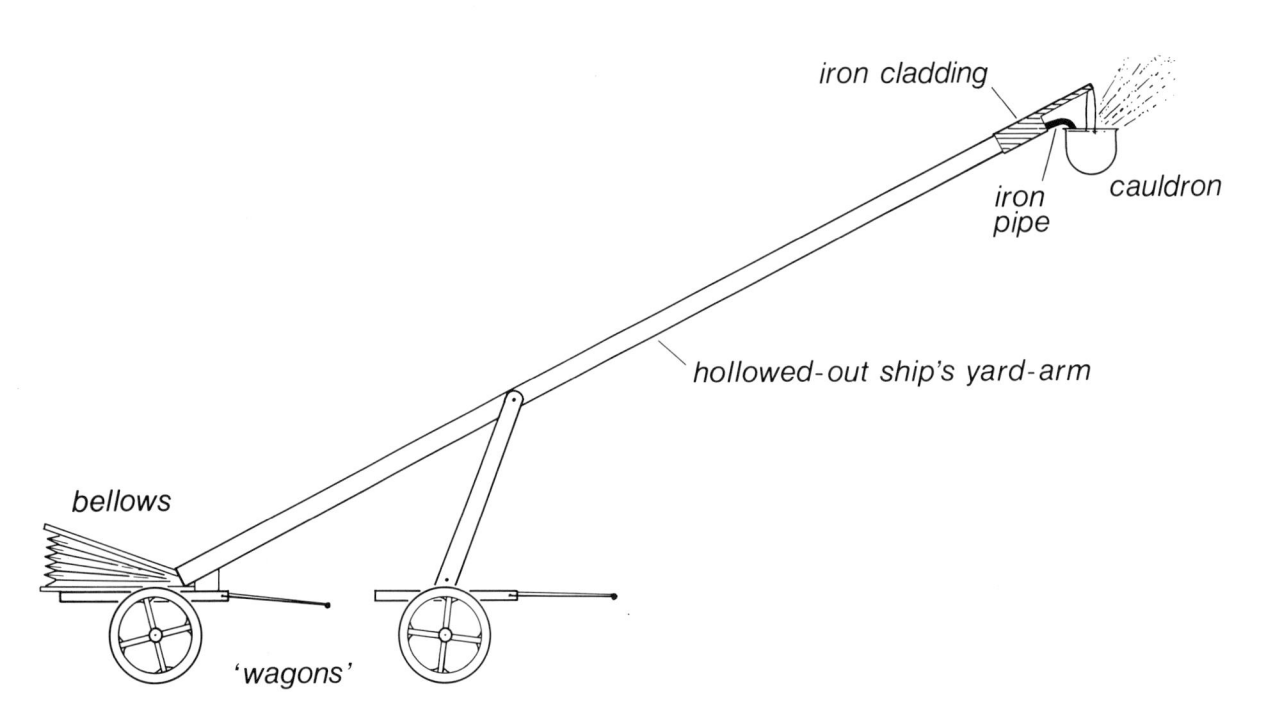

Figure 11. Flamethrower.

siege engines in the works of ancient historians and writers on engineering, ranging from small makeshift contraptions to enormous and very expensive pieces of machinery. There is an interesting cautionary tale (Vitruvius, 10.16.3–4) about one Diognetos, who was employed as resident military engineer by the people of Rhodes. A rival engineer, Kallias, visited the city and in the course of a public lecture described how a siege engine—a movable, fortified tower equipped with a battering ram and various weapons—approaching the walls could be hooked up and lifted inside by means of a tower crane of the *carchesion* type. This impressed the Rhodians so much that they fired Diognetos and appointed Kallias in his place. Soon afterward, however (305–304 B.C.), Demetrios I, known by the nickname of Poliorcetes (the Besieger), attacked Rhodes, bringing with him a siege engine 125 feet (38 m) high and 60 feet (18.3 m) wide, weighing 160 tons. Kallias, who had looked so plausible beside the drawing board, had to admit that he could not build a crane to hoist it. The Rhodians went back to Diognetos and pleaded with him. After a show of reluctance, he was swayed by a delegation of young girls and agreed to help. He devised a simple but effective scheme. During the night he made openings in the wall at the point where the great engine was expected to attack and fixed sloping wooden chutes to project through them. The entire population of Rhodes then rallied round with buckets full of water, mud, and sewage, which they poured down the chutes, creating a small cesspool in front of the machine. When it was moved forward the next day, it sank in up to its axles and could neither be moved up to the wall nor pulled back. Even the heaviest siege engines, though they could not be lifted bodily, could be rendered useless by a tower crane skillfully hooked on to the battering ram with a grappling iron; the point of the ram could be lifted clear of the wall and its swing restricted to a small, ineffective arc. In a seaborne attack on waterside fortifications these same cranes could be used to capsize warships and landing craft as they approached or to pull aside scaling ladders mounted on them.

But the most impressive military technology achieved by the Greeks and Romans was undoubtedly in the area of missile projectors, the catapults used to shoot arrows or hurl stone shot. As Thucydides makes no mention of these weapons, we may be sure that they were not in use before the fourth century B.C. Exactly when they first appeared as a significant element in an army's weaponry is not clear, but by the end of the fourth century they were in use, and there was a period of rapid development and improvement in the third century, most of it financed and authorized by Hellenistic monarchies.

Our evidence for the development of catapult design consists mainly of three treatises and a short fragment, ranging in date from the late third century B.C. to the late first century A.D. In particular, we are indebted to Hero of Alexandria, who, though writing at the end of this period, gives a certain amount of historical background in addition to the contemporary designs.

The earliest weapon he describes was in fact a form of crossbow, known to the Greeks as a "belly shooter" (*gastraphetes*) for reasons that will become clear later. Its purpose was to extend the effective range of its arrows by using a bow that was heavier and stiffer than those normally used by archers. This means that some method of drawing the bow other than a man's arm and shoulder muscles had to be found and also a method of holding the bowstring back when the full force of the bow was on it and then releasing it when the weapon had been properly aimed. All this was accomplished by means of a slider, which ran back and forth in a dovetail groove on the top of the stock of the crossbow (fig. 12a). The slider was pushed forward until the claw of the trigger mechanism was in position over the bowstring so that it could be clamped down on either side of the arrow groove. Then the projecting end of the slider was placed against a wall or boulder, and the archer pressed his stomach against a concave rest at the butt end of the stock so as to push the slider back, pulling the bowstring and bending the bow. By this means a bow with a draw force of more than 100 pounds (45 kg), which is about the maximum for a hand bow, could be used. When the bow was drawn, the slider was kept back in position by pawls on a ratchet (fig. 12b) until the weapon could be raised into the firing position and a missile, which probably had a horizontal notch, placed in the groove against the bowstring. These missiles were sharp-tipped bolts rather than arrows, though feather vanes, called flights, may sometimes have been used for special accuracy. Then, when the weapon was aimed, the lever that held the trigger claw clamped down was pulled back, allowing it to lift and release the bowstring. As there has been some confusion about this, it should be made clear that the slider did not move forward at this stage, only the bowstring and the missile.

Hero notes a number of later improvements. First, it was a cumbersome business to lift the crossbow down between each shot and then raise it again when it was drawn. So instead of the "belly pusher," a winch with a ratchet was used to draw the slider back (fig. 13).

These weapons were developed in size over the fourth and third centuries B.C., and we hear of some monster machines. Some of them threw stone shot instead of arrows, having a sling of woven hair or leather at the center of the bowstring. As the draw force increased, multiple pulleys had to be used as part of the winching mechanism. The record breaker in this category may have had a bow 15 feet (4.5 m) long from tip to tip, which threw a stone ball weighing about 40 pounds

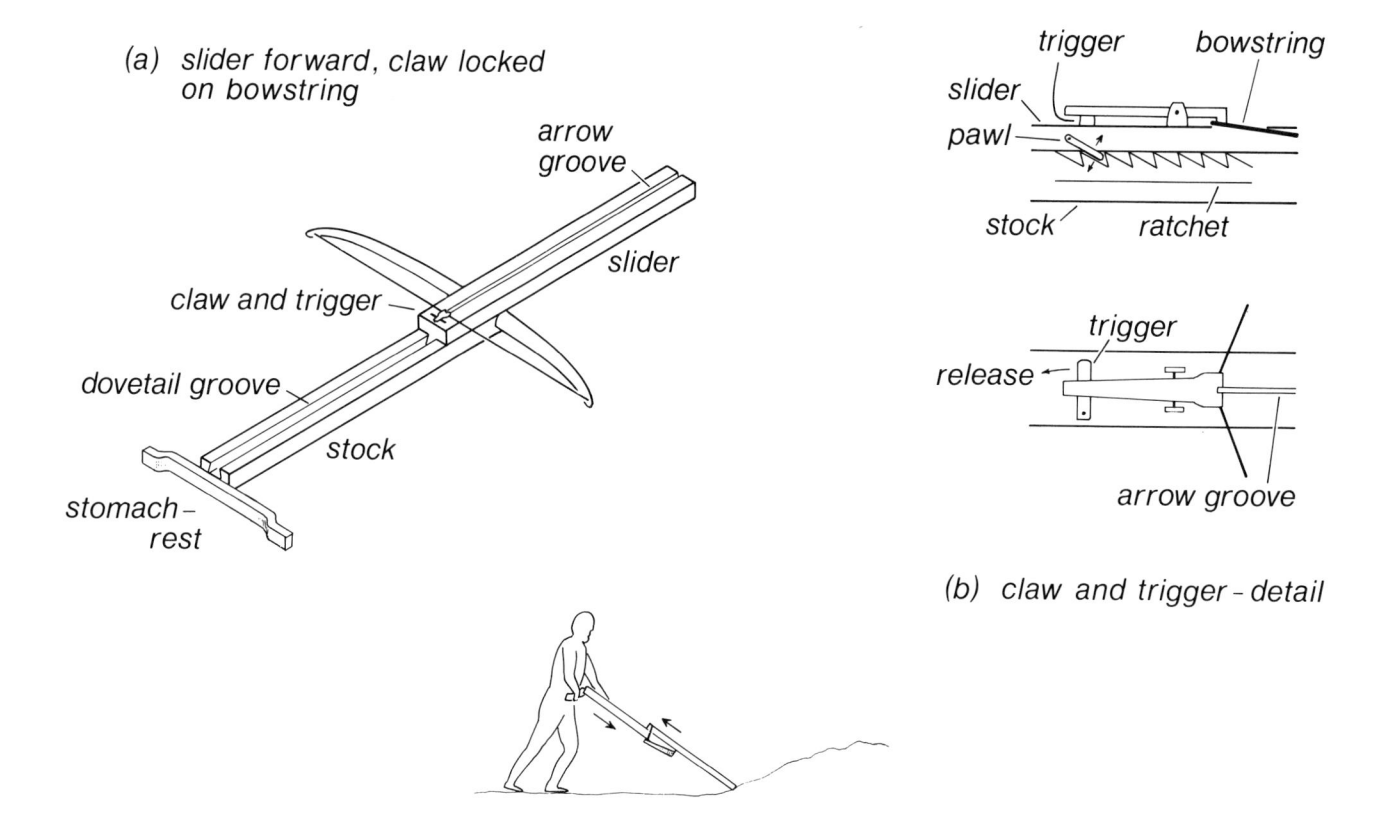

Figure 12. Crossbow (*gastraphetes*, belly shooter).

(18.1 kg). Clearly, the limitation here was the quality of wood available to make the huge bow, though it is possible that other materials such as animal sinew or horn were used to make a compound bow with increased energy storage. But this kind of research was carried out at the craft level, and unfortunately the theoretical writers do not discuss it in detail.

A much more important development came with the introduction of the torsion spring. This consisted of a bundle of cords made from an elastic material, with a wooden arm inserted through the middle, so as to swing in a limited arc from side to side (fig. 14a). When the arm is pulled around in one direction, it twists and stretches the cords on either side of it, pulling them into tension; when it is released, the cords un-twist very rapidly, shortening to their original length and thus swinging the arm with great force. The amount of stretch and the power in the spring (the strain energy, to use the technical term) depend on a number of factors, of which the most important are the nature of the material from which the cords are made, the distance of each individual cord from the center of rotation (fig. 14b), and whether the cords in their released position are straight, nearly straight, or twisted into a helix. These factors are all mentioned by Hero and the other writers in various contexts.

The catapult was constructed with two of these springs, the arms swinging outward on release to move a bowstring joining their tips (fig. 14a). The design of the slider and trigger mechanism was the same as for the

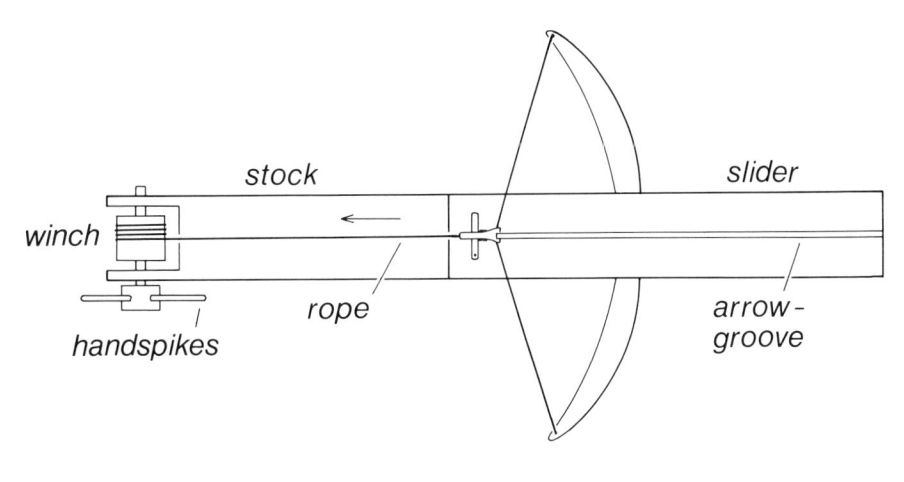

Figure 13. Winch used to draw bow catapult.

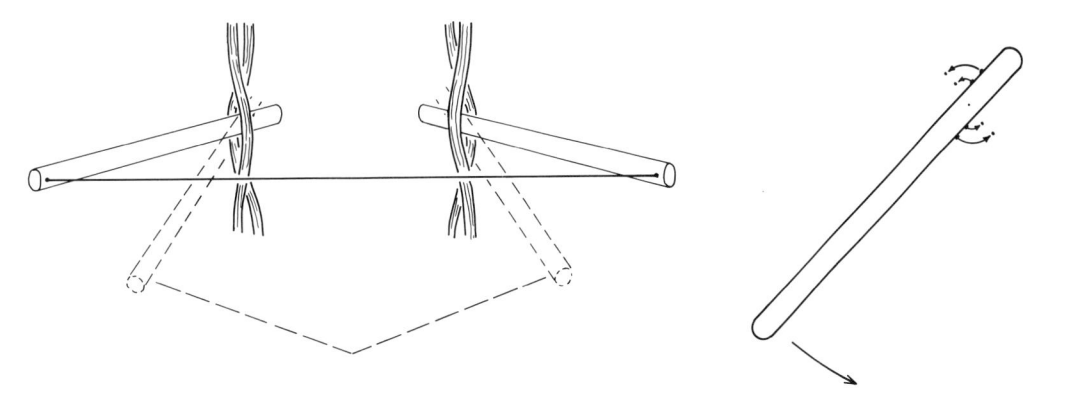

(a) two torsion springs, arms and bowstring

(b) cords further from centre of rotation are stretched more

Figure 14. Torsion springs.

crossbow type, and the earliest torsion spring catapults shot bolts or arrows. From there on we find a number of lines of development that show the ancient engineers to have been thoroughly competent at the experimental, trial-and-error level.

The first question they asked was what material should be used for the spring cords, and how could they best be anchored at the top and bottom? They may have tried hemp or flax in the early stages, but before long they discovered the ideal material—animal sinew, which they called *neuron*. This seems to have been obtained from the larger tendons of various animals, mainly working ones such as oxen. They discovered, no doubt by experiment, that pigs' sinew was not so effective. The tendons were teased out into fibers and then made into a continuous length of sinew rope, presumably by the same methods as those used for making hempen or papyrus ropes. Here, once again, the ancient writers reveal practically nothing about the craft industry, and modern attempts to reconstruct catapults exactly have been frustrated by this particular problem.

There is also the problem of preserving the texture and elastic properties of the sinew over a period of time, which the ancients seem to have succeeded in doing, mainly by steeping in olive oil and taking the tension off the springs when they were not in use. There are also references in the ancient writers to the use of hair as an alternative material. This was presumably horsehair in most cases, although female human hair was highly recommended.

When the elastic material had been made into a continuous length, it was threaded alternately up and down through two holes in the top and bottom of a rectangular wooden frame, passing around short iron rods on the outside (fig. 15a). The arm was held in position while this was being done, and the cord was stretched as tightly as possible. At an early stage it was discovered that if the iron rods were rotated in the opposite direction to the backswing of the arms, the tension in the cords would be increased, both in the drawn or cocked position and

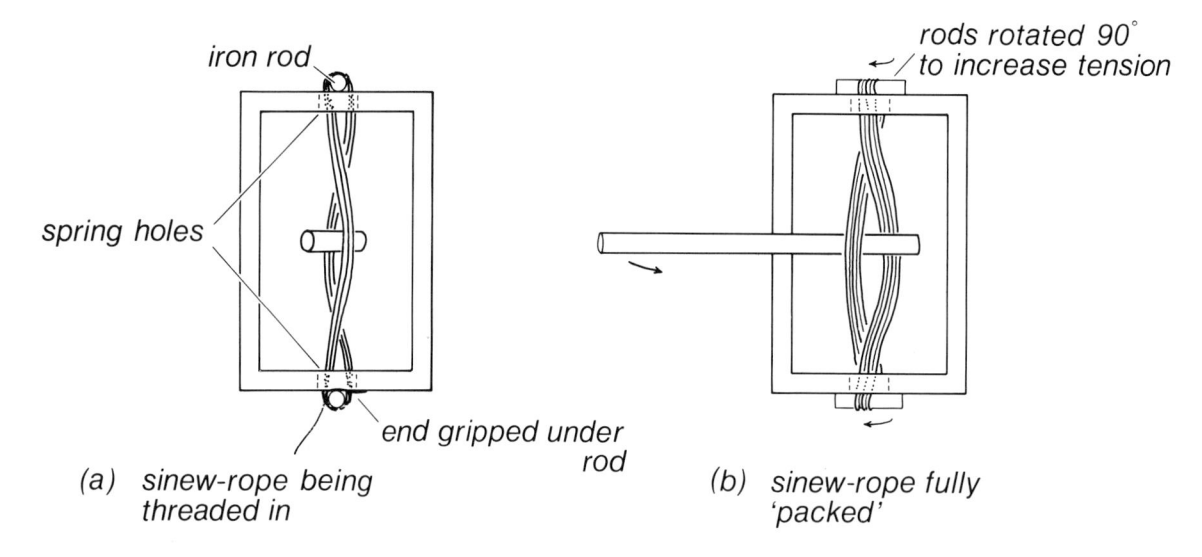

Figure 15. Torsion spring frame with rotated rods.

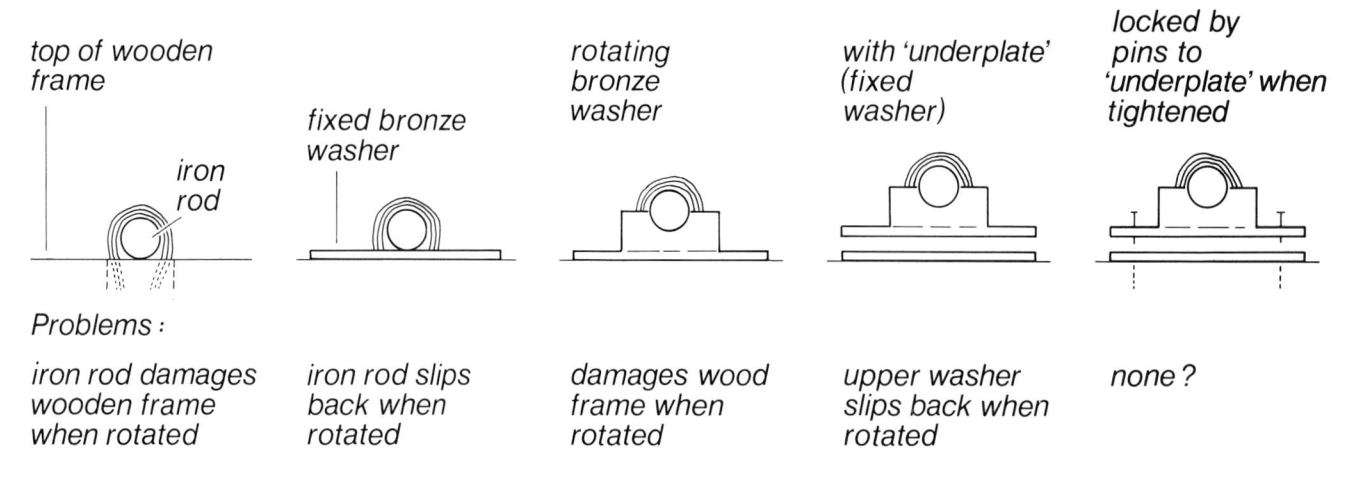

Figure 16. Improvements in washer design of torsion spring catapult.

when the arms were fully forward, and that this improved the performance of the catapult (fig. 15b). Then the weapon makers found that the rotating rods tended to damage the surfaces of the frame with which they were in contact, so they devised washers to minimize this damage and gradually improved the design, as shown in figure 16. The last of these designs involves a very early application of the vernier principle, in which there are sixteen holes in the lower washer, spaced at intervals of 22 1/2 degrees, and three pairs of holes in the upper one, more closely spaced at 15 degrees. This means that there are forty-eight different positions around the circle in which one of the three pairs is opposite a pair in the lower washer and can be locked into it with two pins. The rods, along with the washer in the later models, were rotated by means of a primitive spanner or wrench.

A second series of developments concerned the design of the wooden frames in which the springs were mounted. They were all directed toward one objective—an increase in the arc through which the arms could swing. This, as they clearly saw, would increase the effective power of the springs and the range of the weapon (fig. 17).

Many attempts have been made to estimate the performance of these weapons. The only way to arrive at a reliable estimate is to construct a working model, using precisely the materials available to the ancient

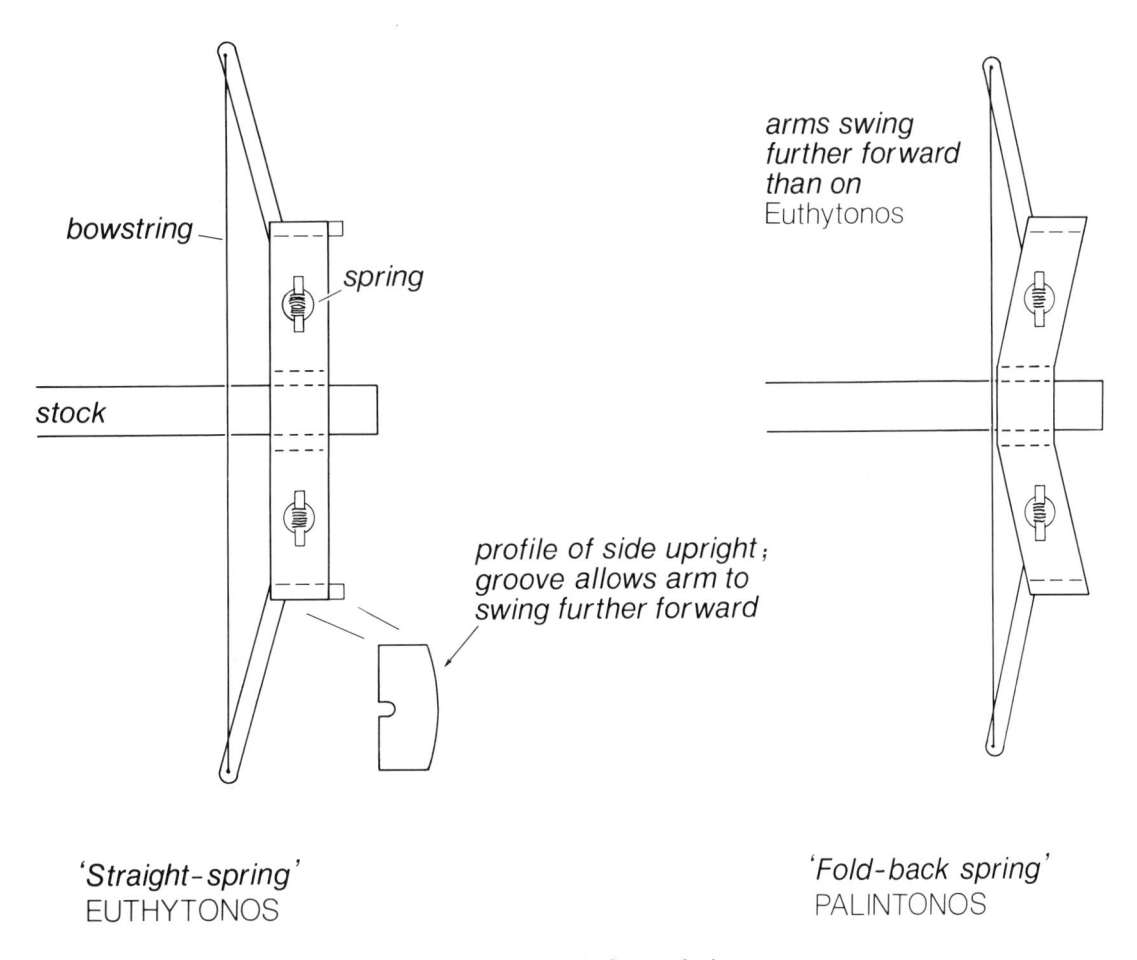

Figure 17. Catapult frame designs.

artisans. A number of attempts at this have been and are being made in various parts of the world, but pending more results it would be reasonable to accept the general view that twin-arm arrow/bolt-shooting catapults had an effective range of about 250 yards (229 m) within which a skilled marksman could reasonably hope to hit an individual standing figure. The missile would travel some distance farther than that—perhaps 400 yards (366 m)—but its velocity would be lower and the aim uncertain at that distance. The range of stone-throwing catapults was probably a good deal less—perhaps about 150 yards (137 m)—but this would depend on whether they were fired on a low trajectory to smash down walls or on a high one to pass over the defenses and fall on the buildings inside.

A number of other improvements were made or attempted in catapult design. The most impressive one was thought out by an arms expert called Dionysios of Alexandria; it was a rapid-firing catapult, the nearest approach in the ancient world to the machine gun. The torsion springs were of the normal type, but the slider was moved forward and drawn back by means of a chain drive on each side. As it reached its forward limit, a projection on the stock operated the trigger claw and locked it onto the bowstring. Then the chains drew the slider back, and an ingenious loading device dropped a bolt from a magazine onto the slider in front of the bowstring. Finally, another projection at the rear end of the stock activated the trigger and fired the bolt. This catapult could probably have been operated by one man, and may have been able to shoot about three times as many bolts in a given time as an ordinary one.

Experiments were also carried out in an attempt to find an alternative elastic material for the springs such as bronze strips or air compressed in a closed cylinder by a piston, but they had little success.

The Romans were less innovative than the Greeks, but more practical. They devised a light, portable type of catapult, which they called a hand catapult (*manuballista*). Its spring frames were made of wrought iron, much smaller than the older wooden machines, and the sinew springs were enclosed in light bronze canisters to protect them from weather damage. Some remains of these weapons have come to light within the last ten years in various areas that once belonged to the Roman Empire.

It was the Romans, too, who made and used the version of the torsion spring catapult that had only one spring and one arm, which swung upward in a vertical plane to throw a round stone shot by means of a sling on the end of the arm. This was known as the "wild ass" (*onager*) and was an altogether cruder machine. It is generally assumed that it was adopted in a period of decline, when skilled craftsmen were no longer available to make more sophisticated machines; indeed, our best evidence for it comes from the fourth century A.D.

WATER ENGINEERING

Archaeological evidence survives for a number of water supply schemes in Greek and Roman cities throughout the Mediterranean world. The earliest significant Greek remains are those of a tunnel cut through a hill on the island of Samos, made on the orders of the tyrant Polycrates in about 530 B.C. Its purpose was to convey water from a spring on the far side of the hill to the city of Samos. It seems to have been rather more than 1,000 yards (1,025 m) long, and just over 8 feet (2.4 m) square in cross section, with a considerable number of vertical shafts up to the surface at irregular intervals. This is a typical example of an engineering project made possible by the concentration of wealth in the hands of a powerful individual and by the recognition of a real need for water supplies that could be guarded against enemy action in a siege.

In the first half of the second century B.C., a very ambitious project was set up by Eumenes II in the city of Pergamum (southeastern Asia Minor). A spring that gave an abundant supply of water was at a higher elevation than the citadel; it was also about 3,300 yards (3 km) away, and the intervening ground was much lower, falling at one point to a level 600 feet (183 m) lower than the spring site. There was clearly no possibility of running an open gravity-flow channel from the source to the citadel, so an inverted siphon or U-bend was used instead. This consisted of a sealed pipeline that rose and fell with the undulations of the land (fig. 18).

This system was many years ahead of its time and posed some formidable problems to its designers and builders. First, there was the choice of materials for the pipeline. At the lowest point of the system the water pressure would be about 260 p.s.i. (18.3 kg/cm²), and that would put an enormous stress on the pipes and joints. Bronze would be out of the question on grounds of cost, and if lead pipes were used their walls would have to be very thick. A number of short lengths of earthenware pipe, with an internal diameter of about 7 inches (18 cm) were found on the site, and this was most probably the material for the whole pipeline, although it is strange that so few pieces remain out of so many. But the system must have been a nightmare for maintenance engineers. If all the pipe sections were made in lengths of about 3 feet (0.9 m), which is highly probable, there must have been more than 2,800 joints, about half of them working under pressures of 100 p.s.i. (7 kg/cm²) or more. From Vitruvius (8.6.8) we gather that earthenware pipes were normally made, as were the surviving fragments at Pergamum, with a wall thickness of about 1.5 inches (38 mm); each length had a tongue about 2 inches (5 cm) long at one end, which was inserted and sealed into a socket in the next length with putty made from quicklime and olive oil. The sections were carried a few feet above the ground by rectangular stone blocks with circular holes in them, of which a considerable number were found on the site. Another problem would be blockage of the lower bends by sediment, which would necessitate the dismantling of the whole system.

The charge has been made against the Romans that they were overtraditional in their approach to water engineering and failed to realize the capabilities of closed-pipe systems. It would be fairer to say that they fully recognized the problems, and when they chose the open-channel method, it was for sound engineering and economical reasons. It involved a high initial capital cost, but was relatively easy to maintain, while the closed-pipe method involved not only a high capital cost, but a heavy commitment for mainte-

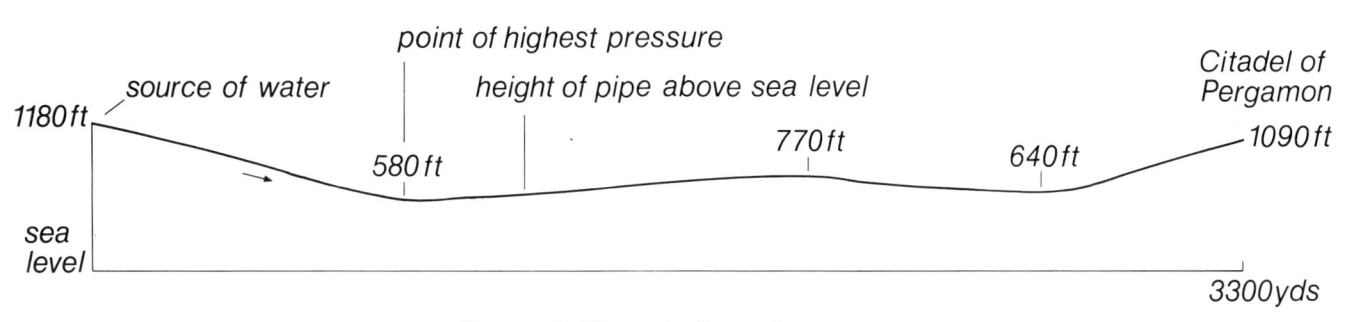

Figure 18. Water pipeline at Pergamun.

nance and repair. When the Romans used it, they did so because it was totally impossible to use anything else, as we shall see.

An examination of the aqueducts that supplied Rome itself, built over a period of some 400 years, clearly shows that the Roman engineers (and there is no evidence to show that Greeks were employed at any stage) were by no means unwilling to try new techniques and materials as they became available. Our knowledge of this system is immeasurably greater than that of any other because in addition to the surviving remains we have the account of Frontinus, the chief water commissioner from 97 to 103 A.D. He was not himself a technical expert but a very conscientious administrator who made it his duty to discover and record as much as he could of the layout and organization of the system.

The oldest supply line was the Aqua Appia, built about 312 B.C., at a time when Rome's position among the Italian cities was by no means secure. For this reason, and also because of the low level of the source, it ran underground for virtually its whole length of just over 10 miles (16.1 km). It supplied the low-lying southern quarters of Rome, its channel being a mere 28 feet (8.5 m) above the level of the Tiber in that region.

A comparison of two later aqueducts, the Aqua Marcia, constructed 144–140 B.C., and the Aqua Claudia, completed in A.D. 47, shows clearly how the technology developed and improved in various respects over two centuries.

First, let us consider the materials and construction of the water channel. The obvious problem with dry-laid blocks of tufa stone, as used for the channel of the Aqua Appia, was that any individual block could be forced outward, fracturing the waterproof lining and causing serious leaks. This was solved in the Aqua Marcia by a simple but effective measure. A semicircular vertical groove was cut in each end of each block, so that each pair of grooves between facing blocks formed a cylindrical hole about 1 inch (2.5 cm) in diameter (fig. 19a). This was filled with a plug of mortar, which effectively keyed them together and prevented lateral movement (fig. 19b). Also, the blocks were held in place with pure lime mortar, which would give moderately strong adhesion. But stone block construction is inevitably expensive and depends on there being a local supply of stone. In the late first century B.C. builders began to use concrete for the water channel, casting it in wooden formwork and facing the outer surfaces to protect them from weather erosion. The Aqua Claudia was mostly built in this way, the older concrete having been improved upon by the use of more regular-sized lumps of aggregate, set in a stronger mortar. There is evidence from about this time for the use of pozzuolana, a volcanic dust that, when used as a cement, makes a very strong and waterproof concrete. The ultimate refinement came with repairs carried out under Hadrian some seventy years later; corners and piers were made of concrete with full brickwork casing, some of them being fine examples of craftsmanship.

The second point of improvement was the surveying and routing of the aqueduct. The entire channel had to be set out with a gradient between 1:200 and 1:400, though some irregularities could be tolerated in the underground sections. Where the channel ran on or just below the surface a trench was cut, the channel constructed, and flat stone slabs were placed over the top to prevent interference and pollution. If the required level was a few feet above ground, a *substructio* was used— a thick wall of rubble faced with cut stones that carried the channel on its top. But using these methods meant having to follow the contours of the land, and in the winding valley of the Anio (Aniene), where several of the aqueducts were situated, this meant making long and expensive detours

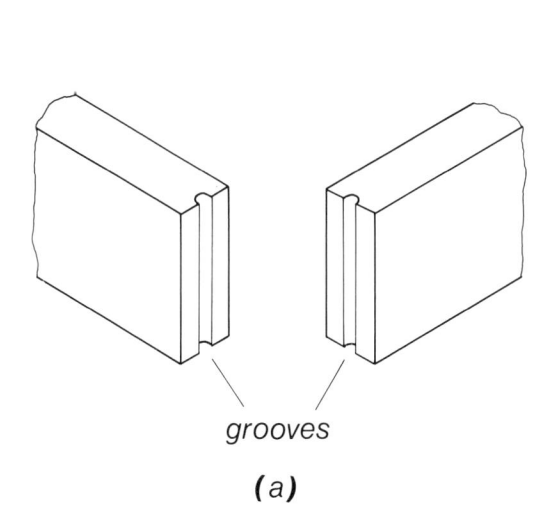

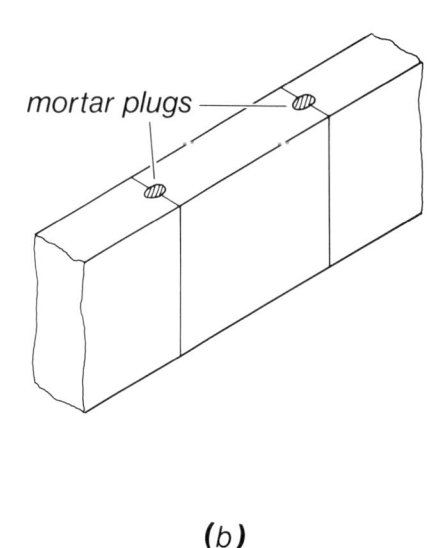

Figure 19. Stone blocks keyed together in construction of Aqua Marcia channel.

away from the direct line. As techniques developed, the engineers became more adventurous in taking short cuts, cutting deeper tunnels through hills and raising higher arched structures over valleys. This also can be seen from a comparison between the Aqua Marcia and the Aqua Claudia, as shown in the table below.

It can be seen at once that although the sources of the two aqueducts are quite close together, the surveyors of the Claudia have managed to reduce its length by about 25 percent, mainly by cutting across a bend opposite Tibur (Tivoli). This accounts for the much greater proportion of the upper section being raised on arches. In the Roman system these structures were all well below the maximum safe height, which the Roman engineers seem to have set at about 150 feet (46 m). There is good evidence to show that where they encountered a valley deeper than this, they used a combination of two systems. A bridge was built to a reasonable height, similar in design to an aqueduct but broader, and was made to carry eight or nine parallel lead pipes linking the summits on either side, with sufficient fall between the inlet and outlet levels to ensure an adequate flow rate (fig. 20). The lowest part of the siphon that ran along the bridge was not in fact level, but was made to slope slightly upward toward the outlet, so that any air pockets would clear

	Marcia	*Claudia*
Approx. linear distance source to delivery	30 mi. (48 km)	28 mi. (45 km)
Total length of conduit	57 mi. (92 km)	42.5 mi. (68.5 km)
Length underground	50 mi. (80 km)	33 mi. (53 km)
Length on substructures	7 mi. (11 km)	6.5 mi. (10.5 km)
On arches in upper reaches	750 yd. (686 m)	5,000 yd. (4.6 km)
Max. height of arches above ground	68 ft. (21 m)	105 ft. (32 m)
Height above Tiber at delivery	125 ft. (38 m)	158 ft. (48 m)

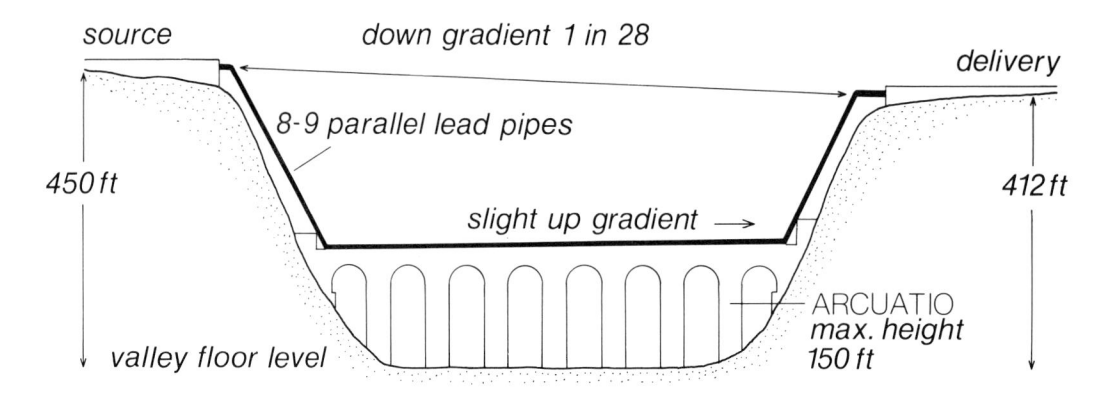

Figure 20. Aqueduct combining bridge and closed-pipe systems.

themselves. This kind of structure was used by the builders of the Gier aqueduct, part of the supply to Lyons in east-central France, and evidence for similar ones has been found in Spain and Asia Minor. They mostly date to the second century A.D., the time of the ubiquitous emperor Hadrian.

Six of the later aqueducts in the Roman system had catch basins, which Frontinus calls covered fish ponds (*contectae piscinae*), about six miles outside Rome. These were settling tanks of no great capacity, not storage reservoirs, since the whole system was designed for a constant rate of flow and met a demand that did not fluctuate much. In fact, there is good reason to believe that supplies to houses and public buildings were allowed to run all the time and were not normally turned off when not in use. From these tanks the channels were carried on arches to the city, three of them (the Julia, Marcia, and Tepula) on the same line of arches. On arrival in Rome they flowed into elevated brick-and-concrete tanks called castles (*castella*) from which the water was distributed. A typical pattern was that of the Marcia. The main supply was divided into three branches; one, which accounted for about 10 percent of its total supply, was *in nomine Caesaris*—at the disposal of the emperor, to assign as he wished. The second branch, taking about half the total, supplied private customers who paid a water tax in return for the service. The third branch, which took up the remaining 40 percent of the water, was for tax-free public uses, the breakdown being as follows:

To 4 military camps, 4%;
To 15 public works (*opera publica*), 4%;
To 12 gifts (*munera*), 9%;
To 133 pools (*lacus*), 23%.

"Public works" was the official term for public baths and lavatories. Public lavatories, which were not very numerous, were mostly situated in the bath buildings; the effluent was carried away from them and into the sewers by water that flowed continuously in a narrow channel past the front of the toilet seats. The "gifts" were almost certainly fountains, donated to particular areas of Rome by public benefactors, and the "pools" were large troughs or basins at which the poorer folk filled their buckets and jugs, sometimes replaced by water spouts set in a wall, known as "springers" (*salientes*). Frontinus notes (2.103) that they had to be kept running at all hours of the day and night.

It was characteristic of ancient science that neither the Greek nor the Roman engineers made any attempt to measure the speed of flow of the water in their systems. They relied instead on static measurements of the

Size	Latin Name	Diameter		Cross Section		Capacity in
		in.	cm	sq. in.	cm²	*Quinariae* (approx.)
5	Quinaria	0.90	2.29	0.65	4.19	1.0
12	Duodenaria	2.18	5.54	3.75	24.19	5.75
20	Vicenaria	3.67	9.32	10.5	67.74	16.33
100	Centenaria	8.21	20.85	53.0	341.93	81.5
120	Centenum-Vicenum	9.00	22.86	63.5	409.68	97.75

cross section of channels and supply pipes, and in fact the Romans evolved a special unit for this purpose, the *quinaria*. The above figures were the most commonly used pipe sizes, the smallest designed to supply one customer, the largest being a "district supply main."

The total delivery of the entire system to the city of Rome was probably between 80 and 120 million gallons (300,000–450,000 m³) per day.

Supplies of running water on this scale were limited to urban settlements, and the great majority of people in the ancient world got their water from wells. This means that they had to raise the water laboriously from depths ranging from 6 to 50 feet (2 to 15 m) up to ground level. The commonest device for doing this, consisting of a winch, rope, and bucket, had been in use for many centuries before the classical period and hardly qualifies as engineering. But from the second century B.C., or perhaps earlier, the Greeks and Romans used the force pump, known to them as the "Ktesibian machine" after its supposed inventor, an Alexandrian Greek of the third century B.C.

Most of the force pumps described by Hero and Vitruvius (and all the surviving examples) are of twin-cylinder design, with the pistons working reciprocally, operated by a rocker arm (fig. 21). The most sophisticated type had bronze cylinders and pistons, with inlet and outlet valves of the disc type; Hero also describes a flap valve that could be mounted vertically on the outside of a cylinder (fig. 22a). Soldering and welding were the most common methods of assembly. Quite a number of pumps survive that display various permutations of these elements; where development can be traced as between earlier and later models, it is usually in the valve design, in which flap valves are mounted at a slight angle to ensure rapid closure (fig. 22b) or stems are fitted to the disc valves and valve guides to control their movement (fig. 22c).

A type that is represented in three of the surviving pumps was made from a tree stump, with lead tubes for cylinders; they correspond exactly to Vitruvius' description. If worked at a leisurely pace, they could have raised almost 5 gallons (19 l) per minute, or 265 gallons (just over 1,000 l) per hour.

Hero of Alexandria describes, not speculatively but as a piece of equipment in regular use, a fire-fighting apparatus that used a two-cylinder force pump made entirely of bronze. It was mounted in a mobile water tank and had an ingenious outlet nozzle that could be turned around or up or down so as to direct the jet in any required direction.

Hero also describes a device that was probably ornamental rather than useful, commonly referred to as "Hero's fountain." It consisted of a spherical bronze vessel with a capacity of about 4 pints (1.9 l) with an outlet pipe let into its top, extending through almost to the bottom (fig. 23). At its

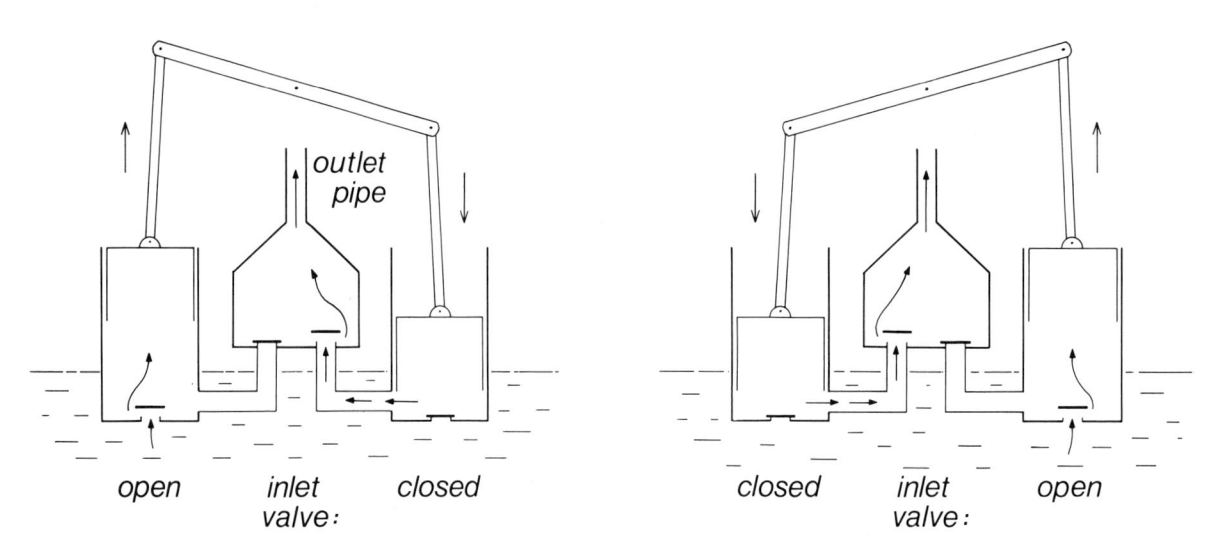

Figure 21. Basic design of force pump.

(a) Hero's valves
flap-valve
lugs prevent displacement
disc-valve

(b) improved flap-valve

(c) improved disc-valve
valve guide stem

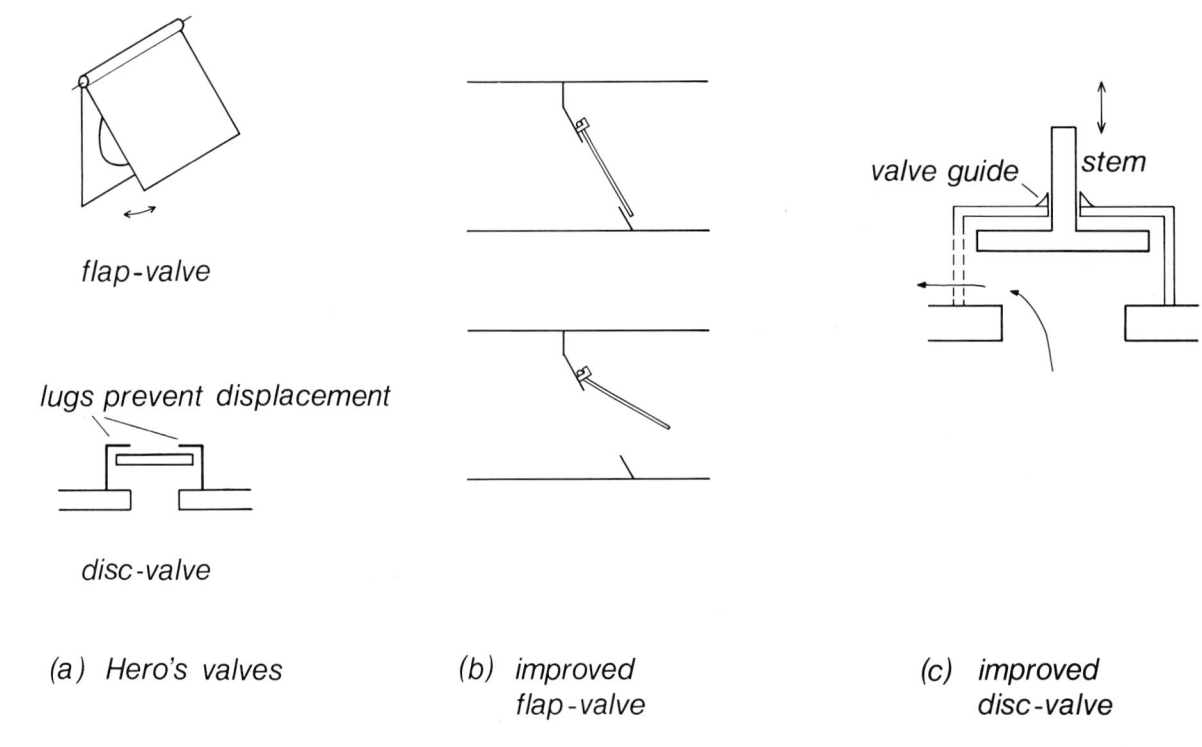

Figure 22. Improvements in valve design of force pump.

top end was an ingenious arrangement with a jet similar to that on the fire engine, but that did not rotate horizontally. When folded down it effectively closed a valve at each end of the crosspiece. A rather crude system was used to compress air into the upper part of the sphere through a no-return flap valve, building up pressure; when this had been done, out of sight of the spectators, the machine was brought out,

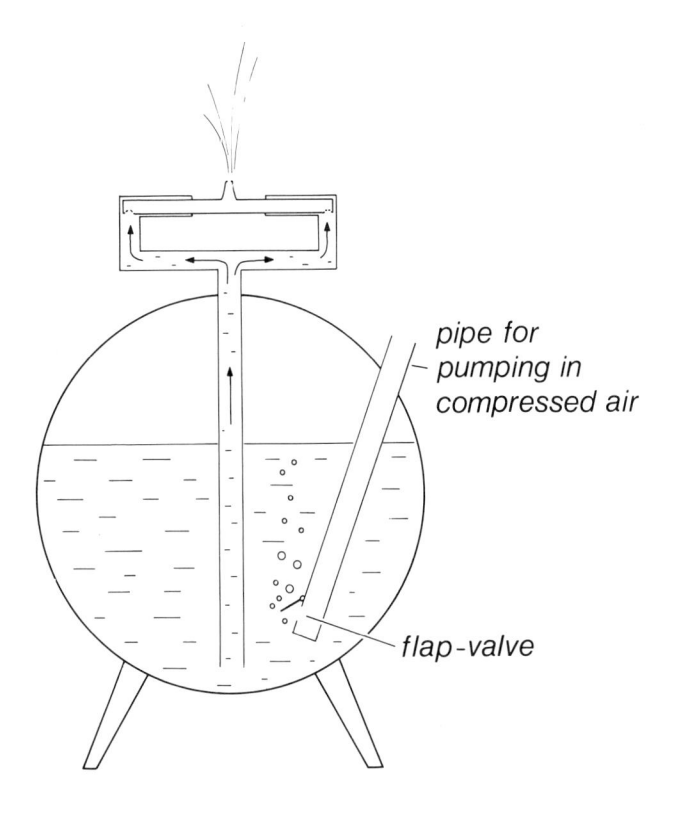

Figure 23. Hero's fountain.

To judge from surviving remains, the most common type was the screw pump (*cochlea*). Vitruvius gives directions for making one (10.6.1–3). The rotor was made from a tree trunk shaped to form an exact cylinder, with a length sixteen times its diameter. Each end was marked out in eight sectors, and parallel lines were drawn along the length (fig. 24a). Then a series of lines was drawn around the circumference at the same distance apart, forming a pattern of squares. Narrow flat strips of osier (willow) were then nailed diagonally across these squares to form a helical ridge that circled the pole about five times (fig. 24b). Vitruvius then says that a similar ridge, starting from each of the seven remaining sector points, was laid parallel to the first, making what is today called an eight-start screw, but the surviving remains of these pumps suggest that there were normally only two ridges, starting from opposite sides. The ridges were then built up to a height equal to the radius of the pole, so that its overall diameter was doubled; in the surviving remains short pieces of flat wood, rather than strips, are used for this. The whole rotor was then enclosed in a casing made with staves and iron hoops, exactly like a straight-sided barrel (fig. 24c). At each stage of construction the interior was treated with pitch to make it watertight.

This type of pump had to be operated sloping at an angle, its lower end immersed in the water supply. Given that the ridges cross the longitudinal lines at a 45-degree angle, the best angle of tilt for the pump, according to Vitruvius, is about 37 degrees. This angle must have been found by experiment, but it turns out to have been quite accurately assessed; some of the most modern screw pumps used for floodwater clearance have their blades at the same angle and operate at almost exactly the same inclination.

Ancient screw pumps were operated by

the jet turned upward, and the water spouted up as if by magic. The same principle is widely used today in garden insecticide sprayers.

Water pumps were used in the ancient world for other purposes besides well-drawing. The most important was the irrigation of cultivated land, usually on a very small scale in vegetable gardens; virtually all cereal growing was by dry-soil cultivation. Mining was carried on throughout the Roman Empire, and many mines were subject to water seepage, which had to be pumped out. Ancient wooden-hulled ships invariably leaked, and the bilge had to be pumped out of them. For most of these purposes a pump was required with a large throughput but with a comparatively low lift; in the case of deep mines, where high output had to be combined with high lift, an ascending series of pumps had to be used.

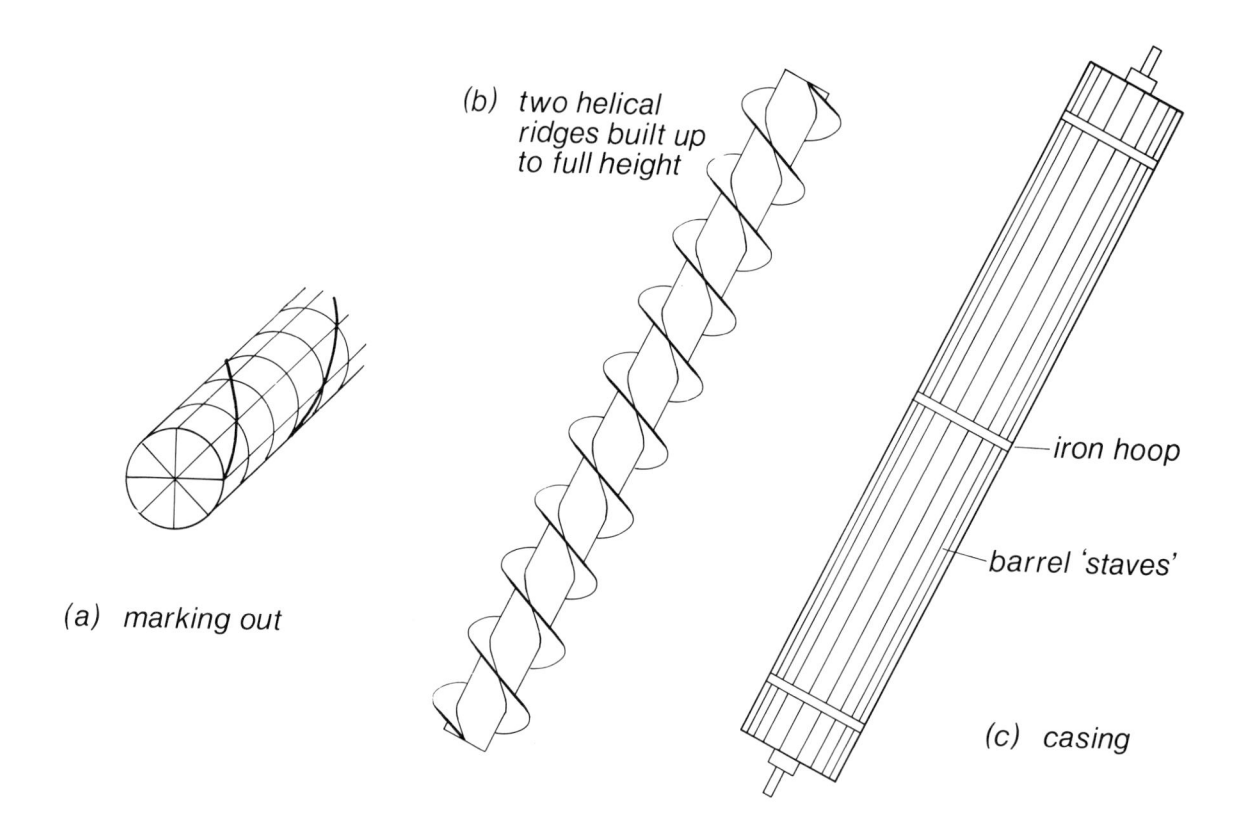

Figure 24. Construction of screw pump.

"men treading." There is no firm evidence to suggest that any kind of wheel or treadmill was fitted, so it seems that the operators turned the barrel with their feet, much as modern lumberjacks roll floating logs on a river, except that the pump operators probably had a handrail to steady themselves with; as against this, they had the disadvantage of having to adopt a lopsided stance in order to roll a barrel that was slanted.

The following table gives a rough idea of the performance of three sizes of screw pump, assuming a reasonable level of mechanical efficiency.

For higher lift the bucket wheel was used. In its simplest form, still to be seen until quite recently in rural areas around the

Length	8 ft. (2.44 m)	10 ft. (3.05 m)	12 ft. (3.66 m)
Diameter	1 ft. (30.5 cm)	15 in. (38 cm)	18 in. (46 cm)
Lift	4 ft. (1.22 m)	5.5 ft. (1.67 m)	6 ft. 7 in. (2.04 m)
Speed	25 rpm	20 RPM	20 RPM
Output per minute	81 gal. (308 l)	128 gal. (486 l)	222 gal. (840 l)
Power required	0.118 HP	0.25 HP	0.53 HP
Provided by	1 man	2 men	4–5 men

Mediterranean, this is simply a large wheel, built on the same principles as a cart wheel but with a larger hub and thinner spokes. Earthenware pots tied to its rim fill as they dip below the water and tip over as they reach the top of their orbit, emptying (with a good deal of splashing and wastage) into a wooden trough or launder, which conveys the water by gravity flow to where it is needed. Here once again we can see over a period of time two significant technological advances by which wastage was reduced and efficiency improved (fig. 25). If such a wheel were worked by one man treading, it might have been turned about four times per minute, giving an output of about 41 gallons (155 l) per min. This represents a power input of just over 0.1 horsepower, which an able-bodied man would have been able to keep up for several hours, raising most of 2,400 gallons per hour.

There is evidence from papyrus documents found in Egypt, dating from about the first century A.D. onward, that animals were used to work irrigation pumps in the Nile flood plain area, most probably of the bucket wheel type. If so, some form of gearing must have been used to enable oxen or donkeys, harnessed to a long pole and walking around in a circle, to turn a wheel in a vertical plane. Unfortunately, the documents give no details of the mechanics, and the machinery itself, being all made of wood, has perished.

ENGINEERING IN MINIATURE

In the ancient machines considered so far, considerable forces were used in the performance of various types of work—pumping, lifting, propelling. But it would be unfair to ignore those achievements in Greek and Roman engineering in which the energies and forces involved were minute but the sophistication of design was quite impressive. And although some of the principles involved were only applied in miniature models, it is probable that if the needs or the motives had arisen, which they apparently did not, various elements in these mechanisms could have been scaled up.

The most striking example is the so-called Antikythera mechanism, a piece of geared machinery found in a shipwreck off the island of Aegilia (Antikythera) in 1901, originally made in the first century B.C. It was in fact a mechanical analogue calculator, which stood just over a foot high and must have looked rather like a rectangular mantelpiece

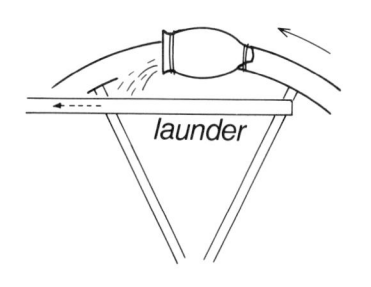

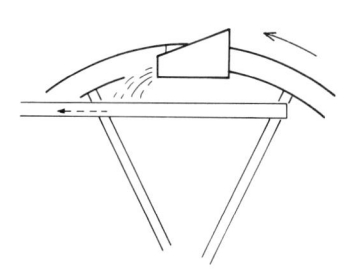

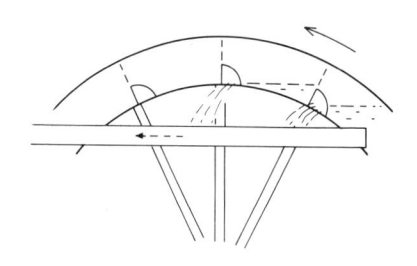

crude earthenware pot

'rectangular grain-measure' (less spillage)

'buckets' built into wheel rim

Figure 25. Improvements in bucket design for water-lifting wheels.

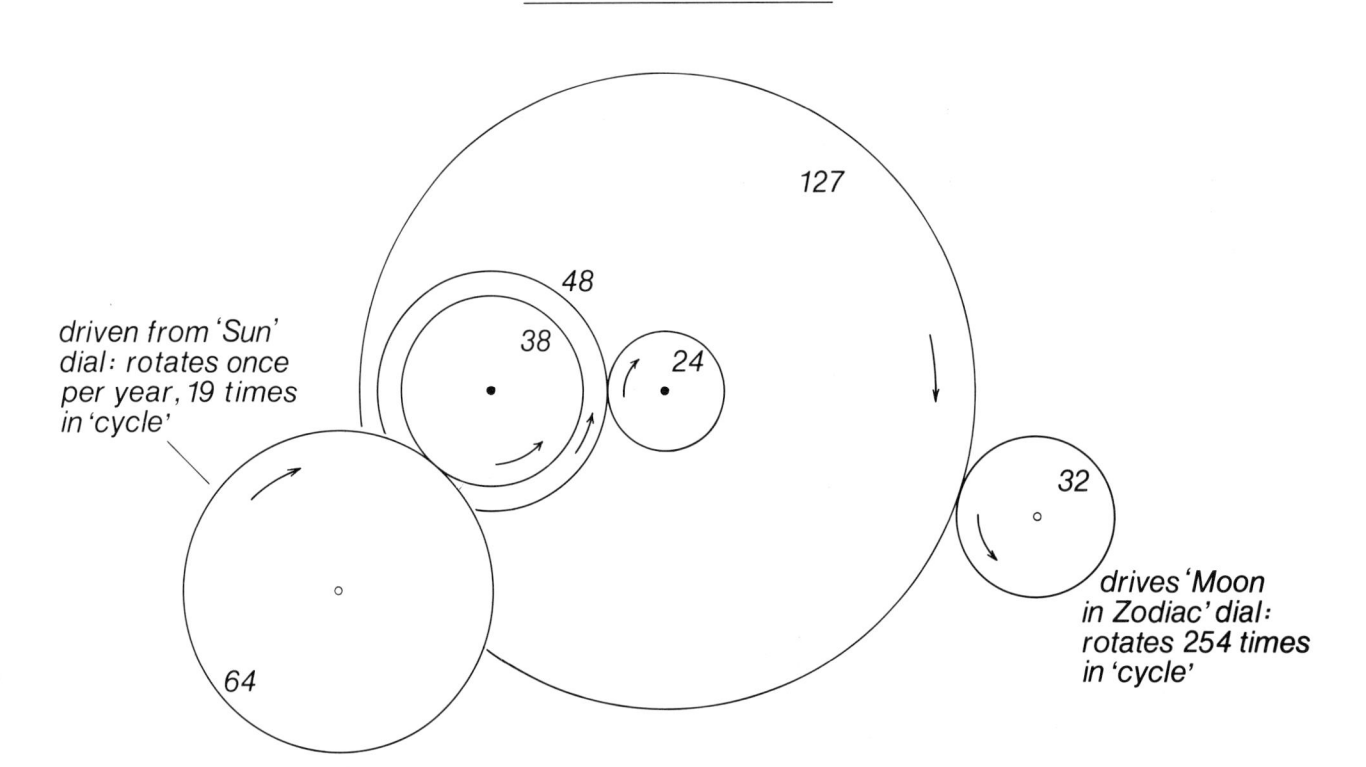

Figure 26. Set of gears from Antikythera mechanism.

clock. A winding handle at one side was used to set the main dial on the front to any required point in the calendar or zodiac circle, and a complicated set of gears rotated a smaller dial that showed the position of the moon in the zodiac. The arithmetic for this was based on the nineteen-year cycle discovered by Meton in Athens ca. 432 B.C., by which the sidereal orbit of the moon around the signs of the zodiac, which takes about 27 1/2 days, and the lunar month (the period from one new moon to the next), which is about two days longer, could be brought into relationship with the solar year. Meton held, in fact, that the period of nineteen solar years was exactly equal to 235 lunar months and 254 orbits of the moon around the zodiac. This involves slight errors, but the accuracy is quite creditable, considering that it was based on naked-eye observations aided by only the crudest of sighting instruments.

The gears that turn the moon-zodiac dial in the Antikythera mechanism are shown in figure 26; the numbers beside each wheel indicate the number of teeth. The overall ratio is 64:38 × 48:24 × 127:32, which is equivalent to 254:19, so that the last spindle turns 254 times for every nineteen revolutions of the first. The arrangement in figure 26 is schematic for the sake of clarity; in fact, the wheels overlap each other so that the last spindle passes through the hollow center of the first and rotates the moon dial in front of the sun dial, just as the minute hand on an old-fashioned (pre-digital) clock is driven through the center of the hour hand.

But there is a much more sophisticated system connected to this. It is a differential turntable, which is turned in one direction by the moon dial drive, and in the same ratio but in the opposite direction by the sun dial drive, in such a way that it subtracts the sun's movement through the zodiac signs from

ENGINEERING

the moon's. This was done in order to drive a dial that indicated the moon's phases, and the need for it arises from the phenomenon of the lunar or synodic month. As the moon orbits the earth, the sun moves around the zodiac circle in the same direction, but more slowly. So, if we start with the sun and moon in conjunction, just before the new moon, and in line with (say) the first point of Aries (fig. 27), we shall find that the moon will return to that same point after about 27 1/2 days, but the sun in the meantime will have moved about 27 degrees around the zodiac and will be approaching the first point of Taurus. The moon then takes about two more days to catch up with the sun and reach conjunction before the next new moon. This longer cycle, the synodic month, occurs 235 times during nineteen solar years. A dial on the back of the instrument was driven by the differential turntable so that it made one complete revolution per synodic month, marking in its progress the new moon, first quarter, and so on.

Who would need such a machine, and how would it be used? It might have been used to predict the positions and phases of the moon in compiling an astronomical calendar or almanac, or it might have been used to work backward or forward from the present time for purposes of astrology, which in antiquity was never clearly distinguished from astronomy. It might also have been used for instructional purposes. Although it was found on a shipwreck, it is unlikely to have been of any use as a navigational instrument; it was almost certainly a piece of scientific equipment that happened to be among the cargo.

From Hero of Alexandria we have accounts of small devices using the principle of the siphon, the expansion of heated air

Sun and Moon in conjunction at first point of Aries

After 27½ days Moon returns to same point in Zodiac

After 29½ days Sun and Moon once more in conjunction

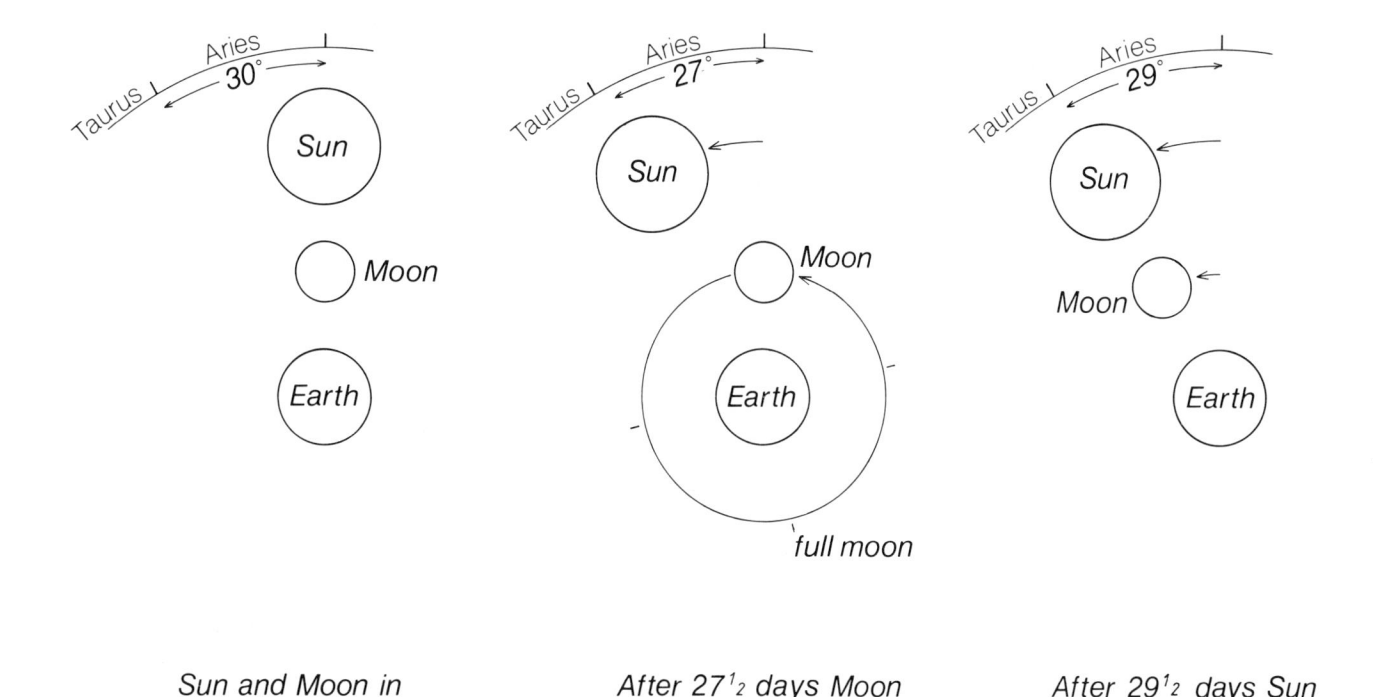

Figure 27. Orbits of the sun and moon as calculated by Antikythera mechanism.

349

and steam, and the cam and lever. A few typical examples will suffice.

In *Pneumatica* 2.3 Hero describes an "altar with dancing figures." The design is shown in figure 28. The round casing of the altar is transparent, being made of horn or glass. As the air in the top section expands when heated by the burning incense, it is forced out through the angled jets near the base and thus causes the platform and its figurines to revolve "as though they were dancing." The principle used is that of the reaction thrust, as in the modern jet engine, but it was not fully understood.

The same principle was used in Hero's steam engine (*Pneumatica* 2.11). The device (fig. 29) was improvised from a cooking utensil (the ancient equivalent of a kettle) and was probably assembled by soldering. In one of the bearings on which the sphere turned friction was reduced to a minimum by the use of a sharp point (*knodax* in Greek) that turned in a cup-shaped socket. The other bearing presents a difficult problem. If it turns freely enough for high speeds, it will almost inevitably leak steam and allow the pressure to fall, and if it is tight enough to maintain a high pressure, the friction will be

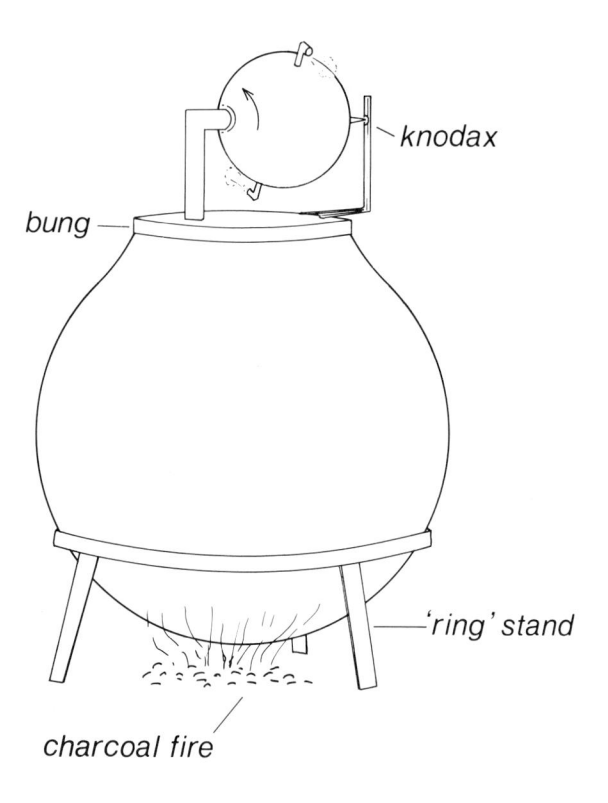

Figure 29. Hero's steam engine.

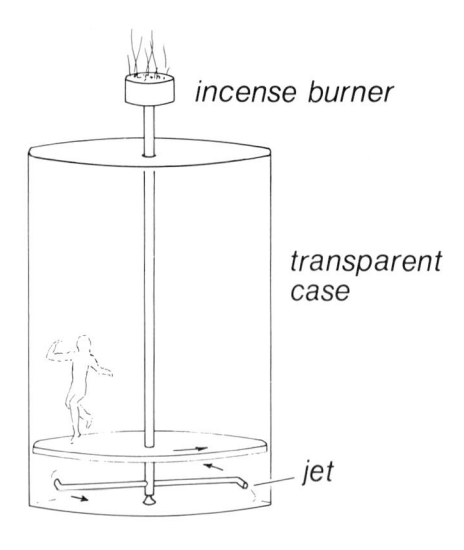

Figure 28. Altar with dancing figures.

enough to slow down the rotation of the sphere. An awkward compromise has to be reached, but Hero seems to have succeeded in doing just that.

The question has often been asked: Why was this steam-powered device not scaled up and used as a power source for practical applications? There are a number of possible answers, the most likely being that by its very nature it has to be run at a high speed; it is also very inefficient. No other method of harnessing the power of steam seems to have been tried.

Apart from jet propulsion, the power generated by the expansion of heated air was harnessed in two other ways to work a small model described in *Pneumatica* 1.38. The doors of a miniature temple were made to open when incense was burned on an altar in front of them. The two methods of operation show some ingenuity. In the first ar-

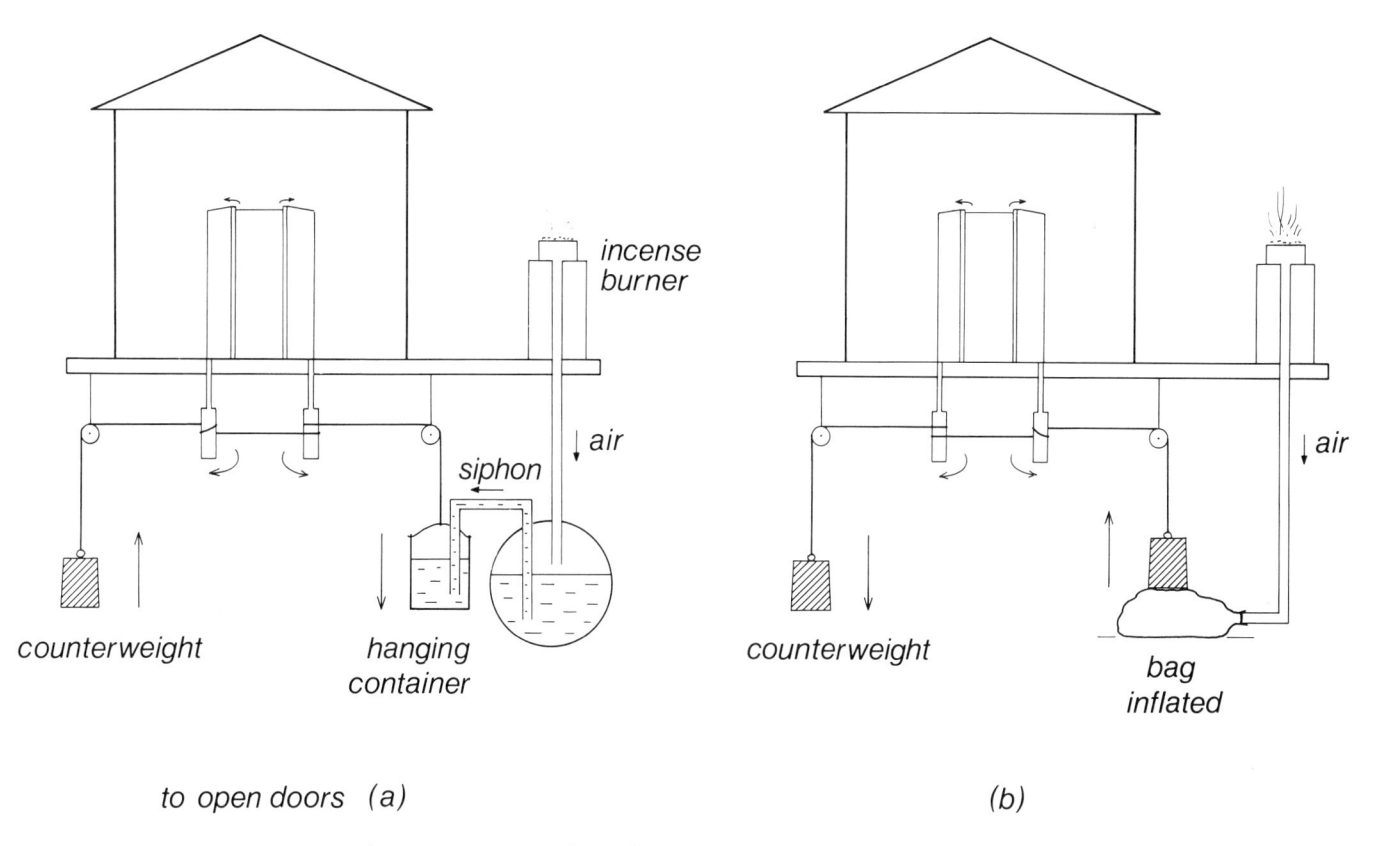

Figure 30. Two methods for opening doors of temple model.

rangement (fig. 30a) the expanding air forces water from the sphere through the siphon tube and into the hanging container, thus increasing its weight beyond that of the counterweight and causing it to descend and open the doors. It must have been quite difficult (Hero alludes rather obliquely to the problem) to regulate the movements of the container so that the siphon outlet was always kept below the surface of the water in it. At the end of his description he makes a very interesting recommendation, that mercury (which he calls *hydrargyron*, liquid silver) be used instead of water in the sphere, since being much heavier it is "easily made more runny by warmth." Mercury was found in natural deposits, and Hero's remark suggests that it was not particularly rare or expensive.

The second design is simpler and cruder (fig. 30b). The expanding air is fed into a "little skin" (*askomation*), which was either the skin of a small animal or a sewn leather bag of suitable size. As this bag inflated, it raised the weight and allowed the counterweight to fall and open the doors. It is strange that Hero did not consider feeding the expanding air into a cylinder and driving a piston, which would have worked much more efficiently. These elements were well known from the force pump. There is a momentary glimpse into the full-scale, real world here, when Hero says that to do away with the need for a counterweight the doors may be made and hung so as to swing open of their own accord, "just as the doors in public bathhouses swing shut of their own accord."

Finally, a very important principle—that of the cam and lever—is used in an "automa-

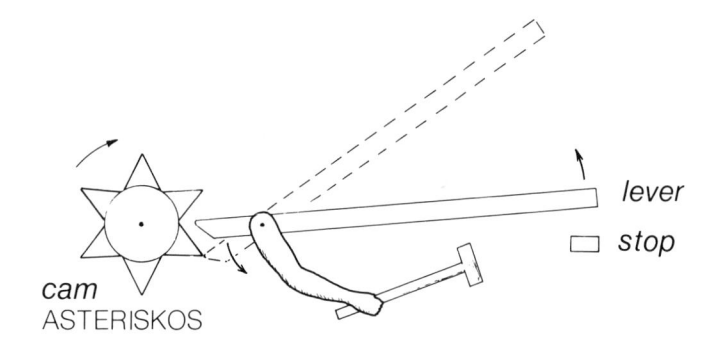

Figure 31. Cam and lever used in automaton theater.

ton theater" described by Hero. The animated scene that is to be presented is the first of a series depicting the legendary Trojan War, in which the Greeks are preparing their ships, using saws, adzes, hammers, and drills. The figurine using a hammer ("and making a noise as in real life") had an arm that was pivoted at the shoulder and was coupled by means of a square shaft to a wooden lever behind the backdrop of the miniature stage (fig. 31). The short, projecting end of this backstage lever was positioned close to a toothed wheel, which Hero calls a "little star" (*asteriskos*), that turned slowly in a clockwise direction. As each tooth came round, the arm of the figurine and the hammer that it held in its hand were raised; when the end of the wooden lever slipped off the tooth, the lever would fall suddenly, and the appropriate noise was made by the other end hitting a stop.

Once again, why was this not scaled up and used for industrial purposes? There is just a possibility that it was, in the fourth century A.D., the *asteriskos* being driven round by waterwheel and the arm being used to work a stone-cutting saw; but the evidence for this is uncertain and unreliable. We are left with the impression of a group of engineers with skill and imagination, backed by proficient craftsmen; but it seems that, in a world in which industry was labor intensive, organized in very small units, and dependent on easily available manual skills, engineers had little part to play except to amuse and entertain.

BIBLIOGRAPHY

SOURCES

Frontinus, *The Stratagems and the Aqueducts of Rome* (*De Aquis*), Charles E. Bennett, trans. (1925; repr. 1969); Hero, *Mechanics*, in Aage Gerhardt Drachmann, *The Mechanical Technology of Greek and Roman Antiquity* (1963); for Hero and Philo on catapults, see Eric William Marsden, *Greek and Roman Artillery: Technical Treatises* (1971); Vitruvius, *On Architecture* (*De Architectura*), 2 vols., Frank Granger, trans. (1931–1934; repr. 1956–1962), or *The Ten Books on Architecture*, Morris Hicky Morgan, trans. (1914; repr. 1960).

STUDIES

J. J. Coulton, "Lifting in Early Greek Architecture," in *The Journal of Hellenic Studies*, **94** (1974); Derek de Solla Price, "Gears from the Greeks," in *Transactions of the American Philosophical Society*, **64**, pt. 7 (1974) (contains bibliography on the Antikythera mechanism); Aage Gerhardt Drachmann, *The Mechanical Technology of Greek and Roman Antiquity* (1963); John G. Landels, *Engineering in the Ancient World* (1978); Eric William Marsden, *Greek and Roman Artillery: Historical Development* (1969), and *Greek and Roman Artillery: Technical Treatises* (1971) (contains full bibliography on catapults up to 1971); John Peter Oleson, *Greek and Roman Mechanical Water-Lifting Devices* (1984) (includes an extensive bibliography on the water pumps); Thorkild Schiøler, "Bronze Roman Piston Pumps," in *History of Technology*, **5** (1980); Joseph W. Shaw, "A Double-sheaved Pulley Block from Kenchreai," in *Hesperia*, **36**, no. 4 (1967); Norman A. F. Smith, "Attitudes to Roman Engineering and the Question of the Inverted Siphon," in *History of Technology*, **1** (1976); K. D. White, *Greek and Roman Technology* (1984).

TRANSPORTATION

LIONEL CASSON

THE CITIES OF GREECE clustered about the shores of the Mediterranean "like frogs on a pond," as Plato put it. And the Romans built themselves so thoroughly about the Mediterranean that they referred to it as "Our Sea" (*Mare Nostrum*). The great body of water lay in the very center of the ancient world, its broad expanse offering the shortest, easiest, and most economical way to get from one place to another. It was inevitable that shipping would become the major mode of transport for both Greeks and Romans.

TRANSPORT BY LAND

Transport by sea did not, however, eliminate transport by land; it merely confined it to an unavoidable minimum. Goods moving between interior points unconnected by navigable streams had to go by land. When winter weather brought shipping to a halt, there was also no alternative but to haul overland.

Efficient movement on land requires roads, and, where the terrain permitted, these came into being in very early times. In Mesopotamia, seat of the early civilizations of Babylonia and Assyria, the flat plains boasted highways between major points by the third millennium B.C. The military might of the Assyrians, who in the first half of the first millennium B.C. were lords of most of the Near East, depended in good part on the fine network of roads they laid to transport their armies. The Persians, who conquered them and took over their realm in the sixth century B.C., inherited the network and improved it.

The roads made possible not only the swift shuttling of military forces but, what was equally vital to a ruler, the swift forwarding of information. Supplemented by a service for supplying changes of horses, the road system enabled government couriers to average almost five miles an hour. Herodotus (8.98; 5.52–53) has a famous description of the splendid organization that the Persian kings maintained for communications between Sardis, a provincial capital in the western part of their empire, and the king's court at Susa:

> Men and horses are stationed a day's travel apart, a man and a horse for each of the days

needed to cover the journey. These men neither snow nor rain nor heat nor gloom of night stay from the swiftest possible completion of their appointed stage. The first man, having covered his, hands the dispatches to the second, the second to the third, and so on, the dispatches going from one to the other through the whole line.

Going day and night, the riders completed the course in about twenty days, covering 100 miles or a little less in each twenty-four-hour span.

The Persian service and others like it were maintained by the Greek monarchs, the Ptolemies and Seleucids, who, in the wake of Alexander's conquest, held sway over great parts of what once belonged to Persia. Then, at the beginning of the Christian Era, the Romans, as a means for consolidating control of their growing empire, expanded the service and altered its nature. The network of roads was extended from the Near East throughout Europe and along the coast of North Africa. The government saw to it, by incorporating existing facilities and building new ones where none existed, that inns and hostelries were available a day's journey apart, generally some twenty-five to thirty-five miles, but closer in difficult terrain where speed of travel was necessarily slower. The Romans' public postal service (*cursus publicus*) relied not on relays of fast-moving horsemen, but rather on single couriers who went the whole distance riding on light wagons. The inns provided, at the end of each day's journeying, in addition to food and lodging, a change of horses.

The Romans built not only more roads but better ones. The Greeks had been content with unpaved surfaces even for their major highways. Not so the Romans: for their through routes they insisted on all-weather roads, and they developed a highly sophisticated technique for building them. The result was a network of fine roads, the like of which was not seen again until the nineteenth century.

To begin with, surveyors laid out as straight a course as was possible. Then a deep bed was prepared with meticulous care, one that would not allow the paving to sink and form depressions; for these, in addition to making for a jolting ride, caught water, which would seep through and undermine the road. The road gangs trenched until they reached firm ground and then filled in with naturally rounded stones embedded in a mass of clay or nonfriable earth. Over this they laid a paving of polygonal stones fashioned from some durable rock such as basalt (silex), granite, or porphyry. The stones were massive, often measuring a foot and a half across and eight inches deep (46 × 2 cm) and they were fitted together as cunningly as a jigsaw puzzle to form an absolutely smooth surface. This kind of road was called a *via silice strata* (road paved with silex), since in Italy, where paving was first carried out, silex—a stone admirably suited for the purpose—was in plentiful supply. The famous Via Appia, which started at Rome and eventually ran 360 miles (581 km) to Brundusium near the toe of the boot, was surfaced for its entire length in this fashion. Italy was the first to acquire paved roads, but by the first and second centuries A.D. they were to be found throughout the empire. There are beautifully preserved stretches, for example, of the paved highway that ran from Antioch to Chalcis ad Belum in Syria.

A main thoroughfare such as the Via Appia would be ten Roman feet wide (about 3.5 inches short of ten English feet, 3.05 meters), providing ample room for carriages to pass abreast. The minimum width for major roads was eight feet (2.44 m). At key points they might widen to three lanes with a combined width of fourteen or even eighteen feet (4 or 5.5 m). And the roads that led into Rome spread out to thirty feet as they approached the city gates.

Next in quality to the *via silice strata* was the road paved with gravel (*via glarea strata*). It was prepared in the same way but not given the crust of paving; the upper part of the bed, worked smooth, became the surface. The Romans saw to it that all their roads, paved or unpaved, were properly drained to avoid the damage that standing pools of water can do. The surface was crowned to throw off rainwater, and continuous ditches along the sides carried it away.

The last step in building a road was the setting up of milestones (*miliaria*). They were placed every Roman mile (some ninety-five yards [87 m] shorter than our mile), and each was inscribed with a figure giving the distance from the road's starting place or, in the provinces, sometimes the distance between one town and the next. These must have been a godsend to weary travelers plodding on foot or in slow-moving carts and wondering how much farther they had to go.

When the road builders encountered a river, if the slopes were gentle enough and the crossing point shallow, they let traffic ford, merely helping out at times by paving the river bottom with flat stones. Where fording was impossible, they bridged, and they were as skilled in raising bridges as in laying roads. On secondary routes they used wood, but on the major arteries of travel they carried the road across on durable structures of stone in the form of an arch or series of arches resting on massive piers. The Via Flaminia, the grand highway that linked Rome with the cities of the Po valley, crossed a river near Narnia, some fifty miles north of Rome, over a bridge the central arch of which stood more than sixty-two feet high (19.30 m) and spanned more than 100 feet (30.46 m). A bridge built in the early years of the second century A.D. still carries traffic over the Tagus River near Augusta Emerita (Mérida) in western Spain; its six arches rise some 245 feet (74.68 m) over the normal level of the water. Roman engineers designed their bridges with long access ramps on either side in order to keep the approaches as nearly horizontal as possible and reduce the grades hardworking draft animals would have to climb.

The prime purpose of Rome's roads was, as in earlier times, the efficient movement of armies and the quick transport of dispatches. Inevitably they were a boon to the local populations, who exploited them for their day-to-day needs. Yet, even on Italy's finest highways, transport of goods was slow, cumbersome, and, as a consequence, prohibitively costly.

As early as the third millennium B.C., men of the Near East had invented both the two-wheeled cart and the four-wheeled wagon, as well as a harness for hitching draft animals to them. The harness was of a type specifically designed for a pair of oxen, the most powerful animals available. Every cart or wagon had, extending from the center of its front face, a draft-pole with a horizontal crossbar (yoke) near the outer end; the oxen were placed one on either side of the pole, and the crossbar was set just in front of their prominent shoulders, enabling them to push against it with all their might.

Oxen are notoriously slow. For transport where speed counted rather than power, the Greeks and Romans supplanted them with teams of mules or horses. Unfortunately, they did so without making any change in the nature of the harness and, since mules and horses lack the ox's jutting shoulders, bound them to the yoke by a band passed over the breast. As the animals threw themselves into the pull, this pressed against the windpipe and impeded them from using their full strength. Only many centuries later, during the Middle Ages, did men finally conceive of the padded horsecollar, which put the pressure on the shoulders and not the breast and made possible an unimpeded pull.

Horses or mules were for hauling passengers or light loads; for bulky and heavy commodities there was no alternative to oxen. But even their capacity was so limited that the cost of moving large amounts of heavy material, such as timber or stone, was astronomically high. There has survived an inscription (Roebuck, 1969) that records the expenses involved in putting up a building at Eleusis, some twelve miles northwest of Athens, in the late fourth century B.C. The marble for the columns came from the quarries at Pentele near Athens. Since these were quite far from the coast, transport by sea was out of the question; the loads had to go by land, a distance of only about fifteen to twenty miles. Here are some entries that reveal dramatically how costly this was:

> We began to bring in a column drum ... it was brought in 3 days; 31 teams transported it.
> We began to bring another drum ... 33 teams transported it; it was brought in 3 days.
> We began to bring another drum ... 27 teams transported it on the first day; on the second day were added 3; it was brought in three days.
> We began to bring 2 drums at one time on a double rig on the tenth of the month; 40 teams transported them on the first day, on the second were added 5; they were brought in 2 1/2 days.

In other words, it took some thirty teams of oxen three days to haul each column drum.

Not only was the motive power painfully slow, but the vehicles themselves were not particularly efficient. One great handicap was the lack of good lubrication. The only types of lubricant to be had, dregs of olive pressings or animal fat, were too costly to be applied liberally; vehicles, especially the lowly working wagons, announced their coming from afar by the tortured squeaking of their wheels. These were shod with iron tires and, since springs were unknown, every unevenness in the road was transmitted to the load; the clattering was as loud as the squeaking.

The massive four-wheeled wagon served for heavy loads. For less ponderous freight, two-wheeled carts were preferred and, for transporting passengers, light carts drawn by a pair of mules or horses. By Roman times there was a full range of passenger vehicles available, from the *cisium,* a simple open cart so common it could be hired from livery stables at the town gates of populous centers, to the rich man's *carpentum,* a deluxe carriage covered by a substantial roof fitted with curtains to close in the sides. For long journeys, there was the *carruca dormitoria* (sleeping wagon), a roomy four-wheeled vehicle, topped with an arched canopy of leather or cloth, somewhat like the American Conestoga (covered) wagons.

In mountainous areas—where there were no roads, good or bad—it was impossible to use vehicles of any sort. There, the earliest form of transport was the porter, who continued to be used, especially in difficult terrain, long after men had turned to pack animals. The first of the pack animals, and the one that was favored most widely in the ancient world, was the donkey; it was patient, hardworking, and—of prime importance—economical to maintain. In the level lands of the Near East, camels also came into widespread use, the Bactrian or two-humped variety among the Assyrians around the beginning of the first millennium B.C. and the dromedary or one-humped among the Arabs about the same time. Vehicles need roads, but camels do not, which made them the mode of transport par excellence for the desert expanses of Arabia and the Middle East.

Riding horses were rarely used by ancient travelers; they were for the army's cavalry units or the government's dispatch carriers. For the voyager who wanted to spare himself the discomfort of jouncing in a springless carriage, the only alternative was to go by litter, a convenience available for hire along with the carriages at the gates of major Roman cities. The traveling litter, like the deluxe carriage, had a canopy and draw curtains: the occupant lolled at his ease as six or eight husky bearers, balancing it on their shoulders, kept up a steady pace. For long journeys, the men could be replaced by a pair of mules harnessed to the carrying poles, one ahead and one behind. A litter was the most painless way to travel, but it was also the slowest.

TRANSPORT BY SEA

One of Demosthenes' law cases involved a pair of partners who financed a shipment of 3,000 jars of wine from Mende in northeastern Greece to a port on the Black Sea at the mouth of the Dnieper River (35.10). All were loaded aboard a single standard cargo carrier, a vessel of modest size driven by the wind and manned by a crew of perhaps fewer than a dozen. Given no bad luck with the weather, it could make the voyage in a few weeks. To transport the jars overland would have been inconceivable: hundreds of pack animals, a regiment of drivers, and all to be fed for months on end. Throughout ancient history, the sea was the preferred means of transport, above all for the three commodities that bulked largest in ancient commerce: grain, wine, and olive oil.

Sea transport did have certain disadvantages. The greatest was that it was not always available. Greek and Roman mariners limited their activity to the period from late spring to early fall. The rest of the year their vessels went into hibernation, the smaller drawn up on the beaches and the larger snugged down in the inner recesses of harbors. This was in part due to the severer weather of winter but also because of the increased amount of cloudiness that occurs during the winter and the periods immediately bordering it. In the days before the invention of the mariner's compass, skippers plotted their courses by prominent landmarks or, when land was out of sight, the sun by day and the stars by night. They gambled on getting clear weather, and the odds were most with them during the summer months. Moreover, the summer provided longer days, which were welcome not only when on the water but in harbor as well; for, to a world that lacked good artificial light, they meant more hours for working cargo. Voyaging during the winter did not entirely stop, but it was always exceptional, such as the hauling of troops to meet an emergency or moving cargo to alleviate a desperate shortage.

A second disadvantage was that almost all water transport depended on the wind. Some few classes of ships were free of such dependence, but most were sailing craft, which in a calm simply could not move. And, even if there was wind, unless it came from the right direction a sailing vessel still could not move. The great majority of Greek and Roman sailing ships, certainly all that were used for large-scale overseas transport, were square-rigged; that is, they carried their sails set at a right angle to the keel. They operated most efficiently with a wind from behind or from the side. If the wind came from the side but from a point somewhat ahead, they were still able to use it, but it involved tacking, which was slow and hard work, and they preferred to wait for a change of direction. If the wind came from ahead, they could not use it at all and either had to wait until it changed or follow a roundabout course in which they managed to keep it more or less on the side.

The last, but not the least, disadvantage was the ever-present possibility of bad weather or—during those periods of history when the seas were not properly patrolled—attack by pirates. Although storms were far less frequent in summer than winter, they did occur, particularly around the beginning and end of the sailing season. The famous storm that drove St. Paul to shipwreck off the island of Melita (Malta; Acts 27) caught his vessel when, taking a chance, it left Crete just after the season had closed.

The ancients were able to escape the vagaries of the wind to a certain extent by using galleys, shallow-hulled vessels powered by multiple rowers as well as by sail. Warships were perforce all galleys, since they could not afford to put themselves totally at the mercies of the wind. But there were also oared merchant craft. They ran the gamut of size, from vessels that were little more than rowboats to certain types that had as many as fifty men on the benches and, in emergencies, could be pressed into service as men-of-war. Merchant galleys were most useful for short hauls, for carrying miscellaneous goods and passengers along the coast or between nearby islands. Whenever they could, they raised sail and exploited the wind, just as sailing ships did. However, during calms, or when the winds were contrary, they had the great advantage of being able to run out the oars and keep moving.

For transport over open water, and especially for transport of bulky or heavy cargo, the carriers were sailing ships pure and simple. From the Middle Ages on, most wooden vessels in the West were made in the way that served shipwrights all during the great age of sail: they erected a skeleton of keel and frames (ribs) and then fastened to this a skin of planks. The Greeks and Romans followed a procedure that was just the reverse. They laid a keel, to be sure, but then built up on this a shell of planks, fastening these to each other in a unique fashion. Setting the planks edge to edge, they linked the edges by mortise-and-tenon joints so close together that, in a well-built craft, they might stand no more than a joint's distance apart.

Then, as a final precaution, each joint was transfixed by a dowel to make sure it would never separate. Into this tightly knit shell a complete set of frames was inserted for stiffening. The result was a hull of extraordinary strength and durability, one that required a minimum of calking and was guaranteed to stand up to years of hard work. What is more, on most merchantmen, the underwater surfaces were given a covering of lead sheathing to protect them from the marine borer, an ever-present pest in the warm waters of the Mediterranean. After Rome's fall, shipwrights ceased to add such protection, and the practice did not return until the eighteenth century, when copper sheathing was introduced.

Ancient ships of all sizes, whether little skiffs or large carriers, were steered not by the stern rudder found on all vessels today but by oversized oars fastened on each quarter. A tiller bar was socketed into the upper part of the loom (the inboard section of the oar's shaft); pushing or pulling on this made the loom pivot within its fastenings, thereby putting the blade at an angle to the hull and directing the ship. The side rudder has often been condemned as inefficient. Quite the contrary: it is not at all inferior in performance to a stern rudder. The latter replaced it in the Middle Ages by offering advantages of another kind.

By the fifth and fourth centuries B.C., the average Greek freighter had a capacity of some 100 tons (90.7 metric tons); indeed, the smallest that was reckoned suitable for overseas hauling was seventy to eighty tons. By the Hellenistic age, shipwrights were turning out steadily larger types. Underwater archaeologists have excavated off the coast of southern France the completely preserved hull of a vessel, dating from the first century B.C., that was 135 feet long and thirty in beam (41.1 × 9.1 m) and had a capacity of over 400 tons (362.8 t). In Roman times, merchantmen of 500 to 600 (453.6 to 544.3 metric) tons were common, and the largest were double that size. The city of Rome imported annually some 135,000 tons (122,470 t) of grain from Egypt; to haul this it employed a fleet of carriers that ran about 180 feet (56.1 m) in length, 45 in beam (13.7 m), and held 1,300 tons (1,179.3 t) of grain in their holds. Once, sometime in the second century A.D., one of these mighty craft, because of a particularly bad spell of weather, was blown off course and ended up in the port of Athens, which, by that time, had subsided into a commercial backwater untouched by the currents of international trade. The ship's arrival created a sensation, as can be seen from a contemporary description that has survived (Lucian, *Navigium* 5):

> What a size the ship was! one-hundred-eighty feet in length, the ship's carpenter told me, the beam more than a quarter of that, and 44 feet from the deck to the lowest point in the hold. And the height of the mast, and what a yard it carried, and what a forestay held it up! And the way the stern rose up in a gradual curve ending in a gilded goose-head, matched at the other end by the forward, more flattened, sweep of the prow with its figure of Isis, the goddess the ship was named after, on each side! Everything was incredible: the rest of the decoration, the paintings, the red topsail, even more, the anchors with their capstans and winches, and the cabins aft. The crew was like an army. They told me she carried enough grain to feed Athens for a year. And it all depended for its safety on one little old man who turns those great steering oars with a tiller that's no more than a stick!

After the fall of Rome, great merchantmen like these did not sail the seas again until the end of the eighteenth and beginning of the nineteenth century, when East Indiamen finally achieved such dimensions.

The most striking proof of the size and capacity of the vessels in the Roman merchant marine are the obelisks that now stand in the city of Rome. Each came there from Egypt on the deck of a ship. Some detailed information happens to have survived about that which brought over one of the largest, the obelisk now standing in front of St. Peter's Basilica in Rome. This weighs, together with its pedestal, close to 400 tons (362.8 t); to counterbalance such a ponderous load on the deck, the ship that carried it was ballasted with more than twice that weight in lentils in its hold. It had, in other words, a total capacity of at least 1,200 tons (about 1,090 t).

All overseas carriers, ordinary size or oversize, were square-riggers. Usually there was a broad mainsail amidships and a very small sail, the so-called *artemon,* perched like a bowsprit sail far in the bows; the mainsail supplied the drive and the *artemon* facilitated steering. The very largest vessels, such as those on the Alexandria–Rome grain run, also had a mizzen. The rig was meager—a far cry from the towering clouds of canvas carried by the great ships of a later age—but it was safe; the ancients preferred security to speed. Underrigged as they were, ancient sailing craft could average no more than between four and six knots with a favorable wind, and half that or less with an unfavorable.

The result was slow transport, slower certainly than on sailing ships of the nineteenth century. In the eastern basin of the Mediterranean the prevailing winds during the sailing season are northerly. Thus, voyages from north to south—say, from Athens to Rhodes or from Asia Minor to the Levant or Egypt—were as quick as voyages could be in ancient times. The run from Neapolis (Naples) to Alexandria, for example, some 1,000 nautical miles, could be accomplished under ideal circumstances in nine days. From Athens to Rhodes was some six to seven. But the prevailing northerlies at the same time condemned a vessel to take twice as long or even more on the way back, since the courses involved a steady battle against the wind. To go from Constantinople to Gaza took five days, to return ten. The voyage from Alexandria to Neapolis, in the teeth of northwesterlies most of the way, involved so circuitous a route in order to get a slant of wind an ancient square-rigger could use that it might take two months and sometimes more.

Northerlies prevail in the western basin of the Mediterranean as well. Here, however, the trend of the coast made them more equable in their effect. An ancient vessel could travel from Rome all the way to Gibraltar in some seven days, and the return would be just as fast.

Today most sailing craft are equipped with some form of the fore-and-aft rig, in which the sail is set parallel to the keel. This system permits more efficient travel against contrary winds than the square rig. Certainly by the second century B.C., and perhaps earlier, at least two forms of this rig were in use among the Greeks and Romans. One was the spritsail—a rectangular sail fitted with a long spar running from the base of the mast diagonally across the windward side of the sail to the peak—and the other the lateen, a more or less triangular sail hung from a very long yard that crosses the mast at a steep angle. These rigs were favored for small craft since, being used for working along the coast or in harbor, such vessels had to deal with winds from all quarters rather than with the steady trade winds that the large carriers could count on meeting in the open waters of the Mediterranean.

The prime purpose of ancient commercial craft was to haul cargo. The cargo that was heaviest, most cumbersome, and hardest to deal with was building stone. The Roman emperors fancied stone in exotic colors for their public buildings and were willing to pay for importing it from Asia Minor, North Africa, Egypt, and other distant places. The sole feasible means of transport, of course, was by ship. Smaller blocks could be loaded inside the hull; big members, such as columns, traveled lashed on deck. This must have been the way the monumental columns in the portico of the Pantheon in Rome made their journey. These monoliths, each 41 feet (12.5 m) long and weighing close to 84 tons (76.2 t) are of granite that was quarried at Syene (Aswan) far up Egypt's Nile, near the First Cataract. They were floated on barges to Alexandria at the mouth of the river, and there hoisted to the deck of one of the big vessels that made the run between Alexandria and Rome. On arrival at the mouth of the Tiber River, they were transferred to barges, brought up the Tiber to Rome, and hauled on wagons or rollers from the dockside to the building site. Many of the columns of the temple complex at Heliopolis (Baalbek) in the Bekaa Valley of Lebanon also came from the same quarry and, though they are much smaller (only about ten tons each), represent an even more remarkable feat. For, after having been transported by ship to a Lebanese port, they had to be hauled, no doubt by multiple teams of oxen, up the slope of the mountains that form the western side of the valley, down the other slope, and then along the valley floor to their destination.

The other cargoes ancient stevedores had to load were a good deal less trouble than building stone. As mentioned previously, the commodities that formed the bulk of ancient commerce were grain, wine, and olive oil. Grain was put into sacks. Wine and olive oil, as well as a number of other products—fish sauce, olives, nuts, honey—were shipped in large clay jars. A good deal is known about these, thanks to the recent discoveries of underwater archaeology. Clay is well-nigh indestructible: it can lie underwater for thousands of years without deteriorating. As a consequence, wrecks of ancient wine or oil carriers signal their presence by a cluster of shipping jars on the sea floor.

Divers have identified hundreds of such clusters and salvaged thousands of jars from them.

For wine, jars that were long and slender and had rather a narrow neck were preferred. They were usually big—over three feet tall—capable of holding five to seven gallons, and weighed some fifty pounds when empty and double that when full. Since they were made of porous clay, resin was smeared over the inside to prevent seepage and, after the wine was poured in, they were plugged with a cork stopper and sealed with clay or cement. Those used for olive oil were more squat and fat and had a wider neck. The jars were stowed in a vessel's hold standing upright in tiers. One well-preserved Roman wreck, a large ship, had a hold that could accommodate four tiers, some 8,500 jars in all. Another wreck, still larger, held five tiers, perhaps 10,000 jars. In order to prevent any movement and consequent breakage, each jar was not only packed so as to nestle closely to its neighbors on all sides but also separated from them with dunnage of resilient twigs.

Loading the shipping jars was a slow process. Although they were sturdy—their clay walls are at least a quarter of an inch thick, and usually more—they were too fragile to be handled in batches by a crane and so heavy that one was all a man could carry at a time. Some 3,000 jars could be accommodated as cargo, even by a freighter of ordinary size. When a load of them arrived at a port, the authorities had to round up an army of stevedores who would tramp over the gangplank in an endless line, each with a jar on his shoulder.

The sailing vessels that crisscrossed the Mediterranean were for carrying cargo, not passengers (the true passenger vessel came into existence no earlier than the nineteenth century). The sole recourse an ancient traveler had was to book passage on a freighter; he had to walk up and down the waterfront looking for a ship scheduled to leave for his destination or for some place along its line of course. When, for example, St. Paul was sent from Caesarea in Palestine to stand trial in Rome, he boarded a vessel making for the south coast of Asia Minor, which happened to be on his line of course; on arriving at the port of Myra (Demre), he had the good fortune to find a freighter from the Alexandria–Rome grain run in the harbor, and he took passage on it.

The city of Rome, starting point for a great many travelers, offered a convenient service that did away with weary tramping along the dockside. Its port was located at the mouth of the Tiber; in the town of Ostia nearby was an ample square surrounded on three sides by a line of small offices. Among these were many belonging to the shippers of various seaports: the shippers of Narbo (Narbonne) had one, those of Carthage another, those of Caralis (Cagliari) in Sardinia still another, and so on. Anyone seeking passage to one of these places merely had to check at the appropriate office.

Since the vessels carried passengers only incidentally, they provided neither food nor services; there were no stewards among their crewmen to prepare meals or tend cabins. Indeed, there were no scheduled meals, and the single cabin that they did have was for the captain, the owners of the cargo or their agents, and select people of importance. Voyagers booked deck passage and went aboard accompanied by their own servants, who were loaded down with bedding and other supplies, including sufficient food and wine to last until the first stop, when more could be purchased. The ships did furnish water. When night fell, the servants prepared a bed on deck, either in the open or under a tentlike shelter. Usually there was a well-fitted galley, and, when the crew was done with it, servants would take turns preparing their masters' meals. Even the finest ships, the great freighters that carried grain from Egypt to Rome, offered no more than any other in the way of amenities. What they did offer was quick passage, so much so that travelers were willing to avail themselves of it though it might mean going out of their way. Emperor Gaius (Caligula), for example, advised someone who was leaving Rome for Palestine not to look for a vessel heading there, but "to take a direct sailing to Alexandria.... The ships are crack sailing craft and their skippers the most experienced there are; they drive their vessels like racehorses on an unswerving course that goes straight as a die" (Philo Judaeus, *In Flaccum* 26).

When Emperor Vespasian returned from Egypt to Rome in the spring of A.D. 70, although he could have chosen any galley in the navy he preferred to take passage on one of these grain clippers. He, of course, would have had quarters in the ship's cabin. When St. Paul boarded one at Myra (Demre), he almost certainly did not; and since there were 276 other passengers, space on deck might well have been at a premium when all bedded down for the night.

HARBORS

Homer, writing probably in the eighth century, in describing the harbor of the Phaeacians, sings of a protected bay on which the only works of man are the shacks where each shipowner stored his sails and rigging, the stone shafts sunk in the sand to which ships were tied, the area where sailmakers and riggers and shipwrights worked, and a shrine to Poseidon. In Homer's time, before the Greeks were launched on the economic development that was to flower in the next two centuries, these were the only types of harbor they had: a spot where, thanks to the natural configuration of the land, the waters were so sheltered that a vessel could approach near enough to shore to be unloaded by small boats shuttling out and back or even by porters wading out and back. Indeed, in many a primitive area such harbors continued in use to the end of ancient times.

The earliest known man-made harbor works of the Greeks is at Delos. This island in the center of the Aegean was sacred to Apollo and hence was the site of great festivals in his honor attended by pilgrims from all over the Greek world. In the eighth century B.C. there was built a mighty mole of rough-hewn stone that jutted out over 300 yards (100 m) from the shore. In the next century such moles were to be found in a number of places, and by the fifth century B.C. the harbors of major Greek seaports had acquired their standard features: moles to ensure a quiet anchorage; stone quays along the shore; open sheds and warehouses behind the quays. Since almost all vessels that used the ports were sailing ships, some harbors provided two basins for their convenience, one on either side of a promontory and more or less oriented in opposite directions. Maneuvering under sail inside a cramped basin is difficult and dangerous, so harbors had fleets of tugboats, sturdy little craft powered by several oarsmen, which took arriving ships in tow and warped them to the dockside.

The Hellenistic age brought increase in size and—a significant addition—lighthouses. The first one to be built, Alexandria's pharos, was so striking an achievement that it became one of the Seven Wonders of the World. It was a lofty tower rising in multiple levels, with a blazing fire at the top that could be seen, it was claimed, thirty miles out to sea. Like all its successors in antiquity, it was a beacon to guide mariners to port and not a signal to warn them away from danger. Alexandria's port was one of those that boasted two basins, the Great Harbor facing east and a lesser harbor facing west; the lighthouse stood near the entrance of the Great Harbor, the inner circuit of which was ringed with quays backed by warehouses.

Greek harbor engineers used stone blocks and exploited whatever advantages nature offered. The builders of Roman harbors had available to them a form of concrete that could set under water, which permitted more flexibility. It enabled them to create harbors where there were no natural advantages at all. In the mid first century, the emperor Claudius launched the construction of the harbor that was to serve the city of Rome for almost half a millennium. On an open beach just north of the mouth of the Tiber his engineers created a sheltered basin about one-third of a square mile in extent by building two great breakwaters of stone and concrete. Near the tip of one rose a lighthouse, a massive structure with three square levels of diminishing size topped by a cylindrical level that housed the fire. A few generations later, Trajan added an inner basin an eighth of a square mile in size; it was lined all about with stone quays, behind which stood rows of concrete warehouses with the capacity to store many tons of grain and thousands of shipping jars. The quays were equipped with cranes to handle cargoes of building stone and timber. The staff of the place included not only a massive number of stevedores, but also a full complement of shipping clerks, small-boat handlers, divers (to recover objects that fell into the water), and others.

ON BAY AND RIVER

Western civilization arose along the great rivers of the Near East, Egypt's Nile and Mesopotamia's Tigris and Euphrates. They offered the dwellers in these areas not only a source of water but a means of transport.

The Nile was particularly useful, for it flows opposite to the direction of the prevailing winds, which blow from the north; boats could float downstream and sail upstream. From the first half of the third millennium B.C. all sorts of craft were to be seen on its waters, from light canoes made of bundles of papyrus reeds lashed together to lordly wooden sailing yachts for the pharaoh or his nobles. The mightiest vessels on the river were probably the mammoth flat-bottomed barges that carried obelisks downstream from where they were quarried far up the Nile. The sail in general use was a square sail, very tall and rather narrow; the height enabled it to catch upper breezes, an important feature inasmuch as the Nile in places flows between high-rising cliffs.

The Tigris and Euphrates are very different from the Nile in nature and perforce engendered the development of very different types of craft. Both rivers have rapids in their northern reaches and many shallows. The wind, blowing from the north as on the Nile, is foul for vessels going upstream. To combat these conditions there came into use a special type of craft, the *kelek.* It was not a boat, but a raft consisting of a wooden frame buoyed by multiple inflated skins; rock-strewn rapids, which would have smashed a log raft or a wooden boat into splinters, simply gave a *kelek* a few punctures that could be repaired in short order. It was common practice to leave from the north with a donkey aboard in addition to cargo, float downstream to the destination, sell the wood of the platform as well as the cargo, deflate the skins, load them on the donkey, and walk back home. In the lower reaches, a favored craft was the *quffa,* a round coracle made of sewn skins stretched over a light frame of branches. They could reach good size; some, powered by four oarsmen, were big enough to carry a chariot or a mass of building stone. Modern versions, made of basketry rather than skins, are still in use and can run 13 feet (about 4 m) in diameter and 7.5 feet (2.3 m) in depth.

The other great rivers of the ancient world, such as the Danube, the Rhône, and the Seine, developed their own styles of craft. On all of them, the most troubling problem was getting upstream. One widely adopted solution was towing. It was usually done, as is still true in Egypt and India and certain other places today, by men rather than animals. The ancient towboat, like the modern, was equipped with a special towing mast. The haulers trudged along a towpath that followed the bank of the river, pulling a towline that ran to the tip of the mast and then down to the stern, where it was secured. On some of the ancient towed boats, for example those that went from Rome's port at the mouth of the Tiber to the city docks some thirteen or so miles upstream, the towline was secured to a capstan on the poop; this enabled the vessel's own crew to winch themselves ahead when the going was especially hard.

SUMMARY

Transport by land was difficult. Governments had organized services that ensured quick transport of dispatches by providing regular changes of riding horses or draft animals, but all other land transport was slow and expensive. Heavy vehicles were pulled by teams of oxen, lighter ones by teams of mules and horses; for the mules and horses more or less the same harness was used as for the oxen, which substantially decreased their effectiveness.

The preferred means of transport, and the sole practical one for heavy or bulky commodities, was by ship. Its great drawback was the limited sailing season, since ancient sailors stayed off the water between November and March. For coastal work, the ancients used merchant galleys and smaller sailing craft, including some driven by certain versions of the fore-and-aft rig, but for overseas transport only the square-rigged sailing ships suited. On important runs—for example, the hauling of Egyptian grain from the harbor of Alexandria to Rome—there were ships of great size capable of carrying 1,200 tons or more. The other two major commodities, wine and olive oil, were transported in massive clay jars; ordinary cargo vessels could take 3,000 jars, larger ones up to 10,000. The ancient square rig emphasized safety over speed; with a favorable wind, ancient sailing ships averaged only four to six knots, with an unfavorable half that or less. In the eastern Mediterranean, because of the prevailing northerlies, voyages from north to south were quick, while going in the opposite direction could take twice as long or more. In the western Mediterranean, the northerlies were not quite as troublesome and vessels made more or less the same speed on the major courses.

By the eighth century B.C. Greek engineers had learned to improve natural harbors by the addition of breakwaters. By the fifth century fully developed harbors were to be found at the major seaports; they had basins, protected by breakwaters, with lines of stone quays and rows of warehouses. By the third century harbors had grown to great size and some boasted lighthouses. The Romans, using hydraulic concrete, were able to build harbors wherever they wanted.

All navigable rivers were pressed into use for transport. In Egypt, the Nile was superbly convenient since, thanks to the prevailing wind from the north, vessels could drift downstream and sail upstream. The Tigris and Euphrates, because of their rapids and shallows, saw the development of specially adapted boats—buoyed rafts and skin coracles. Elsewhere the problem of working upriver was solved by the use of towed boats. These were generally hauled by men rather than beasts.

BIBLIOGRAPHY

SOURCES

Herodotus, *Histories*, Aubrey De Selincourt, trans. (1954); Lucian, *The Ship; or, The Wishes* (*Navigium*), K. Kilburn, trans. (1959); Philo Judaeus, *Philo*, F. H. Colson and G. H. Whittaker, trans. (1929–1968).

STUDIES

George Bass, *A History of Seafaring Based on Underwater Archaeology* (1972); Lionel Casson, *Ships and Seamanship in the Ancient World* (1971), and *Travel in the Ancient World* (1974); Piero Gianfrotta and Patrice Pomey, *Archeologia Subacquea* (1981); Virginia Grace, *Amphoras and the Ancient Wine Trade*, 2d ed. (1979); *The Muses at Work: Arts, Crafts and Professions in Ancient Greece and Rome*, Carl Roebuck, ed. (1969); Charles Singer, ed., *A History of Technology*, II (1956).

CRAFTS AND CRAFTSMEN

ALISON BURFORD

ORIGINS OF THE CRAFTSMAN'S ROLE

The legendary Daedalus (fig. 1)—whose name means "cunning artificer"—at once practical workman and magical contriver of fantastic devices, embodied in the many tales associated with him throughout classical antiquity both the fundamental characteristics of craftsmanship itself and the general public's attitude toward craftsmen and their work. Son of Metion (Forethoughtfulness) and grandson of Eupalamos (the Ready-handed), he was born to craftsmanship; in turn he taught various skills to his own young relations: Icarus, his son who died of overconfidence in his father's artificial wings, and Perdix, his nephew, whom he eventually killed from professional jealousy. His extreme versatility enabled him to invent carpenters' tools, ships' rigging, a new sculptural style, and statues that moved, and to make Pasiphaë's cow, the Minotaur's labyrinth, steam baths, golden honeycombs, and folding chairs. Like skilled workers in the real world, he was both what today would be called "artist" and "craftsman," a distinction that scarcely existed in antiquity—gem cutters and sculptors were *technitai* or *fabri*, technicians or makers, on exactly the same professional footing as blacksmiths or bootmakers. During his working career, Daedalus moved from place to place to work for different patrons, both as their servant and as an autonomous creator of objects that they wanted but could not supply for themselves. And his works inspired admiration mixed with a certain suspicion and fear.

Similar ambivalence toward the skilled worker appears frequently in Greek and Roman literature. Homer described a mixing bowl of chased silver as "the loveliest thing in the world, a masterpiece," and the gods' dwellings as "contrived with cunning device" by "the famed craftsman" Hephaistos, god of fire and forges; but he portrayed the smith god himself as lame and made thickset by working in his smithy (*Iliad* 23.740; 1.607–608; *Odyssey* 8.308–311). In classical Athens Plato was moved to remark of craftsmen that their minds were "as cramped and crushed by their mechanical lives as their bodies are crushed by the manual crafts" (*Republic* 495d–e); this is in con-

Figure 1. Daedalus presents his wooden cow to Pasiphaë while Icarus works at a carpenter's bench cutting mortices with a hammer and chisel; a bow drill lies on the floor. Fourth style wall painting from the House of the Vettii in Pompeii. ALINARI/ART RESOURCE

trast to other comments that betray his appreciation of the crafts. Likewise Cicero in late republican Rome could actively patronize craftsmanship, but still say that "all mechanics are engaged in vulgar trades" with "nothing liberal" (meaning nothing worthy of a free and liberally educated man's intellectual concern) about them (*On Duty* 1.150). The professional manual worker was of course discounted socially and politically, in part because he earned his living by his craft.

But, intellectually speaking, there was common ground between philosophers and craftsmen. While fine craftsmen worked to a great extent by eye, almost instinctively, there were mathematical principles that not only architects and sculptors but also painters and potters could apply to their works so as to achieve the required balance and proportion; the so-called golden section is the best known example. The expert knowledge of craftsmen trained in more mundane crafts also attracted the interest of such men as Socrates. Evidence for communication between theoreticians and technicians comes mainly from the Greek epoch, and from Athens in particular. But its importance at all periods, as a factor in the relationship between commissioners of artifacts and their makers, can be inferred from the prevailing excellence of workmanship and the subtle modifications that maintained stylistic coherence without declining into repetition and stereotype. Moreover, had there not been a discriminating public, finely wrought objects that characterize the heights of craftsmanship in antiquity would not have been made.

TRANSMISSION AND DEVELOPMENT OF CRAFT TECHNIQUES

The achievements of Greek and Roman craftsmen should be assessed in a wider context. The fact is that all the basic techniques they required had already been developed: no fundamental technological advances took place during the Greco-Roman period. The material needs of society remained unchanged with but few exceptions, none of which called for entirely new methods.

But this is not to deny true inventiveness to Greek and Roman craftsmen at their best, in their constant refinement of inherited techniques, and in the dynamism of the variations they continually introduced into their work. There were in any case breaks in cultural continuity, most markedly at the collapse of the Mycenaean civilization, which meant rediscovering techniques such as monumental stoneworking, gem cutting, and even the use of precious metals during and after the Dark Age. And parts of the Mediterranean world only became civilized within the classical period, the Italian peninsula itself being a case in point.

Cultural decline within the Dark Age was by no means all-embracing. Iron, exploited first in eastern Asia Minor, became widely known, and pottery already demonstrated qualities inherent in later Greek art. Then from the eighth century onward contact with Phoenicia, Syria, and Egypt led to the "orientalizing" of Greek art, the introduction of writing, the transformation of small-scale statuary and wooden architecture into the sculpture and monumental building in stone of the classical world, and the development of important changes in armaments and shipbuilding. None of this meant that the Greek technician merely imitated. The strength and liveliness of native tradition in the crafts was already such that he translated Near Eastern and Egyptian designs into something unmistakably Greek and immediately embarked on a quite new line of development.

Thereafter the Greeks were the main purveyors of new ideas within the Mediterranean world. Sometimes it was a two-way exchange, as with the Scythians. In Italy the Etruscans, although gifted with considerable technical expertise of their own in ceramics, imported and imitated Athenian pottery. Greek influences also reached them and other Italic peoples through the Greek settlements in southern Italy and Sicily, but only following the Roman conquests in Greece and Asia Minor after 200 B.C. did Roman art and architecture become extensively hellenized. Native genius was largely merged in the artistic amalgam of classical Greek and Hellenistic styles, but some regional characteristics and preferences prevailed in elements of stone-carved relief and portraiture and in the developing use of fired brick and mortar together with the arch and vault, all known earlier but never taken up by the Greeks.

The establishment of the Roman Empire saw the spread of urban culture into western Europe and parts of North Africa where it had scarcely existed before. Here too, despite the pervasiveness of a general "imperial" style, regional characteristics were not entirely stamped out. Thus the Celts reacted to Roman domination so that, while Gallic potteries could produce ware indistinguishable from that of Arretium (Arezzo, central Italy), Gallic stoneworkers maintained their own tradition in reliefs and sculptures (fig. 7) and the Celtic art of enameling came into the Roman world.

CRAFTSMEN AT WORK

Once the initial rediscoveries had been made, Greek and Roman craftsmen contrived many fresh approaches where further development was possible within the existing confines of the craft. Where development had reached its limit, as in carpentry, they continued to work wood as competently as the joiners, builders, and carvers of previous ages.

The carpenter's skills touched every activity from agriculture to war, from seagoing (fig. 2) to religious observances. He depended on traditional methods; if the replacement of bronze tools by iron made his work easier, it did not essentially alter techniques. But of course changes in shipbuilding occurred, for instance with the evolution of the trireme and the experiments of Hellenistic rulers in constructing ever bigger versions. These, together with the building of large war fleets (among others by the Athenians from the 480s and the Romans from the 260s onward), must have entailed some alteration of shipyard procedure beyond merely increasing the number of workers and the dimensions and quantity of timbers used. Nevertheless, tools and basic carpentering techniques remained essentially the same.

In monumental architecture, on the other hand, timber came to be largely displaced by stone. Yet, strength of tradition meant that even though they now had no practical function some elements of wooden construction were retained by the stonemasons. And carpentry went on being required for very important structural elements such as roof beams, ceilings, doors, and so on.

The stonemason's craft, little practiced in Dark Age Greece, quickly gained importance during the seventh century B.C. Figurines and statuettes were supplemented by life-size and larger statues in stone, and by the early sixth century big stone temples were being built. Methods were derived from the Egyptians, but the replacement of bronze by iron stoneworking tools probably came quite early—and with them the ability to do rather different things—so that adjustments in technique continued to be made with small-scale but telling alterations of style and finish. The concern to find new sources of suitable stone took craftsmen over land hitherto familiar only to shepherds; but the problems of transporting heavy loads meant that even in nearby quarries the mason must cut blocks as close as possible to final dimensions from the quarry face itself. Often accessibility overcame considerations of quality.

This meant calling on the ancillary crafts of surface finishing, for example, stuccoing to give coarser limestones the appearance of marble. If the interiors of houses of the well-to-do and of public buildings had not been faced with expensive marble panelling, they generally were plastered and prepared for further decoration. Few examples of Greek wall painting survive, but some contemporary vase paintings demonstrate its stylistic influence, and comments in the ancient liter-

Figure 2. The carpenter's trade as depicted on the grave stele of P. Longidienus Camillus, a Roman shipwright, who is shown at work on a boat. RAVENNA MUSEUM. *FOTOFAST, BOLOGNA*

ature indicate the esteem in which this craft was held, together with the painters' enduring concern to extend their range of treatment and to exploit new materials. Examples from Pompeian villas demonstrate the elegant fantasies with which later Hellenistic painters indulged their patrons (fig. 1), and some mosaics are clearly designed after earlier paintings.

The use of colored stones for surface decoration, first tried by the Sumerians, developed within the Greek world from modest beginnings in the late fifth century B.C. with pavements of white and colored pebbles set in abstract patterns. Within the next century cube-cut stones were composed in more complicated and naturalistic designs; the rather douce tones of stone tesserae then came to be supplemented by brightly colored pieces of glass, used occasionally in pavements and extensively in walls. Farther west, mosaics were rare until late-republican Romans began to incorporate them into garden shrines, and then into their villas. Thereafter interest in mosaics spread throughout the empire and the craft expanded enormously, so that by the second century A.D. provincial mosaicists were influencing styles in Italy.

Perhaps more than any other craft, metalworking provided contacts among otherwise culturally disparate and geographically remote parts of the ancient world. Many areas lacked metals, so that an extensive commercial network in ores and bulk metals had long existed; trade in items of metal manufacture was almost as important and facilitated the spread of technical developments and stylistic influences. Largely by this means knowledge of ancient Near Eastern and northern European art came to Greek workshops, and Celtic and Germanic work came to the attention of patrons and craftsmen within the Roman world. Although iron gradually supplanted bronze for many tools and weapons, bronze continued to be used not only for ornamental but also for utilitarian objects. Much bronze reached the workshop already alloyed. Its constituents, copper and tin, were always available on the market, too, so that smiths could mix their own bronze, as did the sculptor Phidias for his great statue of Athena Promachos on the Athenian acropolis. Bronze-working techniques (fig. 3) did not undergo major changes; methods already established in the Bronze Age continued to be applied to the manufacture of bronze statues and such tools, weapons, and pieces of armor as were not replaced by iron versions.

While cast iron remained unknown in the ancient Mediterranean world, wrought iron gradually came into use from the late Bronze Age onward. Smiths (fig. 4) acquired the art of hardening iron for the cutting edges of tools and weapons by using metal with a higher carbon content than normal, and so moved toward the production of steel. This process, which may have resulted accidentally from the imperfect reduction of iron ore, was further encouraged by the use of ores naturally rich in manganese from areas such as Thrace or Spain. Nevertheless the smith's equipment—fire, anvil, bellows, molds, hammers, tongs—underwent no drastic transformation.

In some places ores required only surface working to extract them. Where it was necessary to mine, the remains of working show that, as in the silver mines of Attica, shaft and gallery cuttings were fairly carefully made, in the traditions of good quarrymen. Improvements came to be made in equipment, and the application of the Archimedean screw and various types of waterwheels enabled miners to work at levels prone to flooding, as in the mines of Roman Spain. Yields from silver and iron ores were increased by the modification of furnaces. But if earlier methods were less efficient, the high quality of Athenian silver in particular was renowned throughout the Greek world.

TECHNOLOGY

Figure 3. Attic red-figure kylix portraying metalworkers in a bronze foundry: (*top*) workers use rasps to scrape and smooth the legs on a colossal bronze statue of Achilles; (*bottom*) an assistant works the bellows behind a furnace as the artist prepares to release molten metal from the oven into a mold. At right, another assistant works with a hammer on a male figure whose arms have just been attached and whose head lies on the floor ready for fixture. On the walls hang a spare pair of feet and various tools of the trade. First quarter of fifth century B.C. WEST BERLIN, STAATLICHE MUSEEN PREUSSISCHER KULTURBESITZ, ANTIKENMUSEUM INV. NR. F2294.

Figure 4. Attic black-figure amphora depicting a blacksmith in his workshop forging metal with his helper while two customers oversee the work they commissioned, *ca.* 520–510 B.C. BOSTON, MUSEUM OF FINE ARTS, H.L. PIERCE FUND NR. 01.8035

Figure 5. Roman silver-gilt *emblema* dish from the Hildesheim Treasure decorated in high relief with a medallion figure of Athena probably copied from a Hellenistic model. First century A.D. WEST BERLIN, STAATLICHE MUSEEN PREUSSISCHER KULTURBESITZ, ANTIKENMUSEUM INV. NR. 3779.1

The uses of silver and gold were inevitably restricted to finely wrought objects intended for display or cult purposes. Changing tastes in plate were met by inventive modifications of design—engraved, embossed, or in relief (fig. 5). As for jewelry, the fineness of detail achieved in Greek and Hellenistic work equaled the best of the ancient Near East.

One quite new development in metalworking, the minting of coins, took place in about 625 B.C., invented by Greeks and Lydians in western Asia Minor. Coins were made by striking a disk of hot metal (silver or electrum—an approximate four-to-one gold-silver mixture—at first) with a die of hardened bronze carved in much the same way as a seal stone; this method continued to be used with little modification throughout antiquity. The precision of detail in many coins and gems suggests that the cutters must have had either magnifying devices of some kind, or excellent eyesight. Certainly we hear of some very young Roman gem engravers whose eyes would have been at their sharpest.

The constant demand for pottery and the general availability of workable clays made the potter (fig. 9) almost as integral a part of the community as the carpenter and the smith. But the fact that some clay beds were better than others, so that cities such as Athens and Corinth in Greece and Arretium in Italy became major centers of production, meant that trade in terra-cotta goods was quite far-reaching. All clay manufactures required careful attention during firing to ensure that the kiln became hot enough for the correct length of time. Athenian experiments with black glazes on red ground, for instance, necessitated altering the firing temperature two or three times in order to make the clay ground turn red and the glaze stay black. An important development in manufacturing methods was the Hellenistic adaptation of molds, already used for decorative architectural elements and figurines, to the production of relief decorated pottery (fig. 6), in imitation of costlier bronze and silver ware. Lamps also came to be made by this means (fig. 11) throughout the Hellenistic and Roman periods.

The widespread use of glass was for a long time discouraged by high costs due to the apparent scarcity of suitable raw materials and the difficulties of transporting objects made of so fragile a substance. During the Greek period glass was used in small quantities, among other things for decorative detail such as the eyes of statues. Egypt and Syria had been the earliest and remained the most important sources; indeed, the technique of glassblowing, discovered during the first century B.C., appeared first in Syria. It was largely this invention that allowed glass to reach a wider market in the Roman world.

Leatherworking, on the other hand, was like pottery manufacture a widespread and age-old craft. Hides were usually (but, surprisingly, not always) tanned outside the city, by means of various unpleasant liquids. The resulting leather provided equipment of many kinds, from ladies' slippers and soldiers' sandals to workmen's aprons, harness, ships' tackle, shields, leather flasks, and vellum (or parchment as it was later known). Associated with this craft would have been gluemaking, utilizing hides and bones, to supply a material essential to woodworking of all kinds, and the very specialized craft of manufacturing sinew rope, which provided the means of torsion required in siege catapults.

As for textiles, even though home production of woolens remained an important source, workshops came to supply both cloth and ready-made clothing. Both workshop and home producers probably would have depended on the crafts of fulling (fig. 7) and dyeing, the quality of which only hints survive in paintings and in such rare examples as a gold-embroidered purple cloth recently found in a Macedonian royal tomb. The availability of diaphanous fabrics is evident in the literature as well as in sculptures and vase paintings. Such fabrics might have been silks imported from Asia or very finely woven cottons from Egypt. Linen, of which Egyptian workshops continued to be a major source, had uses apart from clothing—as ships' canvas. One of the many abiding mysteries concerning ancient craftsmanship is the almost complete silence in the sources on sailmaking and rope manufacture, both of which were essential to war fleets as well as to the numerous cargo vessels continuously plying the Mediterranean coasts. It serves as a salu-

Figure 6. Terra-cotta fragment of a vase cast from an Arretine ware mold decorated in relief with a depiction of Alexander the Great hunting a lion and signed by the potter M. Perennius Tigranus. Late first century B.C. BY COURTESY OF THE TRUSTEES OF THE BRITISH MUSEUM

Figure 7. Funeral reliefs on a tombstone from Roman Gaul showing a fuller at work: (*left*) treading wool cloth in a tub of water and fuller's solution to release grease and dirt; (*right*) trimming the raised nap with iron cropping shears. *Reproduced from Gustave Julliot,* INSCRIPTIONS ET MONUMENTS DU MUSÉE GALLO-ROMAIN DE SENS (1898). THE NEW YORK PUBLIC LIBRARY

tary reminder that our view of most crafts can only be partial at best.

CRAFT TRAINING AND THE WORKSHOP

Whenever possible, the craftsman taught his skills to his own sons, in the workshop. If he had no suitable children of his own, he acquired apprentices, or bought young slave boys as substitutes; girls may also have learned some crafts, but the evidence for professional craftswomen, free or slave, is exceedingly slight at all periods. The passing on of crafts within the family is exemplified in legend. Phereclus, the Homeric shipwright, was descended from Tekton (Builder) and Harmonides (Joiner), and in the real world Caicus and his three sons worked as carpenters in the Delian sanctuary during the third century B.C.; strong family connections are detectable among shipwrights working on Athenian warships. Many architects were related to carpenters —the Roman Tiberius Claudius Vitalis and his son, or Publius Cornelius Thallus and his father—or to other architects, like Metagenes and his father, Chersiphron, at Ephesus, and some of the official architects at the Delphic sanctuary.

While family connections among metalworkers are hardly known, stoneworkers were undoubtedly born to their craft (fig. 8). The Athenian sculptor Praxiteles, son and nephew of sculptors, had many descendants; other sculptor families may also be traced through several generations. The Argive stonemason Polyxenos cut stone, perhaps in the family quarry, and

375

Figure 8. Inscribed bone tool found in the House of Mikion and Menon, a building excavated at the Athenian Agora, which served as private home and workshop for a family of marble workers. The bone stylus was probably used for making models in wax or clay. Fifth century B.C. COURTESY OF THE AMERICAN SCHOOL OF CLASSICAL STUDIES AT ATHENS, AGORA INV. NO. BI 819

also worked it on the site together with his two sons at Epidaurus. As Plato remarked, potters also taught the craft to their sons. They occasionally signed their work, as did sculptors, often including their father's name, perhaps in acknowledgment of their indebtedness to paternal training. The same may then be true of mosaicists' signatures; and although no painters' signatures survive, literary discussions reveal family interest in that craft too.

The workshop (meaning personnel, not plant) was generally small. Illustrations of workshop scenes suggest that a cobbler's, a furniture maker's, a blacksmith's (fig. 4), or a sculptor's establishment might consist of little more than master and helper. Other crafts required a bigger work force; Athenian vase paintings show eight persons making, decorating, and firing pottery (fig. 9), and the same number working on a large bronze statue (fig. 3). Potteries in Italy and Gaul and brickworks too were doubtless much the same size. Larger groups than this are known, among others the 120 shield-makers owned by metics in late-fifth-century Athens, the unscrupulous Roman governor Verres' collection of smiths and jewelers in the former palace at Syracuse, Crassus' work force of 500 slave carpenters and masons, and armorers in the state workshops of the empire; but they too would have operated in small workshop units, whatever the scale of the overall organization.

Training started early. If, as must often have happened, a craftsman had no children, or if they were inept, he would take on a child apprentice, usually his own or someone else's slave. Some crafts might take several years to learn properly, but a nimble child could be useful; and there are indications that quite young boys could be considered qualified. Roman epitaphs speak of sixteen-year-olds as sculptors (one being compared to Praxiteles) and children of eleven and twelve as skilled jewelers and silver engravers.

Few details of apprenticeship are known, but everywhere the same general considerations would have prevailed. No competent craftsman could afford to have objects sold from his shop if they had not been properly made. Discipline was no doubt strict—for good reason where valuable materials were at risk—but little is heard of this aspect of the apprentice's life, apart from the Roman jurists' quoting, in illustration of a point concerning personal injury, the possibility that a master shoemaker "struck a pupil with a last for not doing correctly what he had shown him," and so "knocked the boy's eye in" (*Digest* 9.2.5.3).

The very nature of certain processes such as mining, quarrying, smelting ores, firing kilns, glassblowing, or forging iron would in itself have presented constant threats to health and safety. In the mines, galleries might collapse or fires meant to encourage ventilation burn out of control; at the surface, smelting could produce poisonous fumes. In every smithy dangers were posed by the handling of molten and red-hot metals, not to mention the carelessly swung hammer. But although at some periods convicts and prisoners of war were condemned to work in mines and quarries, and although in democratic Athens the great majority of silver miners were slaves, this does not indicate any general rigid distinction within the craftsmen's world between those who did the dangerous and dirty work and those who

Figure 9. Athenian pottery workshop as depicted by the Painter of the Leagros Group on a fragment from an Attic black-figure hydria: (*left to right*) an amphora is inspected after being glazed; a craftsman is throwing a large vase on a potter's wheel spun by a boy sitting on a low stool; a pithos that has just been thrown is carried outside to dry before being fired; an old man walking with a staff is probably the proprietor of the pottery; a porter carries a sack of charcoal to the kiln, which is being raked out by a stoker before relighting. MUNICH, STAATLICHE ANTIKENSAMMLUNGEN UND GLYPTOTHEK

supervised with clean hands—between slaves' and freemen's work.

The truly competent craftsman must understand every process related to his craft, however specialized the actual production of goods in the workshop might be. No technical process could be isolated completely. Thus smiths should know how to refine metals or even smelt ore, although they worked far from the actual source of their material. Sculptors often worked on their selected material at every stage, from quarry face to their sculpture's appointed setting. Likewise, carpenters might fell and season their own timber, or at any rate needed to understand the treatment received by the wood they were to convert into axle blocks or ships' planking.

Versatility of another sort also was required of some craftsmen, in that the creator of gold and ivory cult statues, the cartwright, the house builder, the toolmaker, the jeweler, or the armorer all worked with more than one material. The ability of the *architecton* (meaning master craftsman in Greek and Latin, and used of both builders and shipwrights) to coordinate many different craftsmen consisted of more than merely administrative competence; he was the leader of construction and had to be able to judge every process required for completion of the job. All successful production, not only on building sites and in shipyards, depended on communication among the crafts; new developments must often have been prompted by the adaptation of designs from one craft to another.

Workshop tradition controlled but could not stifle the talents of a gifted craftsman. On the other hand, it could not instill talent where none existed or prevent carelessness and poor judgment, of which there are examples enough and for which no doubt undiscriminating customers were sometimes also to blame. Nor could it always ensure success, however carefully the craftsman might make his preparations—hence the apotropaic emblems against evil happenings, such as appear in workshop scenes (fig. 9) and as found in the sculptor Phidias' workshop at Olympia, where he made the great gold and ivory statue of Zeus. However rationalist the intellectual circles that Phidias, the friend of Pericles, moved in himself, he could not counter anxieties about the incalculable elements in the processes of craftsmanship, the unexpected faults found in raw material, or the inherent difficulties of working with fire. The Potters' Hymn, composed at Athens sometime in the classical period, invoking against potters who cheated their customers their bogies Syntrips (Smasher), Smaragos (Crasher), Asbestos (Unquenchable), Salaktes (Shake-to-pieces), and Omodamos (Conqueror of the unbaked), was not just a literary joke but reflected genuine superstitions within the craft. So too masons' preoccupations gave rise to stories that in the Italian quarries of Luna (Luni, Carrara) the places where marble had been cut away filled up of their own accord.

CRAFTSMEN AND THE ECONOMY

Craftsmen depended on regular employment for a decent living wage, but they did not necessarily find it in the same place during their entire working lives. If business declined, they had to move elsewhere to work. This meant that society at large could not always depend in its turn on getting things made precisely at will or immediately upon need.

Skilled workers were not distributed evenly throughout every city, district, or province, nor were their movements easily predictable; they generally tended to concentrate in an area for one reason or another —the availability of good raw materials being one. Thus craftsmen at Corinth were among the leaders in the orientalizing of Greek art during the archaic period, and remained instrumental in Greek architectural development thereafter, too, partly because beds of fine clay and workable limestone lay close to the city and because access to good timber enabled Corinthian shipwrights to dominate their field. At Athens the existence of fine clay and marble together with abundant silver ore played its part in making the city one of the busiest manufacturing centers in the Greek world, just as readily accessible metals, clays, easily worked stone, and timber assisted the crafts to flourish in the cities of Etruria and in Rome itself.

But craftsmen could also depend on trade to bring them their raw materials, and they would doubtless have tended to congregate in centers such as Athens for the commercial advantages alone. However, the nature of trade was such that employment in remote places was by no means ruled out by the lack of requisite materials. Smiths at the sanctuary of Apollo at Bassae (Phigalia), high in the Arcadian mountains, imported iron ore, which they smelted and wrought into objects suitable for dedication.

Craftsmen could be drawn together temporarily for public works. In order to build up the rural sanctuary of Asclepius, the small city of Epidaurus culled most of the required skilled labor from Corinth, Argos, Troezen, Stymphalos, Tegea, Athens, and Paros. Epidaurian craftsmen were only skilled enough to do such jobs as laying the foundation courses of temples, building workshops for sculptors, making simple metal fittings, and so on. Obviously, special projects in one place often created a shortage of skilled workers in another; and if the usual contacts within the craft world were disrupted, as by Athens' defeat in the Peloponnesian War (404 B.C.), skilled workers might go out of circulation. In this very period, Dionysius I of Syracuse gathered skilled workers by advertising far and wide for his preparations against Carthage. Soon after, Ephesus was turned into a vast armaments workshop during the Spartan Agesilaus' campaigns in Asia Minor, but virtually no building of temples went on in mainland Greece for some time thereafter. Public works in Italy and throughout the Roman Empire ran up against labor shortages too. In the second century B.C. the temple of Juno Lacinia at Croton (Crotone) in South Italy could not have its marble roof repaired because no workers were available capable of doing the job. When Pliny the Younger, as governor of Bithynia in Asia Minor, requested architects from the emperor to oversee construction, Trajan replied that he could spare none, as he had not even enough for the projects then in hand at Rome.

Could measures be taken to guarantee the availability of skilled workers? The offer of steady work for regular pay was as good a guarantee as any, and this the Roman army could make, ensuring against dependence on a mobile and unpredictable labor supply by instituting its own corps of craftsmen and technicians in the regular legionary forces. Each legion, writes Vegetius (2.11), "has carpenters, masons, wagon makers, smiths, painters, and other workers . . . for building barracks and . . . making siege engines and so on . . . they also have workshops for shields, cuirasses and bows, arrows, missiles, nets and all types of weapons," and makers of military boots and other equipment. But no authority was responsible for assuring that skilled labor was generally available.

Sometimes the answer was simply to buy more slaves—as in the newly expanding brick and tile industry of late republican Rome, for instance. But that could not be the invariable solution, since an excess of skilled labor, to be maintained whether it was fully employed or not, was for all but the very rich as much of an embarrassment as the want of it. On occasion, large numbers of war captives might be drafted into public works, as at Acragas (Agrigento, in Sicily) during the fifth century B.C.; similarly, convicts were employed in Roman imperial mines and quarries. But unless they had been trained before captivity, such labor could contribute only crude energy, not skill. Although many skilled workers were slaves at some stage in their lives, there was no craft worked exclusively by slaves. Most workshops in every craft would have had a slave or two, while some might be manned entirely by slaves or by freedmen working out the obligation they had to a former owner who happened to have only a business interest in the craft concerned. Some slaves came onto the market already trained, perhaps from workshops that made a regular practice of selling skilled personnel as well as their products.

How widespread the sale of skilled slaves may have been, there is no telling. Nor can we say what was the proportion of craftsmen owners to investor owners of workshops. That all were concerned for profit cannot be denied. The question is whether they were interested in expanding their business, and if so, by what means. If the market allowed, an investor could increase his profits in direct proportion to the number of new slaves he bought. They would either produce more goods or earn him more hiring fees. But what advances were made toward new and more profitable working methods, whereby each man's efforts became more productive? Some would argue, by means of mass production and increased specialization.

Mass production of a kind could be achieved in one of two ways: first, by simply lowering standards, by neglecting traditional workshop practices so as to produce more product per man-day. This would account for shortcuts such as the elongation of painted animals on some Corinthian pottery (fig. 10) so that fewer figures were required to cover the surface, the lamps made from worn molds (fig. 11), the shabby figurines offered by the hundreds, in countless sanctuaries, and the coins struck from worn and

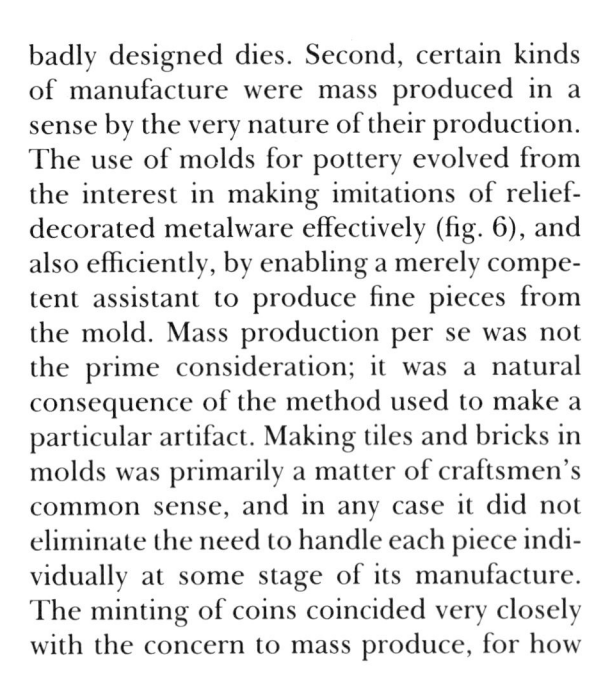

Figure 10. Ripe Corinthian oenochoe painted with orientalizing decoration (38 cm high), *ca.* 625–600 B.C. PARIS, BIBLIOTHÈQUE NATIONALE NR. 4756

Figure 11. Attic mold-made clay lamp decorated with blurred rosettes and a centaur attacking with a club (0.083 m wide). Second half of third century B.C. COURTESY OF THE AMERICAN SCHOOL OF CLASSICAL STUDIES AT ATHENS, AGORA INV. NO. L 5232

badly designed dies. Second, certain kinds of manufacture were mass produced in a sense by the very nature of their production. The use of molds for pottery evolved from the interest in making imitations of relief-decorated metalware effectively (fig. 6), and also efficiently, by enabling a merely competent assistant to produce fine pieces from the mold. Mass production per se was not the prime consideration; it was a natural consequence of the method used to make a particular artifact. Making tiles and bricks in molds was primarily a matter of craftsmen's common sense, and in any case it did not eliminate the need to handle each piece individually at some stage of its manufacture. The minting of coins coincided very closely with the concern to mass produce, for how better could coins be, and be seen to be, consistent in value than to be struck in quantity? Abuse came about from the pressure exerted on the craftsmen by Roman imperial administrators with other aims in view—mass production at all costs—than maintaining quality. In this, they are like officials who instructed helmet polishers at Constantinople in a later time to double their output. Otherwise, positive interest in methods of mass production was slow and slight; no attempt was made to mechanize. Even the Roman army's insatiable demand for nails did not inspire a device that eliminated the need to hand-forge each nailhead separately until well into the imperial period.

Specialization certainly existed, and there was a division of labor within the workshop, making for sensible work routine but not necessarily more manufactured goods per man-day. If as Xenophon suggests some shoemakers in classical Athens confined themselves to cutting out uppers only (fig. 12), this only meant that in large places there was enough business to attract numerous workers and that shoemakers could afford to employ assistants for various stages of manufacture as they learned each aspect of their craft. In small towns and villages a skilled man could not work even at a single craft, but must be a jack-of-all-trades (*The Education of Cyrus* [*Cyropaedia*] 8.2.4–5).

Craft titles have been interpreted as evidence of specialization for the specific purpose of increasing productivity. Certainly, broad categories such as "smith," "potter," "carpenter," "sculptor," or "leatherworker" were supplemented by subtler distinctions such as "statue-eye maker," "gold-leaf worker," "trumpet maker," "purple dyer," "ladies' slipper maker," "spear polisher," "glue boiler," and so on. But the use of such names reflects not a new efficiency in the workshops of classical Athens or Rome so much as a desire on the craftsman's part for some distinction from his fellows within a complex craft community such as grew up in any busy commercial center. The desire for profits did not propel ancient craftsmen out of the workshop into the factory, although it certainly propelled more workers into a greater number of workshops. Even so, the prevailing attitude remained that of the Athenian cloakmaker observed by Bishop Synesius: a regular visitor to Alexandria in the fourth century A.D., he invariably sold out very soon, but seems never to have been moved to expand his business so as to meet demand on his next visit (*Letters* 52).

To what extent were manufacturers also concerned in the distribution of their products? A fair proportion of every craft's manufactures was commissioned directly by the customer and was sold out of the workshop (figs. 4, 12). The Roman jurists indicate what must often have been the case, the need to make it clear who provided the materials (especially if precious metals were required) and who owned the object up to the point of actual delivery, thus providing against damage or theft. But there was always a considerable ready-made market too, not only for cooking vessels and tools, but also for such things as grave-marker reliefs of the purely conventional kind. The successful craftsman could predict local trends and take account of the popular desire to be in fashion; sales would be concluded in the local market or in the shop alongside a conveniently situated workplace.

Goods sold abroad reached their destina-

Figure 12. Attic black-figure vase depicting an Athenian shoemaker at work in his shop cutting a pair of shoes to measure for the boy standing on his bench. OXFORD, ASHMOLEAN MUSEUM

tion by various means. The craftsman might take his own wares to a distant market, as did the Athenian cloakmaker mentioned above, but most trade was carried on by independent merchants. Some would have been speculators buying up a workshop's output and selling it wherever they could; others would have plied between source and distant market regularly enough to be able to commission certain types and styles of products, such as the large or "important" Attic vases that came to rest in the tombs of the Etruscan upper classes. In either case, trading in manufactures was usually a subsidiary interest for merchants mainly concerned with agricultural produce or metals.

The presence far afield of objects of a recognizable regional style might also be due to the "export" or migration of the craftsmen responsible (fig. 15). This is particularly obvious in the Roman imperial period, with the spread of Arretine ware to Gaul from Italy, which was due not only to the migration of workers from Arretium, but also, as in the case of terra-cotta lamp production in various western provinces, to the setting up of branch workshops controlled from a central manufactory in Italy.

Many craftsmen traveled abroad to execute a single commission, or to complete an object that could not be safely transported in one piece, like marble sculptures that could not be finished until set in place; the craftsmen then returned home or moved on to other patrons elsewhere. Some Greek craftsmen known to have worked for Scythian patrons may even have spent time in Scythian settlements, although their usual base of operations would have been one or another of the Greek cities on the northern coast of the Black Sea.

Craftsmen earned their living by their skills. What sort of a living was it? Direct evidence is poor; on one hand there are Athenian records indicating day wages for public works in the classical period, and on the other Diocletian's edict of A.D. 301 fixing a ceiling on prices and wages. Rates of production can be only roughly estimated in a few instances, and since wages and prices can rarely be aligned, it is impossible to say, for example, how many lamps a lampmaker could turn out per day, and at what margin of profit. Payments for temple building at Athens show that sculptors, fine carpenters, and masons all earned about the same—little more than twice the daily allowance made to citizen soldiers on active service—and that citizens earned no more than resident aliens and slaves. The earnings of Phidias, the designer of the Parthenon sculptures and creator of the large gold and ivory cult statue of Athena, were no doubt more generous; but the only comparison we have is the large contract price paid to the Parian sculptor Thrasymedes, who had similar responsibilities for the temple and statue of Asclepius at Epidaurus (his materials being accounted for under another contract). Literary anecdotes indicate what we would expect—that painters and sculptors like Apelles and Lysippos could command very high fees from patrons such as Alexander the Great, for wealthy patrons have always found part of the appeal of commissioning works of art in being able to boast how much they have paid for them.

The Roman evidence is scantier, but Diocletian's edict at least indicates economic distinctions among the crafts that are probably realistic. Pay for stonemasons, carpenters, boatwrights, smiths, and others was fixed at about twice the amount paid to lowly workers, farm laborers, and shepherds; shipwrights, mosaicists, and marble pavers were rated a little higher; wall painters and plaster modelers, at three times, and picture painters, at six times the laborer's wage.

The question then remains what a given wage could buy. Here again the nature of the evidence allows little more than the inference that most craftsmen must have lived very simply. If the painter Protogenes was able to choose to subsist for a time on lentils in order, as he said, to sharpen his artistic sensibilities, most skilled workers, like most of the general population, had no choice in the matter at all.

CRAFTSMEN AND SOCIETY

Although the majority lived simply, craftsmen were concerned to observe, if they could, the customs of society at large by spending money on dedications to the gods and on fitting memorials at their own death. This was true not only of urban workers, but also of the inhabitants of mining communities, geographically and socially the most isolated workers of all. By setting up monuments indicating craft identity and pride of workmanship they were partly defying the prevailing prejudices and partly countering their own feelings of alienation in a society with strong moral antipathy toward professional manual workers. Some communities even excluded them from full citizen rights, despite the fact that they might be citizen-born residents. Those who were slaves suffered all the disabilities of their status in any case. And the inevitable mobility of some craftsmen debarred them from full rights and participation in community affairs wherever they were.

In fact, of the surviving examples of dedications, those from craftsmen make up only a small proportion, and few match those of prosperous members of the general public. But the fact that dedications were made at all is more important than the scale on which they were made. No doubt many craftsmen made simple offerings of tools or perishable products from their own workshops; but among the grandest workers' dedications known are those made by Athenian potters *ca.* 500 B.C. Nearchos commissioned a maiden-statue (*kore*) (fig. 13) from the internationally renowned sculptor Antenor and had it inscribed, "Nearchos the potter dedicated the first fruits of his products to Athena. Antenor, son of Eumares, made the statue." Another potter, Pamphaios, known from many signatures, had himself portrayed holding a piece of pottery in a relief he dedicated to the goddess. It is surprising that there survive no dedications made by Athenian smiths of any kind, or by leather-workers or stoneworkers (with the exception of the mason Archedemos' homely hillside shrine on Mount Hymettus to Pan and the nymphs).

Although few rival Nearchos' offering, dedications from the Roman period are far more numerous and more representative of all the crafts. Some consist of repairs to sacred monuments done at the craftsman's own expense: a British bronzesmith commissioned to make a bronze statue of Mars contributed to its dedication by adding one pound of bronze on his own account; the architect Julius Lacer built a small temple to commemorate his bridge building in Spain.

Craftsmen made dedications almost without exception to deities acknowledged by the general public, not to those particularly associated with the crafts. For example, of the few metalworkers' offerings known, none was made to Hephaistos or his Roman equivalent, Vulcan. A rare instance of a craft-oriented cult is provided by the thank offering made by two quarry workers for having been the first to cut 20-foot monoliths in a Romano-Gallic quarry; the object of their gratitude was not only the widely worshiped woodland deity Silvanus but also "the Numidian mountains" of North Africa, which were presumably accorded cult status by quarrymen precisely because they provided building stone highly esteemed in various parts of the Roman Empire. Otherwise, the need to conform in this as in other respects is clearly apparent in personal records from the mining area of Laurium in

Figure 13. Marble *kore* signed by Antenor and inscribed with a dedication to Athena by the potter Nearchos, *ca.* 520 B.C. ATHENS, ACROPOLIS MUSEUM INV. NR. 681. PHOTO: ALISON FRANTZ

southern Attica, an industrial community consisting mainly of several thousand slaves at the height of its production. Most of the slaves came from regions like Thrace or northern Asia Minor, alien in speech and cultural background, with loyalties lying far from those of the Greek world. Yet they made entirely conventional dedications to Greek deities, in Greek.

Conformity after death was even more eagerly sought for by these same miners, in funeral reliefs of standard type that included no reference to their craft. The one memorial of the fourth century that declares a craft interest is that made by Atotas the Paphlagonian (from northern Asia Minor). Otherwise strikingly conformist in its flawless Greek hexameter verses affirming Atotas' heroic ancestry, this epitaph, headed "Atotas the miner," is one of the few exceptions to the general rule that Greek epitaphs reveal little or nothing of their subjects' careers. Most of the other exceptions are craftsmen's too, but only one accompanying relief, belonging to the shoemaker Xanthippos (fig. 14), reflects occupational interests. Craftsmen in the Roman period were far readier to have professional concerns stated in their memorials (fig. 2), probably not because the antipathy to manual workers had diminished, but rather because the social and political structure was now such that everybody felt the need for fuller identification, craftsmen included. Again, conformity of language and presentation predominates, but many grave reliefs, particularly from Roman Gaul (fig. 7), show their subject in his workshop.

The craftsman's need of a social life could be met by professional solidarity carried over from working hours. This is more apparent in the Roman period, but hints of its existence in the Greek world survive in such dedications as those made by twelve Athenian clothes cleaners to Pan, the nymphs, and the river Achelous, and by eleven miners at Laurium to the hero Heracles. In the Roman world numerous dedications were made by collegia, associations

Figure 14. Grave stele of the Athenian shoemaker Xanthippos, *ca.* 420 B.C. BY COURTESY OF THE TRUSTEES OF THE BRITISH MUSEUM

formed by members of the same or connected crafts for purposes such as celebrating feast days and imperial birthdays, and providing proper funerals for their fellows. They played a part in the life of military craftsmen too: the Belgic tribesman Julius Vitalis, an armorer in the Twentieth Legion, was buried by his collegium of armorers. Each collegium had a rigid official hierarchy, and rising through the ranks was obviously a rich substitute for the public offices to which craftsmen could rarely aspire. Thus the Lydian goldsmith Camillus Polynices administered every office in the Romano-Swiss collegium of carpenters and builders to which he belonged, and the imperial freedman Tiberius Flavius Hilarion held office during thirty-five years of membership in the carpenters' collegium at Rome. But the real value of membership lay in the companionship and respect that could accrue, as is apparent in the Gallic Quintus Candidus Benignus' memorial: "He was a builder of the greatest skill. . . . Great craftsmen would always call him master. . . . No one could excel him. . . . He was sweet-tempered and knew how to entertain his friends—a man of gentle and studious character, and a kindly spirit." So it was that goldsmiths and pavement workers too made offerings to the unity and corporate spirit of their respective collegia.

But however important professional solidarity might be, some craftsmen did find a certain acceptance in society. Not only was the sculptor Phidias an intimate of Pericles', but shoemakers' shops near the Athenian agora served as meeting places for all sorts, including Socrates and Pericles. The anecdote relating their discussions with Simon the shoemaker is confirmed by the actual discovery of his workshop close to the council chamber. Not that the Athenian democracy ever chose craftsmen to lead it; Cleon was called "the Tanner" probably because he derived his wealth from that unlovely craft, not because he himself had graduated from the vats. Architects fell into a somewhat special category: for one thing, as supervisors of public works they were officials of the city that appointed them; for another, they tended to come of good families, however it was that they acquired their architectural skills. Philon served as an Athenian trierarch, and Vitruvius is known to have belonged to a decently middle-class Roman family. Otherwise, connections between the crafts and public life are rarely heard of, apart from the fact that the painter

Loukios Sossios and the mosaicist Publius Aelius Harpokration served as council members at Cyrene (in Libya) and Perinthos (on the Sea of Marmara), respectively. The majority of craftsmen would have appreciated the advantages of having any recognized status, however lowly: the Hellenistic sculptor Theon of Antioch repeated in his epitaph what he had always added to his signatures: the fact that the city of Rhodes granted him, not full citizenship, but merely rights of residence.

INDIVIDUAL ACHIEVEMENT

The woodworker Mannes' epitaph from late-fifth-century Athens reveals not only his Phrygian slave origins and the fact that he served in the army, but also great pride in his own skill: "By Zeus, I never saw a better woodman." What would he or the painter Sossios, "who made the palace at Cyrene glorious among the nations for my surpassing skill," have conceived of as the mainspring of their expertise? Practically speaking, it was the traditional workshop training they had undergone. But no craft's traditions were so rigid that a good craftsman could not make constructive alterations to the pattern he received. Was individual inspiration an element in his craftsmanship, or was fine artistry external to the maker, being magically or divinely instilled?

Although irrational fears plagued craftsmen as much as anyone else in the ancient world, and although for the layman the expert's knowledge was mysterious, craftsmen were not seen as magicians or mere instruments of the gods, who in any case had themselves learned the crafts (from the Titans, "first discoverers" of all techniques). Odysseus' reaction to the amazing and terrifying designs on Heracles' sword belt is to wish that its maker might "never contrive another work *by his genius*" (*Odyssey* 11.609–614). And personal statements of the craftsmen themselves attribute their fine works to good training and the personal expertise gained thereby. It is equally clear from literary discussions that connoisseurs also conceived of artistic inspiration in the modern sense, simply as superb technique. On these grounds alone craftsmen claimed full responsibility for their works and also expressed competitiveness with other practitioners of their craft. The Paphlagonian Atotas declared that in the mines of Attica "no one rivaled me in skill (*techne*)," just as the housebuilder Maximus of Rome was "unrivaled in *techne*," or the Roman freedman the silver and gold engraver Marcus Canuleius Zosimus "excelled in his art." Bakchios had victory in an Athenian pottery contest mentioned in his epitaph, and the rivalry of earlier vase painters was openly expressed by Euthymides on one of his pots: "Euphronios never did it like this."

Personal pride in and responsibility for the work are implicit in the signatures added to many finished objects, ranging from gold and silver plate, buildings, statues, and gravestones to mosaic floors, painted pottery, gems, coins, and even city walls. It is nowhere more explicit than on the marble relief by Alxenor (fig. 15) demonstrating the new (late-sixth-century) technique of foreshortening, inscribed with the exclamation, "You have only to look and see!"

Yet many outstanding examples of craftsmanship had no name put to them. Only a handful of gem cutters' and very few coin designers' names are known, and the majority of painted pots, even at Athens, are unsigned. If some patrons were pleased to have a craftsman associated by name with their commissions, many must have discouraged the practice of signing, although precisely why is not clear. In the case of temple sculptures, Roman imperial monuments, and most coinage the absence of signatures can be attributed to the maker's responsibility being merged in the state's collective concern for the successful outcome of the work. If the unusually daring sculptor Theophilus added his name to the heel of a colossal imperial statue, the makers of the Parthenon pediments must remain content with anonymity and the professional satisfaction of having finished the rear and invisible side of their figures as finely as the side that showed.

BIBLIOGRAPHY

SOURCES

Cicero, *De Officiis* (*On Duty*), Walter Miller, trans., Loeb Classical Library (1913; repr. 1975); Theodore Mommsen and Paul Krueger, eds., *Corpus Iuris Civilis,* 1: *Digesta* (*Digest*), 16th ed. (1954); Homer, *Odyssey,* A. T. Murray, trans., 2 vols., Loeb Classical Library (1919; repr. 1976), and *Iliad,* A.T. Murray, trans., 2 vols., Loeb Classical Library (1924; repr. 1978); Plato, *Republic,* Paul Shorey, trans., 2 vols., Loeb Classical Library (1930; repr. 1978); Pliny the Elder, *Natural History,* 10 vols., Loeb Classical Library (1938–1962), especially vol. 9, H. Rackham, trans. (repr. 1968), and vol. 10, D. E. Eichholz, trans. (repr. 1971).

Synesius, *Letters,* in *Epistolographi Graeci,* Rudolf Hercher, ed. (1873); Theophrastus, *On Stones,* Earle R. Caley and John F. C. Richardson, eds., trans. (1956), and *Enquiry into Plants,* Arthur Hort, trans., 2 vols., Loeb Classical Library (1916; repr. 1968); Flavius Vegetius, *De Re Militari* (*The Military Institutions*), John Clark, trans. (1944); Vitruvius Pollio, *The Ten Books on Architecture,* Morris Hicky Morgan, trans. (1914; repr. 1960); Xenophon, *The Education of Cyrus* (*Cyropaedia*), Walter Miller, trans., 2 vols., Loeb Classical Library (1914; repr. 1968).

References to craftsmen's personal records

Figure 15. Marble stele signed by Alxenor "the Naxian" and found in Orchomenos, Boeotia. Alxenor had probably migrated to Boeotia after the destruction of Naxos around 490 B.C. Late sixth century/early fifth century B.C. ATHENS, NATIONAL ARCHAEOLOGICAL MUSEUM NR. 39

(inscriptions) are given in Alison Burford, *Craftsmen in Greek and Roman Society* (1972) following.

STUDIES

Sheila Adam, *The Technique of Greek Sculpture in the Archaic and Classical Periods* (1966); John D. Beazley, *Potter and Painter in Ancient Athens* (1946); Raymond Bloch, *Origins of Rome* (1960); John Boardman, *The Greeks Overseas,* 2d ed. (1980); Alison Burford, *The Greek Temple Builders at Epidauros* (1969), and *Craftsmen in Greek and Roman Society* (1972); Helen Cockle, "Pottery Manufacture in Roman Egypt," in *Journal of Roman Studies,* **71** (1981); Michael H. Crawford, *Roman Republican Coinage* (1974); Katherine Dunbabin, *The Mosaics of Roman North Africa* (1978); Moses I. Finley, *The Ancient Economy* (1973); Robert J. Forbes, *Studies in Ancient Technology,* 9 vols. (1957–1964), especially vol. 4 on fibers and fabrics, 2d ed. (1964), vol. 5 on leather, 2d ed. (1966), vol. 7 on mining and quarrying, and vols. 8–9 on metallurgy, 2d ed. (1971); Peter Garnsey, Keith Hopkins, and C. R. Whittaker, eds., *Trade in the Ancient Economy* (1983).

W. V. Harris, "Roman Terracotta Lamps: The Organisation of an Industry," in *Journal of Roman Studies,* **70** (1980); John F. Healy, *Mining and Metallurgy in the Greek and Roman World* (1978); Martin Henig, ed., *A Handbook of Roman Art* (1983); Reynold Higgins, *Greek and Roman Jewellery,* 2d ed. (1980), and *Greek Terracottas* (1967); Robert J. Hopper, *Trade and Industry in Classical Greece* (1979); G. B. D. Jones, "The Roman Mines at Riotinto," in *Journal of Roman Studies,* **70** (1980); Colin M. Kraay and Max Hirmer, *Greek Coins* (1966); Helen Loane, *Industry and Commerce of the City of Rome (50 B.C.–200 A.D.)* (1938); Russell Meiggs, *Trees and Timber in the Ancient Mediterranean World* (1983); Claude Mossé, *The Ancient World at Work,* Janet Lloyd, trans. (1969); Joseph V. Noble, *The Techniques of Athenian Painted Pottery* (1965).

Hanna Philipp, *Tektonon Daidala: Der bildende Künstler und sein Werk im vorplatonischen Schrifttum* (1968); Thomas G. E. Powell, *The Celts* (1958; new ed. 1980); Tamara Talbot Rice, *The Scythians* (1957); Francesco M. de Robertis, *Lavoro e lavoratori nel mondo romano* (1963); Martin Robertson, *A History of Greek Art* (1975); Donald Strong and David Brown, eds., *Roman Crafts* (1976); K. D. White, *Greek and Roman Technology* (1984).

CALENDARS AND TIME-TELLING

ALAN E. SAMUEL

THE MOTIONS OF THE EARTH, the moon, and the sun create natural units of time that are apparent to observers at all places on the earth. The rotation of the earth creates the alternation between night and day, and a complete period, measured by twenty-four hours under the present system, is called a day. The circuit of the moon around the earth, completed when the moon returns to the same line made between earth, moon, and sun, takes about 29.5 days. The motion of the earth around the sun, measured as the interval required for the earth to return to the same point in its orbit in relation to the sun—called a year, or more technically, a tropical year—occupies approximately 365.25 days. Greeks and Romans, like most peoples, used all three of these natural units of time, but because they used the periods as they actually occur in the course of the celestial motions, their time measurement was complicated by the variability of the movements or the incommensurability of the durations of one or another.

A calendar is an attempt to create a system that relates months to years. Since a lunar month is 29.5 days long only on average and varies considerably from that average, an actual calendar lunar month may occupy anywhere from twenty-nine to thirty days. That in itself represents no difficulty, for the periods can be determined by observation. The construction of calendars is complicated by the attempt to reconcile months with the year; the nearest number of lunar months that makes up a year is twelve, but the number of days occupied by twelve lunar months, approximately 354 days, is much at variance with the 365.25-day length of the year. If no attempt is made to reconcile the much shorter twelve-lunar-month period with the year of the sun, in a very short time months will change their relations to the seasons. With a discrepancy of over eleven days a year, it requires a lapse of only fifteen years before a winter month falls in the summer. This problem was one of particular importance to Greeks and Romans, for their religious festivals in many instances were related to the seasons, and they required calendrical designations that would ensure that festivals would be held in the right seasons and on the days that the gods expected them.

The most obvious solution is that achieved by a system called intercalation—the adding of an extra month—and quite early, the simplest form of intercalation, the adding of an extra month every other year, was adopted by the Romans and in Greek cities. Thus one lunar year was 354 days, the next 384, for example, creating an average lunar year of 369 days, less than four full days longer than the solar year. This would provide a much slower development of the discrepancy between the lunar year and the seasons, requiring about twenty-five years for a month to shift even a single season, a calendrical disjunction almost acceptable in societies functioning in lands of Mediterranean climate and with experience of much shorter life expectancies than those of modern times.

By the time Greeks and Romans enter our ken, their calendars had been established in their essential natures. Each individual city had its own list of months and its own sequence, some adjacent to each other fitted out with quite different arrangements; others, far apart but related by colonial or ethnic ties, with identical lists. The colonies of Miletus—Cyzicus on the Propontis and Olbia on the north shore of the Black Sea—had the same list and sequence of months as stand in the calendar of the mother city. There were broad divisions in the practice of naming months, parallel to ethnic or dialect divisions amongst Greeks, so that there are month names that are peculiarly Doric, Ionic, or Aeolic in use. Despite differences in nomenclature, however, the construction of lunar calendars as a means of keeping time was essentially the same throughout the Greek world, well down into Hellenistic times, despite variances in detail that arose from individual religious practice or local custom.

The Greeks also named and numbered the days in the month; by such a practice, a day became a date and a specific numbered or named date began at a particular time on one day and ended at a similar time on the next. In the modern-day system a date begins, by convention, at the time of day designated as midnight. The Greeks operated a calendar that followed the moon, so the calendar date began at moonrise on one day and continued until sunset/moonrise the next. In Athens and other Greek cities, the days of the month were divided into three groups and counted off in those three divisions, called decades. The first day of each month was called "new moon," and the remaining days of the first third of the month were called the second, third, and so on of the waxing month, to the tenth of the waxing month. The numbers of the middle third were simply eleventh, twelfth, and so on to the twentieth; while in the last third of the month, the count was initially backwards, progressing from the tenth of the waning month down to the last day of the month, which was called the first and the new. The terminology for the days in this decadal count varied from place to place, and even changed at Athens toward the end of the fourth century B.C.; but in most places in which the count of days can be determined, the count seems to have proceeded on a decadal basis. In some Greek calendars, however, and particularly in the Macedonian, which was in common use all over the Greek world from the time of Alexander, there was no division of the month, and the count proceeded from one to thirty (or twenty-nine, depending on the month).

By Hellenistic times, advances in astronomical knowledge had encouraged the development of cycles to determine appropriate years for the intercalation of the extra month by which the lunar calendar was kept in accord with the seasons. According to later Greek writers, there was an early awareness that biennial intercalation still left a discrepancy between lunar and solar years; the total discrepancy between the two years, without intercalation, was 11.25 days per year, which in an eight-year period amounted to exactly ninety days or three months. Over an eight-year period, therefore, three, not four, months had to be intercalated, and thus an "astronomical cycle" could be devised to control intercalation of three months every eight years. That cycle, which was still not perfect because it did not account for the exact lengths of the number of months that went into eight years, could be and was improved into a sixteen-year cycle. This system, in turn, was improved by the invention in 432 B.C. of a nineteen-year cycle by the Athenian Meton and later refined by the astronomer Callippus in the fourth century B.C.

There is no evidence that any of these astronomical cycles were used to control the civil calendar of any Greek city. They were useful, indeed indispensable, to astronomers, who needed accurate measures of time intervals for the recording and manipulation of astronomical observations, but they had no particular value to ordinary citizens, whose regulation of religious or private life neither required such long-term accuracy nor precluded the occasional adjustment of intercalation to preserve the relationship between the civil/lunar year and the seasons. By Hellenistic times, however, when many refinements of these astronomical cycles were known and other, longer and more precise, cycles had been invented, the attraction of ordinary civil use became almost irresistible. When Egypt, for example, came under Macedonian control, the local twenty-five-year cycle that had regulated the Egyptian lunar religious calendar was adapted by the middle of the third century B.C. to the Macedonian calendar for use by the Ptolemaic administration. In the areas of Syria and the East controlled by the Seleucid kings, the Macedonian calendar was adjusted to make its months coincide with the months of the Babylonian calendar, which was in turn regulated locally by a nineteen-year cycle. The system was in general use in the East, and persisted in an adjusted form in cities all over the eastern regions well into the period of Roman domination.

In Rome, only one calendar was used by the citizens. Whereas the calendar served Greeks as an aid (or hindrance) to correct timing of religious observation and was an instrument to be improved when possible, it was for the Romans something of a religious end in itself, and was treated with some veneration. Still, changes took place, bringing about a significant evolution. Initially, the Romans seem to have had a ten-month lunar calendar, beginning with the month Martius and ending with the month December (which means tenth in its Latin derivation). At some very early stage, two months were added to the beginning of the year (Januarius and Februarius) to make a twelve-month lunar calendar, which, like Greek calendars, attempted to make the lunar year coincide with the seasons by intercalation. The month lengths in the Roman calendar, however, were not strictly regulated by the moon, and the problem of intercalation was therefore different. Four months—Martius, Maius, Quintilis (July), October—had thirty-one days; Februarius had twenty-eight days; and the remaining seven—Januarius, Aprilis, Junius, Sextilis (August), September, November, December—had twenty-nine days. This length of 355 days was fixed, and approximation to the seasonal year was achieved by intercalating a month in the course of the last days of Februarius in such a way as to add either twenty-two or twenty-three days to make the intercalary year either 377 or 378 days. Of the pattern of intercalation we know nothing, and it seems likely that in fact there was no established system but that intercalation was irregular, often arbitrary, coinciding generally with the aim of keeping the calendar year parallel to the year of the seasons. In general it is not known which years in Roman history were intercalary, and the problems of understanding the calendar during the period of the republic create frequent difficulties in establishing a detailed chronology for Roman history.

Julius Caesar instituted a comprehensive reform of the Roman calendar in 46 B.C. In Ptolemaic Egypt, the Greeks had for two centuries used the Macedonian adaptation of the Egyptian civil calendar mentioned above, which was constructed of twelve months of thirty days each, plus five additional days at the end of the year to create a year of 365 days. That this year was one quarter of a day shorter than the seasonal year had long been known, and in fact, Ptolemy III had decreed toward the end of the third century B.C. that a sixth day should be added to the calendar every four years to achieve an average year length of 365.25 days; but the royal order for reform had been ignored. It was this 365.25-day year that Caesar chose as the standard for Rome's calendar. The month lengths were changed to create a 365-day year, and a single day was to be intercalated every four years to the so-called Julian year. The reform created the calendar to which our modern mnemonic device applies: "thirty days hath September, April, June, and November; all the rest have thirty-one, save February, with twenty-eight, except in leap year, twenty-nine." The system was easy enough to order, but not so simple for Roman priests to follow, accustomed as they were to counting inclusively; thus they intercalated 1001001001, for example, instead of 100010001000. In this way the Julian calendar quickly fell out of synchrony with the seasons, and in the reign of Augustus intercalation was omitted to bring the Roman calendar back to the intended relationship with the seasons. From A.D. 8 on, intercalation was resumed (correctly) and the system thereupon proceeded without error.

In the Roman calendar, the first day of the month was called *Calendae,* the *Nonae* denoted the fifth of the month, or the seventh day of a 31-day month, while the *Idus,* Julius Caesar's fateful day, was the 13th in a short month and the 15th in a 31-day month. To designate other than these specific days, the terminology counted backward from any specific point, using Roman inclusive count, so that "the fifth day before the Ides of March" means 11 March. After the Ides, one counted back from the Calends of the following month.

Just as it is usually difficult to locate within the year in terms of the modern calendar the date of an event given as a date in an ancient calendar, so it is no simple matter to relate the year of an occurrence to a year in the current system. That system—in which years designated as A.D. (*anno Domini*) run forward to the present and will continue into the future, beginning with a year 1 as the date of the birth of Christ, and years before that date are called B.C. (before Christ) and run backward getting higher as dates are earlier—was not completed and instituted until well after the end of ancient civilization. In the Greek and Roman areas of the Mediterranean many different systems were used to designate and keep track of years, some concurrently, some at different times from one another. The most common, perhaps, was the designation of a year with the name of a person, one usually holding some official capacity, so that the year would be known as "the year of *X.*" Years were designated by the names of priestesses of Hera at Argos; by the names of the archons in Athens; jointly by the names of the two consuls at Rome; and so on. Every city or region had its own system, at least at first. There had been no improvement on this confusion even as late as the fifth century B.C., for the Athenian writer Thucydides, writing of the beginning of the Peloponnesian War, felt required to give a date according to the year identified by the name of the priestess of Hera at Argos, the Athenian archon, and the name of the Spartan ephor, thus using three designations to identify the year for a wider audience.

Under such a system, dates can only be located in the past or years elapsed between events determined if lists are maintained of the years in their designations. Archon lists in Athens and consul lists in Rome, for example, could provide the requisite information. As far as is known, however, such lists began to be kept formally and publicly only at the end of the fifth century B.C., so the year dates (and therefore the years in the B.C. system that are assigned to events) lose certainty prior to the fifth century. Once the Athenian archon list was established in the fifth century, however, and the sequence of archons became fixed, events could be assigned to archon years, and ancient writers at least were fairly satisfied with the chronology thus established. Other systems, such as the one based on Spartan ephors, also grew up in Greece; and another based on a list of victors at the Olympic Games, the Panhellenic festival celebrated every four years, established a new and somewhat more convenient system. With the convention accepted that the year 776 B.C. should be considered the date of the first games, and therefore the beginning of the system, all dates given in terms of Olympiads can be worked out in terms of our B.C.–A.D. system. Since ol. 1,1 equals 776 B.C., then by simple arithmetic any year can be found—so that, for example, ol. 117,3 is 310 B.C. The list of victors at the games having been drawn up by the end of the fifth century B.C., the use of the system for chronological purposes followed very soon, and prominent Greek historians were using it during the fourth century B.C.

There were other systems used for keeping track of years over long periods of time. The most common were based on eras, or periods of time in which successions of years proceeded from the date of, for example, an important political, military, or religious event. The era in widest use in the Greek East was the Seleucid Era, in which the year 1 was the year in which King Seleucus became governor at Babylon, a year that has been identified as 312 B.C. in the modern system or 311 B.C. according to the Babylonian calendar, used in astronomical reckoning. In a sense, the reckoning by Olympiads is an era system, with the first year, or epoch, being 776 B.C. There were many eras in use at different times in later antiquity, and these various systems existed side by side, to be correlated and reconciled into more convenient tables of events by ancient and modern chronographers.

Antiquity not only enjoyed a variety of different systems for recording the passage of years, but the calendar year also began in different places at different times in the seasonal year. The beginning of a year was usually tied to an astronomical phenomenon, such as a combination of solstice and phase of the moon; the Athenian calendar may have begun on the evening after the summer solstice when the lunar crescent is first visible. Thus it is possible to link an ancient year only approximately with the seasonal year or with a year designated in the modern system. In Athens, the year ran approximately from the beginning of summer to the beginning of the next summer. The Olympic festival came in midsummer, so the Olympiad year began around that time. In the Roman East during imperial times, many calendars used the anniversary of Augustus' birth, 23 September, as the first day of the new year. There were, in fact, almost as many different ways to begin the year as there were systems for organizing and naming the months or for regulating the year.

The calendrical reforms introduced by Caesar and known as the Julian calendar gradually came to dominate most civil timekeeping practices in the Mediterranean region. Although calendars might have different month names and lengths in the different cities of the Roman Empire and might begin at different times in different places, the calendars in use came more and more to adopt the 365.25-day length of the Julian calendar. Ancient hemerologia (lists of months with their lengths) show the equivalences amongst many calendars. Some calendars had months coincident with Julian months; others, like the so-called calendar of Asia, which was prescribed for Rome's Asian cities and which began on 23 September, might or might not contain months of Julian length, so long as the year started on 23 September; still others followed the original pattern of the Egyptian civil year, with twelve months of thirty days each and five to six extra days at the end of the year. A final group followed none of these patterns, operative without a twenty-eight-day month and without the inclusion of extra days at the end of the year; nonetheless the months were arranged in various ways to follow the Julian year. Ultimately the Julian calendar with its Roman month names prevailed everywhere. That calendar, however, still contained a minor discrepancy with regard to the seasons, an error of 11 minutes 14 seconds per year, amounting to three days in four hundred years. To correct this, Pope Gregory XIII in 1582 retarded the calendar by ten days in a single year to account for the accumulated elapsed time and introduced an adjustment in intercalation whereby in the future the leap-year day would be omitted in the century years not divisible by 400, thus eliminating the accumulation of the excess of three days per 400 years. The Gregorian calendar is used in the West today, while the Julian form, unadjusted, remains the pattern by which B.C. years are still reckoned.

With so many different calendars in use in the Greek and Roman world, the conversion of a date given in an ancient calendar is not always an easy matter. Since ancient sources all give dates in terms of one or another ancient calendar, a great deal of effort has been expended to understand the operation of ancient calendars, so that reported dates can be converted in an understandable form. For some calendars, the precise relationship between their months and those of the Julian calendar is known; while for some others the relationship can be set out only approximately. In general, the calendars of the Greek cities are not very susceptible to reduction into exact Julian equivalences, while Hellenistic calendars based on Egyptian or Babylonian calendars can often provide dates with great accuracy. Once the period of the Roman Empire is reached, the institution of the Julian reform ensures that dates can be determined with great accuracy when they are given in terms of the Julian calendar itself or of one of the many calendars based on it.

There were other forms of time reckoning based on periods that do not accord with astronomical phenomena. The best known of these is the week, which is earliest attested as a seven-day period in Jewish usage. The seven-day week was well enough known to Greeks and Romans by Roman imperial times, but it was not commonly used until the third century A.D. as a means of designating days in addition to the number of the day of the month. By this time, the original Hebrew practice of merely enumerating the days of the week had given way to the use of the so-called planetary week, in which the days of the week were given names of the planets. It was, in fact, the increasing use of the planetary week in astrological as well as astronomical work that helped popularize the concept of the week in the first place. It was the seven-day week that ultimately replaced all other artificial divisions of the month, such as the Roman system of the eight-day market week or the division of the month into three ten-day periods, which may have served some formal purposes in the calendrical usage of some Greek cities.

Greeks and Romans also had a need to divide the day into segments, and had various means of designating and measuring elapsed time that could not be astronomically marked. The system of dividing the period from the beginning of one day to that of the next had long been known to Babylonians and Egyptians, and by the time their practice entered the ken of the Greeks, it had become a simple matter of dividing the periods of light and darkness into equal twelve-hour segments. The hours were not fixed lengths, as they are today: Greeks and Romans both divided the period from sunrise to sunset, and from sunset to dawn, into twelve lengths that were equal on any particular day, so that latitude and season affected the length of the hour. As daylight lengthened and nights grew shorter, daylight hours became longer and night hours shorter.

The hours were designated by numerals, and their passage could be followed tolerably well by the transit of the sun during the day and of the stars at night. Sundials, water clocks, star clocks, and shadow tables were used by Egyptians and Babylonians long before the rise of Hellenic civilization, and Herodotus claims that the Greeks learned the use of the sundial from the Babylonians. In any case, that technique of marking the passage of time was known very early among the Greeks. Fixed periods of time could be measured, when desired, by use of an instrument called a klepsydra, a device from which water leaked at a regular rate, so that each emptying produced an identical period of time. The mechanism was used by the Athenians to time speeches at public functions.

By late Hellenistic times, the technology of such mechanisms had developed great potential, for interest in astronomy had led to the development of very complex and precise geared devices, which operated to represent in model form the motions of the celestial bodies. They do not seem to have been machines aimed at predicting the locations of the bodies, and thus were illustrative rather than practical. The ingenuity with which the construction of these machines proceeded, however, makes it clear that Greeks could have produced workable and accurate mechanical clocks had they so desired. But, just as astronomical knowledge that made possible the institution of a more accurate calendar by the late third century could not be enforced on an uninterested population, so the capability for accurate time measurement was not taken up. In calendrical matters as in so many others, Greek practice was dictated by perceptions of practical human needs that were very different from our own.

BIBLIOGRAPHY

Elias J. Bickerman, *Chronology of the Ancient World*, 2d ed. (1980); Friedrich K. Ginzel, *Handbuch der mathematischen und technischen Chronologie*, 3 vols. (1906–1914); Agnes Kirsopp Michels, *The Calendar of the Roman Republic* (1967); Alan E. Samuel, *Greek and Roman Chronology* (1972).

ALPHABETS AND WRITING

RACHEL KITZINGER

THE ANCIENT GREEKS BELIEVED that writing was an important factor in the growth of their civilization. Prometheus, in Aeschylus' play *Prometheus Bound* (442–470), boasts of the gifts he has given mankind:

> Listen to the sufferings of men, how at first they were witless and how then I gave them intelligence and skilled minds. . . . At their beginning men looked with their eyes but saw nothing and with their ears listened but did not hear. Like dreams they muddled through each moment of their long lives. They used neither brick nor wood to make themselves shelter but lived in caves like weightless ants deep in the sunless recesses. They could not tell the signs of winter coming nor of spring with all its flowers nor summer and its harvest. They managed all without thought until I revealed to them patterns, hard to detect, of the stars' rising and setting. The use of numbers, best of all knowledge, I taught them and the composition of letters, how to make them work as memory and mother of the arts. I put the yoke and saddlebag on beasts to be man's slave, to take the burden of his toil; and for his leisure harnessed the horse to chariot and to obey the rein. And without me they could not now raise sail to cross the sea. Such were the devices I invented for mankind.

Along with sailing, agriculture, building, astronomy, mathematics, medicine, and civil jurisprudence, writing represents cultural stability and progress in the Greek mind. It is this aspect of writing—the role it played in the development of ancient civilization—that will be the focus of this essay.

We must first turn to the moment when the Greeks took the alphabet from their eastern neighbors and ask the following questions: Where did the Greek alphabet come from? What were its antecedents in the East? Where, when, and how was it transmitted from the East to Greece? If we then consider the nature of oral culture in Greece before the arrival of the alphabet, we will gain some sense of the changes that writing prompted. With this dramatic step from East to West the alphabet entered the Western world, and the story of its movement into Italy and its adaptation by the Romans to a form very much like our own alphabet and the other alphabets of Europe, is quickly told.

SOURCES AND PRECEDENTS

The most prevalent tradition among the Greeks themselves was that their alphabet came from the Phoenicians. The fifth-century historian Herodotus has this to say on the matter (*Histories* 5.58, George Rawlinson, trans. [1880]):

> Now the Phoenicians . . . introduced into Greece upon their arrival a great variety of arts, among the rest that of writing, whereof the Greek till then had, as I think, been ignorant. And originally they shaped their letters exactly like all the other Phoenicians, but afterwards, in course of time, they changed by degrees their language, and together with it the form likewise of their characters. Now the Greeks who dwelt about those parts at that time were chiefly the Ionians. The Phoenician letters were accordingly adopted by them, but with some variation in the shape of a few, and so they arrived at the present use, still calling the letters Phoenician, as justice required, after the name of those who were the first to introduce them into Greece.

Certainly scholars are now in agreement that one of the tribes speaking a North Semitic language, if not the Phoenicians themselves, passed on their written symbols to the Greeks (see Driver, 1948, for another point of view). Since there is strong archaeological evidence for Greek contact with the Phoenicians in particular, we may accept the Greek tradition on this point as a working premise.

The Phoenician writing system itself had a long history of development before the Greeks borrowed it. It is important to understand the particular structure of the Phoenician system in comparison with other writing systems in the East in order to see what advantages the Greeks inherited with this system and how these advantages allowed the Greeks to make the final step to a fully developed alphabet.

We will look briefly at three of the major scripts in use in the second and first millennia before Christ: Egyptian hieroglyphics, Mesopotamian cuneiform, and finally the North Semitic "near-alphabet." Although the historical relationship between these systems is a vexed subject beyond the scope of this article, we can, without asking questions of interdependence, describe them, so as to reveal how far writing had developed when the Greeks learned it.

Since about the middle of the fourth millennium the Egyptians had been using a script later called hieroglyphics (sacred carvings), which was to remain a complex system mastered only by professional scribes to make religious and state records. With about six hundred signs in common use (and hundreds more to draw upon), the system reproduced the spoken language in three ways. First, a single symbol could stand for an entire word; it therefore represented a unit of meaning in the language, not a unit of sound. Second, a word could also be written through syllabic phoneticization, where the written symbol stood for a consonant plus any vowel, or for a consonant plus any vowel plus another consonant. In addition some of the word signs were used in a third capacity, as determinatives. When placed before another word a determinative channels that word into a category—god, man, mountain, country—to help the reader, who might be misled by the imperfections and ambiguities of the phonetic system, when reading the following word.

Since hieroglyphics included twenty-four simple-syllable signs, the Egyptians could adequately have written their language in a purely phonetic system. They never chose to simplify in this way, however, which they could have done by ridding themselves of the redundant word and complex-syllable signs. At least one reason for maintaining their complex system was its enhancement of the aura of writing and the privileged status of the priestly class.

Closely related in its basic structure to the Egyptian system is Mesopotamian cuneiform, which the Assyrians and Babylonians took over from the Sumerians around the middle of the third millennium and improved upon subsequently. Cuneiform gained its name in modern times from the distinctive wedge-shape of the marks (Latin *cuneus:* wedge) that the writing implements made in clay to form the elements of the script. There is a vast medical, scientific, religious, legal, and poetic literature preserved in cuneiform, the first flourishing of which belongs to the period of Babylonian ascendancy (*ca.* 1700–1530 B.C.). Cuneiform has almost as many signs as Egyptian hieroglyphics (about 600), although fewer of these signs were used with any frequency. It too used three different kinds of symbols: word signs, syllabic signs, and determinatives. However, whereas in the phonetic part of Egyptian the vowels were unexpressed, cuneiform phoneticized both consonants and vowels with one hundred simple syllabic signs (consonant plus vowel; vowel plus consonant) and many more signs for complex syllables. To add to the complication, many of these signs were homophones or polyphones. That is, the same sign could stand for various similar, but not identical, sounds or for syllables with vastly different sounds that were connected semantically. Like the Egyptians, and for similar reasons, the Assyrians and Babylonians did not completely reduce their writing system to the one hundred simple-syllable signs, although these alone would have been adequate to express the language and a gradual process of simplification did take place. An additional reason for retaining the different kinds of symbols was to ensure complete accuracy in reading. The imperfections of one kind of symbol were compensated for by the virtues of another.

The great step forward that both hieroglyphics and cuneiform made over previous systems was the discovery of phoneticization. But neither system was reduced only to phonetic representation; writing remained complex and cumbersome, the property of a limited number of professional writers who mastered the hundreds of signs necessary and showed no interest in making their secret skill available to the general population.

The case is different for our third group of writing systems, those developed in the second millennium to set down the Semitic languages spoken throughout the Middle East and the Arabic peninsula, of which Phoenician was one. While the relationship between these languages and their systems of writing is complicated and not completely known, the inner structure of the systems is similar. They used only simple-syllable signs and so reduced the number of symbols necessary for writing the language to between twenty-two and thirty. The price paid for such simplicity was to leave vowel sounds completely unexpressed: they were to be supplied by the reader as context and knowledge of the spoken language allowed. Semitic languages are suited to such a system because the semantic root of a word consists only of consonants; the vowels express, among other things, changes in tense, person, and voice. For example, the Phoenician word for "king" contains the consonants *m-l-k;* but what vowels were pronounced with these consonants we do not know. (In Hebrew the word is *melech*; in Arabic *malaku*.) Because Semitic writing fails to separate and represent equally consonants and vowels, it does not reproduce fully the spoken language and permits a great deal of ambiguity, which the reader must resolve to understand the text accurately. (There is a modern type of shorthand somewhat like this: APTMNT 4 RNT; only familiarity with the spoken language and idiom allows us to read this as "apartment for rent.") Nonetheless, the advance in simplicity and efficiency that the Semitic systems made over hieroglyphics and cuneiform helps to explain why they spread so far and were adapted to so many different languages: the North Semitic branch to Greek, the Aramaic branch to Hebrew, Arabic, and the Indic scripts.

We can see, then, that when the Greeks learned Phoenician (North Semitic) writing, they inherited a system that had moved a long way toward full efficiency. It remained for the Greeks to take the final step away from a syllabary to a full alphabet by using symbols to represent separately the vowels and consonants that make up a syllable. Although heard as a single unit, syllables must be divided when written to produce flexibility and efficiency in the system. For example, we can write the words *dangle, land, lad, lead, lag, nag, elan, glad,* and so on, with only six different symbols if we represent letters instead of syllables. The Greeks could write with equal economy, in part because the Phoenicians already had a system reduced to pure consonant sounds (and, with glottal stops and semiconsonants, sounds very close to vowel sounds).

At an early stage in their own history—in fact, before they borrowed and improved the Phoenician script—the Greeks had written their language in a syllabic system far less efficient than Semitic writing. Known today as Linear B, this system used at least eighty-nine symbols to express the various vowel-plus-consonant and consonant-plus-vowel combinations that the Greek of that period required, as well as a number of ideograms to duplicate the semantic sense of the word represented in phonetic form. The Linear B tablets, which record the contents of royal storehouses, tributes paid to the king, and offerings to various gods, date from the Mycenaean period (*ca.* 1400–1200).

Because of its comparatively localized nature and confined use, and because of its general inefficiency, the Linear B writing system did not survive the disruption caused by the invasions of the twelfth century that destroyed much of Mycenaean culture. Thus it may be said that at an early date the Greeks "forgot" how to write. It was a fortunate loss, however, for when they developed their second script some 500 years later, they were able to use the Phoenician system to create a script that was a true alphabet. The critical factor in this final step was that for Greek, unlike Semitic, a writer had to represent vowel sounds accurately to reproduce in a comprehensible form the spoken language. For example, a Greek had to be able to write *a-n-a-x* for "king"; *n-x* would have been at best ambiguous, at worst incomprehensible. So, compelled by this necessity it would seem, they created symbols for pure vowel sounds.

We are now in a position to consider the evidence for the borrowing of the North Semitic, probably Phoenician, alphabet by the Greeks. As we have seen, the Greek tradition asserts that the alphabet came from the Phoenicians. But with such an unreliable source as tradition we must look for confirmation in the other kinds of evidence we have available. That evidence is largely archaeological: the remnants of inscriptions preserved on stone, clay, and metal that allow us to reconstruct the progress, chronological and spatial, of letter forms throughout the ancient world. However, the first piece of evidence comes from the names that the Greeks gave to the letters of the alphabet.

Those names were as follows (those in parentheses were to fall into disuse): alpha, beta, gamma, delta, epsilon, (digamma), zeta, eta, theta, iota, kappa, lambda, mu, nu, xi, omicron, pi, (koppa), rho, sigma, tau, upsilon, phi, chi, psi, omega. With the exception of digamma, epsilon, omicron, upsilon, and omega, these names mean nothing at all in Greek but are very close to the names of the twenty-two letters of the Semitic "near-alphabet" (as reconstructed from Hebrew):

aleph, beth, gimel, daleth, he, waw, zayin, heth, teth, yod, kaph, lamed, mem, nun, samek, ayin, pe, sade, qoph, resh, shin, taw, where each letter name has a meaning in Semitic. For example, *aleph* means "ox," *beth* "house," and *shin* "tooth."

In addition, epigraphical evidence shows that the shapes of the letters in very early Greek inscriptions resemble the shapes of North Semitic letters. And the order of the letters in the Greek alphabet corresponds to the order of letters in the Semitic "near-alphabet." Finally, early Greek inscriptions are written from right to left, following the Semitic habit; at a later time the Greeks changed to writing from left to right.

THE PLACE OF BORROWING

The circumstances surrounding the borrowing of the alphabet by the Greeks from the Phoenicians are almost completely unknown. We can imagine that the place must have been a town or settlement where Greeks and Phoenicians were in close contact. That there was one place and one incident of borrowing seems clear from certain ways in which the various Greek alphabets developed soon after the initial borrowing: although they differ from one another in some aspects, they are consistent in their differences from the North Semitic script. That both the teacher and the learner were not fully versed in each other's language is also clear from the inaccuracy and incompleteness in the process of borrowing.

The Greeks and Phoenicians came into contact because both had extended their trade activities into each other's territory. Any of the sites, therefore, where archaeologists have turned up evidence of the simultaneous presence of Greeks and Phoenicians might have served as the place where the forms and names of the letters changed hands (and mouths). If the place was in Greece, it must also have had extensive trade connections with the rest of Greece; this would account for the alphabet's spreading as quickly as it seems to have done. The most likely Greek possibilities are the islands of Cyprus, Crete, Thera (Santorini), or Rhodes, although each hypothesis has drawbacks. Cyprus, for example, had its own script related to Linear B and to Linear A (a Minoan script dating from the seventeenth to the end of the fifteenth century B.C.). This writing system remained in use in Cyprus but never spread elsewhere. Some scholars believe that the presence of an already established system would prevent the borrowing and creating of another. Crete had trade relations with the Phoenicians and with the rest of Greece, but there is no memory in the literary tradition of Crete as the source of the Greek alphabet, although there is a lively tradition for other places.

The discovery in North Syria of a Greek settlement of an appropriate date, at the site of the modern town Al-Mina, has led many scholars to assume that it was either there or at a similar settlement actually in the territory known to the Greeks as Phoenicia that the Greeks learned their alphabet. We can imagine traders from various parts of Greece bringing their goods to a place like Al-Mina and returning with the alphabet in a standardized but only partially formed or partially learned Greek version. One town then passed it on to some of its neighbors and trade connections in a further-developed, local form. In this way there arose in a short time a proliferation of local forms of the alphabet throughout the Greek world, the so-called epichoric alphabets. For example, the Attic alphabet differs from that of Corinth, a near neighbor which acquired the alphabet independently, as much as it does from the alphabet of distant Rhodes, but it resembles the alphabets of other close neighbors, the islands of Aegina and Euboea. Unfortunately, no inscriptions have yet turned up at the site to confirm the Al-Mina hypothesis, which is nonetheless now widely accepted.

TECHNOLOGY

Semitic order	Phoenician	Archaic Greek	Eastern Greek	Western Greek	Etruscan	Archaic Latin	Classical Latin	Roman
1	K ⱡ	A ⱡ	A alpha a	A A	A	ΛA	A a a	A a
2	9 9	ᵹ 8	B bēta b	B	ᵹ	B B	B be b	B b
3	↑	↑ ↑	Γ gamma g	∧ (	⅃	< C	C ce k	C c
							G ge g	G g
4	△	△	△ delta d	△ D	◁	D D	D de d	D d
5	⇂	⇂ ⇂	E ei, epsilon e	E ⋌	⇂	⋌E	E e e	E e
6	Y	⇂ w		F E	⇂	∧ Iʼ	F ef f	F f
		Y	Υ u, upsilon u	Y Y	V	V	V u u,w	V,U,W v,u,v
							Y y y	Y y
7	I	I	Z zēta dz, zd	I	I		Z zeta z	Z z
8	⊟	⊟H h	H ēta ē	⊟H h	⊟	⊟H	H ha h	H h
9	⊕	⊕	⊙ thēta th	⊕	⊗			
10	⅂	I ⋋	I iōta i	I	I	I	I i i,y	I,J i,j
11	Y Y	ⱡ K	K kappa k	K	ⱡ	K	K ka k	K k
12	L	⋀ ⋁	Λ labda l	L ∧	⌐	L	L el l	L l
13	⌇ ᛘ	ᛘM	M mū m	M ᛘ	ᛘ	ᛘM	M em m	M m
14	⅂ ⋋	ᛘ ⋋	N nū n	N	ᛘ	N	N en n	N n
15	⟊	⟊	Ξ ksei ks		⊞			
16	O	O	O ou, omikron o	O	O	O O	O o o	O o
			Ω ōmega ō					
17	↑	↑	ΓΠ pei p	ΓΠ	Π	ΓP	P pe p	P p
18	ⱡ	M s			M			
19	φ	φQ q		Q	φ	φQ	Q qu q	Q q
20	ᑫ ᑫ	ᑫᑫ	P rhō r	P R	ᑫ	P R	R er r	R r
21	W	⋌ ⋋	⌇Σ sigma s	⌇⌇	⋋	⋌S	S es s	S s
22	+ X	T	T tau t	T	T	TT	T te t	T t
			Φ phei ph	Φ	Φ			
			X khei kh	X ks	X	X	X ix ks	X x
			Ψ psei ps	ΨKh	Ψ			

Development of the western alphabets. *Reproduced from Alfred C. Moorhouse, THE TRIUMPH OF THE ALPHABET © 1953 BY HENRY SCHUMAN, NEW YORK*

THE DATE OF BORROWING

If our ignorance about the location hinders the imagination in reconstructing the actual transaction, equally if not more troubling is our uncertainty about the date. Here, opinions of scholars have ranged from the fourteenth century B.C. down to the end of the eighth. Once again the evidence available to us is not conclusive. However, as of the mid 1980s there is a general, though not unanimous, agreement on a century—the eighth—and on the middle of that century rather than the beginning or the end. Perhaps the most

402

persuasive piece of evidence is the absence of any Greek inscriptions that can be securely dated earlier than the end of the eighth century. Although some earlier inscriptions may have been written on a material that has not survived, this possibility cannot explain the total silence from any earlier period, a silence that may yet be broken by further archaeological investigation. Another criterion for dating, that of identifying the period when Semitic letter forms most resemble the early Greek letter forms, is too subjective to be conclusive. However, despite the paucity of reliable evidence, if we take into account the date of the earliest existing inscriptions and of the emergence of other alphabets borrowed from the Greek (Phrygian and Etruscan in particular), as well as the history of the mutual influence between Greeks and Phoenicians, we can settle, however tentatively, on a date around 750 B.C. for the transferral of the forms and names of the Semitic letters to the Greeks. If we accept this date, we must also imagine that the alphabet, once the Greeks learned it, was adapted to the Greek language and spread throughout the Greek world with remarkable rapidity. All we are really assuming, however, is that the Greeks were quick to pick up the mechanics of representing spoken sound in written form. It took them centuries after being introduced to the mechanics to understand and develop the advantages (and disadvantages) of literacy that an efficient writing system, easily accessible to the general population, afforded. This easy accessibility was a major factor in the development and use of the Greek alphabet and distinguished it radically from previous writing systems.

CIRCUMSTANCES OF THE BORROWING

If we have had some difficulty in determining when and where the Greeks got their alphabet, we have at least been helped by a certain amount of evidence. To answer the questions of who, how, and why, we can rely only on our imaginations and our common sense. Since trade provided the context for the borrowing and the spread of the alphabet, we may assume that it was either a merchant or a craftsman who became fascinated by the possibility of recording spoken language in a permanent and transferable form. A merchant may have witnessed and understood the aid to memory and objectivity that writing offers in the recording of accounts and contracts, although none of the surviving early inscriptions shows this use. Especially in trade between people speaking different languages or between those who depended successfully on verbal agreements, the perceived advantage would not necessarily have inspired the requisite mental energy.

A craftsman, on the other hand, when shown the possibility of making his vase or statue "speak" by writing a dedication, or even his own name, on it, might well have been excited by the commercial as well as the aesthetic value of such an invention. In fact, one of the earliest inscriptions that we have in Greek is scratched on a vase to be awarded as a prize in a dancing contest. Found at the Dipylon Gate in Athens, it is dated to about 725 B.C. The first line of the inscriptions reads *hos nūn orchēstōn pantōn atalōtata paizei*; the second is incomplete and illegible. The line is in dactylic hexameter, the meter of oral epic, and means, "Whoever of all the dancers now most gracefully sports..." Scratched on the vase after it had been glazed and fired, the inscription could have been written by anyone—maker, donor, victor, or indeed a stranger showing off his ability to write—but it illustrates one of the earliest and most common uses of writing, one whose value lies in giving a voice of ownership or dedication to an inanimate object.

One scholar has even gone so far as to suggest that it was a poet who first understood that the Phoenicians could record lines of poetry, and was inspired to learn the Semitic letter forms and adapt them to Greek in order to record his own verse. Although this suggestion seems unlikely, given the completely oral nature of verse composition and performance in this period, it makes one implication that may be correct. The most striking innovation that the Greeks made in the Semitic script was the use of separate signs for vowel sounds. They may have been inspired to this step at least in part by the desire to record lines of poetry like the dedication on the Dipylon vase mentioned above, for the metrical pattern of Greek poetry depends on the arrangement of long and short vowels in a line. The early alphabet did not distinguish between long and short *o*-sounds and *e*-sounds (and indeed the Greek alphabet never developed separate letters to distinguish between the long and short sounds of *a, i,* and *u*). Although a writer might assume the reader's ability to determine for himself the length of a vowel through his knowledge of the pronunciation of the word, the presence of the vowel sound itself could not be left completely unexpressed.

ADAPTATION AND MODIFICATION

But we are getting ahead of ourselves. We must imagine a Greek, interested by the sight of the Phoenician writing, asking to be taught the Semitic alphabet. As the Phoenician formed each letter, he would speak its name out loud and make the Semitic-language sound that the letter represented. The Greek would memorize the shape and its name simultaneously. However, many of the sounds the letters stood for would be unfamiliar to him, since the Greek language did not use them. At this point we must assume that the principle of acrophony came into play; that is, instead of associating the true Semitic sounds with the letters, the Greek assigned to each letter a sound familiar to him from Greek that corresponded to the initial sound of the *name* of the letter. In this way he was able to match the letters to Greek sounds and put them together to write Greek words.

This process of appropriation obviously involved a certain amount of creative misunderstanding. For example, the Semitic letter *aleph,* which represents a glottal stop, became in Greek the symbol for the vowel *a*-sound, which, it could be argued, was the sound that seemed to the Greek ear to begin the word "aleph." For similar reasons, the Semitic letter *he,* also a glottal, became both the long and short *e*-sound, and the half-consonant letter *yod* became iota, the *i*-sound. The Semitic letter *waw,* which is also a half-consonant, served two purposes. It was kept as a half-consonant (the short-lived Greek letter digamma), but was also altered slightly in form to serve as the vowel *u*-sound (Greek upsilon).

The transformation of the Semitic *heth* (which became a vowel in some places and an aspirate in others) is a more complicated story. In the version of the alphabet used in Ionia (Western Asia Minor), the Semitic *heth* was heard as an *e*-sound, because the Ionic dialect did not have an *h*-sound. They therefore ignored the initial *h* of the name (or did not hear it) and adapted the letter to a long *e*-sound (eta). Other dialects that did use an aspirate at the beginning of words used this letter for the *h*-sound, which begins its Semitic name. By the end of the fifth century, however, the Ionic use of eta as long *e* had been adopted universally, and the *h*-sound was represented by the asper (c), a rough-breathing mark derived from ⊢, the result of cutting the eta (Θ) in two. (The other half, ⊣, developed into the smooth-breathing lenis mark '.)

With this practical yet ingenious principle of "acrophonics," the Greek alphabet assigned letters to vowel sounds where none had existed in Semitic. (For a different opinion see Gelb [1963].) After the initial stage of adapting the twenty-two Semitic letters to Greek sounds, we must assume at least three more steps in the formation of the Greek alphabet. However, these further stages were not identical in all the places where the alphabet spread after the initial borrowing. So we find in early Greek alphabets a great variety surrounding the letters involved in these changes: the sibilants (sigma, zeta, xi, san), the "additional letters" (phi, chi, psi), and the final letter, omega, a long *o*-sound.

The Phoenician language had four sibilant sounds and letters: *zayin* (like our *z*), *samek* (*s*), *sade* (*ts*), and *shin* (*sh*). Considerable confusion resulted when these letters were adapted to the Greek sibilant sounds. Eventually all Greek alphabets ended up with a letter like the *zayin* in form, but representing a *dz*-sound and with the name zeta (probably derived from the Phoenician letter name *sade*). To represent the unvoiced *s*-sound, some Greek alphabets used a letter that looked like Semitic *shin* but was called sigma (which resembles the Semitic name *samek*), while others used a letter that they called san (possibly after the Semitic *zayin*) and whose form perhaps came from the letter *sade*, in which position as the eighteenth letter it appeared in the alphabets that used it. The alphabets that used san did not use sigma and vice versa. Similarly, some Greeks adopted the shape of the Phoenician *samek* for a *ks*-sound and called the letter xi, perhaps from the name of the letter *sin* (or perhaps by analogy with the new letter chi). Other alphabets did not include the letter xi but produced its sound by writing the two consonant sounds (*k-s*) with separate letters; still others used the sign X (chi) for the *ks*-sound.

At some point fairly soon after the twenty-two letters of the Semitic system were adapted to Greek sounds, three new letters were added to the alphabet, perhaps in Ionia, to represent sounds that had not found a letter in the initial twenty-two. Their shape may have been borrowed from a cursive form of Phoenician writing or adopted from another writing system—Cypriot, for example. Or they may have been freely invented. The letters, Φ (phi), X (chi), Ψ (psi) —aspirated *p* and *k,* and *ps*—appeared at the end of the alphabet everywhere they were adopted but did not initially represent the same sounds everywhere. Although the various early Greek alphabets can be divided into rough geographical areas by their use of these letters, other inconsistencies among them do not follow the same geographical pattern.

In Ionia some time before 660 B.C. omega, the final letter of the alphabet, was invented to represent a long *o*-sound, to match the distinction in the Ionic alphabet between the short *e* (epsilon) and the long *e* (eta). Not all alphabets at first felt the need to distinguish between long and short vowel sounds with separate letters, but eventually they all recognized omega as a letter of the alphabet. With the addition of these four letters we reach the number twenty-six. Two letters of the original twenty-two were abandoned early on by most of the Greek alphabets: the koppa (Q) and the digamma (ϝ); however, both are important for the history of the alphabet's development. Before they disappeared from the writing of Greek, they infiltrated the Etruscan and Roman alphabets, finally showing up in ours as the letters Q and F.

From this necessarily complicated account of the early history of the Greek alphabet we gain some sense of the progress of an invention as sophisticated as writing in the Mediterranean world. In an atmosphere of expanding geographical and intellectual limits, where trade established contact between formerly isolated places, and where the Greeks were discovering and making their own the advances of other civilizations, the alphabet exhibits both the unity and diversity that flower in such circumstances. Whether by accident or by conscious or semiconscious decision, the creation of vowels as separate symbols at the first stage of the Greek alphabet's history was the key to its rapid spread and enthusiastic local variation throughout the Greek world. For the first time, a system of symbols representing speech was efficient enough and adaptable enough to differences in dialect and pronunciation so that writing could be viewed as a tool available to anyone determined to acquire the skill. The Greek alphabet never belonged to a privileged few who gave it the aura of a sacred mystery, of an obscure and hidden code available only to those in power. As each city-state discovered it, made it its own by adapting it to a particular dialect, and passed it on, the alphabet became a reflection of the local language, while at the same time registering the fact that these languages were all Greek. Dialects heard spoken can seem to be different languages; when seen written in a common alphabet they are revealed as variations of a shared possession.

While the Greek alphabet remained differentiated locally throughout the fifth century, there was a gradual movement during the sixth and fifth centuries toward the Ionic as the standard alphabet. The Ionic differed significantly from the Attic alphabet; for example, it used the eta for a long *e* instead of an *h*-sound and the symbols Ψ for the *ps*- and χ for *kh*-sounds, respectively. We cannot be sure why the Ionic became the universally accepted form of the alphabet, but it is tempting to speculate that the Homeric poems were responsible for such standardization. We may be fairly certain that the *Iliad* and the *Odyssey* were first written down using the alphabet of Ionia, where tradition places their source. With the ascendancy these poems acquired in the Greek world came perhaps the authority and prominence of the alphabet in which they were initially written. If this is true, the decree of 403 by which Athens officially adopted the Ionic alphabet and the similar though less official process of adoption throughout the Greek world illustrate the independence of literary influence from the political competitiveness that continually divided the Greek states from one another.

ORAL AND WRITTEN CULTURE

Before tracing the route of the alphabet to Italy we may linger to consider what effect the arrival of the alphabet had on the development of Greek literature and culture. Although it is impossible to speak simply of cause and effect, we can at least sketch some of the changes that literacy brought to literature and speculate about its effect on the intellectual development of the Greeks at least until the end of the fifth century, by which time literacy was well established. Obviously this is a vast topic and only a few suggestions can be made here.

In the latter half of the eighth century, when the alphabet was introduced, the Greeks had already developed an oral literature, examples of which have come down to us in written form, in the *Iliad* and the *Odyssey* and fragments of other epics. The poetic sophistication of these poems exceeds comparable epics from Near Eastern cultures precisely because, it could be argued, they were developed orally over centuries without the intrusion of a cumbersome script. Their form and content offer a glimpse into the workings of a culture completely unfamiliar with the written word, one in which poems are preserved over generations by repetition, handed on from one poet to the next in the course of many performances. But each repetition is not a word-for-word reproduction; rather, each poet, using a common stock of formulaic expressions and a sense of thematic structures inherited from years of listening, retells in metrical form a story he has heard before from another poet. Each telling will be a new variation on an old theme, although the poet may be under the impression that he is re-creating verbatim a poem he has heard before. Poems repeated in this way from place to place and generation to generation carry the memory of the past and thus represent "history" for the listeners. Along with other rituals that the society performs, these recitations are the focus of a sense of community, of a shared culture as it is represented in the narrative of the poems. The poetic style that allows for the kind of "memorization" by which a poet like Homer, when he "sings" the *Iliad*, re-creates extemporaneously a poem of approximately 13,000 lines, mirrors and perhaps to some degree shapes the way of thinking of the poet and of the audience. Some people have argued that the length of the *Iliad* and the *Odyssey* can only be explained by Homer's knowledge of writing. Even if this is true, other characteristics of the poems are entirely due to the long oral tradition that precedes them.

The style is rhythmic and repetitive in its sounds, full of assonance and alliteration. The sentence structure is paratactic: sentence is added to sentence without subordination. Images are concrete and lend themselves to sensual apprehension. The narrative describes human and divine action and speech in a pattern not defined by the linear progression of pages turned, but by the often circular and digressive wanderings of the poet's associative memory. The formulation over centuries of the content of the narrative ensures that to a large degree it conveys, and indeed forms, the values and patterns of behavior within the society, for which it serves as a collective memory.

It is not only the poet whose creative method is grounded in the demands of oral recitation, however. The audience, as it listens, follows the progress of the narrative by a kind of imitative process, an identification with the poet and his words. Through the persuasive power of sound, rhythm, and image, intimacy between teller and listener results in the assimilation of information and values through the spoken word. This intimacy of speech is a feature of oral society that appears in contexts other than the performance of epic narrative. In an oral culture all political and legal processes depend on the persuasive power of those in authority and the ability of men to remember and repeat what has been said in the past. Consider the embassy to Achilles' tent in the ninth book of the *Iliad*, where Phoenix, Odysseus, and Ajax attempt to persuade their comrade to reenter the battle. The future of the Greek army seems to depend on their ability to move him to action. In both Odysseus' and Phoenix's speeches, one of the most forceful means of persuasion is memory of the past. Odysseus recalls for Achilles, word for word, the commands that Peleus gave him nine years before, when he left for Troy, words admonishing him to refrain from strife with his fellow warriors. Phoenix establishes his authority to advise Achilles by recounting the long history of his relationship with the younger warrior and his family. Phoenix also retells the old story of Meleager, which he uses as a paradigm to awaken Achilles to the demands of the present situation. Throughout the *Iliad* Nestor, the adviser to all, gains his authority by his long life and hence his rich memory of past events, which he evokes as the means for understanding the present and for shaping action in it.

In an oral society language cannot be abstracted from the need to argue, persuade, and remember. There is no place for, or possibility of, abstract thought, for the removal of language from the concrete, sensual reality of people's lives, past and present. Thoughts moving counter to the mainstream of culture and tradition, which call into question reality as it is perceived and agreed upon by the population as a whole, can only be preserved through the continuing existence and speech of their originator or their adoption by others who have been persuaded to internalize them into the patterns of their own speech.

Similarly, language gains power only inasmuch as the speaker can persuade the listener of its truth in a form that is also memorable. Much depends on the verbal authority and ability of the speaker. Odysseus in the *Odyssey* is the master of lies, but his lies are never pure fiction; rather, they are rearrangements of his own history or the history of his fellow heroes. They are believed because they make sense in the mouth of the man telling them. In such a society, language cannot free itself of the relationship between speaker and listener, cannot exist outside of the moment of speaking and hearing and remembering. Private thought and private speech cannot exist, at least not in a form that survives the moment of utterance.

These conditions of experience change with the arrival of the written word; not immediately, but inevitably. While some aspects of oral society remained powerfully present in Athens and other city-states throughout the sixth and fifth centuries, writing played an important role both in the political life and in the intellectual and literary life of the Greeks. Although it is artificial to separate political and intellectual development, since the two areas constantly influenced each other, we will look at them separately as far as is possible, following first some events in the intellectual history of the sixth and fifth centuries and then looking at the relationship of writing and speech in fifth-century Athenian democracy.

Among poets, one of the first effects of the written word is the notion of the "author," the poetic or narrative "I." Homer's poems, which were composed in an oral context even though they were written down (when, no one knows; possibly soon after their composition, just as possibly years later), reveal the presence of the poet only in their telling, in the arrangement and juxtaposition of traditional elements. Much like Odysseus with his lies, the poet "sews together" (*rhapsode* means sewer of songs) the traditional elements of his narrative in a way that is distinctive and personal. But the narrator has no voice within the story. The poet remains the anonymous source of memory, an instrument of the Muses who gives the community not only its entertainment but also its history and, to some extent, its moral judgments and sense of values.

In contrast to Homeric anonymity, when we look at a poem by Sappho, one of the lyric poets who flourished in the late seventh and sixth centuries, we find the poet presenting herself as the subject of the poem. The one complete poem of Sappho that survives is a hymn to Aphrodite in which the poet appeals to the goddess for relief from her lovesick state and makes Aphrodite address her directly, by name, in the poem. While the hymn form is taken from the oral tradition and Sappho's song is composed for oral delivery, the intimate and private nature of the poem and the self-consciousness of the poetic persona are quite distinct from the communal concerns of oral poetry. One of the reasons for this new revelation of the feelings and thoughts of isolated (though often repeated) moments in an individual's life, which can be seen in many of the lyric poets, is the freedom that writing gives the poet to compose in isolation, with the knowledge that the poem can be preserved beyond its performance in written form. Sappho still expects her poem to be sung, not read, and the lyric poets in general depended heavily on the forms, diction, and subject matter of songs developed before writing. But writing allowed the poet to reflect on and manipulate these forms and their traditional subject matter with a newfound autonomy; in addition, it liberated the life of the text from the moment of performance.

Writing and Intellectual Change

Because the written word dismantled the kind of interdependence of poet and audience that had existed in the purely oral society, and because it eliminated the need implicit in that relationship to preserve and re-create over and over the traditions and memory of a society, it also helped to revolutionize how people thought. For it allowed the possibility of preserving thought outside of memory, of abstracting it, releasing it from the concrete, and of using language to question assumptions and explore new ways of examining the past and the reality of the present. Without the use of writing, the pre-Socratic philosophers of the sixth and fifth centuries could not have worked out their ideas or developed the objectivity and independence of mind that lie at the heart of their work. Their questioning of what composes the physical world, their speculations about aspects of being and reality not visible to the eye, their determination to discover the permanent laws of the universe were made possible and, at least in part, were inspired by writing. The fact that law codes, for example, were now recorded in writing and therefore made permanent surely contributed to the belief in, and the attempt to discover, constant, observable laws within the functioning of the universe.

Another indication of the link between a new kind of thought and writing is the development, around this time, of prose, a purely written use of language. Although many of the pre-Socratic philosophers continued to write in poetry and started to develop within poetic diction an abstract vocabulary to express their ideas, it is also likely that some, perhaps the sixth-century thinkers Anaximenes and Anaximander of Miletus, were among the earliest experimenters with prose, finding it a form of writing more conducive to the kind of abstract thought they wished to record. This is not to say that writing, whether in poetry or prose, caused the investigations that permitted these philosophers (a title given them in hindsight, to describe their role as the predecessors of Plato and Aristotle) to move intellectually beyond the cosmologies and mythologies of the past. A number of interdependent social, political, and economic factors contributed to this movement: for example, increased contact with the scientific knowledge of the Near East, the development of the polis (the city-state) and its social and political offices, and so on. But writing, both as a symbol of permanence and as a tool for independent, objective thought, was an essential element in the intellectual growth of the period and in the questioning of previous ways of thinking, largely as they were embodied in the Homeric poems and those of Hesiod.

It is not only among the pre-Socratic philosophers, but also among the early logographers (chroniclers) that we find the first reliable evidence for the writing of prose, a style of composition finally fully divorced from the demands of memory and an oral society and suited to the demands of categorization and analysis. Prose writing had its roots in the early use of the written word to replace verse as a means of recording and remembering information, from lists of priests, magistrates, athletic victors, legal codes, and treaties to recordings of the sayings of wise men. From the simple act of recording in prosaic form the chronicles of the past, we can trace through Hecataeus, Hellanicus, and finally Herodotus the emergence of the desire to accumulate, categorize, and analyze that information, test its accuracy, and extract from it patterns of human behavior, all relatively free of the need to prescribe any single such pattern. Here again, the writer, unlike the oral poet, is not bound by the need of his society to elaborate, preserve, and reinforce the categories and patterns that society has created for itself, and so is able to expound what he understands from the point of view of someone outside, looking in.

Hence, we see the birth of that area of intellectual endeavor we know as history. Like philosophic thought, it was made possible by the ability that writing gives to accumulate and preserve observations of the natural and human world, to speculate in analytical and abstract language about causes and systems, and thereby to predict and to test predictions against events as they occur.

The historian's aim was not so much to preserve the past as it was to explain it. Herodotus' *Histories*, written in the third quarter of the fifth century, is the first prose book of great length, and the earliest prose writing to survive; it is twice as long as either Homeric poem. In his circuitous excursiveness, his strong narrative sense, and his avowed reliance on hearsay accounts, we can easily recognize Herodotus' dependence on the oral style and the preservation of knowledge and information in the form of traditional stories to be told and remembered. But we also witness the existence of an objective and abstracting intellect in his attempts to establish by comparison and logical principle the truth of the stories he has heard, in his comparative evaluations of various cultures and their customs, in his search for the causes and patterns of the events he records, and in his rationalizing of myth.

The implied relationship of Herodotus to his audience also has an oral and a written side. We have good evidence that the *Histories* was very popular and that this popularity was gained through public readings of parts of the text. This success was therefore based on the same kind of oral, public recitation that gave the Homeric poems a popular audience but could only apply to segments of Herodotus' work. The book is far too long to be recited in its entirety. Therefore, Herodotus must have written with the knowledge that his work could be appreciated as an integrated whole only by a small, elite, interested, and comprehending group of readers. In his attempt to give unity and coherence to a vast amount and variety of material, Herodotus is fully reliant on the written word, which he is the first to use for such a project, and on readers with a willingness to understand the kind of effect for which such a book strives. As a historian he is, in fact, one of the earliest experimenters with literary form, as well as historical analysis. But a great deal of what he says and how he says it looks back to oral forms of storytelling and is designed to please and to educate a listening public (for which he was reprimanded by Thucydides).

While Herodotus in his *Histories* combines elements of oral and written composition, we can see in the historian Thucydides (born *ca.* 455 B.C., about thirty years after Herodotus) the first example of an author writing exclusively to be read. Thucydides uses writing with full confidence: inspired by the possibility of speaking to the future; willing to trust the reader to discover, through reading and rereading, the truth of the text; unafraid of ambiguity and misinterpretation. He says that his history is to be a *ktema es aiei* (possession for eternity) that predicts patterns of human behavior for the edification of future generations. His style is convoluted, complex, and fast paced. It is intended very clearly for a reading audience and thus is the first prose to survive that pays no attention to the requirements of oral delivery and comprehension but rather seems to show us the author thinking "on paper."

Thucydides recognized the essential role of speech in the history he was writing and reported (whether from memory, hearsay, or imagination we cannot say for certain) the speeches delivered at all the major debates of the Athenians among themselves and with their allies and adversaries. Here too, however, he admits the influence of written history. The speeches are abstracted from their actual delivery, reduced to an appropriate and likely content, perhaps at times invented entirely by the historian on the basis of what should have been or was likely to have been said. They stand in the history as symbolic of arguments that reveal and present the ethos of the speakers and their age. But the voice of the author himself, embodied in the way he juxtaposes speeches with one another and with the narration of events, exposes to hindsight and historical understanding the limits inherent in the speeches that were necessarily bound to the particular circumstances of their delivery. Thus, both writer and reader possess a godlike overview of events that the original speaker and audience, as far as they are depicted, lack. Of the works that have survived from Greece, Thucydides' *History of the Peloponnesian War* is the first text to show in its style and thought the full influence of writing, even though it is the impact of speech on people and events that forms one of Thucydides' main preoccupations as a historian; his writing is deeply influenced by the various artistic and rhetorical forms of the written language.

Writing and Orality in the Polis

The complex relationship between writing and speech that we have been examining in some of the literature of the sixth and fifth centuries can be seen also in various aspects of Athenian political life throughout the same period. The Athenians developed both modes as parallel arts, each essential to the public life of the polis, each, however, attracting and repelling the other like the ends of two revolving magnets. Solon, the Athenian lawgiver active during the first quarter of the sixth century, provides a conspicuous example. When he created a new constitution and set of laws for the Athenians, he had them displayed on large wooden tablets (*axones*) for all to see and refer to, a symbol of their authority and absoluteness, as well as their availability and application to people of all classes and status. But Solon also wrote poetry that expresses the values and assumptions behind his laws. It is at least possible that he intended his poetry to be heard and remembered by the people of Athens, to persuade them of the wisdom of the laws, something he could not trust a mere display in written form to do. In this reliance on poetry and its influence on the audience, he remains firmly planted in the oral tradition.

The Athenians continued to carve lists of magistrates and their achievements, of tributes and victories in public festivals, decisions of the boule and the ecclesia (the council and democratic assembly), new laws, and dedications to the gods on wood, stone, and metal to be publicly displayed. The symbolic value of these inscriptions remained a promise of permanence and of unchanging structure. (It was a value to be seen as well in their visual style, as discussed below.) The written display was also motivated by the assumption that the workings of the government, its legislative decisions and judicial framework, belonged to all citizens to know and use. Everyone was not necessarily able to read the inscriptions, and in fact it is unlikely that many could, but the information was there and the simplicity of the alphabet made it theoretically possible for anyone to learn to read if he or she wished to. The display, therefore, was an invitation to participate; it was not, as in cultures with complex writing systems, a manifestation of hidden, arcane, and remote power.

The visual style of many of these inscriptions reflects their function both as evidence of the democracy's authority and as a way to make public and proliferate information. In the style called stoichedon, which was common in Athens in the sixth and fifth centuries, capital letters were arranged to make rows in both a horizontal and a vertical direction, creating a pattern of order and regularity. There were no divisions between words, sentences, or paragraphs, and little or no punctuation. Often the height of the stone on which the inscription was carved was such that the top lines would be hard to read without strain. The shape of the carved letters has been described by Stanley Morison (*Politics and Script*) as "square, uniform, rational, and perfectly functional." Compared to previous writing styles the stoichedon style is a development in the direction of clarity, while still reflecting the Greek assumption that the essential nature of language is spoken. In the earlier boustrophedon (turning like an ox) style, writing moved in a continuous, back-and-forth line: when one end of the stone was reached, instead of starting against the far end, the next line continued in the opposite direction immediately under the line just written. (The pattern was considered to resemble an ox plowing; hence the name.) Thus if one line moves from right to left, the next moves from left to right, and so on. This continuity came perhaps from a natural instinct to follow the fluidity and continuity of spoken language. The stoichedon style maintains a certain resemblance to speech by not marking word breaks, and so making the inscription legible only by sounding out the letters in a stream and hearing, rather than seeing, the words.

Thus every time the inscription is read, it is spoken and heard by others. Unlike boustrophedon writing, there are line breaks in stoichedon, with the result that each line read from left to right. And the vertical columns also move the eye from top to bottom, but of course letters read column-fashion make no sense. The overall visual effect of these inscriptions is not, foremost, one of a striving for legibility but rather of order and ornamentation, of writing for its own sake as a witness to the acts of the democracy and their public nature. In the public sphere, therefore, the written word is understood in itself as the sign and guarantor of what it contains, of its descriptive and prescriptive content. But apprehension of the content depends on speaking the words that are written, of turning the writing back into speech.

In fact, writing seems to have intruded very little into the day-to-day lives of the Athenians and into the actual functioning of the democracy in the fifth century. None of the democratic institutions depended on the use of writing, with the single exception of ostracism, which again takes advantage of the alphabet's simplicity and accessibility. The practice rested on the assumption that any citizen could write a proper name. In an ostracism, every citizen could vote for the expulsion of any other citizen by scratching the target individual's name on a piece of broken pottery. This fascinating, antityrannical practice would be unimaginable in a society where writing was not considered common property, a sign, like freedom of speech, of each citizen's equal rights. However, it does not in itself argue for a high level of literacy among the population, since it was always possible for someone to ask another to write a name for him.

The evidence for extensive literacy beyond the name-writing level is unconvincing for the fifth and early fourth centuries. Socrates, for example, could talk of buying a text of Anaxagoras in the agora (Plato, *Apology* 14.26), but the price he mentions seems to indicate that he bought a synopsis or pamphlet rather than a full-length "book." The passage cannot be used, therefore, as evidence for booksellers (in our sense of the word) as a common part of the agora's business, at least for the fifth century. In fact, the high cost of producing a papyrus or parchment scroll must have limited the number of full-length texts available to individuals, so that very few people could have owned anything like a library or even a complete text of a simple work of any length. The tradition finds it worthy of mention that Euripides had a private library, which he referred to in writing his plays; it therefore must have been an unusual feature of even a writer's property. In general, ancient writers quote each other from memory, often inaccurately. Schoolboys did memorize poems or speeches from a scroll or wax tablet, but here again it is probably a question of short texts written as an aid to memorization, with the emphasis on the oral delivery of the memorized piece. Texts were not studied in written form in the normal course of a boy's schooling. We can be fairly sure that all reading, whether by someone alone or in company, was for the most part done out loud, and writing, whether on scrolls or wax tablets, used capital letters with no spaces between words, like monumental inscriptions. It is not until well into the fourth century, and then not incontestably, that reading and writing appear to be common activities in the daily life of Athenian citizens.

Thus, while writing was a powerful factor in the democracy's assumption that all citizens had a part in their government, in practical terms the functioning of the democracy did not depend on literacy but on a sophistication of speech that was an inheritance from and development of a purely oral culture. In both the ecclesia and the law courts, the power to persuade a large audience through the skillful use of the spoken word was of paramount importance. Rhetoric was a fundamental part of the education of an Athenian citizen and speech was the standard medium of communication; Athenians were trained, through extensive memorization of poetry and the constant need to listen to and absorb other people's arguments, to use and to hear language on a sophisticated level. Here again, however, writing began to play a part. By the end of the fifth century those involved in law cases who could not rely on their natural or trained eloquence were able to buy speeches written by professional speech writers. These orations they would then memorize and deliver as if extemporaneously composed. Writing thus made the eloquence upon which one's rights as a citizen might depend a commodity available to anyone with the money to pay for it.

The sophistication of the Athenian population's receptivity to the spoken word, and the intimate connection between political activity and rhetoric, can be seen in the great popular art form of fifth-century Athens—tragedy. The tragic plays dramatized and examined contemporary political, moral, and social questions through the medium of the spoken word, borrowing much of their language from the law courts as well as from the oral poetic tradition of Homer. The playwrights wrote their plays: their intricacy, compactness, and complexity of thought and language depend on written composition. But they wrote them for a single performance to a large, listening audience who would not, for the most part, have the opportunity to read the play from a text or see it a second time. It is astonishing to a modern reader that the average Athenian citizen could have absorbed these plays and their intricate structure and argumentation in a single viewing; modern dependence on the written word has deprived most people of the ability to take in and understand language so readily through the ear, rather than the eye.

It is no accident, however, that communication, the use and misuse of language, becomes a constant concern in these plays. This preoccupation can be seen, in part, as the natural result of the close association of speech and political action. In addition, however, it is a response to the sophistic movement, which challenged the grounding of language in a communal, universally accepted morality and value system. And this movement can itself be understood as one of the effects of writing and of the dissolution of an oral society where, as we have seen, language reflects and maintains the traditions of the community.

Indeed, the tragedies themselves display, sometimes directly, the tense interaction of scribal and oral forms. In the *Hippolytos* of Euripides, for example, there is a scene that beautifully illustrates the discordant natures of written and spoken language in the Greek mind. Phaedra, when she wishes to release herself from the shame of loving her stepson, Hippolytos, and at the same time punish him for his almost priggish purity, writes a note falsely accusing him of rape and attaches it to her wrist before committing suicide. Her husband, Theseus, impressed by the ruthless absoluteness of her death and of the written message that has become the voice of the dead woman, can neither recognize the falsehood of the message nor be swayed by the eloquent spoken denial of Hippolytos. Here writing carries a voice beyond the death of its author, but it is false and, because it is detached from the living voice, cannot be questioned; the authority of its unchanging, stark statement allows the lie to go undetected, unthreatened even by a living voice. (There are, of course, other reasons why Theseus does not question the note, which have to do with the relationship between Theseus and Hippolytos.)

Writing and Reason in Plato

Tragedy, then, enhances the strong oral tradition in Athenian public life. At the same time, the playwrights explored some of the problems that arise in a society shifting between oral and scribal habits. The most explicit examination of these problems, however, comes in the work of Plato, whose well-known hostility to the influence of tragedy on the Athenian population is inspired in part by the orality inherent in the form. In his understanding of the matter, the audience absorbed the lessons tragedy taught through the intimate and emotional persuasiveness of dramatic speech, which precluded rational thought.

Plato's own feelings about written and spoken language are complicated and unresolved. In fact, the conflict between speech and writing is articulated as a central problem for the philosopher. As a matter of principle Socrates, Plato's teacher, never wrote a word, because he believed in spoken dialogue as the only means of philosophical instruction; in this practice he depended on the oral tradition in Athenian society. Plato, in the *Phaedrus* (275d; Reginald Hackforth, trans. [1952]), puts into Socrates' mouth the following:

> You know, Phaedrus, that's the strange thing about writing which makes it truly analogous to painting. The painter's products stand before us as though they were alive, but, if you question them, they maintain a most majestic silence. It is the same with written words; they seem to talk to you as though they were intelligent, but if you ask them anything about what they say, from a desire to be instructed, they go on telling you just the same thing forever. And once a thing is put in writing, the composition, whatever it may be, drifts all over the place, getting into the hands not only of those who understand it, but equally of those who have no business with it; it doesn't know how to address the right people, and not address

the wrong. And when it is ill-treated and unfairly abused it always needs its parent to come to its help, being unable to defend or help itself.

Plato wrote extensively, however, and it is only because he did so that we know anything of Socratic or Platonic philosophy. He chose to write in the form of dialogues because, it would seem, that preserved to some degree the active, living relationship between teacher and student, both in the interchange between Socrates and his interlocuters within the dialogue and in the relationship of the reader to the text, where answers are not given but have to be actively pursued by the reader and can only be found through knowledge already acquired.

Yet it can be argued that one of the basic tenets of Platonic philosophy, the theory of Ideas, is derived, consciously or unconsciously, from the perception of the relationship of writing to reality and of writing to speech. True discourse, Plato says, happens when knowledge is *"written* in the soul of the listener." He might have said "when the soul hears," but the metaphor Plato finds for true understanding is writing. So, when he speaks in the *Republic* of the education of the guardians through music, Plato uses the metaphor of learning letters (3.402a–c; Paul Shorey, trans. [1963]):

> It is, then, as it was when we learned our letters and felt that we knew them sufficiently only when the separate letters did not elude us, . . . and when we did not disregard them in small things or great and think it unnecessary to recognize them, but were eager to distinguish them everywhere, in the belief that we should never be literate and letter-perfect till we could do this. . . . And is it not also true that if there are any likenesses of letters reflected in water, or mirrors, we shall never know them until we know the originals, but such knowledge belongs to the same art and discipline? . . . Then, by heaven, am I not right in saying that by the same token we shall never be true musicians, either—neither we nor the guardians that we have undertaken to educate—until we are able to recognize the forms of soberness, courage, liberality, and high-mindedness, and all their kindred and their opposites, too, in all the combinations that contain and convey them, and to apprehend them and their images wherever found.

True knowledge is always only a reflection, a remembering, of the ultimate, unchanging Forms, as good writing is a reflection of living knowledge, of speech. Thus writing provides Plato with a metaphor of something that can always and only be a reflection of something else and is thus incomplete; but, inasmuch as it is an accurate reflection, permanent and unchanging, it is an indispensable metaphor for the difference between the Forms and our perception of them, for the nature of human knowledge.

Plato, by juxtaposing the intimacy of the oral world with the permanence of a philosophical written text, bears witness to the rich interaction that persisted in classical literature and thought between the oral tradition and the relatively young phenomenon of writing. We could go on sketching the Greeks' constant and fertile engagement in this issue. In the fourth and third centuries, however, writing and literacy became far more prevalent, and in the Hellenistic period we find a scholasticism and self-conscious literariness that signals the complete separation of texts from oral delivery. The library at Alexandria, one of the functions of which was to collect texts of, and create commentaries for, all the great literary works of the classical period, is the product of an age that is thoroughly accustomed to the written word. For the Greeks of the archaic and classical periods, however, the aftermath of the introduction of the alphabet brought recognition of the capacity of language and the thoughts it expresses to reach beyond the limits of time, place, and circumstance; and yet that very permanence and abstraction often seemed lifeless, incomplete, inert, and ever dangerous unless infused with the spirit of speech, the "true" language.

THE ROMANS

With the Romans we find a different story. The Romans acquired their alphabet from the Greeks, probably by way of the Etruscans in the seventh century. In our dating that would be shortly after the Greeks themselves received it from the Phoenicians. We can reconstruct with some certainty the history of the alphabet in its journey west, in general outline if not in detail. The Etruscans, a people of unknown race and language, had a dominant influence in Italy from the seventh to the end of the fifth century. They seem to have taken the alphabet from the Greeks of Cumae (Cyme, modern Cuma), a colony established by the Euboean city of Chalcis on the west coast of Italy, very soon after the Cumaeans themselves received it, and certainly before the Greeks had abandoned either the digamma or koppa. The Etruscan alphabet originally had the twenty-two Semitic letters plus four of the additional Greek letters: upsilon, phi, chi, psi.

Before the Etruscans developed this alphabet further, it was borrowed by the Romans. The evidence for the Romans' borrowing from the Etruscans, rather than directly from the Greeks, seems conclusive. In the first place, the Semitic letter names retained in Greek have been abandoned by the time the Romans get the alphabet. In the Roman names, the difference between the closed-syllable names *el, em, en,* and *ar* (preserved in our alphabet) and the open-syllable names *be, ce, de,* and so on, can be explained by the presence in Etruscan of vocalized liquids (l, r) and nasals (m, n). Secondly, one of the ways in which the Etruscans denoted the *f*-sound, the combination of digamma (ϝ) and eta (H, which had an *h*-sound, not an *e*-sound in the Cumaean Greek alphabet) appears in the earliest Roman inscription, on a fibula (brooch) from Praeneste (Palestrina). (An Italian scholar has argued recently that the Praeneste fibula is a nineteenth-century fake. If this is true, it must of course be discounted as evidence for the influence of Etruscan on Roman writing. However, there is adequate evidence from other sources to uphold the theory.) The later practice of dropping the eta and using the digamma alone for the *f*-sound also seems to have been an Etruscan habit. A third piece of evidence comes from the use of the letters gamma and koppa. Etruscans used the gamma (written   , later C) for a *k*-sound; they had no *g*-sound in their language. They used the kappa (K), however, for a *k*-sound before *a,* and the koppa (Q) for a *k*-sound before *u.* The Romans, following the Etruscans, used the gamma for the *k*-sound but also for a *g*-sound. They eventually dropped the kappa, using the *c* (Greek gamma) for a *k*-sound before *a, e,* and *o,* although they kept the use of the koppa before *u.* (The kappa was, however, retained in certain words, like *Kalends*.) Finally, the Romans initially lacked—because the Etruscans did not use it—a sign for *x* (the *ks*-sound), although the Cumaean Greeks had and used such a sign (chi). Early on, the Romans, perhaps after consulting the Greek alphabet, reintroduced the chi for *x,* but placed it at the end of their alphabet.

That the borrowing happened soon after the Etruscans themselves got their alphabet is clear from the fact that the Romans had a *b* and an *o* in their alphabet, which letters were, however, soon dropped from the Etruscan alphabet.

The Romans rejected five of the Etruscan letters. They had no need for the aspirated letters Θ (*th*), φ (*ph*), and ψ (*kh* in the Etruscan Cumaean alphabet); these they turned into symbols for numerals: Θ → Ꞓ → C = 100; φ → C|Ɔ → M = 1,000; ψ → ⊥ → L = 50. They also rejected two of the *s*-sound letters, keeping only the sigma.

Thus after some development the early Roman alphabet was composed of the following: A, B, C (*k*-sound), D, E, F, I (zeta), H, I, K, L, M, N, O, P, Q, P (the original form of R), S, T, V (*u*-sound), X. Later changes involved dropping the zeta, which was not needed in Latin, and eventually putting in its place the G, a variant of the C to make the distinction between the *k*-sound and the *g*-sound, which Etruscan had not needed. A stroke was added to the *ar* (P becoming R) to distinguish it from the P that has evolved from the Greek Π and early Latin Γ. Since the digamma had been used for the *f*-sound, the V had to serve both for the vowel sound *u* and the semiconsonant *w*. The Romans had no need for a *v*-consonant, as the sound did not exist in classical Latin. The emperor Claudius attempted to add a letter Ⅎ, upside-down digamma, to distinguish between the consonant sound *w* and the vowel sound *u*, but his innovation did not catch on. It was not until the Middle Ages that the vowel was written with a U, to distinguish it from the consonant V, and that a new letter, double-*u*, was invented to express the *w*-sound.

In the first century B.C. when Greek words flooded Rome after the Romans had conquered Greece, the Romans took Z and Y (capital zeta and upsilon) from the Greek alphabet and added them to the end of their own in order to be able to transliterate Greek words. It remained for the Middle Ages to invent the J variant of I to represent the consonant *j*-sound, bringing the alphabet to the form that we use.

Development of Literacy and Literature

The story of Roman literacy and the use of writing differs markedly from the Greek. There is little evidence for the use of writing over the four centuries following the borrowing of the alphabet from the Etruscans. What inscriptions have survived record dedications, boundaries, funerary epitaphs, and laws. For example, the Twelve Tables, the earliest Roman law code, was, according to traditional accounts, drawn up and written on tablets of bronze (or perhaps wood) in the year 451–450 B.C. These tablets were displayed in the forum. But there are no surviving literary texts from this period.

While possessing nothing as elaborate or developed as the Greek oral tradition, the Romans had their own fund of orally transmitted songs, hymns, prayers, spells, oaths, and gnomic sayings. Yet, when in the third century we find the Romans using writing for literary purposes, it is not to set down their own lore; rather, it is to translate into the Latin language Homer's *Odyssey*. From its very inception, written literature was informed by Greek models. These models transformed and overwhelmed the native spoken traditions and divorced Roman literature from nonliterary roots. In contrast with the way the Greek oral tradition evolved into a written tradition, the Roman oral tradition presumably remained distinct (with so little evidence it is hard to be certain) and for the most part did not directly influence or blend into the written forms.

A good example of the process by which Greek models took over and shaped Roman literature and its language is the fate of the Saturnian verse, a form of poetic line that seems to have come from the formulaic and ritualistic oral tradition of the Italic tribes. Livius Andronicus used it to translate the hexameters of Homer into Latin. But when Ennius created the Latin hexameter in imitation of the Greek, which he knew from reading Greek epic, the Saturnian was doomed. Even in drama, where there was a strong native tradition, the imitation of Greek models gives to the Roman works a studied literary quality.

Thus writing, which had been employed only in very restricted ways for centuries after its introduction into the Latin language, achieved with relative suddenness a well-defined place and a sophisticated and self-conscious use in molding the Latin language to Greek literary models.

The Romans developed monumental writing into a fine art. Although the beginnings during the republic were slow to develop and unimpressive, from the first century B.C. on inscriptions of great precision, clarity, and beauty were carved on stone throughout the Roman Empire, a symbol of the power and authority of Rome. Thus began the spread of the Latin alphabet to the rest of Europe, where it was never to lose its hold.

From early on in their history the Romans were for the most part literate and, as we have seen, writers achieved sophisticated literary forms and styles. Even so, writing had not gained a strong enough hold in the West not to be threatened with extinction. In the Middle Ages, it fell almost exclusively into the care of the church. And so writing once again became restricted to use by a relatively small group of officials, a circumstance reminiscent of its exclusive use by Egyptian and Mesopotamian scribes but completely foreign to its use in Greece and Rome. It was only through the patient copying of texts by monks that many of the literary works of antiquity survived in the West to be rediscovered in the Renaissance. (Some ancient texts, for example many of the works of Aristotle, were translated into Arabic and Syriac and were preserved in the East, eventually reentering the Western tradition and providing valuable editions of many ancient works, some otherwise unknown in the West.) Outside the church, people once again depended entirely on speech until literacy began to spread anew in the twelfth century.

BIBLIOGRAPHY

HISTORY OF THE ALPHABET AND WRITING

Reginald Austin, *The Stoichedon Style in Greek Inscriptions* (1938); Rhys Carpenter, "The Antiquity of the Greek Alphabet," in *American Journal of Archaeology,* **37** (1933), "The Greek Alphabet Again," in *American Journal of Archaeology,* **42** (1938), and "The Alphabet in Italy," in *American Journal of Archaeology,* **49** (1945); Robert M. Cook and Arthur G. Woodhead, "The Diffusion of the Greek Alphabet," in *American Journal of Archaeology,* **63** (1959); David Diringer, *The Alphabet,* 2 vols. (1948; 3d ed. 1968); Sterling Dow, "Minoan Writing," in *American Journal of Archaeology,* **58** (1954); Godfrey R. Driver, *Semitic Writing from Pictograph to Alphabet,* S. A. Hopkins, ed. (1948, rev. ed. 1976); Benedict Einarson, "Notes on the Development of the Greek Alphabet," in *Classical Philology,* **62** (1967).

Ignace J. Gelb, *A Study of Writing,* rev. ed. (1963); George P. Goold, "Homer and the Alphabet," in *Transactions of the American Philological Association,* **91** (1960); Arthur Gordon, review of Margherita Guarducci, *La cosidetta Fibula Prenestina. Antiquari, eruditi e falsari nella Roma dell' Ottocento,* in *Classical Journal,* **78** (1982–1983); Lilian H. Jeffery, *The Local Scripts of Archaic Greece: A Study of the Origin of the Greek Alphabet and Its Development from the Eighth to the Fifth Centuries B.C.* (1961); Stanley Morison, *Politics and Script* (1972); Holger Pedersen, *The Discovery of Language: Linguistic Science in the Nineteenth Century* (1962); Sir John E. Sandys and Sidney G. Campbell, *Latin Epigraphy,* 2d ed. (1927); Sir Edward Maunde Thompson, *An Introduction to Greek and Latin Palaeography* (1912); Berthold L. Ullman, *Ancient Writing and Its Influence* (1932; 3d ed. 1980), and "How Old Is the Greek Alphabet?" in *American Journal of Archaeology,* **38** (1934); Arthur

G. Woodhead, *The Study of Greek Inscriptions* (1967; 2d ed. 1981).

LITERACY AND ORALITY

John A. Davison, "Literature and Literacy in Ancient Greece," in *Phoenix,* **16** (1962); Jacques Derrida, "Plato's Pharmacy," in J. Derrida, *Dissemination,* Barbara Johnson, trans. (1981); Stuart Flory, "Who Read Herodotus' *Histories?*" in *American Journal of Philology,* **101** (1980); John R. Goody and Ian Watt, "The Consequences of Literacy," in J. R. Goody, *Literacy in Traditional Societies* (1968); William C. Greene, "The Spoken and Written Word," in *Harvard Studies in Classical Philology,* **60** (1951); F. D. Harvey, "Literacy in the Athenian Democracy," in *Revue des Etudes Grecques,* **79** (1966); Eric Havelock, *Preface to Plato* (1963), and *The Literate Revolution in Greece and Its Cultural Consequences* (1982); Eric Havelock and Jackson P. Hershbell, *Communication Arts in the Ancient World* (1978).

Henry Immerwahr, "Book Rolls on Attic Vases," in C. Henderson, ed., *Classical, Mediaeval, and Renaissance Studies in Honor of Berthold Louis Ullman* (1964); Bernard Knox, "Silent Reading in Antiquity," in *Greek, Roman and Byzantine Studies,* **9** (1968); Walter J. Ong, *Orality and Literacy: The Technologizing of the Word* (1982); Leonard Woodbury, "Aristophanes' *Frogs* and Athenian Literacy," in *Transactions of the American Philological Association,* **106** (1976).

BOOK PRODUCTION

SUSAN A. STEPHENS

INTRODUCTION

The bulk of classical literature was produced in Athens, Alexandria, and Rome; therefore, any discussion of book production ought to focus on these centers. Unfortunately, of Athenian, Alexandrian, and Roman books there have been few if any survivors. But the *disiecta membra* of Greco-Roman literature, fragmentary rolls and codices now in excess of several thousand, have been preserved, thanks to the aridity of the climate in the sands of Egypt; 95 percent are in Greek, 5 percent in Latin. While the earliest belong to the fourth century B.C., by far the majority are to be dated on paleographic grounds between A.D. 50 and 300. Some were found intact or nearly intact in tombs or buried in jars, but most had been discarded on town rubbish heaps in antiquity. The material thus found is of course random and in varying degrees of preservation; nevertheless, it provides an excellent beginning for assembling information about ancient books.

Occasional finds in other parts of the Mediterranean augment this material: a carbonized roll containing Orphic hymns found in northern Greece, dated from context to the fourth century B.C.; the Herculaneum papyri, books from a philosopher's library preserved but unfortunately carbonized by the eruption of Vesuvius in A.D. 79, many of which early excavators destroyed in the process of unrolling; the so-called Dead Sea Scrolls, fragments of about 800 leather book rolls found at Qumrân and Murabba'ât; papyri and parchments from the Roman military settlement at Dura-Europos on the Euphrates; and a considerable number of wooden writing tablets from the peripheral regions of the Roman Empire —the most notable of which have been found at Vindolanda in Roman Britain. Statistical analyses of these remains can be combined with two other types of evidence: first, representations of books, readers, and scribes from vase or wall paintings and reliefs; second, references to books and readers found in ancient sources ranging from Homer to Eustathius. These yield a coherent, though by no means complete, picture of the development and significance of the ancient book. Evidence for the early period, for example the introduction and development of the book roll in archaic and classical Athens, is almost entirely lacking.

However, the central question in any discussion of the ancient book is what prompted the change from book roll, the standard format for written material in the Mediterranean world from 3000 B.C. until the second century A.D., to the codex, or the book as we know it. Recent analyses of the remains from Egypt have begun to provide the answer.

THE MATERIALS: PAPYRUS, SKINS, INKS, AND PENS

The variety of early writing surfaces and formats is a tribute to man's ingenuity as well as his perseverance. For permanent records, stone has always been fashionable, though it is difficult to work and not very portable. Clay tablets were also tried; and while they were slightly more portable, they had a tendency to crumble. In large numbers they presented any ancient record office with unenviable storage problems. Lighter tablets made of wood or skins cured in a variety of ways found a vogue among businessmen, schoolboys, or poets for the recording of preliminary or impermanent drafts; for ephemera whatever might come to hand—broken pieces of pottery or bone or wood—could be pressed into service. However, the single most popular writing material in the ancient world was papyrus—so common that from it our modern word "paper" is derived.

Papyrus

Cyperus papyrus is a reed plant native to Egypt; it has a triangular stalk that may grow to a height of from seven to fifteen feet, topped with a feathery crown, stylized representations of which are exceedingly common in Egyptian art. The name itself is derived from Egyptian *papuro*, which has been plausibly interpreted to mean "that of the pharaoh."

As early as 3000 B.C. the Egyptians had learned how to manufacture flat sheets from the plant for use as a writing surface. The most extensive description of this technique comes from Pliny the Elder (*Natural History* 13.74–82), who is, however, inaccurate in a number of points. Observation of actual papyrus rolls, as well as experiment, supplement and correct his account. The triangular stalk was separated with a needle point into thin vertical strips about the thickness of one layer of fibers. The choicest strips came from the center of the stalk, with a gradual diminution in quality as the strips approach the outer cortex. These strips were then spread on a flat surface. First a layer of strips running vertically was positioned with, it appears, sides of the strips touching, but not overlapping, and on top of these was placed a horizontal layer, that is, a layer running at right angles to the underlayer. The two were then pressed together (Pliny specifies a press; modern experimenters use a mallet) in order to break down the cell structure of the fibers and release a glutin that when dried served as the bonding agent. Pliny was mistaken when he states that the bonding agent was Nile water. Since the strips of papyrus once separated will dry out very quickly, Nile water was probably used to keep them moist throughout the preparation process. Sheets formed by this method (*kollemata* in Greek) were then sundried and joined to one another to form rolls. So that a scribe met no impediment to his pen when writing over the area where the sheets were joined, the left sheet was regularly placed to overlap the right for a distance of one or two centimeters. The sheets were pasted together at the area of overlap with a wheat paste to which vinegar was added, probably to impede the growth of mold.

The standard unit of manufacture and sale for papyrus was not the individual sheet, but the roll (*chartes* in Greek; *charta* or *volumen* in Latin). According to Pliny, the roll was normally made up of twenty sheets, and although rolls made up of fifty or seventy sheets are known, Pliny's information is confirmed by a number of sources ranging in date from the pharaonic to the Arabic period. From observation, it appears that the manufactured sheets varied both in width and height; in the Roman period the normal range for the width of a sheet (the only dimension given by Pliny) was 4 to 9 inches (11 to 24 cm); therefore, commercially available rolls would have ranged in size from 23.7 square feet (2.2 m² [4 × 8 in./11 × 20 cm]) to 51.7 square feet (4.8 m² [19 × 8 in./24 × 20 cm]). The consumer would buy rolls, then cut off whatever amount was necessary for shorter items, such as a letter, or paste together two or more rolls if the material to be copied demanded a roll longer than the standard lengths provided.

Rolls were made with horizontal fibers placed on the inside where they could be protected from the constant strain of rolling and unrolling; since the edges on the horizontal fiber side tended to fray, a sheet rotated through 90 degrees, so that its fibers were vertical, was normally glued to the front of the roll (*protocollon*); a similar sheet could be glued at the end of a roll (*eschatocollion*) as well. The *protocollon* served as a protective covering for the whole roll when it was rolled up. The normal writing surface was the interior of the roll, the horizontal fiber side, which might be smoothed with a mallet to remove puckers or ridges. The vertical fiber side, the outside of the roll, was usually left blank, though there are plentiful exceptions to this practice.

Pliny remarks that the qualities esteemed in papyrus were fineness, firmness, whiteness, and smoothness (*tenuitas*, *densitas*, *candor*, *levor*). Again, this has been borne out by observation. Although it has been argued that papyrus was ultimately surpassed by parchment and paper because it was coarser, darker, and more brittle than either, papyrus of the Pharaonic period was characteristically white, or light cream in color, and occasionally some of the Ptolemaic and Roman papyri from Egypt, although they have been subjected to the elements for 2,000 years, are fine in texture and supple enough to be unrolled or unfolded easily, though by far the majority have darkened from age and exposure.

How expensive was the papyrus roll and how easily available was it? Evidence for the manufacture of papyrus outside of Egypt is scanty and of dubious value. It is possible that the plant was introduced or grew natively in many areas of the Mediterranean, especially Palestine and Sicily, but during the period with which we are concerned it was not manufactured commercially outside of Egypt.

Probably the majority of papyrus manufactories were located in or near the delta—the papyrus-growing region—because stalks once dried out were unsuitable for processing. Probably the center of the industry, or at least its distribution center, was in Alexandria. Under the Ptolemies, control of the industry was no doubt centralized, but whether or not such centralization continued in the Roman and Byzantine periods is simply unknown. What is known is that papyrus in large quantities was in more or less continuous supply to the West from at least the fourth century B.C., and more likely from the time when writing was introduced into the Greek world until the Arab conquest. About the retail prices of papyrus Naphtali Lewis (1974, pp. 133–134) concludes:

> During most of classical antiquity, we discover, a roll of papyrus cost the equivalent of one or two days' wages, and it could run as

high as what the labourer would earn in five or six days. Thence, with each step up the economic ladder the magnitude of the price of papyrus recedes proportionately. The Egyptian peasant who paid 200 drachmas for a simple abode was surely not buying papyrus rolls at 2 or 3 or 4 drachmas apiece to satisfy his minimal and occasional needs. But to the villager who paid three or four or six thousand drachmas in cash for his house such papyrus prices could hardly have loomed large. Accordingly, in social milieux more elevated than that of a prosperous Egyptian villager the purchase of papyrus is not likely to have been regarded as an expenditure of any consequence, but to have fallen, rather, into a category comparable to that of our "incidentals," or "petty cash."

Skins

Books could also be made out of the hides of a wide variety of animals that, once cured, were cut into sheets and bound together in some way. Those of younger animals generally provided writing material of a better quality.

Although there were two different methods of treatment—curing or drying in a taut or stretched condition—the initial processes for both were the same. Once the hides were removed from the recently slaughtered animals they were either soaked immediately in a chemical solution to promote the loosening and removal of hair, or the hides were temporarily cured and dried to prevent bacterially induced decay so that they could be set aside for processing at a later time. The soaked hides were then cleansed of hair from the external layer (hence called the "hair side") and of flesh from the inner or hypodermal layer (called the "flesh side"). In the cured hides hair and flesh sides can be distinguished by slight differences in color and by faint traces of hair follicles on the former. This led, in the preparation of codices, to the practice of arranging the sheets so that when the pages were open hair side faced hair side and flesh side faced flesh side. Next, impurities like dirt or grease would be removed, and the hides might be split into two or three thinner layers. The skill with which these processes were carried out ultimately determined the quality of the writing material.

At this point the processes diverge. In the preparation of leathers (tawing and tanning) the skins were steeped in solutions derived from alum, or various vegetable compounds like oak galls, wood barks, or acacia pods to render the hides durable and flexible. In the preparation of parchment, which usually refers to the skins of sheep and goat, and vellum, which refers to that of kid or calf, the skin was stretched on a frame and slowly air-dried in moderate temperatures and out of direct sunlight. When dried, it could be smoothed and treated with pumice or chalk to increase whiteness. Once dried, the skin was stiff and durable, but if, subsequent to this, the skin again became too wet, the fiber alignment produced during the stretching and drying process could be broken down and serious damage to the writing surface might result. Unfortunately, ancient methods of curing hides were not always neatly categorizable. Frequently, hides could be stretched and dried like parchment, and afterward tanning solutions would be applied to both sides in order to make the material water resistant.

Discoveries of fragments of about 800 book rolls (the so-called Dead Sea Scrolls) written on skins provide considerable information about the technical makeup of rolls. Skins were arranged with hair or flesh side uniformly outside or inside, depending on the type of text to be copied (specifications for which were given in detail in rabbinic law). The skins, cut into sheets, were laid side by side and sewn together with animal or vegetable fibers, but inevitably these sewn areas were more conspicuous than in papyrus rolls and consequently scribes did not write over the areas of join.

Leather rolls (*diphthera* in Greek) were used throughout Asia Minor from at least the eleventh century B.C., and were certainly known to the Greeks, but available evidence suggests that rolls made of papyrus were more common. The first evidence of the export of papyrus from Egypt also comes from the eleventh century B.C. In an Egyptian narrative from this period, the adventurer Wen Amon takes 500 rolls of papyrus along with him to Phoenicia for barter. It is possible that the Greeks became acquainted with papyrus when they acquired an alphabet from the Phoenicians. This occurrence can be placed no later than the eighth century B.C., but certainly by the sixth century Greek mercenaries and later Greek merchants were securely established in Egypt, and by this period papyrus would have been available for export.

The Greek word for papyrus is *bublos*, from which *biblion* (book) and ultimately our word *bible* derive. That the Greeks used papyrus rolls in the fifth century is beyond question. Herodotus remarks, for example, that "the Ionians have for a long time called papyrus (*bublous*) skins (*diphtheras*), because they used to use sheep and goat skins when papyrus was in short supply; and still even today many eastern peoples write on such skins" (5.58). Obviously in his day Athenians were writing on papyrus rolls, though leather rolls were not unfamiliar. Colin Roberts (1954) makes the attractive suggestion that to fifth-century Greeks a literary mention of leather rolls would have suggested a remote or primitive past, as when Euripides (frag. 627) speaks of "ink-dipped skins." And Speusippus' complaint in a letter of 343/2 B.C. that the Persian occupation of Egypt caused a shortage of writing material further indicates the importance of papyrus for the Greek world.

The earliest fragment of parchment (*pergamena* in both Greek and Latin) bears a date of 195 B.C.; the fact that it was found at Dura-Europos on the Euphrates tends to support a Near Eastern origin for the material. Pliny's assertion (*Natural History* 13.21), on the authority of Varro, that parchment was invented at Pergamum because a Ptolemy had placed an embargo on the exportation of papyrus to the Attalid Kingdom is almost certainly false. A more plausible explanation of this story is offered by Richard R. Johnson (1970), who argues that the dynastic struggles between Antiochus and the Ptolemies between 173–168 B.C., which culminated in the seige of Alexandria, must have resulted in a shortage of papyrus for all consumers outside of Egypt. Such a reduction in normal supplies might well have forced the Pergamene library to convert to parchment (at least temporarily), the techniques for its manufacture being already well known; and perhaps shipments of parchment were introduced to Rome through the Pergamene delegation headed by Attalus, who was sent there in 168 B.C. Certainly, parchment was used in Rome in the first century A.D. in the form of notebooks as well as in experimental codices.

Inks

Inks were of two kinds. The earlier was used by the Egyptians and was made from carbon, obtainable in the form of soot or lampblack, mixed with a thin vegetable gum that allowed it to adhere. The majority of papyrus rolls were written in this carbon-based ink, which was black or dark brown in color. Because this ink was chemically inert, it neither faded with age nor reacted with the writing surface, and because it was water soluble, it was possible to sponge writing surfaces clean and reuse them. The term for this in Greek was *palin psao* (rub again), from which the name "palimpsest" was derived.

Papyri as well as parchments and leathers could be erased in this way and reused, but most surviving palimpsests are parchment.

A later ink, derived from iron-tannin compounds, was produced by steeping the same kind of vegetable matter that was used in the tanning process, for example oak galls, and mixing it with iron sulfate. Such inks, which were usually brownish in color, might also contain gum arabic to help adherence and various vegetable carbons to make them blacker. Because they adhere to the rather greasy surface of parchment more easily than carbon-based inks, it has often been suggested that iron-tannin inks were invented specifically for writing on skins, but in fact the earliest example of metallic ink in the West has been found on a papyrus dated to A.D. 111.

Both types of ink were used until the seventh century, but in the medieval period, iron-based inks were found to be preferable. While the iron-based inks adhere better to parchment, they are not chemically inert and, in some instances, may produce small amounts of sulfuric acid that can cause serious damage to the writing surface (see, e.g., Metzger, 1981, pl. 20). Colored inks, especially those with a reddish or purple tinge, were used in the illumination of biblical manuscripts, but they do not begin to appear until the fourth or fifth century A.D.

Pens

The Greeks, unlike their Near Eastern precursors who wrote, or rather painted, their letters with brushes made from pliant rushes, wrote with reed pens. The reeds (*kalami*) were dried out, one end cut and trimmed to a point, which was then split to hold a quantity of ink. Eric Turner in *Athenian Books in the Fifth and Fourth Centuries B.C.* (p. 12) regards the introduction of this type of pen as significant for the development of literacy in the West. He observes:

Brush calligraphy, a precise technique, calling for careful control of the hand by the eye, can be acquired only after a long apprenticeship. In countries that practice it, writing is a mystery and a craft, confined, as it was in both Egypt and Assyria, to priests or guilds of scribes. But writing with a pen is an accomplishment anyone may master. In Greece, there are no guilds of scribes guarding a hereditary secret, and the distinction between Oriental and Greek literature is that the latter is the literature of everyman.

Reed pens and occasionally pens made with metal tips have been found in quantity in both the Greek and Roman world. In addition to them, the stylus was developed for writing on waxed tablets.

THE BOOK ROLL

From the beginning of the fifth century numerous illustrations of book rolls appear on Attic vases, often in the hands of readers who are usually identified as poets or schoolmasters hearing their students' lessons. This suggests at least that those who could afford to buy such vases were familiar with books—and therefore Greek literature—and were eager to demonstrate this familiarity. In one of the most famous illustrations the poet Sappho is seated and reading from a book roll (Athens hydria 1260, dated to about 440 B.C.). Her pose may be taken as typical for the ancient reader: she grips the roll with both hands; in her left hand she winds the portion already read, while with her right hand she unrolls the material about to be read. The text can be seen written in tall columns on the inside of the roll. Written vertically on the outside of the rolled-up portions are the words *epea pteroenta* (winged words), which are doubtless intended as a label.

Book rolls like the one Sappho reads were for the ancient world the standard medium for publication. Writing was from left to right (though letters are often randomly placed in representations on vases) and always in capitals. Enlargement of the initial letter of a sentence or section was very rare, but came into vogue for biblical manuscripts probably around the fourth century.

The first examples of the minuscule hands so familiar from medieval manuscripts do not occur before the ninth century A.D. Such book rolls with pretensions to elegance had certain features in common. Words are not divided from each other. The text is written in columns (*selides* in Greek); for prose they were often tall and narrow, sometimes with as few as eight to ten letters per line, as in Demosthenes' *On the False Legation* (*De Falsa Legatione*) (Turner, 1971, pl. 67); for poetry, at least from about the third century B.C., the columns were the width of a single line of verse, such as Menander's *Sikyonios* (see, e.g., Turner, 1971, pl. 40).

While the height of columns of poetry may vary, they tended to be rather shorter in the Ptolemaic and early Roman periods. In prose the column assumes an architectural solidity; scribes often attempt to right justify the margins by using the caret (<) as a line filler. Margins were usually generous above, below, and between columns, and the back of the roll was normally left blank. Marks of punctuation, accents, or indeed any kind of lectional aid, were rarely present in what were considered deluxe editions; rather, they characterized the scholar's book or the student's exercise. Neither line nor column numbering was used, although occasional stichometrics (see, e.g., Turner, 1971, pl. 40) are thought to have been used by some scribes in order to keep a count of lines for which they would be paid. Horizontal ruling for lines or vertical rulings for columns are not normally found on papyrus rolls, though they are present in the leather scrolls from Qumrân and in later biblical manuscripts. However, lead, which would have been the means of making such rulings, is mentioned in connection with books in a number of literary sources. Books might be wound around a wooden, or sometimes an ivory, cylinder, to give them stiffness and prevent any bending along the vertical axis or spine. But it must be added that very few rolls have been found with such support, and in fact, many have been fractured along the spine.

When punctuation did occur it was sporadic and unsystematically applied. Three types normally appeared. First, devices used to separate or to join syllables: these include the diaeresis (¨) placed over an iota or upsilon, usually to divide it from a preceding vowel—often it appears to be ornamental rather than functional; the apostrophe ('), to mark elision or to separate syllables; and the hyphen (-), to link parts of compound words that were unfamiliar. Second, devices used to mark off clauses, sentences, or even sections: these include the dicolon (:), high (·), median (·) and low (.) stop, and a slight gap left in the text. And third, the paragraphus, a horizontal dash, often with an accompanying dicolon, was used in both prose and verse to divide one speaker's part from another.

The paragraphus might also occur in poetry to divide the verse into stanzas or mark the end of a section. Accents, marks of rough or smooth breathing, and marks of quantity can also be found, though much more frequently in poetic texts than in prose.

There are a variety of other sigla, some of which were critical signs said to have been invented by Alexandrian scholars for work on ancient texts, others used by a corrector (*diorthotes*) to indicate omissions, transpositions, or queries; the purpose of still others is unclear. (For a detailed discussion and examples of all these devices, see Turner, 1971.) Abbreviations and ligatures are found in scholarly texts like that of Aristotle's *Constitution of Athens* (Turner, 1971, pl. 60), but not in expensive-looking, well-set-out editions.

Rolls could be labeled in several ways: title and author, and sometimes the number of lines were regularly placed inside the roll immediately below (if space permitted) or to the right of the final column of text. But this was not very convenient when the roll was closed. A tag (*sillybos* in Greek; *titulus* in Latin) written on a separate piece of papyrus or parchment could be glued or otherwise affixed to the back of the roll in such a way that it hung down from the top margin. But this kind of label could easily be lost, as the number of such labels that have been found without any trace of the original roll would indicate. Of course, the owner might write the name of the roll on the outside, across the fibers (which on the outside of the *protocollon* would be running horizontally).

A wall painting from Pompeii suggests that rolls were normally stored vertically in boxes (*kibotos* or *teuchos* in Greek; *capsa* in Latin, see Turner, 1971, pls. 9, 10). For authors whose oeuvre was contained in numerous rolls, these boxes may have served as a rudimentary filing system. M. W. Haslam (1976) has demonstrated a connection between these boxes and the composition of medieval manuscripts. Within a single manuscript, for example, the speeches of Demosthenes might be grouped into several categories—Philippic, *symbouleutic*, public, private, encomiastic. While the speeches within each category remained the same, the relative position of the speeches within the category as well as the actual order of categories might vary from one manuscript to another. He accounts for this by supposing that rolls of individual speeches were regularly stored in boxes labeled by category (Philippic, and so forth), and when scribes copied from rolls to codex, they copied the contents from one box, then moved on to another. The order of boxes then would be random as well as the order of speeches copied, but the categories would remain the same. A similar ordering can be observed for the speeches of Isocrates.

In order to conserve or recycle paper, the backs of rolls were often pressed into service, either after the material on the front ceased to be read or even while the front was still in use. But for literary productions with some pretensions to elegance, writing on the back of a roll would have been avoided. A fragment work of the Roman poet Gallus found in 1978 at Qaṣr Ibrîm in Upper Egypt and dated between 50 and 20 B.C. provides an excellent example of modish publication (see plates published in Anderson, Parsons, Nisbet, 1979).

In contrast, the elder Pliny made much more sparing use of rolls, for he bequeathed his nephew 160 rolls of notebooks written in a minute hand on both sides of the roll ("commentarios centum sexaginta mihi reliquit, opisthographos quidem et minutissimis scriptos," *Letters* 3.5.17). The term *opisthograph* has been applied generally to any roll that has a text copied also onto its back —a fair number of which exist—but opisthographs in which the same scribe has written both sides of the roll are quite rare. One such papyrus is in the Beinecke Library collection at Yale University. Assignable on paleographic grounds to the second century B.C., it holds two speeches of Isocrates—the *Helen* written along the fibers on the inside and the *Plataicus* across the fibers of the outside or back of the roll. The format of the whole is small and compact, as if the scribe intended to save as much space as possible; its overall appearance brings to mind Martial's mention of compact books for the traveler (*Epigrams* 1.2).

How rolls were copied is a matter for debate. It is unclear whether ancient scribes copied by eye or by ear (that is, by dictation, as was the practice in medieval scriptoria); nor is it at all certain that practices among professional scribes or booksellers remained constant over the thousand-year period in which the roll flourished. In those cases where only one copy of a text was required, it would have been more economical for a single scribe to copy by eye from an exemplar, but when multiple copies were required, dictation by one to many was probably more practical. Unfortunately, evidence is ambiguous; if an error appears to result from misreading the exemplar—a phonetic error or mistaking one letter for another—it could as easily have been the fault of a reader dictating to a group as of a single copiest reading to himself as he copied. T. C. Skeat has produced considerable detailed evidence to demonstrate that the *Codex Sinaiticus* and the copy of the *Iliad* in the Pierpont Morgan Library in New York City were the results of dictation, but he thinks it possible that "visual copying and copying from dictation existed side by side" (1956, p. 195).

Generalizations about all ancient manuscripts are impossible; Skeat cautions that "for far too long the question has been debated in the absence of the manuscripts" and that "in such investigations the manuscripts must be treated as individuals—it is useless, for example, to collect errors of a given type from a variety of manuscripts and then lump the results together" (1956, p. 207). Rather, each manuscript must be evaluated independently. With respect to the quality of the texts of papyrus book rolls, observation would suggest that manuscripts that are beautifully written and set out (the equivalent of a modern coffee-table book) are not necessarily the most carefully produced. Professional booksellers were said to proofread their texts, but a manuscript like the British Museum's Bacchylides, which is the source for almost all of his extant poems, shows some corrections but contains so many unnoticed errors that whatever proofreading it experienced cannot have been too careful. This phenomenon was familiar to ancient scholars, who corrected by themselves or through secretaries whatever copy they wished to use from another exemplar.

It is well to remember that the roll was basically an elite means of storing and carrying information. An elegant, well-constructed roll would certainly have been beyond the means of the average denizen of the Greco-Roman world. The prodigal use of space, with wide margins and a back normally unwritten on, reinforces this view. Further, with the exception of those explicitly shown with book rolls in order to identify them as poets, those reading are most frequently schoolmasters or slaves. Roman literature is full of examples in which the learned man is pictured being read to by his slave or dictating to another, but not undertaking these tasks for himself.

In these circumstances the relative incovenience of the ancient book roll in comparison to the modern book is perhaps explicable. But the implications for ancient scholarship—Alexandrian or otherwise—are serious. While such scholars undertook in theory the systematic organization and comparison of data, the practical limitations of the roll require us to call into question both their methods and their thoroughness.

For example, neither scribes nor scholars who used rolls numbered columns, though the practice of column numbering, or docketing, was quite familiar in documentary texts. Therefore, no means of cross-referencing was possible. And, occasionally, if the writer of a scholarly commentary was unable to lay his hands on a reference, he might simply leave a blank in his text where the reference could be placed, in the event that a subsequent reader might happen across it. Practically speaking, it is impossible to use two rolls at one time, which meant that the kind of rapid consulting and cross-checking that is so easy with modern books was impossible. This fact alone accounts for the habit observable in ancient grammarians and scholiasts of gathering the majority of their examples from the beginning of books, for information in the center of the roll was much harder to retrieve.

TRANSITION TO THE CODEX

Rolls would have been used for matters of permanent record and, of course, for publication. Alongside the roll both the Greeks and later the Romans used another format for writing, specifically for ephemeral material, or for preliminary drafts before transfer to the permanent storage of the roll. The writer as he composed, the businessman as he kept his daily accounts, the schoolboy as he copied his lessons were more likely to use a wooden tablet. In Greek called *deltos* or *pinax,* it was commonly formed of two or more pieces of wood joined together either by a clasp or by leather thongs passed through pierced holes. The wood could be written upon directly with pen or chalk or scratched with a stylus, but more usually the center of the tablet was hollowed out to receive wax, colored by pitch; a small raised strip of wood was often left in the middle to prevent the wax from being smudged when the tablets were closed.

The wood tablet is certainly very old—it has been plausibly identified on two Neo-Hittite reliefs of the ninth and eighth centuries, and it may be to such a tablet that *Iliad* 6.169: *en pinaki ptukto* (in folded board) refers. In any case, by the fifth century Greeks used a wooden tablet whitened with gypsum (*leukoma*) for temporary public notices. A number of such tablets joined together were called *tabellae* by the Romans (hence the name "tablet"), but also *codex* or *caudex,* because they were normally made from wood, and if the tablets were small enough to be held in the fist they could be called *pugillares.*

The standard implement for writing on the wax tablet was the stylus, usually made of metal. It had a sharp point for marking the wax and at the other end a flat edge for smoothing it out again, that is, for erasing errors. Hence Horace's admonition to frequently invert your stylus and you will write something more worthy of reading ("saepe stilum vertas, iterum quae digna legi sint scripturus," *Satires* 1.10.72–73) applies to composition in a preliminary form written on wax tablets. The correct relationship between tablets and the finished roll can be seen, for example, from the scholarly habits of the elder Pliny, who on journeys kept a secretary at his side with roll and tablets. The secretary would read to him from a published text (*liber*), that is, a work copied onto a roll and circulated. He himself dictated his own impressions or preliminary notes to a scribe who wrote on the tablets (*pugillares, Letters* 3.5.14–15).

Since there is a practical limit as to how many wood tablets can be joined together and carried in comfort, parchment folded over to imitate the wooden tablet came into use. These parchment pages, called *membranae* in Latin, appear to have been used side by side with the heavier tablets of wood and wax, for Quintilian remarks in *Education of an Orator* (10.3.31) that the use of wax tablets is best for students because they are easier to erase, but parchment is better for those with weak eyesight, though he cautions that dipping the pen frequently interrupts the flow of thought.

Similar notebooks made of papyrus have been found from Dura-Europos on the Euphrates, though these belong to the third century A.D., and a prohibition against using papyrus notebooks because they did not meet ritual requirements appears in a decision quoted in the Jewish law (the Mishnah), from the second century A.D. But such tablets and parchment or papyrus notebooks were for a limited and private use, such as a lawyer jotting down precedents for court, a doctor carrying a list of handy remedies, or a businessman keeping a record of daily accounts. The notebook did not reach into the world of the official scribe or to the copying houses, where the roll was supreme.

But by the end of the first century A.D. there appear to have been tentative attempts to develop or exploit the format of the parchment or papyrus notebook more extensively, and the first codices were born. The mention of the marketing of editions of Roman authors in small pocket codices as a traveler's vademecum in Martial (1.2) is the earliest evidence for such an enterprise, which at least initially seems to have been unsuccessful.

The next attempts to circulate material in an expanded notebook or codex form very likely came from lawyers, doctors, or astrologers, that is, from professionals who were more concerned about the availability of information than with the aesthetic qualities of its presentation. Also, this class of businessman would have been most familiar with the tablet or notebook. Many of the earliest dated codices bear out this hypothesis; these are a manual of philosophy, of medicine, of grammar—texts that are workmanlike rather than calligraphic, intent on using all the available space.

But of course this did not offer competition for the roll as a vehicle for literary production, though statistical analysis of the fragments of Greek literature ranging in date from the first to the fifth century A.D. shows an interesting trend. Approximately 2,000 remnants of book rolls and codices from these centuries have been found. The proportion of codices gradually increases to 2 percent of the total in the period between the first and second centuries A.D., to 18 percent by the beginning of the third century, to 48 percent between the third and fourth centuries, and stands at 73 percent of the total by the end of the fourth century A.D.

The conclusion is inescapable that between the second and fourth centuries A.D. the book roll, which had held primacy of place for a thousand years in Greece and Rome, rapidly lost ground to the new format of the codex. While it is of course a superior means of storing and retrieving information, this cannot alone account for the change— why did it happen at this period and not before? It has been argued that the material dictated the form in which it would be made up; that is, when animal hides cured in some way became more popular in the West, they were more easily assembled into the codex format than the roll. But it may be objected that the Persians used leather rolls, made up like papyrus rolls, only with the sheets stitched instead of glued, for their historical archives, and the so-called Dead Sea Scrolls are in the main written on leather (in fact, one famous example had started to crack and was mended in antiquity with a strip of reinforcing papyrus glued on to patch its break). The use of skins had not therefore required a change of format before the second century. While Pliny the Elder remarks that papyrus had to be rationed for a time under the emperor Tiberius, such shortages appear to have been infrequent and hardly severe enough to dictate a full-scale change in the way of copying and disseminating books.

In fact, professional scribes might well have retarded the development of the codex. Its format consists of individual sheets (one or more) superimposed on each other and folded across the middle in such a way that one original sheet now yields four writing surfaces (or pages) that are one-half the width of the original. This unit is called a gathering, and it may be joined to similar gatherings and the whole secured by stitching. The size of the codex may be varied by altering the number of sheets in the gathering or the total number of gatherings, but the principle remains the same. The outer pages can be protected by binding covers and the result is both durable and sturdy.

Although it is a relatively simple device, it would have posed considerable problems for the professional scribe. Copying onto a roll must have been much easier than into a codex, where, if the number of pages was large, it was impossible to copy successive pages one after the other because on the left side the hand would run against the bulk of the fold or gather, while the right hand as it moved toward the right edge would lack support. In fact, the scribe copying material into the codex needed to copy his pages before they were assembled, first on one side and then the other (that is, onto half of the original sheet) until the middle of the book or gathering was reached, then back again, keeping a correct order. Also, he would need to gauge accurately the number of pages the material required, for it is difficult to insert or remove pages from a codex. If a page is added at the end, there will be a blank page at the beginning; if a single half sheet is added at the end, it will tend to work loose and fall out. However, with a roll sheets may be pasted in or removed at will.

Colin H. Roberts, in a brilliant study written in 1954 and revised with T. C. Skeat in 1983 (*The Birth of the Codex*), suggested that the real impetus for the codex came from an unexpected quarter. He observed that only about 1.5 percent of the some 871 texts of Greek literature that have survived from the second century are written in the codex form. If this is compared with material produced and circulated by the newly emerging Christian sects for the same period, there is a startling difference; of the 172 texts that have survived to date, including New Testament, Old Testament, and Apocrypha, 158 are in the new codex form. This statistic is more striking because there are no examples of the New Testament found written on the inside of a roll, and the few examples of the Old that are found in the roll form can usually be identified as Jewish rather than Christian (by the presence of the tetragrammaton for the name of God, see, e.g., Metzger, 1981, pl. 3). In an essential way then the format of even the earliest Christian material is different from the bulk of contemporary non-Christian writings. This is not to say that the Christians invented the codex. Clearly they did not. Its antecedents, the wax tablet and the parchment or papyrus notebook, were used throughout the Near East and the West. But non-Christian experimentation with the codex form appears scarcely to have begun when substantial numbers of Christian codices burst upon the scene.

Why did Christian communities and scholars adopt this format exclusively in Egypt—and undoubtedly elsewhere? Most certainly to differentiate (originally) the gospel material from the sacred books of Jewish scripture and from works of non-Christian literature. According to Jewish law, the sacred scriptures could be copied only on parchment and only in the roll format, and the oral law (the Mishnah) could not be written in a permanent way at all. But it could, for the purposes of scholarly disputation and study, be written temporarily onto wax tablets or in notebooks. Very likely, followers of Jesus initially regarded his sayings as part of oral law, and quite conscientiously did not commit them to roll form. Later, of course, when the relationship between the Jewish law and emerging Christian beliefs was being defined, any initial distinction in format would serve to reinforce a break with the older code. And because it did not constitute publication in a formal sense, the new format was easily distinguished from the rolls of non-Christian literature—a distinction that was by the fourth century to become a familiar artistic shorthand.

The roll came to be equated with pagan learning, or what was regarded as the best of it—philosophy—while the codex served to identify the Christian. The codex had several other advantages: it was economical and easy to carry, and passages for reading or meditation could be found with a minimum of trouble. Then in the long run the codex, by providing a means of control over material, led to the canonization, or codification, of Christian authorized books, because it is much harder to make undetectable additions or deletions from a codex; with a roll, sheets may be pasted in or removed at whim.

CHRISTIAN BOOK PRODUCTION

Since Christianity was a grass-roots movement, not, at least in the beginning, attached very much to the intellectual elite, it is not surprising to find that New Testament texts were not published in the sense that the classical world understood the term.

These texts do not appear to have been copied by professional scribes in scriptoria, but rather were written in a style that is serviceable, but by no means the equal in calligraphy of the best non-Christian rolls. It has been dubbed "reformed documentary," because its paleographic affinities are to the style in which business documents were normally written (see, e.g., Metzger, 1981, pls. 6, 7, 9).

In good literary production, regularity of letter shape and size is essential; columns of writing have an architectural quality about them—whether tall and narrow, short and broad, or something in between—the solidity of the writing block is maintained. Not so in documentary production. The hands are less calligraphic, less regularly written; often there is word division, indentation, or organization into sections to facilitate reading. One habit of the writer of documents has been cogently linked to the development of manuscript illumination: the practice of enlarging the initial letter of a line or section, even occasionally extruding it into the margin. This tendency, which is so common in later medieval manuscripts of all sorts, is already apparent in the earliest biblical manuscripts written in Greek, which are datable to the second century A.D.

A further elaboration of this technique, which is totally unknown in literary papyri, is the use of red ink to highlight certain letters. This can be first observed in a third-century copy of a gospel from the Faiyūm in which the abbreviation (Pet) for the name of Peter is added in red, perhaps as an imitation of the Jewish practice of writing the tetragrammaton in gold letters. And two other Christian books of the fourth or early fifth century show initial letters enlarged as well as rubricated.

From such relatively humble beginnings, scriptural codices displayed rapid technical development in paleography, in format, and in their bindings that is a harbinger of the Middle Ages. A special writing style for copying biblical manuscripts evolved—the biblical majuscule—so pervasive that even non-Christian books were often written in it. The majuscule with its distinctive rounded letters, each carefully and consistently formed to sit in a notional square, persists into the Middle Ages and beyond. Although later phases of this handwriting style become quite ornate, its earliest manifestations, like the reformed documentary itself, aimed at clarity and ease of reading (e.g., Metzger, 1981, pls. 13, 15). Quite likely, they both originated in the production of books to be read aloud for liturgical purposes rather than for private devotion.

By the fourth century, Christian codices achieved such elegance that they successfully competed with and even surpassed the elegance of non-Christian books. The *Codex Sinaiticus* (Metzger, 1981, pl. 14) is not only the largest ancient codex to survive—a single page is slightly over a foot wide and fifteen inches high—but its four-column format, unique among Christian books, seems to be imitating the classical book roll, especially the tall, narrow column format that predominated in the prose writings of the second century A.D.

One final book—the *Glazier Codex*, which is on deposit in the Pierpont Morgan Library—deserves mention because it provides a clear link between the traditions of book production that had developed at the end of the ancient world with those of early medieval Europe. The *Glazier* is a miniature codex, measuring about five by four inches (12 × 10.5 cm), containing the first half of the Acts of the Apostles written in Coptic. Made of vellum and assigned to the late fourth or early fifth century A.D., it is one of the very few books from this period to have survived intact with its bindings. They are red-brown morocco with wooden boards for covers. Holes have been drilled in the wood to thread through the leather cording that holds on the back. There is also a cover strip to protect the top edges of the page and a wrapping band adorned with bone strips. It is an attractive and elegant little book, but those papyrus codices found buried near the monastery of Pachomius at Nag Hammadi (north of Coptos [Qift] at the point where the Nile turns to flow east) display even greater technical mastery, both in the variety and ornamentation of their covers and bindings and in the proficiency with which they have been bound.

However, the real importance of this codex lies in its back cover. Here is the first true miniature illustration: the ansate cross adorned with a red, yellow, and brown interlace pattern of some complexity, flanked by peacocks with doves and olive branches (plate in Bober, 1967). The ansate cross was par excellence the symbol of Coptic Christian Egypt. It is well known to have been derived from the ancient Egyptian symbol for life, the ankh, which regularly adorned representations of the pharaohs and the gods and in Christian times seems to have survived in textiles as well as in funerary art. This cross is sitting on a base—again a familiar symbol from the pre-Christian period—the *djed* (meaning stable or durable) pillar that frequently supported the ankh and was in Egyptian iconography associated with rebirth, as were peacocks. The doves and olive branches doubtless symbolized resurrection. The whole is executed in such a way as to suggest that the artist is thoroughly familiar with the iconographic tradition and that his subject is neither new nor experimental.

So here at the end of the fourth century are found identifiable elements of later, medieval book illustration, elements that next appear in the late seventh century: the deliberate use of a coherent set of symbols in the illustration, here for resurrection and rebirth; a psychological predisposition to adopt pagan iconography and reform it as Christian; an interlace pattern, which was long thought to have come from the Near East, displaying the very colors that first appear in Irish psalters—red, yellow, and brown; and a very sophisticated, even whimsical, use of color to break up the apparently regular and monotonous pattern of the interlace. That a well-defined iconographic tradition and certain techniques like interlace had gained a secure foothold in monastic book production by the beginning of the fifth century can no longer be disputed, signifying a tradition that was more likely to have been transplanted to western Europe than to have been invented there anew.

BIBLIOGRAPHY

Since much of the earlier work on book production has been superseded, the interested reader is advised to start with the most recently written studies first, particularly those of Colin H. Roberts, T. C. Skeat, and Eric G. Turner. Excellent discussions of previous scholarship may be found in *The Cambridge History of the Bible*, II, G. W. H. Lampe, ed. (1969), and in Colin H. Roberts and T. C. Skeat, *The Birth of the Codex* (1983).

SOURCES

For the convenience of the reader, plate references throughout this article are to handbooks of Bruce Metzger or Eric G. Turner whenever possible. The following are editions of facsimiles and catalogs of Greek and Latin manuscripts: K. Aland, *Repertorium der griechichen christlichen Papyri. I, Biblische Papyri. Altes Testament, Neues Testament, Varia, Apokryphen,* Patristische Texte und Studien, 18 (1976); Albert Bruckner and Robert Marichal, *Chartae Latinae Antiquiores,* I (1954); Joseph van Haelst, *Catalogue des Papyrus littéraires juifs et chrétiens* (1976); E. A. Lowe, *Codices Latini Antiquiores,* I (1934); Bruce Metzger, *Manuscripts of the Greek Bible* (1981); New Palaeographical Society, *Facsimiles of Ancient Manuscripts* (1st ser. 1903–1912, 2d ser. 1913–1930); Roger Pack, *The Greek and Latin Literary Texts from Greco-Roman Egypt,* 2d ed. (1965); Richard Seider, *Paläographie der griechischen Papyri,* I (1967); Eric G. Turner, *Greek Manuscripts of the Ancient World* (1971).

STUDIES

R. D. Anderson, P. J. Parsons, and R. G. M. Nisbet, "Elegiacs by Gallus from Qaṣr Ibrîm," in *Journal of Roman Studies,* 69 (1979); Frank W. Beare, "Books and Publication in the Ancient World," in *University of Toronto Quarterly,* 14 (1945); Theodor Birt, *Das antike Buchwesen in seinem Verhältnis zur Literatur* (1882; repr. 1959), *Die Buchrolle in der Kunst* (1907), and *Kritik und Hermeneutik nebst Abriss des antiken Buchwesens,* in Handbuch der klassischen Altertumswissenschaft, I, pt. 3, Iwan v. Müller, ed. (1913); Harry Bober, "On the Illumination of the Glazier Codex," in *Hommage to a Bookman* (1967); Alan K. Bowman and J. David Thomas, *Vindolanda: The Latin Writing Tablets* (1983).

Guglielmo Cavallo, *Ricerche sulla maiuscola biblica* (1967), and *Libri, editori e pubblico nel mondo antico: Guida storica e critica* (1975); Alphonse Dain, *Les Manuscrits* (1949; rev. ed. 1964); Lloyd W. Daly, *Contribution to a History of Alphabetization in Antiquity and the Middle Ages* (1967); Robert Devreesse, *Introduction á l'étude des manuscrits grecs* (1954); Karl Dziatzko, *Untersuchungen über ausgewählte Kapitel des antiken Buchwesens* (1900); Robert J. Forbes, *Studies in Ancient Technology,* vol. 5, 2d ed. (1964).

M. W. Haslam, "A Problem of Textüberlieferungsgeschichte," in *Liverpool Classical Monthly,* 1 (1976); Herbert Hunger, "Antikes und mittelalterliches Buch- und Schriftwesen," *Geschichte der Textüberlieferung der antiken und mittelalterlichen Literatur,* I (1961); Richard R. Johnson, "Ancient and Medieval Accounts of the 'Invention' of Parchment," in *California Studies in Classical Antiquity,* 3 (1970); Frederic G. Kenyon, *Books and Readers in Ancient Greece and Rome,* 2d ed. (1951); Tönnes Kleberg, *Buchhandel und Verlagswesen in der Antike* (1967); Naphtali Lewis, *Papyrus in Classical Antiquity* 2d ed. (1974); Bruce Metzger, "The Making of Ancient Books," in *The Text of the New Testament* (1964); Kurt Ohly, *Stichometrische Untersuchungen* (1928); Rudolf Pfeiffer, *History of Classical Scholarship,* I (1968).

Ernst Posner, *Archives in the Ancient World* (1972); Ronald Reed, *Ancient Skins, Parchments and Leathers* (1972), and *The Nature and Making of Parchment* (1975); Leighton D. Reynolds and Nigel G. Wilson, *Scribes and Scholars: A Guide to the Transmission of Greek and Latin Literature,* 2d ed. (1974); Colin H. Roberts, "The Codex," in *Proceedings of the British Academy,* 40 (1954), and *Manuscript, Society and Belief in Early Christian Egypt* (1979), with T. C. Skeat, *The Birth of the Codex* (1983).

H. A. Sanders, "The Beginnings of the Modern Book," in *University of Michigan Quarterly Review,* 44, no. 15 (Winter 1938); Wilhelm Schubart, *Das Buch bei den Griechen und Römern* (2d ed. 1921; 3d ed. 1962); T. C. Skeat, "The Use of Dictation in Ancient Book Production," in *Proceedings of the British Academy,* 42 (1956), "Early Christian Book Production: Papyri and Manuscripts," in *Cambridge History of the Bible,* II, G. W. H. Lampe, ed. (1969), "Two Notes on Papyrus," in *Scritti in onore di Orsolina Montevecchi* (1981), and "The Length of the Standard Papyrus Roll and the Cost-advantage of Codex," in *Zeitschrift für Papyrologie und Epigraphik,* 45 (1982), with Colin H. Roberts, *The Birth of the Codex* (1983); O. Stegmüller, "Uberlieferungsgeschichte der Bibel," *Geschichte der Textüberlieferung der antiken und mittelalterlichen Literatur,* I (1961).

Eric G. Turner, *Athenian Books in the Fifth and*

Fourth Centuries B.C. (1952; 2d ed. 1977), "Writing Materials and Books," in *Greek Papyri: An Introduction,* chap. 1 (1968), *The Typology of the Early Codex* (1977), and *The Terms Recto and Verso: The Anatomy of the Papyrus Scroll,* Papyrologia Bruxellensia, **16** (1978); Kurt Weitzmann, *Illustrations in Roll and Codex: A Study of the Origin and Method of Text Illustration* (1947); Carl Wendel, *Die griechisch-römische Buchbeschreibung verglichen mit der des Vordern Orients* (1949); H. Widmann, "Herstellung und Vertrieb des Buches in griechish-römischen Welt," in *Archiv für Geschichte des Buchwesens,* **8** (1967); Franz Wieacker, *Textstufen klassischer Juristen* (1960).

GOVERNMENT AND SOCIETY

Greek Forms of Government

OSWYN MURRAY

ALL HUMAN SOCIETIES can be said to possess a form of government, in that any group in order to survive must possess a form of organization and control over its members for the purposes of corporate action. Forms of government are normally conditioned historically, by such factors as tradition, the nature of the group activities, and the economic and geographical constraints within which the group must operate. They are normally held to be inevitable by the society concerned, whether through nature or divine sanction. They may or may not be justified by a self-conscious ideology or a charter myth; and, once the system has passed away by evolution or destruction, it may or may not be of more than historical interest in exemplifying a principle of wider applicability outside its original context. In addition, the system of beliefs and values enshrined in a social organization may become part of a wider tradition, necessary to the understanding of a whole succession of societies, perhaps over millennia, as far as the present day and even into the future. Forms of government are therefore both historically determined, and so to be viewed as passing phenomena, and also part of a continuing system of thought. Whether that system is itself independent of history, or merely culturally specific over long periods of time, is an important question, to which only a philosophy of history can provide an answer.

Greek societies were at all periods until the Hellenistic age relatively small, face-to-face societies. The city of Athens in the classical period had an adult male citizen population of approximately 30,000 in the fourth century B.C., and perhaps half as much again in the period of its greatest prosperity in the fifth century; no other city of the time is likely to have been much more than half that size. The social composition of Greek societies was (excluding the status of slavery and other forms of serfdom) fairly homogeneous, without great extremes of wealth or a firmly entrenched hierarchy; but there was considerable diversification in economic activity. These societies existed in close contact with each other in a period of rapidly changing circumstances. It is therefore not surprising that, as in the life sciences, this constantly agitated gene pool evolved a greater variety of organizational responses than the earlier monolithic high cultures of the river valleys of Mesopotamia and Egypt; equally it is not surprising that the Greeks developed only partially and late those bureaucratic organizational skills that were characteristic of the oriental despotisms from their origins. Only one other culture of the Mediterranean area was in a position similar to that of the Greeks: the Phoenician communities, originating on the Levantine coast of the Mediterranean and subsequently spreading through North Africa as far as Spain. These exhibit a number of parallels with the Greek experience, whether through independent development or by cultural transmission; but our evidence for the governmental forms of the Phoenician cities is insufficient, being largely confined to their reflection in the annals of their more primitive Jewish neighbors. Direct comparison is therefore seldom possible, and we are not able to say to what extent the Greek achievement is unique, rather than a response to the pressures of urbanization in the Mediterranean area.

Greek societies are in fact the first known to us to have concentrated their attention not on the skills of efficient government and the execution of decisions, but on the actual process of decision making itself. It is in this sense that we can say that the Greeks invented politics: they created and perfected the techniques for the public taking of decisions on a basis of persuasion through rational argument. In the classical period they also developed ways of discussing problems of morality and procedure in relation to politics, which moved from the particular situation to the general principles involved: they invented political thought. In the hands of Plato and Aristotle, discussion of these problems became sufficiently systematic for us to recognize for the first time in history the existence of political theory; that is, speculation based on a set of coherent principles concerning the appropriateness of particular types of institution.

The primacy of the Greeks in the history of Western political and social thought is reflected in the fact that all the most important words and concepts used in political theory derive from the Greek language. This closeness of the Greek experience makes it difficult to view the Greeks historically and to realize that words such as "politics," "democracy," and "tyranny" had very different meanings for them; we should be especially aware of these changes, and their significance in revealing the hidden presuppositions of our own thought. For the study of the origins of our modes of discourse and their transformations serves to reveal our limitations and our hidden assumptions.

The chief difference between our use of this political vocabulary and its original use lies in a fundamental reinterpretation of the subject matter of the theory of politics, associated with the age of Machiavelli and Hobbes. For us politics is the study of forms of domination and control; of organization for effective action; and of conflict between power groups, or their reconciliation with the interests of the whole. Our basic problem remains the freedom of the individual in a theory concerned with his subordination to the group. To the Greeks, questions of power and of control were peripheral; they lacked a theory of sovereignty because they did not need one. The immediate aim of politics was to discover or to aid in the creation of a general will to action. The community (*koinonia*) was paramount, and its fission into conflicting groups was *stasis*, or revolution, a pathological state of breakdown. Greek political systems were designed to subordinate the group to the whole, with the result that the groups that were recognized in the public domain are not peripheral but tend to reflect fundamental divisions of class interest in the Marxist sense. The ultimate aim of politics was to achieve the good life, which was more likely to be defined in terms of leisure or activity than in terms of domination or exploitation. As a result the Greeks only occasionally felt that conflict between society and the individual that is a product of the distance between ruler and ruled. To them it was self-evident that the interests of the individual were those of the community. Thus the original conflict in Sophocles' *Antigone* is a conflict between two sets of social values, religious and political, not (as modern productions of the play usually presuppose) between the individual and the state.

THE ORIGINS OF POLITICAL ORGANIZATION IN GREECE

The earliest known political system in the Greek world is that of Mycenaean society in the second millennium B.C. (about 1600 to 1150 B.C.). Developed Mycenaean culture was organized around towns and palace strongholds, often interrelated with each other. It is clear that the towns were politically dependent on the palaces and that each palace center dominated the surrounding area both politically and economically. A considerable number of apparently separate palace centers can be identified in mainland Greece and Crete, notably at Pylos, Sparta, Mycenae, and Tiryns (Peloponnese); Athens; Gla, Orchomenos, and Thebes (Boeotia); Cnossos, Phaistos, Mallia, and Hagia Triada (Crete). The idea of a general overlordship exercised by the rulers of Mycenae rests on the evidence of Homer and on the fact that the Argolid was the most important area of Mycenaean culture; other evidence suggests rather that each palace center was independent. The type of political organization can be inferred from the evidence of a palace economy; the clay tablets of a small literate bureaucracy show the palace as the center of reception and storage for agricultural produce, luxury goods, and arms. One man, the *wanax*, stands at the head of the system; under him are other officials, the general (*lawagetas*), groups of men who were apparently local officials, called *qasireu* (?*basileus*), and others. A complex system of land tenure seems to have involved the regulation of land distribution from the center. The clay tablets containing lists and brief statements, written in Greek in the syllabic script known as Linear B, have been found at seven sites on Crete and the mainland, enough to suggest that the palace system was widespread. There is also evidence for centralized use of labor in the building of roads, drainage systems, and massive fortification walls. This organization was not, however, an indigenous development, but rather one taken over from the earlier non-Greek Minoan culture in Crete; it derives ultimately from the example of the early palace cultures of Mesopotamia and perhaps Egypt.

The type of oriental despotism reflected in Mycenaean culture is fundamentally unsuited to the geographical and economic constraints on social organization in the Mediterranean basin; with the destruction of the main palace settlements (1200–1150 B.C.) the system disappeared from Greece. Its memory was retained only in the curious double image presented by Greek heroic poetry, which reached its final form in Homer after some three centuries of oral development. In this portrayal of a heroic past all details of the Mycenaean system (including its use of writing) have been forgotten; only the vague memory of a monarchic past remained, alongside a political geography that corresponds reasonably well to that of the Mycenaean age. Otherwise the Homeric picture relates to a quite different political and social system, essentially nonmonarchic and presumably the result of evolution in the Dark Age. It is this system that provided the mechanisms of Greek political life.

Homeric Society

The question of whether the Homeric poems can be used as evidence for a historical society has been much debated, for the poems present a complex picture, which is the result of combining elements of invention with historical forms from different periods. However, three models of political behavior emerge with reasonable consistency; the problem is to determine how far they could have coexisted in one historical period.

The first model is monarchic, and seems to reflect an idealized version of the Mycenaean past rather than any later period. There are few signs that such a power system could have existed widely in the Dark Age, although a magnificent and unique princely burial of the early tenth century at Lefkandi (Euboea), found in 1980, has still to be explained; other "heroic style" burials of kings in Cyprus of the eighth and seventh centuries seem to involve a mixture of Homeric and Near Eastern influences.

In Homer the Mycenaean *wanax* survives as a formulaic title in certain passages, but normally the heroes are called *basileus*. This may well be the same word as that designating certain local officials in the Linear B tablets, but in classical Greek it was the standard word for the status of king. The ancient Greek view of their past did indeed emphasize the universality of kingship as the earliest form of political organization. Aristotle, for instance, defined the heroic *basileia* as a specifically Greek form of kingship that was "by consent, traditional, and legal" (*Politics* 3.1285b); he clearly believed that it had been widespread, if not universal, in early Greece into the historical period.

This picture is now generally rejected. It rests on a literal belief in the continuity of the heroic world with the later period, which modern research has shown to be false. Individual legends about the exploits of these alleged early kings are late and unreliable. More significantly, there are no proper accounts of the decline of kingship and its replacement by other political institutions: here the contrast with Roman myth is striking. In early archaic poetic and legal texts the word *basileus* seems to be used either generically, as the title of a magistrate holding apparently temporary office, or to designate a group of leaders. Given its apparently similar usage in Mycenaean Greek, this suggests that the word implies not monarchy but rather a form of aristocratic control; it was a later confusion between two historical periods under the influence of the Homeric poems that gave the word a new meaning.

Modern studies of early Greece tend to emphasize two other models, found in Homer, as reflecting the historical realities of the late Dark Age. The first offers a picture of the aristocratic *basilees* as a hereditary nobility distinguished from the rest of the community by their style of life rather than any great differences of wealth or power. Every *basileus* stands at the head of an aristocratic family (*genos*), whose economic and physical expression is the household (*oikos*). The *genos* consists of his immediate family, including adult sons and their wives; but the grouping is inherently unstable because, on the death of the head, all property is shared equally among his surviving sons, each of whom then constitutes a separate *oikos*. The wealth of the group is created first through the agricultural labor of the individual and his family, with the assistance of slaves, and second by the proceeds of warfare and piracy.

The leaders of the community may possess inherited status and greater wealth, but they are primarily distinguished by a lifestyle that unites the competitive consumption of agricultural surplus in institutionalized feasting with a military function. The center of the house of the *basileus* is the hall (*megaron*), used for feasting and entertaining those of a social status similar to the host's; the group of warriors defines itself and sets itself off from the community by such practices. The social code thus created rests on competitive feasting and displays of generosity; gift giving (though not direct gift exchange) is an important way of establishing mutual relationships. Links may be created over long distances through guest friendships. The host is obliged to receive a traveler, and to present him with a gift; such ties may be remembered over generations. The resulting groups constitute an elite of warriors, at the service of each other and of the community, which may often support them in return for their protection. The ethic of the group is unitary, not allowing deviation, but competitive rather than cooperative, and essentially individualistic. A man's honor (*time*) is established and maintained through public displays of generosity and of preeminence (*arete*) in all forms of public activity. *Arete* later designated any virtue or excellence, but in early Greek it is used especially of courage or skill on the field of battle; and those who display it are the men of *arete*, the *aristoi*. Homeric poetry explicitly presents itself as the entertainment of such a warrior class at its feasts.

Archaeological evidence can be used to support such an interpretation of Homer; for the late eighth century, before the growth of urban settlement, a number of areas show small independent communities around a larger *megaron*-type building, and burial customs attest the preeminence of the aristocratic warrior and the significance of feasting as a status symbol. A number of parallels in other societies, from Polynesia to Afghanistan and the tribes of northern Europe, have been adduced. Such instances serve to demonstrate the fundamental principle that in subsistence societies, agricultural surplus is often used as a social differentiator; the feast is a social ritual, whether for sharing or for display, and it may often serve to create a class structure and a group identity. In particular the relation between alcohol and warfare is reciprocal, the one providing release and bonding for the other. The warrior group must develop activities for peacetime that continue to prepare it for war: the release of aggression and inhibition through alcohol has a close connection with the psychological effects of fear and tension on the battlefield, and group loyalties forged in the drunken escapades of the officers' mess are an excellent preparation for the hazards of war.

Many of the social and political characteristics of later Greek society can already be discerned in this model of an aristocratic warrior elite, largely self-sufficient, but also at the service of the community. Aristocratic leadership itself persisted even in the most advanced states until the end of the fifth century, and the social and moral attitudes of its origin was perpetuated through the medium of the *Iliad* and the *Odyssey,* which were the basic texts of Greek education throughout antiquity. The institution of the *symposion,* itself a descendant of the Homeric feast, helped to preserve and diffuse the group values of an earlier period. The relation between economy and society in the Greek world remained dominated by the concept of beneficence (*euergesia*), a transference into the public sphere of the relationship between honor, power, and the gift; the result was a system of public economy fundamentally different in conception from modern capitalism, and inexplicable in capitalist terms.

The Polis

The two models so far discussed reflect the past; a third model prefigures the future. In the background of the poetic portrayal of the Homeric aristocracy a more articulated community life is clearly visible. The characteristic social and political organization of the Greek world was the polis, or independent city-state, a phenomenon that has many analogues but no parallels in subsequent history. The polis originated in this period, and in the seventh and sixth centuries was spread by Greek colonization around the shores of the Mediterranean and the Black Sea. By the classical period there were hundreds of such Greek communities scattered "around the sea from the river Phasis [in the Caucasus] to the Pillars of Hercules [Straits of Gibraltar] like ants or frogs around a pond" (Plato, *Phaedo* 109b). Under Greek influence the same type of organization was adopted by other peoples, notably the Etruscans and Romans. Later, in a further wave of settlement after the conquests of Alexander the Great, it penetrated as far as the river valleys of the Nile and Mesopotamia, and even beyond to Afghanistan. Wherever Greeks went they founded a polis; an army on the march could even constitute itself into a polis, as Xenophon's *Anabasis*, his account of the march of 10,000 Greek mercenaries drawn from many different communities through a hostile Persian Empire, reveals. At the start of the *Politics*, Aristotle presents a proof that "the polis exists by nature, and that man is by nature an animal of the polis" (1253a), a phrase that is usually modernized in translation to read "a political animal," which imports the idea of politics as a constant identifiable human activity. Aristotle goes on to demonstrate that those who do not live in a polis are not fully human: the polis is conceived of as both natural and necessary to the full development of man. Politics, as its name reveals, is the study of the organization, function, and aims of the polis, and this article will therefore center on the polis. But no social institution can remain unchanged by time and place, however constant its basic forms may seem; rather than offer a definition of the polis (as many modern theorists have attempted), we must follow its historical development and its changing functions.

Homer provides the first evidence for the existence of the polis, in a number of passages that are perhaps rightly thought to be late in the development of the epic. The account of the ideal land of the Phaeacians (*Odyssey* 6.262–267) describes its physical form:

> Around our city is a high fortified wall; there is a fair harbor on either side of the city, and the entrance is narrow. Curved ships are drawn up on either side of the road, for every man has a slipway to himself; and there is their assembly place [agora] by the fine temple of Poseidon, laid with heavy paving stones in the earth.

The description of the decoration on the shield of Achilles (*Iliad* 18.490–540) includes two cities. In the agora of one a lawsuit is taking place in front of the people in formal assembly, who are restrained by heralds; each elder takes the scepter in turn to offer his judgment. The other city is at war, defending its walls. Even armies on campaign possess such an institutional structure, a place "where was their assembly and their law, and where their altars to the gods were established" (*Iliad* 11.807–808). In contrast, the Cyclopes are completely uncivilized: "They possess neither counsel-taking assemblies nor judgments [*themistes*], but dwell on the tops of high hills in hollow caves, and each one utters judgments for his children and wives, and they take no heed of one another" (*Odyssey* 9.112–115).

Already for Homer the polis has certain physical characteristics: it is an urban settlement with docks and walls, and it has a public meeting place bordered by public temples. The delimitation of the settlement by walls and the existence of a public space at its center presuppose a formal system of government. These developments in urbanization can be dated archaeologically. The site of Smyrna (Asia Minor), settled about 1000 B.C. by Greeks from the mainland, possessed walls by 850, which were remodeled several times in the next century and a half; about 700 the city was redesigned on a regular plan, which must have involved a centralized redistribution of land. Similar signs of public building and public action can be found all over Greece. The town of Eretria was founded on Euboea about 825 B.C., and by the second half of the eighth century major temple buildings existed; in the seventh century the city put up strong walls and engaged in major public works to control the course of the river. The earliest public temples in Greece come from the mid eighth century, and are to be found in most important cities by 700. In the same period in many areas there is a change in the settlement pattern, from isolated small units to the establishment of one central community. The colonizing movement, which began in the late eighth century, involved the formal founding of a new polis by public act from the parent city, which presupposes a conscious acceptance of the polis and its institutions. The arrival of the polis as a settlement pattern and a governmental form can therefore be dated to the century between 850 and 750 B.C.; already by 700 it was taken for granted as the standard form of social organization.

For us it is the use of the public space that is important, and once again Homer can provide the starting point. He mentions two types of communal activity that remained central to the organization of the polis throughout its history: the settlement of legal disputes and the taking of communal decisions.

The development of Greek law cannot be entirely omitted from an account of Greek political institutions, since the lawcourts and the law code were at all periods regarded as part of the political system. Homer describes two types of legal procedure, a primitive public oath-taking test (*Iliad* 23.566–595) and a more complex formal arbitration procedure involving a case of murder, in which the right to pay compensation and the amount to be paid is discussed by the elders in public assembly. Although their decision is not binding on the two parties, it has the weight of public opinion behind it, and they are entitled to an arbitration fee—law is already a source of profit (*Iliad* 18.497–508). Decisions (*dikai*) are made and criticized in accordance with what seems right, not in relation to a divine order.

It is possible to object to the activities of the *basilees*. Homer's judges are responsive to the voice of the people; in *Works and Days* (256–264), Hesiod, the poet contemporary with Homer, personifies the individual judgment as the abstract Justice (Dike):

> She is the virgin Dike born of Zeus, glorious and honored by the gods who dwell on Mount Olympus; and whenever anyone harms her by casting crooked blame, straightway sitting by her father Zeus, son of Kronos, she tells him of the minds of unjust men, until the people pays for the arrogance of its *basilees* who, plotting evil, bend judgments astray and speak crookedly. Take thought of this, you gift-eating *basilees*, straighten your words, utterly forget crooked judgments.

From its origins law and justice were central to the Greek conception of the polis.

The second significant feature of Homeric society for the future of the polis is the method used for taking communal decisions. A public gathering place, the agora, was already an essential part of the Homeric picture of the polis; its use is demonstrated in the narrative. The noble *basilees* take decisions for the community, meeting in a council (boule); these decisions are then ratified before a formal meeting of the people (demos). Two examples will show how well structured the procedure was.

In *Iliad* Book Two Agamemnon decides to test his troops; he orders "the loud-voiced heralds to summon the long-haired Achaeans to the gathering [agora] . . . but first he called a council of the great-hearted elders." Here he unfolds a plan: he will propose withdrawal from Troy, and the other elders must oppose him in assembly. Nestor speaks in favor, and they proceed to the meeting, which is controlled by nine heralds. When the people are seated, Agamemnon takes his *skeptron,* or staff of office, and addresses them standing. Unfortunately the proposal is so popular that it starts a rush for the ships, which is halted by Odysseus, who takes the *skeptron,* the symbol of authority, and uses persuasion on the nobles and compulsion on the others to bring them back to assembly. At this point one of the people dares to speak, and is silenced by Odysseus with a blow from the *skeptron*. A herald secures silence, and Odysseus and Nestor persuade the army to stay and fight; Agamemnon gracefully yields, and dismisses the Achaeans to prepare for battle (*Iliad* 2.48–393).

In the *Odyssey* the young Telemachus calls an assembly on Ithaca to complain about the behavior of his mother's suitors. Again he orders "the loud-voiced heralds to summon the long-haired Achaeans to the gathering. They made the announcement, and they gathered swiftly." Telemachus went to the assembly, and "took his father's seat, and the elders yielded to him." An elder speaks, and asks who called the assembly; Telemachus "stood in the middle of the agora, and the herald Peisenor placed the *skeptron* in his hand"; at the end of an impassioned speech he dashes it to the ground. There follows a long debate in which the behavior of the suitors is discussed; one speaker even appeals to the people to aid Telemachus against them: "Now I cast blame on the rest of the people, seeing you all sitting silent, and not speaking out against the evil suitors in our defense, though you are many" (*Odyssey* 2.1–259).

Both these occasions present a formal assembly with rituals and rules of procedure; both involve genuine discussion between opposing points of view. Only the leaders of the community are expected to speak, but it is clear that the people have a part in the decision-making procedure. The assembly includes at least all male members of the community able to bear arms, and there is no obvious sign of its limitation to a particular social class or property qualification. The lack of a method for deciding between conflicting views points to the purpose of the assembly in creating unity rather than mediating opposition: the Greek assembly was never capable of resolving deep-rooted divisions, which tended to lead to violent confrontation outside the assembly.

The Homeric picture leaves obscure the development of an executive power, not least because that is confused with earlier monarchic elements. But slightly later evidence shows that hereditary or long-term office was not the standard pattern; rather, executive magistrates were normally annually appointed and often not eligible to hold office again; they were also often young members of the nobility, who by their tenure of office became life members of the council. They were therefore normally submissive to the will of the council despite the absence of any formal check on their powers.

It is hard to deny the reality of these political institutions and their physical setting; by the late eighth century the Greek communities had already evolved those political forms that remained distinctive of the polis for the rest of its history. Two features deserve special emphasis. The first is the place of persuasion in politics and law, and the freedom from preconditions involved in that process: rather than appeal to precedent or to human or divine rules, appeal to reason or to a principle of what is just is the norm. Persuasion is as important a function of the Homeric *basileus* as fighting: Odysseus is "the best in good counsel and mighty in war" (*Iliad* 2.273), and other heroes are described as being better at one or the other. The second factor is the absence of a privileged group of experts within the class of *basilees*: all are equally entitled to make decisions or give judgment. The absence of a close connection between religion and the political and legal structures, reflected in the absence of a priestly class, is highly significant; in this sense, at least, politics and religion had always been separate in Greece.

The Concept of Good Order

The period from 675 to 525 B.C. saw the development and articulation of the archaic polis. Politically the traditional aristocracies lost power as their economic status declined through the development of alternative sources of wealth in trade and craft manufacture, and as their function as a military elite was subsumed in new military tactics. It was a period of turbulence and social tensions, in which tradition and custom were no longer felt to be adequate. The conceptual framework within which these problems were resolved remained, however, a unitary one, implying that a consensual solution was possible: the existence of conflict was recognized, but as a form of disorder.

Justice and Good Order are the two central concepts in this characterization of the social order of the polis. The new ideal was already formulated by Hesiod. His mode of political discourse rests on the traditional form of the genealogy: abstract concepts derived from concrete activities in the public domain are personified and treated as members of a divine family. Thus abstraction through personification, if not original to Hesiod (there are a few random examples in Homer concerned with physical states), becomes for him a meaningful system of political relationships, expressing the forms of order and disorder in human society. Zeus, the high god, validates the social order literally, by begetting it: "He married second rich Themis [Custom], who bore the Horai [Norms], Eunomie [Good Order], Dike [Justice], and blessed Eirene [Peace]" (*Theogony* 901–902). In other words, the marriage of divine and human order produces the norms that create the conditions for social order, justice, and peace.

In this hierarchy Themis is already known from Homer as a goddess jointly associated with Zeus in convoking the gatherings (*agorai*) of men (*Odyssey* 2.68) and as the herald of the council of the gods (*Iliad* 20.4); she derives her existence from the plural *themistes* or customary laws of society, just as Dike derives hers from the plural *dikai* or judgments given in accordance with those laws. Conversely "dark *Eris* [Strife] begets painful Labor and Forgetfulness and Famine and tearful Griefs, and Fights and Battles and Slaughters and Murders and Conflicts and Lies and Words and Disputes and Disorder [Dysnomie] and Vengeance, all kin of one another, and False Oath who plagues mortals worst of all when a man willingly perjures himself" (Hesiod, *Theogony* 226–232).

Similarly, Hesiod presents a picture of two cities of men in *Works and Days* (225–247): the city of straight *dikai*, where peace and prosperity reign and war, famine, and vengeance are absent, where the land gives forth its produce and man need not go to sea, and where "the women bear children like to their fathers"; and on the other hand the city of violence (*hybris*), infested with famine and plague, whose army and walls and ships are destroyed by Zeus.

For Hesiod divine and human order are closely related: the benefits of *eunomia* are not only social but also natural, in the bounty of a nature directed by Zeus toward the principle that the virtuous shall prosper. Conversely, the wicked city is afflicted, not just with the consequences of its own disorder but also with punishment by natural disasters controlled by the divine.

The Rise of Tyranny

Aristotle (*Politics* 4.1297b) saw a close connection between military service and political rights in the early polis:

The first type of constitution among the Greeks after kingship was formed from the warriors, initially from the cavalry (for the strength and dominance in warfare belonged to the cavalry; hoplites are useless without a formation, and such skills and tactics did not exist originally, so that the cavalry was the strong arm), but as the cities increased in population and those who carried arms gained importance, more persons gained a share in political power.

The new mass levies of heavily armed troops (hoplites) that evolved in Greece in the early seventh century created a new political class.

The sense of class solidarity and of commitment to the polis was expressed in a new form of poetry in elegiac meter, accompanied by the flute (*aulos*) rather than the lyre (*kithara*) as the Homeric hexameter had been. The language of this poetry draws heavily on Homeric vocabulary, but instead of narrative the dominant discourse is that of direct exhortation to valor; the poetry is didactic, serving to mold a new class to the service of the polis.

It is with the Spartan poet Tyrtaeus in the mid seventh century that the new values of the hoplite class emerge most clearly. The warrior is exhorted to die for his country in a more direct expression of patriotism than is offered by the competitive individualism of the Homeric warrior elite. A man must stand firm with his comrades in the group (Tyrtaeus frag. 11.7–14):

> For you know the destructive work of Ares, god of sorrow, you have experienced all the fury of painful war. You were with those who fled and with the pursuers, young men, you have had your fill of both. Those who dare, standing by one another, to join in the hand-to-hand fighting in the front line lose fewer men and protect the people behind: when they flinch the courage [*arete*] of all is perished.

The word *arete* is redefined to fit a new cooperative ethic; excellence gives way to the idea of courage as endurance in a group situation (Tyrtaeus frag. 12.13–20)

> *This* is excellence [*arete*], this is the finest possession of men, the noblest prize that a young man can win. This is a common good for the city and all the people, when a man stands firm and remains unmoved in the front rank, and forgets all thought of disgraceful flight, steeling his spirit and heart to endure, and with words encourages the man standing beside him. This is the man who is good in war.

The sense of equality and the group ethic involved in the creation of a warrior class no longer confined to an elite, but comprising perhaps a third of the citizen population, was bound to lead to a sense of class consciousness and the rejection of aristocratic domination.

The overthrow by force of an aristocracy is first clearly attested at Corinth about 676 B.C. with the establishment of the tyranny of Cypselus and his son Periander. The phenomenon of tyranny spread to most of the advanced cities around the isthmus, Megara, Sicyon, and Athens, and across the Aegean to Mytilene (Lesbos), Miletus, and Samos; for more than a century tyranny was one of the prevalent forms of government, and among the more important Greek cities only Sparta and Aegina seem to have escaped it. After about 525 tyranny remained a possible option in government under a variety of political circumstances, first for the cities of Asia Minor under Persian control, where tyrants were in effect aristocratic governors on behalf of a foreign power, and then for other cities under military threat. The great Sicilian tyrannies of the early fifth century under Gelon and Hieron, and of the early fourth century under Dionysius I and Dionysius II of Syracuse, were in large measure responses to the military threat from Carthage.

The word *tyrannos* is non–Indo-European and is unknown to Homer. It is probably Phoenician, for its closest cognate is *seran* in Hebrew, a word used of the rulers of the Philistines in the cities of the Levantine coast; others have suggested that it is a Lydian word, on the basis of its first use in Greek by Archilochus (frag. 19) of Gyges, king of Lydia, and of a possible parallel with the Greek name for the Etruscans, *Tyrrhenioi*, who, myth claims, came from Lydia. In any event the word is new, and borrowed from a society where monarchy was more usual. It signals the first certain arrival of monarchy in Greece on a widespread basis since the Mycenaean period.

The word *tyrannos* appears to have possessed originally merely descriptive force; some of the early tyrants (notably Cypselus of Corinth) have attributed to them legends that attest their status as popular heroes. But by the second generation a combination of aristocratic hatred of these usurpers and growing popular demand for political rights turned many tyrants in reality or in the minds of their subjects into stock figures of hatred. The murder of a tyrant became a claim to heroic status, and the expulsion of tyrants by other cities could be seen as a moral duty. The figure of the tyrant entered political mythology as the stereotype of the absolute ruler, unchecked by any moral or legal constraints, devoted to cruelty and sexual license, hated and feared by his citizens. Tyranny was the worst form of government, outside the law, uncontrolled by the community, and exercised by force over unwilling subjects. It served (along with the prevalence of monarchy among many non-Greek peoples considered inferior) to deter the Greeks from allowing any individual to achieve any form of constitutional or extraconstitutional preeminence, at least until the reevaluation of monarchy by political theorists of the fourth century.

Despite this negative image and their failure to conform to the traditional political institutions, the archaic tyrannies contributed significantly to the development of the polis. It was during this period that the power of the traditional aristocracies was broken. The story of the tyrants of Mytilene is reflected in the poetry of their aristocratic opponent, Alcaeus, and shows how the aristocrats gradually lost political control of the city in the face of a popularly appointed leader, and failed to regain control when that leader died; he was replaced by another protector (*aisymnetes*) for a ten-year period. Meanwhile Alcaeus is excluded from the polis (frag. 130):

> I poor wretch live a rustic's life, longing to hear the assembly summoned, Agesilaidas, and the council; what my father and my father's father have grown old possessing among those citizens who wrong each other, from this am I excluded, an exile on the frontiers.

The case of Athens shows how, even when the tyranny had been overthrown by its aristocratic opponents, the leaders were compelled to accept that the political situation had changed, and to acknowledge the real power of a wider group of citizens. Despite their alleged unconstitutionality, the tyrants seem to have caused a centralization of power in their own person, which on their fall was transferred to the city and its institutions.

A similar centralization of artistic patronage radically transformed the relations between society and art under the tyrants. Previously the forms of artistic creativity had been related to the needs of the aristocracy for luxury goods, fine pottery, and entertainment at the symposia; only religious art stood somewhat apart, although it is not clear to what extent temples and shrines were community ventures rather than vehicles for personal display by men of power. With the tyrant individual patron and state merged; not only was the wealth of the city available for the building and adornment of temples and public buildings, but the tyrant sought to create great public festivals for the display of artistic patronage. Thus in Athens the cult of the Mysteries of Eleusis was the focus of much Peisistratid activity; and these rulers also established or brought into prominence the two great public festivals, the Panathenaia and the City Dionysia. The creation of public political art forms such as Athenian tragedy and comedy stems from this activity. Public display and conspicuous expenditure on public buildings were means by which the tyrants maintained their popularity and power; and this was the chief impetus toward the creation of a public art.

The Lawgivers ("Nomothetai")

Tyranny came to be seen as the path opposed to *eunomia;* when the Spartans conducted their campaign to expel tyrants from nearby cities in the late sixth century, they did so as a hoplite state firmly devoted to the political principle of *eunomia*. But that concept itself altered after the age of Hesiod under the influence of another external factor, the advent of writing in Greece.

The Mycenaean syllabic writing system had been awkward and inefficient, suitable only as a memory aid in recording lists of items and simple statements; it implies literacy confined to a restricted bureaucracy and used for specialized functions. During the Dark Age it was forgotten (except in Cyprus). Homer portrays an oral society; writing is mentioned only once, in the story of Bellerophon (*Iliad* 6.166 ff.), but the description is deliberately made vague. Still, the episode shows that the use of writing was once again known to Greece; in fact, the earliest surviving Greek inscriptions (on pottery) date from around 750 B.C. The new system was derived from the Phoenician script, which represented individual consonantal sounds; to this the Greeks added vowels, to create an alphabet that is basically the same as our Western alphabet. This system of approximately twenty-four letters was adopted by all Greek cities over the next generation or two, and passed to Etruria and Rome. It was extremely simple to learn, and the enormous variety of written texts at all levels of literacy surviving from the archaic world implies that writing was never the preserve of a class of experts, but available to and widely used by all but the poorest male members of society. The impact of literacy on Greek political systems is fundamental; two separate "literate revolutions" can be discerned. The first took place among many communities in the seventh and sixth centuries; the second can best be seen in the changes in the Athenian constitution and Athenian public life around the year 400 B.C.

Hesiod had already founded the concept of *eunomia* on a demand for "straight judgments" and an attack on the *basileis*. The most important political change in the archaic age was the removal of the law from the control of the aristocracy through the establishment of *written* law codes, which the magistrate was compelled to follow or whose control was even placed in the hands of the demos, the people as a whole.

The earliest Greek ideas about law revolve around two concepts, *thesmos* and *nomos*. *Thesmos* appears to be the earlier word, or at least to be the more poetic one. It comes to have an archaic sense of solemnity about it; *nomos* is the normal prose word. A *thesmos* is usually conceived of as imposed from outside, while a *nomos* is freely accepted by the group. The gods protect both; but unlike Jewish and Christian ideas, neither was conceived of as emanating from them directly, apart from a few universal laws of humanity known as the unwritten laws (*agraphoi nomoi*). Laws were created by men to serve their purposes, and each community might therefore have different laws. Later laws were made by the political community; but in this period they were often the creation of one man. The position of the lawgiver (*nomothetes*) is not easy to explain: appointed by the people, he has absolute power and absolute confidence in his creation of a (more or less) complete written law code, which is then considered definitive; he appears almost as the founder of a new polis, like the founder of a colonial city. In fact, this may well be the conceptual model, for he emerges first in the colonial cities of the west: Zaleucus of Locri Epizephyrii and Charondas of Catana (Catania) in the mid seventh century are figures whose work was remembered, even if no certain information survives. It was perhaps precisely in colonial cities, which lacked a traditional class of *basileis* to interpret the law, that the need for a written code was first felt.

Crete was also held to be an early source of law, a tradition reflected in the figure of Minos, the legendary king who became judge in the underworld. The earliest surviving written Greek law (*Greek Historical Inscriptions* no. 2) is in fact from Dreros in Crete, from the second half of the seventh century:

> May the god defend this [?]. This has been decided by the polis: when a man has been Kosmos, for ten years that same man may not be Kosmos; if he should become Kosmos, whatever judgments he gives, he himself shall owe double, and he shall be useless [deprived of political rights] as long as he lives, and what he does as Kosmos shall be as nothing. The Kosmos and the Damioi and the Twenty of the polis shall be swearers to this.

A number of important political principles are already established by this text. The polis decides (this is the first clear use of the term *polis* as a strictly political entity); the god (as so often later) is merely invoked to favor the decision. The chief magistracy is in the future to be strictly annual. Infringements are to be punished by a fine, by disqualification from political rights, and by invalidation of the magistrate's acts. The enforcement of this law seems to rest in the hands of other magistrates (or possibly a council). There is no indication whether it was part of a wider set of laws, although it presupposes a community that regulates its political structures by written law.

The Law Code of Sparta ("Rhetra")

Another constitutional enactment of the seventh century establishes the respective rights of the various political bodies in the polis of Sparta; it is our earliest surviving political constitution, and is known as the Rhetra or Great Rhetra (*rhetra* is the Spartan word for an enactment or law). Like most Spartan institutions, it was attributed to the legendary *nomothetes* Lycurgus, and is descibed by Plutarch (*Parallel Lives*, "Lycurgus" 6):

> Founding a shrine of Zeus Syllanios and Athene Syllania, tribing the tribes and obing the obes [territorial divisions], establishing a council of thirty with the rulers, to hold *apellai* from season to season between Babyka and Knakion, thus to bring in and reject; but to the people [to belong the decision] and the power [? this clause is very corrupt]. But if the people speaks crooked, the elders and the rulers to be rejecters.

The text was later thought to be an oracle from Delphi, a tradition as old as Tyrtaeus, who paraphrases and guarantees its main provisions in a poem called by Aristotle the *Eunomia*. It was written in an archaic Spartan dialect that is partially preserved in the text of Plutarch; one crucial clause is garbled, but its general sense can be reconstructed from Plutarch's comments (derived from Aristotle) and from an (admittedly less trustworthy) reworking of Tyrtaeus' lines. In this text the relation between innovation and the regulation of existing bodies is often obscure; for instance, the tribes must be older than the document, but the obes may be a new institution. The grammatical structure of participles and infinitives shows that the main clauses refer to the assembly of the people (*apella*): the aim is to establish the rights of this body in relation to the council and the magistrates (here in fact Sparta's two kings). Times and place of meetings are prescribed, and the procedure of the assembly is established. In Plutarch's narrative the last clause is said to be a later addition, which may well be so, since it appears to conflict with the tenor of the previous sentence. The document shows that in seventh-century Sparta political organization and administrative structures were already well defined, and written law is used to establish new rights for a citizen assembly against the existing political bodies.

Solon of Athens

The only *nomothetes* to speak to us with his own voice is Solon of Athens, who chose to present his views to the public in poetry, much of which has survived; for perhaps the first time, poetry was taken from the privileged world of the aristocratic *symposion* into the public agora: "I come as herald from lovely Salamis, presenting an order of words for song instead of a speech" (frag. 1). Speech, the language of the agora, was not yet written down, but poetry was; and it could also be learned and repeated by others in an oral context. In a culture only just beginning to move from oral to written communication, poetry possessed the power of diffusion through both channels. Solon used his poetry to influence public opinion beyond the political meeting place, in a way that foreshadows the political pamphlets and publicizing techniques of a fully literate age; by this means he attacked the injustices in Athens before his appointment as *nomothetes,* and afterward defended and explained his achievements.

Athens was a deeply divided society. A generation before Solon, in 621/620 B.C., its first law code had been established by Dracon, shortly after an attempt to create a tyranny had failed. Little is known of this code except that it was "draconian," so harsh that it must represent an aristocratic use of law to repress a dissatisfied people. Solon appears in the list of Athenian magistrates as archon for 594/593 B.C., and it is usually held that this was the year of his activity as *nomothetes.*

Before his appointment Solon had attacked the leaders in a poem (frag. 4.1–10) that begins:

> Our city will never perish by the decree of Zeus or the will of the blessed immortal gods; for the great-hearted guardian of a mighty father, Pallas Athene, stretches her hands over us. But the citizens themselves in their wildness wish to destroy this great city, trusting in wealth. The leaders of the people have an evil mind, they are ripe to suffer many griefs for their great arrogance; for they know not how to restrain their greed, nor to conduct decently their present joys of feasting in peace.

Later in the same poem (32–39) he defines his conception of *eunomia* in terms derived from the two cities of Hesiod:

> *Eunomie* makes all things well ordered and fitted and often puts chains on the unjust; she smoothes the rough, puts an end to excess, blinds insolence, withers the flowers of unrighteousness, straightens crooked judgments and softens deeds of arrogance, puts an end to works of faction and to the anger of painful strife; under her, all men's actions are fitting and wise.

The significant advance in this formulation is that Solon sees man as responsible for his own fate: the gods will never destroy the city, and the wickedness of the leaders brings no divine retribution or natural disaster (as in Hesiod), but rather political discontent caused by the opposite of *eunomia, dysnomia.* Before his reforms he presented himself as a radical, attacking the abuses of the powerful; Aristotle quotes a number of passages from the poems, and concludes, "In general he is continually attributing the cause of the conflict to the wealthy" (*Constitution of Athens* 5). Afterward Solon defended himself as a moderate: "I stood between them like a marker-stone [*horos*] in boundary land" (frag. 37.9–10). And he defines clearly the paths that he could have taken, but did not: "What I said, that I accomplished with the gods; I did nothing vainly, nor did it please me to act through the violence of tyranny, or that the noble should have equal share in the rich land of our country with the base" (frag. 34, lines 6–9).

Three themes recur through the poetry of Solon. The first is the theme of *dike,* a justice now conceived of as independent from the gods, but still a necessary constituent of the *eunomia* that is community life: it is curiously unproblematic, and requires not explanation but action to safeguard it. The second theme is that of wealth, itself neutral and a natural desire of man, to be attained in whatever way he can, but leading to abuse (frag. 13.7–13) when someone seeks it at the expense of another:

> I desire to have wealth, but I do not wish to obtain it unjustly: for justice always follows later. The riches that the gods give stay fast with a man from the bottom of the cup to the top; but he whom men honor for his arrogance [*hybris*], does not act rightly; but, trusting in unjust deeds, ends where he would not go, and swiftly is ensnared in delusion.

It is this sort of wealth that leads to the opposite of *dike, hybris*.

The third theme is that of the *nomothetes* and the law as a boundary marker (*horos*). For Solon the working of *eunomia* required the setting of limits to the desire for wealth in the interests of social justice; the task of law was to define the rights and mediate the conflicts between the members of society. It was concerned with the prevention of conflict and with arbitration: even crime and injury required recompense to the victim, not punishment by society. His conception of the task of the social reformer is at once moral and wholly secular. He appeals to no higher authority to justify his laws, which are self-evidently right. Such a rational, non-punitive approach to law was not achieved again until the eighteenth-century English jurist Jeremy Bentham; that this was not the normal Athenian attitude is evident from such texts as Aeschylus' *Eumenides*.

Solon's most important and lasting achievement was to establish a complete code of laws, which served as the basis of the Athenian legal system for the next 300 years at least. The Solonian code was written on wooden axles (*axones*) or pillars, which revolved in frames and were permanently set up for public consultation; it was not formally revised until the end of the fifth century, and even then its principles were still found adequate for the age of Socrates. References to many of Solon's laws survive, and show that the code covered all areas of the law as now conceived: criminal law (homicide, theft, assault), public law (treason, amnesty for exiles, rights to public dinners, taxation, refusal to take part in public life), public morals (prostitution, homosexuality, slander of the dead, expenditure and public display at funerals, vagrancy), family law (legitimacy, inheritance, adoption), land law (boundaries, sharing of water supplies), commercial law (loans, exports), religious law, and legal procedure. The principles of fixed written law and equality before the law were recognized as basic: "I *wrote down* laws [*thesmoi*] alike for commoner and for noble, fitting straight justice to every man" (frag. 36.18–20). A major aspect of this preoccupation was his abolition of enslavement for debt and of a form of serfdom that existed in Attica, in a measure known as the "shaking off of burdens" (*seisachtheia*): the existence of a group of peasant farmers in a state of social or economic dependence on the aristocrats had been one of the chief sources of discontent.

Aristotle highlights the three most democratic features of Solon's reforms as:

> First and most important, the ban of loans on the security of the person; next, permission for anyone who wished to seek redress for those who were wronged; and third, the one which is said particularly to have contributed to the power of the masses, the right of appeal to the jury court—for when the people are masters of the jury ballot they are masters of the state. (*Constitution of Athens* 9.1)

The second of these measures involved a major innovation in legal procedure, the establishment of two classes of action, the *dike*, which could be brought only by the aggrieved party in person, and the *graphe* or written plea, which could be brought by any citizen. Thus writing enabled a class of public actions to be established, either on behalf of the public interest or on behalf of the individual too frightened to act for himself. The creation of mass jury courts (*heliaia*), although at first only to hear appeals from decisions of the magistrates, gave the people control of legal decisions. Solon may not have foreseen the ultimate use of these courts as a political weapon, but he clearly believed that the people, not any class of legal or hereditary experts, should be the final arbiters of justice. For later generations it was the Solonian law code that established him as the founder of democracy.

Solon's legislation (*nomothesia*) also included constitutional reforms that should in principle have made Athens the most advanced example of *eunomia* in Greece. They are not described in detail in his poems, but in fragment 5 the general principle behind them is made clear:

> To the people [demos] I gave as much privilege [*geras*] as is enough, neither taking away nor adding too much to their honor; while those who had power and were famed for their wealth, for them I took care that they should suffer no slight. I stood holding my strong shield over both, and I did not allow either to triumph unjustly.

Geras is the word used in Homer for the distribution of booty among aristocrats; this must have been the first time anyone had suggested that the people also were entitled to *geras*. The most fundamental step in Solon's political reforms was the attempt to relate this *geras* not to birth or inherited status but directly to wealth. He created four property classes based on agricultural produce: the "five-hundred-bushel men" (*pentakosiomedimnoi*), the "cavalry" (*hippeis*, whose land produced more than 300 bushels), the "yoke-fellows" (*zeugitai*, hoplites, with more than 200 bushels), and the *thetes*; it was in theory possible to move from one class to another, as one inscription records. Political duties were distributed in accordance with this classification: the nine archons and the state treasurers were reserved to the highest class, and the *thetes* had merely membership of the assembly and jury courts. The principle adopted reflects the system of eligibility for military service according to ability to provide horse and armor; but extended into the political sphere it represents a crucial shift from aristocracy to timocracy. The significance of the change can be seen in the transfer of executive government from a class called the *Eupatridai*, or men of good birth, to the "five-hundred-bushel men"—a name that involved a deliberate affront to aristocratic values. To ensure that the aristocracy should not use their traditional influence to maintain control of the magistracies, Solon instituted a complex system for election, involving selection by lot from a previously elected larger body.

A similar attempt to protect his reforms from aristocratic interference can perhaps be seen in Solon's establishment of a second council alongside the traditional aristocratic council of the Areopagus (named from the hill on which it met): the new council was composed of 400 men, 100 from each tribe, perhaps chosen by lot. There is archaeological evidence which suggests that it had offices in the agora that included a meeting room and a dining and kitchen complex, implying that it was already expected (as later) that some part of it should be in permanent or at least frequent session. This large council was clearly intended to be a microcosm of the assembly, and to be ensured of freedom from control by the aristocracy through the magistrates; Solon's contribution to the free working of the assembly thus went considerably beyond the provisions seen in the Great Rhetra of Sparta. What business the assembly was expected to discuss is unclear, but it probably included legal appeals from magistrate's decisions—it is usually assumed that assembly and jury courts were not fully separate at this date. A law of Chios about a generation later (*Greek Historical Inscriptions* no. 8) suggests a system modeled on that of Athens:

If he is wronged in the court of the *demarchos* [?let him deposit X] staters [and] let him appeal to the people's council. On the third day after the Hebdomaia let the council be assembled, the people's, under penalty [for nonattendance, or possibly "with power to inflict penalties"] chosen fifty from each tribe. Let it perform the other business of the people, and also all those judgments that may be under appeal of the month.

Here again two councils exist, the people's and (presumably) an aristocratic one; the people's council prepares business for the assembly, and (in this law) is especially concerned with appeals from public magistrates' decisions.

It is unlikely that these constitutional reforms were specifically contained in a separate document of the type of the Great Rhetra. We have no evidence of the separation of different legal subjects like constitutional law or laws concerning magistrates in the fragments of the Solonian laws. Nevertheless, there is evidence of reference to public officials and legal procedures in the laws. It is not therefore plausible to doubt the picture of Solon's constitutional reforms given in Aristotle's *Constitution of Athens* on the grounds that it is a creation of fourth-century political theorists.

Solon's attempt to provide Athens with the most sophisticated political constitution of its time failed completely. Within five years struggles over the archon elections caused no election to be made; after similar episodes a compromise of dividing the archonships among the Eupatrids and groups called the Farmers and the Craftsmen (the three wealthy groups) was attempted. Factions based in different parts of Attica grew up behind three powerful aristocrats, and led to two short periods of tyranny under Peisistratus; after a ten-year exile Peisistratus returned in 546/545 B.C. to establish a permanent tyranny under himself and his sons for thirty-six years. It was not until the end of the sixth century that the *eunomia* envisaged by Solon could return, in a very different form. Nevertheless, the basic structures of the later Athenian democracy, its council and assembly, its lawcourts, and its selection of magistrates at least in part by lot, were established by Solon, and in that sense the Athenians were right to regard him as the founder of their political system as well as of their legal code.

The Organization of Sparta

In the early archaic period the Spartan polis seems to have been exceptional only in being politically and culturally one of the most advanced in Greece; by the end of the sixth century a series of changes had taken place that already made her both unique and the most complete embodiment of the principles of the hoplite polis. This development was disguised under a political myth, according to which every aspect of Spartan society had been instituted by the *nomothetes* Lycurgus. As related by Thucydides (1.18): "After an exceptionally long period of political unrest, Sparta nevertheless achieved *eunomia* in the earliest period, and never experienced a tyranny: they have possessed the same constitution for a little more than four hundred years to the end of this war [404 B.C.]." This myth may at least be significant in that it locates the origins of the Spartan system in time, rather than claiming that it had always existed; for it is clear that its main features presuppose the existence of a hoplite warrior class, however much it may have built on earlier customs: its origins cannot therefore be earlier than about 700 B.C.

In other respects the legend of Lycurgus is unhelpful, for the Spartan system appears to be the result of a conscious process of remodeling and adaptation over perhaps three centuries; by the classical period it presents an image of coherence, impressive both in its structural elegance and in its claim to historical continuity. The modern analyst therefore sees Sparta as an example of a pseudoarchaic society in which innovation is disguised as tradition, while tradition only survives through transformation. Every aspect of the society is justified through its functional coherence with the aims of the society; unlike genuinely traditional or archaic societies, there is little sign of the survival of "irrelevant" institutions. Although not archaic in this sense, the system was essentially conservative, in that one purpose of the Spartan myth was to limit and control innovation. The Spartan polis therefore became frozen in time as a hoplite warrior state, the perfect embodiment of the principle of *eunomia*. The completion of this model of the polis as what Max Weber called "a guild of warriors" may be dated for our purposes to the late sixth century; thereafter such changes as took place were consequences of external or internal forces working toward the dissolution of the ideal.

The catalyst in this development was Sparta's conquest and colonization of the neighboring fertile area of Messenia; this both provided the material basis for raising all citizens to full warrior status and created the necessity for that status to be fully exploited. Not only was the ratio between Spartan citizens and subject population of Helots approximately one to seven (Herodotus [9.28.2] writes of 5,000 Spartans and 35,000 light-armed Helots at the battle of Plataea in 479 B.C.), but, in contrast with most ancient slave populations, the Messenian Helots preserved a certain communal identity; revolts were therefore a continuing feature of Spartan history, and defense against them was the fundamental constraint on the development of Sparta.

Citizenship at Sparta meant membership in the warrior class, and citizens were liberated from all forms of nonmilitary activity. The development of a specifically hoplite mentality directed to obedience and disciplined courage has made Sparta an ideal to later conservative theorists, but they often fail to recognize the price to be paid for this specialization in social function. The creation of a citizen warrior class required a slave-producing class, and the warrior function had thus to be directed as much to internal control as to external military goals. For this reason Sparta was traditionally "slow to go to war" despite the acknowledged supremacy of its army, and committed to a defensive stance in foreign policy; it has been well described as a society organized on militaristic principles, but not organized for military action. The hoplite virtues were in fact internalized and directed to the preservation of a police state, based on the maintenance by force or terror of a form of non-racial apartheid.

In analyzing the Spartan state, it must be recognized that the nature of our sources means that we can only describe a timeless model. Spartan secrecy was proverbial; our main ancient sources do not reach back beyond the fourth century and accept the official Spartan myth of Lycurgus completely. Their authors were also admirers of Sparta, who wished to present it as a contemporary political ideal. The earliest is Xenophon, whose pamphlet on the institutions of Sparta, written in the early fourth century, is uncritical and eulogistic; Aristotle in the *Politics* offers a more balanced but less detailed account; later writers combine the vices of antiquarianism and idealism. Our description must therefore be of a model society, unlocated in time and heavily idealized.

All Spartan citizens were allotted an equal portion of land, to be farmed by the conquered Messenians; the Spartans themselves constituted a military elite of the *homoioi*. This term is often translated "equals," but socially and economically the Spartans were not equal; nobility of birth persisted at all periods, and was connected to inequalities of wealth: it appears that beside the state allotment of land, private possessions persisted. The word *homoios* refers rather to the consequences of the Spartan system of educational training (*agoge*). The Spartans were not "equal," but "uniform," "all alike," imbued with the same set of mental attitudes.

Social cohesion was ensured by an elaborate educational system and by the manipulation of the traditional relationship between commensality and the military function. The ties of kinship were systematically weakened. At birth it was the elders, not (as elsewhere) the father, who decided whether a child should be reared or exposed. From the age of seven all males (except the heirs apparent to the dual kingship) underwent a state-organized training. They were divided into packs under the supervision of older boys, and subjected to a complex progression through grades related to age. At twelve they began to live communally in conditions of ritualized austerity, providing their own bedding and given inadequate clothing and food, which they were expected to supplement by cunning and theft; much of the supervision of the system was left to the older youths. As with the nineteenth-century educational institutions of the Anglo-Saxon elite (themselves partially based on the Spartan model), the system was turned inward to create ever more complex ritual distinctions, expressed in a private language; it instilled conformity for the sake of survival and encouraged the not uncommon tendencies of young male adolescents toward sadism and homosexual relations between older and younger boys.

At the age of twenty those who had successfully passed through the *agoge* moved from an age-group to a peer-group structure: they were eligible for election to the *syssitia* or *andreia*, the commensal groups that were the basis of Spartan social life and military organization. Until the age of thirty the adult Spartan was required to live in these groups, and thereafter, even when married, to eat daily with his group. The *syssitia* were the basic units for military organization. The system is derived from earlier traditions of commensality among warrior groups, extended to cover the whole male citizen body and adapted to the military needs of a hoplite polis.

The substitution of male groupings for the family had a profound effect on the status of women. To some extent women seem to have modeled themselves on the male *agoge;* they were famous for taking part in athletics and for their skill at public choral dancing. But ancient writers clearly thought these institutions incomplete and condemned the lawgiver for not paying enough attention to women. They disapproved strongly of the freedom allowed to Spartan women, their lack of social discipline, and their legal right to own property. Aristotle thought that a major cause of the breakdown of the Spartan system was the fact that by his day two-fifths of the land of Sparta was owned by women (*Politics* 2.1270a). The relative freedom of women was, however, a direct consequence of the devaluation of the family in Sparta, and was a result of their exclusion from the male-oriented system of the *agoge*.

Other excluded groups of citizens are known. Because of the emphasis on equality in warrior status, exclusion from full citizenship was inevitable for such as those who failed to win admission or were unable to maintain their contributions to the *syssitia*, who were defeated and survived in war, or whose heredity was suspect; from time to time the Spartan state rewarded meritorious conduct by non-Spartans, admitting them to subordinate citizen status. The privileges and disabilities of these various groups remain obscure, but by the early fourth century the groups were sufficiently numerous to form the basis for an unsuccessful attempt to overthrow the system in the conspiracy of Kinadon (398 B.C.).

Outside the citizen body, the Spartans made use of noncitizen communities of their neighbors (*perioikoi*), semiautonomous townships the inhabitants of which were required to take part in campaigns, but were not subject to the ritual training or prohibitions against such occupations as trade and craft manufacture imposed by the Lycurgan system. Little is known of their organization, although they seem to have regarded their status as one of privilege and to have been generally loyal; Herodotus implies that their numbers were roughly equal to those of the citizen body. Beyond this group lay the Helots, whose status was that of slaves tied to the land, required to pay half their produce to their masters, subject to permanent curfew, arbitrary murder by the secret youth organizations (*krypteia*), and periodic purges.

The peculiarities of the social organization ensured that the political institutions of the state described above, although advanced for their period in giving great power to the assembly, and although similar in structure to those of most Greek city-states at all periods in possessing the three separate organs of executive magistracy, council, and citizen assembly, lacked any dynamic for development. The council of elders (*gerousia*), elected for life from those over the age of sixty, was in practice confined to members of the leading families. Although its formal function was always defined merely as the preparation of business for decision by the assembly (*probouleuein*), it controlled most aspects of political life with the magistrates. Even when the council was divided and the assembly had expressed itself in favor of a measure, a majority of one vote on the council was sufficient to prevent a measure being allowed to go forward (Plutarch, *Parallel Lives*, "Agis" 9–11); and Aristotle could treat the citizen assembly as having power only to ratify decisions, without apparently the right to reject them (*Politics* 2.7.1272a). This assembly (the *apella*) did, however, retain the basic rights of a warrior assembly, to decide on foreign policy and in particular on questions of war and peace: on many such important occasions it is recorded to have met, heard arguments on both sides, and made the substantive decision. It could therefore possess considerable influence in support of the policies of a particular military leader.

This military leadership was provided by Sparta's unique double kingship, vested by hereditary right of primogeniture in two royal families. The origins of this duality have never been satisfactorily explained; no other Spartan institution reveals a similar division (other basic social units relate to multiples of three or five), but there is no doubt about the functional significance of this double office. The existence of two independent kings enabled the institution to survive the vicissitudes of heredity, when one officeholder might be a minor or incompetent, and the principle of appointing regents was well established. The dual nature of the office seriously weakened the power that any single holder could wield, and therefore meant that it was not often a threat to other institutions: in a dispute with the *gerousia*, the king normally lost.

The main importance of the office was that only a king or his regent could lead a citizen army into battle (naval expeditions were not subject to this limitation). The kings possessed ritual privileges (including exemption as heirs apparent from the *agoge*), which made Herodotus compare them in part to the kings of Persia (6.56–59), but there is no sign here or elsewhere that the kings of Sparta had once possessed formal absolute power. In the fourth century Aristotle rightly described the Spartan kingship as no true monarchy, but a form of hereditary generalship for life (*Politics* 3.1285b). The emergence of great kings (such as Cleomenes, effective tyrant of Sparta in the late sixth century, or Agesilaus, architect of Sparta's decline and fall in the fourth century) runs counter to the traditions of the office. The record of deposition and exile or disgrace of kings for political offenses or military incompetence is striking. The machinery for deposing a king was even institutionalized in a procedure of stargazing to discover whether the present occupant was in fact acceptable to the gods (Plutarch, "Agis" 11).

The other important magistrates in Sparta were the *ephoroi,* a board of five elected annually by the assembly, apparently without distinction of birth. The ephors are not mentioned in the Great Rhetra, but a list of chief ephors (probably fictitious in its early names) claimed to go back to 754 B.C.; the ephor's name served to date the year. The earliest ephor of political importance was Chilon, with Solon one of the "seven wise men" of early Greek folklore, who held office in 556/555 B.C. The ephors presided over the *apella;* conflict between them and the kings was therefore inevitable from time to time, since both competed for leadership of the warrior assembly. There is the possibility that changes of political policy may have been reflected in successive holders of an annually elected office; but its weakness in relation to the permanent position of the kings was compensated for by the possibility of coalition between ephors and *gerousia.* Their powers in relation to the kings were or became great: they could enforce a king's attendance before them, suspend him from office, prosecute him before the *gerousia,* and settle disputes between the two kings. Xenophon (*Constitution of the Spartans* 15.6–7) describes the relationship vividly:

> Everyone rises from his seat at a king's approach, except the ephors when seated on their chairs of state. The ephors and kings exchange oaths each month, the ephors on behalf of the city, the king on behalf of himself. The king's oath is to exercise his power in accordance with the existing laws of the city; the city swears that it will maintain the kingship unshaken, provided the king keeps his oath.

Collapse of the Spartan System

The decline and fall of the Spartan system can be explained in terms of "metal fatigue," the rigidity of an unchanging social code in a changing world; yet it is also true that a system that cannot adapt necessarily alters its character according to external pressures, until it reaches a crucial point of collapse. Even in its own terms the Spartan system had two basic weaknesses.

The first of these was revealed especially in problems of leadership. The training that Spartans underwent resulted in a rigidity of mind that made it difficult for them to cope with other situations. Their refusal to accept anything new is symbolized in their insistence on continuing to use iron bars as currency when the rest of Greece had adopted silver coinage in the early sixth century; yet the venality of Spartan commanders abroad was notorious. The accusation against kings and other commanders of being corrupted by foreign customs was common from the late sixth century on; the Spartan attempt to establish direct control over other cities in the early fourth century was a disaster. The political and military record of the kingship demonstrates the inefficiency of hereditary generalship; a number of highly talented political and military leaders (notably Brasidas and Lysander in the late fifth century) could find no permanent place in the hierarchy. The survival of the Spartan state over three centuries under such circumstances is testimony to the strength of the underlying social system and the myth of military supremacy that it engendered in others. That myth, however, was shattered at the battle of Leuctra in 371 B.C.

The second weakness was finally revealed on the same occasion, and relates to the long-term demographic effects of the Spartan system. According to Aristotle, the city was destroyed by lack of manpower (*oliganthropia*); it is certain that the adult male citizen population declined from about 8,000 in the early fifth century (Herodotus, 7.234) to 1,000 a century later (Aristotle, *Politics* 2.1270a). Some of this decline may be due to the major earthquake in 465 B.C., which set off a ten-year Helot revolt. From the mid fifth century onward Sparta was engaged in almost continuous war: although there were few defeats, and no major natural disasters like the Athenian plague, this must have had an effect on the numbers in a military elite. It is true that Spartan marriage customs were consciously designed to effect a renewal of the citizen body, in that they allowed the sharing of women and the taking of additional wives for the purposes of procreation, and social sanctions were also imposed on bachelors. But the significant fact is that the Spartan state did not succeed in reversing the decline by these or any other means so as to renew the full citizen body. The reason for this may lie in the connection between citizenship and land ownership: it was believed that originally the allotments of land (with their Helot labor force) that guaranteed contributions to the *syssitia* had passed inalienably from father to son, but at some point, apparently in the late fifth century, a "*rhetra* of Epitadeus" had allowed the allotment to be given or bequeathed (though not sold) at the discretion of the possessor. Whether this law is genuine or an attempt to explain a flaw in the system, it is likely that a gift could cover mortgage or entailment, and problems of debt could emerge. This must in part explain the concentration of land in the hands of a few, and therefore the decline in citizen numbers. A combination of demographic factors (birth control to ensure maintenance of social status, despite low life expectancy) and the ability to maintain present standards by effectively disposing of the land at the expense of successors undermined the essential relationship between commensality and membership of the warrior community: state regulation of community life was transformed into the self-interest of a military caste. To compensate for declining numbers, from the late fifth century Sparta made increasing use of armed Helots and *perioikoi*, and rewarded them with forms of semi-citizen status. The conspiracy of Kinadon (398 B.C.) was a sign of the dangers of this course. At the battle of Leuctra the Spartans, apparently still the most powerful and one of the most prosperous states in Greece, mustered 10,000 hoplites from themselves and their allies, and outnumbered their Theban opponents, but the total number of Spartan citizens present was 700. The fact that 400 of these were killed in the battle demonstrates the reality of Spartan courage; but courage alone was insufficient to prevent the myth of their hoplite supremacy being exposed.

After the battle of Leuctra, Sparta lost her Messenian territories and the majority of her Helots; others were freed in her defense. She might once again have become a normal city-state, and she was certainly subject to many of the pressures of the late classical and Hellenistic periods. The concentration of land in the hands of the few continued, and Sparta became effectively an oligarchy, with a small group of full citizens and a large dispossessed class of "inferiors"; the *agoge* broke down. But the Lycurgan myth could never be wholly abandoned. Two successive kings in the third century B.C., Agis IV and Cleomenes III, tried to remedy Sparta's social problems. Their program was essentially the standard contemporary Greek one of cancellation of debts and redistribution of land, but it was expressed in terms of a return to the laws of Lycurgus; it included the creation of a body of some 4,000 citizens with allotments living according to the old principles. The peculiar danger of this particular radical movement was that it could lay claim to being a conservative reform, and so expose the inconsistencies within contemporary oligarchic thought, which admired Lycurgan Sparta while defending the rights of family and property. The resistance of the wealthy resulted in the execution of Agis; a generation later Cleomenes was overthrown by the combination of Macedonian power with the propertied classes of neighboring cities, who feared the example he was giving. Spartan independence was ended, and Sparta became merely a museum in which old rituals continued to be performed for the sake of the tourist trade.

The view of Sparta as a social and political system unchanged for centuries disguises the change in perception of the character perceived. Sparta originated as an advanced hoplite polity whose chief peculiarity was that it had universalized the principle of hoplite status through the exploitation of serf labor. In the classical period it could retain its place as an ideal for the conservative nostalgia of those living in radical cities dominated by men below the hoplite census. It could also be seen as the ideal city of limited franchise confined to the hoplite class, and of rule by an aristocratic council. Later in the Hellenistic period it stood as an example of the stability of the "mixed constitution," in which the combination of monarchy (the dual kingship), oligarchy (the council), and democracy (the assembly) ensured permanence; as such it was an imperfect forerunner of the perfect Roman republican mixed constitution fantasized by Greek theorists from the age of Polybius to that of Cicero.

But the chief importance of Sparta in the history of political thought is not its role as a focus for conservative ideas. Sparta is the most important single influence on the development of political theory in the fourth century; all utopias invented in the ancient and the modern world betray its influence. It was the Spartan example that established certain fundamental preoccupations in utopian political thought. The most basic of these are the ideas that the state is a unity that covers the totality of the interests of its members and that the state has a unified purpose. For Greek theorists the *politeia,* the organization of a Greek polis, covered not only the constitution; it was the totality of social institutions distinguishing it from other cities. This totality was assumed to have a purpose or end (*telos*), and to be constructed on rational principles toward that end. Great emphasis was placed on education for membership (*paideia*), for it was by education that the unformed material of the human being could be directed toward the aims of the community. These aims themselves might be communal, concerning the interests of the state, or individual, concerning the achievement of the highest form of self-expression for the individual—but even here the path to the goal was through communal experience.

The origins of such modes of discourse lie in the Spartan experience. Spartan society was the first and most successful to be organized according to a single principle. The aim of the Spartan *politeia* was the instilling of disciplined military courage (*andreia*) in its citizens, the perfection of the hoplite. Plato might criticize this aim as inadequate, and regard other virtues as more fundamental to society; but in building his ideal republic on the single virtue of justice, he followed the principles established in the real polis of Sparta. Aristotle was more critical of Sparta. In his view, not only was the virtue chosen by it the wrong one, but the evidence of its defeat at Leuctra showed that the means to its goal were deeply flawed. Aristotle chose rather to emphasize the complexity of virtues needed for successful community life, and was aware of the importance of affective communal relations; but he fully accepted the claim that the state was a teleological entity, an organization serving an end.

It is not therefore surprising that both Plato and Aristotle follow the example of Sparta in many details of their systems. Both emphasize the fundamental importance of *paideia* for citizenship: Sparta was the only city in Greece to possess such a state-organized education. They also often made appeal to the institution of commensality, as transformed by the example of Sparta. They were fascinated by the relationship between property and contributions to the common feast. Plato proposes a Spartan model in the *Republic,* and devotes the first two books of the *Laws* to the relative merits of Spartan and Athenian customs of commensality; Aristotle pays great attention to the relation between commensality and land ownership in the *Politics,* explicitly drawing many of his examples from Sparta and Crete. Plato's abolition of the family, his eugenics, and his advocacy of the equality of men and women are derived from study of Spartan institutions; Aristotle's reaction against them combines theoretical objections with a mistrust of precisely those features of Spartan society that had inspired Plato, along with a preference for the general Greek view that women are intrinsically inferior to men. Nothing in the political thought of the fifth century prepares us for this outburst of radical restructuring of Greek social institutions on theoretical principles: without the reality and the myth of Sparta, utopianism would never have been conceived.

THE POLIS AND THE TRANSFORMATION OF PRE-STATE FORMS

Sparta offers a striking example of the way that pre-state forms of social organization were remodeled in the service of the hoplite state. The transformation of pre-state forms within the polis is, however, a wider phenomenon. Three levels of early organization were generally recognized by Greek theorists of the school of Aristotle (most clearly in Dicaearchus, frag. 52). At the highest level, all Greek cities were divided into *phylai:* Dorian cities possessed in origin three *phylai* with identical names, Ionian cities had in general four. The phyle therefore seems to go back beyond the origins of settled polis life to a pre-state period, and the word is usually and misleadingly translated "tribe" or "clan." In the historical period, however, *phylai* were in fact never independent units, but always subdivisions of the body politic, of an inclusive (all citizens belonged to a phyle) and hereditary nature. Moreover they seem to be found only in the polis, or in political organizations clearly affected by the polis; they are not found in the genuinely tribal areas of Greece, where the tribe (*ethnos*), rather than the polis, was the dominant form of social organization. The clearest function of *phylai* in the early polis is military, in that the army was divided into regiments of *phylai*. Below the *phylai* lesser divisions are known with varying names, but of two types: those based on male companionship and function, often involving age classes; and kinship groups, based on real or fictitious family descent.

It is clear that the later existence of such institutions with names reflecting pre-state forms cannot be taken as evidence of substantive continuity, for the identity in nomenclature often disguises a series of conscious changes that have in many cases completely transformed the institutions. This argues either an exceptionally low degree of embedding for such institutions in the social and religious rituals of the Greek polis or an exceptionally high degree of rationality, in the willingness to transform traditional institutions in the service of social and political reform; and, although it is possible that the first type of explanation will work for the *phylai,* the second must be right for the changes visible in other types of association. It does not therefore follow that the Greek polis was actually or originally a tribal or lineage state, but that ethnic fictions were a sign of the rather early date of rationalization of Greek political life.

Manipulation of *phylai* is first clearly attested in the early sixth century, when the tyrant Cleisthenes added a fourth non-Dorian phyle to the three Dorian ones in Sicyon: this particular change can be seen as a means of admitting non-Dorians to political rights without disturbing existing structures. In the mid sixth century an arbitrator from Arcadia, Demonax of Mantinea, was appointed by the Delphic oracle to settle disputes in the colonial city of Cyrene, whose population comprised groups of settlers of different periods and different origins: "He divided them into three *phylai,* the first of the Therans and dwellers-about [the earliest settlers], the second of Peloponnesians and Cretans, the third of islanders" (Herodotus, 4.161). Here too the new phyle division is a means of giving all citizens equal political rights while allowing them to maintain their separate ethnic identities. Since Cyrene was a Dorian foundation, the new system presumably replaced the older traditional tripartite division. Similar changes are known for other cities; for instance, at an unknown but early date Corinth replaced the three Dorian *phylai* with eight based on locality.

Cleisthenes of Athens

The most systematic reorganization of traditional forms of association was undertaken by the Athenian statesman Cleisthenes in the first institutional reforms since Solon, shortly after the expulsion of the Peisistratid tyranny; the reforms are dated to the year 508/507 B.C. We are exceptionally well informed about them, since they remained the basis of Athenian local government and cult organization throughout the classical period, and their workings are revealed by many inscriptions. Cleisthenes' aim was to end regional faction and aristocratic control of Athenian political life and to ensure the free working of the central political structures by placing local government in the hands of the people. It is likely that the immediate provocation of his reforms was an attempt by other aristocrats after the fall of the tyranny to restrict the Athenian Assembly by excluding many Athenians from the citizen list, with the result that his opponents were able to control both elections and assembly against the wishes of the majority. But the reforms went far beyond any immediate political aim, and succeeded in creating a new atmosphere in politics by destroying the traditional forms of aristocratic control.

In place of the four Ionian *phylai* Cleisthenes established ten new ones, whose names and cults were authorized from Delphi. Each phyle consisted of three groups of villages (*demoi*), one group from the "city," one from the "inland," and one from the "coast": these groups were called thirds (*trittyes*). The city covered all that area which, because of its physical proximity, might naturally be expected to take most part in political life at Athens: the central plain between Mounts Aigaleos and Hymettus, down to the coastal area of Piraeus. On the probable assumption that the system remained unchanged into the classical period, we know that there were 139 demes, or legally constituted villages. Each supplied annually a fixed number of councillors to the Athenian Boule, between one and twenty-two, which implies that they were of different sizes, as does the fact that the number of demes in each phyle varied from six to twenty-one. The demes in the countryside were based on existing villages, but in the city they seem to have been rather more arbitrary divisions.

The *trittyes* are now generally thought to have been equal in size, which means that their strict geographical division between the three areas of Attica cannot have been wholly maintained; but it also suggests, as does other evidence, that they should be seen merely as a mixing device, designed to create ten *phylai* of equal size drawn as far as possible equally from the three different areas.

In this reorganization the *phylai* continued to function as military and religious units; the demes were new political institutions.

They had little direct impact on political activities at the center, except in ensuring that the new Council of 500 (boule) chosen by lot, fifty from each phyle (replacing the Solonian Council of 400), was genuinely representative of all areas of Attica and genuinely independent; for in the assembly and at elections there was no "constituency" organization by constituency groups. The main change was at the local level, where the deme assembly with its chief official (*demarchos*) provided local government in a polis the territory of which was too large to be ruled effectively from the center, and which had therefore suffered from a baronial style of local control. In a reaction to earlier aristocratic attempts to limit citizenship, the deme organization now supervised the citizen list: entry on the deme list at eighteen was the official recognition of citizenship. The importance of this aspect of the reform is shown by the fact that, although membership of a deme was initially by residence, it was subsequently hereditary, and the deme-name (demotic) became part of the official designation of every Athenian citizen, in the form "Megacles son of Hippocrates of [the deme of] Alopeke."

The two traditional entities of phyle and deme were thus transformed and welded into a coherent system. Another traditional unit underwent changes at least as radical that exhibit the same tendency. The brotherhoods (*phratriai*) were a typical pre-state form of social grouping: by analogy with other Greek cities they may well have been aristocratic warrior organizations under the control of particular aristocratic clans (*gennetai*). But in the classical period they were characteristic pseudoarchaic institutions. Every citizen belonged to a phratry; membership of the phratry was prior to membership of the deme, for a legitimate Athenian male belonged to a phratry even before birth, in that his father's legal betrothal was witnessed by members of the phratry. Presentation of the young child to the phratry members by his relatives at a formal sacrifice was the first public recognition of his legitimacy; he was again presented at adolescence, and his name was entered on the phratry register. In practical terms membership of the phratry and participation in its cult acts was the direct channel of mediation between individual and community; the phratry was more important to a man than any other single group organization, and the essential proof of citizenship was not in fact inscription on the deme list but evidence of acceptance by fellow *phrateres*.

The phratry had existed in the seventh century, for its members were invoked in Dracon's homicide law in the third instance, after family and kin; but that does not of course imply that the phratry was universal at this time. We possess reference to a law of uncertain date and meaning regulating entry to the phratry, which implies different social levels within the phratry and therefore attests the widening of its membership at some point. More striking is the fact that the phratries had been universalized and standardized: they all worshiped the same two gods, Zeus Phratrios and Athena Phratria, and had the same rituals on the same feast days. They might make individual regulations, but they were under the control of the state, and must therefore in their classical form have been the consequence of a conscious reorganization by the state. This deliberate remodeling of an earlier institution and its ritual framework is closely related to the Cleisthenic reforms. The connection is made explicit by Aristotle (*Politics* 6.1319b):

> A democracy like this will find useful such institutions as were employed by Cleisthenes at Athens when he wished to develop the democracy, and by those setting up the demos in Cyrene; different *phylai* and *phratriai* must be created outnumbering the old ones, and the celebrations of private religious rites must be grouped together into a small number of public celebrations, and every device must be em-

ployed to make all the people as much as possible intermingled with one another, and to break up the previously existing associations.

It is true that a less reliable source (*Constitution of Athens* 21.6) claims that Cleisthenes "left the *gene*, phratriai, and priesthoods untouched." But even if the reform of the phratriai took place later, it is related to the principles behind Cleisthenes' reforms, and represents the completion of his reordering of the traditional types of association.

Demos and Citizenship

The word *demos* is frequent in early Greek political texts, and can designate either the people as a whole or the rest of the people as contrasted with a particular privileged group. In both these situations it possesses a basic ambiguity, for the demos is not necessarily everyone, but all those who can be conceived of as belonging to the politically conscious classes, whether or not they have political rights; in a particular situation it may ignore those members of the community below the threshold of political consciousness. Often before the late sixth century it is in fact evident that the word *demos* refers primarily to the hoplite class, rather than to the entire community.

With Cleisthenes that can no longer be true. Whatever the situation before, the structure of his reforms required a complete citizen list, and therefore implies the recognition that all citizens have equal basic rights. It is perhaps this claim that is enshrined in the setting up of a new ideal in this generation: in place of the ideal of *eunomia* comes the new compound, modeled on the old and therefore an explicit challenge to it, *isonomia*—"equal order."

THE ARCHAIC POLIS

The process of state formation is known from other primitive societies, and commonly begins from a stage dominated by chiefs or "big men" similar to the Homeric *basilees*. Two models of this process have been advanced. The first emphasizes the emergence of an elite and the concentration of wealth into its hands: the state is an organ of oppression created by a developing aristocracy or monarchy in the interests of maintaining and increasing its privileges. The second approach sees the emergence of the state as the response of the community as a whole to a common need for collective action, whether to improve performance or to protect the society and its benefits against outsiders: state institutions arise as the result of the increasingly complex needs of a society.

In the early history of the Greek polis there are some signs of development corresponding to the first model, in the increased differentiation of an aristocracy and in its desire to create and monopolize political and religious offices; but such development was frustrated by the "hoplite revolution." And it is clear that the underlying tendency toward the creation of complex political institutions corresponds more closely to the second model. Political institutions were always seen as serving the community as a whole, in principle if not in practice, and there seems often to have been a basic assumption that all members of the community should have equal political rights.

Reasons for this are not difficult to find: small face-to-face societies are less susceptible to the development of rigid social differentiation. It seems that ownership of land was relatively evenly spread in Greece, and in the archaic period other sources of wealth rapidly emerged; the forces of coercion were either identical with or no match for the citizen army. Although class conflict did exist, it never replaced the idea of the community in the archaic political consciousness. The principle of *eunomia* implied a social order that was not imposed from above, but agreed upon by the community as a whole and accepted as being in conformity with justice.

What is surprising is the degree of rationality exhibited in the relation between political institutions and the elementary structures of archaic society. It has become almost axiomatic to consider early Greece as an example of an organic society whose collective representations were still unified, where there was no separation between different spheres of activity, public or private, and where political activity and institutions were the expression of a collective consciousness and of a web of social relations, rather than an independent sphere with its own rules. If Max Weber was right to believe that Greece created the conception of formal rationality and the independence of politics and political institutions from other forms of social interaction (and some would deny even this), this was a development of the classical, not the archaic period.

This picture requires modification, for the origins of the political rationality are earlier than it allows. In the archaic period there is no direct evidence for the nature of political activity or for the normal working of political institutions: we see them only at points of change or crisis. Yet it is clear that an apparently separate set of political institutions characteristic of the polis can be traced back to the age of Homer, and that a specific political form of discourse was created by Hesiod. Moreover, throughout the archaic period a series of changes in different cities demonstrates reform in accordance with rational political principles, which are able to override traditions based on kin and religious practice. By the end of the archaic period the polis was perceived as a specifically Greek form of rational political order, different from other forms of urbanization: "The polis that lives by order, though small and set on a rock, is greater than mad Nineveh" (Phocylides frag. 4 Diehl). The social solidarity of the archaic polis was not undifferentiated, but already accepted the existence of an independent political sphere; indeed it might be argued that it was politics, not religion, that structured the collective consciousness, as expressed in the rational order of *eunomia*.

THE CLASSICAL POLIS

Discussion of the classical polis is necessarily focused on the city of Athens. This reflects the fact that most of the surviving evidence, whether literary or epigraphic, concerns Athens. But the bias is not a random one; it is clear that political developments at Athens were more radical and more fundamental than elsewhere, and that the Athenian experience represents the ultimate theoretical development of the principles enshrined in the polis. Athens is therefore both profoundly untypical of other cities and a model of their ultimate potential. The development of Athenian political institutions may be divided into two major periods, that of the customary or oral democracy of the fifth century B.C. and that of the constitutional or literate democracy of the fourth century. The characteristics of the customary democracy are reliance on traditional aristocratic leadership, the use of ritual to control and define public meetings, the dominance of the spoken word at those meetings, the public recording in writing and display of various classes of decision, and the supremacy of the will of the people over the written law. The characteristics of the later constitutional democracy are the institutionalization of political leadership, the use of law to control public meetings and of architecture to define them in the place of ritual, the development of techniques of persuasion related to prepared written texts and established rules of rhetoric, the creation of archives and the more systematic public presentation of communal decisions, and the separation of the concept of law from that of the political will of the people.

The Concept of Equality

The first significant turning point in the development of a specifically democratic form of government is the replacement of *eunomia* by a new ideal, *isonomia* (equal order). *Eunomia* of course continued to be regarded as an important political concept. It is still central to Pindar's rather conservative view of political order in the early fifth century, he is capable of attributing it to all constitutionally governed aristocratic states, like Corinth, Aegina, and Thebes. In the late fifth century, discussion of *eunomia* reflects a growing interest in oligarchic and conservative political forms, and is a vehicle for questioning the values of the developed Athenian democracy; the most extensive surviving theoretical discussion of *eunomia*, that found in the *Anonymus Iamblichi* of the late fifth century, inverts this concern by attributing true *eunomia* to democracy. In the fourth century *eunomia* is essentially used to refer to the Spartan constitution and is closely connected with idealizations of it.

Isonomia is a word formed on the same lexical principles as *eunomia*, and was clearly originally invented to emphasize a contrast with the former ideal: "equal order" was to replace "good order." The date and occasion of this rejection of the old ideal are uncertain. It most probably belongs to the Cleisthenic reforms at Athens, where *isonomia* is a current political word from about that period, but there is a possibility that it was invented a decade earlier during the overthrow of the tyranny at Samos (Herodotus, 3.142). It marks a decisive break with the concepts of either an aristocratic or a hoplite polis, and proclaims equal political rights for all; it is described as "placing the power in the middle," that is, in the citizen assembly. *Isonomia* is therefore the first word to designate what were later called democracies. Herodotus offers the clearest account of the resonance of this concept in the earliest known theoretical discussion of different political constitutions. His analysis reflects sophistic views of the mid fifth century, and is given in the unlikely context of a debate among the Persian nobility over the merits and defects of the three traditional Greek varieties of constitution—monarchy, oligarchy, and *isonomia* (Herodotus, 3.80):

> The rule of the mass of the people has first the fairest of all names to describe it, *isonomia*. . . . Under it a ruler is appointed by lot and is subject to a formal scrutiny for his conduct in office, and all questions are discussed in public.

The speaker ends with the magnificent slogan, "In the many lies the whole."

The principles of *isonomia* are, then, open debate in a mass assembly and the removal of power from the aristocracy by establishing random selection and accountability for public office. The process is well illustrated by a series of reforms known from post-Cleisthenic Athens. In 501/500 B.C. the Athenians established an oath to be sworn by the new Cleisthenic council of 500 citizens chosen by lot. The oath survived with various alterations throughout the two centuries of democracy. In its developed version it included general provisions (to act in accordance with the laws, to act in council in the best interests of the polis, to oversee the magistrates) and specific negative promises (to put no illegal measures to the vote, not to hold in prison any citizen except those accused of treason, revolution, or defaulting on tax contracts, and not to take action in a variety of important matters "without a decision of the people in assembly"). Not all of these clauses may be original; nevertheless the institution of an oath reveals the central importance of the new council in the political system.

In the same year a board of ten generals (*strategoi*) was instituted, elected one from each tribe. Their existence must have reduced the power of the polemarch, the traditional annual magistrate charged with supreme command in war. Originally they may have acted merely as a board of advisers, but by 480 they had replaced the polemarch as military commanders. Although they could operate singly, they more often operated as a board or in groups.

After the victory over the Persians at Marathon in 490 B.C., the Athenians activated (or introduced) the law of ostracism, by which prominent Athenian aristocratic leaders could be voted into exile for ten years without loss of property or political rights. For five years from 487 a major public figure was exiled annually; all (except those who had fled to the Persians) were recalled and even elected to high military commands during the Persian War of 480–479. Thereafter the procedure was used more sparingly, to settle major disputes of policy between leaders, until the institution was discredited by a scandal over an attempted revival of the law in 417. Excavations have recovered more than 6,000 potsherds used in the voting procedure, inscribed with the names of both known and unknown members of the aristocratic elite. It seems clear that initially, at least, ostracism was used as a weapon against the traditional ruling class.

Finally, in 487/486 B.C., the practice of selecting the traditional magistrates (*archontes*) by lot replaced direct election. The consequence of this simple reform is revealed by the fact that, whereas previously many a prominent leader is known to have been archon, no important political figure is ever recorded as archon thereafter.

Fifth-Century Athens

The aggressively egalitarian character of these measures reflects the self-confidence of a society founded on the new principle of *isonomia* and the assertion of the power of the citizen assembly over its leaders. Ability to control the assembly lay with those who could both persuade and produce results, such as the radical Themistocles, who established the great port of the Piraeus, turned Athens into a sea power, and steered the Greek alliance to victory over Persia, and the conventional military leader Cimon, who created the Athenian empire, providing state revenues and full employment for the democratic masses.

The culmination of the process begun by Cleisthenes came in 462/461 B.C.; it involved the ostracism of Cimon and the removal from the traditional aristocratic council of the Areopagus of what were claimed to be the "additional powers" that it had acquired. This reform in fact abolished the last check on the democratic political structures from a body that had already lost much of its prestige, being composed of former archons who were now chosen by lot; the Areopagus was left with little more than supervision of certain religious matters and its function as a court for homicide trials. Although the details of the reform are obscure, the tensions it caused are revealed by the fact that its initiator was murdered. Aeschylus' trilogy, the *Oresteia,* performed in 458 B.C., explores the meaning of these events in its portrayal of the fall of a great warrior, the consequences of political assassination, and the purification of the polis through the establishment of a new order of justice embodied in the court of the Areopagus.

The generation from 460 to 429 B.C. was the age of Pericles, whose leadership of the demos was virtually unchallenged: in the words of Thucydides, in this period Athens was "in name a democracy, but in fact the rule of the first man" (2.65.9). His control combined aristocratic and democratic features. He himself was of aristocratic birth, and presented the austere, almost aloof image of a traditional leader, but he maintained his dominance in the assembly through populist measures. He engaged in a public building program that channeled the surplus revenues of empire to the citizens of Athens; many citizens were also given land overseas in colonial military settlements. The benefits of citizenship became so important that in 451/450 B.C. a new restrictive definition was introduced confining it to those born from parents both of whom were citizens; this can have affected adversely only the aristocracy, since endogamy was the rule in all but the highest reaches of society. Pericles was also responsible for the introduction of pay for civil public service (recompense for military service is likely to have begun earlier under Cimon). Both council and jury service were paid at subsistence level. One not very reliable source asserts that the Athenian empire provided at least partial income for as many as 20,000 citizens; these included 6,000 jurors, 500 councillors, and some 700 internal officials, as well as 700 officials for the empire and those who received payment for military service (*Constitution of Athens* 24.3). The relationship between control of the democratic assembly and the revenues of empire assured an aggressive foreign policy, which culminated in the Peloponnesian War (431–404 B.C.).

It was during the Periclean period that the word *demokratia* came to replace *isonomia* as the designation for political arrangements of the Athenian type. It belongs to a new generation of political ideas based on the concept of power, and relates especially to the antithesis of *oligarchia:* "the power of the people" opposed to "the rule of the few"; both are terms descriptive of power relations, and not necessarily favorable in their connotations. These are the two political constitutions opposed to each other in the ideological conflicts of the late fifth century, when Athens had consciously imposed "democratic" political forms on its subjects and Sparta sought equally consciously to support "oligarchies" among its allies.

The death of Pericles in the plague that struck Athens during the early stages of the Peloponnesian War left a vacuum in political leadership, and meant that the assembly became a focus for free political debate between men competing to assert their dominance through it. The rise of the demagogues in this period is perceived negatively by contemporary sources, Thucydides and the comic poet Aristophanes, as the triumph of loud-mouthed, unprincipled, lower-class orators, who seduced the assembly into following them by unscrupulous oratory and extravagant promises. This is of course a caricature; most of the demagogues were men of wealth if not aristocratic, and many possessed important skills in government often lacking in their predecessors: the demagogue Cleon was, for instance, responsible for setting Athens' war budget on a sound basis when it became clear that the Periclean plans were leading to bankruptcy. It is not indeed obvious what differentiated the demagogues from their competitors for the leadership except their aggressively populist style of oratory in the assembly, and this was in turn a direct consequence of the need to persuade an assembly from meeting to meeting in a competitive situation. In short, Athens had become for the first time a polis truly controlled by the assembly, without any check from a traditional leadership. The chief danger in this development was the gap that opened up between the orators in the assembly and the generals required to carry out their plans; previously the same man had proposed and executed policy. In the first half of the war this conflict was fought out between Cleon and the general Nicias; it ended paradoxically in the death of the orator on the field of battle, with the general left as architect of an uneasy peace.

From about 420 B.C. onward the influence of the Sophistic movement is visible in politics. Sophists claimed to teach the "political art," by which they meant primarily the art of persuasion. The common denominator in their various theories was the possibility of separating persuasion from principles. The consequence was a generation of aristocrats whose traditional dominance had been eroded by the rise of the demagogues and whose education had prepared them for the belief that morality and political ideals were merely means to political control. They therefore lacked any commitment to the Athenian political system. As long as they were successful in it, they were prepared to support it; but once their dominance was called in question, they regarded democracy as "obvious lunacy" (as Alcibiades is made to say in Thucydides) and made various attempts to establish their control through constitutional change and violent revolution. This treason of the aristocracy destroyed the Athenian war effort; the first period of Athenian democracy collapsed through its inability to resolve the tensions it created in its leadership structures.

Decision Making at Athens

From the mid fifth century there is good evidence for the procedures of decision making at Athens, since the Athenians recorded many of their public decisions and transactions on stone. The marked increase in such public records at this time is an indication of the consequences of the reforms of 462/461 B.C., in a greater awareness of the importance of public display and accountability. The record is of course selective; only certain categories of business were inscribed on stone. Many others were recorded on papyrus and stored in the public archives. They include, in foreign affairs, treaties and regulations concerning the empire; in religious matters, religious laws, regulations of cult practice, building accounts, and general state accounts (since the temples acted as state banks); and, in internal affairs, decisions concerned with public building, grants of citizenship or civic privileges, decrees concerning colonies, and lists of honored citizens such as the war dead.

The decisions taken by the people of Athens began with a standard formula, "It was decided by the Council and the People"; then the presiding tribe (*prytaneis*), the secretary, the president of the meeting, and the proposer are listed. Amendments or additional proposals put forward follow the main decree, and are headed by the statement "Antikles spoke" or by some such formula as "Archestratos spoke: otherwise as Antikles said, and . . ."; the various different headings may reflect different procedures in detail, but it is not clear that they are always significant.

In addition to this evidence, although no direct record of speeches made in the assembly exists, Thucydides offers a number of highly stylized descriptions of debates, while the comic poet Aristophanes uses the procedures of the assembly as a setting for two scenes. The first, in the *Acharnians*, portrays a debate in which the chief character, Dikaiopolis, seeks to interrupt the business of hearing envoys in order to advocate peace with Sparta; the second, in the *Women at the Thesmophoria*, describes an assembly for women at the festival of the Thesmophoria, where the rituals and the proceedings are a parody of those in the Athenian Assembly.

The Council (Boule)

The Council of 500, composed of male Athenian citizens who had reached the age of thirty, was chosen annually by lot, fifty from each tribe; within the tribes each deme was allotted a number of seats in proportion to its size, and this allocation was not significantly changed in the classical period. It reflected the population distribution at the end of the sixth century, before the growth of the port of Piraeus and the silver-mining towns of the Laurion peninsula, and was not therefore representative of local interests in a direct sense, but merely reflected hereditary deme affiliations. A citizen could serve twice in his lifetime, but no more; from the mid fifth century councillors were paid at subsistence rates. Each tribe was on permanent duty for one prytany, a tenth of the year, living and eating in the circular building known as the tholos, on the west side of the agora; these presidents (*prytaneis*) had as their primary duty that of convening and presiding over meetings of the full council and the assembly; they had seats at the front of the meetings, which they controlled with the help of a slave police force of Scythian archers. One of the *prytaneis* was chosen by lot to serve as *epistates,* president for the day, a post that could be held only once in a lifetime; he had charge of the keys of the temple treasuries, and formally presided at the meetings.

The council met daily apart from holidays and days of ill omen, normally in the council chamber (*bouleuterion*). It received embassies and prepared business for the assembly. Every matter brought before the assembly had to be considered first in the council: sometimes the council would merely put forward a topic for discussion, but more often it would draft a detailed set of proposals to be presented to the assembly. For this purpose it seems that the generals (*strategoi*) regularly attended the council; other politicians might on occasion act through members of the council as intermediaries, or make use of the right of every Athenian citizen to have access to the council and make proposals in person. It seems that the proposer in the council was also the formal speaker in the assembly.

On taking office members of the council underwent a formal scrutiny (*dokimasia*), and were subject to a review of their actions by the succeeding council (*euthuna*) on leaving office. Each meeting was preceded by a series of rituals, which were closely analogous to those performed before meetings of the assembly. It has been calculated that in any generation some 12,000 Athenians, or roughly a third of the male citizen population, would have served on the council: some estimates put the proportion even higher. It is at least certain that the Athenian citizen had the opportunity to partake not merely in decision making, but also in the detailed preparation of business and the administration of the state to an extent that no other known complex society has achieved.

The Assembly (Ecclesia)

The central political institution of fifth-century Athens was the assembly, source of all changes in law and all political decisions. It met regularly, probably at least once in each conciliar month and more often if the council so decided. The place of meeting was an open hillside, the Pnyx, where an auditorium of nearly 2,900 square yards (2,400 m²) was created; this space, the so-called Pnyx I, was in use from about 460–400 B.C. The audience sat on the hillside, looking down on the speakers and, beyond them, the agora and the city of Athens. The space could have contained approximately 6,000 participants, and it is significant that the quorum for a number of decisions was 6,000—in other words, numbers were not counted, but such decisions could only be taken if the assembly were clearly full.

The sources always speak in terms that equate the assembly with the Athenians as a whole; in fact any one assembly can have held only approximately a fifth of the male citizen body. There is no sign that this limitation affected the character of decisions taken, or that any particular group of Athenians dominated the assembly; when all Athenians were forced to live within the city walls during the Peloponnesian War, this does not seem to have altered the composition of the assembly or its working. The varied groups of Athenians living within easy distance of the meeting place probably reflected the general composition of interests well enough, the port workers of the Piraeus being balanced by the farmers of the plain and the hillsmen of Acharnae and beyond.

In principle the fifth-century assembly was sovereign to decide any matter, subject only to the rules for the preparation of business by the council. In practice even this constraint was slight, since the council itself was a microcosm of the assembly, and proposals could be made in the assembly instructing the council to bring a matter forward. The assembly had the right to depose magistrates at any time, and to conduct the elections of new or regular magistrates as it saw fit; it could, for instance, depose generals or elect extra ones at will, though such actions were rare. There was no absolute rule against debating a decision again and reversing it. The sole effective checks on the freedom of the people in assembly related to the need for a quorum in decisions involving honors or penalties for individuals and the possibility of indicating a speaker for proposing a motion against the laws—that is, a motion that was in conflict with laws already existing. Such an indictment (*graphe paranomon*) suspended the decision until the case had been heard in court; it is not, however, known when this procedure was first introduced, and the earliest reference to it is in about 415 B.C. If later it became an important political weapon, used often by competing politicians, that reflects the changed constitution of the fourth century. The fifth-century democracy was regulated by the acceptance of traditional leadership and, increasingly, by the skills of political rhetoric.

The chief constraints on the process of decision making were provided by the ritual framework within which the assembly took place, which ensured a sense of occasion and created an atmosphere in which potential conflicts could be resolved in the creation of a common purpose expressed in the will of the majority. Before the meeting a purificatory sacrifice of a small pig was offered, and its blood was sprinkled around the perimeter of the meeting place. The herald recited a ritual prayer and a curse. The prayer was "that the meeting may go as well as possible, to the benefit of the city of the Athenians and individually of ourselves, and that whoever acts and speaks in the best interests of the Athenians may prevail." The curse was directed against those who took bribes to speak against the interests of the city, betrayed the city, or deceived the council and assembly; it also mentioned a number of historical categories, those who sought to restore the tyranny, negotiated with the Mede, or debased the coinage.

The proceedings were opened by the presiding officer; religious matters had precedence, and then embassies were heard. After the council's draft was read out, the herald asked, "Who wishes to speak?" Initially he called first on those over fifty, and then the rest of the citizens, but later that distinction was dropped. Speakers put on a wreath and spoke from a raised step at the front of the meeting; there was no formal limit on the length of a speech or on the number of times anyone might speak. Decorum was characteristic of the speakers until the late fifth century; Pericles himself is said to have possessed a notably "Olympian" style of public speaking, which doubtless reflects the aristocratic dominance of political leadership. The emergence of the demagogues in the last thirty years of the fifth century brought a new style of rhetoric and of public behavior: although many of the speakers were from the wealthier classes, they cultivated an aggressively populist image and deliberately adopted a manner of speaking that was "forceful and unscrupulous." They shouted and gesticulated in the assembly, and were even accused of speaking when drunk. This change in political style is the subject of Aristophanes' most bitter comedy, the *Knights* (424 B.C.), in which the current popular hero Cleon, thinly disguised as a Paphlagonian tanner, is ousted by a yet-more-degenerate demagogue, a sausage-seller. In reality the demagogic style seems to be a response to the need for speakers to present a clear image to the assembly in a situation of competitive leadership. The behavior of the audience is less well attested. The existence of Scythian archers to keep order suggests that disruptive behavior was not unknown, but there is no evidence of even unpopular speakers finding it difficult to present their views.

The efficiency of the Athenian Assembly should not be underestimated. Meetings began at dawn and were usually over by midday, leaving the afternoon free for a meeting of the council to consider the action necessary on the decisions taken by the assembly. The number of decisions taken in any meeting was high. Perhaps the most important feature of the procedure was that votes were taken by a show of hands (*cheirotonia*), which was estimated rather than counted: there was probably (as later) a means of challenging the estimate, although normally that would not be necessary.

Comparative study by Mogens H. Hansen of the only modern example of direct democracy, the *Landsgemeinde* of certain German Swiss cantons, shows that swift and effective discussion is characteristic of such mass meetings, which will not tolerate irrelevant or verbose speakers, and that estimating votes rather than counting them is a speedy and uncontroversial method of determining majorities. A notable feature of even these modern examples, which operate within a state with a well-organized party system, is that such mass assemblies are not amenable to influence by party organization. It is in fact clear that political parties did not exist in Athens, and that many features of the system were designed to prevent smaller interest groups from being in a position to influence the decisions of the majority. Occasionally conservative minority groups are seen at work, either sitting together in the assembly or combining to attempt to influence lawsuits and elections, but the ineffectiveness of these groups is clear; they became significant only when they were prepared to resort to armed revolution. There is no doubt that more or less fluid groups formed within the class of political leaders, but these groups lacked any formal following and any publicly defined program. Consistency of policy therefore rested on the personality of the speaker and his continuing ability to persuade the people.

Political Discourse

In Athens there were three places of public discourse in which speakers sought to influence a mass audience: the assembly, the lawcourts, and the theater. There is little evidence for styles of discourse in the lawcourts, but a comparison between the assembly and the theater is revealing.

The assembly heard long speeches that offered arguments in favor of different courses of action; when Thucydides came to represent its debates, he chose to systematize the discussion into pairs of speeches opposed to each other, each of which collected together the best arguments that could have been, and perhaps were, used. This antithetical mode of discourse is characteristic of fifth-century representations of argument, where it is often asserted that each argument has its opposite. Such modes of thought have their natural place in the lawcourts, where the facts are normally in dispute; but we must suppose that debates in the assembly were often more complicated than this model might suggest.

The theater was also a place for public discussion: argument is more central to fifth-century tragedy than action. The issues raised are matters of political concern at the deepest level of universality; speeches have the same tendency to organize the arguments into two opposed sets and to include as many arguments as possible in favor of each side, regardless of the minor inconsistencies that may result. Thus the oppositions represented in Sophocles' *Antigone* are set out with a clarity and a completeness that reveals an interest in the argument for its own sake; the idea that the argument is weighted in favor of one side merely imports modern ideas of drama and misrepresents the seriousness with which the moral issue is debated. The speakers present the case; the audience and their representatives, the chorus, must judge the issue. But the discourse of tragedy differs from that of the assembly in two respects: first, there is no need for the argument to lead to any decision on the part of the audience, and, second, the issues raised often reflect tensions between the rational world of the polis and the demands of religion, family, or sex. This reflects the role of tragedy in a festival context, in which norms could be overturned and mythic representations could reflect inner tensions of the social system. Nevertheless, the logical organization of the formal confrontations in Attic tragedy corresponds to the style of rational public argument that the Athenians sought to attain in the assembly.

The Execution of Decisions

The execution of public business was entrusted to boards of officials under the supervision of the council. With certain important exceptions in finance and military affairs, the boards were chosen by lot for a year at a time and were accountable for their actions on leaving office. The number of these boards was large and fluctuating, for any particular task was liable to have a board created for it, however temporary the need might be. The lot disregarded experience and even competence, and was much criticized by philosophers on these grounds, but it was a fundamental principle of the democracy that all citizens should have equal opportunities for duties in office holding. The disadvantages were overcome in two ways. First, since all officials appointed by lot operated as members of a board of between five and twenty citizens, a sufficient degree of collective competence could be guaranteed. Second, the administrative tasks were highly fragmented, and the business of each group was well defined. In this way the Athenians managed to provide for the government of a highly developed society with complex needs in foreign policy and military affairs without recourse to permanent officials, bureaucrats, lawyers, or other professional experts; the record of success of this government over the 200 years of its existence compares favorably not only with other ancient societies but also with the modern bureaucratic state.

Political Leadership

In the fifth century political leadership centered on the main annually elected office, the board of ten generals (*strategoi*), elected directly by the whole people, one from each tribe, and elegible for reelection. Military command was traditionally a preserve of the aristocracy, and the assembly was in origin and in practice the gathering of the fighting men; so this privileged relationship between military command and leadership of the assembly was natural. In the period before 429 B.C. it seems that all important political leaders were generals; but of course not all generals were political leaders. The continuity of tenure of the generalship by prominent leaders like Cimon and Pericles (who was elected continuously over at least thirty years) had one effect on the institution of the generalship: at some point the Athenians decided that the practice of reelecting the same man each year unfairly disadvantaged other members of his tribe. In 440/439 B.C. we find a board of eleven generals, two from Pericles' tribe. In a number of subsequent years, both before and after Pericles' death, the evidence shows that the board of ten contained one tribe with two representatives, and therefore one with none; attempts to show that there may have been two tribes doubly represented on occasion have so far not succeeded. The procedures for obtaining this result are unfathomable, but they must have involved indicating one candidate as more popular than all others. It is typical of the Athenian concern for collegiality that not even here is there any sign of formal presidency or other form of precedence on the board.

The *strategia* as a basis for political leadership came under severe pressure after the death of Pericles. It is true that, like Pericles, the leading politician, Nicias, was elected general every year until his death in 413 B.C., but his control of the assembly was never safe. It is also true that his rival Cleon, despite his lack of experience in military affairs, sought continually to achieve the traditional combined status as leader of the people and general. But later politicians recognized the division between military office and control of the assembly. This was in part a consequence of the more even competition between the new politicians of the post-Periclean age and the increased importance of public speaking; in part it was a result of the pressures of war, which meant that generals were often absent from Athens; in part also there were genuine differences of opinion between the traditionalist generals and the radical but inexperienced politicians who wanted adventurous campaigns. The relationship between generals and politicians became one of mistrust; generals were compelled to undertake enterprises of which they disapproved, and were prosecuted in the courts when they failed to achieve the impossible. It was this atmosphere of mistrust that led to a crisis in the leadership after the Sicilian defeat of 413 B.C. and caused many in the traditional ruling class to favor some form of nondemocratic government.

The Ideology of Democracy

The practice of Athenian democracy was based on clear and coherent principles of political organization. Equality of political rights for all male citizens entailed the central importance of the meeting of those citizens in the assembly, whose decisions could not be limited in any significant way; the council mirrored the assembly, and served its interests before and after its deliberations. But equality of political rights implied also equality in political office; the use of the lot as a random selection process was a fundamental principle of democracy. Efficiency and the fragmentation of power established the need for multiple boards of officials subject to rules of accountability. The lawcourts may be seen as constituting a separate closed system organized on similarly democratic lines, and operating under laws that were essentially the laws of Solon, as modified from time to time by the assembly. But inevitably the lawcourts became involved in the political sphere, both constitutionally, in that they had a role to play in the examination of magistrates, and as a consequence of their use in the rivalries between competing politicians. Only the generalship stands outside the bounds of this coherent system, as an anomaly closely bound to traditional forms of leadership. But the existence of this anomaly points to a fundamental weakness in the ideology of democracy—the difficulty of reconciling the need for political leadership with the principle of absolute equality.

It is clear that the logical coherence of the Athenian democracy owes nothing to political theory, but is a consequence of the rational development of institutions through a process of continuing reform and adaptation. Nevertheless, a number of fifth-century discussions reveal a conscious awareness of the basic presuppositions of the democratic system. One is the passage of Herodotus describing *isonomia,* quoted above. Two others deserve mention.

Thucydides' version (2.37) of the funeral oration of Pericles over those killed in the first year of the Second Peloponnesian War (431 B.C.) expresses the democratic conception of political equality:

> Our constitution does not copy the laws of neighbouring states; we are rather a pattern to

others than imitators ourselves. Its administration favours the many instead of the few; this is why it is called a democracy. If we look to the laws, they afford equal justice to all in their private differences; if to social standing, advancement in public life falls to reputation for capacity, class considerations not being allowed to interfere with merit; nor again does poverty bar the way, if a man is able to serve the state, he is not hindered by the obscurity of his condition. (Richard Crawley, trans. [1874, 1910])

Later (2.40) Thucydides turns to the balance between leadership and mass participation:

> Our public men have, besides politics, their private affairs to attend to, and our ordinary citizens, though occupied with the pursuits of industry, are still fair judges of public matters; for, unlike any other nation, regarding him who takes no part in these duties not as unambitious but as useless, we Athenians are able to judge at all events if we cannot originate, and instead of looking on discussion as a stumbling-block in the way of action, we think it an indispensable preliminary to any wise action at all. (Richard Crawley, trans.)

In Plato's *Protagoras*, Protagoras offers a defense of democracy in the form of a myth that probably reflects the actual thought of this fifth-century Sophist, rather than being Plato's invention. According to the myth, when the gods created the living creatures on earth, they forgot about providing for man and left him naked and defenseless. In pity Prometheus gave him knowledge of technology and the fire necessary for its use; but when men gathered together for self-protection in cities, they found they lacked political skill. Zeus, fearing that they would therefore destroy themselves, sent Hermes to impart shame and justice to them. Hermes inquired how he should distribute these gifts among men (*Protagoras* 322):

> "Shall I distribute them just as the arts were distributed—that is, on the principle that one skilled doctor is enough for many laymen, and so with the other experts? Shall I distribute justice and shame? that, or shall I lend them out to everyone?" "To everyone," said Zeus. "Let them all have their share. Cities could never exist if only a few shared in them, as with the other arts. Moreover, you must lay it down as my law that anyone who is unable to share in shame and justice shall be put to death as a plague to the city."

According to Protagoras all men possess political skill, at least potentially; the task of the Sophist is to educate them for the political life.

Oligarchy

It was this notion of political skill as shared equally by all that was attacked in the late fifth century. Those able to afford the considerable expense of being trained by the Sophists claimed to have greater skill, and therefore greater right to rule; military failure was attributed to the ignorance and folly of the people in political decisions. For their own good and for the sake of the war effort, this reasoning ran, the people should hand over power to those who knew how to use it.

Oligarchy was the historical successor to aristocratic government, as the criteria of birth and wealth fused to create the idea of an elite whose social position justified their control of the state. But the variety of oligarchies was enormous, from the "cabal of a few men" operating at Thebes during the Persian Wars to the Spartan hoplite constitution. The extent to which oligarchy was a theoretical rather than a traditional form of government in the fifth century is obscure. But the earliest known written constitution for an oligarchy in this period suggests a remarkably sophisticated approach to the problems of government.

In the mid fifth century the cities of the Boeotian plain liberated themselves from Athenian control, and between then and 420

B.C. established a complex federal-style oligarchic constitution. This constitution must have been expressed in a formal written agreement or treaty between the various cities, since it both imposed on each of them a standard type of local government and also made provision for a central federal set of institutions. In each city there was a property qualification for full citizen rights; and those entitled to rights were divided among four "councils," one of which served as preparatory council for the other three in rotation; decisions had to be passed by all four groups.

The federal organization rested on eleven "wards," assigned in relation to population; the city of Thebes possessed two wards in respect of its own population, and two in respect of territories subordinate to her; the other cities either constituted a separate ward (as Tanagra) or were grouped together. Each ward produced one magistrate (*boiotarchos*) on the board of eleven, sixty councillors for the central council, 1,000 hoplites, and 100 cavalry, together with an unknown number of jurymen and taxes in proportion. The central meetings of the Boeotian League were held at Thebes, and the Council of 660 was itself divided into four sections sitting in rotation to prepare business for the main council (Thucydides, 5.38; *Hellenica Oxyrhynchia* 11).

The Boeotian constitution is interesting for two features. In its central organization it offers the earliest example of a federal or representative form of government; this type of federal league became particularly important in the Hellenistic period. It also reveals the imposition of a standardized form of oligarchic government in the individual cities of Boeotia, and shows that oligarchy could be regarded as more than the rationalization of historically determined institutions. There are of course many obscurities: although every city limited political rights, they may not have done so on identical principles; and the significance of the repeated four-council organization is unclear.

The Boeotian constitution is reflected in the constitution proposed by the oligarchic regime of the Four Hundred in Athens in 411 B.C.; two documents preserved in the Aristotelian *Constitution of Athens* (30–31) propose a limited political body of 5,000, divided into four "councils." But the Athenian oligarchs never consolidated their rule sufficiently to establish a genuine constitution; they were quickly dissolved into a wider body of the Five Thousand, which merged back into a democracy. Again, on the surrender of Athens in 404 B.C., a Spartan-backed oligarchy led by the Thirty Tyrants was set up, but it resorted to legalized terror to maintain itself and was quickly overthrown in favor of a "restored democracy."

"Stasis"

The conflicts at Athens in the late fifth century revealed a fundamental weakness in the Greek conception of politics. Greek political life was based on the conception of community, and of the communal will. It sought always in politics to create unity. It avoided the establishment of institutions of conflict and of self interest. It also avoided the creation of a body separate from the community but replicating it on the metaphysical plane, the state. It was therefore fundamentally opposed to the principles of modern political thought, based on the Christian doctrine of the fall of man; and it must be admitted to have one major disadvantage. It found it difficult to cope with the will to evil and the natural wickedness of man. Political power was inherently dangerous, for the individual and the community.

Two bogies emerged in Greek political institutions. The first was the figure of the tyrant, absolute ruler and therefore absolutely corrupt. The dangers of this situation could be overcome by fragmenting power and reinforcing the social constraints embodied in the law. The second danger was the breakdown of the social order itself.

Stasis was a situation in which conflict could no longer be resolved within the accepted political structures. It was particularly prevalent in Greece because of the existence of alternative governmental models to suggest that the present procedures were not the only possible ones. Conflict of this type was not merely conflict about the best form of government, because it was basically a disguised form of class conflict. But in terms of political institutions it was correctly described by Thucydides (3.83) as a political disease, in which all normal social constraints broke down:

> Thus every form of iniquity took root in the Hellenic countries by reason of the troubles. The ancient simplicity into which honour so largely entered was laughed down and disappeared; and society became divided into camps in which no man trusted his fellow. To put an end to this, there was neither promise to be depended upon, nor oath that could command respect; but all parties dwelling rather in their calculation upon the hopelessness of a permanent state of things, were more intent upon self-defence than capable of confidence. (Richard Crawley, trans.)

In Athens itself the practical response to this problem was expressed in the closing stages of the civil war of 404 B.C. According to Xenophon (*History of Greece* [*Hellenica*] 2.4.20–21) as the two sides confronted each other in the Piraeus, a priest of the Eleusinian Mysteries belonging to the aristocratic clan of the Heralds and fighting on the democratic side shouted this appeal:

> Fellow citizens, why are you driving us out of the city? Why do you want to kill us? We have never done you any harm. We have shared with you in the most holy rites, in sacrifices, and in splendid festivals; we have danced in choruses with you and gone to school with you and fought in the army with you, braving together with you the dangers of land and sea in defense of our common safety and freedom. In the name of the gods of our fathers and mothers, of the bonds of kinship and marriage and companionship, which are shared by so many of us on either side, I beg you to feel shame before gods and men, and cease to harm our fatherland.

It was on this basis and on the moderation and good sense of the democratic leaders that the amnesty at the end of the war was accepted and the Athenian democracy reestablished.

But the problem of *stasis* and of the instability of political institutions remained central to Greek political thought, and theoretically insoluble. Aristotle's great discussion of the problem in books five and six of the *Politics* produces little more than practical expedients for maintaining the status quo; his real answer lies in the earlier discussion of the political community as fundamental to the polis, and reflects the same attitude as that expressed in the passage of Xenophon above. The problem lies at the heart of the Greek admiration for the permanence of Spartan institutions; it explains the development in the Hellenistic period of a theory of the mixed constitution, which, combining aspects of all types of constitution, might somehow achieve permanence. Despite all the evidence to the contrary, it was precisely this virtue of stability through balance that Greek theorists saw in the constitution of the Roman Republic.

ATHENIAN DEMOCRACY IN THE FOURTH CENTURY

Athenian democracy underwent a fundamental transformation in the course of its restoration; but this transformation is not directly related to the political events, nor is it clearly signaled as a political reform in our sources. It is in fact part of a wider change in civic consciousness, which can best be explained in terms of a shift in political values. In the fifth century it would have been natural to say that the demos, the people in assembly, was the ruler of Athens (or in modern terms the sovereign power); in the fourth century it was generally agreed that the laws were the supreme authority and that the assembly operated in accordance with those laws. The establishment of the rule of law independent of and superior to the political institutions of the state involved a redefinition of the relationship between law and the will of the people, and between law and decision making; it involved an acceptance of limitations on the power of the people and a distinction between the permanence of law and the transience of politics. This change in perceptions undoubtedly reflects a response to what had been seen as basic flaws in the radical democracy of the late fifth century, the supremacy of the assembly and its willingness to disregard the constraints of law. It demonstrates a new realism and moderation in the face of defeat and offers a modification of democratic procedures in the light of oligarchic criticism. The fourth-century democracy was more law-abiding and more stable, and more concerned with social consensus, than the democracy of the Periclean age.

These developments can also be seen as part of a wider phenomenon, the final triumph of literate modes of thought: a democracy based on tradition and ritual gave way to a democracy founded on written rules. It was in this generation that politicians and professional speech writers began for a variety of reasons to preserve their oral performances in the written medium. Rhetoric, the art of public speaking, offered no longer merely a preparation for extempore delivery, but a complete science of language in which the text itself served as record and as medium of instruction. The political act in all its stages became fixed and permanent.

The Revision of the Laws

The laws of Athens were crucial in this process. The laws of Solon, archaic texts written on wooden axles, had never been formally replaced; new laws, inscribed on stone, and passed by the assembly in ordinary session, might be found scattered through the city. In 410 B.C. the Athenians established a commission to revise these laws, and set them up as a code engraved on stone in the Stoa Basileios, the oldest of the Athenian public stoas where the *archon basileus* held his court. This building was discovered by the American School at Athens in 1970, and excavations since have revealed the places and procedures of display of the new law code and its subsequent revisions. The earliest evidence for this activity is the surviving republication in 409–408 B.C. of Dracon's law of homicide, which stood at the head of the Solonian code, and so of the new code. After the usual preamble, it runs:

> The law of Dracon about homicide shall be inscribed by the recorders of the laws [*anagrapheis*] after they have received it from the *archon basileus* jointly with the secretary of the council, on a marble stele, and they shall set it up in front of the Stoa Basileios. The *poletai* shall let the contract according to the law. The *Hellenotamiai* shall supply the money. First Axon. (*Greek Historical Inscriptions* no. 86)

The process of revision took six years, until 404 B.C., when Nicomachus, one of the commissioners, is known to have laid down his office. After the rule of the Thirty, the restored democracy promulgated the final code in 403/402 B.C.: a decree proposed by Teisamenos describes 500 elected lawgivers, whose duty it was to display the laws and take note of proposals for change before promulgating them and inscribing them on the wall "for all to see." As reported in Andocides, *On the Mysteries* (87), in future

> the magistrates may not use an uninscribed law under any circumstance. No decree [*psephisma*] of Council or People shall override a law. No law may be passed against an individual without applying to all citizens alike, un-

less an Assembly of six thousand voting by secret ballot so decide.

The activities continued briefly, for Nicomachus is recorded as having revised also the religious code; his career is given in a speech of Lysias' (*Oration* 30), in which his conduct in office is attacked. But the attitude of the Athenians to this revision is clear. The new code was fixed and permanent. It could be changed only by repeating the procedures whereby it had been established—appointing *nomothetai* who must be members of the jury panels, establishing that the new law did not conflict with existing ones, and displaying it and announcing it in three successive meetings of the assembly. In fact, this procedure was so cumbersome that it had to be modified later; but its general provisions lasted until the overthrow of the democracy by the Macedonians in 322/321 B.C. These provisions are of fundamental importance, for they removed the right of legislating from the assembly. Whereas in the fifth century the words *nomos* (law) and *psephisma* (decree) had been used almost interchangeably for decisions of the assembly, throughout the fourth century a hierarchy of enactments existed: *nomoi* were fixed and permanent, made by special commission; *psephismata* were enacted by the assembly in accordance with those laws. The indictment for proposing a decree contrary to the laws (*graphe paranomon*) became a fundamental limitation on the sovereignty of the assembly; a number of other legal devices were evolved for challenging proposals of the assembly in the lawcourts. Assembly and lawcourts became distinct and independent institutions of political authority: law and government were separated.

The code itself does not survive, but the structure of its political and administrative sections can be recovered. The second part of the Aristotelian *Constitution of Athens* gives an account of the constitution in the author's own day, in the last decade of the classical democracy (332–322 B.C.). This section is in effect a commentary on the relevant sections of the law code, and is arranged according to the divisions established in the code. After a section concerned with qualifications for exercise of citizen rights and youth training, the divisions reflect a legal division into laws concerning the council (and its supervision of the assembly), general laws common to all magistrates, laws under the nine archons, and laws under the other officials (see also Demosthenes, 24.20–23).

From this we may deduce that the law code contained a section defining citizenship, and that thereafter each part of the law was related to the office to which it was considered relevant; the offices in turn were defined through their methods of selection (by lot or by election) and their legal functions. No separate part of the law code dealt with the assembly, which was considered under the heading relating to the council.

Forms of Government in Fourth-Century Athens

Outwardly many of the forms of government remained the same as those of the fifth-century democracy, with the addition of more complex rules of procedure. But there are many signs of the new spirit. Contemporary with the restoration of the democracy is the remodeling of the meeting place on the Pnyx (Pnyx II). Its orientation was reversed, so that the speakers stood before a small cliff toward the top of the hill and the audience sat in a shallow bowl surrounded by a retaining wall, facing uphill. The space thus created was only slightly larger in size than the meeting place of the fifth century, and held perhaps 6,500 or slightly more. This can hardly have been the reason for the reorientation, which lies rather in the desire to create a visually bounded space, not open to the views of city and countryside but rather, through the manipulation of spatial elements, enforcing that sense of separation and solemnity that had previously been achieved through ritual. The assembly was now physically bounded rather than ritually defined, and these physical constraints reflected its willingness to accept legal constraints. The renewal of democratic institutions is also seen in the building of a new council chamber in the agora; significantly, the old chamber became the first official Athenian repository for documents.

The restored democracy also instituted pay for attendance at the assembly. In the first decade of the century this rose from one to two to three obols; by the age of Aristotle it was one-and-a-half drachmas for the main monthly assembly and one drachma for the other meetings. Contemporaries perhaps rightly regarded this development as a competition between the democratic leaders to gain popularity; but only a certain number who arrived first received pay, and it seems to have had the important side effect of limiting and defining the number of meetings.

This process of limitation was perhaps gradual, and the stages are obscure. But by the time of Aristotle there were four regular meetings in each prytany, and the business to be conducted at each was defined by law. The first assembly was reserved for a vote of confidence in the magistrates and for discussion of the food supply and the defense of the state; lists of vacant inheritances and heiresses to be claimed in marriage were read out. The second assembly was assigned to "supplications," appeals or requests for special favors and dispensations by citizens on behalf of themselves and others for reasons private or public. The remaining two sessions were devoted to any business in the order: three religious matters, three matters concerning embassies, and three secular matters. Some business could be taken without a debate or vote if unopposed, by a special quick procedure (*Constitution of Athens* 43). Presumably other matters than these could be raised at any meeting after the officially designated business; there seems to have been no fixed calendar of meetings, which tended to crowd into the last days of a prytany. So the number of meetings ensured that there was seldom delay in transacting important business. It is disputed whether the council also had the power to summon additional emergency meetings, but such meetings would not often have been needed.

Some changes seem designed to reduce the power of the council: the section of the council in permanent session (*prytaneis*) lost its duty of presiding over the assembly and assessing the vote to ten *proboloi* drawn from the council for each meeting, one from each tribe. Other changes attest greater professionalism, such as the institution of annual secretaries and the greater care taken in the drafting of preambles to documents, and in their dating.

Citizenship

The concern for definition and limitation is strikingly attested in the increased importance placed on the status of citizenship. First defined by formal list in the age of Cleisthenes, it had been limited by Pericles' law of 451–450 B.C. to those born of citizen parents on both sides. In the restoration of the democracy proposals had been made on the one hand to limit the franchise by a property qualification and on the other to extend it to those noncitizens who had helped in the return; both were defeated, and the Periclean rule was reenacted for the future. The rules were progressively tightened, so that marriage to a noncitizen, initially invalid for the purposes of establishing legitimacy and citizenship, became actually illegal. By about 340 B.C. a foreign man living with an Athenian citizen as his wife could be sold into slavery and his property confiscated; a foreign woman living with an Athenian man was similarly punished, and her husband was fined 1,000 drachmas. A large number of lawsuits concerned with citizenship around the year 346/345 B.C. attest a major revision of the citizen lists, and the rejection of the claims of many to be citizens; those convicted were sold into slavery. Increasingly the citizen body sought to impose rules of membership on itself.

It also sought to regulate the education of its younger members through state action. By the time of Aristotle, a complex system of youth training under specially designated magistrates had evolved, in which, before enrolling as citizens, young men (*epheboi*) had to undergo military training and guard duties in the frontier forts and garrison towns of Attica for two years (*Constitution of Athens* 42); their names were inscribed on lists by years in the agora. This training, the *ephebeia,* has clear analogies with the Spartan *agoge* and more generally with adolescent rites of passage; it seems to have been systematized perhaps as late as the 330s, but may well be much earlier in origin. The Aristotelian text seems to suggest that all citizens underwent this training, not merely those of hoplite status and above; if so, the institution is a spectacular demonstration of the alteration of civic consciousness in the fourth century, for the training is essentially related to hoplite warfare on land. Many modern scholars have indeed been unwilling to believe that the thetes of Athens also partook in the training, but in later periods citizenship and the *ephebeia* were closely connected in many cities.

Political Leadership

The Athenians of the fourth century possessed no word for politician; instead they referred to the "orators and generals" (*rhetores kai strategoi*). This dual designation reflects the acceptance of the division between control of the assembly and military leadership, which had caused so many problems in the late fifth century. The generals of the fourth century were often professional soldiers, sometimes even foreign condottieri given citizenship to make them eligible for office; they took relatively little part in the political activities of the assembly. This does not of course imply that they were nonpolitical figures. Their advice was often sought and usually followed, they had access to the council and close connections with particular orators, and they were also often active in the lawcourts in prosecution or defense. But control of the assembly was no longer considered part of the function of a general, and the position of general was no longer regarded as necessary to political leadership.

The status of orator was not defined by the holding of an office. Anyone who proposed decrees in assembly or council, who proposed laws before the *nomothetai,* or who took a prominent part in instigating or supporting public actions in the courts might be regarded as a *rhetor.* Often the word carries a derogatory connotation, much like our modern "politician"; speakers will assert that they are ordinary citizens who do not make a habit of presenting proposals or prosecuting. But there was a small group of *rhetores* who might be regarded as professional politicians in two senses. First, they had undergone professional training in rhetoric and were themselves recognized experts in public speaking; second, they devoted a large part of their time to public affairs, and regarded the direction of public policy as the highest activity. Their reward was public honors and esteem; officially at least, acceptance of financial rewards for public advice was punishable with death. The pride of these men in their activities can best be understood from the two great opposing speeches of Demosthenes and Aeschines on the occasion of a proposal to honor Demosthenes with the public presentation of a wreath at the festival of the Dionysia, debated in 330 B.C. before the courts. Each man defended his own record and attacked his opponent's over the last twenty years, on the grounds of consistency, success, and dedication to the interests of the city; behind the mutual recriminations, the degree of stability within the system and the high standards of public responsibility of its leaders are revealed. During a period of high risk and political instability, when most external factors were beyond the control of Athens, the Athenian political system survived with modest success and without provoking major internal dissension.

These principals were supported by a larger number of lesser political figures, who are known to us by their appearance in public speeches or as the proposers of decrees; from this evidence it is clear that prominent men might rely on a small and informal group of associates to assist them in public business. But these two categories do not exhaust the known instances of political participation. There were also large numbers of political actions promoted by citizens otherwise unknown, whose occasional activity cannot easily be connected to any form of group interest. The actual level of participation in the creation of public policy in Athens demonstrates how little the democracy was inhibited by the existence of a professional political class.

Legal control of the *rhetores* was embodied in a number of laws that made the proposer responsible for his activity. He could be prosecuted for proposing a decree against the laws, for proposing a law that was undesirable, and for various forms of malicious prosecution in the courts. These penalties were frequently invoked: more than a hundred cases are known for the small group of prominent *rhetores*.

In the mid fourth century a different type of political leadership emerged, based on the holding of elective financial office to which a man could be reelected annually. The first politician of this type was Eubulus, commissioner of the Theoric Fund, which received the surplus state revenues for redistribution to the people as payments for attending the theater; under his direction the fund was used to divert expenditure from military activity and to build up a reserve. The disastrous Social War (357–355 B.C.), in which the allies of Athens revolted and Athens lost control of the Aegean, led to financial and military weakness and a less aggressive policy. In this period from 355 to 342 B.C. Eubulus rebuilt the reserves and increased public expenditure within the city, exploiting resources like the silver mines and Athenian trade dominance. The rise of Macedon finally broke the consensus on which Eubulus' control had rested, and Demosthenes inherited the benefits of the revived power of Athens.

A second leader of the same type emerged after the defeat of the Greeks by Philip of Macedon at Chaeronea (338 B.C.). The orator Lycurgus controlled the city finances for twelve years, raising the revenues to 1,200 talents a year, investing in major public works both military and cultural, reforming the Athenian dramatic festivals and the navy, and apparently presiding over a renewal of Athenian cultural life and social institutions, whose limits are still unclear.

Both these instances reveal the pattern of the future. Athenian political life had long reflected the relationship between the assembly and the use of public wealth; leaders maintained their position by their ability to create and redistribute surpluses. Traditionally this had been achieved through military activity, conquest providing profit and military service providing pay, while others benefited from the shipbuilding and armaments supply trades. As warfare became more dangerous and more expensive, attention turned to peaceful expenditure on public buildings and festivals, and, of course, to the possibility of building up military power for the future. Financial office had always been reserved for the rich, not so much on the grounds of their ability, but as a safeguard against malpractice in the possibility of seizure of their property. But since shortfall of state revenues was made up by taxation of the rich through a system of liturgies, or compulsory contributions to specific needs, the rich had a vested interest in maximizing state revenues and minimizing high-risk expenditure; they were the natural exponents of a cautious foreign policy and a generous building program. This connection of wealth, a policy of beneficence, and internal expenditure became increasingly dominant in the world of the Greek city-states after the conquests of Alexander, when independent military action was impossible and the people had to rely increasingly on the willingness of the wealthy to undertake political responsibilities and political expenditure. Control of the state by the wealthy was inevitable, and, like many other cities, Athens became in name a democracy but in fact was ruled by the few rich men.

Alternative Ideologies

The failure of oligarchy at Athens and the obvious stability of the new democracy led to the development of alternative ideologies. These were of varying types, but all reflected the desire to reestablish the concepts of privilege and exclusivity that Athenian democracy denied. One type of response has already been described: a form of sentimental pro-Spartan social posturing, which advertised discontent without requiring action. More significant for the emergence of political thought was the growth of utopianism. The political thought of Plato explores alternative principles of social organization with a freedom that registers his dissatisfaction with current realities, but that has had the effect of liberating political theory from the constraints of history for better and for worse. Aristotle benefited from this revolution and attempted to combine the two traditions of political thought.

Less often considered now, but more important at the time, was the development of a theory of monarchy as an ideal government to complete the triad of types of constitution defined according to the number of rulers (one, few, or many). Once thought to be a primitive and barbarian style of government, in the hands of writers like Isocrates and Plato monarchy became a possible ideal, in which one man by his virtuous rule could lead a willing people. There are very few theoretical arguments possible in favor of such a proposition, and all of them were demolished by Aristotle in the third book of the *Politics*. Nevertheless history was to establish monarchy as the most successful form of government for the next 2,000 years, and the possibility that it might have a theoretical basis, and rest on more than tradition, religion, or the rule of force, was the last legacy of the Greek genius for political experimentation.

BIBLIOGRAPHY

SOURCES

Thucydides, *History of the Peloponnesian War*, Richard Crawley, trans. (1874, 1910).

STUDIES

General

Georges Balandier, *Political Anthropology*, A. M. Sheridan Smith, trans. (1970); Bernardo Bernardi, *Age Class Systems* (1985); Georg Busolt, *Griechische Staatskunde*, 2 vols., 3d ed. (1920–1926); Hector M. Chadwick, *The Heroic Age* (1912); Emile Durkheim, *The Division of Labor in Society*, George Simpson, trans. (1933; repr. 1964), and *The Elementary Forms of Religious Life*,

Joseph W. Swain, trans. (1915; repr. 1965); Victor Ehrenberg, *The Greek State* (1932; 2d rev. ed., trans., 1969); Moses I. Finley, *Democracy Ancient and Modern* (1973), and *Politics in the Ancient World* (1983); Meyer Fortes, *Kinship and the Social Order* (1970); Morton H. Fried, *The Evolution of Political Society* (1967); Numa D. Fustel de Coulanges, *The Ancient City*, Willard Small, trans. (1874; 12th ed., 1901); John R. Goody and Ian Watt, "The Consequences of Literacy," in *Literacy in Traditional Societies*, J. R. Goody, ed. (1968); Schuyler Jones, *Men of Influence in Nuristan* (1974); Claude Lévi-Strauss, "The Concept of Archaism," in his *Structural Anthropology*, vol. 1, Claire Jacobson and Brooke Grundfest Schoepf, trans. (1963–1976).

Christian Meier, *Die Entstehung des Politischen bei den Griechen* (1980); Walter Nippel, *Mischverfassungstheorie und Verfassungsrealität in Antike und früher Neuzeit* (1980); Paul A. Rahe, "The Primacy of Politics in Classical Greece," in *American Historical Review*, **89** (1984); Walter G. Runciman, "Origins of States: The Case of Archaic Greece," in *Comparative Studies in Society and History*, **24** (1982); Marshall Sahlins, "Poor Man, Rich Man, Big-man, Chief: Political Types in Melanesia and Polynesia," in *Comparative Studies in Society and History*, **5** (1963); Elman R. Service, *Origins of the State and Civilization* (1975); Quentin Skinner, *The Foundations of Modern Political Thought*, vol. 1: *The Renaissance* (1978); George Steiner, *Antigones* (1984); Max Weber, "The City," in his *Economy and Society*, vol. 2, Ephraim Fischoff *et al.*, trans. (1968); Elisabeth C. Welskopf, ed., *Soziale Typenbegriffe im alten Griechenland und ihr Fortleben in den Sprachen der Welt*, 5 vols. (1981–1985); Karl-Wilhelm Welwei, *Die Griechische Polis* (1983).

The Archaic Polis

Antony Andrewes, *Probouleusis: Sparta's Contribution to the Technique of Government* (1954), *The Greek Tyrants* (1956), "The Government of Classical Sparta," in *Ancient Society and Institutions: Studies Presented to Victor Ehrenberg on His Seventy-fifth Birthday* (1966), and "The Survival of Solon's Axones," in *Phoros: Tribute to B. D. Merritt* (1974); Helmut Berve, *Die Tyrannis bei den Griechen*, 2 vols. (1967); Paul Cartledge, *Sparta and Lakonia: A Regional History 1300–362 B.C.* (1979); George L. Cawkwell, "The Decline of Sparta," in *Classical Quarterly*, **33** (1983); Robert Drews, *Basileus: The Evidence for Kingship in Geometric Greece* (1983); Victor Ehrenberg, "When Did the Polis Rise?" in his *Polis und Imperium* (1965); Moses I. Finley, *The World of Odysseus* (1954; rev. ed. 1965), and "Sparta and Spartan Society," in his *Economy and Society in Ancient Greece* (1981); Stephen Hodkinson, "Land Tenure and Inheritance in Classical Sparta," in *Classical Quarterly*, **36** (1986); Werner W. Jaeger, "Solon's Eunomia," and "Tyrtaeus on True Arete," in his *Five Essays*, Adele M. Fiske, trans. (1966).

David Malcom Lewis, *Sparta and Persia* (1977); Douglas M. Macdowell, *Spartan Law* (1986); Oswyn Murray, *Early Greece* (1980); Pavel Oliva, *Sparta and Her Social Problems*, Iris Urwin-Lewitova, trans. (1971); Martin Ostwald, *Nomos and the Beginnings of the Athenian Democracy* (1969); H. W. Pleket, "The Archaic Tyrannis," in *Talanta*, **1** (1969); Francois de Polignac, *La naissance de la cité grecque* (1984); Mervyn Popham, E. Touloupa, and L. H. Sackett, "The Hero of Lefkandi," in *Antiquity*, **56** (1982); Bjørn Qviller, "The Dynamics of the Homeric Society," in *Symbolae Osloenses*, **56** (1981); Elizabeth Rawson, *The Spartan Tradition in European Thought* (1969); Denis Roussel, *Tribu et cité: études sur les groupes sociaux dans les cités grecques aux époques archaïque et classique* (1976); Eberhard Ruschenbusch, *Solonos Nomoi: die Fragmente des Solonischen Gesetzewerkes* (1966); Peter Siewert, *Die Trittyen Attikas und die Herresreform des Kleisthenes* (1982); Bruno Snell, *Tyrtaios und die Sprache des Epos* (1969); Anthony M. Snodgrass, *Archaeology and the Rise of the Greek State* (1977), and *Archaic Greece: The Age of Experiment* (1980); Chester G. Starr, "The Decline of the Early Greek Kings," in *Historia*, **10** (1961), and *Individual and Community: The Rise of the Polis 800–500 B.C.* (1986).

Eugene Napoleon Tigerstedt, *The Legend of Sparta in Classical Antiquity*, 2 vols. (1965, 1974); John S. Traill, *The Political Organization of Attica* (1974); Michael Ventris and John Chadwick, *Documents in Mycenaean Greek*, 2d ed. (1973); Emily Vermeule, *Greece in the Bronze Age* (1964); Jean-Pierre Vernant, *The Origins of Greek Thought*

(1962; trans., 1982); Henry T. Wade-Gery, *Essays in Greek History* (1958).

The Classical Polis

Gerhard J. D. Aalders, *Political Thought in Hellenistic Times* (1975); Ernest Barker, *From Alexander to Constantine* (1956); Jochen Bleicken, *Die Athenische Demokratie* (1986); George M. Calhoun, *Athenian Clubs in Politics and Litigation* (1913; repr. 1970); John McK. Camp, *The Athenian Agora: Excavations in the Heart of Classical Athens* (1986); Laurence B. Carter, *The Quiet Athenian* (1986); George L. Cawkwell, "Eubulus," in *The Journal of Hellenic Studies*, **83** (1963); Robert W. Connor, *The New Politicians of Fifth-Century Athens* (1971); John Kenyon Davies, *Athenian Propertied Families, 600–300 B.C.* (1971), and *Wealth and the Power of Wealth in Classical Athens*, rev. ed., W. R. Connor, ed. (1981); Kenneth J. Dover, "Anapsephisis in Fifth-Century Athens," in *The Journal of Hellenic Studies*, **75** (1955), "Dekatos Autos," in *The Journal of Hellenic Studies*, **80** (1960), and *Greek Popular Morality in the Time of Plato and Aristotle* (1974); Moses I. Finley, "Athenian Demagogues," in *Studies in Ancient Society*, M. I. Finley, ed. (1974); W. George Forrest, "An Athenian Generation Gap," in *Yale Classical Studies*, **24** (1975).

Simon Goldhill, *Reading Greek Tragedy* (1986); Christian Habicht, *Gottmenschentum und Griechische Städte*, 2d ed. (1970); Mogens Herman Hansen, "Misthos for Magistrates in Classical Athens," in *Symbolae Osloenses*, **54** (1979), "Seven Hundred Archai in Classical Athens," in *Greek, Roman, and Byzantine Studies*, **21** (1980), "Initiative and Decision: The Separation of Powers in Fourth-Century Athens," in *Greek, Roman, and Byzantine Studies*, **22** (1981), *The Athenian Ecclesia: A Collection of Articles 1976–1983* (1983), "The Athenian 'Politicians' 403–322 B.C.," in *Greek, Roman, and Byzantine Studies*, **24** (1983), "*Rhetores* and *Strategoi* in Fourth-Century Athens," in *Greek, Roman, and Byzantine Studies*, **24** (1983), "The Number of *Rhetores* in the Athenian *Ecclesia*," in *Greek, Roman, and Byzantine Studies*, **25** (1984), *Democracy and Demography: The Number of Athenian Citizens in the Fourth Century B.C.* (1985), and *The Athenian Assembly in the Age of Demosthenes* (1987); A. Robin W. Harrison, "Law-making at Athens at the End of the Fifth Century B.C.," in *The Journal of Hellenic Studies*, **75** (1955); F. David Harvey, "Literacy in the Athenian Democracy," in *Revue des études grecques*, **79** (1966); Eric A. Havelock, *Preface to Plato* (1963); Sir James Wycliffe Headlam-Morley, *Election by Lot at Athens*, 2d ed., revised by D. C. Macgregor (1933); Felix Heinimann, *Nomos und Physis* (1945); Charles Hignett, *A History of the Athenian Constitution to the End of the Fifth Century B.C.* (1952).

Arnold H. M. Jones, *Athenian Democracy* (1957); Julius Kaerst, *Studien zur Entwicklung und Theoretischen Begründung der Monarchie im Altertum* (1898); George A. Kennedy, *The Art of Persuasion in Greece* (1963); George B. Kerferd, *The Sophistic Movement* (1981); Jakob A. O. Larsen, *Greek Federal States: Their Institutions and History* (1968); Nicole Loraux, *The Invention of Athens: The Funeral Oration in the Classical City*, Alan Sheridan, trans. (1986); Douglas M. Macdowell, "Law-making at Athens in the Fourth Century B.C.," in *The Journal of Hellenic Studies*, **95** (1975); Peter J. Rhodes, *The Athenian Boule* (1972), "Athenian Democracy after 403 B.C.," in *Classical Journal*, **75** (1980), and *A Commentary of the Aristotelian Athenaion Politeia* (1981); Heinrich Ryffel, Μεταβολή Πολιτειῶν [*Metabole Politeion*]: *Der Wandel der Staatsverfassungen* (1949).

Homer A. Thompson, "The Pnyx in Models," in *Studies in Attic Epigraphy, History, and Topography Presented to Eugene Vanderpool*, *Hesperia*, supp. 19 (1982); Homer A. Thompson and Richard E. Wycherley, *The Agora of Athens: The History, Shape, and Uses of an Ancient City Center*, vol. 14 of *The Athenian Agora*, American School of Classical Studies at Athens (1972); Paul Veyne, *Le pain et le cirque* (1976); Pierre Vidal-Naquet, *The Black Hunter*, Andrew Szegedy-Masak, trans. (1986); Frank W. Walbank, "Monarchies and Monarchic Ideas," in *Cambridge Ancient History*, vol. 7, pt. 1, 2d ed. (1984); David Whitehead, *The Demes of Attica 508/507–ca. 250 B.C.* (1986); Wolfgang Will, *Athen und Alexander: Untersuchungen zur Geschichte der Stadt von 338 bis 322 v. Chr.* (1983).

Alternative Paths: Greek Monarchy and Federalism

MICHAEL GRANT

THE BACKGROUND TO HELLENISTIC MONARCHY

Aristotle (*Politics* 3.9.1285b.7–8) suggested that the Greek city-states had at first been governed by "heroic" monarchies, small-scale continuations of the great kingships of the Mycenaean age. As Oswyn Murray has reminded us (GREEK FORMS OF GOVERNMENT: Homeric Society), it is not now accepted that this can have been a universal phenomenon. Yet discoveries at Lefkandi and in Cyprus, as he points out, do suggest that there were some "Dark Age" kingships, in certain cases under eastern influence (for contrasting views, see R. Drews [1983] and P. Carlier [1984]).

These monarchs no doubt asserted their right to govern and judge by divine right, handed down by the gods from whom they claimed descent. They were assisted, as the Homeric poems suggest, by gatherings of elders, enjoying various degrees of free speech, and by assemblies whose members' opinions had to be listened to, although their main function was to receive and applaud decisions announced from above.

However, as time went on, these diminished monarchs of Dark Age Greece, where they existed, often proved unable any longer to preserve their one-man power in the face of rivalry from their elders and nobles, who could likewise be described as *basileis* (kings; *cf.* Homer, *Odyssey* 8.41). If, for instance, a war broke out, and the kings proved unable to conduct it effectively, this gave the nobles their chance; and so did a disputed or unsatisfactory succession, or agricultural failure. For one reason or another, therefore, the aristocratic upper class of society gradually got rid of the city kings (where there were any to be got rid of), and themselves ruled instead, as a group.

However, there were a number of exceptions. Thus Kyrene, founded by Thera in 632 B.C., remained a monarchy until 456 (although it had lost its secular power earlier; Herodotus, 4.161). Leaving aside, for the moment, Macedonia on the fringes of the Greek world, the most notable, as well as the most curious, of these exceptions was Sparta. There, throughout ancient history, two kings reigned jointly, belonging to the Agiad and Eurypontid families. Each claimed descent from Herakles; and although the origins of the Spartan monarchy were explained in a bewildering variety of different ways—including the possibility that the dual kingship may have gone back to an earlier territorial division, such as between Sparta and Amyklai—it must surely have been extremely early, going back, perhaps, to a date not far removed from the Dorian invasion itself (even if, as seems likely, the kingship did not assume the actual form described to us before the sixth century B.C.). On the military nature of the kings' power and the checks imposed on that power by their duality and other Spartan institutions, see GREEK FORMS OF GOVERNMENT: Spartan *eunomia*.

Most other city-states, however, as we have seen, dispensed with their monarchies (if they had ever had them) in early times. The nobles who succeeded them took over their claims to divine descent and, by virtue of these, asserted their own monopoly of "virtue" (*arete*) and a monopoly also, in consequence, of the power to provide orderly government (*eunomia*), so that disobedience to that power was a sin. But disobedience and questionings nevertheless broke in, from a variety of causes that combined to make the lower classes of society more outspoken. As a result, except in regions such as Thessaly, Kyrene, and Cyprus, which remained outside the mainstream of Greek thinking, aristocratic governments often eventually came to grief. There were various ways in which this could occur. But in a considerable group of advanced city-states what happened was that the aristocratic regimes were overthrown by single individuals, described by the Greeks as "tyrants"—although "dictators" is a less misleading term.

The word *tyrannos*, which, as Murray observes, is probably of Phoenician origin (related to the Hebrew *seran*), was first employed, as far as we are aware, by the poet Archilochos of Paros, with reference to King Gyges of Lydia (ca. 685–657 B.C.; frag. 19). Gyges was a personage who had subverted a previous government by forcible means and had established his own autocratic rule in its place, and that was what, in Greek lands too, the word meant. For the tyrants of Greek city-states had also managed to accomplish precisely the same thing: an individual, by employing violence, broke through onto the Greek political scene and took control in his city.

It may possibly have been in Ionia (under the influence of Lydia) that the institution of tyranny initially emerged among the Greeks. But according to tradition it was their European mainland that supplied the pioneer. He was said to have been Pheidon of Argos, which preceded Sparta as the principal city. Aristotle, however, found him hard to fit into the usual classification distinguishing hereditary kings from tyrants who had seized power by violence, because he was "a king who became a tyrant," that is to say a hereditary monarch who exceeded his constitutional powers (*Politics* 5.8.1310b.4).

More obvious and characteristic tyrants were Kypselos of Corinth (whose accession, despite disagreements, is attributable to ca. 657, soon after the probable date of Pheidon's death), Orthagoras of Sikyon, Melanchros of Mytilene, Peisistratos of Athens, Polykrates of Samos, Thrasyboulos of Miletos, Phalaris of Akragas, and Hippokrates of Gela. Of partially or wholly aristocratic origins themselves, they attacked whatever disaffected noble partisans they could, and claimed that they were not tampering in any of their actions with the traditional laws, but were leaving them intact. Moreover, they were also eager to gain the support of the partly or largely non-aristocratic but not unprosperous hoplite class (already in existence, although the phalanx tactics characteristic of these infantry forces were only gradually developed), who felt that their military importance merited them a larger political say. Tyrants formed significant interstate associations and arranged dynastic marriages. They also enlarged their fleets, and this, together with the wide extension of coinage, enabled them to increase their cities' trade. In addition, they spent a great deal on public buildings and state cults and festivals, with the deliberate intention of concentrating artistic and cultural patronage in their own hands to weaken the conservative appeal of antique ceremonials based on clans and families. To finance these projects, they imposed harbor dues and taxes on sales and agricultural produce. Such measures strained their popularity, but the tyrants of Corinth and Sikyon, so it was said, sought to broaden their political base by offering concessions to the pre-Dorian elements of their populations.

The sons of the first tyrants of these cities, Periander and Kleisthenes, respectively, proved even more successful than their fathers. But those who came after them—and the pattern was repeated elsewhere—began to feel increasingly isolated; for their lack of legitimacy caused grumblings and disturbances, which inevitably made the rulers themselves increasingly suspicious and oppressive, and ever readier to have recourse to armed force, thus earning the term "tyrant" the opprobrious connotation it acquired in the ancient world and still possesses. And so these potentates fell (usually giving way, in the first instance, to wealth-based oligarchies rather than claims based on birth as hitherto). Only on and around the west coast of Asia Minor did tyrants linger on for a time, since they were found convenient by Persian suzerains.

Yet it would be a considerable mistake to think of the fifth century, after most of the tyrants had gone, as a period entirely devoted to the development of republican government. Isokrates and Plato, as Murray tells us, were among those who constructed ideal theories of virtuous monarchy—"the last legacy of the Greek genius for political experimentation"—and even apart from Sparta and Macedonia, important areas were still under monarchic rule, at least for many decades to come. Preeminent among these regions was Sicily, where the internal affairs of most of the largest cities never attained sufficient stability to make orderly constitutional development possible. Thus Hippokrates (ca. 498–491/490) made Gela the island's strongest state. Then at Akragas, which had formerly experienced the "tyranny" of Phalaris, the city reached the zenith of its power under the autocratic rule of Theron (488–472), whose major expansion was greatly assisted by a historic victory over the Carthaginians at Himera (480). His ally in the battle was Gelon, who after succeeding Hippokrates at Gela had become tyrant of Syracuse (485–478), which he made into the greatest power in the entire Greek world. His brother Hieron I defeated the Etruscans off Cumae (474). In ca. 466 the autocratic government was brought down, but it was renewed by Dionysios I (406–367)—the most powerful personage in the entire Greek world—followed, once again, by a moderate oligarchy.

A further noteworthy monarchy during the classical period was the kingdom of the Cimmerian Bosporus, extending on either side of the Straits of Kerch, which separated the Black Sea from the Sea of Maiotis (Azov), and the Tauric Chersonese (Crimea) from the Caucasus. The foundations of the state were established during the 480s, when the Archaianaktids, the ruling house of Pantikapaion—of Milesian or Mytilenean origin—unified the local Greek settlers for protection against their Scythian neighbors. Then in 438 Spartokos I, a Thracian or Thraco-Maiotian mercenary commander, created a highly centralized state, ruled by the dominant Greek or hellenized minority, who derived extensive riches from metalworking, remarkable fisheries, and the export of grain (notably to Athens).

Another monarchy on the Greek fringes was that of Macedonia. It was ancient, and its Argead rulers (more self-consciously than their subjects) claimed Greek descent, despite skepticism from Greeks elsewhere, who mocked the Macedonian language, although it was not so very different from their own. Macedonia more or less decisively entered Greek history when its king Alexander I (obliged to accompany Xerxes in 480) organized a national army. Archelaos (413–399) modernized the kingdom and introduced Greek artists to his new capital at Pella. Then Philip II (359–336) enormously amplified, strengthened, and enriched the Macedonian state and gained control of Greece by defeating its coalition at Chaironeia (338). His son and successor Alexander III the Great (336–323) destroyed the Persian Empire and carried Macedonian power as far as the Indus River.

The monarchies that were characteristic of the Hellenistic world emerged from the confused succession wars that followed Alexander's death. The overseas conquests of Alexander were converted into two major kingdoms, the elaborately bureaucratic state of the Ptolemies in Egypt, encouraging the institution of ruler worship, and the vast, more loosely organized empire of the Seleucids, based in Syria and Mesopotamia. The Ptolemaic kingdom survived, with diminishing power, until the death of Cleopatra VII in 30 B.C.; it was then annexed to the Roman Empire. The Seleucids had already succumbed to the Romans in the earlier part of the same century. Around the peripheries of their imperial dominions, and as a result of their partial fragmentation, a considerable number of other regional monarchies had gradually developed. Asia Minor (where Halikarnassos under Mausolos, 377–353, had set the precedent) provided several important examples. Remarkable developments also occurred in Bactria (northern Afghanistan), where Diodotos I broke away from Seleucid rule to establish what became an imperial kingdom, with Indo-Greek offshoots that survived until the beginning of our era.

Meanwhile, monarchies from earlier epochs revived or survived in other parts of the Greek world as well. At Syracuse Agathocles (317–289) reestablished autocratic rule, and Hieron II reigned for more than half a century as a Roman dependent, though his death (215 B.C.) was followed four years later by Roman annexation. Macedonia itself also remained a kingdom, stabilized inside mainly European territories under the Antigonid dynasty of Antigonos II Gonatas (284/283–239), which prompted new, more liberal monarchic theorizing but was extinguished by the Romans in 167. Unlike, however, the kingdoms of Asia Minor, which mostly became Roman provinces in the following century, the dynasts of the Cimmerian Bosporus survived as clients of Rome until the fourth century A.D.

FEDERALISM

Although so profoundly particularistic in character, the Greek city-states from early times showed some recognition, however inadequate, of the need to work together. The great quadrennial games served this purpose, and so did the wavering growth of Panhellenic ideas, which these festivals helped to sponsor. There was also the institution of official "guest-friendship" (*proxenia*), by which one city-state honored a visitor or resident from another (as early as 625–600 B.C. at Kerkyra [Corcyra]; Meiggs and Lewis, *A Selection of Greek Historical Inscriptions* 4). The development of interstate arbitration likewise played a part.

But more fundamental was the development of federalism in a variety of forms and degrees—that is to say, association between states which, while retaining their own independence pooled and merged their policies, particularly regarding foreign relations, in certain respects. Such federal units varied in the nature of their interstate ties, but possessed a primarily religious character. Among "amphictyones," groups of "dwellers around" who collaborated but lacked any central political or military authority, that of Delphi was the most famous. But before 700 B.C. the Ionian cities, too, had formed a similar organization, the Panionion, with its sanctuary of Poseidon Helikonios on a spur of Mount Mykale, replacing his shrine at Melie, which the Ionian cities destroyed owing to its inhabitants' reluctance to accept absorption. Poseidon was also worshiped at Kalaureia (Poros), the center of an early union comprising the cities of the Saronic Gulf and Orchomenos (Boeotia). Later, however, the philosopher Thales urged closer integration upon the Ionians, in vain (Herodotus, 1.170.3), and it was largely due to this failure that their revolt against the Persians (499–494), despite its ambitious scale, proved ineffective.

In northern Greece there were initiatives of a different character. Thus from the seventh century at least the four cantons of the Thessalian tribal state organized a confederacy under an elected military leader (*tagos*), provided, most frequently, by the Aleuadae, who were the royal house of Larissa. The representatives of the confederacy attended regular religious celebrations at the sanctuary of Athena Itonia near Pharsalos. Federal power and centralization were only spasmodically enforceable, but in the course of the sixth century the league became the major power of northern Greece.

Although there is some dubious evidence in support of an earlier date, the first apparently clear reference to a common decision dates from 511 (Herodotus, 5.63.3). After a subsequent period of decline, Thessaly saw its confederacy fall into the hands of Macedonia (under Philip II) and then Rome (148 or 146).

An outstanding part in the development of early federal institutions was played by Thessaly's southern neighbor Boeotia—though this was only grudgingly admitted by Athenian writers, owing to their dislike of Thebes and its oligarchy. The uncomfortable proximity of Boeotian cities to one another and the longstanding rivalries that had developed between them militated against any form of federal collaboration. On the other hand, the need for some unity against Thessaly and Athens was unmistakable, and with this in mind an agreed distribution of the agricultural resources of the Boeotian plain was only sensible. Thus in due course city delegates began to meet at the religious festival of the Pamboeotia in the sanctuary of Athena Itonia at Koroneia. As early as *ca.* 550, too, the coins of a number of cities display a common type—a round or oval Boeotian shield—which clearly endows the series with a federal character. Some of the earliest of these coinages bear the initials of Tanagra and Haliartos (or Hyettos), while a further issue of similar date, bearing no letters at all, comes from Thebes—an omission that was probably intended to suggest its own supremacy in the league. At the end of the century another city, Orchomenos, produced separate designs, indicating that it resented this inequality.

Because of its hatred for Athens, the Boeotian League sided with the enemy in the Persian Wars, after which it suffered disbandment. It was reconstituted in 447 (*Hellenica Oxyrhynchia* 11), possibly with Orchomenos instead of Thebes as its dominant force for a time; there had been

Boiotarchs by 479 (Herodotus, 9.15). There was no federal citizenship, but a federal council enjoyed sovereign authority (*cf.* Thucydides, 5.38.2). Then, after dissolution in 386 and the successes of Thebes from 379, the league briefly, under Theban leadership, became the leading power of Greece. Following upon the defeat of the Greeks at Chaironeia by Philip II (338), it was reestablished once again—no longer under Thebes, which was ruined—but remained in a subordinate position until dissolved by the Romans in 146. Yet another reconstitution followed, but it was more or less restricted to religious ceremonials.

The Boeotian League, despite promising beginnings, had failed to qualify as a serious or first-class federal experiment owing to the permanent or ever-recurring predominance of one of its cities, Thebes. For the same reason the Peloponnesian League, which became a major force in the sixth century B.C., was not authentically federal, in the sense of being an association of equals, but an "alliance under a hegemon": for despite the independent attitude, for a time, of Corinth, Sparta was always in control, and it was with good reason that the confederacy was described in ancient times as "the Lakedaimonians and their allies" (Thucydides, 5.77; 5.79). Sparta was also the acknowledged leader at the professedly Panhellenic anti-Persian congress of 481 (Thucydides, 1.18.2). The same "hegemonial" description applied, after 478 B.C., to the Delian League, which was run by Athens—as its subsequent conversion into the Athenian Empire indicated clearly enough. When it was revived in the fourth century, technical changes were introduced, but the Athenians, despite a measure of deliberate restraint, were still at the helm. In the Panhellenic League of Corinth (337), Philip II's predominance was glaringly obvious: it was even known as "Philip and the Hellenes." The character of the league of cities of Chalkidike (432 B.C.), dominated by Olynthos, is disputed, but it seems to have severely restricted the independence of the member cities.

Only in a number of more remote or backward territories, as far as pre-Hellenistic times are concerned, were there approaches to confederacies of equals. Thus in Arkadia the cantons and cities, into which the original tribe had been split, formed some sort of association warranting, in the fifth century, the issue of federal coins at Heraia, probably on the occasion of the Arkadian national festival, and after the destruction of encroaching Sparta's power at Leuktra (371 B.C.) a regular league came into being, with its capital at newly founded Megalopolis, created by amalgamating (synoecizing) smaller communities. There was a federal board of fifty officials (*demiourgoi*), elected by the member states in proportion to their size, and a federal Assembly of the Ten Thousand (the *murioi*). However, sufficient unity to endow the league with a stable basis of power failed to materialize.

It was not until the Hellenistic age that groups of communities agreed effectively to sink parts of their political independence in order to become effective federated equals, capable of presenting a competent resistance to external encroachments. This was achieved, in particular, in two territories of the Greek mainland that (like Arkadia) had hitherto remained insignificant. These were Aitolia and Achaia, on either side of the Gulf of Corinth. It proved possible to form confederacies in these regions because the existing communities were backward and feeble, incapable of staving off any outside menace by themselves.

Thus by the later fifth century B.C. the small tribal communities of Aitolia, dwelling not in cities but in small towns or villages that formed a distinctive but not very coherent unit (Thucydides, 3.94 ff.), had created some kind of a loose central association, and by 367 this had attained the status of a league (Tod, *Greek Historical Inscriptions* 137). It was remarkable for its carefully thought out constitutional structure. This was presided over by an annually elected president (general). An assembly, convened at the religious center of Thermon, met regularly twice a year, in addition to whatever special sessions might be required. All adult males, it seems, could vote, although wealthier members carried more weight. Cities were represented in proportion to their numerical strength, but a committee of thirty or forty (*apokletoi*) conducted much of the league's business. Expansion carried membership beyond Aitolia, but remoter communities only possessed civil and not political rights. The confederacy's outstanding success was its singlehanded defense of Delphi against the Gauls (279 B.C.). At the end of the century, despite a reputation for piracy, it was the second power in eastern Europe, after Macedonia, and a Roman ally. But then the Aitolians invited the Seleucid Antiochos III the Great into Greece (192 B.C.), and were deprived of their independence by the Romans.

Across the Corinthian Gulf the cities of the Achaians, often little more than villages, had established some sort of inconsiderable associations from an ancient date, based on a religious center at the shrine of Zeus Homagyrios near Aigion; by the fifth century this constituted a confederacy with common citizenship (Xenophon, *History of Greece* [*Hellenica*] 4.6.1). By 290 B.C. a more durable league had been created, extending eventually over 8,000 square miles and including non-Achaian states, notably Sikyon (251 B.C.).

The constitution was like that of the Aitolians, with variations designed to strengthen the league at the expense of the cities. The president (general), automatically commander-in-chief, was ineligible for immediate reelection. Council membership was restricted to men over thirty. Ten deputies (*demiourgoi*) presided over the assembly, to which all male citizens of the member states belonged (though poorer people, especially those living elsewhere found it difficult to attend). But the voters were not individuals (as in Aitolia) but states—an advance toward representative government (subsequently these states elected a council of representatives). The league became powerful under Aratos of Sikyon, president in alternate years from 245 B.C., who helped Macedonia to destroy the Spartans at Sellasia in 222. Philopoimen (208/207–182) virtually united the Peloponnese, but initiated a period of disagreements with the Romans that eventually, in 146 B.C., caused the dissolution of the confederacy and the deportation of 1,000 Achaians to Rome, including the historian Polybios.

"Although," observes Victor Ehrenberg (p. 131), "in the Hellenistic age the Polis did play its special and important part, fundamentally the federal development meant the end of the idea of the Polis." Federalism had helped to correct the fragmentation imposed by the poleis; but it did not, as it turned out, succeed them. For that was the destiny of the Romans, whose superior military and political organization made short work of the confederacies; the Etruscan League, for example, succumbed piecemeal to the Romans after the fall of Veii (396 B.C.), owing to the absence of any unity stronger than common attendance at the sanctuary of Voltumna.

BIBLIOGRAPHY

GENERAL

Cambridge Ancient History, III, 2d ed. (1982) and VII, 1 (1984); Victor Ehrenberg, *The Greek State*, 2d ed. (1969); Michael Grant, *From Alexander to*

Cleopatra (1982), and *The Rise of the Greeks* (1987); Lilian Hamilton Jeffery, *Archaic Greece* (1976); Claire Préaux, *Le monde hellénistique* (1978); Frank William Walbank, *The Hellenistic World* (1981).

MONARCHY AND "TYRANNY"

Actes du Colloque International sur l'Idéologie monarchique dans l'Antiquité (1977); Frank Ezra Adcock, *Greek and Macedonian Kingship* (1954); Antony Andrewes, *The Greek Tyrants* (1956); P. Carlier, *La royauté en Grèce avant Alexandre* (1984); Lucien Cerfaux and J. Tondriau, *Le culte des souverains dans la civilisation gréco-romaine* (1957); R. Drews, *Basileus: The Evidence for Kingship in Geometric Greece* (1983); Moses I. Finley and D. Mack Smith, *History of Sicily*, rev. ed., C. Duggan, ed. (1986); N. G. L. Hammond, *A History of Macedonia*, I (1972), II (1978); J. T. Hooker, *The Ancient Spartans* (1980); S. Hornblower, *Mausolus* (1982); William Woodthorpe Tarn, *The Greeks in Bactria and India*, F. L. Holt, ed., 3d ed. (1985).

FEDERALISM

R. J. Buck, "The Formation of the Boeotian League," in *Classical Philology*, **67** (1972); John M. Cook, *The Greeks in Ionia and the East* (1963); J. Ducat, "La confederation béotienne et l'expansion thébaine a l'époque archaïque," in *Bulletin de correspondance hellénique*, **97** (1973); George Leonard Huxley, *The Early Ionians* (1966); Jakob Aall Ottesen Larsen, *Greek Federal States* (1968); Marta Sordi, *La lega tessala fino ad Allessandro Magno* (1958).

ROMAN FORMS OF GOVERNMENT

E. STUART STAVELEY

FROM A CONSTITUTIONAL ASPECT the history of Rome falls into three distinct phases: primitive monarchy, Republican government, and monocratic authoritarianism. It is true that both the insistence of Roman writers in tracing the origins of most Republican institutions to the regal period and the successful attempt of Augustus to represent his new Principate as *republica restituta* (the Republic restored) have encouraged the view that this sequence of governmental forms was a natural progression; and indeed it undoubtedly portrays an element of continuity vouchsafed by a respect for tradition. But the changes effected in *ca.* 510 B.C. (the traditional date for the transition from monarchy to Republic) and in the Augustan Age must be recognized as something more than the mere modification in balance permitted under an unwritten constitution. They were in fact abrupt and fundamental.

MONARCHY

The primitive king of Rome differed from those of most Greek cities in one important respect: he claimed no divine descent and no hereditary title. Each successive monarch was selected on his merits. This difference is probably to be explained in terms of the heterogeneous nature of Roman society. Whereas clan chiefs in many of the close-knit Greek communities readily agreed to afford permanent preeminence to one or two families, the Roman heads of family (*patresfamiliae*), being of more diverse racial origin, no doubt opted for greater flexibility. As in early Greece, however, the scope of the king's power was dictated by what was the paramount need of the time—firm leadership and coordinated action in war. In the military sphere that power was absolute, but in the purely domestic sphere it was circumscribed in practice by a respect for the autonomy of the gentes (clans) in ordering the affairs of their dependents.

Almost as old as the institution of monarchy itself was the Senate. There is no reason to question the tradition that this body was recruited by the first king from among the very patresfamiliae who had assented to his appointment: hence, according to one interpretation of the phrase, the corporate title *patres conscripti* (literally, family heads called into service) by which senators were known. This body acted as a regal council. Strictly speaking, it had no constitutional powers and only such authority as flowed from the social status of its members. But, to judge by the undeniable antiquity of the formula *auctoritas patrum,* its advice carried considerable weight. Furthermore, in the early stages of the monarchy at least, it played a vital role in the selection of successive kings. In strict theory, the regal power was conferred by the god Jupiter at the ceremony of the *inauguratio,* but in practice the choice lay with the senators; for it was their nominee, the so-called *interrex,* who, no doubt after consultation with his colleagues, put forward a name for the god's approval.

King and Senate were the only significant constituents in the monarchical system of government. The Roman tradition, it is true, would add a third—the people (*populus*), which allegedly met in a formal assembly of thirty local kinship groups known as curiae and which even recorded a vote on such issues as the endorsement of the king's appointment. But the sources here are undoubtedly in error. Certainly, members of the gentes did occasionally gather in their several curiae during the regal period, but, whether the purpose was to permit them to bear witness to a domestic family transaction such as an adoption or actually to the installation of a king, their role, like that of the assemblies of Homeric legend, was almost certainly passive.

The sixth century saw a modification of regal institutions and almost certainly a widening of the scope of monarchical authority at the expense of the gentes and indeed the Senate. Tarquinius Priscus (traditionally 616–579 B.C.) is alleged to have assumed power after a coup and without the interposition of an interregnum. How his successor, Servius Tullius (578–535 B.C.), came to be appointed we are not told, but the accession of the last king, Tarquinius Superbus (534–510 B.C.), suggests the establishment of a dynastic claim. This break with tradition was associated with the rapid emergence of Rome as a trading center within the Etruscan sphere of influence and with the consequent weakening of the structure of the agrarian-based society. The city's new prosperity had attracted large numbers of immigrants experienced in trade and handicrafts, and in these circumstances it was natural that a candidate who recognized their interests and responsibilities would eventually prevail.

Some have likened the last three Roman kings to the Greek tyrants of the seventh and sixth centuries, and indeed clear parallels can be drawn. Both derived support from elements previously excluded from political influence. Both can claim to have extended centralized control and thus to have nurtured, or even given birth to, the concept of citizenship. Thus, in the Rome of the Tarquins, as in the Athens of Peisistratos, a national religion was fostered that tended to overshadow the cults of the local clans and to provide a focus of devotion for all the citizenry. King Servius, too, acted much as did Greek tyrants or their immediate contemporaries in establishing a national census, in setting up new locally based administrative tribes, and in replacing the army's feudal contingents with a new force recruited from the population at large on the basis of a property qualification. But it would be misleading to carry the comparison with early Greece too far. Unlike most of the tyrants, the last kings of Rome did not emerge from within the aristocracy as victors in a bitter factional struggle, and for that reason they were not similarly tempted to launch an outright assault upon aristocratic power. The Senate was slightly enlarged to embrace a wider spectrum of interests, but its dignity and authority were preserved and respected. Even the new Servian tribes, unlike those created by Cleisthenes in the aftermath of the Athenian tyranny, were unitary territorial divisions, many of them actually taking their name from the landed family that was dominant within them.

Why then did the monarchy collapse at the end of the sixth century? The tradition stresses the propensity of the younger Tarquin toward overbearing and oppressive rule, and, since the Roman dread of kingship that prevailed for so many centuries must surely have been born of experience, it may reasonably be believed. But of what may well have been a far more crucial factor it says little. Toward the end of the sixth century the Etruscan League suffered a series of serious military reverses with the result that there was a relapse in the trading activities of all its associated states. Although the onset of the recession was gradual, the city of Rome, itself the hub of the Etruscan trading area and strategically placed at a crossing of the Tiber, must have been among the first to feel the effects. Thus, in worsening conditions of overpopulation and underemployment incursions into personal freedom that in prosperous times might have been suffered or even have gone unnoticed could easily have been viewed or represented as tyrannical. Likewise, an aristocracy that had been prepared to endure some diminution of influence in the national interest could have been tempted to reassert its rightful authority. It is likely, therefore, that the economic recession that hit Rome at this time had a major impact not only upon her future political course but also upon her form of government. Whereas in Athens an expansion in trade led inevitably to a widening of suffrage, to the development of democratic institutions, and eventually to mob rule, in Rome by contrast, to her lasting benefit, the decline in Etruria's fortunes permitted her traditional ruling class to reassume control.

Peculiarly among ancient states Rome managed to acquire a national identity, even a sense of national mission, without being forced in the process to throw overboard her natural leaders. Consequently, with the collapse of the monarchy and the establishment of the Republic Rome entered upon a period of stable, responsible, and effective government that has rarely been paralleled in the history of man.

THE REPUBLIC IN THE MAKING

The Aftermath of Revolution

That the Roman monarchy came to a sudden end and was not absorbed into a system of aristocratic government as was the monarchy in certain Greek city-states is now very widely accepted. Tarquin was driven from Rome in a coup organized by members of a resurgent Latin aristocracy. But, though the tradition is thus far trustworthy, it cannot be entirely believed when it suggests that the mechanism for alternative government was already firmly in place at the moment of Tarquin's expulsion. Here, with a misplaced emphasis upon the antiquity and continuity of Roman institutions, the sources prove unreliable. An *interrex*, they say, was immediately appointed to preside over a new form of popular assembly—a centuriate assembly —which had been fashioned some years earlier by Servius Tullius to parallel the new structure of the army. The centuriate assembly then proceeded to elect two chief magistrates, or consuls, who each were endowed with the equivalent of regal authority and held office in tandem for one year. Eligibility to this magistracy was to be restricted to an aristocratic elite known as the patriciate, whose members were allegedly direct descendants of the original senators and of a few later recruits.

Elements of this traditional account may

be salvaged, notably the concepts of annuality and duality. Even the latter has been called into question on the ground that no obvious parallel for the dual magistracy can be found in the institutions of other Latin communities. Yet it is surely perverse to query originality in a people who attained such unique preeminence. Several possible explanations of the institution of dual command may be found in the history of Rome itself. A simple one is that Rome faced a military threat on both her northern and southern flanks. Another is that the appointment of two executives with equal powers and the right of veto was a deliberate attempt to prevent the development of excessive power in the aftermath of the monarchy. It was certainly seen and valued as such throughout the Republic, even though with typical Roman ingenuity the more inconvenient consequences of the arrangement were obviated by the system of the "turn," whereby in normal times consuls who found themselves in Rome at the same time agreed to discharge their more important civil functions in alternate months.

Other elements in the tradition's version of events are less creditable. It may be doubted, for example, whether the new magistrates inherited the absolute and limitless power of the monarch. Their authority was designated as *imperium*, a term that had an essentially military connotation; and, although *imperium* came in time to be interpreted as conferring an undefined measure of civil jurisdiction, it nevertheless displayed characteristics that distinguished it clearly from the charismatic power associated with the kings. It was symbolized by a totally different set of insignia, for example, and it was recognized from the earliest years of the Roman Republic as being susceptible both to a process of grading and to restriction by statute. Furthermore, the magistrates' *imperium* was conferred not by a show of divine will, as had been regal power, but through an affirmation of consent on the part of those over whom it was to be exercised. It seems improbable that there was an electoral assembly already in place at the time of Tarquin's fall, but the very fact that such an assembly, when it did emerge, was modeled upon the structure of the army suggests that from the outset the *imperium* of the consul depended upon the avowed approval of Rome's military personnel.

It is most unlikely too that the new magistracy was ever a patrician preserve. The at one time orthodox doctrine that the patriciate originated in monarchical times and was an aristocratic elite distinguished by race or status has recently lost favor and is being increasingly replaced by the view that it was an artificial caste formed probably in the early years of the Republic for political ends. That at that time it made some attempt to monopolize the consulship in practice is indeed possible, even though the evidence of the early magisterial lists lends such a view little support. But that it ever established a monopoly of office based on law is inconceivable.

The Structuring of the Republican State

The period of military rule that followed the expulsion of Tarquin is likely to have been of short duration. With Rome not only under attack on several fronts but also suffering from internal strains induced by recession and overcrowding, it was inevitable that the new leaders should become increasingly involved in domestic issues and in the maintenance of public order. It cannot have been long before an attempt was made to establish the new regime on a broader and more stable footing. The sources themselves say nothing about such a restructuring, but two important developments, datable perhaps to the 480s, can be discerned that may well have formed part of the same constitutional package.

One was the establishment of a popular assembly whose chief function was to elect the annual magistrates. This body was in effect an extension of the centuriate army of Servius Tullius, which had comprised a legion of 6,000 divided into sixty fighting units of 100 men each, known as centuries. It was formed by making use of the basic centuriate structure and by either extending the existing military centuries or creating new ones to serve for all adult males who whether by reason of age or lack of the necessary property qualification were not in the army. Eventually, though not perhaps in the fifth century, the total number of voting centuries in this new assembly was brought to 193.

Two features of the centuriate assembly (*comitia centuriata*) are particularly noteworthy. In common with other Roman assemblies of earlier and later origin, it operated on the principle of the group vote. Under this arrangement the votes of individual citizens were used merely to determine the sense in which the vote of the particular group in which they were enrolled would be cast, and it was the tally of the votes of the groups themselves that determined the final outcome. The second is that the centuriate assembly was a markedly timocratic structure, which afforded heavy weighting to the wealthier voters. This was in part due to its origins. Recruitment into the Servian legion had been based on the ability to finance the provision of personal arms, and of the sixty centuries of the legion no fewer than forty had been drawn from the highest of the five property classes. But those who set up the political assembly in the fifth century appear to have deliberately espoused the principle —later unashamedly praised by Cicero— that the weightiest voice should be given to those with the greatest financial stake. In the new political assembly the sixty centuries reserved for those qualified by age and property to serve in the legion were duplicated to accommodate older citizens in the same property group, and a total of only fifty centuries (out of 193) was created for the large numbers of citizens in lower categories. Thus when the assembly eventually reached its full strength, a simple majority was attainable by the votes of the first property class (eighty centuries) and the cavalry elite (eighteen centuries).

This centuriate assembly soon began to function in both the legislative and jurisdictive spheres, but its first responsibility was to confer *imperium* upon the consuls, a responsibility that had previously been discharged by the army. At the outset its power may have been restricted to the simple acceptance or rejection of names put forward by retiring magistrates, but it is unlikely to have been long before it began to exercise a genuine right of choice.

The other major development of this time was the establishment of a formal structure for the new Republic in the shape of what was generally termed the "patrician state." That the patriciate in some sense underpinned the new constitution is strongly indicated. Until the end of the Republic the senior officers of state were known as the "patrician magistrates"; the patricians too laid undisputed claim to what was anomalously called the *auctoritas patrum*, effectively the right of veto over electoral and legislative activity; and, perhaps most significant of all, the patricians assumed control of the institution called the "interregnum," reserving the right when the occasion arose both to appoint an *interrex* and to provide one from their own number. Who the patricians were and how they were able to establish such unchallengeable claims must remain a matter for speculation, but the following is a not improbable scenario.

The patriciate was a caste formed in the early fifth century exclusively from among senatorial families who with some justice could claim to represent the patresfamiliae of the old Latin aristocracy. Hence perhaps the title—*patricii*—that they adopted. Since membership was no doubt dependent upon current influence, they could rely on the support of numerous clients as well as on a sizable number of citizens who had come to regret the association with Etruria and to cherish the ideals of the earlier Latin society. Their principal aim was to end the unsatisfactory and potentially dangerous period of military rule and to establish themselves as the permanent guarantors of a new and sound governmental order. It was not their intention to play an active role themselves each year in selecting magistrates. The chain of magistracy, once forged, was to be self-perpetuating in that the consuls of one year were to be responsible for presenting the names of potential successors to a newly formed popular assembly. But, if ever the chain of magistracy were broken, the patricians were to be at hand as the ultimate repositories of power to reforge it through the institution of the interregnum.

It may be thought that the establishment of constitutional forms designed to satisfy the aspirations of an aristocratic elite accords ill with the creation of a popular assembly constructed according to the timocratic principle. But such a view is based on a serious misunderstanding of the nature of Roman society at this period. In Solonian Athens—and even in the Rome of Servius Tullius—the introduction of timocratic institutions may be construed as an assault on narrow-based aristocratic privilege. Not so, however, in fifth-century Rome, when as a result of the recession many in the high property bracket became increasingly dependent on the agrarian economy and its values. Perhaps if the patriciate had itself actively sought to monopolize office, the centuriate assembly would not have been a wholly suitable instrument; but certainly it could be relied upon to elect a steady stream of responsible men of aristocratic descent.

Of particular interest in this connection is the text of the Licinio-Sextian law of 367 B.C., which provided that "at least one consul each year should be a plebeian." Contrary to the view of many, the clear import of this measure is not that the assembly was thereby liberated from a previous requirement that it should appoint patricians; rather is it that its freedom was for the first time circumscribed by a ruling that it appoint plebeians (nonpatricians).

Plebeian Institutions

While the official institutions of the Roman Republic were thus being formalized, another movement was taking root in Roman society that was to make a major impact on constitutional development. The poor and overcrowded population of the city was induced by severe economic hardship to unite in an effort to put pressure on Senate and magistrates to improve its lot. From as early as 494 B.C. the poor began to hold mass meetings and to appoint spokesmen to represent their case. These officers were called tribunes, and, although perhaps at first appointed ad hoc, they came very quickly to constitute an annually elected panel of ten. They lacked official standing at this stage, but they derived an immunity from the law, and thus considerable authority, from the pledge to protect them that was solemnly sworn by their electorate.

In 471 B.C., at the prompting of Lucius Publilius Volero, this movement set about ordering its affairs in two important respects. First, it reacted to the recent creation of the "patrician state" by specifically excluding all patricians from its offices and its deliberations. It thus transformed itself into what was essentially a "plebeian" movement. Second, it reorganized its decision-making procedures by abandoning the mass meeting and forming a new assembly, hereafter known as the *concilium plebis,* in which voting was conducted, as in the official centuriate assembly, on the group-vote principle, but in which the units of vote were the Servian territorial tribes, currently numbering twenty-one. This body could claim to be representative of the various districts included within the Roman domain, and for as long as all were within easy access of the city it had no inbuilt bias toward the interests of the wealthy.

Strengthened by this new order, the plebeian body soon began to pose a serious threat to the government in that it constituted a state within the state. The plebeians in mass decided upon corporate action which the authorities found it difficult to resist, while the tribunes deliberately used their inviolability to shield those who sought to flout the consuls' authority. In a Greek city such developments might well have led to serious stasis and to a consequent undermining of the entire social and political fabric. In Rome, however, a common sense of purpose and a determination to pursue first the national interest led inevitably to a policy of compromise and to the eventual absorption of plebeian institutions into the official body politic.

The principal feature of this accord was the legalization of the tribunes' inviolability, for at one stroke the plebeian officers were thus given official status and brought within the orbit of the unitary state. This inviolability also soon became the basis of two further well-established tribunician rights: the right to help a plebeian against the arbitrary exercise of a magistrate's power (*ius auxilii*), which may not have been so extensively used as when in the early years the tribunes represented a revolutionary movement, but which probably by the mere threat of its use effectively guaranteed the development of criminal trials before the people and the demise of summary jurisdiction; and the right of veto (*ius intercessionis*), which gave them powers to obstruct all legislation, and later even senatorial decrees, and which was but a logical extension of the *ius auxilii*. It was also probably at the same period, the mid fifth century, that the plebeian assembly was officially recognized as an instrument entitled to legislate on behalf of the entire Roman *populus*. The right was at first made conditional upon the grant by the patricians of *auctoritas*, but, as this sanction was applicable to centuriate legislation also, the enactments of the *plebs* were in theory made equivalent to laws of the *populus*. Later, in 287 B.C., when the tribunes could no longer be said to represent a sectional interest, even the need for this *auctoritas* was removed, and the assembly was thereafter totally unfettered.

Nothing so well exemplifies the extraordinary capacity of the Roman governing class for flexibility and invention as the manner in which they adapted what at first had been the institutions of a semirevolutionary body into integral and invaluable constituents of the state machinery. By the close of the fourth century the tribunes appeared to have lost their raison d'être. Rome's expansion into Latium had brought relief from her economic ills, and the plebeian leaders could no longer plausibly claim to be the champions of a disaffected element in society. In such circumstances the tribunate and other plebeian institutions might well have died a natural death. The Roman government, however, perceived their usefulness and actively encouraged their survival. The urban-based office of tribune, with a representative and easily managed assembly to hand, was seen to be the ideal instrument for coping with routine legislation at a time when Rome's growing overseas commitments were making ever heavier demands upon the consuls; while the unchallenged powers of the tribunate, especially the veto, were welcomed by the corporate oligarchy as providing them with an additional effective check upon any abuse of *imperium*, or even any excessive show of independence, on the part of an ambitious member of the executive. With the Senate's encouragement, therefore, the office soon became the virtual preserve of young members of the governing class who were about to embark on orthodox political careers.

New Offices and Powers

The absorption of the plebeian organization at the end of the fourth century was but one means by which Rome provided herself with additional instruments of government. Almost from the outset of the Republic the need was felt for such instruments, and as Rome spread her tentacles across Italy and, from the third century onward, overseas, that need became ever more acute.

The initial reaction to the problem was the simple one of creating new magistracies. One such was the office of censor, a dual magistracy filled for a period of eighteen months every five years, which was first introduced *ca.* 443 B.C. to relieve the consuls of certain of their domestic responsibilities. These included the vital tasks of producing updated property ratings for the citizenry and revising the senatorial roll. Unlike the consuls, the censors did not themselves wield *imperium*, having no military functions; but they were elected by the senior assembly, the centuriate, and on account of their quinquennial election and the importance of their duties they developed in time into the most highly respected officers of state.

Another, though less prestigious, new office of early origin was the quaestorship. Tradition has it that a quaestor had been appointed even in regal times to act as the king's criminal investigator, but the institution of a regular magistracy filled annually by popular election dated from the mid fifth century when first it became common to hear criminal cases before the centuriate assembly. The quaestor at this stage assumed the new but related role of public prosecutor. Like other minor magistrates, he was elected not by the timocratic and somewhat cumbersome centuriate body, but by an assembly of the *populus* that voted by tribes and was closely modeled upon the *concilium plebis*.

Into a different category, in that it was not designed to satisfy any regular administrative need and in that it was an extraordinary office, falls the dictatorship. Sources differ as to whether the first dictator was nominated in order to provide Rome with a single military overlord at a time when there was a need for a unified command, or whether his appointment was designed to inspire terror and to extract obedience from the populace at a moment of domestic crisis. The latter explanation appears the more likely if only for the reason that he was named at dead of night and was deemed to be endowed with *imperium* under mystical circumstances and without popular sanction. But, once the institution of dictatorship had been devised, it was used over a period of almost three centuries to meet a whole variety of emergencies with which the regular magistrates were either unable or supposedly unfitted to deal. The tenure of the office was limited to six months, and, since for this reason, among others, it was better adapted to the special needs of a city-state than to those of an imperial power, it fell into disuse after the Second Punic War. Its immense constitutional significance, however, lies in the fact that it committed Rome at a very early stage to the concept of a graded *imperium*. The dictator was deemed to have precisely twice as much power as the consul and, to advertise the fact, was afforded a retinue of twenty-four lictors, or attendants, in contrast to the consul's twelve. This probably did not mean, as some scholars have maintained, that on appointment he automatically and invariably assumed responsibility for the actions of the consuls and the lesser magistrates: it does mean, however, that he was entitled to assume that responsibility if and when he chose.

This policy of providing for governmental needs by the creation of altogether new magistracies was soon abandoned. From the fourth century the Romans turned to solving their problems both by enlarging the size of existing magisterial colleges and by conferring new duties upon them. The quaestorial college is a notable case in point. Over the Republican period the number elected annually swelled from a mere one to no fewer than twenty, and they were assigned diverse responsibilities, as for example in the spheres of finance, the military commissariat, and even junior naval command, which bore no relation to their original investigatory and judicial functions. The aediles, too, who as plebeian officers became instruments of government along with the tribunes when the plebeian organization was reconciled with the official establishment, were in 367 B.C. increased in number from two to four by the creation of a pair of so-called curule aediles who were to be elected by the entire *populus;* and to them were assigned a multiplicity of functions including the responsibility for organizing public games, for controlling the urban food supply, for supervising public works, and even for managing the urban police and fire services.

From the constitutional point of view the most significant development was the decision to increase the number of annual magistrates endowed with *imperium*. This was a move dictated by Rome's ever-growing military commitments as well as by the increasing burdens involved in administering the civil law. Already in the period 445 to 367 B.C. there had been a curious episode when the Romans had in certain years abandoned the dual consulship and had conferred the consular *imperium* instead upon a group of military tribunes with consular power (*tribuni militum*) varying in number from three to six. The motives for this maneuver have been variously interpreted as military, political, or administrative, but, whatever the truth, one sure result must have been to convince the Senate of the advantages of sharing the workload at the top. When therefore the experiment of the consular tribunate was abandoned and the dual magistracy was restored, it was decided to provide the consuls with a third, yet unequal, colleague. He took the title of "praetor," which had originally been applied to the consuls themselves; and, although he was at first envisaged, and indeed used, as an additional commander in the field, he soon began to confine his activities to the administration of civil law in Rome. To mark his junior status the Romans once more invoked the concept of the graded *imperium*: they afforded the new praetor just six lictors and thus signified that, while holding independent responsibility, he was subject to the greater authority of the consuls (who were attended by twelve lictors) whenever they chose to exercise it.

This precedent, once set, was followed on a number of further occasions. As Rome spread her contacts in Italy, another praetor was added (*ca.* 242 B.C.) to deal with contractual disputes between Romans and aliens; and later, when Rome began to establish provinces overseas, first in Sicily, then in Sardinia and Spain, the problem of providing military governors was resolved by adding yet further praetors to the college, until by the first decade of the second century the number of annual magistrates endowed with *imperium* had reached eight.

At this stage in the development of the empire Rome changed course once more. The policy of augmenting annual colleges of magistrates, which certainly worked well enough for the lesser administrative posts, was seen to have serious shortcomings where *imperium* was involved. From the political standpoint, of course, the nobility viewed with some concern the prospect of a dilution of the higher echelons of the governing oligarchy that would inevitably result from a progressive and continuing increase in the number of senior magistrates elected annually. But there were also more serious considerations which more nearly affected the national interest. There was a damaging waste of talent and experience involved in any system that looked to confer heavy responsibilities upon new recruits and to deny the state the services of men of proven worth who had reached the top of the political ladder. Furthermore, in those provincial areas that remained unsettled and were the scene of continuing military activity there were obvious disadvantages in an enforced annual change of command. The Senate's answer to this problem was to embrace the principle of power divorced from office.

This concept, it must be said, was not altogether new. It in fact dated from the late fourth century when during the Second Samnite War Rome had for the first time become involved in military action that was neither localized nor confined to the campaigning season. At the siege of Neapolis (Naples) in 327 B.C. it had become apparent that Rome could only benefit from a continuity of command and the retention of the services of the ruling consul in the field. The Senate, therefore, had taken advantage of the flexibility offered by a largely unwritten constitution by asking the assembly to extend the consul's *imperium* (by the process of *prorogatio*) beyond the date at which he was due to lay down his office. In this way had been born the concept of promagistracy, which was to play so important a role in the development, and indeed the ultimate collapse, of Republican institutions and which was to become the main prop of the imperial regime that followed. The promagistracy allowed the holder to exercise an *imperium* equal in strength to that which was attached to the equivalent office without its being restricted by the principle of annuality. Indeed, in the early years before Sulla the only effective qualification that distinguished the promagistrate's authority from that of the magistrate himself was that it could not lawfully be exercised within the bounds of the city of Rome.

The possibility of a resort to promagistracy was soon recognized as a solution to more than one of the Senate's problems. It had obviated the need to increase still further the pool of regular military commanders after the recruitment of the first praetor in 366 B.C., and it had perhaps smoothed the way for even that magistrate's permanent secondment to jurisdictive duties. It had also helped to resolve the problem caused by the occasional need to recruit an able and proved commander at a time of military crisis, a need that had traditionally been met by the clumsy and unsatisfactory expedient of appointing a dictator with a limited six-month tenure. When, therefore, in the second century Rome was faced with rapidly expanding military and administrative commitments overseas, the promagistracy appeared to provide a perfect answer. It enabled the Senate to abandon the proliferation of senior magistracy and gave it freedom to assign the most suitable personnel to the various provinces for as long as it deemed expedient. This is not to say that the governing of provinces by promagistrates at once became the norm. The Senate's first aim was to cast off the shackles of rigidity. Some of the praetors continued to serve in the provinces, though they did tend progressively to be diverted to the presidency of new permanent criminal courts. Consuls, too, could and frequently did assume military command during their years of office in troubled areas of the empire. But, as the overseas territories multiplied, promagistrates were henceforward used on an increasing scale.

THE REPUBLIC AT ITS HEIGHT

The Greek historian Polybius, writing in the second century from the point of view of a foreign observer, described the Roman constitution as one "than which it was not possible to find a better." It represented for him the ideal of the mixed constitution, a combination of democracy, monarchy, and aristocracy, which in people, consuls, and Senate could boast three sovereign elements, and in which the powers of each element were balanced against those of the others with a scrupulous regard for equilibrium. A brief survey of the role played by each in the middle Republic should enable us to judge the accuracy of this assessment.

The People

In theory the Roman *populus* did indeed enjoy sovereign powers. All legislation depended on their assent, given freely either in the tribal assembly of the whole people or in the *concilium plebis,* two bodies that in these days of a dwindling and politically irrelevant patriciate were virtually indistinguishable. In elections, too, the people exercised a free choice over a range of candidates, eventually even winning the right in the second century to cast their votes by secret ballot. The senior magistrates, it is true, were chosen by an assembly that was heavily weighted in favor of the wealthy. But it should be remembered that it was an assembly voting by tribes that elected the magistrates below the rank of praetor, and that after the establishment of a regular career pattern, or *cursus honorum,* election to junior office was a necessary precondition of further political advancement.

In practice, however, the people had far less authority than might at first appear. They had no right to initiate legislation and they had no direct control over lists of candidates. They were also debarred from participating in any open debate either on the content of proposed legislation or on the merits of electoral candidates; for, although it was open to the presiding magistrate, and occasionally other interested parties, to call and address meetings (*contiones*) in the immediate run-up to a vote, those who attended could do no more than listen and had no opportunity for an exchange of views. Even after a vote had been taken, the declared will of the people could technically be frustrated either by the interposition of a veto from a hired tribune or by an announcement of unfavorable omens emanating from the presiding magistrate himself or from the influential college of augurs. But by far the most formidable obstacles to a truly democratic expression of the popular will were those presented by the structure and the voting procedures of the assemblies.

The senior assembly in Rome, that which throughout the Republic had responsibility for electing consuls, praetors, and censors, and which was called upon to endorse the most important decisions of government, such as those involving war and peace, was the centuriate. Until the third century, as has already been remarked, the highest property class and the cavalry elite could combine their 98 voting units (out of a total of 193) and thereby determine the outcome of any vote. When the tribes were brought up to their final tally of thirty-five in 241 B.C., it was decided by the nobility, probably for reasons of political advantage, that the centuries of this all-important first property class should be coordinated with the tribes in the sense that the citizens enrolled in each century should all be drawn from the same tribe. This reform necessarily implied a reduction by ten in the number of centuries allocated to the first class (80)—seventy being a multiple of thirty-five—and as a result the combined voting strength of the first class and the cavalry now fell nine votes short of an absolute majority. But this relatively minor adjustment did not materially affect the balance of interest within the assembly. The propertied class still had decisive control, and, as Cicero pointedly remarked, there were more people enrolled in his day in one single century of the proletariat than in the entire group of seventy first-class centuries. This imbalance was further accentuated by procedural rules which in practice deprived the lower-rated citizens even of an opportunity to record their votes. Voting and the announcement of results were conducted class by class beginning from the top; and, possibly purely on account of the time factor involved in taking a vote, it was the accepted rule in Rome that in multiple elections a candidate should be declared elected as soon as he was declared to have carried a bare absolute majority of the total voting units, and, further, that voting should cease altogether as soon as a number of candidates equal to the number of offices to be filled was declared elected. Not only did these rules sometimes produce a different result from that which would have been produced if voting and declarations had been allowed to continue, but they also ensured that those who were enrolled in the centuries of the lower property classes were on most occasions effectively disfranchised. In these circumstances it is hardly likely that they bothered to attend the vote.

In the two tribal assemblies, the *concilium plebis* and the *comitia populi tributa*, which were responsible for the majority of legislation and for the election of the minor magistrates, there was of course no such inbuilt bias in favor of wealth. Here, however, the operation of the group-vote principle conspired to produce very much the same effect; for, as the Roman domain was extended in Italy and as new tribes were formed to accommodate these citizens domiciled in comparatively distant areas, it inevitably followed that an increasing number of tribes came to be represented in their respective voting units at the assembly in Rome only by those who could afford the time and the means to travel. At the elections for minor magistrates, which were for the most part held at the same time as consular elections, it is likely, therefore, that voters were predominantly those who had come to Rome primarily to attend the centuriate assembly. At a legislative vote, except on very rare occasions when feelings ran high—as, for example, during the tribunate of Tiberius Gracchus—attendances are likely to have been sparse and to have been calculatingly predetermined by the promulgator of the proposed measure.

It must be conceded that the principle of the group vote as applied to the tribal system had one great merit, which no doubt gave it appeal to governing class and citizenry alike. It enshrined the representative principle by precluding the possibility that any comitial decision would be taken solely on the votes of those who chanced to be domiciled within easy reach of the place of assembly and by ensuring that the voice of every tribal area, however thinly represented at the vote, would carry equal weight. That it did so appears to have been a mere accident of history, since at the time when the tribal assemblies were originally set up all the citizens lived within easy access of the city. But there is evidence enough that this representative principle was later consciously embraced by the nobility as sacrosanct. When in 312 B.C. the independent-minded censor Appius Claudius attempted to counter its effectiveness by permitting rural dwellers to register in urban tribes, his opponents acted swiftly to undo his arrangements; and it is reasonable to suppose that the nobility sponsored the aforementioned reform of the centuriate assembly in the next century with a view to introducing what they saw to be the advantages of the tribal group vote into the operations of the main electoral body.

Whether the Senate endorsed the representative principle in Roman voting for its own sake is debatable. What is certain is that it also had its own less disinterested reasons for doing so. It would not have served its purpose to allow a situation to develop in which a potentially decisive body of voters might be canvassed and addressed in the mass. That would have carried with it the danger that candidates or magistrates might be tempted to resort to methods bordering on the demagogic. It would also have struck a severe blow at the very essence of the electoral campaign as it had traditionally been conceived in Rome, a campaign geared not toward persuasion and the conversion of the uncommitted but rather toward garnering political clients and delivering existing potential support. The fact that the Roman domain was divided into well-defined tribal areas must have been seen as an invaluable asset in assisting this process, for it made it possible for those seeking electoral support to concentrate their efforts economically where most they were needed. Even in the dying years of the Republic Cicero during his electoral campaign was advised to acquire as a matter of priority a map of Italy "marked out in tribal divisions."

It should be said that the populace showed few signs of being dissatisfied with the arrangements made for voting, whether it be in centuriate or tribal assemblies. Unlike the citizens of many Greek city-states, who were predominantly traders and as such individualists and searchers after self-expression, the Roman electorate of the middle Republican period was composed largely of farmers who were readily disposed both to respect authority and to support any system of government that manifestly served the national interest. What is more, though their power to influence events was limited, they yet derived substantial benefit from the mere possession of their voting rights. Thus votes canvassed and duly delivered could be, and no doubt frequently were, traded for benefits received or benefits yet to come—benefits, it may be said, that accrued not only to the wealthier individuals who journeyed to Rome to cast a vote but also to the entire communities and townships of which they were members. The group vote and the representative principle it enshrined virtually guaranteed that no corner of the Roman citizen area would be without its champions in the influential circles of the nobility. It was indeed in anticipation of securing these corporate benefits of patronage that the people of Italy set such store by full rights of suffrage at the time of the Social War (91–87 B.C.).

Popular sovereignty, then, in Polybius' sense was in practice more of a fiction than a reality. Voters in general were induced to attend assemblies not by the appeal of personalities, of policies, or even of specific legislative proposals, but rather by ties of gratitude to those who sought their votes. Yet this is not to deny that the popular vote made a vital contribution to the smooth running of the Republican system of government. It was important in that it encouraged active patronage and offered some guarantee to all citizens that their interests would not be ignored. It was important too in that it imposed upon candidates and would-be legislators the absolute necessity of winning the support of that substantial body of fellow nobles without whose active cooperation they could not succeed in delivering the vote they needed. It was thus indirectly an insurance against the capricious use of authority by any one individual, and an insurance also against the protracted domination of the Roman political scene by a narrow faction.

The Consuls

For Polybius the consuls represented the despotic or monarchic element in the Roman constitution, and he was right to the extent that as holders of *imperium* they wielded an authority that theoretically knew no definition. Originally appointed for the main purpose of taking overall command on a field of battle, they soon stretched the concept of *imperium* to cover a range of specific civil powers. Among the most important of these were the right of arrest and summary jurisdiction, the right of edict, the right to summon popular assemblies and to initiate legislation, the right to preside at elections and to nominate candidates, and the right of precedence in putting motions before the Senate. In the course of time, however, restrictive legislation, political pressures, and even in some cases the mere weight of precedent combined seriously to emasculate their authority. At a very early stage a law that conferred upon all citizens a right of appeal effectively deprived them of their criminal jurisdictive powers and resulted in the transfer of all responsibility in criminal cases to the centuriate assembly. Again, as has been seen, the very effectiveness of the plebeian movement in the fifth century imposed notable restraints upon the consuls' freedom of action, and the resulting compromise, which afforded recognition to the tribunes' inviolability and powers of obstruction, ensured that those restraints were afforded legitimacy. In the field of choosing their successors, too, they suffered an early setback as the newly constituted centuriate assembly grew in confidence; for, whereas originally the consuls may have merely nominated as many candidates as there were places to be filled, the custom soon became established that they should accept the candidacy of any who professed himself willing to stand and who could demonstrate that he had the necessary legal qualification. In theory, they appear to have retained the absolute right to refuse the candidature of anyone they chose, and even indeed to refuse to announce the result of an electoral vote; but this right was invoked only exceptionally and is evidenced only in the lawless years of the dying Republic.

On the face of it the consuls' other rights remained unimpaired, although their exercise was of course always subject to the threat of collegial veto inherent in the concept of duality and equal power (*par potestas*). But even here one has to interpose an important qualification. The consuls owed their political advancement, and in particular their present high office, to efforts made on their behalf by large numbers of fellow nobles. It follows that, unless they were prepared to violate a code which set very great store by the obligation to repay a service, and unless they were prepared in the process to sacrifice their future political careers, the consuls could not take strong and independent action which did not have substantial senatorial backing. It is therefore no exaggeration to say that, though armed with extensive executive powers, they were in practice no more than the instruments of senatorial will.

The Senate

Whatever claims may be made for the principle of popular sovereignty or for the limitless executive authority inherent in the concept of *imperium*, it was in practice the Senate that effectively directed the government of Rome throughout the long and successful period of the middle Republic. In this there is something of a paradox, for alone of the three constitutional elements listed by Polybius the Senate could claim no legal basis for its powers. It is true that the small patrician group within the Senate still retained the *auctoritas patrum,* or the effective right of veto, over all proceedings in the centuriate assembly, and it is likely that this traditional right vested in but a part of its membership was welcomed and valued by the whole Senate in that it served to strengthen any claim that it may have made to be regarded as the ultimate guardian of the constitution. But this was of little practical value and was scarcely, if at all, responsible for the Senate's preeminence. That may be ascribed to two causes. One was that the Senate was unique in being the only institution that enjoyed any permanence at Rome and that could therefore bring some cohesion both to the mechanics of government and to the formulation of policy at a time of rapid expansion and constantly changing demands. The other was that it commanded considerable respect both from the magistrates who were drawn from its ranks and, more particularly, from the electorate at large in the light of its successful record in steering Rome through a series of major domestic crises and foreign wars to her present peak of greatness.

Senators retained their rank for life, with the sole qualification that they could exceptionally be stripped of it by the censors for misconduct. Most succeeded to it by heredity, but it was attainable also, as was the highest level of magistracy, by those new men of talent who managed to draw attention to themselves and to prove themselves worthy of promotion. Consuls and ex-consuls had always been automatically members of the Senate. Then by the Ovinian law of *ca.* 300 B.C. censors had probably been required to enroll all who had held what were known as the curule magistracies (not only the consulship but also the praetorship and the curule aedileship). And at a much later date the gates were opened first to tribunes of the *plebs,* and eventually under Sulla to quaestors. The Senate, therefore, was unique among the aristocratic councils of the ancient world. In contrast to the closed and in many cases short-lived oligarchical synods of the early Greek city-states, the Roman Senate could always draw new strength from a constant, though never dramatic, infusion of fresh blood. It was indeed that rare phenomenon, perhaps most closely paralleled in modern times by the British House of Lords—an all-in-one repository of new talent, political experience, and that selfless devotion to duty which is the hallmark and priceless asset of a virile hereditary aristocracy.

The Senate's role in taking decisions dated from the earliest years of the Republic. It was the Senate that had decided what particular circumstances necessitated the appointment of a dictator, and it was usually on the Senate's advice that the consul had acted in making the nomination. It was the Senate that during the period 445 to 367 B.C. had determined each year whether the situation called for the appointment of consuls or of consular tribunes, and, in the event of its opting for the latter, how many of them there should be. It was the Senate that somewhat later had devised the expedient of prorogation of *imperium*; and, although the first promagistracy was instituted by the assembly, it was the Senate that had very soon assumed the responsibility for deciding when and in what area a prorogation was desirable and for determining how long it should remain in force. By the early second century, therefore, it was exercising virtually unquestioned control over the allocation of specific commands and of overseas provinces to magistrates and promagistrates alike. Over the years, too, countless other tasks accrued to the Senate, which gave it almost complete freedom to direct the course of foreign policy. These included a responsibility for determining the size of the military levy and the disposition of the legions, for controlling the release of state funds from the public treasury, for framing the charters under which new overseas dependencies would be governed, for receiving the submissions of foreign embassies, and for deciding the terms of reference and the makeup of legations sent out by Rome. Nearer to home its permanent status led it to assume a much needed responsibility for dealing with longstanding problems affecting the interests of citizens and Italians, and so to pass regulatory decrees that served almost as mandatory guidelines to the magistrates in the exercise of their *imperium*. A general decree of 186 B.C. banning organized Bacchanalian cults throughout Italy is a famous case in point. All these duties were undertaken out of expediency or sheer necessity and with the tacit consent of the vast majority of the citizenry. They thus developed into established prerogatives within the framework of the unwritten constitution, sanctioned by that formidable authority we term tradition, known to the Romans as ancestral custom (*mos maiorum*).

Yet the Senate's preeminence did not rest solely upon a catalog of special extralegal prerogatives. These certainly helped to cement its influence and to increase the pressure it could bring to bear upon a potentially wayward magistrate; but its authority rested also in no small measure upon the very considerable influence that it wielded as a body in determining the political fortunes of those who were its members. It could make use of its powers to punish any magistrate who thwarted its will by denying him the right to march through Rome in triumph after a military success, or, in later times, by depriving him of the opportunity to hold a promagisterial command, to which most consuls aspired as a source either of military renown or of financial profit. But probably more significant, if less commonly recognized, was the claim the Senate could make upon a magistrate's compliance with its wishes which resulted directly from its own services in advancing his political career.

There is a common misconception about the way in which elections were fought in Republican Rome, in that candidates are generally assumed to have relied for success almost entirely upon their own efforts and those of an immediate circle of friends. This is most unlikely to have been the case. Certainly, elections in Rome bore no resemblance to elections in modern democracies, where candidates stand on a well-advertised political program and can rely on the full backing of a party machine. The lack of any means of mass communication, together with a voting system that in effect precluded the majority from casting a vote, would have rendered such a modern-style campaign totally impracticable. Yet it would be quite wrong to conclude on this account either that candidates did not require assistance on a large scale or indeed that their general political stance and their views on specific issues, which must have been common knowledge within the inner circle of the nobility, were wholly irrelevant to their chances.

The political *clientela* of a Roman noble was concentrated very largely in his own tribal areas. It was his own *tribules* whom he is particularly credited with courting during a campaign, and it was to his own *tribules* alone that he was legally permitted to direct veiled electoral bribes in the form of free entertainment and the like. If he belonged to a political coterie, or if as a new recruit to the nobility he was sponsored by a coterie, he could presumably also count upon the support of the clients of powerful allies who belonged to tribes other than his own. But so long as senators in general were ready to involve themselves disinterestedly in elections this could rarely have sufficed. To have a reasonable chance of electoral success a candidate needed at least a modicum of active support from not a few uncommitted senators, and to that end he had to make efforts to impress them with his talent, his personality, and, perhaps more than is commonly believed, his policies. This heavy reliance on senatorial backing probably helped to ensure that in most years the consuls were in tune with majority opinion in the Senate. Where a difference did arise, however, the Roman code of political ethics dictated that in the last resort it should be resolved in the Senate's favor. Consultation with the Senate became the established norm, and at least before the end of the Punic Wars it would have been regarded as a serious breach of etiquette for a consul either to introduce legislation or to take any other important initiative without senatorial blessing.

The firm grip that the Senate maintained over all aspects of policy making and magisterial action guaranteed the stability of the Republican system of government. Without it the dangers inherent in the concept of shared *imperium* and in the delicate and complex arrangements for checks and balances would most surely have led sooner than they did to inaction and eventually to anarchy. As it was, by assuming the role of arbiter and ultimate decision maker the Senate nullified the risk of conflict and effectively transferred the magisterial right of veto to itself.

THE REPUBLIC IN DECLINE

To the eye of Polybius at the period when he wrote, the Republican system of government appeared strong and intact. In retrospect, however, it is possible to detect clear signs of decline already in the first half of the second century. At first the process of disintegration was gradual and without marked effect, but after the stormy tribunate of Tiberius Gracchus in 133 B.C. it began to accelerate dramatically, with the result that Rome was plunged almost before it knew it into a protracted period of violence, near-anarchy, and eventual civil war. How, then, did this come about?

The standard answer to this question is that the Republican constitution, designed as it was for the governance of a city-state, was totally unsuited to Rome's new role as mistress of an overseas empire. Territorial expansion, it is argued, made the maintenance of the existing power structure impossible and called for the establishment of a totally different constitutional framework within which the determination of policy and its execution would be concentrated in a single organ of government. But such an answer, given in the knowledge of how Rome's problems were eventually solved through the Principate, is not sufficient in itself, nor is it entirely convincing. Rome enjoyed the advantage of an unwritten and flexible constitution, and had for three hundred years capitalized on that flexibility with considerable skill and ingenuity to meet new and often dangerous challenges both external and internal. The room for maneuver that such an informal structure affords is well illustrated in modern times by the example of Great Britain, whose unwritten constitution has vouchsafed her far more stable and durable government than that enjoyed by any of her European neighbors, and that despite the formidable challenges presented successively by the Industrial Revolution, the acquisition and subsequent abdication of a worldwide empire, and recent profound changes in social attitudes. It is not, therefore, too much to believe that Rome could have responded to the various problems thrown up by her new imperial commitments without undergoing constitutional upheaval. Radical changes might certainly have been necessary, including possibly, among other things, the abandonment of some of the checks and balances that were built into the existing system, the strengthening of the executive authority of the consuls vis-à-vis that of other holders of *imperium*, and even some modification of the principle of annuality in certain areas. But, given the will on the part of the Senate and, above all, the broad consensus among the citizenry that such changes were demanded by events, all this and more might well have been achieved without any material undermining of the Senate's dominant role as the taker of policy decisions.

If this assessment is correct, then it is a failure within the Senate that must be held accountable for the Republic's decline and eventual collapse. At just the moment when its leadership and resourcefulness were most required it seems to have lost both its way and its will to act. The lapse was one from which it found it impossible to recover. The image painted by the sources is of an institution that thereafter became increasingly less self-confident and that floundered ever more desperately amid mounting pressures to regain the authority to which it had fatally forfeited its claim. It is notoriously difficult to analyze and explain such transformations in the attitudes and in the effectiveness of a corporate body, but three possible contributory factors deserve mention. One was the inevitable sense of tiredness and relief, combined with a mood of self-congratulation, that followed Rome's eventual victory in the protracted life-and-death struggle with Carthage. A second was the demoralizing, and some would say corrupting, influence exerted upon senators by newfound contacts with the culture and manners of a decadent Greek civilization. According to Cato the Elder, whose election to a famous censorship in 184 B.C. proved that he was no maverick, this was a cancer that ran deep within the Roman nobility and that posed a threat both to its moral fiber and to its patriotic zeal. A third factor was something more tangible—the damage done to the clearsightedness and impartiality of the majority of senators by their own growing personal implication in the financially lucrative operations of empire. There are signs that already before the Second Punic War senators were in danger of being diverted from their responsibilities in government by involvement in business enterprises, since attempts were made at that time to restrict their extramural activities by law. In the second century the opportunity for developing these interests was correspondingly greater, and, if even the traditionalist Cato the Elder himself became indirectly involved in marine insurance, there can have been few among senators who were able to resist the temptation. The danger here was clearly twofold: first, that the senator at a most crucial time for Rome would devote less than his full attention to the affairs of state; and second, that he would allow his judgment both in determining policy and in forming personal associations to be influenced by narrow, commercial interest.

These same weaknesses which diverted the Senate from treading the path of much-needed and radical constitutional reform were responsible also for a relaxation of its control over the executive. One of the major problems thrown up by overseas expansion was that of the irresponsible provincial governor who, being insulated by distance from the Senate's supervisory eye, felt emboldened to abuse his authority often to his own financial advantage. This could no doubt have been solved in the early stages by swift and retributive action; but the Senate's response in establishing the appropriate criminal procedures was both belated and tentative, and, when eventually it set up a permanent court to deal with these cases, it was rendered largely ineffective by the partiality of the senatorial juries who sat upon it.

There was a gradual and almost imperceptible decline also in the Senate's corporate influence over elections. This was evidenced by an increase in electoral corruption, which was never brought satisfactorily under control, and it was evidenced too by an intensification of factional conflict within the nobility, which was not unconnected with the fact that there was now a less scrupulous scrutiny of candidates' merits by disinterested senators. The effect was particularly damaging at a time when so many weighty political problems required urgent attention, because any decline in the indebtedness felt by the magistrates to the Senate as a body spelled for it a significant loss of policy control. The advocacy of policies thus fell increasingly to individuals and to the political groups to which they adhered. Predictably, proposals for much-needed reform therefore carried less weight than would have been the case if they had been introduced on the initiative of a senatorial majority. Indeed, such proposals frequently ran into fierce obstruction from political opponents who begrudged the credit and the increase in potential electoral support that they feared might accrue to their authors as a result of their enactment. The Senate's disinvolvement and self-induced loss of control over policy were thus a recipe for inaction at just the time when firm action was most needed.

In circumstances such as these it could only be a matter of time before accepted constitutional procedures were forced to give ground before the urgent need to solve a political crisis; and it was the tribune, Tiberius Sempronius Gracchus, who in 133 B.C. made the first and fatal breach in the armory of *mos maiorum*. His concern was with the major problems, military, social, and economic, that had been created by the continuing drift of ex-soldier farmers from their rural farms to the city; and, anticipating stiff opposition to his proposals for reversing this trend, he opted to take his measure to the *concilium plebis* without first making the customary application for senatorial approval. The Senate, already conscious that its authority was slipping away from it, reacted immediately by hiring another tribune to interpose his veto against the bill, whereupon Gracchus responded by flouting all precedent and having the offending tribune deposed in midterm by the assembly that had elected him. Battle was now well and truly joined. The tribune went on effectively to challenge in the assembly the Senate's time-honored control over state finance and then took the unusual, and in recent times unprecedented, step of standing for a second term. The Senate in turn rejoined by resorting to the expedient of declaring a state of emergency, which it had not done since the demise of the dictatorship, and passed a decree purporting to instruct the consuls to defend the constitution by whatever means they should deem necessary. Tiberius Gracchus and many of his followers were then attacked and put to death in the first show of street violence that Rome had seen for almost four centuries.

Although the Senate may be said to have won this preliminary skirmish, it did so at some considerable cost. Tiberius Gracchus had thrown down a serious challenge to the Senate's authority, and the events of 133 B.C. taken together had laid open to public debate for the first time the whole issue as to where the seat of real power within the Republican system of government should reside. Henceforward the Senate found its position undermined further not only by the activities of independent-minded magistrates, but also by the force of constitutional argument. Even within its own ranks there grew up a deep divide between those who chose to champion the Senate's traditional role (*optimates*) and those who proclaimed the until now unfamiliar doctrine that asserted the overriding supremacy of the popular will (*populares*). The majority in both camps were motivated more by personal interest than by any deep-rooted convictions on constitutional principle, but they pursued their ends with a vigor and persistence that greatly accelerated the Republic's decline.

In conducting their campaign the so-called *populares* were greatly assisted by a significant development in Rome's tribal assemblies, which stemmed from the gradual depopulation of the rural areas. Many of those who during the later second century migrated to Rome appear to have retained membership in the rural tribe in which they were registered while still domiciled in the country. Consequently, as their numbers grew—and they did not have to grow by very many—these immigrants were soon in a position to outvote the few fellow tribesmen who happened on any occasion to have traveled to Rome. The effect of this development on the *concilium plebis* was dramatic. For the first time since the fourth century Rome found herself with an active legislative body that bore some resemblance to the assembly of Athens—a body whose key voting personnel were concentrated in the city and could therefore be subjected to the pressures of direct persuasion, bribery, demagogic promises, and even, as the Republic wore on, the threat of armed intimidation. At the same time and in direct consequence, the tribunate, for so long the willing tool of the nobility, was encouraged once again to assume its quasi-revolutionary role and to serve as a vehicle for those who for whatever reason sought to carry measures into law in the teeth of senatorial opposition. It is possible that this trend could have been checked if vigilant censors had taken steps to reassign the entire immigrant population to the four urban tribes; but there is no suggestion that they made a serious attempt to do so, and, however obvious the dangers may appear in retrospect, it is likely that conservative senators as well as radicals were superficially attracted in these times of great political tension by the opportunity to bypass the time-consuming process of contacting clients and delivering the rural vote.

The availability of this urban-based assembly encouraged the *populares* in the first place to propound the doctrine of popular sovereignty and enabled them in the event to translate their theory into practice. Because the assembly could often be persuaded to deliver what the Senate refused to deliver they were able to undermine the Senate's authority still further by seducing at least temporarily to their cause those influential individuals or groups who sought to advance their own short-term interest. One such group was the newly emerged class of wealthy businessmen (*publicani*) who undertook state contracts in the provinces and performed other lucrative services in the imperial sphere. Needless to say, their long-term interest lay in stable government, but it was not always too difficult to persuade them to condone legislation promoted in the popular assembly if its effect would be to enhance their short-term profit. Another such group, whose capacity for influencing the course of events was that much greater, comprised those men of excessive ambition who, however disdainful they may have been of the populace, were yet ready to grasp at power from whatever hand might offer it. Into this category fall the great military dynasts of the first century, men such as Marius, Pompey, and Caesar, who among them engineered the final collapse of Republican government.

Thus far nothing has been said about the part played by the Roman army and its commanders in inducing the anarchy of the late Republic. If the analysis given above is correct, this may not have been the basic cause of constitutional instability that many scholars would have us believe. It was, however, the major contributory factor in precipitating ultimate collapse. During the early and middle years of the Roman Republic the legionary army had been recruited from among the property-owning classes, but this basis of recruitment, suitable as it had been for a city-state, was ill adapted to the demands of an overseas empire. Farmers could not easily afford to spend more than one or two campaigning seasons away from their farms, and it had been the burden of putting in long periods of service abroad that had caused many in the second century to sell their land and gravitate to the city. Out of necessity, therefore, the property qualification for legionary service had been progressively lowered, and this process reached its logical conclusion with the Marian reform of 107 B.C., which threw the army open to volunteers irrespective of wealth. In the circumstances of the time this proved to be a development fraught with danger. The farming personnel of the old army had had much in common with the governing class, which they helped to sustain in the assembly, and of which as political clients they were the beneficiaries. The Senate and the system of government of which it was so integral a part had thus provided a natural focus for their loyalty. It was not so with the new "proletarian" army of the late Republic. The Senate had in any case already lost much of that respect which once had been universally paid to it, but it now went on to sacrifice even that which remained by its total failure to recognize the new armies as a state responsibility and by its consequent refusal to make any satisfactory permanent provision for comparatively impoverished soldiery on their disbandment from service. This was a failure that was induced in part by inertia, but it is also to be explained both by the Senate's disapproval of the army reform itself and by its pique at a series of subsequent measures authorizing recruitment that were carried by the assembly without prior consultation. Inevitably, therefore, new recruits were driven to look elsewhere for champions of their cause. They turned in fact to their own commanders, men who were for the most part all too ready to respond.

Had *imperium* been restricted to the annual magistrates, as in the early Republic, this link of dependence between armies and their commanders might not have constituted so grave a threat, since the principle of annuality itself might well have afforded protection enough against the abuse of military power. In the promagistracy, however, and in the concept of power divorced from office, the Republic had unwittingly forged an instrument for its own destruction. The promagistrates wielded the authority of the equivalent magistracy, they wielded it at a distance, and they wielded it without being subject to the normal restraints that the principle of a collegiate magistracy imposed. Furthermore, as Rome's commitments grew, sheer necessity dictated that commanders should assume responsibility for far larger concentrations of men than once had been customary, and that they should exercise their *imperium* over an area far larger than that defined by a single administrative province. The commissions to wage war on Mediterranean piracy that various commanders received during the last century of the Republic provide a good example of such wider powers; for they rested upon what was termed an *imperium infinitum*, an *imperium* that could be exercised without any restriction of movement and that empowered its holder to recruit troops and commission supplies in a selection of provinces technically governed by other promagistrates. A new development, too, was the long-term command, a promagisterial *imperium* granted not, as once had been the practice, for so long as the Senate thought fit, but rather for a stated number of years. This could be as many as five, as in the case of the Gallic command conferred on Caesar in 59 B.C., and even then could be subject to extension. This trend also was dictated by military expediency and by the need to give a commander a guaranteed time span over which to plan his strategy, but in the Republic's last years the principle was often abused by political protagonists in both camps with a view to giving their particular champion a military advantage.

The opportunity for ambitious and power-hungry leaders to strike up close associations with large armies was quite clearly enhanced by these developments in the structure of military command, and the power that was thus put in their hands by loyal legions anxious for material reward was immense. They could in effect dictate their own political terms and make a mockery of any ordered civil government whether controlled by the Senate or by the popular assemblies. But such a threat of veiled dictatorship was not the only one presented by the rise of the military dynast. There was room in the empire for more than one powerful army devoted to its own commander, and it soon became only a matter of time before Rome was embroiled in bloody civil conflict between political rivals.

While these changes in the military power structure were taking shape, politicians in Rome continued to fight an ideological battle that appeared to become less relevant with the passing of each year. There was a tendency by those on both sides of the divide to attempt to encode their own interpretation of constitutional propriety, and so to replace a system of government based largely upon tradition by one that had the backing of statute law. On the *popularis* side the process began almost with the death of Tiberius Gracchus. His brother Gaius introduced a measure that by implication provided legal justification for the deposition of a magistrate, and he sought similar legal justification, though this time not successfully, for the tenure of successive tribunates. Somewhat later the principle of popular sovereignty began to be entrenched in laws of the assemblies through the insertion of a clause that bound senators or magistrates, and occasionally both, to swear obedience to the measure in question on oath. Steps were taken, too, to curb the Senate's time-honored privilege of granting dispensation from the law. And, perhaps most significantly of all, an effective challenge was put up to the Senate's prerogatives in appointing provincial governors, sanctioning the prorogation of their *imperium*, and determining their period of tenure. The first step along this road was taken in 123 B.C., when the Senate was required by law to name the provinces for which the consuls would be responsible after their year of office in advance of their election and thus before their actual identity was known. The second was taken in 107 B.C., when the *concilium plebis* was induced to confer an important war command upon Gaius Marius in defiance of the Senate's own arrangements. Thereafter the precedent was followed with increasing frequency.

Not unnaturally the traditionalists, or optimates as they were called, were less eager to resort to law. Their reaction in the early years was to use their newfound weapon of the *senatus consultum ultimum* whenever constitutional precedent was seriously challenged; but, although this usually proved to be an effective short-term defense, its frequent use tended to provoke armed conflict and to provide the proponents of popular sovereignty with fresh ammunition for their ideological battle. For this reason Lucius Cornelius Sulla, when in 81 B.C. he had emerged as victor in Rome's first civil war, decided to mount a more radical counterattack. Using the interregnum in deference to the basic doctrine of the "patrician state," he secured his own appointment to a new form of dictatorship which knew no prescribed time limit. He then proceeded to promulgate what amounted to a written constitution, which embodied in statute many of those features of pre-Gracchan Republican practice that he regarded as conducive to stability. In Sulla's ideal state the Senate was to be the key, controlling body, as it had been in the middle Republican years. It was brought up to full strength through new recruitment, and arrangements were made for it to be constantly supplemented in the future by means of the automatic promotion to senatorial rank of each annual board of quaestors, now enlarged to twenty. It was given as of right the advance veto over legislative proposals, which earlier it had exercised only by universal consent. Furthermore, since all the praetors were allotted permanent duties in Rome during their year of office in the field of criminal jurisdiction, it was in theory given even greater discretion than ever before over the appointment of provincial commanders, who were now to be almost exclusively promagistrates. The consuls Sulla envisaged as reverting to the role of compliant senatorial agents, and he attempted to ensure this by enforcing a stricter fixed magisterial career (*cursus honorum*) and by prescribing minimum intervals between offices. As for the *concilium plebis*, which had been such a thorn in the side of the Senate and had passed so much unwelcome legislation over the past half century, his object was to neutralize it partly by means of the Senate's newly acquired power of advance veto and partly by emasculating the office of tribune which had spearheaded the assault. Here his most imaginative move was to discourage the ambitious from holding the tribunate by legally debarring all who did so from any further political advancement.

Within two years Sulla abdicated his dictatorship and retired into private life. Within ten years almost the entire Sullan structure had been dismantled, largely through the agency of a new generation of dynasts who used the veiled threat of military force first to flout the new constitutional rules and then to effect their repeal. It is quite futile to attempt to apportion the blame for this reversal between the Senate itself and other social groups. As Caesar must later have recognized when he dubbed Sulla a "political illiterate," the very concept of the Sullan constitution was itself fatally flawed. It certainly encapsulated several facets of a system of government that had once enjoyed unquestioning acceptance, but, as was implied by the very need to introduce formal rules, that consensus which is so essential to the stability of a constitution based upon *mos maiorum* was now totally lacking. When viewed against the background of recent political developments, Sulla's constitution was inevitably regarded by most sections of contemporary society as serving a sectional interest. Without an iron hand to uphold it it was destined to meet the same abrupt fate to which any formal system of government is so readily prone when it lacks majority support.

If the Senate thus artificially resurrected by Sulla could provide no focus for loyalty, no more of course could the urban-based tribal assembly, whose newfound authority rested upon a somewhat warped interpretation of the doctrine of popular sovereignty. Being more malleable than the Sullan Senate, it was perhaps more readily tolerated by those powerful men and groups who stood to reap temporary advantage from its support. But such an irresponsible and unrepresentative body could never win their respect. The army and its leaders viewed it with contempt, while the great mass of Roman citizens living outside the city, and not least the newly enfranchised Italians, saw its influence as a threat to the traditional system of patronage which in the past had served them well.

If the successful achievements of Rome before the fall of Carthage illustrate the great advantages of an unwritten constitution, the protracted agonies of the Republic in the years thereafter reveal its one inherent weakness—a capacity for survival beyond its natural term of usefulness. As the protagonists on both sides of the ideological spectrum juggled with the rules of procedure in the post-Gracchan period, they sought justification for their actions in the spirit of the ancestral constitution. What all but a few failed to recognize was that so intangible and so variable a concept as *mos maiorum* draws life only from the respect which is at any time afforded to it. When Julius Caesar delivered his coup de grace to the ailing Republic in 49 B.C., that respect, and with it much of the framework of the unwritten constitution itself, had long since ceased to exist.

THE PRINCIPATE

On seizing power after the war with Pompey, Caesar paid scant regard to Republican forms or practice. Recognizing that Rome's salvation at this stage could lie only in a monocratic concentration of power, he effectively abandoned the principle of collegiality at the top and decided to base his authority on a neodictatorship in the Sullan mold. This office he assumed at first on the basis of annual renewal and then, more realistically, on the basis of a life tenure. Since it carried the right to twenty-four lictors and thus gave him an authority greater than that of any other magistrate, he used it unashamedly to turn the regular magistrates into his own subordinate executive agents. He himself took successive consulships and eventually assumed the right directly to appoint one-half of the other senior officers of state. The Senate, certainly, was to play an important, though very different, role in Caesar's new order; for, to judge by his policy of recruitment, he envisaged it as potentially a representative forum for many cosmopolitan interests which until now had effectively been disregarded. But it was stripped of its traditional decision-making prerogatives, which were assumed by Caesar himself; and the perhaps overdue process was begun of transferring some of the more burdensome administrative functions of the Senate to semipermanent prefects, who formed the embryo of what in time was to become a complex professional bureaucracy subject to central direction.

The abruptness of the changes that Caesar introduced and the threat that they constituted to the susceptibilities and aspirations of the governing class led to his assassination. Events soon proved, however, that the move toward more autocratic government was irreversible. Within two years of his death his nephew and heir, Octavian, later to be known as Augustus, had acquired a similar dictatorial *imperium* in company with Mark Antony and Marcus Aemilius Lepidus, an *imperium* that established the three triumvirs as potential overlords of the regular annual magistrates and gave them sweeping powers in the field of legislation and of magisterial appointment. The grant was originally for a five-year term, but this had little practical meaning because the powers were renewable, and through a curious quirk of Republican tradition, the five-year limit implied no more than a guaranteed period of tenure and carried with it no obligation to renounce the powers when the period expired.

It still remained, however, to establish a principle on which a new form of government could be based. Caesar had not been given the time to develop any plans, dynastic or otherwise, that he may have had; and the effects of this omission are to be seen clearly in the renewal of civil conflict that followed his death. It fell, therefore, to the young Octavian, who in 31 B.C. emerged after a war with Antony as the undisputed master of Rome, to restore constitutional stability by means of fundamental changes in the structure of government. For this task he was ideally equipped. He had under his command a vast legionary army, much of it inherited from Caesar, which looked to him for resettlement and a guarantee of its future livelihood. He also enjoyed, perhaps in greater measure than any Roman before him, that moral authority and esteem which the Romans called *auctoritas* and which in effect empowered a man to take independent action without having to pay overmuch regard to the question of its legitimacy. This he derived in part, of course, from the sheer size of his potential military support, but he derived it too from a variety of other factors —from the popularity that accrued to him as Caesar's heir, from his long list of political honors exemplified in the triumvirate and a continuing succession of annual consulships, from his successful presentation of himself as the champion of Italy against unwelcome Eastern influences in the war against Antony, and perhaps too from the fact that so many saw in his victory the promise of a prolonged respite from the civil disturbances and armed conflicts that had plagued Rome for a full hundred years. Finally, he enjoyed a third, very considerable advantage in that with Caesar's example before him he was in a position to learn from his mistakes. He no doubt saw clearly that the need to resolve the collapse of constitutional authority by concentrating decision-making and executive powers in the same hands was paramount, but he was also quick to recognize that Caesar's fate had been the direct result of his readiness to break too abruptly with traditional forms and to trample somewhat insensitively upon sectional interests. He was thus able to avoid falling into the same trap, and to this end he appears to have set himself two objectives. The one was to ensure that virtually all the powers by which he sought to establish personal control could be justified by reference to Republican precedent, however recent. The other was to limit major institutional changes to those that could be clearly shown not to damage the true interests of potentially influential social groups. The measure of his success in achieving these objectives is attested not only by the durability of the system of government that he established, but also by the seeming readiness of so many of his contemporaries to believe his own claim, made toward the close of his life, to have established "a restored Republic."

The Augustan Constitution

Octavian formally laid down his extraordinary powers, though not his consulship, in 28 B.C. In the following year he took the title of Augustus and, no doubt by prearrangement with the Senate, received from its hands a provincial command of such extensive proportions as to give him a responsibility for governing more than half the overseas territories of the empire, including almost all those that had standing armies. This command was conferred upon him initially for a guaranteed period of ten years and was subsequently renewed at intervals during his lifetime. During the first four years the *imperium* that was needed for this commission was derived from his tenure of the consulship, to which in the tradition of Caesar and the triumvirs he continued to be elected in successive years. But in 23 B.C., recognizing that this continued tenure was not in the best Republican tradition and that it damaged the opportunities for other members of the nobility to attain the highest office, he gave up the consulship and continued to discharge his provincial responsibilities in the role of a proconsul.

Although the sheer size of Augustus' province and his long security of tenure were unprecedented, his position differed from that of his Republican predecessors essentially in degree rather than in kind. As we have seen, there had already been established a trend in the first century B.C. toward giving promagistrates ever larger territorial responsibilities and longer guaranteed tenure of their commands. The practice had also been established of allowing promagistrates to delegate their *imperium* to senatorial legates of their own choosing, and this provided Augustus with the precedent for appointing governors, answerable to himself, for all the individual provinces within his particular domain. Only in two respects may Augustus have violated Republican tradition, and because they technically affected only his authority outside Rome these violations are unlikely to have caused serious offense.

First, he was specifically freed from the obligation to lay down his *imperium* on entering the city of Rome. As this was traditionally the only automatic method of divesting oneself of a promagisterial command, the dispensation effectively guaranteed him life tenure. This was a reality which his successors did not feel the need to conceal when they waived the pretense of periodic renewal. Second—and this is not entirely undisputed—he appears to have taken an *imperium* superior in strength to that enjoyed by the several other proconsuls who were appointed by the Senate to govern the remaining provinces of the empire. Such a provincial *imperium maius* had been no more than mooted in late Republican times, and there had been a precedent only in the period immediately following Caesar's assassination, but Augustus could reasonably have argued that the trend toward wide-ranging commissions had already made it an inevitable development. The *imperium maius* was in effect a form of dictatorial authority limited to the provincial sphere, which gave Augustus the authority to impose his will upon other proconsuls should the need arise. In Augustus' case it was perhaps viewed as no more than a necessary substitute for the executive authority of consul, which traditionally had been used as a channel for the Senate's broad directives on provincial administration, and which had rested not on superior *imperium*, but on the greater *auctoritas* that went with the highest office.

The decision to drop the consulship in 23 B.C. also left Augustus without any authority at Rome. To rectify this situation he appears to have assumed two additional major powers. Beyond dispute is his assumption for life of the tribunician power (*tribunicia potestas*). From this he could derive, among other things, the right to initiate legislation and the right to interpose a veto; but, although he and his successors chose to lay considerable stress upon it, it is probable that its value was more psychological than real. It served to put Augustus in the mainstream of the *popularis* tradition and thus to allay the fears of all groups whose interests that tradition once had served. A few years later it is likely that he also assumed for life the consular power (*consularis potestas*). This was something more substantial, and from it could well have been derived several of the more important prerogatives that the Princeps ("the first," as the emperors were called) is known to have exercised, among them a right of edict, jurisdictive powers, the right to conduct a census and to review the senatorial roll, and the right to become directly involved in the nomination of consular and praetorian candidates and thereby to exert influence upon the major elections. Given the general desire to avoid a return to the urban chaos of the late Republican years, it is improbable that the assumption of such a power, albeit without precedent, would have caused great offense. The concept of power divorced from office was after all itself a Republican one, which had been accepted as early as the fourth century with the creation of the promagistracy; and Augustus' fellow nobles, who were now more interested in the dignity of high office than in the power it conferred, are likely to have welcomed the conferment of a permanent consular power as a very acceptable alternative to his tenure of successive consulships.

Such, then, were the principal powers that underpinned the supreme position of Augustus and all his successors in what became known as the Principate (the rule of the first man). In his own personal account of his achievements Augustus wrote that he received no powers that were inconsistent with *mos maiorum*. The strict constitutionalist might wish to challenge this claim, particularly if Augustus did indeed hold an *imperium maius*. But it is unlikely that he intended seriously to mislead on a matter where the facts were there for all to see. The common perception was that he had scrupulously avoided following Sulla and Caesar in assuming offices such as an unlimited dictatorship that were totally inconsistent with Republican tradition or its natural development. The uniqueness of Augustus' position rested not on the extraordinary nature of his powers, but rather upon the accumulation of so many in his own hands—an accumulation that was made more feasible and more acceptable by a significant extension of the concept of power divorced from office.

It has been the contention of many scholars that the Principate was conceived not as a form of monarchy, but rather as a diarchy, in which power was to be shared between Princeps and Senate. Superficially, this concept of diarchy draws support from the fact that the Roman Empire was divided between the so-called imperial provinces, which the Princeps governed on a quasi-permanent basis through the agency of his appointed legates, and the senatorial provinces, to which the Senate nominally continued to appoint its own promagistrates on a regular basis. Yet this analysis is largely irrelevant and misleading. The Senate, certainly, had a vital role to play in the Augustan scheme of things. It was the Senate which was to inherit many of the prerogatives of the Republican assemblies, and it was therefore the Senate which was to be responsible for conferring upon the Princeps his various powers and which was to be the ultimate source of their legitimacy. For this reason alone it was of the greatest importance for the credibility of the Principate as Augustus conceived it that the Senate should be held in high regard and that it should regain much of the dignity and respect that it had enjoyed when the Republic was at its height. But veneration and real power do not necessarily go hand in hand. Whereas in the middle years of the Republic the Senate had been the decision-making body and those who held *imperium* had been its instruments, the situation during the Principate was almost exactly reversed. The Princeps not only had the lifelong authority to control the membership of the Senate, which he did not hesitate to exercise freely; he also enjoyed an overriding *auctoritas* which was enough to ensure that even the expression of a wish was treated as a command.

In one area of government, that of legislation and elections, Augustus made a most significant break with tradition. After some experimentation with Republican forms in the early years, he transferred all the legislative functions of the *populus* and *plebs*, which since the fifth century had been fulfilled by the tribal assemblies, to the Senate, and he gave to the decrees of the Senate the force of law. Further, there is strong evidence that he reduced the time-honored electoral activities of the centuriate assembly to a mere formality, and that he handed over the effective say in the appointment of consuls and praetors to a new select body composed of the members of the Senate and of the more prominent among that class of wealthy non-senators who constituted the so-called equestrian order. It is a tribute to Augustus' genius and to his understanding of the most cherished desires of every section of society that such an abrupt abandonment of the once loudly acclaimed principle of popular sovereignty should have evoked scarcely a voice of protest. There was, no doubt, a general recognition that the urban-dominated assemblies that had featured so largely in the last years of the Republic had little to recommend them. Their activities had been a source of frustration and irritation to the rural citizenry, whom they did not begin to represent, and they had been welcome to the urban masses themselves only insofar as they had allowed them to trade their voting power for benefits in cash and kind. Romans domiciled outside the city, therefore, may well have viewed the transfer of legislative functions to the more representative Senate with some relief, while the urban populace, once it was assured by the Princeps' permanent tenure of the tribunician power of his continuing tutelage, may have had little reason to pine for a right of suffrage which had brought with it as many hazards as it had rewards.

In the matter of the major elections Augustus' decision may well have been dictated to a large extent by the sheer apathy of the voters. Even during the Republic the mass of the potential electorate had never taken much active interest in the outcome of elections, and those who had traveled to Rome to vote had done so almost exclusively as a service to a noble patron. It follows that, once the delicate balance of influence existing between individual noble families had been disturbed by the impact of the Julian family on traditional loyalties, and once the wealthier element in Italy had become accustomed to looking upon Augustus as its potential protector and patron-in-chief, there was a greater reluctance than ever to participate in an exercise that had ceased to have any meaning. Nor was the governing class itself likely to have been displeased with this development. From its point of view the elections had long since come to be seen as essentially trials of strength reflecting the size and the amenability of its respective *clientelae*, and it must surely have been happy to rid itself of the unrewarding and burdensome chore of a canvass that no longer served its traditional purpose. After the lifting of the restrictions imposed by Caesar and the triumvirs the nobles are likely to have been well pleased to be offered once again the opportunity to fulfill what they saw as their destiny, and it should have suited them well to confine their electoral canvass to those who were of their own rank. Indeed, it could well be argued that election by fellow senators encapsulated the essence of middle Republican practice, since in those times despite popular suffrage and comitial participation the most effective single determinant of electoral success had probably been the ability of the candidate to enlist the support of his noble colleagues.

The inclusion of elements of the equestrian order (knights, *equites*) in the new select electoral body calls for a word of comment. It is possible that Augustus wished his new creation to be seen as a microcosm of the Republican centuriate assembly, and that he gave a voice to influential *equites* in recognition of the sometimes controversial role which men of that class had played in the electoral contests of the late Republic. If so, he appears to have miscalculated the extent of their interest. Owing to their own lack of enthusiasm their participation in the major elections was short-lived; and there is evidence enough that at least from the time of Gaius (Caligula) the decisive votes on these, and indeed on all other, elections were cast by the senators alone.

Post-Augustan Developments

The period from the death of Augustus in A.D. 14 to the final collapse of the Roman Empire in the West covers a span of over 400 years. That it can be treated so briefly here in what amounts to little more than an epilogue is to be explained by the fact that its principal interest for the student of government lies in the emergence and development of a complex administrative bureaucracy. There are, however, three features of the post-Augustan Age that have a particular bearing on constitutional forms and so merit attention.

One was the continuing trend, established even in Augustus' day, toward phasing out the executive functions of the traditional magistrates and toward transferring their responsibilities to new nonelected officials who were not bound by the principle of annuality and who could be selected specifically on the strength of their expertise. Some Republican offices actually ceased to exist. The tribunate, for example, lost its raison d'être with the abandonment of the *concilium plebis* and with the assumption of tribunician power by the Princeps. The censorship also atrophied when the Princeps chose regularly to invoke the censorial power which was latent in his consular *imperium* and to delegate its essential functions to his own nominees. Quaestors and aediles were retained for minor administrative functions, although the more important responsibilities of the latter, such as control over the supply of food and over police, were transferred to semipermanent officials known as prefects or procurators. Even the major magistrates waned rapidly in importance, praetors losing some jurisdictive functions to the new imperial and senatorial courts, and consuls being reduced to the performance of honorary duties and to the fairly nominal right of initiative within the Senate, which in any case always yielded in precedence to that of the Princeps himself. Exceptionally, however, it seems to have been the deliberate policy of successive emperors to preserve the dignity of these top offices and even to increase their number. The college of praetors probably grew to eighteen (from twelve) in the principate of Tiberius, and at the same time a fairly regular practice was established of replacing the eponymous consuls of the year in midterm with one or more pairs of substitutes or *suffecti*. This proliferation of consuls and praetors is probably to be explained in the early years by the Princeps' concern to avoid electoral contests that might be too keenly fought within the Senate and at the same time to satisfy the earnest wish of as many nobles as possible to attain to the highest dignity. Later during the Principate the same policy was continued both because tenure of the consulship or praetorship remained a precondition of elevation to the ever-growing number of important provincial commands and prefectures, and also because the Princeps found it convenient to use election to these offices as a mark of special favor.

As the magistrates were divested of their responsibilities the actual work of government fell increasingly upon permanent officials. Some of these emerged from among the freedmen staff of the Princeps' own household and were displaced by members of the official bureaucracy only at the time of Hadrian; a majority were drawn from the newly reorganized equestrian order, which became progressively more professional as a standard career based upon a foundation of military service became established; while a few, where both tradition and qualifications dictated, were appointed from among the senators. Two of these officials in time assumed quasi-governmental authority. One was the prefect of the city (*praefectus urbi*), always a senator, who from quite early days was given ultimate responsibility for the governance of the city of Rome. The other was the prefect (frequently the two prefects) of the praetorian guard (*praefectus praetorio*), who began life as an equestrian officer commanding troops stationed in Italy; in the later empire this prefect developed into what one source describes as an officer "little less than royal" as the complexity of imperial government forced the Princeps himself to withdraw ever more from a direct decision-making role. Usually an equestrian until A.D. 230 and thereafter a senator, he effectively combined in his own person the roles of active military commander, prime minister, and chief justice rolled into one. Whatever may have been the outward appearance, however, he is likely to have remained a delegate in strict law and to have derived his *imperium* from the consular authority of the Princeps.

A second significant feature of the post-Augustan Age was the steady decline of the Roman Senate both in its contribution to government and in its public esteem. One reason for this was the progressive displacement of the old nobility in its ranks by parvenues who owed their advancement to imperial preferment. Another was the growing awareness and acceptance of its impotence that was bound to follow any shattering of the Augustan illusion. Augustus himself had studiously avoided any action that might show up the Senate's true weakness. He had given the Senate jurisdictive powers over its own members; he had deliberately refrained from exerting too obvious an influence over the conduct of elections by too free a use of personal commendation; and, although his own proposals for legislation were endorsed as a matter of course, he had created the illusion of consultation by setting up a cabinet of advisers on which senators were heavily represented. His successors, however, either could not, or did not attempt to, match his tact. Already by the second century a mere letter, or even a speech, of the Princeps was recognized as an accepted legalized vehicle of political initiative. In elections, too, senatorial freedom of choice was restricted by a much freer use of commendation by the Princeps as well as by his greater control over nominations; and it is clear from Pliny the Younger that even by Trajan's day the Princeps was openly recognized to have an absolute control over appointments to the consulship at least. This broadening of practice into law is well illustrated by two sources. Cassius Dio, writing of the Augustan Age, is content to remark that in the matter of elections "nothing was done of which the Princeps disapproved." The jurist Ulpian, who describes the situation as it was in the early third century, expresses himself more bluntly. "The appointment of magistrates," he writes, "is the concern of the Princeps."

The Senate was also damaged by the steady encroachment of professional equestrians upon functions that had traditionally been reserved for its own members. This was no more than an inevitable development which resulted from the fact that the equestrian career provided the skills and experience that alone equipped a man for the specialized responsibilities of empire, and it was one that was actually fostered by the unwillingness of the new breed of senators to undergo the discipline of preparation for senior magistracy by way of a military tribunate and junior administrative posts to which their Republican counterparts had readily submitted. Senators therefore gave way to equestrian procurators in many areas of administration at home and overseas; they were replaced by equestrian jurisconsults in Hadrian's inner cabinet, or *consilium*; and even in the sphere of military command they found themselves at quite an early stage working alongside able and professional equestrian prefects, who increasingly came to be given responsibility for directing operations in the empire's minor trouble spots. The logical culmination of this process was the decision taken by Gallienus in A.D. 260 to divorce the civil governorship of the provinces from the provincial military commands and to confer the latter upon equestrians. The very safety of the empire may have depended upon the armies being led by men with the professionalism that only the rigors of the equestrian military career (*militia equestris*) provided; but, for the Senate, to be deprived of its long-held reputation as a breeding ground for Rome's generals was a fatal blow. Thereby it lost its sole remaining claim to respect, and it quickly degenerated into little more than a city council.

As Marcus Aurelius and others clearly recognized when they sought to counter the consciousness of senatorial impotence by cultivating a show of deference, this decline in the Senate's powers and standing was of some considerable constitutional moment. Whatever may have been the practical reality, the Augustan system of government had been built around the theory that the Princeps received his several powers as a gift from the Senate. It follows that any marked deterioration in the Senate's popular esteem spelled particular danger for the very stability of the Principate itself. It was certainly a major, though by no means the only, contributory factor in precipitating the crisis of the empire in the third century and in effecting the transformation of the Principate into an open monarchy.

It is then to the concept of principate itself and to its inherent weaknesses as revealed by the passing of years that we must finally turn our attention. Without doubt it was a basic flaw in the Augustan constitution that by reason of its very nature it could incorporate no formal provision for an ordered transmission of power. The difficulty was quite simply that in the absence of any avowed monarchical principle there was no constitutional status to be bequeathed. The problem of how to ensure a smooth succession after his death was one that caused Augustus himself acute concern, and he devised a twofold solution. First, he arranged for some, though not all, of his various powers to be conferred by the Senate prior to his death upon his chosen nominee. These comprised a grant of tribunician power for a period of years and a promagisterial *imperium* that equaled his own. Second, he deliberately restricted his choice of nominees to those who could claim unquestionably to be members of his own Julian family. In the special circumstances of his own times, when a reversion to Republican chaos was still a real possibility and when the precedent of one-man rule had not yet been firmly established, such a solution may have been the only one possible. It preempted any revolt within the Senate on his death by presenting it with its own fait accompli, and it guaranteed the nonintervention of the army in recognizing its still overriding loyalty to the Julian name. For all that, it was very much an ad hoc solution, and it had the unfortunate consequence of establishing a pattern that threatened to undermine the very credibility of that principle of senatorial choice which was the kingpin of the Augustan system. The element of dynasticism that was inherent in Augustus' planning, together with what was a requirement in practice that the Senate should confer powers upon the nominees of future emperors, however manifestly unsuitable they should be, effectively depreciated the Senate's role and sapped its self-confidence to such an extent as to render it unfit to respond to the challenge when the inevitable moments of crisis arrived.

Despite this inherent weakness the Principate survived in recognizable form for two centuries, there being but one reversion to civil war, in A.D. 69, when the death of Nero and the collapse of the Julio-Claudian line precipitated a power struggle between the commanders of rival provincial armies. That it did so survive was probably due in the early years to the relative stability provided by dynasticism, which was implicit in the Augustan arrangements and which was even more openly embraced in the Flavian cause by Vespasian after A.D. 71. Then, after the death of Domitian in A.D. 96, good fortune played a hand by providing Rome with a succession of emperors whose ability and achievements earned them the loyalty and respect of the armies in their own right, and who, being childless, managed peaceably to overcome the problems of the succession through the pursuit of a policy of adoption. But the mental instability of Commodus, his excessive abuse of power, and his eventual assassination in A.D. 192 plunged the empire once more into disarray and, with the Senate reduced to impotence, finally exposed the hollowness of the legal fiction upon which the Principate had been constructed.

A great deal had changed within the Roman Empire since the days of Augustus. Apart from the progressive decay of the Senate and other urban institutions, the army itself, which, if not the instrument of power, had yet been the ultimate guarantor of the Augustan Principate, had undergone a profound transformation. Changing patterns of recruitment combined with the pursuit, by Hadrian in particular, of an active policy of imperial decentralization had conspired to turn the unitary and largely Italian-based army of Caesar and Augustus into a series of independent and powerful provincial armies that represented the interests of the areas in which they served. The former owed unswerving loyalty to their Julian commanders, whom they regarded as their patrons and their champions. The latter derived their security from within their own native environment and so tended to regard the Princeps, if he were not one of their own, as irrelevant to their needs. By the end of the second century, therefore, the elaborate structure of the Principate, which had so happily reconciled autocracy with Republican tradition and which had proclaimed a primacy of one man based upon a combination of legal power, *auctoritas,* and potential military support, had long outlived its usefulness.

Facing up to this reality the emperors of the third century showed themselves increasingly disposed to lay aside pretense and to embrace unashamedly the principle of absolutism. It may be that all but one continued to observe the nicety of seeking a formal senatorial grant of powers, but in all other respects they tended to ride roughshod over tradition and to hold themselves above the law. This open avowal of monarchy, however, did nothing itself to render the Principate any more stable. Indeed, during the ninety years from the death of Commodus to the accession of Diocletian Rome saw no fewer than twenty-six different emperors at the helm, as rival armies warred with one another for the role of kingmaker and as successive emperors failed to establish any credible claim upon their subjects' loyalty other than their own fragile military reputations. The task of restoring some measure of stability had to await the arrival of the Illyrian emperors toward the end of the third century, who with strong provincial backing were able to cling to power sufficiently long to take appropriate action.

The principal architect of constitutional change was Diocletian (A.D. 284–305), and his solution had two main constituents. First, he aimed to minimize the danger of future conflict over the succession by evolving the concept of a shared imperial power. His own original system of the tetrarchy, which provided for the empire to be divided among four rulers, two of senior and two of junior rank, did not itself endure, but it did at least establish a pattern that formed the basis of similar arrangements in the fourth century and that eventually found expression in the division of the Roman Empire into two totally independent entities. And second, he strove to provide the Principate with a new legitimacy by seeking a solid and acceptable foundation for centralized absolutism in the concept of theocracy. To this end he followed his predecessor, Aurelian (A.D. 270–275), in donning the purple and the crown, in cultivating the mystique and unapproachability of divine majesty, and in declaring himself to be lord and god (*dominus et deus*).

A generation later, Constantine built upon the foundation he had laid by openly espousing the dynastic principle and proclaiming his own monarchical authority to be ordained by the grace of the Christian God. This radically new concept of the imperial power did not succeed in restoring total harmony. It did, however, reestablish the emperor as a natural focus for the loyalty of all Roman citizens to a degree not known since the earliest days of the Principate. In the eastern half of the empire the doctrine of divine right continued to support imperial authority for more than a millennium, while in the west it survived the ravaging of migrating hordes and the crumbling of Roman power itself to reemerge as the acknowledged basis of the Holy Roman Empire.

BIBLIOGRAPHY

SOURCES

Augustus, *Res Gestae Divi Augusti* (*Acts of the Divine Augustus*), Peter A. Brunt and John M. Moore, intro., comm., and trans. (1967); Cassius Dio Cocceianus, *Dio's Roman History*, Earnest Cary, trans., on basis of version by Herbert B. Foster, 9 vols. (1914–1927); Cicero, *De Republica, De Legibus* (*On the Republic, On Laws*), Clinton M. Keyes, trans. (1928); Livy, *The History of Rome* (*Ab urbe condita*), B.O. Foster *et al.*, trans., 14 vols. (1919–1967); Polybius, *The Histories*, Evelyn S. Shuckburgh, trans., 2 vols. (1962); Suetonius, *Lives of the Twelve Caesars*, John C. Rolfe, trans., rev. ed (1928).

STUDIES

General

Frank Adcock, *Roman Political Ideas and Practice* (1959); S. A. Cook, Frank Adcock, M. P. Charlesworth, eds., *Cambridge Ancient History*, 12 vols. (1923–1939); Kurt von Fritz, *The Theory of the Mixed Constitution in Antiquity*, 2d ed. (1975); Abel H. J. Greenidge, *Roman Public Life* (1901; repr. 1970); Mason Hammond, *City-State and World State in Greek and Roman Political Theory until Augustus* (1951; repr. 1966); Léon Homo, *Roman Political Institutions from City to State*, M. R. Dobie, trans., 2d ed., (1962); Wolfgang Kunkel, *An Introduction to Roman Legal and Constitutional History*, J. M. Kelly, trans., 2d ed. (1973); Jakob A. O. Larsen, *Representative Government in Greek and Roman History*, 2d ed. (1966); Karl Loewenstein, *The Governance of Rome* (1973); Francesco de Martino, *Storia della Costituzione romana*, 5 vols., 2d ed. (1972–1975); Ernst Meyer, *Römischer Staat und Staatsgedanke*, 3d ed. (1964).

Theodor Mommsen, *Römisches Staatsrecht*, 3 vols. in 5 (1887–1888; repr. 1952–1953), trans. as *Le droit public romain* by Paul F. Girard, 7 vols. in 8 (1889–1896); A. O' Brien Moore, "Senatus," in August F. von Pauly and George Wissowa, eds., *Real Encyclopädie der klassischen Altertumswissenschaft* (1893–1972); E. Stuart Staveley, *Greek and Roman Voting and Elections* (1972); Chaim Wirszubski, *Libertas as a Political Idea at Rome during the Late Republic and Early Principate* (1950).

Monarchy and Republic

A. E. Astin, *The Lex Annalis before Sulla* (1958); Aurelio Bernardi, "Patrizi e plebei nella costituzione della primitiva repubblica romana," in *Rendiconti Istituto lombardo di scienze e lettere*, **79** (1945–1946); Jochen Bleicken, *Das Volkstribunat der klassischen Republik* (1955; 2d. ed. 1968); Arthur E. R. Boak, "Extraordinary Commands from 80 to 48 B.C.; A Study in the Origins of the Principate," in *American Historical Review*, **24** (1918–1919); George W. Botsford, *The Roman Assemblies* (1909; repr. 1968); Jérôme Carcopino, *Sylla, ou La monarchie manquée* (1931); D. Cohen, "The Origin of the Roman Dictatorship," in *Mnemosyne*, **10** (1957); Ugo Coli, "Regnum," in *Studia et Documenta Historiae et Iuris*, **17** (1951).

Robert Develin, "Comitia tribute plebis," in *Athenaeum* (Pavia), n.s. **53** (1975); Victor Ehrenberg, "Imperium Maius during the Roman Republic," in *American Journal of Philology*, **74** (1953);

Plinio Fraccaro, "The History of Rome in the Regal Period," in *Journal of Roman Studies,* **47** (1957); Kurt von Fritz, "The Reorganisation of the Roman Government in 366 B.C. and the so-called Licinio-Sextian Laws," in *Historia,* **1** (1950); Emilio Gabba, *Republican Rome, the Army, and the Allies,* P. J. Cuff, trans. (1976); Matthias Gelzer, *The Roman Nobility,* Robin Seager, trans. (1969); Wilhelmina F. Jashemski, *The Origins and History of the Pro-consular and Pro-praetorian Imperium to 27 B.C.* (1950); Hans Kloft, *Prorogation und ausserordentliche Imperien 326–81 v.Ch. Untersuchungen zur Verfassung der römischen Republik* (1977); Hugh Last, "The Servian Reforms," in *Journal of Roman Studies,* **35** (1945).

Kurt Latte, "The Origin of the Roman Quaestorship," in *Transactions of the American Philological Association,* **67** (1936); Christian Meier, *Res publica amissa* (1966); Arnaldo Momigliano, "An Interim Report on the Origins of Rome," in *Journal of Roman Studies,* **53** (1963); Robert E. A. Palmer, *The Archaic Community of the Romans* (1970); Jean Claude Richard, *Les origines de la plèbe romaine* (1978); Ronald T. Ridley, "Notes on the Establishment of the Tribunate of the Plebs," in *Latomus,* **27** (1968), and "The Origin of the Roman Dictatorship," in *Rheinisches Museum für Philologie,* **122** (1979); Richard E. Smith, *The Failure of the Roman Republic* (1955; repr. 1975).

E. Stuart Staveley, "Tribal Legislation before the *Lex Hortensia,*" in *Athenaeum,* **33** (1955), "The Constitution of the Roman Republic 1940–1954," in *Historia,* **5** (1956), "The *Fasces* and *Imperium Maius,*" in *Historia,* **12** (1963), and "The Nature and Aims of the Patriciate," in *Historia,* **32** (1983); Jaakko Suolahti, *The Roman Censors* (1963); Lily R. Taylor, *Party Politics in the Age of Caesar* (1949; 2d ed. 1961), and *Roman Voting Assemblies from the Hannibalic War to the Dictatorship of Caesar* (1966); G. Tibiletti, "The Comitia during the Decline of the Roman Republic," in *Studia et Documenta Historiae et Iuris,* **25** (1959); F. W. Walbank, "Polybius on the Roman Constitution," in *Classical Quarterly,* **37** (1943); Pierre Willems, *Le sénat de la Republique romaine,* 2 vols. (1878–85; repr. 1968).

Principate

Jean Béranger, *Recherches sur l'aspect idéologique du principat* (1953); Peter A. Brunt, "The Lex Valeria Cornelia," in *Journal of Roman Studies,* **51** (1961), and "The Lex de Imperio Vespasiani," in *Journal of Roman Studies,* **67** (1977); John Buchan, *Augustus* (1937); Jérôme Carcopino, "L'hérédité dynastique chez les Antonins," in *Revue des études anciennes,* **51** (1949); Martin P. Charlesworth, *The Roman Empire* (1951); Guy E. F. Chilver, "Augustus and the Roman Constitution 1939–50" in *Historia,* **1** (1950); John A. Crook, *Consilium Princips: Imperial Councils and Counsellors from Augustus to Diocletian* (1955); Jesse R. Fears, *Princeps a diis electus: The Divine Election of the Emperor as a Political Concept at Rome* (1977).

Mason Hammond, *The Augustan Principate in Theory and Practice* (1933; 2d ed. 1968), "The Transmission of Powers of the Roman Emperor from the Death of Nero in A.D. 68 to that of Alexander Severus in A.D. 235," in *Memoirs of the American Academy in Rome,* **24** (1956), and *The Antonine Monarchy* (1959); A. J. Holladay, "The Election of Magistrates in the Early Principate," in *Latomus,* **37** (1978); Laurence L. Howe, *The Praetorian Prefect from Commodus to Diocletian (A.D. 180–305)* (1942); Arnold H. M. Jones, *Studies in Roman Government and Law* (1960; repr. 1968); Hugh Last, "*Imperium Maius:* A Note," in *Journal of Roman Studies,* **37** (1947); B. Levick, "Imperial Control of Elections under the Early Principate," in *Historia,* **16** (1967).

André Magdelain, *Auctoritas principis* (1947); Fergus Millar, "The Emperor, the Senate and the Provinces," in *Journal of Roman Studies,* **56** (1966), and *The Emperor in the Roman World, 31 B.C. to A.D. 337* (1977); Edward T. Salmon, "The Evolution of the Augustan Principate," in *Historia,* **5** (1956); D. C. A. Shotter, "Elections under Tiberius," in *Classical Quarterly,* **16** (1966); Gianfranco Tibiletti, *Principe e magistrati repubblicani* (1953); R. Villers, "La dévolution du principat dans la famille d'Auguste," in *Revue des Études Latines,* **28** (1950); Zvi Yavetz, *Plebs and Princeps* (1969).

Greek Class Structures and Relations

STANLEY M. BURSTEIN

DIVISION INTO CLASSES or status groups is characteristic of all complex societies and ancient Greece is no exception. The study of social stratification and the attempt to understand the phenomena involved, particularly that of social class, has therefore been one of the major concerns of the disciplines of sociology and social history. Particularly influential have been two definitions of a class, one posed by sociologist Max Weber, who defined classes as "groups of people whose opportunities in life were determined by the market situation," and the other by Karl Marx and his successors, for whom a class was "a social group with a particular function in the process of production" (Burke, 1980). Common to these and other similar definitions is the fact that whether relations between classes are assumed to be essentially peaceful (Weber) or marked by conflict (Marx), class is viewed as a neutral phenomenon, not predetermined by law. By contrast, membership in a status group, according to Weber, is ascribed, meaning a person's position in society is determined by his status or honor, which is "acquired by birth, defined legally and might carry power and privilege with it" (*ibid.*).

Class divisions existed in ancient Greece, and Greek thinkers recognized their importance. Thus, Aristotle (*Politics* 3.1279b.6–40), following Plato, observed that in the end all societies could be said to be divided into two unequal and often hostile groups, the rich and the poor. In so analyzing society, Aristotle broke with a strong Greek tendency to see society as composed not of a series of hierarchically arranged classes but, as M. I. Finley phrased it in *Ancient Economy and Society*, of "a spectrum of statuses" marked by unequal honor and privileges. Chief among such statuses were male and female, free and nonfree, citizens and noncitizens, and noble and nonnoble. No sense of class solidarity therefore could or did exist between free male citizens rich or poor and their nonfree or free noncitizen counterparts, since only the former were members of the polis, or a community that provided the context for all Greek social, economic, and political relations.

The predominance of this view of society in Greek thought is reflected by the moral character of Greek social terminology in which high- and low-status individuals are regularly characterized as the good (*agathoi* [good] or *aristoi* [best]) and the bad (*kakoi* [bad] or *poneroi* [burdensome]), and a properly run society is one in which the "good" rule over the "bad." Thus, even Aristotle, the most "scientific" of Greek social analysts, categorized constitutions based solely on class considerations in this way, stating that the oligarchy or rule by the few rich was a perversion of aristocracy, a constitution in which power was allocated according to the status and individual merit of the members of its governing class.

The study of the social history of modern societies uses statistical information on many interrelated phenomena, including population, income distribution, and price fluctuations. Such data are not available to historians of ancient Greece. A definitive history of class relations in ancient Greece is therefore not possible, but an analysis of data found scattered in literary and nonliterary sources does permit the determination of the main trends of Greek social history.

All of the more than 600 known Greek city-states (poleis), whether tiny communities with a few hundred citizens and a few square miles of territory or large cities such as Athens with its thousands of citizens and almost 1,000 square miles of territory, were predominantly agrarian communities in a poor country whose citizens were first and foremost landowners and warriors. Throughout Greek history land was the preeminent form of wealth and the right to own land was the most jealously guarded privilege of citizens, the privilege that most sharply divided them from noncitizens. Aristotle's contention that Greek society was divided into two basic classes, the rich and the poor, means that the fundamental social division within a polis was not that between the propertied and the propertyless, as Marxists would argue, but between large and small property owners. Thus, when Solon divided the Athenian citizen body into four wealth-based census groups, even the lowest group, the *thetes,* whose position in Homeric society was so poor that Achilles in the *Odyssey* (11.489–491) says that he would prefer being a *thete* to a landless man to being the king of the dead, were assumed to own property that could produce up to 200 *medimnoi* (310 bu./10.9 m³) of agricultural produce per year.

In one of the rare instances where statistical information is available concerning the distribution of wealth in a Greek city-state, the male citizen population of Athens in 412 B.C. numbered about 20,000, and a proposal to disfranchise propertyless Athenians would have affected 5,000 people. By contrast, limiting the franchise to those possessing sufficient wealth to qualify for hoplite service (having an estimated annual income of between 200 and 300 *medimnoi*) would have resulted in a citizen body of 12,000. In other words, when Athenian fortunes during the Peloponnesian War were at their nadir, only 25 percent of the citizenry was landless while 60 percent possessed at least a moderate amount of property. Of the remaining 15 percent, only a small minority could be classified as "very wealthy," and Davies' 1981 study has shown that in 412 B.C. those qualified to undertake military liturgies, a duty imposed by law only on the wealthiest citizens, numbered only 400 individuals or 2 percent of the Athenian citizen population.

Athenian society, in a reflection of the norm prevailing among Greek cities, was pyramidal in shape. The base was formed by a comparatively small number of landless individuals and a large group of small property owners. The rest of the pyramid consisted of a small class of moderately wealthy citizens—that class whose presence Aristotle assumed essential to the maintenance of a sound constitution—and a tiny class of the very rich who provided the city's political and social leadership and on whom fell such fiscal burdens as Athens cared to levy, primarily the performance of liturgies and the payment of *eisphora,* the extraordinary property tax.

The legitimacy of this ordering of society was never seriously challenged. Even in Athens during the height of the so-called radical democracy in the fifth and fourth centuries, citizens usually chose their leaders from the minority of the very rich. Nevertheless, social tension and conflict are among the most prominent features of Greek history, and the reasons are clear. For much of Greek history the gap between the rich and the poor was not great: in Solon's division of the Athenian citizenry the minimum census for the highest social class, the *pentakosiomedimnoi*—the so-called 500-bushel men—was only two and one-half times that of the maximum for the *thetes.* However, a number of factors, including the general economic poverty of Greece, the character of the Greek laws of inheritance and debt, and the lack of a genuine free market in land, affected in important ways the membership of these two groups. Although under normal conditions opportunities for upward social mobility for all but a few lucky or unusually enterprising individuals were extremely restricted or nonexistent, the possibility of downward social mobility even to the extent of the loss of citizenship or even freedom itself was ever present for significant numbers of Greeks. Not surprisingly (instances are abundantly documented in the remains of aristocratic Greek literature), when economic and political conditions permitted a few upwardly mobile individuals to become leaders, the result was sneers and cries of outrage from those whose status was thus challenged. Such snobbish complaints are not, however, evidence of the sharp and bitter internal confrontation, which Greek writers call *stasis,* that existed in cities where conditions threatened large numbers of people with downward social mobility.

GREEK SOCIETY IN THE HOMERIC POEMS

The basic elements of Greek social structure were already in place in the society depicted in the *Iliad* and the *Odyssey,* but the question of dating has been debated. The two epics claim to relate events of the Mycenaean age, that is, of the period before *ca.* 1100 B.C., when the culture disappeared, but detailed study by twentieth-century scholars has resulted in a different conclusion. The poems themselves are believed to be the production of oral poets working sometime between the mid eighth century and mid seventh century B.C. Of the realities of both the Mycenaean age as revealed by archaeology and the Linear B tablets and of the polis-based society of the archaic period these poets seem equally ignorant. Instead, the social background against which the action of the two epics is played seems to coincide most closely with the conditions of the late Dark Ages, that is, with those of approximately the ninth century B.C.

Gone is every trace of the elaborate scribe-administered palace society of the Myceanean age with its palace hierarchy headed by a *wanax* (king), multiple forms of land tenure, extensive craft specialization, and widespread use of slaves. Equally absent is the nomadism Thucydides in *The History of the Peloponnesian War* (1.2) claims to have been typical of the period of migrations during the Dark Ages, and the poleis that formed the stage for social activity during the succeeding archaic and classical periods have not yet come into existence. Instead, Greek society as depicted in the Homeric epics is local, small scale, and agrarian. Men are first and foremost "eaters of bread," although stock raising and meat eating are more prominent than in later Greek history. Towns are few and insignificant. The mythological Phaiakia, visited by Odysseus and the nearest approximation of an urban settlement, is essentially a utopia located at the ends of the earth, and it even appears to be primarily a residential center for the area's principal aristocratic landowners. Archaeology has confirmed this picture of a small-scale, nonurban Greece in the ninth century B.C. since excavation has shown that the important Dark Age site of Lefkandi in Euboea was a small but prosperous village of at most 160 occupants.

The social structure presupposed by the Homeric epics was correspondingly simple. Membership in a community meant belonging to an *oikos,* a self-sufficient household based on an agricultural economy. The citizenry consisted of the male heads of such households, which contained various dependents, mainly relatives and slaves. The slaves were primarily female house servants, obtained mostly as a result of war and kidnapping. Their status was not invariably hereditary since the offspring of a freeman and a slave woman was free but of lesser status than the children of his wife (*Odyssey* 14.199–212). At the top of this society was a small elite class of warriors, called by Homer *heros,* composed of a limited number of chieftains (*basileis*) who might rule one or more villages and whose wealth was measured by their estates, herds, and flocks. Additional allotments of land (*temene*) were placed at their disposal by their communities in recognition of their role as leaders and protectors. With these resources, they could maintain large households, and lesser warriors were attracted by their repute as war leaders and providers of booty.

About the majority of the population below this elite and their dependents, the *Iliad* and the *Odyssey* provide little information. The nearly contemporary poems of Hesiod, particularly *Works and Days,* which illuminates conditions in late Dark Age Boeotia, suggest that it consisted of members of similar but smaller agricultural households, the more prosperous of which might include a slave or two in addition to work animals and other livestock. Alternative socioeconomic roles were few and precarious, in part because the weakness of governmental institutions meant that society could not guarantee the security of individuals lacking the support of kin or other protectors, and also because the economic demands of such small and largely self-sufficient communities could not support—with the rare exception of a figure such as the smith mentioned by Hesiod (*Works and Days,* 493)—full-time craftsmen and other specialists. Hence the conduct of trade and the provision of needed nonagricultural services and craft products seems largely to have remained, as conservative Greek thinkers contended throughout Greek history that it should remain, in the hands of outsiders such as the ubiquitous Phoenicians of the Homeric poems and of marginal members of the community itself, primarily *thetes.* These latter, who formed the bottom of Homeric society, were either landless or belonged to households that were so weak and impoverished that they were forced to survive by becoming dependents of stronger and more prosperous neighbors, or by working for them on whatever terms they could obtain, or alternatively by attempting to pursue the more precarious occupations that normally were the preserve of outsiders.

The generally low level of wealth and the small scale of Dark Age Greek society meant that status divisions were sharp and the possibilities for upward social mobility were limited. The Homeric elite comprised a small aristocracy whose power was based on their wealth and the effective monopoly of the military, political, legal, and religious roles in their society. They were, in the epic phrase, "Zeus-born *basileis*," whose mythical genealogies asserting divine descent validated their claims to aristocratic status. They shared a culture and way of life with special forms of address, rules of etiquette, lists of appropriate and inappropriate activities, and social rituals. One such ritual was the mutual gift exchange that forms so prominent a part of aristocratic life in the *Odyssey*; in particular, it permitted conspicuous displays of wealth on such critical occasions as weddings and funerals and served to emphasize the social division between aristocrats and non-aristocrats. It is true that such a *hero* as Odysseus might, if he chose, perform routine agricultural and household tasks or undertake a trading voyage in order to obtain metals essential to his way of life. But, as was true of the rich in all periods of Greek history, the essential difference between the Homeric aristocrat and even a prosperous non-aristocrat such as Hesiod was that the former did not have to labor to survive and the latter did (as Hesiod emphasizes again and again in his poetry). Thus, the mere suspicion that Odysseus might be a common merchant threatened to exclude him from aristocratic Phaiakian society. Similarly, that an individual such as Hesiod's father could recoup his fortunes by migrating from Asiatic Kyme to Boeotia and purchasing a piece of marginal land, or that a calling from the Muses and Hesiod's own talent could introduce his son to the world of the aristocracy, merely proves that occasional individuals could improve their social position even in Dark Age Greece. Similarly, the fact that aristocratic women and children kidnapped or captured in war could become slaves or that an aged and weak former *basileus* such as Odysseus' father Laertes could be reduced to working his own small plot like any *thete* demonstrates that there were circumstances in which even aristocrats could lose high status, or, as Odysseus' experience in Phaiakia indicates, regain it through a good marriage.

Still, the evidence as a whole indicates that such examples of social mobility were unusual in a society in which land, the primary form of wealth and the ultimate basis of a person's status, changed hands rarely. The Homeric epics with their open sympathy with the values of the aristocracy contain little hint of any discontent with this state of affairs. Thus, the one discordant note in them, the protest of Thersites, is brutally rebuffed to the delight of the whole army at Troy. Hesiod (*Works and Days* 39. 202–213), with his grumbling at the demands of the "bribe-devouring *basileis*" and his grim fable of the hawk and the nightingale (*ibid.*, 202–213), suggests the contrary, that there already existed in the late Dark Ages that potential for social conflict which was so characteristic a feature of archaic Greece.

ARCHAIC PERIOD (*ca.* 750–500 B.C.)

The approximately two and one-half centuries of the archaic period saw great changes in every aspect of Greek life. Population increased strongly and rapidly. The polis system appeared and spread as population shifted from independent small settlements such as Lefkandi to new and more compact urban centers such as Eretria on Euboea. Coincidental with these changes in the basic pattern of Greek life was vigorous economic growth as evidenced by the steady increase of such items of conspicuous expenditure by new poleis and rich citizens as temples, city walls, fountain houses, and statuary. At the same time the introduction of coinage toward the end of the period began to change the character of wealth and economic activity itself, while the substitution of hoplite warfare with its need for large numbers of nonnoble infantry for the older and more individualistic cavalry warfare of the heroic age permanently altered the military and social balance of power in the new poleis. For some the revolutionary changes of the archaic period brought wealth and power, but for many the end of the Homeric social order brought insecurity and distress, so that it is not surprising that these centuries were ones of frequent and bitter social conflict.

For the aristocracies of the new poleis the archaic period was in many ways a golden age. The weak rulers of the Dark Ages were replaced by hereditary aristocracies whose members took vigorous advantage of the economic opportunities of the period, as is revealed by the Homeric *Hymn to Apollo* (147, 155) reference to the "long-robed Ionians" who come to Delos with their "swift ships and great wealth" and Strabo's (*Geography* 8.6.20) allusion to the Bacchiads' harvesting the revenues generated by the commerce of Korinth. The creation and proliferation of the great athletic festivals, the flourishing of the symposia and the lyric poetry that was so intimately connected with it, the appearance of decorated pottery and other imported and domestic luxury goods, and the idealization of male and female beauty and refinement evidenced by the numerous *kouroi* and *korai* of archaic statuary and by Semonides of Amorgos' (frag. 7.67–70 Edmonds) bitter denunciation of the beautiful but indolent "mare-woman" who refuses to work and is a "burden to her husband/ unless he happens to be a tyrant or a prince,/ the kind whose heart is delighted by such things," all bear witness to the elegance and sophistication of aristocratic life and to the need for wealth to support the conspicuous expenditures associated with it.

If the archaic period was the golden age of the Greek aristocracy, it was also the period in which their domination of Greek society first came under serious challenge. "Wealth is the man,/ no poor man is good or honored," the late-seventh-century Lesbian poet Alcaeus (frag. 360 Campbell) wrote. Yet at the same time that the adoption of hoplite warfare undermined the military basis of aristocratic supremacy, economic growth made possible not only the elaboration of the aristocratic way of life but also the appearance of a small class of nonnoble rich for whom aristocratic Greek society offered no status commensurate with their wealth. Opportunities for gaining wealth existed, and both nobles and nonnobles took advantage of them. Thus, Herodotus (*Histories* 4.152) alludes to the fortune made by Kolaios of Samos as a result of his opening up the metal trade with Tartessos (southern coast of Spain), as well as to that of Sostratos of Aigina, which archaeology suggests was derived from trade with Etruria. Others profited from, to list only the most obvious: mercenary service in Egypt and the Near East, slaving, and piracy (which still had a certain air of the heroic about it as late as the sixth century B.C.). The development of luxury crafts associated with the conspicuous spending of the archaic aristocracies and the new poleis brought wealth to such men as the metalworkers Theodoros and Rhoikos of Samos, the Megarian engineer Eupalinos, and a perfumer whose affected manners Anakreon ridiculed (frag. 387 Page). Whatever the source of their wealth, the demands of such nonnoble rich for admission to the closed circles of the aristocratic classes of the Greek cities provoked ridicule and then fear when their claims found supporters among ambitious but disaffected members of the aristocracy itself. They were willing to form marriage alliances with monied nonnobles, a practice in which the mid-sixth-century B.C. Megarian poet Theognis (*Elegies* 53–60, 183–192) saw not only treason to the aristocratic class but also a threat to the survival of the traditional social order itself.

Recent interpretations have rightly emphasized the dynamic, creative aspects of the archaic period in contrast to the preceding Dark Ages; and as a result they have tended to locate the causes of its bitter social and political conflicts in the frustrated aspirations of the comparatively few new rich and the prosperous small farmers who formed the core of the poleis' new hoplite armies. The ancient sources suggest otherwise, indicating that it was the threat of significant downward mobility for many people that fueled the crises that the new rich and their aristocratic allies exploited.

No ancient analysis of the causes of the problem exists or probably ever existed, but enough hints survive in the sources to discern at least some of the roots. Cancellation of debts and redivision of land, representing perhaps a fresh slate for a troubled society, were ever the demands of Greek revolutionaries, and they point to a scarcity of land on the part of a portion of the population in newly emerging city-states and to a dysfunctioning of the Greek law of debt. Hesiod advised men to pay their debts (*Works and Days* 403–404)—good advice, for in most cities the law threatened defaulters with slavery. Hesiod (*Works and Days* 377) also advised men to have only one son; again the advice was good since Greek inheritance law prescribed equal division among all eligible male heirs, a rule that threatened impoverishment for families with numerous sons, or loss of status; and repeated division of farms reduced the size of land parcels below that necessary to support a household.

In such situations, avenues of escape were limited. The proliferation of new socioeconomic roles that accompanied the growth and expansion of the polis system offered some alternatives, for instance, in crafts, but the opportunities afforded by them should not be exaggerated. The number of artisans was always small; Burford reports (1972) that the ceramic industry of Athens never employed more than 125 potters even at its peak, and many of those were slaves or free foreigners. Moreover, rewards were poor and status was low. Xenophon (*Education of Cyrus* 8.2.5) notes that in small towns artisans could barely support themselves and then only by practicing many trades; elsewhere he wrote that even when successful, the artisans' way of life made them poor citizens, unfit for the military and political functions so essential to the life of the polis (*Household Management* 4.2–3). In addition, in coastal cities and islands fishing was possible, as was petty trade; according to Aristotle (*Politics* 4.1291b.24) the poorer citizens of Aigina adopted such pursuits. Finally, archaic Greece was still in many ways a tribal society in which the horizontal divisions of status and class were crosscut by the vertical ties of solidarity created by kinship and personal obligation. Poorer members of the community might turn to their more fortunate kin or friends for short- or long-term aid, but the price paid, especially in the latter circumstance, might be high—the transformation of a once-free citizen into a dependent of his richer neighbors to whom he rendered services and tribute for the privilege of remaining on his land. This probably happened in seventh-century Attica in the case of a class of peasants called *hektemoroi* or "sixth-parters" from the one-sixth due on their produce.

Only by taking advantage of what American historians call "shipboard mobility" could one completely escape, by seeking temporary but possibly lucrative employment abroad, mainly as a merchant or mercenary like, for example, Sappho's brother in Egypt. Or one could immigrate to one of the new Greek colonies where plots of land probably larger than those available at home were given out. There was even the possibility of becoming a member of a new colony's aristocracy, the *gamoroi*, or land sharers as they were called at Syrakuse. The spectacular spread of Greek colonies around the shores of the Mediterranean, North Aegean, and Black Sea basins between the mid eighth and the late sixth centuries B.C. bears eloquent testimony to the great number of Greeks who chose this difficult avenue of escape.

For the poleis and those who chose not to risk everything by abandoning their native cities in the hope of a new start elsewhere the results were unfortunate. Emigration, withdrawal from farming, or acceptance of dependent status reduced the number of households whose resources in men and property the polis could call on in time of need and accentuated the differences between the rich, in whose hands land tended to concentrate, and the poor, for whom revolution and the establishment of a tyrant to redress their grievances often seemed the only hope. Thus, Solon (frag. 32; 36.18–25) believed he disappointed many supporters who expected him to use his office as lawgiver to establish a tyranny in order to divide the lands of the rich among the rest of the citizens. Elsewhere such restraint was not the rule, and the exploitation of the misery of the poor by ambitious aristocrats, often supported by private armies of mercenaries and by frustrated nonnoble hoplites, resulted in tyrannies in many of the major cities of Greece during the seventh and sixth centuries B.C. They swept away the old aristocracies of blood, replacing them with new aristocracies based on wealth and connections with the tyrant.

A different solution to the problems of the archaic period was attempted by Sparta: conquest. Apparently faced by the twin problems of a growing population and inadequate agricultural resources, Sparta in the eighth century B.C. conquered first the remainder of Lakonia and then her western neighbor Messenia. In both areas the inhabitants were reduced to the status of Helots, held to be enslaved to the state with the hereditary obligation of paying tribute equal to one-half their crop; in return they were promised they would not be sold away from their homes. These lands, together with the right to be provided support by the Helots living on them, were distributed among Spartan warriors, thereby increasing the wealth of the Spartan aristocracy. Those Spartans who protested their exclusion from the division of the conquered territory, particularly that of Messenia, the so-called *parthenioi*, were exiled to southern Italy where they founded the colony of Taras (Taranto).

A revolt of the Messenians in the mid seventh century B.C. forced a major reorganization of Spartan society and resulted in the unique Spartan social system that lasted in varying degree for three centuries. Although complex in detail, the underlying premises of the reform were simple. Status distinctions between Spartans or citizens of the polis of Sparta and non-Spartans inhabiting the territory ruled by Sparta were strengthened, and distinct socioeconomic and political functions were assigned to each group. Thus, the abundant agricultural wealth represented by Lakonia and especially Messenia and the labor of their numerous Helot subjects permitted the Spartans to withdraw from all economic functions, which were turned over to the *perioikoi*, free inhabitants of semiautonomous towns in Lakonia and Messenia, thereby freeing Spartan males to specialize in the military and political aspects of polis life and women to devote themselves to bearing and rearing children. Although no attempt was made to equalize landholding in Sparta or to strip the Spartan aristocracy of its special privileges, which may have included a monopoly on eligibility for membership in the *gerousia*, the Spartan council, the public effects of such social and economic distinctions in Spartan society were muted.

In their public life all Spartans were to be, as they called themselves, "equals." Assignments of *kleroi*, lots of Messenian land and Helots, assured all Spartan warriors the minimum economic resources necessary to fulfill their roles as citizens, and rules forbidding the sale or transfer of the lots served to prevent concentration of land in the hands of the richer Spartans and to insulate the poorer Spartans against the threat of downward mobility. Sumptuary rules for the public (as opposed to the private uses of wealth) and the requirement that all Spartans undergo the same rigorous upbringing and participate in the activities of such social groups as the men's clubs, the *syssitia,* that crosscut the older kinship groups lessened the sting of real disparities in wealth among Spartan citizens. The right of all Spartan warriors to attend the assembly and be elected to the city's chief magistracy, the ephorate, balanced the special privileges of the Spartan aristocracy and the two kings. Restrictions on the use of coinage and contact with outsiders further protected the system against change with the result that for over two centuries Sparta enjoyed internal stability and military power unparalleled in the rest of Greece.

Greek thinkers incorrectly but understandably contended that the Spartan system was modeled directly on that of the Dorian cities of Crete, for there enslaved populations were also ruled by warrior aristocracies whose wealth was their spear, sword, and shield. As in Sparta the various social groups in Crete were divided by sharp status divisions, which are amply documented in the literary sources and especially in the numerous epigraphical remains of Cretan law codes, including the Gortyn code, which was inscribed in the late sixth or early fifth century B.C.

At the bottom of Cretan society were two groups, chattel-slaves and the *woikees* (a term implying attachment to an *oikos,* household). About the former little can be said. One of the standard Cretan terms for them, *chrysenetoi* (gold-bought), suggests that they were primarily obtained by purchase. The latter were apparently the enslaved descendants of Bronze Age Minoans who, like the Spartan Helots with whom they were compared in antiquity, maintained their own separate communities and customs—Aristotle (*Politics* 2.1271b31–33) says they continued to use their own laws—and paid a tribute to their Dorian masters in return for the privilege of remaining and working on their land. The free Greek population was divided into two groups: the full citizens, whom the Gortyn code calls simply "freemen" and who alone belonged to the men's clubs, membership in which was required for citizenship and from whom the magistrates were elected; and the *apatairoi* who, as their name, "those without comrades," suggests, were excluded from the social institutions of the elite and the privileges that were associated with them. Whether, like the Spartan *perioikoi,* they enjoyed in compensation a monopoly of economic functions is unknown. Cretan law accentuated the sharpness of these status divisions, as the Gortyn code reveals, by assigning different penalties for similar offenses depending on the status of the individuals: higher ones for offenses committed against a citizen by individuals of lower status and vice versa.

At the same time Cretan legislators attempted to stabilize their society and its social structure. To prevent the concentration of land in the hands of a small class of rich individuals with the attendant problems of downward mobility, they restricted the free alienation of land by emphasizing the need to follow strict rules of agnatic succession (that is, on the father's side) in the case of childless families and imposing on female heiresses obligations similar to but less extreme than those required by the Athenian institution of the epiklerate. This provided the rule that in default of a male heir, a daughter became the vehicle for transmitting her father's property to the son of her marriage with her nearest male kinsman.

Legislation forbidding the *woikees* the possession of arms or participation in the closely related activities of the gymnasia (Aristotle, *Politics* 2.1264a21–23) served to keep the subjects on whose labor the system depended weak, while by retaining their customs the laws accentuated the difference between them and the *apetairoi*. Thus they prevented the development of any feelings of solidarity between the two principal noncitizen groups on the island. Aristotle (*Politics* 6.1319a11–13) alludes to other examples of the use of law to attempt to insulate various Greek cities against the problems of the archaic period, some of which went so far as to try to stabilize their citizen bodies by absolutely forbidding the sale of a certain portion of one's estate. By far the best-known and most creative use of law for such purposes is to be found in the work of the Athenian lawgiver Solon.

Like other archaic cities, pre-Solonian Athens was ruled by a hereditary aristocracy, the Eupatrids, who alone were eligible to hold political office and whose prosperity is indicated by the splendors of Geometric and Proto-Attic pottery and the early Athenian dedications at Delphi. According to Aristotle (frag. 384 Rose), the remainder of Athenian society was divided into two status groups, farmers and *demiourgoi* (public workers), the latter term apparently being used in the general sense to refer to nonagricultural specialists rather than only to craftsmen. Solon's encouragement of foreign craftsmen to settle in Athens and his law requiring craftsmen to teach their sons their skill on pain of forfeiting their right to old age support from them suggests that still in the early sixth century B.C. there was no large body of native Athenian artisans. The success of the Athenian aristocracy in uniting under the rule of Athens the comparatively large territory of Attica without creating a suppressed and rebellious subject population such as bedeviled Sparta spared the city many of the problems that beset other poleis during the seventh century B.C. By the time Solon was appointed sole archon and lawgiver in 594 B.C., however, aristocratic Athens was threatened with class war.

Thanks to the survival of significant fragments of Solon's poetry and the accounts of Aristotle and Plutarch, the situation in Athens is much better known than that of other Greek cities, although much still remains unclear. According to Aristotle (*Constitution of Athens* 2.5) the crisis was long in the making and rested on two facts: the extreme concentration of land in the hands of the aristocracy and the worsening plight of two groups of poor Athenians, the *hektemoroi* and debtors. Athenian law made both groups liable to sale as slaves in case of their defaulting on their payments. Solon's reference (frag. 28b; 36. 8–11 Edmonds) to attempts to repatriate Athenians sold justly or unjustly and a bitter denunciation of fellow aristocrats' greed for gold and silver strongly suggests that at least some aristocrats ruthlessly took advantage of the law or ignored it in a desire to obtain the wealth essential to maintaining a lavish way of living.

Solon was appointed archon and lawgiver to resolve the problem of the *hektemoroi* and the debtors, and it occupies center stage in both ancient and modern accounts. As a result two facts essential to the long-term success of his reforms tend to be obscured: first, his reforms imply that the majority of Athenian farmers were neither *hektemoroi* nor debtors and, second, his creation of a new wealth-based upper class, the *pentakosiomedimnoi*, indicates that some prominent supporters were drawn from the group of nonnoble rich who aspired to a role in Athenian society hitherto denied them. Solon was neither a revolutionary nor a democrat. Although his reforms, aimed at establishing a just and stable society in which each social group could securely enjoy the privileges and rights appropriate to it, they satisfied neither the extremists among his supporters, who had hoped that he would become tyrant and enrich them at the expense of the aristocrats as happened elsewhere, nor the "traditionalists" among his opponents, who begrudged the least sacrifice of their privileges. Solon's reforms were essentially conservative in character and intention. Far from being eliminated, inequality was reaffirmed as the central fact of Athenian social organization. Nevertheless, the means chosen to achieve this end were radical and the shock registered by Solon's aristocratic critics is understandable. A reorganization of the Athenian citizenry into four new groups, *pentakosiomedimnoi*, *hippeis*, *zeugitai* (apparently the small farmers who served as hoplites), and *thetes* replaced the old divisions of Eupatrids, farmers, and *demiourgoi*. The status of *hektemor* and the punishment of slavery for indebtedness were abolished; judging from the fact that down to the Peloponnesian War the majority of Athenians were self-sufficient farmers, both the *hektemoroi* and debtors retained control of the land they lived on.

The right to hold office remained limited to the top two Solonian classes, but to facilitate the integration of the nonnoble rich, wealth as measured by the produce of one's estate and not by birth determined which of the Solonian classes an individual was enrolled in. Class was thus substituted for status as the determinant of political privilege in Athens and the aristocratic monopoly of public life was erased. Sumptuary rules eased the aristocrats' need for the conspicuous expenditures, especially those connected with weddings and funerals, that had fueled the crisis of 594 B.C.; and legislation strengthening the epiklerate (*epikleroi* were fatherless, brotherless heiresses) and permitting childless citizens to adopt an heir slowed the tendency of landownership to be concentrated in the hands of the rich.

Politically, Solon's reforms were a failure since they did not prevent Athenians a generation later from coming under the rule of the tyrant Peisistratos and his sons. Socially, however, the picture was different. For the rest of the sixth and much of the fifth century B.C. class tensions were strikingly absent from Athenian history. Despite the attempts of fourth-century B.C. theorists such as Aristotle (*Constitution of Athens* 13.4) to interpret the emergence of the Peisistratid tyranny in terms of the strife between rich and poor, it appears to have arisen primarily from divisions within the upper class itself, and the tyrants seem to have taken no significant actions against members of that class provided they did not actively oppose their rule. The same is true for the reforms of Kleisthenes, which likewise did not challenge the monopoly on political office granted by Solon to the two top census groups.

CLASSICAL PERIOD (*ca.* 500–336 B.C.)

Unlike the archaic period, the classical period was not a time of great innovation but one in which the Greeks exploited to the fullest the potentialities of the political, social, and economic institutions that had developed during the preceding two and one-half centuries. This was particularly true of Athens, where the disaster of the Persian invasion of 480–479 B.C. was followed by half a century of unparalleled growth and prosperity.

The fleet that had helped to turn back the Persians enabled Athens after the war gradually to build an empire that ultimately encompassed most of the islands of the Aegean basin and many of the cities of the Black Sea and the west coast of Asia Minor and thus made the city the preeminent political power and commercial center in the Greek world. At home the population, both citizen and noncitizen, expanded rapidly. The city of Athens together with its port of Piraeus were rebuilt in a new and more splendid fashion. Literature and art flourished, and, most important of all, so did the democracy that, building on the reforms of Solon and Kleisthenes, became in the fifth century a system in which for the first time it was possible for almost the entire male citizen body to participate in the government of its own city.

With the fifth century B.C. came also the birth of political theory in Greece and the first explicit analyses of society as composed of classes and of political systems as instruments of class domination.

> I do not commend the Athenians for choosing the kind of government embodied in their constitution, because they have elected to give knaves [*tous ponerous*] the advantage over honest men [*tous chrestous*]. . . . First, I will say this. They are right in deciding at the very beginning that the poor and the common people [*oi penetes kai o demos*] ought to prevail over the rich and well born [*ton gennaion kai ton plousion*], because it is the common people who drive the ships that make the city strong. (pseudo-Xenophon, *Constitution of Athens* 1.1–2; trans. T.S. Brown)

As the hostile remarks of the so-called Old Oligarch, the anonymous author of the oligarchic pamphlet on the *Constitution of Athens* preserved among the works of Xenophon, indicate, aristocratic intellectuals assailed the democracy for inverting the natural order of things, for forcing "honest men," whom he defines as the "rich and wellborn," to submit to the rule of "knaves," the demos. This was no longer a term for the whole citizen body, as in Homer, but for the poor (primarily the two lowest Solonian census groups, the *zeugitai* and especially the *thetes*) and apparently the artisans, workers, and merchants who Plato claimed made up the assembly (*Protagoras* 319b–323a). In Athens, her critics charged, men were free to be whatever they wished, and the result was injustice and social and political chaos since privileges were granted to all on a basis of equality instead of to each according to his merit. If Athens were a properly run city, the anonymous critic continued, only "the ablest men [would] write the laws. . . . Honest men will chastise the rogues, and honest men also will be the ones to give advice on matters of state. . . . The common people, to be sure, would immediately be subjected by the aristocrats" (pseudo-Xenophon, *Constitution of Athens* 1.9). Plato would have agreed with the Old Oligarch since his recipe in the *Republic* for the end of class strife and the establishment of social peace and justice involved the reorganization of poleis so that political and military functions would be monopolized by a hereditary aristocracy of intellect and merit and those engaged in economic pursuits, the demos of the Athenian democracy's critics, would have no voice in its own governance.

In actuality, however, the sources suggest that the fifth century was a period of social peace in Athens. The two oligarchic regimes that briefly ruled Athens in 411 B.C. and 404–403 B.C., the Four Hundred and the Thirty, were each the result of conspiracies developed by small groups of conservative aristocrats and intellectuals who used intimidation and violence to seize power during moments of exceptional political weakness and demoralization. Although they claimed to rule in the name of the "rich and wellborn," their excesses quickly cost them the little aristocratic support they had enjoyed, while much of the upper class actively supported the democratic counterrevolutions that overthrew them, and with reason. An aristocrat who criticized an Athenian for earning his living in the agora or otherwise harassed his social inferiors might find himself the object of a suit before unsympathetic jurors, but no significant action was taken against the aristocracy as a class or against their property. The archon began his term of office by promising that at the end of his year everyone would possess the property he had at its outset; and although by 412 B.C. 5,000 Athenians—more than the citizen populations of many poleis—were landless, the demand for cancellation of debts and redivision of the land of the rich, so common in the fragmentary evidence for the other periods of Greek history, is absent from the richer documentation for fifth-century B.C. Athens. The one act supposedly directed against the aristocracy, the law moved by Perikles in 451 B.C. limiting citizenship to the children of Athenian parents (some aristocrats were the products of foreign intermarriages), was probably the result of a general Athenian desire to strengthen the distinction between citizen and metic at a time when the nature of cosmopolitan life was tending to blur it. This desire is also evidenced by the resistance of Athenians to grant aliens the right to own land or win citizenship (even if, like the orator Lysias, they helped defend the democratic cause against the Thirty). In fact, far from acting against "the rich and wellborn," the democracy, as even the Old Oligarch (pseudo-Xenophon, *Constitution of Athens* 1.3) had to admit, preferred to choose its leaders from them. Indeed, recent study has revealed that this was true even of such notorious targets of conservative polemic as the demagogues Kleon and Kleophon, whose nicknames "The Tanner" and "The Lyremaker" refer not to their practicing those trades themselves but owning shops in which slave craftsmen produced those products. Similarly, the less controversial Nikias, the commander of the ill-fated Athenian invasion of Sicily in 415–413 B.C., derived much of his wealth from slaves whom he hired out to persons who had leases to work the silver mines at Laurion.

The social peace of fifth-century B.C. Athens was a reflection of the fact that this century was a period of unusual opportunity for the poor. Thus, Aristotle (*Constitution of Athens* 7.4) refers to a dedication on the Acropolis boasting that the dedicant, having begun life as a *thete*, rose to the status of a *hippeis*, the second highest of the Solonian census classes. So sharp a change in status must have been rare even in fifth-century Athens, but the prosperity of the period is undeniable. In large part Athens' prosperity was due to its empire and the growth of the city and of Piraeus that accompanied it. In the same passage in which he observes that in a small city a craftsman could barely eke out an existence, Xenophon noted that in a large city, such as fifth-century B.C. Athens, he could earn a good living even if he specialized in only one aspect of a craft. More important, however, were the opportunities available to the class of *thetes* as a whole. Faced with an impoverished old age after the Peloponnesian War, Eutheros replied to a suggestion of his friend Socrates that he take a job as a rich man's overseer by saying that he could not bear slavery—the necessity to obey the orders of another person (Xenophon, *Memorabilia* 2.8). And for most of the fifth century B.C. *thetes* did not have to face that necessity.

Despite the existence of a substantial landless minority, no system of wage labor developed in Athens. Such labor instead was provided by slaves, as is indicated by Thucydides' remark that 20,000 slaves, mostly trained in the crafts, fled Athens during the latter part of the Peloponnesian War (Thucydides, 7.27.5). As the Athenian democracy's critics pointed out, it was Athens' empire that made this situation possible. By the 420s B.C. Athens' revenues from tribute and other sources may have totaled 2,000 talents per year, an enormous sum. It was equivalent at fifth-century B.C. rates (a skilled worker earned one drachma per day) to twelve million man-days' work. Except for a portion placed in reserve, this sum was spent on public activities: maintenance of the fleet, pay for political service, and construction projects. Conservative critics such as Aristotle (*Constitution of Athens* 24.3) claimed that these expenditures allowed as many as 20,000 Athenians to live in comfort, but this was an exaggeration. In particular, pay for political service was intermittent and low—three obols, the equivalent of one-half of a day's wages, was given for jury service. At best, therefore, it was a useful supplement for a person with other sources of income. More significant were service in the fleet, which provided thousands of Athenians during the annual cruises or campaigns with pay equal to that of skilled workmen, and the great building program on which, as the Erechtheum accounts indicate, numerous Athenian men worked as independent laborers alongside slaves and metics. Perhaps even more important were the opportunities for "shipboard mobility" afforded the Athenian poor by the empire itself. Figures preserved in various sources suggest that over 10,000 Athenians, the majority of them *thetes* and *zeugitai* if the plans for the foundation of the Athenian colony at Brea (*Greek Historical Inscriptions* 49B, 39–42) are typical, may have taken part in the colonies and cleruchies founded during the fifth century B.C. By so doing, these poor citizens were able to improve their status to a degree not possible if they had remained at home.

The good times and, to some extent, the social peace that had characterized them ended, at least temporarily, with Athens' defeat in the Peloponnesian War in 404 B.C. The disappearance of the empire deprived Athens of the revenues that had supported the democracy and forced numerous Athenians who had prospered as colonists or cleruchs to return to an impoverished Athens. Such, indeed, had been the fate of Socrates' friend Eutheros, who had lost the overseas property that had supported him. Examples of economic hardship were prominent in comedies such as *Lysistrata,* which Aristophanes wrote during the last ten years of the Peloponnesian War, and became more frequent in the literature of the early fourth century B.C. A climax is reached in Aristophanes' *Assemblywomen (Ekklesiazousai),* with its proposals for the establishment of a community of property, and *Wealth (Ploutos),* with its strident picture of a world gone wrong in which the good are poor and the unjust rich.

Not surprisingly, evidence of tension between classes at Athens, so rare in fifth-century sources, is common in those of the fourth century B.C. Thus, Isocrates' *Exchange of Property* (*Antidosis* 159–160) complains that wealth, which was a source of pride and prestige during his youth in the fifth century B.C., exposed one to harassment and lawsuits in the fourth. Legal speeches from the difficult years of the early fourth century B.C. confirm his sense of unease with their allusions to legal actions instituted for the purpose of confiscating the property of the rich because of the democracy's need to find money for payments to citizens and their equally insistent claims that rich defendants gladly expended their wealth in the performance of liturgies from which the poor profited. Despite the loss of empire, Athens retained many advantages, including the silver mines at Laurion and a position as the commercial center of the Aegean. When the city regained a degree of prosperity during the fourth century B.C., social tensions eased, and the position of the "rich and wellborn" as leaders of Athenian society became more secure. This is revealed by Demosthenes' allusions to the new splendor of their homes as compared with those of their ancestors in the fifth century B.C. (*Demosthenes,* 23.207–208), by the advice given him that his suit against Meidias was hopeless because Meidias was rich (21.151), and by the comfortable and refined life-style that forms the background of so many of the comedies

Menander wrote during the late fourth century B.C.

Outside of Athens sources suggest that fifth-century conditions were less happy. Nonetheless, individual opportunities did exist. Metics could serve in the army and as rowers in the Athenian fleet, and along with other non-Athenians they conducted much of the commerce within the Athenian empire. Likewise the Theban law mentioned by Aristotle (*Politics* 3.1278a.25–27) requiring that anyone who practiced a trade had to wait ten years before participating in political life indicates that even in that oligarchic noncommercial city a small class of upwardly mobile non-aristocrats was beginning to appear. In the end, however, no city possessed the economic resources that made possible Athens' social peace, so that elsewhere in Greece relations between the classes seem to have been more tense (pseudo-Xenophon, *Constitution of Athens* 3.10–11). Actual outbreaks of class violence appear to have been rare before the Peloponnesian War. Then, however, in their attempts to win the war, both Athens and Sparta exploited class tensions in the cities, the Athenians by assisting democratic factions with strong support among the poor, and the Spartans by helping oligarchic groups centered in the aristocracies—with results that are all too visible in Thucydides' graphic accounts of the unsuccessful oligarchic coups at Kerkyra (Corfu) in 427 and Samos in 411 B.C. and the bloody purges of the city's aristocracies and the confiscation of the estates of those killed and exiled that followed the purges (*Peloponnesian War* 3.70–84; 8.21; 8.73).

If anything, conditions worsened in the fourth century. The recommendation of the military writer Aeneas Tacticus (*ca.* 144) that the rulers of a besieged city should guard against betrayal by the masses and by debtors clearly points to the continued existence of serious class tension during the first half of the century when Sparta's enemies, particularly Athens, as in the fifth century, exploited the fact that support for Sparta was concentrated in the oligarchically inclined aristocracies of the Greek cities. References to instances of class violence are common in the sources, but the experience of one city must serve as the example for many.

In 364 B.C. Herakleia Pontika (Ereğli), a city on the north coast of Asia Minor, was ruled by an oligarchy of three hundred aristocratic landowners who had overthrown the democracy that governed the city since the late fifth century B.C. only to be faced by strong agitation for cancellation of debts and redistribution of land. In desperation, the oligarchs invited Klearchos, an exile serving as a commander of mercenaries with a local Persian satrap, to return and stabilize the situation. Once in the city, Klearchos used his mercenaries to become tyrant and to massacre and confiscate the estates and liberate the slaves of his aristocratic opponents. (Those who escaped endured an exile that lasted until 281 B.C.) Herakleia's fate was shared by numerous cities on the Greek mainland, on Sicily, and in southern Italy, and the hordes of exiles created by such revolutions were a source of social disruption throughout the Greek world. Its severity can be seen from the fact that even after the huge losses suffered by exiles serving as mercenaries during the campaigns of Alexander the Great, 20,000 assembled in Olympia in 324 B.C. to hear Aristotle's son-in-law Nikanor announce Alexander's order that they were to return home. It is no wonder that oligarchic regimes throughout Greece welcomed Philip II's organization in 338 B.C. of the League of Korinth, which made guarantees against redistribution of land, cancellation of debts, and freeing of slaves for the purpose of revolution.

Not even Sparta was immune, although, as usual, the city's development was unique.

Aristotle (*Politics* 2.1270a.18–26) noted that in the second half of the fourth century the Spartan system, which was established three centuries earlier, was in a state of decay. The comparatively broad-based military society of the early classical period had been replaced by a narrow oligarchy marked by wide disparities of wealth and privilege. Fully privileged citizens numbered less than one thousand and the concentration of land in the possession of the rich was extreme (with fully 40 percent of it being owned by women). The majority of Spartans, without land to support them, had experienced severe downward mobility and had lost not only their land but also their coveted status of full citizenship; they now belonged to the embittered class of *hypomeiones,* inferiors, who occupied an ambiguous position between the full citizens and the *perioikoi*.

The roots of the problem went back into the fifth century. The wars of the late fifth and early fourth century made permanent the decline in manpower caused by the great earthquake that devastated Sparta in the 460s B.C., while the great influx of wealth that resulted from Sparta's victory in the Peloponnesian War and the exploitation of its empire in the succeeding decades encouraged a small group of rich families to expand their land holdings by acquiring vacant *kleroi* (estates). This process was facilitated by a law, probably to be dated to the end of the fifth century and ascribed to the ephor Epitadeus, that allowed the free transfer of *kleroi* by gift or will. Already in the 390s the potential for serious class conflict was revealed when the Spartans nipped in the bud a conspiracy involving Helots, *perioikoi*, and "inferiors" organized by an ambitious and embittered "inferior" named Kinadon who gave as his motive the desire "to be inferior to none in Lakedaimon" (Xenophon, *History of Greece* [*Hellenika*] 3.3.11). Two decades later the process was accelerated, with the results described by Aristotle. An independent Messenia was reestablished following the disastrous Theban defeat of Sparta at Leuktra in 371 B.C., and numerous poorer Spartans were thereby impoverished since they were deprived of the Messenian *kleroi* and Helots on which they had depended to maintain their status as fully privileged citizens.

HELLENISTIC PERIOD (*ca.* 336–30 B.C.)

A new period of opportunity for Greeks outside of Greece opened with the thirteen-year reign of Alexander the Great. By his conquest of the Persian Empire, Alexander destroyed a state system that had regulated affairs in the Near East for over two centuries. Alexander himself never had the opportunity to implement whatever plans he may have had for the organization of his empire. Only after a generation of internecine war among his generals did a political system in which Greeks were to play an important role emerge in Asia.

Traditionally the Hellenistic period has been viewed as one in which Greek and non-Greek societies and cultures blended to form a new cosmopolitan civilization. Recent studies, however, have made it clear that the reality more closely resembled the Athenian orator Isocrates' dream of a conquered Asia where natives, reduced to the status of helots, worked to support Greek colonists, those exiled and poor Greeks who had so disturbed the peace of the fourth-century cities. Far from blending to form a new culture, Greek and native societies existed side by side in the new Hellenistic kingdoms. In Egypt and Asia, status, specifically ethnicity, and not class determined social position and privilege. Whether or not Alexander envisaged an empire governed by a mixed elite of Macedonians, Greeks, and non-Greeks, in Ptolemaic Egypt and Seleucid Asia Macedonians and Greeks alone belonged to the ruling elite. As a result, during the third century thousands of Greeks endorsed Theocritus' claim that "as a paymaster Ptolemaios is the best for a freeman" (*Idyll* 14.59) by immigrating to the east to fill the new cities and military colonies Alexander and the Seleucids had founded in Asia or to settle in one of the three Greek cities of Egypt or to receive cleruchies in the Egyptian countryside. Although a minority amounting to less then 10 percent of the total population of the Hellenistic kingdoms, Greeks and Macedonians monopolized the higher levels of political and economic life in the east and prospered for the most part modestly, as can be seen from the charming picture of middle-class life in Alexandria drawn by the poet Theocritus in *Idyll* 15. Some, such as members of the court, prospered mightily, as is revealed by their numerous honorary inscriptions and the magnificent homes that have been excavated, for example, at Ai Khanum in Afghanistan.

Throughout the Hellenistic and succeeding Roman periods in Egypt and Asia membership in the ruling elite required certification as a Greek citizen. As apartheid was not characteristic of Hellenistic society, this meant in practice that it came ultimately to be composed not so much of individuals of Greek birth as of Greek culture, that is, of those who received a Greek education culminating with the completion of civic, religious, and military education (*ephebia*) and enrollment on the citizen rolls of a Greek city. All others were subjects, and depending on the status assigned to a particular ethnic group in the several Hellenistic kingdoms its members enjoyed different privileges and were subject to varying degrees of restriction on their freedom of movement and to varying levels of taxation and criminal punishment. Discrimination even extended to the point that, as the first-century A.D. Jewish writer Philo (*In Flaccum* 78)
noted, the law specified that different types of whips be used on Greeks and Egyptians when they were flogged. Not surprisingly, therefore, social conflict during the Hellenistic period tended, especially from the late third century on, to take the form of revolts by subject peoples to restore native rule rather than struggles between classes within the Greco-Macedonian citizenry of the kingdoms.

By contrast the Hellenistic period in Aegean Greece was marked by a steady widening of the gap between the "rich and wellborn" and the poor, with the result that tension and sometimes open strife erupted between social classes. Although the governments of Greek cities were increasingly democratic in form, most were controlled by aristocratic oligarchies whose often enormous wealth can be seen in the creation of numerous new festivals, the appearance of new and more luxurious types of houses (Vitruvius, *On Architecture* 6.7.4), and, most strikingly, by the many honorary decrees that thanked them for using their own funds to pay for services and amenities that the cities could not afford. Even Athens succumbed to the trend toward concealed oligarchy. True, its democracy survived efforts to disfranchise the poor during the brief period of oligarchic government imposed by Antipater in 322 B.C. that followed Athens' defeat during the Lamian War, and again during the ten-year administration of Kassander's agent Demetrios of Phaleron. Nevertheless, the elimination of the liturgy system, and the transfer to the major magistracies of the responsibility for public expenditures once provided by it, effectively limited the holding of those offices to the narrow circle of the very rich who could afford the required payments. At the same time, the spread of formal literary and rhetorical education among the rich further sharpened the division between them and the poor. This is illustrated by the transformation in Athens of the *ephebia* from a mandatory two-year period of military training beginning at the age of eighteen to a voluntary one-year term of public service, the nonmilitary aspects of which included lectures by members of the various philosophical schools. As a result the number of *ephebes*, which in the fourth century annually numbered over 400, plunged during the third century to less than—and sometimes far less than—100 per year.

While the aristocracies of the Greek cities prospered, the condition of the poor worsened, particularly during the early Hellenistic period when Alexander the Great and his successors suddenly released the accumulated treasures of two centuries of Persian rule and ignited an inflation that severely affected the poor. This inflation also affected artisans, for their wages seem actually to have fallen throughout the Hellenistic period. Renewed calls for a "clean slate," that is, for the cancellation of debts and the redivision of the land of the rich among all citizens, are well attested even in the fragmentary sources from which the history of the Hellenistic period has to be written.

Cities resorted to various devices—debt moratoria, subsidized purchases of grain to hold down the price of bread, and even in the case of Rhodes (Strabo, 14.2.5) the assigning of the care of the poor to individual members of the governing oligarchy as a liturgy—in the attempt to moderate the crisis. Its severity is clearly revealed by the example of third-century B.C. Sparta.

According to Plutarch (*Agis and Cleomenes* 5), land concentration and the closely connected rise in the disfranchisement and indebtedness of poorer Spartans had by the middle of the third century advanced to the point that of the 700 remaining Spartans only 100 possessed land and most of the rest were in debt. Hellenistic intellectuals such as the utopian writer Iamboulos located their ideal classless and strifeless societies at the ends of the earth; three remarkable Spartan kings, Agis IV (*ca.* 244–241 B.C.), Kleomenes III (235–221 B.C.), and Nabis (*ca.* 206–192 B.C.), found their ideal in the romanticized past of Lykurgan Sparta and its society of warrior "equals." Restoration of Sparta to that past and of its power and glory was their goal. To that end they implemented a series of radical reforms that, in addition to the restoration of the Lykurgan discipline, included the cancellation of debts, the reestablishment of the system of *kleroi* and their allocation to landless Spartans, and the expansion of the citizen body by the enfranchisement of certain metics. Ultimately, even some freed Helots were enfranchised.

The excitement the Spartan revolution aroused among debtors elsewhere in Greece is clear from the sympathetic account of the reformer kings Agis and Kleomenes by their contemporary, the Athenian historian Phylarchos (whose work Plutarch used as the basis for his *Agis and Cleomenes*). Later, the hostile treatment of Kleomenes III and Nabis by the second-century B.C. historian Polybius reveals the fear and hatred the revolution generated among Greek oligarchs who saw movements in sympathy with it spring up in their cities in the 220s B.C. and again in the 190s B.C. In the end, however, the aristocracies retained and strengthened their control of their cities by finding powerful protectors, first in the 220s B.C. in the person of Antigonos III Doson of Macedon, and in the second and first centuries B.C. in Rome, whose aristocratically dominated senate found in the Greek aristocracies congenial agents for the achievement of Roman goals in the Aegean basin. Rome's support was all the stronger because the Greek aristocracies' democratic opponents rallied successively to the cause of each of Rome's various enemies in the east, from Philip V of Macedon to Mithridates VI of Pontos.

BIBLIOGRAPHY

Good introductions to the theoretical and methodological problems involved in the study of the social history of ancient Greece are provided by: M. M. Austin and Pierre Vidal-Naquet, *Economic & Social History of Ancient Greece* (1977); Peter Burke, *Sociology and History* (1980); Moses I. Finley, *The Ancient Economy* (1973), and *Economy and Society in Ancient Greece,* Brent D. Shaw and Richard P. Saller, eds. (1981); Sally C. Humphreys, *Anthropology and the Greeks* (1978); Max Weber, *The Agrarian Sociology of Ancient Civilizations,* Richard I. Frank, trans. (1976).

Since World War II a number of general surveys of Greek society and its institutions have been published. Among the most useful are: Antony Andrewes, *The Greeks* (1967); Frank J. Frost, *Greek Society* (1971; 2d ed. 1980); Andrew Lintott, *Violence, Civil Strife, and Revolution in the Classical City* (1982).

Although comparatively less attention has been devoted to the ideological aspects of Greek social history, a number of general studies do exist, important examples of which are: M. T. W. Arnheim, *Aristocracy in Greek Society* (1977); Alison Burford, *Craftsmen in Greek and Roman Society* (1972); Geoffrey E. M. De Ste. Croix, *The Class Struggle in the Ancient Greek World* (1981); Walter Donlan, *The Aristocratic Ideal in Ancient Greece* (1980); Moses I. Finley, *Politics in the Ancient World* (1983); Arthur R. Hands, *Charities and Social Aid in Greece and Rome* (1968); Johannes Hasebroek, *Trade and Politics in Ancient Greece,* L. M. Fraser and D. C. MacGregor, trans. (1933); David Whitehead, *The Ideology of the Athenian Metic* (1977).

Since World War II by far the most extensive and creative work in the area of Greek social history has been devoted to the Dark Ages and archaic periods. For some of the most important resulting studies see: Alcaeus, in *Greek Lyric,* I, David A. Campbell, ed. and trans. (1982); Anakreon, in *Poetae Melici Graeci,* Denys L. Page, ed. (1962); Antony Andrewes, *The Greek Tyrants* (1956); David Asheri, "Laws of Inheritance, Distribution of Land and Political Constitutions in Ancient Greece," in *Historia, Zeitschrift für Alte Geschichte,* 12 (1963); *The Cambridge Ancient History,* III, pt. 3 (1925; 2d ed. 1982); Thomas J. Figueira, *Aegina: Society and Politics* (1981); Moses I. Finley, *The World of Odysseus* (1954; rev. ed. 1978); Frank J. Frost, "Tribal Politics and the Civic State," in *American Journal of Ancient History,* 1 (1976); pseudo-Xenophon, *Constitution of Athens,* in Truesdell S. Brown, *Ancient Greece* (1965); Simonides, in *Greek Lyric,* II, J. M. Edmonds, ed. and trans. (1924; repr. 1964); Solon, in *Greek Elegy and Iambus,* I, J. M. Edmonds, trans. (1931); Humphrey Michell, *Sparta* (1952); Anthony M. Snodgrass, *Archaic Greece* (1980); Chester G. Starr, *The Economic and Social Growth of Early Greece, 800–500 B.C.* (1977); Ronald F. Willetts, *Aristocratic Society in Ancient Crete* (1955).

In the resurgence of interest in the social history of ancient Greece the classical period has not been neglected, although scholarly attention has focused mainly on Athens. Starting points for further study are provided by: Stanley Mayer Burstein, *Outpost of Hellenism: The Emergence of Heraclea on the Black Sea* (1976); John K. Davies, *Democracy and Classical Greece* (1978), and *Wealth and the Power of Wealth in Classical Athens* (1981); Victor Ehrenberg, *The People of Aristophanes,* 3d rev. ed. (1962); Arnold H. M. Jones, *Athenian Democracy* (1957); Donald Lateiner, "An Analysis of Lysias' Political Defense Speeches," in *Rivista storica dell'antichità,* 11 (1981); Claude Mosse, *Athens in Decline 404–86 B.C.* (1973); Valentine Rose, *Aristotelis Fragmenta* (1886).

Good introductions to some of the main problems of the social history of the Hellenistic period are: Roger S. Bagnall, "Egypt, the Ptolemies and the Greek World," in *Bulletin of the Egyptological Seminar,* 3 (1981); Paul L. MacKendrick, *The Athenian Aristocracy 399 to 31 B.C.* (1969); Mikhail Rostovtzeff, *The Social and Economic History of the Hellenistic World* (1941); Benjamin Shimron, *Late Sparta: The Spartan Revolution 243–146 B.C.* (1972); William W. Tarn, "The Social Question in the Third Century," in his *The Hellenistic Age* (1923; repr. 1968).

Roman Class Structures and Relations

RICHARD P. SALLER

INTRODUCTION

Rome changed dramatically in the millennium from the regal period to the later empire, as its boundaries expanded and it became wealthier, with a more sophisticated culture. Naturally, these developments deeply influenced Roman society: the important categories of social rank changed, while the society became more highly differentiated. And yet some of the most basic features remained constant. Roman society was always starkly hierarchical, with the position of its privileged members formally recognized by the state and marked out in public by special dress. From the humble these privileged Romans expected overt displays of deference, most obvious in the rituals of the patron-client relationship. The poet Martial (*Epigrams* 2.68) wrote of his patron's demand to be addressed as *dominus et rex* (lord and king), titles that even early emperors avoided as arrogant and unnecessarily provocative. Though the terms varied from period to period, the humiliating, public subordination of the weak and humble to the great was found in every age.

Concomitant with this advertised social hierarchy was the absence of any serious egalitarian ideology of the sort we are so familiar with today. In a famous passage in his *On the Republic* (*De Republica* 1.43) Cicero explains the basic flaw of democracy in which each citizen has equal rights: "Equality itself is unfair, since it makes no distinctions in accordance with social rank (*dignitas*)." The same sentiment is found in other Roman authors of other periods (for example, Pliny the Younger, *Letters* 9.5). Of course, these writers were members of the privileged strata, and it might be expected that the humble took a different view. In fact, a different view is found in some Christian authors who for the first time put in writing, on a substantial scale, the feelings of the less fortunate in Roman society. They clearly resented what they perceived to be abuses by the rich and powerful, but there was never (to our knowledge) any widespread call for the demolition of the hierarchy and the privileges implicit in it, no widespread, serious thought, for instance, about the abolition of slavery.

The preceding remarks raise a point that

deserves emphasis: information about pre-Christian Roman society comes almost entirely from literary works composed by members of the elite who showed little interest in their social inferiors. This is reflected in modern historical scholarship, which has concentrated on the privileged, literate Romans. Recently, historians have paid more attention to the masses in the city of Rome and especially in the countryside. Nevertheless, the sources place narrow limits on what can be said with confidence about humble Romans, and this essay will devote a disproportionate amount of space to the privileged classes, which constituted much less than 1 percent of the population in classical times.

An account of Roman society can be given in terms of three types of social categories: order, status, and class. Orders are categories whose membership is formally defined by the state, such as the patriciate and plebs in early Rome, and later the senatorial and equestrian orders. Status groups are less precise categories based on the social estimation of a man's honor, or, to put it another way, people's perception of a man's prestige. In different societies that estimation will be influenced by different factors, such as respectability of family or education. There is no agreement among historians about the definition of class, but the principal class divisions, based on a man's place in economic production, are between owners of the means of production and nonowners, and then in the former group between those who live in leisure off the labor of others and those who work with their own means. Thus a great landowner using slaves or tenants to work his estate would be in one class, the peasant working his own small plot in another, the tenant in yet another class, and then the slave, who owned not even his own labor power, in the lowest class. Though these classification systems divide society in somewhat different ways, the criteria for assigning men to an order, status, or class are not wholly dissimilar in each. In particular, wealth was of fundamental importance in assessing a man's position in all three systems.

There has been increasingly rancorous debate recently about which of these systems is best for analyzing Roman society. This essay will use all three, in the belief that some aspects of Roman society are best understood in terms of class, some in terms of status, and some in terms of orders (which the Romans themselves focused on). Certainly the social hierarchy depended on class exploitation throughout Roman history, but within that context many conflicts and attitudes stemmed from status.

THE EARLY REPUBLIC

In the conventional historical accounts of early Rome (ancient and modern) the two main themes are military conquest and domestic social conflict in the form of a struggle by the plebeians to secure political and economic concessions from the dominant patricians. The problem for the modern skeptical historian is that much of the conventional account of this social conflict, based on the writings of Livy and Dionysius of Halicarnassus, is wholly unreliable. The writing of history at Rome began only centuries after the great events of the "Struggle of the Orders" occurred. The earliest Roman historians had had some documentary evidence at their disposal, particularly records of legislation, but historians such as Livy did not confine themselves to this meager material. They used their imaginations to elaborate far beyond what could be deduced from the evidence, producing a schematized, oversimplified account of the social history of early Rome. This has obliged modern historians to sift out the reliable from the unreliable elements of the conventional narrative, in reconstructing their own versions of the early social conflicts. Scholars continue to engage in this endeavor today, with wildly varying results depending on what each scholar chooses to identify as reliable. Some have even discarded the notion of struggle altogether. The following conservative account, based largely on legal evidence, makes no attempt to survey all of the hypotheses of modern scholars.

The most extensive and dependable document on early Roman society is the fragmentary law code known as the Twelve Tables, traditionally dated 451–450 B.C. In it the basic divisions in Roman society are discernible: patricians and plebeians are distinguished and prohibited from intermarrying; the Comitia Centuriata, in which citizens were separated into groups according to wealth, is mentioned; and slaves and freedmen are subjected to special rules. In addition, one of the dominant types of relationship between the classes, the patron-client bond, is protected as sacred.

As soon as an effort is made to move beyond this relatively solid starting point, the disagreement among historians begins—even over the basic question of definition of patricians and plebeians. Most would argue that the patricians were a closed circle of privileged families who claimed a monopoly of high office and priesthoods in the early Roman Republic. Thus the patriciate was a hereditary order that tried and failed to cut itself off as a caste from the rest of the population through the ban on intermarriage with plebeians in the Twelve Tables. The plebs are usually said to consist of all nonpatrician Romans. It has been argued that the social structure of the citizenry of early Rome was more complex, made up of three components: the patricians and their dependents (together constituting the *populus*) and then the plebs. The evidence for this challenging viewpoint is slender, and it presents difficulties: for instance, the ban on intermarriage is most easily understood in a context of two and only two mutually exclusive orders.

The Romans believed that the division between patricians and plebs went back to the founding of the city. There are strong reasons for skepticism about the legend associated with it. Nonpatrician names appear in the lists of kings and early consuls, suggesting that a closed circle of privileged families was not clearly defined from the beginning. The fact that in later times the *interrex* (the caretaker official between consuls) had to be a patrician makes it reasonably certain that the patrician order dates back to the regal period. A reasonable guess is that after the expulsion of the last king *ca.* 510 B.C. the existing patrician families attempted to close their order and to establish a monopoly of political, religious, and legal privileges. The attempt culminated in the ban on intermarriage in the Twelve Tables, which would have made them an exclusive ruling caste, but the ban was repealed after five years by the *Lex Canuleia* and the patrician monopoly of other privileges was gradually broken.

A corollary of this view is that the plebeian order emerged as a response on the part of the rest of the citizenry to patrician claims to exclusiveness, privilege, and authority. It is easy to envisage the early republican development of the plebeian "state within the state" (particularly the tribunate and the assembly or *concilium plebis*) in this context. By its very nature as a catchall, the plebs comprised men from all economic classes, from poor peasants and artisans to prosperous landowners who had not been able to establish their membership in the patriciate for one reason or another (perhaps an insufficiently distinguished lineage). The different class interests can be clearly discerned in the three types of issues pressed by the plebs. The wealthy plebeians were primarily concerned with establishing their right to hold high office, denied by the patricians though perhaps not explicitly in law. The mass of humble plebeians, for whom officeholding was not within the realm of possibility, were far more interested in the basic economic issues related to subsistence. Finally, the establishment of constitutional and legal rights was an issue that presumably affected rich and poor plebeians alike.

The disparate nature of plebeian interests must have been one of the reasons for the failure of the plebs consistently to unite in order to challenge the dominance of the patricians, who were a small minority. In addition, the influence of patricians over their plebeian clients must have discouraged a section of the plebs from pressing their demands. Only five times in more than two centuries, according to tradition, did the plebeians make use of their most effective weapon against patrician power, the secession, that is, withdrawal from the city. During the first century and a half of the republic plebeian successes were political and legal: the organization and recognition of plebeian institutions, the tribunate, and the plebeian assembly, in the first half of the fifth century B.C.; the publication of substantive law in the form of the Twelve Tables; and the election of plebeians to the consular tribunate and quaestorship in the second half of the fifth century.

The most far-reaching single success for the plebs came in 367–366 B.C. in the Licinian-Sextian laws, which also neatly illustrate the underlying class divisions within their ranks. The laws had political and economic aspects. For the benefit of wealthy and ambitious plebeians, their right to hold the highest magistracy in Rome, the consulship, was guaranteed. The concerns of poor plebeians were met by measures for debt relief and for limiting the amount of public land that any single Roman could occupy. Land distribution and debt were contentious issues between rich and poor Romans throughout the duration of the republic.

As Rome expanded in Italy part of the newly conquered land was designated public land (*ager publicus*), which could be occupied by Roman citizens for minimal rent. The powerful managed to lay claim to a disproportionate share of the land, which prompted the poor at various times to seek a more equal distribution either by laws granting individual plots to humble citizens or, as in the Licinian-Sextian legislation, by limiting the amount of land any single wealthy Roman could occupy, in order to free part of it for others.

The recurrence of debt as an inflammatory social issue is no surprise in view of the harshness of Roman institutions and laws of debt, particularly *nexum* and *manus iniectio.* For peasant farmers living at the level of bare subsistence, which is common in an undeveloped agricultural economy, bad years required that they starve or borrow from the wealthy, who were able to store surplus. The poor peasant might take out a straight loan, to be repaid with interest after the following harvest. But since his production was only marginally above his needs in good times, it was likely that the next harvest would not provide enough beyond his needs to pay off his debt with interest. Several consecutive poor harvests could be disastrous. If the poor man were unable to repay the loan, he faced the legal procedure described in the Twelve Tables, *manus iniectio* (literally, the laying on of a hand). Under this procedure the creditor was entitled to seize the debtor and, if no one came forward to pay the debt, to sell him into slavery abroad or to inflict capital punishment. In contrast to modern debt law with its mild civil procedure, default on debt in Rome was a crime with the gravest consequences.

To avoid the *manus iniectio* procedure for default, a poor man taking a loan could put himself into debt-bondage under his creditor—a condition called *nexum* in which the debtor paid the interest and perhaps the capital with his labor. The differences between *nexum* and *manus iniectio* should be stressed: *nexum* was the result of taking a loan and involved bondage in Rome; *manus iniectio* proceeded from failure to repay a loan and resulted in death or sale into slavery outside of Rome. (Roman citizens could not be kept as chattel-slaves in Rome.)

In the context of these harsh debt laws, the Licinian-Sextian reform provided only temporary relief. Interest paid to creditors before passage of the law was applied against the capital, the remainder of which was to be paid in three annual installments. The law did nothing to ameliorate the precarious position of subsistence farmers, who continued to be forced into debt, nor did it alter the oppressive debt laws. Consequently, debt resurfaced as a social and political problem repeatedly in the decades following the reforms, and new laws were passed to limit interest rates and to provide for the repayment of debts.

Through the Licinian-Sextian laws, then, the plebeians won notable political and economic concessions from the patricians, and more were gained in the following decades. The plebeian elite gradually won access to nearly all the important magistracies and priesthoods (the censorship in 351 B.C., the praetorship in 337, and the priesthoods in 300). For the poor plebeians the *Lex Poetelia* (ca. 326 B.C.) abolished the institution of *nexum*. The impact of the law is far from clear. On the one hand, the Roman law of debt remained harsh: default was still regarded as a crime for which the penalty granted by a court could be personal execution (that is, the creditor could take control of the debtor's person and force him to work off the debt in bondage). On the other hand, it seems clear that in the later Roman Republic and early Roman Empire the peasantry was not by and large a tied peasantry, as it was under the late Roman colonate. So it may be that the abolition of *nexum* represented a not negligible advance in the independence of a section of the poorest plebeians.

The year 287 B.C. is traditionally identified as the date of the end of the Struggle of the Orders. By a final secession the plebs forced the patricians to acknowledge that the decisions of the plebeian assembly (*plebiscita*) had the force of law for the whole state. Some radically skeptical historians today, rightly pointing out the highly schematic nature of the ancient accounts of the Struggle, have dismissed it altogether. But in general outline it seems plausible: the sources of tension and conflict are very similar to those found in better documented archaic Mediterranean societies. The institutions of debt-bondage in the Near East were not very different in their results from Roman *nexum*. The principal issues of contention in Solonian Athens were more or less the same as those in Rome: codification of the law, abolition of debt-bondage, and breaking the monopoly of office held by a limited circle of aristocratic families. The vital difference between archaic Athens and Rome is that the Solonian and later reforms produced an independent Athenian peasantry able to achieve thoroughgoing democracy, whereas at Rome the citizen masses never gained control of the state despite the legal validity of *plebiscita*. This raises the question of whether the plebeians really achieved a victory in the Struggle of the Orders.

Far from losing power in the Struggle, the patricians preserved it by sharing it with wealthy plebeians. In this way they co-opted the leaders of the opposition without whom the humble plebeians had no one to raise or press their interests in the assemblies. Before the admission of plebeians to high office, the patrician-plebeian division cut across class divisions. From the later fourth century B.C. onward, the patricians and wealthiest plebeians together formed a nobility that coincided with economic divisions in society and was open to newcomers with the necessary resources. This ability to absorb new men into the aristocracy—at first rich plebeians and the elite from other Italian municipalities, and then the rich and powerful from the provinces—contributed to Rome's impressive social and political durability over centuries.

EXPANSION AND THE GROWTH OF WEALTH

With wealthy plebeians no longer ready to press the interests of the poor in order to win support for their own goals, the lower classes were relatively quiet for the century and a half after 287 B.C. Almost constant warfare also contributed to social stability in the short term. The spoils of victory were enormous and, as long as they were shared, adequate to keep most Romans satisfied. Aside from booty, part of the newly conquered land was used for the settlement of colonies, thus satisfying the land hunger of poorer Romans. Whatever the overt intention behind colonization in this period—it may well have been military security—the effect was to move tens of thousands of Romans to new areas, thus relieving the pressure on land in Latium. This population movement took place largely without a political struggle at Rome. The notable exception was the action of the populist tribune of 232 B.C., Gaius Flaminius. Though senatorial approval of legislative bills was no longer strictly necessary, it had remained customary. Flaminius pushed through the assembly a law providing for individual (*viritim*) grants of land in the Po valley without the senate's approval, and so provoked an outpouring of senatorial hostility.

After the decisive defeat of the Carthaginians in the Second Punic War, the Roman military machine established Roman dominance across the Mediterranean with a speed that was striking to contemporary Greeks. This very success produced enormous social and cultural changes within Roman society that undermined the traditional sources of military manpower and eventually the republic itself. As a result of conquests much of the accumulated wealth of Mediterranean lands flowed into Rome. Though all soldiers might hope for a share of the booty, the profits were concentrated overwhelmingly in the hands of the propertied classes: as generals and officers they received a lion's share of the booty; as governors they could use their power to extort large sums from subject peoples; as members of tax collection companies they lined their pockets with massive profits from collecting the state's tribute.

The influx of wealth served to exaggerate the differences between rich and poor. Part of the riches were expended on luxury items to be displayed in an attempt to buy or preserve social status. Competition in conspicuous consumption was surely one of the causes of the increasing disregard of social norms among aristocrats in their drive to acquire even greater riches. In response, sumptuary legislation was passed in the early second century to control lavish expenditure by citizens (for instance, laws limiting the size of banquets), but they had little effect.

More important for its influence on the social structure of Italy is the fact that much of the profit was invested in Italian land to provide a continuing income. Since there was not enough good land still unoccupied in Italy, this investment required the dispossession of small landowners on a considerable scale. The conquests also provided the rich with a new and more profitable source of labor in the form of slaves. Slavery had been part of the economy of Italy before the Second Punic War, but the wars of conquest in the second and first centuries B.C. produced a massive population movement that changed the shape of the social structure dramatically. It has been estimated that by the Augustan Age there were three million slaves working in Italy—more than 40 percent of the total population.

Insofar as the wars yielded large numbers of cheap slaves, Roman peasant-soldiers had to struggle to retain their place in Italian agriculture. The pressures on many peasants to sell their small plots were irresistible. The age-old precariousness of their existence worsened as year after year large numbers of them were sent out of Italy for army service. As a rough guide, it has been estimated that more than half of Italian adult males may have served for more than five years of their lives during the second century B.C. Until 170 B.C. the process of dispossession of the peasantry was offset to some degree by settlements of colonies, but after this date the policy of colonization was abandoned by the senate for several decades. Consequently, the level of social discontent rose as the size of the rural proletariat grew.

The decades after 167 B.C. (where Livy's narrative breaks off) are relatively poorly documented, but a few symptoms of the underlying social tensions can nevertheless be detected. The census figures for these decades show a declining number of citizens with enough property to be eligible for military service. As long as the wars abroad offered hope of considerable booty, military recruitment was not difficult. The war against Spanish tribes, which reopened in 154 B.C., was, however, long, tiresome, and unprofitable. The resistance to levies of consuls came to a head in 151 and 138 B.C. with the unprecedented jailing of the consuls by the plebeian tribunes in an effort to protect men from conscription. These were small indications that ordinary citizens were less willing to spend years fighting without regard to their own interests in wars that enriched principally the upper classes.

This increasing assertion of an independent will is also apparent in laws of 139, 137, and 131 B.C. providing for secret ballots in the assemblies. Before these reforms the elite could watch the voting of their followers and dependents to be certain that they voted as instructed. Cicero later asked rhetorically, in *On Laws* (*De Legibus* 3.34), "Who does not believe that the ballot law took away all influence from good, propertied men?" He is, of course, exaggerating the effects of ballot reform. Means of circumventing the laws were found and the influence of the aristocracy over the voting masses continued, but with diminished force as a result of social and economic developments. Though the process is difficult to document, it seems clear that the displacement of the peasants and their migration—some to cities, others to the countryside as casual laborers—must have disrupted the traditional vertical ties holding Roman society together (particularly patron-client and landlord-tenant bonds). Patrons and clients by no means disappeared, but there was a growing group of poor voters who would respond to appeals on the basis of class interest, men unrestrained by propertied patrons and later labeled by Tacitus "the vile plebs" (*Histories* 1.14).

For a time the aristocracy was able to suppress the discontent of the increasingly alienated masses. By the very nature of the political system, leadership in reform had to come from senatorial magistrates, and peer pressure discouraged senators from taking up the cause. Gaius Laelius (died after 130 B.C.), recognizing the undesirable effects of the replacement of peasants by slaves on the land, considered bringing forward a bill for land distribution, but his senatorial friends convinced him to drop it.

REFORM IN THE LATE REPUBLIC

The necessary aristocratic leadership emerged to champion the popular cause in the teeth of fierce senatorial opposition in 133

B.C., the year marking the beginning of a century of domestic upheaval that ended in the collapse of the republic. The most prominent figures were Tiberius Gracchus (tribune in 133 B.C.) and his brother, Gaius (tribune in 123 and 122 B.C.). The motives of the Gracchi and their senatorial opponents have been hotly debated by modern historians. Some view their land reforms as inspired by a conservative desire to reinforce the declining military manpower reserves in the countryside; others believe that the Gracchi were ambitious, selfish politicians willing to do anything to win a popular following; still others see the brothers as committed leaders of the poor in the class struggle. Those historians who think the issue was essentially political argue that opposition among senators had little to do with protection of their own economic interests, but was provoked by the unorthodox political methods of the Gracchi; for other historians the hostility is to be explained by the threat to aristocratic possession of public land presented by the reforms. Fortunately, the motives on either side, which may have been mixed and which today are concealed beneath the exaggerated rhetoric of the time, are not vitally important here.

Whatever his personal motives, Tiberius Gracchus must have appealed to the humble citizens on the basis of their own class interests—otherwise it is impossible to understand why the tribal assembly decided to proceed against the powerful authority of the senate and to approve the reforms. The words of Cicero, one of the earliest surviving sources for the Gracchan program, reflect the class division between the rich and the masses: "Tiberius Gracchus proposed an agrarian law; it was pleasing to the people (*populus*); the fortunes of the humble appeared to be established; the propertied, good men were strongly opposed to it, because they both saw that discord was aroused and, since the rich (*locupletes*) would be moved from their traditional possessions, they judged that the state would be deprived of its champions" (*On Behalf of Sestius* [*Pro Sestio*] 103). The resentment of a circle of senators was in fact so intense that the political infighting escalated to the point of violence. When Tiberius sought an unconventional second term as tribune, he was killed in mob violence by a band of senatorial vigilantes.

Despite Gracchus' death, the senate did not try to repeal his popular measures in the assembly. The new law provided for a limit on individual holdings of public land (500 *iugera*, or 312 acres, plus 156 acres for each child); excess holdings were then to be distributed to the poor in lots of 30 *iugera* (about 19 acres) or less by a land commission. Our main sources consistently indicate that the rural poor (not the urban proletariat) were the supporters of Gracchus and the intended beneficiaries of the distribution, but they disagree on the matter of whether only Roman citizens or all Italians were eligible to receive a plot. Most historians have taken the view that if the citizen assembly was voting in its self-interest, the distribution must have been limited to citizens. But recently it has been shown that on previous occasions Romans had been willing to include Latins and Italians in land distributions after first giving them citizenship, a legal prerequisite for ownership of Roman land. On this view, the transfer of some Italians to the Roman citizen body may explain the angry response of local Italian aristocrats who anticipated greater difficulty in meeting Roman demands for troops with a declining local manpower base. Alternatively, hostility may have been aroused by the land commission's encroachment on land that was *ager publicus* but had been long held by Italian aristocrats. In the end the Roman and Italian elites were apparently successful in obstructing the activities of the land commission, and it might have seemed that they won a victory. From a financial point of view the interests of the propertied class were largely protected, but from a political perspective the events of 133 B.C. proved that the constitutional machinery was incapable of settling the differences between rich and poor short of violence.

When Gaius Gracchus was elected tribune ten years after his brother and reelected in the following year, he pressed for a more wide-ranging reform program, addressing not only the class issue raised by his brother, but also problems that had emerged from distinctions of order in the intervening decade. Like his brother, Gaius sought to meet the needs of the rural poor with a revival of distributions by the land commission. In addition, he secured legislation for the foundation of colonies in Italy and on the site of Carthage. The latter was the first Roman colony outside Italy and was a forerunner of others that eventually eased tensions in Italy arising from a shortage of land.

The urban poor in Rome had shown no great interest in being resettled on farms; rather, their principal concern was the supply of basic foodstuffs at reasonable prices in Rome. The variations in availability of grain through the agricultural cycle and between years caused wild fluctuations in prices, which could prove disastrous to urban dwellers on the edge of subsistence. As Rome grew into an urban center of hundreds of thousands, a huge city by premodern standards, the grain supply became a recurring source of political tensions. Gaius Gracchus attempted to deal with the problem by having the state build storage facilities, in order to smooth out fluctuations in supply, and sell grain at subsidized prices.

Gaius did not restrict his reforms to the class interests of the poor. Two other measures served to increase the separation of the two leading orders of the state, senators and equestrians. Before 129 B.C. these two groups of wealthy citizens were mixed together in the highest census classification, the eighteen *centuriae* of those granted a "public horse" for cavalry service. By a law of 129 B.C. senators and their families were excluded from these *centuriae*, making the remaining nonsenatorial wealthy members a clearly distinct order. The most prominent members of this second order were *publicani*, the public contractors whose sense of common interests made them a formidable special interest group. Gaius favored the *publicani* with a law giving them the lucrative job of collecting tribute in the recently annexed province of Asia. The whole order of equestrians (knights, of whom many were not *publicani*) benefited from Gaius' transfer of the privilege of jury service from senators to themselves.

This measure remains problematic for historians on two counts. First, it is unclear whether the jurors were drawn from equestrians in the narrow sense of those with a public horse (supplied and maintained by the state) or all nonsenatorial citizens who possessed not less than 400,000 sesterces; second, it is uncertain whether only juries for cases of extortion by senatorial officials were affected or other juries as well (if such existed at the time). Whatever the answer to these problems, the extortion court was the focus of tension between the two elite orders for the next fifty years until a compromise was reached in 70 B.C. whereby both orders provided jurors. The power of equestrian juries to condemn senators after a provincial tour of duty was a potential source of unhealthy influence, as demonstrated by the notorious case of the consul Publius Rutilius Rufus in 92 B.C. An equestrian jury unjustly convicted and exiled him allegedly for extortion but really because as a senatorial legate of the governor of Asia he aided the governor in suppressing abuses by greedy equestrian tax collectors. Despite such a blatant miscarriage of justice, it is important not to exaggerate the conflict between the two leading orders: it was not fundamental in the way that the division between rich and poor was. Senators and equestrians were tied together by kinship and friendship, by common cultural interests, and, above all, by a shared goal of protection of their propertied interests. Tensions occasionally surfaced in regard to jury service or public contracts, but the senatorial and equestrian orders consistently stood together against threats to the social order and property rights.

A different and more serious conflict based on legal status had flared up a few years before Gaius' tribunate. The land law of Tiberius Gracchus made possession of citizenship a more acute issue among the Italian allies (though the precise reason is not altogether clear). In response to Italian unrest Fulvius Flaccus, consul of 125 B.C., proposed a bill offering the Italians a choice between full Roman citizenship and remaining independent with the additional protection of the Right of Appeal (*ius provocationis*). The bill did not find support in the senate or the voting public and was abandoned. The strength of Italian feeling toward this intransigence was revealed by a futile revolt by the frustrated Latin colony Fregellae. The rebellion was quickly crushed and the colony razed, but the issue remained for the reformer Gaius. The sources, though not altogether consistent and clear, suggest that Gaius called for the grant of citizenship to those of Latin status, and then Latin status for the Italian allies. With his other reforms Gaius appealed to the self-interest of one section of voters or another, but his franchise bill would have benefited only those outside the citizen body. Consequently it failed, and more generally Gaius' popular support was undermined by the populist counterproposals of the tribune Livius Drusus. Drusus' proposals, which turned out to be insincere demagoguery, were enough to stop Gaius' attempt to win a third term as tribune. When Gaius, accompanied by an armed band, tried to prevent the repeal of his legislation in 121 B.C., violence once again broke out and he met the same fate as his brother.

The Gracchan reforms, unsuccessful in the short term, revealed with stark clarity the basic divisions in Roman society and the conflicts that had to be resolved over the following century before social stability could be reestablished. The land-military manpower nexus came to the fore again within a generation in the activities of the great general Gaius Marius. In order to raise troops for his campaign against the Numidian king Jugurtha, Marius dropped the traditional property requirement in his recruitment of citizens in 107 B.C. This was the final step in a long trend toward the recruitment of poor citizens in the army. The enlistment of the rural poor (both the proletariat and those just above the minimal property requirement for the fifth class in the centuriate assembly) might have presented no danger if the senate had arranged for their land hunger to be satisfied upon discharge. The insensitive senate, however, left it to Marius to take care of his veterans. Through the agency of the tribune Lucius Appuleius Saturninus, Marius secured the agrarian legislation needed to settle his men. In the end Saturninus became too radical and violent for the taste of Marius, who at the senate's request used force to suppress him. Marius was not the man to challenge the republic itself, but he revealed how a popular, successful commander with the support of a tribune could propose legislation that would provide land grants for his soldiers—a combination of constitutional and raw power against which the senate was ultimately helpless.

THE CIVIL WARS

The matter of citizenship for the Italians had been left unsettled by Gaius Gracchus and

Livius Drusus. Some Italians managed surreptitiously to have their names placed on the roll of citizens, provoking a Roman law in 95 B.C. that established an inquisition to identify offenders. As a result, Italians' resentment against their exclusion from the citizen body mounted until another tribune, Livius Drusus (son of the aforementioned), took up their cause in 91 B.C. His attempt to put together a coalition of interests within the electorate to vote for the grant of citizenship met with strong opposition and collapsed when he was assassinated. Left with no peaceful alternative, the Italians took up arms in the "Social War," so called because it pitted Rome against her Italian *socii,* or allies. It was not a conflict over basic class interests, and this is no doubt the reason why the war could be brought to an end after a few years of bloody fighting with the Romans conceding citizenship (despite their habit of refusing to compromise in war).

The outcome of the Social War set the stage for the first round of full-scale civil war between the Roman senatorial generals, Marius and Sulla. In order to limit the influence of the new Italian voters in the assembly, they were enrolled in a minority of the tribes. A tribune of 88 B.C., Publius Sulpicius Rufus, in an effort to rectify the inequitable distribution, sought the support of Marius, who in return was to receive the lucrative eastern command against Mithridates through a law proposed by the tribune. One of the senate's traditional obstructionist methods, the suspension of public business, was used to try to prevent the legislation from being passed. The response was mob violence to drive off the obstructors. Up to this point the incident followed a pattern seen before: constitutional move and countermove escalating to mob violence. On this occasion, however, Sulla, an obstructor who had been deprived of the eastern command and driven from Rome, refused to accept the result of the mob action. He joined his troops in Campania and, by hinting that the change of command in favor of Marius would deprive them of the opportunity to plunder Asia, convinced his soldiers to march against Marius in Rome. In the subsequent fighting, Sulla's army established his dominance long enough for him to regain his command. As soon as Sulla left for the east, Marian forces retook Rome in a bloodbath, only to lose it to Sullan forces again in another bloodbath five years later. On the surface this round of the civil wars was a struggle between two ambitious senators, not a class struggle. But at a deeper level it is clear that the civil war would not have happened without a context of social unrest: the consuls lost control of the constitutional procedure in Rome because of urban violence, and Sulla was able to use his army against the city owing to the troops' lack of regard for the general welfare of the state. That land hunger was a significant factor lurking behind the overt aristocratic competition is shown by the bloody aftermath of Sulla's final victory. With the excuse of eliminating his enemies, Sulla proscribed scores of senators and hundreds of equestrians, confiscating their property. The numbers were so high because large tracts of confiscated land were needed to satisfy the veterans. In short, Sulla established the precedent of using an army loyal to its general to further personal political ambitions through violence, while the poor soldiers discovered civil war to be a means of obtaining a redistribution of Italian land for their own benefit. The latter clearly acted out of self-interest, not a sense of class consciousness: small farmers as well as rich forfeited land to the Sullan settlers, a process that replaced an old class of discontented landless with a new one.

Sulla recognized that the republic could not survive if others followed his precedent, and so before resigning his dictatorship he instituted a series of reforms designed to stabilize the state and to restrain ambitious individuals like himself. Senatorial commanders were prohibited from leaving their province with their army without senatorial approval; tribunes' powers to veto and to propose legislation were restricted, while tribunes themselves were barred from running for higher magistracies (a deterrent to the ambitious who might have contemplated using or abusing the office). The net result of the reforms, it was hoped, would be the reinforcement of the senate's dominant, conservative role in politics, but they were unlikely to be effective as long as competitive politicians could appeal to an electorate and a soldiery with serious social grievances. In the words of the distinguished historian Ronald Syme (1939), "Sulla could not abolish his own example."

During the three decades following Sulla's retirement the Roman propertied classes cooperated to suppress scattered overt threats to the social hierarchy from below. The first came shortly after Sulla's death and was the result of his disturbance of land ownership. Called upon by dispossessed farmers in Etruria, the consul of 78 B.C. Aemilius Lepidus took up their cause and challenged the senate's authority with an army, demanding various reforms. The senate saw to it that Lepidus' uprising was crushed, but did so by entrusting an extraordinary command to the young Pompey (Gnaeus Pompeius Magnus). This ambitious politician used his army again later in the decade to suppress a social rebellion of a different kind, the slave uprising under the leadership of Spartacus (73–71 B.C.). The seriousness of the latter revolt is indicated by its duration and the fact that ten legions became involved in putting it down. A decade later trouble surfaced again in Etruria. The ancient sources treat it as one manifestation of a broad conspiracy organized in Rome in 63 B.C. by the unsuccessful senator Catiline, but some historians have recently doubted this. Cicero, consul in 63 B.C., is the main contemporary source for the conspiracy and had an interest in magnifying its extent in order to increase his own credit for suppressing it. With this in mind, some historians today argue that the wide scope and cohesion of the conspiracy were largely figments of Cicero's rhetoric. However that may be, the urban side of the plot, if there was one, came to nothing, and the only significant revolt was raised in Etruria by disgruntled peasants, joined by Sullan veterans unhappy with the poor quality of land granted to them. These desperate men, formed into two legions by Catiline and in some cases carrying only pointed sticks as weapons, fought to the bitter end in a hopeless contest against a fully equipped consular army.

None of these uprisings had any real chance of success against the organized state forces, largely because in the absence of a unifying ideology the lower classes could put up only scattered, hastily organized opposition. Spartacus and his fellow slaves were fighting to return to their native lands, while the peasants and veterans in Etruria were struggling for a decent plot of land, pointedly excluding slaves from their cause (Sallust, *The War with Catiline* 56.5). There was apparently no serious thought of a social revolution in which all lower classes could unite in the hope of a new social order. How little the various groups of poor citizens perceived themselves to have common interests is well illustrated by the fate of the land distribution bill proposed by the tribune Publius Servilius Rullus in 63 B.C. As consul Cicero was able to have the bill defeated and to protect the property of the rich by manipulating poor urban voters with the argument that since they had no desire to face the hardships of farming themselves, they had no reason to support the interests of their rural counterparts.

If the upper classes stood together against threats to property from below, they did not cooperate to resist alteration and repeal of parts of the Sullan reforms. After some dissension the senate fully restored the powers of the tribunate in 70 B.C. Though the restoration was not expected to be subversive, the resulting loss of senatorial control over appointments to military commands was soon apparent. The tribune of 67 B.C., Aulus Gabinius, proposed an extraordinary command for Pompey to deal with the serious problem of piracy, which had badly disrupted trade in the Mediterranean and, in particular, Rome's food supply. The senate, unwilling to see repeated extraordinary commands in the hands of ambitious politicians like Pompey, tried to obstruct Gabinius' bill by putting up tribunes to veto it. The urban populace was in no mood to tolerate constitutional niceties in the midst of a food shortage: their threat of violence against senators, and Gabinius' threat to have opposing tribunes removed from office, frightened off potential opposition and the command was given to Pompey. After his striking success against the pirates, Pompey was given another extraordinary command against Mithridates VI by a popular law of the following year. That law was passed without serious incident, perhaps because senators wished to avoid another confrontation.

The opposition to Pompey was reserved for 62 B.C., when the general returned victorious from the East. For two years a group of conservative senators succeeded in preventing Pompey from securing a land bill to settle his veterans and ratification of his political arrangements in the East. Despite Pompey's deeply felt desire for respect from the old senatorial families, the opposition of the politically conservative optimates drove him to an agreement in 60 or early 59 B.C. with the populist politicians Gaius Julius Caesar and Marcus Licinius Crassus in what became known as the First Triumvirate. Some historians from antiquity and later take this agreement to signal the end of the republic. That is an exaggeration, but the agreement did represent a large step in the senate's loss of control of events and particularly army commands. Caesar was elected consul for 59 B.C. and with the aid of the tribune Vatinius brought a series of bills before the assembly, including a land bill for Pompey's veterans and other poor citizens and a change of assignment for himself from the forests of Italy to Cisalpine Gaul and Illyricum (to which Transpadane Gaul, or that part of Italy north of the Po, was shortly added). The obstructionist methods previously used by the senate to restrain populist politicians were tried again: Caesar's colleague as consul, Marcus Calpurnius Bibulus, attempted to bring the proceedings to a halt on religious grounds, but was driven from the assembly by the strong-arm tactics of Pompey's veterans in need of land. As a result, the veterans were decisive in seeing to it that the land bill was passed, and Caesar received the Gallic command that a decade later provided both the spark for civil war and the resources with which Caesar won.

During Caesar's two five-year commands in Gaul urban violence in Rome escalated as populist senators became increasingly aware of the power to be acquired from a combination of legislative programs in favor of the urban poor and political organizations among them. The leading figure was Cicero's enemy Publius Clodius Pulcher. After having himself adopted from a patrician into a plebeian family in order to be eligible, Clodius won the tribunate for 58 B.C. In the years prior to his election the senate had evidently seen potential dangers from the disaffected urban masses and tried to prevent trouble by banning *collegia* (neighborhood and religious cult associations, which could be used politically against senatorial authority) and by offering more subsidized grain to the urban citizenry. As tribune, Clodius proposed legislation to reverse the 64 B.C. ban on *collegia,* to provide a grain dole without any charge to all urban citizens, and to prevent the use of religious obstructions by higher magistrates against tribunes' activities. The bills were passed, giving Clodius a broad popularity among the urban masses and a means of organizing armed violence in the city beyond any level previously seen. In response, another senator, Titus Annius Milo, recruited his own gang. Rome had experienced urban riots before the 50s, but not in recent times with the persistence that in that decade repeatedly disrupted assemblies and in two years prevented consular elections from being held for months until after the beginning of the usual term of office. The climax was reached in early 52 B.C. when Milo's gang killed Clodius, whose body was then cremated by his urban supporters, who used the senate house as a pyre. As in the crises of the 70s B.C., the senate was forced to turn to Pompey to restore order, this time as sole consul. Peace was established by his troops and Milo went into exile, but the stage was set for the struggle between Pompey and Caesar in two respects. Pompey was beginning to cooperate with a group of conservative senators determined to bring Caesar down, and Pompey's prestige was now so high that Caesar was unable to accept any diminution of his own position that might leave him second in *dignitas* to Pompey. Despite the wishes of the vast majority of the senate, Caesar's enemies refused compromise and in 49 B.C. drew Pompey into the civil war that proved fatal to the republic. Caesar's veteran legions, enriched by Gallic booty and looking forward to donatives and land, fought for Caesar's victory, apparently unhindered by thoughts of a higher loyalty to the state.

THE FALL OF THE REPUBLIC

As in the civil war of the 80s, the destruction of the republic in the 40s was the result of competition between leading senators for position and prestige; but, as before, the competition would not have reached a ruinous level of violence if the soldiers had not followed these aristocrats, on whom they depended for land and booty. The part of the urban masses in the demise of the republic has been rated by some historians as relatively unimportant. It is true that the urban mob's power in violent confrontations was no match for trained troops and that the urban riots, though disruptive, would not by themselves have been fatal to the republic. Nevertheless, had it not been for urban violence at certain critical junctures (for example, in 88, 67, and 52 B.C.), the senate might have maintained its control of the constitutional machinery through various obstructionist techniques and, consequently, its influence in the all-important selection of commanders. Thus urban as well as rural poor played critical parts in the sequence of events leading to Caesar's crossing of the Rubicon in 49 B.C.

Many in Italy believed Caesar to be siding with the disaffected and saw his victory as one on behalf of the oppressed. There were calls for abolition of debts, which had been exacerbated by the currency shortage during the civil war. But Caesar's victory was a factional one and his reforms were a mixed blessing for the poor. On the one hand, a year's rent was remitted for inhabitants of Rome and past interest payments were allowed to count against as much as a quarter of the capital borrowed—benefits to the indebted of all classes. On the other hand, Caesar reduced drastically the number of recipients on the urban grain dole (from 320,000 to 150,000). Like previous victorious generals, Caesar had to settle his veterans. Sulla had made the mistake of doing this by dispossessing existing Italian landowners and so perpetuating unrest in the countryside. Caesar also granted his veterans land in Italy, but took the further step of moving large numbers of rural and urban poor to land in the provinces.

Caesar was assassinated in 44 B.C. in spite of his moderation in reform and his clemency toward his opponents. After his assassins were defeated in 42 B.C., there was an open fight for political power between factions of his followers. His heir, Octavius (Augustus), won at the cost of enormous suffering. Caesar's policy of clemency was ignored in favor of Sulla's expedient precedent of proscribing many rich Italians in order to seize their property. In addition, whole towns were dispossessed and their land given to veterans. The anguish caused by this process is poignantly expressed in the first and ninth eclogues of the poet Vergil, one of the many whose land was confiscated. Vergil's Meliboeus is portrayed in a state of wretched anxiety, uncertain where he will go after being forced off his land in a world in such turmoil that mothers no longer care for their young (*Eclogue* 1.11 ff.).

THE AUGUSTAN PRINCIPATE

After his victory, Augustus, a consummate politician, set about dealing with the roots of political and social upheaval in Italy. For the rural poor he continued Caesar's program of overseas colonies. After the settlement of the civil war veterans, he established a regular program of land distribution to soldiers on retirement, to be paid for by a 5-percent inheritance tax on citizens. Though the wealthy grumbled, this was a small price to pay to shift the veterans' reliance on commanders to the state. More than a quarter of a million free adult males were resettled outside of Italy in this process from 45 to 8 B.C. —a demographic shift that largely relieved the pressure on Italian land resulting from its concentration in the hands of the rich and the importation of slave labor. Provincials no doubt suffered loss of property, but (from the ruler's point of view) at least the discontent was moved away from the center of political power. Augustus sought to eradicate the endemic urban violence, in part by more systematic attention to the basic needs of urban dwellers and in part by more systematic use of force: permanent government machinery was established to manage the importation and distribution of grain and a standing police force (the urban cohorts) was organized for the first time in Rome.

These measures served to ease social unrest among the poor in Rome and Italy, producing an equilibrium for centuries. The sense of legitimacy desired by Augustus for his new regime, however, could come only from the support of the elite orders. During the civil wars it had been expedient to reward supporters with admission to the senate, as a result of which Augustus found himself with a bloated senate of doubtful respectability afterward. Augustus could not of course resuscitate the old republican noble families killed off in the wars, but he did try to reestablish the standing of the senatorial order by instituting a new property requirement of one million sesterces for senators (higher than the old one, which had not distinguished them from *equites*), by purging unworthy members from the senate, and by prohibiting demeaning marriages between members of the senatorial order and freedmen. These new measures revived respect for the traditional ordering of society. If the senate did not enjoy real political power under the principate, senators could console themselves with individual honors and the thought that their position at the top of the social hierarchy was recognized and reinforced.

Augustus marked out a more distinctive position in the new regime for the second order as well. As in the republic, the equestrian order comprised citizens with property worth 400,000 sesterces (whether the grant of the public horse was also necessary is open to debate). The "flower of the order" in the republic were the tax farmers (*publicani*), who had no official position in government but were highly visible and esteemed because of their political influence as a special-interest group. Augustus began to appoint equestrians to public and private administrative posts in his service so that the honor and prestige of the leading men of the order came to depend directly on the emperor. In addition, Augustus sought to raise the standing of the order as a whole through a revision of the equestrian roll and the revival of ceremonial parades to review equestrians in Rome (the *transvectio*).

The early imperial historian Velleius Paterculus wrote of the enthusiastic reaction to Augustus as the figure who restored respect for traditional authority, religion, and property rights (*History* 2.89). His view was colored by his obsequiousness to the throne, but it is true that social stability prevailed for more than two centuries after Augustus' reforms. This stability and the greater wealth of information invite the historian to examine the relatively static social pyramid of the principate in more detail (rather than analyzing a series of crises, as for the republican period).

THE IMPERIAL SOCIAL ORDER

The Senatorial Class

The leisure class of the empire was made up of the top three orders: senatorial, equestrian, and curial (local town councillors). The senatorial order included senators, their families, and descendants to the third generation. The size of the senate stabilized at about 600. If the population of the empire was of the order of fifty million, then the senatorial order constituted only a few thousandths of one percent of the population, in which was concentrated enormous power and wealth. Although the senate as a whole lost most of its power under the emperors, individual senators were still entrusted with high office and the major military commands. The trend of ever-greater accumulations of wealth continued from the republic. Senators like Pliny the Younger who considered themselves modestly well off had twenty times the minimum senatorial census requirement, yielding an income some 2,500 times that of a family living at the level of subsistence. The notoriously wealthy senators such as Seneca the Younger possessed fortunes more than ten times as large as the younger Pliny's. Imperial writers assumed that these fortunes took the form of vast estates, supplemented by money out in interest-bearing loans and hoarded precious metals. Recently some historians have argued that despite the social stigma attached to involvement in commerce senators also derived income from trade and industry. Senators certainly did market the products of their estates (including some manufactured items such as bricks and tiles) and also indirectly profited from urban craft production by collecting rent from urban buildings, but there is no clear evidence for the regular participation of senators in commercial enterprises unrelated to their property. As Cicero wrote in a much-discussed passage in *On Duty* (*De Officiis* 1.150 f.), agriculture was the most worthy occupation for a freeman. He did not mean that gentlemen worked the land themselves—indeed, farmers and herdsmen were despised and ridiculed as rustics (*agrestes*). The senator's estates were worked by slaves or free tenant farmers, and managed by slave overseers.

All senators were supposed to be endowed with the three aristocratic qualities of high birth, wealth, and moral excellence, but some were better endowed than others, producing stratification even within this small order. Those with consular ancestors (*nobiles*) claimed a particularly elevated status, given recognition by emperors through grants of patrician status and the ordinary consulate.

The Equestrian Class

Equestrians have been labeled by some modern historians as "the middle class" and characterized as businessmen, but they were not perceived in this way in antiquity. For the historian Dio Cassius (*Roman History* 52.19.4) they were aristocratic citizens slightly less dignified than senators because they possessed the three aristocratic virtues in lesser degrees. Like senators, equestrians had to be of reputable birth, embodied from the reign of Tiberius in the rule requiring free birth in the previous two generations; and like senators, they were primarily men of landed wealth, not a bourgeoisie immersed in commerce. As the number of official positions for equestrians grew during the principate, they came to resemble senators more insofar as they derived honor from officeholding. Because the order included a broader group than senators, the internal stratification based on officeholding went further. By the late second century A.D. there was a formal hierarchy of epithets: excellent (*egregius*) for procurators, most accomplished (*perfectissimus*) for the senior prefects, and most eminent (*eminentissimus*) for the praetorian prefects. These appellations distinguished equestrians from senators, called most renowned (*clarissimi*), but by the early third century A.D. equestrians were no less honored. Indeed, in court protocol the praetorian prefect was placed above all senators except the urban prefect. Most equestrians, however, were much less elevated, never holding imperial office (there were only a few hundred offices for thousands of equestrians): equestrian rank, visibly advertised by the golden ring, simply set them off as the one-tenth of one percent (or so) of the population who had the required wealth, respectability, citizenship, and connections with the imperial court for membership.

The Curial Class

The third order of the local notables (curials) has been described, with good reason, as the backbone of the empire. Its members enjoyed a symbiotic relationship with the central government, which protected their position and property in return for vital support in administration. It has been doubted whether members of this order should be described as "aristocrats," but the label is appropriate in a broad sense because they thought of themselves as superior to the masses by virtue of the three aristocratic qualities of wealth, respectable birth, and moral excellence. They had to meet a property requirement, known to have been set at 100,000 sesterces in the northern Italian town of Comum (Como), but perhaps different elsewhere. It was hoped that municipal councillors (*decuriones*) could be recruited entirely from propertied men of leisure, but in some small towns such men did not exist in sufficient numbers. In these places, according to the third-century jurist Callistratus (*Digest* 50.2.12), traders (*negotiatores*) could be admitted to the curial order, but only as a last resort after all honorable men (*honesti viri*) had been recruited. Men of low status, including auctioneers, undertakers, and freedmen, were firmly excluded as unworthy.

Wealth was required of decurions for pragmatic reasons as well as those of status. The local magistracies were unpaid, and in return for the honor of being elected, magistrates were expected to pay for public buildings, games, and distributions of food, and to manage the collection of imperial taxes. This last responsibility was especially important: on the one hand, it offered decurions the opportunity to shift the tax burden to the ordinary working people in the community; on the other hand, if the local official could not collect enough to meet imperial requirements, the difference had to be paid out of the official's personal fortune. The pressure of these financial demands on the curial order increased and sharpened stratification within it, as the first men (*primores viri*) used their power to escape obligations, thus leaving a disproportionate burden of expenditures for the less wealthy decurions. The development is impossible to document in detail: references to the financial difficulties of modest decurions begin to appear in the legal evidence of the Antonine age (A.D. 138–192), and by the fourth century a privileged inner core of the council came to be officially designated as the ten leading men (*decemprimi*).

The three leading orders were separated by differences of citizenship, culture, and language, but the essential unity of their basic values and economic interests was recognized by the time of Hadrian in their collective appellation, the more honorable (*honestiores*), in contrast to the mass of the more humble (*humiliores*). As earlier in Rome's history, legal privileges were rearranged accordingly to correspond better with class divisions. While the Romans were conquering their empire and massively exploiting the vanquished, the criterion of citizenship was a significant determinant of legal rights. Under the principate, as the empire became increasingly integrated and citizenship was more widely distributed throughout the provinces, the *honestiores-humiliores* distinction replaced the old Roman–non-Roman distinction as the decisive factor in the assignment of formal legal privileges. Despite Aelius Aristides' assertion, made in the second century A.D., that all inhabitants of the empire were equal before the law, the legal system explicitly gave the testimony of *honestiores* greater credibility and exempted them from the brutal treatment meted out in court to *humiliores* (flogging, torture, and aggravated capital punishments such as crucifixion and exposure to wild beasts).

Working Freemen

The great majority of the empire's inhabitants were classified as *humiliores*—an amorphous group of working freemen about whom few generalizations can be made. Probably more than three-quarters of them worked the land in varying conditions, depending on the system of land tenure in force, the demand for labor, and agricultural methods. These rural laborers can be divided into two classes: those who owned their own farms and those who worked the land of others. Such a division no doubt oversimplifies the situation, since there must have been many peasants who tilled tiny plots of their own and supplemented their income by working for wages in peak seasons on neighboring large estates. Little is known of the independent smallholders, since they have left no written records and the leisure classes were not interested in them as tenants or as voters in the now moribund assemblies. It is usually assumed that the dispossession of peasants continued for some of the same reasons discussed in relation to the republic—most notably, land grabbing by rich, powerful neighbors, and the usual financial difficulties faced by peasants. This view may well be right, but it must be remembered that it is based on scattered testimony and a priori assumptions rather than clear evidence of a general trend. Furthermore, it has been pointed out that large landowners may have wished to see some smallholders remain at least on marginal land as a source of casual labor for slave-worked estates.

The position of tenant farmers is somewhat better known, though just how widely they were employed is a matter of debate.

Since there is no reason to believe that slave or wage labor was widely used in the fields in most provinces, it is probable that tenants were the principal source of labor on the estates of the rich. Exploitation of their labor took various forms, with some paying fixed rents and others paying a share of the crop. Though juridically free, these farmers could find themselves subject to the estate owner for economic and social reasons. Tenants who fell into debt did not become *nexi*, as in early Rome, but if they were found guilty of default on debts, a judge could require them to satisfy the creditor through compulsory labor. In other cases the lack of tenant farms elsewhere or simple inertia may have discouraged peasants from using their freedom of movement to avoid abuse and excessive exploitation by their landlords. A famous inscription from imperial estates along the Bagradas River (Medjerda, in Tunisia) provides invaluable evidence for this. Imperial procurators leased large tracts from the emperor's estates to wealthy men (*conductores*), who in turn subleased family plots to tenants obligated to pay rent and to work several days per year on the main estate of the *conductor*. The inscription (Lewis and Reinhold, vol. 2, 1955, 183 f.) preserves a plea from the subtenants to the emperor Commodus (A.D. 180–192) for protection from abuses at the hands of the *conductor*. They complain that the *conductor* in collusion with the procurator has used soldiers to force them through beatings to work extra days despite their possession of citizenship, and they threaten to leave their land if the abuses continue. The emperor gave the peasants' plea a sympathetic hearing, but then left the collusive procurator, said to be receiving gifts from the *conductor,* to remedy the problem. The inscription illustrates several important features of imperial society: the collaboration between local notables and government officials to exploit the rural laborers, the violence used by the wealthy to intimidate their work force, and the reluctance of the tenants to move. It is also interesting to note that the tenants believed the emperor would help them, but emperors, even in cases where their attention could be attracted by the humble, are unlikely to have been very effective protectors at such a distance.

In a major treatment of ancient class conflicts De Ste. Croix (1981) argues that beneath the superficial stability of the principate the condition of the rural *humiliores* gradually worsened in a trend that led to the institution of the colonate and ultimately to the collapse of the empire in the West. The basic reason was that, as slaves became more expensive and slave production less profitable, the propertied classes increased their oppressive exploitation of the humble free. In the later empire of the fourth century these humble workers lost their freedom of movement when the emperors bound them to their land as coloni. In short, the republican development from use of citizen bondsmen to chattel-slaves was now reversed.

There is some truth in this thesis, but as a general proposition it is difficult to prove. During the republic, when humble citizens exercised political leverage through assembly votes and military service, they won certain limited concessions and legal rights (abolition of *nexum* and the right of appeal). Under imperial rule the vote became worthless, and the army was a privileged, professionalized minority rather than a citizenry under arms. Without leverage the condition of poor citizens was gradually depressed until they became simply *humiliores*. But it must be remembered that humble citizens constituted only a small fraction of the working class prior to the reign of Augustus. The provincial masses never enjoyed privileges and rights as citizens, receiving citizenship in A.D. 212 only after it had been debased. As for the argument that peasants had to be exploited more intensively to make up for declining profits from slave labor, an alternative view is plausible: if land in fact was concentrated in fewer and fewer hands, the propertied classes may have maintained their extravagant way of life by exploiting larger estates less intensively. In sum, the evidence for a worsening condition of the rural working class as a whole during the principate is inconclusive.

The urban *humiliores* are known from scattered references in literary sources and from tombstone inscriptions. Living conditions for the working classes of the cities were generally bad: they suffered from cramped living quarters, poor sanitary conditions, periodic fires, and food shortages. Nevertheless, it is possible to distinguish different social levels within the population. Manufacturing and trade in the urban centers were generally conducted on a small scale by men who were small-fry in comparison with senators but prosperous in the context of the urban proletariat. Some were well enough off to own a few slaves to work alongside them and at the end of their lives to afford substantial funerary monuments. More lived only marginally above subsistence levels: in good times they could afford to pay exiguous monthly dues to a funeral club (*collegium*) to ensure a humble, individual burial for themselves, but in bad times they rioted to protest the price of grain. Beneath this stratum were the utterly impoverished who eked out a living through casual work and doles; their corpses were thrown into anonymous mass graves.

A large section of the free urban population in Rome—probably a majority of the prosperous artisans—were ex-slaves. Freedmen as a group clearly show the limitations of any analysis of Roman society based solely on classes. They were found in every economic class: a few imperial freedmen were among the wealthiest private citizens in the empire with fortunes of hundreds of millions of sesterces, while most were poor urban dwellers. The latter group appears to have been socially integrated with their freeborn counterparts, to judge by the pattern of intermarriage between free and freed poor in Rome. Some were tied as clients to their former masters by obligations of work and respect, while those who purchased their freedom with money saved through work were legally independent. The servile origins of those who reached the leisure class were not forgotten: they were barred from membership in the three aristocratic orders and had a special municipal priesthood (*seviri* or *augustales*) set aside both to honor them and to distinguish them from the freeborn elite. The importance attached by Romans to order and status emerges most clearly in the hostility aroused by wealthy, powerful freedmen of the emperor. The senatorial and equestrian orders bitterly resented what they perceived to be an inversion of the social order when emperors allowed their ex-slaves to wield greater power and influence than their social betters. Senators who had to court imperial freedmen for favors were degraded to the point of being "slaves of slaves" (Epictetus, *Discourses* 4.1.148). Much of the overt political conflict during the principate was rooted in these distinctions of status rather than class.

Slaves

At the bottom of the social hierarchy were the enslaved human chattel. Since slavery is described elsewhere, it is necessary only to comment briefly on how slaves fit into the analysis of classes. Slaves are said to have constituted a separate class on the grounds that they owned none of the means of production, not even their own labor. A class analysis of slavery, however, provides only a limited understanding of the institution. As in the free and freed populations, the reality for slaves was one of various statuses.

Though slaves did not have the legal capacity to own property, in practice a fortunate few had slaves of their own and considerable fortunes at their disposal. One imperial slave is alleged to have paid the emperor Otho (A.D. 69) a million sesterces, a senatorial fortune, to secure appointment to a very lucrative servile position as a chief accountant or *dispensator* (Suetonius, "Otho," *Lives of the Twelve Caesars* 5.2). Many slave artisans in the cities were free to engage in business transactions as long as their masters received a cut of the profits. At the other end of the spectrum, many rural slaves were given only the minimum of food and clothing necessary to keep them working, and some were kept bound in chains with no hope of manumission.

Social Mobility

After this account of the imperial social hierarchy in static terms, mobility and relations between classes deserve brief mention. Two important factors influencing the chances of mobility in a society are demographic trends and the potential for accumulation of wealth. Historians have long been aware that during the principate there was a constant flow of new families into the senatorial order. Despite Augustus' attempts to encourage Romans to have children, senators failed to produce sons to take their places in the senate at the extraordinary rate of 75 percent per generation. Thus in every generation most senatorial positions were open to new men. The mobility was largely lateral, in that the replacements were drawn from the local aristocracies of Italy and then the provinces. By the late second century most senators were of provincial origin, and yet the senatorial aristocracy managed to maintain its traditional character, partly because the new men shared the general values and culture of the old senatorial families and partly because they were co-opted into the order by senatorial patrons who handed on to them the specific traditions of the senate. Membership in the equestrian order also spread in the provinces during the principate by way of the same web of patron-client and friendship connections. This movement into the two highest orders, well under way by the end of the republic, was a vital process for the political, social, and cultural integration of the empire, and resulted in the empire's durability.

The mobility discussed so far was for those who already possessed considerable wealth. For the masses upward mobility was a matter of accumulating enough money to enter the ranks of the propertied elite. But in a society in which most economic production was based on inherited land, prospects for enrichment were poor. When humble men dreamed of becoming rich, they envisaged an inheritance or the discovery of treasure, not the founding of a successful business enterprise. Some traders and artisans in the cities did achieve a modest level of prosperity, but in Rome these were more likely to be freedmen with skills than the poor freeborn. Freedmen may also have had greater opportunity for enrichment because they were in a better position to attract bequests from wealthy ex-masters in return for services. The most important means of mobility for the rural freeborn was probably army service. The government depended on soldiers' arms and rewarded legionaries with the privileges of *honestiores* and the grant of land or a substantial sum of money on retirement. Only a small fraction of the rural population could take advantage of this opportunity, and a very few were lucky enough to be promoted to the centurionate (the cadre of top professional military officers) and even equestrian procuratorships. The latter, along with the successful imperial freedmen, comprised the handful of men allowed spectacular rises in status by imperial institutions.

SOCIAL STABILITY IN THE PRINCIPATE

After examining the Roman social order, the modern observer may wonder how relative stability prevailed during the principate in the midst of enormous inequalities and sometimes violent exploitation of the poor. Various factors may be suggested, though they cannot be assigned a precise weight. As in the republic, the poor derived no solidarity from any class consciousness. Members of the humble classes joined the army and, in return for privileges, provided the force necessary to protect the regime and property rights. Rather than seeking to improve their condition by a common struggle with their peers, many of the poor sought to protect and improve themselves through patron-client ties to the rich. The value of such ties in reducing social conflict is indicated by Tacitus' division of the urban plebs into two categories: the solid citizens, including those bound to the aristocratic houses as clients, and the vile plebs (*Histories* 1.4).

Some historians have made much of the distinctions of order within the upper class, suggesting that emperors used the equestrian order, dependent directly on themselves, to undermine the power of senators. It is true that increasing numbers of equestrian officials were appointed during the principate, but these equestrians did not replace senators as commanders of the great armies for two centuries after Augustus' reign. Moreover, the very method of making appointments shows that emperors had no intention of developing a new administrative class independent of or opposed to senators: the system (or lack thereof) required that equestrians have the support of senatorial patrons in order to secure a post from the emperor. The emperor did need loyal aristocratic administrators, but such men could be found among senators, most of whom were just as dependent on the emperor's favor as their equestrian counterparts. Occasionally senatorial resentment was aroused toward overly ambitious equestrians such as Tiberius' praetorian prefect Sejanus, but generally senators and equestrians were joined by bonds of friendship, patronage, common education and culture, and a shared interest in the preservation of the social order.

The relative stability of the principate, however, could not be preserved in the face of increasing frontier pressures from the late second century and the political turmoil of the third century. By the end of the third century stable government was restored, but at the cost of a larger army and a central government requiring higher taxes. The pressures and changes resulted in the increasing alienation of the senatorial order in Rome from imperial government. During the frontier and civil wars emperors could less and less afford the luxury of making appointments from a small pool of senatorial amateurs. Emperors from Marcus Aurelius (A.D. 161–180) on increasingly turned to more experienced equestrians, until Galerius (A.D. 305–311) reportedly eliminated all senators from military commands. Senators continued to occupy some imperial posts in the later empire, but they no longer were the chief source of the most powerful administrators, as they had been for more than eight centuries. In the second and third centuries the economic interests of senators and the emperor began to diverge. As long as most senators had come from Italy and had their wealth in tax-exempt Italian land, there was no basic conflict of financial interests between the emperor and senators who cooperated to exploit the provincials. The potential for conflict began when provincials whose land was liable to tribute entered the senate, and it increased in the later empire with generally increased taxes and the renewed taxation of Italy. In this context senators devoted considerable effort to avoiding government demands for taxes and army recruits from their estates.

The Late Empire

As senators withdrew, equestrians were called upon to fill the highest administrative and military positions. They were members of the propertied class, like senators, but from the emperor's point of view had the advantages of being more numerous, hence a larger pool of talent, and less conscious of a group identity and interest than senators.

Decurions, as the mediators between central government and the taxpaying masses, were heavily affected by the intensification of taxation in the later empire. They were at once hated by the common people as brutal tax collectors and financially pressured by the imperial government to meet demands for more money. The pressure grew so fierce that decurions tried to run away from their responsibilities, prompting the emperors to issue legislation tying them to their councils. The deterioration in their position is unmistakably reflected by the late fourth century in their liability to flogging, a punishment earlier reserved for *humiliores*.

After the imposition of more systematic and heavier taxation (*capitatio-iugatio*) in the late third century, much of the rural work force was tied in place. It is unclear exactly how the tax reform and the tied colonate were connected. The latter may have been a by-product of the new tax system—the government's attempt to placate large landowners who complained that they could not pay heavy taxes if their tenants did not remain on their land. It is also uncertain whether the colonate was just one step in the gradual deterioration in the status of the rural work force. Alternatively, it may have been a response to the poor people's increasing opportunity to change landlords in a time of labor shortage. Imperial legislation shows that as long as labor was in short supply and landlords were seeking new tenants, the bondage could not be enforced effectively by the government. This is just one aspect of the growth of the importance of patronage in the countryside. Rural patronage had always existed, but intensified government efforts to control the movement of peasants and to enforce heavier taxes increased the value to the peasant of the protection of powerful patrons—even if his small plot had to be forfeited to the patron in the bargain.

In places the pressure on rural workers became too much to bear: some crossed the frontiers to join the Germans, others escaped into the hills to live as bandits. The oppression may have provided the background for a series of revolts from the late third to the fifth centuries by men in Gaul and Spain known as the Bacaudae and identified as "rustics" in the sources. Although the evidence for them—and particularly for their motives—is sparse, imprecise, and heavily colored by the class biases of their opponents, their rebellions serve to highlight the weakening social fabric in the western half of the empire that neither increased government machinery nor the recently triumphant church could restore. On the contrary, without a technology capable of increasing production, the growing, nonproductive government and church organizations could only demand more and more from fewer workers in an atmosphere of increasingly brutal oppression. Consequently, when Roman rule in the West collapsed a millennium after the foundation of the republic, we may doubt whether many among the lower classes mourned its passing.

BIBLIOGRAPHY

SOURCES

Aelius Aristides, *The Ruling Power*, James H. Oliver, ed. and trans. (1953); Appian, *Roman History*, Horace White, trans., 4 vols. (1912–1913); Cicero, *De Officiis* (*On Duty*), Walter Miller, ed. and trans. (1913); Cicero, *De Republica* (*On the Republic*) with *De Legibus* (*On the Laws*), Clinton

W. Keyes, ed. and trans. (1928), *Letters to Atticus,* D. R. Shackleton Bailey, ed. and trans., 7 vols. (1965–1970), and *Letters to His Friends,* D. R. Shackleton Bailey, ed. and trans., 2 vols. (1977); Dio Cassius Cocceianus, *Roman History,* Earnest Cary, ed. and trans. (on the basis of the version of Herbert B. Foster), 9 vols. (1914–1917); Dionysius of Halicarnassus, *The Roman Antiquities,* Earnest Cary, ed. and trans. (on the basis of the version of Edward Spelman), 7 vols. (1937–1950); Juvenal, *Sixteen Satires,* Peter Green, trans. (1967).

Naphtali Lewis and Meyer Reinhold, *Roman Civilization,* 2 vols. (1955); Livy, *Early History of Rome (Ab Urbe Condita)* books 1–5, Aubrey De Selincourt, trans. (1960); Martial, *Epigrams,* Walter C. A. Ker, ed. and trans., 2 vols. (1920–1925); Petronius Arbiter, *Satyricon,* William Arrowsmith, trans. (1959); Pliny the Younger, *Letters,* Betty Radice, trans. (1963); Plutarch, *The Lives of the Noble Grecians and Romans,* John Dryden, trans. (Modern Library ed. rev. by A. Hugh Clough, 1932); Sallust, *The War with Catiline* and *The War with Jugurtha,* John C. Rolfe, ed. and trans. (1921); Seneca, *Ad Lucilium Epistulae Morales (Letters),* Richard M. Gummere, ed. and trans., 3 vols. (1920–1925); Tacitus, *Annals of Imperial Rome,* Michael Grant, trans. (1956).

STUDIES

General

Perry Anderson, *Passages from Antiquity to Feudalism* (1974); Peter A. Brunt, *Italian Manpower 225 B.C.–A.D. 14* (1971), and "A Marxist View of Roman History," in *Journal of Roman Studies,* **72** (1982); J. A. Crook, *Law and Life of Rome* (1967); John H. D'Arms, *Commerce and Social Standing in Ancient Rome* (1981); G. E. M. De Ste. Croix, *The Class Struggle in the Ancient Greek World* (1981); Moses I. Finley, *The Ancient Economy* (1973), and, ed., *Studies in Ancient Society* (1974); Peter D. A. Garnsey, ed., *Non-Slave Labour in the Greco-Roman World* (1980); Keith Hopkins, *Conquerors and Slaves* (1978), and *Death and Renewal* (1983); Arnold H. M. Jones, *The Roman Economy,* Peter A. Brunt, ed. (1974); Ramsay MacMullen, "Social History in Astrology," in *Ancient Society,* II (1971); Ronald Syme, *The Roman Revolution* (1939); Paul Veyne, *Le pain et le cirque* (1976); Timothy P. Wiseman, *New Men in the Roman Senate, 139 B.C.–A.D. 14* (1971).

Republic

Ernst Badian, *Publicans and Sinners* (1972); Peter A. Brunt, "The Army and the Land in the Roman Revolution," in *Journal of Roman Studies,* **52** (1962), "The Roman Mob," in *Past and Present,* **35** (1966), and *Social Conflicts in the Roman Republic* (1971); Moses I. Finley, "Debt-bondage and the Problem of Slavery," in *Economy and Society in Ancient Greece,* Brent D. Shaw and Richard P. Saller, eds. (1981); Martin Frederiksen, "Caesar, Cicero and the Problem of Debt," in *Journal of Roman Studies,* **56** (1966); Matthias Gelzer, *Die Nobilität der römischen Republik* (1912), trans. by Robin Seager under the title *The Roman Nobility* (1969); Andrew W. Lintott, *Violence in Republican Rome* (1968); Claude Nicolet, *L'Ordre équestre à l'époque républicaine (312–43 av. J.-C.),* 2 vols. (1966–1974).

J. S. Richardson, "The Ownership of Roman Land: Tiberius Gracchus and the Italians," in *Journal of Roman Studies,* **70** (1980); Robin Seager, "Iusta Catilinae," in *Historia,* **22** (1973), and, ed., *The Crisis of the Roman Republic* (1969); Israel Shatzman, *Senatorial Wealth and Roman Politics* (1975); David Stockton, *The Gracchi* (1979); Arnold Toynbee, *Hannibal's Legacy,* 2 vols. (1965); Susan Treggiari, *Roman Freedmen during the Late Republic* (1969).

Early Empire

Peter A. Brunt, "Princeps and equites," in *Journal of Roman Studies,* **73** (1983); Peter D. A. Garnsey, "Aspects of the Decline of the Urban Aristocracy in the Empire," in *Aufstieg und Niedergang der römischen Welt,* Hildegard Temporini, ed., II:1 (1974), "Independent Freedmen and the Economy of Roman Italy under the Principate," in *Klio,* **63** (1981), and *Social Status and Legal Privilege in the Roman Empire* (1970); Mason Hammond, "Composition of the Senate, A.D. 68–235," in *Journal of Roman Studies,* **47** (1957);

Keith Hopkins, "Elite Mobility in the Roman Empire," in *Past and Present*, **32** (1965); Ramsay MacMullen, *Enemies of the Roman Order: Treason, Unrest, and Alienation in the Empire* (1967), and *Roman Social Relations 50 B.C. to A.D. 284* (1974).

Beryl Rawson, "Family Life among the Lower Classes at Rome," in *Classical Philology*, **61** (1966); Meyer Reinhold, "Historian of the Ancient World: a Critique of Rostovtzeff," in *Science and Society*, **10** (1946); Mikhail I. Rostovtzeff, *Social and Economic History of the Roman Empire*, 2 vols. (1926; 2d rev. ed. by P. Fraser 1957); Richard Saller, *Personal Patronage under the Early Empire* (1982); Arthur Stein, *Der römische Ritterstand* (1927); Paul Veyne, "Vie de Trimalchion," in *Annales: économies, sociétés, civilisations*, **16** (1961); Paul R. C. Weaver, "Social Mobility in the Early Empire: the Evidence of the Imperial Freedmen and Slaves," in *Past and Present*, **37** (1967); Zvi Yavetz, *Plebs and Princeps* (1969).

Late Empire

Peter R. L. Brown, *The World of Late Antiquity, A.D. 150–750* (1971); Arnold H. M. Jones, *The Later Roman Empire 284–602*, 3 vols. (1964); E. A. Thompson, "Peasant Revolts in Late Roman Gaul and Spain," in *Past and Present*, **2** (1952).

Slavery

THOMAS E. J. WIEDEMANN

SLAVERY (*douleia* in Greek; *servitus* in Latin) was a social institution that defined the relationship of certain individuals toward others as one of absolute dependence in every sphere of life. It was thus a "peculiar institution," insofar as all other unequal social relationships theoretically reserved certain rights to the weaker party: thus wives might be subject to their husbands, or tenants to their landlords, but an ancient society would emphatically reject the idea that husbands or landlords had the right to deal with their wives or tenants just as they pleased. Slaves on the other hand were property: we may properly speak of "chattel-slavery." The total dependence of a slave on his master was somewhat more like that of a child on his father, and in the ancient world, as in more recent slave-owning societies, a master would articulate his superiority by addressing a slave as "child" (*pai* in Greek; *puer* in Latin). The crucial difference was that a son or daughter would grow up to attain the status of an adult citizen or a citizen's wife, while a slave had no right ever to expect any improvement in his status. In practice, a small but significant proportion of Greek and Roman slaves were given their freedom sooner or later. But this was a free gift on the part of their masters (who under certain circumstances might revoke that gift); no moral claims that a slave might have on his master could alter his total lack of rights in theory. The slave was his master's "property." For reasons of humanity as much as of self-interest, most masters may in practice have treated their slaves no worse than their wives, children, free servants, or tenants; and in the comparatively primitive economic conditions of antiquity, slaves frequently had an easier and more secure economic existence that landless laborers or even smallholders. Nevertheless slavery as a system theoretically permitted institutionalized violence and exploitation to a degree that was unlimited (and in practice therefore both impossible to achieve and pointless).

Since the rise of the abolitionist movement in the late eighteenth century, scholars of antiquity have had to come to terms with the fact that the Greeks and Romans, in so many respects an inspiration to later ages, did not merely tolerate slavery—as many other agrarian-based cultures have done—

but actually allowed it to reach unprecedented proportions. The frequency of references to slaves and slavery in Greek and Latin literature (compared with, for example, Hebrew literature) suggests that the Greek and Roman civilizations were based on slavery to an extent to which other preindustrial civilizations were not. This was worrying for those who wished to defend the superiority of classical civilization. Some tried to argue that the germs of an abolitionist movement did exist in antiquity. To do this they had to misinterpret as condemnation the theoretical remarks of some Greek Sophists and Roman jurists who stated that slavery was a social, not a natural, institution. Others, believing in the inevitability of moral "progress," suggested that the excesses of slavery were curbed more and more in the course of time by state intervention, particularly the protective legislation of Roman emperors. It was claimed that two great moral forces arising out of ancient civilization, Stoic philosophy and Christianity, "humanized" slavery; some historians even argued that the victory of Christianity in late antiquity led directly to a decline in the importance of slavery. Another school of historians has been more interested in economic than moral issues. They have argued about how important slavery actually was (often, unfortunately, in terms of the "numbers game"—attempts to estimate the numbers and proportion of slaves at different times and in different places in antiquity. The evidence is so sparse and so difficult to interpret that only informed guesses are possible); they have "blamed" slavery for the ancient world's failure to achieve the economic takeoff that the capitalist world has attained in the last two centuries; or they have suggested that slavery was a system of exploitation characteristic of human societies at a certain stage of development, only to be replaced in due course by other systems of economic exploitation, equally unjust in their own way—feudalism and capitalism. This last was the interpretation adopted by Karl Marx, and his stress on slavery as primarily an economic system has resulted in an enormous amount of research on the subject by Marxist ancient historians in East and West. Not surprisingly, given the moral issues that usually attend a discussion of slavery, argument between those who "maximized" and those who "minimized" its importance has been heated and occasionally acrimonious.

A number of distinctions may be useful. First, slavery can be analyzed as a system, an "ideal type" implying certain patterns of behavior common to all societies in which it is a recognized institution. These potential elements may be described without chronological or geographical distinction. However, this "ideal type" took different forms in different societies. Athens differed from other Greek states, and archaic Rome differed from Italy in the first century B.C. or in late antiquity. While the institution of slavery was an option available to all societies in the ancient world, how it was applied differed radically in terms of both scale and functions. Such differences were not between different types of slavery, but between different societies. A society in which production is geared to the consumption of the household—like most ancient societies—will do quite different things with its slaves from one in which production is geared to an international capitalist market.

It follows that we should next distinguish between slavery as a social system and those elements of it that enabled it to become a form of economic exploitation. To see slavery primarily as an economic institution has led to an undue emphasis on slaves as producers, and even to seeing slaves as an economic "class" analogous to the nineteenth-century European proletariat. Although many, and at some times most, slaves were involved in agricultural or craft production, this was only one of the potential functions of slavery as a system. If slavery was quantitatively or qualitatively more important from an economic point of view at some periods of antiquity than at others, then this can only be explained in the context of the social and economic development of antiquity as a whole. In fact the emphasis on slavery as *the* ancient economic system has diverted attention from other forms of economic exploitation that were more widespread in most times and places in antiquity —those of tenants or serfs.

But the ancient literary sources themselves put more emphasis on discussing slavery than the institution's economic importance may have warranted. Greek thinkers tended to arrange their arguments in terms of "polar opposites": alternatives such as "good or bad," "male or female," "young or old," "rich or poor" (the Greek language makes such ways of organizing an argument particularly attractive). Since one of the interests of Greek thinkers (the dramatists of the fifth century B.C. and their successors, the philosophers) was the question of political and moral freedom, and slavery was the obvious "polar opposite" to being a free citizen, the slave/free polarity became arguably the most important framework used by Greeks to analyze their own societies. Thus there is an enormous amount of writing about the unfreedom of slaves; there is comparatively little about the restrictions faced by other groups such as women or resident noncitizens (metics). In particular, this made it extremely difficult for Greeks even to think about other forms of economic dependence like tenancy or serfdom. Yet serfdom was widespread in many Greek states. Greek colonists at Heraclea Pontica (Ereğli, on the shores of the Black Sea) and possibly at Syracuse treated the indigenous population as serfs, and there were similar categories of agricultural workers in Crete, Thessaly (the *penestai*), Sicyon, and Sparta (the Helots). Many ancient writers and some modern scholars assimilate these groups to slaves; there was no Greek word for "serfs" as a separate category (the second-century A.D. lexicographer Pollux has to list them under the heading "between freemen and slaves"), and even as brilliant a thinker as Plato (*Laws* 776b–778a) gives the impression that he cannot see any difference between slavery and the serfdom endured by Sparta's Helots.

It is therefore worth stressing that the differences are crucial. When the Spartans conquered Messenia in the seventh century B.C., they imposed on the conquered communities the economic burden of surrendering half their agricultural produce and the ritual obligation to send mourners to attend the funerals of their Spartan masters. Not only, however, did they not become the "property" of those individual Spartans to whom their land was allotted, but they did not become the "property" of the Spartan state either. They could not be sold; they continued to live in family communities of their own; and they retained the other half of the food they produced. They were not slaves, but a conquered population. When Spartan hegemony over the Peloponnese was broken by the Thebans at the battle of Leuktra in 370 B.C., the Messenians were given their independence and were immediately recognized as a free community by the rest of the Greek world. There is plenty of evidence for the brutality of Spartans against the Helot population (including random killings); but these atrocities were directed against an enemy community, not against slaves. The relationship is illustrated by the story that each year the Spartan authorities formally declared war on the Helots to justify any murders that would be committed.

Roman writers, following Greek literary traditions, found it equally difficult to describe serfdom amongst non-Roman peoples except as a form of slavery. One example is Tacitus' surprise that the early Germans had "slaves" who lived in their own houses working their own parcels of land with their families, rather than as domestic servants within the master's household (Wiedemann, no. 20).

The emphasis on slavery in Greek and Roman philosophy and sociology illustrates the extent to which it was perceived as a state of total lack of rights. Stoic philosophers might allow slaves a capacity for moral virtue, and Christians for salvation in Christ; but the reason why they singled out slaves was precisely because the slave's status was as far removed from the free citizen's as it was possible to get without ceasing to be human. The slave was on the margin of human society, like the barbarian; hence the idea developed by Aristotle that barbarians were slaves by nature. A slave was perceived as someone who was socially "dead," deracinated either as a result of capture in war, having been abandoned by his parents at birth, or being descended from a slave. Consequently the slave had no claims on the community for the means to live; if someone within the community gave him his "life" by taking him into his household as a slave (Latin writers derive the word *servus* from *servatus,* someone "saved" as opposed to killed in war), then that life was a free gift granted by the master. In the circumstances of the ancient household-based economy, there was of course practically no chance for an outsider to survive at all unless he found a permanent place within a particular unit of production, a household.

The converse of the proposition that all slaves were outsiders was that insiders could not be enslaved. Communities that allowed debtors to be sold as slaves (archaic Rome, Athens before Solon, the early Germans as described by Tacitus) required that these slaves be sold abroad—no one could be held as a slave within the community of which he had been a citizen. Roman law went so far as to insist that a foundling of free birth could not become the slave of those who brought him up: if his free birth could be proved in a court of law, he had to be set free (the *vindicatio libertatis*). Nor was self-sale (slavery might well be preferable to freedom, if one were starving) recognized as a legal ground for enslavement, unless it had been undertaken to defraud an unsuspecting buyer. And no one could legally become a slave as a result of kidnapping or capture by pirates (although the Roman authorities never managed to stamp out such activities entirely).

The slave's whole existence was therefore considered a gift on the part of the master, who had saved him from death as a rightless captive or an exposed infant. Slavery can consequently be seen as a mechanism for integrating outsiders into a society. Just how frequently a society is prepared to take the next step, turning a slave into a free person or even a citizen, depends on a number of wider factors. Greece, throughout the historical period, was a poor country suffering from chronic overpopulation; hence comparatively few slaves appear to have been freed, and only under the most exceptional circumstances was an ex-slave granted citizenship. But procedures for freeing slaves did exist. In Athens, there was the *dike apostasiou,* technically a court case against a runaway slave; but if the master declined to appear, the accused slave was formally acquitted and declared to be free. Inscriptions from Delphi and Boeotia show that the conditions masters imposed upon slaves in return for granting them their freedom might be strict: continuing service for a stated number of years (*paramone,* "staying with" the old master or someone specified by him), the payment of a sum of money to provide a substitute slave, or even the provision of the ex-slave's own child to take her place (Wiedemann, nos. 23–26).

At Rome the freeing of slaves (manumission) was so much more frequent that it amazed Greek observers. The Roman state needed soldiers to fight its wars; the Roman elite needed dependents to support them in the struggle for political power and status. Rome was always more willing to grant citizenship to outsiders, and freed slaves became Roman citizens. Although Augustus felt that manumissions had become so frequent that they had to be restricted (the *Lex Aelia Sentia,* A.D. 4), Romans believed that slaves who had faithfully served their masters could expect to be manumitted at about the age of thirty. They may of course have put this principle into practice rather less regularly than they themselves thought they did. One effect was that Rome was a racially mixed society. There might be prejudices against "barbarians" on grounds of culture, but not on grounds of "blood" or "race." It should be noted that in practice only domestic slaves (the urban household) were likely to be freed; most agricultural slaves labored until they died. Roman law also carefully defined the relationship of dependence between ex-slaves (freedmen) and their old owners (patrons, "substitute fathers"). The freedman owed his patron respect and financial and political support; in return the patron would defend his interests, for instance, in legal cases. But he also had to promise to provide his master with a stated number of days each year to work for him or provide services (for example, as a hairdresser). Thus manumission did not mean that the ex-slave was free of obligations, and we find many jobs—as craftsmen, physicians, childminders (*paedagogi*) or teachers of the patron's children—being performed by slaves or freedmen without distinction. The managers of particular farms (*vilici*) might be slave or freed; the difference was that only freed slaves had a legally recognized identity, so that it would be advantageous to use a freedman for certain business deals (as a procurator). And if a master fell in love with a female slave and wished to marry her, he would have to free her first to give her a legal identity: no pre-Christian law code recognized that slaves, as nonpersons, could enter into matrimonial unions. (Needless to say, slaves had no rights to reject the sexual advances of their masters.)

Perhaps the clearest symbolic indication that a slave had no identity of his own in the eyes of society was that he had no right to keep the name he was known by prior to enslavement. In the Greek and Roman world, as in other slave societies, the slave bore the name that his master assigned him when he acquired him (in the case of slaves born within the household, the name was given by the owner, not the parents). Greek masters might give their slaves names indicating their geographical or ethnic origin (Geta, Daos, Lydos, Syros); certain slave names were commonly reserved to slaves of particular races (thus Greeks would call Phrygian slaves "Manes" or "Midas," and Paphlagonians "Tibios"). Owners might also give their slaves names based on that of some god to whom they had a particular attachment (Demetrios, Dionysios), or anything else that took their fancy (Dikaios, "he who is just"; Eros, "sexual desire"). For Romans, Greek names were associated with luxury and sophistication: many Romans therefore gave Italian-born slaves Greek names (just as they might give slaves of eastern or northern origin Latin names). When a Roman slave was manumitted, his servile name became his *cognomen* (the name by which a citizen was usually referred to); but his personal and gentile (family) names would be those of the master who had freed him. Thus the orator Marcus Tullius Cicero, when he acquired his slave secretary, gave him the name Tiro (meaning a new recruit in an army); on manumission, the freedman became "Marcus Tullius, Marci libertus, Tiro": his official name identified him as the freedman (*libertus*) of Cicero, where a freeborn citizen was identified in terms of his father ("Marci filius"). The names borne by Roman freedmen can therefore reveal something about who freed them; this is particularly useful for dating imperial freedmen, since the exact years of their patron-emperors' reigns are known. On the other hand, very few Latin servile names disclose anything certain about a slave's place of origin: Greek or Latin names are not necessarily an indication of Greek or Italian origin (this vitiates any attempt to calculate the proportion of slaves originating from any particular area).

If the arbitrary imposition of a name symbolized the slave's lack of an independent social identity, his subjection to his master was also made clear in more concrete ways. Since the slave's existence was held to depend on the master's will, it followed that in theory a master had every right to use or abuse his slave as he wished. A slave had to do any job that his master set him, no matter how unpleasant, and he had an obligation to the master who had "saved" him to do it well. Moral philosophers like Seneca might sympathize with those who had suddenly fallen into slavery and were not fit enough to carry out their servile duties properly, or applaud a youngster of aristocratic Spartan birth who, after being enslaved, preferred suicide to emptying chamberpots; but they were clear that slaves who performed their tasks well were simply fulfilling their obligations, and had no right to expect any reward as if they were conferring a benefit (*beneficium*).

The fruits of a slave's labor were his master's; thus an owner could lease his slave to someone else, or he could allow his slave to go and work by himself on condition that he remitted part of his income. (Such slaves were frequent in Athens, where they were called *khoris oikountes*, "living on their own.") If a slave was involved in a business deal, then any money he made was his master's; if he was left anything in a will, it belonged to his master. In practice, slaves would be allowed to build up some private savings, with which they might in time buy their own freedom. That was not a right, but a privilege, which could be withdrawn. A slave at Delos cursed his mistress for depriving him of his savings; no legal redress was open to him. Roman law did recognize that a slave had a claim to his savings; in archaic Rome, all property rights were considered to be vested in the paterfamilias, the head of the family, but he might transfer parts of the family property to dependents like sons or slaves. Such personal property was called *peculium* (a "little herd," since most wealth was in the form of cattle). A slave would be allowed to buy his freedom with his *peculium*, to do business with it, or give it to another member of the same household; he retained it if he was transferred into the ownership of another. But it was not his property, and his master would feel entitled to confiscate it if he misbehaved.

If someone harmed a slave, then the court awarded compensation to the owner, not to the slave; this was not in itself degrading, since compensation for injuries to a free dependent (a child or woman) would also be paid to the head of the family, not the person injured. But what did indicate the inferiority of the slave was that Greek and Roman law codes invariably assessed injury to a slave as deserving less compensation than exactly the same injury done to a free person. Thus the fifth-century B.C. law code from Gortyn in Crete prescribed compensation of two drachmas per day for the illegal imprisonment of a free person, but only one drachma for that of a slave. The fifth-century B.C. Roman law code, the Twelve Tables, evaluated compensation for a broken bone at 300 bronze asses (coins or metal bars) for a free person, but only 150 for a slave. Roman law also specified that a third party might be held responsible for harming a slave (that is, the value of his owner's property) in other ways: by inciting him to steal or damage his master's property, to run away (which was a form of theft), or to waste his time by encouraging the slave to consult sorcerers or attend public shows. The third-century A.D. jurist Paulus adds, "or else causes a slave to live in ostentatious luxury or to be disobedient or persuades him to submit to homosexual acts" (Wiedemann, no. 11). In all such cases the law was concerned to protect an owner's property, and only incidentally the well-being of a slave. Since that property right was absolute, it could be alienated by gift or by sale, and the vendor had the power to impose binding conditions, which the law guaranteed. Such conditions might be to the advantage of the slave: the new owner might be required to free the slave within a stipulated number of years, or promise that he would never employ the slave (if female) as a prostitute. (The emperor Vespasian decreed that if such a condition was broken by a subsequent owner, the woman automatically became free: Wiedemann, no. 194.) But such conditions might equally be to the slave's detriment. The *Digest* contains many references to clauses in wills or sales contracts forbidding the new owner from manumitting a slave before a certain period of time has elapsed (normally to ensure that the slave would continue to be available to serve some third person, perhaps a child), or indeed forever, as a punishment. An emperor might allow such a clause in a will to be set aside, but only if he was satisfied that the testator had been beside himself with rage at the time, and that it was clear that he had become reconciled to the slave again (Wiedemann, no. 199). It was the testator's rights, not the slave's, that were protected.

If an owner's rights were absolute, then it followed that he was also responsible for any misdeeds committed by his slaves against third parties. He was liable to pay compensation for any damage done; hence the vendor of a slave had to guarantee that there were no outstanding claims against him. Roman law allowed the owner of a "noxious" slave the alternative of handing him over to the injured party.

It will be clear that since slaves did not exist as independent social beings, they could not in theory appear in courts of law. Other groups such as women, children, and noncitizens also could not appear in their own right, but a citizen could appear on their behalf. No one could appear on behalf of a slave (apparent exceptions such as the Athenian *dike apostasiou* or Roman *vindicatio libertatis* prove the rule, since these were procedures to establish that the person in question was in fact free). In actual practice, there were procedures to protect slaves from excessive ill-treatment even at the hands of their own masters: but such procedures carefully avoided putting the master's rights over his slave into question. Thus an Athenian law permitted any citizen to lodge an accusation with the Thesmothetai (board of judges) against anyone who treated another person, whether free or slave, in a humiliating or illegal way (Wiedemann, no. 183). This law had the effect of protecting slaves; its purpose was to punish arrogant behavior (*hybris;* hubris) against whoever it was directed. Arrogance was notoriously characteristic of would-be tyrants and therefore a danger to Athenian democracy as a whole. In general, both Greek and Roman restrictions on a master's right to maltreat his slaves had to be based on an appeal to religion, not to the courts.

Roman laws and imperial decrees repeatedly affirm that slaves who attempted to bring any kind of charge or complaint against their masters were to be punished severely without being heard. Only under highly exceptional circumstances were courts prepared to listen to charges brought by a slave against a freeman—indeed, the owner's rights in his slave were held to imply that slaves, like wives or children, could not be forced to give evidence against their own masters. The exceptions were treason against the state (including cases of *vis publica,* violence used for political ends) and ritual impurity, particularly in cases involving unchaste Vestal Virgins. In times of civil war, or when emperors were weak or insecure, there was a great temptation to ignore these restrictions on slave testimony, but the theory was remarkably tenacious. Thus when the emperor Augustus felt that he had to submit slaves to interrogation to elicit evidence of treason on the part of their masters, he first "bought" the slaves for himself or the public treasury (Wiedemann, no. 179). Augustus was however responsible for the one major breach in this principle: his legislation making adultery a criminal offense (*Lex Iulia de adulteriis coercendis* of 18 B.C.) provided for the interrogation of the slaves of either of the accused. This transferred to the state the rights of investigation that traditionally belonged only to the head of the household concerned (the wife's husband or father).

In the instances where a slave's evidence was accepted, Roman and Greek law regularly provided for, if it did not actually require, this evidence to be given under torture. Roman legislators specified that the torture of a slave should only be undertaken as a last resort, when certain proof could not be obtained otherwise (Wiedemann, no. 178). The level of brutality and violence in the ancient world was high, by present standards. But what horrifies the modern reader of a law court speech in which an accused Athenian argues his innocence by offering to have his slave testify under torture is not the callous indifference to the physical pain inflicted on someone who was, after all, a member of the same household (Wiedemann, no. 177). It is rather that the use of torture symbolized the fact that slaves were seen as only marginally human. Like other marginally human groups—children and barbarians—they could not be trusted to speak the truth. Just as reasonable discourse (*logos*) was the appropriate way to deal with fellow Greeks, so the violence (*bia*) proper to subhuman animals was the appropriate way to deal with these marginal groups. (Aristophanes joked that *pais,* meaning child or slave, came from *paiein,* beating.) Torturing a slave to obtain court evidence exonerating his master symbolized the unlimited extent of the latter's rights over him.

It should be repeated that there is no evidence that brutality against slaves was standard practice, or that branding a slave or shackling him or putting him to work in a treadmill was approved of, other than as a punishment for specific delicts. But any sanctions against acts of brutality had to be extralegal. Several ancient writers tell the story of a slave owned by the wealthy Roman Publicus Vedius Pollio who dropped an expensive crystal goblet while his master was entertaining the emperor Augustus at dinner. Pollio was so angry that he ordered the slave, who was a mere boy, to be thrown into a fish tank containing man-eating eels. Augustus was horrified by this and had the slave set free on the spot, Pollio's other crystal cups smashed in his presence, and the fish tank filled in (Wiedemann, no. 190). The ancient sources are unanimous in condemning Pollio: if a Roman wanted to punish his slave with death, he was expected to hold a formal meeting of his household friends (*consilium*) first, and evidence suggests that the actual execution had to be carried out by state or municipal officials. It was these officials who had the right to feed slave criminals to the beasts in the public arenas possessed by every respectable Roman city; Pollio in his rage was arrogating to himself the rights of his community.

Killing a slave without due process was homicide, but no one questioned the master's right to punish misbehavior. The second-century A.D. physician Galen reports that he had to treat several wealthy friends for bruises they had incurred by hitting their slaves. As a warning against such fits of anger, he reports (Wiedemann, no. 198):

> The story is told that the emperor Hadrian struck one of his attendants in the eye with a pen. When he realised that he had blinded him in that eye, he called the slave to him and offered to let him ask him for any gift to make up for what he had suffered. When the victim remained silent, he again asked him to make a request of whatever he wanted. He declined to accept anything else, but asked for his eye back—for what gift could provide compensation for the loss of an eye?

No doubt most people succumb to anger from time to time; but a slave owner was answerable to no one for the injuries he inflicted on his slave, and a slave had no right of redress. Violent punishment symbolized the slave's place at the margin of human society, no matter how responsible or powerful his position may in reality have been.

In fact it was the slave's very marginality that allowed freemen to use him in positions of responsibility without feeling that he would threaten their power. This was particularly true of slaves belonging to the state or (in Rome) to the imperial household (*domus Caesaris*). Because a slave had no family ties, and no one except his owner had any claims on his loyalty, Greek and Roman municipalities preferred to use slaves rather than freemen to look after official records and even to enforce the law. Fifth-century Athens was policed by a group of slaves called the "Scythian archers"—an apparent paradox, since slaves were carefully excluded from the citizen's privilege of participating in warfare. One reason for using slaves was that policing was an unpopular and sometimes dangerous job, requiring a level of discipline that free citizens were loath to accept. States and municipalities bought slaves to perform other unpleasant tasks involving unusual hours of work, such as refuse collection. But Scythian slaves—outsiders by ethnic origin as well as social status—were ideal as a police force because they were thought to have no links with any particular citizen. If their ignorance of Greek impeded communication (as revealed in the jokes about these policemen in Aristophanes' *Women at the Thesmophoria*, 930–1125 and *Lysistrata*, 435–452), it was also thought to minimize the danger of corruption. Slaves also provided some administrative continuity in a democratic state like Athens, where the civic officials changed annually: hence they were ideal as state accountants or superintendents of public buildings (including temples). But although they might be granted a substantial allowance (a state accountant in third-century B.C. Athens received three obols daily, compared with the two obols granted to disabled and needy citizens), they remained slaves: "The presidents of the council . . . are to punish the slave in charge of the council chamber by whipping in accordance with what his wrongdoing deserves" (Wiedemann, no. 163).

The Romans also had slaves to assist state and municipal magistrates and look after public buildings like temples, roads, and aqueducts. Frontinus, at the end of the first century A.D., gives a short account of the slaves responsible for the upkeep of Rome's water supply (Wiedemann, no. 167). He identifies two groups, one of 240 belonging to the Roman state, and one of 460 belonging to the imperial household.

The slaves of the emperor's household deserve special consideration. The Caesars, like all wealthy families, used slaves and freedmen in positions of responsibility to manage their own estates as well as other property for which they were responsible. Since their estates were vast, their freedmen managers and procurators had greater responsibilities than those of other households. But it was a difference of quality as well as quantity: the emperor was responsible not only for his family property (*res privata*), but also for funds that he held in his capacity as a magistrate, or state official (the *fiscus*, as opposed to the state's *aerarium*). Free citizens were initially unwilling to surrender their independence by serving another citizen in a managerial capacity; the Julio-Claudian emperors consequently had no alternative but to turn to members of their own household to assist them in the financial administration of the empire. By the end of the first century A.D., free citizens of the equestrian order were prepared to work for the emperor as secretaries or fiscal officials; and such civil servants—men like Pliny and Tacitus—were appalled at the power and influence that had been wielded by freedmen like Pallas, Narcissus, and Icelus in the times of Claudius and Nero. During the reign of Claudius, these "fiscal" slaves were even allowed unprecedented legal privileges, such as the right to marry citizen women (Wiedemann, no. 168). It is not surprising that some individuals might actually choose to become slave or freedmen dependents of the emperor (*Oxyrhynchus Papyri* 46.3312, dated second century A.D.; Wiedemann, no. 169). Emperors of course continued to employ slaves in sensitive positions precisely because they had no loyalty to anyone other than their master; thus they maintained a private bodyguard of slaves from Germany. In late antiquity, eunuchs were given particularly important positions in the imperial household. Eunuchs are the marginal group par excellence: not only have they no social identity by background, but their inability to found a family means that even if freed, their only social link would be to their master. The control eunuchs exercised over access to the emperor in late antiquity may well have been a sign that the emperor, like the eunuch, was on the margin of human society—except that in his case, it was the upper margin, that between human society and the divine.

The divine world was one area from which slaves could not be excluded. There were of course certain cults that were specifically associated with the political community, and slaves, like other noncitizens, were excluded from these cults. But otherwise it was accepted that the religious impulse was unaffected by slave status. When Cassandra, brought to Greece as a slave, is about to prophesy, the chorus in Aeschylus' *Agamemnon* comments (1084): "The divine power remains even in the heart of one enslaved." Slaves, so long as they spoke Greek, might become initiates of mysteries such as those of Demeter at Eleusis; and the regulations of the Benevolent Society of Diana and Antinous from Lanuvium (Lanuvio) in Latium (second century A.D.; Dessau, *Inscriptiones Latinae Selectae* 7212) show that slave and free participated on equal terms.

It was this recognition of slaves' religious needs that enabled masters to accept practical limitations on their theoretically absolute rights. No master could possibly have given way to the wishes of a slave; but he might have thought it prudent to give way to those of a god who had taken a slave under his protection. There are so many references to shrines designated as places of asylum or sanctuary for slaves who claimed that they were being ill-treated by their masters that we are entitled to consider this an essential element of ancient slavery. Allowing disgruntled slaves to change masters did not threaten slavery; on the contrary, it helped make it legitimate by recognizing that slavery could sometimes be intolerable (and normally, therefore, should be accepted by the slave).

The theory that a slave was the absolute property of his master allowed only one-sided solutions to any conflict between them. The master could get rid of the slave by selling, freeing, or executing him. But the slave had no right to get rid of his master. He could of course murder him, directly or through sorcery. Although we should be wary of assuming that slaves generally hated their masters any more than servants in other societies have done, Greek and Roman writers could certainly wax rhetorical on the theme of "the enemy within the household," and Roman law thought it necessary to impose vicious punishment on all slaves in a household who failed to stand by a master who was being attacked. Simply to run away was equally dangerous, although it occurred in every slave society; there are many examples of legislation to facilitate the return of runaways, letters asking officials to search for runaways, and public notices describing particular runaways and offering rewards for their return. One of the letters written by the Apostle Paul asks one Philemon to be lenient toward a runaway slave called Onesimos whom Paul had persuaded to return to his master. If practical measures to prevent flight failed, the Romans had recourse to religion (the prayers of the Vestal Virgins were thought to root runaways to the spot). There is even an example of an insurance scheme against the risks of having one's slave run away (Wiedemann, no. 217). Under none of these circumstances could unilateral action by the slave be tolerated by society.

There was however one course open to a slave: to flee to a sanctuary, as mentioned above. "The best thing for me to do is to run to the Temple of Theseus for refuge and stay there until I manage to find someone to buy me" (Wiedemann, no. 223). We note that Theseus' protection will not free his Athenian slave from his status as a slave: it merely finds him a new, possibly more humane, master. At some shrines, slaves would not be transferred to a new owner, but would remain as the slaves of the deity whose protection they had invoked (it is not clear how their previous owners were compensated). But invariably someone (priests or magistrates) had to look into the slave's complaints, and only if these persons— themselves no doubt the owners of slaves— decided that the slave really had been treated unreasonably would the change of master be permitted. Roman law also contains references to the responsibility of magistrates (the city prefect at Rome, governors in the provinces) to investigate complaints of ill-treatment by slaves who had fled to temples; this was in no sense a "trial," but an act of piety to the god invoked. Under the principate, statues of emperors were counted as sacred, and slaves tended to take refuge there; in late antiquity, Christian churches provided sanctuary in the same way.

Those elements of slavery thus far considered were potentially present in all ancient (and other) slave societies. But the different functions performed by slaves—the tasks they were set to do in any particular place and time—reflected all sorts of historical and economic factors that had little to do with slavery as such.

The evidence for the Mycenaean period is difficult to interpret; Linear B tablets from both Knossos and Pylos reveal that the royal households abstracted agricultural and craft produce from a considerable number of persons called *doero*, which seems to be the same as the classical Greek word *doulos*. In some respect they were certainly like chattel-slaves: they belonged to someone (a man or a god), they might be sold, some of their names indicate an external place of origin. On the other hand, they were able to intermarry with persons of other statuses, and seem to have been allocated plots of land on the same basis as free men. It might be safer to suppose that these people were serfs rather than chattel-slaves in the strict sense.

With the Homeric period there are no problems: slaves (*dmoes*), invariably deracinated outsiders captured in war or bought from traders, are found in the households of kings and heroes doing whatever jobs are difficult and unpleasant. The number of menials is an index of a great man's wealth and fame; slaves, especially women, are not there merely to clean, wait at table, look after the children, fetch and carry, and serve as concubines; they are there as a conspicuous sign of luxury. In terms of productive work, slaves did many of the things that free persons did too; women would weave and sew in the company of their mistresses. One area that appears to have been the special preserve of slaves was pastoralism. The *Odyssey* mentions slaves looking after cattle, goats, and pigs. These were "marginal" occupations in antiquity—not only because the hours and responsibility made them unpleasant, and attacks by robbers or wild beasts made the job dangerous, but also because pastures were "marginal" places, uncultivated woods and mountains far from the city, and herdsmen were cut off from social life for months at a time. Thus these jobs were suited to slaves, not freemen.

With the beginnings of a more democratic or egalitarian social life in Attica and some other parts of Greece in the sixth century B.C., there was a considerable increase both in the numbers of slaves and in their role in the productive sector, especially in agriculture. The legislator Solon (*ca.* 600 B.C.) was remembered not so much for his constitutional reforms as for abolishing the right of the rich to enslave debtors and sell them abroad. (Some scholars think that this category of bondsmen, the *hektemoroi,* was originally a servile class similar to the Spartan Helots.) While this guaranteed the freedom of the Athenian smallholder, it encouraged the rich to look elsewhere for a labor force to work land that they could not work themselves. While slaves were not suitable for seasonal work (since they required sustenance the year round, while a laborer could be hired just for the harvest), they were ideal for crops that required labor most of the year, like vines. Chios, famous for its wine, was also noted for the large number of chattel-slaves there.

During the classical period, the great Greek cities all had large numbers of slaves working on the land or in industry; but slaves must not be identified here with the "proletariat" hypothetically associated with an incipient industrial revolution. It was because these cities were wealthy that they could afford slaves, onto whose shoulders part of the burden of production could be shifted. If there had been fewer slaves available, the same productive work would have been done by free persons (just as Greek writers pointed out that domestic chores were done by women in households too poor to afford slaves). Owning a slave would increase a master's economic security, not merely by enabling him to abstract the surplus profits of his labor; it also meant that in a world where professional or craft skills were at a premium, he would always be able to count on the services of a permanent member of his household—kin, neighbors, and hired craftsmen were notoriously unreliable. But freemen and slaves shared the same skills; they worked side by side in the fields, or pottery workshops, or on construction sites. The accounts of the costs of temple building show that freemen and slaves were paid the same rate (a slave would of course have had to hand part of his wages over to his owner).

One area where the labor force seems to have consisted almost entirely of slaves was mining; conditions in the Athenian silver mines at Laureion were appalling, and life expectancy short—but so they were for all miners in antiquity, free as well as slave. Evidence from the Roman world, especially the regulations for a mine at Vipasca (Aljustrel, in Lusitania [Portugal]: *Inscriptiones Latinae Selectae* 6891), shows that miners might be freemen. (The Romans frequently condemned criminals to work in the mines; these persons, called *servi poenae*, "the slaves of their punishment," were in no sense chattel-slaves.) On the other hand, slaves might also be made to do work that we consider high status, but which involved a considerable element of risk—such as banking. Pasion (Isocrates, *For The Banker* [*Trapeziticus*]) had a noted banking career, and was one of the few ex-slaves to be granted Athenian citizenship.

The large proportion of slaves to the total population (perhaps up to one-third) in certain cities of fifth- and fourth-century B.C. Greece was not so much the cause as the result of the wealth of these cities. Freemen were made more conscious of the absolute division between them and their slaves; and slavery (*douleia*) began to be used as a political and moral metaphor. Those who could afford to keep slaves to do their work for them did so in order to show that they were wealthy; but their wealth was based not only on the exploitation of slaves but also on other sources: political officeholding, successful warfare, rents from tenants or (in the Hellenistic states of the Near East) serfs.

In the Roman world, there was an analogous reason why the rich opted to exploit the labor of slaves. During the fourth century B.C., in the aftermath of the Gallic invasions of central Italy, Rome reasserted its leadership over the other Latin cities, and then over the rest of central Italy, at the cost of turning toward militarism to an extent equaled by few other states in human history. But in return for being prepared to fight on campaigns that went on for year after year, the ordinary Roman peasant farmer insisted on security against unlimited exploitation by the wealthy: sometime in the 320s B.C., debt bondage was formally abolished. Although creditors could continue to force debtors to work for them in order to pay off their debts (*addictio*), they now had to look elsewhere for a work force they could treat as permanent. The same wars of conquest meant that the Romans were provided with as many slaves as they could use. (This does not imply that ancient wars were merely large-scale slaving expeditions.) By the middle of the second century B.C., central and southern Italy had become "slave societies." It was by no means the case that the free peasantry disappeared, as some ancient writers asserted (except perhaps in those areas that Rome confiscated from Italian communities that had made the mistake of supporting Hannibal during his invasion of Italy in the Second Punic War). But slaves were certainly preponderant in some sectors of the economy, in particular viticulture and pasturage, and those handicrafts that catered to two new "markets" created by Roman imperialism: the requirements of the capital city and the army.

The enormous increase in the number of slaves (perhaps to two million, a third of the population of southern and central Italy), many of them of free origin and enslaved as a result of the collapse of law and order in the eastern Mediterranean in the late Hellenistic period, meant that the ideal of master and slave as members of one harmonious household had no reality in fact: the inhumanity with which masters treated their slaves (sometimes even failing to provide for them at all) resulted in slave rebellions, including three major ones: two in Sicily, under the leadership of Eunus (*ca.* 135–132 B.C.) and Salvius (104–101 B.C.), and one in Italy, led by the gladiators Spartacus, Crixus, and Oenomaus (73–71 B.C.). Ancient writers saw these rebellions as responses to specific injustices. It is quite wrong to consider them revolutionary attempts to abolish slavery as such: the Sicilian rebels set up a Hellenistic kingship to rule over the Greek cities on the island, and the aim of Spartacus' followers (insofar as it was not simply to plunder Italy) was to fight their way across the Alps to their places of origin outside the reach of the Roman Empire.

Ancient sources suggest that the importance of slavery in Italian agriculture declined from the first century A.D.; the end of Rome's wars of conquest meant that fewer persons were enslaved and had to be integrated into the households of Italy, and the ending of compulsory military service for Italians meant that landowners were readier to let their land be worked by free tenants rather than slaves. By late antiquity, the status difference between theoretically free tenants (*coloni*) and agricultural slaves had virtually ceased to exist. Neither group could leave or be sold apart from the land they worked. This was serfdom (although of a sort still far from the "feudalism" of medieval northwestern Europe). It did not imply that slavery had been abolished, especially as a means of displaying wealth and status. Christian senators in the eastern as well as in the western empires continued to own slaves to provide domestic services; if some Roman senators owned thousands of slaves, this does not mean that slavery was more important as an element in the process of production, but simply that these senators had more wealth to display than any classical Greek aristocrat. The barbarian warlords in the post-Roman West behaved no differently. There is some evidence that Christian theologians encouraged masters to take seriously their moral obligation to free slaves who had served them faithfully (on the precedent of Old Testament injunctions to free Jewish debt bondsmen in Sabbatical years); and the custom followed by Frankish magnates of manumitting a slave at their death on condition that he pray regularly for their souls may go back to late antiquity. The treatment of slaves may have been more or less harsh in different periods of antiquity, manumission more or less frequent, and the tasks assigned to slaves various in nature; but it did not occur to anyone, pagan or Christian, that the institution as such could be dispensed with.

BIBLIOGRAPHY

SOURCES

Thomas Wiedemann, ed., *Greek and Roman Slavery* (1981), a sourcebook containing the most important texts on the subject in English translation.

STUDIES

Reginald H. Barrow, *Slavery in the Roman Empire* (1928); Iza Biezunska-Malowist, *L'esclavage dans l'Égypte gréco-romaine*, 2 vols. (1974–1977); Keith R. Bradley, *Slaves and Masters in the Roman Empire* (1984); William W. Buckland, *The Roman Law of Slavery* (1908; repr. 1969); Paul Cartledge, "Rebels and Sambos in Classical Greece," in *Crux* (1985); Moses I. Finley, ed., *Slavery in Classical Antiquity* (1960), and *Ancient Slavery and Modern Ideology* (1980).

Yvon Garlan, *Les esclaves en grèce ancienne* (1982); Peter Garnsey, ed., *Non-slave Labour in Graeco-Roman Antiquity* (1980); Keith Hopkins, *Conquerors and Slaves* (1978); M. H. Jameson, "Agriculture and Slavery in Classical Athens," in *Classical Journal*, **73** (1977/78); Isaac Mendelsohn, *Slavery in the Ancient Near East* (1949); Orlando Patterson, *Slavery and Social Death* (1982); W. D. Phillips, Jr., *Slavery from Roman Times to the Early Transatlantic Trade* (1985); Susan Treggiari, *Roman Freedmen during the Late Republic* (1969); Joseph Vogt, *Ancient Slavery and the Ideal of Man*, Thomas Wiedemann, trans. (1974); Paul R. C. Weaver, *Familia Caesaris* (1972); William L. Westermann, *The Slave Systems of Greek and Roman Antiquity* (1955).

Greek Law

DOUGLAS M. MACDOWELL

WAS THERE SUCH A THING AS GREEK LAW? The Greek cities of the classical age were for the most part independent states. Each city made its own laws, and a law made in Athens was not valid in Corinth; occasions when one city interfered in others and imposed laws on them (as in the Athenian empire of the fifth century B.C.) were exceptional.

It appears then that we should not speak of Greek law but of Athenian law, Corinthian law, and so on. Nevertheless, some modern scholars have maintained that Greek law can be regarded as a unity, because it is possible to identify some legal principles and practices that were shared by different cities. For example, it was a common rule that a woman could not contract a legal marriage without the consent of her father or other male relative. Yet examples of this sort are not really sufficient to justify our regarding Greek law as a single system. To take a modern parallel, the law forbids bigamy in virtually all countries in Europe and America, though not in Asia; yet we do not on that account regard all the legal systems of Europe and America as a unity. Since moral beliefs and conventions easily cross political frontiers, it is not surprising if, at a particular period, different states have similar laws. But a general presumption of similarity is more misleading than helpful. It is unsafe to assume that a law existing in one Greek city existed also in other cities unless there is evidence for it. All too often there is no such evidence.

Indeed, for many cities we have no information about their laws at all. Elsewhere the evidence is patchy. In some places laws were inscribed on stone; we have a few complete inscriptions and many fragmentary ones. The greater part of the evidence is literary, and most of it comes from the place where most literature was produced, Athens. Its interpretation requires the skill of the literary and textual critic as well as the skill of the historian; still, it is possible to reconstruct a fairly comprehensive picture of Athenian law. Most of this essay concentrates on Athens. But, to illustrate other possibilities of legal systems in Greece, some attention is devoted first to what is known of law in the earliest period, and then to Crete and Sparta, whose laws are known to have had some especially interesting and unusual features.

THE HOMERIC AGE

No Greek city had a written code of law before the seventh century B.C. But law need not be written. Any community that has an established procedure for deciding disputes between individuals, or for punishing those who offend, can be regarded as having a legal system; and in Greece it is possible for us to detect traces of legal procedures in the earliest literature, the Homeric poems. Of course these poems do not give us a complete account of law in early Greece, but as we read the *Iliad* and *Odyssey* we can notice the ways in which offenders are treated and the procedures that are used for settling disputes. Different procedures occur in different parts of the poems. That may be because parts of the poems were composed at different times or in different places. When we find a particular procedure mentioned in Homer, we cannot attribute it to a precise date or place, but we can reasonably assume that it was in use somewhere in the Greek world before the seventh century.

A good example of variety of treatment for a single offense is provided by homicide. If one man killed another, one possible consequence was a vendetta between their families: the family of the killed man proceeded to take revenge by killing the killer (or another member of his family), and so on indefinitely, as each family tried in this way to establish its superiority in honor. Another possibility was that the killer might go into exile and live unmolested in another city or country. A third possibility was that the killed man's family might accept a payment of recompense (*poine*) from the killer, in the form of gold or some other valuable commodity. Instances in the *Iliad* show that all three penalties—death, exile, and payment—were in use, but they do not enable us to say with confidence whether all were available at the same time nor whether, if they were, it was the killed man's family or the killer himself who could choose which was to be adopted in a particular case.

For deciding disputes, the simplest method was an appeal to the king. One of the functions of a king was to be a judge or "knower" (*istor*); it was believed that he knew better than other men what was right, because he was inspired by Zeus. Besides, he had power, so that he could enforce his judgment against an offender who was reluctant to accept it. But in practice, of course, some kings must have given bad judgments. Comments on kings' judgments in Homer are generally complimentary, but a contrasting picture is given in another early poem, Hesiod's *Works and Days* (33–39, 258–264), where Hesiod urges his brother to reach agreement privately and not to seek justice from "gift-devouring kings" who give "crooked judgments." The king in this case must have been the ruler of Thespiai, the Boeotian city in whose territory Hesiod's village of Askra was situated. The passage is good evidence for the simple judicial procedure that was still in use in Boeotia around 700 B.C.: a man who was in dispute with another could appeal to the king, and the king gave his decision. But it also illustrates how easily a sole judge could be suspected of prejudice or corruption.

So it is not surprising that even in Homer another kind of judicial procedure has already made its appearance, one in which the verdict does not rest entirely in the hands of one man. This is trial by a number of elders or leading men. The best example occurs in Homer's account of the elaborate pictures on the marvelous shield of Achilles, as part of the description of a city at peace.

> In the assembly place were people gathered. There a dispute had arisen: two men were disputing about the recompense for a dead man. The one was claiming to have paid it in full, making his statement to the people, but the other was refusing to receive anything;

both wished to obtain trial at the hands of a judge. The people were cheering them both on, supporting both sides; and heralds quietened the people. The elders sat on polished stones in a sacred circle, and held in their hands sceptres from the loud-voiced heralds; with these they were then hurrying forward and giving their judgments in turn. And in the middle lay two talents of gold, to give to the one who delivered judgment most rightly among them. (Homer, *Iliad* 18.497–508)

This famous description of an early trial has been the subject of much scholarly controversy. It is clear that the object of dispute is the payment of recompense for the killing of a man. It seems that the killer, who admits that he committed the homicide, has put down some payment and claims that nothing more is required of him, but the victim's relative refuses to take it. Presumably he demands some different penalty, either that a vendetta should continue or that the killer should go into exile. The two men make speeches, and then each elder in turn delivers his judgment. The elder who delivers judgment "most rightly" is to receive a reward of two talents of gold, and presumably his judgment is the one that will decide the case. But who is to decide which elder's judgment is right? The best answer to this puzzle seems to be that the right judgment is the one that receives the most applause from the crowd of spectators. That is why the trial is held in a place of public assembly and the two men make their speeches to the people, not just to the elders: public opinion will really decide the case. This passage shows us the forerunner of the democratic jury. The judgment is formulated in words by an elder, but in effect it is the people's judgment.

CRETE

The Cretans were believed in classical times to have been the first Greeks to have laws, which Minos, the legendary king of Knossos, was supposed to have drawn up with inspiration from Zeus. These laws, or at least some of them, were still in use in the fourth century B.C. To judge from the account in Plato's *Laws,* their main purpose was military: men were required to undergo certain physical and military training, and to have their meals together in messes. Slightly fuller accounts of the Cretan constitution are given by Aristotle and Strabo, including more details of the organization of the messes and the upbringing of boys, and also some information about the election of a council of elders and of ten principal magistrates (*kosmoi*). But it remains obscure how far this system extended. The number of cities in Crete was very large, traditionally either ninety or one hundred. Although some cities controlled others at various times, it is misleading to regard the whole island as a single state. Perhaps the laws that other Greeks attribute to "the Cretans" were really only the laws of Knossos, the most important city. These laws should therefore be considered as separate from the most substantial evidence we have about law in Crete, which belongs not to Knossos but to another city, Gortyn.

The great inscription found in 1884 at Gortyn in central Crete is the largest single text of laws that survives from any Greek city. It was inscribed in the fifth century, but that does not mean that the laws in it were all new at that time; its purpose may have been to bring together in one public place all the laws on certain matters that were to be in force thenceforth, including some of long standing as well as new amendments. It is not a complete legal code, for it omits some of the most obvious subjects such as homicide and theft; possibly the rest of the code was inscribed on another wall that has not survived. What it contains is a series of laws on various personal and familial subjects, including marriage, sexual offenses, inheritance of property, and ownership of slaves.

It reveals a society with substantial differences in the legal status of individuals. There was the free citizen or "comrade," who belonged to a "comradeship" (*hetaireia*); there was the "noncomrade" of inferior status (*aphetairos*); and there was the serf or slave (*oikeus* or *doulos*). What difference there was between a serf and a slave, if any, is a question disputed by modern scholars. One possibility is that serfs were families permanently attached to an estate and could not be sold like slaves. There were also other categories, which we cannot define precisely. The law about rape is one that shows the principal distinctions of status fairly clearly, although the relation among the monetary denominations of the fines is obscure.

> If anyone rapes a free man or free woman, he shall pay a hundred staters; and if a noncomrade, ten; and if a slave rapes a free man or free woman, he shall pay double; and if a free man a male or female serf, five drachmas; and if a serf a male or female serf, five staters. If a man seduces by force a domestic slave-woman, he shall pay two staters; but if she has already been seduced, one obol by day, and if at night, two obols. (*Law Code of Gortyn* 2.2–15)

Much of the inscription is about family property. A wife could have her own property, which she was entitled to keep if her husband died or the marriage was dissolved.

> If a husband and wife are divorced, she is to have her own property, which she came with to her husband, and half of the produce, if there is any from her own property, and half of whatever she weaves in the house, and five staters if the husband is the cause of the separation. (*Law Code of Gortyn* 2.45–54)

She could then be married again. When a man died, his house in the city with its contents and his farm animals were inherited by his sons. The rest of his property was to be divided in the proportion of two parts for each son, one part for each daughter or adopted son. A daughter could be given her portion when she was married, without waiting for her father's death. If the deceased man left no living children or grandchildren or great-grandchildren, his property passed to his brothers or their descendants; failing them, to his sisters or their descendants. Failing even them, there were further provisions governing the right to inherit, although their interpretation is disputed. But what was not possible was for a man to bequeath his property to an heir of his own choice; the rights of the family, in a wide sense, prevailed over the preference of an individual.

A situation of particular interest arose if a man died leaving a daughter but no sons. In that case the daughter became the holder of her father's property (*patroioukhos* or heiress), and her marriage became a matter of special importance because her husband, although he did not become the owner of the property, would have the use of it in practice and her children would eventually inherit it. The law therefore required her to be married to the nearest male relative, her father's brother (his eldest brother, if he had more than one); failing that, to her father's brother's son; failing that, to another man of the same tribe (phyle). Priority was thus given to keeping the property within the family. The law goes into considerable detail to lay down the procedure to be followed in various eventualities: if the heiress was not yet old enough to be married (she could be married at the age of twelve), if the nearest relative was not yet old enough to marry, if the heiress was already married to someone else, and so on.

Because every Greek city had its own laws, we may not assume without evidence that any particular detail of the laws of Gortyn was also to be found in the laws of any other city. Nevertheless it is likely that many cities did have laws more or less similar to these, because they were based on social customs and structures that were widespread in the archaic and classical ages, especially the solidarity of the family and the distinctions between citizens, noncitizens, and slaves.

SPARTA

The strangest laws in classical Greece were those of Sparta. Their origin is mysterious. By the fifth century B.C. it was believed that laws were introduced several centuries earlier by a man named Lykourgos (in Latin spelling Lycurgus), and were based on the laws of Minos in Crete, with various improvements. Some modern scholars accept this, but many reject Lykourgos as being merely a mythical figure and hold that the distinctive laws of Sparta were not established before the seventh century. A further difficulty is that the laws attributed to Lykourgos were for a long time unwritten and so may have been subject to gradual change. In the fourth century Xenophon and others maintained that the decline in the Spartans' population and power was due to their failure to keep to the laws of Lykourgos; but it is hard to know how much of Xenophon's account of those laws is historically accurate, and how much is an idealized picture of what he thought the laws ought to have been. This is the so-called Spartan mirage.

There is no doubt that the lives of Spartan citizens were controlled by a code of extraordinary strictness, designed to produce fit and expert soldiers. Newborn babies were inspected by tribal elders, who had authority to decide whether a baby was healthy enough to be reared, or was to be exposed to die as unfit. From his seventh year onward a boy underwent the system of public education known as the *agoge,* a harsh training in fighting and endurance. Throughout the period from his seventh to his thirtieth year he was not permitted to live with his family, but resided in a group of boys or young men in austere conditions. After his thirtieth year he could reside in his own house, but not dine there; every Spartan man had to be a member of a mess and contribute to its common meals. From his twentieth to his sixtieth year he had to perform military service when required, and to keep himself trained and fit. All this was enforced by law; anyone who failed to perform the training and service, or to contribute to a mess, was punished by loss of his citizenship. For lesser offenses, the five ephors, magistrates who were elected annually, had virtually unlimited authority to impose minor penalties for any conduct they considered unbecoming for a Spartan.

But the Spartan citizens to whom this code applied were only a small proportion of the population of Lakonia. In this population distinctions of status were of the utmost importance. Some inhabitants of Sparta were free but not citizens; these included former citizens who had lost their citizenship, and Helots who had been freed for serving Sparta well in war. We know several names for categories of free noncitizens, such as *neodamodeis* and *mothakes,* of which the exact definitions are doubtful. Lakonia also contained many "cities" (most of them no more than villages in size) besides Sparta. The inhabitants of these other places, who were known as *perioikoi* (in Latin spelling *perioeci*), were subject to Spartan control and had to serve in the Spartan army when required, but they were free, not slaves, and presumably arranged their own local affairs by their own laws, of which we know nothing. A more oppressed class was that of the Helots. These were primarily agricultural laborers, producing food for the Spartans as well as for themselves. They were not exactly slaves, since the individual Spartans whose land they worked could not sell them. Yet they were almost entirely without legal rights. Every year the Spartan authorities made a formal declaration of war on the Helots, and legally this enabled any Spartan to put any Helot to death with impunity. Thus the Helots could be compelled to obey orders, and were not much better off than slaves.

Spartan law about property is a notorious problem. Plutarch declares that Lykourgos imposed equality of landholding by dividing the land of Sparta (as distinct from the land of the *perioikoi*) into 9,000 lots of equal agricultural value; this number of Spartan families was maintained until the end of the fifth century, when a new law, proposed by one Epitadeus, made it possible for a man to give away his lot of land, or to bequeath it by will, so that after a while most of the land passed into the hands of a few wealthy men and the others were left landless. This account has some puzzling features. Plutarch fails to explain how some Spartans became richer than others if they all held land of equal value, and how the lots of land were passed from one generation to another if one man had several sons and another man none; these and other difficulties have led some scholars to reject the whole account. But it can be defended by postulating further arrangements not mentioned in Plutarch's brief summary: it may be that, even though the lots of land in Lakonia were equal and inalienable in the earlier period, some Spartans became richer by acquiring land in Messenia in addition; it may be that there was an administrative procedure for reallocating a lot left with no heir to a family having two heirs. But even if it is true that equality of landholding was maintained for some time, by the fourth century it had quite broken down, evidently because of the law proposed by Epitadeus.

> Some of them are in the position of owning too much property, while others have very little indeed; consequently the land has come into the hands of a few. This also is badly arranged by law; for he [the legislator] quite rightly made it dishonorable to buy property or to sell what one has, but he permitted those who wished to to give it away and to bequeath it, and yet the result is bound to be the same either way. Also, nearly two-fifths of the whole country belongs to the women, because there are many heiresses, and because of giving large dowries. It would have been better if no dowry or a small one or even a medium-sized one had been fixed. As it is, one can give the heiress to whoever one wishes; and if one dies without making a will, whoever one leaves as heir gives her to whoever he wishes. (Aristotle, *Politics* 1270a16–29)

This passage of Aristotle attaches much importance to women. Women seem to have had greater independence in Sparta than elsewhere; and the freedom to bequeath property, including the freedom to give it to a woman and to give a propertied woman away in marriage to any unrelated man, was much greater in Sparta than in Athens, Gortyn, and other cities. The rights of the family in matters of property had virtually disappeared. In this respect Sparta was more "progressive" than other cities; it is interesting that Aristotle saw it as one of the worst features of Spartan law.

ATHENS

Athens is the only classical Greek city from which we have enough information to give us a reasonably full account of its legal system. Even here the information is far from complete. Only a few texts of laws have survived, either inscribed on stone or quoted in literature. For many facts we rely on about a hundred law court speeches, composed by Demosthenes and other orators; in all of these the speaker is arguing on one side of a case, so that the statements about law may be incomplete and unreliable.

Drakon is said to have drawn up the Athenians' first written code of law in the late seventh century. Only his law on homicide continued in use for a long time (and even it probably received some amendments); the rest of his laws were superseded in the early sixth century by the legislation of Solon. After democracy was established, many additions and changes were made and caused some confusion, until at the end of the fifth century a comprehensive review and reinscription of the laws was carried out. Most of the information we have belongs to the period after this review.

Civil Status, Marriage, and Inheritance

In the law of status an important change was made in 451 B.C. Previously a man was an Athenian citizen if his father had been so, but in that year the law was altered, on the proposal of Perikles, so that Athenian parentage on both sides was required for citizenship, and marriage between an Athenian and an alien was not permitted.

By the fourth century the population included a substantial number of aliens, who were free but not Athenian citizens. An alien who had permission to reside permanently in Athens was called a metic (*metoikos*). He could not hold office or take part in politics, nor could he own land in Attike (unless given that right as a special privilege); but in private affairs his rights and duties, which included the duty of military service, differed little from those of a citizen. However, aliens could not normally hope to become citizens. The offer of citizenship to anyone who volunteered for service in the navy, made at a crisis of the war in 406, was unique; otherwise naturalization was a privilege only given as an unusual honor to an individual by special decree. On the other hand, it was possible for a citizen to be temporarily or permanently disfranchised (*atimos*) as a penalty for an offense. This excluded him from political activity, but in other ways his position was not quite the same as a metic's; unlike a metic, he was excluded also from speaking in a lawcourt, but he does not seem to have been prevented from owning land or from marrying an Athenian woman.

The other class within the Athenian population was the slaves. Legally a slave was just an item of property owned by a citizen or by a metic, or in a few cases by the state. But it was possible for a slave to be liberated by his owner and given the status of a metic.

Athenian women were legally under the care and control of their male relatives. The lord (*kyrios*) of a woman was normally her father until she was married and her husband thereafter, although if her father or husband died another male relative would take responsibility for her. A marriage had to be arranged by the woman's father (or other *kyrios*) with the prospective husband; it was not valid unless preceded by a formal betrothal (*engye*) in which the father gave his daughter to her husband. He was not legally required to give a dowry with her, but it was usual to give one, either a sum of money or an item of property, of which the proceeds would be used for supporting her. If a dowry was given, the law did require that it should be returned if the marriage came to an end. Divorce was straightforward. A husband could, if he wished, just send his wife back to her father, and that terminated the marriage. Alternatively her father could take her away from her husband. However, it is not clear that it was legal or practicable for a wife to obtain a divorce without the consent of either her husband or her father. A woman who was either divorced or widowed could be married again, but it was not legal to have two husbands or two wives at the same time. However, a man could have a concubine (*pallake*) as well as or instead of a wife.

A child was not legitimate unless his parents had been formally married. This was important for the inheritance of property. If a man died leaving legitimate sons, they inherited the property, sharing it equally; illegitimate sons had no claim. If a son predeceased his father, leaving a son of his own, the grandson inherited. If there were no sons or grandsons but there was a daughter, she became an *epikleros*, similar to the Gortynian *patroioukhos*. We may translate the word as "heiress," but strictly an *epikleros* did not own the property; it just remained with her until she had a son (a grandson of the deceased man) to inherit it. Meanwhile the control and use of the property was in the hands of her husband. The rule was therefore that the nearest male relative of the deceased man (the order of precedence was brother, nephew, uncle, cousin on his father's side, and failing them a relative on his mother's side) was entitled to claim her in marriage. If he was already married, he could divorce his wife to marry the heiress. But if he did not want to marry her, he had to give up the property, too; he could not take one without the other, but had to allow both to be claimed by the next nearest relative. From all this we see that the solidarity of the family retained considerable importance in Athens, even as late as the fourth century. The wishes of an individual woman, on the other hand, were of no account. She had no legal right to choose her husband, but had to go to the nearest relative who claimed her. An interesting case of two heiresses is described by Andokides. This passage shows that it was considered creditable to keep the family together by marrying an heiress, even if little or no property came with her; but it makes no mention of love or personal suitability as a reason for marrying.

> Epilykos, son of Teisandros, was my uncle, my mother's brother. He died in Sicily without male offspring, but leaving two daughters, who were to pass to Leagros and me. The family's affairs were in a bad way; the visible property which he left amounted to less than two talents, but the debts were over five talents. Still, I invited Leagros to meet me in the presence of members of the family, and said to him that to behave like relatives in such a situation was the thing for good men to do. "It's not right for us to prefer another estate or a successful man, and look down on Epilykos's daughters. After all, if Epilykos were alive, or had left a large amount of money when he died, we should expect to have the girls, because we're the nearest relatives. So, whereas in that case we should have done so because of Epilykos or because of his money, as things are we'll do it because of our good character. So you put in a claim for one, and I will for the other." (Andokides 1 [*On the Mysteries*] 117–119)

Nevertheless the legal rights of the family were gradually weakened. In the earliest times, it seems, the property of a deceased person could always be claimed by his nearest surviving relative; he could never choose his heir. But even before the time of Solon a way had been devised by which a man without sons could choose as his heir someone who was not his nearest relative: before his death he could adopt someone, who thereby became his son for legal purposes. Solon extended this possibility by allowing a man to adopt a son by a will, taking effect only at his death. This proceeding was something quite different from adoption in modern times; it was not an arrangement for rearing children, but an arrangement for inheritance, and the person adopted was commonly an adult. It was subject to various restrictions. A man who had a son could not disinherit him by adopting someone else. Nor could a daughter be deprived of her rights as an heiress. But what a father with an only daughter quite commonly did was to adopt her husband as his son; that precluded any relative from claiming her in marriage after his death. Complete freedom to leave one's own property to any heir one chose, although it existed in Sparta in the fourth century, did not reach Athens before the Hellenistic period.

Offenses Against Persons and Property

Another area of law in which the family remained important was homicide. If a person was killed, whether deliberately or by accident, it was no longer permissible in classical Athens for his family to take the law into their own hands by killing the killer; instead it was their responsibility to take legal action. Proceedings for homicide were more elaborate than for other offenses. Their purpose was not only to avenge the killing and deter other killers, but also to protect the community from religious pollution (*miasma*) arising from contact with a person guilty of bloodshed. First the family had to make a proclamation ordering the alleged killer to keep away from public and religious places. Next they made application to the *basileus*, the arkhon (archon) or magistrate who had responsibility for various religious matters. He held three preliminary hearings, each in a separate month, and then arranged for a full trial in a fourth month. All trials for homicide were held in the open air, so that all those present might avoid the pollution of going under the same roof as a killer. Different kinds of homicide were judged in different places by different juries. The council of the Areopagos tried only cases in which someone was accused of killing an Athenian citizen intentionally with his own hand. Men called the *ephetai*, who were perhaps but not certainly some of the members of the Areopagos, sat at the Palladion (a temple of Pallas Athena) to try persons accused of unintentional homicide, or homicide of a noncitizen, or complicity in homicide committed by someone else's hand, and at the Delphinion (a temple of Apollo and Artemis) to try persons who admitted that they had killed but claimed that the killing was lawful, for example because it was done in self-defense. The penalty for intentional homicide was death or permanent exile from Attike with confiscation of property; for unintentional homicide, exile that could be ended by permission of the killed person's family. This distinction based on the offender's intention is of great importance in the development of jurisprudence, because it is one of the earliest attempts to take account legally of motives as well as acts. Aristotle makes some interesting comments on it.

> Whenever a person hits another or kills him or does anything of that sort with no previous deliberation, we say that he did it unintentionally, on the ground that intention lies in deliberation. For instance, it is said that on one occasion a woman gave a man a philtre to drink, and afterwards he died from the philtre, but she was acquitted for no other reason than that she did not do it deliberately. For she gave it to him for love, but she failed to achieve this aim; so they decided it was not intentional, because she did not give him the philtre with the thought of killing him. So here the intentional is classed with the deliberate. (Aristotle, *Magna Moralia* 1188b29–38)

The attempt to distinguish degrees of guilt by motive was extended to other offenses, including personal assault and damage to property. Thus a distinction was made between *aikeia* or battery, which was just hitting someone, and a more serious offense called *hybris*. *Hybris* is difficult to define, and has been an object of renewed study in recent years. "Arrogance" is not a satisfactory translation; it is rather a kind of self-indulgence, gratifying one's own desires without regard for the wishes and rights of other people. Many different kinds of behavior might exhibit it, and the text of the law about *hybris* makes no attempt at all to define it, but leaves it to the court to decide whether any particular act is *hybris* or not. But it appears that personal assault was the kind of act most likely to be regarded as *hybris* in law. It is a case of assault that gives rise to some comments made by Demosthenes, and these reveal how it is primarily the offender's attitude and state of mind that distinguish *hybris* from battery.

> It was not the blow that made him angry, but the dishonor; to free men it is not the being hit which is serious—though that is indeed serious—but being hit with *hybris*. There are many things which the hitter might do, some of which the victim might not even be able to describe to someone else, in his stance, in his look, in his voice, when he acts in *hybris*, when he acts as an enemy, when he hits with the fist, when he hits on the face. That is what stirs men, that is what makes them forget themselves, if they are unaccustomed to insults.
> (Demosthenes 21 [*Against Meidias*] 72)

Disputes about property may well have been commoner than any other kind of legal case. They included claims for a piece of land or a house, a slave, an animal, movable objects like furniture and equipment, or simply a sum of money. If it was just a dispute about who owned the item concerned, the winner of the case became the rightful owner and obtained possession, and that was all. If, on the other hand, the accusation was one of deliberate theft, the penalty could be severe; for certain categories of theft, including stealing at night and stealing a sum of more than fifty drachmas, the penalty was death. Perhaps more often the accusation was the intermediate one of "damage" (*blabe*). This term was used in a very wide sense. It covered not only physical damage to an item of property, but any action causing loss of property or money. We know of some cases in which the alleged damage consisted simply of failure to repay a loan. But the laws about damage prescribed payment of double the amount of the damage if it was committed intentionally, or of the simple amount if it was committed unintentionally. This explains why a creditor, instead of just claiming payment of a debt, would prosecute the debtor for damage: if he could convince the jury that the money had been withheld intentionally, he stood to gain twice as much.

Obligations to the State

Under the Athenian democracy a good deal of law naturally concerned public affairs. Constitutional law is not considered here, but it is appropriate to notice some laws concerning the public duties of individual citizens. Every male citizen and metic was liable from his eighteenth to his sixtieth year to be called up from time to time for military or naval service. Various excuses were acceptable, including membership in a chorus for a festival or responsibility for collecting a tax; but anyone who absented himself without an acceptable excuse, or who during a campaign deserted his post or "threw away his shield" to run away, could be prosecuted for cowardice. The penalty was disfranchisement. Rich men had also to perform another kind of service, liturgies. This name (*leitourgia*) was given to various appointments that involved spending considerable sums of money, for example as a trierarch maintaining a ship in the navy, or as a *khoregos* making arrangements for a chorus at a festival. The appointments were supposed to be given to the richest men, who were best able to afford the expense. If a man who was appointed wished to claim that someone else not performing any liturgy was richer than himself and therefore ought to be appointed in his place, what ensued was one of the strangest of Athenian legal proceedings: a challenge to exchange (*antidosis*). The protester challenged the other man either (if he admitted being richer) to take over the liturgy, or (if he claimed to be poorer) to hand over the whole of his property in exchange for that of the challenger, who would then perform the liturgy himself. If he refused to do either, a trial was held at which the jury decided which of them was to perform the liturgy.

The most serious public offense was attempting to overthrow the democratic constitution and seize control of the state oneself. A law about subverting the rule of the people and setting up a tyranny prescribed outlawry as the penalty; the offender was to be treated as an enemy of Athens, whom anyone was permitted to kill with impunity. Betrayal of Athenian interests to a foreign enemy was another serious offense; the penalty was death or exile, combined with confiscation of property and exclusion from burial in Attike. Death was the penalty also for a speaker in the ekklesia (ecclesia, meaning assembly) who misled or deceived the Athenian people, or proposed a course of action that was contrary to the Athenians' interests because he had accepted a bribe from their enemies. Anyone who had information about any of these kinds of treason was expected to go straight to the boule (council) or the ekklesia to denounce the offender, without waiting to go through the ordinary procedure of summoning him to appear before a magistrate. The boule and ekklesia then decided what should be done; in very serious instances the ekklesia itself would try the case. This was the procedure called *eisangelia*. In the fifth century *eisangelia* was used also for some religious offenses. In the fourth century the ekklesia still heard some religious cases, but in these it did not make the final decision: if a person was accused of wrongdoing in connection with a religious festival, the ekklesia heard speeches from the prosecutor and the defendant and gave a preliminary verdict, but no penalty was imposed until the case was tried by a jury. This was the procedure called *probole*. Other religious cases, mainly those in which someone was accused of impiety (*asebeia*), were tried by a jury.

Trial by Jury

Of all the Athenian contributions to the development of law, the most important was the establishment of a system of trial by jury. In early times most cases were tried by a single arkhon, or perhaps by six of them (the *thesmothetai*); the council of the Areopagos tried cases of homicide and a few others. It is obvious that an individual arkhon will sometimes have given a prejudiced or wrongheaded verdict; in particular, in a period when the arkhons were all aristocrats, they may often have favored aristocratic litigants against non-aristocrats. Early in the sixth century a great step forward was taken by Solon, one of whose reforms was to allow a litigant dissatisfied with an arkhon's verdict to appeal to a body called the *eliaia* (*heliaia*). The *eliaia* is generally thought (though there is no explicit evidence and the matter is disputed) to have been at that period simply the assembly of all citizens, the ekklesia, meeting under a different name for the purpose of trying cases. (Later the name was used for an individual court, especially the one presided over by the *thesmothetai*.) But as the population increased and appeals became more frequent, it must have become impracticable for the whole assembly to consider them all; and someone at some time— we know neither the name nor the date, except that it must have been between Solon and Perikles—had the brilliant idea that a limited number of ordinary citizens could be regarded as representing the whole citizen body. If we regard a jury as being essentially a number of ordinary persons with no special qualifications or expertise, whose views can therefore be assumed to be identical with the views of the general population, this was the occasion when juries were invented.

By the second half of the fifth century, for which there is more evidence, we find the system well established. Many details are revealed by Aristophanes' comedy about jurors, *Wasps,* performed in 422 B.C. Each year volunteers were invited, and a list of 6,000 jurors for the year was made up. The jury for each case was drawn from this list. At the time of *Wasps* the same jurors formed the court of a particular magistrate for the whole year; but it was found that this made bribery too easy, and in the fourth century there was a complicated arrangement, described in detail in Aristotle's *Constitution of Athens* (*Athenaion Politeia*) for drawing lots to assign each juror to a court each day. Different sizes of jury were used for different types of case, according to their importance, but no case had fewer than 200 jurors, and some had 1,000 or more. In the fourth century odd numbers, such as 201, were used to avoid a tie in the voting. Each juror was paid three obols for each day on which he sat to try cases. This was not a large sum; an able-bodied man could generally earn more by work of other kinds. There was consequently a tendency for the volunteers to be old men who were no longer able to do other kinds of work; the juror's pay could serve as an old-age pension. That is the state of affairs Aristophanes satirizes in *Wasps;* by comic exaggeration he makes his chorus of jurors very ancient and decrepit, veterans of the Persian Wars fought nearly sixty years before. Undoubtedly this was a weakness of the system, because it meant that the juries were in this respect not quite typical of the whole body of citizens.

The chairmen of the various courts were the arkhons and other appropriate magistrates, such as the market officials (*agoranomoi* and *sitophylakes*) for cases concerning trading in the market. Their position was formal; unlike a modern judge, they did not sum up the evidence or advise the jury about the law. The jury members were entirely responsible for deciding questions both of law and of fact. First the prosecutor and then the defendant made a speech; in some cases each was permitted to speak twice. Each was allowed the same length of time for speaking, measured by a water-clock (*klepsydra*). The amounts of time allowed for different kinds of case were laid down by law, more time for the more important kinds, but no trial took more than one day. Each litigant was expected to speak for himself; he was not allowed to pay a lawyer to speak on his behalf. However, if he lacked confidence in his own oratory, two other expedients were available: he could get a speechwriter to compose a speech for him to deliver, or he could get one or more friends to deliver supporting speeches within his allowance of time. If he wished the jury to hear the texts of laws or other documents, he could have them read out in the course of his speech. The same applied to the evidence of witnesses; in the fourth century it became normal for evidence to be written out in advance and read to the jury at the trial.

At the end of the litigants' speeches the jury voted at once, without further advice or deliberation. The majority decided the verdict. The method of voting was by placing pebbles, or later bronze disks, in urns for conviction or acquittal; various devices enabled a juror to conceal which way he voted. In some cases it was necessary also to fix a penalty or an amount of compensation to be paid to the prosecutor. For this purpose each litigant delivered another speech, making a proposal, and the jury voted again to choose between the proposals. The commonest kind of penalty was payment of money; more serious penalties were disfranchisement, exile, or death, sometimes combined with confiscation of property and exclusion from burial in Attike. Imprisonment was seldom used as a penalty; the main use of the prison was to hold men awaiting trial or execution.

Magistrates, Prosecutors, and Cases

Even after the introduction of juries, the arkhons and other magistrates remained an important part of the system. They retained the power to impose fines for minor offenses connected with their own spheres of activity; for example, a magistrate responsible for organizing a festival could fine anyone who behaved in an improper or disorderly manner at the festival. The maximum fine that a magistrate could impose on his own authority, certainly in some cases and probably in all, was fifty drachmas. If he thought a heavier penalty necessary, he had to refer the case to a jury for trial.

A private individual wishing to initiate legal proceedings had to apply to the appropriate magistrate. One of Solon's innovations was to allow anyone who wished (*ho boulomenos*) to initiate proceedings in cases where an offense was regarded as affecting the community as a whole. This established a distinction between a private case (*dike idia*, often called simply *dike*), brought by a prosecutor who complained that he had suffered some wrong personally, and a public case (*dike demosia*), brought by anyone who wished (or, for some offenses, any citizen who wished) on behalf of the general public. The offenses for which public cases could be brought were primarily ones like cowardice on military service or embezzlement of public money, which obviously affected the whole community equally. But they also included some offenses against individuals. Some were offenses in which an individual victim might be unable to take legal action himself, such as maltreatment of an orphan; others were ones that, although directed against a single victim, were regarded as so serious that they offended everyone, such as *hybris*. In general any fine or other penalty imposed on the defendant in a public case had to be paid to the state, in a private case to the prosecutor, but in some cases the payment was shared.

The device of encouraging volunteers to prosecute was an ingenious one for getting offenders brought to justice in a community that had virtually no police force. Yet it did give rise to some abuses. In practice, prosecutions would seldom be brought by individuals who had nothing to gain by them. To encourage prosecutions, therefore, the prosecutor in some public cases, if he won his case, was given as a reward a proportion of the fine or property confiscated from the offender. In other cases there was no financial reward, but the prosecutor might hope to gain a reputation as a public figure bringing offenders to justice, or he might prosecute as a way of doing harm to a political opponent. Blackmail was also possible: a man might threaten to bring a prosecution unless his victim paid him to refrain from it. Men who made a habit of prosecuting for their own dishonorable purposes became known as "sycophants" (in modern English the word has acquired a different meaning). Sycophants seem to have flourished in the late fifth century, when the plays of Aristophanes contain many jokes about them. To discourage unjustified prosecution, a law was introduced imposing a penalty on a prosecutor, in most kinds of public cases, if he either obtained less than one-fifth of the jury's votes or abandoned the case before the trial; the penalty was a fine of 1,000 drachmas, with (at least in some cases) partial disfranchisement in addition. It was also possible to prosecute a man for being a sycophant. Clearly the Athenians had difficulty in giving enough encouragement to volunteer prosecutors without giving them too much.

There were several kinds of public cases, used for different kinds of offenses. The most usual kind was called *graphe.* This name means "writing," and the origin of it is probably that the charge had to be put in writing, at a time when charges in private cases were still oral; but the name continued in use even after it had become the rule to put the charge in writing in private cases too. The law about *hybris,* which is one of the few laws to have been preserved in a fairly complete form, gives some information about the *graphe* procedure.

> If anyone treats with *hybris* any person, either child or woman or man, free or slave, or does anything illegal against any of these, let anyone who wishes, of those Athenians who are entitled, submit a *graphe* to the *thesmothetai.* Let the *thesmothetai* bring the case to the *eliaia* within thirty days of the submission of the *graphe,* if no public business prevents it, or otherwise as soon as possible. Whoever the *eliaia* finds guilty, let it immediately assess whatever penalty seems right for him to suffer or pay. Of those who submit private *graphai* [this phrase is strange; the text may be corrupt] according to the law, if anyone does not proceed, or when proceeding does not get one-fifth of the votes, let him pay 1,000 drachmas to the public treasury. If a money penalty is assessed for the *hybris,* let the person be imprisoned, if the *hybris* is against a free person, until he pays it. (Law quoted by Demosthenes 21 [*Against Meidias*] 47)

The following is a list of other kinds of public cases.

1. *Apagoge.* The prosecutor began by arresting the defendant and taking him to the prison. This procedure was used against thieves and other malefactors, especially those caught in the act, and also against persons who were convicted or accused of homicide and were seen in places where they were not allowed to be.

2. *Ephegesis.* This was the same as *apagoge,* except that the prosecutor, instead of arresting the defendant himself, brought the magistrates (normally the officers called the Eleven) to him and told them to make the arrest.

3. *Endeixis.* This also was similar to *apagoge,* but the prosecutor first delivered his charge to the magistrate, and arrested the defendant afterward, if at all; sometimes no arrest was made. This procedure was used against disfranchised men who were seen to be in any of the places, or to be performing any of the functions, that were forbidden to them.

4. *Phasis* was used for various offenses connected with trade, property, or mining. The prosecutor, if he won the case, received half the amount that the defendant was condemned to pay, and the procedure was consequently a favorite with sycophants.

5. *Apographe.* The prosecutor submitted a list of property which, he claimed, the defendant retained in his possession although it ought to have been forfeited to the state. If he won the case, he was rewarded with a proportion of the value of the property; the proportion is said to have been three-quarters, but this seems very high and the figure has been questioned.

6. *Eisangelia* was a name used for several kinds of case: a case initiated by a denunciation to the ekklesia or the boule, usually for treason or some other serious offense against the state; a case for maltreatment of an orphan or an heiress; and a case in which a public arbitrator was accused of misconducting an arbitration. In these cases, unlike other public cases, the prosecutor did not suffer a penalty if he abandoned the case before trial or obtained less than one-fifth of the jury's votes.

7. *Probole.* The case had a preliminary hearing in the ekklesia before going for trial by a jury. This procedure was used mainly for cases concerning religious festivals.

8. *Dokimasia* was a procedure for checking that a man was not disqualified from being a citizen, or from holding an office, or from

speaking in the ekklesia. Any objection that he was disqualified could be put forward by anyone who wished during the hearing, without any previous charge or notice.

9. *Euthyna.* At the end of his term of office, every magistrate or official was subject to examination of his conduct in office. The public auditors could accuse him of stealing or misusing public money, and anyone who wished could accuse him of any other improper use of the office.

Private cases had fewer procedural varieties than public cases, but there were some that are worth noting. The exceptional nature of homicide cases has already been mentioned. *Diadikasia* was a procedure used when a right (for example, to claim an inheritance) or an obligation (for example, to perform a liturgy) was disputed between two or more persons. Its distinctive feature was that there was no prosecutor or defendant; all the claimants were on equal terms.

Many private cases were subject to arbitration (*diaita*). Privately arranged arbitration had always been possible, but in 399 B.C. an official system of arbitration was introduced. Its purpose was presumably to avoid the trouble and cost of a full trial by jury in cases that could be brought to an agreed settlement without one. The public arbitrators were ordinary citizens of fairly advanced age: every citizen had to serve as an arbitrator in his sixtieth year. Cases were assigned to arbitrators by lot. The arbitrator heard the litigants' arguments and evidence and then, if he could not get them to agree, gave his verdict. Either litigant could appeal against the verdict and demand a full trial; thus arbitration did not deprive anyone of the right to be tried by a jury if he wished. If the case did go to a jury, the statements of witnesses and other evidence produced at the arbitration were sealed up in jars and brought out again at the trial. No evidence could be presented at the trial that had not been presented at the arbitration. The purpose of this rule was presumably to ensure that each litigant would present his case fully to the arbitrator.

Another innovation at the turn of the fifth and fourth centuries (the first case was in 400) was the procedure called *paragraphe*. It was a procedure for objecting that a prosecution was being brought in a way forbidden by law. The objection might be simply that a different legal procedure ought to have been used. Or it might be that no prosecution was admissible for the alleged offense or complaint because it was excluded by a time-limit or other rule. The procedure was that a separate trial was held to consider the objection; here the roles of the litigants, and consequently the order of their speeches, were reversed, because the defendant in the original case was the prosecutor in the *paragraphe*. If he won the *paragraphe* trial, the original case lapsed; if he lost, the trial of the original case proceeded in the normal way on another day. An older procedure for attempting to stop a trial was called *diamartyria*. It consisted of a formal statement by a witness of some fact that made further legal proceedings inadmissible. It continued in use in the fourth century in inheritance cases, in which a declaration that a man was the legitimate son of the deceased would exclude anyone else from claiming the property.

In the middle of the fourth century some other important changes were made. At this period, it seems, increasing maritime trade between Athens and other parts of the Greek world led to a demand for speedier justice for traders. To provide this, a new kind of mercantile case (*dike emporike*) was introduced. It was open to merchants and shipmasters, whether they were Athenian or not, for any dispute arising out of a trading agreement that had been made in the Athenian market or that concerned a voyage to or from Athens. The cases were "monthly"; the meaning of this remains a subject of scholarly disagreement, but the preferable interpretation seems to be that applications to bring such cases were accepted in every month, except in the four summer months when merchants would wish to make use of the best weather for voyages. Even if that interpretation is wrong, at any rate it seems clear that the aim was to provide prompt decisions, and to avoid keeping travelers waiting in Athens for long periods. The attempt to make justice more expeditious appears to have been a success, since soon afterward some other kinds of cases, mainly financial, were made "monthly" too. Two features of mercantile cases are particularly worth noticing. One is that they had to be based on written contracts; this indicates that written documents had now become normal in commercial affairs. The other is that no distinction was made between Athenian and non-Athenian merchants and shipmasters; this shows that distinctions of nationality and citizen status were becoming less important.

The Importance of Athenian Law

As a whole, the Athenian legal system in the fourth century B.C. was the most elaborate and advanced that had yet been developed by any people, as far as our knowledge goes. This was not because the Athenians devised different rules of conduct from other Greeks. On the contrary, their views of right and wrong behavior do not seem to have differed greatly from those elsewhere in Greece, and were certainly less original than those of the Spartans. The progress they made in giving legal definition to moral beliefs was less than might have been expected in a city inhabited by Socrates, Plato, and Aristotle. By far their most important legal achievement was in the field of procedure. They entrusted the administration of justice to the people. Every important decision was in the hands of ordinary citizens with no special expertise, and yet the system worked. Admittedly some decisions were made that were later seen to have been wrong; the condemnation of Socrates for impiety is the most notorious instance. But even that condemnation was probably an accurate reflection of public opinion at the time. With both its weaknesses and its merits, the Athenian system stands for all time as the supreme example of democratic justice.

BIBLIOGRAPHY

SOURCES

Andocides (Andokides), *On the Mysteries,* in *Minor Attic Orators* I, K. J. Maidment, trans. (1941); Aristotle, *Politics* [and] *Magna Moralia,* in *The Complete Works of Aristotle: The Revised Oxford Translation,* Jonathan Barnes, ed., 2 vols. (1984); Athenian inscriptions in *Inscriptiones Graecae* I, II, 4th ed. (1930); Demosthenes, *Against Meidias* III, J. H. Vince, trans. (1935); Homer, *The Iliad of Homer,* Richmond Lattimore, trans. (1977); Hesiod, *The Works and Days,* Richmond Lattimore, trans. (1959); *The Law Code of Gortyn,* Ronald F. Willetts, ed., (1967).

STUDIES

Erich Berneker, ed., *Zur griechischen Rechtsgeschichte* (1968), including full bibliography for the years 1924–1966; Arnaldo Biscardi, *Diritto Greco antico* (1982); Robert J. Bonner, *Lawyers and Litigants in Ancient Athens* (1927); Robert J. Bonner and Gertrude Smith, *The Administration of Justice from Homer to Aristotle,* 2 vols. (1930–1938); Eva Cantarella, *Norma e sanzione in Omero* (1979); David Cohen, *Theft in Athenian Law* (1983); Edward E. Cohen, *Ancient Athenian Maritime Courts* (1973); Moses I. Finley, *Studies in Land and Credit in Ancient Athens* (1952), and *The Use and Abuse of History,* chap. 8 (1975).

Michael Gagarin, *Drakon and Early Athenian Homicide Law* (1981); Philippe Gauthier, *Symbola* (1972); Louis Gernet, *Droit et société dans la Grèce ancienne* (1955); Mogens Herman Hansen, *Apagoge, Endeixis and Ephegesis against Kakourgoi, Atimoi and Pheugontes* (1976), *Eisangelia* (1975), and *The*

Sovereignty of the People's Court in Athens in the Fourth Century B.C. (1974); Alick Robin Walsham Harrison, *The Law of Athens*, 2 vols. (1968–1971); Charles Hignett, *A History of the Athenian Constitution* (1952); Signe Isager and Mogens Herman Hansen, *Aspects of Athenian Society in the Fourth Century* B.C. (1975).

John Walter Jones, *The Law and Legal Theory of the Greeks* (1956); Arnold Kränzlein, *Eigentum und Besitz im griechischen Recht* (1963); Justus Hermann Lipsius, *Das attische Recht und Rechtsverfahren*, 3 vols. (1905–1915); Douglas M. MacDowell, *Athenian Homicide Law in the Age of the Orators* (1963), *The Law in Classical Athens* (1978), and *Spartan Law* (1986); Martin Ostwald, *Nomos and the Beginnings of the Athenian Democracy* (1969); Fritz Pringsheim, *The Greek Law of Sale* (1950); Peter John Rhodes, *The Athenian Boule* (1972); Eberhard Ruschenbusch, Σόλωνος νόμοι (1966), and *Untersuchungen zur Geschichte des athenischen Strafrechts* (1968); David M. Schaps, *Economic Rights of Women in Ancient Greece* (1979); Ronald S. Stroud, *The Axones and Kyrbeis of Drakon and Solon* (1979), and *Drakon's Law on Homicide* (1968); Hans Julius Wolff, *Die attische Paragraphe* (1966), and *"Normenkontrolle" und Gesetzesbegriff in der attischen Demokratie* (1970).

HELLENISTIC LAW: EDITORIAL NOTE

Bibliographical information for Hellenistic law can be obtained from Claire Préaux, *Le monde hellénistique (323–146 av. J.-C.)*, I (1978), pp. 63–65, and F. W. Walbank, A. E. Astin, M. W. Frederiksen, and R. M. Ogilvie, eds., *The Cambridge Ancient History*, VII, Part 1, *The Hellenistic World*, 2d ed. (1984); see index, s.v. "law, lawcodes," and corresponding sections of the bibliographies. Pages 572–573 list writings on law and the administration of justice in Egypt, which provides the most abundant evidence for Hellenistic times. Especially important on this subject are Raphael Taubenschlag, *The Law of Greco-Roman Egypt in the Light of the Papyri 332* B.C.–*640* A.D., 2d ed. (1955; repr. 1972), and M. J. Wolff, *Das Justizwesen der Ptolemäer* (1962).

See also Jozef Modrzejewski, *Le monde hellénistique* (Introduction bibliographique à l'histoire du droit et à l'ethnologie juridique, J. Gilissen, ed., VII, 1965); Jozef Modrzejewski and Detlef Liebs, eds., *Symposion 1977: Vorträge zur griechischen und hellenistischen Rechtsgeschichte* (1977, 1982); Virgilio Ilari, *Guerra e diritto nel mondo greco-ellenistico fino al III secolo* (Guerra e diritto nel mondo antico, I, 1980).

Roman Law

ALAN WATSON

THE DEVELOPMENT OF ROMAN LAW is one of the most significant, original, and enduring achievements of the human spirit. The Roman achievement lies both in the creation of legal rules that have long evoked admiration, and also in isolating the idea of law from other concepts such as morality, religion, or economic welfare. To a remarkable extent Roman law appears neutral, not directed toward or based upon other "goods." Hence its rules and institutions have provided an outstanding resource for selective borrowing even where Roman religious and political ideas are discounted.

Law is not an end in itself but can only be a means toward other ends. It is not even easy to conceptualize legal ideas as something in their own right, distinct from other societal ideas. Slavery, for instance, is a societal institution; a law of slavery exists only to clarify the societal ideas and to regulate conflicts. Issues such as who can be enslaved, whether any master can free any slave, and the status of freed persons depend (or should depend) on economic, political, and social considerations, not on law. But these considerations come to be crystallized in law. Legal rules are used as a shorthand for these societal values in order to resolve disputes more readily. The legal rules come to have a life of their own.

It is part of the achievement of Roman law that from the earliest recorded time the law seems to exist in its own right. Already in the Twelve Tables, the code of the mid fifth century B.C., law appears sharply differentiated from morality and religion. But with autonomy of law comes categorization of law. The dividing line drawn between one branch of the law and another will often have important consequences—for further analysis and legal development and for the outcome of the lawsuits—yet is largely arbitrary and derives to a considerable extent from the legal tradition and not from other societal factors. As early as the Twelve Tables, for instance, public law and private law were regarded as separate entities, and the former was mostly excluded from the code. Thereafter Roman jurists showed little interest in public law, an attitude that carried over to lawyers in the civil law systems and persisted until very modern times. Legal reasoning and tradition, not economic considerations, dictated that for the Romans sale and barter would be very different contracts, and that the contract of hire should encompass three very different types of legal relation: the right to use another's property for a fee, the right to another's services for a fee, and the right to have a specific task performed for a fee. So powerful has the impact of Roman legal thinking been on the later Western world that only recently and only in some countries, such as Germany, has it been recognized that a contract for labor services (Dienstpacht) is a very different thing from hire of a thing (Miete) and involves very different obligations.

LAW OF THE KINGS AND THE TWELVE TABLES

According to tradition, Rome was founded in 753 B.C. and until 509 was ruled by kings who, according to nonlegal writers, were responsible for much legislation mainly in sacral and family law. Most modern scholars deny the existence of such legislation, but it seems plausible: first, because the rules ascribed to this period show the father with more restricted powers than was the case in the early republic and therefore do not reflect the expectation (and invention) of later Romans; second, because it has not proved possible to show convincingly any grounds for subsequent fabrication; and third, because the careful, laconic style of the Twelve Tables indicates a long tradition of drafting.

The demand for codification in the early republic is said to have stemmed from the grievances of the plebeians, who could not know the law and felt exploited by the patrician magistrates. The patricians, in an attempt to block or delay reform, organized a delegation to Greece to study the law of Solon. If the tradition is accurate, the plebeians lost the battle. The Twelve Tables deal almost only with private law, a very little criminal law, and the law of disposal of the dead. The powers of the magistrates are not delineated, and the code does not deal with forms, whether for trials or for contracts or for freeing slaves. Without other knowledge, the Twelve Tables would not be protective of rights. And there is no real sign of Greek influence. In contrast to modern codifications, no attempt was made to set out the law systematically: rather, the code contained only clarifications of the law or innovations. Thus, dowry, which had long existed, is not dealt with, and the law of slavery appears only incidentally. There are seven known provisions on prescription—the acquisition of rights by lapse of time, a new institution—but otherwise there is nothing about acquisition of property (as distinct from transfer, which also is not fully dealt with). The first set of ten officials, *decemviri*, appointed to set down the law produced ten tables of law in 451 B.C.; a second set was appointed to complete the work and they did produce a further two tables, but they turned tyrannous. To this second set is attributed the rule that a patrician could not marry a plebeian, which was overturned by the Canuleian law of 445 B.C.

SOURCES OF LAW IN THE REPUBLIC

Law does not emerge easily out of societal conditions: it has to be institutionalized. That is, it must be endorsed by one of the recognized means of lawmaking. The more satisfactory the sources of law, the easier it is to have legal rules of high quality that are responsive to societal needs. The Roman genius for law is above all a genius for developing flexible sources of law.

No doubt in the earliest period law was largely customary, but in historic times, both in the republic and in the empire, custom was not a fruitful source of law. Very few rules are attributed to it, there is no theory of its lawmaking capacity, and we are told by the emperor Constantine that it cannot prevail against statute or reason. The unimportance of custom is a good indication of the fruitfulness of the other sources of law.

The Twelve Tables were, of course, legislation. But in normal times legislation was used sparingly, and usually for private law the organ of legislation was the Council of the Plebs (*concilium plebis*). Apart from the Canuleian law the most important private laws in the republic were: the Aquilian law of about 287 B.C., which above all regulated damage to property; the Atilian law of about 210, which provided for the appointment by the praetor and a majority of the tribunes of the plebs of a tutor to a fatherless child who otherwise would have no guardian; the Cincian law of 204, which restricted large gifts; the Plaetorian law of 193/192, which gave remedies when a person under twenty-five was defrauded; and the Atinian law of about 150 B.C., which provided that the ownership of stolen property could not be acquired by long usage until the property had come back into the hands of the person from whom it was stolen.

The individually elected higher magistrates could not legislate, but they could issue edicts setting out how they would act within their sphere of competence during their term of office. Strictly these magistrates could not make law but those in charge of law courts could refuse to grant an action where one was provided by civil law, they could allow a remedy where none was provided, and they could reinterpret the law. The most important magistrates in this regard were the praetors, especially the urban praetors and perhaps also the peregrine praetors, although the boundary lines between their jurisdictions is not clear. It became established that when a praetor was elected he would issue an edict containing his intentions in a number of clauses, which were mainly of two types: individual edicts setting out that the praetor would grant an action in particular circumstances and sometimes, in the absence of a relevant edict, model forms of action called *formulae*. Since praetors were elected for only one year at a time and could not be reelected, and since the edict was valid only during their term of office, each year saw the possibility of much reform since praetors did not need to obtain further support for their edict. In practice they took over much of their predecessor's edict, but often with changes. The praetor's edict was the most important vehicle of legal change in the republic: the praetors, for instance, remodeled the whole of the law of succession, and were largely responsible for the law of contract, especially the highly significant consensual contracts.

The curule aediles (those entitled to a curule chair as a symbol of rank of office) had jurisdiction over streets and marketplaces and issued important edicts governing the sale of slaves and beasts, the keeping of wild beasts (often for games) near public places, and suspending things over, or letting them fall on, public places.

One feature of Roman lawmaking that at first sight is extremely puzzling is the importance attached to the opinions of the jurists, that is, persons who held no official position but were experts in giving unpaid legal advice to private individuals, to the lay judges, and to magistrates, and who were of high social standing. Why, too, we may wonder, did the jurists themselves find satisfaction and honor in giving opinions that often conflicted with the opinions of their fellows?

Originally the interpretation of law was in the hands of the College of Pontiffs (pontifices), all the members of which were patricians. It was thus important for those who were well connected and who wished to be pontiffs to know the law. The opinion of the college was authoritative and each year one member was chosen to be the spokesman.

The position was one of great significance. Plebeians could become pontiffs after the Ogulnian law of 300 B.C., and in time the pontiffs lost their monopoly of legal interpretation. But people of social importance continued to seek to be pontiffs and to give legal advice, although individually and no longer authoritatively, and this practice was treated with respect.

In time the jurists began to produce books of varying types. The first major step was the *Tripertita* by Sextus Aelius Paetus, who was consul in 198 B.C. This contained the provisions of the Twelve Tables, a commentary on them, and a description of the relevant forms of action. Quintus Mucius Scaevola, consul in 95 B.C., is said to have first divided the civil law into categories or classes (*genera*), and he produced the first commentary on the civil law, in eighteen books. This seems to have been old-fashioned and to have covered only topics that could be dealt with by statute or pegged to a discussion of statute. He also wrote many other books. Other jurists wrote commentaries on particular topics, on the edict, and even compiled collections of their answers to legal problems, real and hypothetical. By the first century B.C. prominent jurists were knights rather than senators.

SOURCES OF LAW IN THE EARLY EMPIRE

Augustus restored the use of legislation, but primarily through the Comitia Tributa, not the Council of the Plebs. He had a number of laws enacted concerned mainly with family law and the manumission of slaves. Subsequently, few statutes were passed except under Claudius (A.D. 41–54), who, as a true lover of the republic, legislated through the Council of the Plebs. By the end of the first century legislation had died out.

No change was made in the right of the magistrates to issue edicts, but they ceased to innovate and made only a few minor alterations. The emperor Hadrian (A.D. 117–138) gave the jurist Salvius Julianus the task of consolidating the edict of the urban praetor. Julian made a substantial alteration in the organization and a minor one in substance, but thereafter no change could be made.

Augustus gave selected jurists the right to issue replies on his authority. The import of this change is unclear but it would bring lawmaking by jurists more under his control. (A modification to this, again unclear, was introduced by Hadrian.) The jurists wrote more and more books and, largely as a result of their writings, the first 250 years of the empire are known as the classical period of Roman law. Great innovations had died with the republic, and subsequent jurists dedicated their efforts to ever-greater refinements. Bestowing authority on jurists to make law allows for flexibility and continuing suggestions for improvement, but it has a serious defect. In the absence of a system that ranks the jurists, there is no authoritative way of determining the outcome when a point of law is disputed. Many problems argued by the jurists in the early empire were settled only by Justinian. Prominent in the disputes were the rival schools—probably true teaching establishments—of the Sabinians and the Proculians, who seem separated by no ideological divide.

One juristic work, the *Institutes* of Gaius (second century A.D.) deserves particular mention, partly because it is the only classical work to survive largely complete and intact, partly because it served as the main model of Justinian's *Institutes* and hence became the structural basis for most modern civil codes. This is an elementary textbook for beginning students and is in four books: Book One covers sources of law and persons; Book Two property and succession;

Book Three intestate succession and obligations; and Book Four the law of actions.

By about A.D. 230 the writing of juristic books had virtually come to an end. New sources of law came into being in the empire. Decrees of the senate (*senatus consulta*) gradually came to have lawmaking force and by the time of Hadrian they could be directly applied as law.

The emperor could issue edicts, like any magistrate, and since his jurisdiction was universal they could be on any matter: the *constitutio Antoniniana* of A.D. 212, which gave Roman citizenship to all free inhabitants of the empire, was an imperial edict. His decisions in lawsuits (*decreta*), though technically binding only in the particular case, were treated as authoritative in others, and collections of these decisions were made. Instructions (*mandata*) issued to governors and other officials were also authoritative for succeeding generations. Most significant of imperial constitutions (legislative enactments) for future development were the rescripts (*epistulae*), replies sent to private individuals who had asked for a ruling by the emperor on a point of law.

SOURCES OF POSTCLASSICAL LAW

Between the death of Severus Alexander (A.D. 235) and the accession of Justinian I (527) a number of external factors had an impact on the legal tradition. Until at least the end of the reign of Diocletian (305) the attempt was successfully made to retain classical law despite the intervening political and economic chaos. Constantine the Great moved the center of the empire to Constantinople in the Greek East and introduced Christianity as the state religion. Subsequent centuries saw the loss of the Latin West. But what the period has in common is the nonproduction of innovative juristic works and in their place the centrality of imperial rescripts. There were some juristic books, of course, but they are abridgments of elementary commentaries on earlier works, or they are collections of earlier texts. A problem for using imperial rescripts was the difficulty of finding the one that clearly applied to the given situation. An unofficial collection, the *Codex Gregorianus*, appeared in 291, another, the *Codex Hermogenianus*, in 295; neither has survived. The *Codex Theodosianus*, compiled and published (438) on order of Theodosius II, has survived; it is an official collection of all the general imperial constitutions, brought up to date, since the reign of Constantine.

Theodosius II issued the famous Law of Citations in A.D. 426. This made authoritative all the writings of five of the classical jurists, Ulpian, Paul, Papinian, Modestinus, and Gaius. Other jurists cited by them also had weight. When the five expressed differing opinions, the will of the majority was to prevail. When they were equally divided the opinion supported by Papinian was to win. When they were equally divided and Papinian had expressed no opinion the judge could follow whom he wished. This does not mark a low point of jurisprudence as is often suggested. Rather, it ranks the jurists of more than two centuries before, and makes important their opinions when a point was still unsettled. Naturally, any imperial rescript would take precedence, and these would be drafted by jurists who had become imperial functionaries. Thus, a contemporary lawyer, or one in the more recent past, writing in the name of the emperor, would take precedence over the great jurists of the past.

THE WORK OF JUSTINIAN

Justinian I joined his uncle Justin (who had risen from the ranks) as coemperor of the

Eastern (Byzantine) Empire in 527 and, on the latter's death in the same year, he became sole emperor. He immediately began to restate the law. His first step in 528 was to set up a ten-man team including Tribonian (quaestor in 529) and Theophilus, a professor, to prepare a collection of imperial rescripts drawn from the three previous codes and later enactments. They were to bring the rescripts up to date and make desired alterations. This first *Code* was published in 530 and has not survived.

Justinian turned to juristic writings and as a preliminary he resolved some of the disputes of the classical writers by promulgating the *Fifty Decisions,* which have not survived as a collection. In December 530, he instructed Tribonian to choose a commission, and he in fact appointed sixteen men. They were to make extracts from the great jurists of the past and to arrange them in fifty books, divided into titles according to subject matter. The commissioners were to choose the best view on every point, and cut out all dissension along with everything that was superfluous or obsolete or that was already in the published *Code*. Contrary to a widely held view, they were not given the power to change the substance of the texts. The commissioners retained at the beginning of each extract the name of the jurist and the work from which it was taken: more than one third of the *Digest,* as it is called, is taken from Ulpian, and a further sixth from Paul. Justinian claims that almost 2,000 books were read and reduced to one-twentieth of their length. The *Digest* was published in 533. Thus were the writings of the great jurists reduced to a manageable whole. To keep them that way, and also to preserve the *Digest*'s authority, Justinian forbade all commentaries and allowed only direct translations into Greek.

While work on the *Digest* was under way, Justinian ordered the preparation of a new elementary textbook, the *Institutes;* this task was entrusted to Tribonian, Theophilus, and Dorotheus. The work was to be based on elementary works of classical jurists, especially Gaius' *Institutes*. The *Institutes* of Justinian are in four books: Book One contains sources and persons; Book Two deals with property and testate succession; Book Three with intestate succession, contracts and quasi contracts; and Book Four with delict and quasi-delict crimes and actions. The *Institutes* came into effect on 30 December 533, the same day as the *Digest*.

All this while, from 529, fresh imperial constitutions were issued; and instructions were given for a new *Code*. This was issued in 534 in twelve books subdivided into titles in which the rescripts are arranged chronologically. Like the *Digest* and *Institutes,* the second *Code* has survived.

Although the work of codification was complete, new rescripts continued to be issued, now known as the *New Constitutions* or *Novellae*. At a much later date, the *Digest, Institutes, Code,* and *Novellae* came to be called the *Corpus Juris Civilis*.

ACTIONS

A legal remedy existed only where there was an appropriate action. The two main types of procedure up to and including classical law were both in two stages. The oldest type, the *legis actio* procedure, contained a small number of forms that had to be used in front of the praetor or other elected magistrate. Each form could be used for a variety of claims. They were so formal that after their demise Gaius (probably mistakenly) believed that a party who made a mistake in the wording lost his case. The second stage, in front of a judge or arbiter after the praetor had given his approval, was less rigid. The *legis actiones* were gradually replaced between the third century B.C. and the first century A.D. by the formulary procedure.

The first stage here, before the praetor, led to his issuing a *formula*, a formal statement of the claim that if proved before the judge led to the condemnation in damages of the defendant. For an action ordinarily to be available the alleged facts had to fit within the scope of an existing *formula*. Thus, for a long period an action under the *formula* for sale would be successful only if there was an actual contract of sale; if the agreement was not of sale, but something akin, or if the contract was void, the action would fail. But the praetor filled in many gaps either by inserting a fiction—the action was to proceed as if something were the case when it was not —or by giving an ad hoc remedy, an action on the facts. Some of these last became standardized, particularly for damage to property. From the early empire onward there gradually developed a more bureaucratic system of procedure, the *cognitio*, with official judges.

THE LAW OF PERSONS

Marriage and Divorce

In early Rome reciprocal promises of betrothal were made by the contract of *sponsio* on behalf of the bride and groom, but before the beginning of the second century B.C. the promises ceased to be actionable. Nonetheless betrothal had some legal effects: from the time of the betrothal relatives of the pair were in-laws, and sex by the woman with another man was adultery. By the fourth century A.D., the fiancé gave the woman a gift to ensure the marriage, a gift that he forfeited if he did not marry her; if she would not marry him she had to return a multiple of the gift.

There were two types of marriage. In the earlier, marriage *cum manu*, the wife came into the power, the *manus*, of her husband or of his father if he were still alive. In marriage *sine manu* the wife remained in the power, the *potestas*, of her own head of family if he were alive, and otherwise remained independent. *Manus* was created in three ways. *Confarreatio* was a religious ceremony involving a cake of spelt (*far*, a kind of wheat), and it required the presence of the *pontifex maximus*—chief priest—and a *flamen dialis*—one of the three major priests responsible for consecration and sacrifice—hence its use must have been restricted to the top level of society. *Coemptio* was an imaginary, possibly once real, purchase of the bride by a modified form of *mancipatio*, which was the form of transfer reserved for certain important kinds of early property. A wife who was not married with either of these formalities came into the power of her husband by *usus*, use, after a year unless she stayed away for three nights. The Twelve Tables contained a provision whose point was the intentional avoidance of *usus* by absence of the wife. So the second type of marriage, *sine manu*, was also early. It was frequent by the beginning of the second century B.C., and, as a result of deliberate misinterpretation of another provision of the Twelve Tables, marriage *cum manu* became virtually obsolete early in the first century B.C. *Confarreatio* was restored early in the empire but only with religious effect. No ceremony was needed for marriage *sine manu*, but celebrations including the leading of the bride to her husband's home were usual. Marriage required agreement, and this was commonly evidenced by a dowry.

Only marriage between Romans or with someone from a state that had been granted the right of intermarriage with Romans constituted full civil law marriage. Marriage between patrician and plebeian was forbidden by the Twelve Tables, but was permitted again by the Canuleian law of 445 B.C. Marriage between persons of senatorial rank and freed persons was frowned on in the republic, but was first actually prohibited for senators and their descendants by Augustus. Later, Jews and Christians were forbidden to marry. Slaves could not contract any marriage. Close relationship was also a bar, but the prohibited degrees varied from time to time. Originally, second cousins could not marry, but by the first century B.C. first cousins could. Uncles and nieces, aunts and nephews could not intermarry until a *senatus consultum* permitted marriage with a brother's (though not sister's) daughter so that the emperor Claudius could marry Agrippina the Younger. Almost four centuries later the old law was restored, with the death penalty for such incest. By the time of Augustus the female had to be at least twelve years old, but whether she had reached puberty was irrelevant. The Proculians required that the male be fourteen, but the Sabinians demanded actual puberty, to be determined by physical examination.

The consent of the paterfamilias of the bride and of the groom was required, as was the consent of the parties, although in early law the wishes of the woman were legally irrelevant. Where the woman was independent, the consent of her tutor was needed when the marriage was to be *cum manu* from the outset (but not otherwise); it was also needed for any dowry.

Except where it was *cum manu*, marriage had little impact on the status of the parties. In early law the husband could punish his wife, but for serious offenses it was her family that judged her and, with the husband's consent, put her to death. The main consequence of a valid Roman marriage was that the children were born into the power (*patria potestas*) of the husband or his father.

Divorce was permitted to the husband in early Rome only on specific grounds: adultery, tampering with keys, poisoning a child (abortion?). She or her father then had no right to the return of the dowry. If the husband cast her off for any other reason he had to give her one half of his property, the remainder being forfeit to the goddess Ceres. This continued until about 230 B.C., after which it came to be established that a husband (and a wife, too) could divorce for any reason. It then became sensible for the parties to make their own arrangements for the return of the dowry if the marriage failed. Otherwise, on divorce the dowry had to be returned but the husband could retain fixed fractions, if for instance there were children, or the wife had committed adultery. No action or formalities were required for divorce, unless the marriage was by *confarreatio*, in which case a reverse ceremony was needed. In the Christian Empire Constantine enacted that on divorce an offending wife would be deported and a husband could not remarry. If he did, the ex-wife could seize the second wife's dowry. Justinian enacted that if a wife divorced her husband, except for specified reasons, she would be confined in a nunnery for life and all her property would be forfeit. Nonetheless the divorce was valid.

Partia Potestas

Children born in a civil law marriage were in the power, *potestas,* of their father or remoter male ancestor, and so remained all their lives unless the *potestas* was ended by death or by emancipation. The *pater* had enormous power. He could put children to death for just cause (proven apparently by an investigation by the family council) or could sell them into slavery; his consent was necessary for their marriage; and he could bring about their divorce. A father who abused his power might be punished, and eventually after the Twelve Tables some powers, such as the right to sell into slavery, were restricted. Originally only the *pater* (or a woman who was independent) could own property, although it was customary to allow descendants and slaves to have a private fund, the *peculium,* which they might use as if it were their own though technically it belonged to the *pater*. When dependents made contracts with third parties the benefits accrued to the *pater*, but he could not be sued in disputes over the contract. This was obviously inefficient for trade, and the praetor eventually allowed actions to third parties against the *pater* in certain cases: where the dependent had a *peculium* then up to the limit of the *peculium* and also to the extent that the *pater* had benefited; where the *pater* had authorized the third party to contract; when the *pater* had set someone up in business or put him in charge of a ship. Augustus permitted a son, so long as he remained a soldier, to dispose of military earnings by will, and this exceptional case was gradually widened until a son was effectual owner of all military earnings (*peculium castrense*). Constantine extended this to earnings from certain public offices and he also gave children ownership of property left them by the mother though the father retained the use of it during his lifetime.

Patria potestas was also acquired by adoption, of which there were two forms. *Adrogatio* was used when the adoptee was independent. After investigation by the pontiffs into its suitability the matter went before the Comitia Curiata, a legislative body whose decision was in fact a law. Since only males above puberty could appear before the Comitia, only they could be so adopted. Adoption of this type was not to provide a loving home for an orphan baby, but was mainly political, to preserve a family from extinction; but it did, of course, involve the extinction of the adoptee's family line. Adoption of the other type, which was used when the adoptee was already in *patria potestas*, arose from a deliberate misinterpretation of a provision of the Twelve Tables that said if a son were sold three times—probably a reference to *nexum*, an old form of bondage of freemen—he would be free from his father's power. The father transferred him by a modified *mancipatio* to a friend who released him; this was repeated twice, and then the friend either reemancipated him to the father (so that he would be outside *patria potestas*) or retained him. The friend then claimed to be the father, the father did not counterclaim, and the praetor adjudged the son to the adopter. In time it was accepted that only one sale was necessary for a similar transfer of daughters or remoter descendants. The same procedure could be used for emancipation, the deliberate freeing of children from paternal power. In later law, at least, this was common.

Guardianship

Both males and females under puberty who were not in *patria potestas* had a tutor, a guardian whose office was treated as a very serious duty. As early as the Twelve Tables a tutor might be appointed by will, but only by the paterfamilias and only to those who became independent on his death. Failing this, the tutelage went to the nearest male agnates, relatives linked through males, who had themselves reached puberty. The nearest agnates would inherit the pupil's property if he died, but it should be noted that the tutors had no control over the person of the pupil. The Atilian law of about 210 B.C. allowed the praetor at Rome and a majority of the tribunes of the plebs to appoint a tutor to a pupil who had none. A further statute extended this to the provinces, and there was further provision for appointment of a special tutor when there was a lawsuit between the pupil and the existing tutor.

To act as tutor was a public duty and could not be refused except for specific excuses. While the pupil was *infans*, literally "unable to speak" and so be understood, until the fifth century A.D. he could not legally act, and the tutor alone had to act; when the child was older, the tutor's consent was needed for all legal acts of the pupil that might result in loss to the tutor. The Twelve Tables gave an action for theft from a pupil's account against an agnatic tutor for double the amount he had embezzled, but it was available only at the termination of the tutelage; there was another action for fraud by a testamentary tutor (one designated by a father's will) which could be brought during the tutelage. Later, probably in the third century B.C., arose the action on tutelage, the *actio tutelae,* which is perhaps the oldest of the good faith actions—those actions in which the judge is instructed to condemn the defendant to pay a sum equal to "what he ought to give or do in accordance with good faith."

From the earliest times, women who were independent and above the age of puberty also had tutors who were appointed as they were for children. But the women themselves had the power of administration, and the tutor's job was restricted to giving his consent to certain acts. The arbitrariness of this was recognized and various devices were introduced to enable women to change obstructive tutors.

Lunatics and their property were placed under the curatorship of their nearest agnates by the Twelve Tables. A prodigal who wasted an inheritance that he had received on intestacy, and later any prodigal, could be placed under curatorship and prohibited from dealing with his property. The Plaetorian law of 193/192 B.C. provided a fine for anyone who defrauded someone under the age of twenty-five; it also gave the minor a defense if he was sued by someone who was defrauding him. The praetor in time gave the minor a remedy for any transaction in which he might suffer loss. Later in the second century A.D. it became customary for a minor to have a curator; if he had, the minor was not liable in any transaction for more than he gained unless the curator had consented.

Slavery

For much of its history, Rome was a slave state in the sense that slaves were the main means of production. Yet little law emerged peculiar to slavery. The main ways of acquiring slaves were by capture from a people who did not have a treaty of friendship with Rome, or by birth to a slave mother that one owned. Exceptional cases are illuminating. A child was born free whose slave mother was free at any time between conception and birth. By the *senatus consultum Claudianum* if a master forbade a woman to cohabit with one of his slaves and the woman persisted, then she and any children could be enslaved by a decree of a magistrate. Or the woman could make a bargain that she would remain free but any children would be slaves. Again, by the Twelve Tables a thief caught in the act would be enslaved. So would those who avoided the census to escape conscription. A person above majority who had himself sold as a slave in order to share in the price also actually became a slave.

A slave could own nothing, and anything he acquired belonged to his owner even if he were allowed a *peculium.* If he committed a delict then (like a son) he could be given by the master to the victim in lieu of paying damages, a form of limited liability called noxal surrender. During the republic there were no legal limitations on the master's right to punish; gradually restrictions crept in, but they were always limited and relatively ineffective.

There were three ways of freeing a slave that conferred citizenship as well as liberty. The slave might be enrolled in the census, so long as it was taken, as if he were a citizen. Or someone, with the connivance of the master, might wrongly claim before the magistrate that the slave was free and the master would put up no defense. These were dodges, but the Twelve Tables allowed slaves to be freed by will. In this last way alone, the slave could be freed conditionally, and the heir was allowed to do nothing to inhibit the slave's eventual freedom. Restrictions were imposed on this type of manumission—perhaps the most common—by Augustus. Slaves informally freed in the republic remained slaves but were protected by the praetor; eventually their freedom was recognized but they did not become citizens.

Freed persons, but not their children, were subject to certain disabilities at public law. In addition they had certain duties to their former masters, including restrictions on suing their patrons; the payment of promised days of work; and, in varying degrees, payment of property on death.

THE LAW OF PROPERTY

Legal genius is largely a matter of drawing the most appropriate distinctions, and the Romans showed their skill nowhere more than with property. A first distinction was between things under divine law and things under human law. Under divine law were *res sacrae,* things such as temples dedicated by order of the Roman people to the gods above, and *res religiosae,* things dedicated to the gods of the underworld, namely tombs. *Res sanctae* were in an intermediate class, to some extent under divine law, and were like the gates and walls of cities: climbing on them entailed the death penalty. Things under divine law could not be owned. Under human law were public and private things. Public things were owned by the state, things such as roads, harbors, and navigable rivers. Riverbanks were private but their use was public. Some things were classed not as public but as common to all, such as air, the sea, and running water. There was dispute as to whether the seashore above high water mark was public or common to all. Things were further classified as corporeal or incorporeal, a distinction whose sole importance was that incorporeal things could not be transferred by the legal method that required actual physical delivery (*traditio*).

The main division among things that could be privately owned was into *res mancipi* and *res nec mancipi,* a division also important for transfer of ownership. *Res mancipi*—a classification that was early fossilized—were things important in an early agricultural community: Italic land, the four oldest land servitudes, slaves, cattle, horses, mules, and asses (the Proculians included the animals of draft and burden only when they were broken-in). These *res mancipi* could be transferred only by *mancipatio* or *in iure cessio.*

Mancipatio was a formal ceremony requiring the presence of the transferor, the transferee, five male witnesses who were Roman citizens above puberty, and another who held a bronze scale. The transferee grasped the object of transfer, struck the scale with a bronze or copper ingot, and said, "I declare this slave [for instance] to be mine by the law of the citizens, and let him have been bought by me with this bronze and this bronze scale." The transferor said nothing and his silence showed his acquiescence. Obviously the ceremony goes back to a time before coined money, and required the actual weighing of the money. The ceremony contained an inherent warranty—not, oddly, for the transfer of ownership, but that if the transferee were lawfully evicted, that is, if the thing was taken from him, the transferor would pay him double the price stated in the *mancipatio.* The action lay only if the price were paid or security given, but it could not be directly excluded by agreement of the parties. A dodge developed, though, of stating a ridiculously low price in the *mancipatio.* A similar warranty existed when the acreage of land was wrongly stated in the *mancipatio.*

Transfer by *in iure cessio* could be used for

all kinds of property, including incorporeals. It was a fictitious lawsuit in front of the magistrate in which the transferee claimed to be owner, the transferor put up no defense, and the magistrate adjudged the thing to the transferee. Unlike ordinary lawsuits, this decision actually transferred ownership and its effect was not just between the parties.

Mancipatio and *in iure cessio* gave ownership only to Roman citizens, as did *usucapio,* a form of prescription that occurred when someone had undisturbed control of land for two years or of movables for one, provided his control began in good faith, and that the thing was not stolen property and was capable of private ownership. In postclassical law a very different system was used. Possession for ten years—twenty if the owner was not in the same province—extinguished the owner's title without giving the possessor ownership. Even before Justinian, however, this possession did give ownership.

Res nec mancipi could be transferred by *traditio,* actual physical delivery, and this was available to foreigners. However there was some lessening of the strict requirement of physical delivery. There was delivery *longa manu,* by the long hand, when goods stored in a warehouse were sold and the seller gave the buyer the key within sight of the warehouse; and delivery *brevi manu,* by the short hand, when the transferee was already in possession. *Traditio* did not transfer ownership of *res mancipi,* but if other requirements were fulfilled the recipient would gain ownership by usucapion after one year (or two for land). The Publician action, perhaps of the first century A.D., allowed the recipient to recover the property from anyone during the intervening year as if the year had run.

There were other, less important, ways of acquiring ownership. By *occupatio* one took physical control of something that did not have an owner. *Specificatio,* the making of a new thing out of materials belonging to another who did not consent, say wine out of grapes, gave ownership, but the owner of the materials would usually have an action for compensation or even for theft. *Accessio* occurred where property of one person became inseparably joined to more important property of another. *Thesauri inventio,* treasure trove, was property hidden so long that the owner could no longer be traced. At first, this went to the landowner, but under Hadrian it was established that the landowner and finder shared equally.

The Romans also distinguished between ownership and possession. Generally speaking, a person had possession when he had physical control of a thing, even through an intermediary, and intended to keep it. Possession was important, not only as a requirement for usucapion, but because it was itself protected by remedies called interdicts. When ownership was in question the person who had possession, or was put into possession because of the interdicts, would be the defendant in any lawsuit, and it was only the plaintiff who had to prove his case in order to win. Usually, but not always, interdicts protected the present possessor: thus, by the interdict called *utrubi* possession was in effect awarded to the person who had had possession neither by force, nor by stealth, nor by grant at will for the longest period in the preceding year. When someone held control but not in his own name, particular rules came into force. Thus, a pledge creditor to whom the thing had been delivered did possess, a lessee did not, and a tenant for life did. A grantee at will did, but his claim to possess did not prevail against the grantor.

Possession was both a matter of fact and law. One gained possession when one took control with the requisite intention. And one retained possession so long as one did not relinquish the intention, provided the intention was not unrealistic and no one else had taken control.

Property might also be subject to burdens. Some of these operated only between neighboring land, whether by operation of law or by arrangement. Several restrictions of the former type were contained in the Twelve Tables; for instance, five feet of land around the boundaries could not be usucapted, overhanging trees could be lopped by the neighbor up to fifteen feet from the ground, and nuts or fruit that fell onto neighboring land could be collected. Again, the code gave an action if work had been done on a neighbor's land as a result of which rainwater might now cause damage. There was also a remedy by which one might demand security for damage threatened by a neighbor's defective property.

The most significant rights over neighboring property are servitudes, whose prime characteristic is that they are attached to the land, and survive despite changes in ownership. A servitude had to fall within a recognized class, and the four earliest—the right of way, the right to drive beasts, a combined right of these two, and the right of aqueduct—were *res mancipi*. Other well-known servitudes were the right of light and to let the rainwater from one's roof fall on a neighbor's land. With the sole exception of *oneris ferendi* servitudes could not impose a positive obligation on the owner of the servient land, but by *oneris ferendi* he could be compelled to keep a wall that acted as a support of adjoining property in good condition. Servitudes could only be exercised for the benefit of neighboring land, and had to be so used as to create as little disturbance as possible.

Property could also be burdened by real security. The oldest form is probably *fiducia*, the transfer of ownership of a *res mancipi* with a clause requiring good faith from the creditor. This was a good security for the creditor because, since he became owner, he had a strong right against anyone who got control of the property. It could also be good for the debtor since, because the creditor had such strong protection, the creditor did not need to insist on physical control, and the debtor in possession could continue to work his slaves, beasts, or land. In *pignus*, which could relate to all kinds of property, the debtor transferred possession but not ownership to the creditor. The creditor, if he lost possession, had a special Servian action to pursue the thing from the debtor or from anyone else. When the debtor paid and the thing was not returned, the debtor could bring the normal action, *vindicatio*, for ownership of the security, or a contractual action. *Hypotheca* was a variant on *pignus*—the texts use the terms interchangeably—in which not even physical control was delivered. The creditor's rights to sell the pledge in the event of nonpayment of the debt varied from time to time.

Finally there were burdens that are sometimes termed personal servitudes. Usufruct (*usus fructus*) was the right to enjoy the use and fruits of a thing for one's lifetime without impairing the substance. *Usus* was the much more limited right to enjoy the use but not the fruits; and *habitatio*, the right to live in a particular building, was a variety of *usus*.

THE LAW OF SUCCESSION

By the time of the Twelve Tables succession could be by will as well as by intestacy. Heirs were classed as *necessarii, sui et necessarii,* and *extranei*. The first were slaves of the deceased, appointed by will, and with no power to refuse. This was important because by Roman law an heir was responsible for all debts even when they exceeded the inheritance. The second were those persons in the power of the deceased who became independent on his death; they, too, had no power to refuse. Both *necessarii* and *sui et necessarii* became heirs automatically at the moment of death. All other heirs were *ex-*

tranei; they had the right to refuse and became heirs only when they accepted the inheritance by a formal act or by acting as heir. In early times the heir became responsible for the *sacra,* the private religious duties of the deceased, but this came to be regarded as burdensome, and Publius Mucius Scaevola, the *pontifex maximus,* was himself responsible for inventing a dodge to avoid the *sacra.*

When there was no will, succession was regulated at first by the Twelve Tables. For the freeborn, *sui heredes* (those who became independent by the death) took first. Failing these, the nearest agnate (a person related through males); and failing the agnate, the *gentiles,* members of the clan. The identification of the nearest agnate was made very narrowly, so that if he died or refused the inheritance it did not go to the next nearest agnate, but to the *gentiles.* If a freedman died intestate, his *sui heredes* succeeded, failing whom his patron. In the first century B.C. the law of intestate succession was remodeled by the praetor's edict, and basically gave rights first to children, including those given in adoption, next to blood relatives up to the sixth (and in one situation, the seventh) degree, and then to husband or wife.

As early as the Twelve Tables wills could be made in three ways: *in procinctu* when the army was drawn up in battle array, and when no formalities were required; before the Comitia Calata, which met only twice a year for this purpose, and where the will was a legislative act; and *per aes et libram,* which developed from the practice of using a modified form of *mancipatio.* The first two died out early on, although Julius Caesar reinstituted a military will. In the *testamentum per aes et libram* a figurehead acted as if he were transferee, but the inheritance went to the named heir, and the named legatees and tutors accepted without reference to the figurehead. The praetor modified this in the late republic: if a written will were produced, with the seal of those necessary for a *mancipatio,* then the praetor gave possession to the person named as heir. Other forms of will came into being in postclassical times.

Only a sane Roman above puberty could make a will, and until Hadrian's time a woman could only if she had undergone a change of family (that is, been married *cum manu*); even then the consent of her tutor was required. A will was effective only if an heir was instituted who was competent and who accepted. Only Roman citizens could be instituted heirs, with the exception that the slaves of Romans could also, whether they were slaves of the testator (provided they were given their freedom) or of another. Unborn descendants could be instituted: indeed if they were born after the will was made and they were unprovided for, the will became void. The Voconian law provided that a person in the first class on the census, the wealthiest, could not appoint a woman heir. This lost its significance with the decline of the census and the introduction of trusts. To avoid the danger of the designates institute not becoming heir, the testator could appoint a substitute, or a line of substitutes, to take if he did not. Where the institute was a *suus heres* of the testator and under puberty, the will could be so written that the substitute would take even if the institute took but died before puberty.

In addition to the appointment of an heir a will could contain legacies, trusts (*fideicommissa*), and the appointment of tutors. Legacies, like institutions, had to be written in proper form and they were of different kinds depending upon the words used. The two most important kinds were legacy *per vindicationem,* by which the legatee became owner as soon as the will was effective, and legacy *per damnationem,* in which the heir was ordered to give the legacy to the legatee. If he failed, the legatee had a personal action against him. Trusts at first had no legal force and were binding only on the conscience of the heir. They were used primarily where the beneficiary was legally barred from inheriting. Augustus enforced them in some cases and they came to be legally effective. In some situations codicils (later additions to a will) were recognized as having legal force.

THE LAW OF CONTRACT

Roman law is most highly regarded for its contract law even though the Romans did not develop a theory of contract but only individual types of contract. For an agreement to be a contract it had to fall within a particular type, say sale, and then it had the legal characteristics of that type. With the sole exception of *stipulatio,* the earliest of the contracts that could be used for any lawful business, the individual contracts were all defined by their function. Yet the Romans classified them by their form as verbal, literal, real, and consensual.

Verbal Contracts

Verbal contracts are those that require set spoken words or a set pattern of words to be effective. The most important was *stipulatio,* where the promisee orally asked "Do you promise . . . ?", and the promisor replied "I promise." The verb used had to be the same in question and answer, the promise had to correspond to the question, and no delay could intervene between question and answer. Originally only one verb, *spondere* (which suggests a sacral origin) could be used, but from quite early times any verb could be used. The contract was one of so-called strict law. The parties were supposed to mean what they said and only what they said. Hence it was difficult to imply unspoken terms. More important, the promisor was still bound even if he had entered the contract only as a result of fraud or extortion. This was remedied by praetors in the first century B.C. Around 80 B.C. the praetor Octavius gave an action for extortion (*metus*) for four times the value involved; he restored the injured party to the position he would have been in but for the extortion; and he gave a special defense of extortion (*exceptio metus*) if the wronged promisor was sued. The last is particularly interesting. An *exceptio* is a clause inserted into pleadings when the defendant accepts the accuracy of the plaintiff's claim, but insists another appropriate factor has to be taken into account. The *exceptio* had to be specifically pleaded. In 66 B.C. Gaius Aquilius Gallus gave the *actio de dolo,* action for fraud, for simple damages, but only if there was no other remedy, and also an *exceptio doli.* He defined fraud so narrowly that there had to be negotiations between the parties; hence the action was a contractual remedy. Since an action was available for fraud in other contracts, the *actio de dolo* was invented for fraud in the strict law, as contrasted with good faith, contracts. Within a short time the scope of the action for fraud was widened.

Not all stipulations were valid. A stipulation was void if it was illegal, immoral, or impossible, or subject to such a condition. Nor could one be made for performance to a third party. A stipulation to be performed after the death of one of the parties was void as impossible, but the advantages of such an agreement (for life assurance, for instance) led to the dodge that if the promise were framed "to give me when I am dying," then it was valid as becoming effective at the last moment of life.

But a stipulation could be used to cover all the terms of another type of contract, say sale, in which case the contract was one of *stipulatio;* or some terms of another contract, say warranties against eviction and latent defects in sale. One standard use was as personal security where the guarantor promised to pay the same—or a lesser but not greater—debt than the principal debtor, and the creditor could exact from either. There were three main forms depending on the verb used in the stipulation: *sponsio, fidepromissio,* and *fideiussio.* The rules here are complicated, but the basic picture is that so many rules developed to protect the guarantor that the two earlier forms ceased to be effective, and *fideiussio* emerged early in the empire, without the restrictions.

In early law performance did not discharge a contract. There had to be a similar act of extinction, in this case called *acceptilatio*. When this ceased to be necessary, perhaps as early as the late third century B.C., *acceptilatio* remained, but as a method of discharging a stipulation (when the parties so agreed) without performance.

There were two other verbal contracts. *Dotis dictio* was one method of promising a dowry and had the peculiarity that nothing was said by the promisee. It could only be promised by the bride, her paterfamilias, or a debtor of the bride. *Iusiurandum liberti* was an oath given by a new freedman that he would perform the services to his patron that he had promised before manumission. It is the only contract of historical times that involved an oath.

Literal Contracts

There was only one literal, that is, written, contract, and a great deal about it is obscure. It was also a contract of strict law and it existed by the early first century B.C. but is probably older. Rather than being an original contract it was instead a way in which one contract was changed into another. The creditor wrote fictitiously in his formal account books that an existing debt had been repaid and then made another entry fictitiously stating that a loan of the same amount had been made to the same debtor or another. Thus the old contract was extinguished and a new one created. Only Romans could be creditors but there was a dispute between the Sabinians and the Proculians as to how far foreigners could be debtors. The contract died out, perhaps in the third century A.D. with the demise of account books.

Justinian in his *Institutes* but not in the *Digest* treats of a literal contract. If someone writes, he says, that he has received money when he has not and two years pass, then if he is sued he cannot put up the defense that he never received the money. This is not really a contract, but amounts to saying that if a person granted an I.O.U. and let it stand without challenge, then after a period of time he is barred from denying he took the loan.

Real Contracts

The real contracts, contracts *re*—literally "by the thing," meaning by delivery—show that the categorization by form does not correspond to historical development. The oldest real contract, very different from the others, is *mutuum,* loan for consumption. A strict law contract dating from the third century B.C., it was unilateral since only the borrower was bound, and he had to return the exact equivalent of what was lent. No interest was enforceable by the action although interest could be arranged for through a separate stipulation. The action in this instance and also for the literal contract was the *condictio,* described below. In the first century A.D. the *senatus consultum Macedonianum* provided that no remedy was to be available to someone who lent to a son in power, even after the son became *sui iuris* (in one's own right).

The very different *commodatum* was loan for use in which the borrower did not become owner and would not suffer the loss if the thing were destroyed or damaged unless he had failed to show the degree of care that was regarded as appropriate. The contract was introduced by a praetorian edict in the first century B.C., but inexplicably there was also a civil law action for what was proper according to good faith.

As early as the Twelve Tables there was an action for double damages where a depositee failed to return the article deposited. Whether we should see a contract in this or an action akin to theft is a matter of dispute. But early in the first century B.C. the praetor issued an edict giving double damages against someone who failed to restore a thing deposited with him as a result of a house falling down, shipwreck, or fire, but only simple damages against his heir who failed to restore or a depositee in other circumstances. Oddly, there also developed a civil law action. Normally the depositee was liable only for fraud.

Consensual Contracts

The consensual contracts—contracts that come into being simply by the agreement of the parties and that require no formalities—are one of the great Roman inventions. There are four of them: hire; mandate; partnership, which comes from the law of succession; and sale, with roots in *mancipatio* and *stipulatio*. They have little in common in their origins except that, as consensual contracts, an action was provided for them by the praetor's edict.

Sale (*emptio venditio*) required agreement, a price, and a thing to be sold. No formalities were required, but for important transactions evidence would be provided by writing or by giving earnest money (*arra*), a deposit, which could also serve as part payment. This *arra* had no specific legal function. Justinian changed the law here: if the parties agreed that the contract was to be put into writing there was no contract until the writing was completed and formalized and either party could withdraw without penalty provided no *arra* had been given; if *arra* had been given, then if the buyer withdrew he forfeited the *arra,* or if the seller withdrew he had to restore the *arra* and as much again.

Since agreement was needed, error that blocked agreement prevented the sale from coming into being. Such error was sufficient if for instance it was about the identity of the thing sold, or was the so-called *error in substantia*. The last is rather obscure but seems to mean error as to the material the thing is completely made of, such as bronze for gold (but not gold alloy for gold), or error as to the sex of slaves. A lesser error left the sale valid but there would be an action available if the error was the result of misrepresentations by the seller: for the difference in value if the misrepresentation were innocent, for all subsequent loss if the misrepresentation was deliberate.

The price, according to the Proculians, who prevailed, had to be in coined money. The Sabinians had wished to extend sale to cover the legally inadequate rules of barter. The price also had to be certain in the sense that it had to be knowable, and it had to be seriously intended—a disguised gift was not a sale. A new rule was apparently introduced by Diocletian (284–305 A.D.) only to disappear until it was restored by Justinian, that the sale of land was void if the price set was less than half the true value. There also had to be a thing to be sold: hence if a slave was sold who was already dead the sale was void. There could be a sale of a future thing, for instance of a growing crop. If this sale were construed as *emptio rei speratae*, a purchase of a hoped for thing, then the sale came into effect only if the thing came into being; if as *emptio spei*, "purchase of a hope," then the expectation was what was bought, and the sale was valid even if no thing came into being. Originally there could be no sale of anything incapable of human ownership, such as a temple, but eventually it was accepted that such a sale was valid, in the sense that an action on it might be brought.

The buyer was obliged to pay the price on time and, if he were in delay, interest and the seller's expenses. The seller's obligations were more complex. He had to keep the thing safe until delivery, deliver possession, give guarantees against eviction and hidden defects, and be free from fraud. As we have seen, ownership was transferred only by delivery, but under sale risk passed to the buyer as soon as the contract was perfect. The seller still in possession therefore was liable if he did not show proper care, but the standard of care demanded is not certain, and may have varied. Oddly, the seller did not have to make the buyer owner. It was enough originally that he delivered the thing in good faith. So it became customary for the buyer to take a stipulation that his enjoyment would not be legally disturbed, and by a series of steps that culminated in the second century A.D. this guarantee came to be implied in the sale. Likewise at first there were no innate guarantees against hidden defects, but they were often taken by stipulation. The curule aediles, who had control over the streets and markets, issued an edict giving an action where beasts or slaves had been sold and the declaration of defects was false or had not been given. Eventually, the warranty against latent defects was implied in all sales.

Hire (*locatio conductio*) may almost be described as a residual category after sale, covering every type of bilateral agreement where there is a money price on one side. As does hire in many modern Western systems, it thus covers hire of a thing, of a piece of work to be done, and of services. In hire of a thing the lessor had to give the lessee the use of the thing for the agreed period. If the thing was not fit for the purpose of the lease the lessee was excused from paying rent, and if the lessor unnecessarily caused the thing not to be used, then the lessee could sue for all resulting loss. In hire of a piece of work to be done the person hired agreed to produce a certain result on a thing delivered by the hirer; for instance, training a slave of the hirer to be a doctor, or to deliver the hirer's wheat to Rome. The person hired was liable for any loss caused to the thing even if he were not negligent unless the injury was the result of external force or robbery with violence. Hire of services was less important than it is today since much work would be performed by slaves, and when the services of another's slave were hired this would usually be hire of a thing. The so-called liberal arts such as the teaching of philosophy, giving of legal advice, and surveying, were regarded as too noble to be the object of a contract.

Partnership (*societas*) had a long history before the introduction of the consensual contract. As early as the Twelve Tables, *sui heredes* who did not divide up the inheritance were partners (in all their assets, necessarily) but not as the result of contract. Then the praetor gave a *legis actio* for others who wished to form such a partnership. Even when consensual partnership came into being, the standard case was partnership of all the assets of the partners; obviously not a mercantile arrangement, but for close relatives who worked a farm together. But other lesser partnerships were available, including partnership of one transaction, which is unknown in modern law but useful for a society that does not accept direct agency, that is, where an obligation entered into by the agent becomes the obligation of his principal. Each partner had to contribute something, whether work or assets, and each had to have the right to some share of profits. Unless the partners agreed otherwise they would share equally in any profit or loss. The partners were liable to each other only for fraud, it being regarded as a person's own fault if he chose a negligent partner. Unlike modern partnership, Roman partnership was almost entirely turned inward and controlled the relationship between the partners. A partner's contract on partnership affairs with a third party was a contract between him and the third party who could neither sue nor be sued by the other partners.

Mandate (*mandatum*) was the gratuitous undertaking to do something on behalf of a friend, and the contract came into existence sometime in the second century B.C. If the undertaking was to enter a contract with a third party, then any resulting contract was between the third party and the person acting as mandatory. Hence mandate was not direct agency. Until performance was started, either party could withdraw from the contract. The mandatory was entitled to be reimbursed for any loss and expenses, and he was normally liable only for fraud.

Only the foregoing are described as contracts in Gaius' and Justinian's *Institutes,* but the *Digest* has a title on what later came to be called the innominate—not specifically named—contracts. These fall into two types. The first occurs where there is a standard type of situation, and where specific legal rules have come to govern an institution that does have a name such as *permutatio* (barter) or *aestimatum* (sale or return). The second, described by the jurist Paul in the second century A.D., occurs when there is a bilateral agreement for each to give or do something, and an action would lie to one who performed his side of the bargain. As early as the republic, the praetor also protected pacts in the sense that he allowed them to act as a defense although not as the basis of an action. There were subsequent developments.

There were also situations akin to contract but not to delict that gave rise to actions "as if from contract." The most important of such actions were the *actio negotiorum gestorum,* action for work done, and the *condictio*. The former lay when someone acted, without authorization but reasonably, on behalf of another. The actor could recover any expenses up to the value of the property saved. It was also the action where an authorized person acted for another in court, and the action for or against the *procurator,* the general agent. The *condictio* was an action that lay whenever, as a result of a transfer, the defendant owned something that he ought to give to the plaintiff: for instance, if the plaintiff had by mistake paid to the defendant something he did not owe him, or if the plaintiff had for an agreed reason given something to the defendant, and the reason was not forthcoming. An anomalous case was the *condictio* to recover stolen property because the plaintiff had remained the owner.

THE LAW OF DELICT

Delicts were private wrongs but much of what we consider criminal law was covered by them. Only four delicts, theft, robbery with violence, damage to property, and verbal or physical assault were dealt with in the *Institutes* of Gaius and Justinian.

As early as the Twelve Tables *furtum,* theft, was divided into manifest and nonmanifest. The former meant that the thief was caught in the act, and originally if he were a slave he was beaten and thrown from the Tarpeian Rock; if a freeman he was beaten and adjudged to the victim as a bond servant. Later, by the edict the penalty for manifest theft was four times the value of the stolen property. For nonmanifest theft the penalty was always double the value of the stolen property. Until the second century A.D., by a clause of the Twelve Tables, a thief at night could always be killed.

The physical requirement for theft was not carrying away but wrongful touching. This caused practical problems when only part of a larger whole, say some wine from a cask, was removed since the action lay for a multiple of the value, not of the owner's interest. The problem was compounded in that if the thief intended to use the thing only temporarily, he was still liable for theft of the whole thing. The necessary wrongful intention had to be to make a gain, but there were some doubtful borderline cases.

The Twelve Tables instituted a ritual search for stolen property and if any was found the theft was treated as manifest. The edict introduced an action for a fourfold penalty where a search was refused. If stolen property were found on someone's property without a formal search he was liable for a threefold penalty whether he was the thief or not (*furtum conceptum*), but in his turn he had a right of action for the same amount against the person who placed it there. These actions, established by the Twelve Tables, were repeated in the edict.

Rapina, robbery with violence, was instituted as a separate delict by the praetor Marcus Licinius Lucullus (76 B.C.), with an action for a fourfold penalty. *Damnum iniuria datum*, wrongful damage to property, was dealt with by the Aquilian law of 287 B.C., although in part that merely consolidated earlier legislation. It was in three chapters, of which the second is out of place. That dealt with the situation in which by stipulation a friend of the creditor acted as alternative payee, payment was made to him, and he released the debtor by *acceptilatio*, but did not hand the money over to the creditor. Until the introduction of mandate there was no contract between him and the creditor, hence this delictal action.

Chapter one of Aquilian law gave an action where a slave or herd animal was wrongfully killed, and it lay for the highest value the slave or animal had had in the past year. Wrongfully at first meant without rightful cause, but before the end of the republic it meant that the killing was malicious or negligent. The damages were doubled if the defendant denied liability. In the early empire the action was interpreted restrictively and lay only if the defendant had killed, not if he had merely furnished a cause of death. The latter was the case for example if a midwife handed a drug to a pregnant slave, and the slave herself drank it. In such an instance the praetor routinely gave an action on the facts.

Chapter three of the law gave an action for other damage to inanimate and animate things alike caused by wrongful burning, snapping, or breaking, and it lay for the loss that became apparent within thirty days. The reference to thirty days came to be neglected, and this chapter, too, came to be restrictively interpreted.

Iniuria, personal injury, was the object of three clauses of the Twelve Tables, whose meaning is not entirely clear. For *membrum ruptum*, presumably a serious bodily injury, the victim could inflict the same injury unless a compromise was reached. For *os fractum*, a broken bone, the action was for 300 asses (copper coins) if the victim were a free man, 150 if a slave. Probably this was the minimum for this subcategory of *membrum ruptum*. For minor assaults the action was for twenty-five. Depreciation of the value of the money made the awards absurdly low and in the third century B.C. a general edict of the praetor made the assessment flexible. This effectively destroyed the distinctions between the categories, and the action was eventually extended to verbal assaults. Other edicts followed, giving actions for specific situations: public insult; following a matron, young boy or girl, or removing a chaperone contrary to good morals; assaulting another's slave contrary to good morals, primarily by beating him or having him tortured; and *iniuria* to someone in power whose paterfamilias was absent.

In addition to the four main delicts there were a number of others of which *metus* and *dolus* have been mentioned. Others included an action for double damages for taking in another's runaway slave or deliberately making him worse, physically or morally, and one for wrongfully cutting down another's trees.

When a slave or son committed a delict without the master's knowledge, the action normally gave the master the choice of paying the whole amount of the condemnation or delivering the wrongdoer to the victim in so-called noxal surrender. This amounts to an early form of limited liability, as does the similar provision in the *actio de pauperie* when an animal caused injury and could be said to be at fault. The aediles also gave an action where a wild animal was kept near a road and did damage.

Finally, there were four situations akin to delict where an action was given for an obligation arising as if from delict. These were: where a judge made the case his own (whatever that means); against the owner of a dwelling when something was poured or thrown from his dwelling (even without the owner's knowledge) and caused damage; for allowing something to be placed or suspended from eaves or a projecting roof when its fall could cause injury; against a ship's captain, innkeeper, or stablekeeper for any theft or fraud committed in the ship or building by an employee.

THE SUBSEQUENT HISTORY OF ROMAN LAW

More than any other system, Roman law has had an impact on very different societies, in very different economic, political, and geographical conditions.

The first large-scale borrowing and adoption occurred among Germanic tribes in what had been part of the West Empire. The Visigothic king Alaric II issued the *Lex Romana Visigothorum* in 506 for his Roman subjects (or for all his subjects); it was composed of extracts from Roman pre-Justinianic sources such as the Theodosian Code and an epitome of Gaius' *Institutes*. At roughly the same time the Burgundians, probably under King Gundobad, issued the *Lex Romana Burgundionum* also for their Roman subjects, but this comprised statements of legal rules, not extracts. In 654 the Visigoth Recceswind repealed the *Lex Romana Visigothorum* and issued the *Lex Romana Recesvindiana* that applied to all, Romans and Visigoths alike. But it was Justinian's compilation that was to be the main vehicle for transmitting Roman law to later ages.

In the Greek East, Theophilus, a compiler of both the *Digest* and the *Institutes*, issued a version of the latter that is about six times as long and is known as the *Paraphrase*. Other compilers wrote works on the *Code*, and later an unknown jurist made a large work out of commentaries on the *Code*. Around 740, at a time of falling legal standards, the first official Byzantine codification appeared. This, the *Ecloga*, was based primarily on the *Institutes*. Other works appeared, but the most famous is the *Basilica* of Leo VI the Wise, Byzantine emperor (886–911). This is in sixty books divided into titles in each of which are collected, with changes, the appropriate passages of the *Digest, Code,* and *Novels,* and sometimes of the *Institutes*. Around 1345 a judge, Harmenopoulos, issued his *Hexabiblos*, which was based on a number of minor works; in 1835 this was decreed to be law in force in Greece until a civil code could be issued. The modern Greek civil code came into force only in 1946, heavily influenced by the German tradition, which was itself based on a different approach to Roman law.

In the West intimate knowledge of Justinian's compilation soon ceased, but a revival began in Bologna in the late eleventh century. Shortly thereafter Irnerius (*ca.* 1055–*ca.* 1130) made Bologna a center to which flocked students from many parts of Europe to study Roman law. Irnerius and his school—of which the most famous are his four successors, Bulgarus, Martinus, Jacobus, and Ugo—are known as the glossators because their main works were marginal glosses on the texts. Many glossators taught outside Italy, including Vacarius in England and Placentinus at Montpellier. Later glossators, such as Azo, wrote commentaries, *Summa,* on the *Code* and *Institutes.* Accursius in the first half of the thirteenth century produced an edition of the gloss that became standard and is known as the Great Gloss. It was for long included with both manuscript and printed versions of the compilation.

By the late thirteenth century the main centers of Roman law learning were in France, but Italy was soon to regain the mastery. A new approach was being taken, mainly to adapt the Roman rules to contemporary practice. The most famous jurists, now known as commentators or post-glossators, included Petrus de Bellapertica, Cinus de Pistorio, Baldus, and above all Bartolus (died in 1357) of whom it became for centuries a catchphrase: "No one is a jurist who is not a Bartolist."

Roman law as a learned academic subject was of necessity taught in universities. The customary law of the individual territories, largely unwritten and lacking in international appeal, could not compete there. Hence formal legal education stressed Roman (and canon) law and generally dismissed other elements of local law. Lawyers, whether practical or theoretical, draw their legal argument from wherever they can and so Roman law, and the way it was understood by jurists, came more and more to permeate legal systems.

The process was reinforced in any territory—which was most of those in western Europe—that accepted Justinian's compilation in whole or in part as part of the law of the land or at least as directly highly persuasive. This reception was very slow and its progress varied from place to place. In northern France, for instance, it did not reach its fullest extent until the Napoleonic Code came into force in 1804. In the end only English law could be said not to have become "civilian" and even that borrowed much of the substance of Roman law. In the seventeenth century, largely as a result of Humanist studies that revealed the extent to which Roman law was not classical, there was a revival of interest in other aspects of local law. This led to the phenomenon of "institutes" of local law that were primarily modeled in size, structure, and (above all) substance on Justinian's *Institutes.* Thus, topics such as public law and commercial law which were not in Justinian's *Institutes* were also excluded from these local compilations. In their turn these local bodies of law formed the models for modern European civil codes. Thus it is that the private law of modern European countries such as France and Austria seems much closer to that of Justinian than to their own private law of, say, the sixteenth century.

In modern times Roman law spread far beyond Europe, mainly as a result of colonization: for instance to South Africa and Ceylon (Sri Lanka) with the Dutch; to Quebec, Louisiana, and parts of Africa with the French; and to Latin America with the Spanish and Portuguese (although in the nineteenth century the French *code civil* there became the dominating influence).

BIBLIOGRAPHY

EARLY LAW

Alan Watson, *Rome of the XII Tables, Persons and Property* (1975).

HISTORY

Herbert F. Jolowicz and Barry Nicholas, *Historical Introduction to the Study of Roman Law,* 3d ed. (1972).

TEXTBOOKS

William Warwick Buckland, *A Textbook of Roman Law,* 3d ed., Peter Stein, ed. (1963); Joseph Anthony Charles Thomas, *A Textbook of Roman Law* (1976); Alan Watson, *The Law of the Ancient Romans* (1970).

SUBSEQUENT HISTORY

Hermann Kantorowicz, *Studies in the Glossators of the Roman Law* (1938); John Henry Merryman, *The Civil Law Tradition* (1969); Paul Vinogradoff, *Roman Law in Medieval Europe,* 2d ed., F. de Zulueta, ed. (1929); Alan Watson, *The Making of the Civil Law* (1981).

Greek Administration

CHESTER G. STARR

As the survey of greek history in the present work has shown, the ancient Aegean world was politically divided into a large number of independent, small states called poleis. Many districts in the less developed regions of western and northern Greece, indeed, continued to be tribally organized, although Aristotle (*Politics* 1.2.1253a) solemnly pronounced that "man is by nature an animal intended to live in a polis." Culturally and religiously, on the other hand, Greeks everywhere shared a common structure of thought and values, man-centered, rational, logical.

In these tiny states, which may be compared to one-celled amoebas, political, religious, and social activities were conducted in a simple way, geographically focused in an open area usually called an agora. Administrative needs were not likely to be extensive or to require the creation of elaborate bureaucratic systems; the one Greek polis that evolved in this respect was Athens in the classical period. Yet various public functions did come to require some machinery of control in virtually all states. Here we shall first survey the emergence of those functions in archaic Greece (roughly 750–500 B.C.). Thereafter our evidence permits us to look at classical Athens in greater detail before turning to the much more developed bureaucracies of the Hellenistic age which followed Alexander's conquest of the Near and Middle East. Our concern in this section is not with the legislative, judicial, and executive organs of Greek poleis in themselves but rather with the execution of public affairs as distinguished from policy-making, i.e., the rise of procedures and structures to implement and supervise the execution of the decisions and directives of government.

ARCHAIC GREECE

The polis crystallized as a consciously organized political system during the eighth century B.C. in the more advanced areas of Greece, economically and socially speaking. In its fundamental essence it was never conceived as an extent of territory, although its boundaries could be drawn on a map, but rather as a group of citizens feeling themselves bound together under the rule of law. As the late seventh-century poet Alcaeus (Page frag. 426 *Sappho and Alcaeus* 1955) put the point, "It is not stones nor timber or the craft of craftsmen, but wherever there are men knowing how to defend themselves, there are walls and a polis." Later Aristotle (*Politics* 4.11.1295b and 3.9.1280b) observed, "A state aims at being, as far as it can, a society composed of equals and peers . . . for the sake of attaining a perfect and self-sufficing existence."

The most visible mark of this spiritual unity was the obligation of all citizens to revere the patron deity of the body politic, as well as other gods and heroes of the community. Each state had a central hearth dedicated to the goddess Hestia, and a prime requirement in the foundation of a colony was the transport of fire from that hearth to kindle the protective fire of the new settlement. It is in the religious field, accordingly, that the first function of government emerged to produce administrative structures. During the preceding Dark Age worship had apparently been conducted at open-air altars, but by the eighth century simple shrines were being erected; by 700 B.C. wealthier Greek communities began to construct true temples, at first of wood on stone foundations but then increasingly entirely of stone.

The purpose of a temple was to serve as a box to protect the statue of the deity there worshipped, but religious sanctuaries also came to house a great variety of dedications, or offerings. Rhodopis, a famous courtesan who plied her profession at the Greek trading post of Naucratis in Egypt and there enticed the brother of the poetess Sappho, wished to leave a memorial of herself in Greece and sent to Delphi a tithe of her possessions in the form of "a quantity of iron spits, such as are fit for roasting oxen whole. . . . They are still to be seen there, lying of a heap" (Herodotus, 2.135). Such a dedication of iron spits was discovered at the Argive Heraeum (Heraion). Bronze caldrons, often adorned with majestic griffin heads, were presented to Olympia down to the seventh century, when the needs of the Greek states for hoplite (infantry) armor diverted supplies of bronze to more mundane purposes. A tithe of the booty of interstate war or of piracy might also be used to erect a statue or to present trophies of victory. Foreigners as well made presents to Greek shrines. The Hellenistic inventory of the temple of Athena at Lindos on the island of Rhodes lists a linen corselet given by the Egyptian pharaoh Amasis as well as gifts by Datis and Artaphernes, generals of the Persian king Darius I, although some scholars consider these a pious fabrication. Herodotus records seeing at Delphi a throne from Midas of Phrygia (*ca.* 738–696 B.C.) and goblets, bowls, and other objects of gold and silver given by Lydian kings from Gyges (*ca.* 685–657 B.C.) to Croesus (*ca.* 560–546 B.C).

Both the requirements of public cult and the need to protect these treasures led to an expansion of the personnel serving the temples. In earlier days the kings of the Greek tribes had conducted sacrifices, although Homer knows of priests for specific deities; when the kings disappeared at the beginning of the historic era they were replaced by priests, who directed superintendents of sacrifices and other specialists. Seers who divined the will of the gods by observing the flight of birds, meditating on dreams, or inspecting the entrails of sacrificial victims, also became more professional; a family of seers, the Iamids, served the shrine of Zeus at Olympia for centuries.

Stewards of the growing wealth of the temples and treasurers under various titles were also required. Almost certainly the first public records of expenditures and inventories were those maintained by these religious officials; as we shall see in a later section, religious financial records were eventually carved at Athens and elsewhere on stone in lasting form. It was the erection and maintenance of temples that necessitated the major expenses of the incipient poleis of the eighth and seventh centuries. The burdens involved in providing cult utensils (the use of which was carefully regulated by a law at Argos); and victims for sacrifices were much heavier than could be met by the occasional revenues from temple-owned land. In constructing his ideal state Aristotle (*Politics* 7.10.1330a) assigned a full quarter of its revenues to religious purposes.

It should, however, be observed that priests in ancient Greek states were essentially public officials, much like churchwardens or, as a secular equivalent, members of school boards. On behalf of the community they oversaw the proper celebration of sacrifices, processions, and other ceremonies to honor and appease the gods of the state; but the details of the cult were in the hands of professionals. At the great shrine of Demeter at Eleusis the priests initially belonged to the Eumolpid and Kerykes clans, but very often priests were chosen from aristocratic families by public vote. In any one polis the priests of the various gods did not form a college, nor did the priests of a deity such as Athena have an overarching unity from one polis to another. Even in the religious field, in sum, we cannot speak of a true bureaucracy in the archaic era.

Military Administration

Early in his *Laws* (626a) Plato casually observes that "every polis is in a natural state of war with every other," a statement that throws into vivid relief the international anarchy of the world of the polis. From the beginning of conscious political organization in the Greek world wars took place incessantly. Usually these struggles were to acquire a debated fringe area, as in an eighth-century war by which Corinth sheared off part of its northern neighbor Megara, or the fierce contention of Eretria and Chalcis in Euboia over the fertile, if small, Lelantine plain.

From this area of public activity arose a second function requiring a certain amount of administrative personnel. After the disappearance of the kings, the generals of a Greek state were normally elected officials, serving for only a year with the title of *polemarch,* or strategus. Would-be tyrants found such posts a very convenient jumping-off point for securing more lasting power. Military operations otherwise did not require specific administrative provisions. Once the phalanx style of fighting, based on heavily armored infantrymen (hoplites), had become dominant in the early seventh century, anyone who could afford the necessary armor was expected to serve, and communal pressures presumably made any formal draft arrangements unnecessary. Since wars were fought in the summer along state frontiers and involved often only one battle, soldiers also provided their own food.

The generals did need certain specialists. Expert seers ascertained the pleasure of the gods, but the military commanders could take or leave this advice as they wished. To keep the phalanx in step as it marched into battle a skilled player of the aulos—an oboe-like pipe—was needed, as is shown on one of the first portrayals of hoplites on a Corinthian vase. After the battle the victorious side erected a trophy and also disposed of the spoils, including the armor of the dead and other items; a law ascribed to Solon about 600 B.C. speaks of a group of professional booty-purchasers. Especially when the Greeks came to fight the Persians and other wealthy opponents loot was as important a product of victory as in Roman or early modern history.

Naval activity throughout history has required some form of expenditure to build and maintain ships and has consequently forced the development of public agencies to provide and to man the vessels. Down to almost the end of the sixth century Greek states did not engage in naval battles, but Sparta, Corinth, Athens, and other poleis did occasionally find it necessary to transport troops by sea or to send envoys to the island shrine of Delos. At Athens there are obscure references to a system of *naucraries,* administrative districts each of which had to provide a ship and presumably its crew. At least one of these *naucraries* was identified with a coastal district (Colias), and probably the ships in question were owned by private citizens, much as in the early naval organization of Norman England based on the Cinque Ports, each of which could be required to provide a certain number of private ships for fifteen days a year. A naucraric fund at Athens is also attested; how it was nourished is unclear.

Community Services

As industry and commerce burgeoned in the Greek states from 700 onward and civil unity became more evident, true cities eventually appeared that, mainly after 600, were nodes of political, social, and economic life. Thus a third function of public activity produced a requirement for some type of offices to carry out a wider range of decisions of governmental agencies and to provide internal security and services for the community. Homeric kings had made do with household managers and a vague group of aides called *therapontes* but had no need for archives and secretaries. From the seventh century onward, however, treaties were inscribed on stone or bronze tablets; internal conflict between aristocrats and non-aristocrats led to the consolidation of laws, which also were published at times on stone either as specific rules or as general codes. Judges in Crete and elsewhere had their *mnemones* (remembrancers, memory-clerks), who appear by 500 often to have additional responsibilities in registering private contracts. Although the presence of secretaries or scribes is not well illuminated in the archaic era, they must have developed to some degree to meet the varied obligations of publishing or preserving documents. Herodotus (3.142–143) also mentions a prominent citizen of Samos as possessing a record of state expenditures, or perhaps more accurately those of the tyrant Polycrates; and treasurers called *kolakretai* at Athens disbursed funds from the naucraric fund.

Certainly the rise of tyrants in the turbulent seventh and sixth centuries helped to promote the rise of public expenditures. The mercenaries who protected their rule had to be paid; the poets who embellished their courts expected presents; temples and also secular buildings were erected as profusely as revenues permitted. At Corinth, Megara, Samos, and Athens tyrants provided more regular water supplies to the growing urban populations; Pisistratus of Athens defined the boundaries of the agora and presumably walled Athens itself (though no trace of this wall south of the Acropolis has yet been found). At Corinth the Cypselid tyrants constructed a slipway across the isthmus by which the small vessels of that period could be hauled from the Saronic Gulf to the Gulf of Corinth and thus avoid the dangerous journey around the southern rocky promontories of the Peloponnesus; harbor works in the form of extensive breakwaters also began in the archaic period.

The payment of scribes, mercenaries, sculptors, and other specialized professionals required money; or to put the matter in reverse order, the extraordinarily rapid spread of the custom of striking coins may have been facilitated by these demands. Coinage itself traditionally began in Lydia shortly before 600; by the end of the next century hundreds of Greek mints, both in the Aegean and in the far-flung colonies, were in existence. Many states struck staters, tetradrachmas, and other denominations in silver only occasionally, but mints such as that of Aegina issued currency in abundance as an international means of exchange.

How did the treasurers of the poleis get the silver or actual coinage in order to spend it on temples, naval stores, mercenaries, and other purposes? By and large, citizens did not like to pay direct taxes. Land taxes existed at times, but at Athens only under the Pisistratid tyranny did farmers have to pay 5 percent (or in another account 10 percent) of their crops to the state. Poll taxes were likewise avoided except for resident aliens and sometimes slaves. As a consequence states had to rely largely on tolls at their ports, sales taxes in their markets, and a wide variety of fees, as for using public weights, and also the fruits of justice in the form of fines and guarantees. Cyzicus, a Milesian colony, granted to one man exemption from all taxes save fees on slave-dealing, horse-dealing, public scales, and perhaps ferry tax (Solmsen, *Inscriptiones Graecae* [hereafter *IG*], 4th ed., 51); one must wonder from what other dues he was thus spared. Athens was fortunate enough to have its own silver mines in the Laurium district, which were being exploited before 500; the tyrant Pisistratus had commanded the resources of Thracian mines.

Mints demanded specialized workers as well as directors; the collection of taxes or fees and tolls also involved some personnel. The methods of accounting for receipts and expenditures may have been borrowed from temple practice, but required sundry professional scribes and accountants as well as treasurers. Very little of the resulting administrative structure is illuminated well from the archaic period. On the whole state revenues from all sources were very limited, but so also were public functions. By the close of the era the principle that supervision of public activities above the level of ordinary religious and clerical personnel should be carried out by amateurs for limited periods was firmly established in all Greek states.

CLASSICAL ATHENS

Across the fifth and fourth centuries the Greek state that is best known is Athens. Once the Persian invasion had been defeated by sea and by land the Athenians seized their opportunity to become first leaders, then masters of the Aegean. Even after its empire had been crushed during the Peloponnesian War, Athens remained the economic and cultural center of the Greek world. Accordingly, antiquarian scholars from the fourth century onward devoted a great deal of attention to describing Athenian history and institutions. The major surviving work of this type was the product of the effort by Aristotle and his students to survey a great number of Greek states in preparation for his major treatise, the *Politics*. In 1890 the *Constitution of Athens* (*Athenaion Politeia*, conventionally abbreviated *Ath. Pol.*) was discovered almost intact on papyrus rolls in upper Egypt. Although this work is certainly by a student rather than by Aristotle himself, it is a product of the later fourth century and gives a clear picture of the structure of Athenian government at that time; in his *Politics* proper (4.15.1299a; 6.5.1321b) Aristotle surveys more generally the responsibilities and agencies of administration.

Athens was democratic throughout this period, and its citizens expected to be informed of the conduct of public business. Decrees of the assembly, decisions of the council, financial records, and a large volume of other material were accordingly put before the eyes of the public—either painted on walls, written on whitewashed wooden boards, or carved on stone steles. A remarkable amount of the latter form of publication has survived, either intact or more often in fragmentary form. Both the accidents of survival and a rather erratic judgment as to what to put on stone sometimes leave the modern student puzzled or with incomplete evidence, but the epigraphic material provides fascinating light on the day-to-day operations of Athenian public bodies.

General Administrative System

The functions of the state continued to be those of the archaic era—religious, military, and general administrative—but in classical Athens they became far more complex, detailed, and increased in variety. The cult of Athena was now magnificently housed on the Acropolis and required a number of priests, priestesses, musicians, heralds, sacrificers, even washers who bathed the statue of Athena once a year in the sea, and laundresses of the robe that was renewed every four years. From the time of the Pisistratid tyranny, moreover, state control over other major cults such as that of Artemis at Brauron or Demeter at Eleusis became more pronounced. By the fourth century the mysteries of Demeter were supervised by two representatives of the old priestly clans but also by two priests elected by the assembly. For some cults priests continued to be appointed from certain families, but for many public election was now the rule. The ceremonies of the Greater Panathenaea every four years were conducted by ten state commissioners who served from one celebration to the next; other processions and annual rites were in the hands of a different board, which changed every year.

Religious protection of the community remained basic to its good health and wise decisions. Each meeting of the assembly began with a prayer, sacrifices, and a purifying circumambulation of the assembled citizenry by a *peristiarchus*. Half of the meetings of the assembly each year took up as their first item "sacred matters"; after each celebration of the Dionysiac festivals, including the plays, the assembly had a special convocation to vote whether the responsible officials had performed adequately.

Military and naval matters provided ever-shifting problems that required more anxious and continuous attention. The draft of citizens for the army was now conducted by posting the age classes called for a specific occasion on whitened boards in the agora at the shrine of the Eponymous Heroes (those for whom tribes were named); failure to respond to the call or subsequent cowardice in battle was prosecuted in special suits. Sailors and marines for the navy could also be drafted from the lower classes, although mercenaries were often hired throughout the fifth and fourth centuries (but not slaves except in dire emergencies). Maintenance of the great walls of Athens as well as the extensive system of outlying forts and signal towers was in the hands of a special board of *teichopoioi*. The building of ships was specifically ordered by the assembly, which elected naval architects and their treasurers. The Athenian navy was a heavy burden both in its requirements for rowers and in expenses for building, maintaining, and storing warships; these problems will be surveyed below in the consideration of Athenian finances.

The bustling economic activity of the Athenian markets and the port of Piraeus spawned an ever more extensive pattern of rules and corresponding bodies of officials for their proper application. By the fourth century Athenian law courts had a system of trials for commercial disputes that ensured their solution within a month, and the vital grain supply was carefully regulated to assure adequate seaborne supplies for the urban agglomerations of Athens and the Piraeus. Athenian democracy also sought to cope with social problems in various ways.

Payment for attending the assemblies and the festivals gave some aid to the poor by the fourth century, and more direct assistance was provided for invalids and the children of Athenians who died in war; from the days of Pericles the council, boards of magistrates, and the jurors (who had to be over the age of thirty and so were senior citizens) also received pay. The field of education, however, remained in private hands except for the military training of males (the ephebes) from the age of eighteen to twenty under the direction of a *kosmetes* and ten guardians, and in the supervision of gymnasia for athletic activity; Athens never went as far in this respect as did Sparta.

Structure of the System

Aristotle (as the author of *Ath.Pol.* will be called here) counts eleven changes in the Athenian constitution across its legendary and historical development, but these alterations were largely in the character of the governing authority. By the date of *Ath.Pol.* the very complex system of government in Athens could be precisely described. Its rules and methods of procedure, however, were only partly fashioned in decrees; much seems to have been an almost unconscious reaction to the growth of Athenian economic and social life.

The assembly (ecclesia) has been likened to a dynamo as the ultimate generator of public decisions, but in turn the council (boule) of 500, elected by lot for one year, can be called its regulator. By classical times the nine archons, who previously had been the chief executive officials, had been limited to restricted, often purely formal realms of action including sacrifices, festivals, and special law suits. In their place the council, the board of ten generals (strategoi, elected not by lot but by vote each year), and the popular leaders called demagogues helped to steer the assembly on more or less continuous lines of policy.

The regular administrative functions of the Athenian state were controlled by boards usually of ten commissioners chosen by lot for one year; the principle that any citizen could fill any post continued to dominate Athenian thought. True, the boards were directly supervised by the council, and before entering office all officials were examined by law courts in a process called *dokimasia*, primarily to determine that they were citizens, had treated their parents well, and had served on military expeditions when called up (these requirements are those attested for archons, but probably were generally applied). At this time, undoubtedly, the lame, halt, blind, and intellectually inadequate citizens could be set aside. Military officials, treasurers, the public architect, the supervisor of water supplies, trainers of the ephebes, some priests, ambassadors, and others, however, were always chosen by vote; special building programs had their own architect, supervisor, secretary, and sometimes treasurer.

Among the regular boards, one may cite as an example of the very specific chores assigned to each group the duties of the *astynomoi* (*Ath.Pol.* 50):

To keep control over the flute-girls, harp-girls, and lyre-girls, and see to it that they are not hired for more than two drachmae; if several persons are anxious to hire the same girl, they cast the lot between them and assign her to the winner. They also see to it that none of the dung-collectors deposits the dung within ten stadia [about one mile] of the city walls. They prevent people from encroaching with their buildings on public roads, from constructing balconies protruding into the road, from making drainpipes with a discharge into the street from above, and from having windows opening into the street. And they remove the corpses of people who die in the streets, having state slaves at their disposal.

Market commissioners (*agoranomoi*) ensured that all articles offered for sale were pure and unadulterated; other officials checked weights and measures; and from a recently discovered inscription of 375–374 B.C. (Stroud, 1974) we now know that public slaves called testers (*dokimastes*) both in Athens and in the Piraeus had to approve the validity of all coinage. Whereas in earlier times there had been ten *sitophylakes* (grain commissioners), by the time of *Ath.Pol.* twenty were required for Athens and fifteen for the Piraeus to control the price of grain and the weight of loaves of bread. A board of eleven guarded prisoners and carried out executions, either by hemlock as in the case of Socrates, or by nailing condemned criminals to wooden planks at the seashore. Five road commissioners used public slaves to keep in good condition the roads, which had been laid out in the Pisistratid tyranny. When one adds all the boards named in *Ath.Pol.* it is clear that an extensive part of the Athenian citizenry served in office each year, and the annual rotation of posts produced as a consequence a very broad knowledge of administrative procedures.

The council, assembly, and many officials also needed to keep their records and conduct business. For this purpose there was a varied group of secretaries and assistant secretaries often checked by controllers (*antigrapheis*). Below these were slaves and resident aliens as scribes, but the suspicious character of Athenian democracy forbade even the ordinary clerical staff from serving any one board for more than one year; a true bureaucracy was not yet possible.

The polis has been likened to a one-celled amoeba, yet under a microscope even an amoeba displays a remarkable complexity of structure. So too Athens had not only a general system of organization, in which the city proper was not sharply distinguished from its rural surroundings, but also a wide range of brotherhoods (phratries), local cult societies, and family groups that exercised power over many aspects of life that today have become subject to the purview of public bodies. There were also in Athens over 100 demes, local units of government that had been assigned significant functions in the reforms of Cleisthenes just after 508 B.C. Like the polis itself, the deme was fundamentally a group of citizens who inherited their membership despite their physical location, should they have happened to move after 508, but the relatively static character of ancient rural life meant that the demes continued to be also geographical entities that were largely directed by their wealthier members. The demarchs, or deme rulers, ensured local order, watched over public buildings, provided draft groups, and above all admitted young males at the age of eighteen to the registers of citizens. Since demes often owned lands, they also had to have treasurers as well as priests for local shrines. Each year a group of forty citizens was chosen by lot to serve as traveling judges in the demes; they tried minor suits up to the value of ten drachmas (about a week's pay for a skilled worker).

Any administrative system requires eternal vigilance to make sure that assigned tasks are carried out efficiently and in good time, and to provide checks against the distortion of favoritism, bribes, and embezzlement. Athenian democracy, while noble in general theory, was very cautious in actual practice, but this side of government is best discussed in the financial sphere.

Financial Administration

Beyond the invaluable pages of *Ath.Pol.* the financial side of Athenian administration was widely discussed in antiquity, a suggestion of its importance. Xenophon wrote a tract, *Ways and Means,* to propose methods of increasing revenues in the difficult days after the end of the Athenian empire; a work passing under the name of Aristotle, *Financial Management* (*Oeconomica*), is largely a collection of dubious stratagems to gain funds (not exclusively or even primarily Athenian); speeches by Demosthenes and other fourth-century orators analyze the especially challenging problems of maintaining the navy in that era; and a truly remarkable variety of epigraphic records survives.

Records of contributions and building expenses as well as inventories exist for the shrines of Delos and Delphi as well as even for Sparta; but the most extensive set of sacred and secular financial documents is that of Athens and its patron deity, Athena. In 454 the treasury of the Delian League was moved from the shrine of Apollo on Delos to the Athenian Acropolis, where it was protected by the ten treasurers of Athena. In return the goddess received one mina per talent of the yearly contribution (*phoros*) or tribute of each dependent state in the empire; from 454 to 415 these sums, one-sixtieth of each state's payment, were registered on stone steles, which have largely been recovered in modern times.

Five years after the shift of the treasury the Athenian Assembly voted that Athena receive 3,000 talents of the accumulated reserve so that she could be suitably housed in a new temple, to replace the one burned by the Persians. The Parthenon, the fruit of imperialism, was the most expensive temple ever erected in classic Greece, costing more than the total expenditure in the next century to build the temple of Asclepius at Epidaurus, its famous theater, and all the other structures at this great shrine. For the Erechtheum, begun later in the fifth century, records of payment to the stone-masons are preserved in detail; whether citizen, resident alien, or slave, all workers received the same wages.

Not only does the epigraphic evidence reveal the receipts and expenses of the treasurers of Athena; there also survive a number of inventories of valuables guarded in the *opisthodomus* or rear room of the Parthenon (which could be locked). Among the fifth-century series 74 Lampsacene staters and 27 1/6 Cyzicene staters are scrupulously registered year by year (Meiggs and Lewis, *Greek Historical Inscriptions* 59) because these electrum (gold-silver alloy) coins were not as easily expended as the standard silver tetradrachmas issued in profusion by the Athenian mint. In the next century the inventories present a veritable arsenal of weapons, including 318 boxes of arrows (probably for the new-style catapults then coming into use). At the rural shrine of Artemis at Brauron inventories solemnly list the clothes dedicated to the goddess by girls upon their marriage (Solmsen, *IG*, II, 2d., 1514).

During the later decades of the fifth century and well into the fourth century the Athenians grouped the resources of most of the other public cults under the direction of five or six elected Treasurers of the Other Gods and drew heavily on their reserves during the Peloponnesian War. These deities at times owned lands that were rented out under the watchful scrutiny of the council; one record of such a lease even carefully registers the sale of mud from a ditch on one estate as fertilizer (*IG* I, 2d., 94).

Secular financial records include a variety of decrees of the assembly, ordaining certain expenditures and allocating specific revenues for those purposes. Thus the cult of Apollo was supported by a tax of two drachmas on the cavalry, one on hoplites, three obols on archers, to be collected by the demarchs from the citizens and by the ten elected masters of archery from the archers; the proceeds were turned over to two members of the council serving as treasurers of Apollo (*IG* I, 2d., 79). The state silver mines at Laurium were formally leased for three years if in operation, or for ten years if newly opened. The repression of revolts by Samos and Potidaea gave rise to published accounts of the expenditures required to put down the uprisings. One of the most detailed financial records on stone is a very lengthy inscription recording the sale of property owned by Alcibiades and other Athenians condemned in 415 for profaning (mocking) the sacred mysteries of Eleusis; in these lists even the disposal of a brazier for two obols finds its place (Meiggs-Lewis 79).

Regular revenues of the state continued to be almost entirely indirect taxes except for poll taxes on resident foreigners and slaves. A toll of 2 percent was collected at the port, and a sales tax of 1 or 2 percent in the markets; special *praktores* received the fines emerging from the activity of the courts; auctions of land were taxed; even the hides of sacrificial animals were sold and produced revenues of nearly two talents (12,000 drachmas) in 334–333. In general the collection of indirect taxes was contracted out to *telonai*, who had to provide guarantors. By the fourth century these awards as well as public leases and rents were granted by a board of ten *poletai* in the presence of the council, and payments were duly handed over to ten *apodektai*, who by 411 seem to have replaced the *kolakretai* as the officials who distributed revenues to the various treasuries in accordance with standing orders. Whenever a tax-farmer or lessee of state property made a payment, his obligation was erased from the appropriate document as official record of receipt.

Normal state income was far from adequate to cope with the expenses of a number of public functions, including the annual torch races and plays at the Dionysiac festivals as well as the maintenance of the galleys (triremes) of the fleet. These obligations were met by the system of liturgies, extraordinary burdens assumed for one year by Athenians and even resident aliens with property worth more than three talents. Each trireme thus had a trierarch appointed by the generals, who in the palmy days of Athenian empire oversaw for a year the maintenance and operation of the ship without serious expenditure of his own; but across the fourth century trierarchs also had to meet many of the costs of their ships. Joint trierarchs had begun to appear in the last, desperate years of the Peloponnesian War; by a law of 358–357 a system of grouping the well-to-do in twenty *symmoriai*, each with sixty members, helped to distribute this burden, but the speech of Demosthenes *On the Symmories* reveals how difficult was the financial problem of keeping the largest Greek navy of the time in operation. The needs of war also could lead to a decree of the assembly directing the levy of a special tax (*eisphora*) on the rich; here too the wealthy were grouped in symmories, the leaders of which had to secure the payments of their colleagues. More voluntary gifts (*epidoseis*) of grain, money, weapons, and other useful items helped to cope with emergencies and were officially honored by public decrees. Athenian citizens of the upper classes, in sum, paid very heavily in large lump amounts for the privilege of avoiding regular direct taxes.

Aristotle (*Rhetoric* 1.4.1359b) and Xenophon (*Memorabilia* 3.6.5) concur in insisting that leaders of the Athenian state must understand finances and secure a balance between receipts and expenditures. Yet there never was a concept of a unified state budget; specific revenues were pledged to specific needs under the control of treasurers for the military funds, the festival fund, invalids, and other areas of expense, and so "the Athenians did not record on stone the inflow and outflow of their revenues, domestic or imperial" (Ferguson, *Treasurers*, vii). From the epigraphic material it is clear that mistakes in addition were common; although the Greeks knew the abacus, it does not seem to have been widely used. The records themselves are very puzzling. Why the sale of the goods of the profaners of the Mysteries should have been set forth in such extensive, permanent form is a riddle to us, although there may have been reasons in the political temper of the time to justify this publication. Again, the treasurers of Eleusis suddenly inscribed their expenditures for just one year in such minute detail that even the price of nails used to repair the sandals of a slave is recorded. It has been observed that if they had done this every year, by the end of the fourth century no one would have been able to get into the sanctuary.

Very often publication of receipts, especially at sanctuaries, was in connection with a special event, such as the construction of the complex at Epidaurus or the rebuilding of the temple of Apollo at Delphi after its destruction by fire in 383. Here the list of contributions solemnly notes the gift of one-and-a-half obols by one citizen of Phlius, a sum scarcely adequate to cover the cost of inscribing his name. Nor were all financial records to be found in public archives. The keeping of documents at Athens became regularized in the Old Bouleuterion (thereafter called Metroon) from the end of the fifth century; but an earlier decree of the assembly requires the presentation of contracts "by the priests, commissioners of sacrifices, or anybody else who knows," in reference to the fact that private bankers often kept such documents (Meiggs-Lewis 58).

However haphazard and erratic the financial records of Athens were, very careful supervision of the receipts and expenditures of the state was maintained. Every official holding moneys was subject to audit in every prytany (one-tenth of the council year) by accountants (*logistai*) chosen from the council; at the major meetings of the assembly satisfaction with the conduct of the magistrates had to be voted; and release from office was far more difficult than entry. At the end of a magistrate's term, that is, a board of ten auditors and their staffs investigated his conduct during his term of office, and any irregularities were presented by another board to the courts, which in any case had to formally discharge the magistrate from his position. Further, the auditors sat in the agora the next three days after completing their task, and any citizen could present his own complaint; as one student of Athenian administration observes, "a veritable tyranny was exercised over magistrates" (Glotz, *La cité grecque,* 268). To be sure, private influence can always produce public corruption, and Aristotle (*Politics* 3.6.1279a) dryly observes that men seek office to gain profit; but our evidence for Athens suggests that the scope for maladministration was severely limited. Where we hear of exploitation on a large scale the cases usually involve the mistreatment of dependent states during the age of the Athenian empire.

One last aspect of Athenian financial administration deserves note. The burdens of the navy, social payments from the festival fund, and other responsibilities weighed so heavily upon Athens as the fourth century proceeded that a manager (*dioecetes*) of finances came to be appointed almost regularly. Eubulus thus supervised the festival fund continuously from 354 to 350 and restored order to state finances, the level of which he raised to a new peak; from 338 on the statesman Lycurgus was reelected three times for four-year terms as virtually a professional administrator. From the work *Financial Management* attributed to Aristotle we can see that many other Greek states had trouble in the fourth century in balancing their budgets and had to resort to very crude methods of confiscation and exaction; but here too a cadre of professionals probably came into existence, if on a lesser scale than at Athens. This group was to be utilized by the monarchs of the Hellenistic age.

THE HELLENISTIC WORLD

After Alexander carried out his meteoric conquest of the Persian Empire, 334–323 B.C., Greek political and economic life entered a far more complex phase. In the Near East highly developed bureaucratic structures employing scribes of clay tablets, papyrus, and other materials for records of royal administration ran back into the third millennium B.C., as has recently been attested again by the remarkable discoveries in the palace of Ebla in north Syria. The Persian court, as heir to the ages, had a royal chancery for proclamations, edicts, diplomatic correspondence, and even a daily register of all actions of the Great King; at Persepolis two collections of clay tablets have been found that itemize the stipends of workers at the palaces and also authorize the payment of travel allowances. Throughout the empire the satraps provided regular reports to the central government, and the king's agents investigated loyalty and subversion for their master.

Much of this system passed on into the service of the Hellenistic monarchs who divided Alexander's empire among themselves in the bitter Wars of the Successors (Diadochi) down to 301, but their administrators came from the Greek world. Trained at home in the petty problems of the polis, these officials showed great ability in broadening their scope of activity. For the Antigonid dynasty of Macedonia our evidence is too scanty to discuss individually, but for the Ptolemies of Egypt and Seleucids of the central Near and Middle East as well as for the minor kingdom of Pergamum information is more abundant.

Ptolemaic Egypt

Ptolemy I (formally king 305–282) was the most astute of Alexander's marshals. After the death of the great Macedonian conqueror, Ptolemy I seized control of Egypt and bribed the official taking Alexander's body back to Macedonia to divert it instead to Alexandria. Thereafter he managed to defeat all efforts by the other Macedonian generals to invade Egypt but himself sought no more than control of his own base and also commercial ports and islands in the eastern Mediterranean. However, how much time he had to also reorganize Egyptian administration to secure his internal revenues is unclear; certainly some of the fundamental rules and regulations were the work of his son Ptolemy II Philadelphus (r. 282–246). For both of the first Ptolemies the objective was to tighten and reenforce a system already in existence; apart from the capital of Alexandria and the old trading post of Naucratis only one Greek city, Ptolemais, was founded, lest the tissue of rural life be disturbed.

By the time of Alexander's entry, Egypt had been a unified state for almost 3,000 years, a string of green thrown down across the North African desert on either side of the Nile River. Yet periodically in that long era Egypt had fallen asunder, and its agricultural wealth had suffered from internal disorder, which led to neglect of the canals and of the security of the peasantry.

The first Ptolemies sought to correct the weaknesses of the system that had shown themselves during repeated revolts against Persian rule, and to gain the loyalty of their subjects by careful attention to the native religious structure: more temple-building took place under the Ptolemies than for many preceding centuries. Nevertheless, the Ptolemies converted the formerly independent priesthoods into agencies of the government, which took away temple lands in return for regular support of religious activities. The rulers also made very little use of natives in administration, which was entrusted essentially to Greek professionals; of all the Ptolemies only the famous Cleopatra VII could speak the language of her subjects. In general the internal aim was to continue to treat Egypt as a royal household in which the subjects labored to provide as much of the agricultural and other production of Egypt to the Ptolemies as possible. This wealth was used to support the rulers' diplomatic and military position in the Hellenistic state system.

The base of Ptolemaic bureaucracy was the village (*come*), which was supervised by a comarch and elders. Beside the comarch, a village secretary (*comogrammateus*) kept the archives, provided the voluminous reports required by higher echelons, and engaged in massive correspondence; in particular the secretary compiled each year a detailed list of all occupants of the village, their possessions, their animals, and the land they held, together with an assessment of its quality. These inventories were forwarded to the nome (provincial) capital, where a nomarch or later a strategus controlled administration and a nome secretary consolidated all the village lists for transmittal to the capital in Alexandria. On the nome level an official called *oeconomus* watched over all financial matters, but was himself checked by auditors; often there also was a superintendent of police. The nome itself could have subdivisions into toparchies with a supervisor (*epistates*) and secretary.

Unfortunately the papyri that provide detailed light on almost every aspect of local government do not survive for the central bureaucracy in Alexandria. The Ptolemies posed as patrons of Greek culture and learning, and we are accordingly reasonably well informed about the directors of the famous Library of Alexandria and the activity at its sister research institute, the Museum, as well as about court life in the fulsome praise by Theocritus and other poets. The general administration consisted of a principal minister to advise the ruler, a *dioecetes* for fiscal matters (and often thus the most important bureaucrat at the court), a chief justice, priests of the cults of the deified Ptolemies, and military and naval personnel.

The *dioecetes* Apollonius, who served under Ptolemy II, does turn up frequently in the archives of his estate manager, Zenon. The central office of Apollonius had a subsecretary to keep the daybooks, a secretary for letters, and at least seven accountants (each with up to ten assistants), as well as a counterscribe or auditor for each. One of Apollonius' offices alone used sixty rolls of papyri in ten days; several offices together consumed 434 rolls in no more than thirty-three days.

When one turns to the evidence in local archives of requests, orders, and regulations from the nomes and Alexandria it is evident that Ptolemaic Egypt was the best example of a bureaucratic state in antiquity. As estate manager Zenon kept every scrap of paper (there are over 2,000 papyri in the Zenon archive, now scattered throughout European and American museums) to attest his minute supervision of Apollonius' holdings. Two documents survive from Roman times, written by an official as acting strategus of a nome to himself as regular secretary of the nome, requesting certain actions. At times the directives from on high have an amusing characteristic, as in the very specific order sent down from Alexandria in the days when the Ptolemies were no more than Roman puppets (112 B.C.; Hunt-Edgar, *Select Papyri* 416):

> To Asclepiades. Lucius Memmius, a Roman senator, who occupies a position of great dignity and honor, is sailing up from Alexandria to the Arsinoite nome to see the sights. Let him be received with special magnificence, and take care that at the proper spots the guest-chambers be prepared . . . and that the titbits for Petesouchus and the crocodiles, the conveniences for viewing the Labyrinth, and the offerings and sacrifices be provided; in general take the greatest pains in everything to see that the visitor is satisfied.

To describe in detail the financial system elaborated by the Ptolemies and their servants to exploit the riches of Egypt would require a whole volume in itself; one may refer to specialized modern studies or to the elaborate provisions promulgated under Ptolemy II for the collection of taxes on the production of wine and oil. It was not a planned economy in the modern sense, i.e., a structure of dynamic character, but certainly every aspect of production was thoroughly regulated and reported.

In the raising of grain, to give only one example, the seed was furnished by the state to the farmers on royal lands (who could not leave their native village during the agricultural season), and crops were inspected while they were growing. At harvest time a tax-farmer, a village official, and the farmer himself carefully watched over the threshing floor to make certain that the state got its due share of at least one-half the crop but also, theoretically, that the farmer was not defrauded; the role of the tax-farmer was to guarantee full collection, making up any deficit himself but receiving any surplus plus a bonus. Then the grain was transported down the Nile, a matter requiring a formal contract and statement of quality, to Alexandria for the use of the court and army and for sale abroad through Rhodes and other ports. Some dues were payable internally in cash; the Ptolemies coined on a different standard than the Attic weights used by Alexander and most Hellenistic monarchs, thus keeping Egypt a closed economic sphere monetarily as well as by the use of tariffs and even import bans. The revenues were garnered by a system of state banks up and down the Nile, again to be forwarded to Alexandria. Monopolies existed for many products, including linen, papyrus, oil, and wine; a salt tax was accompanied by an obligation to buy a certain amount. All told, over 150 different kinds of taxes and fees are known in Ptolemaic Egypt through the survival of receipts given on papyri and on pottery shards (*ostraca*); even selling pumpkin seeds in a village square required a license. Labor services were also required in abundance to keep up the canals, to plant and tend trees, and to transport grain, stone, and other items.

The Ptolemaic bureaucratic structure was never completely uniform and regular, even in theory. The foreign possessions of the Ptolemies were generally run on a looser rein, and upper Egypt (the Thebaid) differed significantly from the Hellenized Fayum, which provides much of our information. The general outlines were inherited from pharaonic days and were largely determined by the physical character of a land that depended on the annual Nile floods; the Greek officials serving the king added more conscious rationalization of resources and introduced some improvements, as in the quality of seed and animals, new plants, and the use of iron tools.

For a time the Ptolemies enjoyed great wealth, but their administrative system was already creaking by the reign of Ptolemy III (246–222). Even under the *dioecetes* Apollonius a surprise check on one occasion found seven talents—42,000 drachmas, a significant sum—missing from a chest; by the second century embezzlement, corruption, and violence led toward chaos, partly because the family feuds of the dynasty by this date had become severe and protracted. Whereas a *dioecetes* in the later third century had instructed his *oeconomici* primarily to check local production of grain, animals, linen, and other items (Hunt-Edgar 204), Ptolemy VIII Soter II, his sister Cleopatra II, and his niece Cleopatra III (both of the latter married at one time or another to the king) issued in 118 B.C. a lengthy "amnesty to all their subjects for errors, crimes, accusations, condemnations, and offenses of all kinds" (Hunt-Edgar 210)—a document that catalogs in horrifying detail the exploitation of the subjects by the use of false measures, application of force, requisitioning, and other violations of standing regulations.

To a remarkable degree outraged subjects appealed for redress to the king by petition and letters, and often the rulers earnestly tried to assure that justice was actually dispensed; but the Greeks who directed the machinery of government and theoretically provided checks in tax-farming and other areas could subvert their good intentions. Peasants accordingly turned to sullen sabotage of the system by permitting the canals to deteriorate, and at times fled to the marshes of the Delta or even revolted. Much of upper Egypt was independent during the early decades of the second century B.C.

For the last century and more of technical Egyptian independence the Ptolemies were really caretakers of the land, supported by the Romans as far as external threats were concerned; but the laissez-faire character of the Roman Republic did not lead to internal interference with Ptolemaic mismanagement or the suppression of the ever more unruly mob of Alexandria, which once even lynched a Roman visitor who killed a cat. If one looks back to the meticulous structure of checks in classical Athens the conclusion seems inevitable: the more absolute a bureaucratic structure becomes, the less likely it is that any form of vigilance can prevent corruption and the exploitation of subjects who cannot voice their discontent in meaningful ways.

The Seleucid Dynasty

Seleucus I ruled (311–281) vast territories from the western, Hellenized coast of Asia Minor as far as modern Afghanistan and Turkestan; his fringe territories in India he had bartered about 304 for 500 elephants, which helped him win the crucial battle of Ipsus in 301. Seleucid power was exercised over areas that varied widely in structure and level of development. In mountainous districts there were client kingdoms and dynasts; huge temple estates existed, especially in Asia Minor; throughout the realm the Seleucid kings earnestly founded Greek cities and military colonies to knit together their state.

Although these cities imprinted a strong Hellenic stamp in Asia Minor and Syria for centuries to come, they were less successful in helping the Seleucids maintain the unity of their realm. Part of the eastern territories broke away to form the independent kingdom of Bactria, and the Parthians, formerly Siberian nomads, steadily nibbled away at other eastern districts, occupying even Mesopotamia in 141 B.C. From the west the boots of Roman legionaries tramped ruthlessly over the Hellenistic world; Antiochus III (r. 223–187) was defeated by the Romans in a war in 192–188, and thereafter the Romans supported every opponent of the Seleucids until finally Pompey set aside the last king of the dynasty in 64 B.C.

In their prime, however, the Seleucid kings built an administrative system based on the Persian model, but since we lack the papyri so common in Egypt its details are not as easily seen. The central government had a chancery to issue orders and letters; areas directly under the kings were grouped in more than twenty satrapies or *strategiae*, each of which was divided into three or four eparchies, and these in turn into *hyparchies* or other local units. Beside the administrative staff proper, each satrapal capital had an *oeconomus* to direct the collection of a variety of dues from royal estates farmed by virtual serfs and also from the state mines; sales taxes, customs, and a salt tax are also known. The Greek cities, although permitted local self-government by assembly, council, and priests, often were controlled in reality by a royal governor and had on occasion to provide mandatory contributions to the royal treasury. Probably Seleucid revenues at their peak exceeded those of the Ptolemies, but the needs of the Seleucid monarchs were correspondingly greater.

Other States

In the interstices of the complex Hellenistic state structure, based primarily on the relations of the three major dynasties, there was room for a great number of other, smaller states. Some were ancient Greek poleis, including Byzantium at the mouth of the Black Sea; Athens, which sank into somnolent philosophical meditation; and the bustling, vigorous trade center of Rhodes. This latter community was wealthy enough to support a program of social aid that kept the poor contented, and so permitted its narrow governing oligarchy to rule in peace. Rhodes also had a significant navy, the dockyards of which were carefully protected: when Philip V of Macedonia sent agents to fire the Rhodian navy they were easily apprehended by the guards. Even minor poleis, however, now had complex systems of administration. Cicero (*For Flaccus* 19) incidentally describes the municipal bank of Temnos in northwest Asia Minor as "very businesslike and most proficient in paperwork. Not an obol can change hands without the intervention of five praetors, three quaestors, and four bankers, elected there by the people." Records of sanctuaries also became more common; those of Delos provide our best light on wages, prices, and the value of land in the Greek Aegean during the Hellenistic era.

Among the smaller kingdoms the one centered on the rocky peak of Pergamum is the best known. Originally it was a tiny state, created in 282 B.C. by the revolt of the Seleucid eunuch treasurer Philetaerus; his relatives, the Attalid family, ruled on to 133 and eventually were masters of a great deal of western Asia Minor by currying favor with the Romans. The Attalids deliberately imitated Ptolemaic fiscal policies to secure the maximum revenues from the timber and pitch of Mount Ida, state silver and copper mines, royal woolen factories, and the manufacture of parchment; agricultural production was assisted by the improvement of plants and animals. Epigraphic evidence illustrates the control exercised over the capital itself, which extended to provisions for cleaning the streets. Another document recapitulates an agreement with mutinous mercenaries who were to be paid for ten months of the year, exempted from taxes while in service, and provided grain and wine at fixed prices.

Again like the Ptolemies, the Attalids used their revenues in part to support literature and the arts. The Pergamene Royal Library was second only to that of Alexandria; poets and scholars were patronized; to commemorate the defeat of the Gauls of central Asia Minor Attalus II created a great altar at Pergamum (which is now in East Berlin) and also a massive monument in Athens. In the end, however, Attalid power yielded to Roman mastery; the last Attalid bequeathed his wealth and rural lands to Rome in 133. His subjects revolted in a great social upheaval against Roman control, but in vain. By 129 the Romans created the province of Asia and included in it the city of Pergamum itself, which Attalus III had sought to leave free.

The complex, professional bureaucratic systems of administration erected by Hellenistic monarchs, greater and lesser, could provide extensive revenues to the kings for courtly ostentation, support of arts, letters, and science, and international rivalries; but they generally were marred by the basic principle that the systems were for the benefit of the rulers, not the ruled. Patriotism in any meaningful sense could not exist in states where a governing upper class of Greeks exploited masses of natives of different speech and custom. Hellenistic government and law were always conducted in

Greek, not Aramaic, and only in Judaea did a native tongue continue to produce its own literature. The one monarchy that caused the Romans the most trouble was the Antigonid dynasty of Macedonia, which did not suffer from such a division. In most other districts of the Near and Middle East the administrative machines really weakened, rather than reenforced, any possibility of remaining independent of Roman power. In the end perhaps the most illuminating structure of administration in Greek history was that erected bit by bit in classical Athens.

BIBLIOGRAPHY

SOURCES

Alcaeus, *Greek Lyric* I, David A. Campbell, trans. (1982); Aristotle, *Constitution of Athens (Athenaion Politeia) and Related Texts*, Kurt von Fritz and Ernst Kapp, trans. (1950), and *Politics*, Ernest Barker, trans. (1948, 1951, 1962); Cicero, *Pro Flacco (In Support of Flacco)*, vol. 10, C. MacDonald, trans. (1977); Herodotus, *Histories*, Aubrey De Selincourt, trans. (1954); Arthur S. Hunt and Campbell C. Edgar, trans., *Select Papyri*, 2 vols. (1932–1934); Russell Meiggs and David Lewis, eds., *A Selection of Greek Historical Inscriptions* (1969); Benjamin D. Meritt, Henry T. Wade-Gery, and Malcolm F. McGregor, *The Athenian Tribute Lists*, 4 vols. (1939–1953); Felix Solmsen, *Inscriptiones Graecae ad inlustrandas dialectas selectae*, 4th ed. (1930); Marcus N. Tod, ed., *A Selection of Greek Historical Inscriptions*, 2 vols. (1947–1948).

STUDIES

Andreas M. Andreades, *A History of Greek Public Finance*, I (1933); M. M. Austin and Pierre Vidal-Naquet, *Economic and Social History of Ancient Greece* (1977); Roger S. Bagnall, *The Administration of the Ptolemaic Possessions outside Egypt* (1976); Elias S. Bickerman, *Institutions des Séleucides* (1938); C. Blinkenberg, *Lindos*, II (1941); August Boeckh, *Die Staatshaushaltung der Athener* (1817; 3d ed., 1886; Eng. trans. *The Public Economy of the Athenians* by George C. Lewis [1842], by Anthony Lamb [1857]); Alison Burford, "The Purpose of Inscribed Building Accounts," in *Acta 5th Epigraphical Congress* (1967), and *The Greek Temple Builders at Epidauros* (1969); Georg Busolt, *Griechische Staatskunde*, 3d ed. (1920–1926); Paul Collomp, *Recherches sur la chancellerie et la diplomatie des Lagides* (1926); Roger A. De Laix, *Probouleusis at Athens* (1973).

Victor Ehrenberg, *The Greek State* (1960); William S. Ferguson, *The Treasurers of Athena* (1932); M. I. Finley, "Le document et l'histoire économique de l'antiquité," in *Annales* (1982); Charles W. Fornara, *Archaic Times to the End of the Peloponnesian War* (1977); Gustave Glotz, *La cité grecque: le développement des institutions* (1928; rev. ed. 1968); Bernard P. Grenfell, ed., *Revenue Laws of Ptolemy Philadelphus* (1896); Esther V. Hansen, *The Attalids of Pergamum*, 2d ed. (1971); Bernard Haussoulier, *La vie municipale en Attique* (1884); James W. Headlam, *Election by Lot at Athens*, 2d ed. (1933); Arnold H. M. Jones, *Athenian Democracy* (1957); Boromir Jordan, *The Athenian Navy in the Classical Period* (1975); Ulrich Kahrstedt, *Studien zur öffentlichen Recht Athens*, 2 vols. (1934–1936); K. Köster, *Die Lebensmittelversorgung der altgriechischen Polis* (1939); Colin M. Kraay, *Archaic and Classical Greek Coins* (1976).

Tullia Linders, *The Treasurers of the Other Gods in Athens and Their Functions* (1975); Ernst Posner, *Archives in the Ancient World* (1972); Claire Préaux, *L'économie royale des Lagides* (1939, 1979); Peter J. Rhodes, *The Athenian Boule* (1972); Michael I. Rostovtzeff, *A Large Estate in Egypt in the Third Century B.C.* (1922), and *Social and Economic History of the Hellenistic World*, 3 vols. (1941); Geoffrey E. M. De Ste. Croix, "Greek and Roman Accounting," in *Studies in the History of Accounting*, ed. A. C. Littleton and B. S. Yamey (1956); Chester G. Starr, *Economic and Social Growth of Early Greece, 800–500 B.C.* (1977), and "The Early Greek City State" and "The Decline of the Early Greek Kings," in Chester G. Starr, *Essays on Ancient History* (1979); E. S. Staveley, *Greek and Roman Voting and Elections* (1972); R. S. Stroud, "An Athenian Law on Silver Coinage," *Hesperia*, **43** (1974); Rudi Thomsen, *Eisphora* (1964); Alfred Zimmern, *Greek Commonwealth*, 5th ed. (1931).

Roman Administration

JOHN FERGUSON

THE PERIOD OF THE KINGS

For the earliest period of Roman history we are reliant on archaeology, which is a limited source for administrative structures, and on tradition, which is liable to accretion.

Archaeology tells us of continuous settlement of the future site of Rome from the early Iron Age, with separate communities of shepherds and farmers on the Palatine Hill first, and shortly after on the Esquiline, Quirinal, and perhaps Caelian. There is indication from the tradition of early religious practice that these four merged into a single community (Varro, *On the Latin Language* 5,8.45–54). Archaeology also tells us that Etruscan pottery and, more important, Etruscan building techniques reached Rome in the last quarter of the seventh century. This coincides with the tradition of an Etruscan monarch from 616 B.C.

Tradition tells of an earlier kingship, and ascribes to the legendary founding father Romulus a civic structure of three tribes, Ramnes, Tities, and Luceres, each divided into ten curiae or extended families, and these into about ten gentes or families. The names of the tribes are Etruscan in form, but they may be Etruscan forms of preexisting names. In addition Romulus is said to have appointed a senate or council of elders of 100, which expanded to 300 across two centuries and a half; the figures cannot be taken literally, but indicate historical growth. The curiae, which seem to have become neighborhood groups or wards, met in the Comitia Curiata to ratify the choice of a new king, and to confirm or refer back the decisions he made on the advice of the council.

The king was nominated by an interrex, or temporary head of state, chosen from the senate for five days. If the curiae did not ratify his choice the process continued till they did. The office was thus elective for life. The king was religiously the chief minister of state, charged with maintaining the *pax deorum,* the divine favor, with the support of pontifices ("bridge-builders," priests), flamines (priests of special cults) and augurs (soothsayers who observed the omens). He was commander-in-chief of the armed forces, and was generally responsible for foreign relations. He was head of the legislature, both in making and executing the law;

that this was effective is shown in the extraordinary phenomenon of the absence of blood feuds. He was responsible for state finances, which were relatively uncomplicated, the licensing of a salt monopoly, land rents, customs dues, fines, and occasional special levies in emergency. For these last two functions the king had the support of quaestors or investigators.

Reforms were traditionally ascribed to Servius Tullius. The three old tribes were abolished and replaced by twenty new tribes, four urban (taking their names from four of the hills) and sixteen rural (named after the gentes, but geographical in structure). Landowners were divided into five classes based on gradation of property value; those who fell below the minimum qualification were known as *capitecensi* (the polled) or *proletarii*. Each of the three tribes previously had provided a thousand infantry to the army; cavalry (*equites*) were enrolled but played no part in military tactics. Under the new dispensation the *legio*, legion or levy, comprised 6,000 infantry divided into sixty *centuriae*, centuries or units of 100 drawn not from the new tribes, but from the classes, most from the highest, next most from the lowest. The *equites* were also involved in the reforms, being increased to sixty companies of thirty. From this military reorganization sprang a new political institution, the Comitia Centuriata, meeting, because it was military in origin, outside the city boundaries. Each century recorded its own majority vote, and then voting was by centuries. This meant that the cavalry and upper class could outvote the poorer citizens. Already in the state the divisions between rich and poor were emerging. It is hard to say whether the Comitia Centuriata began to function under the kings. If not, it did very shortly after.

Another division was that between patricians, the aristocracy who formed the senate, and plebeians, the mass of people in city and country. The exact nature of the division between them is not clear. Birth had something to do with it; the plebeians did not belong to the gentes, and some were foreigners and immigrants. Geography was a factor—the Aventine and the Velabrum were plebeian areas—and wealth was another: already in the countryside larger estates were contrasting with peasant holdings, and in all such situations the rich tend to become richer, and the poor poorer. Alongside this were the accidents of history. But the plebeians were excluded from civil and political rights, essentially from the right of marriage (*connubium*) and the right of property (*commercium*). The Servian reforms brought the plebeians into the political structures by including them in the Comitia Centuriata, but this was largely to keep them away from effective power.

AFTER THE REPUBLICAN REVOLUTION

The ousting of the last Tarquin (Tarquinius Superbus), traditionally *ca.* 510 B.C., was an ousting of kingship as well as of a particular tyrant. Henceforward, except in a religious context, the word *rex*—king—was ill-omened.

The revolution made little immediate difference to the mass of the people. Like many revolutions, it meant the passage of power from the very few to the few. The powers of the king remained in the hands of the new leaders, the praetors, who were later called consuls or colleagues. But there were differences. There were, from the first, two leaders; both had *imperium*, army command and civic authority, and they served as a check on one another. They were elected by the Comitia Centuriata, now on the nomination of the senate, who took care to confine the choice to their own ranks; they received *imperium* from the Comitia Curiata. Further, they served for one year only. Penal jurisdiction and financial administration passed increasingly to the quaestors, but the new officials retained the rods and axes as the symbol of corporal and capital authority. They eschewed the purple toga associated with kingship, but retained a purple band on their garment. They surrendered religious authority to the *pontifex maximus,* high priest, and *rex sacrorum,* "king of the sacred rites," both new offices. Correspondingly with these changes their military and political importance was high.

In times of crisis recourse might be had to a single person in authority, now called dictator, with the office of Commander of the Infantry; he was expected to appoint a second-in-command, Commander of the Cavalry. His term of office was limited to six months, or the period of crisis.

THE CONFLICT OF THE ORDERS

The administrative structures did not greatly change over the next centuries. What happened was that the plebeians organized themselves into a body that could challenge the exclusive occupation of the seats of power by the patricians: when we have discounted the imaginative details recorded by the historians, the main facts are certain.

For twenty years or so it seems from the names that a number of plebeians were chosen as consul, many of Etruscan origin, but from 486 B.C. the aristocrats, led by the Fabii, asserted themselves strongly. These facts make it unlikely that the first confrontation was as early as the traditional date of 494 B.C.

The weapon of the plebeians for collective bargaining was secession—departure en masse from the city—an act which, if not countered, would irrevocably weaken the armed forces during a period of military conflict between Rome and her neighbors. Five such acts of secession are recorded in the traditions, from 494 to 287. They were not all historical, but they form a record of recurring confrontation.

In the fifth century the plebeians made considerable advances. First, right at the outset came the establishment of their own officers, called tribunes of the plebs, originally perhaps two in number, but by mid century ten, and protected by a solemn oath on the part of the plebs. They were not technically magistrates, that is, state officials. They were elected by a popular assembly (*concilium plebis*), which originally lacked constitutional authority but was recognized by 471 B.C. They had the right to convene this body, and they held the right of veto over actions of the magistrates. Their powers were thus mainly negative.

Second, the middle of the century saw the first written code of laws, the Twelve Tables, enacted by the Comitia Centuriata, binding on all, patricians and plebeians, published, and in basic but comprehensive terms regulating both public and private life.

Third, the Valerio-Horatian Laws of 449 B.C. (named after the consuls of that year) established yet another assembly, the Comitia Tributa, of the whole people, patricians and plebeians, organized by tribes, to deal with minor public business. The laws gave some legality to the enactments of the *concilium plebis,* although exactly in what conditions is obscure. They established a right of appeal against oppressive action by magistrates. And they established the sacrosanctity (inviolability) of the tribunes of the plebs.

Fourth, four years later the Canuleian law established the right of plebeians to intermarry with patricians.

Finally, in 443 censors were appointed for the first time, and thereafter at irregular intervals, to check and maintain the official lists of citizens.

THE FOURTH CENTURY

The fourth century was a period of crisis. Externally, roving Gauls swept through the Alps and in *ca.* 387 B.C. sacked Rome; the recovery was one of the first examples of Rome's extraordinary resilience in defeat. Economically, heavy interest rates and bond-servitude were increasingly oppressive.

The patricians were in numerical decline. The history of the fifth century records fifty-three patrician families; only twenty-nine of these continue into the fourth. War and social exclusiveness were taking their toll.

The rich plebeians were challenging the political power of the patricians. In 367 the tribunes Gaius Licinius and Lucius Sextius passed legislation, possibly ensuring that one consul should be plebeian (in which case it was not always observed), certainly making it possible for this to happen. The noble families are now extended in number: The gens Licinia, gens Sextia and gens Genucia join the exclusively patrician aristocracy, followed by the gens Popillia, gens Marcia, and gens Plautia. Then in 339 plebeian consul Quintus Publilius Philo, subsequently dictator, carried legislation opening further offices to the plebeians and limiting the patrician veto.

The poor plebeians wanted to be free from bond-slavery. Licinius and Sextius tried to limit large estates and make extra land available for small allotments. Legislation in mid century checked the power of usury; the Poetelian law of 313 ended imprisonment for debt.

The expansion of Roman influence in central Italy through alliances and wars was now under way. It led to one piece of legislation that carried major implications for the future. This was the *ius Latii*, the rights of Latium or Latin rights. From 338 B.C. the people of Latium enjoyed the rights of marriage (*connubium*) and property (*commercium*) under Roman law. It is less clear whether other rights that existed later, such as the acquisition of full citizenship on migration to Rome, date from the fourth century.

Much the same time saw the development of the closely similar *civitas sine suffragio*, citizenship without the vote, applied to communities in Campania—Capua, Cumae, Suessula, and Acerrae—as well as to some outside: Formiae and Fundi, and perhaps Caere. The communities are called *municipia*, municipalities, meaning that their members accepted the *munus* (duties and obligations) of being Roman citizens. They were thought of as being in some sense Roman.

THE DEVELOPED REPUBLICAN CONSTITUTION

Under the developed constitution executive power lay in the hands of the senate, not theoretically since it had no legislative powers, but in practice through its decrees (*senatus consulta*). The senate comprised those who had served as senior magistrates; once they had entered the senate they were there for life.

The magistrates were elected, and held office for a year only, although in 326 and 307 B.C. we have records of the extension of office at the discretion of the senate, to act "on behalf or in place of" (*pro consule* or *pro praetore*). This was vital for the future. They were unsalaried, and therefore only the rich could afford to stand. Power was officially in the hands of two consuls (as they were now called), but the increasing complexity of business involved others. The *praetor urbanus* was responsible for the administration of justice in Rome. Four aediles, originally a plebeian post, later involving patricians as well, were now state officials charged with the general care of the city, traffic, water supply, food supply, market practices, and religious observances. Four quaestors administered the finances; they were to increase in number in future centuries. Censors were appointed from time to time for their special tasks, and a dictator, with wide powers but a limited term, in emergency.

The ambitious politician would probably serve in the army for ten years, and then would pass, with suitable intervals, through the offices of quaestor, possibly for plebeians tribune of the plebs, possibly but not always aedile, then praetor and consul. There was a minimum age of twenty-eight for quaestors, forty for praetors, and forty-three for consuls; this was defined in 180 B.C. but may reflect earlier practice. This was the *cursus honorum,* the proper succession of offices. Legislation in 342 had banned pluralism—holding more than one office at a time—and had prescribed an interval of ten years between two consulates. Censors were invariably chosen from ex-consuls.

The magistrates were supported by other officers. The praetor might be aided by *reciperatores,* to examine detailed evidence; he would send prefects (*praefecti*) to administer justice outside Rome. In 311 B.C. a kind of ministry of naval warfare was started with two officials in charge of the maintenance of the fleet. There were numerous minor officials, clerks, escorts, heralds, messengers, and others. These were known, at least later, as *apparitores* or attendants, and were mostly drawn from the freedmen or former slaves.

There remained four assemblies. The Comitia Curiata was by now politically insignificant but retained some formal duties. The Comitia Centuriata held the main official power, with the ultimate rights in matters of war and peace, life and death, and the election of magistrates. The Comitia Tributa increasingly took on other state business; the admission of landless citizens by an imaginative reform on the part of the great Appius Claudius in 312 made it a more democratic body than the others, and the tribal structure made it less unwieldy. The *concilium plebis* (Assembly of the People) officially had legislative power by the Valerio-Horatian legislation of 449 and the Hortensia law of 287, but without patrician support it would hardly be effectual, whatever the legal position.

THE EXTENSION OF ROMAN ADMINISTRATION

In the third and second centuries Roman power spread throughout Italy and in various ways all round the borders of the Mediterranean. The policy of expansion was not deliberate. If Rome was a dragon, she was a reluctant dragon. There were plenty of opportunities in the first half of the second century for Rome to take over Greece, but she repeatedly withdrew. The simple fact was that the structures that governed a city-state were inappropriate to an empire, and the governing oligarchy did not want to take on responsibilities that might have required them to share their power with a wider group.

The initial acquisition of new overseas responsibilities was met by the appointment of additional praetors. Somewhere about 242 B.C. a second praetor was established to deal with legal business involving foreigners. In 227 two more were brought into being to administer the government of Sicily and Sardinia, and in 197 two more to cover Hither and Further Spain. The number of quaestors was also increased but we do not know exactly how and when. A second quaestor was appointed to Sicily in 210, and it is reasonable to assume that new quaestors were established for the new provinces.

To extend the number of praetors further would have been to weaken the closed circle of the aristocracy. Consequently no new overseas provinces were admitted for fifty years from 197 B.C. But by the middle of the century pressures in Greece and North Africa had become impossible to withstand. The senate therefore reverted to the experimental and occasional device used earlier, and extended the term of office of consuls and praetors for one year to enable them to act as provincial governors *pro consule* or *pro praetore*. This became a regular part of the administrative system. Although office was normally for one year, it might be extended in emergency. Such action made possible the takeover of Macedonia and Africa as new provinces in 147–146 and the acceptance of the astonishing bequest of the kingdom of Pergamum to Rome in 133 B.C.

The governor's main duties were the defense of the frontiers and the maintenance of law and order. His staff was not large: one or more quaestors for financial control, a lieutenant (*legatus*) for the armed forces appointed by himself; other personal adherents, often gaining political experience and position, for minor administrative duties; and the necessary clerks and secretaries, who would be freedmen. Within the provinces there might be a considerable measure of self-government, and even official independence for some privileged cities (such as Messana in Sicily), which was more than nominal since it involved exemption from taxation. The rest of the provinces were tributary. This was justified either as war indemnity after conquest, or as representing the total right of the people of Rome to the property of conquered subjects.

There was, however, no standard system of taxation. There were diverse sources of money: a land tax, sometimes (as in Sicily and Sardinia) an actual tithe of the harvest; a poll tax; a tax on each head of cattle grazing on public land; harbor dues on goods passing in and out; revenues from rent of public land; and indirect taxes of various kinds. The governor's staff was insufficient to organize tax collection; it was left to the local authorities, who used private contractors or *publicani*, the publicans of the Authorized Version of the New Testament, either locally or, later, increasingly from Rome itself. These made over the due sum to the treasury at Rome, keeping for themselves as much as they could from overcollection.

Other states around the Mediterranean were linked to Rome formally by treaty as allies (*socii*) or, less formally, as friends (*amici*). When in 196 B.C. Flamininus declared the freedom of the Greeks as *amici*, the relationship was officially partnership, but in fact was dependence, the relation of a *cliens* to his *patronus* in an aristocratic society. The rulers of these nominally free states, known as client kings, were registered at Rome in a catalog of friends (*tabula amicorum*); their territories offered convenient buffer states to the Roman possessions.

The formal structures of home government showed little change. With the extension of territory the number of tribes was raised to thirty-five in 241 B.C., but stopped there. New citizens were thereafter distributed among the tribes, which ceased to be geographical entities and became administrative conveniences. There were slight adjustments made in the Comitia Centuriata; Dionysius of Halicarnassus called them democratic, but the changes were marginal. With military campaigns now distant from Rome, induction into office was moved in 153 B.C. from 15 March to 1 January to enable governors to take up position well before the campaigning season.

Although the formal change was slight, the composition of the ruling class had altered. In 179 B.C. the senate comprised 99 patricians and 216 plebeians. In 172 both consuls were plebeians. But this meant only that there was a new group within the closed circle, not that the circle was open. In the first two-thirds of the second century the consulship was confined to twenty-five families, with only five exceptions. These new men (*novi homines*), had to be outstanding themselves, and had to attract aristocratic support. They included Marcus Porcius Cato and Gaius Laelius.

POLYBIUS ON THE DIVISION OF ROMAN ADMINISTRATIVE POWER

The Greek historian Polybius, who was brought to Rome as a prisoner of war in 168 B.C. and stayed to be a friend of Scipio Aemilianus and an admirer of all things Roman, has a full appraisal of the Roman administration at this time (6.3–18).

He begins his account with the three kinds of state—kingship, aristocracy, and democracy—and argues that the Roman constitution and administration combined all three principles in the part played by consuls, senate, and plebs.

The consuls are at the head of all public affairs. All other magistrates except the tribunes are subordinate to them. It is they who promulgate *senatus consulta*. It is they who summon the assembly, introduce bills, and implement the decisions. In matters of war their authority is virtually absolute, including their control of public funds. Their power, considered of itself, is monarchical.

The senate controls all revenue and expenditure. They hold ultimate jurisdiction in all criminal offenses in Italy. They are responsible for foreign relations, receiving embassies, declarations of war. To foreign delegations Rome seems an aristocracy.

The plebs—the people—have the power to confer honors and inflict penalties. They appoint to office. They have the power of adopting or rejecting laws. They deliberate on war and peace. These are three key powers that make the constitution ultimately democratic.

The three orders are dependent on one another. The consuls need the senate in order to fulfill their plans, for example to supply their troops. They need the plebs to ratify treaties, and they are subject to the judgment of the plebs on laying down office. The senate requires the ratification of the people for its decisions, and a veto from a single tribune renders it impotent. Similarly, the people depend on the senate, for example for employment, and upon the consuls, under whose authority they stand in time of war.

This interaction, Polybius claims, is the secret of Roman success. At times of danger it leads to a united and invincible determination. In times of peace the orders keep check on one another. However, the practice did not match the theory. It is just to say that there were monarchical, oligarchical, and democratic elements in the constitution, but they were in marked imbalance. Republican Rome was an oligarchy.

THE BREAKDOWN OF THE REPUBLICAN ORDER

The century from 133 to 31 B.C. saw the collapse of the old order in crisis and civil war. The ill-fated reforms and the deaths of the Gracchi; the seven consulships and seesaw career of the anti-senatorial Gaius Marius; the rising of the Italian allies; the ruthless dictatorship of Lucius Cornelius Sulla; the briefly blazing portents of Marcus Aemilius Lepidus (78 B.C.) and Quintus Sertorius; the slave wars; the coup d'état of Gnaeus Pompeius Magnus (Pompey the Great); conspiracy by the disaffected Lucius Sergius Catilina; the rise of Julius Caesar; the parceling out of power among Pompey, Crassus, and Caesar; civil war between Pompey and Caesar; the new triumvirate of Octavian (the future Augustus), Mark Antony, and Lepidus; the final confrontation between Octavian and Antony—these are only some of the clashes against which the administrative system was powerless. And all the time in the background the Celtic forces might be on the move, or skilled and subtle rulers such as Jugurtha in North Africa, Mithridates VI Eupator Dionysus in Pontus, and above all Cleopatra VII of Egypt might be playing on Roman weaknesses to their own profit.

The problems were in part economic. The elder Pliny said that large estates had proved the ruin of Italy. Tiberius Gracchus tried to limit the enclosures of public land to their legal maximum of 300 acres (500 *iugera*), perhaps with additions for children, and to increase the number of smallholders by distributing allotments of up to 18 acres (30 *iugera*). Despite his death at the hands of aristocratic gangsters he seems to have had some success, as the census figures, reflecting the new property holders, rose by 75,000 between 131 and 125 B.C. His brother, Gaius, went further, proposing overseas colonization, and also, recognizing that an urban proletariat would remain, seeking to stabilize the price of corn at Rome. He too was killed. The Gracchi had used methods either unconstitutional or untraditional. Tiberius had bypassed the senate, ignored a veto, had a fellow tribune deposed, and stood for a second term as tribune in successive years. By the time Gaius was elected for a second term this had become legal. But Gaius made head-on attacks on the abuse of senatorial privileges, and when he no longer had the protection of sacrosanctity he gathered round him what looked like a private bodyguard. Martial law was proclaimed, Gaius resisted by force and was killed. The constitution had effectively ceased to function.

A second new feature was the power of the wealthy bourgeoisie, the second highest economic class, the *equites*, so called originally because they were wealthy enough to provide the cavalry. By the second century they were composed of those outside the ruling aristocrats but with a fortune of 400,000 sesterces. They were interested in money making, not political power. The growth of empire enabled them to increase their wealth through the tax-contracts; many invested in land; many provided the capital for business enterprises. They could not however avoid some political involvement, and Gaius Gracchus transferred the juries that tried extortionate provincial governors from the senators to the *equites*. These courts became the shuttlecock in a power struggle and were batted to and fro between the classes, for although the *equites* did not seek to sit in the seats of power, they wanted the aristocracy under control.

A third issue was discontent among the Italian subjects of Rome. They had remained loyal to Rome during the Second Punic War. Now they began to claim the right of franchise, that is, Roman citizenship. Failing to attain it by constitutional means, they rose in violence. In 90 B.C. the franchise was conferred on those who had remained loyal, and perhaps on those who abandoned violence. A year later this was extended to all free men south of the Po, and the old Latin status was conferred on those north of the Po. There was a problem, however. To avoid being swamped by the new citizens the senate enrolled them in a limited number of tribes only; our sources differ as to how many. This occasioned discontent; within five years it was changed and the rights of the new and old citizens made identical. Sulla actually enrolled new senators from the wealthy Italians. It was the first of those steps that renewed the governing and administrative body from outside Rome.

A fourth factor, perhaps the largest of all, was the power of a victorious general. Gaius Marius was an *eques* who was a somewhat ambiguous dependent of the aristocratic Caecilii Metelli. He showed himself an able military officer, attained the offices of quaestor and praetor, and enhanced his position by an aristocratic marriage. He achieved the consulship in 107, and with it military command in Africa. Military threats from the north caused his reelection each year from 104 to 101. His reappointment in 100 was inevitable; his final office was in 88. Marius is important because he reorganized the army, admitting *proletarii* or *capitecensi*—citizens whose wealth was less than the minimum required for the lowest of the five classes of the centuriate organization—and thus creating a force with personal ties to its commander. A charismatic individual with an army behind him and some support from different civil elements (in Marius' case a minority of aristocrats, the *equites* generally, and some radical demagogues) could defy the constitution.

His great right-wing opponent, Lucius Cornelius Sulla, simply used his army to march on Rome in 88 B.C. and achieve power as dictator, killing those who stood in his way. Ironically, Sulla was seeking to restore the old system. He insisted on retroactive approval of his most outrageous acts. In the administrative field he restored to an enlarged senate the courts that judged political corruption, and gave it firmer control of overseas governors. But before long he abdicated. His most lastingly significant contribution to the future administrative system was the introduction of non-Roman Italians into the senate, but he hardly saw the ultimate implications of this step.

Gnaeus Pompeius Magnus (Pompey the Great), after rising by violent and unconstitutional means to be elected consul in 70 B.C., went on to signal triumphs in the East. He achieved a sweeping expansion, settlement, and reorganization of the provinces and client kingdoms, new and old, which was of enormous administrative importance since it established the permanent framework of Rome's rule throughout this huge area. But he disbanded his army on his return and was dependent on the wealth of Crassus and the rising power of Caesar to achieve his ends. These three held the effective power in their triumvirate, but they still worked through the existing machinery. Crassus was killed in the East, and Pompey, having undermined the constitution, presented himself unsuccessfully as the defender of the senate against Caesar.

Gaius Julius Caesar, late in coming to leadership, undertook ten years campaigning in Gaul, which extended the bounds of Roman rule far beyond the Mediterranean area. His subsequent legislation as dictator, from 45 B.C., shows no systematic attempt to improve the constitution, but nevertheless included a wide range of individual reforms. Two reforms contained particularly significant administrative implications, the grant of citizenship to Cisalpine Gaul and elsewhere, and the enrollment of non-Italians in the senate, which he increased to 900.

The old order was neither powerless nor powerful. Marcus Tullius Cicero, a "new man," consul in 63, who achieved power by his oratory, had tried to foster stability by the *concordia ordinum,* a united front from the aristocracy and the *equites.* His famous boast "Cedant arma togae, concedat laurea laudi" (Let arms yield to the toga, military laurels to civic glory) was a temporary illusion. The conspirators who killed Caesar had no policy. A new triumvirate of Mark Antony with his military power, the perhaps underestimated Lepidus who became *pontifex maximus,* and Octavian (the future Augustus), Caesar's great-nephew, who bore the prestige of his name allied to subtle ambition and wise delegation, swept them aside, murdered Cicero and others, and reaffirmed the power of arms.

THE AUGUSTAN
ADMINISTRATION

Out of the continuing turmoil of civil war, Octavian, adopted heir of Caesar, emerged triumphant as sole ruler, backed by the power of the armies. Military victory in 31

B.C. was followed by a solemn but illusory restoration of the republic in 27, when he assumed the title Augustus.

He had to retain personal power over the administration while preserving the image of republican constitutionality. His powers were constitutional, only they were accumulated and permanent. From 31 to 23 he was consul, giving him military and legislative authority. But he needed the office to reward his loyal supporters and to satisfy the senatorial aristocracy. The pillars of his power were two, the *proconsulare imperium* and the *tribunicia potestas,* the former giving him the command of the armies and the governance of provinces, the latter sacrosanctity and control of legislation. He assumed for a time (together with his lieutenant Marcus Agrippa) the office of censor, and gradually reduced the senate to 600 again. New recruits to the order came from ex-quaestors, but only those with a high property qualification and an unblemished record of public service. He also retained in his own hands powers of nomination to office.

One great change was symptomatic of the reality behind the facade. Fairly early in his reign the emperor instituted a *consilium principis* (Committee of Senate), comprising the two consuls, one representative from each of the other colleges of magistrates, and fifteen members chosen by lot, to prepare the business of the senate and form a liaison committee between the senate and himself. In A.D. 13 not long before his death he transformed this by the permanent accession of three members of his own family and his own right to co-opt whomever he wished from his *amici*. The *consilium principis* thus became the emperor's own committee and a means of bypassing the senate altogether. Bryce's dictum that "every Monarchy becomes in practice an Oligarchy" has its application to the Roman Empire.

Augustus, without establishing a systematic bureaucracy, greatly improved the quality of administration by developing a form of civil service. He made personal appointments of *curatores* or *praefecti* in charge of different departments of state. These were career posts, salaried and permanent. The incumbents were selected impartially from the first two classes. This was perhaps the single most important administrative change. Support for administration came from the emperor's private staff of freedmen (ex-slaves), working as secretaries or accountants. They were to become more powerful in the future. The Praetorian Guard, perhaps 4,500 strong, acted as the emperor's bodyguard and as his orderlies with a variety of functions. Their commanding officer was thus of great influence. Augustus minimized dangers from this quarter by having two commanders as a check on each other, and appointing from the *equites* only. The *equites* thus had a career structure open before them: military service, junior procuratorships in the provinces, and then a few top-ranking posts such as governor, head of a department, or prefect.

The armies on which Augustus' power depended might be an instrument of usurpation. He cut their strength from sixty legions to twenty-eight, while developing the auxiliaries from occasional levies into a standing force. The greatest concentrations of legions were remote from Rome, eight on the Rhine frontier and seven on the Danube, three in Syria, three in Spain, and two in Egypt. His policy was not basically expansionist; it was to ensure that his world was at peace within secure frontiers. To this last end he aimed at establishing frontiers on the Danube and the Elbe. In Germany the annihilation of a force of 20,000 led him to fall back on the Rhine. The extraordinary quality of the Pax Romana is seen in that southern Gaul had a mere 1,200 troops. The settlement of ex-soldiers in "colonies" all round the empire added security and helped romanization; there were some eighty such foundations between the death of Caesar and the death of Augustus.

The administration of the empire was tactfully divided between emperor and senate. The senate was responsible for Rome and Italy, Sicily, Sardinia, Corsica, Southern Spain (Baetica), Illyricum, Macedonia, Achaea, Asia (i.e., western Asia Minor), Bithynia (northwestern Asia Minor), Crete and Cyrene, and Africa. Later, it lost Sardinia, Corsica and Illyricum and gained Cyprus and Gallia Narbonensis. Augustus had Egypt (where senators were forbidden to go), Syria, Gaul, the rest of Spain, the Danube provinces, Galatia, Cilicia and Judaea. But the emperor also had *imperium maius,* wider authority, which gave him ultimate power over all the provinces; he kept this mailed fist in a velvet glove. The imperial governors were carefully chosen from ex-consuls or ex-praetors, with prefects from the *equites* for Egypt and some lesser provinces. They were salaried and served for several years. Improved communications gave them readier contact with the center. Senatorial governors usually served for a year only.

Financial reform was a high priority. The abuses of the old system are amply indicated by Cicero's pamphlets against Verres and by his correspondence. Julius Caesar had not been a man to tolerate this. We do not know his plans in detail, but he clearly intended to be personally responsible for the imperial finances, and placed his own slaves or freedmen in charge of the mint and indirect taxes (*vectigalia*). It is noteworthy also that he arranged for the tithe in Asia to be paid directly in cash by the provincials without the intermediary of the *publicani.* His death in 44 B.C. brought renewed problems, and the civil wars of the next thirteen years created the conditions for heavy exactions, by Cassius in Laodicea, Tarsus, and Rhodes, for example, or by Antony in the eastern provinces.

For Augustus the first need was to establish the facts. A survey of the empire was carried out; a late author, Aethicus, says that it was systematic, comprehensive, and took over sixty years. This is certainly wrong, but it evidently took place. The evidence for a single comprehensive census is effectively limited to one provincial author, the evangelist Luke. But we know of provincial censuses, as in the Gauls in 27 and 12 B.C. and A.D. 14–16, and it is probable that the establishment of new provinces began with a census. Censuses were carried out either by the governors or by officers specially appointed. The function of a census included a record of population in age-groups, and of property and valuation.

It seems that the taxation system was different in imperial and senatorial provinces. The senatorial provinces were "stipendiary." The main tax was a fixed sum distributed over the body of taxpayers. The imperial provinces were "tributary." The main tax was a land tax (*tributum*) varying with the value of the land. Tax collection in the imperial provinces was in the hands of specially appointed officers called procurators.

Augustus instituted no change in the state treasury except to transfer it from the hands of quaestors to those of praetors. His own privy purse was enormous, and it covered many of the costs of central administration.

Modern authors have sometimes spoken of the dyarchy or dual rule of Augustus and the senate. It is a tribute to the tact and skill of Augustus that they have done so. In truth the old order had gone. The emperor ruled, but the senate still had its place in the administrative system.

THE SUCCESSION

Augustus had schemed, without too many scruples, to keep the succession to autocratic power within his own family. The deaths of his two grandsons scuppered this scheme. Instead he adopted Tiberius, son of his wife Livia by her first husband, and undoubtedly the ablest person available. Tiberius, curiously uncertain of himself, gave to the senate the chance of restoring the republic. They responded by voting him all the powers of Augustus, and thereafter talk of such restoration was never practical politics. For half a century power was kept within the Julio-Claudian family with its imperial prestige. Nero's death brought back the old pattern of military commanders fighting for power. From "the year of the Four Emperors" (A.D. 69) Vespasian emerged supreme, and was succeeded in the new Flavian dynasty by his sons, Titus and then Domitian. Domitian's assassination in 96 brought further uncertainty, but thereafter for nearly a century a combination of deliberate policy and the accident of childlessness saw the adoption by the ruling emperor of his best successor. It was an age that even Edward Gibbon praised, the age of Nerva, Trajan, Hadrian, Antoninus Pius, and Marcus Aurelius. It is ironical that Marcus Aurelius, the idealized philosopher-king, should have restored the policy of filial succession in the interests of the worthless Commodus. From the renewed chaos emerged a fresh dynasty, the Severi. Lucius Septimius Severus, the founder, knew where real power lay. His dying advice to his sons was "Don't fall out; pay the soldiers and despise the rest." In the "hell of a half century" that followed the death in A.D. 235 of Severus Alexander the army was indeed the emperor-maker. At one point it actually put the empire up for auction to the highest bidder; the millionaire who was foolish enough to buy it paid with his life a few weeks later.

CHANGES IN THE PROVINCES

During the Julio-Claudian period there were some provincial changes. Britain was added to the empire by conquest. Cappadocia, Thrace, the Cottian Alps and the two Mauretanias, formerly client kingdoms, acceded with the death of their rulers. Administrative adjustments created new provinces in Raetia and Pamphylia. The general administrative structures held.

The great expansion took place under Trajan, whose campaigns added Dacia (roughly present-day Romania), Armenia, Assyria, Mesopotamia, and Arabia, though Hadrian wisely withdrew from the most easterly provinces.

The distribution of the legions at about the time of the accession of Hadrian (A.D. 117/118) is illuminating. There were three in Britain, four backed by a fleet on the Rhine frontier, ten along the Danube together with a fleet, eight along the eastern frontier with fleets in the eastern part of the Black Sea and the Mediterranean, two in Egypt, one in the rest of North Africa, one in the whole of Spain, and a fleet covering either flank of Italy. The concentrations of legions mark at once the danger points and the points of expansion; the situation in the East reflects the rise of Parthia. There is no finer demonstration of the "immeasurable majesty of the peace brought by Rome" (Pliny the Elder, *Natural History* 27.1.1.3) than the fact that a single legion, based at Lambaesis, policed the whole of North Africa from the Atlantic to the borders of Egypt.

Some of the strength of the Roman Empire lay in the considerable autonomy of the municipalities. A number of municipal charters have survived. The general structure of local government is oligarchic and conservative, but such as to give a solid sense of local pride. The normal pattern shows two chief magistrates, elected annually, corresponding to the consuls at Rome, two aediles, a senate or council of a hundred, and an assembly.

Augustus had made tours of inspection in the empire, and in doing so had kept provincial governors up to scratch. His successors on the whole did not, and this could lead to abuses, especially on the part of petty officials. Hadrian was the most indefatigable traveler among the emperors: he spent more than half his reign outside Italy. By contrast his successor, Antoninus Pius, no less careful of the well-being of provincials, scarcely left Italy, but sat like a benevolent spider in the center of his web.

Claudius, who had a sense of history, realized that as Rome had been strengthened by bringing the Italians into partnership, so now she would be strengthened by developing a similar relationship with the provincials. Too sensible not to proceed gradually, he granted citizenship to towns in Noricum and Mauretania, and introduced a number of Gauls into the senate: we have a record of the humane and enlightened speech whereby he defended this last measure against criticism. Nero too granted citizenship to the Alpes Maritimae. At this time we begin to find Spaniards, such as Seneca, prominent in Roman society and politics. Vespasian and his sons introduced into the senate individuals from Gaul and Spain, and granted Latin status to magistrates in some or all of Spain, a halfway house to full citizenship, and a recognition of progress and token of goodwill. Trajan, Hadrian, and Marcus Aurelius were themselves all of Spanish origin, and Antoninus' family was from Gaul.

The practice of granting Latin status continued in the second century. Hadrian extended its scope to embrace a larger number of the governing class in the municipalities. The culmination of this policy came in A.D. 212 when Caracalla granted Roman citizenship to virtually all the free inhabitants of the empire. A cynical view suggests that it was to increase tax revenues. The emperor's own speech stresses that he is bringing more worshipers to the gods on whose favor Rome depends.

DEVELOPMENTS IN ADMINISTRATIVE ORGANIZATION

One major change took place in the structures of the state, although it hardly touched the realities of power. Under Tiberius the election of magistrates was transferred from the Comitia to the senate, and the Comitia de facto ceased to have a legislative function; the reign of Nerva witnessed its demise. The third part in Polybius' balance of powers had ceased to possess even a nominal existence.

Under Claudius an opportunity arising out of his predecessor's overspending was taken to rationalize the structure of financial administration. The result was that financial power was coordinated in the emperor's hands.

Claudius also greatly improved the efficiency of the civil service by a departmental structure: *a libellis* dealing with petitions, *ab epistulis* with correspondence, *a rationibus* with finance, and *a studiis* acting as librarian and privy seal. The freedmen in charge of these, Pallas, Narcissus, and others, were immensely powerful, immensely rich, immensely corrupt, and immensely efficient. The old aristocracy regarded these ex-slaves as upstarts. Under Trajan and Hadrian this work was transferred to *equites* and was administered as part of the machinery of state rather than as part of the emperor's private estate. Hadrian further simplified business by separating Greek from Latin correspondence; this made for efficiency, but was perhaps the first chink in the unity of the empire.

The reign of Domitian (81–96) saw a practical change of some importance. He virtually ignored the senate, even for form's sake, and won the bitter hatred of the senators. The veil was stripped from the realities of power. If anyone had power beside the emperor it was the "friends of the emperor" (*amici principis*) who met in the council (*con-*

silium principis). Juvenal (*Satires* 4.37–149) has an unforgettable picture of such a gathering summoned to determine the fate of a big fish. The word is *orbem*, which can mean the circumference of the fish or the world, and the question is *conciditur?* "Is it to be chopped in pieces?" Early in the third century Macrinus (the first *eques* to become emperor, A.D. 217–218) and Elagabalus (emperor 218–222) did not even go through the motions of allowing the senate to vote them into power, though they did condescend to notify the senate, which was forced to acknowledge the fait accompli. The emperor was responsible for all legislation: many of the senate were absent on their country estates.

A more positive development took place under Hadrian. He led Salvius Julianus to codify the edicts of the praetors into a systematic whole, a vital stage in the development of Roman law. This type of work was carried on, notably by Papinian and Ulpian under the Severi. Legal experts were by now playing a vital role in the *consilium principis*.

DIOCLETIAN

By the last part of the third century A.D. it was clear that neither the machinery of empire as established by Augustus nor the developed autocracy could cope with the economic and military crises that assailed them on all sides. The Balkan soldier Diocles, who took office in 284 as Diocletian (Gaius Aurelius Valerius Diocletianus), gave much thought to the problems. He was a man of vision and energy, a planner, for better or worse a bureaucrat's dream.

Diocletian organized a tetrarchy of emperors to share the vast responsibilities of government and defense: two senior with the title of Augustus, himself based in Nicomedia (Izmir) being responsible for the East, and his partner, Maximian, based in Mediolanum (Milan), for the West. Each had a junior colleague or Caesar, Galerius in the East, based in Sirmium (Sremska Mitrovica) and Thessalonica (Salonika), and Constantius I Chlorus in the West, working from Trèves (formerly Augusta Trevirorum, now Trier). It will be noted that Rome had no part in the scheme. Each was supported by a Praetorian prefect. This was designed both for more efficient administration and for secure succession. The Augusti were to retire after ten years, the Caesars would become Augusti, and new Caesars would be appointed. Diocletian abdicated loyally in A.D. 305 and forced the reluctant Maximian to do the same. The scheme, brilliantly logical, foundered on human ambition, family pride, and the accidents of history. Constantius died. His son Constantine I the Great and Maximian's son Maxentius, passed over as Caesars, asserted themselves. Maximian came out of retirement and resumed the title of Augustus. It is needless to go into the chaotic details; out of the situation a single autocrat reemerged in the person of Constantine.

Diocletian's realization that large entities created more problems than they solved led him to reform provincial administration. In order to provide more stringent supervision and to reduce the power of governors, he roughly doubled the number of provinces by halving their size. The Christian convert Lactantius, using the very word of Juvenal's earlier satire, says that they were "chopped into slices." Italy lost its privileged position and was treated with the rest of the empire. There was some division of civil and military powers. The new provinces were organized into twelve (or thirteen) dioceses, each governed by a *vicarius*, responsible to the Praetorian prefects, and supported by two finance officers drawn from the *equites*.

Diocletian's other major administrative innovation was financial. He had to face the result of galloping inflation and the depreciation of coinage. His first answer was to raise what bullion he could and issue a more reliable coinage throughout the empire. He tried to cope with inflation by the logical approach of dealing directly with the causes; the result was his famous edict detailing maximum prices over a vast range of goods from cabbages to crinolines and services rendered by virtually everyone from barbers to barristers. The penalty for infringement was death, but the policy was doomed from the start. Goods disappeared from the shops, and a flourishing black market developed. Again logic had to give way to human weakness. Diocletian also established an equitable system of taxation, based on land and involving its productive capacity and the number of those working on it.

CONSTANTINE

By the time Constantine achieved sole power, in 324, any pretense that the empire was not an autocracy had gone with the winds of time. The imperial court was itself a complex organization. There were four ministers in charge of the main offices of state. The quaestor of the sacred palace (*quaestor sacri palatii*), was responsible for petitions and edicts; he had the support of a vast army of clerks. The master of the offices (*magister officiorum*), controlled the secretariat, the imperial couriers, the imperial audiences and the bodyguard. The companion or count responsible for dispensing the sacred money (*comes rationalis* [later *comes sacrarum largitionum*]), was in charge of mines and mints. The companion or count of the private estate (*comes rei privatae*), administered the imperial lands. Meetings of the Privy Council involved a corps of ushers and a corps of notaries, whose head held a position of influence. The imperial bodyguard was supported by officer cadets. There was a large domestic staff including the eunuchs in charge of the bedroom suite.

The Roman Senate no longer had any part to play. It became effectively the city council of Rome under the chairmanship of the *praefectus urbi*. The *consilium principis* remained in a revised form, chosen by the emperor, including the chief officers of state, entitled the Sacred Consistory, and standing in the emperor's presence; this may have had an incidental effect of expediting business. The Praetorian Guard was disbanded and Praetorian prefects, now civilian officials, were judges and finance officers. Diocletian had already assigned one to each tetrarch. Under Constantine there were, it seems, three in the West and two in the East, but eventually they reverted to four, responsible for the Gauls, Italy, Illyricum and the East. The *vicarii* and the provincial officials were responsible to the emperor through these.

Constantine's greatest administrative innovation was the transfer of the capital in 330 from Rome to Byzantium, refounded as New Rome or Constantinopolis—Constantine's City—a new capital for the newly Christian empire. This brilliant vision ensured the survival of the Roman Empire for another thousand years. It also accelerated the eventual split between East and West that still survives among the Christian churches.

SURVIVALS

The greatest surviving influence of Roman administrative organization is undoubtedly through Roman law, whose full codification was due to Justinian in the sixth century A.D. Roman law remains the basis of much of later European law.

The Holy Roman Empire of the Middle Ages was a serious attempt to restore the glories of ancient Rome, but it was more a matter of prestige than of detailed administrative survival or imitation. There have been deliberate essays in the imitation of Roman institutions, notably in the French and American revolutions.

In some ways the most interesting survival of Roman administration lies within the Roman Catholic church (and in measure the Eastern Orthodox church), which took on the structure of diocese and vicar, where the pope holds the place of the emperor, and the College of Cardinals holds the position of senate or *consilium,* where the councils follow the procedures of the Roman Senate; even the dress of officials recalls the ancient Romans. The religious historian Adolf Harnack once said, "The Empire has not perished, but has only undergone a transformation. . . . The Roman Church is the old Roman Empire consecrated by the Gospel."

The great achievement of the Roman Empire was to give to a larger area of Europe certainly, and probably the whole world, a longer period of untroubled peace than at any time in the history of mankind either before or since. Military conquest was followed by government by consent. To this last there were two major contributory factors. One was the combination of a centralized and unifying administration, with genuine local responsibility in the municipalities. The other was the extraordinary capacity of the Romans to assimilate new citizens from all over the world and accept them into their power structures. Both of these carry lessons for the present and the future.

BIBLIOGRAPHY

SOURCES

Martin Percival Charlesworth, ed., *Documents Illustrating the Reigns of Claudius and Nero* (1939); Kitty Chisholm and John Ferguson, eds., *Rome, the Augustan Age: A Sourcebook* (1981); Cicero, *Orationes,* Albert Curtis Clark and William Peterson, eds., 6 vols. (1905–1918), and *Epistulae,* William Smith Watt and David Roy Shackleton Bailey, eds., 3 vols (1958–1982); Hermann Dessau, *Inscriptiones Latinae Selectae,* 5 vols. (1892–1916); Dio Cassius, *Roman History,* Earnest Cary, trans., 9 vols. (1970); Diodorus Siculus, *Library of History,* Charles Henry Oldfather *et al.*, trans., 12 vols. (1946–1967); Dionysius of Halicarnassus, *Roman Antiquities,* Earnest Cary, trans., 7 vols. (1970).

Victor Ehrenberg and Arnold Hugh Martin Jones, eds., *Documents Illustrating the Reigns of Augustus and Tiberius,* 2d ed. (1955); Abel Hendy Jones Greenidge, Agnes Muriel Clay, and Eric William Gray, *Sources for Roman History 133–70 B.C.,* 2d ed. (1960); Ernest George Hardy, *Six Roman Laws and Three Spanish Charters* (1911–1912); Arnold Hugh Martin Jones, *A History of Rome through the Fifth Century,* 2 vols. (1968–1970); Juvenal, *The Satires,* John Ferguson, ed. (1970); Lactantius, Samuel Brandt and Georg Laubmann, eds., 2 vols. (1890–1897); Naphtali Lewis and Meyer Reinhold, *Roman Civilization: Sourcebook,* 2 vols. (1966); Livy, *From the Founding of the City,* Benjamin Oliver Foster *et al.*, trans., 14 vols. (1966); Michael William McCrum and Arthur Geoffrey Woodhead, *Select Documents of the Principates of the Flavian Emperors A.D. 68–96* (1961).

Polybius, *The Histories,* William Roger Paton, trans., 6 vols. (1967), and *Scriptores Historiae Augustae,* David Magie, trans., 3 vols. (1930); Edith Mary Smallwood, ed., *Documents Illustrating the Principates of Nerva, Trajan and Hadrian* (1966), and *Documents Illustrating the Principates of Gaius, Claudius and Nero* (1967); Suetonius, *Works,* John Carew Rolfe, trans. (1914); Tacitus, *Annals,* Henry Furneaux, ed., 2 vols. (1884), and *Historiarum Libri,* Charles Dennis Fisher, ed. (1910); Varro, *On the Latin Language,* Roland Grubb Kent, trans., 2 vols. (1967).

STUDIES

Frank Frost Abbott, *A History and Description of Roman Political Institutions,* 3d ed. (1911); Frank Frost Abbott and Allan Chester Johnson, *Municipal Administration in the Roman Empire* (1926); Alan Edgar Astin, *The Lex Annalis before Sulla* (1958);

Ernst Badian, *Foreign Clientelae 264–70 B.C.* (1958), *Roman Imperialism in the Late Republic* (1968), and *Publicans and Sinners* (1972); Thomas Robert Shannon Broughton, *The Magistrates of the Roman Republic*, 2 vols. (1951–1960); Peter Astbury Brunt, *Italian Manpower 225 B.C.–A.D. 14* (1971); James Bryce, *Studies in History and Jurisprudence*, 2 vols. (1901); Max Cary and Howard Hayes Scullard, *A History of Rome*, 3d ed. (1975); Robert Combès, *Imperator* (1966).

John Anthony Crook, *Consilium Principis* (1955), and *Law and Life in Ancient Rome* (1967); Arnold Mackay Duff, *Freedmen in the Early Roman Empire* (1928); Tenney Frank, *An Economic Survey of Ancient Rome*, 5 vols. (1933–1940); Albino Garzetti, *From Tiberius to the Antonines* (1974); Matthias Gelzer, *The Roman Nobility*, Robin Seager, trans. (1969); Michael Grant, *From Imperium to Auctoritas* (1946); Abel Hendy Jones Greenidge, *Roman Public Life* (1901); Mason Hammond, *The Augustan Principate* (1933), and *The Antonine Monarchy* (1959); William Emerton Heitland, *The Roman Fate* (1922), and *Last Words on the Roman Municipalities* (1928); Herbert Hill, *The Roman Middle Class in the Republican Period* (1952); Léon Homo, *Roman Political Institutions from City to State*, Marryat Ross Dobie, trans. (1929).

Laurence Lee Howe, *The Praetorian Prefect from Commodus to Diocletian* (1942); Arnold Hugh Martin Jones, *Studies in Roman Government and Law* (1960), and *The Criminal Courts of the Roman Republic and Principate* (1972); Clinton Walker Keyes, *The Rise of the Equites in the Third Century of the Roman Empire* (1915); Karl Loewenstein, *The Governance of Rome* (1973); David Magie, *The Roman Rule in Asia Minor*, 2 vols. (1950); Theodor Mommsen, *The Provinces of the Roman Empire from Caesar to Diocletian*, William Purdie Dickson, trans., 2 vols. (1886), and *Römischer Staatsrecht*, 3 vols. (1887); Claude Nicolet, *L'Ordre Equestre à l'époque républicaine*, 2 vols. (1966); Robert Maxwell Ogilvie, *A Commentary on Livy Books 1–5* (1965); Henry Michael Denne Parker, *The Roman Legions*, 2d ed. (1958).

Hans-Georg Pflaum, *Les procurateurs equestres sous le haut-empire romain*, 2 vols. (1950), and *Les carrières procuratoriennes equestres sous le haut-empire romain*, 2 vols. (1960); James Smith Reid, *The Municipalities of the Roman Empire* (1913); Michael Rostovtzeff, *The Social and Economic History of the Roman Empire*, Peter Fraser, trans., 2d ed., 2 vols. (1957); Howard Hayes Scullard, *Roman Politics 220–150 B.C.*, 2d ed. (1973); Israel Shatzman, *Senatorial Wealth and Roman Politics* (1975); Adrian Nicholas Sherwin-White, *The Roman Citizenship*, 2d ed. (1973); Eastland Stuart Staveley, *Greek and Roman Voting and Elections* (1972).

George Hope Stevenson, *Roman Provincial Administration* (1939); Ronald Syme, *The Roman Revolution* (1939); Lily Ross Taylor, *Party Politics in the Age of Caesar* (1949), *The Voting Districts of the Roman Republic* (1960), and *Roman Voting Assemblies* (1966); Graham Webster, *The Roman Imperial Army* (1969); Timothy Peter Wiseman, *New Men in the Roman Senate 139 B.C.–A.D. 14* (1971).

Interstate Relations

SHALOM PERLMAN

DIPLOMACY AND INTERSTATE RELATIONS in Greece and Rome were characterized by one basic principle: the demarcation between diplomacy and foreign policy was not quite clear because there was no separation of powers within the government of the Greek polis or the Roman state; moreover, no permanent institutions or bodies dealing with interstate relations were established. Although the Greeks and the Romans created almost all the machinery for conducting interstate relations (dispatch and protection of envoys, nomination of special *proxenoi* in Greece and election of *fetiales* in Rome, definition of the terms of bilateral and multilateral treaties, including arbitration), they never considered it necessary to give permanence to these bodies and procedures. The *fetiales* were a permanent *collegium,* but their tasks and duties in interstate relations were limited; even before the principate, when their tasks were taken over by the emperor, the envoys—*legati*—played an important part; it was only under the late empire that the Roman emperors established an advisory office of specialists on foreign affairs, expert in the knowledge of old treaties and precedents. It is therefore not surprising that except for the term *proxenoi* the Greeks did not create any special vocabulary to denote those who participated in diplomatic negotiations, or that they did not create special terminology for treaties but used such words as *presbys* (elder) to denote envoy and *spondai* (libation or sacrifice) for truce and treaty; similarly, the Romans used *legatus* (deputy) also for envoy and *sponsio* (guaranty, promise) for truce.

In the Greek polis diplomacy and decisions on relations with other states were decided upon by the council and the assembly: "The deliberative element is sovereign on the issues of war and peace, and the making and breaking of alliances" (Aristotle, *Politics* 4.14.3; 1298a 4–6). This was the reason for open diplomacy, although there was certainly a difference between democratic Athens and oligarchic Sparta or imperial Rome in this respect. Small states such as Athens sometimes may have been afraid of secret negotiations between larger states. Thucydides noted instances of secret promises and secret negotiations by Sparta (1.58.1; 1.101.2; 4.22.1; 5.44.2; 5.45), and the Persian king complained that each Spartan ambassador spoke a different language, that is, no two ever made corresponding representations (Thucydides, 4.50). But even in Sparta the final decision was with the council and assembly. The Macedonian and Hellenistic kings as well as the Roman emperors could conduct secret negotiations and make quick decisions, thus gaining an advantage, which sometimes provoked the envy of a Greek politician.

GREEK INTERSTATE RELATIONS

Greek political attitudes embodied particularism—the belief that each political group has a right to pursue self-interest and independence without regard to the interests of larger groups—and a zealous guarding of the autonomy and freedom of the polis. In spite of this, interstate relations developed quite early and were facilitated by natural ties among the Greeks and by the continuous efforts to prevent, or at least to mitigate, warfare among the Greek states. A common language facilitated direct negotiations between the Greek states and although there were differences in the dialects in which signatory cities published a treaty at home, Spartan envoys had no difficulty in making themselves understood in Athens, nor did Athenians in Thebes. Common religious beliefs and practices provided opportunity for interstate meetings and for the establishment of rules of warfare and generally observed truces. Thus, before the outbreak of the Peloponnesian War, the Corinthian envoys could justify their claims against the Corcyraeans: "These, then, are the considerations of right which we urge upon you—and they are adequate according to the institutions of the Hellenes" (Thucydides, 1.41.1.).

Early Greek interstate organizations were the amphictyonies, religious leagues comprising a number of tribes or other discrete population groups residing in the area of a famous shrine (*amphictyones,* dwellers round about), under the tutelage of its god. Each league was devoted to the care and protection of the temple and the maintenance of worship within it. This entailed a sharing of both practical and religious responsibilities, and so protocols, tolerances, and similar, essentially interstate, matters had to be agreed upon. Consequently, such a league commonly came to exert considerable influence in political as well as religious affairs, assuming the administration of periodic games and other major functions, and negotiating oaths of nonaggression, mutual defense, and joint offense (oaths that in the event almost invariably were violated as particularism superseded mutualism). The most famous, powerful, and long-lived amphictyony was that originally composed of twelve tribes in the area of Delphi, who sent deputies or representatives to meet at the Delphic temple of Apollo in the spring, and at the temple of Demeter in the village of Anthela, near Pylae (Thermopylae), in the autumn. Other amphictyonies included those of Calauria in the Saronic Gulf and of Onchestos in Boeotia, both devoted to temples of Poseidon; that of Delos, devoted to Apollo; and that comprising twelve Ionian states on the coast of Asia Minor devoted to Poseidon Helikonios, whose place of assembly, Panionion, was at Mycale. In time, the stronger states began to exercise predominant influence, thus causing friction, intervention, and even change of membership. Philip II of Macedon became a member of the Delphic amphictyony in 346 B.C. This amphictyony continued until Roman times, and changes in its membership were made by Augustus and Hadrian.

The contribution of the amphictyony in Greece was in the provision for a truce during common festivals, and in rules for more humane conduct during war, sanctioned by an oath, as Aeschines relates in his speech *On the Embassy* (115):

> I read their [the amphictyonies'] oaths, in which the men of ancient times swore that they would raze no city of the amphictyonic states, nor shut them off from flowing water either in war or in peace; that if anyone should violate this oath, they would march against such an one and raze his cities; and if anyone should violate the shrine of the god or be accessory to such violation, or make any plot against the holy places, they would punish him with hand and foot and voice, and all their power. To the oath was added a mighty curse.

Another interstate arrangement based on the consciousness of Greek kinship and aimed at promoting truce and amity developed round the great Panhellenic festivals and games (Olympic, Pythian, Isthmian, and Nemean) and the accompanying *panegyreis* (festal assemblies), which were so colorfully described by Isocrates in his *Panegyricus* (4.43):

> Now the founders of our great festivals are justly praised for handing down to us a custom by which, having proclaimed a truce, and resolved our pending quarrels, we come together in one place, where, as we make our prayers and sacrifices in common, we are reminded of the kinship which exists among us and are made to feel more kindly toward each other for the future, reviving our old friendships and establishing new ties.

These early attempts did not prevent warfare, which was almost endemic in Greece and was often entered into without warning: " 'Peace' as the term is commonly employed is nothing more than a name, the truth being that every state is by law of nature engaged perpetually in an informal [*akeryktos* (not announced by a herald)] war with every other state," says Plato in the *Laws* (1.626a). Hence the small Greek states often sought protective alliance with larger states; such alliances were often themselves an "exchange of peace for war" (Xenophon, *History of Greece* [*Hellenica*], 7.4.10).

In the fourth century B.C. the search for peace and for interstate relations based on justice became more pronounced. This can be seen in the attempt to define the difference between truce (*spondai*), "the dictation of terms to the conquered by the conquerors after victory in war," and peace (*eirene*), "a settlement of differences between equals" (Andocides 3, *On the Peace with Sparta* 11). The search is also evidenced by the introduction of the annual Festival of Peace by the Athenians in memory of the victory and peace of 375 B.C. In this period expediency and advantage in interstate relations, which had been so stressed in the fifth century, give way to a growing consciousness of a distinction between justice and advantage.

ROMAN INTERSTATE RELATIONS

The reasons for and the course of the development of Rome's relations with other states and nations were quite different from those of Greece. Romans may have felt kinship with the Latins, but not with any other tribes or states either in Italy or outside it. Rome's expansion was, therefore, built on predominance, which aimed at total absorption into the Roman state; although various legal and constitutional forms were devised, Rome did not leave much freedom or independence to the states she absorbed. It was only at a time when there was no real challenger left to Rome's imperial power that Augustus established the *Ara Pacis* (Temple of Peace), the symbol of Pax Romana.

On the other hand, Rome was by far more

generous in her grants of citizenship than was a Greek polis. Rome very early granted extensive privileges of *conubium* (the right to contract marriage without loss of Roman citizenship by the offspring) and of *commercium* (the right to make commercial contracts according to Roman laws and enforceable automatically in Roman courts). Early in the first century B.C. (90/89) Roman citizenship was conferred not only on the Latins, but also on all the other Italians who until then had been subordinate allies of Rome (*socii et amici populi Romani*). This process was continued in north Italy and in those parts of the western provinces in which romanization made great progress until in A.D. 212 Roman franchise was extended to the whole empire. This difference in interstate relations was well put by the emperor Claudius in a speech before the senate in A.D. 48: "Was there any cause for the ruin of the Lacedaemonians and the Athenians, though they were flourishing in arms, but the fact that they rejected the vanquished as aliens?" (Tacitus, *Annals* 11.24).

The most important contribution made by Rome to interstate relations was the establishment of an order based on the "law of nations" (*ius gentium*), that is, international law, and on observance of its formulas, especially in declaration of war and conclusion of treaties. Rome was not interested in equality or in the preservation of the rights of states, but was meticulous in appearing to abide by correct legal procedure as an expression of the rule of justice. Whereas the Greeks spoke in interstate relations of the "common laws of the Hellenes" at most, the Romans considered that "that which natural reason constituted among all men is preserved equally among all nations and is called *law of nations*" (Gaius, *Institutes* 1.1.1). Although Rome certainly did not neglect the real political advantages of the state, she prided herself on "preserving justice even toward the lowest" (Livy, 42.47).

ROMAN *FETIALES*, GREEK *PROXENOI*

The main application of *ius gentium* in interstate relations was in the legal provisions for declaring war and making peace. The Romans developed a quite elaborate system of formulas and rituals regarding the declaration of war and the conclusion of peace, which were put into practice by the collegium of *fetiales*, the only Roman permanent body dealing with interstate relations. The twenty *fetiales* were not required to make policy decisions or to conduct negotiations, but only to carry out strictly defined legal proceedings. The observance of these proceedings was regarded as a safeguard for keeping good faith among nations by providing legal distinction between what the Romans called just and pious war and brigandage.

In the case of declaration of war, it was the task of the *fetiales* to make the grievances of Rome known to the enemy; if no satisfaction was given within a fixed time and the senate decided on war, it was their task to recite certain formulas on the border of the enemy's territory and hurl a spear into his land; if, because of distance, this was impossible the ceremony was performed near the column of war (*columna bellica*) in Rome. In case of peace, after the terms had been agreed upon, the *fetiales* read them aloud and sacrificed a pig as confirmation of the oath sworn at the time, which laid a curse on Rome in case she was the first to break the peace.

The institution that was developed in Greece to facilitate interstate contacts was that of *proxenia*. This was the only term specifically coined by the Greeks in the vocabulary of interstate relations; its meaning is "state-friend." The earliest mention of a *proxenos* is at the end of the seventh century B.C., and the word is used today for "consul." *Proxenia* probably developed from personal ties of friendship and hospitality (*xenia*) between members of different states; an example may be seen in one "Xenias, a man of Elis who was a personal friend [*xenos*] of Agis and the state-friend [*proxenos*] of the Lacedaemonians" (Pausanias, 3.8.4). A famous *xenia* relationship is that between Pericles and the Spartan king Archidamus (Thucydides, 2.13.1). The Spartan envoy to Persia is called *xenos* of the Persian king by Plutarch ("Artaxerxes" 22.3).

The *proxenos*, unlike a consul, was not a citizen of the state that appointed him, but of the state in which he was appointed; thus, the Athenians Cimon and Callias served as Spartan *proxenoi* in Athens and the above-mentioned Xenias was the Spartan *proxenos* in Elis. Although *proxenia* may have sometimes been hereditary in a family and the formula of conferment was usually "to him and to his descendants," it was certainly not permanent and *proxenia* could even be withdrawn. A *proxenos* was often appointed in recognition of the help he gave to visiting ambassadors and in expectation of future services. It was for this reason that leading politicians were appointed as *proxenoi* and because of these connections they in turn often served as envoys to the appointing state. These politicians often considered the appointment to be of help in promoting their political careers in their own countries. The *proxenos* was, then, active in promoting good relations with the appointing state and often even identified with the internal regime of the state he represented; thus, in 403 B.C. the restored Athenian democracy renominated *proxenoi* in Thasos who were revoked by the oligarchic regime of the Thirty Tyrants.

The *proxenos* usually received the ambassadors from the appointing state and facilitated their contacts with the appropriate political bodies of his own state. Moreover, the *proxenos* usually served as protector and intermediary in legal and economic matters for the visiting citizens of the other state. (In the *Birds* of Aristophanes [1,021–1,022], an Athenian asks upon arriving in Cloudcuckoobury, "Where are the *proxenoi*?") In Rome a special magistrate, the *praetor peregrinus*, was in charge of these services for visiting foreign citizens. Roman nobles proudly exercised the tasks of patrons of foreign communities or rulers (Livy, 42.38).

Still, in spite of the fact that the *proxenos* often identified with the internal regime and the foreign policy aims of the appointing state, there was rarely a problem of breach of loyalty to his own state; the order of loyalty was first of all to his own state and then to that which appointed him. This general trend is well expressed by Plato (*Laws* 1.642b):

> O stranger of Athens, you are not, perhaps, aware that our family is, in fact, a *proxenos* of your State. It is probably true of all children that, when once they have been told that they are *proxenoi* of a certain State, they conceive an affection for that State even from infancy, and each of them regards it as a second motherland, next after his own country.

The *proxenos*, therefore, could not be made responsible by the state he represented; although he may have been of great help in promoting interstate contacts, he did not have any official diplomatic status.

ENVOYS

Both the Greeks and the Romans appointed envoys to conduct negotiations with foreign states. These envoys were not permanent representatives but were chosen ad hoc as necessity arose, usually in collegia of between three to ten in the same way as regular magistrates. In Greece envoys were chosen by the council and assembly from among the active politicians; in Rome they were chosen by the senate from among men of senatorial rank. A special commission of ten envoys was usually sent out by the Roman Senate to help the commander in the field with the settlement of the affairs of a defeated or conquered country.

Envoys were usually expected to secure treaties, friendships, and alliances, but they were rarely—in Rome practically never—given plenipotentiary powers, which, in any case, were only extended powers to conduct negotiations. The results of negotiations always had to be ratified by the sovereign body, whether the council and assembly or the senate. Usually instructions were given to the envoys. In the Greek polis instructions were sometimes very vague, in contrast to Rome, where they were sometimes even given in writing. On return from a mission envoys often put their political weight and influence into efforts to persuade the sovereign bodies to ratify the results of their negotiations. The envoys were responsible for their mission and although this responsibility was not always well defined, envoys were sometimes tried and punished both in the Greek polis and in Rome when they failed in their mission or agreed to conditions unacceptable to the ratifying body.

Envoys from foreign states were received by the sovereign bodies of the state according to an accustomed procedure. In times of war enemy envoys were not admitted in the polis, but negotiations could then be started by a herald (*keryx*) or by special arrangement; in Rome a special procedure was devised for such cases. In every case envoys were protected and given safe exit even in times of war; however, inviolability of envoys was less observed in Greece (although heralds were sacrosanct) than in the Hellenistic world and in Rome, where failure to observe it was regarded to be transgression of the law of nations. Refusal to receive Roman envoys was regarded by the senate as casus belli and a similar refusal by the Roman Senate was an indication of hostile intentions.

Although there was no permanent diplomatic service in Greece or in Rome, there was almost constant movement of envoys, which made interstate contacts almost uninterrupted; and although they were not very successful in preventing wars, these missions helped in lessening interstate friction and discord. Roman embassies sometimes helped in promoting agreement by diplomatic interference in internal quarrels of the other state. With the expansion of the Roman Empire, there was less need for envoys and negotiations until a strong Persia and the German states on the borders caused the revival of old Roman methods and procedures. The first instance was the surrender of the Roman standards captured by the Parthians from Crassus in 54 B.C., achieved by diplomatic means in the time of Augustus. In the fourth and fifth centuries A.D. the Romans tried unsuccessfully to stave off by diplomacy the invasion of German tribes.

GREEK TREATIES AND AGREEMENTS

Greek particularism on the one hand, and the attempts at predominance and the organization of larger units including a number of states on the other, influenced the character and the contents of the treaties entered into by the Greek city-states. Truce agreements (*spondai*) or treaties of peace (*synthekai*) that put an end to war and included provisions on territorial matters, regulated the status of former or present allies, and included clauses providing for arbitration, and—albeit rarely—for economic matters, were not uncommon in Greece. Not less important were the treaties setting up a defensive alliance (*epimachia*) or an offensive-defensive alliance (*symmachia*).

Interstate arbitration did not develop in Greece into an organized or widely accepted procedure. The notable instances are those of the second half of the fifth century B.C., beginning with the inclusion of a clause about arbitration in the peace between Athens and Sparta in 446/445 (Thucydides, 1.140.2). But it seems that in connection with the outbreak of the Peloponnesian War the proposal of arbitration was rather an exercise in propaganda than an attempt to solve the conflict. This can be seen from the accusation by the Corinthians against Corcyra (Corfu) of the misuse of the proposal for arbitration (Thucydides, 1.28.2; 39.1–2). Similar propaganda can be seen in the complaints by Philip II against the Athenians that they refused proposals for arbitration (pseudo-Demosthenes, 7.7; 12.11; 14–15; 17).

During the Peloponnesian War a clause for arbitration was included in the one-year truce in 423 B.C., in the Peace of Nicias, and in the treaty between Argos and Sparta in 418. These treaties did not last long and the arbitration clause was never implemented. Still, there were at least two conflicts in which arbitration was tried several times: the quarrel in 418 between Argos and Sparta concerning the Cynurian territory and a conflict in A.D. 25 between Sparta and Messenia concerning the *ager Dentheliates* (Tacitus, *Annals* 4.43.5).

It is not surprising that a strong state would reject proposals that it submit to arbitration; on the other hand, such a state would try to impose its arbitration on others when it was in its interests. This was the policy pursued by the Hellenistic kings and later by Rome.

There cannot be any doubt that economic matters played an important part in interstate relations in antiquity. Economic matters were often regulated and decreed by the hegemonial polis, or the imperial city, but clauses on economic matters were sometimes included in interstate agreements. The Thirty Years Peace concluded in 446/445 B.C. between Athens and Sparta may have included a provision for the freedom of trade (thus justifying the Megarians' complaint, which became one of the causes of the Peloponnesian War). Three agreements between Sparta and Persia in 412/411 included the terms for Persia's financial support for the maintenance of Sparta's fleet. Athens was interested in two regions outside her league: Macedon, from which she imported timber and where she wanted to protect the economic interests of her allies, and the Hellespont (Dardanelles), from which Athens and her allies imported grain.

Economic and other conflicts in civil matters between citizens of different states were regulated by *symbola*—agreements between two city-states that defined the legal procedure to be followed and the place in which a trial should take place.

The defensive alliance (*epimachia*) put on the contracting parties the obligation to furnish military aid in the case of an attack by a third party. It was a nonaggression treaty, and the difference between *epimachia* and *symmachia* is well defined by the Corinthians after the treaty between Athens, Argos, Mantinea, and Elis in 420 B.C. was concluded:

> The Corinthians, however, although allies [*symmachoi*] of the Argives, did not accede to the new treaty—even before this when an alliance [*symmachia*], offensive and defensive, had been made between the Eleans, Argives, and Mantineans, they had not joined it—but said they were content with the first defensive alliance [*epimachia*] that had been made, namely to aid one another, but not to join in attacking any other party. (Thucydides, 5.48.2)

Symmachia is defined as "comradeship in arms" and the first mention comes from the sixth century B.C. Although it was a bilateral treaty on the basis of equality, it soon developed into a hegemonial alliance in which one polis became the leader (*hegemon*) in war. Thus, in the fifth century B.C., the two great hegemonial leagues were the Lacedaemonians and their allies and the Athenians and their allies. Although they differed in their origins and in their organization, the two leagues were attempts at creating larger political, military, and even economic units under the leadership of one polis. The final decision (even if it was not the sole decision) on the league's policy was in the hands of the hegemonial, or imperial, city (for in both cases the league developed into an *arche* [empire]), which entailed interference in the internal affairs of the allies, prevention of secession, and subjection of the rebels as well as economic and military exploitation. In the long run this undermined the stability of interstate relations, and the rivalry between the hegemonial leagues in the fifth and fourth centuries added to the spread of warfare in Greece. A good example of instability arising from relations and rivalry among hegemonies is the account of the peace between Athens and Sparta in 375/374 given by Diodorus Siculus (15.38.4): "For the Lacedaemonians and Athenians, who had constantly been rivals for hegemony, now yielded one to the other, the one being judged worthy to rule on land, the other on the sea. They were consequently annoyed by the claims to hegemony advanced by a third contender and sought to sever the Boeotian cities from the Theban confederation."

An attempt to lessen the risks of outbreak of war because of hegemonial predominance can be seen in what becomes in the fourth century B.C. an almost regular form, the Common Peace (*koine eirene*). Although it was first imposed by the Persian king with the help of Sparta in 386 B.C., it soon became a form used by the Greeks themselves, even as part of new hegemonial alliances.

The Common Peace treaties established the principle of equality in autonomy and freedom of all the city-states, great and small alike; various terms prohibited interference in the internal affairs of another polis, and forbade subversion of existing constitutions from without. During the fourth century, treaties outside the Common Peace also included provisions that safeguarded existing constitutions against subversion and overthrow by outside interference. Examples are the treaty between Athens and Iulis in 362; the *symmachia* between Athens, Arcadia, Achaea, Elis, and Phlius in 362/361; and the *symmachia* between Athens and Thessaly in 361. The Common Peace was a general peace treaty, because it aimed at the inclusion of all the Greeks (although at first not those cities of Asia Minor that belonged to the Persian king nor the three islands that remained in Athenian hands), whether they legally became a party to it or not.

Although clauses providing for punishment of those who transgressed the Common Peace were included, the implementation of the treaty was in the hands of one of the great states (Sparta or Athens), who made use of it in order to promote their own interests. Sparta tried to build up her hegemony while implementing the King's Peace, and Athens, although Common Peace principles were incorporated in the Second Athenian Alliance of 377 B.C., soon returned to the policy of political, military, and economic interference in the affairs of the member states. Philip II in his policy of expansion into Greece also made excellent use of Greek interstate diplomacy to secure his and his descendants' hegemony.

Another development in interstate relations in the fourth century B.C. was the *isopoliteia* treaty establishing equality of citizen rights between the contracting states. The first such treaty was that between Keos and Eretria in the first quarter of the fourth century. Previous grants of citizenship were unilateral, either as privilege to single citizens or conferred by one city on another. But in all these cases, including the *isopoliteia* treaty, the rights of citizenship could only be exercised by taking up residence in the other city. And although *isopoliteia* agreements became more frequent in the Hellenistic period, they facilitated intermarriage and trade at a time when, with the decline of the city-state, citizenship rights were no longer of great political significance.

The decline of the influence of the great hegemonial cities facilitated the development of *sympoliteia* (confederacy of states). Confederacies were already established in the fifth century B.C., but the most active period of the Arcadian, Achaean, Aetolian, and Thessalian confederacies was in the third and second centuries. The basis of the *sympoliteia* was a tribal unit (*ethnos*) in which there was a small number of city-states unable to gain predominance by themselves. The local government was not annulled in the *sympoliteia*. There was a joint central government, but citizens also preserved citizenship in their polis; the federal citizenship conferred on all civil rights, such as rights of trade, acquisition of property, and intermarriage. The member city-states and *ethnoi* were generally represented on the central council and in the central collegium of magistrates. Expansion outside ethnic boundaries involved the confederacies in international power politics until their absorption by Rome.

ROMAN TREATIES AND AGREEMENTS

Like the Greeks, the Romans distinguished between temporary interstate agreements such as armistice (*indutiae*) or preparatory truce (*sponsio;* in Greek *spondai*), which were usually entered into by commanders in the field to provide for the burial of the dead and the first diplomatic exchanges (contacts) before negotiations were started.

Foedus was the permanent treaty of alliance and amity. The Romans distinguished between two kinds: *foedus aequum* and *foedus iniquum*. The first was based on equality in terms of obligations, providing for mutual military assistance; it guaranteed territory, full autonomy, and independent coinage; no Roman garrison was to be installed, but the contracting state undertook to furnish military help to Rome. The second, *foedus iniquum*, usually included cession of territory to Rome and, above all, restrictions on the conduct of foreign policy. Although *foedus* was usually entered into after a war, Rome later dictated terms of *foedus iniquum* when it served foreign policy, as in her demands on Antiochus III in 193 B.C. The king's envoys complained in Rome:

> The king wondered what possible reason the Romans had for ordering him not to meddle in certain European affairs, to renounce his claims to certain cities, and not to exact from some the tribute owing to him: such demands were unprecedented when a pact of friendship between equals was being negotiated; they were the demands of conquerors settling a war, yet the envoys sent to the king at Lysimacheia had presumed to dictate to him precise instructions on these matters. (Diodorus Siculus, 28.15.2)

Foedus iniquum was the main tool for establishing Roman predominance in Italy and the method, at least, was applied outside as well. It and all other treaties had to be ratified by the Roman Senate and, when necessary, changes were introduced in the terms negotiated by the envoys. As in Greece, the treaties entered into by Rome contained clauses of enforcement based on religious sanction expressed in the oath or by the imprecation of the *fetiales*.

CONCLUSION

In spite of the lack of a professional diplomatic service, both the Greeks and the Romans created a great number of varied methods for making interstate contacts and starting interstate negotiations. Envoys and heralds moved quite freely, procedures for their dispatch and reception were developed, and on the whole their immunity was observed. Interstate agreements and treaties were developed, both bilateral and multilateral, not only in order to make peace after a war, but also in order to prevent conflicts and provide the machinery for keeping a general peace. Moreover, rules that would guarantee the maintenance of good faith between states, based on the concept of justice, were made the basis of interstate relations. Together with attempts at arbitration and confederacy, this was no mean achievement.

BIBLIOGRAPHY

SOURCES

Aeschines, *The Speeches of Aeschines*, Charles D. Adams, trans. (1919); Andocides, in *Minor Attic Orators*, K. J. Maidment and J. O. Burtt, trans., vol. 1 (1941); Aristophanes, *The Birds*, Benjamin B. Rogers, trans. (1924); Aristotle, *Politics*, H. Rackham, trans. (1932; rev. 1944), and *The Athenian Constitution (Athenaion Politeia)*, H. Rackham, trans. (1935); M. M. Austin, *The Hellenistic World from Alexander to the Roman Conquest* (1981); Vittorio Bastoletti, ed., *Hellenica Oxyrhynchia* (1959); Hermann Bengtson, ed., *Staatsverträge des Altertums*: vol. 2, *Die Verträge der griechisch-römischen Welt von 700 bis 338 v. Chr.* (1962); Hatto H. Schmitt, *Die Verträge der griechisch-römischen Welt von 338 bis 200 v. Chr.* (1969); Cicero, *De Republica, De Legibus (On the Republic, On Laws)*, Clinton W. Keyes, trans. (1928; 1977), *De Officiis (On Duty)*, Walter Miller, trans. (1913); and *De Finibus Bonorum et Malorum (On the Chief Good and Evil)*, H. Rackham, trans. (1914; 1921); Demosthenes, *Olynthiacs, Philippics* (and other works), James H. Vince, trans., 2 vols. (1926; 1930; 1932; 1962).

Diodorus Siculus, *The Library of History*, C. L. Sherman, trans. vol. 7 (1952); Charles W. Fornara, *Archaic Times to the End of the Peloponnesian War* (1977; 1983); Gaius, *Institutes of Roman Law*, Edward Poste, trans., E. A. Whittock, ed., 4th ed. (1925), and *The Institutes*, Francis de Zulueta, trans., 2 vols. (1946–1953; repr. 1958–1963); Herodotus, A. D. Godley, trans., 4 vols. (1920–1928); Hyperides, in *Minor Attic Orators*, K. J. Maidment and J. O. Burtt, trans., vol. 2 (1954); Isocrates, George Norlin, trans., vols. 1–2 (1928–1929), and La Rue van Hook, trans., vol. 3 (1945); Arlette Lambrechts, *Tekst en uitzicht van de Atheense proxeniedecreten, tot 323 v.C.* (1958); Naphtali Lewis, ed., *Greek Historical Documents: The Fifth Century B.C.* (1971); Livy, *From the Founding of the City*, various trans. and eds., 14 vols. (Loeb Classical Library, 1919–1967); Russell Meiggs and D. Lewis, *A Selection of Greek Historical Inscriptions to the End of the Fifth Century B.C.* (1969); Pausanias, *Description of Greece*, W. H. S. Jones, trans., vol. 1 (1918); Luigi Piccirilli, *Gli arbitrati interstatali greci, I: Dalle origini a 338 a.C.* (1973); Plato, *Laws*, R. G. Bury, trans. (1926); pseudo-Plato, *Definitions*, John Burnet, ed. (1906).

Plutarch, *Moralia*, F. C. Babbitt, trans., vol. 3 (1931), and *Parallel Lives*, Bernadotte Perrin, trans., "The Life of Solon," vol. 1 (1914); "The Life of Pericles," vol. 3 (1916); "The Life of Artaxerxes," vol. 11 (1926); Polybius, *The Histories*, W. R. Paton, trans., 6 vols. (1922–1927); G. Rotondi, *Leges publicae populi Romani* (1912); Servius, *Qui feruntur in Vergilii carmina commentarii*, 3 vols. (1881–1887; repr. 1960, 1961); Robert K. Sherk, *Roman Documents from the Greek East* (1969); Cornelius Tacitus, *The Annals*, John Jackson, trans. (1931; 1951–1956); Thucydides, *History of the Peloponnesian War*, Charles F. Smith, trans., 4 vols. (1919–1923); Marcus N. Tod, *A Selection of Greek Historical Inscriptions*, 2 vols. (1933–1948); Michael B. Walbank, *Athenian Proxenies of the Fifth Century B.C.* (1978); J. Wickersham and G. Verbrugghe, *Greek Historical Documents: The Fourth Century B.C.* (1973); Xenophon, *Hellenica (History of Greece)*, C. L. Brownson, trans., 2 vols. (1918–1921; 1947–1950).

STUDIES

Sir Frank Adcock and Derek J. Mosley, *Diplomacy in Ancient Greece* (1975); E. Badian, *Foreign*

Clientelae, 264–70 B.C. (1958); Elias J. Bickerman, "Remarques sur le droit de gens dans la Grèce classique," in *Mélanges Ferdinand de Visscher*, III (1950); P. Bonk, *Defensiv- und Offensivklauseln in griechischen Symmachia-Verträgen* Ph.D. diss. Bonn (1971); J. Calabi, *Richerche sui rapporti fra le poleis* (1953); Werner Dahlheim, *Struktur und Entwicklung des römischen Volkerrechts im dritten und zweiten Jahrhundert v. Chr.* (1968); P. Gauthier, Symbola, "Les étrangers et la justice dans les cités grecques," in *Annales de l'Est*, Memoire, **42** (1972); W. Gawanthka, "Isopolitie, ein Beitrag zur Geschichte der zwischenstaatlichen Beziehungen in der griechischen Antike," in *Vestigia*, **22** (1975).

A. Giovannini, "Untersuchungen über die Natur und die Anfänge der bundesstaatlichen Sympolitie in Griechenland," in *Hypomnemata*, **33** (1971); F. Gschnitzer, "Proxenos," *R. E.*, suppl. **13** (1974); F. Hampl, *Die griechischen Staatsverträge des 4. Jahrhunderts v. Christi Geb.* (1938); A. Henry, "The Prescripts of Athenian Decrees," in *Mnemosyne*, suppl. **49** (1977); Alfred Heuss, "Die Völkerrechtlichen Grundlagen der römischen Aussenpolitik in republikanischer Zeit," in *Klio*, **31** (1933), and *Abschluss und Beurkundung des griechischen und römischen Staatsverträges* (1967); Sir David Hunt, "Lessons in Diplomacy from Classical Antiquity," in *Proceedings of the Classical Association*, **79** (1982); P. Karavites, "Capitulations in Greek Interstate Relations," in *Hypomnemata*, **71** (1982); Bruno Keil, *EIPHNH* [*Eirene*], *eine philologisch-antiquarische Untersuchung* (1916).

D. Kienast, "Presbeia," in *R.E.*, suppl. **13** (1974); G. V. Lalonde, *The Publication and Transmission of Greek Diplomatic Documents* (diss., University of Washington, 1971); Jakob A. O. Larsen, *Representative Government in Greek and Roman History* (1955), and *Greek Federal States: Their Institutions and History* (1968); Victor Martin, *La vie internationale dans la Grèce des Cités (VIe-IVe s. av. J.-C.)* (1940); Derek J. Mosley, "Envoys and Diplomacy in Ancient Greece," in *Historia Einzelschriften*, **22** (1973); E. Olshamer, ed., *Antike Diplomatie* (1979); Coleman Phillipson, *International Law and Custom of Ancient Greece and Rome*, 2 vols. (1911).

A. von Premerstein, "Legatus," in *R.E.*, **12** (1924); Anton H. Raeder, *L'Arbitrage international chez les Hellènes* (1912); J. W. Rich, "Declaring War in the Roman Republic in the Period of Transmarine Expansion," in *Collection Latomus*, **149** (1976); Timothy T. B. Ryder, *Koine Eirene, General Peace and Local Independence in Ancient Greece* (1965); B. Schleussner, *Die Legaten der römischen Republik* (1978); Eugen Taubler, *Imperium Romanus: Studien zur Entwicklungsgeschichte des römischen Reichs* (1913); Marcus N. Tod, *International Arbitration Amongst the Greeks* (1913); K. H. Ziegler, "Das Volkerrecht der römischen Republik," in *Aufstieg und Niedergang der römischen Welt*, **1.2**, H. Temporini, ed. (1972).

Wars and Military Science: Greece

J. K. ANDERSON

HOMERIC WARFARE

The ancient Greeks looked upon Homer as the first authority on the art of war, and the modern historian can do no better than to follow their example. In Homeric warfare, kings, motivated by love of glory and love of plunder, lead their armies to the sack of cities—Troy itself, before which the Achaeans battle for ten years against Priam's people and their allies, or smaller towns, which fall to raiding parties. In the *Iliad* (6.414–427), Andromache reminds her husband, Hector, that

> Noble Achilles slew my father and sacked the well-peopled city of the Cilicians, Thebe of the lofty gates. He slew Eetion, but reverenced him and did not spoil his body, and burned him together with his finely wrought armor. . . . Seven brothers I had in the palace, who all in one day entered the house of Hades. For swift-footed noble Achilles slew them over the shambling oxen and bright-fleeced sheep. My mother, who once was queen below woody Plakos, he brought hither with other spoils, and straightway freed, taking ransom uncountable.

To his wife's entreaties that he should withdraw from the battle, Hector replies that this would shame him before the "Trojans and Trojan women with trailing robes," and foresees the day when "holy Ilium shall perish, and Priam, and the folk of Priam of the good ashen spear," and Andromache will be carried into slavery in Greece, in Argos to weave at another woman's loom, and "carry the water of Messeis or Hypereia," and men will say, as they watch her weeping, "This is the wife of Hector, who was the best fighter of the horse-taming Trojans, when they fought around Ilium" (*Iliad* 6.440–465).

Tradition told how the cities of the Greek princes were destroyed in their turn, in the third generation after the Trojan War. The archaeological record shows that the wealthy civilization of the Bronze Age ended, not only in Greece but elsewhere in the eastern Mediterranean, in a time of violence and destruction extending from the thirteenth into the early twelfth century B.C. In this period many royal fortresses were burned and their wealth dispersed. Many cities named in the epic tradition, including

Troy itself and Mycenae, the home of Agamemnon, the leader of the Greeks, may be identified with known sites whose destruction is proved archaeologically.

The cities of the Bronze Age and their wealth perished apparently at the hands of invaders. For several centuries during the Early Iron Age Greece was thinly populated and impoverished. During this time traditions of the more glorious past must have been passed on from generation to generation, especially among the descendants of the old possessors of the Greek mainland, who had migrated to the west coast of Asia Minor and the adjacent islands. In the second half of the eighth century B.C., commerce, wealth, and civilization revived, and at this time or soon after poets of genius (probably not the single "Homer" to whom the later Greeks gave the credit) created the *Iliad* and the *Odyssey* in something like the form in which we have them. Other stories of the Trojan War and of the returns of the heroes were told by lesser men in other epics that are now lost.

The epic poets do not describe a regular siege of Troy. The Greek expedition landed and beached its ships some miles from their objective, a walled city on a low hill. The invaders encamped near their ships, and for ten years both sides repeatedly sallied out to do battle in the floodplain of the Scamander River, lying between the city and the camp. Battles in epics are decided by the prowess of individual heroes, often directly inspired by the gods, whose intervention reminds the modern reader that poets do not confine themselves to strict realism in their narratives. Both armies include large, anonymous masses of infantry, but we generally only glimpse them when the poet spares half a line to say that they skirmished, or fought each other, or were slaughtered by some great hero as he drove them in rout, "slaying ever the hindmost."

Men of rank and name, who are generally of princely descent, and often kings, are "horsemen" or "knights." "Squires," usually of inferior birth, drive the chariots in which the warriors ride to battle. In the *Iliad* only Diomedes and Odysseus are described as riding on horseback, when they make a night raid on the Trojan camp, slay the Thracian king Rhesus, and lead away his team of chariot horses, leaving the chariot behind because of the impossibility of removing it without raising an alarm (*Iliad* 10.465–565). Both heroes, like all the other leaders on both sides, are elsewhere represented as riding in chariots.

Typical is the passage that describes the preparation for battle on the day following the killing of Rhesus. Agamemnon, the leader of the Greeks, arms himself and commands his men to prepare for battle; the knights order their charioteers to bring their horses to the ditch that guards the camp, and themselves follow soon after. Meanwhile, Zeus from the heavens rains down blood in sign of the slaughter that is to follow (*Iliad* 11.47–55).

The first weapon of the hero is the spear. Often he carries two, intending to throw one or both, but spears are also used at close quarters. Spears may be flung from chariots with deadly effect, as when Diomedes, driven into battle by Nestor, kills Hector's charioteer by a spear-cast (*Iliad* 8.118–121). But more often the warrior leaps down from his chariot before hurling his missile, and he never fights hand to hand from his chariot, either with spear or with sword.

The sword, which can cut as well as thrust, may be used to follow up a successful spear-cast. Or, the man who has thrown his spear in vain may draw his sword in a last desperate attempt, as does Hector, whose own spear has rebounded from the shield of Achilles, when he resolves to die not ingloriously. Achilles meets him with a superior weapon as he comes on, and thrusts his spear through the vital spot that is uncovered by his armor, "at the throat, where the life is most swiftly destroyed" (*Iliad* 22.289–327).

Although the sword is second to the spear, it can still rip up a man's belly, or send a head spinning from the shoulders to roll in the dust, helmet and all. Among offensive weapons the bow is held in little esteem; it is the weapon of treacherous Pandarus, or cowardly Paris who shoots from ambush and wounds more often than he slays (*Iliad* 4.85–140; 11.368–383).

Defensive armor includes the helmet, shield, and bronze cuirass; also the leg armor that gives the "well-greaved Achaeans" their special epithet. Scholars have attempted for a century to fix the date of the composition of particular epic passages by identifying armor and weapons described in them with pieces from dated archaeological contexts. But the results are disappointingly inconclusive. The well-built fortress of Troy itself, sandy Pylos, and Mycenae rich in gold belong to the Late Bronze Age, and the epics consistently tell of bronze weapons and armor, mentioning iron only rarely and incidentally. But these things by themselves prove no more than a vague generalized tradition passed down over the centuries. Proof that the poets of the eighth century had exact detailed knowledge of Bronze Age warfare eludes us, and when it comes to demonstrating that this or that detail belongs to the poet's own world rather than that of the heroes, we are not much better off than the ancient commentators on Homer. "Like the clear note when the trumpet rings out blown by savage foes who beleaguer a city, even so was the clear voice of Achilles," says the poet (*Iliad* 18.219–221), and an ancient scholar comments that "the poet knows the trumpet, though the heroes do not." The modern archaeologist will agree; but he can also show that both the poet and the heroes knew bronze cuirasses, shields "equal in every direction" (that is, round), and silver-studded swords. It is true that the swords, cuirasses, and shields of 700 B.C. are not identical with those of 1200 B.C., but when words might fit either who can be so bold as to say definitely whether the epic is preserving a fragment of the past or presenting that past in terms familiar to the poet and his hearers? The helmet of Damasos, "with bronze cheekpieces," that failed to save its wearer from the spear of Polypoites (*Iliad* 12.182–186) might be matched from a fourteenth-century tomb near Knossos or by a quite different helmet found in an eighth-century warrior's grave near Argos.

The boar's-tusk helmet that Meriones lends to Odysseus for his midnight foray (*Iliad* 10.261–265) could until recently be confidently claimed as one object that appeared in the archaeological record of the Bronze Age, and no later. But the recent discovery of fragments of worked boar's tusk, presumably from such a helmet, in the cremation burial of a warrior of the Early Iron Age, has raised the possibility that even as late as the eighth century such an object might have been preserved as an heirloom in some family of aristocratic warriors. It is significant that the poet gives the helmet of Meriones a provenance going back several generations.

Much more than types of armament is doubtful. The catalog of ships (*Iliad* 2.484–762) that lists, in a form inconsistent with the details of the narrative, the contingents making up the Greek host before Troy, has been claimed to be an actual list drawn up first by Bronze Age bureaucrats and subsequently versified and handed on by oral tradition. It has also been regarded as more probably an attempt by some poet to collect and set in order local traditions that ascribed to this or that hero of the Trojan War a dwelling in one or other of the ruined townships whose true history had been forgotten by the time that reviving civilization reawakened in the Greeks an interest in their past.

There has been much argument as to whether Homeric warfare represents the actual tactics of the Bronze Age, or of the time when the epics were composed, or of no time at all, being a creation of poetic fantasy intermingled with traditions of different periods. The last answer is probably the best; yet we should not suppose that the poets invented a type of warfare altogether so remote from reality that the fighting men to whom they sung would have found it absurd.

As has been said, Homeric battles are decided by the knights, and the knights ride in chariots to, from, and about the battlefield. Thus, when Hector hurried to encounter Ajax (*Iliad* 11.531–538), his charioteer

> lashed the fair-maned horses with the whistling whip. And they, starting from the blow, quickly bore the swift chariot into the midst of the Trojans and Achaeans, trampling upon corpses and shields. With blood was bespattered the whole axle underneath, and the rails round the chariot, sprinkled with gouts from the horses' hooves and from the tyres. Their master was eager to enter the throng of warriors and to break it.

But chariots do not enter the throng and shatter the enemy ranks by their impetus. The warrior leaps down, and with his feet firmly planted on earth generally uses his weapons to much more advantage than men who are still riding in their chariots. Thus Agamemnon "leaped from his chariot and stood in the way" of Bienor and his charioteer Oileus, slew them both and left them with their breasts shining white, since he had stripped them of their armor, and went on to meet two sons of Priam, "one well-begotten, one a bastard, riding in one chariot; and the bastard was charioteer.... Him Agamemnon hit above the nipple through the chest with his spear, but Antiphos [the wellborn] he struck beside the ear with his sword and hurled from the chariot" (*Iliad* 11.90–110).

While the hero fights, his charioteer should keep his chariot close behind him, to provide a speedy means of retreat if he is wounded or faced by overwhelming odds, or summoned to another part of the field. The Homeric chariot is thus used very differently from the historical scythed chariots of the Persians, designed to gallop into opposing masses of men and cut their way through; or the chariots of the Old Testament (1 Kings 22:31–35; 2 Kings 9:16–26), mobile platforms for archers. Scholars have therefore claimed that the poets of the Greek epics did not understand anything about the real use of chariots in warfare because they lived in an age when battles in Greece were fought on foot. The supporters of this argument hold that war chariots were used in Greece during the Bronze Age, but then disappeared for several centuries. They were then supposedly reintroduced into Greece from elsewhere and used for racing. The poets knew of the Bronze Age war chariots through tradition and therefore brought chariots into their battles, but in a manner, it is argued, wholly unrelated to reality.

Chariots had certainly existed in Bronze Age Greece as early as the late sixteenth century B.C., when the earliest known Greek representations of them appear on tombstones set up over the royal graves of Mycenae, and on a gold ring from the treasures in those graves. A century or so later chariots formed a major part of the armed forces of the Greek-speaking kings who then ruled the palace of Knossos in Crete. The palace archives list several hundred chariots, not all fully assembled, and by associating them with armor indicate that they were military vehicles, but do not tell us how they were used.

Pictures on the walls of the palaces of mainland Greece, and painted vases, show that chariots were familiar in the fourteenth and thirteenth century B.C. Usually their occupants are represented as unarmed, and a painting from the palace of Tiryns shows an unmilitary use of the chariot that seems surprising—to carry young women to watch a hunt. But sometimes spearmen, with helmets and round shields, are shown riding in chariots or standing in front of them. The spears are not nearly long enough to reach an enemy beyond the front of the chariot team, and the chariots themselves (like those of the *Iliad*) are lightly constructed and would not provide a stable platform from which to fight hand to hand. Spears could of course be thrown from the chariot, but two spears would soon be used and there is never any indication in the pictures of a reserve supply of weapons. So, although we have no clear picture of chariots in battle, it makes sense to suppose that the spearmen would have leaped down to fight on foot, like Homeric heroes. When one reflects on the weight of armor, the heat of the Greek sun, and the value of tactical as well as long-range mobility, the use of chariots in this way does not seem to be a foolish waste of a pair of horses, an elaborate vehicle, and a skilled driver.

Only the gold ring from Mycenae, already mentioned, shows a bow being used from a chariot, and that in a stag hunt, not a battle. By contrast, in contemporary Egypt the bow is the weapon of the chariotry. The monuments of the pharaohs of the nineteenth and twentieth dynasties show long lines of Egyptian chariots galloping into action, each with a driver, and an archer beside him. At the battle of Kadesh, fought by Ramses II against the Hittites in about 1288 B.C., such a line of chariot-borne archers is represented facing a line of Hittite chariots, each of which carries three men: a driver, a spearman, and a shield bearer who has probably been added to the crew for the express purpose of protecting the other members from the Egyptian arrows. But this measure proves ineffective: the Hittites and their teams are being shot down at a range at which spears are useless. Presumably, in the circumstances of this particular action the spears would have been thrown if the Hittites had come close enough; but there is no indication of a reserve supply. Elsewhere Hittites are shown who have dismounted from their chariots to attack an Egyptian camp on foot; perhaps here we have the clearest indication of Hittite tactics.

After the end of the Bronze Age there are no more Greek pictures of chariots for several centuries. But that is probably not significant, for there are few pictures of anything. So the argument that chariots themselves did not exist because artists did not represent them is unsafe. When pictures of chariots again appear on Greek vases, in the second half of the eighth century B.C., they show peculiarities of construction and harness that distinguish them from contemporary Near Eastern chariots, and better suit the supposition that they are the descendants of those of the Bronze Age than the theory that they have been introduced from outside. On large vases made to stand as monuments above men's graves there appear lines of chariots carrying armed men. Perhaps these represent funeral processions; funeral games, including chariot races, may have followed. For the funeral of Patroclus before Troy, the *Iliad* describes both a procession (23.127–137) and a chariot race (23.262–650). Vase paintings also show warriors standing between pairs of horses, probably chariot teams, and much more rarely on horseback. Battle scenes including chariots and horses are also rare, but at least one shows chariots used in the Homeric manner. It is possible that the artists are illustrating ancient stories, as later Greek vase painters did, but it is at least equally possible that they are depicting a contemporary world in which aristocratic rulers modeled their lives to some extent on the heroic ideal.

That ideal's chivalry did not extend to

mercy to all prisoners and captives, or respect for women as such. When Helen comes toward Priam and his counsellors on the walls of Troy, the old man's courtesy is beyond reproach (*Iliad* 3.146–170). But Andromache can expect no such courtesy on the day when she falls into Greek hands, and other captive women are treated as chattels, given away as prizes at the funeral games, or distributed like other loot in the division of spoil. When fair-cheeked Briseis is taken from Achilles, the hero's wrath is roused by the injury to his pride, rather than by his feelings for the girl herself: women, gold, and fine armor build up the esteem of a mighty warrior and the respect with which the world regards him.

Armor is stripped from the slain bodies of enemies. A dead man's friends and retainers must venture their own lives to recover his corpse so that it may receive its due, the funeral fire, but there is no religious obligation to pay the last rites to slain enemies. When Odysseus boasts over the body of Socus that the dead man's parents will not close his eyes, but the carrion birds will pluck them out, flapping their wings in flocks about him, the poet is evidently not outraged (*Iliad* 11.452–454). Andromache remembers the generosity of Achilles to the body of Eetion, but when the same Achilles has the corpse of Hector in his power and outrages it and drags it behind his chariot, it is the sympathy of the gods for the dead man that is aroused, rather than their anger against the violator.

Hector's body is eventually ransomed, and enemies who beg for mercy on the battlefield may also be spared death for ransoming. But there is no obligation to accept a proffered surrender. Achilles, when he reenters the war after the death of his friend Patroclus, says that he will no longer show mercy as once he did, and bids a Trojan suppliant die without complaining, "for Patroclus also is dead, who was a far better man than you are" (*Iliad* 21.97–113). Even after a man's surrender has been accepted his life is not safe; twelve Trojan captives are sacrificed to appease the shade of Patroclus (*Iliad* 23.175–176). Admittedly the poet does speak of these sacrifices as "evil deeds."

The Homeric warrior is truly chivalrous in his desire to excel in valor and seek fame by gallantry in the battlefield. Achilles, knowing himself doomed to an early death, demands his recompense of glory. Hector goes out to battle in order to avoid disgracing himself before the Trojans and their long-robed women. The warrior's code is most nobly expressed by Sarpedon, king of the Lycians, when he reminds his companion Glaucus that their people honor them with "the chief seat and portions of meat and brimming cups" and rich estates, and that in return they should fight in the forefront of the battle (*Iliad* 12.317–321):

> So may some one of the closely armored Lycians say: "Not ingloriously do our kings reign over Lycia, and eat the fat flocks and drain the honey-sweet wine. But their strength too is noble, since they fight among the noblest of the Lycians."

He concludes by reminding his friend that death awaits the coward no less than the brave man, and urges him to battle, where "we shall give to some man cause for boasting, or he to us."

THE HISTORIC PERIOD

A few passages in the *Iliad* seem to give glimpses of a different style of warfare, conducted by disciplined bodies of infantry. Thus the poet compares the advance of the Greek army to a wave that gathers itself far out at sea and comes on in silence until it breaks, foaming on the rocks. The officers lead, and the common soldiers follow as though voiceless (*Iliad* 4.422–432). Once again, the passage cannot be fixed in historic time, because files of disciplined infantry are sometimes shown in the art of the Late Bronze Age. But these words were certainly heard with approval from the seventh century B.C. onward by Greeks who had been trained in the discipline of the hoplite phalanx—a battle line of armored spearmen, drawn up in close order usually eight ranks deep, and moving forward in step. Those Greeks who had seen something of the Near Eastern "barbarians" will also have relished the following verses in the passage, in which the Asiatic host of the Trojans and their allies is compared to flocks of bleating ewes waiting to be milked.

For their part, the Asiatics, in whose armies archers and spearmen, horsemen and foot soldiers were scientifically combined, found the Greek system of making war absurd. Herodotus (7.9.2) relates their attitude:

> They find out the fairest and most level piece of ground, come down on to it, and fight. In consequence, even the victors come off with great loss. About the vanquished I do not even comment. They are actually annihilated. Since they all speak the same language, they ought to employ heralds and ambassadors to make up their differences, and resort to anything rather than to battle. However, if it were absolutely necessary for them to make war upon each other, they ought to find out the ground upon which each side is most inaccessible, and make trial of that.

Herodotus puts this speech into the mouth of a Persian prince who is urging King Xerxes to invade Greece. While there is no reason to suppose that this particular Persian ever used this particular argument, the historian had himself been born in a Greek city on the edge of the Persian Empire, and had traveled extensively in Asia in the middle of the fifth century B.C., about a generation after the great war with Xerxes. He may well have heard such criticisms directed against his countrymen.

But in fact this style of fighting, which had been generally prevalent in Greece for two centuries by the time of Herodotus, was not so unreasonable. Greece is a land of mountains that run out into the sea in bold headlands and continue across it in chains of islands. The mountainsides are covered with forest, or with dense scrub clinging to the limestone rock. Among these mountains are pockets of farmland, some of them upland valleys of a few acres, others plains of many square miles. In the middle of the eighth century B.C. this countryside was peopled by villagers who scratched a living from one harvest to the next and were ruled by an illiterate hereditary aristocracy. By the middle of the seventh century groups of villages had coalesced into towns to which commerce and small-scale industry were bringing the wealth that was necessary for civilized life. But each town still needed the olive oil, wine, and barley from its farmland; and to keep their political independence the citizens had to be prepared to defend that land.

To guard the frontiers where they were most inaccessible might indeed seem the obvious strategy. Hunters and herdsmen made their living in the hills. The state might have established an effective first line of defense by recruiting companies of archers or javelin men, lightly equipped for mountain warfare, and stationing them in forts to defend the passes. But such garrisons would have been useless unless they were kept up permanently. From the heart of a city's territory to that of its neighbor was often less than a day's march, and unless the frontier guards were on duty the enemy would be through the passes before the defenders had mobilized. Permanent frontier guards were impossible. No early city-state had the resources or the administrative organization needed to keep a strong force of regular soldiers in the field. Besides, a standing army recruited from the poor was politically dangerous. In fact, Greek history offers several examples of political leaders who seized power with the help of bodyguards voted to them by their fellow citizens.

If the frontier could not be defended, an invading enemy must be met in the heart of the city's territory. Cities themselves could be fortified. In some places Mycenaean citadels were still defensible, and new fortifications were being built. As early as the eighth century B.C., Smyrna (İzmir) on the west coast of Asia Minor had a massive wall of sun-dried brick, which was certainly not unique. However, unless the complete destruction of a city was sought, it was seldom necessary to undertake a siege. Victory in the field was usually sufficient to secure limited war aims. If a beaten army took shelter behind its city walls, the victors could do damage to farms, orchards, and vineyards, with effects that might last for a generation. At the same time, they could enrich themselves by driving off stock and slaves and carrying away movable property, including even the tiles from farmhouse roofs. Merely to beat down and trample the standing barley might be enough. Few cities in the early sixth century B.C. could have endured, as the great commercial seaport of Miletus did, the destruction of the harvest for eleven successive years (Herodotus, 1.17.1–18.2). As late as the early years of the Peloponnesian War (from 431 B.C.) the Spartan King Archidamus II hoped to bring Athens to terms by annual invasions and the destruction of the crops. Athens, like Miletus, was able to hold out even after a permanent base was established in Attica by Agis II, the son of Archidamus, because it commanded the sea. But against smaller and less favorably situated states the strategy of devastation continued to be practiced with effect.

So to defend the land the citizens turned out in person. At least, all citizens turned out who could afford to equip themselves with weapons and armor. The poor were not wanted; an unarmored man throwing stones (even from a sling) or swinging a cudgel would have only a nuisance value as a skirmisher, and his presence would weaken the line of battle. On the other hand, the rich, although they would certainly be required to serve and might be chosen as leaders, were no longer the only ones who could equip themselves adequately. By the middle of the seventh century B.C. spears, swords of iron, helmets, cuirasses and greaves of bronze, and great round shields of wood or leather, with heavy bronze rims, were within the reach of the craftsman or of the smallholder who could plow his own land with a yoke of oxen. Formed into a close-ordered phalanx, these armored spearmen, or hoplites, could bear down on men who fought individually in the old style. Nor could the phalanx be broken either by chariots or by mounted men, who had by the seventh century generally replaced chariots on the battlefield. The development of hoplite armies therefore favored systems of government in which the franchise was open to the middle class. Narrowly "aristocratic" institutions were characteristic of those parts of Greece, notably the plains of Thessaly, where cavalry prevailed. Democracy was found in maritime states, because sea powers needed rowers for the galleys and recruited them from the poorer citizens. They therefore were more liberal in extending political privileges without property qualifications.

Naturally, political and military developments did not take place everywhere in the same way, or at the same time. Nor were the different items of hoplite equipment introduced simultaneously as parts of a single "weapon system." The earliest Greek pictures of the phalanx are on vases decorated by the Corinthian artist we know as the Macmillan Painter, who was active about 640–630 B.C. His hoplites wear plate cuirasses very similar to an actual example found at Argos in a grave of the late eighth century. The warrior who was buried in this grave certainly did not fight as a member of a phalanx; on the other hand, since the subject was beyond the powers of most archaic artists, we cannot be certain that the first phalanx was no earlier than the earliest surviving vase paintings of phalanxes. Probably the "bronze men from the sea"—Ionian Greek and Carian mercenaries who in about 664 B.C. helped to establish the Egyptian Twenty-sixth Dynasty (Herodotus, 2.151–152)—were already trained in the discipline without which, as Aristotle was to observe more than three hundred years later (*Politics* 4.1297b17), the hoplite army was worthless. But the exact date of the first hoplite phalanx remains uncertain.

Hoplite warfare determined not only political institutions but the Greek system of education. The gymnasium, unknown outside the Greek world, was designed to develop the physique of boys who would be soldiers as well as citizens. It is, however, remarkable that although in the phalanx hoplites fought as members of a united body, Greek athletics emphasized individual excellence, and team sports were almost unknown. Coordinated drill probably began at eighteen, when boys became ephebi and entered into military training, which at Athens (about whose institutions we are best informed) eventually came to include two years' garrison duty. Once trained and formally enrolled as adult citizens, men remained liable for military service until the age of sixty. In wartime they might be required to turn out at a moment's notice, bringing with them three days' rations of barley meal, onions, and cheese.

At Sparta neither the gymnasium nor the *ephebeia* existed as such. The upper class, the Spartiates, were taken from their families at the age of seven and passed from one official organization to another until they reached manhood. As adults they belonged to military messes, whose daily rations were supplied from the members' farms, tilled not by themselves but by the Helots, conquered local peasants. In consequence, the Spartiates could occupy their whole lives with military training, and acquired a professional skill that set them apart from the rest of the Greeks. A story preserved only in late sources (Plutarch, "Agesilaus" 26; Polyaenus, *Strategy* [*Strategemata*] 2.1.7) but dating from the early fourth century B.C. tells how Sparta's allies complained to the great King Agesilaus that Sparta contributed a disproportionately small number of men to the allied army. Thereupon the king paraded the army, and gave the order "Fall out, the potters!" "Fall out, the blacksmiths!" Then the masons, the carpenters, the shoemakers, and so through different trades until at last the Spartiates were left almost by themselves. In this way the king demonstrated that, however few men Sparta contributed, her share of soldiers was disproportionately large.

The story serves as a reminder that hoplite armies were not made up exclusively of farmers. But it seems that Socrates, the journeyman sculptor-turned-philosopher whose gallant conduct on the battlefield is repeatedly mentioned, was an exception among craftsmen who were required to serve as hoplites. Xenophon, a former pupil of Socrates and a distinguished professional soldier, notes that agriculture hardens a man's body for military service, and proves the farmer's superiority by saying that if a war came the farmers would vote to go out and offer battle, while the townsmen would vote to remain within the fortifications (Xenophon, *Household Management* (*Oeconomicus*) 6.6–7).

From Xenophon's writings, and from later military handbooks (which are, however, chiefly concerned with the Macedonian phalanx), something of hoplite drill can be learned. The essential maneuver was to form the phalanx, or line of battle, from the column of march by halting the leading unit and bringing up the following files to form on its left. Each file leader was an officer, at least in the Spartan army, commanding as well as leading his own file; so the front rank of the phalanx was formed of officers, just as the cutting edge of a blade was formed of hardened steel. The following troops gave weight to the blow.

Something of the feelings of the front rank of an advancing phalanx can be learned from Thucydides' description (5.71.1) of the battle of Mantinea, fought in 418 B.C.

> All armies behave in the following manner. In closing with the enemy, they tend to be pushed out toward their own right wings, and both armies outflank the enemy's left with their own right, because, out of fear, each man pushes his unshielded side as close as possible to the shield of the man who is drawn up on his right, and thinks that the best precaution consists in the denseness of the closing up. The front-rank man on the right wing is first responsible for this, because he is always eager to put his own bare side out of reach of the enemy, and the others follow him, through the same fear.

In the packed mass, with the men of the front rank closing up against their neighbors and the file that each led pressing on behind him, there was no room for individual skill at arms. Plato's *Laches* opens with a discussion of the art of fencing in hoplite armor, which is represented as a novelty at the supposed date of the dialogue, about 420 B.C. To Nicias, the rich gentleman soldier, it seems that this skill, like riding and other outdoor sports, provides healthy exercise for young men. He even allows that it may have some value in an actual battle after the ranks are broken, when the chances of pursuit and retreat lend themselves to individual encounters. However, the veteran professional Laches will have none of it, and demonstrates the uselessness of this art by saying that the Spartans, who are acknowledged to be the best soldiers in Greece, reject it altogether (*Laches* 181c–184c).

As the armies closed, the men of the front rank and perhaps their immediate followers could thrust overarm with their spears against the eyes or throats of the enemy first rank. They would also try to bear the enemy down by pressing shield against shield, and their followers added their weight until one side or the other gave way. If his spear was dropped or broken, the hoplite drew his sword. (Those of the Spartans were little more than daggers, which may have been more effective in the close press.) But the spear was the essential weapon; the Greek said "taken by the spear," not "won by the sword."

As for the shield, its weight and the manner in which it was carried made it more suitable for fighting in formation than for individual combat. The left arm was thrust up to the elbow through a central loop, and the left hand held a grip located just inside the rim. The size of the shield, generally rather under three feet in diameter, was thus governed by the length of the forearm, and as Thucydides indicates, the hoplite could not easily bring his shield across to cover his own right side. Nor could he use it to protect his back; so the runaway usually discarded his shield. The Spartan mother's command to her son to come back "with his shield or upon it" has become proverbial.

If two hoplite phalanxes did grapple, the result, while less destructive than the Persian critic claimed, was likely to be grim enough. Xenophon describes the battlefield after Agesilaus' victory at Coronea in 394 B.C., "the ground reddened with blood, bodies lying friend and foe together, shields pierced through, spears splintered, daggers unsheathed, some lying on the ground, others in bodies, others still gripped fast" (Xenophon, *Agesilaus* 2.14). However, it was not unusual for one army to lose its collective nerve before actually coming to blows, and instead of merely edging sideways, to turn and run. In that case there would be discarded shields and weapons on the battlefield, but few corpses.

Since the immediate objective was limited to gaining control of the battlefield, the victorious army did not normally attempt pursuit. Weapons and bodies would be collected. The victors' own dead would either be buried on the battlefield, or brought home, sometimes after cremation. Those of the enemy would be stripped, but not outraged, and returned to their fellow citizens when the latter sent heralds requesting permission to pick up their dead. Thereby they formally conceded the victory. Nicias once learned, when his men had been reembarked after a successful seaborne operation, that two dead bodies had not been found. He chose to allow the enemy, who had in other respects been thoroughly defeated, a formal victory, rather than to leave his fellow citizens unburied (Thucydides, 4.44.5–6).

Captured armor was, from an early period, often dedicated at great religious sanctuaries such as Olympia. The custom also developed, probably not earlier than the beginning of the fifth century B.C., of erecting a trophy (from *tropaion*, turning point) at the place where the enemy had been turned to flight. Such trophies originally consisted of tree trunks to which a captured helmet, shield, and cuirass were attached. The first permanent trophy of stone was erected by the Thebans after their victory over the Spartans at Leuctra in 371 B.C.

Cavalry, riding small, unshod horses bareback, could not break a hoplite phalanx and therefore could not decide the issue of a campaign. However, they had auxiliary functions. Mounted hoplites, who rode to the battlefield but fought on foot, are shown on vase paintings of the seventh and sixth centuries B.C. from Athens, Corinth, and elsewhere. They may have formed picked mobile troops, inheriting something of the aristocratic tradition of Homeric chariot warfare. But a small body of men, however select, could not have withstood a whole phalanx in the field, and the majority of citizens, who had to march as well as fight, no doubt resented the horsemen's privileges. Mounted hoplites therefore disappeared before the classical period, although their memory was perhaps preserved by historical survivals such as the retention of the name *hippeis* (horsemen) for the infantry bodyguard of the Spartan kings.

True cavalry, who fought on horseback and did not use the horse merely for transport, also developed in Greece during the seventh and sixth centuries B.C. The cavalry of Assyria and of Lydia provided a model, and these civilized Asiatic powers were influenced in their turn by the Scythians and other nomadic peoples. Ancient cavalry, lacking the security of saddles and stirrups, preferred missile weapons. Mounted archers and javelin throwers were both employed in Asia, and such cavalry formed the most important part of the Persian army, whose conquest of Asia from the Indus to the Aegean Sea during the third quarter of the sixth century B.C. made a confrontation of Greek with "barbarian" inevitable. However, the Greeks, few of whom were good archers even when standing on their own feet, never developed horse archers to match those of the Asiatics. Mounted archers appear on a few early works of art from Crete, the home of the only famous Greek bowmen, and in the classical period the Athenians employed a company of Scythian horse archers, apparently chiefly as military police. But the citizen cavalry of Athens and that of other Greek states was armed with javelins or, since throwing the javelin required special skills, which young part-time soldiers did not always trouble to learn, with spears used for thrusting.

Hunting is recommended by Xenophon (*On Horsemanship* 8.10) as a means of practicing the use of weapons while riding across country. But where the rideable ground was heavily farmed this was not practical. Attic vase paintings of the sixth century B.C. show boys on horseback using javelins against deer and boar, but in Xenophon's own time (fourth century B.C.) it was usual to hunt on foot. Xenophon also recommended (*Hipparchicus* 1.26) the establishment of athletic contests to encourage military skills, and pictures on prize amphorae of the fourth century B.C. show that javelin throwing from horseback was at that time one of the events in the Panatheraic Games. This competition, however, was never introduced at Olympia.

Cavalrymen also carried swords. Battle-axes, although known in Asia and among the Scythians, were not used in Greece. Vase paintings and sculptures usually show Greek cavalrymen unarmored but this is probably an artistic convention. A few of the horsemen of the Parthenon Frieze (*ca.* 440 B.C.) have helmets and cuirasses, and it may be supposed that this much armor at least was generally worn in battle. In *On Horsemanship*, written probably in the second quarter of the fourth century B.C., Xenophon recommends elaborate armor for man and horse, but this seems to reflect what he had seen in Persia rather than normal Greek practice.

Cavalrymen, like hoplites, equipped themselves at their own expense, although at Athens, from at least the late fifth century B.C., a subsidy was paid toward the cost of the horse. The cavalry was therefore an aristocratic body, formed chiefly from the young men of the richer landowning families. The tyrants who governed Athens during much of the sixth century B.C. regarded aristocratic families other than their own as rivals, and relied on Thessalian cavalry. After the expulsion of the tyrants by a Spartan army in 510 B.C., the Athenian hoplite force was greatly expanded, but the cavalry was neglected. Then, following the Persian Wars of 480–479 B.C., the Athenians set about creating an effective citizen cavalry force that was a thousand strong by 431 B.C., at the outbreak of the Peloponnesian War against Sparta and its allies. When Pericles abandoned Attica to the invading Peloponnesian army, and withdrew the population into the fortifications of the city, the cavalry alone took the field. Besides skirmishing successfully with the enemy's horsemen, the Athenian "knights" harassed marauders and, carried on warships refitted to serve as horse transports, took part in raids on the enemy coast. However, in the great pitched battle of Delium (424 B.C.) the Athenian cavalry proved less effective than that of the Boeotians.

Delium was fought because the Spartans had been forced onto the defensive by Athenian operations around the Peloponnesian coast. The Athenians believed that their own army could now take the field and challenge their Boeotian neighbors. They were defeated by the superior tactical skill of the Theban general Pagondas. The Athenian hoplites formed the usual phalanx, eight deep, and, charging "at a run," broke the left of the enemy line, where contingents from different Boeotian cities were likewise drawn up in the usual manner. But Pagondas had massed the Thebans themselves twenty-five deep in the right wing, and the weight of this formation bore the Athenian left back after a hard struggle. Meanwhile the Athenian right had fallen into confusion in the process of encircling the broken contingents of the enemy's left, and now fled in panic at the sight of a party of Boeotian cavalry, whom they mistook for the vanguard of a fresh army, emerging over a hill. In the rout, the Boeotian cavalry were particularly effective in cutting up the fugitives (Thucydides, 4.89–99).

The column massed to break one wing of the enemy's phalanx was henceforth the distinguishing feature of Theban tactics. When the Spartans, after the defeat of Athens at the end of the Peloponnesian War (404 B.C.), sought to extend their domination over Central Greece, the Theban column was repeatedly opposed to the Spartan line. At the Nemea River in 394 B.C. the Spartans used the tactical mobility conferred by their superior discipline to outflank the enemy's left, and then moved across the battlefield from side to side, cutting up the separate contingents of the Thebans and their allies as they came straggling back after a charge that had routed the allies of the Spartans. But when in 371 B.C., at the battle of Leuctra, the Spartans attempted to repeat the maneuver they were defeated by the Theban Epaminondas. In previous battles the Theban column had been on the right wing. Epaminondas placed it on the left, directly opposite the Spartans themselves. When the latter attempted their outflanking movement behind a cavalry screen, the Theban cavalry drove the screen in upon its own infantry, and before the Spartans could regain their order the main mass of the Theban infantry was upon them. After a desperate struggle in which the Spartan king Cleombrotus I and his principal officers fell, the Theban column crushed the part of the Spartan line that was opposed to it. The Theban "Sacred Band" of three hundred picked men, led by Pelopidas, played a major part in the victory.

Sparta never recovered from the disaster at Leuctra, but Thebes, now opposed by Athens as well as Sparta, failed to establish her leadership over Greece and gradually declined after Epaminondas was killed on the field of his second great victory at Mantinea in 362 B.C. This battle left Greece in confusion, with Sparta trying to recover the territories that had been liberated from her by Epaminondas. Thebes was in control of Boeotia in central Greece but checked by Athens, and by the mountaineers of Phocis to the west, who used the accumulated treasures of Apollo at Delphi to raise large mercenary armies. Many Greeks hoped for a leader who would establish peace among the city-states and perhaps lead a united Greece to the conquest of Persia.

Such a leader eventually appeared in Philip II of Macedonia (359–336 B.C.). As the probable creator of the Macedonian phalanx, whose soldiers carried a sixteen-foot pike (*sarissa*) instead of the hoplite's spear, and as an innovator in siege warfare, Philip forged the instrument with which his son Alexander the Great conquered the East. He also gave his army a secure economic base by exploiting the gold and silver mines of Mount Pangaeus, which passed under his control after his capture of Amphipolis in 358 B.C. Perhaps even more important, although less securely attested, was the transformation of a pastoral economy into an agricultural one, resulting in the creation of a peasant class from whom the rank and file of the new phalanx were recruited. Officers, and a fine cavalry force, were drawn from the ancient Macedonian aristocracy. Philip stands at the beginning of a new age; but in coordinating large masses of infantry with cavalry he may be considered the sucessor of Epaminondas, whose tactics he probably studied when, from 367 to 364 B.C., he was detained as a hostage at Thebes.

The armies of the Greek city-states were still largely composed of citizen hoplites, down to the Macedonian conquest of Greece (battle of Chaeronea, 338 B.C.). But the fourth century B.C. saw an increasing use of professional mercenaries. From the time when the Egyptian Twenty-sixth Dynasty had been established with the help of "bronze men from the sea" (*ca.* 664 B.C.) the rulers of the Near East, including, in the fifth century B.C., the Persian satraps of Asia Minor, had hired Greek hoplites, mostly from Arcadia, as bodyguards and garrison troops. In 401 B.C. the Persian prince Cyrus the Younger added more than ten thousand such mercenaries to his Asiatic levies in an attempt to dethrone his brother Artaxerxes II. These Greeks were substantial citizens, hoping to make fortunes in the service of a generous Asiatic prince, according to Xenophon, whose *The March Up Country* (*Anabasis*) is a firsthand account of this expedition. Their failure did not discourage other Greeks from entering the service of the king of Persia himself, of his satraps, and of the Egyptians, who revolted from Persia in 405 B.C. and maintained their independence until 340 B.C. Some Greek generals, including the Athenian's Chabrias and Iphicrates, distinguished themselves in these wars and also served their own states well, and the Spartan king Agesilaus raised money for Sparta's wars in Greece by leading armies of liberated Helots in the Egyptian service. (Sparta had first used such "newly enfranchised" troops against the Athenian possessions on the north coast of the Aegean under Brasidas in 424 B.C. Thereafter they were increasingly used for distant expeditions, including Agesilaus' own campaigns in Asia in 396–394 B.C.). By the time of Alexander the Great's invasion of Asia (334 B.C.) the most formidable part of the Persian forces in the west was a corps of Greek mercenaries under Memnon of Rhodes. Greek mercenaries also did good service to King Darius III at the decisive battles of Issus and Gaugamela. Although condemned by Alexander's propagandists as traitors to the common cause of Greece, they may have regarded themselves as defenders of liberty against the Macedonian conqueror.

Mercenary cavalry was not of great importance before the Hellenistic age, but the growth of professionalism that resulted from the increasing use of mercenaries led to the creation of effective light infantry. During the Persian wars the battles of Marathon (490 B.C.) and Plataea (479 B.C.) had shown that hoplites could charge through arrows, and even endure prolonged arrowfire while remaining stationary, provided they kept their close order upon favorable ground. But during the Peloponnesian War several actions (notably the Athenian victory of Sphacteria in 425 B.C.) showed that hoplites could be destroyed by mobile troops armed with missiles on ground that did not allow them to keep their order. To be effective, such troops had to be individually skilled in the use of their weapons, and also drilled to cooperate in open order; hence the need for professionalism. The most effective of the new professionals were the peltasts, javelin men who took their name from the *pelta,* a light, crescent-shaped shield of wicker used by the mountaineers of Thrace. Thracian peltasts are ridiculed by Aristophanes in the *Acharnians* (425 B.C.), but were hired on several occasions by the Athenians, their most notable exploit being the massacre of the defenseless inhabitants of Mycalessus in 415 B.C. by some Thracians who were being shipped home after reaching Athens too late to be dispatched with reinforcements to the siege of Syracuse.

Iphicrates, the son of an Athenian shoemaker, created by harsh discipline and rigorous attention to detail a professional force that established the reputation of the peltast during the Corinthian War of 394–386 B.C. His greatest success—the destruction, on ground favorable to hoplites, of an entire Spartan regiment—counterbalanced the victories of King Agesilaus. Thereafter peltasts were widely used by both sides, not only for skirmishing but for guarding mountain passes and so denying the enemy access to the level plains, a strategy that the early city-states had been unable to undertake for want of regular light infantry. Field fortifications, walls, and stockades planned to allow rapid sorties and retreats and so to enable defending peltasts to make full use of their mobility, also came into use; an interesting example, dating probably from the late third or early fourth century B.C., survives in the so-called Dema Wall, guarding the pass between Mounts Aegaleos and Parnes in Attica.

For all the modifications that warfare between Greek city-states underwent between the seventh and the fourth centuries B.C., it remained largely an affair of citizen soldiers, armed as hoplites and having as their first object the capture or the defense of agricultural land. Such warfare, with its formal conventions, fought between enemies who were deeply conscious that they shared a common language and common gods, was less marked by humanity toward prisoners and noncombatants than might have been expected. Fettering of captives is mentioned more than once by Herodotus. By an act of poetic justice the Spartans who had been defeated at Tegea (mid seventh century B.C.?) were set to work in the fields chained in the same fetters that they themselves had brought for their expected captives. At a later date Sparta and Argos had an agreement for the ransoming of prisoners; but we learn of it only in connection with the story of how the Spartan king Cleomenes I tricked some Argives who had taken sanctuary in a sacred grove into coming out, in the belief that they had been ransomed. They were then put to death (battle of Sepeia; ca. 494 B.C.). Cleomenes completed the massacre by burning the grove with those Argives who had remained in it. Such acts were generally thought to incur divine vengeance—Cleomenes died disgraced and mad a few years later—and sanctuaries were frequently respected. Agesilaus is praised by Xenophon for granting a free retreat to a party of Thebans who had escaped to a temple after the battle of Coronea (394 B.C.).

Prisoners, who might be sold as slaves or ransomed by their friends, had a commercial value. But to secure, feed, and house large numbers of prisoners required administrative machinery that the city-states simply did not possess. Thucydides (7.87) has left a famous picture of the sufferings of thousands of Athenian and allied prisoners in the stone quarries of Syracuse after the disaster of 413 B.C. Confined in a narrow unroofed space, without protection from the burning sun or the night frosts, without sanitation, with only a miserable allowance of grain and water, they were not even able to dispose of the corpses of those who died of wounds and sickness. Some seven thousand men were packed together in filth and the stench of decaying bodies. After seventy days the survivors were sold into slavery, except the Athenians themselves and such Sicilian and Italian Greeks as had sided with them, who had to endure for eight months in all. Yet it is also reported that some Athenians were released for repeating to their captors the choruses of Euripides, and one may question whether the sufferings of the remainder were not due to mismanagement and want of organization as much as to deliberate cruelty.

Large numbers of prisoners were sometimes massacred out of hand, like the crews of the Athenian fleet destroyed by Lysander at Aegospotami in 405 B.C. At Plataea in 427 B.C. the garrison surrendered upon the promise that the Spartan commander would "punish the guilty, but nobody contrary to justice." The prisoners were, however, all put to death, being unable to reply satisfactorily to the question whether they had done anything in the present war to help the Spartans and their allies (Thucydides, 3.52–68). Four years earlier the Plataeans themselves had, with more justification, put to death a hundred and eighty Theban prisoners, the survivors of a force that had tried to seize Plataea in time of peace. Thucydides notes (2.5–6) that their bodies were given up to their friends for burial.

Sparta's shortage of manpower made Spartan prisoners especially valuable as bargaining counters. Two hundred and ninety-two Lacedaemonians, including a hundred and twenty of the Spartiate aristocracy, were captured by the Athenians on Sphacteria in 425 B.C., and it was resolved to "guard them in chains until some treaty was reached, and if the Peloponnesians invaded the land before this to put them to death" (Thucydides, 4.41.1). On other occasions the Athenians were less merciful in their treatment of prisoners. The cases of Mytilene and of Melos have been given special prominence by Thucydides (3.27–50; 5.84–116). In the Mytilene case (427 B.C.) the Athenian assembly originally voted to put to death all the males of military age and sell the women and children into slavery; but a second decree (which reached the Athenian commander on the spot just in time to prevent his carrying out the first) restricted the death penalty to "rather more than a thousand" of those most responsible for their city's revolt. The remainder were spared slavery, although their land was divided among Athenian settlers. At Melos (416 B.C.) the Athenians did kill the grown men and enslave the remainder of the population. In both cases they were motivated by a desire to terrorize their tributary states. But Lesbos was an Athenian ally that had revolted; the sole offense of the Melians was that they had refused to join the Athenian League, although as islanders they fell within the sphere of Athenian sea power.

SIEGE WARFARE

As early as the ninth century B.C. the Assyrian kings possessed formidable siege trains, including scaling ladders, movable screens to protect sappers, and wheeled towers containing battering rams at ground level and archers above. Stories of these wooden monsters, filled with armed men, may have inspired the Greek tale of the wooden horse of Troy, and the bronze head of a battering ram, of archaic Greek workmanship, has been found at Olympia. But it is probable that the ram was dedicated by a city that had captured it in the course of a successful defense. At all events, early Greek city-states had neither siege trains on the Assyrian scale nor the elaborate fortifications needed to resist them. Asiatic city walls were guarded by projecting towers from which the defending archers could deliver flanking fire; the attackers moved their engines forward under cover of the fire of their own archers. But when hoplites stormed a wall defended by hoplites, and neither side was supported by archers, a high wall thick enough to provide the defenders with a platform on which to stand was all that was absolutely necessary, although additional defenses might be provided, especially at the gates. On the François Vase, painted in about 560 B.C. by the Athenian artist Cleitias, is a picture of one of the gates of Troy. Like the armor of the heroes who sally out through the gate, the fortifications reflect the warfare of Cleitias' own time rather than of the Bronze Age. A straight rampart, built of regular blocks, is crowned by rectangular battlements. Between them are piled round stones of a suitable size for throwing. The gate itself is set in a frame of massive beams, suggesting that the blocks of which the wall is built do not represent ashlar masonry but sun-dried brick. One side of the gate is open; the other is closed, and the artist has shown its construction of heavy vertical planks secured by diagonal braces. Hinges (not shown in the picture but known from other evidence) were simple pivots, revolving in sockets in the threshold below and the lintel above. A low sill prevented the gate from opening outward, and a massive wooden bar, housed in a recess in the wall at one side of the gate, was drawn across and its end secured in a hole in the wall on the other side to prevent the gate from being pushed inward when it was closed.

Such defenses, provided that they were adequately manned, would stop hoplites, but not an Asiatic siege train. About a generation before the time of Cleitias the Lydian king Alyattes captured the Greek city of Smyrna by piling a huge earthen siege mound against its mud-brick defenses. Arrowheads of bronze and iron, recovered in hundreds from the earth of the mound, are evidence of the barrage that covered the approach to the walls.

A Greek general who intended to capture a fortified city might try to gain one of the gates by surprise or treachery. When such methods failed, the besiegers tried to starve the defenders into surrender.

Thucydides, in his account of the siege of Plataea, gives the fullest description of a classical Greek siege. Surprise and treachery failed in 431 B.C., and in 429 B.C. the city was regularly besieged by the Peloponnesian army under King Archidamus II of Sparta. The besiegers first ravaged the countryside, cutting down the trees and using the timber to build a stockade around the city. They then heaped a siege mound against the walls, working in shifts day and night. The defenders countered first by raising upon the part of the wall facing the mound a wooden superstructure, covered with hides as a protection against fire arrows. Next they dug away the base of the mound, which they reached first by breaching their own wall and then through a countermine. Meanwhile, the attackers brought up "engines"—battering rams, probably protected by movable sheds or towers. The defenders broke off the heads of the rams by dropping across them heavy beams that were fastened by chains so that they could be drawn up again. Finally, the assailants were frustrated by the construction of an inner wall at the threatened point. After an unsuccessful attempt to set the city on fire, the siege was converted into a blockade. A double ditch was dug round the city, and the excavated earth was fashioned into sun-dried bricks from which inner and outer walls were built. The space between the walls was roofed over to provide a walkway that passed at intervals through guard towers where the sentries could shelter.

This circumvallation did not prevent a daring breakout, which saved a large part of the garrison, but those who remained were eventually starved into surrender (Thucydides, 2.71–78; 3.20–24; 3.52–68).

Since the Athenians supplied part of the garrison of Plataea, including a company of archers, Athenian skill and firepower might be given the credit for the repulse of the less ingenious Spartans and Boeotians. But in conducting sieges the Athenians were no more successful. Artemon, the engineer who assisted Pericles at the siege of Samos in 440 B.C., was credited with the invention of engines that were in fact used by the Assyrians centuries earlier. But he failed to take the city by assault, and is remembered chiefly because the comic poets still made fun of him twenty years later. During the first part of the Peloponnesian War the Athenians reduced Potidaea, Mytilene, and Melos by famine. Their own defeat at the siege of Syracuse (415–413 B.C.) resulted chiefly from their failure to complete a line of fortifications designed to blockade the city on its landward side. At no time did they attempt to take Syracuse by assault.

In 406 B.C. Syracuse, threatened by a Carthaginian invasion that had already destroyed the Greek cities along the south coast of Sicily, submitted to the military dictatorship of Dionysius I (d. 367 B.C.). Dionysius revolutionized siege warfare by the introduction of catapults, and in 397 captured the Carthaginian island fortress of Motya (Mozia) by building a causeway along which huge siege towers were moved forward under cover of catapult fire. These towers overtopped the city walls, equaling the height of the six-story apartment blocks behind them, which the defenders had turned into fortresses. The storming of the city was launched from the towers.

Dionysius' catapults perhaps only fired large arrows, capable of penetrating armor. Stone-throwers powered by the reaction of tightly twisted cables and hurling balls of up to sixty pounds in weight were later developed. To counter the new methods, engineers added to the defense towers with embrasures for catapults and massive batteries of the heavier stone-throwers. Outer defenses, including ditches and palisades, were covered by the fire from these batteries, which were expected to outrange the besiegers' artillery, since the latter fired from ground level, and those of the defenders from elevated positions. City walls were carried well beyond the actual inhabited area, in order to hold the crests of ridges and other important natural features. Again Dionysius was a pioneer. He enclosed within fortified lines extending for many miles the plateau of Epipolae, which overlooks Syracuse on the landward side and was the scene of much of the fiercest fighting during the siege of 415–413 B.C. The plateau narrows to a point at its western extremity, nearly five miles inland. Here was constructed the fortress of Euryalus, whose rock-cut ditches and subterranean galleries form the most elaborate surviving system of ancient fortifications. Dionysius must have fortified this key position, but in its present form Euryalus probably reflects the designs of Archimedes, whose engineering skill baffled the Romans when they besieged Syracuse during the Second Punic War (214–211 B.C.).

In Greece proper, Epaminondas kept Sparta in check by fortifying the cities that were liberated by his victory at Leuctra (371 B.C.). Messene, whose stone walls and towers are largely preserved, is one of the most impressive ancient sites in Greece. At Mantinea the mud-brick fortifications have largely disappeared, but their plan has been recovered. Specially notable at both cities are the elaborate arrangements made to defend the gates, which are approached through passages made by overlapping the ends of the wall, or through outer courts commanded on all sides by the fortifications.

The safety of the gates and their protection against surprise and treachery is the chief concern of a military handbook written shortly before 350 B.C. by an author whom we know as Aeneas Tacticus. (He was perhaps the mercenary captain Aeneas of Stymphalus who is mentioned in Xenophon's *History of Greece* [*Hellenica*]). Of the siegecraft made possible by the introduction of the catapult he seems almost unaware. It was Philip II of Macedonia who, after the middle of the fourth century B.C., showed Greece the power of an organized siege train. Philip took more cities by treachery, or as the indirect result of his victories in the field, than by storm; in his greatest sieges, at Byzantium and Perinthus (later Heracleia, now Marmaraereglisi) in 340 B.C., he failed. But in siege warfare, as in other things, he forged the instrument with which his son Alexander the Great conquered Persia. Alexander's siege of Tyre (332 B.C.) repeated on a greater scale Dionysius' siege sixty-five years earlier of Motya (Mozia), a Phoenician fortress city built on an island that was stormed with the help of gigantic wheeled towers pushed forward along a causeway under covering fire delivered by the besiegers' catapults.

Alexander's successors, notably Demetrius Poliorcetes (the Besieger) practiced his methods on a still larger scale, and from the Hellenistic world they were passed on to Rome.

NAVAL WARFARE

The nature of Greek naval warfare was determined by the development, well before the beginning of the historical period, of the war galley as a specialized type of fighting ship. Merchant ships had rounded hulls, broad beamed in proportion to their length, in order to contain as much cargo as possible. Their crews were small in number; there might be enough men on board to work the ship into and out of harbor by means of oars, but the merchant ship normally moved under sail. A single mast carrying one large square sail seems to have been used before the Hellenistic age, when additional masts and spritsails made their appearance. In the Mediterranean ships rigged in this way could usually count on seasonal winds before which they could run to their destinations. Accommodation, including arrangements for cooking, was sufficient to allow the crew to live on board for days without disembarking, and although they had no compasses, merchant captains were prepared to venture out of sight of land. There was no need for a Greek ship bound for Egypt or Cyrenaica to hug the coast of Asia, touching the territory of the possibly hostile Phoenicians.

Warships, by contrast, were long, narrow, and propelled at comparatively high speeds (perhaps seven knots for short bursts) by large numbers of oars. They carried light sails to ease the task of the rowers on long voyages, but stowed them ashore before going into action. Since the rowers were crowded together in order to pack as many oars as possible into the length of the ship, they had no room to cook or sleep, and fleets of warships therefore preferred to stay close to shore and land their crews every evening if possible.

On naval warfare in the Greek Bronze Age we are inadequately informed. Part of the sequence of wall paintings from the "West House" at Acrotiri on Thera (Santorini) (*ca.* 1500 B.C.) has been interpreted as depicting a naval expedition, and in about 1190 B.C. Rameses III of Egypt won a naval victory over the Philistines and other "Sea Peoples," some of whom had connections with the Aegean area. In the *Odyssey* Odysseus tells of raids on the Nile Delta, but scholars dispute whether these are based on traditions of the Late Bronze Age or reflect the exploits of Greek pirates of *ca.* 700 B.C. Whatever the case, the raiders fight no naval battle, but disembark from their ships and are met on land by the king of Egypt and his army. Nor do the poets describe sea fights in connection with the Trojan War itself, although Ajax fights from the decks of the beached ships in order to defend them from Hector after the Trojans have broken into the Greek camp. Pikes for sea fighting are, however, mentioned by the poets, and they and their audiences may therefore have been familiar with encounters between ships on the high seas.

Homeric ships were propelled by oars fastened by thongs to tholepins (oarlocks were unknown). A mast, carrying a single sail, could be lowered into a cradle when the wind was unfavorable or the ship entered harbor. Forecastle and poop were decked over, and from the poop the helmsman operated the single large steering oar. Some sort of raised gangway connected forecastle and poop; otherwise the ship was left open. Ships were generally beached, stern first, on any convenient sheltered beach, although docks are mentioned in the *Odyssey* as part of the amenities of the city of the Phaiacians. In the catalog of ships (*Iliad* 2.484–762) the smallest vessels, those of Philoctetes, carry fifty men; the largest, those of the Boeotians, 120. Smaller vessels, with twenty oars, appear in the narrative. In all cases, the rowers are freemen, the "companions" of the kings and captains. They possess their own weapons and armor, and are in fact members of the anonymous mass of foot soldiers who make up the bulk of the army when fighting on land.

Since the poets, perhaps deliberately, avoid excess of detail, their descriptions can generally be made to fit the archaeological evidence for either the Late Bronze Age or the Geometric period of Greek art (down to *ca.* 700 B.C., the approximate date at which the epic poems are generally believed to have been composed). The Geometric period did, however, produce two major developments in naval architecture that the poets do not mention. From the ninth century B.C. on, vase paintings regularly show the bows of war galleys ending in a long pointed ram, level with the waterline; and from about a century later they show ships with two banks of oars, that is, with a second line of rowers seated on benches raised above those of the first. Originally, it seems, the lower oars were worked over the gunwale, the upper ones from the raised deck; but by the end of the eighth century the sides of the ship had been raised, so that the lower oarsmen were completely enclosed and pulled their oars through portholes. The tholepins of the upper oars were fixed to the raised gunwale, and a narrow deck, covering only the centerline of the ship, linked the poop and the forecastle and provided a fighting platform for spearmen and archers. Parallel developments in Phoenicia are illustrated on reliefs from the palace of King Sennacherib of Assyria (705–681 B.C.).

Greek Geometric vase paintings do not show battles of ship against ship, but beached ships whose crews skirmish, either from the decks or after disembarking, against enemies on the shore. These pictures recall, but do not seem to represent, the defense of the Greek ships by Ajax in the *Iliad.* Whether they represent other lost epic stories or contemporary warfare is disputed.

The beginnings of naval warfare proper were placed by Thucydides (1.13.4) shortly before the middle of the seventh century B.C., when he records a naval battle between the Corinthians and their colonists in Corcyra (Corfu). Thucydides believed that early naval battles were decided by the marines, armed as hoplites, who served on the ships' decks. Until late in the sixth century the principal type of warship seems to have been the penteconter, with fifty oars arranged in two banks. The much more powerful trireme was probably invented in the seventh century but seems not to have come into general use until shortly before the Persian Wars. The rowers, approximately 170, each pulled a single oar. They sat at three levels, thalamite within the hull, zygite, and thranite. An outrigger (*parexeiresia*) held the tholepins about two feet outboard. The zygite and thalmite oars were worked through ports in the hull. Measurements of still-existing docks indicate that triremes were about 115 to 120 feet (35 to 36.6 m) long and 15 to 16 feet (4.6 to 4.9 m) wide, including the outriggers. The hull was low and had a shallow draft, but exact dimensions are conjectural.

Thucydides (1.13.2) reports that triremes "are said" to have been built at Corinth earlier than in any other Greek city, but at the time of Xerxes' invasion (480 B.C.) the Athenian fleet was by far the largest on the Greek side. It was a recent creation (486 B.C.) financed by a lucky strike in the state silver mines that, upon the proposal of Themistocles, was employed for naval construction instead of being divided among the citizens.

For the campaign of 480 B.C. the Persians employed fleets built and manned by their subjects in Phoenicia, Egypt, and the Ionian Greek cities of Asia Minor. The Persian warships heavily outnumbered those of the Greeks, and were also lighter and more able to maneuver. The Greeks therefore chose to fight in confined waters, and won a decisive victory when Themistocles tricked the Persians into engaging the Greek fleet in the Straits of Salamis. The battle was decided by the use of the ram to sink or cripple enemy warships.

During the next sixty-odd years, until a disastrous sea battle in the Peloponnesian

War, described below, the Athenian fleet was supreme in Greek waters and on occasion carried the war against Persia as far as Cyprus and Egypt. It was based upon the excellent natural harbors of the Piraeus, whose fortifications, built by Themistocles, were joined to those of Athens by the Long Walls. The crews were drawn from the "seafaring mob" (*nautikos okhlos*) of the port, chiefly Athenian citizens of the poorer classes, whose political influence increased along with the military importance of the fleet. Galley slaves were unknown in the ancient world, although at times of crisis slaves were occasionally set free to serve in the galleys. Rich men were required from time to time to serve as trierarchs. Besides commanding, with the help of a professional steersman to give sailing directions, the trierarch fitted out for sea a hull that was allotted to him by the state, and found and paid the crew. Each rower normally received three obols (half a drachma) a day, at a time when the drachma was the standard day's wage for a skilled master craftsman. In a single campaigning season the trierarch would spend in pay alone about the equivalent of an upper-middle-class dowry. But a still heavier financial burden fell on the allies of Athens—the small islands and coastal cities of the Aegean, which had originally contributed willingly to maintain the Athenian fleet against Persia rather than provide ships and men themselves. After the Persian danger was removed, they found themselves the Athenians' subjects.

During this period the Athenians, some part of whose fleet was constantly at sea, were enabled by practice to develop superior skills and so to make even more effective use of the ram. Two maneuvers are particularly noted by the ancient sources. In the *diekplous*, when two fleets were approaching each other in line abreast, the ships of the fleet with the better crews dashed through the intervals in the enemy's line and then swung round to catch the enemy while they were still trying to turn. In the *periplous*, the ships of the better fleet literally rowed rings around the enemy, seeking an opportunity to ram.

During the first phase of the Peloponnesian War (431–421 B.C.) the superior skill of the Athenian crews ensured victory, even over numerically superior fleets in western waters far from the Athenians' home bases (Phormion's victories off Naupactus, 429 B.C.). The capture of Pylos by the Athenian fleet in 425 B.C. drew the Spartan army from Attica to the defense of its own territory, where the presence of a permanent Athenian garrison, maintained from the sea, was expected to encourage a revolt of Sparta's Messenian serfs. Athenian sea power not only secured Pylos but forced the surrender of nearly three hundred Spartan hoplites, the survivors of a larger force that had been unwisely landed on the neighboring island of Sphacteria. Using these prisoners as bargaining counters, the Athenians concluded the advantageous Peace of Nicias in 421 B.C., but overextended their power by sending in 415 B.C. a great expedition against Syracuse in Sicily. Although reinforced, the Athenians were unable to take the city, and their army was eventually trapped after the accompanying fleets were forced to fight a naval battle in the confined waters of the Great Harbor of Syracuse (413 B.C.). Here, as at Salamis nearly seventy years earlier, lightly built warships were beaten by heavier opponents in waters where there was no room for maneuver; only this time it was the Athenian fleet that was crushed.

News of the Sicilian disaster encouraged Sparta to renew the war, and the maritime subject-allies of Athens to revolt. Spartan fleets, financed by the Persian satraps of Asia Minor, were able to carry the war into Ionia and to threaten the vital sea route along which Athens imported grain from the north coast of the Black Sea.

Athens was able to maintain the war for some years, and to win repeated naval victories, although at times forced to liberate slaves to serve as rowers, and to send the aristocratic young cavalrymen on board as marines. Increasing desperation is also shown by a proposal to mutilate captured enemy crews by cutting off their thumbs so that they could no longer hold an oar. Athens and Sparta competed for the services of mercenary rowers; finally the Spartan admiral Lysander was able to outbid the Athenians by raising pay to four obols with money supplied by the Persian prince Cyrus, whose confidence he had gained. In 405 B.C. Lysander destroyed the last Athenian fleet at Aegospotami in the Hellespont (Dardanelles), and the next year Athens was starved into surrender.

The fourth century saw a partial revival of Athenian sea power, initially financed by Persia after Sparta lost the support of King Artaxerxes II by assisting the rebellion of his brother Cyrus. The administration of the trierachies was reformed, so that the financial burden was shared among partnerships, rather than carried by individuals. Technical developments later in the century included the introduction of the quadrireme, an increase of manpower over the trireme that was achieved not by adding a fourth level of oars (which would have been unstable) but by adding an extra man to one or more oar levels. The quadrireme most probably had oars on two levels, each pulled by two men. The quinquereme, a further development, may have had oars on three levels—two men to an oar on the upper two, and single rowers at the oars of the lowest level.

Athens was still the greatest sea power in Greece at the time of the Macedonian conquest (338 B.C.) but thereafter declined rapidly. The fleets of the Successors, who ruled the kingdoms into which Alexander the Great's empire was divided after his death (323 B.C.), were led by gigantic warships whose oar power is expressed as sixteen, twenty, thirty, or even forty. It is generally agreed that these figures reflect the use of large oars, or sweeps as they are technically known, each pulled by many rowers and arranged on one or more levels. They were decked over, and served as fighting platforms for large numbers of marines. They probably also carried batteries of catapults. These "superdreadnoughts" were clumsy and extravagant in manpower. States with an ancient maritime tradition, like Rhodes and Carthage, preferred quadriremes and quinqueremes, and Rome built fleets of quinqueremes in order to overcome Carthage. Small warships, modeled on those used by the Adriatic pirates, were introduced by Philip V of Macedonia (battle of Chios, 201 B.C.), and similar light Liburnians, as such ships were called, played a major part in the defeat of the fleet of Antony and Cleopatra at Actium in 31 B.C. Antony's fleet included triremes led by a "ten-power" warship. With the destruction of this fleet the Hellenistic era of naval warfare closes.

BIBLIOGRAPHY

GENERAL

Sir Frank E. Adcock, *The Greek and Macedonian Art of War* (1957); Yvon Garlan, *War in the Ancient World: A Special History* (1975); Arnold W. Gomme, *A Historical Commentary on Thucydides,* I (1959); Anthony M. Snodgrass, *Arms and Armour of the Greeks* (1967); Jean-Pierre Vernant, ed., *Problèmes de la guerre en Grèce ancienne* (1969).

HOMERIC WARFARE

Gudrun Ahlberg, *Fighting on Land and Sea in Greek Geometric Art* (1971); J. H. Crouwel, *Chariots and Other Means of Land Transport in Bronze Age Greece* (1981); Hilda L. Lorimer, *Homer and the*

Monuments (1950); Homer, *The Iliad of Homer*, Richmond Lattimore, trans. (1977); Anthony M. Snodgrass, *Early Greek Armour and Weapons* (1964).

LATER GREEK WARFARE ON LAND

John K. Anderson, *Military Theory and Practice in the Age of Xenophon* (1970); John D. Best, *Thracian Peltasts and Their Influence on Greek Warfare* (1969); Guy T. Griffith, *The Mercenaries of the Hellenistic World* (1935); Nicholas G. L. Hammond, *A History of Macedonia*, I (1972); Nicholas G. L. Hammond and Guy T. Griffith, *A History of Macedonia*, II (1979); Victor D. Hanson, *Warfare and Agriculture in Classical Greece* (1983); Herodotus, *Histories*, Aubrey De Selincourt, trans. (1954); Charles Hignett, *Xerxes' Invasion of Greece* (1963); Herbert W. Parke, *Greek Mercenary Soldiers from the Earliest Times to the Battle of Ipsus* (1933); W. Kendrick Pritchett, *Ancient Greek Military Practices*, Pt. 1 (1971), and *The Greek State at War*, Pt. 2 (1974); Sir William W. Tarn, *Hellenistic Military and Naval Developments* (repr. 1966).

PRISONERS OF WAR

Pierre Ducrey, *Le traitement des prisonniers de guerre dans la Grèce antique* (1968).

SIEGE WARFARE

Arnold W. Lawrence, *Greek Aims in Fortification* (1979); Eric W. Marsden, *Greek and Roman Artillery: Historical Development* (1969), and *Greek and Roman Artillery: Technical Treatises* (1971); Frederick E. Winter, *Greek Fortifications* (1971).

NAVAL WARFARE

Lionel Casson, *Ships and Seamanship in the Ancient World* (1971); John Morrison and R. Williams, *Greek Oared Ships* (1968).

Wars and Military Science: Rome

GRAHAM WEBSTER

THE ORIGINS OF ROME AND HER ARMY

The origins of the Roman army go back to the time when the peasants of the small communities on the Tiber marches freed themselves from Etruscan domination. The brilliant civilization of the Etruscans left a generous legacy to Rome, which its people were always reluctant to acknowledge. This included a sense of order and organization, superb craftsmanship in iron and bronze based on the rich mineral deposits in their territory, and the techniques of large-scale drainage, hydraulics, and building construction.

Rome, the chief settlement under the Etruscans, was changed from a group of primitive villages into an urban community with monumental buildings on the newly drained marches. The early history of Rome is obscure and subject to the accretions of myths. One of these, used by Roman historians, was the reign of kings, as Tacitus records in the very first sentence of his *Annals*. The myths fashioned these kings into tyrants; their overthrow and the release from the weakening Etruscan yoke was hailed as the first great stage toward political freedom. The truth is impossible to disentangle, but Etruscan influence was very strong and one of the Roman kings, Servius Tullius, was possibly an Etruscan.

He was the first to provide Rome with a defense wall and to reform the army into hoplites in the Greek mode. They had the great advantage of the Etruscan fine craftsmanship in metal based on the rich mineral deposits of Etruria. It seems possible that the basic political organizations of Rome were due to the Etruscans, since to keep control they had played the plebs against the king and his nobles. Out of this arose the durability of control that became a permanent feature of Roman government and justice.

The people had their voting assembly (Comitia Centuriata), which also served as a basis for the annual recruitment into the citizen army. After the expulsion of the kings *ca.* 500 B.C., the nobles attempted to install an oligarchic tyranny, which led to a series of plebeian revolts. This forced a codification of the law *ca.* 450 B.C., set out as the Law of the Twelve Tables. But the most important concession was the right of the plebs to elect ten tribunes of the plebs with the power to veto an unjust act, a power jealously guarded thereafter. It survived into early imperial times. Augustus made a public show of abiding by the old republican constitution and insisted on annual election to this office, which was recorded on his coins and monuments.

The army began as an organization based on citizenship. It had the advantage of finely wrought armor and weapons, which were necessary in the tight formation fighting of the Greek phalanx of the period. But the one important skill Rome failed to acquire from the Etruscans was seamanship and the development of naval warfare, which she was forced to learn by necessity in the Punic Wars against Carthage. But by sheer logical pragmatism, the new idea was introduced of using ships as fighting platforms, a very successful tactic, for its main element was that of surprise.

In the centuries that followed, Rome, slowly and often painfully, dominated the tribes of Italy, almost one by one. Some prudently became allies and levied units to assist the citizen legions. They failed, however, to obtain any political recognition until it was forced from an ultraconservative senate by the bitter Social Wars of 91–87 B.C. The Roman army developed and matured, as a result of the peculiar qualities of the people of Rome. But more important was their sense of purpose that amounted almost to a feeling of destiny, although this was only formulated much later under Augustus. The solid achievements were the results of the Roman temperament and the ability to adjust to adversity. These qualities were very important for the army since it never became a static body clinging to outdated methods, as did so many armies in later times. Whenever the Romans faced a new tactic or weapon, they immediately adopted it. They survived a number of disasters that could have crippled a lesser people; Rome only stiffened her resolve, adapted to the new enemy and fought back. Thus they survived the disaster of Caudine Forks in 321 B.C., the fearful humiliation of the capture of Rome itself by the Gauls *ca.* 390 B.C., and the painfully long struggle against the great power and superior tactics of Hannibal. They not only survived but also always learned by their defeats.

THE EARLY ARMY

For descriptions of the early army one has to rely on the historians Livy and Polybius. Livy is in some ways unsatisfactory, not only because just part of his great work has survived, but also because he wrote under the aegis of Augustus, who wanted the propaganda lessons of the past to stand out clearly. Thus, the reasons he gives for defeat and victory are usually based on Rome's breaking an old custom, or law, or her failure to seek the support of the gods, or the reverse. Thus the taking of Veii after a long siege was, according to Livy, due to the killing of the Roman ambassador by the besieged, and he fails to record the extraordinary engineering feat that undermined the city defenses. Livy considered the fall of Rome to be the result of a Roman ambassador's engaging the Celts in battle, and so on. The lesson here was that Rome could only fulfill her great destiny by showing proper respect for the law and the gods. Apart from this, the information Livy gives about the organization of the army *ca.* 340 B.C. (8.8) is of great value, although some of his figures are suspect.

Polybius was a Greek with an acute eye and a fine intelligence, who had the great advantage of being a member of the Scipionic circle, which provided him with access to details of all the campaigns. He was very impressed by the organization and discipline of the army, which contrasted with the irrationality of the Greeks in these matters. His history was in fact written for his countrymen in an attempt to explain the success of the Romans, especially in warfare. His highly detailed account of it *ca.* 200 B.C. (Book 6) remains the prime source about the army of that time. He deals not only with the organization, but also with the weapons, including the different types of javelins (*pila*) and armor. His remarkable description of the camp has allowed later commentators such as W. Roy in his *Military Antiquities of the Romans in North Britain* (1793) to draw it out as a plan in all its detail

Polybius first describes the annual enrollment for citizens under forty-six years old. Every able-bodied man was expected to serve sixteen years in the infantry or ten in the cavalry. The twenty-four military tribunes, who were appointed, first divided the assembled host by lots into four parts, which became legions, each 4,200 strong. All the men then took the oath of loyalty (*sacramentum*) to their commanders. At a later assembly the men were selected for their positions in the three battle ranks. These consisted of men differently armed and equipped and divided into ten maniples, each with two centurions and standard-bearers. In the first line were the *hastati*, armed with two *pila* with hardened points, protected by a large shield (*scutum*) and a leather cuirass to which was fashioned a bronze breastplate. A distinctive feature of these troops was the large plume of purple and black feathers attached to their helmets, which increased their height by eighteen inches.

The other two ranks, the *principes* and the *triarii* (the third ranks) carried large spears (*hastae*) for throwing. The three ranks were screened by the lightly armed *velites*, drawn from the poorer citizens, who carried *pila* and a circular shield. The cavalry force was 300 strong, divided into ten *turmae*, all recruited from the equestrian order. What may seem to be a rather cumbersome battle line based on property distinction was gradually simplified to the standard type of legionary of the late republic.

What amazed Polybius above all was the organization and discipline of the army; and it was to have the same effect much later on another outsider, Josephus, who studied it in the mid first century A.D. He was especially impressed by the manner in which the army set up their camps. In this the Romans were unique in the ancient world since armies of this period were usually billeted in towns; they built camps that were carefully laid out like urban centers. The concept of order and discipline in such an important matter was peculiar to Rome. Polybius describes how first the tent line and positions of the principal tents were set out with flags on a level piece of ground in a regular manner so that everyone was instantly familiar with the layout. Spaces were left for the horses, baggage animals, and baggage, and in the central area for the military stores. A space of 200 feet between the outer lines of tents and the defenses allowed for rapid deployment, provided room for cattle and spoil taken from the enemy, and gave assurance that hostile missiles would not reach the tents.

Guards for the night were appointed and the watchword circulated. Any soldier found failing in his duty suffered the severe punishment of being beaten by his fellowmen, often suffering permanent injury. Other offenses, such as stealing or cowardice, were similarly punished. If a whole unit was found guilty, every tenth man was selected by lot for beating, and the rest were fed on barley instead of wheat and forced to pitch their tents outside the camp. Polybius then lists the awards for bravery in the field and goes on to detail the soldiers' pay on figures that are difficult to correlate to any known standard.

THE ARMY ADAPTS TO OVERSEAS SERVICE

While Rome was campaigning against the other peoples of Italy, it was possible for her citizen soldiers to return to their homes at the end of each season. Only the exceptionally long siege of Veii obliged some of the men to remain on duty through the winter. The senate, recognizing this difficulty, was obliged to make special payments and to provide suitable warm clothing. This was the first recognition that under certain conditions the men could no longer be treated as unpaid citizen volunteers. As soon as it became necessary to send legions abroad, as happened in the Punic Wars, there was no question of their return at the end of a season, and men began to enlist with a long term of service in mind.

The army was now offering the opportunity for a military career. Although there were still the annual intakes, men often reenlisted immediately on discharge. This practice led to the creation of a professional army, which is well exemplified by Livy's account of the career of Spurius Ligustinus (42.34.1–15). This man enlisted in 200 B.C. and after twenty-two years of service was made first centurion (*primus pilus*) of the *Legio*. With a core of long-serving soldiers in his troops, a general of exceptional ability could secure their loyalty and make demands on them far beyond the normal practice. They were expected to take long and rapid marches and were trained for sudden tactical changes in the battle line during combat. These were usually necessary to surprise the enemy or to exploit its weaknesses, which became apparent only after a battle had started.

What is so remarkable about the Romans is their ability at times of crisis to produce men of great military genius. For example, Marcus Furius Camillus led Rome's army out of the great trough of despair after the Gauls, with speed and sheer ferocity, had descended upon and taken Rome, sweeping the army aside. New weapons, defensive armor, and tactics were introduced, but Rome had to wait over a hundred and fifty years before she was revenged at Telamon (Talamone) in 222 B.C. when another army of invading Gauls was crushed between the converging Roman forces. But any satisfaction was soon dispelled by the greatest crisis Rome ever faced. Hannibal invaded Italy in 218 B.C. and inflicted the crushing defeat of Cannae two years later. In every way the great Carthaginian general and his army were far superior to anything Rome possessed.

HANNIBAL IN ITALY

Hannibal and his troops had been together for a long time, and the Punic army had been welded by experience into a remarkable fighting machine capable of enormous feats of endurance. The Carthaginians had developed subtle tactics for use in battle, far removed from the crude clash of infantry typical of the ancient phalanx. But Hannibal was also a careful man and unwilling to commit his army to a direct attack on the city of Rome. He calculated that he could in time wear down Rome's resistance to the point of surrender. But he underestimated the tenacity of the Roman people and their total inability to accept defeat. The old reactionaries under Quintus Fabius Maximus were for sitting tight and waiting for Hannibal to tire or get impatient. But there was another spirit abroad through the influence of the Scipios, who had a wider vision, a concept of a total war strategy. Rome was already committed to an army in Spain under the two elder Scipios, but they were defeated and killed in 211 B.C.

THE GREAT SCIPIO AFRICANUS

The young Publius Cornelius, son of one of the Scipios in Spain, had shown great courage in battle as a military tribune, and in an act of remarkable political prescience he was given the *imperium* (the power to raise and maintain an army) and sent to Spain with an army to cut off Hannibal's supplies. After a winter spent gaining the confidence of his army, now joined to the surviving fragments, Scipio decided on a bold stroke. As the Carthaginian armies were scattered, he calculated he could make a successful surprise attack on their main base at New Carthage. His army marched 200 miles in six days, keeping pace with the fleet so that both arrived together. Before the citizens could summon any aid from one of the Carthaginian armies, he mounted a fierce attack on the walls. However, in the evening he noticed that the waters of a large lagoon on the north side of the city had receded on the ebb tide, assisted by a strong wind. He sent 500 men across with ladders, and the unprotected walls were scaled, the city taken, and with it a vast quantity of supplies and booty. Scipio's next task was to destroy the Carthaginian armies in Spain. On his first encounter at Baecula (Bailen, 208 B.C), he adopted Hannibal's tactics at Cannae; instead of the traditional three lines, Scipio put his light troops in the center and his legionaries on his wings, hoping to envelop the enemy. But Hasdrubal, then commander, was able to disengage his main force, withdraw without any significant losses, and eventually make his way to Italy.

Scipio was now learning faster than his men were able to adapt to his new tactics. But at Ilipa, he was successful in the same maneuver against the other Hasdrubal, son of Gisgo, and held his center while he executed a brilliant turning movement on the right wing, which he led himself. As Liddell Hart has written, "Military history contains no more classic example of generalship than this battle. Rarely has so complete a victory been gained by a weaker over a stronger force and the result was due to a perfect application of the principles of surprise and concentration." In Spain Scipio was able to develop his tactical skills and innovations. He trained his army in new battle formations and reequipped his men with the fine Spanish sword *gladius*. The brilliance of Scipio in Spain had turned the scales. Although Hasdrubal attempted to join his brother in Italy, he was crushed at the river Metaurus and Hannibal was forced to leave Italy in 203 B.C.

It was inevitable that the two great generals Scipio and Hannibal should eventually meet. This happened in North Africa in 202 B.C. at Zama, where Scipio was victorious. The details of this crucial battle unfortunately remain obscure. Most historians assume that Hannibal's weakness in cavalry prompted him to draw Scipio's horses away from the battlefield by ordering his own cavalry to retire in apparent confusion. Hannibal then put his faith in his veterans, but held them back from the early stages of the fighting. However, it seems that the retreating front lines created a confusion that Scipio was able to exploit. Even so, the issue may have been in doubt had not the Roman cavalry suddenly returned to fall on Hannibal's rear. That day the gods favored Scipio.

THE GROWTH OF THE PROFESSIONAL ARMY

The day of the highly trained and professional soldier had indeed arrived. The new battle tactics of rapid mobility and surprise became realities. It was also the death knell of the old phalanx. The battle where this was amply demonstrated was at Pydna in 168

B.C., when Aemilius Paullus defeated Perseus and ended the Third Macedonian War. Unfortunately, the Polybian account is fragmentary and it is impossible to reconstruct the details. Rome's allies crushed the left wing of Perseus, and the legionaries were able to outflank and split open the Macedonian phalanx.

Rome's enormous expansion in a short period produced difficult social and political problems. Within half a century of the Punic Wars and the capture of the large Carthaginian Empire, Rome had assumed a dominant position over most of the East. The main reason for this rapid expansion was the political collapse of the Macedonian and Seleucid empires. Rome had become involved in alliances with cities and states, who saw her as a protector against predators in lawless times. Rome had no policy of her own, certainly no imperial ambition, and appears to have drifted into a succession of wars through her commitments to rich trading cities like Pergamum and Rhodes. By *ca.* 130 B.C. Rome had control over the Illyrian coast of the Adriatic, the whole of Greece and Macedonia, the west end of Asia Minor, most of Spain, and part of North Africa. This expansion brought Romans into contact with the riches of the East and the opportunities of considerable wealth. Many able citizens of the upper and middle classes now became deeply involved in trade.

These changes had a serious effect on the old standards of Roman morality and rural simplicity. They also affected recruitment for the army. The large overseas service commitments had taken the young men away from the farms and the old pattern of the simple soldier-farmer vanished. Men joined the ranks attracted by the prospect of rich booty, rather than committed to service to the state. Rome was invaded by a mass of cheap slave labor and there was a strong drift of the smallholders and landless peasants into the city, thereby swelling the proletariat. Urgent social reforms were imperative, yet the stubborn *nobiles* resisted all moves toward this end. The consequence was the bitter Social War and the rise of the powerful generals Marius and Sulla and the civil war they engendered.

THE GREAT GENERALS

Scipio Africanus had very clearly shown the advantages to the state of a general with exceptional ability and qualities of personal leadership, but there were also dangers, perhaps not so obvious at the time. His troops had become devoted to him and naturally looked to him as a client did to his *patronus* for just rewards for their services. Scipio accepted this role and entered the political battle in an attempt to secure land for his men and also for the poorer citizens, to reduce the ever-growing problems of the Roman proletariat. But the Scipios and their friends found their schemes totally opposed by the stiff reactionaries led by Marcus Porcius Cato, a stern old-fashioned moralist and an extremely wily politician. Cato's adroit use of slander and innuendo discredited the Scipios. Africanus retired from public life and died in 183 B.C.

As the second century progressed, the need for social and political reform grew and, with it, increasingly bitter internal strife. Reforms were attempted by the two Gracchi, the brothers Tiberius and Gaius, grandsons of Scipio Africanus. The opposition to Tiberius was so hostile that in 132 B.C. it culminated in a riot, when he and 300 of his followers were lynched in the Roman Forum and their bodies flung into the Tiber. His brother, Gaius, a more able politician, continued his struggle and managed to obtain a grain law for distributing corn to the proletariat of Rome at a fixed price. He also had a law passed requiring the state to provide full clothing to soldiers, instead of having the cost deducted from pay, and also to prohibit recruitment of those under seventeen, which shows that laxity had crept in under pressure of finding recruits. But when Gaius attempted to extend the franchise to the long-suffering allies from the other tribes of Italy, opposition stiffened and he suffered defeat.

So concerned were his opponents that they passed an emergency decree (*senatus consultum ultimum*) which authorized the senate to take any steps to safeguard the state. Immediately a group of armed men attacked Gaius and his followers, 300 of whom were killed or arrested and immediately executed. The Gracchan party—and with it the pressure of reform—was effectively eliminated. The oligarchs triumphed and became even more determined to clamp down on any further attempts to change the status quo. In 111 B.C., Rome blundered into the war against Jugurtha of Numidia and suffered a serious defeat in 109 B.C. A great family that had risen to power in post-Gracchan times were the Metelli. Now one of them, Quintus Caecilius Metellus, was given command and took to Africa a protégé of his clan, Gaius Marius, an ambitious equestrian from an undistinguished family of Arpinum.

Gaius Marius

Marius was a rough physical character but a man of great courage, a natural soldier with an overwhelming sense of his own destiny. His confidence in himself and his ability for hard work marked him out and he was fortunate in making a match with Julia, a member of a family of ancient lineage, the Caesars. Julia was to become the aunt of the great Julius Caesar. Marius first saw service in Spain and his outstanding conduct was noticed by Scipio Africanus. The war against Jugurtha was hard and difficult and Marius labored in the field with his men, winning their admiration and affection. He forced Metellus to allow him to return to Rome for the election of the consuls in 107 B.C. He told the plebs that he was the only one who could bring Jugurtha to battle and defeat him, and such was his popularity and power over them that he was swept into the consulship in spite of all the senate's attempts to block him.

He could not raise new legions that year, as the two already recruited were with Metellus. So he requested and got a *supplementum*, the authority to raise extra troops, probably about 3,000 men. The senate thought he would use the normal levy (*dilectus*) and thereby damage his reputation with those with property qualifications, who had just elected him consul and had already been hard-pressed by the need for troops earlier in the year. Marius started to recruit in the usual way, calling especially for veterans. At the last moment before embarkation he called for volunteers from the *capite censi*, that is, the proletariat with no property qualifications, promising victory, spoils, and glory (Sallust, *The War with Jugurtha* [*Bellum Jugurthinum*] 85.48). This was not the dramatic step some modern historians have made it out to be, since with the decline of the small landowning class, the property qualification had been steadily reduced in the preceding generations. But it was the final step: Marius may have been desperate for recruits and the intake through his *dilectus* inadequate, so in desperation he had opened the door wider and had a flood of eager recruits, more than he needed or had been authorized.

He hastily embarked, knowing that many would fail to meet his high standards in a tough training program, but at least he would have enough in the end. A member of the expedition was his quaestor (business and financial officer), Lucius Cornelius Sulla, who came from a patrician family that had fallen on hard times. It was Sulla, ironically enough, who captured Jugurtha through the treachery of Bocchus, king of the Moors, but of course Marius took the credit and the triumph. Thus was sown the great jealousy and enmity between the two men, which was to have dreadful consequences for Rome.

Marius and the Invasions of Italy

A greater task now awaited Marius. Two large tribes of Celto-Germanic origins, the Cimbri and Teutones, were migrating and had invaded the lands of a Roman ally north of the Alps. They had swept aside a Roman army sent to turn them back. The horde, some 300,000 men, turned west into Gaul, where they were joined by other tribes, including the Ambrones. Two more Roman armies were defeated in 109 and 107 B.C., but in 105 came an even worse disaster, the battle of Arausio (Orange), where two consular armies were annihilated with the loss of 20,000 Romans, the greatest catastrophe since Cannae. Although the path into Italy was now open, the Germans crossed into Spain. The fear of the Celts had remained in Roman minds since the Celtic capture of Rome *ca.* 391 B.C. In its anxiety to use Marius, the hero of the hour, to protect Italy from a similar fate, the senate overlooked the rule that ten years should elapse between consulships and appointed him for a second term. He was also allowed in this emergency to raise an army as he had done before, without regard to property qualification.

His first task was to toughen up and train his new army, stiffened no doubt by his African veterans. The men were forced to do long marches in full kit and take part in battle training as if they were on a campaign. While waiting for the Germans, the troops dug a new canal at the mouth of the Rhône to speed up the delivery of supplies. The Teutones and Ambrones eventually appeared, but Marius allowed them to pass by and followed at a distance, awaiting a favorable opportunity to do battle. This occurred near Aquae Sextiae (Aix), where Marius chose the site for his fortified camp with great care, above a long slope of uneven ground, forcing the enemy to charge uphill. He also made sure the great horde was split by challenging the Ambrones on their own at a time when they were gorged with food and drink.

His battle tactics were to become standard legionary practice. He lined up his men in battle order and ordered them to stay quiet and still until the Germans were within javelin range; then the legionaries threw their long *pila* in two volleys into the closely packed mass, bringing confusion to the first ranks. Next the legionaries drew their short swords and plunged in wedge formation into the enemy, forcing the Ambrones so tightly together that they were unable to swing their long swords. At the critical point, when the Germans attempted to withdraw and rally, Marius had planned the simple surprise of hiding part of his army in a wood behind the enemy. At a signal this force emerged, attacking the Germans in the rear, pushing them uphill against the legionaries above. They broke and fled; the Roman cavalry pursued, cutting them down. About 100,000 men are said to have fallen. The German camps were looted and all the booty given to Marius, such was the great respect in which he was now held by his men. The Cimbri crossed the Alps and were defeated in Vercellae, northern Italy, by the combined armies of Marius and Quintus Lutatius Catulus, but unfortunately the accounts of this battle are obscure.

MARIUS AGAINST SULLA. Marius may have saved Italy from a barbarian invasion, but his political incompetence and bullying tactics split the senate into rival factions, creating disturbances and at length revolt. The need to reform the senate and legislature became more pressing, and the Italian armies were still clamoring for the franchise. The assassination of a would-be reformer, Marcus Livius Drusus, started the Italic War of 90 B.C. This amounted to a civil war since many of the allies had seen long service in the army and by their successes forced the reluctant senate into parting with the long-desired franchise. Sulla had achieved notable successes in the East and in the Italic War. He became consul and was given the command against Mithridates VI, king of Pontus, an ambitious ruler who had extended his kingdom and threatened Roman allies and interests. Marius, although retired from military activity and aging, had set his heart on an eastern conquest. His jealousy of Sulla started a civil war, bringing Roman against Roman. Thus began the long and bitter internal strife that was to last fifty-seven years, ending with the rise of Augustus and the sheer exhaustion of the Roman people.

Marius was a very unpleasant character, totally indifferent to human life and suffering, capable of cutting down any who stood in his way, however noble their origin. He has often been credited with army reforms, but he was a practical man lacking imagination and inventive genius. He fully understood the need for leadership, training, and discipline and identified himself with his men, sharing their hardships in the field. At some stage the old unwieldy three battle lines of men merged into one, but this was probably a natural process as the property qualification ceased to be significant. Plutarch credits him with a change in the construction of the *pilum,* substituting a wooden pin for an iron one, but it already had a soft iron shank which bent under impact.

It was a succession of brilliant generals ending in Marius and Sulla that gave the Roman army its resilience, flexibility, and, above all, faith in its own superiority. But this powerful weapon was soon blunted in the cruel attrition of the civil wars, the bloody shambles in which the greatest of all Roman generals, and of all time, was to demonstrate his extraordinary gifts—Julius Caesar.

Julius Caesar

What made Julius Caesar such a military genius? The answer must lie in the man himself, his origins, and his early life. He came from one of the most ancient patrician families in Rome, the Julii, but for several generations they had been undistinguished and only moderately wealthy. Caesar was enormously ambitious and driven by almost superhuman bouts of energy. Forced by his straitened circumstances to plan his political advancement through his wealthy allies Pompey and Crassus, he was hungry for a fortune and the independent power it could give him. The opportunity came unexpectedly when he was appointed governor of Cisalpine Gaul in A.D. 58 and, on the sudden death of his colleague in Transalpine Gaul, was given that province as well. The scene was set for his Gallic adventure.

THE GALLIC WARS. Caesar was above all a brilliant opportunist and he immediately saw an opportunity for conquest with its subsequent wealth and booty. From the crushing of the Helvetii onward his plan was to provoke tribes to take sides, either against him or as an ally. But it was a dangerous game and his motives could easily be misconstrued in Rome, so he wrote careful dispatches to the senate and later supplied his commentaries, the main intention of which was to justify his actions. He suddenly discovered he had great abilities as a field commander, a keen mind, and the capacities to judge possibilities and take instant action. Caesar realized that the most important factors in a war were not only decisive action taken at great speed, but also devoted troops with the skill, ability, and will to carry out difficult, almost impossible, orders. His army was built up, trained, and welded into a fine fighting machine by feats of endurance and the heat of many battles until his legions had an aura of invincibility and a total confidence in their commander.

Caesar did not introduce any new equipment or tactics, but he was able to demonstrate the effective use of friendly Gallic and German allies, especially in cavalry. In Spain the rebel Quintus Sertorius had shown the qualities of Spaniards when well trained and led, and a unit of Spanish cavalry had actually been enfranchised by Gnaeus Pompeius Strabo for its notable service in the siege of Asculum (Ascoli Piceno) toward the end of the Social War. Caesar merely took this practice a stage further, and in so doing gave a new meaning to the *auxilia*, which were soon to become an integral part of the Roman army.

THE AGE OF OCTAVIAN, LATER CALLED AUGUSTUS

The civil wars that followed the assassination of Julius Caesar involved several armies with allegiances to different leaders. At the end of it all, Octavian, Caesar's grandnephew, found himself with sixty legions and the problem of how to discharge such a large number of hardened soldiers. He retained the *imperium* and those selected to remain in the army took the oath to him. Augustus (Octavian) was to take these and other drastic measures because the citizens of Rome and their allies were by now so weary of the wars that they were desperate for a peace of any kind. Augustus proceeded to gain absolute power, step by step, taking every constitutional means to ensure its legality.

His most important decision was the size of the army, and he showed truly remarkable prescience in selecting the number of twenty-eight legions. Additional legions were created at later dates by circumstances Augustus could never have foreseen. His attitude toward the *auxilia* was more cautious, as some nationals were still reluctant to serve too far from their homelands. Gradually this was solved by drafting new recruits, regardless of their ethnic character, to any unit needing men. Exceptions to this practice of absorbing foreign soldiers into the regular army were made for those with traditional fighting methods, such as the Balearic slingers or Hamian archers, and other specialists like the Tigris boatmen who could ply their craft in shallow water.

The Fleets and the Rome Cohorts

Augustus also inherited a large number of ships of various kinds and sizes. The civil wars had shown him the great value of an organized fleet in the eastern Mediterranean. He took the ships and sailors he needed and built naval bases at Misenum, Ravenna, and Forum Julii (Fréjus), and later this arm was to expand to the great rivers the Rhine and Danube. The fleets remained, however, an inferior service. Another innovation of Augustus was the creation of the Rome Cohorts, which consisted of nine cohorts of the Praetorian Guard, three urban cohorts "to control slaves and those citizens whose natural boldness gives way to disorderly conduct, unless they are overawed by force" (Tacitus, *Annals* 6.10–11), and seven cohorts of *Vigiles*, Rome's fire-fighting force. The Rome Cohorts were from their origins organized as part of the army, and were to become an important factor in the process of military promotion, especially for tribunes and centurions. Also, their pay scales were much higher than in the legions and the length of service was only sixteen years, compared with the twenty-five of legionaries. This meant that the veterans or *evocati* were available for further services in other branches of the army.

The Army as a Permanent Force

Under Caesar the army had become a highly efficient and professional body, well fed and officered. Augustus had the more difficult task of transforming it into a permanent peacetime force able to defend the frontiers of Rome, which now extended to the Atlantic, the Rhine and Danube, the Black Sea, and the deserts of Syria, North Africa, and Egypt. This remarkably successful transformation was not achieved without severe setbacks in Germany, Illyricum, and Pannonia. Augustus had one great failure in misjudging the temper of the German people. His original scheme was to make the Elbe the frontier, but this was prevented by the treachery of Arminius and the slaughter of three legions under Publius Quinctilius Varus, a bitter blow which affected Augustus deeply.

The concept of a static peacekeeping army was new to Rome, but Augustus, with his remarkable abilities, grasped it thoroughly. He saw the need not only for the troops to be spaced out carefully in the outer provinces, but also for establishing alliances with friendly rulers to maintain the peace beyond them. He appreciated that diplomacy could be more effective and much cheaper than war. To this end he exercised great skill in selecting kings and queens for this duty and by holding their children in Rome, ostensibly for their education but in reality as hostages. But his greatest triumph, perhaps, was to achieve peaceful coexistence with the Parthians. None of this could have been achieved without understanding that the key to the whole problem of military control was one of communication. Only by securing routes from Italy to all parts of his vast empire could Augustus move his army units quickly when necessary and maintain a rapid transmission of information. But his farsightedness did not end here, for he could also see how these measures were necessary for the expansion of Roman trade into these areas and beyond.

THE EARLY EMPIRE AND ITS DEFENSES

The early empire saw the development of this basic scheme into more and more detailed provision of roads, bridges, and permanent military establishments with security of supplies and sources of materials. The development of the frontier or *limes,* as it is known, was a slow process of adjustment to new threats and subsequent consolidation, but the judgment of Augustus had been sound and few additions were made. One of these was Britannia, invaded by Claudius in A.D. 43. When he was found cowering behind a curtain by the Praetorians, Claudius was a person of little standing, an imperial misfit and totally overlooked by the senate, which declared all the acts of the emperor void and was about to set up a new republic; some senators were even discussing the succession. Faced with such hostility in Rome, Claudius saw Britain as an opportunity to divert public attention and to gain a military reputation and the loyalty of his frontier armies. The conquest of Britain proved to be a costly mistake, but once Rome was committed, it could not readily relinquish the effort, which was to absorb three and, at times, four legions.

Claudius and the Flavian Emperors

It was Claudius, however, who made the *auxilia* more attractive with the promise of the franchise on honorable discharge. He was sympathetic toward the equestrians and much improved their promotion ladder through the auxiliary commands. Thus conditions for officers and men improved gradually and living conditions in the forts and fortresses became more comfortable. It is probable that Vespasian, an experienced field officer, made further improvements, and the layout of forts seems to become more standardized at this time. A serious upset was the civil war of A.D. 69, so well documented by Tacitus. Legions fought legions and some of the Gallic units defected in the creation of an abortive Gallic empire. Two new legions were formed out of the sailors of the Italian fleets. About the same time Rome was engaged in a bitter struggle with the Jews, which led to a detailed account by Josephus; this has become one of the more important sources on the army in action, including a graphic description of the siege of Jerusalem.

Dacia and the Wars of Trajan

It was under Domitian (A.D. 81–96) that the first serious threat developed on the Danube through folk movements beyond the frontier, population pressures, and the rise of Decebalus, king of Dacia. Although the emperor succeeded in deferring a serious war by diplomacy, it was only a temporary relief, and a heavy concentration of legions was needed on this frontier, which led to problems elsewhere. The garrison in Britain, for example, was reduced to three legions and Caledonia was abandoned. The matter was only resolved by the invasion of Dacia by Trajan. Although there is no account of this war, the finely carved column of Trajan gives highly detailed but disconnected scenes, only a few of which offer any historical commentary; but although some of the details are suspect, the column remains a magnificent picture book of the army on campaign. Trajan (A.D. 97–117), a military man obsessed with war, plunged Rome into a wasteful campaign against Parthia and gained vast territories, mainly of desert, at the heavy cost of severe losses of men and of plagues brought back to Europe by his debilitated troops.

HADRIAN'S ARMY REFORMS

Hadrian (A.D. 117–138), in effect Trajan's chief of staff, was a thoroughly pragmatic Roman and horrified by this dreadful waste. He initiated a policy of marking out the limits of the empire with new and stronger defense lines, the most imposing of which is the seventy-two-mile wall in Britain that bears his name. Hadrian also realized that the future strength and vigor of Rome lay in the frontier zones, so he encouraged economic growth and the development of urbanism in these areas. He spent most of his time as emperor in tirelessly traveling to all parts of his domain to put matters right. He tightened up military discipline, cutting out abuses and what he considered to be unnecessary extravagances. Like Marius, he worked and dined with his men and shared their conditions in the field and the camp.

The period of Hadrian marks a watershed in the history of the Roman army. Up to this time the army had been an attacking force seeking to engage the enemy in open battle, where its superiority in equipment, tactical organization, discipline, and high morale would ensure overwhelming victory. The forts and fortresses were training bases and comfortable winter quarters, and their defenses were well planned and perfectly adequate, since long and difficult sieges were never contemplated. During this time, the legions had been through several serious crises, especially on the Danube, where they had faced a highly superior mounted force in the Sarmatians, who possessed fine-scale armor that also covered much of their horses. Two important factors were being understood: one was the need for greater mobility; the other, the need to be able to concentrate large forces rapidly at threatened points.

From the time of Hadrian more cavalry units were formed, and he continued the practice, begun under Domitian, of doubling the size of some existing *alae* (wings of the army). For sudden emergencies the *vexillationes* were being created. These were armies formed by detachments taken from the legions and *auxilia* to form task forces. These were, in embryo, the mobile field armies which were to have such significance at a later period. For the demands of the Dacian wars Trajan raised irregular native units from friendly peoples; these men appear on Trajan's Column, naked to the waist, armed only with clubs. These units were called *numeri* (numbers of men). In the course of the second century they and their mounted counterparts, the *cunei* (wedges), were to find permanent places in the army. Unfortunately, due to the absence of inscriptions, the details of their size and organization remain unknown. The character of the Roman army was changing. It was becoming more and more defensive.

THE WINDS OF CHANGE UNDER SEVERUS AND HIS SUCCESSORS

The changes introduced by Severus were to have far-reaching effects, although this may not have been appreciated at the time. Not only was the army strengthened and enlarged but the grip of central control on government and provincial administration was also much increased. The soldiers were given greater privileges and exemptions from taxes and other obligations demanded of civilians. The merchant class and town dwellers bore the brunt of heavier taxes and a closer watch on and control of their organizations. The old Roman traditions of a free society with an urban life-style supported by the splendid public buildings that had been built and maintained by private beneficence had become matters for the historians. One can trace from this period, and even before, the evidence of decay in city life and its monuments. Requisition of goods and services by state officers became the normal practice, especially in the frontier zones. The changes made by Severus were at least effective in enabling his dynasty to hold the empire together, albeit precariously, until Severus Alexander was killed by his troops in A.D. 235 for attempting to negotiate with the Alemanni, who were menacing the frontier.

The soldiers saw this as cowardice and promptly replaced him with Maximinus, a career officer, son of a Thracian peasant. There followed a period of breakdown of central control and a lack of any political stability at a critical time when the frontiers were under serious threat from barbarians on the move. The Danube was under pressure from the Goths and Vandals, then moving south, while the Rhine was crossed by the Alemanni and the Franks. In the East the weakness of the Parthians was exposed by the Persians expanding to the west under the succession of strong rulers who founded the Sassanian Empire. This ended the precarious treaty relationship Rome had established and held at some cost. The Sassanians brought with them a powerful religion based on the Mazdean belief, which they sought to proselytize among the Iranians.

FURTHER PRESSURES ON THE FRONTIER

The events of the third century are difficult to follow since the surviving historical evidence is so poor. Herodian's account ends with the year A.D. 238, and besides these there are only the unsatisfactory summaries of the fourth-century historians and the fictitious late sections of the *Historia Augusta*. Our greatest loss are the first thirteen books of Ammianus Marcellinus, whose great *History* began with Nerva (A.D. 96); the books that have survived start with the year A.D. 353. Although the evidence is scanty it seems clear that the pressure on the frontiers, although intermittent, was becoming more and more serious. The barbarian tribes themselves were under threat from others pressing behind them. No longer were they merely raiding for cattle and booty, which could be carried back to their homeland; they now were anxious to cross the frontier and settle within the Roman defenses.

There was, however, another factor that may have exacerbated these problems. It had been the practice of Rome since the time of Trajan to enlist barbarian levies in the service of the army; some of these became permanent units as infantry *numeri* or cavalry *cunei,* and it is possible that replacements continued to be recruited from barbarians beyond the frontier. This presented opportunities for well-paid employment, which could have been another factor drawing some of the tribes into the frontier areas.

The Breakdown of Central Control

The frontier armies could no longer hold back this mounting flood. After the murder of Severus Alexander there was a rapid succession of emperors. The weakness he had displayed was a lesson well learned by the soldiers. If the man they elected proved to be inadequate, he was promptly removed by his own men or, more likely, by jealous rivals. From A.D. 235 to 284 there were twenty emperors created in this manner, but there were many more usurpers; of this number only Trajanus Decius (A.D. 249–251) was actually killed in battle, and he had been forced by threat of execution by the soldiers to accept the purple in the first place. The emperor who survived longest was Gallienus, who reigned for fifteen years (A.D. 253–268), until he was murdered by his staff officers during the siege of Mediolanum (Milan).

Another effect of the disintegration of sections of the frontier and the collapse of central authority was that some of the provincials took matters into their own hands. Postumus in A.D. 259 proclaimed himself head of a Gallic empire (including the other western provinces), the fulfillment of an ancient dream still harbored by the Gauls. A rapid succession of Gallic usurpers managed to hold back the barbarian tide until the new empire collapsed in A.D. 274, when Gaul was returned to the imperial fold by Aurelian.

RECOVERY UNDER AURELIAN

This new emperor had been a cavalry commander and was a man of outstanding ability. He succeeded in defeating several invading armies and claimed on his coins to be the Restorer of the World (*Restitutor Orbis*). Aurelian had time also to make some administrative reforms and build the great wall, which bears his name, twelve miles in circuit around Rome. This may not have been necessary then but was symptomatic of the times. One of the reactions to the devastating movements of the barbarians deep into the empire was for the cities to protect themselves. It was correctly assumed that none of the peoples on the move would wish to spend time on a long siege, or had the equipment or technique to do so. The large cities of the Rhineland and Gaul built themselves defenses in some haste, often demolishing public buildings and funeral monuments to provide the stone, thus inadvertently preserving for posterity many fine pieces of sculpture. These new walls were usually on a much smaller inner circuit than those early modest constructions that had surrounded the whole city. The smaller area was easier to defend and the defenses could be built more rapidly. They had high curtain walls and projecting towers at intervals, and corners and gates where archers had a field of fire along the circuit and bolt-firing spring guns could be mounted if they were available.

Military Reactions to the Pressures

In the early empire the army had been equipped with both bolt-firing and stone-hurling *ballistae* for use in open warfare. By the late third century it became necessary to equip civil and military defenses with these weapons to keep enemy masses away from the walls. In the East the idea of large artillery pieces had either survived from Hellenistic times or been redeveloped. Parts of a ten-pound (10 Roman lbs. = 3.27 kg) stone-hurler have been found at Hatra in Mesopotamia, where it had been mounted on the top of a tower. Although the evidence is still very slight, logic would suggest the construction of artillery of larger size and in greater number for mounting on the towers and bastions to disperse large groups of attackers.

The army was at times forced to take the food and facilities they needed from cities and at such times could become as ruthless as the barbarians. The severe stress caused rapid inflation and a currency crisis marked by enormous issues of inferior coins, resulting in the practice of making payments in kind rather than in cash. Soldiers were given food and clothing but had to depend for money in the form of donatives from emperors dependent on their support. A tendency developed for the army to be divided between the static frontier garrisons, served by older inferior troops, and the younger and more active who were drafted into mobile *vexillationes* for rapid deployment where needed. A few strong emperors like Aurelian managed for a time to restore a kind of unity, but the empire needed a greater man with a gift of organization and the strength to carry it out.

DIOCLETIAN

Rome was fortunate in Diocletian (A.D. 284–305). As a pragmatist he recognized that such a large empire with territories facing different problems could no longer be governed by a single central authority. His answer was to divide it into East and West, each with coemperors and a Caesar acting as deputy, a system to become known as the tetrarchy. This was a sensible arrangement providing all four remained loyal to each other. There were serious internal troubles and revolts in Egypt in A.D. 295 and in Britain and part of Gaul where Carausius, a fleet commander, declared himself emperor in A.D. 287. The breach was healed by Constantius I, the father of the great Constantine I, at that time Caesar in the West. By *ca.* A.D. 300 the tetrarchy was in full control and the barbarians held in check. Diocletian survived for twenty-one years before he retired to his great fortified palace at Split. He made serious mistakes, under pressure from Galerius, in obliging his colleague Maximian to retire also and in appointing new Caesars, thus ignoring the sons of his old and new Augusti. The army of the West proclaimed Constantine successor to his father, thus precipitating a civil war, from which Constantine emerged as master of the whole empire. He and his family successors retained firm control until *ca.* A.D. 360.

Diocletian subjected the army to wide-reaching reforms. Over the years the number of men in the old legions had shrunk until they were about half their size; by doubling the number to seventy he brought them back to strength. The most important source of information about the units of the late army is a document known as the *Notitia Dignitatum.* This enigmatic document presents very serious problems, including its date. It is an incomplete list of army commands and of junior offices and the units attached to them arranged in the provinces in which they served. Some of the new legions were named after the patron gods of the tetrarchs: the *Ioviani, Herculiani, Solenses, Martenses*. These legions were equipped with small barbed darts (*martiobarbuli*), vicious weapons against both men and horses. Many of the old auxiliary units had also survived but had become static garrisons with hereditary recruitment, a natural development of the Severan reforms. Most units served in the same fort for several generations, and the families of the men and their officers became landowners or tenants and lived off the land they were defending; some of these units were also named after their forts. Diocletian created a select mobile army which traveled with him and included new cavalry units, the *Equites Promoti, Equites Comites* and the *Scholae*, who were the imperial guards. There was also a picked unit, the *Lanciarii*, equipped with the *lancea* (a light type of lance), as opposed to the heavy *contus* used originally by the Sarmatians.

CHANGES UNDER CONSTANTINE THE GREAT

Constantine created a new crack infantry regiment known as an *Auxilium*, which included the *Cornuti* and *Bracchiati*, raised from Gauls and Germans. The frontier policy was also changed by Constantine, who based units in fortified cities within frontier zones, with artillery permanently mounted in the projecting bastions. Main lines of communication were fortified with small *burgi* and *praesidia*. These were small watchtowers and posts that could be used by units on the move, kept well stocked with provisions and munitions, and presumably armed by a small permanent garrison to prevent enemy access.

By the middle of the fourth century the army can be said to be divided into two main type of soldiers: the mobile armies (*comitatenses*), often billeted in towns, and the static frontier armies (*limitanei*). Many of the individual units contained a surprisingly small number of men, the old imperial auxiliary units of 500 men by then reduced to about 150, or even less. The officers were all military men and the alternating military-civil career structure of the early empire was forgotten. The revolution initiated by Severus was complete.

THE HOUSE OF VALENTINIAN I AT THE CLOSE OF THE FOURTH CENTURY

The empire was under reasonably firm control under the emperors of the house of Valentinian I. New measures forced landowners to supply peasants to fill the gaps in the army ranks; the presence of barbarian invaders on the frontier was accepted and their services enlisted as allies. This was an old Roman practice of making tribal kings into clients and having them defend the frontiers. Those who had already settled within the empire were called *laeti* and *dediticii*, although the precise nature of this arrangement is not known. Others, known as *foederati*, were given allowances and treated almost as army units. The beginning of the end came with the disastrous battle of Hadrianopolis (Adrianople, Edirne) in A.D. 378, in which Emperor Valens was killed and two-thirds of the eastern mobile army lost. This signified the final collapse of the Roman Empire.

THE EMPIRE DISINTEGRATES

In A.D. 406 hordes of Germans and Vandals swept across the Rhine and flooded into Gaul and Spain. Britain was cut off and in attempting to fend off Saxon and Pictish invaders set up her own rulers. By adopting the Roman policy of allowing some of the newcomers to settle on condition they protected the rest of the country, the Britons managed to preserve a shadowy resemblance of a Roman province for another century. But the West submerged into the petty kingdoms of the early Middle Ages. Rome was sacked by the Visigoths in A.D. 410 and again by the Vandals in A.D. 455. The western and central areas had gone forever but the Eastern Empire survived.

The Eastern Empire Survives

The collapse of the Western Empire under the weight of the barbarian invasions was not matched in its Eastern counterpart. The fifth century was a period of internal troubles and religious bickering, which seriously weakened the central authority. However, the Eastern Empire survived, mainly due to its economic strength, but also because of the lack of any serious threat from Parthia. A strong revival came with the accession of Justinian in A.D. 527. He was a very competent administrator, but he was also possessed by ambition for imperial grandeur. Justinian was fortunate in Belisarius, an outstanding field commander who gained large conquests in Italy and North Africa. For a time the Mediterranean had the semblance of the old united empire; but this proved to be ephemeral. Nevertheless, the emperor had succeeded in stabilizing and strengthening the empire of Byzantium, and it became the bastion of Christianity against the rising tide of Islam. Ironically, this advance was held until the city fell to the Crusaders in A.D. 1208.

BIBLIOGRAPHY

STUDIES

Anthony R. Birley, *Marcus Aurelius* (1966), and *Septimius Severus* (1971); Conrad Cichorius, *Die Reliefs der Traianssäule* (1896; rev. ed. 1900); Peter Connolly, *Greece and Rome at War* (1981); Paul Couissin, *Les armes romaines* (1926); Alfred von Domaszewski, *Die Rangordnung des römischen Heeres*, Brian Dobson, ed. (1967); Michael Grant, *The Fall of the Roman Empire: A Reappraisal* (1976); Arnold Hugh Martin Jones, *The Later Roman Empire, 284–602* (1964); Lawrence Keppie, *The Making of the Roman Army* (1984); Johannes Kromayer and Georg Veith, *Heerwesen und Kriegführung der Griechen und Römer* (1928); Edward Luttwak, *The Grand Strategy of the Roman Empire* (1976); Henry Michael Denne Parker, *The Roman Legions* (repr. 1958); H. Russell Robinson, *The Armour of Imperial Rome* (1975); George R. Watson, *The Roman Soldier* (1969); Graham Webster, *The Roman Imperial Army* (1969; 3d ed. 1985).

LIBRARY
MONROE BUSINESS INSTITUTE